Tunica Archaeology

PAPERS OF THE PEABODY MUSEUM OF ARCHAEOLOGY AND ETHNOLOGY
HARVARD UNIVERSITY • VOLUME 78

TUNICA ARCHAEOLOGY

Jeffrey P. Brain

With contributions by

T. M. HAMILTON

ARTHUR SPIESS

PEABODY MUSEUM OF ARCHAEOLOGY AND ETHNOLOGY

HARVARD UNIVERSITY, CAMBRIDGE, MASSACHUSETTS

1988

DISTRIBUTED BY HARVARD UNIVERSITY PRESS

Cover: *Village des Tonicas*, watercolor sketched by Dumont de Montigny between 1728 and 1742. This may be a representation of Trudeau, but the reference to the temporary fort of Loubois, built during the Natchez campaign of 1730, suggests that the village is the one occupied by the Tunica immediately prior to their move to Trudeau. In any event, the depiction would be typical of a Tunica village of the period. (Courtesy Bibliothèque de l'Arsenal, Paris)

© 1988 by the President and Fellows of Harvard College
ISBN 0-87365-204-5
Library of Congress Catalog Card Number 87-72043
Printed in the United States of America

*This volume
is dedicated to
James A. Ford
and
Philip Phillips
who led the way
in exploring
many of the same sites
and problems*

Contents

viii

Tables

Foreword

In many ways this volume is a conclusion: it is the end of the "Trail of the Tunica," and also the second of two volumes of an archaeological project that began rather haphazardly nearly twenty years ago. Oh yes, there ultimately were research designs of one sort or another and the prioritizing of research goals, but let's not fool anyone—it all really began in December 1969, with a letter addressed to me by my dear old friend, Stu Neitzel. That letter, which was temporarily buried in some Directorial desk debris, was unearthed some months later, and then Jeff Brain was sent to Louisiana to look over the materials that he would call the "Tunica Treasure." But that's an old story, well told in the introduction to volume 1.

We turn here to the archaeological retrieval of the other parts of the story—the happenings both before and after the Trudeau interlude for the Tunica. And as Jeffrey Brain has told it, the volume also serves to bring together a mélange of half-forgotten, and what seemed then only partially related, pieces of data. But I think he has done much more. At least for me this book is a wonderful tapestry of people, places, and things. We come across Henry Collins in 1927 promulgating the Direct Historical Approach, the same Henry Collins whom I would invest with an Honorary Fellowship in the Lower Mississippi Survey some fifty years later at the Smithsonian.

And then there's a lanky young Jim Ford, eagerly taking up the torch passed by Henry and in the mid Thirties seeing and identifying for the first time Tunica archaeology. In 1939 Ford would join with Phil Phillips and Jimmy Griffin in the Lower Mississippi Survey. With the coming of the postwar period Phil would devote a long chapter in their classic 1951 Lower Valley report to critical evaluation of historical/ethnographic connections, but with some trepidation. Following my work at Lake George, I would in 1962 uncautiously start a plunge into historic archaeology and write a paper on the topic viewed from the Lower Valley, spurred by some of the discoveries set forward below. The Tunica were still out there in the canebrakes when in 1963–64 I'd take aim at their near-neighbors, the Taensa. But then their time would come: the Tunica Treasure, Leonard Charrier, and Stu Neitzel would see to that. So that's how we got here.

But there are as well so many golden moments of the past that this volume invokes from my own rather desultory fieldwork of the mid-Sixties through the late Seventies; a time when museum administration was foremost in my mind. My first involvement with historical archaeology began in 1961 with a July visit to see the Russell family collection of artifacts at their small farmhouse, almost under the shadow of the Yazoo Bluffs. I was following up a much earlier visit by Phil Phillips. But more importantly I had just made my own discovery in the State Museum in Jackson, Mississippi,

then curated by Stu Neitzel. There I had come across some obviously historic period artifacts from the Russell site such as we'd *not* found at Lake George. Mrs. Russell was caught up with my obvious delight at viewing these very significant finds. As I was leaving, after photographing the collection with the help of one of my students, she thrust a mid-nineteenth-century book into my hand. It wasn't archaeological, just old, but she very much wanted me to have the volume. I still do; it's on a shelf not far from where I write this note: a fine momento of that meeting.

A decade later I would meet my first Tunica face to face. I journeyed to Marksville in the summer of 1971; Stu was back at home, and the Tunica project had now begun in earnest. Stu took me to meet his old friend, Joe Pierite, Sr., Chief of the Tunica, who lived nearby. There at the Tunica-Biloxi Trading Post I photographed the very interesting nineteenth-century Tunica materials that had been recently excavated and then curated by Chief Joe. I was aided in this project by my student, Alan Toth, then Louisiana State Archaeologist, and an eight-year-old youngster whom I dragged away from summer fun on Cape Cod. The recording task took longer that day than expected; it usually does. Thus it was nearly 9 P.M. when we pulled into a well-known catfish eatery in Jonesville, Louisiana, on the bank of the Black River. Not daunted by the late time or the strange place, my son John then happily put away a whole fried catfish; nothing daunts him today either as an ensign on the USS *Lockwood*. Fieldwork has its virtues.

But there is much more to Tunica archaeology than fond memories of the fun in the field collecting those data bits. Jeffrey Brain has tied together all these myriad pieces of information (one might want to call it a "conjunctive approach," or maybe even "multidisciplinary") in a finely integrated picture of the Tunica and their marvelously complex saga of movement and continuity. It is a real monument to the concept of what he now terms "ethnohistoric archaeology." Many of our friends and colleagues have contributed much to this monument, as Jeffrey has amply documented.

Whatever this work be called, the Lower Mississippi Survey is proud to present this truly joint effort: a summary volume with its very superior melding of data from the documents, written and graphic; the artifacts, native and trade; the excavations, large and small; and the conceptions, clear and concise. The field of Historic Archaeology is surely enhanced by this extremely thorough examination of the history of the Tunica. But such good research and fine publication take time, support, and trust. These have been given to us in an unstinting fashion, for which one can only express deep and long-lasting appreciation: Thanks, Phil.

Stephen Williams

Acknowledgments

One of the bonuses of archaeological field research is the opportunity to meet and work with a wide variety of people who enrich the project in so many ways. It is a pleasure to acknowledge the friendships and contributions of these kindred souls.

I begin by recognizing the Tunica, without whom the study in the following pages could not have been attempted—indeed, would not have been. It is their story that is told, and ultimately it is to them that this study is dedicated.

Nor would the study have materialized and developed to this point without the support of my closest colleagues, who have had such a profound effect upon my professional career and personal development and who were actively involved in most phases of the program: Philip Phillips, Stephen Williams, John S. Belmont, Ian W. Brown, Vincas P. Steponaitis, and Robert S. Neitzel. My debt to these friends can never be repaid, but I hope they find in these pages some measure of the value of their participation.

Many other professional archaeologists aided our research at various times. Foremost among these has been William G. Haag, the dean of Louisiana archaeology. As one-time state archaeologist, he actively supported our projects in Louisiana, and, ever the perfect host, he surrendered his home to us on countless occasions. Alan Toth and Kathleen Byrd, subsequent state archaeologists of Louisiana, have been equally instrumental in the success of our study, as have Stephen Perry and Deborah Woodiel of the Louisiana Department of Culture, Recreation and Tourism, and the members of the Louisiana Archaeological Survey and Antiquities Commission. Also to be noted for their individual contributions are Tommy Birchett, Jean-François Blanchette, George Castille, David Dye, Dan Morse, Robert Neuman, William Spencer, and Bill Wright.

The bulk of this volume could not have been realized without the assistance of the archaeological field crews. The many individuals who participated in the various projects are credited in the appropriate sections. Their contributions were vital to the success of those projects and I am grateful to them all. Especially to be acknowledged are Ian Brown and Vincas Steponaitis, whose long-term involvement and dedication were fundamental to the continuity of the program.

Professionals in related fields who added their expertise to many aspects of the study included geomorphologist Roger T. Saucier, ethnohistorian Patricia K. Galloway, and historians Ann Reilly Jones and Patricia D. Woods.

Avocational archaeologists, when given sufficient encouragement, can be of considerable assistance, volunteering both labor and information. Of the many who rallied to our projects, the contributions of the following are acknowledged with special thanks: Janet and Alan Bailey, Ed Dean, Polly Dement, Kyle Herring, Burt Jaeger, Carroll Kelley, Bill Mills, John Rogers, and Jackie Sarrett. Leonard J. Charrier, the finder of the "Tunica Treasure" (and therefore the instigator of the entire study), was an important participant in many of the projects described in the following pages.

Others who were vital to the implementation of the various field investigations were Elbert Hilliard of the Mississippi Department of Archives and History; Larry Crane and Mrs. Lawrence H. Fox of the Louisiana Department of Culture, Recreation and Tourism; Kirk Carney and Wylie Harvey of the Louisiana Office of State Parks; and C. Paul Phelps, Ross Maggio, and Burt Dixon of the Louisiana Department of Corrections.

Professional help of another sort that was crucial to some phases of the program was provided by the legal community. At one time or another, the following lawyers were involved in formal legal actions, as well as informal negotiations, on behalf of the author and/or the university. Fred G. Benton, Jr., Michael L. Hughes, Lee C. Kantrow, Donald Juneau, and James A. Sharaf. Let it be noted for the record that these gentlemen gave generously and freely of their time.

Perhaps the most satisfying of new friendships in the field are those forged with people who may have little initial interest in archaeology per se, but who nevertheless come to accept and encourage one's efforts. The encouragement often takes the form of a special relationship that is vital to the success of a project. Especially to be mentioned in this regard are Gordon Cotton, whose good humor and knowledge of local lore frequently have relieved our labors around Vicksburg, Mississippi, and Nora Marsh, the mistress of Weyanoke Plantation, who epitomizes the very best of Louisiana hospitality.

Funding for the various field projects was provided by both public and private sources. Grants from the National Endowment for the Humanities and the National Geographic Society, supplemented by gifts from Mr. Landon Clay, Mrs. Wilhelmina Phillips, and Mr. and Mrs. John F. Hendon supported earlier phases of the work. Contracts from the Louisiana Office of State Parks paid for the last two seasons at Trudeau. During the later investigations, material assistance and labor were provided by the Louisiana Department of Corrections.

All of this help would have been quite superfluous without the permissions of the landowners to investigate the sites located on their property. It is, therefore, with deep appreciation that the permissions of the following individuals and organizations are acknowledged: the heirs of the Rowe estate, Mrs. Lee V. Russell, the Burroughs family, the International Paper Company, and the state of Louisiana.

The field activity would be for naught, of course, if the results were not disseminated in usable form. Thus we come to the very pleasant task of acknowledging the contributions of yet another class of exceptionally talented people. Richard Bartlett, former director of the publications department at the Peabody Museum, designed the book. Overall editorial supervision and production were initiated by Robyn Sweesy and completed by Mary Strother with conscientiousness and caring exceptional in modern publishing. Whatever consistency of style and clarity of expression exist in these pages are directly attributable to the superb editing of Joan Kathryn O'Donnell, whose empathy made the relationship a most enjoyable learning experience. The illustrations are the products of many skilled hands. Most of the artifacts were photographed by Hillel Burger, the Peabody Museum staff photographer, although a few were photographed by Alan Toth and Stephen Williams. The field photographs of the investigations were taken by Toth and Ian Brown. The linework was drawn by Victoria Olmstead, Lisa Anderson, Alexandra Schultz, and Nancy Lambert-Brown. It was Nancy who translated Bartlett's design into reality with great sensitivity to the requirements of both aesthetics and scholarship. To all of these talented people I offer my profoundest thanks.

Even the most profound gratitude, however, is not sufficient to express my appreciation to Philip Phillips, who made the publication possible. To him the book is dedicated.

Jeffrey P. Brain
Cambridge, Massachusetts
January 1988

Introduction

The part played by Tunican peoples in the aboriginal history of the Lower Mississippi Valley would thus appear to have been very great and to render a knowledge of their position and affinities of unusual importance.

Swanton 1919, p. 8

This volume is the second part of a two-volume set. The first volume, *Tunica Treasure* (Brain 1979), presented an extraordinary collection of European and native artifacts from a mid-eighteenth-century Tunica Indian village site in Louisiana. That collection was the genesis of this study of the Tunica, providing the crucial datum, or point of reference, for the archaeology and history of this most interesting and important people.

The primary purpose of this volume is to present the data derived from archaeological investigations performed under the direction of the author during the ten-year period from 1972 to 1981. This work consisted of a series of projects undertaken in Mississippi and Louisiana, during which a number of sites were excavated. In addition, pertinent earlier excavations conducted by other researchers were reanalyzed. The common theme of this research was to elucidate the Tunica past through archaeology. This volume, then, focuses on the Tunica as they are identified in the archaeological record from late prehistory to the modern era. The Tunica have an unusually high archaeological profile, even as they are traced through four centuries and across four hundred miles of the Lower Mississippi Valley. The diachronic perspective of our research revealed a dynamic story of movement and transformation.

Tunica Archaeology is a case study of culture contact and change, and specifically of acculturation as experienced by an American Indian ethnic group. Acculturation is defined here as that series of actions and reactions that transformed the Tunica from a prehistoric aboriginal group into an assimilated segment of modern America. The archaeological identification and exposition of this process forms the very core of this study.

Any study of culture change requires the establishment of continuity as the nexus within which the change occurs. Since this study is concerned with the acculturation of a specific ethnic group, continuity really becomes a demonstration of ethnicity. The survival of the Tunica as an identifiable group throughout the historic period represents a classic case of ethnic persistence (Spicer 1971).

In these pages, "Tunica" refers to a perceived ethnicity rather than a state of biological or cultural purity. The Tunica have had a long history of living among and intermarrying with other peoples. This admixture is reflected in their recent incorporation and recognition by the United States government as the Tunica-Biloxi tribe, a nomenclature that recognizes only the most notable Indian amalgamation and, therefore, but a portion of the genetic reality. Despite the admixture—and it is likely that any significant group of people who survived four centuries of contact and change accepted refugees from less fortunate, disintegrating groups—it is clear that historically the dominant element has always been Tunica, and the group is designated as such in the contemporary documentation. Such persistence must have been subject to some modifications, of course, but a continuity of basic ideational and, until recently, linguistic traditions must be recognized. This continuity is labeled simply Tunica, in tribute to the people's own long-maintained perception of ethnicity: in Tunican, the word Tunica is a corruption of a phrase that means "the people" (Swanton 1911, p. 306; Haas 1950, 1953).

Although the Tunica were a known historical reality and persist as an ethnographic presence (Hodge 1910; Leitch 1979), a testimonial to their ethnic continuity and survival, we have had no knowledge of how they changed and survived. Neither the written documentation nor the oral traditions of the Tunica themselves gave sufficient insight into or explanations for the continuity. Archaeology was the only significant alternative for explicating the Tunica past.

The bulk of this volume consists of a series of archaeological site reports. In order to correlate them, it is necessary to identify the Tunica archaeologically. For a group known to be of mixed cultural and genetic heritage, this is no small matter. The perseverance of a name, a language, a tribal organization, and even a mind set may all be hallmarks of ethnicity, but they are difficult if not impossible to define archaeologically. As was often noted by contemporary observers, the Tunica were much like their neighbors in the hard matters of material remains. Fortunately, however, there were some exceptions to this general observation. When the archaeological record is examined, artifactual distinctions appear which set the Tunica apart. In these distinctions we find a thread of continuity, at least during the crucial era of contact and change in the sixteenth to eighteenth centuries.

In these pages, therefore, the goals are to document Tunica continuity and to achieve some understanding of the reasons for Tunica survival under circumstances that caused the destruction of so many other tribal groups. Once these goals were established, the question became how best to achieve them. The following sections of the introduction comprise a discussion of the theoretical background, a review of the development of culture change studies, and a presentation of the methodological approach to be used in this study of the Tunica.

Theoretical Background

As its title proclaims, this book is an archaeological study. The meaning behind this declaration must be established; it concerns both what archaeology is and what it can do (Salmon 1982).

Having grown up in the "traditionalist" school of archaeology, with its limited but useful objectives, and having been exposed to the "new archaeology," with its equally limited but useful objectives, I found that neither approach to the past completely fulfilled the goals described above. I needed to deal with a particular people through time and to attempt to understand how they survived and maintained their identity through that time. The issue was relevance—to that people, and to humanity in general. Relevance, in short, regarding the practice and applicability of archaeological inquiry (Ford 1973). An alternative approach was in order.

Given the knowledge and objectives of the time, the so-called traditional approach was a valid and useful way to do archaeology (Belmont and Williams 1965; Willey and Sabloff 1980), and it would serve no purpose to review its inadequacies here (see the initial critique by Taylor [1948]). Strongly historical, it relied upon inductive procedures. Although these attributes are still valuable in archaeological investigation, it must now be granted that other ways to do archaeology also exist.

The scientism of modern life finally intruded into the study of the past in the 1960s, giving birth to the "new archaeology" (a nomenclature that should be quietly shelved, in light of subsequent and ongoing theoretical developments; hereinafter it will be referred to as "scientistic archaeology"). Scientistic archaeology was a very good development, for it forced a rethinking of theories, methodologies, and even goals of research. Its contributions have been enormous, especially at the methodological level, but the rigid hypothetico-deductive nomothetic paradigm, with its emphasis on ecological functionalism and neoevolutionism, simply does not apply satisfactorily to the goals of this research.

It may even be observed that scientistic archaeology is losing favor generally and has failed in its bid to become the permanently established doctrine of archaeological procedure. A number of reasons for this failure exist, among them the rapid fragmentation of the revolutionary initiative into a number of competing approaches. Binford was the messiah, but there was no Saint Paul to pull everyone into line. Even early in the revolution major divergences occurred (see Flannery 1973), and the gaps continue to widen although basic philosophical tenets and many theoretical stances are still shared. The essential problem that alienated so many, however, was the rigidity of paradigms that forced false dichotomies and that were proclaimed in strict, uncompromising polemic (even the term "new archaeology" expressed the complete replacement of the old). Such hard lines are typical of revolutions, but are unfortunate in their tendency to throw out the baby with the bathwater. It was not an advance to denigrate historicism, for example, since particularism and chronology are the very core of archaeology; it was valid, however, to criticize the traditionalist position that these were the only relevant concerns for the study of the past. Few would, or should, seriously claim that the theoretical approach of scientistic archaeology is bankrupt, and indeed its contributions must be acknowledged by even the most hidebound of traditionalists. But because after extensive experimentation many of the promises of scientistic archaeology have yet to be fulfilled, it is reasonable to seek alternatives.

Theories are limited, and for this reason they may have short life spans. This is especially true of cultural theories, which tend to be products of their own times and places and reflect the concerns of the theorists and their cultural milieu. We should be prepared to interpret the past according to contemporary paradigms that address those concerns. Analyses risk being ignored if they do not help current generations understand their roots, or other perceived relevancies of the past, in order to better cope with the present. It follows, therefore, that there is no eternally correct way to do archaeology. Instead, a series of theories and paradigms may be employed that are appropriate and relevant to the intellectual priorities of a given situation. Simply put, "new theories replace old ones not because the old are disproved, but merely because they lose favor" (Glassie 1975, p. 13). It is important to note that ours is a cumulative discipline; although it is subject to changes in orientation and even basic philosophical attitudes, its past accomplishments must not be forgotten. A shrewd approach to the past utilizes the theories and analytic techniques that are most appropriate to the objectives and data at hand, whether they derive from discarded or current paradigms.

Archaeology currently is going through yet another revolution—surely but one more in its continuing quest for the past. Some American and British archaeologists, reflecting a skeptical attitude toward scientistic values in the modern world, are exploring other approaches. This new revolution has the potential to be of the same magnitude as those that have preceded it, although its effects have yet to be fully realized. In the new thinking, scientism has been challenged by a return to historicism and humanism, although these are of course cloaked in new theoretical mantles.

The most important of the current innovations are loosely grouped under the general rubric of "structuralism" (or semantic variations thereof). Ironically, just as Leslie White (1949) had reacted against the anthropocentrism of the prevailing school and argued for a science of culture, or "culturology," that gave birth to scientistic archaeology, the structuralists have argued for a return to anthropocentrism. Rather than formulating and testing general laws of human behavior, the structuralists emphasize the idiographic aspects of historicism and humanism. Precisely those areas discarded by the scientistic archaeologists, then, are revived by the structuralists, who are unabashedly reactionary in championing historicism and humanism as the appropriate stances for archaeological research. This development is a direct result of the failure of the functionalist-evolutionary approach to achieve those general laws and, I suspect, of the realization that the scientistic approach in general did not satisfy the objectives of many archaeological inquiries, not to mention the philosophical preferences of the inquirers themselves (Trigger 1984; Gould 1985). The new ferment in archaeological theoretics is indeed every bit as innovative and important as that of twenty years ago. It is just as searching as the many schools of thought encompassed by scientistic archaeology, and just as promising. Presumably this thinking, too, shall pass after a period of intense polemic; one hopes that it first will contribute a certain advance toward our ultimate goal of reconstructing the past.

The structuralist approach is not entirely new to archaeology (Longacre 1970, p. 137), but only recently has its growing popularity been accorded substantial publication (e.g., Deetz 1974, 1977, 1983; McKay 1976; Hall 1977; Fitting 1977; Gould 1980, 1985; Tilley 1981; Leone 1982; Hodder 1982a, 1982b, 1983; Wells 1985). At this still formulative stage there is considerable variability in the theory and operation of structuralism, as is evident in the use of alternate terms such as "symbolic archaeology," "cognitive archaeology," and "contextual archaeology." However, although their formulations may be modulated by varying degrees of compromise, all the practitioners of structuralism share the common characteristic of reaction against the basic tenets of scientistic archaeology.

The core concept of structuralism is the search for principles of organization of a past culture as these may be recognized in material remains. The particular historical context must be explained in terms of its internal ideology or unifying symbolic structure. Ideology is considered causal in human history, and a cognitive approach therefore is necessary in archaeological study if the goal is to understand human history in human terms. This attempt to "make the past human" (Deetz 1983) is one of the more attractive aspects of the structuralist approach.

A major problem with structuralism, however, is how to extract the ideological from the material or even to relate the two, much less confirm the reality of the relationship. Structuralists maintain that material symbols do not merely reflect ideological behavior but assume an active role in determining ideology: the overt manifestations may obscure true reality because their actual purpose may be to create an ideal reality. While the truth of this proposition may be demonstrated ethnographically, the concept is difficult to apply to archaeological research and would seem to demand more than is reasonable from the data. Even when an ideological-material correlation is proposed, verification appears to rest solely on empathy: "Statements about the past are not therefore ultimately to be judged by whether or not they can be tested, or by the outcomes of such

tests, but in terms of the conceptual, logical relationships presented between the data and its theorisation, i.e. the internal coherence of any particular study" (Miller and Tilley 1984, p. 151).

Such an intuitive approach has a certain anthropocentric allure, but the results must be considered speculative in even the most elegant and reasonable cases presented to date in the North American literature (e.g., Hall 1977; Deetz 1977). The problem of verifiability renders structuralism completely unacceptable to the scientistic school and is difficult even for the more tolerant. Logical argumentation is a valid process in the accumulation of knowledge and can contribute toward explanation, but it must be exercised only with a conscious realization of our own biases (Leone 1982). Pursued from slightly different empathetic perceptions, any given case might well result in alternative interpretations that could be demonstrated with equal plausibility. Nevertheless, the structuralist approach is to be encouraged, for it explores areas too long ignored in archaeological studies.*

In its present formulation, however, the structuralist approach is not well designed for the exploration of the past, especially from the perspective of this study. Its primary problem is an inability to deal satisfactorily with time and change. Ian Hodder, the chief proponent of the approach, illustrates it most successfully with ethnographic examples. When the attempt is made to apply it to archaeological data, the contexts are generally synchronic reconstructions; even when two or more sequential contexts are compared, there is little or no attempt to explain the changes that occurred between them (e.g., Hall 1977; Deetz 1977; Wells 1985).

This crucial lack of dynamic historicism has led some recent investigators to turn to Marxism, either in concert with structuralism as the structural-Marxists (e.g., Tilley 1981; Leone 1982; Miller and Tilley 1984) or in the purer form of neo-Marxism (e.g., Conrad and Demarest 1984, pp. 212–215). Although in both cases the approach has been apoliticized, Marxism is a very loaded concept to introduce into the theoretical melee. In any case, it certainly appears to be too restrictive for general archaeological theory and really is appropriate only for the study of complex sociocultural contexts. The important point for present consideration is these scholars' recognition that if a structuralist approach is to be useful in archaeology it must be combined with historicism.

In a recent article, James Deetz (1983) made exactly the same point. Although basically a structuralist, he acknowledged that a "dose of historiography" is a necessary complement. But most importantly of all, he argued eloquently for a paradigmatic pluralism that would include a scientistic component. He, too, seeks the larger patterns that are the goal of all cultural scientists, even if they are arrived at by means other than the strict scientific method. Presented in reasonable tones of compromise rather than harsh polemic, his plea

---

* Conceptual or symbolic matters were studied from the very beginning of professional archaeology in this country (e.g., Squier and Davis 1848; Squier 1851) and continued as a legitimate field of inquiry well into this century.

falls on the sympathetic ears of this writer. There appears to be little profit in an exclusive approach: the ideal goals of scientistic archaeology, at the one extreme, or structural archaeology, at the other, are probably equally elusive. In any event, if we are ever to make progress in interpreting the past we must be free to adopt any philosophical attitude and employ every theoretical or methodological device that would seem appropriate to the objectives and data of a specific problem, mindful all the while of their individual inadequacies as well as strengths. The complexities of the archaeological record "negate the sharp distinctions that archaeologists have drawn between inductive and deductive approaches and between the explanation of specific historical sequences and the elaboration of theories of human behavior and sociocultural process" (Trigger 1984, p. 295). To draw any philosophical or theoretical boundaries around the problems that we face is to constrict the size of the window that we open to the past.

All of the above has been presented to acknowledge that the philosophical stance in these pages is oriented more toward humanism and historicism than scientism. This stance is to be understood neither as a rejection of the scientistic approach to archaeology nor as a merely reactionary position, but as a conscious selection of what appear to be the appropriate theoretical positions and methodological procedures for achieving the goals set forth for this study. The overall approach taken here is eclectic. It draws from traditional archaeology an empirical concern with the reconstruction of culture history and past lifeways, it shares with structural archaeology the search for internal explanatory factors, but it also accepts from scientistic archaeology the premise that the ultimate goal is pattern recognition and processual interpretation. It may be inductive and particularistically synthetic, but if it fails to suggest larger patterns and processes of relevance, and hence hypotheses to be tested deductively, then it has not served its purpose. The idiography is a means to nomothetic ends: in order to generalize, it is first necessary to particularize (Hickerson 1970, p. 7; Trigger 1982, p. 14). Thus, this study emphasizes historicism and humanism but does not deny scientism. This position is clearly stated by Trigger (1984, p. 289):

The understanding, within the limits that archaeological data will permit, of what has happened to specific groups of people in the past is a matter of great humanistic as well as scientific interest.

And it is confirmed by Nadel (1953, p. 200):

Yet that all explanations, from whichever point they start, should converge, that they should be compatible and build up the "scheme of reality at large"—this is the ideal (and postulate) of scientific understanding.

Culture Contact and Change

This volume presents an archaeological case study of the acculturation of one American Indian group from prehistoric times to the modern era. The particular purpose is to investigate the consequences of European-Indian contact, specifically the impact of the Euroamericans* and their cultural traditions upon the Tunica. Although the terms "culture contact" and "culture change" are used in these pages, it is essential to remember that it is people who were in contact and who effected the changes.

The Tunica have successfully adapted to changing circumstances and have survived. Their survival makes it important to plot the actual course of change. This is not a study of cultural evolution (or neoevolution), a now overextended concept. In fact, parts of the sequence described in later pages could even be termed devolution, although that concept does not sufficiently encompass the situation either. It is simpler and more accurate to refer only to culture change, which may be neither consistent nor directional. Nor, therefore, is it predictable.

If there is one universal law, it is that things do change. As a result, every sequence of culture change must be documented and interpreted with the objective of identifying those individual processes that might ultimately be found to have predictive value. This study of the Tunica seeks to expose such a sequence in its historical and archaeological particulars. Although the focus is on a single sequence of change, the goal is to establish useful generalizations for multilineal models of culture change even within a culture area (cf. Steward 1955). Important questions are whether the change occurred gradually and continuously or in brief, distinct episodes, and whether external or internal stimuli were responsible. Consideration of the former question requires the dimension of time available only in archaeological and historical data, while the latter requires the discrimination of causal factors and processes of change.

The identification, measure, and interpretation of culture change generally have been considered within the basic dynamic categories of migration, diffusion, and independent invention (see Wauchope 1956; Spicer 1961; and Trigger 1968, pp. 39–46, for systems of classification distinguishing types of contact and change within these categories). Through a case study of culture contact between an indigenous ethnic group and intrusive sociocultural systems, it will be demonstrated in these pages that many of the causes and processes of change were due to external stimuli that include the movements of peoples and the diffusion of ideas. But it will also be argued that internal principles of adaptation were a profound force in shaping the actual course of change. The purpose here will be to identify those stimuli, whether internal or external in derivation, that appear to have been operative in a particular context, and to reveal the resulting processes of change.

Culture change that is stimulated primarily by strong and continuing external influence from another sociocultural context often follows a course referred to in the anthropological literature as "acculturation" (e.g., Redfield, Linton, and Herskovitz 1936; Herskovitz 1938; Linton 1940; SSRC 1954; Vogt 1957; Spicer 1958, 1961, 1962; Foster 1960; Beals 1962; Walker 1972; Bee 1974, pp. 94–119; Padilla 1980; Tollefson 1984). The inaugural article by Redfield, Linton, and Herskovitz (1936) provided the core definition of acculturation (ibid., pp. 146–150): "Acculturation comprehends those phenomena which result when groups of individuals having different cultures come into continuous first-hand contact, with subsequent changes in the original cultural patterns of either or both groups." Later researchers generally have followed this definition with varying degrees of modification.

In 1953 the Social Science Research Council (SSRC) Summer Seminar on Acculturation confirmed the basic premise that acculturation is "culture change as it is generated by culture contact" and emphasized that it is "initiated by the conjunction of two or more autonomous cultural systems" (SSRC 1954, p. 974). The latter emphasis reflects an important shift in focus. For Redfield and his colleagues the culture trait was the unit of analysis for determining acculturation: traits were transferred from one group to another and, passing through a cultural filter, were accepted, rejected, or modified. The SSRC formulation, however, replaced culture traits with cultural systems as the unit of analysis. Thus, the very nature of the autonomous cultural systems involved in the contact situations was of primary importance. Systems were analyzed in terms of their "openness" versus "closedness," their "rigidity" versus "flexibility," and their overall ability to adapt under conditions of change. While separately each unit of analysis has obvious limitations, a consideration of both would be useful in acculturation studies. In other words, the transmission and integration of traits must be analyzed within the structural context of the participating sociocultural systems.

Since acculturation is defined as culture change that takes place when two peoples possessed of significantly different cultures live in long and intimate contact with each other, it has been assumed by most students that both peoples are affected by the acculturative process. This is most certainly true, although the degree of reciprocity may be unequal. For many scholars a complete acculturation study therefore must include the changes that occurred in both participating groups. It may be recalled, however, that Redfield, Linton, and Herskovitz's original definition specified that the changes could

---

* As used here, the term "Euroamerican" refers to peoples of European origin and their descendants in North America.

occur in "either or both groups," although the authors did assume a two-way process.

In fact, most acculturation studies have been concerned with the contact of Europeans and nonliterate peoples in Oceania, subsaharan Africa, or aboriginal America during the period of the European discovery of the world. In most if not all of these instances, the Europeans (or their heirs) assumed a dominant position over the contacted populations. The domination was primarily technological, and the technology was commanded by sophisticated sociopolitical, military, economic, and even religious organizations that could at times force changes upon the native peoples with whom they were in contact. From this position of dominance, the intruders were able to be more selective in controlling deviations from their own sociocultural traditions. Their position was reinforced by their advantage of unusual mobility, which allowed them to "reacculturate" by maintaining close connections with their own traditions and constantly restoring their cultural purity. As a result, while the European populations certainly experienced varying degrees of culture change in contact situations, it was invariably the contacted peoples who experienced the most change. This inequality of relationship and difference in the degree of ultimate change is what is meant by acculturation in these pages (see also Drucker 1958, p. 4; Foster 1960, p. 7; Berry 1980, p. 10; but compare Jennings 1976, p. 13, and Waselkov and Paul 1981).*

In acculturation as understood here, it is the contacted, subordinated peoples who generally present the more dynamic examples of the processes and results of culture change and who therefore tend to become the focus of case studies. In these pages, the focus will be on Tunica acculturation to the prevailing Euroamerican systems acting upon them through time. The presence of the Euroamericans and their role in this process are acknowledged and analyzed, but the changes that they, too, experienced are not.

Given this focus, it might seem simpler to avoid the use of the term acculturation altogether and to refer only to culture change as manifested by the degree to which the Tunica sociocultural system was modified by the infusion and acceptance of foreign (Euroamerican) elements. Such a perspective, however, does not specify the conditions and dynamics of acculturation that are so important to understanding the story of Tunica survival. This archaeological study of culture change therefore incorporates the following three criteria of acculturation:

1. Conditions for change that were brought about by prolonged and continuous contact between the Tunica and the generally more dominant Euroamerican sociocultural systems.

2. Continuous processes of dynamic interaction that resulted in the transference and integration (adoption and/or adaptation) of elements from the dominant systems to the Tunica.
3. Successful completion by the Tunica of an acculturative sequence from the precontact period to the present, all the while preserving some of their ethnicity.

We term this process "successful" because despite its often negative impacts, acculturation represents survival.

The principal problem with most acculturation studies is that they were intended to be applied to living peoples. Many criteria, therefore, especially those dealing with individual and psychological acculturation, are inappropriate for archaeological data. Since most acculturation studies have concentrated on living sociocultural contexts, they generally have been synchronically oriented and have lacked historical depth. For this reason, acculturation is usually studied as a condition—a result rather than a process—although in theory ongoing processes may be observed. Only when a significant temporal dimension has been introduced will the significant processes of acculturative change be revealed. It is, of course, the dimension of time that is archaeology's main contribution to acculturation studies.

The consideration of culture change, including acculturation, has been a major focus of archaeological study (e.g., Williams 1966; Brown 1979a; Wells 1980; Waselkov and Paul 1981; Hobler 1986). The ability of archaeology to provide the dimension of time along which a sequence of culture change may be measured makes it a unique laboratory for the exposition of processes as well as results. But although archaeology does add a historical perspective to the subject, the data are limited in quality and explicitness (SSRC 1954, p. 995). As noted, many of the criteria of acculturation studies cannot reasonably be applied in archaeological cases. Therefore, criteria must be selected that can be fulfilled with archaeological data. These data are confined primarily to material remains, of course, and they must be identifiable and measurable.

The basic problem is the archaeological identification of a sociocultural continuum, which must be established before change may be documented by comparing segments of the continuity. In this case, the continuity is that of a particular group through time. It is therefore necessary to identify ethnicity in the historical and archaeological records. Fortunately, the Tunica are explicitly mentioned in the contemporary historical documentation, and it is possible to place them with reasonable geographical accuracy at closely bounded locales through time. For a study of culture change and acculturation to be based on fact, however, and not on speculation, it is necessary to identify specific archaeological contexts at each of those locations.

It is probable that in the absence of documentary evidence most cases of ethnicity would be difficult to verify archaeologically: they would appear primarily as distinctions of wealth, status, and other indications of social class. But the stark contrasts between the varied native cultural traditions of the eighteenth century, many

* Examples of contact between sociocultural systems manifesting relatively equal interaction and transmission of traits and resulting in similar levels of change are referred to as "transculturation" (for use of the term see Malinowski 1945; Ortiz 1947; Beals 1962; Rouse 1962; cf. "transculturation" as used by Hallowell 1963).

of which were still relatively intact, promise the possibility of archaeological identifications. This is especially true of the Tunica, who intruded into a number of different contexts and may be recognized in each case by distinctive assemblages of material culture. The difficulties and potential pitfalls of identifying ethnicity from material culture remains alone are an acknowledged problem. With sufficient historical controls and the establishment of a matching archaeological continuum, however, identification becomes solidly grounded in the known facts and provides a sufficient base from which to proceed.

Material culture remains also provide primary data, again in concert with historical documentation, for the measurement as well as identification of culture change. But differences in material culture do not reflect the whole story of change in a given continuum (Brown 1979c, 1979d), especially in the more severe form of change referred to in these pages as acculturation. That changes were occurring in other sociocultural spheres is assumed, but a close correspondence between changes in material culture and other nonmaterial patterns cannot be expected as a general rule. The manifestation and effects of an innovation must have been quite variable; nevertheless, study of material culture may produce a rough measure of the degree of acculturation that has occurred in a given case (Brain 1979, pp. 270–274). Interpretation of some of the processes of change, however, requires the identification and measure not only of material culture traits, but also of their integration and context within the cultural system (Redfield, Linton, and Herskovits 1936 vs. SSRC 1954). These are archaeological problems that must be explored. In the next section, it will be argued that the best way to explore them is within the conceptual framework of ethnohistoric archaeology.

Ethnohistoric Archaeology

"Ethnohistoric archaeology" is the nomenclature adopted here to identify the archaeology of the American Indian during the historic period. It is an approach designed for archaeological research but which incorporates historical and ethnohistorical, as well as archaeological, data and methodologies in the exploration of the past. These various components and their conjunction in ethnohistoric archaeology must be described before the approach is applied to the case of the Tunica.

For general purposes, archaeology may be defined here as the recovery and analysis of material remains of past human activities, and the interpretation of the behavior that may explain them. It is not "ethnography with a handicap of time" (Simmons 1970, pp. xvii–xviii), for it cannot pretend to acquire the intimate detail of nonmaterial aspects of the past that the ethnographic present offers, and it has as its greatest advantage the perspective of time. While synchronic reconstructions are suitable objectives in archaeological research and ethnographic analogies are important interpretive devices, as discussed below, it is the diachronic study of the past that best utilizes the potential of archaeological data and methodologies.

Archaeology shares the perspective of time with history. But the study of history, or historiography, attains through its documentary data base some measure of the intimacy of ethnography. The combination of the two disciplines in historical archaeology is therefore obvious and desirable (Leone 1972, p. 26; Dymond 1974, p. 99; McKay 1976), especially when contemporary historical and archaeological data may be closely related. In prehistoric—or ahistoric—archaeology, studies result largely in hypothetical developments and conjectural reconstructions. In historical archaeology, however, the addition of documentary details can mitigate the conjectures and strengthen the hypotheses if the archaeological context can be sufficiently identified with the historical information. Historical archaeology tends to focus on the idiographic. This focus does not mean that historical archaeologists must eschew a scientific approach (South 1976), but it also does not mean that they must apologize for achieving historical goals.

Historical archaeology may be minimally defined as "archaeology carried out on sites of the historic period" (South 1976, p. 25). Since this definition could be understood to include classical archaeology, egyptology, sinology, and so forth, it would be more appropriate for our considerations to restrict the field to "the archaeology of the spread of European culture throughout the world since the fifteenth century and its impact on indigenous peoples" (Deetz 1977, p. 5; see also Schuyler 1970). There are scholars in North America who would ignore indigenous peoples and limit the study to Europeans and their genetic heirs, or at least to those who recorded their own history (e.g., Noël Hume 1970,

p. 6). This is not the sense adopted here, but it reflects a schism that exists within the field.

Historical archaeology as practiced in this country is essentially a development of the past fifty years, and it has gained maturity only in more recent decades. Its official founding was in Euroamerican studies, and it was viewed as an auxiliary to historical research (Harrington 1955). Concurrently but quite independently, however, an interest in the protohistoric and historic archaeology of the American Indian developed within anthropology. The resulting arguments over whether historical archaeology is history or anthropology, and whether it deals with the Euroamerican or the Indian, have raised acrimonious debates (e.g., see the series of dialogues published in the journal *The Conference on Historic Site Archaeology Papers*, especially vol. 2, part 2 [South 1968]).

Although it is accepted here that both Euroamericans and Indians quite properly are subjects of historical archaeology within the broader definitions given above (see also Fontana 1965), it is important to distinguish between them not only because of the separate disciplinary backgrounds drawn upon to study them but also because of the fundamentally different data bases, procedures, and objectives used. This dichotomy is not exclusive, nor is it a denial of the sort of rapprochement of data bases, procedures, and objectives explored further below. It merely serves to recognize where historical archaeology has come from and where it might be going, and most of all that there is more than one way to do it—just as in the mother disciplines it serves.

The practice of historical archaeology in North America is defined here as a field of study concerned with two kinds of archaeological contexts (Williams 1962): those of the Euroamericans who were capable of recording their own histories, and those of peoples—in most cases Indian—who had significant contacts with literate Europeans and for whom relevant historical documentation therefore may exist, although it was essentially recorded by others. While both subfields share the same spatial and temporal dimensions and often overlap in the research goals of particular projects, they are distinguished by their intellectual traditions and modes of operation as well as their focus on culturally different human subjects.

The first subfield has been identified as "historic sites archaeology" (Harrington 1952; Larrabee 1969, p. 70; Schuyler 1970, p. 84; Orser 1979b). Founded in historical studies, it is often subdivided into categories differentiated according to historic episodes: colonial, frontier, industrial, and so forth. As a handmaiden to history, historic sites archaeology strives to add another dimension to the study of the Euroamerican past in this hemisphere. Such studies must be conducted with due consideration of the methods as well as objectives of the respective disciplines. This is a crucial point. Historical archaeology is a field in which the research methods of the historian are combined with those of the archaeologist. In historic sites archaeology the task is made somewhat easier because researchers are usually empathetic to their own historical backgrounds, but to be truly successful that researcher must understand the methods of both historiography and archaeology. Thus, historical archaeology should not be conceived simply as archaeology carried out on sites of the historic period but rather should require the use and critical evaluation of historical documentation in the course of archaeological procedures (cf. Wilson 1975; South 1976).

In the second subfield of historical archaeology, the use and evaluation of written documents becomes even more critical, and thus for procedural as well as substantive purposes it seems important to make the distinction. The subject is the American Indian, but the relevant historical documentation is contained almost exclusively within records prepared by Euroamericans. There is a great difference between the content and interpretation of documents written within a cultural tradition and those that describe another (Trigger 1982, pp. 14–15). This brings us to the consideration of ethnohistory.

Ethnohistory is a method for dealing with the problem of using and interpreting historical documents that were written by people who recorded, purposefully or not, data about another people of different cultural tradition. Certain biases are inherent in most records written about one's own people, and it may be anticipated that even more distortion will occur when others are the subject. The presence of the cultural filter in the recording process logically requires a cultural refiltering in the interpretation. This translation process is embodied in the concept of ethnohistory, and its techniques have been consolidated in what is known as the ethnohistorical approach.

The ethnohistorical approach initially was formulated to deal with the vast corpus of Euroamerican documentation about the American Indian and has subsequently embraced a worldwide domain. As characterized by Mildred Wedel, the basic methodology is "the investigation of written records that, first, have been critically examined and evaluated in order to determine their kind and degree of validity and that, secondly, are then viewed with the insights of one knowledgeable in anthropology" (Wedel and DeMallie 1980, p. 110). Ethnohistory, then, is not simply a melding of ethnology and history but represents a more basic interface between ethnography and historiography: it is the historical study of those usually studied by anthropologists and who have no recorded past of their own (Dorson 1961, p. 16; Washburn 1961, p. 31; Sturtevant 1966, p. 6; Hudson 1966, p. 53; Wedel 1976, p. 3; Wedel 1979, p. 183; Wedel 1981, p. 2). It is a methodology for extracting ethnic and cultural information from historical documents, although the documents originally may not have been intended to convey such information.

In the above definition of ethnohistory,* ethnographers do their own historiography. The evidence is derived not from personal observation but from what others—and they not even anthropologists—have learned and documented about nonliterate indigenous peoples. Although ethnohistorical studies can be, and have been, undertaken in Euroamerican contexts (e.g., Lurie 1961; Sturtevant 1966; Dobyns 1972; Brown 1974; Adams 1974, 1976; Handler and Lange 1978), generally the investigations of such contexts are left to the fields of sociology, social history, and history, in which the particular insight of the ethnologist is not necessary. The distinctions between these fields, each of which requires special methods and awareness, are crucial. As summed up by Bruce Trigger (1982, p. 3),

[ethnohistory] has developed as the study of change among indigenous peoples, as opposed to history, which studies the activities of Europeans both before and after they settled elsewhere in the world. This distinction can be rationalized as a methodological one. The techniques that are required to study the history [of] nonliterate groups are different from those needed to study more complex societies that have abundantly documented their own past.

But, as Trigger has also indicated, ethnohistory is more than a methodology. Its objectives are determined by the respective data bases brought to bear upon the subject of nonliterate societies. An ethnohistorical study is characterized by a perspective that employs both the synchronic sensitivity of ethnography and the diachronic dimensions of historiography as applied to a particular group of people (Dark 1957, pp. 233, 251). The objective is "a cultural and/or historical study of an ethnic group as a whole (or a study of some aspect of that culture or history) either at a particular point in time or through a period of years that may extend into centuries" (Wedel and DeMallie 1980, p. 110). Although synchronic reconstructions are important, the emphasis of ethnohistory is usually on diachronic patternings of change within a sociocultural continuum (e.g., Hickerson 1970, p. 7; Euler 1972; Schwerin 1976; Axtell 1981, p. 5; Wedel 1982). This emphasis reflects the origins of ethnohistory in acculturation studies of the 1930s (Keesing 1939; Trigger 1982, p. 4) and the development of the "direct historical approach" (Baerreis 1961; Sturtevant 1966, p. 9; Wedel and DeMallie 1980, p. 112). The latter technique, however, was created by archaeologists for specifically archaeological problems. It will be discussed below and is mentioned here only to establish its intimate relationship with ethnohistory (Galloway 1986).

None of the original basic definitions of ethnohistory cited above includes archaeology as a necessary component (see also Wheeler-Voegelin 1954; Fenton 1966; Carmack 1972; Euler 1972; Schwerin 1976; Orser 1979a, 1979b; Axtell 1981; Trigger 1982). When archaeology is mentioned, it is generally relegated to a supporting role (Trigger 1982, p. 12). "This is purposeful because while archaeology is often serviced by the same sources

---

* Note that ethnohistory is not defined here in the sense of a people's own beliefs about their past, which constitute oral tradition or folk history (Hudson 1966), although such data can be used in ethnohistorical research.

that service ethnohistory (as when documents make the archaeological reconstruction more complete) and while ethnohistories themselves are often used as sources of analogs in archaeological interpretation, the relationship is not critical. Ethnohistory exists as a methodology completely independent of archaeology" (White 1977, pp. 103–104; see also Wedel 1977, p. 8). In those studies in which ethnohistory and archaeology intersect, however, an exciting meeting not only of data but also of methodologies and, ultimately, results may be anticipated. When, as in this study, the primary data are archaeological but an ethnohistorical approach is still taken, the combination may be defined as the ethnohistorical approach to archaeology, or simply "ethnohistoric archaeology" (Baerreis 1961; Hickerson 1970, p. 20; Brain, Toth, and Rodriguez-Buckingham 1974; Spector 1977; Brown 1977, p. 166; Blitz 1985, p. 46).

The utilization of ethnohistorical data in archaeological studies is not new (Eggan 1952). It was first formalized in the direct historical approach which, however, confined itself to identifying historic ethnic groups with prehistoric archaeological sites (Judd 1929; Swanton 1932; Stirling 1932, 1940; Collins 1932a, 1932b; Ford 1936; Wedel 1938, 1940; Strong 1940; Steward 1942). Although such an objective is obviously worthy, it does not fully realize the potential of the approach (Wedel 1977, p. 7). Bridging history and prehistory, ethnohistory and archaeology, the direct historical approach can serve two very useful purposes. First, it can establish an ethnic continuum, and, second, it can identify a base for that continuum in the prehistoric record. Primary analogies may then be used to help reconstruct and interpret aspects of that record. These are all valid and valuable applications of ethnohistorical data to archaeological studies.

The concept of ethnohistoric archaeology, however, involves more. It incorporates the basic procedures of the direct historical approach, as well as its emphasis on ethnic continuity, but it focuses on tracing that continuity through time, following the course of culture change as revealed in the archaeological, ethnographic, and historical records. Such a conjunctive and diachronic approach to a dynamic continuity offers the best prospect for ascertaining patterns of change and the processes behind those patterns. But it is the methodology for achieving these goals that constitutes the raison d'être for the concept of ethnohistoric archaeology.

Methodologically, ethnohistoric archaeology is not a simple matter of meshing ethnohistorical and archaeological data sets (Wedel 1976; Carmack and Weeks 1981). It is conceived as a more sophisticated multidisciplinary integration of both the data and methodologies of ethnography, historiography, and archaeology (Brain, Toth, and Rodriguez-Buckingham 1974, p. 284). The procedure brings to bear all the relevant data—that is, the most reliable data as finally adjudged through critical evaluation. Ideally, the data sets should complement one another, and they should match frequently enough to confirm that they are derived from the same sociocultural context. Irregularities in correlations between data sets also will occur, and these apparent contradictions must be reconciled. Achieving these ends

requires the various methodologies to be understood at least to the extent that the pitfall of naively using spurious data is avoided. In this way, the multidisciplinary conjunction of data and methodologies illuminates and corrects the past, so that interpretations can provide more accurate and comprehensive reconstructions of lifeways and processes of change.

Such a multidisciplinary study of the past has been advocated at least since the direct historical approach was formally articulated (Steward 1942, p. 341). Many archaeologists subsequently have described similar conjunctive studies but have not formalized them (e.g., Krause 1944, p. 304; Laguna 1960, p. 200; Williams 1962, 1966; Krause 1972, p. 106; Adams 1974; Spector 1974, pp. 2–8; Spector 1975, p. 270; Kutsche, Van Ness, and Smith 1976; Mainfort 1979, p. 313; Willis 1980; Carmack and Weeks 1981; Tong 1982; Mason 1985; Fitzhugh 1985, pp. 2–5; Kilmarx 1985). Others have discussed such studies under a broad definition of ethnohistory (Euler 1972; Handler and Lange 1978, p. 221; Axtell 1981, p. 7). At least one ethnohistorian (Wedel 1976, pp. 7–12, 23–26, 32), however, recognizes the distinction between archaeology and the stricter definition of ethnohistory followed here and recommends "blending" the two for certain studies, although she refers to the conjunction as "ethnoarchaeology" (Wedel and DeMallie 1980, p. 111). Many archaeologists have adopted this nomenclature for the concept (e.g., Bauxar 1957; Oswalt and VanStone 1967; James and Lindsay 1973; Gregory 1973; Townsend 1974; Stanislawski 1974; Adams 1976; Bishop and Ray 1976). This is not the meaning of ethnoarchaeology as defined by most other archaeologists, however, and it is important to make the distinction since ethnoarchaeology, as described below, is a perfectly valid procedure in its own right and should not be confused with other approaches (White 1977).

In ethnoarchaeology as it is generally understood—also sometimes known as "living" or "action" archaeology (but not to be confused with "experimental" archaeology)—the archaeologist does ethnography for purposes of archaeological interpretation (Gould 1974, 1978, 1980, 1985). It is a procedure as old as archaeology itself, the novelty being that the archaeologist is involved firsthand with the gathering of ethnographic data for the generation of appropriate analogs. The overall goal is to document correlations between patterns of human behavior and material culture in a present ethnographic context in order to provide inferences for reconstructing past behavior from archaeological material remains (Donnan and Clewlow 1974; Ackerman and Ackerman 1974; Binford 1978; Kramer 1979; Hodder 1982a; Gould and Watson 1982; Krause 1985). The inferences most often take the form of secondary analogy, or comparisons between similar cultures in similar environmental situations (e.g., Watson 1979, p. 277), although some researchers would limit the procedure to primary analogies within a single archaeological-historical continuum (Oswalt 1974, p. 3; Gould 1985, p. 643). This latter practice comes close to the concept of ethnohistoric archaeology, except that the emphasis is on ethnographic data alone and the principal objective is the development of ethnographic analogies for

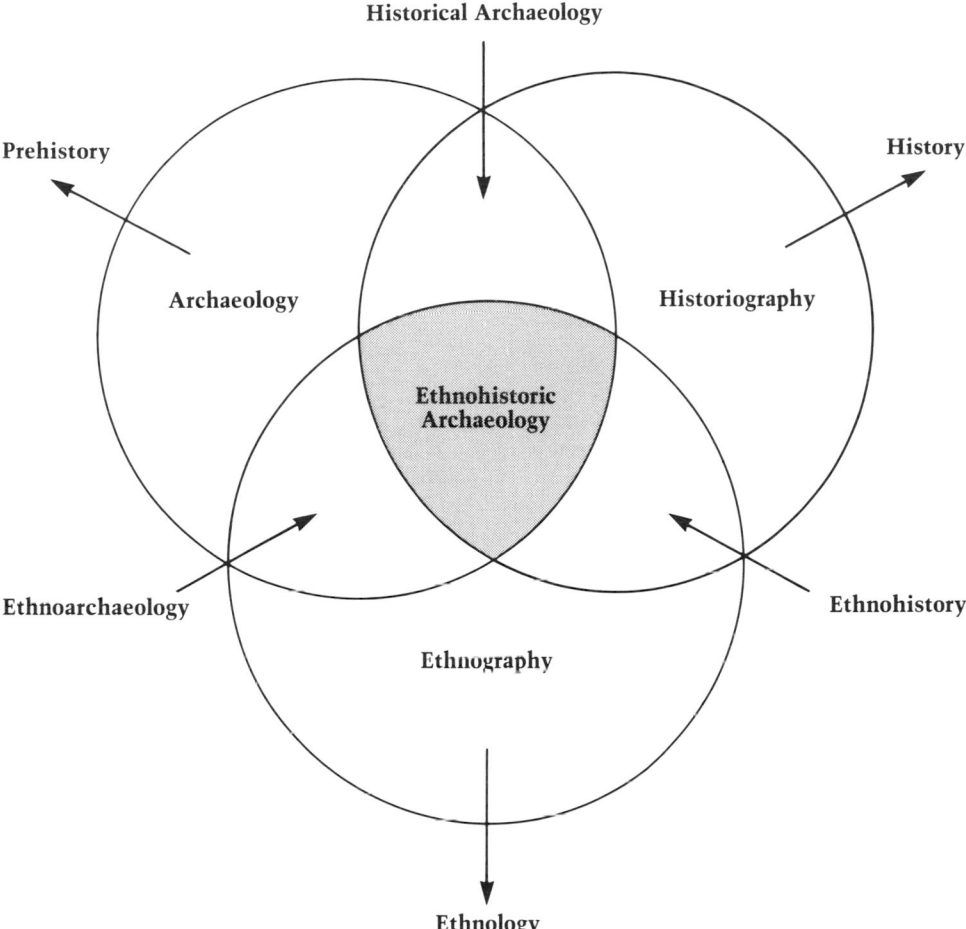

Figure 1. The position of ethnohistoric archaeology in the study of the past (adapted from Brain, Toth, and Rodriguez-Buck-ingham 1974, fig. 1; cf. Adams 1974, fig. 2, and Adams 1976, fig. 54 for similar but significantly different representations.

interpretive purposes. This approach is, indeed, a perfectly valid independent procedure for archaeological interpretation, equivalent to ethnohistory and the analogies of the direct historical approach—and like them, ethnoarchaeology may be comfortably encompassed within the concept of ethnohistoric archaeology.*

Since ethnohistoric archaeology has already been included in ethnohistory, on the one hand, and in ethnoarchaeology, on the other, it might reasonably be asked why we do not simply leave the concept within a broad definition of one or the other and refrain from cluttering up our terminology still further. The answer is best given with reference to figure 1. Although in a schematic representation lines are drawn more sharply than is ever the case in reality, the illustration nevertheless serves to distinguish the relative positions of the multidisciplinary fields of study: ethnoarchaeology, ethnohistory, and historical archaeology. Only at the

interface between these—an interface that really represents a conjunction of the primary disciplines of ethnography, historiography, and archaeology—does ethnohistoric archaeology exist. Recognition of this conjunction allows the formulation of more precise definitions of ethnohistory, ethnoarchaeology, and historical archaeology, and makes explicit the distinctive character of each of these approaches, as well as the nature of the analytical links between them. As a synthetic conjunctive approach that is both flexible and selective in the choice of methodologies and data sets, ethnohistoric archaeology is a powerful tool with which to explore the past.

Ethnohistoric archaeology, then, is defined as a purposeful conjunction of the data and methodologies derived from ethnography, historiography, and archaeology. (Although membership in the union is theoretically equal, it must be acknowledged that archaeology plays the central role in this study.) The approach is further defined by a focus on specific ethnic groups and the attempt to trace the synchronic and diachronic patterns that characterize those peoples through time, with particular emphasis on discovering the dynamic processes of culture change.

---

* Ethnoarchaeology plays a minor role in this study, however, because the present Tunica are so acculturated that few analogies may be suitably applied to archaeological data some centuries removed.

Procedure

In the following pages, the program and results of this study of Tunica archaeology are described. The impetus to the whole research project was the "Tunica Treasure" (Brain 1979), a remarkable collection that established an archaeological datum for the Tunica of the mid-eighteenth century. Although it was recognized as a valuable synchronic point of reference, its real value is as a stage in the diachronic study of culture contact and change. Such a study obviously requires data from more than one stage, and so the research focused on tracing the Tunica back into prehistory and forward to the modern era. A combination of data bases is used to reconstruct stages along this continuum, but the heart of the volume consists of a series of archaeological site reports.

The emphasis on archaeology represents not only the bias of the author and the major contribution of this report but the central premise that only archaeology can provide the continuity for tracing the entire course of culture change experienced by an indigenous ethnic group. Such an archaeological continuum violates historical boundaries in the study of its subjects and enters the prehistoric past. Where the historian sees only dichotomy between prehistory and history, the archaeologist seeks continuity. Prehistory and history are but two aspects of the study of a native people who, unlike the European intruders, have inhabited both domains. Although the focus in this volume is on the period of early European contact, the events of this period cannot be studied adequately without the best possible knowledge of the Tunica's prehistoric background, which provides a comparative base against which the developments of the historic period may be measured.

The primary intent of this volume, then, is to document archaeologically the stages of Tunica acculturation. The objective is to identify a series of Tunica occupations through time and to attempt to recognize the degree of culture change evident in the archaeological record of each occupation. This is, then, an archaeological study of material remains: of artifacts both intrinsic and contextual, of configurations, and ultimately of behavioral patterning. Utilizing ethnohistorical data, the processes behind those patterns will also be explored.

Although this study traces the Tunica from precontact times to the present, its focus is on the eighteenth century, that critical time of transition from American Indian to European sovereignty in the Lower Mississippi Valley for which the archaeological and historical documentation is most extensive. Unlike those studies of acculturation that are concerned with the reciprocal relationships between two or more peoples in contact, the attention here is on the acculturative processes as they may be observed in the history of a single people. The primary objective is to determine how and why the Tunica survived while so many others did not. Was their survival due merely to chance, or to something more fundamental? This question will haunt these pages.

This project became, then, not merely a study of how the Tunica changed but of how they changed in a manner that secured their survival as an ethnic group. Hypothetical solutions require the recognition in the record explored by ethnohistoric archaeology of those attributes that enabled the Tunica to make the right choices, and therefore the necessary changes (whether "right" or not), that contributed to their survival. A basic goal from the beginning was to ferret out a common theme, an underlying ideology that would serve as an explanatory device. It was not assumed that different generations would share the same world view, but it was expected that there would be some continuity between generations.

It is at this level that structuralism could make a modest contribution. The archaeological, historical, and ethnographic records might offer clues that indicate why certain choices were made that determined the processes governing the course of change. The pluralistic and conjunctive approach of ethnohistoric archaeology offers the broadest possible perspective for structural studies through the integration of the archaeological data with contemporary documentation and/or primary ethnographic analogy (Brown 1974; Schwerin 1976; Gould 1980; Carmack and Weeks 1981; Hodder 1982a). Moreover, the focus on a single sociocultural continuum can control variables and identify those internal structural characteristics that are enduring and thus presumably of fundamental significance. It is this search for what Deetz (1983, pp. 28–29) calls the "deeper organizing principles" or "internal dynamics" of a people that constitutes the limited structural approach adopted in these pages. To be successful, there must be a strong emphasis on the historical, the particular, and the contextual.

This study may be characterized as historicist, particularist, contextual, and structural. But it is above all a humanist study, based on this writer's conviction that all research, certainly in the social sciences, should contribute to the overall human welfare: that even arcane archaeological studies should not lose sight of their subjects and should be relevant beyond the confines of the discipline. In order to realize this basic humanitarian ideal, it is necessary to isolate, describe, and explicate those phenomena that reflect the most salient aspects of a people in any given context and relate them to the larger community of mankind. The reason for the multidisciplinary approach is to elucidate in as much detail as possible, and interpret as powerfully as possible, the history of that people and their place in the overall human continuum. Ethnohistoric archaeology encompasses all of the traditionally defined concepts for exploring the past and thereby achieves a functional link in the broad narrative of a people's history.

The particularly satisfying aspect of this research is its relevance to the modern-day Tunica, who not only have maintained their ethnicity but also have expressed a great interest in their past (Butler 1978). In tribute to their interest, the major objective of this study is a reconstruction of the Tunica's odyssey through time and space. It is hoped that the particularism exposed here will not be "trivial, uninteresting, and boring" (Binford 1976, p. xi). In fact, it is anticipated that the insights derived from this study will have a larger significance (Hickerson 1970, p. 7; McKay 1976; Trigger 1982, p. 14): that although the particulars will differ, both the approach utilized and the interpretations made regarding the Tunica will prove useful in other studies. Or, as already simply stated by Philip Phillips (1955, p. 247):

Thus, paradoxically, archaeology in the service of anthropology, concerning itself necessarily with the position of unique events in space and time, has for its ultimate purpose the discovery of regularities that are in a sense spaceless and timeless.

This study is presented in three parts. Part 1 establishes the historical identity of the Tunica and constructs a chronology from the documentation. It places the Tunica through time as they moved from one locale to another, and will be found to agree well with the archaeological evidence presented in part 2. Part 2, in turn, describes new data that constitute the foundation and major contribution of this study. The presentation illustrates a simple example of the direct historical approach as the archaeological record is traced backward in time along the already established historic continuum. It also presents the detail that identifies the Tunica archaeologically and that elucidates particulars of their past not available in the historical literature.

The data of parts 1 and 2 are brought together in part 3 to establish a series of synchronic episodes that reconstruct Tunica lifeways at various stages through time. It is in the comparison of these synchronic units in sequence that the diachronic trends become evident. The relationships within these trends characterize the dynamic aspects of the continuum and provide some clues for the interpretation of Tunica survival.

Part One: Historical Background

The importance of studying the archaeology of more recent documented periods is partly that coordination with historical statements gives a far more detailed, truly absolute time-scale than prehistory will ever achieve in its "text-free" innocence.

Dymond 1974, p. 83

A basic objective and necessity of archaeological research is to order the data in proper chronological sequence. Because the archaeology of the historic period has the advantage of an independently determined chronology, the European calendar, the archaeological record need only be identified with the historical. That crucial correlation will be demonstrated in part 2 of this study. First, however, the historical datum must be established. In the following pages, the historical presence of the Tunica will be identified, and the tribe will be placed at various locales through time.

The Tunica were one of the more important historic tribes in the Lower Mississippi Valley. Not only were they among the larger and better organized of the valley tribes, they also had a curious history of migrating from place to place at irregular intervals. The scale of these movements, and their identification with historic events, was of sufficient magnitude to suggest that the Tunica could provide a firm reference point and integrating factor for the protohistoric and historic archaeology of the valley, as well as a study of acculturation under widely differing circumstances.

The several migrations of the Tunica, and the tribe's intermediate places of settlement, were known historical and ethnohistorical facts when the project began. Before it was refined and confirmed archaeologically, the following sequence of events could be reconstructed (fig. 2):

- At the time of first European contact, Tunican ancestors lived in the upper Yazoo Basin of northwestern Mississippi, where they were discovered by De Soto in 1541.
- Sometime before 1682, the Tunica moved to the lower Yazoo Basin, where they were found by the French.
- In the first decade of the eighteenth century, the Tunica again moved farther downriver, to the vicinity of the Red River confluence where they resided in several different locations.
- Finally, toward the end of the eighteenth century, the Tunica moved once more, this time across the river to central Louisiana, where some of their descendants live today.

The plan of research described in these pages was formulated with this historical outline as a guide. From the beginning, the objective was to construct a series of vignettes that closely defined in time and space a particular ethnic group, the Tunica, at various stages of acculturation resulting from contact with alien cultures. For such a study to be successful, it obviously is necessary to commence with a critical reanalysis of the historical documentation that will provide a framework for integrating the historical and archaeological data (Galloway 1986).

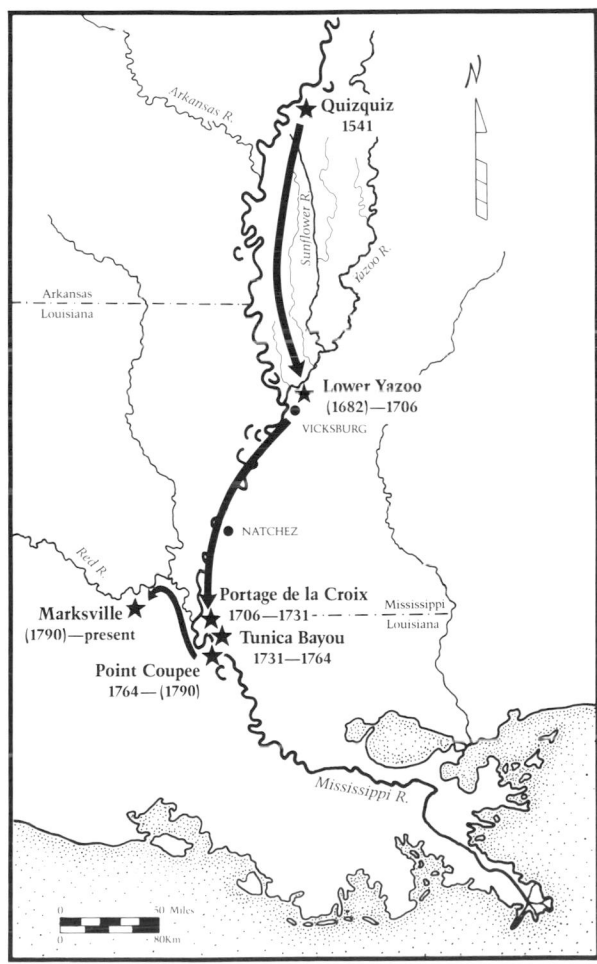

Figure 2. Migrations of the Tunica from northwestern Mississippi to central Louisiana.

Historiographic Overview

Historical documents may be divided into two categories: textual (official histories, reports, memoirs, journals, manifests, inventories, and other written accounts) and graphic (pictorial and cartographic). Both are subject to complex problems of interpretation and require in-depth historiographic analysis.

Before a historical document can be used with any degree of confidence, it is necessary to establish certain facts. The important attributes of a document are the following:

1. Authenticity. It must be ascertained that the document is an authentic work and not fiction, either in whole or in part (this latter discrimination is the most difficult and often the most crucial). It is also necessary to determine whether the document is in its original form or is a copy or some other secondary rendering. It is essential to be aware that plagiarism of texts and maps was a common practice well into the last century.
2. Reliability. The reliability of the reporter and the reportage also must be critically evaluated. The reporter(s) must be identified if at all possible in order to assess both familiarity with the subject and motivations for the report. These considerations obviously affect the nature and accuracy of information contained in the document and determine how that information may be used.

With these criteria in mind, the corpora of texts, maps, and pictures pertinent to this study are reviewed briefly before being employed for substantive or interpretive purposes.

THE TEXTS

Recorded history began in the Lower Mississippi Valley with the sudden appearance of the De Soto entrada in the spring of 1541. The Spaniards traveled within the valley for two more years. Descriptions of the expedition during this period are found in four chronicles: those of Rodrigo Ranjel, Luys Hernandez de Biedma, the anonymous Gentleman of Elvas, and Garcilaso de la Vega. The variable merits and reliabilities of these documents have been examined in depth by many researchers and need not be reviewed here considering their minor role in the story of the Tunica. It is sufficient to note that some useful statistical and descriptive information may be derived from these sources when certain guidelines are followed (e.g., Brain, Toth, and Rodriguez-Buckingham 1974, pp. 239–243). In the present study, the translations of Edward Bourne (1904) were used for Ranjel, Biedma, and Elvas, while Varner and Varner (1951) were followed for Garcilaso, although the text of the original 1723 edition was also consulted.*

The De Soto entrada occasioned the first documentation of the Lower Mississippi Valley and its native inhabitants. This event does not mark the beginning of the fully historic period, however, since it was not repeated. In fact, no further European contact is recorded until the French finally established a continuing presence at the end of the seventeenth century. While European influence (biological, if not cultural) must have occurred during the 130-year interregnum, it is undefined historically. This nebulous period of possible but undocumented contact is referred to here as the protohistoric period.

Marquette and Jolliet, the first Frenchmen on record to have penetrated the Lower Mississippi Valley (French 1850, pp. 279–297; Margry 1879, vol. 1, pp. 253–270), did not venture below the mouth of the Arkansas River. Therefore, although their expedition is of great historical interest as a harbinger of things to come, its contribution to this research is only tangential and is of value primarily for the several maps that place a number of tribal names on the northern frontier of the study area.

The French Dominion in the Lower Mississippi Valley was officially proclaimed in 1682 with the expedition of René Robert Cavalier, Sieur de La Salle. The La Salle papers (French 1846, pp. 45–98; Margry 1879, vol. 1, pp. 433–616; ibid., vol. 2, pp. 181–193, 206–212; Cox 1922; Galloway 1982) are of undoubted historical and ethnohistorical value, although one must beware of a spurious document attributed to Henri de Tonti (1697), entitled *Dernières découvertes dans l'Amérique septentrionale de M. De la Sale; mises au jour par M. le Chevalier Tonti, gouverneur du fort Saint Louis, aux Islinois*. This work, filled with palpable errors and impossible statements, is clearly a fictitious expansion of Tonti's own narrative, but the author has not been identified. In any event, since the 1682 expedition purposely avoided the Tunica, the primary contribution of the La Salle documents to this research is statistical information on tribal locations, as well as general background.

The missionary orders were next on the scene. As a group, the Jesuits generally are excellent sources of ethnohistorical information. They were very interested in native customs, not only religious matters, and made every effort to learn the languages. Usually highly educated by the standards of the day, the Jesuits produced a voluminous and generally reliable body of reportage

---

* Historians have always been leery of Garcilaso, and at least one modern scholar argues that his account is at best a fictionalized elaboration of the other narratives of the expedition (Henige 1987). While Henige's case is impressive, some details in *La Florida* do appear factual. The caveat remains, however: Garcilaso must be used with great care.

(Thwaites 1900). Unfortunately, they were a minor presence in the Lower Mississippi Valley, as is attested by the fact that parts of only four volumes of the seventy-three-volume *Jesuit Relations* (ibid.) are devoted to this area (see also Delanglez 1935). A happy exception was Father Paul du Ru, whose *Journal* (Butler 1934) is a concise, factual account of Pierre LeMoyne d'Iberville's voyage up the Mississippi and contains many observations concerning the native groups that were encountered. But Iberville turned around at the Taensa and so the Tunica were not visited, although their presence was known. Father Gravier is the only Jesuit of record to have visited the Tunica during the early years of contact, but he was preceded by his brothers in Christ, the Seminarians from Quebec (the Recollets). It is thus by the hands and pens of the Seminarians that the first known visits to and descriptive passages about the Tunica were recorded.

The volumes of letters and reports published by John Gilmary Shea (1852, 1861) are our primary source for the Seminarians and their observations. These are for the most part quite reliable and contain much useful descriptive information since the fathers generally were interested in getting to know Indian ways in order to accomplish their work (although statements on religion obviously must be evaluated carefully).

Our potentially most valuable historical source, however, apparently left us nothing. Father Antoine (also known as Albert) Davion maintained a mission among the Tunica off and on for some two decades (Brain 1979, p. 260). Although he was often in Mobile, he spent many years among the tribe, who in turn remembered him fondly. Davion admitted to having difficulty learning their language, but he must have absorbed much about Tunica customs and lifeways as they were at the time of early French contact. Unfortunately, he recorded nothing about his charges. The documents in the Séminaire de Québec that were examined by this author during a visit in 1979 were found to be uninformative (e.g., ibid., app. C.1), and three letters in the Archives du Séminaire des Missions Etrangères in Paris are short, almost illegible, and equally lacking in ethnohistorical detail (Charles O'Neill, S.J., personal communication, 1978). In Mobile the only documentary evidence of Davion is his signature in the baptismal records of the diocese (Richebourg G. McWilliams, personal communication, 1978).

With the single exception of Davion, the missionary effort died out rapidly in the first few years of the eighteenth century. We must turn, therefore, to the lay sector for the bulk of our information from this point on. The explorers, colonists, traders, and administrators—as well as the occasional cleric—in the Lower Mississippi Valley were a varied lot, with equally diverse motivations. Their reports must be evaluated with studied consideration of their backgrounds, positions, and biases.

The principal reporters whose memoirs, journals, and other documents are referred to in this volume are listed chronologically below, according to their periods of activity in Louisiana. Brief comments on the reliability of these personages and their products are included, along with other pertinent information.

Jacques Gravier (1688–1698, 1698–1706, 1708). Father Gravier was a Jesuit missionary in the Illinois country, which was considered a part of Louisiana. In 1700 he made a trip through the Lower Mississippi Valley and visited a number of the native tribes. True to his Jesuit training, he was very observant and recorded details of aboriginal life in his journal (Shea 1861, pp. 115–163).

J.-B. La Source (1698–1699). Considerable confusion surrounds this individual. John Gilmary Shea (1861) misidentified him as the Reverend Dominic Thaumur de La Source, who was only a boy of six in 1699; J.-B. La Source was a lay adult with a different first name (only his initials have survived, but J.-B. usually stood for Jean-Baptiste). All that is known about him is that he accompanied the Seminarians on their first tour of the Lower Mississippi Valley in 1698–1699. Fortunately, he was literate, unusual for a layman of the period, and wrote a letter describing his experiences (ibid., pp. 79–86). He was a keen observer and seems quite reliable.

Pierre LeMoyne d'Iberville (1699–1702). Iberville, the "hero of Hudson Bay," voyaged to Louisiana three times during these years and successfully founded the Louisiana Colony for France. The Iberville journals, kept during all three voyages, are valuable documents for this period of exploration. They contain numerous descriptions of the Indians, their locations, and their customs; there is little information about the Tunica, however, since Iberville himself did not visit them. Iberville also recorded information from his brother, Jean-Baptiste LeMoyne de Bienville, and from Henri de Tonti. Overall, the accuracy and reliability of the journals have withstood the test of time and comparative study. The fine annotated translations of Brasseaux (1979) and McWilliams (1981) are used here.

André Pénicaut (1699–1721). The Pénicaut narrative is especially valuable because of the author's widespread activities during the first decades of the colony. A firsthand account, its descriptive value is enhanced immeasurably by Pénicaut's aptitude for Indian languages. It must be used with care, however, for it is unreliable statistically, containing errors of chronology. We are fortunate in having available the critically annotated translation by McWilliams (1953).

Jean-Baptiste LeMoyne de Bienville (1699–1724, 1732–1743). Bienville was Iberville's younger brother, but unlike Iberville he remained in Louisiana as explorer, soldier, administrator, and thrice governor (or commandant general) of the colony. It is unlikely that the young colony would have survived as well as it did without the leadership of this highly competent individual. His general success with Indian relations during the early years (regrettably not repeated during his final administration) was crucial, as was demonstrated by the Natchez massacre, a disaster that occurred during the decade Bienville was absent from Louisiana and that was directly attributable to incompetent administration. Bienville, of course, was deeply embroiled in politics on a broad front, as well as with the petty squabbles of a floundering colony. Nevertheless, his reports and other papers reveal him to have been a perceptive and reasonable person. Read in context, the documents provide a vast amount of information, much of which pertains to the Indians under Bienville's charge (Rowland and Sanders 1927–1932; Rowland, Sanders, and Galloway 1984).

Pierre Charles Le Sueur (1700–1701). Le Sueur, a Canadian explorer and trader who accompanied Iberville on his second voyage to Louisiana in 1700, was authorized to work copper and lead mines that he had discovered some years earlier in what is now southeastern Minnesota. Accordingly, he traveled up the Mississippi River in 1700 accompanied by André Pénicaut, spent the winter exploiting the mines, and then returned downriver in the spring of 1701. A journal (Le Sueur 1700) and letters are preserved in the Delisle papers in the Archives Nationales in Paris. Le Sueur was an extraordinarily keen observer, especially concerning details of geography. The accuracy of his observations is revealed in the remarkable Delisle 1702 map (see fig. 20).

Bernard Diron d'Artaguiette (1717–1742). Bernard was one of three Diron d'Artaguiette brothers who were active in Louisiana between 1708 and 1742 and have often been confused with each other (de Villiers 1922, pp. 33–34; Kernion 1926, p. 35; Rowland and Sanders 1927, vol. 1, pp. 56–57; McWilliams 1953, pp. 120–121). This Diron d'Artaguiette came to the colony in 1717 and is best known for serving as inspector general of Louisiana and commandant at Mobile. His presence in the colony is documented as late as 1742 (he was not the d'Artaguiette burned at the stake in 1736 by the Chickasaw—that was his brother Pierre). Bernard's most important contributions to history were an original map of the Mississippi (the data for which were recorded in 1719, although the map was not actually drawn up until 1732) and a journal account of a tour of inspection made up the Mississippi in 1722–1723 (Mereness 1916, pp. 15–92). The descriptive and statistical information contained in these documents appears to be very reliable.

Jean-Baptiste Bénard de La Harpe (1718–1723). La Harpe was an educated man who was lured to Louisiana during the heyday generated by John Law's Company of the West. Although he came as a concessionaire and trader, his greatest contribution to history was as an explorer. Based on firsthand observations of the country and its inhabitants, both Indian and colonial, his accounts contain a wealth of reliable information, as has been substantiated by the critical evaluations of Mildred Wedel (1971, 1974). Most of his time, however, was spent far west of the Mississippi. A map attributed to La Harpe, or at least based in part on his observations, confirms the accuracy of his information (La Harpe ca. 1720). The most important La Harpe document for this study is the *Journal Historique de l'Etablissement des Français a la Louisiane* (Boimare 1831; see also Cain,

Koenig, and Conrad 1971). In its present form, however, this work appears to be an anonymous compilation that draws upon Iberville, Bienville, and Le Sueur for descriptions of events prior to La Harpe's arrival in the colony. Despite the question concerning its pedigree, this "journal" may be used with care.

Antoine Simon Le Page du Pratz (1718–1734). Le Page du Pratz was another colonist brought to Louisiana by the grandiose scheme of John Law. For eight of his sixteen years in the colony he was a concessionaire at Natchez, and he came to know his indigenous neighbors well, even participating in their ceremonies and learning their language. His *Histoire de la Louisiane* (1758) reports on the Natchez and other Indians with sympathy and insight unusual for the time (Tregle 1973). In his own words, he strove for truth and accuracy, and although he has been called gullible and even "whimsical" (Winsor 1887, p. 65), he is considered by Swanton (1911, p. 4) to be the principal authority for the ethnohistory of the period, especially concerning nonmaterial details. It is important to avoid the 1774 English edition of his work, which has omitted much material found in the original edition concerning Indian customs.

François Dumont de Montigny (1719–1738). Dumont, a soldier and concessionaire, lived at Natchez for a while and accompanied La Harpe on his exploration up the Arkansas. The original 1753 edition of his *Mémoires Historiques sur la Louisiane* was used in this study and is considered by Swanton (1911, p. 4) to be second only to Le Page du Pratz in terms of reliable ethnohistorical content (note that there was something of a rivalry between Dumont and Le Page du Pratz). Swanton even considers Dumont to be perhaps slightly more accurate on matters of material culture, a judgment with which this writer would concur. Dumont also authored an epic poem (de Villiers 1919, 1931), the manuscript of which is illustrated by numerous watercolor sketches which, although ingenuous, contain much ethnological data. One of them graces the cover of this volume.

Pierre François Xavier de Charlevoix (1721–1722). Father Charlevoix, known as the "first historian of New France," was also the foremost historian of the French period. He was fully aware of the necessity for accurate and critical presentation and was historiographically correct when he used other sources. His *Histoire*, a model of historical reporting for the period, was based in part on personal observation, as evidenced by his *Journal*. Both documents were published together in three volumes under the title *Histoire et Description générale de la Nouvelle France avec le Journal Historique d'un Voyage fait par ordre du Roi dans l'Amérique Septentrionale* (Charlevoix 1744). The original edition and an annotated translation (O'Neill 1977) were used for this study.

Paul du Poisson (1727–1729). Father Poisson was one of the few Jesuits to labor for the Lord in the Lower Mississippi Valley. His mission was among the Arkansas, until he met martyrdom while on a visit to the Natchez during the fateful November of 1729. The one document we have from the hand of Poisson is a marvelously detailed and worldly letter that contains a considerable amount of information about the geography and inhabitants of the valley (Thwaites 1900, vol. 67, pp. 276–325). The information is firsthand and may be considered unusually reliable.

Jean-Bernard Bossu (1751–1762, 1770–1771). Bossu was a professional soldier with literary pretensions and a keen eye for detail; his observations on the Indians are often insightful and sympathetic (he was even adopted by the Arkansas/Quapaw). In his enthusiasm for the subject, however, Bossu often uncritically and cavalierly inserted passages concerning earlier events that were derived from other published sources and heresay. In the case of the published borrowings, his versions are rarely an improvement. A further caveat is that Bossu became embroiled in the political strife of the colony and his comments on the colonial administration must be considered exceptionally biased. Of his two books (1768, 1777), the first is perhaps the more factual, but the lesser-known later volume contains important information and commentary. The annotated translations of Feiler (1962) and Dickinson (1982) are used here, as well as the original editions.

With the exception of Bossu, the later French writers recorded only passing references to the Tunica. The primary data are statistical and include census figures and locations. One writer during the last years of the French regime was the Chevalier Louis Billouard de Kerlérec, whose principal contribution to posterity was a fact-finding mission down the Mississippi in 1758 (de Villiers 1907).

Before leaving the French Dominion, a further note of caution must be interjected. Nineteenth-century pseudohistories, such as *History of Louisiana* by Charles Gayarré (1885), are to be avoided or used only with great care. As was recognized by a contemporary, they characteristically are "mainly composed of transcripts from original documents, woven together with a slender thread of narrative" (Winsor 1887, p. 65): composites of texts that generally are unattributed and may be ruthlessly abridged or badly translated. The great nineteenth-century compendia of historical texts published by B. F. French (1846–1875) and Pierre Margry (1879–1888) are more useful references, but even they have been found to be severely flawed. Margry presented transcriptions of the original documents, but many errors of copying and omissions of significant segments of text have been noted (McWilliams 1953, p. xviii; Beers 1957, p. 109; Nasatir 1974, p. 5; Wedel 1974, pp. 11–12). The translated texts published by French are also often fragmentary, and the translations themselves are frequently faulty and sometimes contain material not in the original documents (McWilliams 1953, p. xiii; Beers 1957, p. 97; Wedel 1974, pp. 11–12). Such spurious additions can be filtered out only by going back to the original

documents—a procedure, needless to say, that is universally recommended by practicing historiographers (see Beers 1957 as an aid to such research).

Twentieth-century examples of reliable historical collections include the *Mississippi Provincial Archives: French Dominion* (Rowland and Sanders 1927–1932; Rowland, Sanders, and Galloway 1984), which are characterized by precise translations and useful annotations (Galloway 1981). The documents consist primarily of correspondence, directives, inventories, and reports created by the many functionaries of the colonial bureaucracy. As such, they provide a very important counterpoint to the private records of the journalists and memoirists.

Excellent secondary sources for the history of French Louisiana are available and may be consulted profitably for purposes of interpretation and for general background concerning the motivations and actions of the *ancien régime* in the colony. The foremost of these sources include Giraud (1953–1974), Crane (1956), McDermott (1965, 1969), Caruso (1966), Eccles (1972), Howell (1973), Woods (1980), and Galloway (ed., 1982).

Contemporary English writers recorded very little about the Indians of the French Dominion in Louisiana, which demonstrates the overall success of the French in excluding the English from their colony. The two most significant eighteenth-century English source books on the subject, by Daniel Coxe and James Adair, do not even mention the Tunica but do provide some important historical and ethnohistorical background. Coxe's *A Description of the English Province of Carolana, by the Spaniards call'd Florida, and by the French La Louisiane* was published in 1722 and is concerned primarily with England's claim to the Mississippi Valley. Although it provides much information about the geography and native inhabitants of the valley, it is based on secondhand reports and contains many errors of fact. It is, in short, an unreliable source for these matters. Adair's *The History of the American Indians* is a more valuable ethnohistorical document. Published in 1775, it is the single most important eighteenth-century volume about the Indians of the Southeast (Washburn 1973, p. 96). Adair lived among the Indians, primarily the Chickasaw, for some forty years (ca. 1735–1775). Although he does not make direct reference to the Tunica, he is an unusually reliable source of information on southeastern Indians in general, and specifically on the neighboring Chickasaw, Choctaw, and Natchez tribes.

English works describing the brief period of British sovereignty (1763–1779) in the Mississippi Valley after the French Dominion are basically statistical documents that contain few useful descriptions of the Indians (e.g., Pittman 1770; Hutchins 1784; Rowland 1911; Gordon 1916). More recent historiographic commentaries on this period include Alvord and Carter (1915, 1916) and Rea (1970b, 1973b). The Spanish period (1763–1803) also is characterized by a lack of useful documentation, and there are few references of any kind to the Tunica (Kinnaird 1946a, 1946b, 1949). Finally, the American period (after 1803) is notable for ignoring the Tunica almost completely—until anthropological interest awakened late in the nineteenth century.

THE MAPS AND PICTURES

Contemporary French, English, and Spanish maps also constitute a source of information vital to this study, and as historical documents they, too, must be subjected to rigorous analysis. But the analysis is of a different order from that required for most textual documents because maps are graphic representations or abstractions of spatial reality and commonly are composites of data on a large scale (Harley 1968; Heidenreich 1976). As noted by R. A. Skelton (1965, p. 4), maps are

the end-product of a complex series of processes—assembly of information from various sources and in different forms, both graphic and textual; assimilation to the mapmaker's geographical ideas, to transmitted cartographic patterns, or to his political interest; and the resultant stages of compilation, control, adjustment, and copying.

Our research has located scores of published and unpublished sixteenth- to nineteenth-century maps that pertain to the Lower Mississippi Valley (see also Holmes 1963, 1965 for a catalog of archival collections). There is, of course, a vast range of quality—that is, accuracy—evident in these maps. Some are useless, the rest of varying degrees of reliability. Some cartographers were competent, a few without peer, but there were also far too many who plagiarized and distorted the renderings of others. The most serious problem, aside from outright fabrication and inadvertent error, is the perpetuation of obsolete information borrowed from earlier maps. It is therefore necessary to determine the date and author of a map and the sources of information on which it was based in order to assess its credibility. The value of each map must be weighed according to personal, cartographic, and historical circumstances. An obvious golden rule is to seek out firsthand information, and the crux of the following discourse will depend foremost upon maps that were drawn by observers who were on the scene. The maps will be supplemented with contemporary textual references by the same and other persons. In the case of lacunae or inconvenient fits, other information deemed relevant, but perhaps less reliable, will be introduced with appropriate caveats.

Fortunately, historical cartography is well developed with respect to maps of the Southeast (e.g., see Thomassy 1860; Winsor 1887, pp. 79–86; Delanglez 1943, 1945, n.d.; Cumming 1958, 1966; De Vorsey 1971, 1982). Comments on critical analysis and evaluation therefore are deferred to the discussions in the text or the figure captions of particularly relevant map sections.

Pictorial representations of Lower Mississippi Valley Indians before the advent of photography are very rare indeed. The watercolors of Alexandre DeBatz and François Dumont de Montigny and the engravings made from the sketches of Antoine Le Page du Pratz constitute the entire known eighteenth-century corpus. Only two of these, one watercolor each by DeBatz and Dumont de Montigny, depict Tunica subjects: they are featured as the cover illustrations for this two-volume set on the Tunica. Although they may lack artistic merit, they contain valuable cultural information on Tunica dress, appearance, settlement patterns, site plans, architecture, and customs. We can only regret that the Tunica did not inspire more numerous artistic representations.

Periods of Tunica History

The following discussion is arranged according to ethnohistorical periods (cf. the strictly historical periods in Brain 1979, pp. 267–269, table 18). These periods, which are simply a convenience for presentation purposes, do reflect general events important to the history of the Lower Mississippi Valley (ibid., pp. 256–266) and are keyed to significant changes in the location of the Tunica (table 1).

Period I includes the initial European exploration by De Soto from 1541 to 1543 and the ensuing protohistoric period. Within it lie the origins of the Tunica in northwestern Mississippi. Period II, 1672–1706, is the time of early French contact, when the Tunica lived on the lower Yazoo River. Period III refers to the consolidation and climax of French Louisiana in the years 1706 to 1731. During this period, the Tunica controlled the Portage de la Croix near the confluence of the Red and Mississippi rivers. Period IV corresponds to the decline of the French Dominion from 1731 to 1764. It was apparently a golden age for the Tunica, however, in their new location on Tunica Bayou. Period V, 1764–ca. 1800, was the time of the British and Spanish regimes, when the Tunica were resettled near Pointe Coupée. Period VI, post-1800, refers to the assumption of American sovereignty and the final move of the Tunica to Marksville, Louisiana.

Table 1. Locations of the Tunica as derived from the historical documentation.

Date	Period	Location	Euroamerican Sovereignty
	VI	Marksville	American
1800			
	V	Pointe Coupée	English/Spanish
	IV	Tunica Bayou	
	III	Portage de la Croix	French
1700			
	II	Lower Yazoo	
1600			
	I	Upper Sunflower	Spanish

PERIOD I: UPPER SUNFLOWER

After more than two years on the trail, the De Soto entrada finally reached the Mississippi River. The chronicles describe a dispirited army, one decimated by numerous skirmishes and the twin disasters at Mauvila and Chicasa, which destroyed supplies as well as men and horses. The splendidly accoutred army that had landed in Florida in the spring of 1539 was reduced by the spring of 1541 to a tattered band that was desperately seeking escape from the whole terrible adventure. The Spaniards therefore headed for the Mississippi River, which they seemed to know would take them to the Gulf of Mexico and a return to Spanish dominions.

The army discovered the Mississippi after entering the native "province" of Quizquiz (fig. 3). The exact

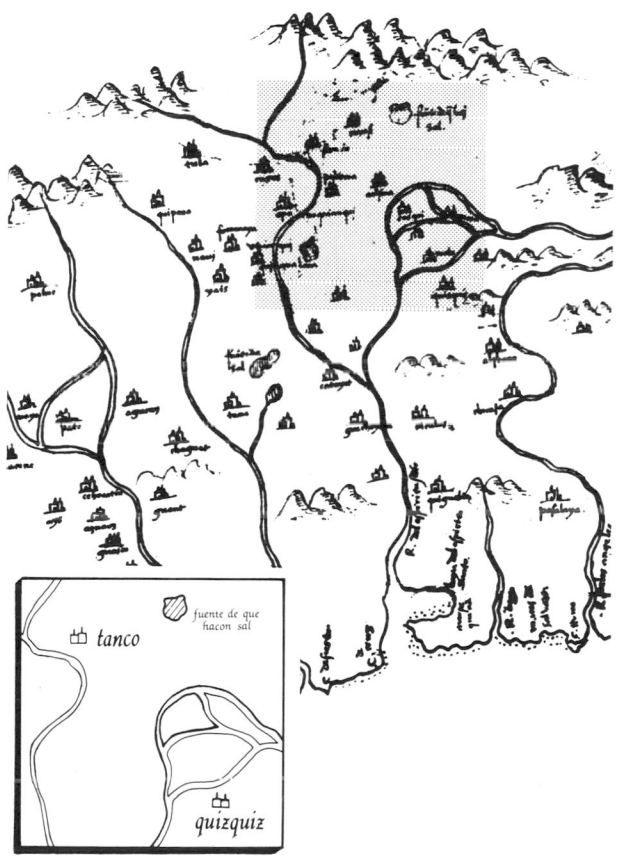

Figure 3. Section of the "De Soto" map, probably drawn by Alonso de Santa Cruz in 1544 or soon thereafter (Boston 1941; Delanglez 1945, pp. 61–62; Cumming 1958, p. 94). The map does contain information about the interior regions of the Southeast that could only have come from the De Soto expedition. Note "Quizquiz," located on the east bank of the *R. del espiritu santo,* and "Tanco," or Tanico, west of the river near a *fuente de que hacon sal.* (Archivo General de Indias, Seville)

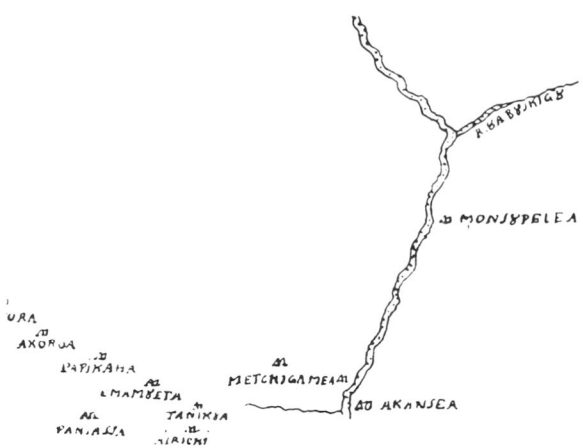

Figure 4. Section of the Marquette map of 1676. The "Tanikᵔa" are shown west of the Mississippi River. (St. Mary's College, Montreal)

location of this province has been the subject of considerable controversy (see Brain 1985), but several theories place it in the upper Sunflower region of the Yazoo Basin in northwestern Mississippi (see fig. 2) (Swanton 1939, 1952; Brain, Toth, and Rodriguez-Buckingham 1974; Brain 1984; Weinstein 1985). Quizquiz is vital to our considerations since it has been hypothetically identified as the ancestral hearth of the Tunica (Brain, Toth, and Rodriguez-Buckingham 1974, pp. 262, 283). Substantiation of this hypothesis is presented in the archaeological section (part 2) of this volume, but the historical documentation also provides compelling support. Although the De Soto chronicles alone are not specific enough for precise geographic determination of Quizquiz and Tunica origins, they are complemented by later documentation and Indian oral traditions.

Unfortunately, the oral traditions of the Tunica are of little help in pinpointing their origins. They offer only a mythical account of emergence from a mountain, near which they settled (Haas 1950, pp. 19, 141). If there is any substance here, it is only that the earliest tribal memory may not be of the valley proper. It is tantalizing to speculate that the reference could be to the Ouachita Mountains, for there is a possible Tunican connection with that topography. To explain, it is necessary to return to the earliest historical records.

Although it is argued here that the people of Quizquiz mentioned in the De Soto narratives were ancestral to the later Tunica, another clue in that primary documentation must not be overlooked. After crossing the river and exploring the provinces on its western bank, De Soto decided to continue farther west and left the valley. After a few days of actual travel, the conquistadores came to the "province of salt" (probably somewhere in the vicinity of Hot Springs, Arkansas), the principal town of which was recorded as "Tanico" (Varner and Varner 1951, p. 454; Bourne 1904, vol. 1, p. 135; ibid., vol. 2, p. 147). The possibility that Tanico was cognate to Tunica has been noted by other scholars (Swanton 1911, p. 306; Swanton 1939, p. 52; Swanton 1946, pp. 14, 29, 54; Dickinson 1980, p. 2).

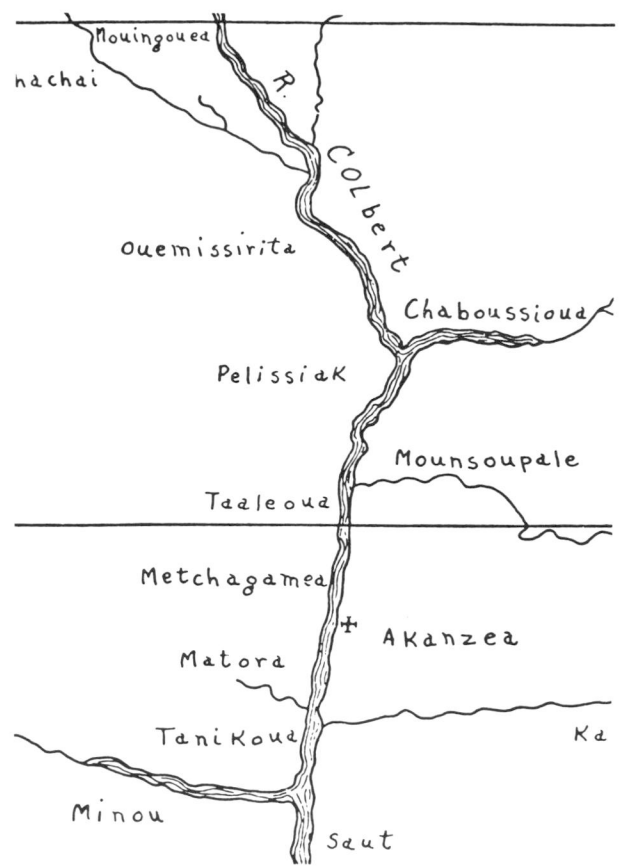

Figure 5. Section of a map attributed to Jolliet and made circa 1679. It is very similar to the Marquette 1676 map, and again the "Tanikoua" are placed west of the Mississippi. (Bibliothèque Nationale, Paris)

The first French accounts 130 years later would seem to confirm the continued existence of the Tanico in the same general region. Crude maps credited to Marquette (1676) and Jolliet (1679) place the "Tanikᵔa" and "Tanikoua" west of the Mississippi River (figs. 4–5). In 1687, both Douay (Shea 1852, p. 219) and Joutel (Margry 1879, vol. 3, pp. 409–410) refer to the Tanico or "Taniquo" in what must have been southern Arkansas (although there is some question about the authorship of the Douay narrative, there is no reason to doubt the facts where they are corroborated by Joutel). The latter orthography is of considerable interest, for it approaches the "Tonniqua" found on the 1701 and 1703 maps of the great cartographer Guillaume Delisle (figs. 6–7). These unusually accurate maps place the Tonniqua far up the Ouachita River near the "*Lacs . . . du Sel.*" The same maps show the "Tonicas," the usual French name for the Tunica, in their proper contemporary home on the lower Yazoo River. The Coxe map published in 1722, but based on much earlier information, may be unreliable in its geographic details; nevertheless, it provides a crucial bit of orthographic evidence, placing Tanico far up a western river and the "Tounica" on the Yazoo (fig. 8).

The Delisle map of 1718 substitutes Tonicas for Tonniquas on the Ouachita, and "Tonikas" for Tonicas who

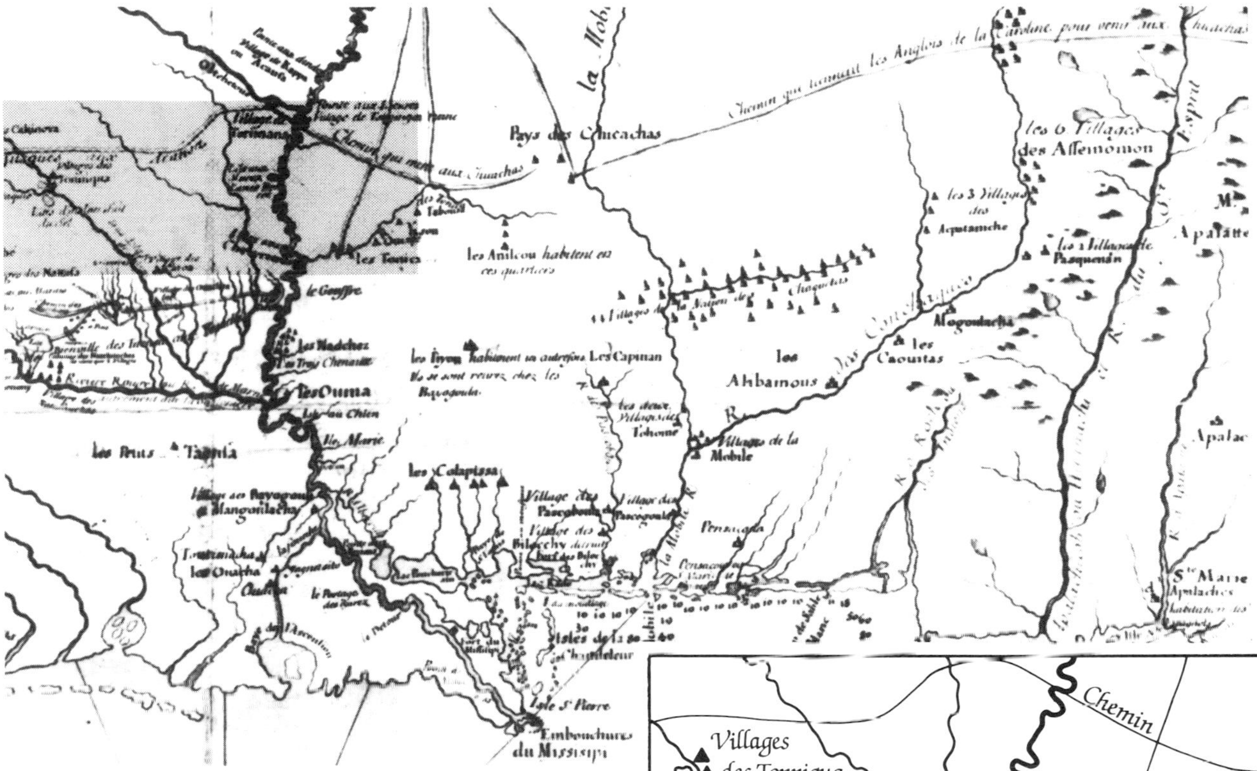

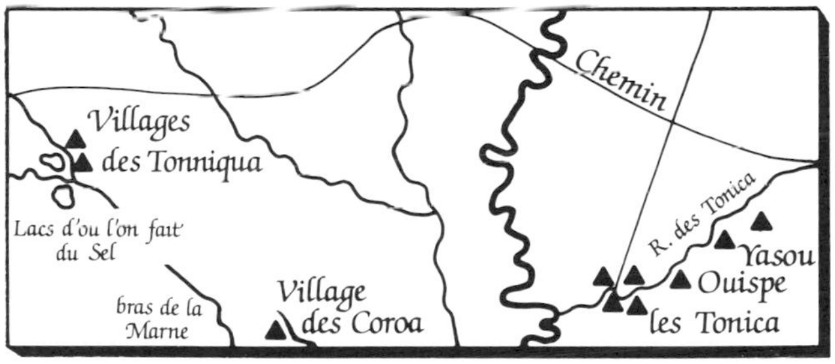

Figure 6. Section of the Delisle map of 1701 (drawn by Guillaume with the aid of his father, Claude). This original map is notable for the delineation of trails, especially the English path from Charleston to the Chickasaw and beyond. The Tunica are placed on the lower Yazoo River at the end of one of these trails, and the "Tonniqua" are situated near another trail west of the Mississippi and across the Ouachita River from *Lacs d'ou l'on fait du Sel*. Note similarity to the legend on the De Soto map in figure 3. (Bibliothèque Nationale, Paris)

Figure 7. Section of the Delisle map of 1703 (attributed to Guillaume; for the part played by his father, Claude, in the preparation, see Winsor 1887, p. 80; Delanglez 1943; and De Vorsey 1982). The map is based on La Salle data corrected by the information from Iberville and Le Sueur that was used in drawing the 1701 and 1702 Delisle maps (figs. 6, 20). Again, the "Tonniqua" are placed well up the Ouachita River. (Yale University Library, New Haven)

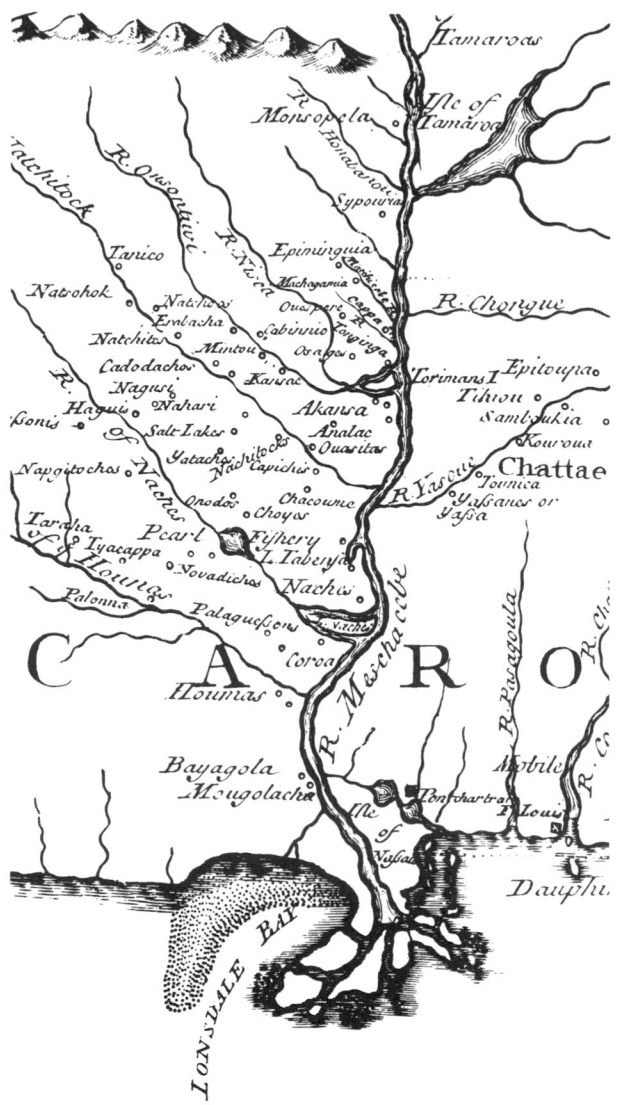

Figure 8. Section of the Coxe map published with his 1722 treatise. A curious map, it reveals much unique and incorrect information. It is unclear what its sources might have been, but they date to early in the century: the "Tounica" are correctly shown on the lower Yazoo River, and the "Tanico" are placed on a western river identified as the "R. Natchitock," presumably the Ouachita. (LMS Map Library, Peabody Museum of Archaeology and Ethnology, Harvard University)

Figure 9. Section of the Delisle map of 1718. One of the cartographic landmarks for eastern North America, this map is also famous for delineating the route of De Soto, although on what authority is not known. Whatever the source, it is of great interest to note that the western "Tonicas" are placed on the route, recalling the "Tanico" of the De Soto map (see fig. 3). (Yale University Library, New Haven)

by that time had moved from the Yazoo (fig. 9). This map also traces the expedition of De Soto, and the Ouachita Tonicas are placed directly on the route. Although it is not clear what Delisle's source might have been (Cumming 1958, p. 186), the so-called "De Soto map" (Boston 1941) shows in remarkably similar configuration "Tanco," or Tanico, on the upper reaches of a western river near a *"fuente de que hacon sal"* (see fig. 3).

All of this must be more than coincidence, and clearly there is some connection to be drawn. The Tonniqua-Tonicas-Tonikas problem of the Delisle maps may indicate that the names were interchangeable and may reflect the known presence of the historic Tunica at saltworks west of the Mississippi (Swanton 1911, p. 307; Swanton 1946, pp. 197–198, 738, 819). But the apparent etymology from Tanico also would seem to reinforce the idea that the particular choice of location was occasioned by a more intimate and deep-rooted bond (see Nuttall 1821, p. 257, for an early recognition of this kinship). While the Tunica themselves may not have been descended directly from Tanico, they were probably a remnant of a larger group identified here as "Tunican," which in the sixteenth century included both Tanico in east-central Arkansas and Quizquiz in northwestern Mississippi.

That the people of Quizquiz were the direct ancestors of the eighteenth-century Tunica is supported by more recent historical and ethnohistorical documentation. Nineteenth-century studies of tribal migration legends indicated that "Tunica Oldfields" was in northwestern Mississippi (e.g., Gatschet 1884, p. 40). Specifically, "Chickasaw and Choctaw tradition places 'Tunica old-fields' on the Mississippi river near Friar point, not many miles below the present Helena, Ark., which would indicate that they had formerly lived in the neighborhood" (Swanton 1911, pp. 306–307; see also Swanton 1946, p. 54). Further substantiation would seem to be explicit in the official 1830 demarcation of the last Chickasaw-Choctaw boundary line, which is described as running "through the Tunica old fields, to a point on the Mississippe [sic] river, about twenty-eight miles, by water, below where the St. Francis river enters said stream, on the West side" (Kappler 1973, pp. 1,035–1,036). This boundary line is indicated on modern USGS quadrangle maps, and in fact it still serves as a boundary separating the present-day counties of Coahoma and Tunica. The line bisects Tunica Oldfields, or Quizquiz, as defined in these pages, although it runs on the northern side of what is considered to be the archaeological core area (see part 2). According to the river channel in the early nineteenth century (Fisk 1944, sheet 22, pl. 6), a point twenty-eight miles south from the St. Francis confluence, by water, would fall slightly below the present line and in the middle of the core area.

The hiatus in the historical record of the Lower Mississippi Valley between the De Soto entrada and the initial explorations of the French lasted for more than a century. Sometime during this protohistoric period, at least one group of the remnant populations left the domains of Quizquiz–Tunica Oldfields and resettled on the lower reaches of the Yazoo River.

PERIOD II: LOWER YAZOO

At the time of first French contact, a tribal group that we shall know henceforth as the Tunica proper was located on the banks of the Yazoo River near its confluence with the Mississippi. Their presence was noted in several accounts of the La Salle expedition, but since the Tunica were considered enemies by the Quapaw, with whom La Salle had concluded an alliance—*"la paix faite et la possession prise"*—the Cavalier thought it prudent to avoid contact. Accordingly, the expedition bypassed the Yazoo, but at least the Tunica were identified by the name they were to bear throughout the historic period (although careless orthography rendered this as "Ionica" and "Tourika" in some of the accounts, the procès-verbal of the expedition specifies "Tonika"). Even Tonti, the most accomplished explorer of the Mississippi Valley during the next two decades, seems not to have established contact with the Tunica until others had already done so. He records only that the Tunica and allied tribes lived on the Yazoo ten leagues from the Mississippi (French 1846, p. 82).

La Salle's epic voyage spurred a flurry of cartographic activity as France sought to validate her claims. As may be expected from an exploration into so vast an unknown territory, the resulting maps were somewhat deficient in geographic accuracy (although according to De Vorsey [1982] it seems that the excessive distortion of the lower course of the Mississippi found on the earliest maps was intentional). Nevertheless, as early as 1684 the Tunica are clearly indicated as living along the banks of a river that can only have been the Yazoo, and their position is confirmed in subsequent maps to the end of the century (figs. 10–16). Possibly as early as 1697 Alexandre de Rémonville, who had "first hand knowledge of the Mississippi" (Giraud 1974, vol. 1, p. 15), noted that the "the first Tunica village is 3 leagues up that river [Yazoo], the large village is 4 leagues higher up" (de Rémonville 1715, in reference to a period at least fifteen years earlier).

The first recorded French visit to the Tunica occurred in January 1698, when an expedition of missionaries from the Séminaire de Québec descended the Mississippi in search of souls to save. The most successful mission was established among The Tunica, and the initial references are most explicit regarding their location: "The first village is four leagues from the Micissipi inland on the bank of a quite pretty river" (Thaumur de la Source in Shea 1861, p. 80). The missionary, Father Davion, has left us no useful information, but fortunately his presence brought others to visit who had more thought for posterity. In 1700, Le Sueur placed the Tunica seven French leagues up the Yazoo (Margry 1881, vol. 5, p. 401), Pénicaut agreed in principle (McWilliams 1953, pp. 33–34), and Father Gravier elaborated by stating that they were "four leagues by water and two leagues by land" (Shea 1861, p. 132). Father Gravier's distinction of the mode of travel is a piece of information vital to the archaeological identification discussed in part 2 of this volume.

The maps left by the missionaries consist of rude sketches (figs. 17–18), but even so they are more accurate than the official 1699 map of Gentil(?) (fig. 16).

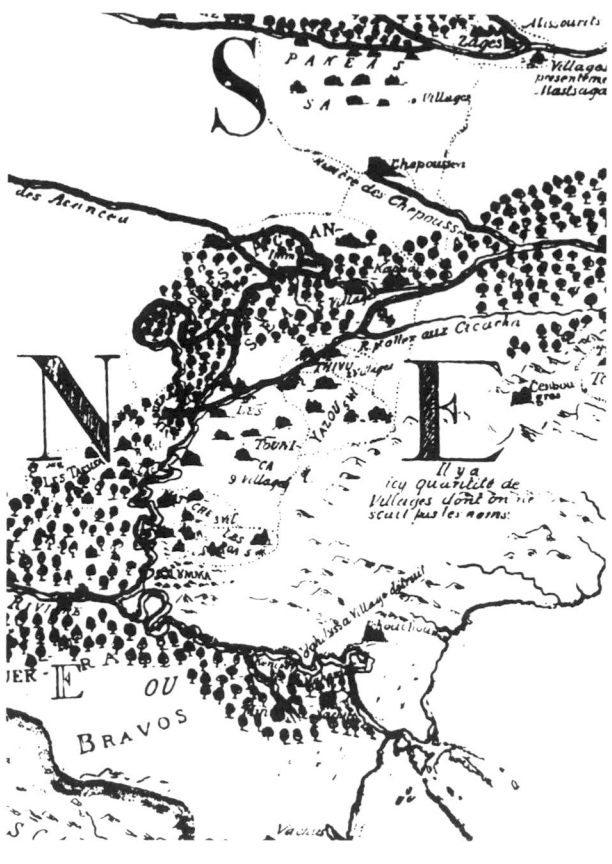

Figure 10. Section of the Franquelin map of 1684. This map was the earliest to incorporate information from the La Salle exploration. The curious distortion of the course of the Lower Mississippi River was probably a purposeful misrepresentation by La Salle to gain support for his second expedition (De Vorsey 1982). Nevertheless, the "Tounica" are placed accurately relative to the distortion. (LMS Map Library, Peabody Museum of Archaeology and Ethnology, Harvard University)

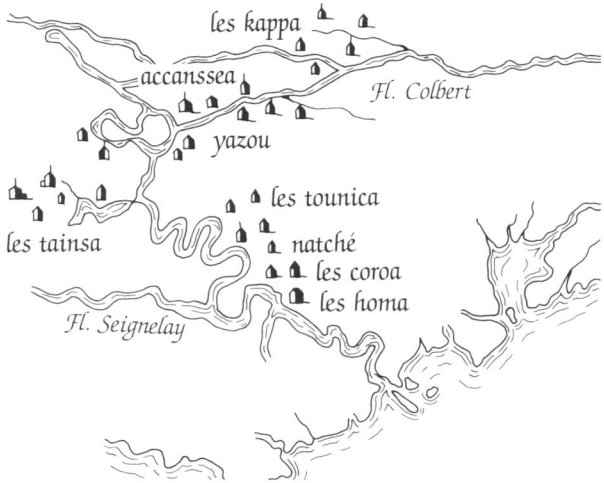

Figure 11. Section of the Minet map of 1685. Minet was the official engineer and cartographer of the second La Salle expedition, and he had access to an original map, now lost, of the first expedition. In this rendition, he clearly follows Franquelin 1684 in accepting La Salle's distortion of the course of the Mississippi River. The "Tounica" are somewhat misplaced but are still in a reasonable position relative to other named groups. (After the original which appears in the Bibliothèque Nationale, Paris)

Figure 12. Section of the Franquelin map of 1688. In this map, the Mississippi is still badly distorted but the Tunica and their neighbors are more accurately located relative to each other. The data may have been derived from Henri de Tonti, who traveled the Mississippi numerous times during this period. (Division of Maps, Library of Congress, Washington, D.C.)

Figure 13. Section of the Coronelli map of 1688 (Coronelli 1688a). This map also perpetuates La Salle's distortion of the course of the Mississippi River, but it is notable in the prominence accorded the "Tounica," although the scale of the map precludes accurate placement. (Newberry Library, Chicago)

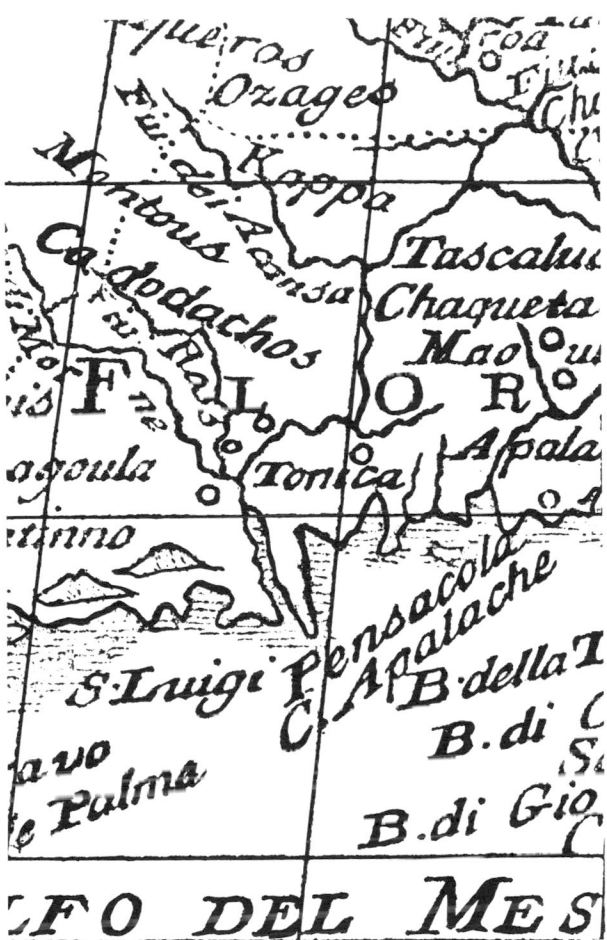

Figure 14. Section of a map attributed to Coronelli, also dated 1688 (Coronelli 1688b). If the attribution and dating are correct, this map shows a profound and immediate change in Coronelli's perception. Although it is not known what the change might have been based on, the Mississippi River flows a far more accurate course and the "Tonica" retain their preeminent position. (Map Library, School of Geoscience, Louisiana State University, Baton Rouge)

Figure 15. Section of the de Louvigny map of 1697. This map confirms that prior to Iberville's explorations new data (possibly provided by Tonti or de Rémonville) were available that placed the Mississippi River in its proper course. The "Tonica" are located on the Yazoo River, although not in the order usually given relative to neighboring tribes. (After the original which appears in the Division of Maps, Library of Congress, Washington, D.C.)

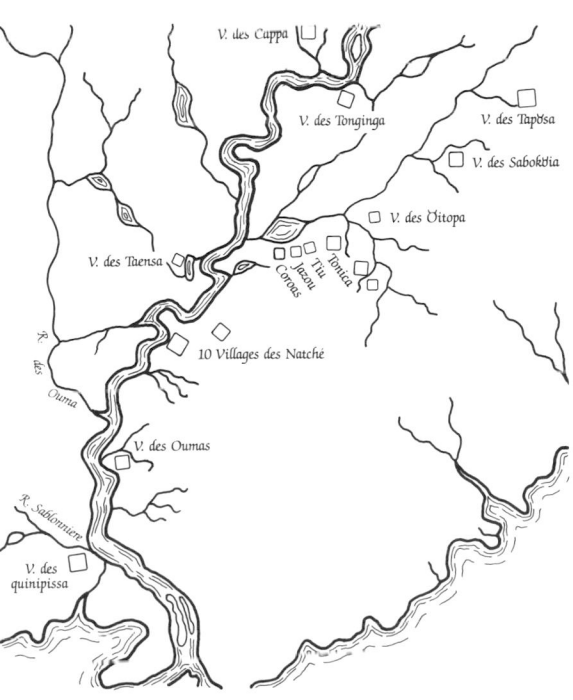

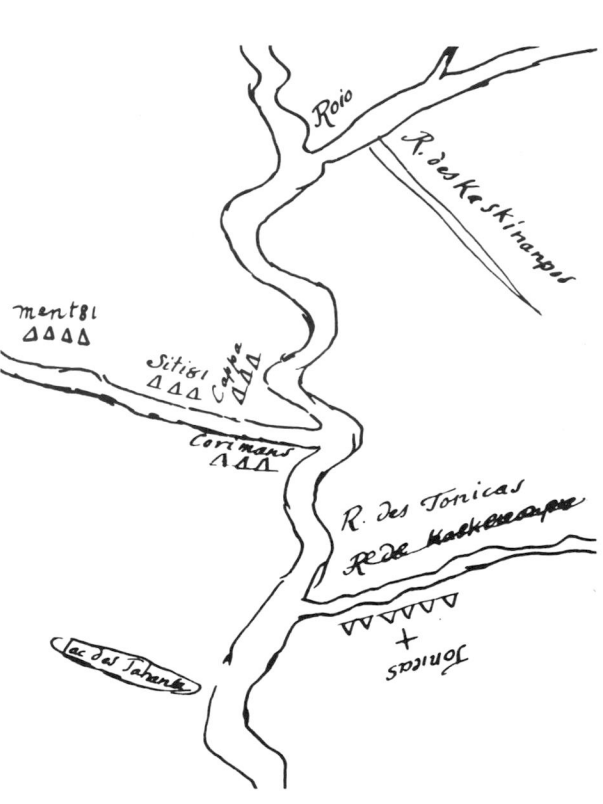

Figure 16. Section of a map dated 1699, tentatively attributed to Gentil. This map is of great interest in that it preserves some of the distortions of earlier maps but incorporates some of the new data from the Iberville expedition. The "Tonica" are clearly placed on both the Yazoo and Ouachita rivers. This map was redrawn by Nicolas de Fer in 1701. (Bibliothèque Nationale, Paris)

Figure 17. Anonymous map drawn circa 1698. This map is in the collections of the Archives Nationales in Paris; another copy is the Séminaire de Québec. On internal evidence these maps date to 1698. An improved version of the map, also in Québec, is dated 1699 and attributed to Father Bergier, S.J. (Baillargeon 1965, p. 206). Although a very rough sketch, the map accurately locates the "Tonicas" on the lower Yazoo River. (Archives Nationales, Paris)

Two maps drawn by Henri de Tonti in 1700 presumably are based on his extensive knowledge of the Mississippi Valley but display little more cartographic skill and no more useful information than the missionary maps. (One of the Tonti maps is a preliminary sketch [1700a], the other a finished version [1700b]. It is worth noting that there are many differences in details between the two, although considering the scale of the maps, the schematic rendering, and the poor quality of the copies available for study, the differences are insignificant.) Another map drawn about 1700 includes data from Iberville and portrays a marked advance in knowledge, especially of the Tunica (fig. 19). The real cartographic breakthrough, however, was brought about by those master mappers, Claude and Guillaume Deslisle (father and son). Guillaume Deslisle placed the Tunica correctly in his map of 1701 (see fig. 6) and then detailed their position in an incredibly precise map of the Lower Mississippi Valley the following year (fig. 20). The more general 1703 and 1718 maps maintain their general position (see figs. 7, 9).

Although the Tunica moved from the Yazoo soon after these initial contacts, they are still located there in many later maps (e.g., Moll 1715; Chatelain 1719a, 1719b; Buache 1724). This is mentioned only as a caveat: all of these maps are simply secondary renderings of various Delisle maps and display no new information regarding the Lower Mississippi Valley.

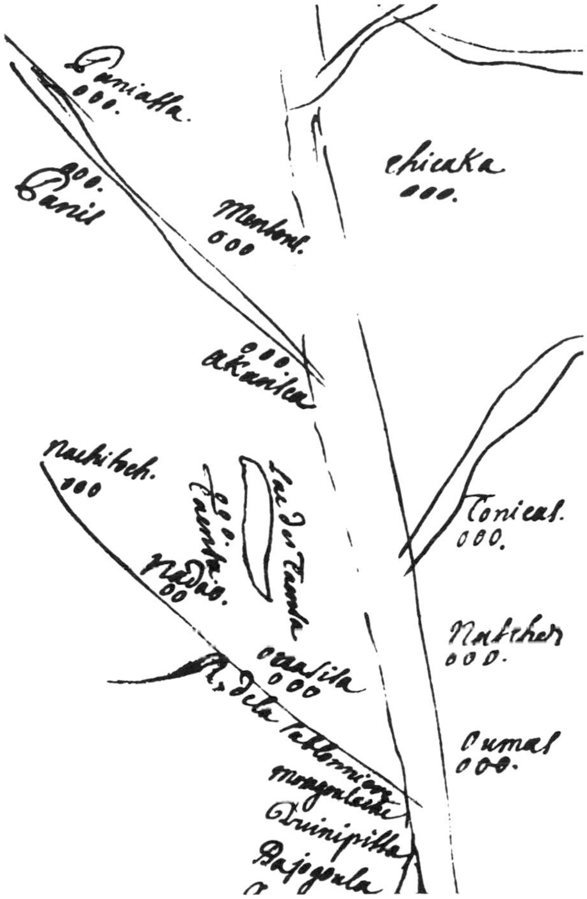

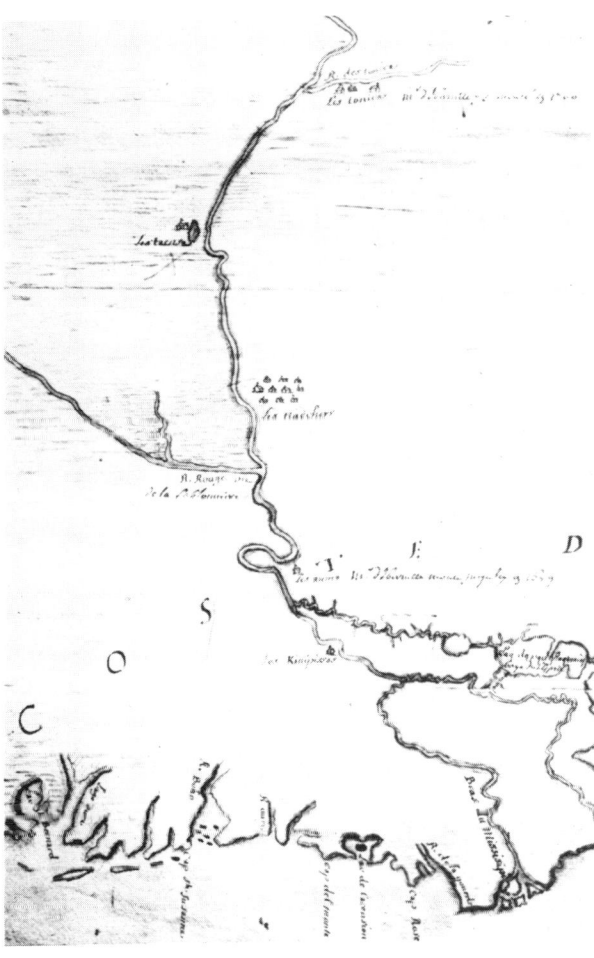

Figure 18. Anonymous map drawn circa 1699. Although this map is even cruder than the one illustrated in figure 17, it displays slightly updated information and was probably rendered in 1699 or soon thereafter. (Séminaire de Québec, Québec)

Figure 19. Section of an anonymous map drawn circa 1700. This map acknowledges a debt to Iberville, and although it still contains some archaic information, it places the river course and tribal locations far more accurately than do any other depictions up to that time. (Bibliothèque Nationale, Paris)

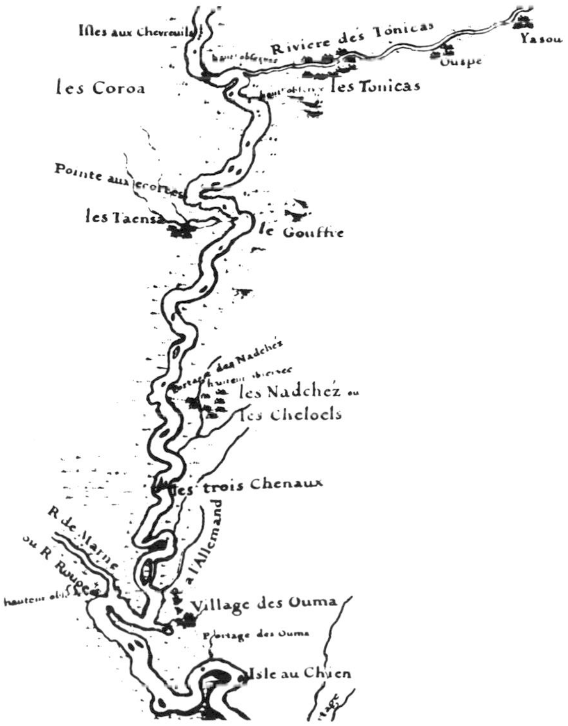

Figure 20. Section of the Delisle map of 1702. This exquisitely detailed map is a landmark for Lower Mississippi Valley cartography, eclipsing even the famous Delisle 1718 map. The cartouche credits Le Sueur for the information on which it is based. The "Tonicas" and their neighbors are placed with unparalleled accuracy. Note also the "Village des Ouma" opposite the mouth of the Red River where the Tunica resettled a few years later (cf. fig. 23). (Bibliothèque Nationale, Paris)

Nevertheless, some later maps are useful for confirming the exact location of the Tunica on the Yazoo. Although the Tunica were no longer present, tribes with whom they had lived, most notably the Yazoo, remained in place until 1730. Therefore, later more precise descriptions of the locations of these companion peoples apply equally well to the Tunica when they were on the Yazoo. The most important of these is the Broutin, de Vergés, and Saucier map of 1740 (fig. 21), which locates the Chakchiuma village of 1736, previously occupied by the Yazoo and Tunica. The course of the Yazoo River was drawn with an accuracy that may be recognized on modern topographic maps, and on the left bank the position of the Tunica-Yazoo-Chakchiuma village is precisely indicated, as is the French Fort St. Pierre (1718–1729). This latter establishment postdated the Tunica occupation, but it provides an important datum for the exact location of the combined Indian village.

Fort St. Pierre was situated four leagues inland from the Mississippi and two musket shots distant from the Indian village, according to Pénicaut in 1718 (McWilliams 1953, p. 216). In 1721 Charlevoix gave another measurement, noting that the village was a league from the fort (Charlevoix 1744, vol. 3, p. 413; O'Neill 1977, p. 131). La Harpe, in 1722, was even more specific:

La rivière des Yasons court depuis son entrée jusqu'au fort Saint-Pierre dans le nord-nord-est, ensuite sur le nord-quart-nord-ouest une demi-lieue, et s'en retournant par le nord jusqu'à l'est-quart-nord-est une autre demi-lieue jusqu'à de petits écors de pierre sur lesquels sont situés les établissemens des nations Yasons, Courois, Offogoula et Onspée. (Boimare 1831, pp. 310–311)

Diron d'Artaguiette in 1723 (Mereness 1916, p. 51) and Father Poisson in 1727 (Thwaites 1900, vol. 67, p. 317) confirmed that the Indian occupation was a league from the fort. The archaeological evidence for the identification of the principal Indian village in relation to Fort St. Pierre will be presented in part 2, below.

The Indian occupation ended in the 1730s, when the last of the Yazoo tribes disappear from the historic record. The Quapaw on the lower Arkansas and the Chickasaw and Choctaw in the hills to the east were to remain in place for a century more, but the Yazoo region was finally bereft of permanent Indian occupation. Our study does not end here, however, for the Tunica had already moved from the Yazoo to a haven far to the south.

PERIOD III: PORTAGE DE LA CROIX

The early French explorations that established the new colony of Louisiana were bold thrusts, but they had a vacillating commitment from the French court. Until the LeMoyne brothers—Iberville and Bienville—successfully established a viable French presence at the turn of the seventeenth century, they were a touch-and-go operation.

The establishment of the French in Louisiana stirred the ire of the English, who set the Chickasaw, already brought into the English sphere, upon the Lower Mississippi tribes. The ensuing disturbances were to have a profound effect upon many aboriginal groups. The Natchez, for example, were ultimately rendered unreliable in their alliance to the French, and even the Choctaw were not secure. Among the Yazoo River tribes, the Yazoo and Koroa finally opted for the English. Only the Tunica remained loyal, and they decided to migrate

Figure 21. Section of the Broutin, de Vergés, and Saucier map of 1740. This fine map combines the knowledge of the best cartographers of the period in Louisiana. The *Village Chatchioumans*, site of the earlier Tunica-Yazoo village, may be located with precision on modern topographic maps. (Bibliothèque Nationale, Paris)

south to a location closer to French protection when the Chickasaw began to press hard early in the eighteenth century. Of course, there must be more to the story than has been recorded, but it is clear that the presence of the French missionary Davion among the Tunica singled them out as a target of English-instigated Chickasaw aggression. It is equally obvious that their regard for the missionary and/or his economic (if not spiritual) value to them brought the Tunica closer to the French settlements downriver.

The date of the Tunica migration from the Yazoo was probably 1706. Pénicaut says it was in 1709 (McWilliams 1953, pp. 129–130), but he is notoriously unreliable in matters of chronology. La Harpe gives the 1706 date (Boimare 1831, pp. 100–101; Cain, Koenig, and Conrad 1971, p. 54), and although he was not present in the colony at the time there is supporting evidence that his information is correct. In a letter dated 2 January 1705, Father La Vente wrote Father Tremblay that "the Tonicas of Father Davion are moving down river 80 leagues" (Tremblay to Laval, 4 April 1705, Archives du Séminaire de Québec, N122; Charles O'Neill, personal communication, 1978). It is unlikely that the Tunica delayed their move for very long after this decision, the catalytic event apparently being Chickasaw retaliation for the capture of an English slaver. According to La Harpe, this was a threat that the Tunica did not feel strong enough to resist, and so they emigrated from the Yazoo.

The Tunica moved to the vicinity of the Red River–Mississippi River confluence. They resettled on the left bank of the Mississippi in a region known to this day as the Tunica Hills, presently comprising western Feliciana Parish, Louisiana, and the southwestern corner of Wilkinson County, Mississippi. The region had been occupied by the Houma, who may have preceded the Tunica in descending the river from the Yazoo and thus in a sense "blazed the trail." La Harpe recounts that the Tunica took the Houma by surprise, killed more than half the tribe, and chased the rest away. Pénicaut gives a bloodless account in which the Tunica simply reoccupied the village already vacated by the Houma. Although the violence of La Harpe's story was a common occurrence during these troubled times, it is probable that Pénicaut's version is more nearly correct—if for no other reason than that it accords better with known Tunica actions under similar circumstances in other times and places. Furthermore, even though Pénicaut may have had problems with chronology, his is a firsthand account. In any case, the important point here is that the Tunica resettled in the Houma village.

The location of the Houma-Tunica village is described in considerable detail by many visitors. The best descriptions are found in the records of the initial contacts by Iberville in 1699 and 1700 (French 1875, pp. 79–82, 96; Margry 1881, vol. 4, pp. 174–178, 265, 269–270; Butler 1934, p. 26; McWilliams 1953, pp. 26–27; McWilliams 1981, pp. 67–69; Cain, Koenig, and Conrad 1971, p. 12; Brasseaux 1979, pp. 53–56). The general consensus of all the accounts is that the Houma village was found near a great bend in the Mississippi where the Red River entered on the west and a portage crossed the neck of the bend on the east. The village

itself was said to be situated about two leagues from the southern terminus of the portage—named the Portage de la Croix by Iberville—and on the summit of a steep hill near a little lake. To the north, a bayou connected the lake to the Mississippi some two leagues above the Red River confluence. Father Gravier, who descended the Mississippi River in 1700, gave the additional information that the northern approach to the Houma was a good league and a half from the river landing and confirmed that "the village is situated on the crest of a mountain, rugged and precipitous on all sides" (Shea 1861, p. 143). In the same year, Tonti also stated that the northern end of the portage was one and a half leagues from the village, but noted as well that it was four leagues from the mouth of the Red River (Delanglez 1939, p. 226). These descriptions are complemented by the minutely detailed Delisle 1702 map, which pinpoints the location of the "Village des Ouma" with unparalleled precision (see fig. 20).

The historical references to the Tunica resettlement of the Houma village have been given above; they are confirmed by descriptions of the village during the Tunica occupation which are most reminiscent of (if not as detailed as) those describing the Houma village. In 1716, de Richebourg recorded that the Tunica "*sont sur des terres très hautes*" (French 1851, p. 251) and Bienville, quoted by La Harpe, completed the description by providing the information that the tribe lived on the shores of a lake on the east side of the Mississippi two leagues above the Red River (Boimare 1831, p. 124; Cain, Koenig, and Conrad 1971, p. 96). In 1719, La Harpe himself visited the Tunica and similarly recorded that the village was near a lake on the east side of the river, but three leagues above the Red River (Margry 1888, vol. 6, p. 246), although in 1722 he gave the distance as two leagues. He also measured three leagues from the southern end of the portage to the village. Two years later, in 1721, Father Charlevoix agreed that "the village is beyond the lake, on a pretty high ground [*assez élevé*]," and added the important information that "there are two other villages of this nation at a little distance from this [village]" (Charlevoix 1744, vol. 3, p. 433; French 1851, pp. 173–174; O'Neill 1977, p. 160). Diron d'Artaguiette (1916, pp. 44–45, 88) also seemed to find that in addition to the principal village there was at least one other. Father Poisson was more explicit in 1727: there was a small village at the southern end of the Portage de la Croix, as well as the principal village, Grands Tonicas, two leagues away (Thwaites 1900, vol. 67, p. 305). In January 1731, Abbé Barthellon (1731) also apparently visited Petites Tonicas, lending credence to the existence of more than one Tunica village during this period.

It is reasonable to conclude that the Tunica initially settled at the previous location of the Houma and maintained their principal village there until 1731, during which time satellite occupations were spun off. This is a vital point since the exact location of the main Houma-Tunica village has not yet been confirmed archaeologically, despite the unusual excellence of the historical documentation. However, intensive investigations in the general locale have unearthed small settlements apparently dating to the Tunica period (see part 2).

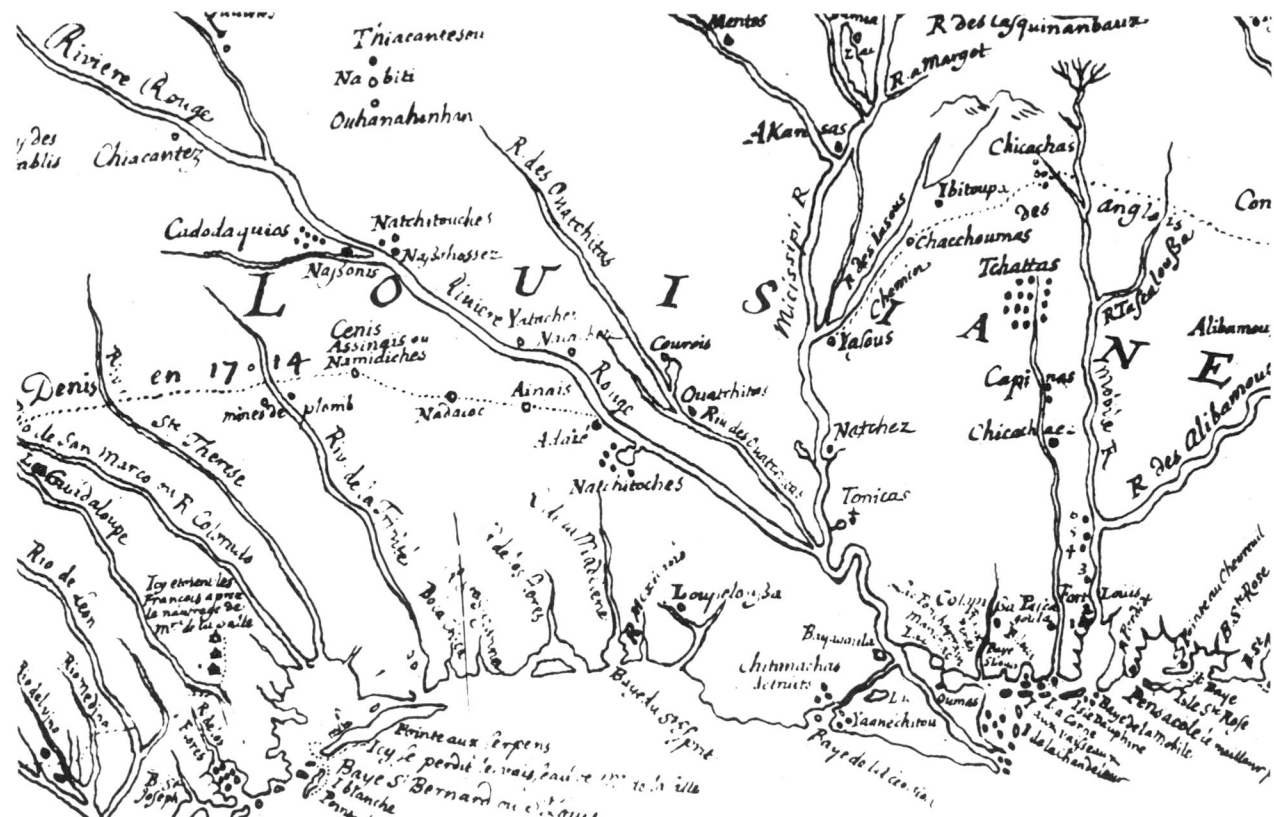

Figure 22. Section of the Le Maire map of 1716. Although lacking the detail of Delisle 1702 (fig. 20), this map clearly places the Tunica in the former location of the Houma, and even the lake is indicated. While Le Maire is not known to have visited the Mississippi, he made an effort to collect the most recent data. This map (or unknown maps from which it was derived) served as a source for the famous Delisle 1718 map (see fig. 9). Particularly noteworthy is the tracing of trails, especially the route of St. Denis to the Southwest in 1714 and the *chemin des Anglois* from "Carleston" to the "Yasous." At least two renderings of this map are known to exist in the Bibliothèque Nationale in Paris. They are virtually identical concerning the Lower Mississippi Valley, except that in the other version "Tonicas" is written as "Tonikas." (Bibliothèque Nationale, Paris)

Contemporary maps provide additional evidence for the growth of a dispersed Tunica settlement pattern during this period (1706/1709–1731). The earliest known map that correctly repositions the Tunica after their move from the Yazoo is that of François Le Maire in 1716 (fig. 22), which clearly places them in the former location of the Houma. Le Maire had made an effort to collect updated information on tribal settlements, and although he did not visit the Mississippi his accuracy in this case, at least, is confirmed by the textual records already cited. Even more conclusive is an anonymous map in the Bibliothèque Nationale of Paris (fig. 23). New Orleans is indicated, so this undated map must have been drawn after 1718. It should be said that the map was "redrawn," since it is a copy of Delisle 1702, but it has been updated and the "Tonicas" have been substituted for the "Village des Oumas" in Delisle's original. Although the map reflects important changes in tribal locations, it represents but a correction of the record and adds no significant new cartographic information.

Many other maps also show the general Tunica presence in the Tunica Hills locale but offer no detail on the actual settlement pattern (Vermale 1717; Delisle 1718; La Harpe ca. 1720; de Beauvilliers 1720; Anonymous 1721; Devin 1721, 1732; D'Anville 1732 [see fig. 66]; Crenay 1733; and numerous French and English maps of later years that need not be cited here because they contain outdated information or are based on secondary sources). There are a few maps, however, that suggest that the Tunica had more than one village in their new location. Bernard Diron d'Artaguiette indicated three villages on his original map of 1719 (Diron d'Artaguiette 1732) (fig. 24), and Ignace François Broutin also charted more than one village for this period in his map of 1731, which is such a vital piece of evidence in the following section (see fig. 25). It must be noted that none of the satellite villages shown on these maps precisely matches the archaeological finds discussed in part 2, but the existence of a settlement pattern that included outlying villages and hamlets is confirmed by the archaeology.

The Tunica lived in this locale until June 1731, when one of those disasters characteristic of the period overtook them (Brain 1977, pp. 12–13). Some surviving Natchez warriors and their allies sought revenge against the Tunica for their support of the French during the recent Natchez rebellion. In a surprise attack on the principal village, the Natchez killed a number of Tunica, including their great chief, Cahura-Joligo. Soon thereafter, the remnants of the tribe moved to a new location on the southern edge of the Tunica Hills near a small tributary of the Mississippi still known as Tunica Bayou.

Figure 23. Section of an anonymous, undated map of the Mississippi River. It is clearly an updated copy of the Delisle 1702 map (see fig. 20) made after New Orleans had been founded in 1718. The "Tonicas" inhabit the exact location of the *Village des Oumas* given in the earlier map. (Bibliothèque Nationale, Paris)

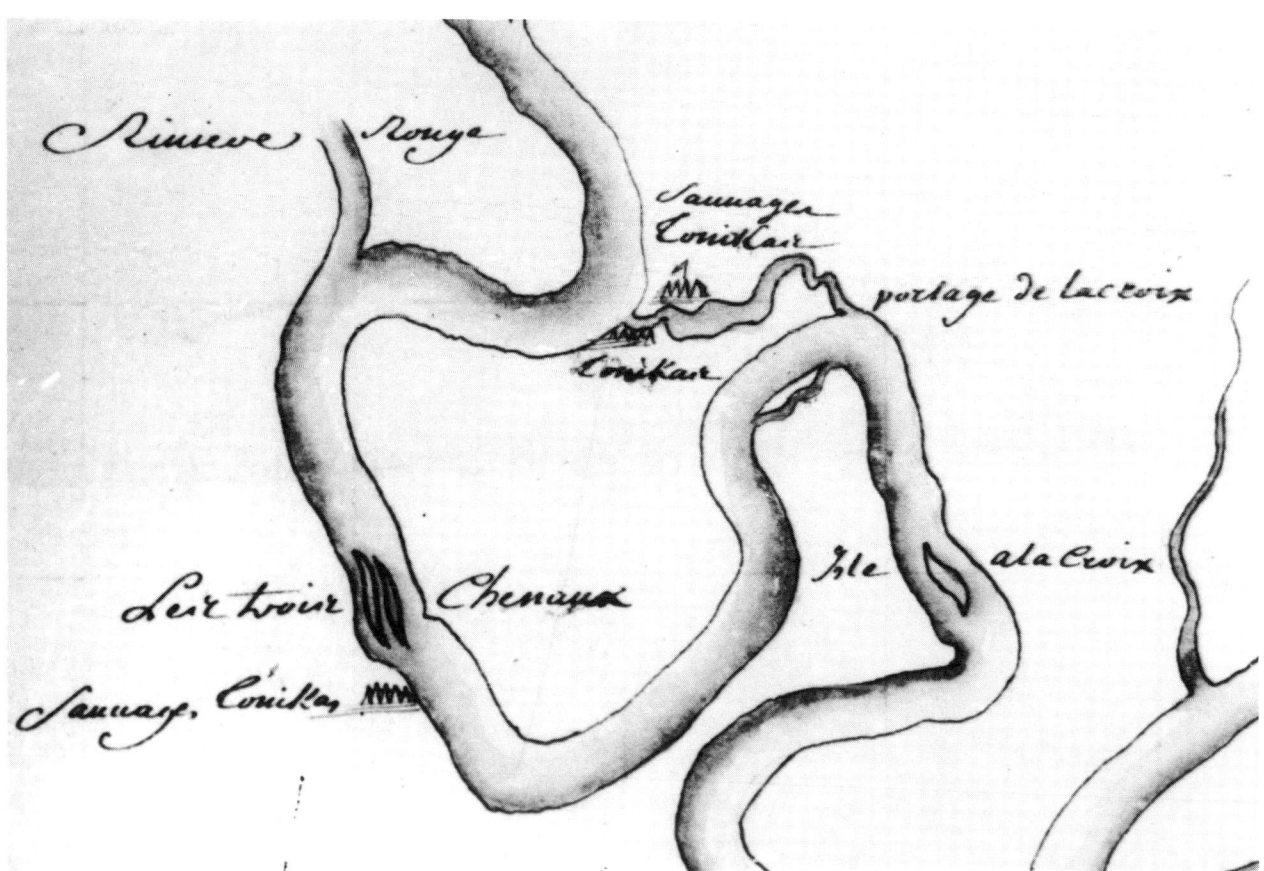

Figure 24. Section of the Bernard Diron d'Artaguiette map dated 1732 but based on observations made in 1719. The map is a very important contribution to the cartography of the Mississippi Valley because it is an original exposition drawn from first-hand experience. Three "Tonikas" villages are located; the principal village is presumably the one on the north side of the lake, flying a pennant. (Bibliothèque Nationale, Paris)

PERIOD IV: TUNICA BAYOU

Tunica Bayou was but a short distance from the tribe's former location, and since by now the Tunica were such an established presence, as well as the only major tribe on the Mississippi south of the Arkansas, no later visitor seems to have felt it necessary to record their exact location in the written documentation. In fact, the only textual references that give any indication of the whereabouts of the Tunica during this period (1731–1764) are those of Vitry in 1738 (Bridges and Delanglez 1964, p. 260), an anonymous officer in 1739 (Claiborne 1880, p. 67), Vaudreuil in 1750 (Rowland, Sanders, and Galloway 1984, vol. 5, p. 48), Bossu in 1751 (Bossu 1768, p. 35; Feiler 1962, p. 30), and Kerlérec in 1758 (de Villiers

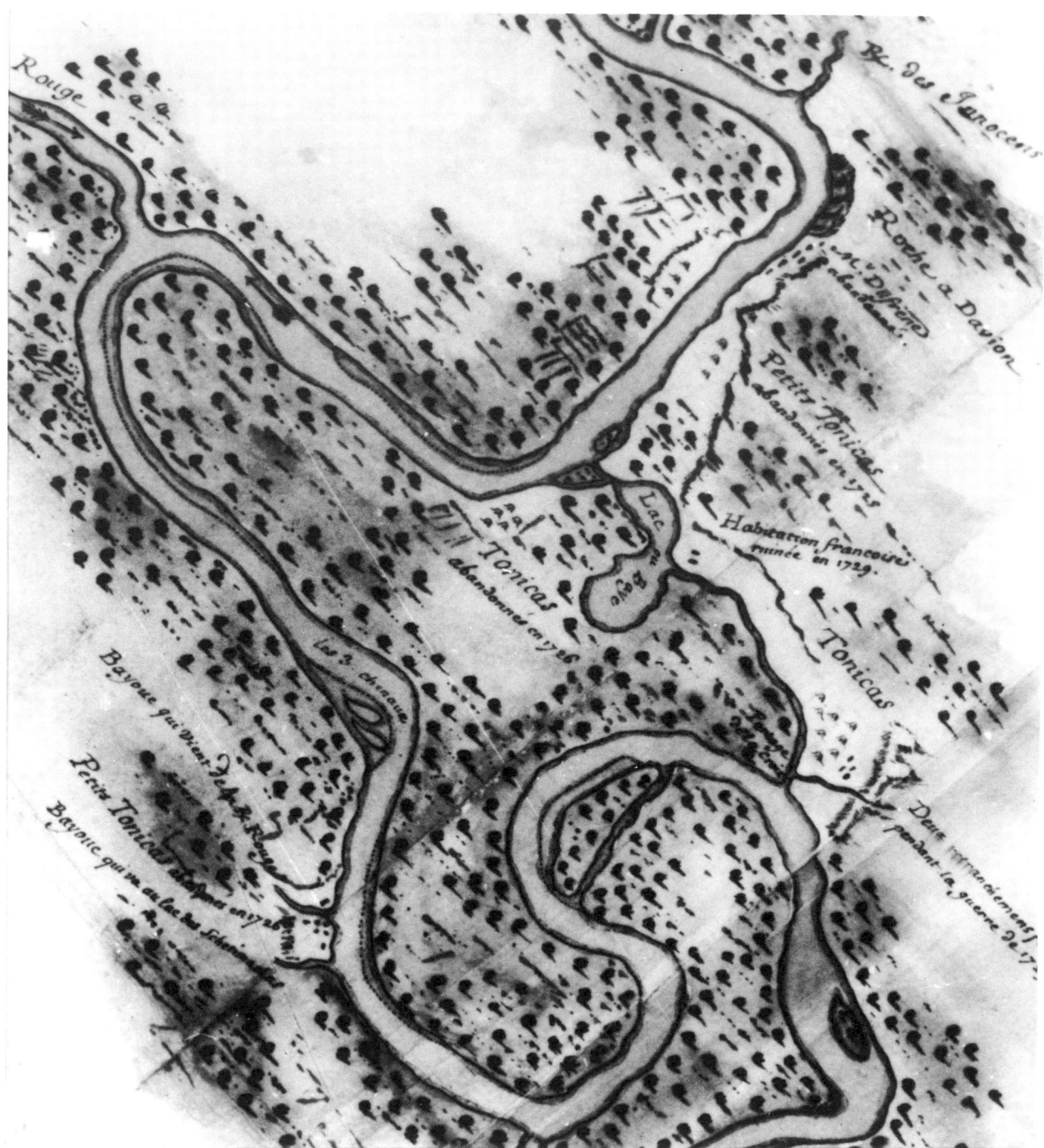

Figure 25. Section of the Broutin map of August 1731. The Tunica village is placed well south of where it was formerly located on the shore of the *Baye des Tonicas* (see also fig. 26): it now appears in the vicinity of Tunica Bayou at the archaeological site known as Trudeau. Note also the locations of other earlier Tunica villages; which indicate the more dispersed settlement pattern that prevailed before the concentration at Trudeau. (Bibliothèque Nationale, Paris)

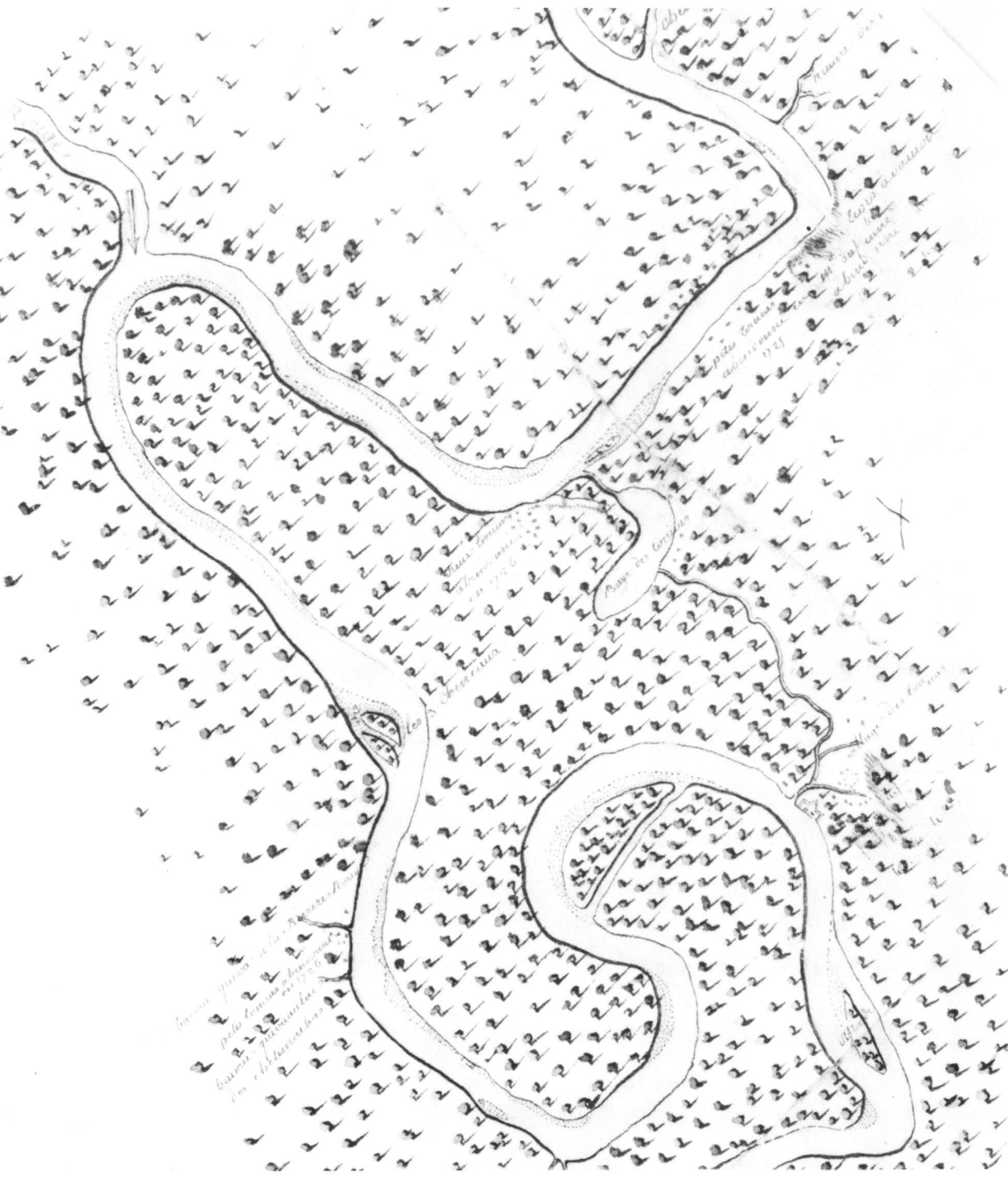

Figure 26. Section of a map attributed to Gonichon, based on the Broutin map of 1731. Note the precise detail with which the Tunica village is drawn and placed in its topographic surroundings. The site plan appears to be an arrangement of houses in a circular pattern in a field, although outlying structures are also indicated across the bayou (see cover illustration and fig. 84). Nearby, on the river bank, a fort is indicated—presumably one of the French posts frequently mentioned in the records as being placed among the Tunica. In late 1731 just such a post was commanded by Sieur Juzan (Brain 1979, app. C.2). (By courtesy of the British Library, London)

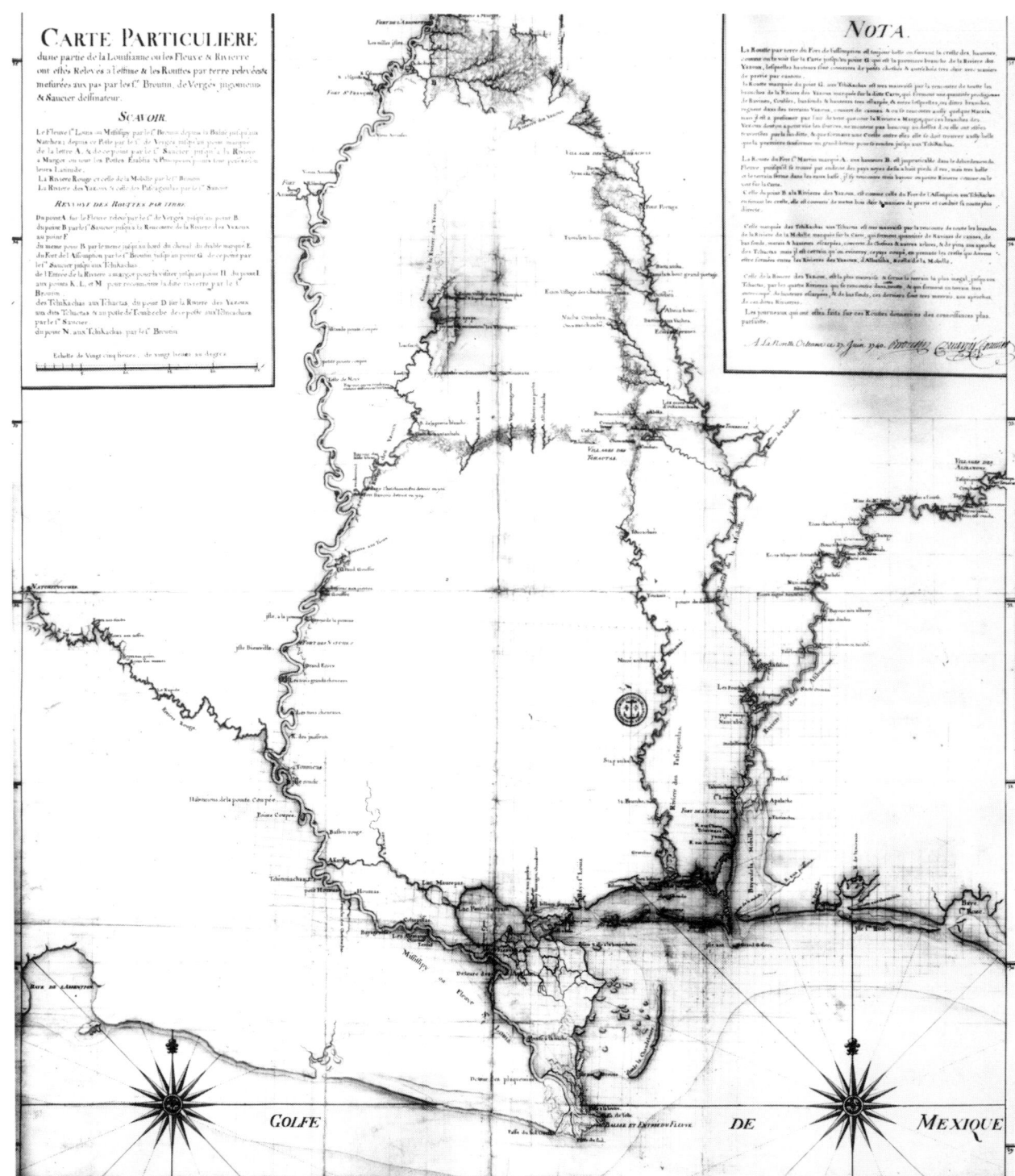

Figure 27. The Broutin, de Vergés, and Saucier map of 1740. This is one of the great eighteenth-century maps, and it stands as a landmark in Louisiana cartography. (Bibliothèque Nationale, Paris)

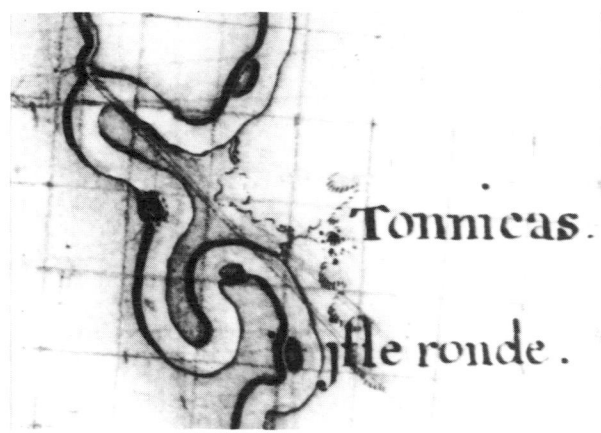

Figure 28. Section of the Broutin, de Vergés, and Saucier map of 1740. Broutin contributed the data for the Lower Mississippi Valley, and although this rendering is quite different from earlier versions it gives essentially the same information. It confirms the location of the "Tonnicas" village on Tunica Bayou, around a hill detached from the first line of bluffs defining the beginning of the Tunica Hills. (Bibliothèque Nationale, Paris)

1907, pp. 74–75), but these are not sufficiently specific to do more than confirm a general locale. The historical identification of the new Tunica village, then, rests solely upon cartographic evidence.

The best maps of the Mississippi Valley for this period are linked by a single individual, Ignace François Broutin. Broutin's credentials are impeccable: he was considered able and diligent in the performance of his varied duties as surveyor, architect, concessionaire, sometime commandant at the Natchez, and engineer-in-chief of the colony (Wilson 1969). In these various capacities he made numerous trips up and down the Mississippi between New Orleans and Natchez. His professional training and familiarity with the natural and cultural geography of the valley are reflected in his precise cartographic work. As early as 1728 it was noted that "Monsieur Broutin is at present doing the surveying from the lower part of the river to this place [New Orleans] and he will do the rest when he goes up to the Natchez . . . being very well acquainted with operations of this sort. He takes all possible pains and . . . appears to be a good fellow, devoted to his profession" (Rowland and Sanders 1929, vol. 2, p. 596).

Broutin's first map was based on these earlier surveys and subsequent voyages on the river. The map is dated August 1731 and obviously was intended to reflect the situation at that precise moment in time, for the Tunica are clearly shown to have relocated to the vicinity of Tunica Bayou (fig. 25). Broutin's skill is evident in this map and in the others he had a hand in making.

A second map also drawn in 1731 is attributed to Gonichon. However, it is obviously another rendering of the Broutin map, and, in fact, Gonichon was Broutin's draftsman. This map is even more interesting in the detail it gives of the new Tunica village and surrounding topographic features (fig. 26). Even the site plan of the village is indicated and is consistent with the sketch of

a Tunica village drawn by Dumont de Montigny during the general period (see cover illustration, this volume).

Another very important map that combined the best cartographic talents in the colony at the time was issued by Broutin, de Vergés, and Saucier in 1740 (fig. 27). It delineates all the important geographic features of Louisiana from the Balise to Fort de l'Assomption and from Natchitoches to Fort Toulouse. Despite the scale, the map is exquisitely detailed and, unlike most compilations, is a rich source of primary information. The Mississippi River from the Balise to Natchez was the work of Broutin, but the rendering is not simply a modification of his earlier map(s) to fit the new scale: there are subtle changes in the course of the river, as well as other features, and new information has been added. Fortunately, the Tunica Hills region is given especially detailed attention (fig. 28). The Tunica are precisely located on Tunica Bayou where it comes out of the hills, and a prominent bluff feature is incorporated within the village. This portion of the map is so accurate that it may easily be matched with a modern topographic map, even allowing for the fact that the Mississippi has since taken away the lower course of Tunica Bayou and the site is now perched precariously on the present bank of the river (see fig. 54).

The importance of the Broutin, de Vergés, and Saucier map is attested by the fact that it was the standard for the remainder of the French Dominion. At the very end, in 1763, it was updated by Demandeville. Unfortunately, the rendering of the Tunica location is somewhat simplified (fig. 29), but the settlement is still clearly in place at this date. As a matter of cartographic interest, but little historical value, a slightly modified ver-

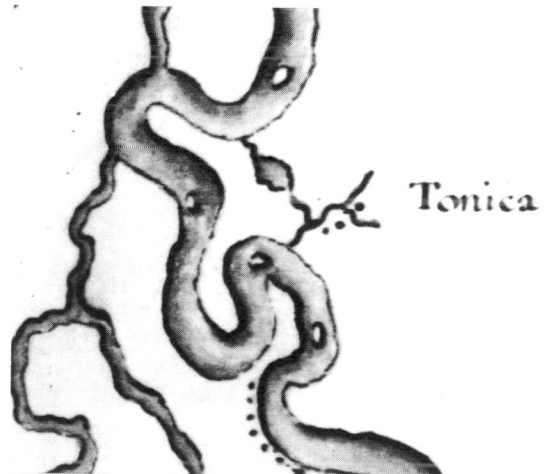

Figure 29. Section of the Demandeville map of 1763. This fine map represents the state of the cartographic art at the end of the French regime: it is a composite that drew upon the earlier work of Devin, Broutin, Gonichon, de Vergés, and Saucier, as well as data developed by Demandeville. The part depicting the Lower Mississippi River reveals no new information and is but a simplified version of the Broutin, de Vergés, and Saucier 1740 map. However, this map does establish that the Tunica were still on Tunica Bayou in 1763 (Bibliothèque Nationale, Paris)

sion of this map was reissued by Broutin's son in 1764 at the beginning of the Spanish regime (Rodriguez Casado 1942, pl. 15).

Of more historical interest, although of little cartographic value, are a number of other maps drawn during the last thirty years of the French Dominion. Although not as detailed as those already discussed, and therefore not as useful for identifying the precise location of the Tunica village during this period, they nevertheless provide independent confirmation of the general provenience. One of these maps is of particular interest because it is probably attributable to Alexandre DeBatz (ca. 1732) (fig. 30). If he was the cartographer, the map may have

been made in the spring of 1732 when DeBatz traveled upriver to the Natchez and stopped off among the Tunica. During this trip he drew the sketches for his famous set of watercolors (Bushnell 1927), including the one of Bride-les-Boeufs (Brain 1979, cover illustration; fig. 208, this vol.). DeBatz was brought to the colony as the draftsman of Pierre Baron, who was briefly (1729–1731) engineer-in-chief of Louisiana. Subsequently, and for most of his thirty-year career in the colony, DeBatz became a well-known and highly regarded architect and engineer (Wilson 1963). Therefore, although the map under consideration here is but a crude sketch, it may be considered reliable. The Tunica

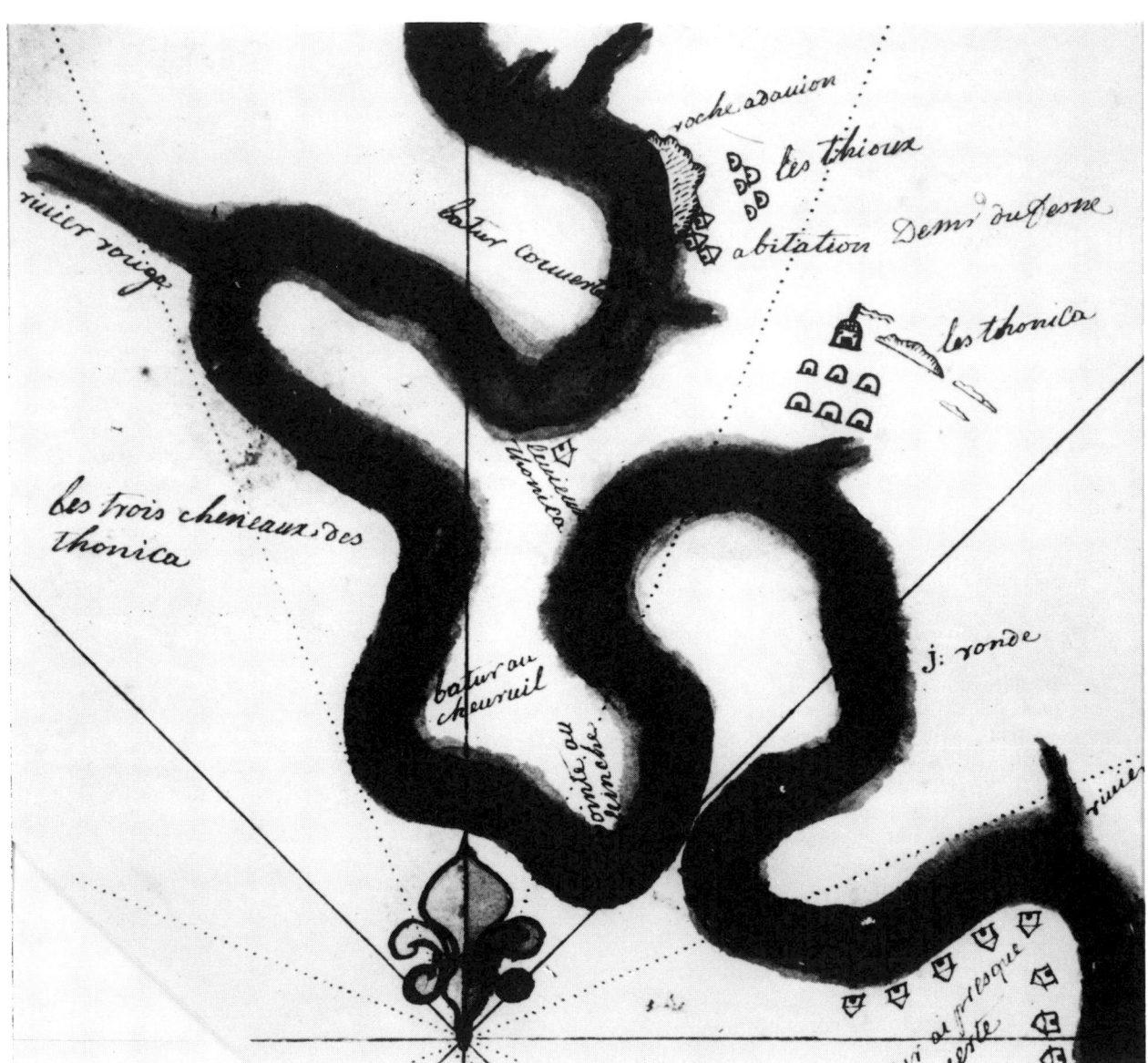

Figure 30. Section of a map attributed to Alexandre DeBatz. Although the style is not like other known DeBatz maps (de Villiers 1921; Wilson 1963), nor the calligraphy as elegant, the compass rose is very similar to that drawn on the DeBatz map of 1747 (ibid.), and the unusual spelling of "Thonicas" is found on the Bride-les-Boeufs watercolor (see fig. 208). Since this map is also a watercolor sketch, it would seem to match, although it is to be regretted that the same commitment to accurate detail was not followed (perhaps because this field sketch was not subsequently "*redigez à Nouvelle Orleans*"?). If the map was part of this series, then it was drawn in 1732. (Bibliothèque Nationale, Paris)

village is clearly positioned south of the old Portage de la Croix, on a major tributary (presumably Tunica Bayou), and near some bluffs.

Generally, however, the contemporary maps are not even this specific. The most famous and widely circulated are the most useless for the present study. Examples include Bellin's "Carte de la Louisiane, cours du Mississipi et pais voisins," which was published by Charlevoix (1744) and reissued in many other editions as late as 1757; Dumont de Montigny's "Carte de la Louisiane, Colonie française avec le cours du fleuve St. Louis," published in his *Mémoires Historiques sur la Louisiane* (1753); and Le Page du Pratz's "Carte de la Louisiane" (dated 1757), published in his *Histoire de la Louisiane* (1758). In all cases, the publication dates are much later than the dates of the accounts, and even though the Bellin and Le Page du Pratz maps were updated, their scale precludes more than the observation that the Tunica are generally placed in the Tunica Hills–Tunica Bayou region. In 1764, however, Bellin published a map that showed the Tunica Hills in some detail and incorrectly placed the Tunica in their pre-1731 position, which makes all of Bellin's maps suspect.

As might be expected since the English were successfully kept off the Mississippi, English maps of the period contribute little to this study. The well-known Popple 1733 and Mitchell 1755 maps were, perforce, based on outdated information concerning the Lower Mississippi area (Cumming 1958, pp. 101, 199, 224). An interesting exception is the Bowen 1748 map, self-proclaimed to have been "drawn from original draughts, assisted by the most approved maps and charts." Whatever the sources of Bowen's information, they were uncommonly accurate for the Tunica: despite an unconventional rendering of the course of the Mississippi River, the Tunica are clearly and properly placed in position on Tunica Bayou (fig. 31).

By the Treaty of Paris in 1763, England finally gained control of all Louisiana east of the Mississippi River. In 1764, she began to assert her sovereignty and the 22nd Regiment, under the command of Major Arthur Loftus, was sent up the Mississippi to take possession of Fort Chartres in the Illinois country. On the morning of 20 March, while slowly working against the current in a narrow channel abreast the high bluffs marking the north end of the Tunica Hills—a landmark known as the Roche à Davion, but soon to be referred to as Loftus's Cliffs—the expedition was fired upon from the shore (Rea 1973a). The ambushers were Indians, among whom the Tunica were later acknowledged to be predominant. The exposed British could not even see their concealed attackers; unable to reply and taking casualties, they turned about and retreated to New Orleans.

Apparently fearing reprisals—for the angry British had fired on their village during the retreat downriver—the Tunica fled to Mobile (Brasseaux 1979, p. 114). Thus, in a time of stress their migratory disposition once again asserted itself. The Tunica soon returned to the Mississippi (as discussed in the following section), but their occupation of the Tunica Hills–Tunica Bayou region had ended. Only their name remained to remind us of their tenancy.

In the "latter end" of the year 1765, the English Lieutenant John Ross was commissioned to make a new survey of the Mississippi River. His map, published in 1775, was based on earlier French maps but was "improved" by his observations. The French maps at his disposal were clearly not the most up-to-date: in the pertinent section of his map (fig. 32), the Tunica are placed at their old location near the north end of the Portage de la Croix, a designation, moreover, not used on the more recent French maps. It is unlikely that the Tunica would have ambushed the British convoy on their own doorstep, where instant retaliation might have been expected should the attack have failed. In any event, as revealed below, the Tunica had by this time been relocated farther to the south, so this information must be discounted as outdated. On the other hand, Ross refers to the more recent location of the Tunica near the southern end of the portage as their "ancient village," implying that it was abandoned and thereby confirming the historical data.

Figure 31. Section of the Bowen map of 1748. For English cartographers of the period, Bowen was unusually well informed about the Lower Mississippi Valley. Although the Mississippi River is rendered in a rather unique style, there is no confusion regarding the accurate placement of the "Tonikas." (Map Collection, Harvard College Library, Cambridge)

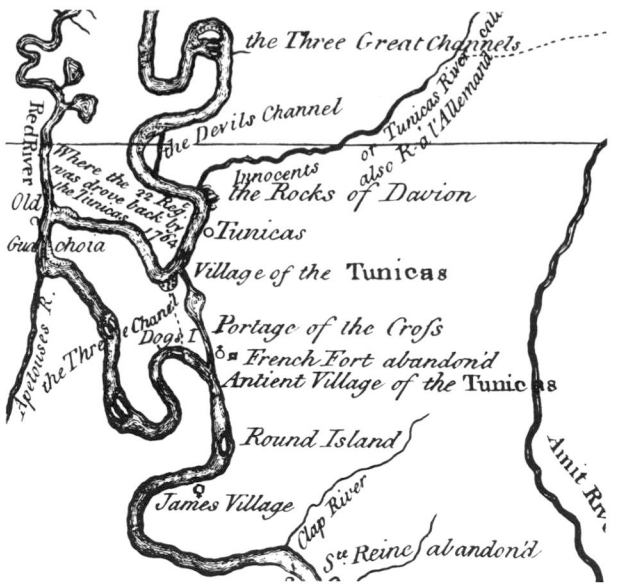

Figure 32. Section of the Ross map published in 1775. This map was based on a 1765 survey and earlier French maps. The placement of the Tunica "where the 22 Reg. was drove back" is presumably derived from old French sources, and Ross supplies the new information that the Tunica Bayou locale had apparently been abandoned. The nearby French fort may be the same one depicted on the Gonichon 1731 map (see fig. 26). In the collections of the U.S. Army Corps of Engineers in Vicksburg, Mississippi, there is a photostatic copy of an anonymous English map of West Florida dating to the same period, which essentially duplicates this information on the Tunica and is probably a revised copy of the Ross map. (LMS Map Library, Peabody Museum of Archaeology and Ethnology, Harvard University)

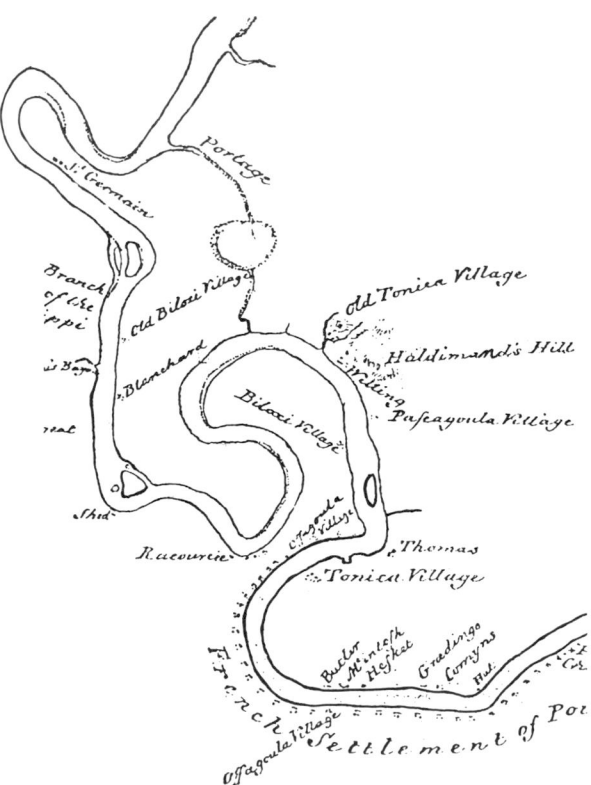

Figure 33. Section of a map made by George Gauld, British Admiralty Surveyor. Although dated 1768 in the Louisiana State University map library, it was probably drawn in the spring of 1774 (Ware 1982, pp. 161–162). Note that the bluff next to "Old Tonica Village" is referred to as Haldimand's Hill and the establishment at its base is identified as Willing. The Tunica are shown at their new location opposite the upper end of the French settlement of Pointe Coupée. (Map Library, School of Geoscience, Louisiana State University, Baton Rouge)

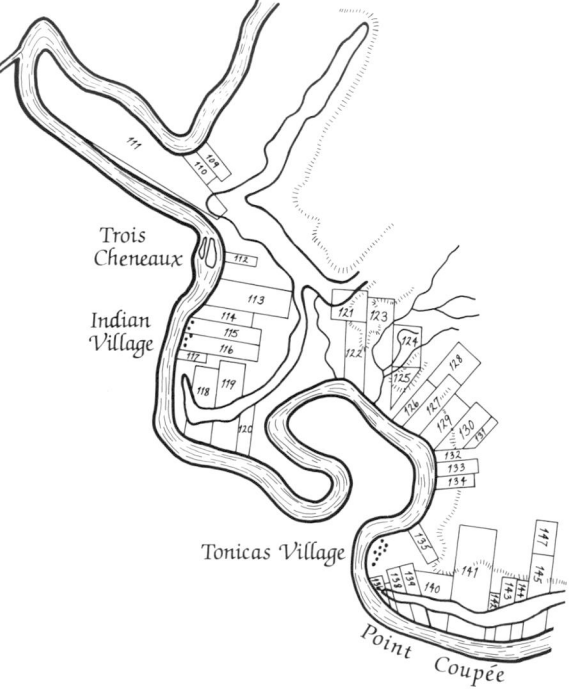

Figure 34. Section of the Wilton map of 1774. This first detailed map of British land grants along the Mississippi was surveyed by William Wilton for Peter Chester, governor of West Florida. Grants 123 (Henry Fairchild), 124 (Herbert de Munster), and 125 (General Frederick Haldimand) shared the location of the "Old Tonica Village." The encroachment of the Mississippi River subsequently took a considerable part of Fairchild's tract and most of Haldimand's, and the Tunica village site was eventually incorporated into what has since become known as Trudeau Plantation. (After the original which appears in the Map Collection, Mississippi River Commission, Vicksburg)

By way of postscript, it is useful for nomenclatural purposes to describe the subsequent history of this last seat of the Tunica in this region. The British did not let such prime land lie abandoned for long. As a reward for their service during the late war, many soldiers were given land grants in the new territories. Brigadier General Frederick Haldimand was one such grantee, and he received at least four tracts totaling 3,000 acres. One grant of 500 acres, awarded in 1768, included part of the "Old Tonica Village" (figs. 33–34). Haldimand apparently gave the land to James Willing (Willing 1772; Carpenter 1847), who in turn seems to have transferred it to Oliver Pollock while they were serving the patriot cause in the area during the Revolution. Their brief tenures were recognized, however: Tunica Bayou was known for a time as Willing's Bayou (e.g., Ellicott 1962, pp. 124, 178), and a small tributary on the south side of the village site is known to this day as Pollock's Bayou (see fig. 54). In a notarized deposition taken in

Philadelphia in 1801, Pollock sold to his brother Jarret this land "known under the name of Old Tunica Village, near the Bayou Willing, the same which the grantor bought nearly twenty years ago of James Willing" (Pollock 1801). It seems, however, that Pollock had not retained legal title to the land throughout those twenty years. He apparently vacated the land, probably because of his great debts incurred in the cause of the Revolution (Kinnaird 1946a, p. 88) and his disfavor with the Spanish government, and it was seized by the Spanish after they captured West Florida. A 1788 survey by Carlos [Charles Laveau] Trudeau, surveyor general during the Spanish regime, shows that the Haldimand tract had been abandoned (fig. 35). Not coincidentally, Trudeau was granted that tract in December 1788 or January 1789. Trudeau soon died, however, and his widow resold the land to Pollock on 2 March 1789. In spite of the brief ownership, the name Trudeau has identified the property—and the Tunica village site—ever since.

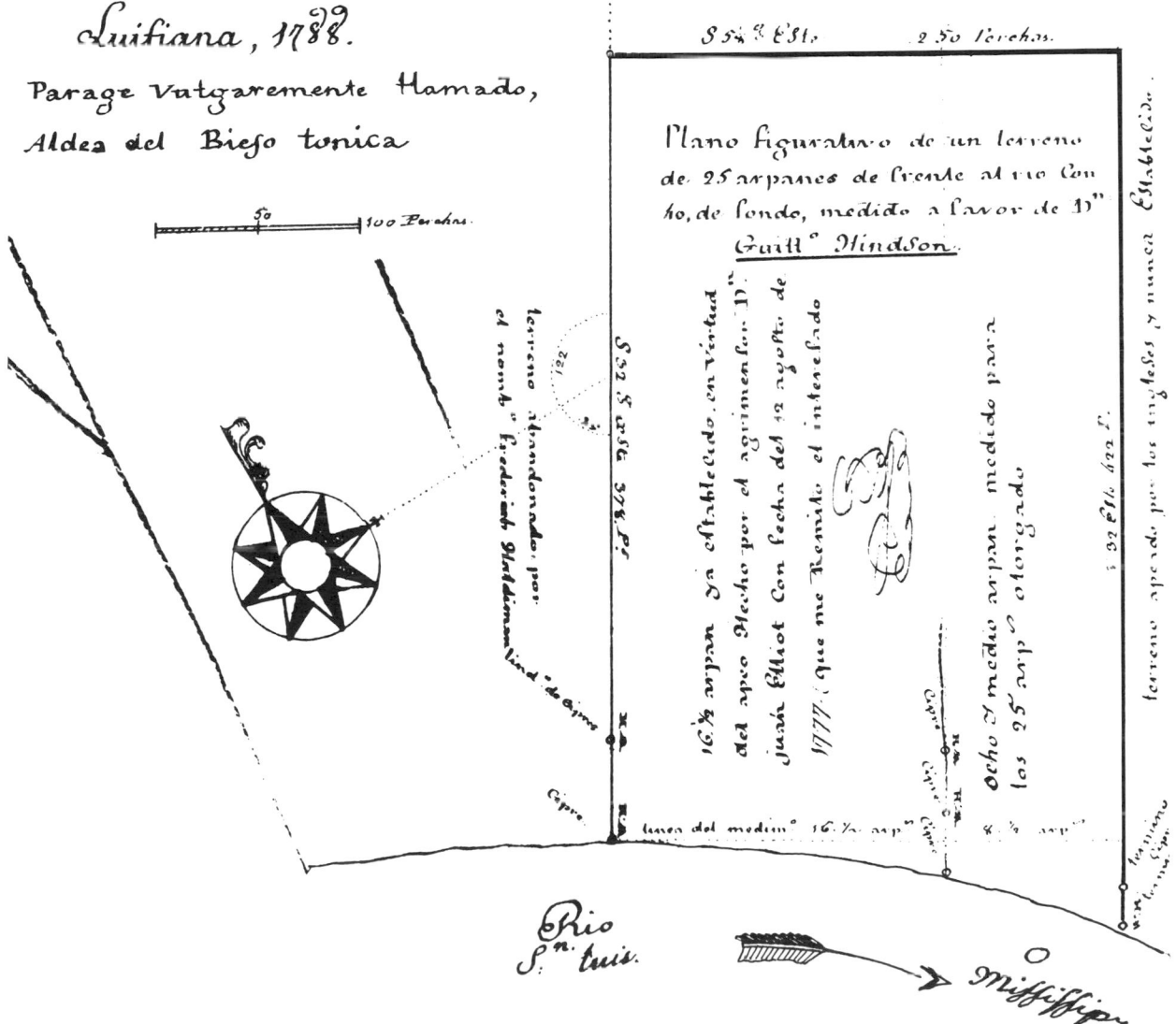

Figure 35. Survey plot made by Carlos Trudeau in 1788. The land "commonly called the site of the Old Tonica" is identified as having been abandoned by Frederick Haldiman (*sic*). (Archivo General de Indias, Seville)

PERIOD V: POINTE COUPÉE

After the ambush of the Loftus expedition in March 1764, the Tunica had fled from the Mississippi to Mobile. Early in April, however, they sought the protection of the new Spanish regime in New Orleans (Brasseaux 1979, p. 114). Jean-Jacques-Blaise d'Abbadie, governor of the transition administration, granted permission for the Tunica to resettle on the Mississippi, and apparently they were temporarily established near Bayou Lafourche (ibid.). By July, however, they seem to have moved to the vicinity of Pointe Coupée (ibid., p. 122), not far downriver from their earlier settlement on Tunica Bayou. That same month, the Tunica made their peace with the English and "New Tonicas" was founded on the east side of the river in English territory, but neighboring the French settlements at Pointe Coupée on the Spanish side of the river (Rowland 1911, p. 267).

Curiously, the Ross map, drawn over a year later in 1765 (Ross 1775), does not show the new Tunica village, although a European establishment named "James Village" is indicated in the vicinity (see fig. 32). However, the map drawn by Philip Pittman the same year, entitled "A Draught of the River Mississippi from the Balise up to Fort Chartres" and published in his 1770 volume, clearly identifies the Tunica in the new location (fig. 36). Pittman was recognized by his contemporaries as a highly competent and accurate surveyor (Rea 1973b), and his map was the first to give a completely new English version of the Mississippi. In his accompanying text, Pittman described the Tunica settlement as being "on the east side of the river, and about two miles above the last plantation of Pointe Coupée (Pittman 1770, p. 35).

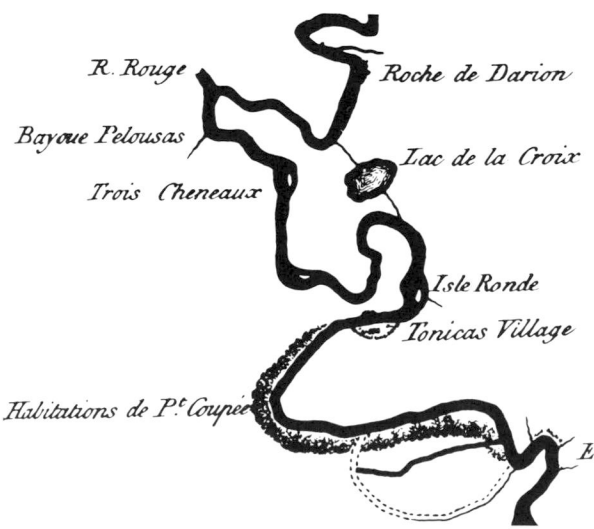

Figure 36. Section of the Pittman map of 1765 (published 1770). Although there are many superficial similarities to the Ross map of the same year (see fig. 32), in this map the course of the Mississippi River appears to be more accurate and the information regarding the location of the Tunica is more up-to-date. (LMS Map Library, Peabody Museum of Archaeology and Ethnology, Harvard University)

On his tour of inspection of the new territories in 1766, Captain Harry Gordon of the Royal Corps of Engineers measured the distance from the center of the Tunica village to the beginning of the Pointe Coupée settlement at one and a half miles (Mereness 1916, pp. 488–489; Alvord and Carter 1916, p. 311). The Durnford 1770, Gauld 1774, and Wilton 1774 maps illustrate the relationship in greater detail (figs. 33, 34, 37). The Gauld and Wilton maps also show the nearby tract that had been granted to Mrs. Margaret Thomas. Mrs. Thomas was the wife of Lieutenant John Thomas, British Indian agent for the district and himself the recipient of a land grant from the Tunica (Rea 1970a, pp. 30, 34–35). Thomas's record that the Tunica village was a league above the Spanish post at Pointe Coupée (ibid., p. 13) therefore should have been based on intimate knowledge. The location of the post is plotted on the Gauld and Wilton maps, and on the Des Barres map of 1779 (fig. 38).

Comparing the Durnford, Gauld, Wilton, and Des Barres maps, it is evident that the Tunica were being increasingly hemmed in by European settlement. Writing ca. 1780, Thomas Hutchins confirmed that the upper plantations of Pointe Coupée had reached a point opposite the Tunica village (Hutchins 1784, pp. 44, 95). Already, European infringement on Tunica lands had been reported (Rea 1970a, p. 20), and it must have been very clear that the Tunica's days at this prime location were numbered. The last reliable record of Tunica presence at this particular site is found in a deposition taken in December 1784 (Rivas 1786).

Although there are later references to the presence of Tunica peoples in the general neighborhood (e.g., Davis 1806, p. 96; Ashe 1808, pp. 323–324; Schultz 1810, pp. 157–158; Rowland 1930, p. 209), it is probable that even if accurate these reports describe only temporary encampments of individuals who returned to their old haunts for trading or other purposes. For before the century was out the Tunica had moved once again, finally abandoning the Mississippi as their permanent abode, and had resettled up the Red River on Avoyelles Prairie.

It must be noted that this segment of the Tunica odyssey will forever remain a historical record unsupported by archaeological confirmation. A comparison of the eighteenth-century maps with a modern topographic map reveals the reason for the archaeological blank: encroachment of the Mississippi River during the past two hundred years has claimed the former location of the Pointe Coupée village site, and probably any temporary camps as well. Once again, all that remains is the name, as preserved in the nearby Tunica Swamp and Tunica Island.

PERIOD VI: MARKSVILLE

In order to consolidate their borders, the new European regimes—the English on the east and the Spanish on the west—attempted to lure the Mississippi Valley tribes to secure locations in their respective domains.

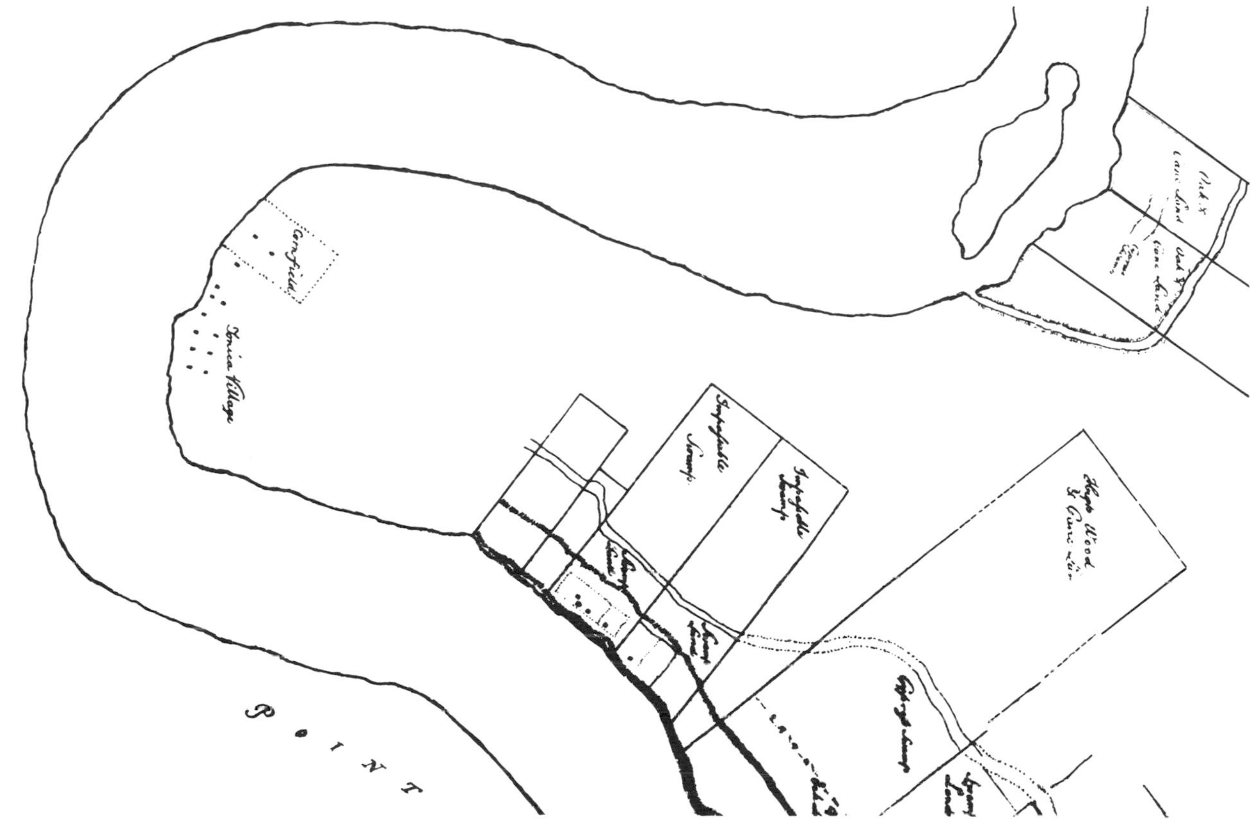

Figure 37. Section of the Durnford map of 1770. The Tunica village is clearly shown in its location near Pointe Coupée. Of particular interest is the apparently linear pattern of the site plan and the nearby communal(?) cornfield. (Map Collection, Mississippi Department of Archives and History, Jackson)

Figure 38. Section of a map published by Des Barres in 1779 (possibly based on an original by General George H. V. Collot). This map details the location of the "Toniac" village and its growing encirclement by Franco-Spanish and English settlements (cf. figs. 33, 34, 37). (Map Collection, Harvard College Library, Cambridge)

Although the policy was soon ignored because the tribal remnants were too impotent to be of value and, from the perspectives of their new masters, too inconstant to be trusted, the precedent had been established.

The Spanish were granting land on the Red River to Indians as early as the 1760s (Whelan and Pearson 1983, p. 31). In 1771, John Thomas noted the initial success of this policy among Mississippi River tribes: "Several smaller groups had separated from these tribes and were settled on the Red River" (Rea 1970a, p. 13). The Tunica might have followed a similar pattern of resettling in groups, but since it was their custom to move as a tribe it may be supposed that they followed tradition, at least to the extent that the principal village was relocated as a unit. When this official move occurred is unrecorded, but it must have been soon after 1784—perhaps as early as 1786. A Spanish report dated 1788 seems to indicate that the Tunica are no longer on the Mississippi (Kinnaird 1946a, p. 250). The 1788 Filhiol map of the Red and Ouachita rivers does not locate the Tunica at all (Williams 1982), although another map of the same date places them on the west side of the Mississippi near Avoyelles Prairie (Bonne 1788). The Tardieu map of 1796 clearly shows that the Tunica were no longer permanently established on the Mississippi (fig. 39), and their absence was confirmed the following year by Ellicott (1962). At the time of the assumption of American control, the Tunica were firmly in place at Avoyelles (Brackenridge 1814, p. 82; Warden 1819, p. 530; Gallatin 1836, p. 115; but cf. Rowland 1930, p. 209), and by the second or third decade of the nineteenth century even any last temporary encampments on the Mississippi had been abandoned (Bradbury 1904, p. 238; Thwaites 1900, vol. 65, p. 267; Wilhelm 1835, p. 102).

Figure 39. Section of a map dated 1796, engraved by Tardieu. There are both French and English versions of this map which differ in some minor details (presumably engraver's errors). They agree, however, in confirming the absence of permanent Tunica habitation on the Mississippi although their name is still prominent. (Map Collection, Harvard College Library, Cambridge)

It is not known what formal arrangements were made for acquiring the land at Avoyelles. The Tunica might have simply moved in, or they could have purchased the property from the Avoyelles Indians or some other group. There is a persistent legend in their own folklore, however, that the tract was obtained through a Spanish grant (Haas 1950, pp. 137–145). This seems entirely likely, given the precedents already set, although no documentation has survived to support the claim. Nevertheless, the Tunica have remained in situ for the last two centuries, at least to the extent that a core group has lived on the tribal lands in what has since become known as the town of Marksville (fig. 40).

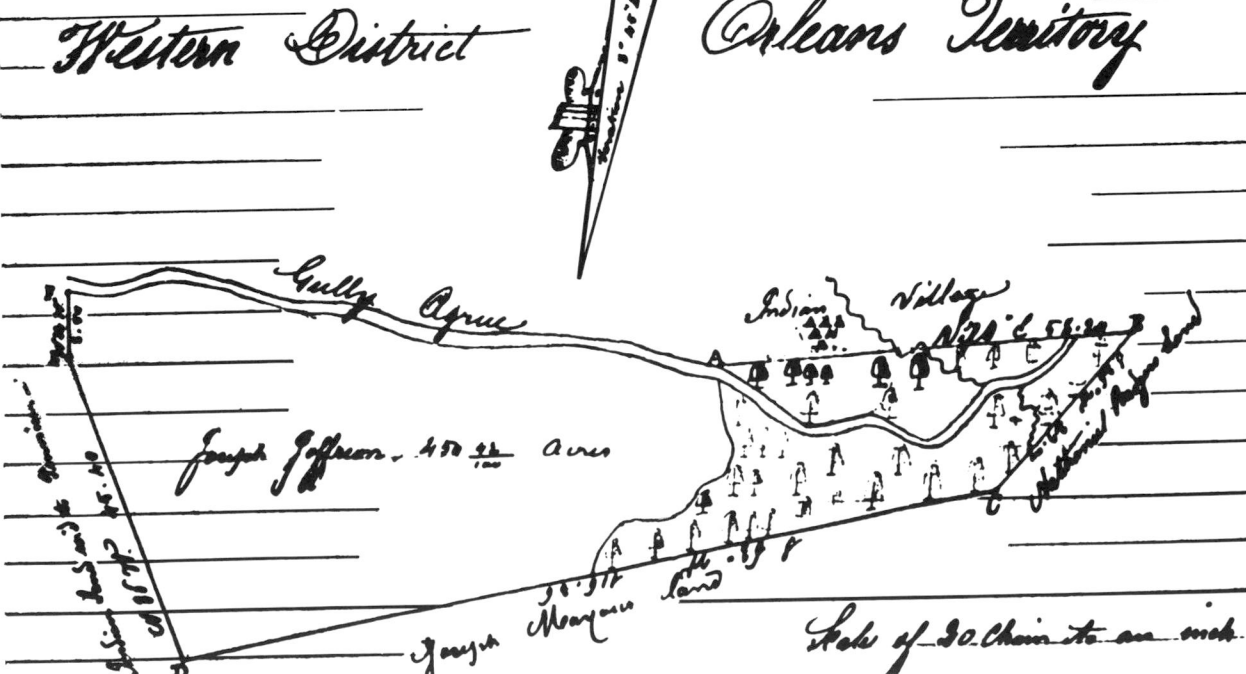

Figure 40. An 1870 confirmation of an earlier land survey in the town of Marksville (Joffrion 1870). The Tunica Indian village is clearly shown north of the Coulée des Grues ("Gully Agrue"), where descendants are to be found to this very day. (Map Collection, Mississippi River Commission, Vicksburg)

Summary

When this research project began, the Tunica were a historical presence who were known to have lived in the Yazoo Basin when first contacted and subsequently were recorded at several locations in the vicinity of the Red River, including their final settlement at Marksville, Louisiana. Documentary and cartographic research carried out during the course of the project has refined the sequence of, and provided somewhat more precise placements for, the various pre-Marksville settlements. Nevertheless, none of these was confirmed: that is, archaeological evidence was required to prove village provenience and Tunica habitation. James Ford (1936) had hypothetically correlated some archaeological remains with the Tunica but had not secured the ethnic identification. A primary objective of the following pages is to confirm Ford's hypotheses and demonstrate other correlations along an ethnic continuum.

Part Two: Archaeological Investigations

Part 1 of this volume detailed the known documentation on the locations and movements of the Tunica, but although they were a historical presence, they were inadequately placed. In part 2 we overcome that lack of precise geographical reference by following the archaeological trail of the Tunica as revealed by this project. Due to the nature of archaeological data, we also learn much about the material culture of the Tunica, as well as that of some other peoples (for the discrimination is important). This knowledge provides a foundation for the ethnohistorical reconstruction attempted in part 3. Part 2, then, represents the most important contribution of this volume, for it presents new data developed during ten years of investigations of the Tunica.

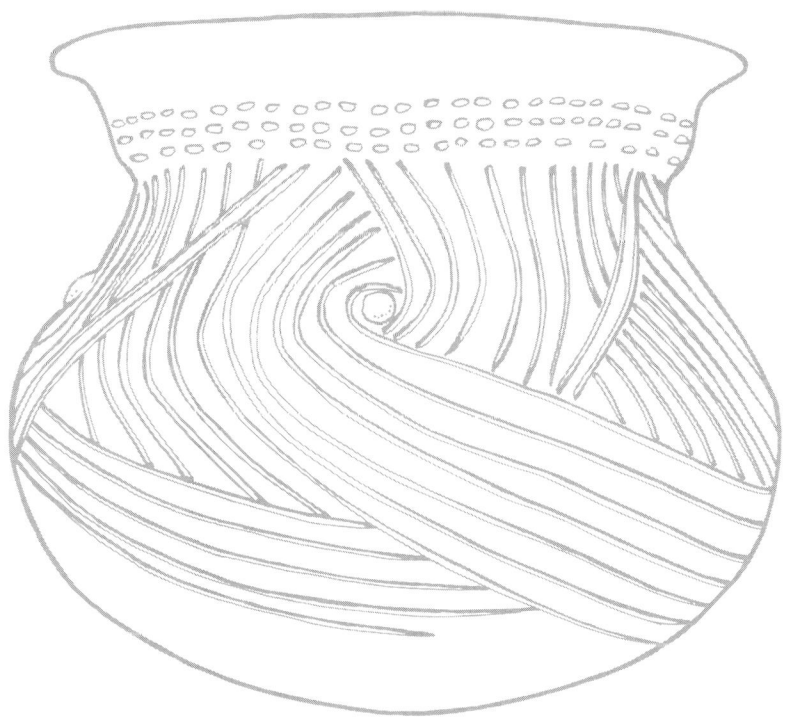

Background

The archaeology of the Tunica is indebted to more than a century of research in the Lower Mississippi Valley. Specific contributions are discussed in the appropriate sections that follow. It is prerequisite, however, to put the work in context by first tracing the broad outline of aboriginal culture history that has been established through modern archaeological investigations in that portion of the valley under consideration.

HISTORY OF THE ARCHAEOLOGY

The archaeology of the Mississippi Valley, as elsewhere in the country, was founded in the antiquarian studies of the nineteenth century. The relatively spectacular aboriginal remains of the newly opened territories, however, especially excited the imaginations of those so inclined to notice—the valley was a primary battleground of the "mound builder" controversy—and it attracted the most inquisitive minds of the period. Ephraim G. Squier and Edwin H. Davis, Montroville W. Dickeson, and Clarence B. Moore were the best, and even by the standards we apply today made substantial contributions, some of which will be noted below.

The era of modern archaeology in the Lower Mississippi Valley began with the excavation of the Deasonville site in 1929 by Henry B. Collins, Jr. Although Collins's foray was brief, his influence on Lower Mississippi archaeology was profound. Not only was the site report (Collins 1932a) a model of reportage for the times, it was also a seminal work that presented the program of archaeology adopted by the next generation of Lower Mississippi Valley archaeologists. It may seem incredible that so modest a publication—an article of only twenty-two pages—should have had such an impact, and in itself it probably did not. The influence instead was personal. Assigned by the Mississippi Department of Archives and History to work with Collins at Deasonville was a young Mississippian, James A. Ford. An attentive student, Ford had already been doing archaeological research, and he carried on Collins's ideas. Most of the innovations set forth in the Deasonville report were espoused by Ford and thus became major tenets in the growth of modern archaeology under his direction. Although a few unsound theories were incorporated in these articles of faith, the foundations of modern practice had been laid.

The first major building block, in fact the cornerstone, in the edifice of Lower Valley culture history was Ford's *Analysis of Indian Village Site Collections from Louisiana and Mississippi* (1936). In this work Ford described collections composed primarily of lowly potsherds from small, insignificant sites (in addition to large, well-known ones), emphases which were proposed by Collins. Furthermore, Ford was doing more than just descriptive archaeology: he was comparing and correlating his data as well. He defined complexes of artifacts and placed them in time and space, and the first regional chronology was born. In addition to two periods of prehistoric complexes, Ford attempted to identify other complexes with known historic tribes. Among these ethnic identifications was a "Tunica complex" (ibid., pp. 98–110). Although his formulation is subject to considerable revision, as is discussed in the following pages, this was the first archaeological resurrection of the Tunica.

Ford had provided a basic culture-historical interpretation for the archaeology of the southern portion of the Lower Valley. Neatly complementary, another study soon appeared that focused on the upper reaches of the valley. While Philip Phillips's ambitious study, entitled "Introduction to the Archaeology of the Mississippi Valley," was mainly a literature search, it provided a comprehensive introduction to the subject (Phillips 1939). For the first time, the known archaeology was synthesized on a large scale, cultural units were formulated and described in detail, regional chronologies were constructed, and causative (or processual) developments were analyzed. Ethnic correlations again were attempted; because of the northerly focus of the study, these were generally considered within the framework of a basic late prehistoric cultural pattern that was coming to be known as "Mississippian." It is of special relevance to our present concerns that Phillips accepted, albeit with some reservations, Ford's Tunica complex and related it to Mississippian remains from eastern Arkansas (ibid., pp. 719–721). Although the correlation was admitted to be tenuous, the connection will be proven valid.

In 1939, Ford and Phillips decided to team up. Enlisting James B. Griffin, they formed the Lower Mississippi Alluvial Valley Survey (subsequently abbreviated to Lower Mississippi Survey, or simply LMS). Their purpose was to follow up on the earlier work and, specifically, to develop archaeological data in the area studied by Phillips comparable to that which Ford had gathered from southern Mississippi and northern Louisiana. The regions actually surveyed were the bottomlands of northeastern Arkansas, northwestern Mississippi, and contiguous portions of Tennessee: an area rich in archaeological remains but poorly known professionally, although pothunters had been mining it for more than a century. One of the objectives of the fieldwork was to investigate the origins of the Mississippian culture. This goal was not realized satisfactorily (and is still a major problem; see Smith n.d.), but the investigations did establish a solid archaeological data base comparable to Ford's earlier work. Pre-Mississippian as well as Mississippian complexes were defined, and the broad outline of culture history for the area was reconstructed. The resulting volume (Phillips, Ford, and Griffin 1951) is rightly recognized as a landmark in Lower Mississippi Valley archaeology (see Brain 1969, pp. 17–19, and Brain n.d. for further discussion of the innovative contributions of this important study).

A second landmark study, which became the new standard, was published by Phillips in 1970. It updated the earlier studies and recast the culture history of the entire valley into a detailed series of regional chronologies, providing the means for correlating events in the archaeological record and asking questions about development, interaction, and process. Subsequent works have refined the record and answered some of those questions with a modicum of success (e.g., Brain 1971, 1978a, 1978b, n.d.; Schiffer and House 1975; Smith 1978, n.d.; Morse and Morse 1983; Williams and Brain 1983). An increasingly important theme in some of these studies has been the part that the Tunica played in the late prehistoric, protohistoric, and historic events perceived in the archaeological record of the Lower Mississippi Valley. This theme becomes an all-consuming interest in the present volume.

LATE PREHISTORIC CULTURE HISTORY

For the purposes of this study, the brief review of prehistoric aboriginal culture history may be confined to the Mississippi period—that is, after A.D. 1000 (for a fuller discussion of the prehistoric background see Williams and Brain 1983, chs. 11, 12). The dynamics of events during this period were heavily influenced by the Mississippian culture, characteristic traits of which had penetrated into regions occupied by Tunica ancestors. Although the latter are not distinguishable in the archaeological record until late in the Mississippi period, there is sufficient evidence to connect them intimately with the Mississippian culture.

The native cultural tradition in the southern part of the Lower Valley during late prehistory has been identified as Coles Creek–Plaquemine, from the names of the two sequent cultures that define the tradition (Brain 1978a, n.d.; Williams and Brain 1983). The Coles Creek culture took form from antecedents during the middle of the first millennium A.D. By the beginning of the second millennium, Coles Creek was at a climactic stage of development from the Yazoo Basin southward. It was characterized by large populations scattered in dispersed settlement patterns and small mound-and-plaza ceremonial centers; a subsistence base that probably included agriculture but depended at least as much on hunting, fishing, and gathering the products of the rich environment; and distinctive complexes of ornaments, tools, and pottery containers.

Beginning during this period, and continuing with increasing intensity but differing manifestations during the ensuing centuries, was an input from the different cultural tradition upriver that is referred to as Mississippian culture. This culture was similar to Coles Creek in that the pyramidal mound-and-plaza form of ceremonial center was an important feature, but its mounds and thus its centers tended to be much larger. Agriculture, relying primarily on the corn-bean-squash triad, also was emphasized to a much greater degree, and the populations were denser and more nucleated. Finally, the artifactual complement was distinctively different. The earliest indication of Mississippian influence on native Coles Creek culture is found in the adoption by the latter of certain modes of pottery manufacture, most distinctively the use of live-shell tempering, and of new vessel forms such as jars. These are general Mississippian traits, and they diffused widely. Then, sometime in the twelfth century, specific contact from the great Cahokia site in west-central Illinois becomes evident. This time, actual artifacts presumably made at Cahokia or one of its satellites appear at sites in the Yazoo Basin on the northern frontier of Coles Creek culture. The known geography of the contact reveals an affinity for sites located at strategic locations, especially at major riverine junctions. It has been suggested that this preference may reflect an economic motivation for the contact and represents an attempt to control trade routes (Brain 1978a, n.d.; Williams and Brain 1983). Whether or not the hypothesis is sound, the geographic pattern seems to have striking parallels to a similar set of preferences and motivations that were to be exhibited by the Tunica centuries later.

Shortly after the Cahokia contact, which seems to have been a relatively short-lived phenomenon, a terrific change occurred in the Yazoo Basin and contiguous regions. Vast amounts of energy suddenly were devoted to the construction of large mound sites, centers far bigger than any that had existed before. At the same time, other Mississippian traits were adopted, including a greater emphasis on corn agriculture and a wide array of artifact types. There was continuity as well as change, however, and basic settlement patterns, general subsistence strategies, and many artifact types continued to be derived directly from Coles Creek traditions. The resultant cultural hybrid has been referred to as the Plaquemine culture (Brain 1978a, n.d.; Williams and Brain 1983). Like so many hybrids, Plaquemine was a vigorous product of its mixed heritage, and the earliest phases—e.g., Winterville in the Yazoo Basin, Routh in the Tensas Basin, and Anna in the Natchez Bluffs— exhibit a florescence in local cultural development. It was a time of broad interaction and innovation. The recombination of new and old elements has all the earmarks of a revitalization movement (Wallace 1956), although it would be foolish to speculate on the exact nature of the phenomenon until more data are accumulated.

The Plaquemine culture continued to flourish in the south, and the continuities may be traced right up to the Natchez and other historic tribes. The Yazoo Basin, however, became increasingly Mississippianized through time—as attested especially by its artifactual inventory—and the latest prehistoric and protohistoric phases are clearly more Mississippian than Plaquemine in character. It is in the northern Yazoo Basin during the protohistoric period that we find the first hint of the Tunica.

ARCHAEOLOGICAL CONTINUITY AND THE DIRECT HISTORICAL APPROACH

It will be argued in the following pages that an archaeological continuum identified as Tunica can be traced from northern Mississippi to central Louisiana, and that this continuum correlates well with the historical sequence described in part 1. The coincidence of the archaeological and historical records allows the formulation of a series of data sets tightly defined through time and space. The research potential of such a series is obvious and has been cited often (e.g., Steward 1942, pp. 339–340; Eggan 1952, pp. 43–45; Baerreis 1961, p. 70; Fontana 1965, p. 65; Williams 1966, p. 25; Leone 1972, p. 26; Euler 1972, pp. 203, 205; Brain, Toth, and Rodriguez-Buckingham 1974, pp. 232–234; Wilson 1975, p. 336; Mason 1976, p. 361; Wedel 1977, p. 7; Blitz 1985, p. 60; Hobler 1986, p. 19). The greatest potential for the anthropological study of a sequence of culture change occurs when a specific people can be documented over an extended interval of time:

If we are ever to have more than general insights into the nature of European-Indian acculturation in the Southeast, it will be necessary to investigate changes through time in specific ethnic groups. What is necessary is to work with the sequentially related settlements of specific [peoples]. We must, for example, have information on the nature and progress of acculturation among the Kashita not only for 1715, but also for 1680 and 1780. (Hally 1971, p. 63)

The same diachronic perspective has been emphasized elsewhere, but in the few cases actually attempted the difficulties of establishing the archaeological continuum have intruded (for recent examples see Ezell 1961, p. 146; Haag 1967, p. 121; Brose 1971; Krause 1972, p. 106; Craig and Peebles 1974, p. 85; Mason 1976, p. 359; Milanich 1978, pp. 84–85; Jones 1978, p. 179; Brown 1982, p. 184; Brose, Jenkins, and Weisman 1982, pp. 327–328; Dobyns 1983, pp. 338–343; Smith 1984, p. 14). The problem is not as severe in the case of the Tunica, however, and a continuum stretching across 400 miles and 400 years is secured through the application of the direct historical approach (Wedel 1938, 1940; Strong 1940; Stirling 1940; see also Eggan 1952; Williams 1981a).

The Archaeological Continuum

Since the time of the earliest historical reference, a number of late prehistoric–protohistoric Mississippian sites have been known to have existed in the region of sixteenth-century Quizquiz in the upper Yazoo Basin. But the accumulated data, although considerable, were not sufficient to support the identification of the Tunica with historic Quizquiz. For this reason, we undertook a reanalysis of the earlier collections of Phillips, Ford, and Griffin (1951), and followed it with a brief survey of the region in 1977 (Brown 1978a). The objectives of the fieldwork were to locate (or relocate) protohistoric

sites, to identify specific Tunican artifactual diagnostics, and to evaluate the archaeological potential of those sites that produced the diagnostic artifacts. A number of promising sites were marked for excavation, but that crucial stage has not yet been reached. Nevertheless, the data are sufficient to support a strong case for Tunica origins in this region.

Whatever befell the people of Quizquiz and their neighbors during the century following the De Soto entrada was of such disastrous magnitude that the native polities simply ceased to exist, and only remnants of the populations survived. The Tunica were one such remnant, and they apparently settled as refugees on the banks of the lower Yazoo River, where they were found by the early French explorers at the close of the seventeenth century (see fig. 2). Their principal settlement there was suspected to be the Haynes Bluff site in Warren County, Mississippi; proof was forthcoming with the excavation of Haynes Bluff and other surrounding sites in 1974. The accumulated evidence provides a valuable reference for the initial French contact period.

When the Tunica moved to the Red River region they initially settled among the Houma, in what has since been known as the Tunica Hills. Although the location of the principal village has not yet been established definitely, an ancillary settlement, Bloodhound, was excavated in 1977. Dating to the period 1706–1731, midden deposits and a contiguous cemetery revealed considerable data on the more extensive French contact during the first third of the eighteenth century. The aboriginal artifacts from Bloodhound and the nearby Angola Farm site excavated in 1934 by James A. Ford also serve as an important archaeological link, firmly relating the lower Yazoo and Trudeau occupations.

The Trudeau site, occupied by the Tunica from 1731 to 1764, was the provenience of the Tunica Treasure collection. This provenience was verified during excavations in 1972, and further investigations were carried out in 1980 and 1981. Together, the collection and supporting information from the excavations provide a firm mid-eighteenth-century datum for the Tunica. They also document the success with which the Tunica responded to the French presence during this period.

There is a break in the archaeological continuum for the last third of the eighteenth century. The historical documentation records that the Tunica left Trudeau and the Lower Mississippi Valley in 1764 after they participated in the ambush of the Loftus expedition. Following a brief sojourn in the vicinity of Mobile, Alabama, they returned to the Mississippi and eventually settled some 15 km south of Trudeau near Pointe Coupée. Unfortunately, that location is now in the middle of the Mississippi River, quite beyond archaeological recovery. This loss is especially to be regretted, for it denies us knowledge of the Tunica reaction to the brief British and Spanish sovereignties.

At some time prior to the assumption of American control of the region in 1803, the Tunica made a final move as a tribal entity: this time from the Mississippi, up the Red River, to the Marksville Prairie in Avoyelles Parish, Louisiana. Here they have remained ever since, although splinter groups frequently have broken away. And here the archaeology picks up again, significantly, in the hands of the Tunica themselves. With the help of local diggers (professional and otherwise), the Tunica have participated in the excavation of their own ancestors on several occasions in the recent past. All of the burials that were exhumed dated to the first half of the nineteenth century. The artifactual contents of the graves illuminate the life-style of the Tunica at that period, while the mortuary practices preserve traditional patterns that reinforce the archaeological continuity.

Some Tunica still live on the tribal land in Marksville. This uninterrupted succession provides the link to the archaeological past and forges an ethnic continuum through time and space. Demonstration of this continuum is the substance of the following pages. Using the direct historical approach, we follow the continuum backward through time in order to establish the Tunica identity of the archaeological remains.

The Direct Historical Approach

The possibilities of applying a direct historical approach in the Lower Mississippi Valley were recognized very early. In fact, the approach is clearly described, although not specified by name, by the founders of modern archaeology in the valley (Collins 1927a, 1927b, 1927c, 1932a, pp. 17–18; Collins 1932b; Walker 1935, p. 1; Ford 1936, p. 6). Phillips (1939, pp. 675–684) also recognized the potential. But interest soon waned, partly because of difficulties in bridging the historic-to-prehistoric transition (ibid.). A more important reason, however, was that the long and rich prehistoric record that was being revealed began to absorb most of the attention. After all, the direct historical approach could only be expected to help elucidate the late prehistoric data, and the Lower Valley was found to have experienced many millennia of great developments that far overshadowed the historically known peoples and their comparatively meager accomplishments. New methodologies had to be developed to deal with these earlier developments, and the direct historical approach was put on the shelf. The potential of the approach has not been forgotten in Mississippi Valley studies, however (e.g., Brown 1982; Giardino 1984; Neuman 1984, pp. 4, 252), and, as noted by Phillips (1939, pp. 719–721), the Tunica provide one of the best opportunities to apply it.

The use of the direct historical approach in these pages represents a limited application of its theoretical promise—limited in that the primary objective is simply to make the archaeological identification and connection back through the historic record into the prehistoric. (Broader interpretive issues are not a concern until part 3, when the more comprehensive concept of ethnohistoric archaeology is the guiding principle.) But the procedure can be declared a success if a continuum can be established by correlating the archaeological contexts with the descriptions contained in the historical documentation. In other words, specific archaeological remains must be identified as Tunica.

The difficulties of correlating narrowly defined locales with the broad descriptions usually found in the documentation have been experienced by the many researchers who have attempted the enterprise. The Lower Mississippi Valley presents the same difficulties (e.g., Haag 1965, p. 316; Giardino 1984; Guevin 1985). Even two of the largest and most important tribes, the Quapaw and the Natchez, have only recently been given precise geographic locations through archaeological investigation (Ford 1961; Neitzel 1965, 1983; Brown 1982, 1984; Brain 1982; Brain, Brown, and Steponaitis n.d.). As a smaller tribe, and one known to have lived in several different regions during the historic period alone, the Tunica could be expected to present a considerable locational problem. In their favor, however, is their high archaeological profile, especially evident as they intruded farther south into regions that exhibit cultural remains very different from those left by the Tunica.

The specific identification of remains as Tunica brings us to the consideration of ethnicity. There have been other efforts to define "peoples" in archaeological data (Rouse 1965, 1972, pp. 61–101), and there are situations in which ethnic specificity might logically be attempted—in fact, must be (e.g., Quimby 1942b; Mason 1976; Wedel 1977; Goodyear 1977; Schuyler 1980; McGuire 1982; Tong 1982; Horvath 1983; Giardino 1984; Guevin 1985). This is one of those situations, for the purpose of this study is to document culture change through time as it occurred within a single ethnic continuum. Ethnic identification, however, is a difficult, even perilous, problem for archaeologists (see Quimby 1942b, p. 273 for a Lower Mississippi Valley example). The problem is compounded by the inability to investigate language, sociopolitical structure, ideology, or phenotype (not necessarily racial characteristics)—those most intimate but intangible tokens of a group's identity, which generally are not sufficiently preserved in the archaeological record. There remains only material culture, and the configurations in which it is found. While it is recognized that pitfalls abound for the unwary (Quimby 1957; Bishop and Smith 1975, p. 54; Bishop and Ray 1976; Mason 1976; Brown 1977; Hodder 1978, pp. 3–12; Mainfort 1979; Kelly and Kelly 1980; Jeter 1982a, pp. 114–115; Horvath 1983; McGuire 1983; Mason 1985; Blitz 1985, pp. 47–55), it is argued here that these archaeological data may be used in ethnic identification if sufficient care is exercised in the analysis and correlation (e.g., see Bishop and Smith 1975, p. 61; Penman 1983).

Logical degrees of reliability in the use of material culture for ethnic identification may be established as a starting point. Obviously, European (or Euroamerican) artifacts are useless for distinguishing between aboriginal groups unless one or more of the following points obtains:

1. A group is known to have received such items only from specific national or special interest groups who distributed sufficiently distinctive artifact types: for example, dedicated presentation medals or unusual modifications of common artifacts (Quimby 1958, p. 331; Brain 1979, pp. 178–181).
2. The group is known from documentary evidence to have preferred certain kinds of artifacts, as distinct from the preferences of other groups.
3. The artifacts were left in configurations especially distinctive of the activities of a known ethnic group.

Aboriginal artifacts, on the other hand, may be expected to be somewhat more reliable indicators of ethnicity if either of the following is true:

1. The artifacts of one group are sufficiently different from those made by another group.
2. The configurations of artifacts differ significantly from one group to another.

The more of these stipulations that are demonstrated in a particular context, the more conclusive will be the case for ethnic distinctiveness.

The basic premise in using material culture for ethnic identification is that the most ethnically sensitive artifacts would be of native manufacture. The potentially most useful artifact category is pottery. Ubiquitous and susceptible to modification, it is therefore suitable for broadly comparative stylistic analysis. Lithics have proven to be of lesser value in ethnic discrimination, but they are not to be neglected. Even negative evidence is important: it is found that the Oliver lithic complex discussed in the following pages, for example, is definitely not a Tunica characteristic. Nonartifactual traits such as burial practices, subsistence strategies, and settlement patterning have even more potential for ethnic identification, as will be considered further in the development of the study. But for present purposes—that is, the tracking of an ethnic group through large segments of time and space—the requirement of abundant and particularistic archaeological evidence is best fulfilled with pottery. It must be cautioned, however, that although pottery may provide a crucial index for distinguishing ethnic groups, its use for such purposes must be carefully defined.

As a fundamental unit of archaeological data for the late prehistoric periods in the Lower Mississippi Valley, pottery has been subjected to rigorous analysis and classification. Basic ceramic traditions have been recognized, and types and varieties of plain and decorated wares segregated (see app. A.1). The types and varieties reflect stylistic differences that usually distinguish relatively circumscribed segments of time and space. These taxa thus have become basic defining characteristics of archaeological components of cultural phases. Since most of the evidence has been prehistoric, there has been little consideration of the ethnic identification of a type or variety, although the question has been raised in historic contexts (e.g., Quimby 1953; Ford 1961). Theoretically, such discriminations should be possible, and to further the possibility the concept of "sets" has been introduced.

As described by Williams and Brain (1983, pp. 89–90, 313–314), a pottery set is a classificatory unit that crosscuts types. Sets are composed of contemporaneous varieties from one or more types that share certain ware modes and overall decorative intent. As such, a set is a device for distinguishing the pottery of a particular time and place, and therefore, by logical extension, the people who made it. Especially large sets are subdivided into subsets with temporal and spatial dimensions equivalent to a cultural phase. A set or subset may, or may not, equal the total ceramic complex of a phase; in our experience, more than one is usually present, especially in the later prehistoric and historic periods (and always present, by definition, when two or more peoples inhabit the same place at the same time, unless all have been acculturated to the same pattern of material culture). Not all varieties present in an archaeological component of a phase need be assigned to a set if, as in the case of obvious imports, they are best perceived as independent entities; a corollary is that varieties that are members of a set may be found independently outside of the particular spatial-temporal locus in which the set was defined. Sets, then, are to be regarded as a convenience, not a rigid requirement of classification. Their convenience lies in the fact that they are synthetic units that are more suitable and more easily used for comparisons at the level of distributional correlations than are either types and varieties, on the one hand, or complexes, on the other. Ultimately, sets are the most appropriate units for ethnic identifications.

In this study, the greatest number of sets—the most "complex" assemblage—comes from Haynes Bluff, which is also known to have the most mixed ethnic composition. It is also the primary connection in this sequence between the prehistoric and historic periods. The ceramic assemblage from Haynes Bluff is similar to that from the nearby Lake George site through the late prehistoric period (Williams and Brain 1983, chs. 10–12). But Lake George was abandoned by the beginning of the protohistoric period, whereas Haynes Bluff continued to be occupied through the protohistoric and early historic periods. Haynes Bluff is thus a vital datum for establishing the ceramic complexes that define the end of the aboriginal record in the lower Yazoo region, a point at which the sets can be sorted out and described (see app. A.2) before the pottery traditions that they represent become adulterated, disused, and finally lost.

The pottery complexes that characterize the late prehistoric through historic periods in the lower Yazoo are diagrammed in figure 41 as assemblages of sets and individual varieties. Many different ceramic traditions and ethnicities are represented in these assemblages, but included among them is one tradition and one ethnicity that can be identified as Tunica.

The archaeological identification of an ethnic group acknowledged to have been somewhat varied in its biological and cultural composition is not easily accomplished. It therefore should come as no surprise that the native Tunica pottery tradition from the late prehistoric period to the mid-eighteenth century consists of more than one set. An evolution occurs in the proportions of Tunica diagnostics through time and space, so that each complex is slightly different (fig. 42). The changing incorporation into the total assemblages of elements from other traditions further complicates the picture. The continuity is evident nevertheless, and is clearly expressed by the one prevailing constant among decorated wares: Winterville Incised, *var. Tunica*. It is argued that this variety is as good an ethnic identifier as is Fatherland Incised, *var. Fatherland* for the Natchez (Quimby 1953). Whether or not it was actually made by the Tunica, *Tunica* does seem to be consistently associated with them (Brain 1979, p. 234; see discussion in app. A.2, this vol.). This ceramic trail, however, can

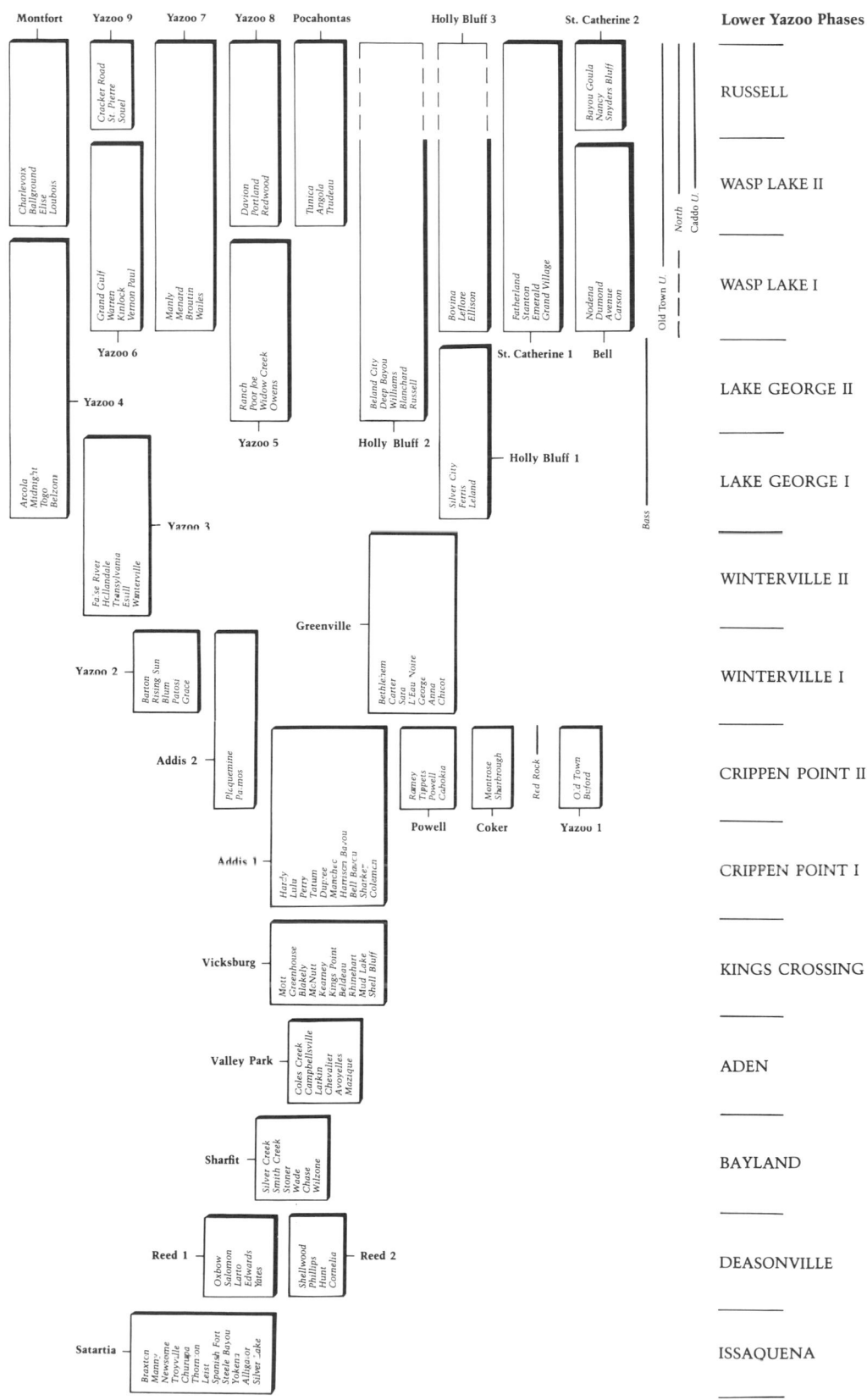

Figure 41. Traditions, complexes, and sets of aboriginal pottery varieties in the lower Yazoo region.

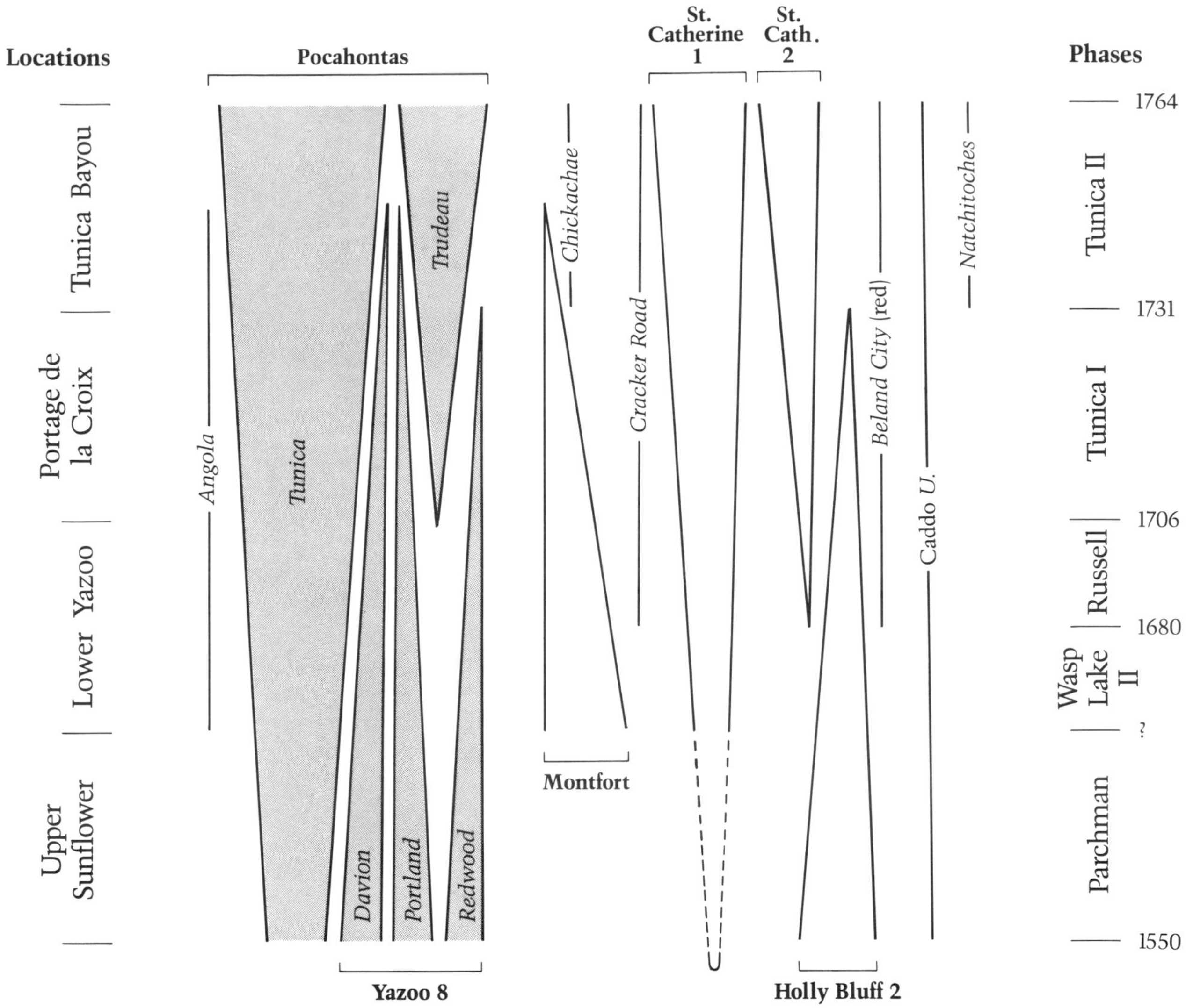

Locations · Pocahontas · St. Catherine 1 · St. Cath. 2 · Phases

Figure 42. Schematic diagram of the changing composition of aboriginal pottery assemblages at Tunica sites through time and space. Synchronically, each complex is somewhat different, especially in the proportions of elements, but diachronically the continuities are clearly evident. The continuum represents a dynamically evolving assemblage of pottery, the core tradition of which was Tunica.

be followed only for the Quizquiz-Trudeau segment, for after the Trudeau occupation the native craft generally seems to have disappeared.

To recapitulate, an archaeological continuum identified as Tunica can be traced across 400 miles of space during 400 years of often dramatic culture contact and change (fig. 43). The key to the continuum is ethnic identification arrived at via the direct historical approach. The first step is adequately established by the living Tunica themselves, who for nearly two centuries have maintained in situ a recognized tribal home which logically links them to the remains of their early nineteenth-century ancestors. These remains are described below under the heading of the Pierite site, the most recent archaeological datum of the Tunica. Although

the graves contained only Euroamerican artifacts, aboriginal traits are preserved in the pattern of the mortuary customs. In fact, these burials exhibit some customs still practiced in modern Tunica funerals (Brain 1976). They are preceded by the eighteenth-century burials at Trudeau, a connection which is further strengthened by the presence of certain specific artifacts of French origin that are present at both sites. These traits, however, could have been shared by other ethnic groups, so the Pierite-Trudeau connection rests primarily upon historical identification—that is, on confirmation that Trudeau was the principal mid-eighteenth-century village of the Tunica by contemporary documents and maps that pinpoint the Tunica occupation at that precise location (see figs. 25–29). From this point on, however, the historical documentation becomes ever more uncertain and the archaeological evidence therefore assumes ever greater importance.

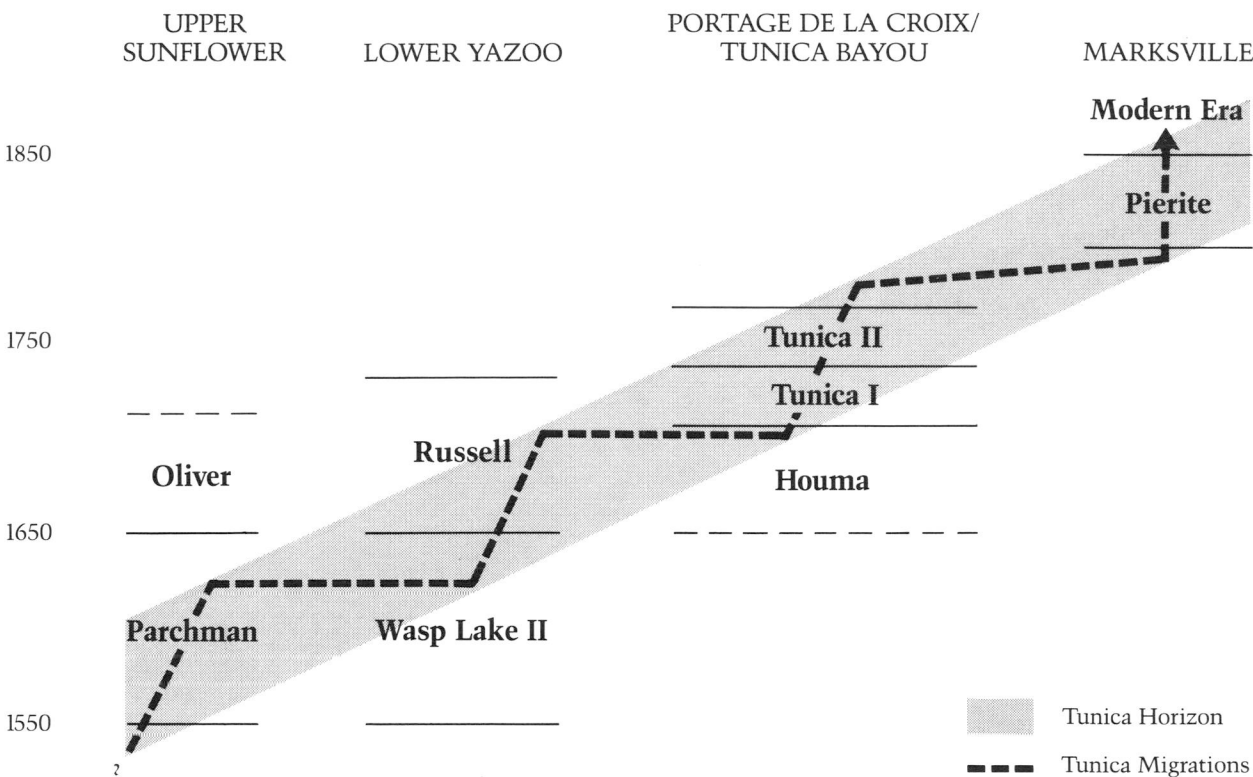

Figure 43. Archaeological phases of Tunica progression.

Identified as a Tunica occupation, Trudeau is the prime archaeological datum for this study. At the time of the Trudeau occupation, the Tunica still retained much of their aboriginal material culture. Indian pottery, especially, was common (Brain 1979, pp. 224–247). When Caddoan and Natchezan trade wares are set aside, the great majority of pieces (seventy-five percent in the Tunica Treasure) are clearly assignable to the Mississippian pottery tradition, and most of these exhibit modes characteristic of the Pocahontas set, which is presumed to be the last practice of Tunica ceramic arts (see app. A.2). The identification of the Pocahontas set with the Tunica is not merely a case of default. Although it is recognized that ethnic attributions of material culture are tricky at best, it is surely no coincidence that Winterville Incised, *var. Tunica*—the most important diagnostic of the Pocahontas set—is found at all Tunica locations from Trudeau to the earlier eighteenth-century sites in the Portage de la Croix and lower Yazoo regions, and even at protohistoric sites in the Quizquiz region (see fig. 42). As the trail blazed by *Tunica* is followed backward through time, there is an increasingly intimate association with the closely related Yazoo 8 subset. In fact, it is the recognition and isolation of a complex in the lower Yazoo defined by *Tunica* and Yazoo 8 that makes possible the leap back into the prehistoric past. The Natchezan and Caddoan elements found at the later sites are replaced by Yazoo traditions of uncertain ethnicity but strong Mississippian character. This changing but consistently trending pattern provides the artifactual guide for identifying Tunica sites and relating them in sequence using the direct historical approach. The sequence of sites will then be used in part 3 to measure culture change with particular emphasis on the processes of acculturation.

Marksville

Marksville refers to the location occupied by the Tunica during the past two centuries. Actually, the Tunica inhabited a number of sites in Avoyelles and Rapides parishes during this period, but Marksville seems to have been the only one continuously occupied. It remains the tribal center to this day, although only a few members of the tribe still live there. Some archaeological data are available from this land.

PIERITE

Pierite (28-H-17) is the LMS designation given to archaeological remains on the traditional Tunica tribal land in Marksville, Louisiana (figs. 44–45). The site is also referred to in the files of the Louisiana Archaeological Survey as Indian Village (16AV21), and in publication as the Coulée des Grues site (Gregory 1978). This land has been occupied continuously by the Tunica and related groups for approximately two centuries, and in addition to the habitations, other structures, fields, and cemeteries presently in use, there is considerable evidence of abandoned locations. These include house sites and graveyards whose occupants have long

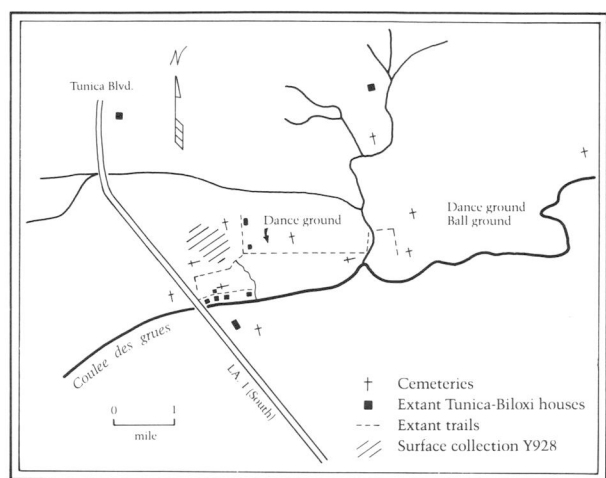

Figure 45. The Pierite site (28-H-17) (adapted from Gregory 1978, fig. 2).

been forgotten but are presumed to be Tunica ancestors. During the period 1950–1971, a number of nineteenth-century Indian burials were uncovered, and most of the artifacts were preserved in the custody of the Pierite family. The potential for establishing a nineteenth-century link between the large corpus of eighteenth-century archaeological data and the modern Tunica brought the LMS to Marksville in July 1971 to inventory and photograph the Pierite collection (Williams 1971), and again in March 1976 for a brief survey.

Previous Excavations

The interments exposed between 1950 and 1971 consisted of nine or more individuals and were found in at least two locations. The first burial was found not on present tribal land but on contiguous private property to the south that had once been occupied by the Indians. The other burials were recovered from a cemetery (or cemeteries) on the tribal land. Description of the burials follows three episodes of excavation that are identified by the principal excavators: Robert Neitzel, Michel Smith with the assistance of the Pierites, and Leonard Charrier. The quality of information derived from each episode is as varied as are these individuals and the contents of the graves themselves.

The Neitzel Burial. The first recorded historic Indian burial at Pierite was found on the land of Robert S. Neitzel in November 1950. Neitzel was not only a neighbor and friend of the Tunica but also an archaeologist. When a plow disturbed the grave, Neitzel recognized the signs and proceeded to investigate (Williams 1962, p. 56). The following information comes directly from Neitzel (personal communication, 1977).

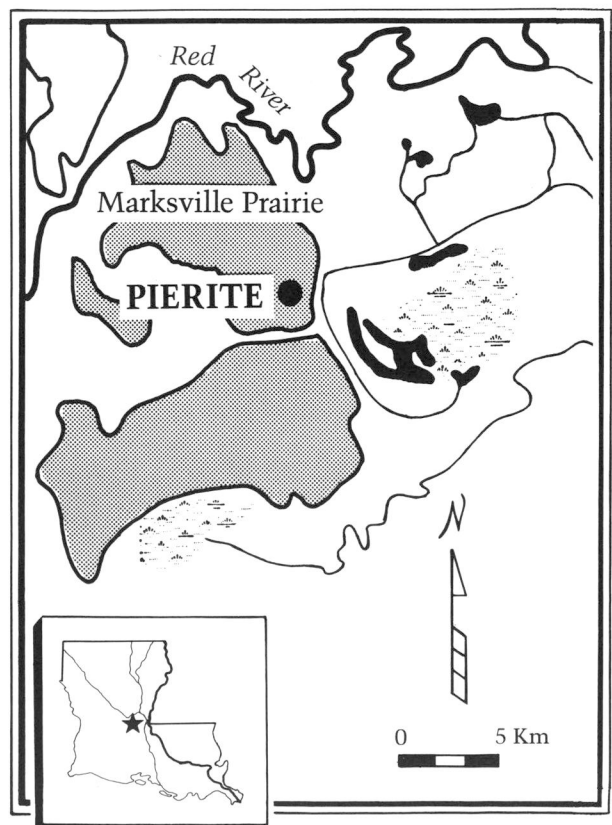

Figure 44. Location of the Tunica in Marksville, Louisiana.

The grave contained the coffin burial of a single adult male in supine position with head oriented to the east (fig. 46). The skull rested on a large case knife, a gun lay along the right side of the body with the stock near the head, an iron kettle had been placed in the pelvic area, and three strips of beaten silver—evidently originally sewn onto a shirt—were found across the chest.

The gun was the most diagnostic artifact in the grave. Neitzel recalled that it was a rifled flintlock with an octagon barrel forty-four inches (111.8 cm) in length and a curly maple stock. The pieces were identified by experts at the National Rifle Association as a "1780 Pennsylvania rifle."[*] The barrel was curated at the Marksville Museum and the silver ornaments were given into the custody of Horace Pierite, but the whereabouts of the knife and kettle are unknown. The skeletal remains were reburied at the site in a small cypress box made by Horace Pierite and Joseph Pierite, Sr.

Neitzel tentatively dated the burial to the 1840s, apparently because of the presence of a coffin, but we now know that crude coffins were used at least as early as Trudeau. Moreover, 1840 seems rather too late considering the date of the rifle. Sixty years would be an exceptionally long life span for a mechanism that presumably saw frequent usage, and it is unlikely that this gun was an unserviceable antique at the time of deposition. Rather, the archaeological record clearly indicates that Tunica custom generally dictated that favored functional items accompany the dead in interment. It seems likely, therefore, that this burial should be dated closer to 1800.

The Smith-Pierite Burials. In the early 1960s, a series of burials was excavated on present tribal land by the Tunica themselves. The actual excavation was performed by Chief Joseph A. Pierite, Sr. and his brother Percy B. Pierite, with the help of Michel Smith, a neighbor who had had some training in archaeological techniques. The first burial was discovered by accident in an eroding field and was partially exposed by Smith and the Pierites before they requested help from Louisiana State University (LSU). Excavation was completed and the burial recorded by archaeology students from the LSU Department of Geography and Anthropology. Subsequently, at least four—and possibly six or more—additional burials were located in the same vicinity and excavated by Smith and the Pierites. Chief Joe often explained that his archaeological activities were grounded in his interest in ancient traditions and tribal identity: the burials "were excavated so that the Tunica-Biloxi and their children might re-establish and strengthen their ties to their past" (Gregory 1975).

[*] This identification was provided through the good offices of the LMS, which was working in the lower Yazoo region at the time. A graduate student member of the field party who was quite knowledgeable about antique firearms read a newspaper account of the discovery and hastened to Marksville to offer his advice. The newspaper had not named Neitzel, and the graduate student had no idea of his archaeological qualifications, which led to an amusing meeting enshrined in the folklore of Lower Valley archaeology (Williams 1981b, p. 7; Brain and Brown 1982, p. 15). Nevertheless, all turned out happily and the gun was identified.

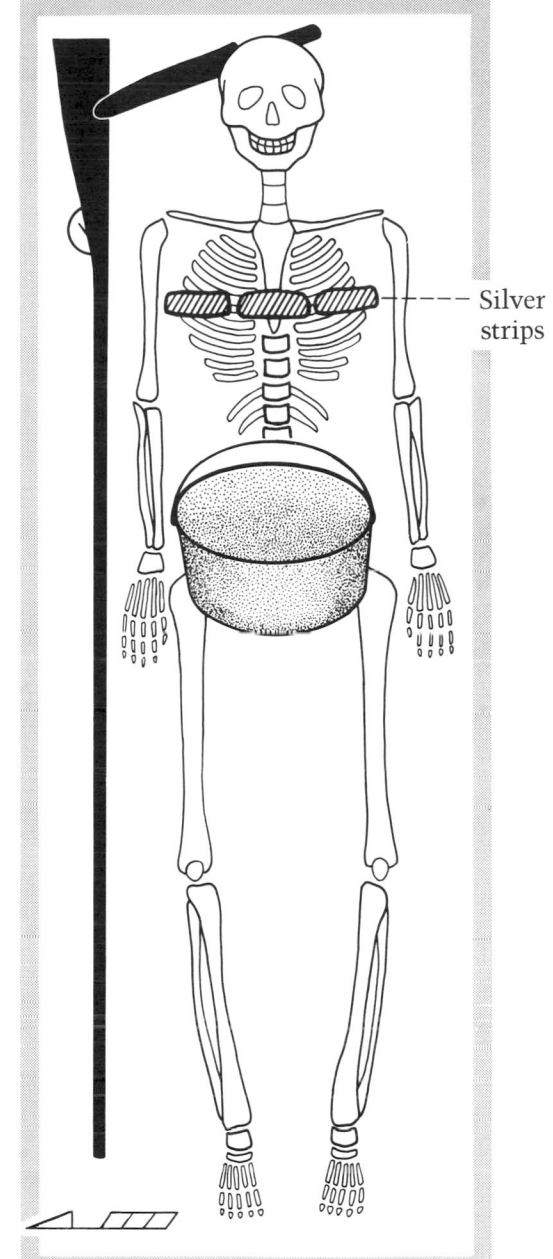

Silver strips

Figure 46. Reconstruction of the Neitzel burial from Pierite: a supine adult male with head oriented to the east (from a photograph by R. S. Neitzel).

The first burial was recorded by Hiram F. Gregory (1961, 1978). Unfortunately, his two accounts differ in a number of details, but a general picture of the burial may still be reconstructed (fig. 47). It consisted of a single individual—an adult male in extended supine position with head oriented to the northeast—placed in a crude coffin of cypress bark nailed together with machine-cut nails. The body had been dressed in a shirt of red-and-green paisley that apparently had been embroidered with white seed beads, most notably in a band below the waist and on a round spot on the back. Other

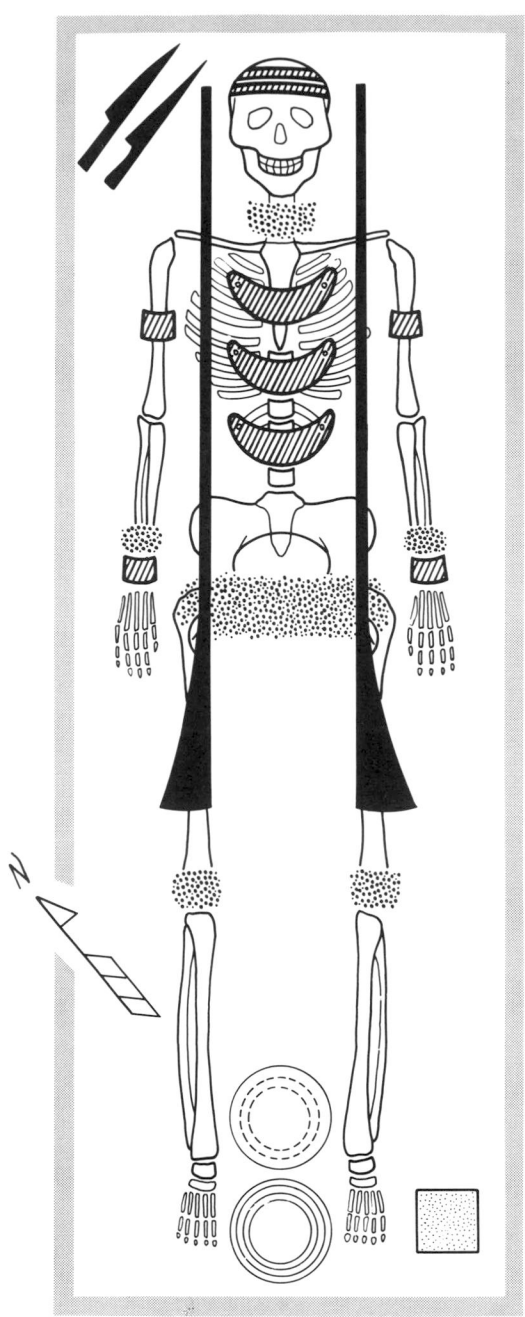

Figure 47. Reconstruction of Smith-Pierite burial 1 from Pierite (from Gregory 1978).

Nonornamental artifacts accompanying this burial included two muskets ("rifles"?) that were cradled in the arms, one on each side of the body, stocks at the pelvis. Lying on the torso, but probably originally placed on top of the coffin, there seem to have been three iron kettles (at least two of which were Type A, Variety 1 in the classification of Brain 1979, pp. 135–136), a single-bit American-poll axe, an adze, a hoe, a harpoon point, a pair of stirrups, pieces of at least one bridle bit, and possibly a spike and a pewter cup (not listed in Gregory's 1961 field report or illustrated in Gregory 1978, fig. 4). Two long knives may have been placed in the coffin by the upper right side of the head, but again these are not mentioned in the 1961 report. On the other hand, only the 1961 report states that a broken glass bottle and a pewter(?) pitcher were found below the knees. At the feet, between the ankles, were two blue shell-edge "soup" bowls, the smaller sitting in the larger, over which had been inverted a brown-green-black-and-white annular mocha bowl. According to the 1978 article, a second stack of four polychrome hand-painted floral dishes was also present. Incidental finds in the area of the feet were a short length of brass chain, and both black and white seed beads; near the left foot was a small metal box.

The box contained prized personal items: a long brass "stock" (butt?) plate that apparently fit one of the guns, a brass powder horn, an iron tablespoon, a (bone-handled?) folding knife, at least two silver bracelets, a mass of small (brass?) straight pins, a cake of rouge, and a number of black and white seed beads (perhaps embroidery from a pouch for the knife). In Gregory's 1961 report a large "woodscrew," a straight razor, and an unidentified metal comb-like object were also recorded, and his 1978 article lists a brass spring. The biggest discrepancy concerns the silver coins apparently stacked in one corner: the 1961 report says there were eight (one French five-franc piece, one American fifty-cent piece, and six Spanish and Mexican coins of unstated denomination), dating from 1802 to 1857, while the 1978 article mentions only five "mill dollars" of French, Spanish, and American mint, dating between 1760 and 1803! In his dissertation, Gregory dated the coins "to about 1840" (Gregory 1973, p. 154). Unfortunately, the coins were divided up between Smith and the Pierites and are no longer available to resolve the problem.

Depending on which series of coins was associated with it, this burial was certainly interred after 1803, and possibly after 1857. The other artifacts are consistent with an early nineteenth-century date, especially if the only ceramics were the shell-edge and mocha; if they included the polychrome floral (as described below), however, the date is probably after 1820. In any event, it would appear that community affluence—at least as represented by the chiefs, as the silver gorgets and headbands identify this person—continued well into the nineteenth century, and perhaps until as late as the Civil War. If the burial occurred earlier in the century, then the chief obviously had acquired the most current ceramic styles as soon as any of his non-Indian neighbors. If the assemblage dates after 1857, the chief may not have been quite so fashionable but was nevertheless well endowed with worldly goods.

concentrations of white beads were found about the knees, lower arms, and neck; also at the neck was a single-strand necklace of black-red-and-white striped beads. Four(?) silver arm bands had been sewn onto the shirt, three large silver crescentic gorgets were suspended on the chest, and two silver headbands adorned the forehead (Gregory 1978, fig. 3). At least one buckle was found at the knees, and possibly four. According to the 1961 report, two brass "hawk" bells were also found at the knees, and four small plain brass buttons were in the chest area.

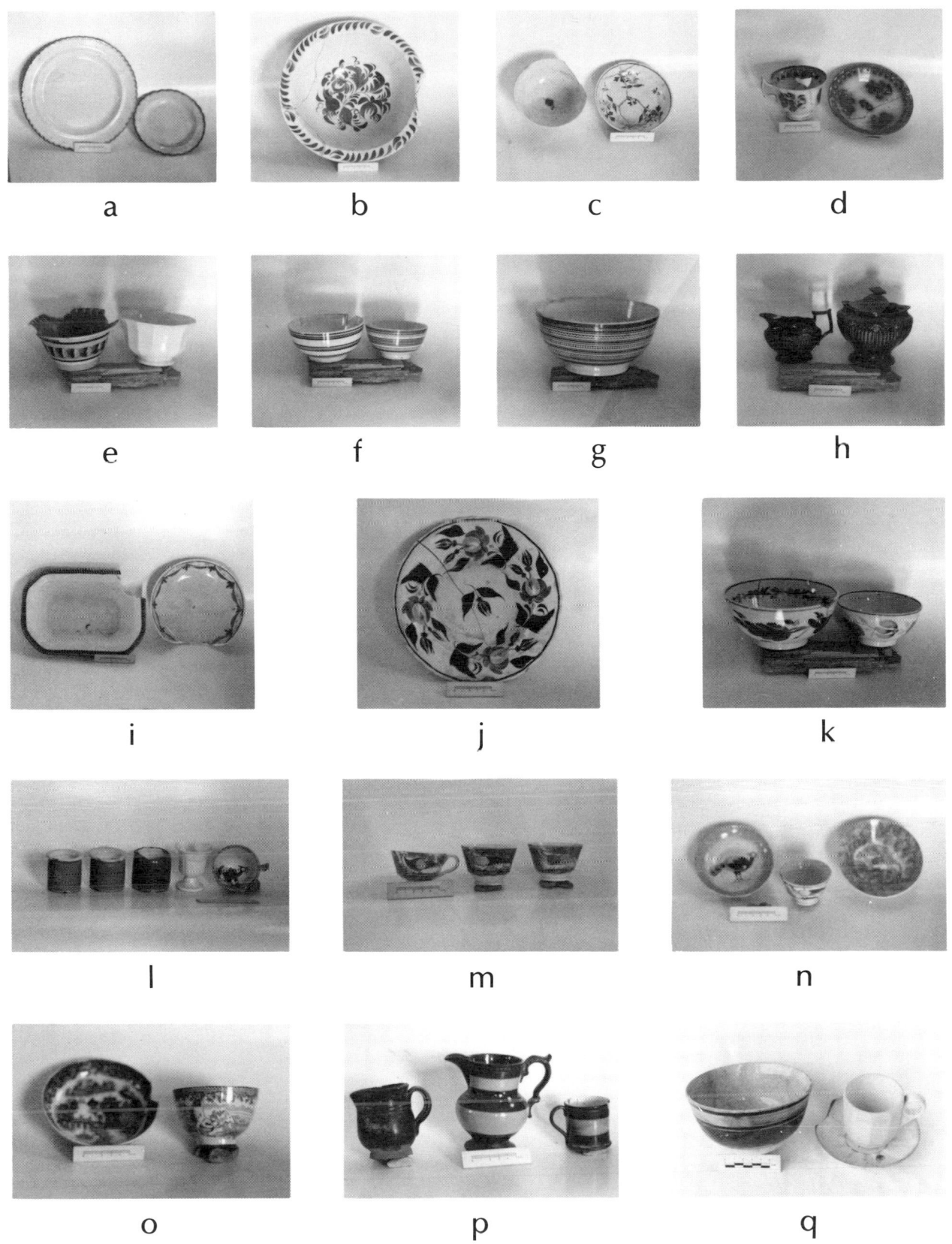

Figure 48. Euroamerican ceramics from the Smith-Pierite burials. (LMS photographs 1971) (approx. 1:10)

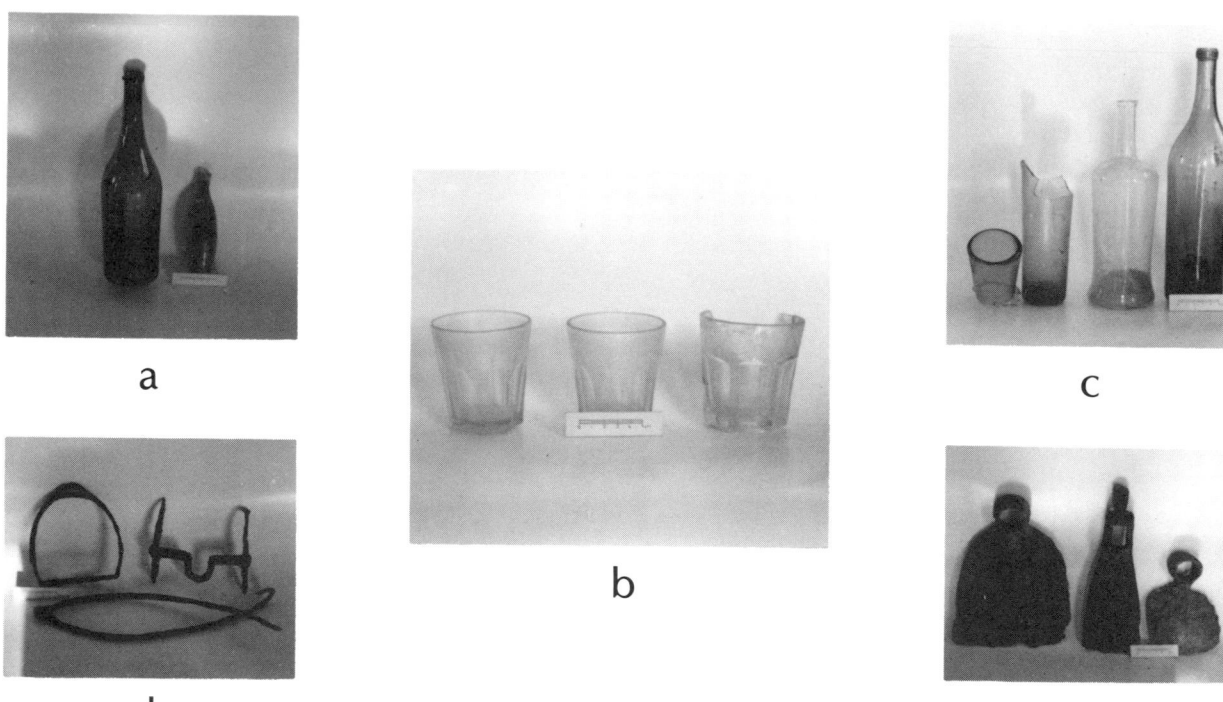

Figure 49. Euroamerican glassware and metal artifacts from the Smith-Pierite burials. (LMS photographs 1971) (approx. 1:10)

The same comments apply to the other Smith-Pierite burials, except that they must be applied more generally to the community as a whole (for surely not all the burials could have been chiefs). Unfortunately, no records were kept on the excavation of these burials and even grave lots were not segregated, so the exact number of individuals is unknown. It appears that there were four to six burials; even if there were more, the wealth of artifacts rivals Trudeau. In addition to the ceramic dishes listed in table 2 and illustrated in figure 48, there were glass bottles, tumblers, and beads; iron kettles and tools (fig. 49); at least one brass kettle and a brass bell; numerous silver ornaments including earbobs, bangles, bracelets, and brooches; and more guns.* Datable items were made in the late eighteenth and early to mid-nineteenth centuries, or ca. 1775–1860. The graves were made after 1800, with most of the burials probably being interred closer to mid-century.

The Charrier Burials.

In the spring of 1971, at least three additional burials were excavated at Pierite by Leonard J. Charrier with the encouragement, if not active participation, of Chief Joseph Pierite, who retained the artifacts. Charrier had gained much experience exhuming Tunica burials at Trudeau (Brain 1979), and by this time he understood the necessity of keeping detailed records. Thus, we have good information on the first and third of these burials (there were apparently

* This inventory and a photographic record were made in July 1971 by Stephen Williams and Alan Toth. A representative collection of these artifacts was donated to the Smithsonian Institution in 1975 (cat. nos. 475840–475848). It includes an especially good sample of nineteenth-century glass bead types.

no artifacts with the second, and so it was not recorded).

Charrier burial 1 was an adult in supine position with the head oriented just north of east (fig. 50). In comparison with the other Pierite burials, it was accompanied by a relatively modest assortment of artifacts. Foremost among these was a polychrome pearlware bowl painted with a bold floral design (fig. 50a); an iron tablespoon had been placed in the bowl. Also present was a large (whiteware?) platter. Over all of these items an iron kettle had been inverted. These artifacts were found in the vicinity of the pelvis. The only other item was a single white glass bead that had been suspended from the neck. This burial may have been interred around 1830 and, judging from the artifacts, might have been a female.

Charrier burial 3, on the other hand, was definitely an adult male of some consequence. The body apparently had been placed in a coffin, as indicated by fragments of cypress and a ring of nails around the edge of the grave; it was oriented in an unusual north-south position, with the head to the south (fig. 51). The status of this individual was indicated by a silver headband and two circular silver gorgets. Next to the gorgets were a number of silver brooches. Also on the chest were an ornate brass handle and a gunstock with silver fittings. An entire gun lay along the left side of the body, the stock near the head. Around the lower legs had been placed a wine bottle and a perfume bottle, a cow bell, a case knife, an oblong metal canister, and a stirrup (its mate was found near the head). A Davenport bowl had been inverted between the feet. Numerous glass beads appear to have been strung to make a necklace and a bracelet for the right wrist.

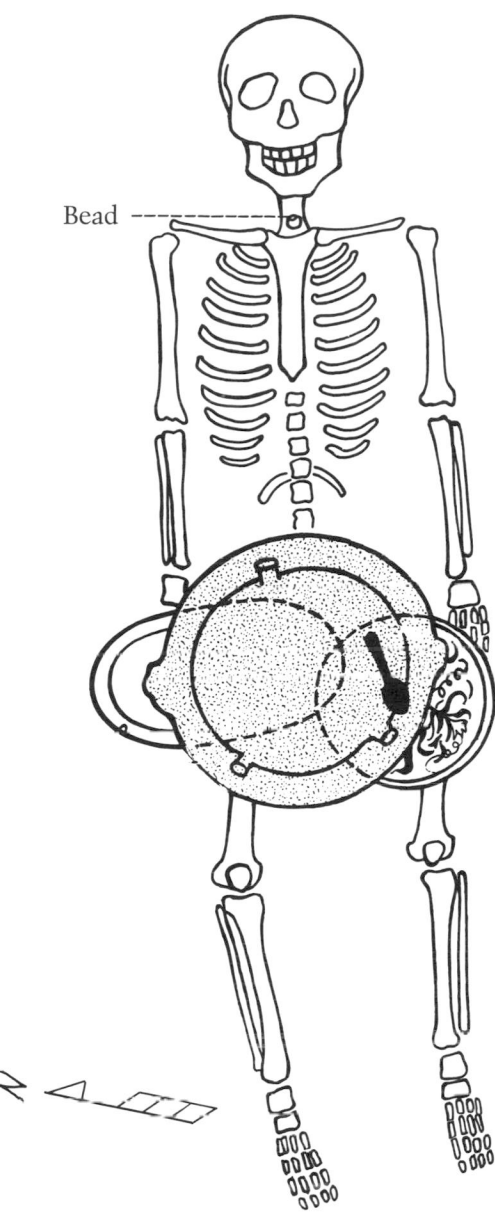

Bead

a

Figure 50. Reconstruction of Charrier burial 1 from Pierite (from a field sketch by L. J. Charrier). a, polychrome hand-painted pearlware bowl. (1:3)

Based solely on the shape of the wine bottle, Charrier burial 3 dates after 1800. The general assemblage would be appropriate for the first third of the century, but of course it could date later. Potentially the most important piece for dating purposes, the Davenport bowl, unfortunately was missing at the time of the inventory. The Davenport pottery was active from 1793 to 1887 (Godden 1964, p. 189), a period longer than that during which the cemetery was used, but a particularly distinctive potter's mark might have defined a terminus post quem within this span.

Summary of the Burials. The Pierite burials date to the first half of the nineteenth century. The first probably was interred soon after the Tunica moved to Marksville, around 1800, and the cemetery apparently remained in use until about the time of the Civil War.

If typical, these burials hardly indicate an impoverished population. In fact, they compare favorably to Trudeau in quantity and variety of artifacts. The items are of good quality and are representative of fashionable contemporary styles (e.g., Webb 1962; Gregory and Webb 1965; Greer 1967; Schuetz 1969). Of course, at least two of the individuals exhumed were probably chiefs, but there is no evidence that the graveyard in which they rested was restricted to such personages; in fact, a larger segment of the population was certainly represented. Known cemeteries on the tribal land today are generally family plots, and it would be reasonable to suppose that this custom had some antiquity. The Smith-Pierite and Charrier burials, then, may represent the remains of an economically and politically prominent Tunica family of the early nineteenth century. The Neitzel burial may represent a poorer member of society, but even he was provided with the basic accompaniment of grave goods.

Table 2. Euroamerican ceramics from the Smith-Pierite burials unearthed at the Pierite site (28-H-17) in the 1960s. Ceramics are arranged chronologically according to probable period of manufacture.

BEFORE 1800

Tin-glazed earthenware
    Blue-and-white plate (fig. 48c)   1
    Blue- or green-and-white pots[a] (fig. 48l)   3
Lead-glazed earthenware
    Coarse redware mug (fig. 48p)   1
    Refined redware
        Jackfield creamer and sugar bowl (fig. 48h)   2
        Polychrome annular pitcher and mug (fig. 48p)   2

1800–1830

Pearlware
    Blue shell-edge plates, bowl, server (fig. 48a, i)   7
    Blue transfer-printed cup and saucer (fig. 48o)   2
    Polychrome hand-painted floral bowls, cup, and
    saucer[b] (figs. 48i, k; 50a)   5
    Polychrome annular
        Simple banded bowls (fig. 48f–g)   3
        Mocha bowl (fig. 48q)   1
        Finger-painted bowl (fig. 48c)   1

1830–1860

Whiteware
    Plain (molded) bowls, egg cup, cup, and saucer[c]
    (fig. 48c, e, l, q)   6
    Gray transfer-printed plate and bowl[d] (fig. 48n)   2
    Brown hand-painted floral bowl   1
    Blue hand-painted floral plate   1
    Flow blue hand-painted floral cup and saucer (fig. 48d)   2
    Polychrome hand-painted floral plate and bowl
    (fig. 48b, j)   2
    Polychrome sponged (spatterware) and hand-painted
    (birds) cups and saucers (fig. 48l–n)   7

[a]These are small delft pots that are blue or green on the outside and white on the inside. Made for pharmaceutical purposes, they seem to have had an unusual longevity for delft ware and were produced well into the nineteenth century (Noël Hume 1970, p. 111).

[b]The cup and saucer and one bowl have fine-line designs painted with a subdued palette of earthen tones and probably date to the first half of this period; the other two bowls have bright bold patterns and are more likely to date to the last half.

[c]These may date after 1850. The cup and saucer are marked "Superior White Granite" and "W. Adams & Sons." According to Godden (1964) and Chaffers (1968), this maker's mark was in use until 1864.

[d]Two blue transfer-printed sherds in the collection, and presumably found during excavation of the burials, bear identifiable maker's marks. One has a "Hyacinth" pattern and was made by "P.B.&H." (which stands for Pinder, Bourne, and Hope) during the period 1851–1862 (Godden 1964). The other, with a "Cintra" pattern, was made by "J.H.," a mark used by five Staffordshire potters, all active between 1852 and 1867 (ibid.).

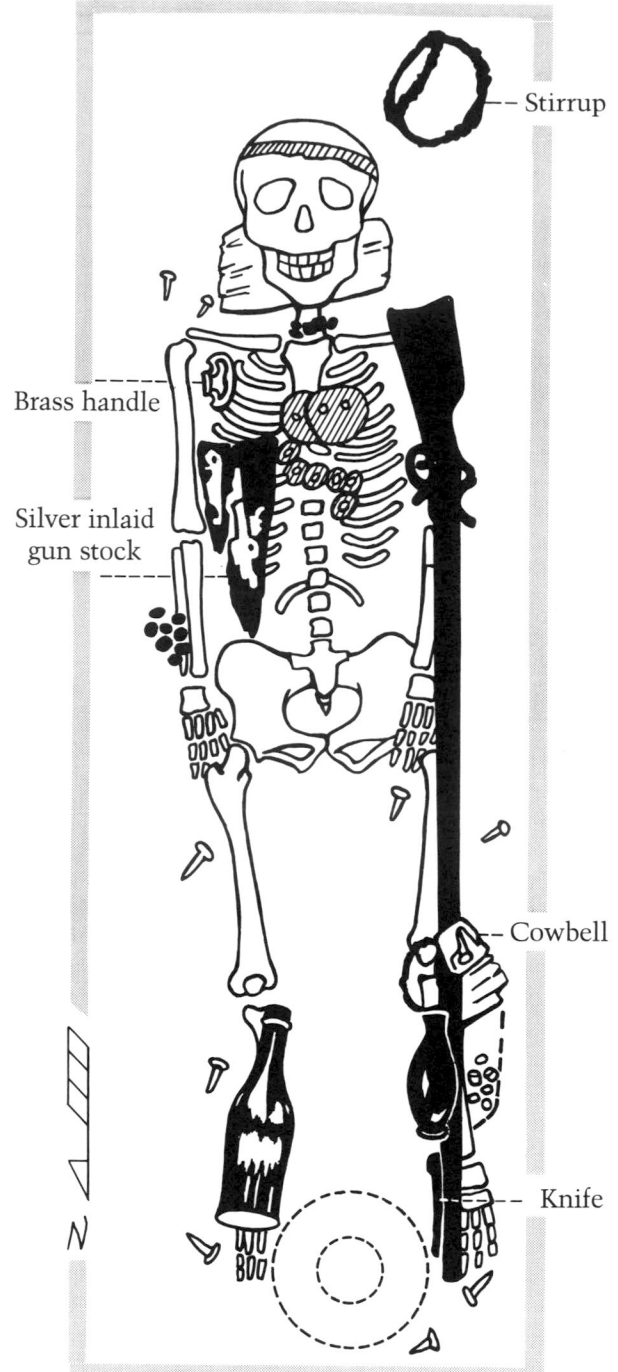

Figure 51. Reconstruction of Charrier burial 3 from Pierite (from a field sketch by L. J. Charrier).

Figure 52. Aboriginal and Euroamerican ceramics collected ▶ from an abandoned house site at Pierite (collection Y928). a, Addis Plain; b, yellow-and-white faience; c, blue-and-white faience; d, lead-glazed earthenware, Type A; e, lead-glazed earthenware, Type D; f–g, creamware; h, pearlware; i–m, polychrome hand-painted pearlware; n, blue transfer-printed pearlware; o, blue shell-edge pearlware; p–q, polychrome mocha annular pearlware; r–t, polychrome finger-painted annular pearlware; u, blue hand-painted pearlware; v, blue-and-white porcelain. (1:1)

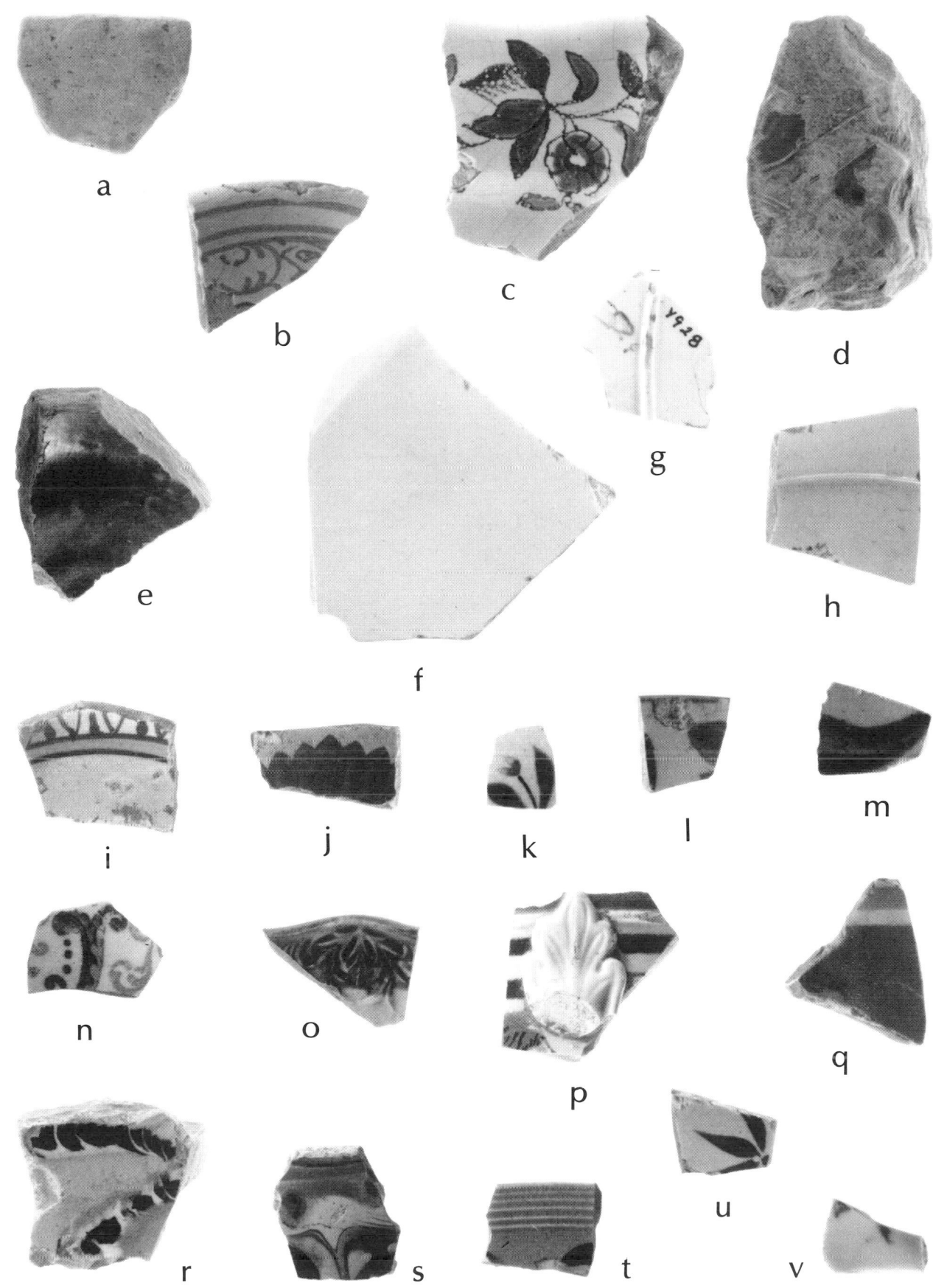

The 1976 Survey

Having been occupied continuously for two centuries, the Pierite site exhibits abundant artifactual remains on the surface. During a brief visit in the spring of 1976, Ian Brown, Robert S. Neitzel, and the author gathered a small collection of artifacts (LMS cat. no. Y928) from a plowed field in the middle of the site (figs. 52–53). These artifacts appeared to be concentrated at an abandoned house site. Judging from the contents of the collection, and assuming it to be representative, this residential locus must have been one of the earliest occupied by the Tunica after their arrival in Marksville. The mean date of the collection falls earlier than the burial assemblage and is heavily weighted to eighteenth-century and very early nineteenth-century types (table 3).* In fact, the tin-glazed and lead-glazed earthenwares have exact counterparts in the Tunica Treasure. The 1976 surface collection, then, provides a vital archaeological link between Trudeau and Marksville, reaffirming the continuity left unestablished by the historical hiatus.

In summary, although there were no aboriginal artifactual identifiers among any of the archaeological material from Pierite that could be used to determine ethnicity, it may be presumed that the remains are those of the Tunica since the land was theirs during the time of deposition. Furthermore, the burials show a continuation of Tunica mortuary practices, and the 1976 collection from the earlier habitation area does contain eighteenth-century artifacts of types known from Trudeau.

* The earliest censuses taken after the assumption of American control in 1803 record that as many as fifty to sixty Tunica lived in this village at the time (see fig. 222; table 79). Note that the assemblage is much richer than those of approximately contemporary Indian sites located farther up the Red River (Whelan and Pearson 1983, pp. 31–36).

Figure 53. Base of a late eighteenth-century olive green glass bottle from an abandoned house site at Pierite (collection Y928). (1:1)

Table 3. Surface collection Y928 of artifacts from an abandoned house site at Pierite.

ABORIGINAL

Pottery:

Addis Plain, *var. Feliciana* (fig. 52a)	1

EUROAMERICAN

Ceramics:

Tin-glazed earthenware	
White	2
Blue-and-white (fig. 52c)	1
Yellow-and-white (fig. 52b)	2
Lead-glazed earthenware	
Type A (fig. 52d)	1
Type D (fig. 52e)	1
Creamware	
Plain (fig. 52f–g)	35
Pearlware	
Plain (fig. 52h)	8
Blue shell-edge (fig. 52o)	1
Blue transfer-printed (fig. 52n)	4
Blue hand-painted floral (fig. 52u)	1
Polychrome hand-painted floral (fig. 52i–m)	6
Polychrome annular	
Simple banded	6
Mocha (fig. 52p–q)	2
Finger-painted (fig. 52r–t)	4
Whiteware	
Plain	5
Gilt-edge	1
Gray painted	1
Gray transfer-printed	3
Porcelain	
Blue-and-white (fig. 52v)	1

Glass:

Olive green (fig. 53)	5

Iron:

Hoe	1
Nail	
Type unspecified	1
Miscellaneous	2

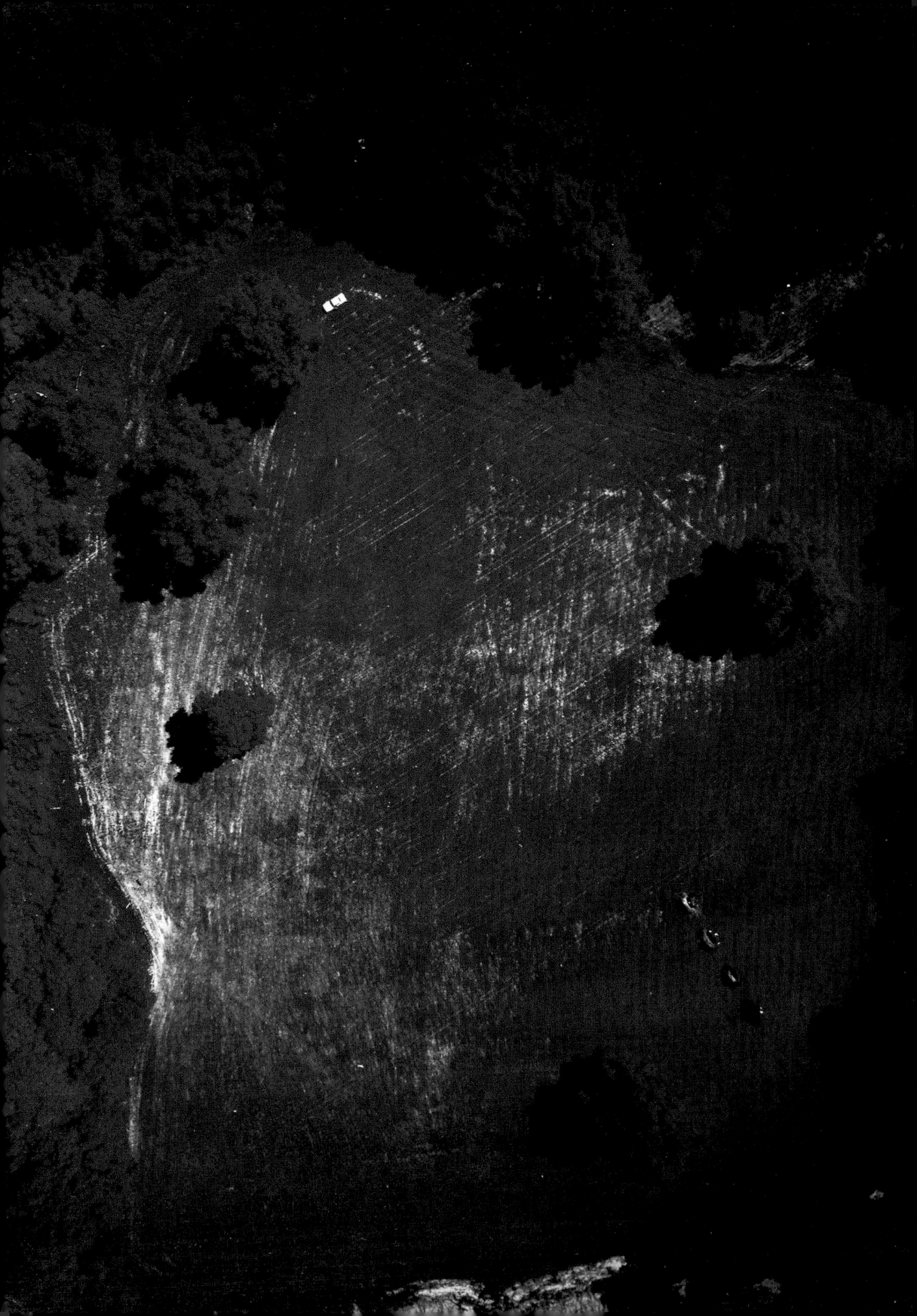

Tunica Bayou

Tunica residence on Tunica Bayou was concentrated on the bayou's south bank at a location that was approximately 1 km from the Mississippi River in the mid-eighteenth century. The nucleus of settlement was a village site that has been given the designation "Trudeau." The Trudeau site has been the object of a considerable amount of archaeological investigation, as well as unauthorized digging.

TRUDEAU

The Trudeau site (29-J-1) was the principal occupation and cemetery area of the Tunica during the period 1731–1764. At present, Trudeau is situated on the east bank of the Mississippi River in West Feliciana Parish, Louisiana (fig. 54). The site is bounded by the Mississippi River on the southwest, by Tunica Bayou on the northwest, and by Pollocks Bayou on the southeast. The northeastern edge is arbitrarily, but quite definitively, determined by a railroad grade that was cut in 1905 (figs. 55, 57).

Geomorphologically, the site is composed of alluvial and eolian deposits. Most of the site is flat sandy loam bottomland created by the fluvial boundaries during an ancient sequence of events. On the western part of the site this early alluvium is overlaid by a recent natural levee which the Mississippi has been building since the eighteenth century. Strata cuts near the river confirmed the sequence: prior alluviation, old ground surface contemporary with the eighteenth-century occupation, recent natural levee accumulation (fig. 55 and color plate).

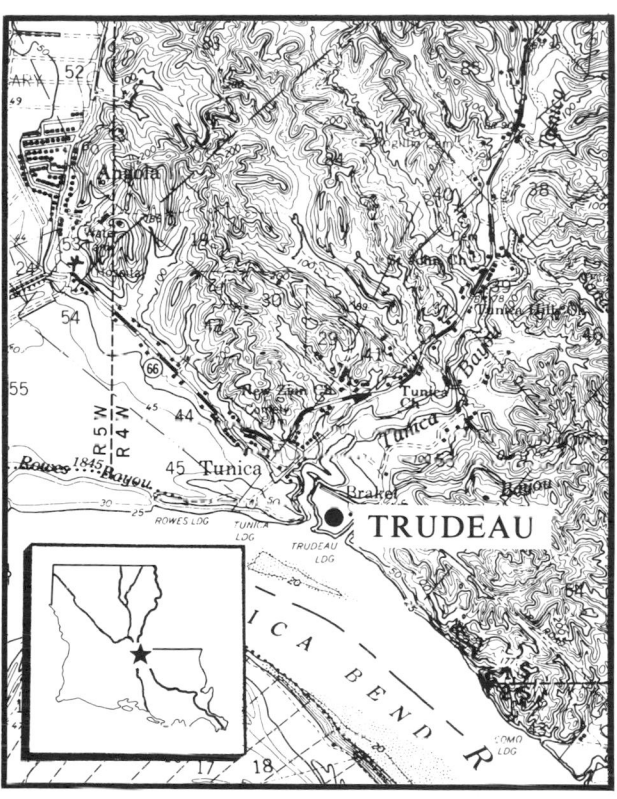

Figure 54. Location of the Trudeau site (29-J-1) in West Feliciana Parish, Louisiana.

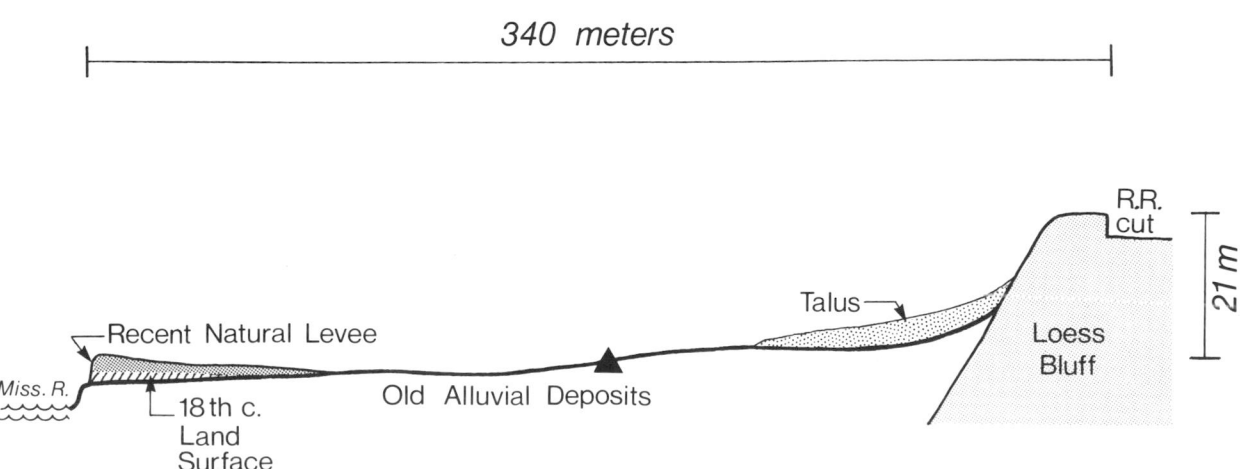

Figure 55. Simplified geomorphological profile of the Trudeau site. (vertical:horizontal approx. 16:1)

Infrared aerial photograph of the Trudeau site. The circular pattern around an open plaza is clearly visible, as is the slight extension to the north (where the automobile is parked) (see figs. 83–84). Excavations in the lower right were dug to explore both geological processes of site formation and recent levee building by the Mississippi River (bottom). (Courtesy Mississippi River Commission, U.S. Army Corps of Engineers, photo no. P2004)

The eastern part of the site is dominated by a small loess bluff remnant, talus from which covers the alluvial deposits for a short distance around the base.

Most of the cultural evidence is found in the middle of the site—the upper portions of the bottomland and the talus—but significant finds are also known from the summit of the bluff. The site probably has been continuously utilized, if not continuously inhabited, since the eighteenth century. Records of ownership can be traced back to within five years of the Tunica occupation, and although no specific usages are recorded until recent times, various agricultural pursuits are reasonably inferred for this prime land. During the past half century the bottomland is known to have been planted with a mixed succession of crops; it has been used most recently for haying. The only known economic use of the bluff has been occasional timbering and cattle foraging.

Human occupation of Trudeau after the Tunica left is given only cursory reference in late eighteenth- and early nineteenth-century historical documents (e.g., Gauld 1774; Hutchins 1784, p. 45; Pollock 1801). These accounts indicate that there may have been temporary encampments by other Indian groups and Euroamericans, but apparently no permanent settlement. To date, there has been no archaeological confirmation of this phase. On the other hand, there is considerable artifactual material from the mid- to late nineteenth century at two locations on the site. The nature and quantity of artifacts confirm that houses were located there about a century ago, but this occupation was not preserved in local records or oral tradition.

The most recent occupation of the site was in the eastern portion at the base of the bluff, where a small three-room tenant house was built at the beginning of the present century and occupied by a succession of black families. The last occupant died on the premises in 1965. The house stood abandoned until we disassembled it in 1980 (Gibson 1984, pp. 51–53). An associated barn, or "crib," immediately to the north had already disappeared, as had any other outbuildings. These occupations resulted in some surface damage to the site.

Throughout the entire last two centuries the bottomland probably remained open—that is, without extensive large growth. Easily cleared, it was frequently reused and was under cultivation, perhaps intermittently at first, but continually for at least the last century. Fortunately, most of the plowing was done with equipment that disturbed the soil to a depth of only about six inches. Twice in recent years, however, the field was broken with a "pan" plow that could reach a depth of twelve inches.

Potentially more destructive has been the pasturing of cows, which denuded the bluff and terraced it with paths. The ensuing erosion is manifest in the talus at the base of the bluff. This talus may have been beneficial, however, in covering and thus preserving earlier strata. Recent alluvial deposits are minimal, except for the natural levee on the western end of the site, despite the fact that it is not unusual for high water to back up as far as the base of the bluff.

The most serious damage has been caused by the meandering action of the Mississippi River, which during the nineteenth century probably took some small outlying Tunica settlements to the west; it then retreated, sparing the main part of the site. On the eastern side, the railroad cut caused considerable damage, essentially removing about half of the bluff. That the Tunica had used this natural feature is grimly attested to by local folklore, which preserves the recollection that "kettles and skulls came bouncing out" as the steam shovel cut through.

In 1967 the land was leased to the "Charter Nine" hunting club, whose members, residents of Baton Rouge, used the land only seasonally for the next thirteen years. This absenteeism set the stage for the excavations that began in 1968, a phase that included trenching for a gas pipeline across the northern corner of the site, as well as the notorious activities of Leonard J. Charrier. Trudeau has also been the object of a considerable amount of professional archaeological attention.

Previous Investigations

The archaeological site of Trudeau was first discovered and reported by Captain W. P. Hall in the early 1880s. Hall had been commissioned by the Davenport Academy of Science (now the Putnam Museum of Davenport, Iowa) to make collections of archaeological materials during his travels on the Mississippi River. In May 1885 he presented to the Academy a large collection that included "two very old rusted copper or brass kettles and three vessels of glazed earthen ware apparently European" (Davenport Academy of Science 1885). The accession catalog entry goes on to describe the recovery of these artifacts and other items in such detail that the good captain must have been in attendance on the occasion:

The two Brass Kettles and the Glazed Pottery and Beads (glass) were found in a mound said to have been four feet high but cultivated about 150 years and worn down. Situated on a point of land between two bayous—Tunica and another about 200 yards from the water each way. It is near Bayou Tunica P.O.; the place is called "Tunica Bend Landing", West Feliciana County.

The larger Kettle was lying on its side, the head of one of the two skeletons found was in the Kettle. The small kettle, as also the pottery Vessels were all lying inverted close by the large Kettle.

The large beads were about the neck of the skeleton and the small ones about the ankles and feet. The two skeletons were close together; heads in opposite directions.

The Iron "Harpoons" were close by. The Brass Bands and Rings or Bracelets were with and some encircling the arm bones.[*]

---

[*] Inquiry to the Putnam Museum in 1986 revealed that the artifacts could not be located, with the possible exception of eleven copper (brass?) bracelets, ten kettle fragments, and what appears to be part of a musket trigger guard (Janice Hall, personal communication, 1986).

This description is consistent with Tunica burials of the mid-eighteenth century, and the precise location can only be Trudeau. A particularly interesting disclosure is the reference to the small mound, which no longer exists. Apparently it was a victim of the plow and had already been "worn down" in Captain Hall's day. The mound may have been a feature dating from a prehistoric occupation of the site, or it might have been only a particularly prominent colluvium on the talus slope; in any event, it is unlikely to have been of Tunica origin, although obviously it was used by the tribe.

The next professional notice of Trudeau was that of the ubiquitous C. B. Moore. His description is brief but again leaves no doubt about the identification of the site described under the heading "Site at Trudeau, West Feliciana Parish, La." (Moore 1911, p. 376):

> *Immediately at Trudeau Landing is a farm with a residence somewhat back from the river. At one side of this house is black soil, indicating former aboriginal occupancy. Through part of this ground ran a small road, from the side of which, we were informed by the occupant of the house, an intelligent colored man, a brass kettle had been uncovered by wash of rain. While digging into this place, after the discovery of the kettle, we were told, various objects of iron or of steel were unearthed, and also a pipe, probably of catlinite [fig. 56], which we obtained.*

> *Seven trial-holes put down by us near where the kettle had been discovered, failed to come upon graves, though dwelling-site debris was encountered in places.*

Moore's lack of enthusiasm is evident: this was a small, featureless site (note that there is no mention of Hall's mound), and obviously historic as well. Moore soon steamed on upriver, missing the exciting potential of this remarkable site.

It was more than half a century before the site's potential was fully realized and acted upon. In the late 1960s a local treasure hunter, Leonard J. Charrier, rediscovered Trudeau and dug more than a hundred burials and other features. His industry was rewarded with an extraordinary collection of aboriginal and European artifacts, the so-called Tunica Treasure (Brain 1970, 1979).* Unfortunately, the unprofessional removal procedures destroyed all the important details of context beyond general provenience. In order to salvage some contextual information, a series of investigations was carried out at the site in 1972, 1980, and 1981.

---

* By way of conclusion to "The Tale of the Tunica Treasure" (Brain 1979, pp. 2–32), it may be noted briefly that the Tunica-Biloxi tribe joined the legal fray over ownership of the collection in 1981. After extensive due process, the Tunica Treasure was finally given into their hands by the local parish court in 1986 and confirmed by the state supreme court in 1987. At this writing, the tribe has been granted sufficient funds by the federal government to construct a museum on the tribal lands in Marksville to house the artifacts.

Figure 56. Catlinite pipe from the Trudeau site (Moore 1911, fig. 1). (1:1)

The 1972 Excavations

The Lower Mississippi Survey conducted limited test excavations at Trudeau during the period of 7–29 August 1972 (Brain 1973). The LMS crew consisted of Jeffrey P. Brain (field director), Ian Brown, Gilman Parsons, Vincas Steponaitis, and Daniel Potts. Funding was provided by research grants from the National Science Foundation and National Geographic Society. The purpose of the investigation was to verify that this site was the provenience from which the Tunica Treasure collection had been removed and, in that case, to establish the archaeological context.

Adequate proof constituting verification of the site required three discrete sorts of evidence: archaeological retrieval of artifactual material comparable to that already contained within the Tunica Treasure collection, in-ground evidence in the form of recently dug holes testifying to the removal of the collection, and the example of an undisturbed situation (preferably a burial with accompanying grave goods). Finally, it was hoped that in the course of these investigations the archaeological context of the collection could be defined within the natural and cultural formations at the site.

The primary site datum was strategically located beneath a large, shady pecan tree and identified with a capped steel pipe. The coordinates of all excavations are in reference to this point. The below-ground tests consisted of sixteen excavation units, ranging in horizontal dimensions from 1 × 1.5 m to 2 × 4 m. Depths varied according to the situation, but in no case was it necessary to dig deeper than 1.5 m. These excavations were placed in six separate locations where it was concluded that the information sought could be recovered most expeditiously (fig. 57). The locations were chosen through a combination of Charrier's information, visual observation, electronic instrument survey, and educated guesswork. Each series of excavations was relatively productive and contributed useful information, so that the most important of the overall objectives were successfully achieved.

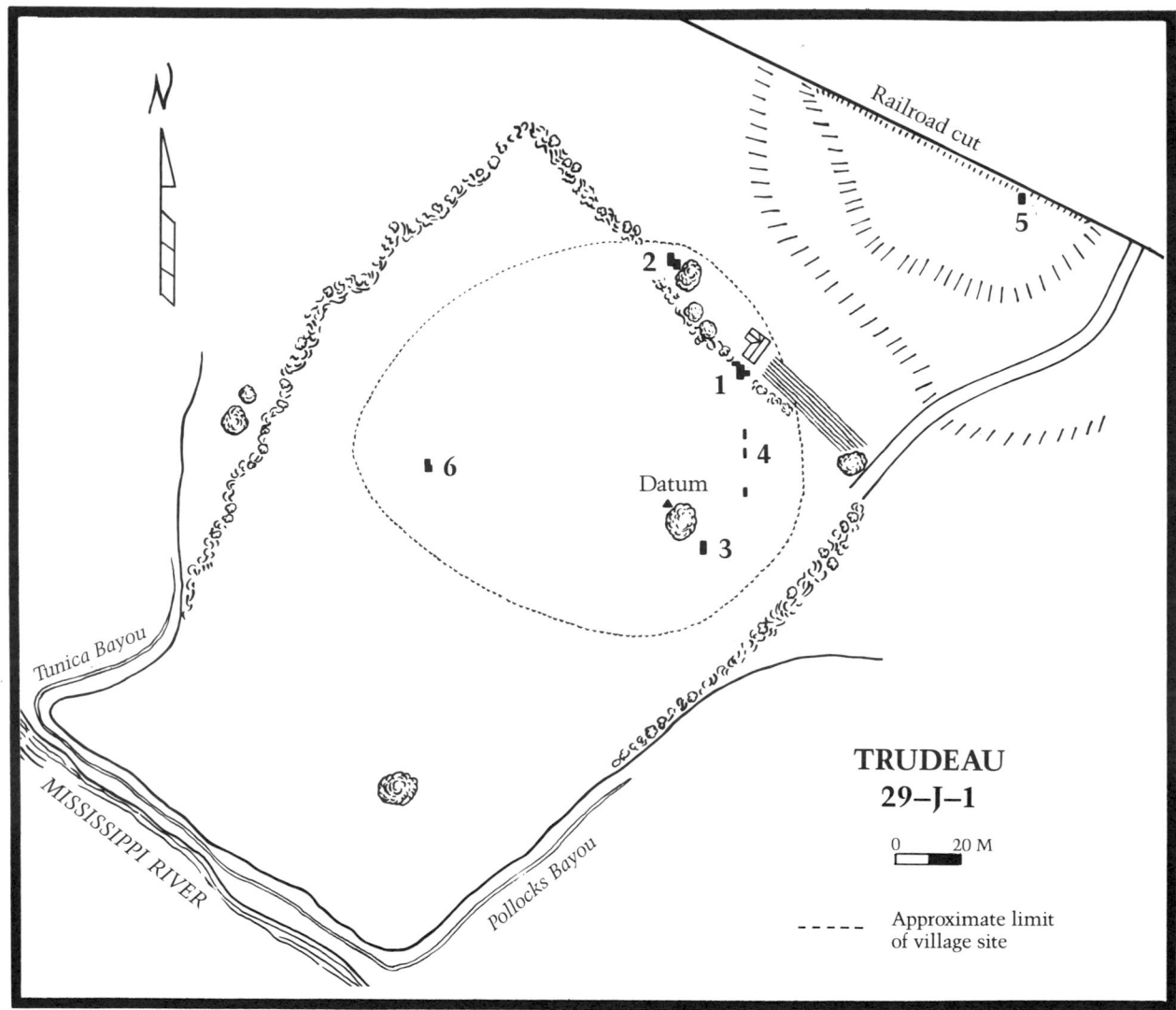

Figure 57. Sketch map of the Trudeau site and locations of the 1972 test excavations by the Lower Mississippi Survey.

At all locations, materials appropriate to a mid-eighteenth-century Indian occupation were discovered. Furthermore, most specimens (although fragmentary) were similar—many even identical—to artifacts included within the Tunica Treasure. The best sample came from location 3, where a trash pit containing a large amount of refuse was found. Two smaller trash pits were discovered at location 4, and scattered midden as well as trash pits were present at location 1. Locations 1, 2, and 5 produced evidence of recent disturbance: specifically, of crude pits dug from the present ground surface to an average depth of approximately 1 m. These pits were cleaned out and found to contain fragments of human bone and scattered artifacts, indicating the former presence of burials with associated grave goods. In most cases, portions of the original burial pits also could be observed. At location 6 an undisturbed burial was found which provided the final necessary bit of proof that Trudeau was indeed the provenience of the Tunica Treasure.

LOCATION 1

The vicinity of the abandoned tenant house (fig. 57) was said by the collector, Leonard J. Charrier, to have been one of the richest locations in terms of number of burials and abundance of their accompaniments. Since this intelligence was born of considerable experience, it seemed logical to concentrate one set of tests there in order to verify this recent activity, and perhaps even find a feature that Charrier might have missed.

A series of contiguous excavation units (V701–702, V706–709) was established at this location. These units ranged from 1 × 1.5 m to 2 × 2 m in horizontal dimensions, although one unit (V707) was expanded irregularly in order to excavate completely a looted grave pit (fig. 58). Excavation unit V701 was never actually opened up, as sufficient information about this location was accumulated from the other units. V709 was the number assigned to the balks left standing between units V702, V706, and V708 during excavation; these were

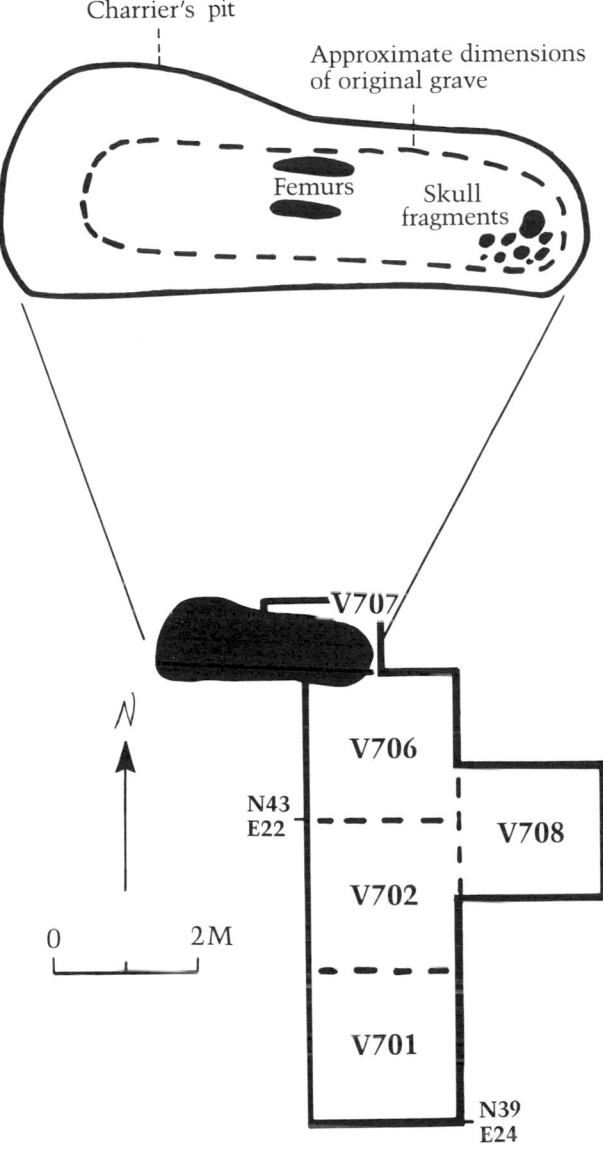

Figure 58. Plan of excavations at location 1, Trudeau, and detail of looted grave.

This humus stained the underlying bluff talus a rich brown color, which shaded imperceptibly to a light brown and then, finally, within 15–20 cm, to the natural color of the loess. The talus was replaced by alluvial deposits at approximately 60–75 cm below ground surface.

The geomorphology and cultural history were straightforward. Ancient alluvial deposits had been overlaid by loess talus which at one stage in its formation had weathered a distinct soil horizon. This horizon contained cultural materials and other evidence of human activity, as did the overlying loam. Recent disturbance mixed the contents of the two strata, but the cultural stratigraphy nevertheless may be interpreted with some confidence from the physical evidence. The old humus zone was clearly an occupational surface. That it dated to the eighteenth century was determined beyond doubt by the content of features that intruded into the underlying subsoil. These included at least three aboriginal trash pits. The largest of these, intersected by excavation units V702, V706, and V708 (figs. 58–59), contained an assortment of mid-

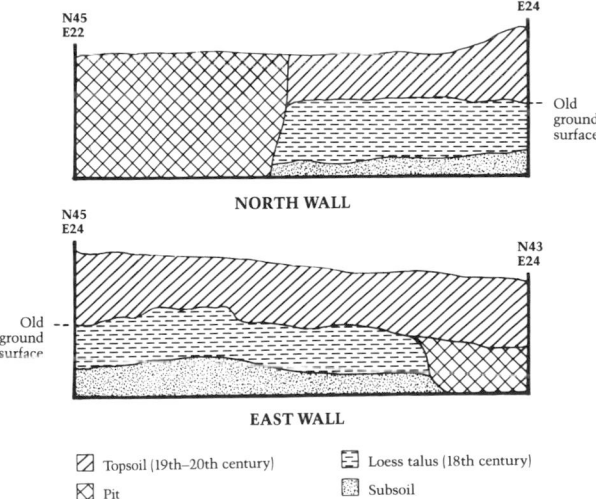

▨ Topsoil (19th–20th century)			▤ Loess talus (18th century)	
▧ Pit			░ Subsoil	

Figure 59. Stratification and stratigraphy of excavation unit V706 at location 1, Trudeau. Note the old ground surface which contained most of the in situ eighteenth-century cultural materials, except for intrusions such as the old pit shown in the east wall. The recent pit in the north wall was determined to have been a looted grave.

later removed to clear a trash pit. The total horizontal area excavated, then, was approximately 14 m². Maximum depth from ground surface was 75 cm, or about 40 cm above datum.

The stratification at this location was consistent in all units, although individual strata varied slightly in thickness from place to place and occasionally were disrupted by ancient and modern features. The basic stratification encountered is diagramed in figure 59 and described here in sequence from the surface down. The first stratum consisted of a gray loam heavily mottled with charcoal and ash and containing occasional lenses of loess talus from the bluff. Generally quite disturbed, this stratum had a high organic and cultural content. Beneath it appeared an old ground surface that had been exposed long enough to develop a thin humus zone.

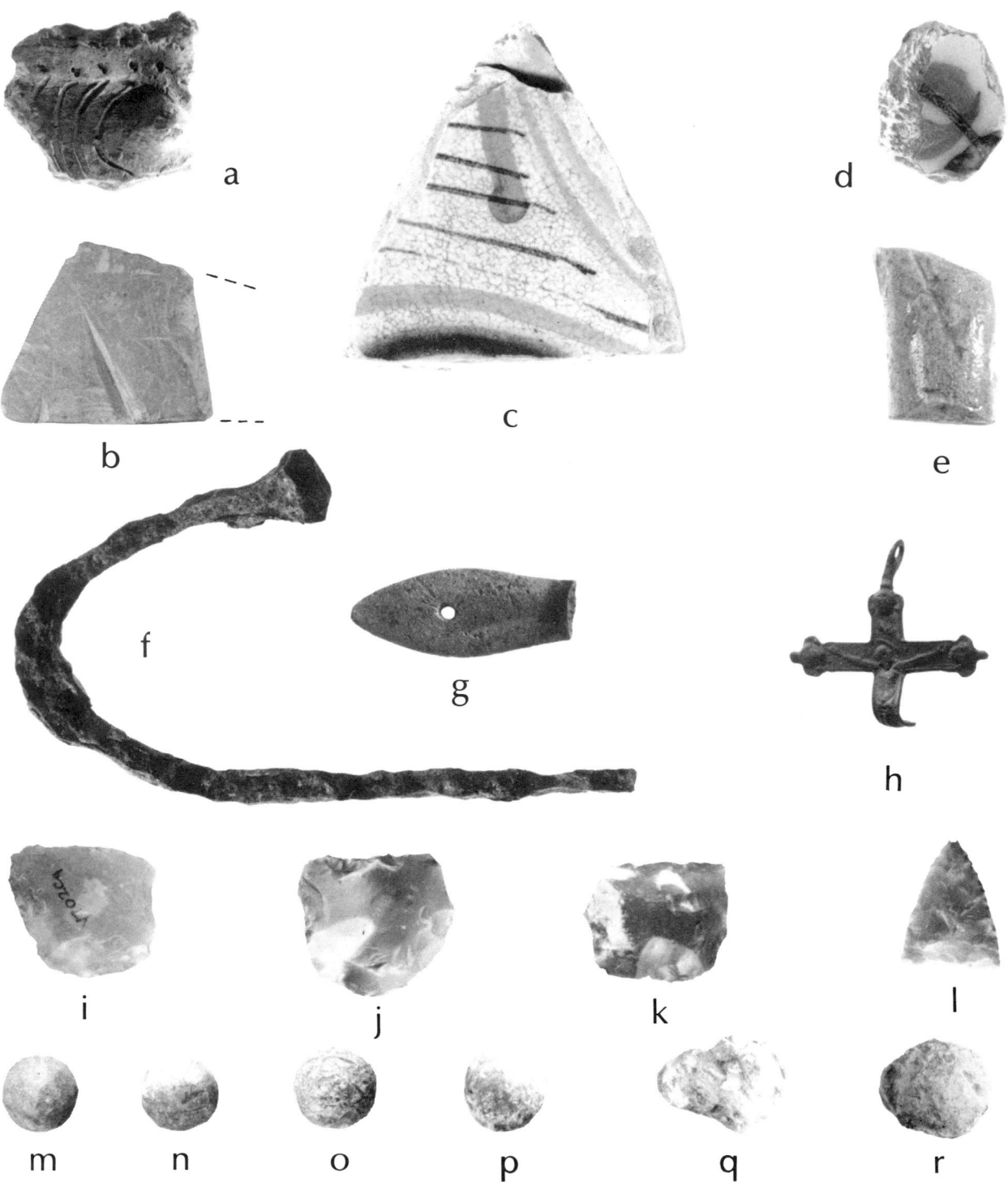

Figure 60. Miscellaneous eighteenth-century artifacts from location 1, Trudeau. a, Winterville Incised, *var. Tunica*; b, catlinite pipe fragment; c, polychrome (yellow-green-purple-white) faience; d, blue-and-white faience; e, lead-glazed earthenware, Type B; f, handwrought iron spike; g, brass trigger guard tang; h, brass crucifix; i–j, spall gunflints; k, blade gunflint; 1, Nodena Lanceolate, *var. unspecified* point; m–p, 28-*calibre* lead musket balls; q–r, distorted lead musket balls. (1:1)

eighteenth-century artifacts (fig. 60; table 4). The feature and the food remains that it contained, as well as the presence of at least one posthole nearby, suggest that this was a habitational locus. Due to the later disturbance, however, no definite structures were identified. That the later disturbance was also of an occupational nature is demonstrated by the abandoned tenant house. Nineteenth- and twentieth-century artifacts were found in great abundance throughout the gray loam topsoil. This occupation was long and con-

Table 4. Aboriginal and European artifacts from feature 2 at location 1, the Trudeau site (29-J-1).

ABORIGINAL

Pottery:

Winterville Incised, *var. Tunica* (fig. 60a)	1
Barton Incised, *var. Trudeau*	1
Mississippi Plain, *var. Pocahontas*	5
Fatherland Incised, *var. Nancy*	1
Addis Plain, *var. Addis*	8
Baytown Plain, *var. Vicksburg*	2
Baytown Plain, *var. Valley Park*	1

Organics:

Corn cobs (burned)[a]	—
Mammal bone (including several Bovidae)	11

EUROPEAN

Earthenware:

Pipe bowl (dark ceramic, not kaolin)	1

Glass:

Olive green	1
Bead	
IIA7	1

Iron.

Wrought nails	
Type I	1
Type V (fig. 60f)	1
Type unspecified	2
Miscellaneous	2

Gun parts/munitions:

Spall gunflint (fig. 60j)	1

[a] Many fragments, all of which appear to be from eight-row cobs. No kernels were found, and the charring of the cobs may have resulted from their use as fuel: perhaps the pit was originally a smudge pit.

tinuous, and its deposits were thoroughly mixed with talus from the bluff, creating a thick layer of midden. The midden also included a substantial number of eighteenth-century artifacts that had been churned up from the underlying stratum (fig. 60).

The most recent disturbance, of course, was the activity of Leonard J. Charrier. His interest was not in the mundane middens of the living but in the sepulchers of the dead, and his work was evident at this location. In the north wall of excavation unit V706, a recent pit was found to have been dug down through the cultural strata and into subsoil (fig. 59). Suspecting that this

feature was evidence of a disturbed burial, we expanded the excavations and soon verified our suspicions at a depth of approximately 75 cm from the surface (fig. 58). The burial apparently had been that of a single adult, lying in supine position with the head to the east. Only a few fragments of bone remained and but a single artifact: a piece of iron kettle found in the extreme western part of the pit. That most of the major accompaniments of this burial were placed at the feet rather than the head is also indicated by the fact that Charrier's pit bulged out considerably at the western end, apparently to provide him with more working room.

In summary, location 1 provided a good sample of artifactual materials, many of which replicated items in the collection; evidence of a recently looted burial; and considerable information on the archaeological context of the eighteenth-century occupation at the site.

LOCATION 2

Charrier pinpointed this location as one where he had located a "rich" burial, but which (for reasons not shared with us) he had closed up after minimal disturbance. The known presence of an in situ burial with accompaniments, plus the prospect of establishing Charrier's intrusion into it, were sufficient encouragement to concentrate part of our efforts here.

Two 2-×-2-m excavation units (V703, V704) were placed where Charrier remembered the burial to have been, just a few meters northwest of a large pecan tree. After removal of the topsoil in both units, the natural loess talus was carefully troweled for features, but none was observed. Those excavation units, therefore, were abandoned, and another (V705) was established on the southeastern side closer to the tree (figs. 57, 61). When

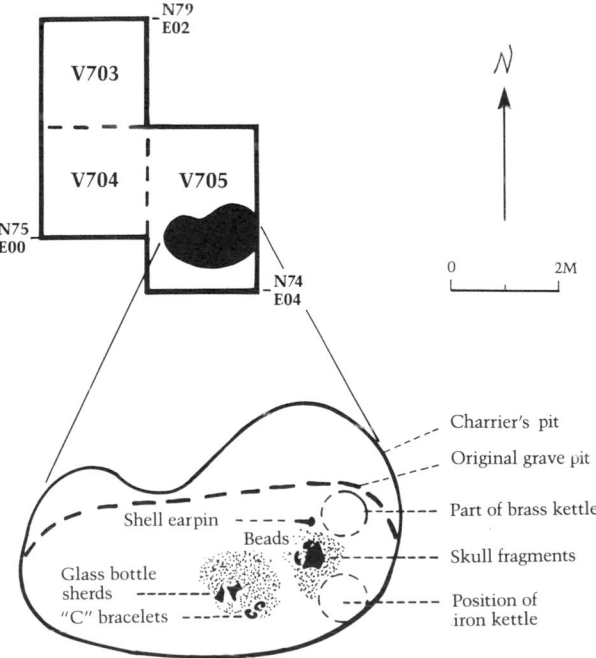

Figure 61. Plan of excavations at location 2, Trudeau, and detail of the looted grave.

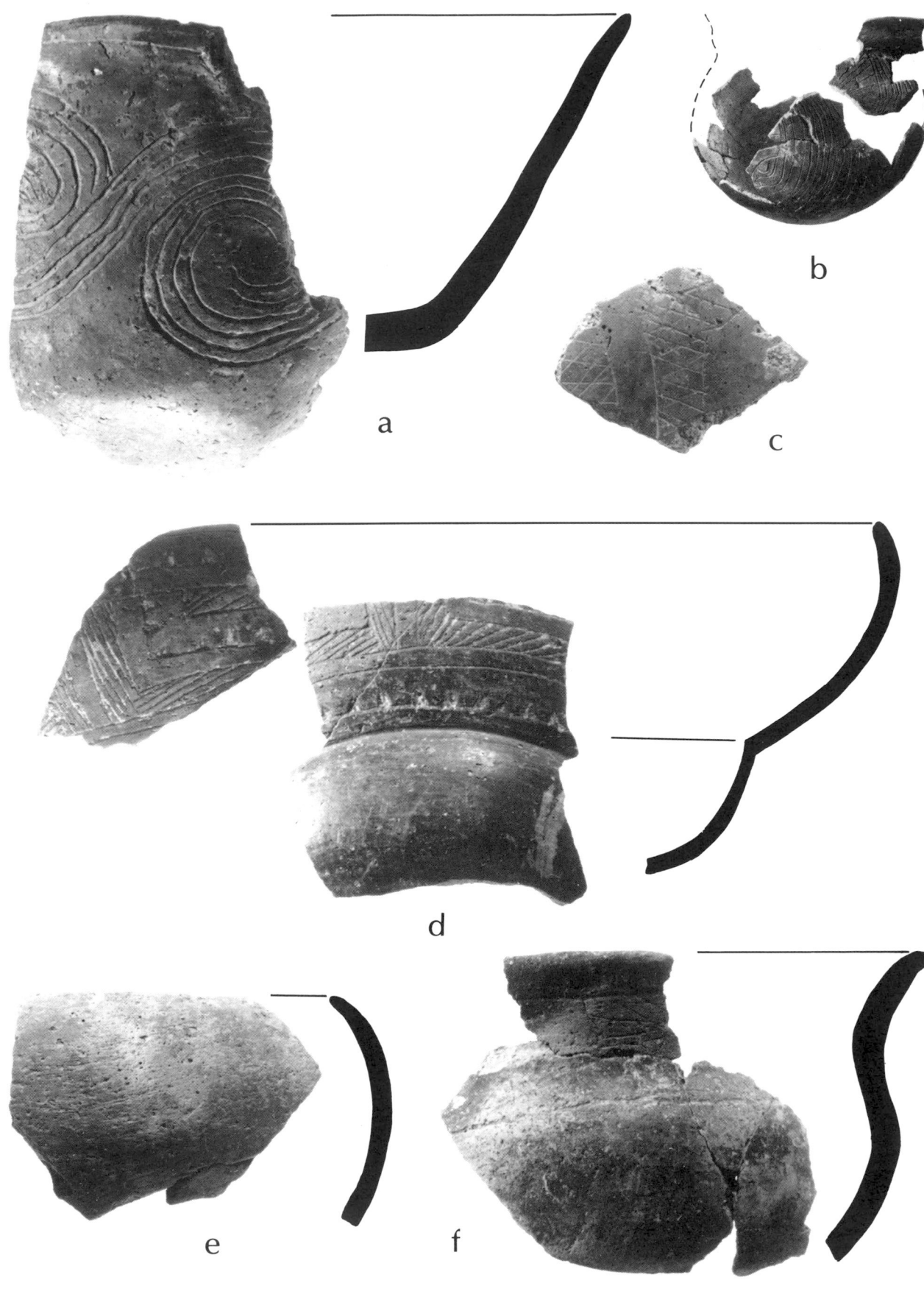

a

b

c

d

e

f

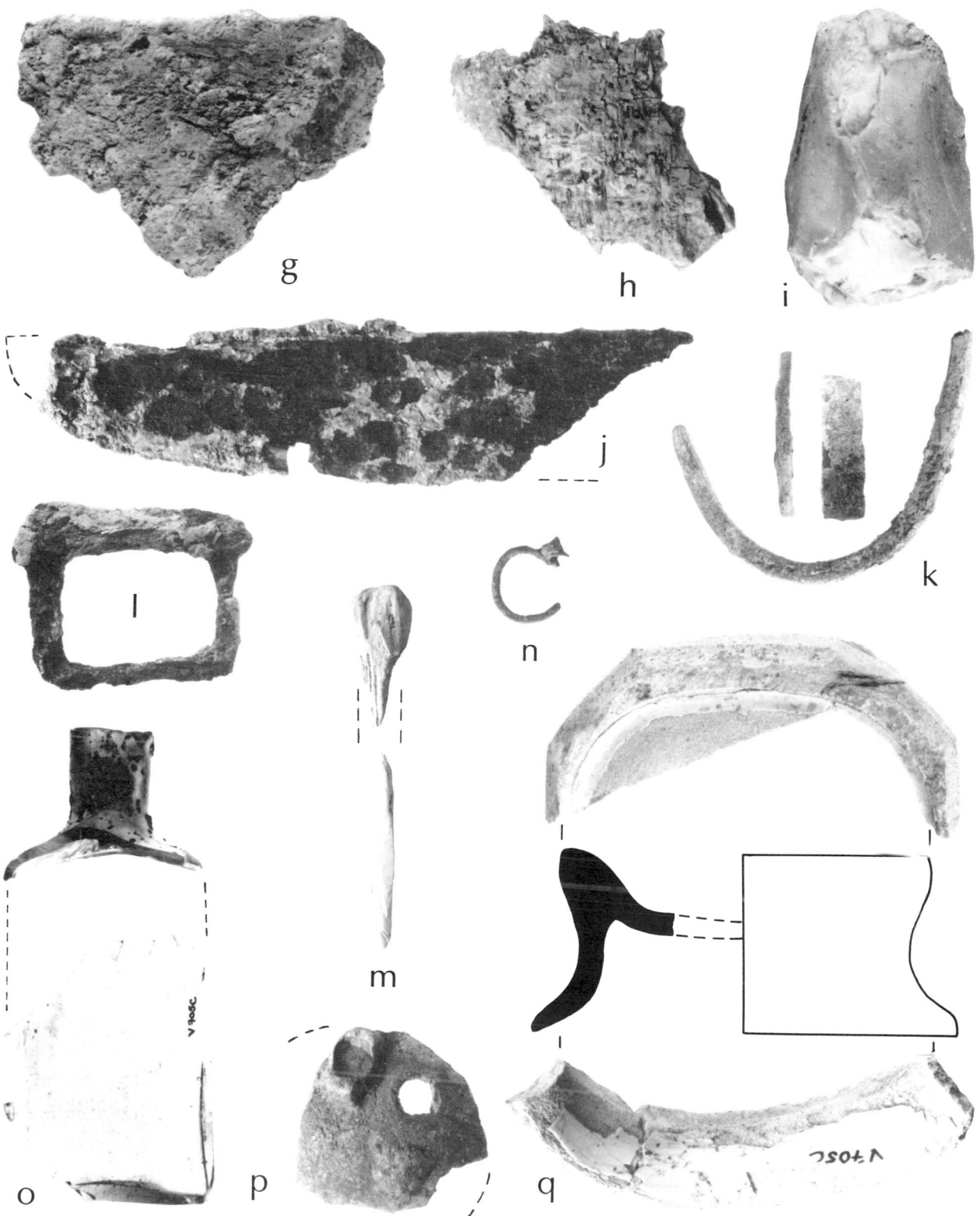

Figure 62. Some of the artifacts from the looted grave in excavation unit V705, location 2, Trudeau. a, Cracker Road Incised, *var. Cracker Road*; b, Winterville Incised, *var. Tunica* (fragments of vessel in the Tunica Treasure collection and from the excavations); c, f, unclassified Caddoan engraved; d, Natchitoches Engraved, *var. Natchitoches*; e, Chicot Red, *var. Grand Village*; g, fragment of iron kettle; h, fragment of brass kettle with basketry impressions; i, chert chopper-scraper; j, case knife blade; k, fragments of brass C-bracelets; l, iron buckle; m, conch shell earpin; n, silver earring; o, light blue-green glass case bottle fragments; p, brass Flowerkey bell; q, blue-and-white faience *salière*. (1:1, except b, 1:3; o, 1:2)

Table 5. Aboriginal and European artifacts from the looted grave in excavation unit V705 at location 2, Trudeau.

ABORIGINAL		IVA1[b]	1,854
		IVA2	22
Pottery:		WIA1	8
		WIA2	2
Winterville Incised, *var. Tunica* (fig. 62b)	1[a]	WIB1	8
		WIB3	1
Cracker Road Incised, *var. Cracker Road* (fig. 62a)	1	WIC1	7
		WIIA3	1
Natchitoches Engraved, *var. Natchitoches* (fig. 62d)	1	WIIA4	2
Unclassified engraved (Caddo) (fig. 62c, f)	2	WIIA11[c]	3
		WIIB2	28
Chicot Red, *var. Grand Village* (fig. 62e)	1	WIIC1	1
		WIIC2[c]	1
Lithics:		WIIIA4	1
Chert chopper/scraper (fig. 62i)	1	*Iron:*	
Red ochre	3		
		Kettle (fig. 62g)	1
Organics:		Wrought nails	
		Type unspecified	13
Shell earpin (fig. 62m)	1	Case knife blade (fig. 62j)	1
Basketry (fig. 62h)	1	Buckle (fig. 62l)	1
EUROPEAN		*Silver:*	
Earthenware:		Earring (fig. 62n)	1
Faience		*Brass:*	
Blue-and-white (fig. 62q)	1	Kettle (fig. 62h)	1
Glass:		C-bracelets (fig. 62k)	3
		Bell	
Light blue-green case bottles (fig. 62o)	2	Flowerkey (fig. 62p)	1
Beads			
IA1	4		
IB2	37		
IIA5	8		
IIA6	57		
IIA7	391		
IIIA1	1		

[a]Numbers indicate whole artifacts represented.
[b]Some of these may be IIA1.
[c]New varieties: see appendix E.

the topsoil of this unit was removed, part of a recent intrusion was clearly revealed along the southern edge. V705 was expanded another meter to the south until the entire outline of the intrusive pit could be traced. This feature then was excavated as a whole.

The upper part of the pit revealed considerable evidence of the recent disturbance. The fill was very loose and contained a high admixture of topsoil. The cultural content, too, consisted as much of trash from the nearby tenant house as it did of eighteenth-century artifacts. Most of the latter were subsequently found to match or join other pieces at the bottom of the pit. There could be no question that there was disturbance and that it was recent; that it was caused by Charrier may be presumed by his identification of the location.

The bottom of the pit was reached at a depth of 1 m from the ground surface (elevation from datum: +65

cm). Lying on it were the remains of a burial. Despite Charrier's protestations, this burial had been badly disturbed; very few elements remained in original position, and none of the artifacts—with the exception of such small items as beads—was intact. Perhaps because it was fragmentary, a surprisingly large amount of material was left in the grave (this being Charrier's definition of "minimal disturbance"?). Although we have no knowledge of what was removed previously, enough remained to reconstruct an already quite adequate assemblage.

The known artifacts—those from the actual grave and/or pit fill—are listed in table 5 (note that the table does not give the number of fragments in each category but rather the number of whole artifacts as reconstructed from the fragments). Many are also illustrated in figure 62. Of special interest are the six aboriginal pots, which include examples from the Tunican, Natch-ezan, and Caddoan traditions. Fragments from four of these vessels were received separately from Charrier, and all joined fragments from the excavations, proving Charrier's earlier presence. Furthermore, pieces of the Winterville Incised, *var. Tunica* pot from both the excavation and Charrier joined a partial vessel in the Tunica Treasure (Brain 1979, p. 234), thus tying together the site, the collector, and the collection beyond any further doubt.

Other artifacts included European containers: one iron and one brass kettle (the latter preserving a piece of native basketry with over-four, under-one weave [Brain 1979, p. 253]), at least two French "case" bottles (ibid., p. 93), and a small faience saltcellar (*salière* [Genêt 1980, pl. 63c]– a most appropriate and intriguing item considering the prominence of the Tunica in the salt trade!). European ornaments are represented by thousands of glass beads, of which there are at least twenty varieties (Brain 1979, pp. 100–113), three C-bracelets (one each of types 4, 6, and 7; ibid., pp. 193–194), a German silver earbob (ibid., p. 163), and other odds and ends as listed in the table. The only aboriginal ornament to survive is a marine conch shell columella earpin of the usual knobbed type (ibid., p. 252).

The original positions of some of these artifacts could be determined and are illustrated in figure 61. The overall configuration of this reconstruction seems quite typical. The grave was that of a single individual interred with the head to the east. The few fragments of skull and mandible establish that the individual was a young adolescent, approximately eleven years old (the second permanent molar, preserved in place in the mandible, is fully formed but had not yet erupted, or was only just beginning to break through the skin and shows no wear). That the sex was female is indicated by the gracility of the bones and confirmed by the presence of a large number of pots and kettles; by the hundreds of blue and white seed beads around the skull, suggesting the feminine trait of weaving beads into the hair (Dumont de Montigny 1753, vol. 1, p. 137); and by the shell earpin, which is a female diagnostic (Brain 1979, p. 252)

Location 2, then, represented a valuable contribution to the objectives of our excavations and provided important primary archaeological data about the site and the collection.

LOCATION 3

In the search for promising locations to test, we relied partly on independent instrument surveys in hopes of discovering undisturbed features. Among the positive readings was one locus 17.5 m southeast of datum where the magnetometer and metal detectors discriminated a large feature with high metallic content. Thus encouraged, we established location 3 (the instrument readings actually were no better than several others recorded, but the location was made doubly attractive by a large pecan tree that was to provide partial shade for the excavations).

The coordinates of the excavations were S12–16 and E12–14, an area that was divided into two excavation units: V710 and V711 (fig. 63). V710 was opened up

first, and after the topsoil was removed a large semi-circular pit was observed in the southeastern quarter. Clearly, the other half of the pit was to be found in excavation unit V711, the placement of the excavations having neatly bisected it. It was decided to explore the pit in two stages: first to isolate and investigate it in V710, and then to open up the remaining half in V711.

Any expectations we may have entertained that the pit contained a burial were shortly dispelled. But we were not entirely disappointed, for we had found instead a large trash pit that appeared to have a very high cultural content. After the natural undisturbed subsoil had been removed from the rest of V710 to a depth of approximately 1 m, the pit itself was approached from the north side and dissected bit by bit. When this half of the pit had been entirely removed, the profile in the south wall of V710 (fig. 63) showed that it was approximately 190 cm in diameter and 120 cm deep. Working from this profile, we removed the remainder of the pit in V711. Stratification was well defined, and so individual layers (A–D, as illustrated in fig. 63) were taken out one at a time. Their contents were cataloged separately in anticipation that they would elucidate details in the interpretation of the cultural stratigraphy. This anticipation was unwarranted, however, as pieces of the same artifacts often were found scattered throughout all the layers. Thus, the cultural content of the pit may be discussed as a whole.

The trash pit was extremely rich in cultural materials, including a large assortment of aboriginal artifacts and food remains, as well as an excellent sample of European items (table 6). The inventory of native potsherds displays most of the usual varieties of the principal protohistoric-historic types in the Lower Mississippi Valley. The Tunican, Natchezan, and Caddoan ceramic traditions are well represented, and there is also ethnically unidentified material present that probably originated in the Yazoo Basin. The few prehistoric potsherds are incidental inclusions and probably were scraped up with the more recent refuse as the pit was filled. They do attest, however, to the earlier occupation of Trudeau by late Coles Creek and Plaquemine peoples.

The lithic tool assemblage is surprisingly substantial considering the large assortment of European tools present. There is no reason to suspect that any of them are displaced from the earlier occupations. In fact, those that can be identified, such as the "triangular" knife (fig. 64ii), are diagnostically late. A worked deer antler tine, which probably had been employed as a flaker, provides further evidence that stone technology was still being practiced at the time that the trash pit was in use. Other bone tools are pieces of long bone that have been cut and shaped, and that exhibit polish and wear striations on the ends suggesting that they were employed as hide scrapers.

The European artifacts display a rich array of domestic items, tools, and ornaments. Ceramics include both faience and majolica, and all six established types of lead-glazed earthenware (Brain 1979, pp. 44–73). Of special interest for purposes of stratigraphic interpretation is a Type C, Variety 1 bowl (fig. 65i), pieces of which were found throughout the trash pit—an indi-

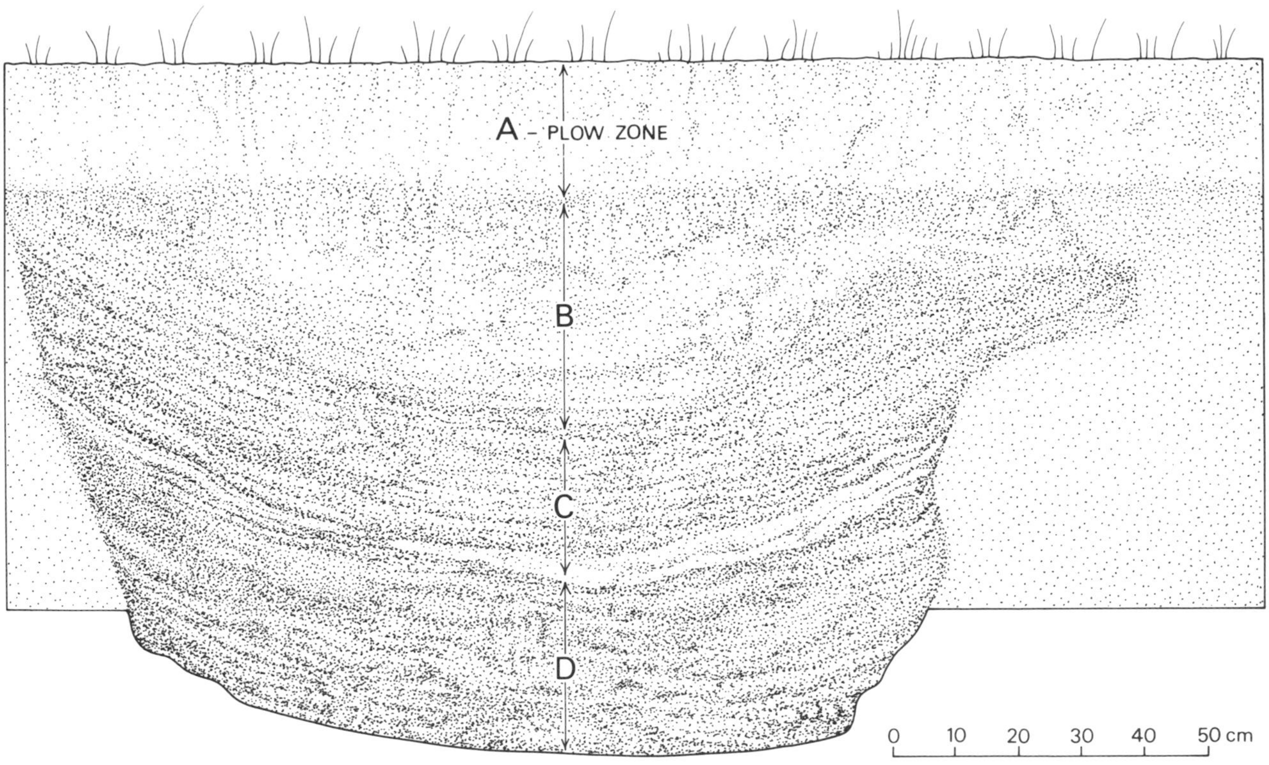

A – PLOW ZONE

B

C

D

0   10   20   30   40   50 cm

b

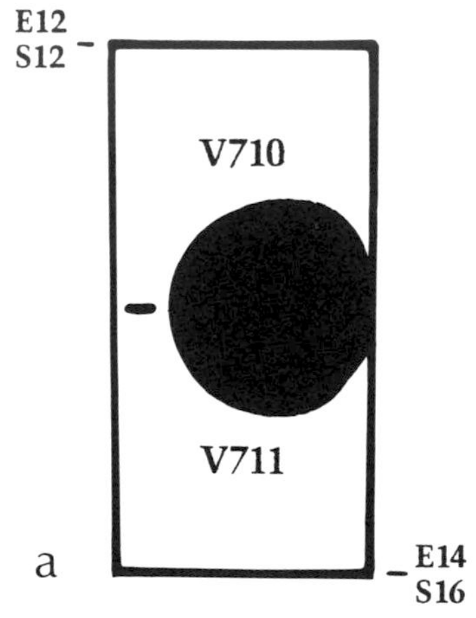

E12
S12

V710

V711

E14
S16

a

c

d

Figure 63. Trash pit V710/711 at location 3, Trudeau. a, plan of excavations; b, cross section of trash pit in south wall of excavation unit V710 and the four major divisions in the stratification by which the contents of the pit in V711 were removed; c, south wall of excavation unit V710 showing cross section of trash pit before lowermost layer was removed; d, trash pit after being completely cleaned out, displaying an almost geometrically circular shape.

Table 6. Aboriginal and European artifacts from the trash pit in excavation units V710/711 at location 3, Trudeau.

ABORIGINAL

Pottery:

Winterville Incised, *var. Tunica* (fig. 64a–e)	81
Barton Incised, *var. Trudeau* (fig. 64f–i)	78
Barton Incised, *var. Portland* (fig. 64j)	10
Tunican Mode	2
Mississippi Plain, *var. Pocahontas*	563
Mississippi Plain, *var. Montfort*	2
Cracker Road Incised, *var. Cracker Road* (fig. 64aa)	3
Fatherland Incised, *var. Bayou Goula* (fig. 64w–y)	11
Fatherland Incised, *var. Nancy* (fig. 64t–v)	32
Fatherland Incised, *var. Snyders Bluff* (fig. 64q–s)	104[a]
Natchitoches Engraved, *var. Natchitoches*	2
Unclassified engraved (Caddo)	4
Unclassified plain (Caddo)	2
Fatherland Incised, *var. Fatherland* (fig. 64k–p)	116[b]
Fatherland Incised, *var. unspecified* (fig. 64z)	12
Maddox Engraved, *var. unspecified* (fig. 64ff)	1
Unclassified incised (Addis) (fig. 64dd)	8
Unclassified engraved (Addis)	1
Chicot Red, *var. Grand Village*	15
Addis Plain, *var. St. Catherine*	121
Leland Incised, *var. Russell* (fig. 64ee)	6
Owens Punctated, *var. Beland City* (fig. 64bb–cc)	2[c]
Addis Plain, *var. Feliciana*	72
Addis Plain, *var. Skillikalia*	22
Anna Incised, *var. Anna*	1
Carter Engraved, *var. Carter*	2
L'Eau Noire Incised, *var. L'Eau Noire*	1
Plaquemine Brushed, *var. Plaquemine*	12
Mazique Incised, *var. Manchac*	6
Addis Plain, *var. Addis*	313[d]
Coles Creek Incised, *var. Mott*	2
Pontchartrain Check Stamped, *var. Pontchartrain*	5
Baytown Plain, *var. Vicksburg*	11
Baytown Plain, *var. Valley Park*	38
Larto Red, *var. Larto*	1
Evansville Punctated, *var. unspecified*	1
Unclassified incised (Baytown)	6
Baytown Plain, *var. unspecified*	29
Pipe bowl of Addis ware (fig. 64gg)	1

Daub: 251

Lithics:

Unclassified chert projectile points (fig. 64hh)	2
Native gunflint	1
Triangular knife (fig. 64ii)	1
Unclassified knife (fig. 64jj)	1
Chert adze (fig. 64kk)	1
Utilized chert flakes/pieces	17
Unutilized chert flakes/pieces	45
Chert pebbles	88
Quartzite hammerstone/chopper	1
Ground quartzite	3
Utilized sandstone	4
Pumice	16
Limonite	40
Hematite	11

Organics:

Bear canine (fig. 64mm)	1
Worked bone/antler (fig. 64nn)	4
Mussel shell spoon (fig. 64ll)	1
Faunal remains[e]	—
Vegetal remains[f]	—

EUROPEAN

Earthenware:

Faience

White	5
Blue-and-white (fig. 65a)	3
Polychrome (fig. 65b–c)	2
Brown	1

Majolica

Blue-and-white	1
Green-and-white	1
Green-and-blue-and-white (fig. 65d)	1
Black-and-blue-and-white (fig. 65e)	1

Lead-glazed

Type A, Variety unspecified (fig. 65f)	2
Type B, Variety 2	1
Type B, Variety unspecified bowl (fig. 65g)	4
Type B, Variety unspecified (fig. 65h)	11
Type C, Variety 1 (fig. 65i–j)	25[g]
Type C, Variety unspecified	1
Type D, Variety 3 (fig. 65k)	2
Type E, Variety unspecified (fig. 65l)	1
Type F, Variety unspecified platter (fig. 65m)	1
Type F, Variety unspecified	2
Unclassified[h]	2
Unglazed	5
Kaolin pipestem	1

Table 6 continued

Table 6 (continued).

Stoneware:

Westerwald (fig. 65n)	2
Grès (short-necked bottle) (fig. 65o)	1

Glass:

Clear	
Wine glass (fig. 65p–q)	5[i]
Tumbler (fig. 65r)	1
Bottle	5
Olive green (fig. 65t–u)	122
Light blue-green (fig. 65s)	24
Beads	
IIA1	1
IIA6	2
IIA7	1
IIB1	1
IIB2	2
IIB10	1
IVB4	3
WIIIA4	1
Unclassified wire-wound	1
Ornament	
Small purple-and-white inset	1

Iron:

Lug from Type F, Variety 1 copper kettle (fig. 65uu)	1
Wrought nails	
Type I (fig. 65ww)	41
Type III (fig. 65zz)	2
Type IV (fig. 65yy)	14
Type V (fig. 65xx)	6
Type unspecified	31
Axe (fig. 65vv)	1
Pike head (fig. 65rr)	1
Folding knife blade (fig. 65ss)	1
Strap (building hardware?) (fig. 65tt)	1
Wire coil	1
Buckle	1
Fishhook	1
Miscellaneous	52

Copper:

Tinkling cone (fig. 65z)	1

Brass:

Pin (silver-plated?)	1
Bells	
Flowerkey	2
Tinkling cones (fig. 65y, aa–cc)	4[j]
Necklace(?) (3 strands of wire twisted together)	1
Wire fragments (fig. 65x)	4
Sheet metal fragments	15
Braid	1

Gun parts/munitions:

Musket barrels (fig. 65qq)	2
Brass trigger guard, Type C (fig. 65dd)	1
Brass side plate, Type C (fig. 65ee)	1
Lead musket ball, 28 *calibre* (fig. 65oo)	1
Lead musket balls, distorted (fig. 65pp)	3
Lead pistol ball (fig. 65oo)	1
Lead shot (fig. 65nn)	2
Spall gunflints	
Musket (fig. 65ff–ll)	12
Pistol (fig. 65mm)	6

[a] Most are from two vessels: a bowl and a bottle.
[b] Eight of these are on Feliciana ware.
[c] These are red slipped outside of the punctated zone; the only other known occurrence of this variety with the added mode of red slipping is from the Haynes Bluff site (see table 63 and app. A.1).
[d] One sherd contains a piece of olive green glass.
[e] See appendix H.
[f] A variety of charred materials including wood, cane, peach pits, and seeds (but no corn).
[g] Twenty-four of these are from one bowl, and the scattering of these sherds throughout the entire trash pit, from the uppermost levels to the lowest, reveals that the observed stratification has no significance for cultural stratigraphy.
[h] These sherds have been burned beyond recognition.
[i] Two of these have an etched design.
[j] Two could have been cone-shaped arrowheads, but it is unlikely that such items were needed at this period.

Figure 64. Aboriginal artifacts from trash pit V710/711 at location 3, Trudeau. a–e, Winterville Incised, *var. Tunica*; f–i, Barton Incised, *var. Trudeau*; j, Barton Incised, *var. Portland*; k–p, Fatherland Incised, *var. Fatherland*; q–s, Fatherland Incised, *var. Snyders Bluff*; t–v, Fatherland Incised, *var. Nancy*; w–y, Fatherland Incised, *var. Bayou Goula*; z, Fatherland Incised, *var. unspecified*; aa, Cracker Road, *var. Cracker Road*; bb–cc, Owens Punctated, *var. Beland City*; dd, unclassified incised; ee, Leland Incised, *var. Russell*; ff, Maddox Engraved, *var. unspecified*; gg, pipe bowl of St. Catherine ware; hh, chert biface; ii, chert triangular knife; jj, chert knife blade; kk, chert adze; ll, mussel shell spoon; mm, bear canine; nn, antler flaker. (1:2)

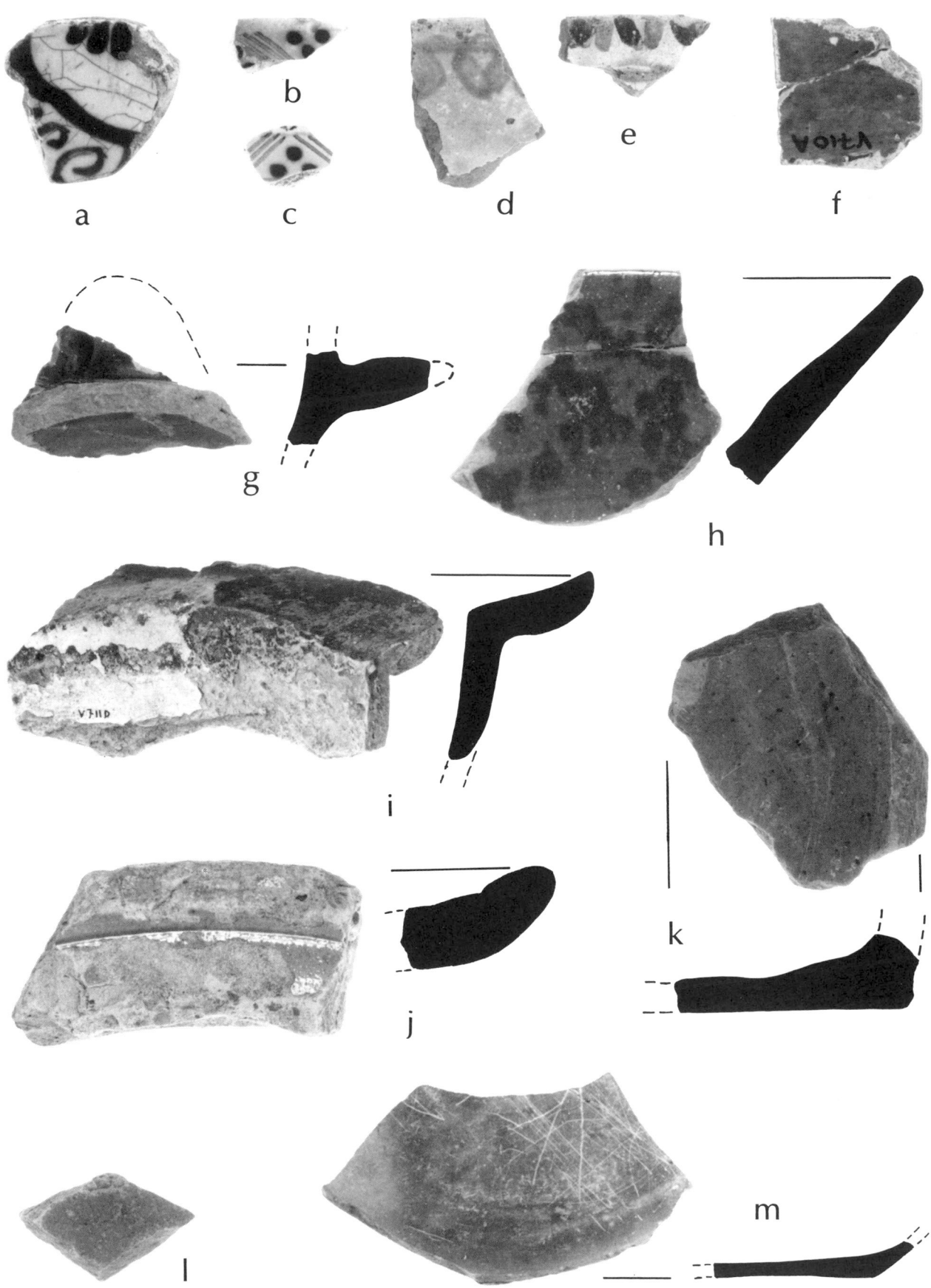

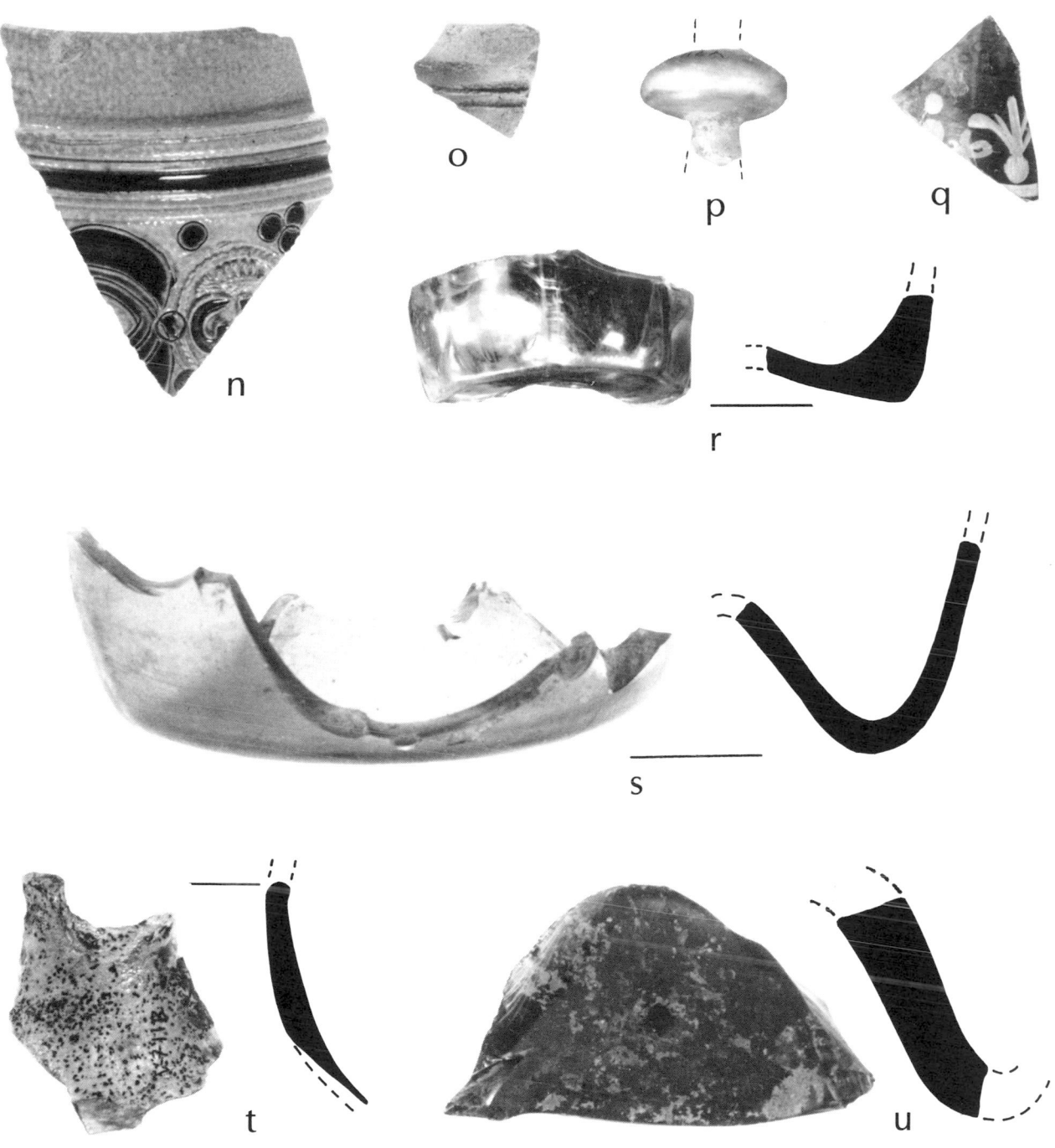

Figure 65. European artifacts from trash pit V710/711 at location 3, Trudeau. a, blue-and-white faience; b–c, polychrome (yellow-blue-red-white) faience; d–e, polychrome (green-blue-white, black-blue-white) majolica; f, lead-glazed earthenware, Type A; g–h, lead-glazed earthenware, Type B; i–j, lead-glazed earthenware, Type C; k, lead-glazed earthenware, Type D; l, lead-glazed earthenware, Type E; m, lead-glazed earthenware, Type F; n, Westerwald stoneware; o, Grès stoneware; p, stem of wine glass; q, etched clear glass; r, base of glass tumbler; s, base of light blue-green glass bottle; t, neck of olive green glass bottle; u, base of olive green glass bottle; v, kaolin pipe stem; w, brass Flowerkey bell; x, brass wire; y–cc, copper and brass tinklers; dd, brass trigger guard, Type C; ee, brass side plate, Type C; ff–ll, spall gunflints for muskets; mm, spall and blade gunflints for pistols; nn, lead shot; oo, lead pistol and musket balls; pp, distorted lead musket balls; qq, iron musket barrel; rr, iron pike head; ss, folding knife blade; tt, iron strap; uu, iron lug from Type F, Variety 1 copper kettle; vv, axe; ww, handwrought iron nail, Type I; xx, handwrought iron nail, Type V; yy, handwrought iron nail, Type IV; zz, handwrought iron nail, Type III. (1:1, except m, qq–rr, tt–vv, 1:2)

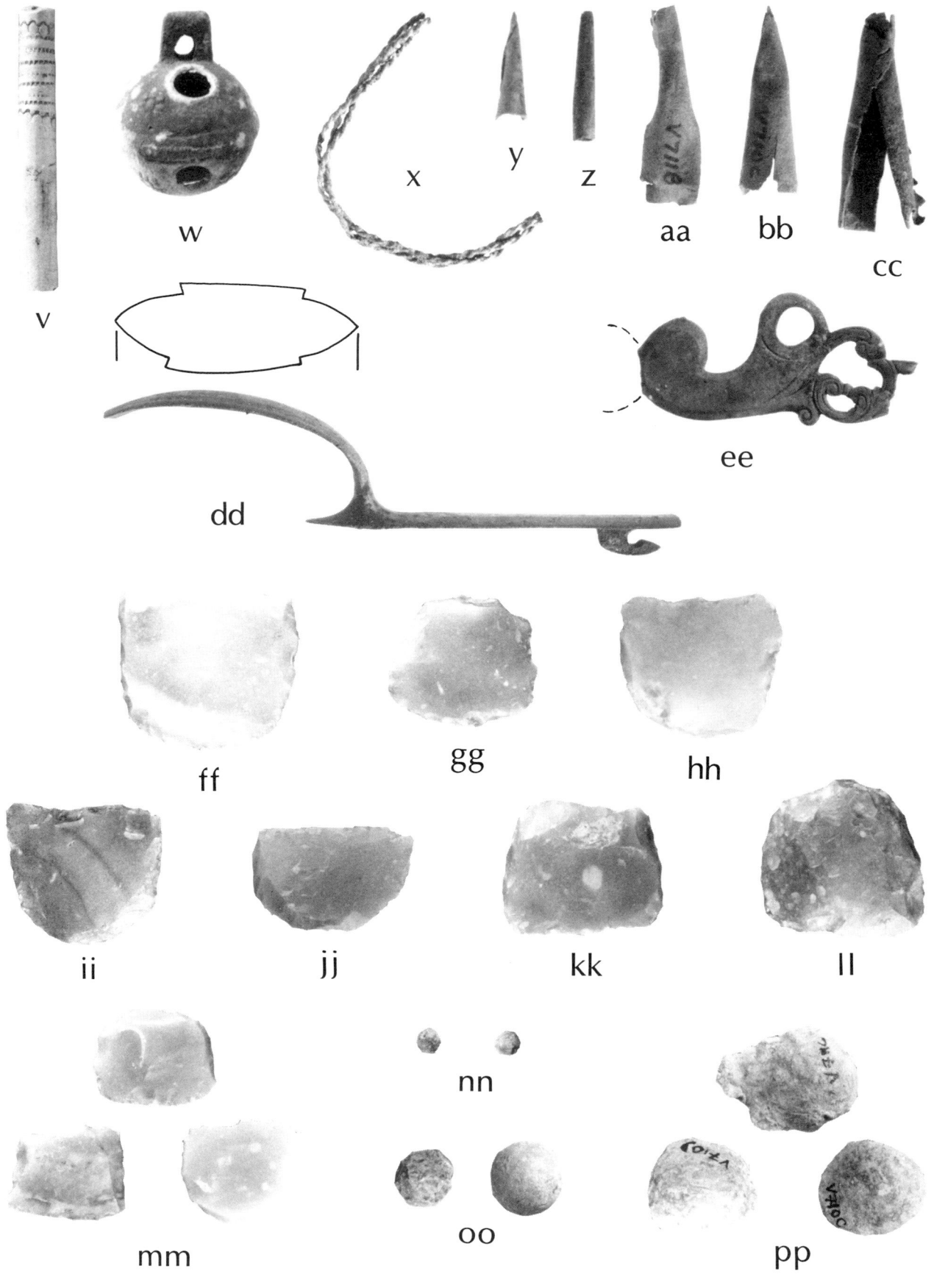

v

w

x

y

z

aa

bb

cc

dd

ee

ff

gg

hh

ii

jj

kk

ll

mm

nn

oo

pp

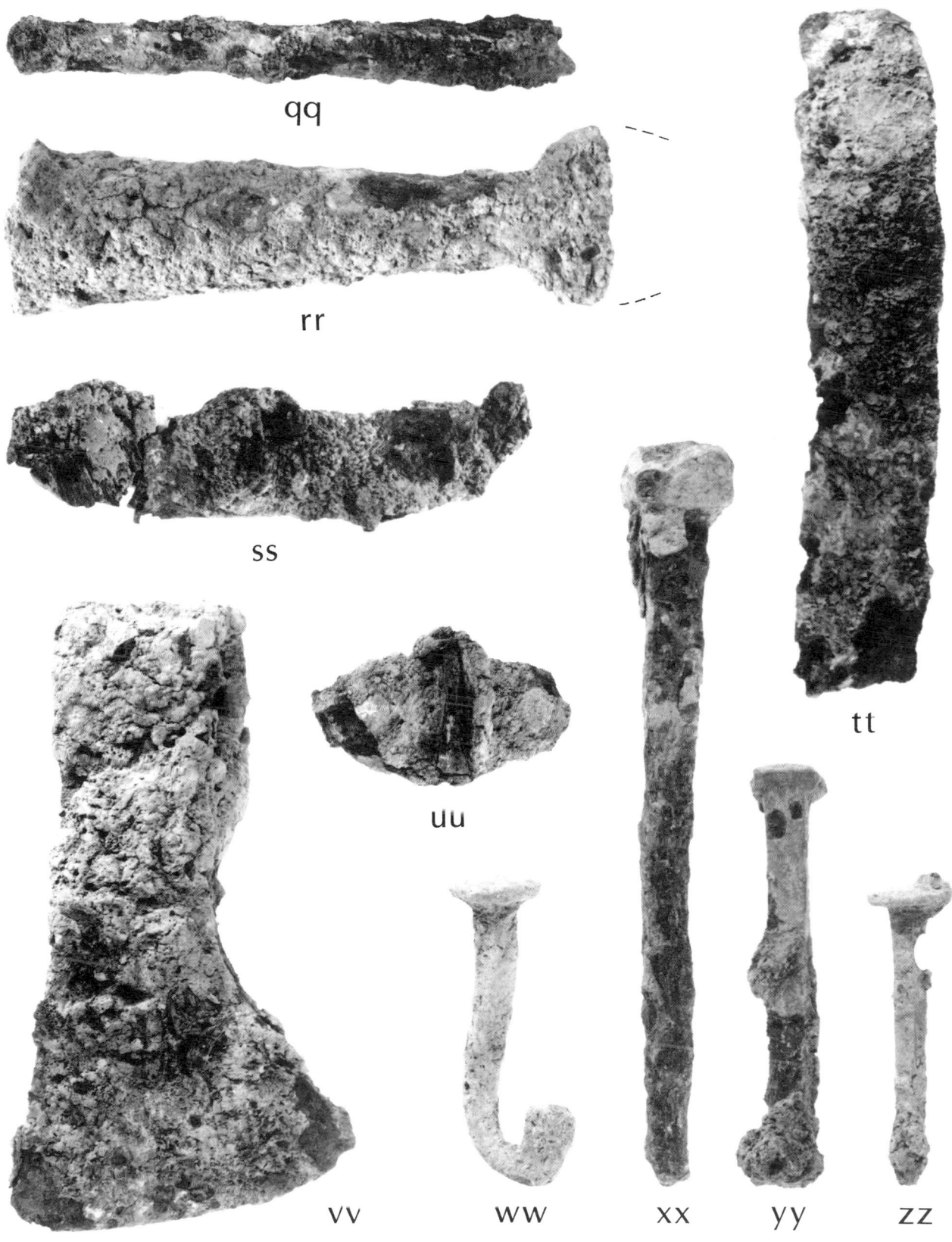

Figure 65 (continued).

cation that the feature was in use for a relatively brief period (i.e., that the stratification observed was not temporally significant). Stonewares are represented by one piece of French Grès and two of German Westerwald. One of the latter is a sherd from a "GR" mug (fig. 65n), which at the time of excavation provided distinctive artifactual evidence connecting the site and the Tunica Treasure collection (Brain 1973, fig. 2; Brain 1979). The Grès, being of French origin, is even more convincing evidence.

The glass bottles, especially a fragment of a very unusual light blue-green bottle (fig. 65s; Brain 1973, fig. 2; Brain 1979), also contributed to the artifactual proof. The large number of olive green bottle sherds suggests that there was no lack of alcoholic beverages,* and that there were even the proper means for drinking them is shown by the tumbler and wine glass (the latter a delicate handblown example with an ornate stem and a floral design etched on the bowl).

Considering the large number of artifacts in other categories, the number of glass beads is exceptionally small. Clearly, beads were deposited with the dead, or were simply lost, but in general they were not intentionally thrown away. The particular varieties represented suggest that the pit may have been filled during the earlier occupation of Trudeau, that is, before mid century.

The quantity of metal discarded is perhaps the greatest surprise. It might have been expected that some additional constructive use would have been found for the axe, pike, knife blade, nails, gun parts, and other miscellanea, even though they were damaged (fig. 65). Some of the items were even functional: many of the nails and other smaller iron items, as well as the brass bells and some of the lead ammunition (and even many of the gunflints), appear to have been perfectly good when they were disposed of. Even if the pit were in use during the early part of the occupation, as suggested by the beads, it would seem that the Tunica at Trudeau were not troubled by any scarcity of metal or metal artifacts, and in fact could afford to be quite profligate in dispensing with same.

The impression of affluence also is communicated by the faunal remains, the analysis of which (app. H) revealed a strong emphasis on large mammals: deer, bison, and bear. No small mammals and very few fish or birds were found. The most important of the birds was the domestic chicken. The Tunica are known to have raised chickens for trade (Charlevoix 1744, vol. 3, p. 433; Bridges and Delanglez 1964, p. 260) and apparently had no scruples about adding them to their own cuisine, unlike their erstwhile neighbors, the Houma (Shea 1861, p. 146). Primarily, however, if the contents of one trash pit are representative, the Tunica seem to have depended upon deer, bear, and buffalo. Deer and bear were plentifully available in the nearby Tunica Hills,† and bison could be found in the Louisiana bot-

* In 1758 Kerlérec visited the Tunica at Trudeau and decried "the drink that has been so liberally lavished upon them for more than twenty years" (de Villiers 1907, p. 75).

† In fact, bears have been recorded in recent memory in the Tunica Hills—one of their last wild refuges in the Lower Mississippi Valley.

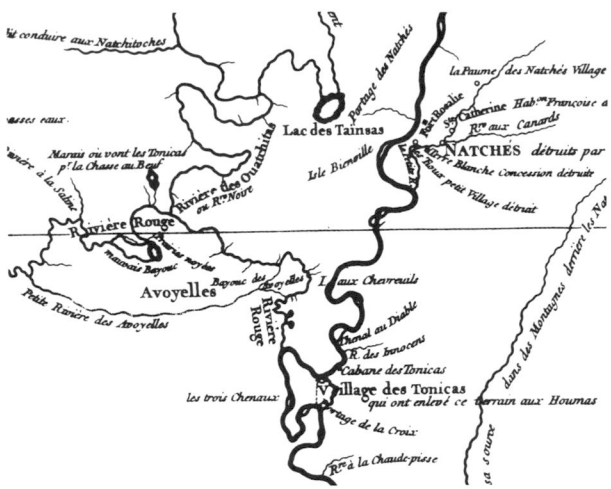

Figure 66. Section of the D'Anville map of 1732. Note the legend at the junction of the Red and Black rivers: "*marais ou vont les Tonicas p! la Chasse au Beuf.*" Perhaps the Tunica were led in these hunts by Bride-les-Boeufs (see fig. 208). (Map Collection, Harvard College Library, Cambridge)

tomlands across the river. There are numerous references to the presence of bison along the Red River and its tributaries (Broutin 1731; Bellin 1764), and the favored hunting ground of the Tunica was in the vicinity of Larto Lake near the confluence of the Black and Red rivers (fig. 66). Le Page du Pratz (1758, vol. 2, p. 67) notes that bison usually were hunted during the winter months, and analysis of the teeth from the trash pit indicated that the deer were killed in the late winter or early spring (app. H).

The V710/711 trash pit, then, was probably filled during the springtime. Although stratification of deposits was observed, the interval of time that the pit was in use appears to have been brief: Chi-square analysis of artifact and bone distributions did not reveal significant differences between stratigraphic subdivisions; pieces of the same artifact were sometimes found throughout the entire pit; and the seasonality of the deer, buffalo, and bear kills coincides. It may be that the pit usage was a single event, in the loosely defined archaeological sense—perhaps a case of spring-cleaning by one or more households. Whatever their number, the contributors were obviously well-to-do in the native context of the times. And although it may be inappropriate to generalize from a single example, it would seem that the Tunica had greater access to large mammals than did their prehistoric predecessors: "When they killed a buffalo, they would eat it. When they killed deer, a wild hog (or) a bear they would eat it" (Haas 1950, p. 157, describing favored foods according to Tunica oral tradition). This gourmandise may reflect both the success of Tunica entrepreneurism and the generally low population relative to the food supply, which allowed the Tunica to ignore a significant portion of the available resources in the environment. It must also be noted that it was only at this very late date (during the protohistoric-historic periods) that the bison suddenly extended its range into the Lower Mississippi Valley (Allen 1876, p. 228; Rostlund 1960).

The major results of the excavations at location 3 were the confirmation that Trudeau was a village site as well as a cemetery, and the knowledge that the Tunica were as profligate in life as in death when it came to the disposal of their material wealth. Also of interest is the fact that despite all the European trade goods, native artifacts and technologies still were strongly represented.

LOCATION 4

The eastern margin of the site between locations 1 and 3 was claimed by Charrier to have been one of the richest burial areas that he encountered. Hoping, therefore, to find evidence of his activities—and perhaps an undisturbed burial or other feature that he may have missed—we established location 4. In addition to pursuing these overall objectives of the excavations, we perceived the opportunity to determine more precisely the nature and extent of the site on this side, where the recent tenant occupation had obscured the earlier surface. For this reason we laid out what may be considered an extensive series of excavations in terms of the limited scope of the operation. The basic excavation was a 1-m-wide by 30-m-long trench, the narrow dimensions of which were selected in order to test the maximum horizontal space between locations 1 and 3. The trench was divided into ten 1-×-3-m excavation units

designated V720–729. Because more promising results were obtained at other locations, only three of these units actually were excavated before the trench was abandoned. These three were V723, V727, and V729, the respective coordinates of which were N9–12/E24–25, N21–24/E24–25, and N27–30/E24–25 (see fig. 57).

The natural stratification in all three excavation units was the same. Beneath a thoroughly mixed topsoil approximately 15 cm thick, the alluvially deposited subsoil was encountered. All cultural materials (prehistoric, eighteenth-century, and nineteenth/twentieth-century) were confined to the topsoil, except where features intruded into the subsoil. All old surfaces had been completely destroyed, presumably by shallow plowing, and their contents jumbled together in the topsoil. The only discrete archaeological contexts were the intrusive features: two trash pits, the bottoms of which had been preserved in the subsoil matrix.

The cultural contents of the topsoil were predominantly eighteenth century, although there was also a considerable representation of more recent materials from nearby nineteenth- and twentieth-century house sites. Because of the absence of original contexts and the similarities of the assemblages, the eighteenth-century artifacts from all three excavation units at location 4 are presented together in table 7. Of particular interest are the strong representation of Natchezan pot-

Table 7. Eighteenth-century aboriginal and European artifacts from the topsoil of excavation units V723, V727, and V729 at location 4, Trudeau.

ABORIGINAL			EUROPEAN	
Pottery:			Lead-glazed	
			Type B, Variety 1	1
Mississippi Plain, *var. Pocahontas*	5		Type B, Variety unspecified	5
			Type C, Variety unspecified	2
Fatherland Incised, *var. Snyders Bluff*	2		Type D, Variety 1 (fig. 67d)	1
			Type F, Variety unspecified	1
Fatherland Incised, *var. Fatherland*	2			
Chicot Red, *var. Grand Village*	1		*Glass:*	
Addis Plain, *var. St. Catherine*	4			
			Olive green	4
Addis Plain, *var. Feliciana*	1		Light blue-green	5
Addis Plain, *var. Addis*	15		Beads	
			IIA1	1
Daub:	1		IIA7	1
Lithics:			*Iron:*	
Unclassified chert projectile point	1		Wrought nails	
Utilized quartzite	1		Type unspecified	5
Utilized chert flakes	4		*Silver:*	
Unutilized chert flakes/pieces	6			
Chert pebbles	31		Earring (fig. 67f)	1
Organics:			*Brass:*	
Human bone	2		Bell	
EUROPEAN			Fishkey (fig. 67g)	1
Earthenware:			*Gun parts/munitions:*	
Faience				
White	6		Blade gunflint (fig. 67n)	1

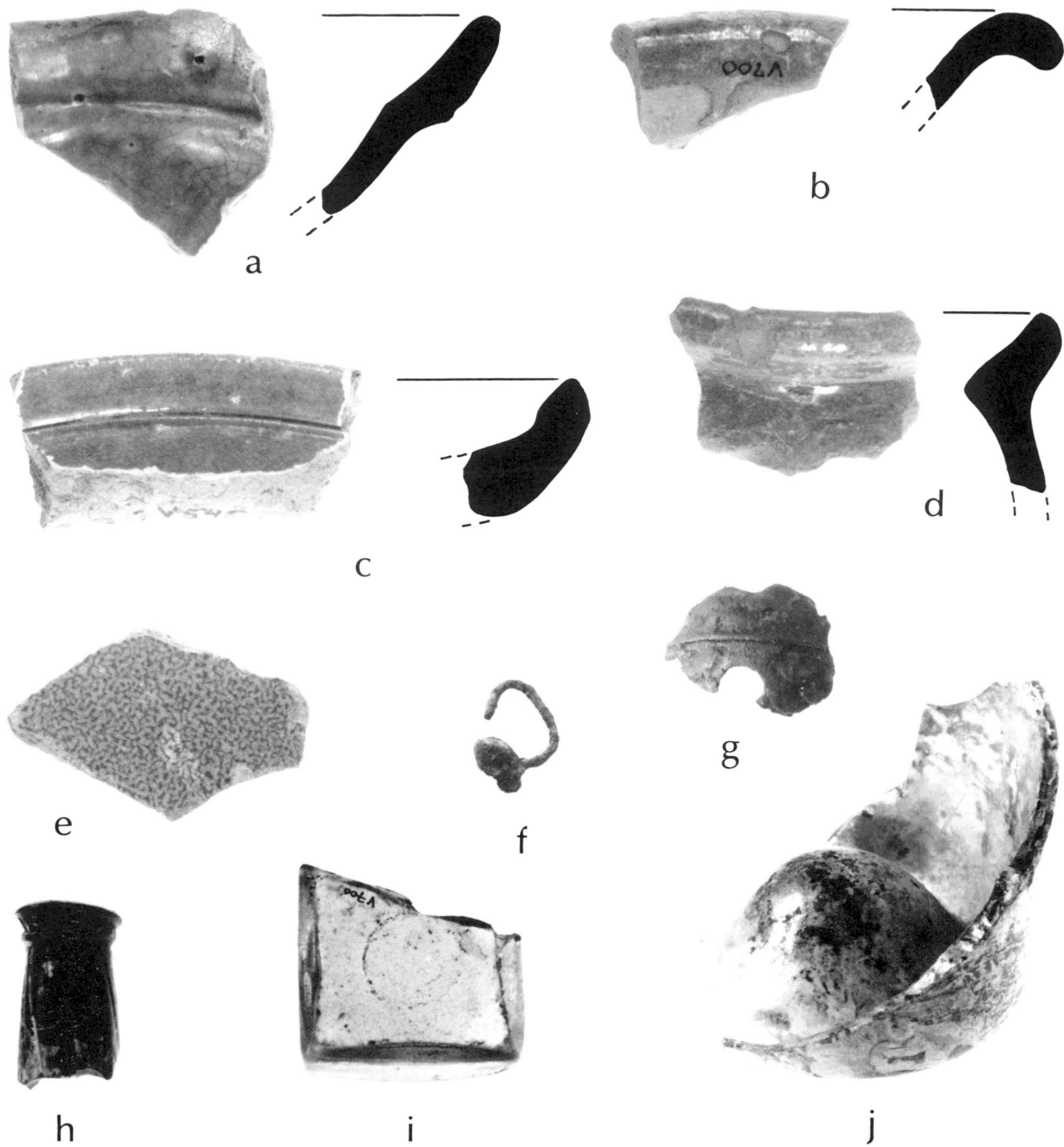

Figure 67. Miscellaneous artifacts from various locations at Trudeau. a, lead-glazed earthenware, Type A; b, lead-glazed earthenware, Type B; c, lead-glazed earthenware, Type C; d, lead-glazed earthenware, Type D; e, Bellarmine stoneware; f, silver earring; g, brass Fishkey bell; h, olive green glass bottle neck; i, light blue-green glass case bottle base; j, olive green glass bottle base; k, Owens Punctated, *var. unspecified*; l, Fatherland Incised, *var. unspecified*; m, conch shell earpin; n, blade gunflint; o, Cracker Road Incised, var. *Cracker Road*; p–q, flattened lead musket balls; r, chert pebble celt. (1:1, except h–j, 1:2)

tery and the absence of Tunica diagnostics (Mississippi Plain, *var. Pocahontas* by itself cannot be assumed to be Tunica). Also to be noted are the presence of daub and of human bone fragments. The daub suggests the former existence of a structure somewhere in the vicinity, while the bone serves as a reminder of the mortuary aspect of the site and may well be detritus from Charrier's despoilations. Compared with the aboriginal materials, the European artifacts are unusually abundant (comprising half the assemblage when the unutilized lithics are discounted). They also display a considerable variety of ceramics and include such special items as the silver earring, Fishkey bell (Brown 1979b, p. 198), and blade gunflint (fig. 67).

k
l
m
n
o
p
q
r

Figure 67 (continued).

The two trash pits, however, contained no European artifacts and as many prehistoric as historic aboriginal potsherds (table 8). But both pits were small—the V723 pit was approximately 80 cm in maximum diameter and 23 cm in depth from current ground surface; the

---

Table 8. Aboriginal artifacts from trash pits in excavation units V723 and V727 at location 4, Trudeau.

	V723	V727
Pottery:		
Mississippi Plain, *var. Pocahontas*		2
Fatherland Incised, *var. Fatherland*	1	
Mazique Incised, *var. unspecified*	1	
Addis Plain, *var. Addis*		2
Baytown Plain, *var. Valley Park*		1
Baytown Plain, *var. unspecified*		1
Daub:	1	
Organics:		
Bone	6	24

V727 pit measured only 30 × 50 cm and was 35 cm deep—and their sparse contents further reduced the chances of obtaining an adequate sample of cultural materials. There is no reason to doubt that these were eighteenth-century features; in fact, the presence of *Pocahontas* and *Fatherland* in this context requires such assignment. The relative poverty of these trash pits in comparison with other contemporary features is notable.

Location 4 was the least enlightening of all the locations tested. But because the original excavation plan was greatly abbreviated, it also was tested minimally. Despite expectations, no evidence of burials was encountered, although the pieces of human bone found near the surface may well attest to their former presence. The most noteworthy result of the excavation is the evidence of habitation, as indicated by the trash pits, the daub, and the general character of the artifactual assemblage in the topsoil (i.e., the variety and quantity of ceramics vs. the lack of beads). The presence of some rare, even valuable, items suggests a degree of affluence consistent with observations elsewhere on the site.

LOCATION 5

Location 5 was established on the summit of the bluff remnant (see fig. 57) in order to elucidate the archaeological contexts that might still be preserved on this natural feature despite the extensive disturbance and erosion. A mortuary aspect was known: Charrier claimed to have dug out a number of burials from the summit. He remembered nothing remarkable about these burials, although it was expected that interment at this location would have had special significance if the bluff was used as a substitute for an artificial mound. As a check on Charrier—his veracity, as well as his activity—we selected a location that apparently included both a looted burial and one identified as only "slightly disturbed." An excavation unit, V715, was laid out to encompass these two features. The original dimensions of V715 were 2 × 3 m, but these were expanded 1 m to the north and irregularly to the west as the burial features were followed out (fig. 68). The excavation unit lay between the coordinates N95–99 and E113–116; its elevation was approximately 20 m above site datum.

Once the pit of the looted burial had been cleaned out, a few disarticulated human bones were found scattered across the bottom at a depth of 110–120 cm. Enough bones and teeth were preserved to determine that the grave had contained a single preadolescent individual probably nine to ten years old at time of death. Orientation was east-west, with the head to the east. The only original cultural items remaining in association with the burial were two very small white beads (IIA1*), a chip of clear blown glass, three fragments of sheet brass (encrusted with charcoal on one side, indicating that they were from a kettle that had once been in the grave), traces of vermilion, and a small amount of cedar bark. Three other important artifacts also were discovered: a 1958 United States silver quarter and two cigarette filters, which provide conclusive evidence of the recency of the despoilation.

Unfortunately, the "slightly disturbed" burial was found to be plundered as badly as the looted one. A few scraps of bone, mostly from the skull and mandible, were in a state of complete disarray. They were concentrated in the eastern end of the pit, however, suggesting that the burial's orientation was consistent with the usual pattern. The teeth and jaw indicated that the individual was a young to middle-aged adult; a conch shell columella earpin (fig. 67) found in association indicates that the burial was probably that of a female. The only other artifacts were unidentified fragments of iron, a limonite mold where an inverted iron kettle had rested near the head, a piece of olive green bottle glass, and a small sherd of Type B lead-glazed earthenware. The latter is almost certainly from broken vessel C-22 in the Tunica Treasure (Brain 1979, p. 50).

During the course of the excavations, a layer flecked with charcoal and daub was noted near the surface. A handwrought iron nail was found embedded in this layer, and it was theorized that there was also a habitational/ constructional context on the summit. This theory was revived during the 1980 survey, as similar evidence was collected from other points nearby; the former presence of a structure was confirmed in 1981.

In summary, the excavations at location 5 provided not only basic archaeological data but additional evidence of Charrier's recent activity and a nearly certain

* See Brain 1979, pp. 98–100 for glass bead classification and numbering system.

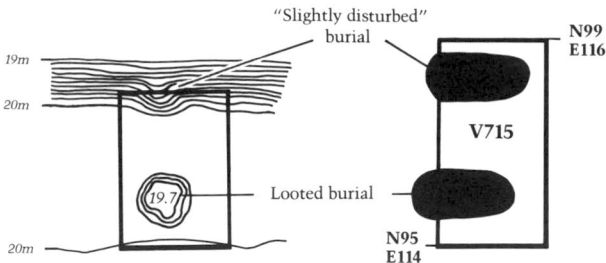

Figure 68. Contour map and plan of excavation unit V715 at location 5, Trudeau.

link with the Tunica Treasure collection. Archaeological contexts at the site were further defined, and the exciting prospect of a habitational/constructional layer on the bluff summit was revealed. As elsewhere on the site, both mortuary and habitation aspects are represented, but it was not determined whether these were of a significantly different order from those in the field below.

LOCATION 6

The instrument survey referred to earlier (see location 3) followed an unrestricted sampling procedure. Because of the limited time available, we were not attempting a comprehensive survey but were merely trying to find locations that might have undisturbed features. Fortunately, although purely by chance, there were a number of positive responses to the electronic probes. One of the strongest of these was pinpointed at a distance of 77 m on a line of 283 degrees from datum (see fig. 57). The magnetometer indicated a large anomaly containing a considerable amount of iron. Metal detectors confirmed the presence of the metal and determined that it was buried fairly deep (i.e., that it was not surface trash). As this appeared to be our best chance to find an undisturbed burial, we set up a 2-×-2-m excavation unit (V730) over the epicenter of the instrument readings. At a depth of 80 cm from the surface (−145 cm from datum) the top of a human skull was found in the northwestern corner of the excavation. The rest of the body lay to the north, so a second excavation unit (V731) was added in that direction. The dimensions of V731 were 1.5 × 2 m, sufficient working space to isolate and completely exhume the burial.

The burial was found to be that of a single individual interred in a grave pit that intruded into the natural alluvial deposits from the old ground surface (since destroyed at that location). The position of the body was supine, as usual, but the orientation was with the head to the south (fig. 69). Although somewhat small (height estimated at approx. 150 cm), the individual was fully mature at death—a young adult perhaps twenty-five to thirty years old, judging by tooth wear. Sex was impossible to ascertain with certainty from the very poorly preserved bones. The pelvis was completely gone, the long bones showed developed musculature but little distortion, and the mastoids were delicate, although probably in proportion to the overall small size of the individual. The only clue is provided by the artifacts, which are entirely male oriented.

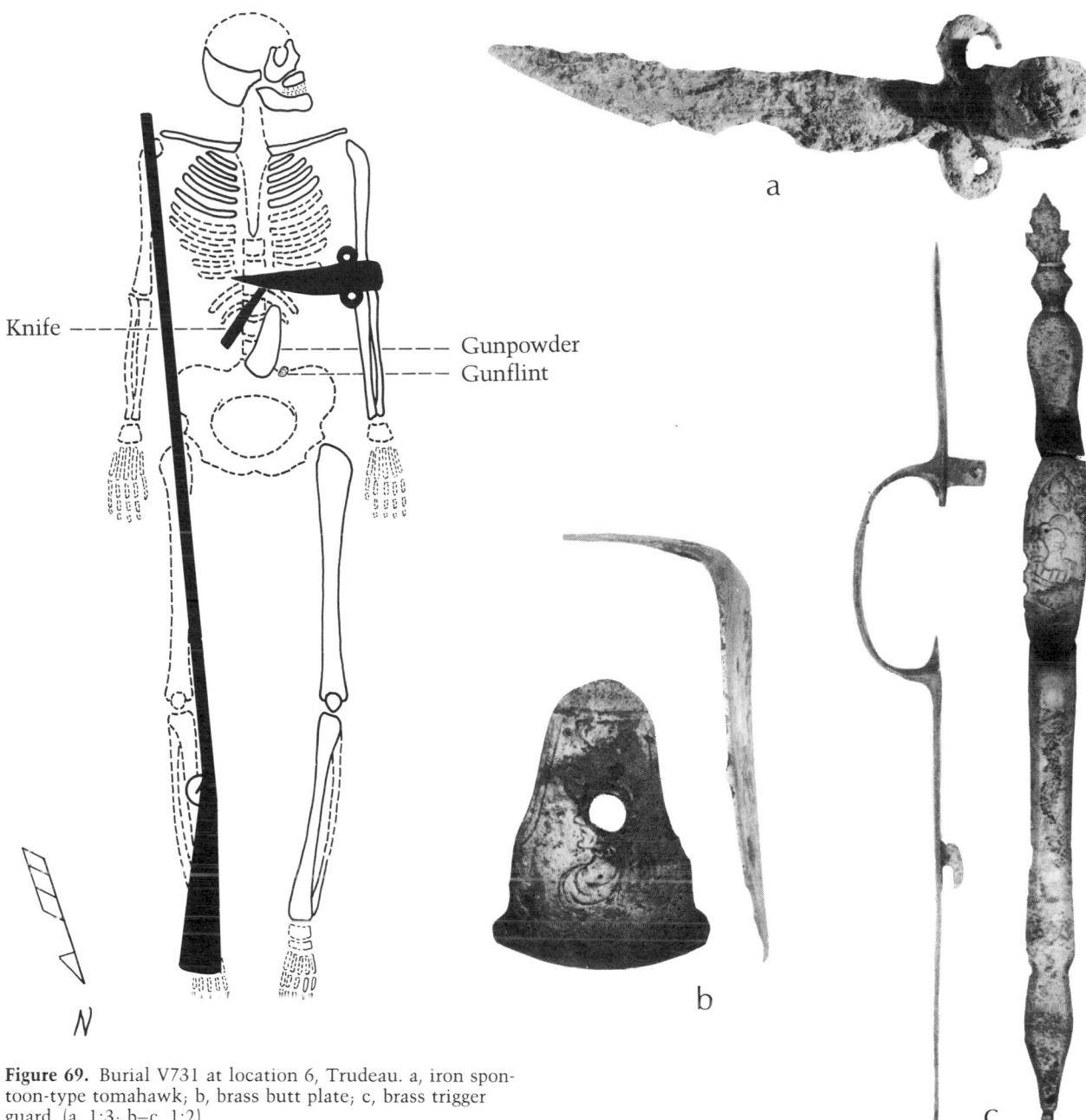

Figure 69. Burial V731 at location 6, Trudeau. a, iron spontoon-type tomahawk; b, brass butt plate; c, brass trigger guard. (a, 1:3; b–c, 1:2)

The principal artifact in the grave was a musket, which was placed over the right arm and leg of the body, the stock resting on the feet (fig. 69). The barrel was of good quality and had a gauge of 28 *calibre* (app. G.2; Hamilton 1980, p. 59), the larger standard trade gun size. The brass furniture is common grade, similar to Type C (Hamilton 1979, p. 212), but exhibits unusual decoration (fig. 69a–b). Hamilton suggests that this gun was assembled from used parts and restocked with a high-grade barrel. The piece was functional and charged when placed in the grave, and an extra gunflint and small amount of gunpowder were found in the abdominal region of the skeleton.

The most interesting artifact is a spontoon-type tomahawk (fig. 69c; see H. L. Peterson 1965, pp. 24–26;

Russell 1967, fig. 72). It was found on the chest of the skeleton with the haft lying on the left forearm. The only other known example of this particular tomahawk form is from burial 7 at the Angola Farm site (see fig. 132b), and it is probable that it is an early eighteenth-century French style, perhaps diagnostic of Louisiana.*

The only other identifiable artifact was a folding (clasp) knife found lying next to the gunpowder and gunflint. All of these items probably had been enclosed in a pouch

---

* The unusual form is reminiscent of a halberd or pike head, which might have provided the ultimate inspiration. Both pikes and halberds were listed by La Salle in 1684 as requisite for his proposed expedition to take possession of Louisiana (Cox 1922, vol. 1, p. 187).

or other perishable container when placed in the grave (rather like burial 7 at Bloodhound Hill). Two unidentifiable bits of iron were discovered near the western edge of the grave pit and may have been fragments from the musket.

No more artifacts of metal, ceramic, or glass were present—not even a bead. This limited inventory was something of a surprise, conditioned as we were to the variety and quantity of artifacts found elsewhere on the site. Perhaps this particular individual, unimpressive in stature, was not a person of consequence. Or his death may have occurred early in the occupation of Trudeau, before the greatest accumulation of European goods took place. This earlier dating is suggested by the gun, the tomahawk, and the similarities to the Bloodhound burial. Temporal placement does not explain the southward orientation, however, which is unique among all other documented Tunica burials before, during, or after Trudeau in time.

In summary, then, this burial appears to be atypical in several respects. Furthermore, the artifacts do not exactly match items in the Tunica Treasure collection, although an eighteenth-century context attributable to the Tunica is consistent with the facts. We felt confident that this undisturbed burial with appropriate artifacts fulfilled the third major requirement to authenticate Trudeau as the Tunica Treasure site.

SUMMARY OF THE 1972 EXCAVATIONS

The test excavations at the six locations described above provided sufficient evidence to prove beyond any doubt that Trudeau was the provenience of the Tunica Treasure. Furthermore, a considerable amount of primary archaeological data was accumulated, and it was established that the site had been a village as well as a cemetery. We had not defined the exact limits of the cultural areas, however, nor had we been able to measure the extent of damage that the site had suffered during Charrier's activities. These considerations were to be the focus of the next stage of investigations.

The 1980 Survey

In 1980 the LMS returned to Trudeau at the invitation of the Louisiana Office of State Parks, which had acquired the land in 1978. The purpose of the investigations was to determine the current condition of the site and to assess its potential for major archaeological excavation. At the very least, it was expected that additional information on the context of the Tunica Treasure would be gathered.

The procedures used for the assessment of Trudeau in 1980 were organized into two major approaches: (1) a comprehensive archaeological surface survey, and (2) an electronic subsurface survey. The archaeological survey was carried out by a crew from the LMS composed of Jeffrey P. Brain (field director), Ian Brown, Richard Fuller, and John Kudlik, with the assistance of Robert S. Neitzel (fig. 70). The electronic survey was contracted to Geophysical Survey Systems, Inc. (GSSI) of Hudson, New Hampshire; the actual field and analytic work was performed by Daniel Stanfill. Labor for clearing and other support activities was provided by the nearby Louisiana State Penitentiary at Angola. Debbie Woodiel, archaeologist for the Office of State Parks, was instrumental in developing and aiding the project, especially in coordinating with other state agencies. The entire field portion of the investigation was conducted during a four-week period in May/June 1980.

ARCHAEOLOGICAL SURVEY

The archaeological survey of Trudeau was conducted during the entire four-week period of fieldwork, with the exception of three days necessarily committed to the electronic survey discussed below. The three primary objectives of the archaeological survey were establishing a control grid, drawing a detailed contour map, and surface collecting all cultural data.

The first priority was to establish our controls. Efforts to relocate our 1972 datum pipe were unsuccessful, apparently because it had been dislocated by plowing or intentionally removed during the intervening eight years.

Figure 70. The Trudeau 1980 field crew: Robert S. Neitzel, Richard Fuller, Jeffrey P. Brain, John Kudlik, Ian Brown.

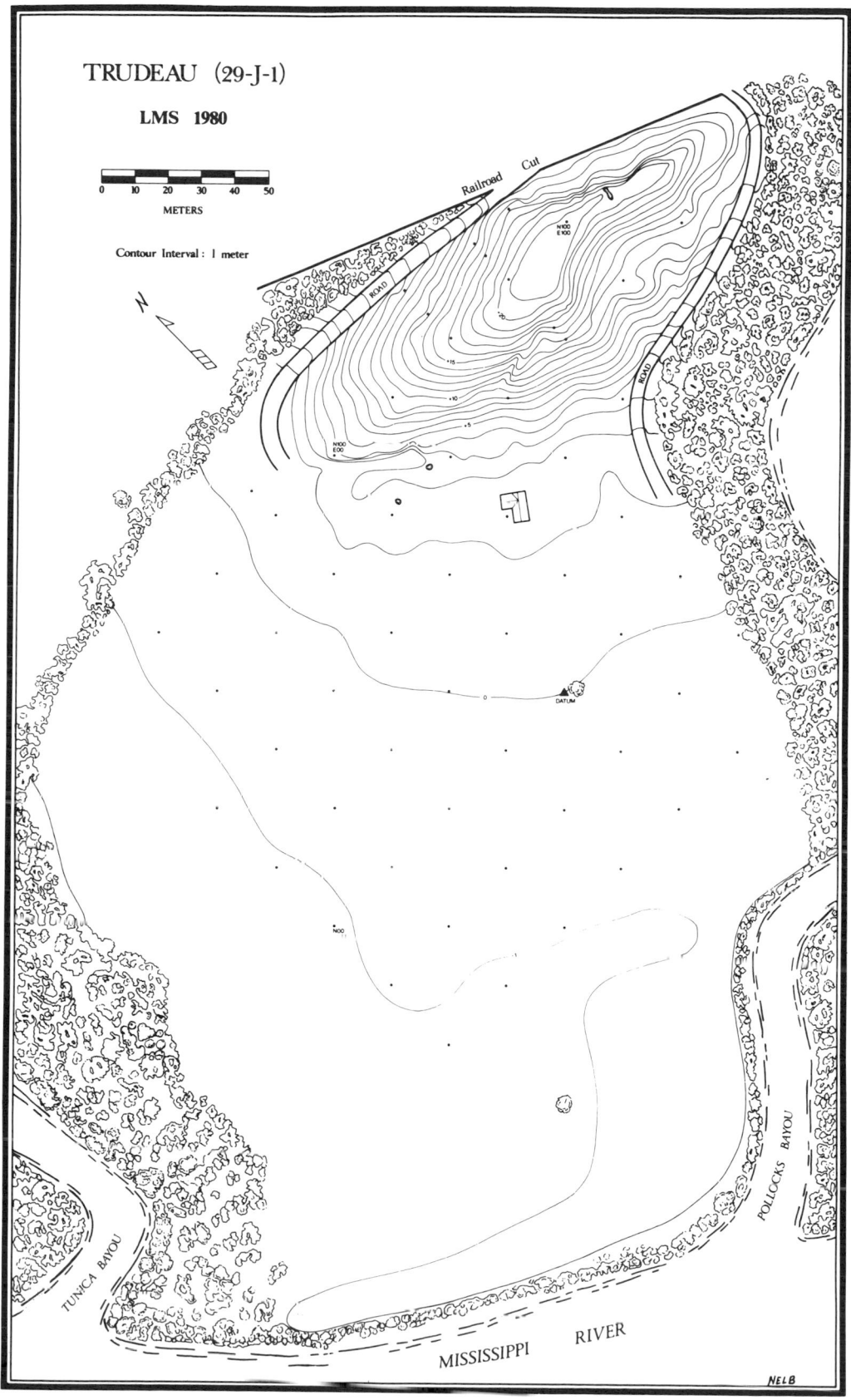

Figure 71. Contour map of Trudeau with 25-m control grid used during the 1980 survey.

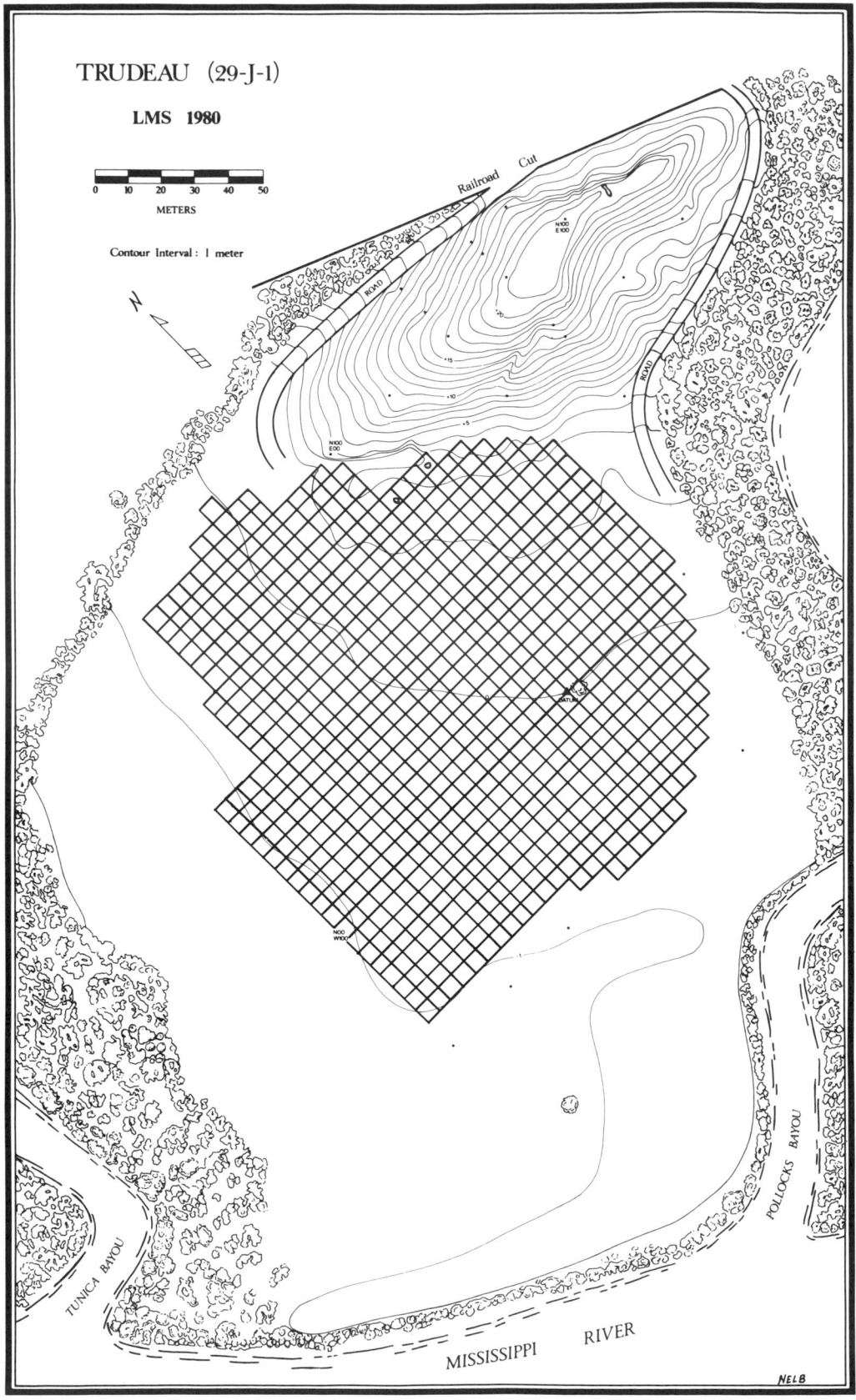

Figure 72. Archaeological survey grid of 5-m² collecting units in the field at Trudeau.

Figure 73. Surface collecting a 5-m square in the field at Trudeau during the 1980 survey.

Fortunately, however, a secondary reference point on a nearby pecan tree survived, and it was possible to place the new datum pipe in the approximate vicinity of the old (and thus correlate the respective grids). All measurements at the site are in reference to this single point, which is marked by a capped galvanized pipe set in concrete (a secondary point was similarly marked at N100/E00). From the datum, north-south and east-west baselines were run out and marked with an engineer's transit theodolite and metal tape measure. In the same fashion, additional lines were extended from the base lines at 25-m intervals, until a coarse grid was established (fig. 71). Wooden stakes were set at each 25-m interval and identified according to distance and cardinal point orientation from datum. Thus, for example, stake N25/E50 is 25 m north and 50 m east of datum. Flags, which were color coded by 25-m units, were then placed at 5-m intervals between the stakes. The entire portion of the field believed to contain the historic eighteenth-century settlement was marked off in this manner. The resulting grid was composed of 5-m squares that became the basic units for collecting artifacts and other cultural data from the surface (figs. 72–73). Survey lines also were run up to the summit of the bluff remnant, where a 2-m grid was established for finer control of this small but important part of the site. Coincident with this transit survey, a contour map of the site and its immediate environs was begun, work on which continued during the course of the fieldwork (fig. 71).

The surface collection of cultural data had two goals: first, to determine the perimeter of the site; and second,

to reveal areas of artifact concentrations (hopefully occupational loci) on the site itself. Originally, a random ten percent sample of the 5-m squares in the large bottomland field was planned, but ultimately we were able to collect every square and even expand the grid as cultural materials were found to extend farther to the northwest than had been anticipated. Each square was carefully scrutinized (even on hands and knees when conditions dictated) by experienced field survey archaeologists (fig. 72).* All cultural materials observed, including modern items, were picked up and bagged. Immediately, field catalog cards were filled out on which were recorded preliminary artifact identifications and counts, as well as other pertinent information such as collecting conditions and positions of significant artifacts. Each square, and therefore collection, was assigned an arbitrary number in the B1 catalog series (B1-1 through B1-740†), which was reserved for the surface collecting of the gridded field. Other finds outside the grid, whether in the field or on the bluff, were located precisely in reference to the datum and natural features, and were given sequential B numbers starting with B2.

---

* As part of the preparations at the site prior to our arrival, the field had been cleared and disced sufficiently for optimum collecting conditions to prevail: enough rain had fallen, and vegetation regeneration was just beginning.

† The weird sequence of numbering (see fig. 79 et seq.) was occasioned by the expansion of the grid to the northwest in accordance with the distribution of cultural materials.

Figure 74. Coles Creek pottery collected at Trudeau during the 1980 survey. a, Coles Creek Incised, *var. unspecified*; b, Mazique Incised, *var. Kings Point*; c–d, Pontchartrain Check Stamped, *var. Pontchartrain*; e, Anna Incised, *var. Australia*; f, Harrison Bayou Incised, *var. Harrison Bayou*; g, Mazique Incised, *var. Manchac*; h–i, Plaquemine Brushed, *var. Plaquemine*. (1:1)

Artifacts. The artifacts recovered from the surface of Trudeau during this survey revealed that the human occupation of the site covered a span of approximately one millennium but was not continuous throughout this time. The earliest occupation dates to the late Coles Creek period, ca. A.D. 950–1200. The ceramic materials are similar to those diagnostic of the Spring Bayou and Mayes phases of the Marksville area to the west (Belmont 1978). The relatively high proportion of Pontchartrain Check Stamped, however, suggests affinities to the early occupation at the Bayou Goula site to the south (Quimby 1957). Illustrations of some of the Coles Creek ceramics are presented in figure 74. The total sample is tabulated in table 9, and artifact distributions are plotted in figures 79 and 80. The most recent occupation comprised, of course, the nineteenth and twentieth-century house sites on the north and east sides of the field (see figs. 85–86). But although they certainly are of interest and useful for comparative studies, neither the prehistoric Coles Creek occupation nor the historic nineteenth- and twentieth-century components are the focus of this research. Because of the overlapping boundaries in surface distributions, in fact, it has been necessary to factor out carefully the earlier and later occupations in order to get a clear view of the eighteenth-century one.

The eighteenth-century Tunica occupation, despite its brevity, is the dominant component at Trudeau. Artifactually, it has left the largest number of diagnostic items. (Note that while *var. unspecified* examples of the common late prehistoric plainware Addis Plain are listed in table 9 because their distributions most closely parallel the distributions of the Coles Creek diagnostics, Addis was made throughout the late Coles Creek-Plaquemine-Natchez tradition. Many of these items could have been made during either of the aboriginal occupations at Trudeau and thus cannot be used for diagnostic purposes.) The total sample of eighteenth-century aboriginal and European artifacts is presented in table 10, and a selection is illustrated in figures 75–78.

In the aboriginal category, pottery forms the bulk of the remains. As known from previous evidence (Brain 1970, 1973, 1979), three native ceramic traditions are represented: Tunican, Natchezan, and Caddoan. There is also a significant group of potsherds that cannot be identified ethnically with confidence on the basis of present knowledge. In terms of sample size, the Tunican and Natchezan traditions are about equally represented. Always the smallest group, the Caddoan ceramics

Table 9. Coles Creek artifacts found at Trudeau during the 1980 survey.

Pottery:

Anna Incised, *var. Australia* (fig. 74e)	1
Plaquemine Brushed, *var. Plaquemine* (fig. 74h–i)	3
Beldeau Incised, *var. Bell Bayou*	1
Harrison Bayou Incised, *var. Harrison Bayou* (fig. 74f)	1
Mazique Incised, *var. Manchac* (fig. 74g)	1
Addis Plain, *var. Addis*	57
Addis Plain, *var. unspecified*[a]	418
Mazique Incised, *var. Kings Point* (fig. 74b)	6
Pontchartrain Check Stamped, *var. Pontchartrain* (fig. 74c–d)	22
Avoyelles Punctated, *var. unspecified*	1
Coles Creek Incised, *var. unspecified* (fig. 74a)	1
Evansville Punctated, *var. unspecified*	4
Baytown Plain, *var. Vicksburg*	438
Baytown Plain, *var. Valley Park*	6
Baytown Plain, *var. unspecified*	9

Lithics:

Alba Stemmed, *var. Scallorn* point	1

[a] These potsherds are tabulated here because their distribution (fig. 80) coincides most closely with the distribution of the Coles Creek ceramics, but considering the longevity of the type Addis Plain it must be expected that an unknown percentage of these date to the eighteenth century.

nevertheless are greatly underrepresented compared with the other samples. The reasons for this imbalance are unknown, but are probably attributable to the vagaries of small sample size.

The Tunican pottery includes the local varieties of Mississippi Plain—*Pocahontas* and *Montfort*—and a very limited selection of decorated sherds. The most prominent among the latter are the twelve sherds of Winterville Incised, *var. Tunica*. The absence of Barton Incised, *var. Trudeau* is inexplicable, but again may be due to small sample size. The only decorative technique employed besides incision was punctation.

The Natchezan tradition is well represented by the standard decorated types and varieties. Once again, curvilinear incising is the principal decorative mode, but red slipping is a major secondary treatment.

The definite Caddoan sherds number only ten. The most diagnostic is a single sherd of Natchitoches Engraved, which unfortunately was found in a disturbed context on the side of the bluff. Among the remaining sherds, only one classifiable type can be recognized:

Maddox Engraved. It is comforting to note that even in so small a sample the identifiable types (Natchitoches and Maddox) exactly match those present in the Tunica Treasure collection (Brain 1979, pp. 243–244).

The unassigned category of ceramics includes such lower Yazoo types as Cracker Road Incised and Leland Incised, which display Natchezan-like designs but have distinctively different wares. These types may reflect continuing contact with the Yazoo or may be heirloom pieces from the period of that occupation. The Chicot Red, *var. unspecified* has small amounts of bone added to the paste, a mode common in Caddoan ceramics (Suhm and Jelks 1962, pp. 7–153) and exhibited in at least one sherd of Maddox Engraved from the site. Red slipping is not a common Caddoan decorative treatment, however, especially at this time (ibid., pp. 51, 101, 131, 139). *Feliciana* is a new variety of Addis Plain that denotes the addition of crushed bone to the paste, as described above for Chicot Red. *Skillikalia* is a sand-tempered variety that seems to have been quite widespread during the early historic period.

Figure 75. Aboriginal artifacts of the eighteenth century collected at Trudeau during the 1980 survey. a–b, Winterville Incised, *var. Tunica*; c–e, Fatherland Incised, *var. Fatherland*; f, Natchitoches Engraved, *var. Natchitoches*; g, pipe stem of St. Catherine ware; h, Nodena Lanceolate, *var. Russell* point; i, Mississippi Triangular, *var. Madison* point; j, chert pebble celt. (1:1)

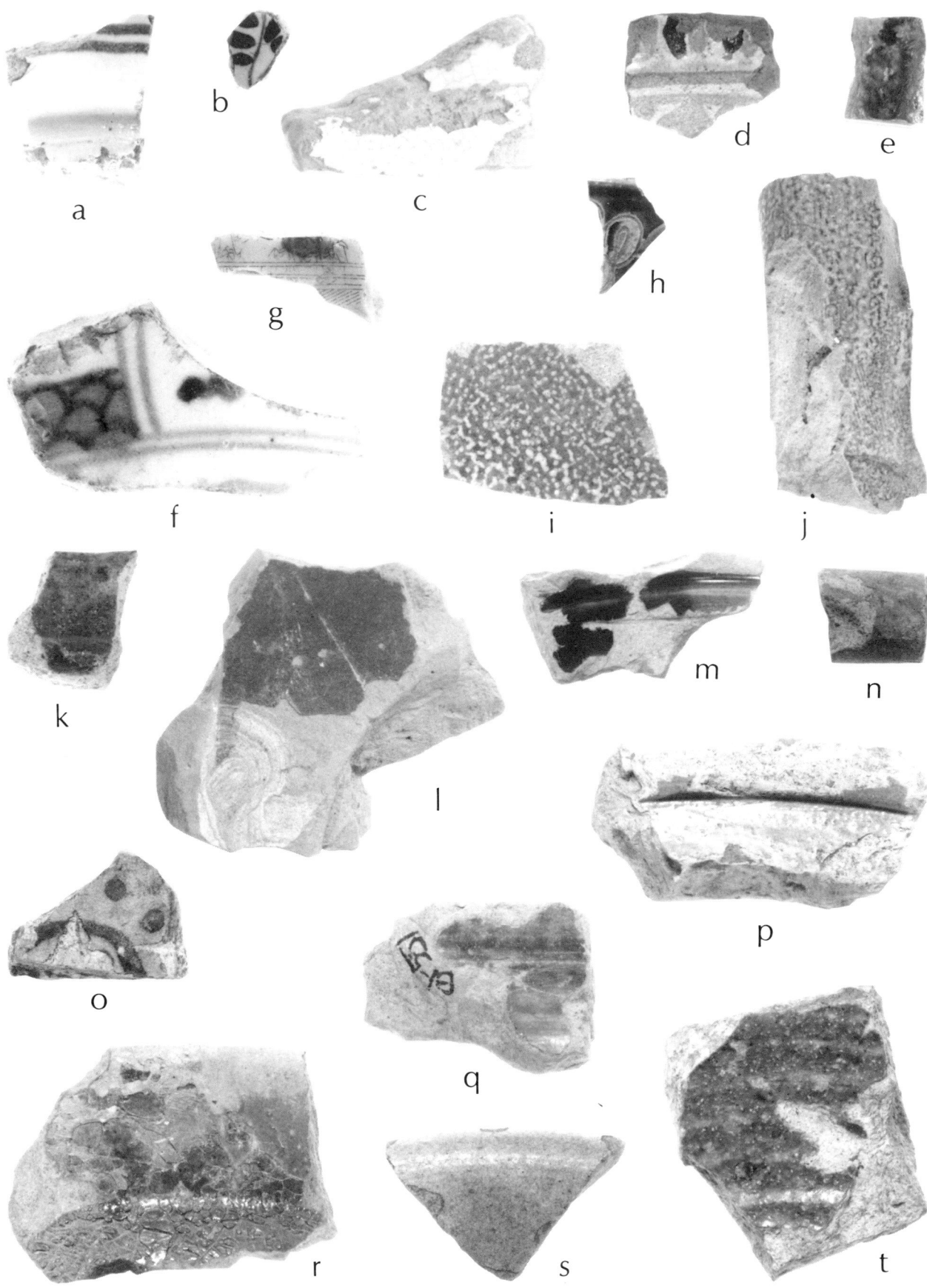

The nonceramic artifacts are limited to lithics, and include both chipped and ground stone tools. Chipped stone predominates, the most common items being simple flakes and pieces of chert, the sharp edges of which were utilized for cutting and scraping. These were tools of convenience: exhibiting minimal effort of manufacture (although 12 out of the 55 were heat treated), they were used briefly for a particular operation and then discarded. More sophisticated chipped stone tools are rare, only three projectile points and one pebble celt (or adze) being found. The points are all late varieties of Mississippian types. The *Russell* point and one *Madison* are made from the common tan chert, while the second *Madison* is of an unusual translucent mottled gray chert. The pebble celt is made of a fine-grained gray chert. The presence of these artifacts is confirmation that European technology had not completely replaced the tool inventory of the mid-eighteenth-century Tunica, at least during part of their occupation at Trudeau. The ground stone items include hammerstones, palettes, and abraders. Many, if not all, of these implements also must have been in use during the Tunica occupation.

In the European category, ceramics again bulk large and are the most varied and informative group of artifacts. Three general classes of ceramics are present: earthenware, stoneware, and porcelain. As noted, within these classes exists a considerable range of variation, which provided much useful information.

The earthenwares are divided into tin-glazed, lead-glazed, and unglazed. Among the tin-glazed, the three major European traditions are represented: faience, majolica, and delft. As would be expected in a French contact situation, faience sherds are the most numerous, although the figures may be misleading. The great majority of sherds are plain white tin-glazed, which at present generally cannot be assigned to a specific tin-glazed tradition. Many might be delft, or even majolica, but because we cannot be certain they fall by default into faience, the logical assumption. With the decorated tin-glazed ceramics we are on safer ground. Twenty-three sherds are faience, seven appear to be majolica, probably Mexican in origin, and only one is certainly delft (fig. 76a–e). Most of the types are represented in earlier samples from the site.

As in the other samples, the lead-glazed earthenwares form the largest subclass, with a total of 260 sherds (fig. 76k–t). Of these, all but eight may be classified in Types A–F of the system established for the Tunica Treasure (Brain 1979, pp. 45–73). Of the eight sherds that could not be classified, six belong to a new type (a very coarse, light buff earthenware, similar to the "Spanish Olive Jar," but with a bright apple green glaze on the interior surface), and two are simply burned beyond recognition. Types A–F are thought to be of French manufacture.

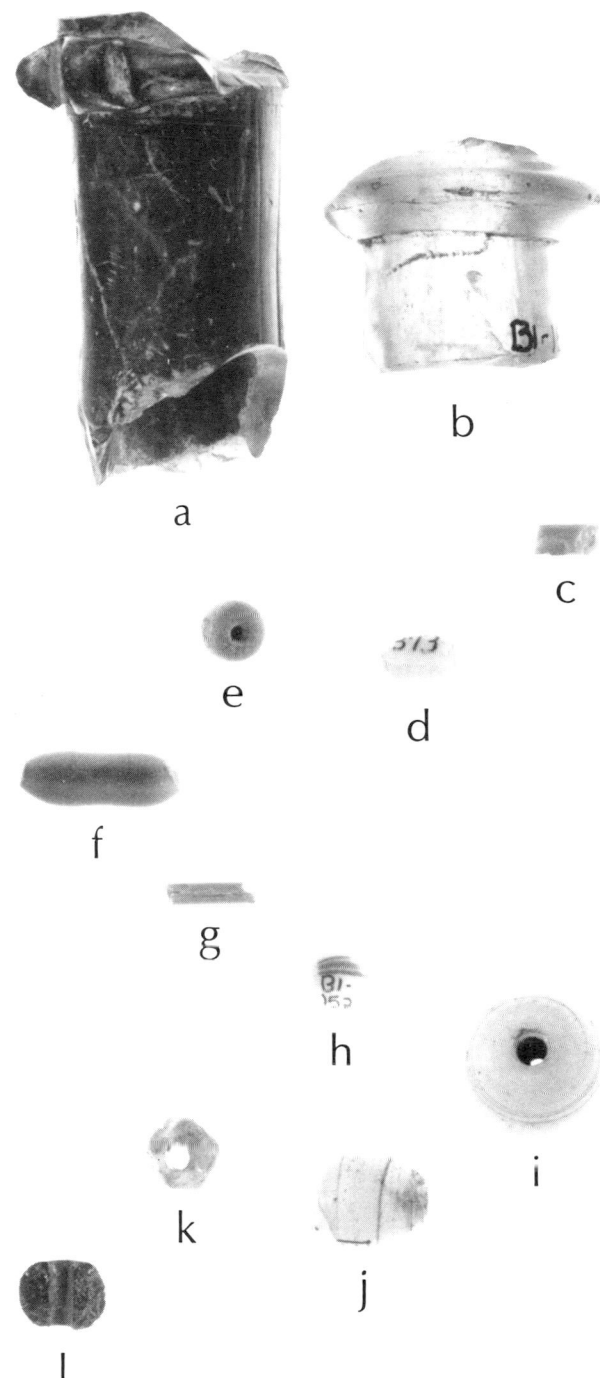

Figure 77. Glass artifacts collected at Trudeau during the 1980 survey. a, olive green bottle neck; b, light blue-green bottle neck; c, IB2 bead; d, IIA1 bead; e, IIA7 bead; f, IIA15 bead; g, IIIA1 bead; h, IVB3 bead; i, WIA1 bead; j, WIC1 bead; k, WIIA3 bead; l, unclassified wire-wound bead. (1:1)

Figure 76. European earthenwares, porcelains, and stonewares collected at Trudeau during the 1980 survey. a–b, blue-and-white faience; c–d, blue-and-white majolica; e, powder purple delft; f, blue underglaze porcelain; g, red-and-green overglaze porcelain; h, Westerwald stoneware; i–j, Bellarmine stoneware; k, lead-glazed earthenware, Type A; l–m, lead-glazed earthenware, Type B; n–p, lead-glazed earthenware, Type C; q–r, lead-glazed earthenware, Type D; s, lead-glazed earthenware, Type E; t, unclassified lead-glazed earthenware. (1:1)

Table 10. Eighteenth-century aboriginal and European artifacts found at Trudeau during the 1980 survey.

ABORIGINAL

Pottery:

Winterville Incised, *var. Tunica* (fig. 75a–b)	11
Unclassified incised (Pocahontas)	6
Tunican Mode	2
Mississippi Plain, *var. Pocahontas*	101
Winterville Incised, *var. Loubois*	1
Mississippi Plain, *var. Montfort*	24
Owens Punctated, *var. unspecified*	1
Parkin Punctated, *var. unspecified*	1
Mississippi Plain, *var. unspecified*	4
Cracker Road Incised, *var. Cracker Road*	6
Fatherland Incised, *var. Nancy*	2
Fatherland Incised, *var. Snyders Bluff*[a]	4
Natchitoches Engraved, *var. Natchitoches* (fig. 75f)	1
Unclassified incised (Caddo)	3
Fatherland Incised, *var. Fatherland* (fig. 75c–e)	21
Fatherland Incised, *var. unspecified*	14
Maddox Engraved, *var. unspecified*	6
Unclassified incised (St. Catherine)	7
Chicot Red, *var. Grand Village*	3
Addis Plain, *var. St. Catherine*	66
Leland Incised, *var. unspecified*	16
Chicot Red, *var. unspecified*[b]	6
Addis Plain, *var. Feliciana*	23
Addis Plain, *var. Skillikalia*	87
Pipestem of St. Catherine ware (fig. 75g)	1

Lithics:

Mississippi Triangular, *var. Madison* points (fig. 75i)	2
Nodena Lanceolate, *var. Russell* point (fig. 75h)	1
Pebble celt (fig. 75j)	1

EUROPEAN

Earthenware:

Faience	
White	48
Blue-and-white (fig. 76a–b)	12
Green-and-white	3
Polychrome	2
Brown	6
Majolica	
White	4
Blue-and-white (fig. 76c–d)	3

Delft	
Powder purple (fig. 76e)	1
Lead-glazed	
Type A (fig. 76k)	18
Type B (fig. 76l–m)	107
Type C (fig. 76n–p)	49
Type D (fig. 76q–r)	62
Type E (fig. 76s)	10
Type F	6
Unclassified (fig. 76t)	8
Unglazed	42

Stoneware:

Bellarmine (fig. 76i–j)	14
Westerwald (fig. 76h)	4
White salt-glazed	1
Unglazed	4

Porcelain:

Chinese export (blue-and-white underglaze) (fig. 76f)	1
Unclassified (red-and-green overglaze) (fig. 76g)	2

Glass:

Clear	4
Olive green (fig. 77a)	110
Light blue-green (fig. 77b)	47
Beads	
IB2 (fig. 77c)	1
IIA1 (fig. 77d)	5
IIA7 (fig. 77e)	1
IIA15 (fig. 77f)	1
IIIA1 (fig. 77g)	1
IVB3 (fig. 77h)	1
WIA1 (fig. 77i)	2
WIC1 (fig. 77j)	2
WIIA3 (fig. 77k)	1
Unclassified (fig. 77l)	2

Iron:

Wrought nails	
Type unspecified (fig. 78e–g)	119
Miscellaneous (fig. 78a–d, h)	62

Copper/brass:

Miscellaneous	3

Gun parts/munitions:

Pistol flintlock (fig. 78i)	1
Gunflints (fig. 78l–o)	31
Lead musket balls (fig. 78j–k)	4

[a]Includes one with St. Pierre (pink paint) Mode.

[b]All on Feliciana ware.

The unglazed earthenware sherds are not classifiable further. Most, if not all, are probably from unglazed parts of lead-glazed vessels, as totally unglazed earthenwares are rare.

As was typical of the period, the stoneware (fig. 76h–j) is predominantly Rhenish (Bellarmine and Westerwald), although the greater number of Bellarmine sherds is unexpected. It is not due simply to the larger average size of Bellarmine jugs, for differences between the individual sherds clearly show that a number of vessels are represented. In addition to the German products, one sherd of English white salt-glazed stoneware (from a fine pitcher or bowl) and four unglazed sherds (probably from common utilitarian pieces of French origin) were found.

The three sherds of porcelain (fig. 76f–g) are the first to come from Trudeau. European only in the sense that they were brought to North America through the mechanisms of European contact, all three sherds originated in the Orient. One is poor quality blue underglaze Chinese export of undetermined type. The other two, from the same vessel, are red-and-green overglaze and may have come from Japan rather than China.

Another important group of European artifacts consists of items made of glass (fig. 77), of which there are two basic classes: containers and beads. Of the container class the most important numerically are bottles, from which there are 157 sherds. These are divided into two subclasses based on color: olive and light blue-green. All of the olive green glass sherds, which constitute more than two-thirds of the sample, seem to be from the so-called "wine" or "rum" bottles so typical of the eighteenth century. These bottles are round, with high kickups (indented bases) and long slender necks. The few sherds that are distinctive enough to convey formal attributes suggest that the bottles they came from were made in France (although there are some peculiarities: e.g., the rim of the bottle depicted in fig. 77a). While no English or Dutch bottles of this type can be identified definitely, it may be expected that they are also included in the sample (as they were in previous collections from the site). The light blue-green bottles are represented by two types: round and square (also known as "case"). Both types are French in origin.

Another kind of container apparently present in this sample is evidenced by the four sherds of clear glass. They are lead glass, indicating that they came from dinnerware such as tumblers or wine glasses. The relative thickness (2–4 mm) suggests that tumblers are the more likely artifact.

Glass beads were remarkably rare surface finds during the 1980 survey. Although beads are not the most visible of artifacts, a total of seventeen is a very small sample considering the hundreds of thousands of beads that had already come from the site. Popular mortuary artifacts, they must not have been lost or discarded in the course of daily activities with equal frequency. Despite the size of the sample, a range of variation is present. There are six varieties of drawn beads: IB2, IIA1, IIA7, IIA15, IIIA1, and IVB3; and at least three varieties of wire-wound beads: WIA1, WIC1, WIIA3, and two

unclassified specimens (see table 10). All of these beads are typical of the mid-eighteenth century in Louisiana. In fact, the average of the mean dates of all the classified varieties is A.D. 1744.5 (see Brain 1979), while the average of the mean dates of the diagnostic varieties is 1746.7, within a year of the 1747.5 mean date of the known occupation of Trudeau. Although the sample is small, then, it very accurately assesses the date of the site. (It also strengthens our hope that when such samples are found at other sites they will be equally determinative.)

The last major group of European artifacts is metallic. By far the most numerous of these are the handwrought iron nails, of which there are at least 119 (only identifiable fragments were counted). These nails appear to conform to the common eighteenth-century French "rose head" type, and usually display the three facets typical of French nails in Louisiana (see app. F.1). An explanation for the relatively large number of nails is discussed in part 3. Smaller things such as chests, boxes, coffins(?), and other portable items were also made with nails, of course, but most of the nails in the collection are too large for anything but structural purposes. It may be that nails served a variety of functions for the Tunica, especially as hand tools of various sorts (see Brown 1979d for further discussion).

Other iron artifacts that can be identified among the badly corroded fragments are such utilitarian items as kettles and knives (both case and folding), and personal accessories including a button and a buckle (fig. 78). Curiously, only one piece of copper and two of brass were found, and these are so small as to be unidentifiable, although they probably came from kettles.

The remaining identifiable European artifacts have to do with the all-important guns and munitions. The only actual gun part recovered is the flintlock from a pistol (fig. 78i). Neither national origin nor model has been recognized, but the lock appears to be eighteenth century. Munitions are represented by four lead musket balls of standard French trade gun *calibres* (diameters range from 13 to 15 mm), and thirty-one gunflints or flakes therefrom. The flints are of both the blond and gray varieties associated with French sites, and include both spall and blade types at a ratio of 16 to 3. The lack of gun parts may be a vagary of the sample, but in the case of the munitions, the low number of balls to flints may be due to the usual off-site expending of the former and the common domestic service of the latter. Of the twenty-one whole flints, fifteen showed extensive use and wear patterns that cannot have come from use in gun locks. At least eight look as though they had been used with strike-a-lights, and three more were very badly burned, as if they had fallen into a hot campfire.

The total sample of diagnostic eighteenth-century artifacts collected from the surface during the 1980 survey numbers slightly more than 1,200. It is interesting to note that at this stage of Tunica acculturation, the European artifacts outnumber the native by a margin of two to one. The distributions of all the eighteenth-century artifacts reflect the spatial dimensions of the Tunica occupation, as discussed below.

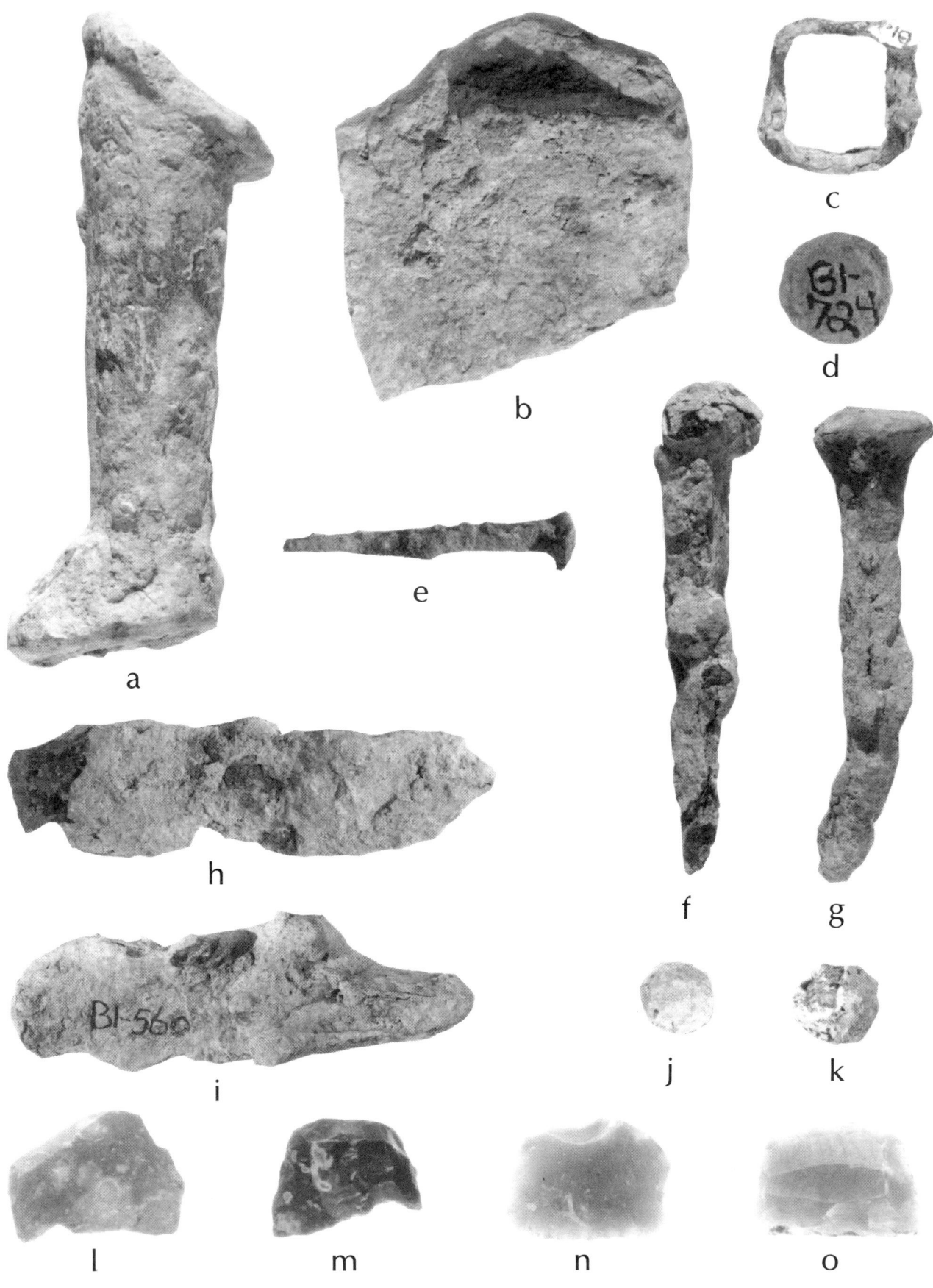

Artifact Distributions. The surface distributions of the artifacts at Trudeau are very informative. Once the classes and types of both the aboriginal and European traditions had been sorted out, some interesting patterns began to emerge.* The most important of these are plotted in figures 79–84.

On the basis of the classification described above, the aboriginal artifacts were divided into two discrete and discontinuous occupations: prehistoric Coles Creek and historic Tunica. The Coles Creek occupation appears to have been nearly as intensive as the Tunica, in terms of numbers of artifacts, but was not as extensive. It was concentrated in the northern corner of the field (figs. 79–80).

Exhibiting a distinctively different configuration, the Tunica occupation covered a larger part of the field and also extended onto the summit of the bluff. The distributions of the native artifacts in the field describe a roughly circular pattern, with low artifact density in the center (fig. 81). This pattern would seem to define a village plan with houses arranged around an open plaza, a layout known to have been used by the Tunica (see cover illustration).

The Mississippian pottery and stone tools, probably Tunica in origin, were found to be distributed fairly evenly around the circle, although decorated sherds were concentrated in the southeastern quadrant. The pottery from the Natchezan and Caddoan traditions was distributed similarly, indicating that native pottery (no matter what its origin) was used indiscriminately throughout the village, presumably by the Tunica themselves (i.e., there were not distinct "Natchez" or "Caddo" households). Utilized stone and daub also show a relatively even distribution around the circle, although nonhuman bone fragments were concentrated in the western half (fig. 82). Considering the small size of the sample, no special significance is attached to the latter imbalance.

The basic plan established by the aboriginal artifacts was reinforced by the distributions of the historic eighteenth-century European artifacts (fig. 83). Despite the general conformity, however, there are some intriguing distinctions between various artifact categories. The earthenwares, for example, are rather evenly distributed around the entire circle, but the greatest variety is found in the southern part of the site (south of datum). This is particularly true of the tin-glazed wares: the majolica,

for example, was found only in this area. On the other hand, stonewares were concentrated on the northern side of the field, and the only European sherd found on the bluff summit was the single example of white salt-glazed stoneware. Bottle glass and beads were found to have a relatively even distribution around the circle, but, as in the case of the tin-glazed earthenware, the greatest variety of beads (and thus the fancier examples) was found in the southern half of the field. Metal artifacts, including gun parts and munitions, were as evenly distributed as any other major group, although a certain bias toward the southeastern and northern corners may be discerned.

A composite map of the distributions of the historic aboriginal and European artifacts presents a detailed plan of the eighteenth-century Tunica occupation in the field at Trudeau (fig. 84). In addition to the basic circular pattern described by the artifacts and village debris, certain locations stand out as "hot spots": places with an unusual number and variety of cultural remains.* The two most important hot spots can be seen on the circle's southeastern side and in its northern extension. The reason for the latter departure from the basic circle could not be determined from the surface evidence, but the existence of the extension was emphasized repeatedly by all classes of artifacts, both aboriginal and European. Whatever it represents, it definitely was a feature of the Tunica occupation—a very intriguing disconformity.

As already noted, the Tunica occupation—as opposed to the earlier Coles Creek component—was not confined to the field. The summit of the adjacent bluff also was utilized, although the full nature of the utilization was not ascertained. Structural remains were encountered: there were many daub fragments on the surface, and a heavily burned layer was observed just beneath the surface along an eroded edge. Together with the presence of burials confirmed in 1972, this evidence indicates that the summit was used in much the same fashion as the field—that is, as both mortuary and construction site. It may be reasonably hypothesized that some difference in importance was attached to the two locations. Indeed, although few artifacts were found at the summit during the survey, the significance of this location is indicated by the sherd from a white salt-glazed stoneware bowl or pitcher, the finest European ceramic known to have come from the site.

Because all cultural remains were retained during the surface investigation of Trudeau, a large sample of artifacts was amassed from the nineteenth- and twentieth-century occupations (fig. 85). Since they are not pertinent to the focus of this study, these artifacts are

---

* As part of site preparation prior to our arrival, the overgrown bottomland field was cut and disced in order to facilitate the archaeological and electronic surveys. Since the field had been plowed many times before, we were not fearful of disturbing anything but did wonder if another plowing would significantly alter the surface patterning of cultural materials as compared with the general site configuration observed in 1972. We need not have been concerned. We learned that during this century, at least, the field had been plowed in all directions—thus effectively neutralizing any bias for creep in a particular direction—and one more random pass would not matter.

* We considered whether these "hot spots" could possibly be evidence of Charrier's activities rather than those of the Tunica: i.e., could they be backdirt areas from the looted grave pits? There is an absence of human bone on the surface, however, and Charrier's notes, albeit meager, do not suggest that he worked the most important of these spots.

◄ **Figure 78.** Iron artifacts and munitions collected at Trudeau during the 1980 survey. a–b, kettle fragments; c, buckle; d, button; e–g, handwrought nails; h, folding knife blade; i, pistol flintlock; j–k, lead musket balls; l–n, spall gunflints (note extensive uneven wear patterns on l and m, probably from use with strike-a-light); o, blade gunflint. (1:1)

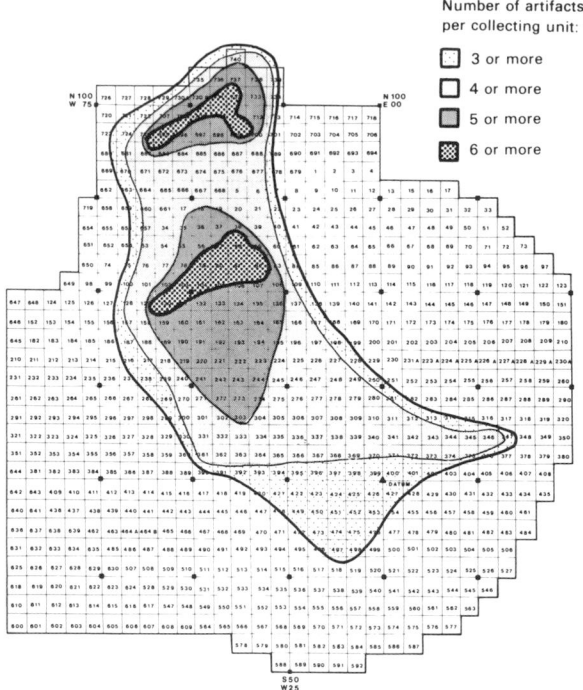

Number of artifacts per collecting unit:

☐ 3 or more
☐ 4 or more
▨ 5 or more
▨ 6 or more

Figure 79. Surface distribution of diagnostic Coles Creek artifacts collected at Trudeau during the 1980 survey.

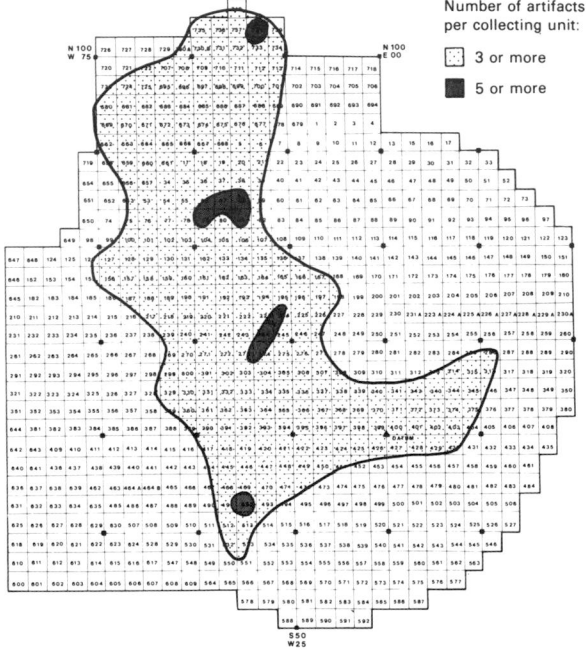

Number of artifacts per collecting unit:

▦ 3 or more
▨ 5 or more

Figure 80. Surface distribution of Addis Plain, *var. unspecified* pottery collected at Trudeau during the 1980 survey. Note that the general configuration is similar to that in figure 79.

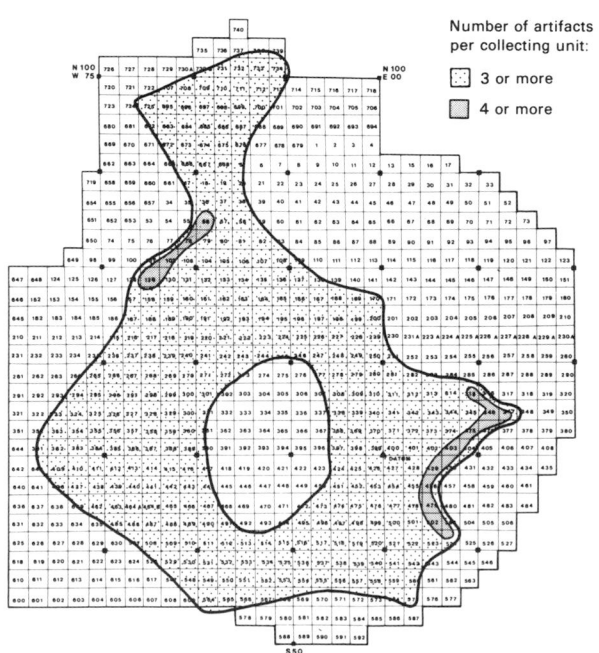

Number of artifacts per collecting unit:

▦ 3 or more
▨ 4 or more

Figure 81. Surface distributions of eighteenth-century aboriginal artifacts collected at Trudeau during the 1980 survey. Note the generally circular configuration with lower artifact density in the center.

Figure 82. Surface distributions of lithics, bone, and daub collected at Trudeau during the 1980 survey. Although not specific to occupation, the closest correlation is with the eighteenth-century settlement. Concentrations may indicate possible house sites.

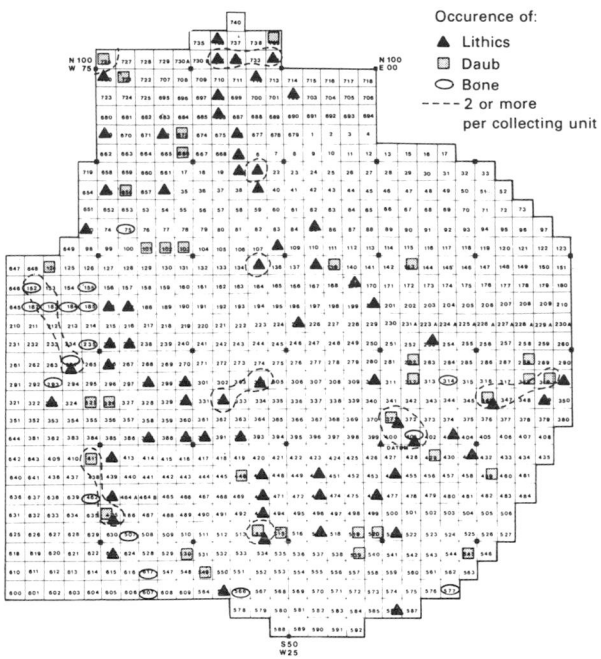

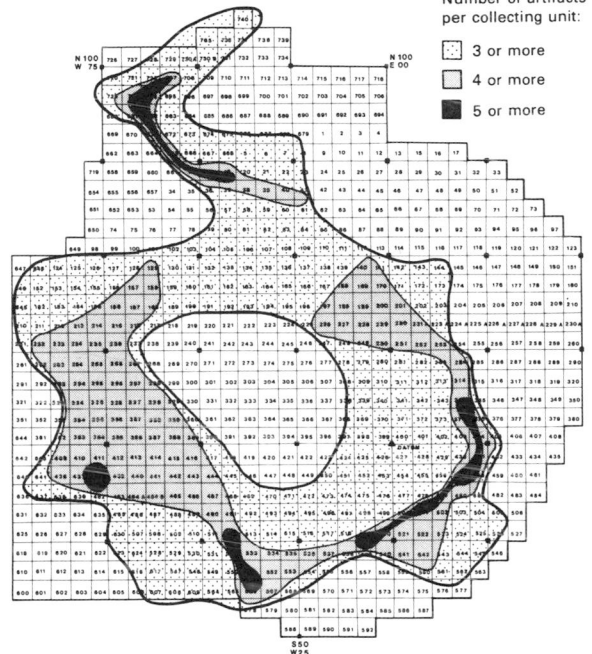

Figure 83. Surface distributions of eighteenth-century European artifacts collected at Trudeau during the 1980 survey. The same general circular configuration is displayed in figure 81.

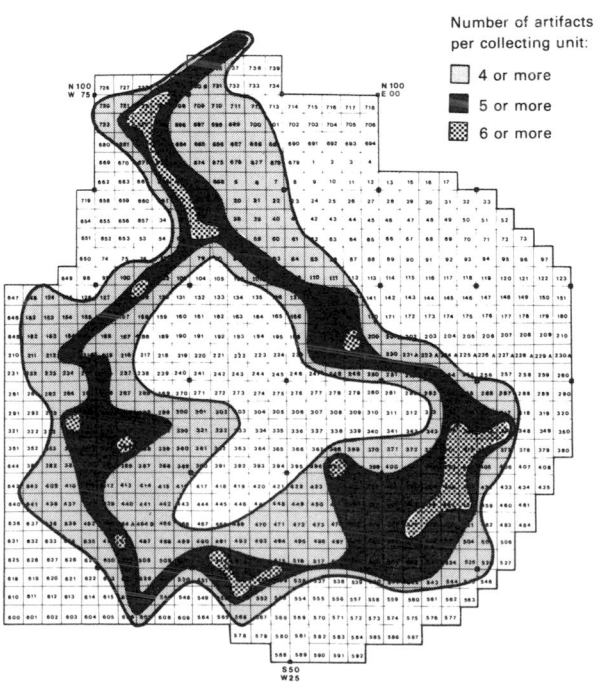

Figure 84. Composite of the aboriginal and European artifact distributions from the eighteenth-century occupation at Trudeau (figs. 81, 83).

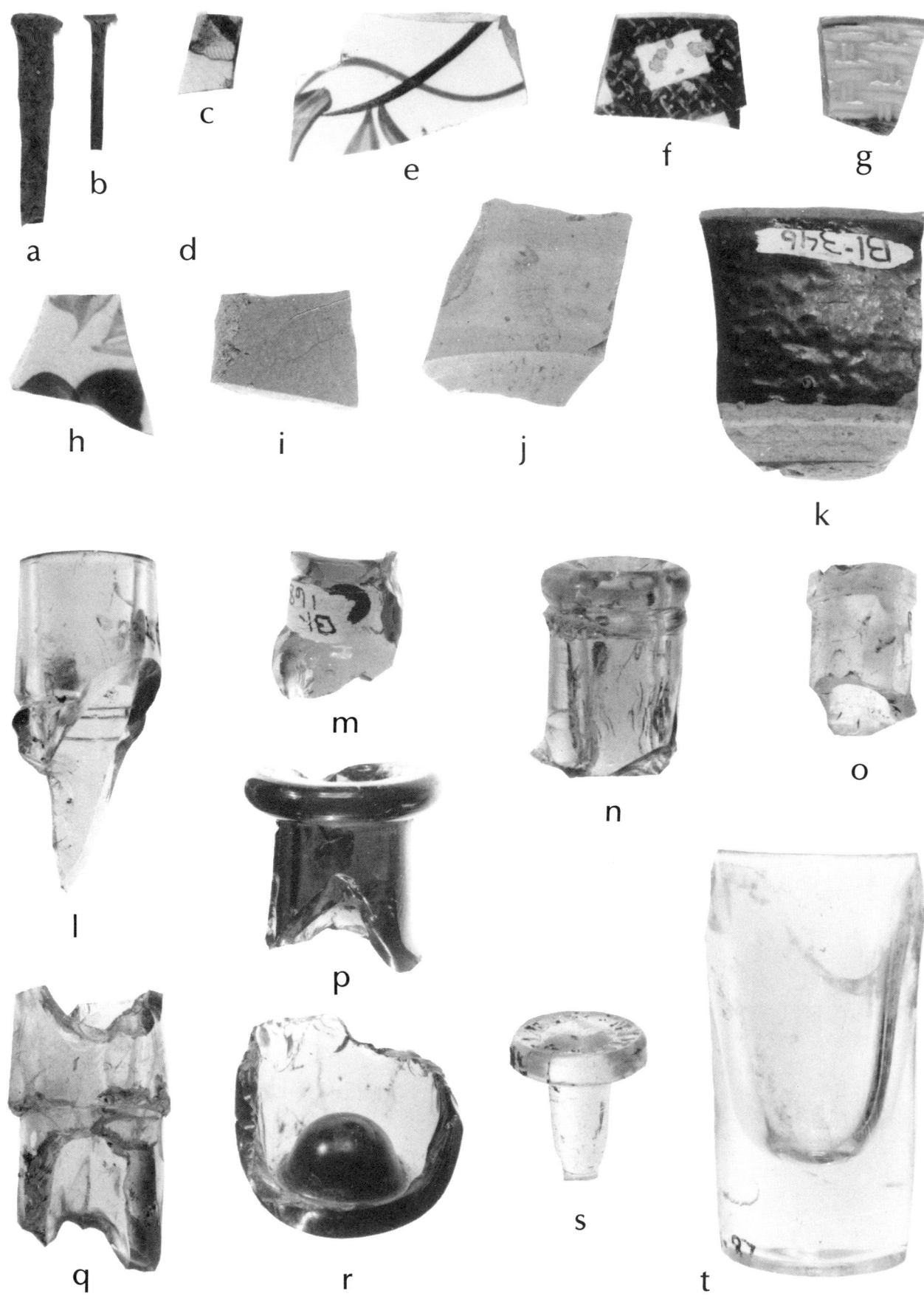

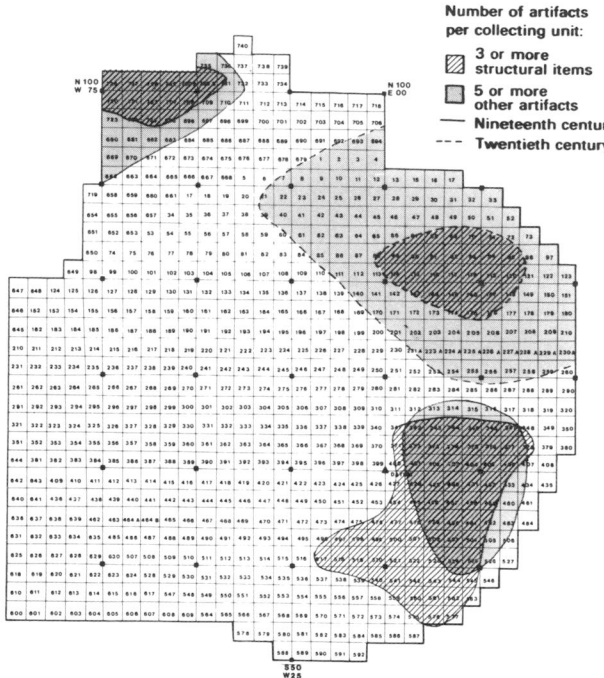

Number of artifacts
per collecting unit:

⊘ 3 or more
   structural items
▨ 5 or more
   other artifacts
— Nineteenth century
--- Twentieth century

Figure 86. Surface distributions of nineteenth- and twentieth-century artifacts collected at Trudeau during the 1980 survey. Note that three distinct loci are evident.

not described here. However, their distributions on the site (fig. 86) are important for establishing the recent human occupations. There are two nineteenth-century loci, one each on the northern and southeastern sides of the field. Judging from the nature of the artifacts, these were house sites occupied during the mid to latter part of the century by small freeholders. The twentieth-century occupation is found on the northeastern side of the field at the base of the bluff and included the tenant house, which was removed during our investigation. At all three loci, the more recent occupations overlay portions of the eighteenth-century component, so artifacts from very different traditions were found together on the surface. It therefore was necessary to sort the historic European and American artifacts with great care in order to arrive at accurate distributions for the various occupations.

ELECTRONIC SURVEY

The subsurface survey of Trudeau was carried out with two different electronic systems: magnetometry and "subsurface interface radar" (SIR). Magnetometers have been used with varying degrees of success in our archaeological investigations (Steponaitis and Brain 1976; Brain, Brown, and Steponaitis n.d.), but they played a minor role in 1980. Trudeau seemed to offer an ideal venue for a test of the sophisticated new SIR system, and its use was emphasized in the electronic survey.

As its name clearly indicates, the SIR system employs the principles of radar detection adapted to underground applications. The SIR system we used consisted of four

components hooked up to a 12-volt power source (fig. 87). The power was supplied by a vehicle that also served to transport the equipment during the survey. The four components were a transducer, a control unit, a tape recorder, and a graphic recorder. The transducer, a mobile antenna, is connected to the control unit by cable. The transducer used at Trudeau was a prototype (model 3102) that had been specially developed for archaeological investigation.

The SIR system performs an advanced impulse radar procedure that gives an electronic subsurface profile. In operation, the transducer transmits an electromagnetic impulse into the ground as it is moved along a predetermined line (a "transect") on the surface of the site. When the impulse strikes an interface between two materials of differing electrical properties—whether natural soils, cultural features, or even artifacts—some of the impulse energy is reflected and the rest continues through the ground to other interfaces. The reflected signals are received by the transducer, which transmits the information back to the control unit where it is monitored on an oscilloscope, recorded on magnetic tape, and printed out on the graphic recorder. The unique aspect of this procedure is the ability to generate automatically a continuous printout of subsurface features. The graphic record is designed to be a complete high-resolution profile, not a point-by-point sample from which extrapolations are made. Ideally, it is a close approximation, electronically expressed, of the actual interfaces that would be seen in a vertical wall of a trench dug along the path of the transducer.

The same 5-m grid established for the controlled surface collecting of Trudeau was used for the electronic survey, but it was expanded to cover a greater area (fig. 88). For this part of the investigation, the operational component of the grid was not the series of 5-m squares but the lines separating them, which became the transects guiding the path of the transducer. In order to avoid the survey stakes and flags, the transects actually were run 50 cm to the west of each north-south line, and 50 cm to the south of each east-west line.

Several transects were run out well beyond the grid originally established for archaeological control in order to verify the cultural limits of the site and to gain some insight into the natural stratification of the soil. The summit of the bluff remnant also was transected. Since the summit was suspected to have been an important place during the Tunica occupation, it was gridded at 2-m as well as 5-m intervals, in hopes of achieving more detailed information about any features that remained. In pursuit of the same objective of greater detail, we resurveyed a 10- × -10-m portion of the field grid at 1-m intervals (see fig. 31). This area was beneath the old tenant house, which was known to have been in place for at least eighty years and thus was the one place on the site that we could be certain had not been disturbed by recent events.

The results of the SIR survey were very intriguing (Brain 1980, pp. 23–32). The graphic printouts along the transects in the field appeared to display numerous sub-

◀ **Figure 85.** Nineteenth- and twentieth-century artifacts collected at Trudeau during the 1980 survey. a–b, cut iron nails; c–h, decorated earthenware; i–k, stoneware; l–r, glass bottles; s, Lea & Perrins glass bottle stopper; t, shot glass. (1:1)

Figure 87. The subsurface interface radar (SIR) system employed in the field at Trudeau in 1980. Moving the antenna along a transect of the control grid, and components mounted in vehicle (inset).

surface features, many of which were tentatively identified by professional analysts as being of cultural origin. An example of the preliminary interpretation of the printout of a transect is illustrated in figure 89. This information was then correlated with similar data in contiguous parallel and crosscutting transects to reconstruct possible features in three dimensions (figs. 90–91). It will be noted that the overall patterning con-

formed well to the apparent site plan reconstructed from the surface distribution of artifacts. The SIR survey of the bluff summit also seemed to confirm the presence of the remnants of a burned structure and its contents. Overall, the preliminary assessment was very exciting. The next step was to match these electronic indications with actual features through a program of selective excavations.

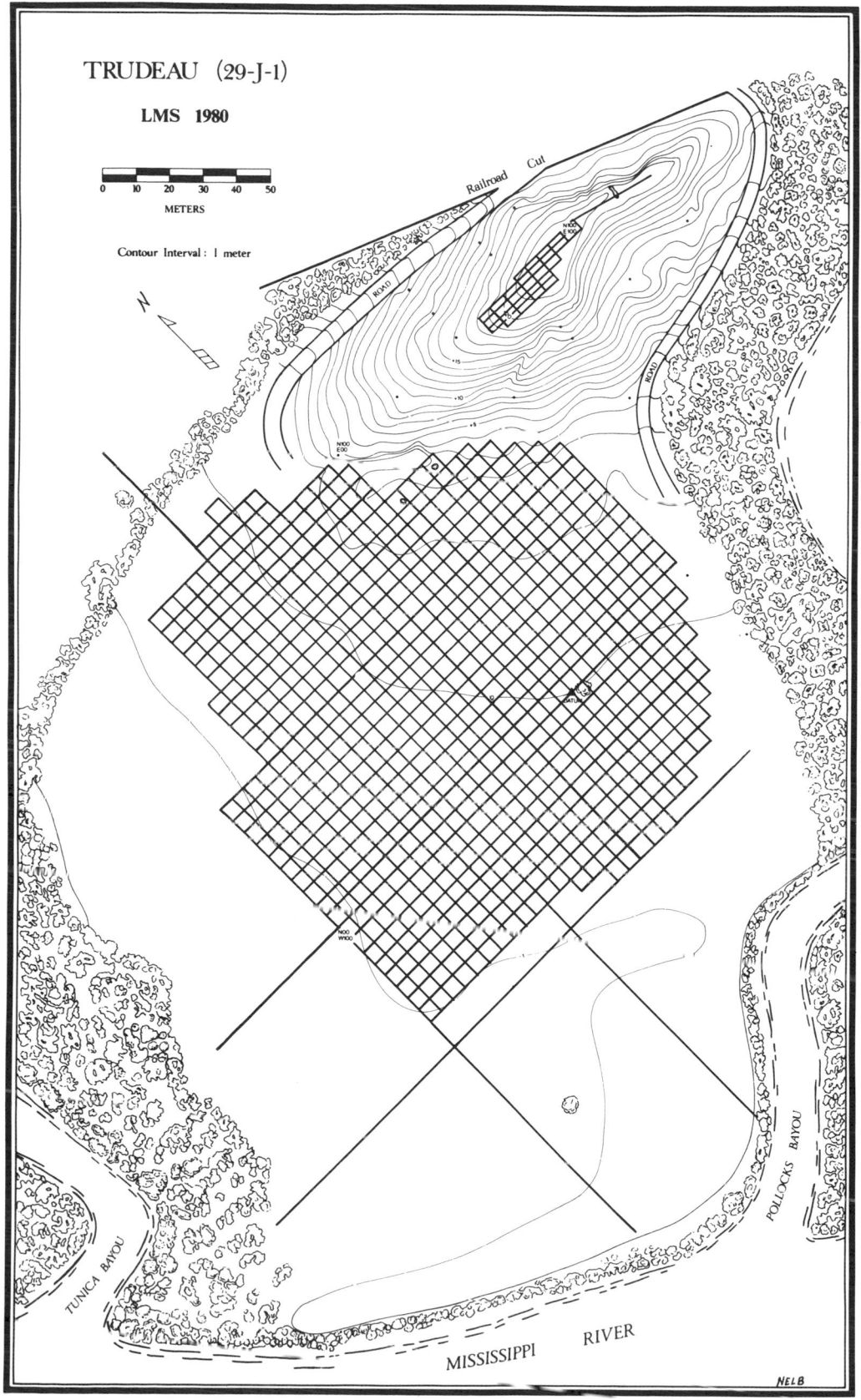

Figure 88. Transect grids for SIR survey at Trudeau. In addition, a 10-m square at the location of the tenant house was transected at 1-m intervals.

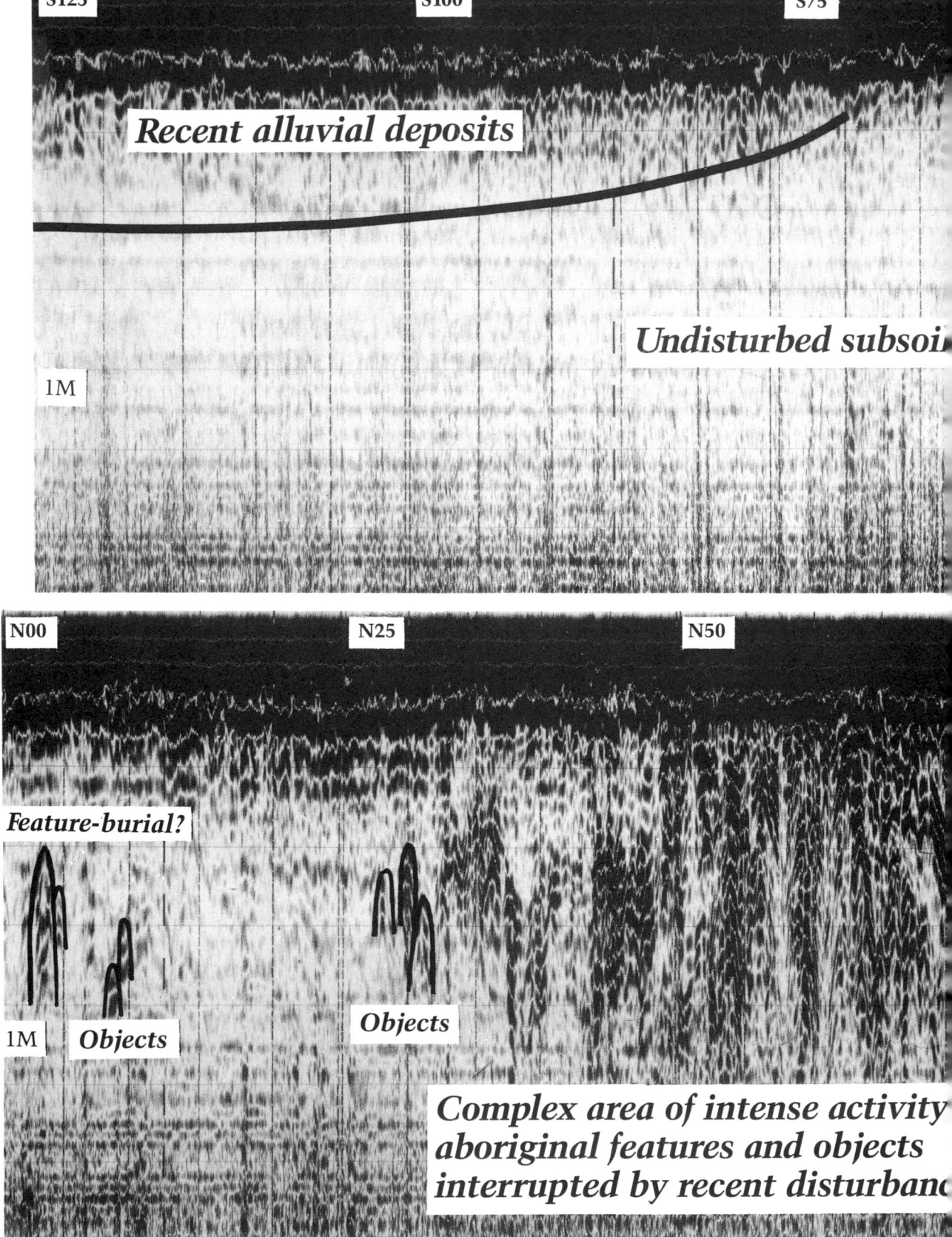

Figure 89. SIR printout of the W50 transect between S125 and N150, Trudeau. Potential features and their interpretations are note

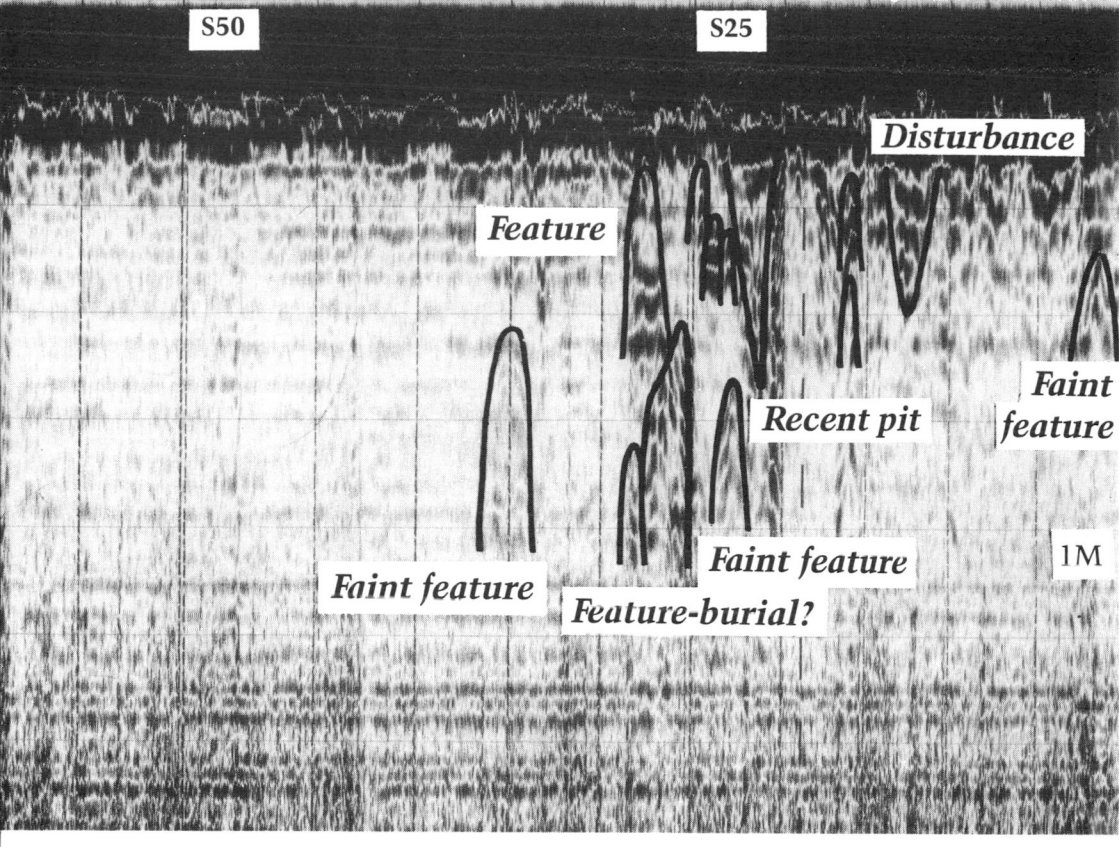

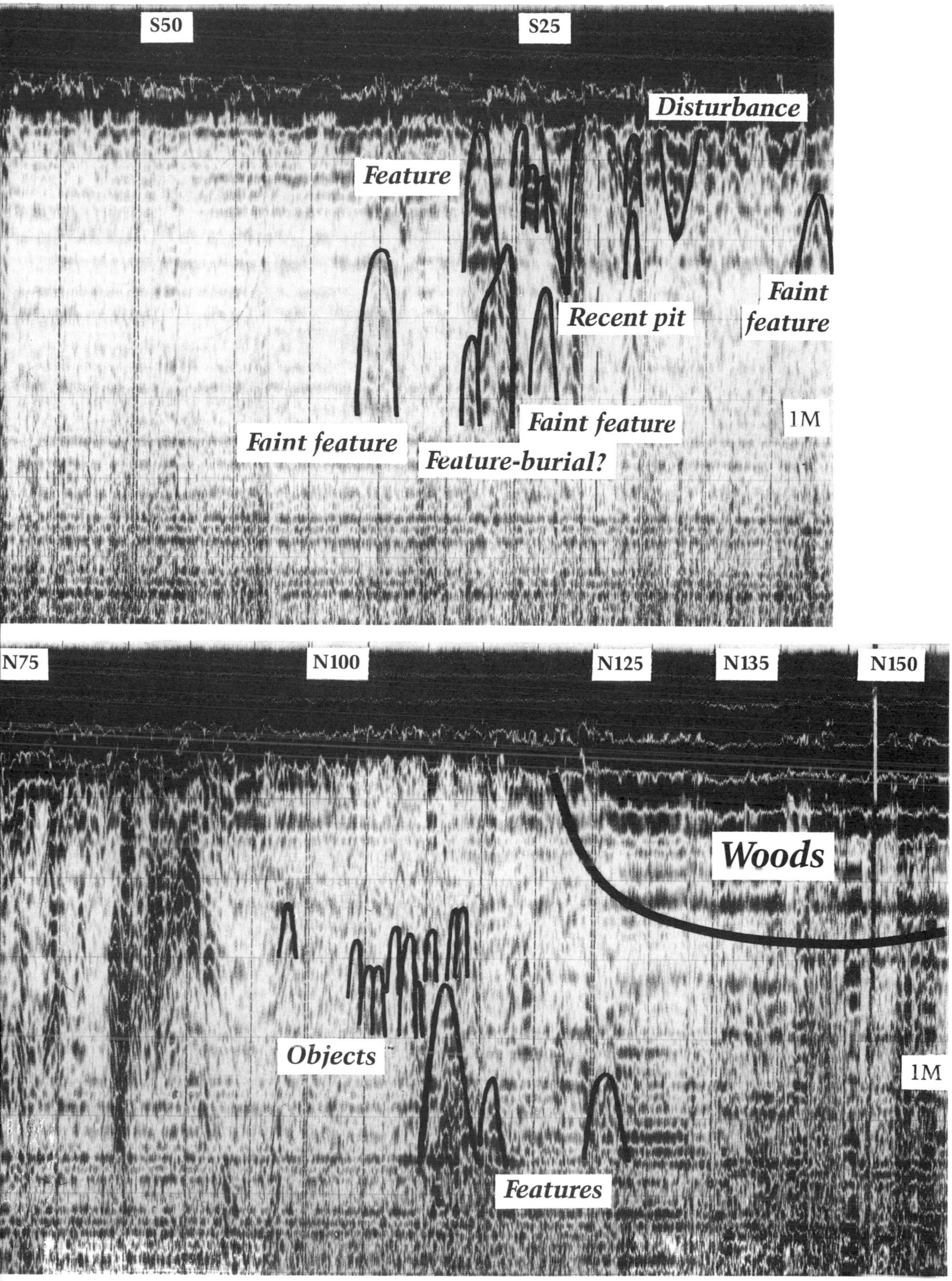

S50   S25

Disturbance

Feature

Recent pit

Faint feature

Faint feature

Faint feature

Feature-burial?

1M

N75   N100   N125   N135   N150

Woods

Objects

Features

1M

Figure 90. Diagram of the results of the SIR survey in the field at Trudeau. The lines indicate positive detection of features along the transects. Multiple parallel lines indicate the presence of superimposed features at a location.

Figure 91. Reconstruction and interpretation of the apparent subsurface features detected in the field at Trudeau during the 1980 SIR survey.

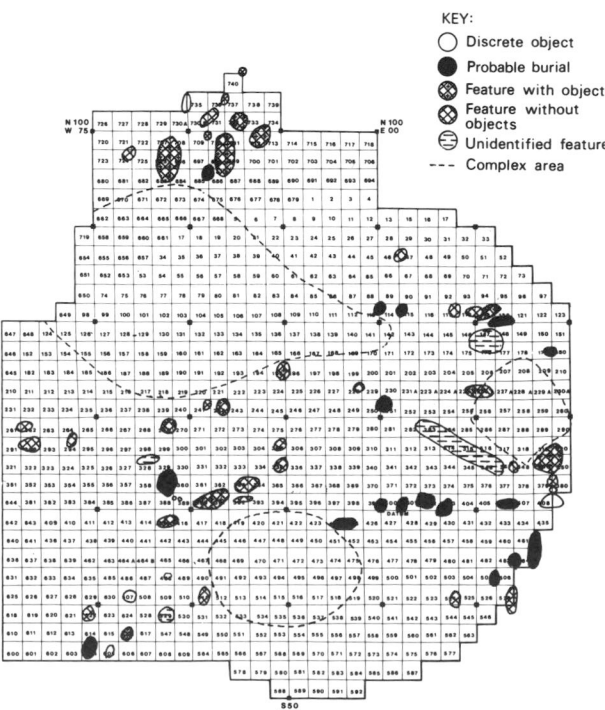

The 1981 Excavations

The 1981 excavations were designed primarily as a follow-up to the 1980 SIR survey. Our first objective was to test the initial interpretations of the apparent subsurface features recorded on the printouts. Accordingly, the bluff top and six locations in the field were selected that revealed numerous and varied electronic signals (figs. 91–92). Second, we anticipated that as the expectations were confirmed (or revised) and refined, we would develop a crude lexicon of electronic signals, which could then be used to "read" the great corpus of 1980 SIR transects. Such subsurface knowledge of the site would be an invaluable aid, of course, to the discrimination of features for future excavation.

Unfortunately, the radar did not live up to our expectations, although it was found to have a limited capability for distinguishing gross geological disconformities. Despite this disappointment, the excavations succeeded in developing a wealth of archaeological data. Much new information about the culture history and physical structure of Trudeau was gained, and the potential of the site for future archaeological investigation is now much better understood.

The Lower Mississippi Survey returned to the site in the fall of 1981, began excavations on 19 October, and finished work on 27 November. The core crew consisted of Jeffrey P. Brain, Ian Brown, Richard Fuller, Diane Silvia, and Thomas Maher. Labor for the clearing and gross movement of dirt was made available by the

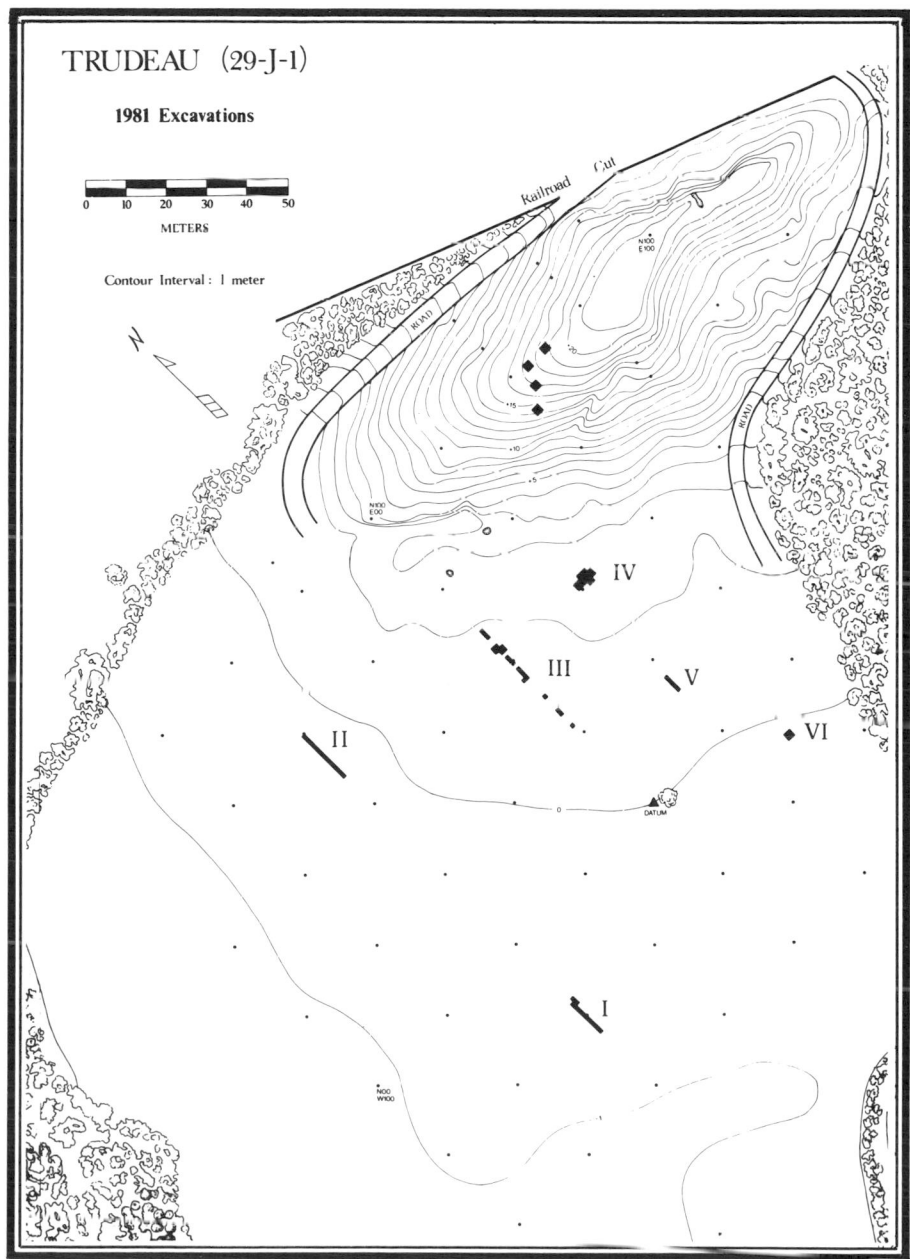

Figure 92. Locations of the 1981 excavations at Trudeau.

Louisiana State Penitentiary at Angola. The SIR system was brought back in order to make a more detailed reconnaissance of the locations to be excavated and to serve both as an aid to the investigations and as a permanent subsurface record. The electronic technician was again Daniel Stanfill, who had established his own company, Detection Sciences Group.

Excavations were placed on the bluff top and at six locations in the field (fig. 92). Because the SIR system could not be brought in until the second week of the operation, excavations were begun on the bluff top, where the shallowness of the deposits rendered effective radar discrimination a marginal proposition and resurveying could not be expected to improve our knowledge significantly.

BLUFF TOP

The 1972 and 1980 investigations of the bluff top on the north side of the site (fig. 93) had revealed strong evidence of a burned structure located just beneath the surface over an area of several meters to the south and east of the N100/E75 coordinates (Brain 1980, pp. 21, 32). The associated cultural materials testified to a mid-eighteenth-century dating for the structure, and its location on the bluff top suggested that it might have been of unusual importance. Because Trudeau lacks artificial mounds, it had long been surmised that the natural bluff remnant served as a natural mound at the site. Any structure at its summit therefore might be expected to have fulfilled a function similar to that of other aboriginal mound-top buildings. Our excavations were designed to test this theory.

A total of four 2-×-2-m excavation units was excavated at this location (fig. 94). These units were designated B56, B59, B75, and B93. Units B56, B59, and B75 were excavated in order to define the limits and nature of the burned structure; B93 was investigated specifically to test some of the more intriguing anomalies detected during the 1980 SIR survey.

During the 1980 survey, the radar antenna was pulled along a course between 25 and 50 cm south of each east-west line. In 1981, therefore, the soil directly beneath the transects was excavated very carefully in order to determine if specific artifacts or features could be correlated with the electronic signals. Although B93

Figure 93. View of the bluff remnant at Trudeau from south-southwest.

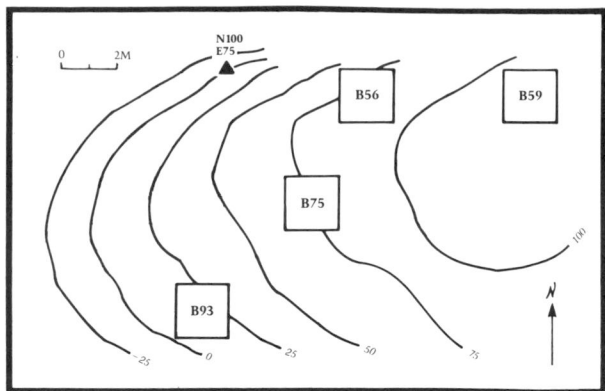

Figure 94. Bluff top excavation plan, Trudeau.

was excavated especially for the purpose of testing the radar, the methods used in excavating this unit were also followed in the examination of B56 and B75. The first step in each case was to excavate the southern three-fourths of the unit down to subsoil (fig. 95). The soil was removed in two natural levels: humus (A), and base of humus to subsoil (B). Once the southern three-fourths had been removed, a section drawing of the north wall was made as a guide for the next step: excavation (with trowel or smaller implement) of a 10-cm-wide unit according to the two natural levels described above. Artifacts were mapped both horizontally and vertically, and another wall section was drawn. The same procedure was repeated with the next 10-cm slice (40 cm in B75), and finally the remainder of the unit was excavated like the first part and given the same catalog designations. Despite the care with which the path of the radar was dissected, there were no definite correlations of artifacts with the electronic signals.

The stratification of deposits on the bluff top was found to be humus, cultural layer, subsoil (fig. 96). The humus was approximately 10 cm thick and consisted of a gray silty loam mottled with daub and charcoal. Cultural materials included both eighteenth- and nineteenth-century artifacts. Beneath the humus in B56, B59, and B93 was a light brown clayey silt that was probably an earlier surface of the bluff. Overlying it in the southwestern quarter of B56 and throughout B75 was a heavy concentration of daub and charcoal. Aside from the daub, structural features were limited to a post mold along the western wall of B75 and a pit about 30 cm deep in the southwestern corner of the square.

The bluff top was moderately rich in artifacts (table 11), and these were especially abundant in the clay and daub layers of B56 and B75. Of special interest is the large number of handwrought nails (fig. 97), which may have been used in construction. Also notable is the preponderance of tin-glazed earthenware (including the one piece of delft from the excavations) over lead-glazed, and of clear or light blue-green glass over olive green. Although the horizontal and vertical positions of all excavated artifacts were carefully plotted, no significant patterns of distribution were observed either within or between the individual units. For the site as a whole the most significant observation is the complete absence of pre-eighteenth-century artifacts.

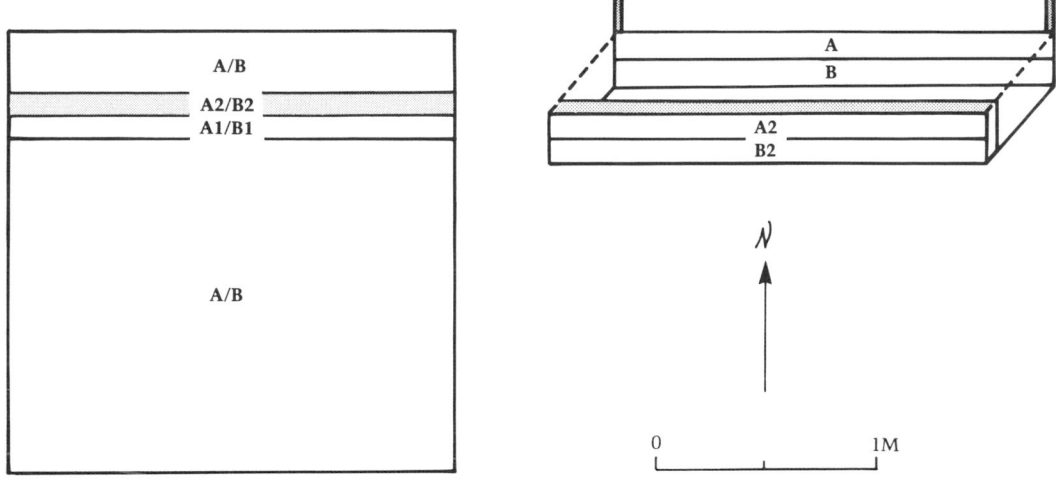

Figure 95. Diagram of excavation techniques for investigation of SIR signals at Trudeau.

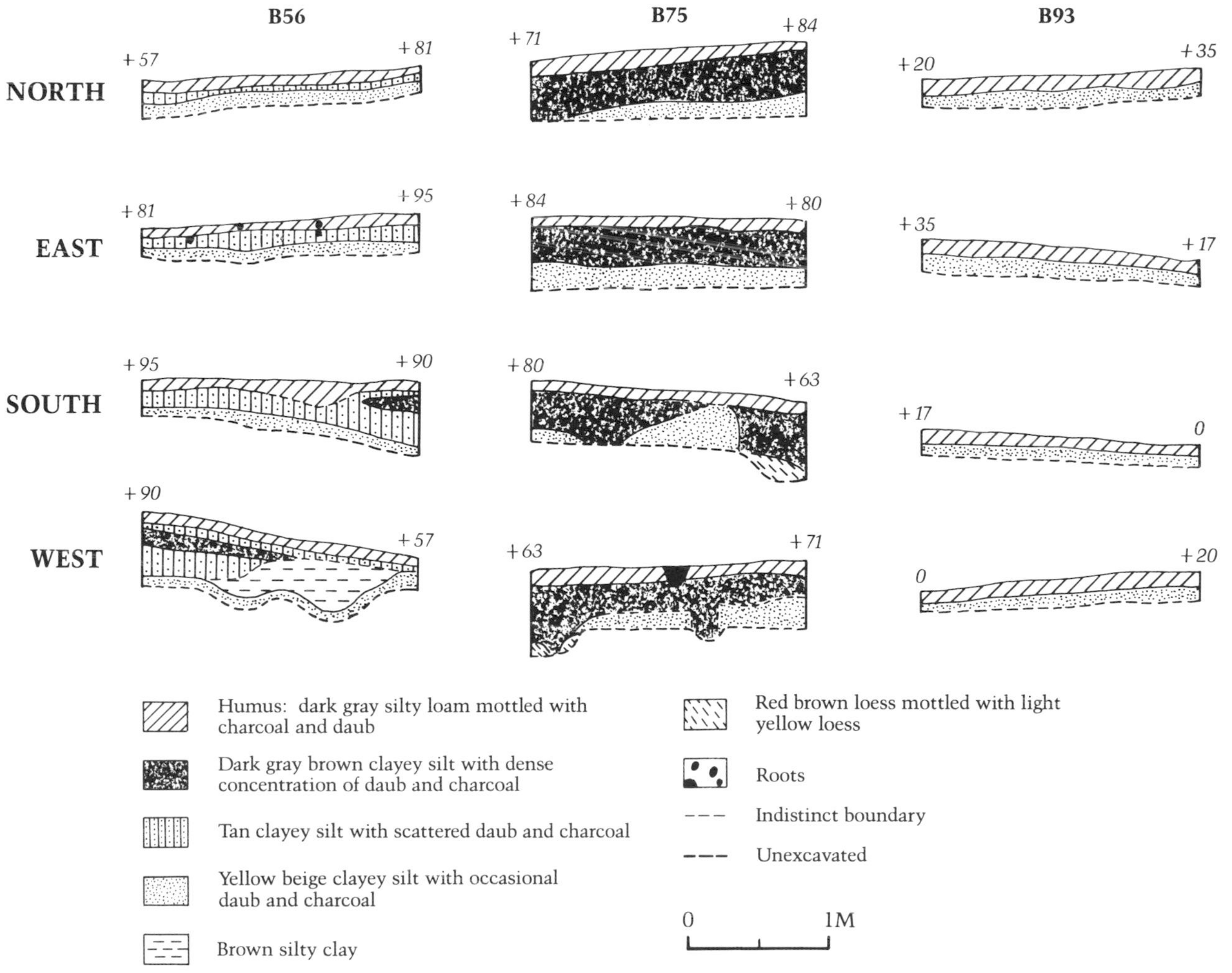

	B56	B75	B93
NORTH	+57 ... +81	+71 ... +84	+20 ... +35
EAST	+81 ... +95	+84 ... +80	+35 ... +17
SOUTH	+95 ... +90	+80 ... +63	+17 ... 0
WEST	+90 ... +57	+63 ... +71	0 ... +20

Humus: dark gray silty loam mottled with charcoal and daub

Dark gray brown clayey silt with dense concentration of daub and charcoal

Tan clayey silt with scattered daub and charcoal

Yellow beige clayey silt with occasional daub and charcoal

Brown silty clay

Red brown loess mottled with light yellow loess

Roots

--- Indistinct boundary

--- Unexcavated

0   1M

Figure 96. Stratification of bluff top excavations at Trudeau.

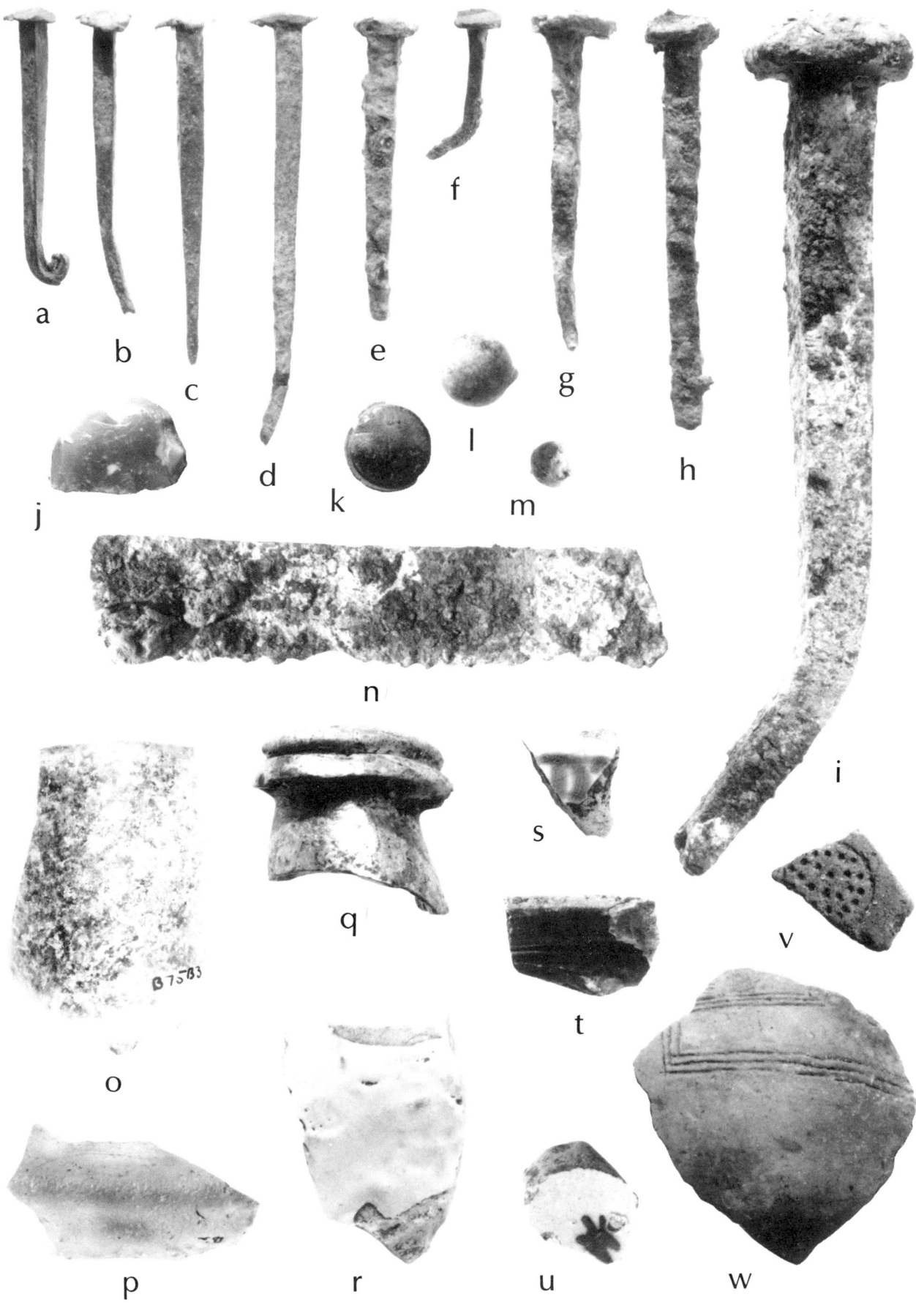

Table 11. Eighteenth-century aboriginal and European artifacts from the bluff top at Trudeau.

ABORIGINAL

Pottery:

Winterville Incised, *var. Tunica*	2
Mississippi Plain, *var. Pocahontas*	14
Fatherland Incised, *var. Fatherland* (fig. 97w)	5 [a]
Fatherland Incised, *var. unspecified*	2
Maddox Engraved, *var. unspecified*	1
Addis Plain, *var. St. Catherine*	1
Owens Punctated, *var. Beland City* (fig. 97v)	1
Addis Plain, *var. Feliciana*	1
Addis Plain, *var. Skillikalia*	1
Addis Plain, *var. unspecified*	4
Pipe bowl fragments [b]	2

Daub: [c] —

Lithics:

Unutilized chert flakes/pieces	25
Ground stone	2

Organics:

Human bone	2
Mammal bone	562
Bird bone	13
Fish bone	5
Shell	4
Charcoal	161

EUROPEAN

Earthenware:

Faience

White (fig. 97r)	3
Blue-and-white (fig. 97s, u)	2

Delft

Powder purple	1

Lead-glazed

Type C (fig. 97t)	2
Unglazed	2
Kaolin pipe bowl	1

Glass:

Clear (fig. 97o)	10
Olive green (fig. 97q)	9
Light blue-green (fig. 97p)	10
Light green	1

Iron:

Wrought nails

Type I (fig. 97a–c)	114
Type II (fig. 97d–e)	28
Type III (fig. 97f–g)	14
Type IV (fig. 97h)	10
Type V (fig. 97i)	1
Type unspecified	51
Saw blade (fig. 97n)	1
Miscellaneous	9

Pewter/lead:

Miscellaneous	2

Brass:

Button (fig. 97k)	1

Gun parts/munitions:

Iron tang	1
Gunflints (fig. 97j)	2
Lead musket balls (fig. 97l)	4
Lead pistol ball or large shot (fig. 97m)	1

[a] Four sherds from the same vessel.
[b] One fragment in form of kaolin pipe.
[c] Large quantity from burned structure.

The excavations at the bluff top did confirm the presence of a burned eighteenth-century structure. The lack of features and jumbled appearance of the daub layer indicated that the location explored was to the side of the structure, which had probably stood in the area subsequently destroyed by the railroad cut (see fig. 92). The loss of this structure is unfortunate, because the presence of both nails and daub indicates that a combination of aboriginal and European construction techniques may have been represented. Such innovation would add to the building's significance, which is already indicated socioculturally by the kinds and proportions of European artifacts. The structure must have served some special function among the Tunica: the large number of food bones argues for a chief personage's residence, but the presence of the human bone from B75 and of the burials found by Charrier suggests the possibility of a temple/charnel house.

Figure 97. Eighteenth-century European and aboriginal artifacts from the bluff top at Trudeau. a–c, handwrought iron nails, Type I; d–e, handwrought iron nails, Type II; f–g, handwrought iron nails, Type III; h, handwrought iron nail, Type IV; i, handwrought iron nail, Type V; j, spall gunflint; k, brass button; l, lead musket ball; m, lead pistol ball or large shot; n, iron saw blade; o, fragment of clear wine glass; p, fragment of light blue-green glass bottle; q, neck of olive green glass bottle; r, white faience; s, u, blue-and-white faience; t, lead-glazed earthenware, Type C; v, Owens Punctated, *var. Beland City*; w, Fatherland Incised, *var. Fatherland*. (1:1)

LOCATION I

Location I was selected because the SIR survey showed what was tentatively interpreted as a variety of objects and features concentrated within a very tight cluster (see figs. 89–91). Because so many discrete and distinctively different signals were recorded in such a limited area, it seemed an ideal test of the anticipated electronic lexicon.

Following the radar transect, a 1-m-wide trench was laid out between S20 and S30. This trench was divided into ten 1-m² excavation units designated B130–139 (figs. 98–99). For reasons explained below, a 1-×-2-m excavation unit (B115) was added later to extend the excavations at the northeastern end of the trench.

The plow zone in each of the trench sections of location I was removed as level A. Below this zone we were unable to follow the natural stratification, so we resorted to a strategy of removing arbitrary levels. The

Figure 99. View of location I excavations from the northeast, Trudeau.

B level consisted of 15-cm arbitrary units in B130 and B131, and 25-cm units in all of the remaining trench sections. Following excavation of the B levels, strata cuts were made in the central and southern portions of the trench.

As elsewhere in the field, the basic geomorphology at location I was found to have been formed by a complex series of alluvial depositions (fig. 100). Beneath the plow zone was a thick layer of brown silt. This layer, about 15 cm thick in B130, expanded to over 70 cm in B138. Pockets of dark brown clayey silt occurred all along the southern end of the trench. Beneath the silt was a layer of white to yellowish brown sand. Quite thin in the southern portion of location I, this layer attained a thickness of about 40 cm in the middle of the trench. It was heavily interbedded with mottled gray and brown silty clay lenses in the northern end of the trench. Elsewhere, the silty clay soil occurred as a rather thick zone beneath the sand. In B134 and B135 a lens of charcoal could be seen at a depth of about 120 cm below the present ground surface. Nothing of cultural relevance was associated with this lens and so it is presumed to have been caused by natural agencies.

Only two intact cultural features were encountered at location I, and both dated to the historic occupation. The first was a small layer of primary midden that was observed along the western wall of B138 and B139. Everywhere else, the eighteenth-century occupation surface had been destroyed by the plow, and most of the associated artifacts (table 12) were confined to the plow zone. The second, and most important, aboriginal feature was an intrusive grave pit (burial Beta) in the northern end of the trench.

The aboriginal pit containing the artifacts associated with burial Beta was first observed at the base of the B level in excavation units B130 and B131 (fig. 101). The outline of this pit, oriented northeast-southwest, was quite clear at this level, but in subsequent levels the fill was indistinguishable from the surrounding soil. The grave had originally been excavated through an extremely complex geological layer of interbedded sands and clays (fig. 100). Only at a depth of about 80 cm below the ground surface did the outline of the grave once again become visible. In order to isolate the pit, investigations were expanded to the northeast with the

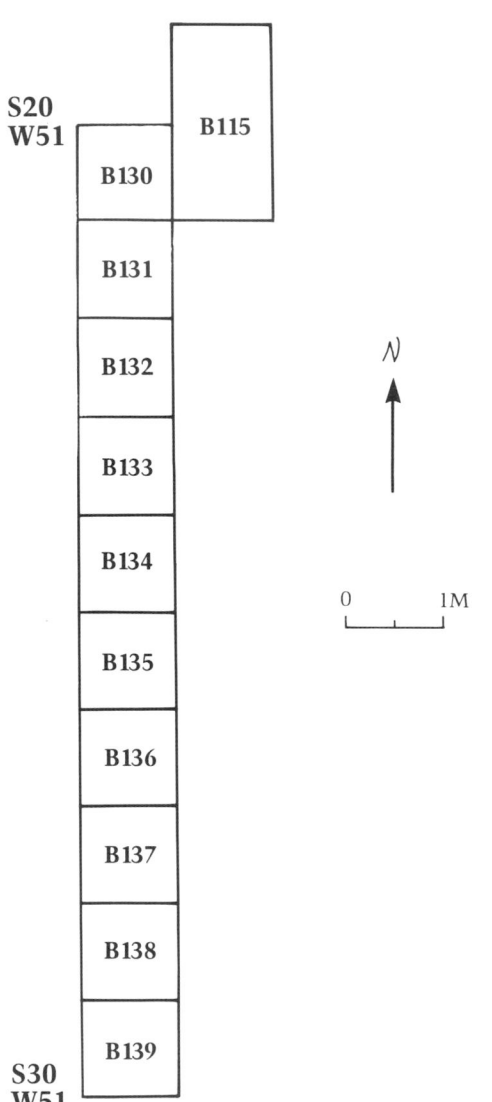

**S20
W51**

B115

B130

B131

B132

B133

B134

B135

B136

B137

B138

B139

**S30
W51**

N

0   1M

Figure 98. Plan of excavations at location I, the Trudeau site.

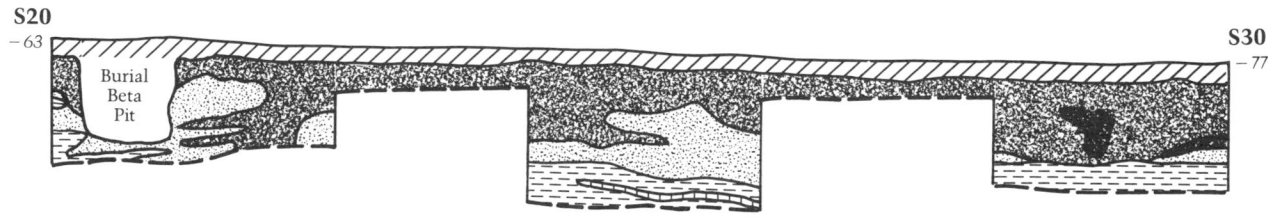

EAST WALL

S20
−63

Burial Beta Pit

S30
−77

WEST WALL

S30
−78

S20
−62

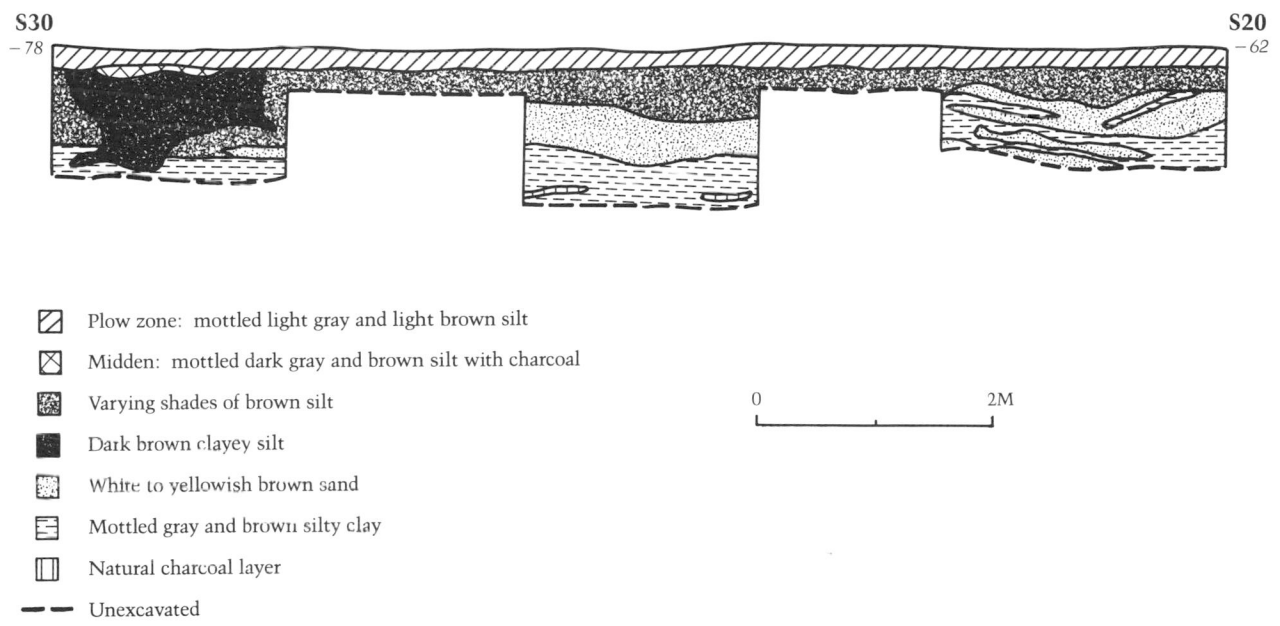

☒ Plow zone: mottled light gray and light brown silt

☒ Midden: mottled dark gray and brown silt with charcoal

☒ Varying shades of brown silt

■ Dark brown clayey silt

☒ White to yellowish brown sand

☒ Mottled gray and brown silty clay

☐ Natural charcoal layer

— — Unexcavated

0   2M

Figure 100. Stratification at location I, Trudeau.

excavation of B115. Following removal of the plow zone, the burial pit was excavated to the same level as in the adjoining trench sections.

From the base of the plow zone to about 20 cm above the subsoil the fill was extremely hard and basically sterile. Soil at the base of the pit continued to be compact, but differed in that it was rich in historic artifacts. The general horizontal positioning of the artifacts is depicted in figure 102. Finds included the lid of an iron pot, many seed and necklace beads, typical cast brass buttons of the period, lead shot, lead musket balls, numerous pieces of at least one Type C musket, a Flowerkey bell, and other items (fig. 103; table 13). Also scattered throughout the fill were charcoal and flecks of vermilion. Several teeth from an infant were noted, but otherwise bone was lacking in the deposits. Human remains were absent even at the base of the pit. The excavation of the portion of the pit in B130 offered a solution to this curious situation: the body had been removed in historic times.

The remains of a bark mat were found on the floor at the southwestern end of the pit, and at the extreme end was an in situ double-stranded necklace. This ornament clearly had once encircled the head of the interment. The individuals who removed this skeleton, presumably the Tunicas themselves, were quite careful when digging up the skull. The head originally had been oriented to the southwest. There was a clear demarcation where the bark ended, revealing that the head and upper torso were the only parts of the body to be placed on a bark matting. Several centimeters below the necklace beads was a fairly dense concentration of white seed beads. These probably were either sewn into the hair or onto a piece of fabric lying beneath the head. A cluster of six buttons was found in the chest area of the individual.

Even though the northeastern end of the burial pit exhibited heavy disturbance, a reconstruction of the original placement of artifacts was possible. White seed beads occurred along the left arm and hand, probably

Figure 101. Burial Beta at location I, Trudeau. View of burial pit from the southwest.

adorning a sleeve. A cluster of lead shot also occurred at the position of the left hand, with musket balls at the right hand, a situation similar to that observed with burial Alpha in location III. A button and bell similarly were associated with the right hand. Gun hardware was located on all sides of the lower extremities, while the pot lid mentioned above was found adjacent to the right hip.

In the absence of bone, the sex and age of the individual remains uncertain. The size of the grave itself indicates an adult, and the presence of armaments suggests a male. However, seed beads in the hair share parallels with a female burial at Bloodhound Hill, while the presence of an infant's teeth indicates the probability of a multiple interment. Despite the uncertainties concerning age and sex of the individual(s), we now have strong evidence for the practice of exhumation among the Tunica, as demonstrated by the fact that the grave was reentered within the limits of the original pit and by the careful removal of the bones and most of the artifacts.

In summary, although the eighteenth-century surface had been destroyed, the presence of daub and the quantity and diversity of artifacts in the plow zone indicate that location I was an important residential locus for the Tunica during their occupation of Trudeau. The presence of the grave is consistent with our knowledge of the overlapping of settlement and mortuary patterns

at the site. Of special interest, however, is the fact that the grave had been exhumed long ago, presumably by the Tunica themselves (certainly not as recently as Charrier). None of this cultural information could be correlated with the radar signals that prompted the selection of this location. The only certain correlation was with the natural sand layer, especially the complex interbedding in the vicinity of burial Beta.

LOCATION II

The 1980 SIR survey had indicated that this general area was one of extreme subsurface complexity: rather than discrete anomalies, the electronic signals displayed intense and continuous activity (see figs. 89–91). There was even some indication of superposition of some signals. The suspicion was that this was a residential area and that the signals detailed structural remains and other major features of a concentrated occupation. The superposition of signals even suggested that more than one occupation surface might be present, and because the 1980 surface collections had revealed that diagnostic Coles Creek artifacts were centered on this portion of the site (see fig. 79), it was anticipated that the apparent electronic stratification reflected cultural stratigraphy of at least two components.

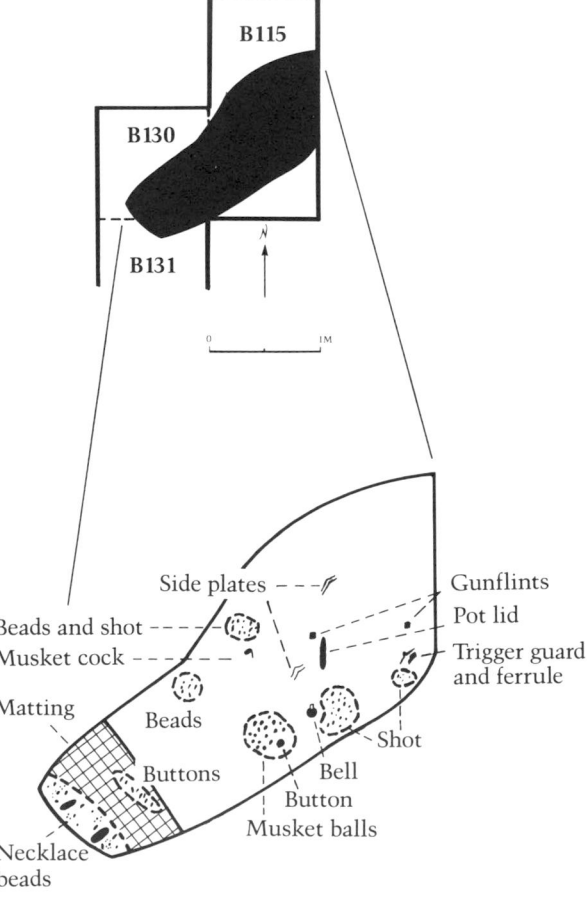

Figure 102. Plan of burial Beta and detail of grave, location I, Trudeau.

Table 12. Aboriginal and European artifacts from location I at the Trudeau site, exclusive of burial Beta (see table 13).

ABORIGINAL

Pottery:

Winterville Incised, *var. Tunica*	1
Unclassified incised (Pocahontas)	2
Mississippi Plain, *var. Pocahontas*	50
Mississippi Plain, *var. Montfort*	8
Fatherland Incised, *var. Snyders Bluff*	3
Fatherland Incised, *var. Fatherland*	8
Fatherland Incised, *var. unspecified*	8
Unclassified incised (St. Catherine)	4
Chicot Red, *var. Grand Village*	1
Addis Plain, *var. St. Catherine*	11
Addis Plain, *var. Feliciana*	12
Addis Plain, *var. Skilhkalia*	6
Addis Plain, *var. unspecified*	94
Mazique Incised, *var. Kings Point*	1
Baytown Plain, *var. Vicksburg*	9
Baytown Plain, *var. Valley Park*	3

Daub: 14

Lithics:

Mississippi Triangular, *var. unspecified* point (fig. 120q)	1
Native gunflint (fig. 120n)	1
Unutilized chert flakes	4
Unutilized chert flakes/pieces	114
Ground stone	4
Hematite	3
Limonite	1

Organics:

Calcined mammal bone	15

EUROPEAN

Earthenware:

Faience	
White	7
Blue-and-white	1
Majolica	
Blue-and-white (fig. 122d)	2
Lead-glazed	
Type A	10
Type B	16
Type C (fig. 122f)	5
Type D	2
Type E	6
Type F	5
Type unspecified	9
Unglazed	10

Stoneware:

Unclassified	1

Glass:

Clear	4
Olive green	31
Light blue-green	13
Light green	2
Beads	
IIB10	1
IVB3	1

Iron:

Wrought nails	
Type I	1
Type unspecified	4
Miscellaneous	27

Lead:

Miscellaneous	1

Copper:

Tinkling cone (fig. 122n)	1
Miscellaneous	7

Brass:

Tinkling cone	1

Gun parts/munitions:

Brass musket side plate (fig. 122t)	1
Brass musket butt plate (fig. 122v)	1
Gunflint	1
Lead musket ball	1

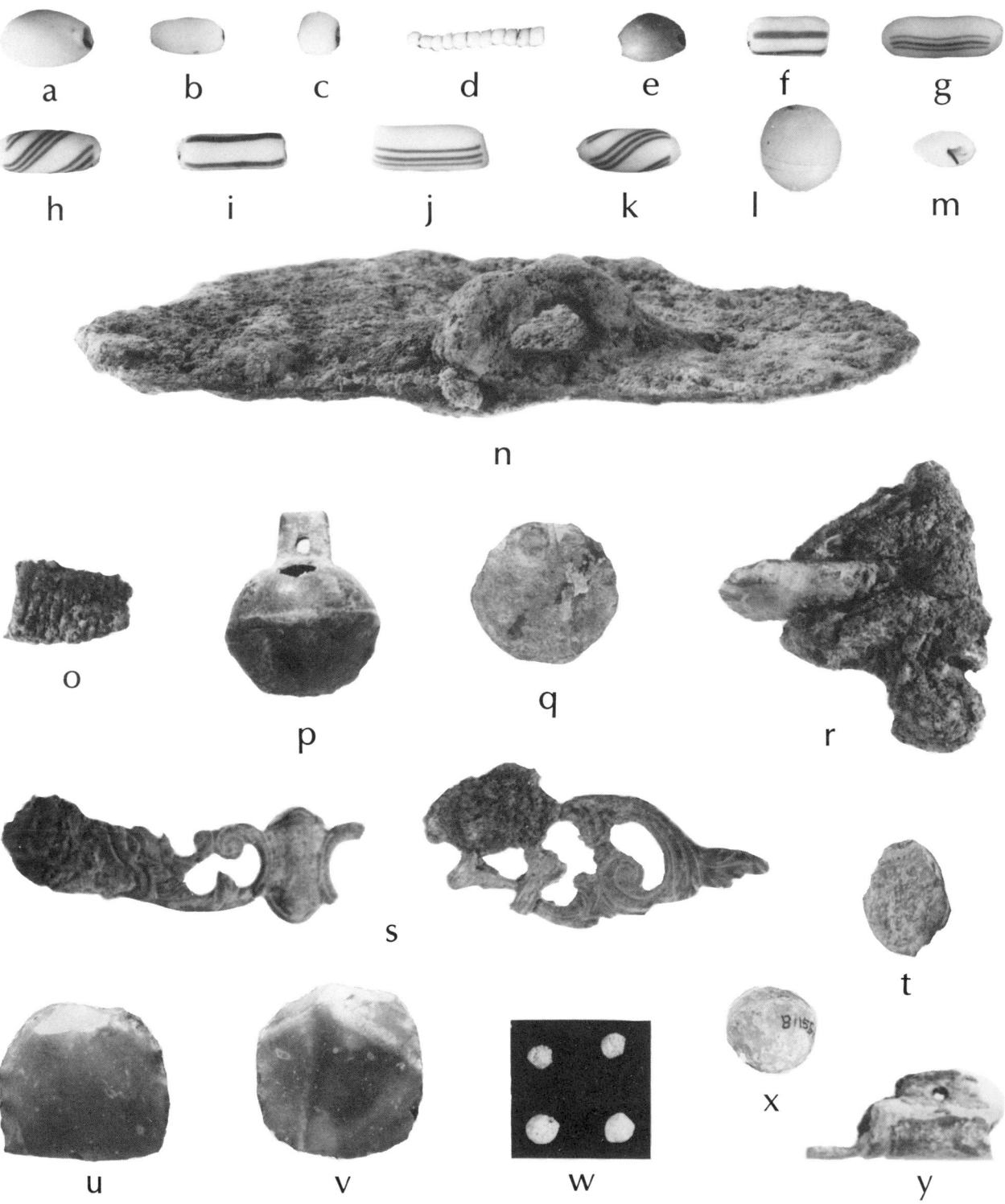

Figure 103. European artifacts associated with burial Beta at location I, Trudeau. a–d, IIA1 glass beads; e, IIA10 glass bead; f, IIB2 glass bead; g, IIB10 glass bead; h, IIB13 glass bead; i, IVB2 glass bead; j, IVB3 glass bead; k, IVB4 glass bead; l, WIA1 glass bead; m, WID1 glass bead; n, iron pot lid; o, iron coil; p, brass Flowerkey bell; q, brass button; r, iron musket cock with flint; s, brass side plate; t, brass escutcheon; u–v, spall gunflints; w, lead shot; x, lead musket ball; y, brass ferrule. (1:1)

Table 13. Aboriginal and European artifacts associated with burial Beta and in grave pit fill at location I, Trudeau.

ABORIGINAL		Light blue-green	1
		Beads	
Pottery:		IIA1 (fig. 103a–d)	200
		IIA10 (fig. 103e)	2
Barton Incised, *var. Trudeau*	1	IIB2 (fig. 103f)	3
Mississippi Plain, *var. Pocahontas*	12	IIB10 (fig. 103g)	2
		IIB13 (fig. 103h)	2
Mississippi Plain, *var. Montfort*	1	IVB2 (fig. 103i)	1
		IVB3 (fig. 103j)	2
Fatherland Incised, *var. Fatherland*	2	IVB4 (fig. 103k)	9
Fatherland Incised, *var. unspecified*	1	WIA1 (fig. 103l)	4
Unclassified incised (St. Catherine)	1	WID1 (fig. 103m)	1
Addis Plain, *var. St. Catherine*	2		
Addis Plain, *var. Feliciana*	1	*Iron:*	
Addis Plain, *var. unspecified*	22		
		Wrought nail	
Baytown Plain, *var. Vicksburg*	1	Type unspecified	1
		Coil fragments (fig. 103o)	5
Daub:	7	Pot lid fragments (fig. 103n)	2
		Miscellaneous	42
Lithics:			
		Brass:	
Unutilized chert flakes/pieces/pebbles	526		
		Buttons (fig. 103q)	8
Organics:		Bells	
		Flowerkey (fig. 103p)	1
Calcined mammal bone	1	Saturn	1
Human tooth fragments	3		
Cloth fragments	2	*Gun parts/munitions:*	
Basketry fragment	1		
		Fragments of Type C musket (fig. 103r–t, y)	35
EUROPEAN		Gunflints (fig. 103u–v)	3
		Lead musket balls (fig. 103x)	13
Earthenware:		Lead shot (fig. 103w)	147
Lead-glazed		*Miscellaneous:*	
Type B	1		
Type F	1	Vermilion	—
Glass:			
Clear	1		
Olive green	6		

A trench 1 m wide by 15 m long was laid out at location II (fig. 104). For purposes of excavation, this trench was divided into fifteen 1-m² units (B100–114), which were excavated in sections of three units each. The middle and end sections (B100–102, B106–108, B112–114) were excavated first, providing a guide to the investigation of the intermediate sections (B103–105, B109–111). Although every effort was made to follow natural levels, there nevertheless was some mixing of deposits in the sections excavated first.

The plow zone ranged between 15 and 30 cm thick (fig. 104) and consisted of a light brown silt mottled with pockets of light gray silt. Beneath the plow zone was a layer of mottled brown sandy silt of approxi-mately equal thickness, although in the northern end of the trench it expanded to at least 60 cm. This soil layer rested on top of a sand zone, which consisted of thin lenses of fine yellow compacted sand interbedded with white medium-grained sand layers and deposits of coarse sand mixed with gravel. It was this thick zone of heterogeneous alluviations that had so excited the radar: the varying water contents of the different sand matrices contrasted sharply both with each other and with the heavier soils above and below. Beneath the sand zone were thick beds of gray and brown clay.

Nearly all cultural features had been destroyed by the plow. A wall trench and plank stains, probably relating to a recent structure, were found at the bottom of the

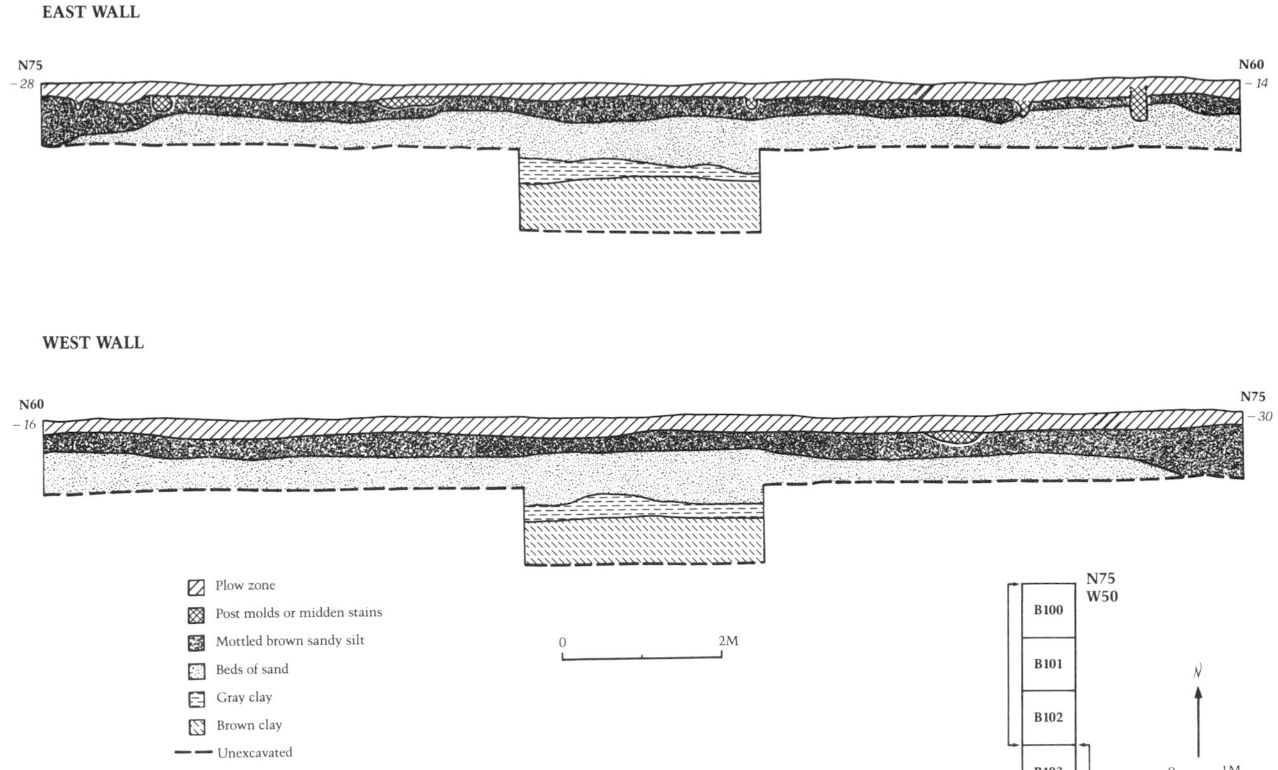

EAST WALL
N75
-28
N60
-14
WEST WALL
N60
-16
N75
-30
Plow zone
Post molds or midden stains
Mottled brown sandy silt
Beds of sand
Gray clay
Brown clay
Unexcavated
0
2M

N75
W50
B100
B101
B102
B103
B104
B105
B106
B107
B108
B109
B110
B111
B112
B113
B114
N60
W50
N
0
1M

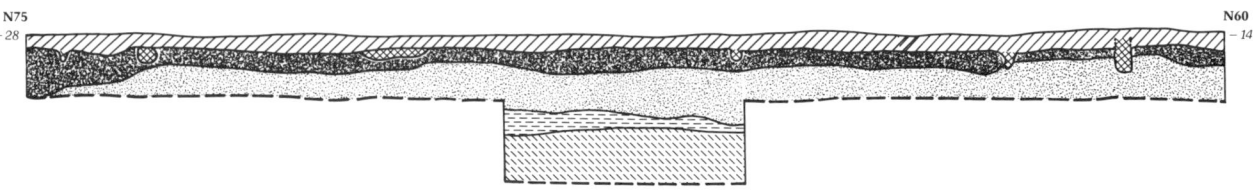

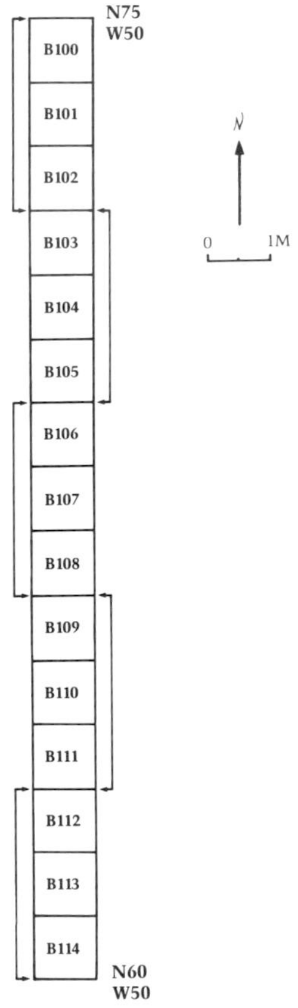

Figure 104. Plan of excavations and stratification at location II, the Trudeau site.

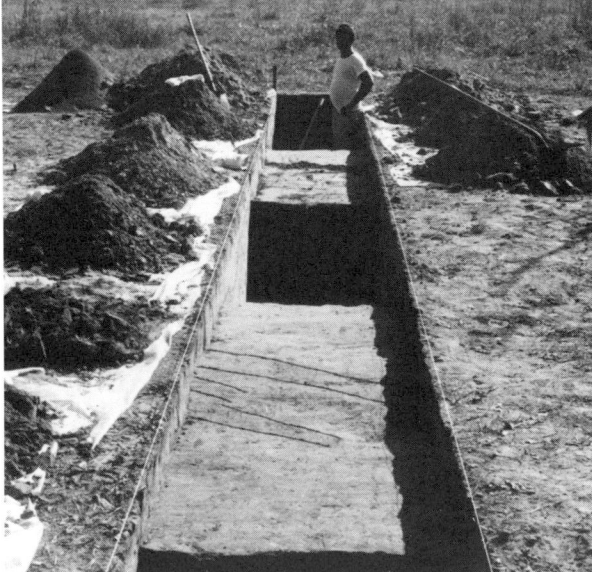

Figure 105. View of location II excavations from the north, Trudeau.

plow zone in the northern part of the trench (fig. 105), and several small patches of midden and the bottoms of six post molds intruded into the top of the mottled brown silt layer. With the exception of these intrusions, all artifacts were recovered from the plow zone (tables 14–15). Again, the evidence attests to the presence of at least two cultural components: Coles Creek and historic. The large number and variety of aboriginal and European items assignable to the latter component, as well as the presence of post molds, daub, and primary

Table 14. Aboriginal and European artifacts from the plow zone at location II, Trudeau.

ABORIGINAL		EUROPEAN	
Pottery:		*Earthenware:*	
Winterville Incised, *var. Tunica*	3	Faience	
Barton Incised, *var. Trudeau*	3	White	2
Unclassified incised (Pocahontas)	7	Brown	3
Mississippi Plain, *var. Pocahontas*	87	Majolica	
Mississippi Plain, *var. Montfort*	1	White	1
Mississippi Plain, *var. unspecified*	1	Lead-glazed	
		Type A	14
Fatherland Incised, *var. Bayou Goula*	1	Type B	21
Fatherland Incised, *var. Nancy* (fig. 120f)	7	Type C	8
Fatherland Incised, *var. Snyders Bluff*	2	Type D	2
		Type E	1
Unclassified engraved (Caddo)	2	Type F	2
		Type unspecified	8
Fatherland Incised, *var. Fatherland*	15	Unglazed	16
Fatherland Incised, *var. unspecified*	24	*Stoneware:*	
Maddox Engraved, *var. unspecified*	1		
Unclassified incised (St. Catherine)	12	Unglazed	1
Chicot Red, *var. Grand Village*	6	*Glass:*	
Addis Plain, *var. St. Catherine*	61		
Addis Plain, *var. Feliciana*	38	Clear	3
Addis Plain, *var. Skillikalia*	67	Olive green	57
Addis Plain, *var. unspecified*	1,082	Light blue-green	8
		Beads	
Plaquemine Brushed, *var. Plaquemine*	1	IA2	1
Avoyelles Punctated, *var. Kearney*	1	IA3	1
Coles Creek Incised, *var. Mott*	4	IIA6	2
Coles Creek Incised, *var. unspecified*	1	IIA7	3
Evansville Punctated, *var. unspecified*	1	IVB1	1
Harrison Bayou Incised, *var. unspecified*	1	IVB4	1
Mazique Incised, *var. Kings Point* (fig. 120k)	11	WID1	1
Mazique Incised, *var. unspecified*	1		
Pontchartrain Check Stamped, *var. Pontchartrain*	30	*Iron:*	
Unclassified incised (Vicksburg)	4		
Baytown Plain, *var. Vicksburg*	311	Wrought nails	
Baytown Plain, *var. Valley Park*	97	Type unspecified	7
Baytown Plain, *var. unspecified*	14	Miscellaneous	148
Daub:	36	*Lead:*	
Lithics:		Miscellaneous	3
Bayogoula Fishtailed, *var. Bayogoula* point (fig. 120p)	1	*Copper/brass:*	
Native gunflint	1		
Quartz scraper	1	Miscellaneous	7
Utilized chert flakes/pieces	5	*Gun parts/munitions:*	
Unutilized chert flakes/pieces/pebbles	359		
Ground stone	3	Iron cock from musket lock (fig. 122x)	1
Hematite	6	Brass side plate, Type D (fig. 122u)	1
Organics:		Brass ferrule (fig. 122r)	1
Calcined mammal bone	12	Gunflints	2
Turtle carapace	1	Gunflint flakes	7
Charcoal	4	Lead balls and shot (fig. 122y)	3

Table 15. Aboriginal and European artifacts from features below the plow zone at location II, Trudeau.

ABORIGINAL

Pottery:

Mississippi Plain, *var. Pocahontas*	3
Fatherland Incised, *var. Fatherland*	1
Fatherland Incised, *var. unspecified*	1
Addis Plain, *var. Skillikalia*	1
Addis Plain, *var. unspecified*	25
Baytown Plain, *var. Valley Park*	1
Daub:	2

Lithics:

Unutilized chert flakes/pieces	27

EUROPEAN

Earthenware:

Unglazed	2

Glass:

Olive green	1

Iron:

Wrought nail	
Type unspecified	1

midden deposits, substantiate that this was a primary residential locus during the Tunica occupation. The relatively large number of Coles Creek artifacts also confirms the presence of a component of that culture. Unfortunately, the archaeological contexts of both occupations have been obliterated: the Tunica by two centuries of agriculture, the Coles Creek by both the plow and the Tunica. Clearly, there was no significant geological separation between the two, as is indicated by the near absence of Coles Creek artifacts directly beneath the plow zone (table 15) and the absence of any cultural materials at all below that. Once again, the subsurface complexity recorded by the radar was found to be entirely geological in origin.

LOCATION III

As was the case with location I, location III's selection was prompted by the presence of a series of radar signals that appeared to indicate a variety of discrete objects and other anomalies (Brain 1980, fig. 30). Again it was anticipated that the results would contribute toward an electronic lexicon of cultural objects and features and, furthermore, would serve as a check on the series investigated at location I.

Excavations in location III were originally limited to a 1-m-wide trench extending 10 m from N45 to N55

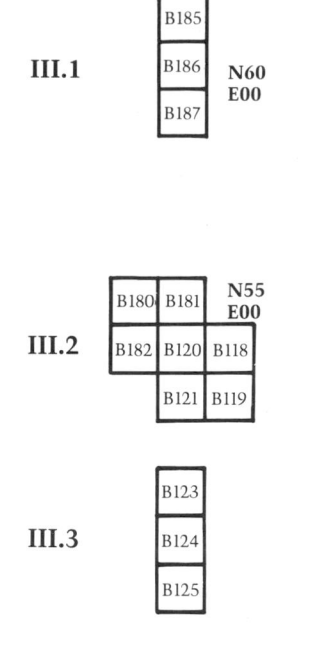
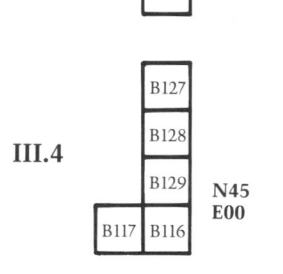
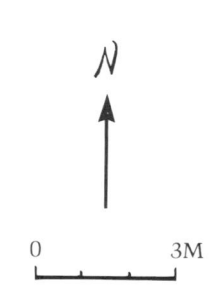
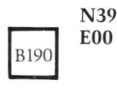
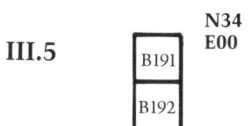
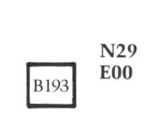

Figure 106. Plan of excavations at location III, the Trudeau site.

(fig. 106). The northern and southern portions of this trench were expanded to isolate burial pits and an old occupation surface. Subsequently, additional excavations were opened to the north and south of the original trench in order to test other SIR determinations. In all, twenty-two 1-m² units were excavated in location III. These excavation units fall into five discrete clusters, which will be discussed in order from north to south.

Location III.1 consisted of three 1-m² units (designated B185–187) positioned over a possible pit feature. The plow zone in each of the 1-m² units was removed as the A level. The B level was excavated as a 10-cm arbitrary level below the plow zone. The entire trench was then leveled off at 56 cm above datum (level C), which entailed approximately 10 cm of earth removal in B185, 5–10 cm in B186, and 0–5 cm in B187. Finally, another 10-cm level (level D) was excavated, taking the trench down to +46 cm.

The stratification in these three units (fig. 107) was similar to that observed in location II. Beneath the plow zone, which again ranged between 15 and 30 cm thick, was a layer of mottled brown sandy silt of varying shades and consistency. It was about 15 cm thick in the northern end of the trench and dipped down to a depth of 60 cm in the southern end. Once again, a layer of white to yellowish brown sand occurred beneath the silt, followed by mottled gray and brown silty clay. As at location I, there is some suggestion here that the sand and clay layers were interbedded.

Artifacts were confined mostly to the plow zone (table 16), but some were found in a number of features and post molds intruded into the B and C levels (fig. 108; table 17). At the base of the plow zone one feature and three post molds appeared. Two of the post molds

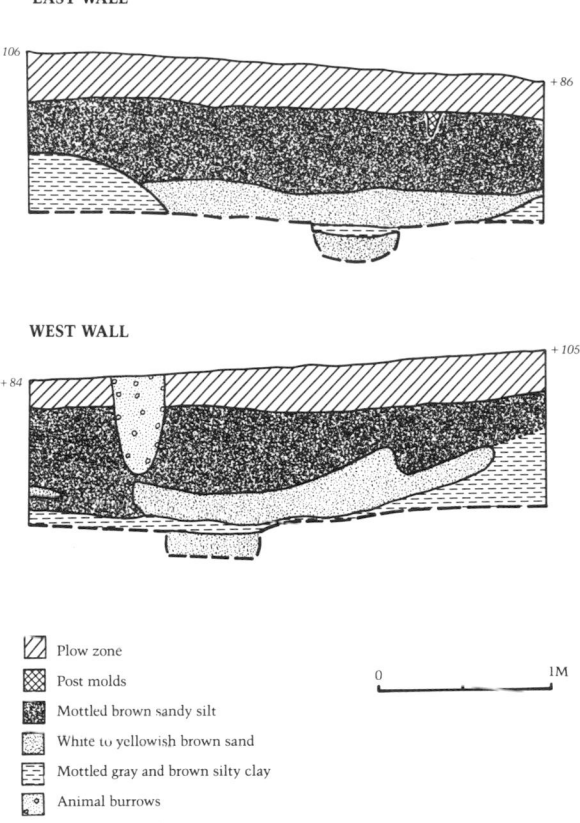

Figure 107. Stratification at location III.1, Trudeau.

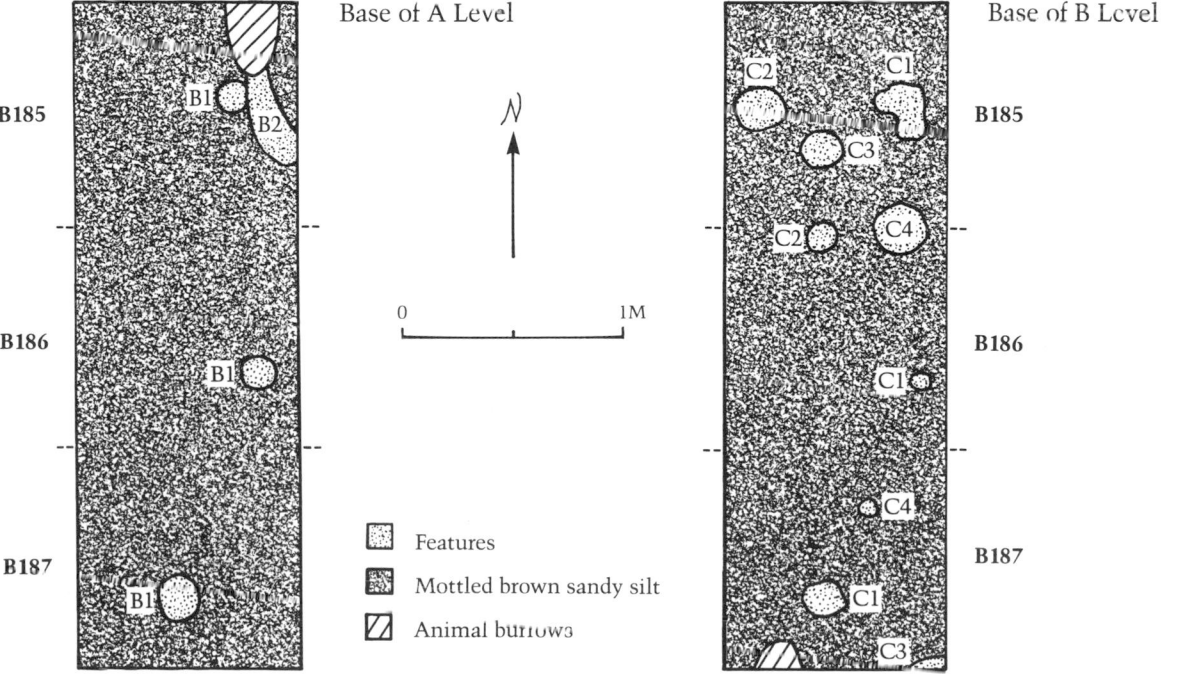

Figure 108. Plan of excavations at location III.1, Trudeau.

Table 16. Aboriginal and European artifacts from the plow zone at location III.1, Trudeau.

ABORIGINAL		EUROPEAN	
Pottery:		*Earthenware:*	
Winterville Incised, *var. Tunica*	4	Faience	
Barton Incised, *var. Trudeau*	3	Blue-and-white (fig. 122b)	1
Unclassified incised (Pocahontas)	1	Unclassified	1
Mississippi Plain, *var. Pocahontas*	50	Majolica	
Mississippi Plain, *var. Montfort*	3	White	1
Mississippi Plain, *var. unspecified*	1	Lead-glazed	
		Type A	2
Fatherland Incised, *var. Snyders Bluff*	1	Type B	13
Fatherland Incised, *var. unspecified*	4	Type C (fig. 122g)	2
Maddox Engraved, *var. unspecified*	1	Type D	5
Unclassified incised (St. Catherine)	4	Type F	3
Chicot Red, *var. Grand Village*	2	Type unspecified	1
Addis Plain, *var. St. Catherine*	15	Unglazed	2
Leland Incised, *var. unspecified*	1	*Stoneware:*	
Addis Plain, *var. Feliciana*	12	Bellarmine	1
Addis Plain, *var. Skillikalia*	5		
Addis Plain, *var. unspecified*	99	*Glass:*	
Plaquemine Brushed, *var. Plaquemine*	1	Olive green	10
		Light blue-green	2
Mazique Incised, *var. Kings Point*	1	Beads	
Pontchartrain Check Stamped, *var. Pontchartrain*	1	IIA1	1
Unclassified incised (Vicksburg)	2	IIA7	1
Baytown Plain, *var. Vicksburg*	8	*Iron:*	
Baytown Plain, var. *Valley Park*	5	Wrought nails	
Daub:	47	Type unspecified	2
		Miscellaneous	88
Lithics:		*Copper:*	
Utilized chert flakes/pieces	2	Wire	1
Unutilized chert flakes/pieces/pebbles	139		
Hematite	1		
Organics:			
Calcined mammal bone	30		
Charcoal	43		

(B185B1 and B186B1) continued into the C level, where six additional ones were detected. The only feature encountered in this area (B185B2/C1) consisted of a water-laid deposit of light to medium gray silt. At the base of the B level this feature blended with post mold B185B1/C1, reaching a total depth of approximately 31 cm. In all, nine post molds and one unidentified feature were observed over an area of 3 m², a rather dense concentration of architectural remains. None of these, however, can be considered adequate explanation for the radar anomaly initially interpreted as a possible pit feature.

Seven 1-m² units were excavated in location III.2 (fig. 106). Trench sections B120 and B121 were opened first to investigate a group of discrete anomalies. In both units, everything from the present surface to the +35 cm level was removed as level A. This level varied between 30 and 40 cm in thickness and included all of the plow zone and a portion of the mottled brown sandy silt layer beneath it (see fig. 111; table 18). A feature that appeared at the base of the plow zone subsequently turned out to be a recently disturbed burial pit (undoubtedly a product of Charrier's activities). In order to isolate this feature, designated burial Delta, excavations

Table 17. Aboriginal and European artifacts from features below the plow zone at location III.1, Trudeau.

ABORIGINAL

Pottery:

Mississippi Plain, *var. Pocahontas*	3
Fatherland Incised, *var. unspecified*	1
Addis Plain, *var. St. Catherine*	1
Addis Plain, *var. unspecified*	3
Baytown Plain, *var. unspecified*	1
Daub:	6

Lithics:

Unutilized chert flakes/pieces/pebbles	6
Ground stone	1

Organics:

Calcined mammal bone	7
Charcoal	2

EUROPEAN

Earthenware:

Lead-glazed	
Type F	1

Glass:

Olive green	1
Beads	
IIA1	1
IIA6	1

Iron:

Wrought nail	
Type unspecified	1
Miscellaneous	1

Gun parts/munitions:

Gunflint flake	1
Lead shot	1

The recent fill (B1) was removed in quarters, as depicted in figure 109. Soil was sifted through quarter-inch mesh screen and window screen. Teeth and fragments of bone were scattered throughout the deposit, but most of the artifacts and human remains were found at the base of B118B1. Included were long bones, rib fragments, and pieces of the skull and pelvis. These bones were either scattered by Charrier or thrown in first when he refilled the pit. The only possible in situ remains were the proximal ends of the left ulna and radius, which were still articulated with a distal fragment of the left humerus. These were in the undisturbed portion of the burial pit and were sufficient evidence to determine the position and orientation of the burial (described below).

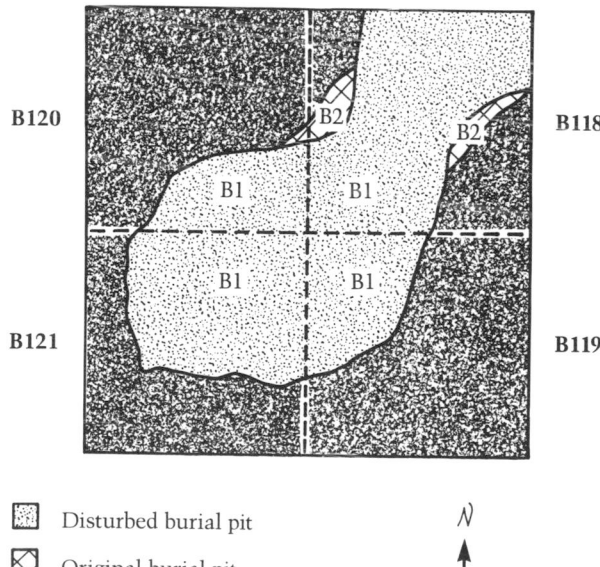

☒ Disturbed burial pit

☒ Original burial pit

☒ Mottled brown sandy silt

N

0 _____ 1M

Figure 109. Burial Delta at location III.2, Trudeau. View of burial pit from the south, and plan of excavations.

were expanded to the east. Two additional 1-m² units (B118, B119) were opened up following the methods described above.

The outline of the disturbed burial pit is illustrated in figure 109. Soil that comprised the recent fill was heavily mottled and contained heterogeneous patches of beige silt, tan silty sand, and gray midden. Pieces of bone and aboriginal potsherds were scattered throughout, as were recent and historic European artifacts. Along the eastern and western edges of the pit were two small patches of mottled gray and tan sandy silt loam (B118B2). These stains were all that was left of the original burial pit.

Table 18. Aboriginal and European artifacts from the plow zone at location III.2, Trudeau.

ABORIGINAL		*EUROPEAN*		
Pottery:		*Earthenware:*		
Winterville Incised, *var. Tunica*	6	Faience		
Barton Incised, *var. Trudeau*	8	White (fig. 122a)		1
Unclassified incised (Pocahontas)	6	Blue-and-white		2
Mississippi Plain, *var. Pocahontas*	124	Brown		7
		Majolica		
Mississippi Plain, *var. Montfort*	13	White		1
Owens Punctated, *var. unspecified*	2	Lead-glazed		
Mississippi Plain, *var. unspecified*	2	Type A		7
		Type B		32
Fatherland Incised, *var. Bayou Goula*	1	Type C (fig. 122e)		9
Fatherland Incised, *var. Snyders Bluff*	5	Type D		11
Fatherland Incised, *var. Fatherland*	8	Type E		2
Fatherland Incised, *var. unspecified*	26	Type F		5
Maddox Engraved, *var. unspecified*	2	Type unspecified		3
Unclassified incised (St. Catherine)	13	Unglazed		5
Chicot Red, *var. Grand Village*	5			
Addis Plain, *var. St. Catherine*	40	*Stoneware:*		
Leland Incised, *var. unspecified*	3	Bellarmine		2
Addis Plain, *var. Feliciana*	30	*Glass:*		
Addis Plain, *var. Skillikalia*	14			
Addis Plain, *var. unspecified*	2	Clear		5
		Olive green		46
Plaquemine Brushed, *var. Plaquemine*	1	Light blue-green		8
Coles Creek Incised, *var. Mott*	2	Bead		
Evansville Punctated, *var. unspecified*	1	IIA7		1
Mazique Incised, *var. Kings Point*	2	*Iron:*		
Unclassified incised (Vicksburg)	2			
Baytown Plain, *var. Vicksburg*	33	Wrought nails		
Daub:	116	Type IV		1
		Type unspecified		2
Lithics:		Miscellaneous		96
Utilized chert flake	1	*Copper:*		
Unutilized chert flakes/pieces/pebbles	325	Tinkling cone (fig. 122o)		1
Ground stone	3	Miscellaneous		7
Hematite	1			
Organics:		*Brass:*		
		Miscellaneous		4
Calcined mammal bone	244	*Gun parts/munitions:*		
Charcoal	39			
		Gunflint (fig. 122bb)		1
		Gunflint flakes		6
		Lead musket balls		2
		Lead sprue		1

Table 19. Aboriginal and European artifacts from the looted grave pit of burial Delta at location III.2, Trudeau.

ABORIGINAL		EUROPEAN	
Pottery:		*Earthenware:*	
Mississippi Plain, *var. Pocahontas*	28	Faience	
Fatherland Incised, *var. Bayou Goula*	1	White	2
		Lead-glazed	
Fatherland Incised, *var. Fatherland*	1	Type A	1
Fatherland Incised, *var. unspecified*	3	Type B	4
Unclassified incised (St. Catherine)	2	Unglazed	5
Addis Plain, *var. St. Catherine*	6		
		Glass:	
Addis Plain, *var. Feliciana*	9		
Addis Plain, *var. Skillikalia*	5	Olive green	6
Addis Plain, *var. unspecified*	87	Light blue-green	1
		Beads	
Coles Creek Incised, *var. unspecified*	1	IIA1	200
Pontchartrain Check Stamped, *var. Pontchartrain*	2	IIA2	1
Baytown Plain, *var. Vicksburg*	8	IIA5	365
		IIA6	2
Baytown Plain, *var. Valley Park*	2	IIA7	334
		WID4	4
Daub:	12	WIIA7	33
		Unclassified	1
Lithics:		*Iron:*	
Unutilized chert flakes/pieces/pebbles	48	Kettle fragments	2
Limonite	1	Wrought nails	
		Type unspecified	4
Organics:		Miscellaneous	205
Calcined mammal bone	20		
Charcoal	13	*Brass:*	
		Bells	
		Flushloop (fig. 122m)	9
		Miscellaneous	3
		Gun parts/munitions:	
		Lead musket balls	3
		Lead shot (fig. 122y)	4
		Lead sprue	1

With the exception of a number of seed beads (IIA1, and one IIA5) grouped around the articulated bones described above, there were no in situ artifacts in the pit. However, a large quantity of material was recovered in the fill (table 19). Hundreds of beads had been left behind, including varieties IIA1 and IIA5 (very small), IIA7 (medium), and a few small wire-wound faceted beads of burgundy color. The IIA1 beads tended to be more clustered than the others, and they also were more often adjacent to bones. The IIA7 beads were not only the most common variety encountered but also had the broadest distribution in the fill. Some of the specimens were associated with rib bones. Other artifacts included nine small Flushloop bells, kettle fragments, numerous pieces of rust from iron artifacts that had been removed, musket balls, and sherds of glass and earthenware. Considering the rich collection of artifacts that was left behind, the removed portion must have been impressive indeed.

Although burial Delta had been completely disturbed and almost entirely destroyed, the following interpretations may be offered. It could be determined from the bones that this had been the inhumation of a young adult, laid to rest in a supine position with the head oriented to the northeast. From the remaining artifacts it is not possible to be certain of the sex of this individual, although the musket balls suggest that it may have been a male.

Table 20. Aboriginal artifacts from the prehistoric occupation surface at location III.2, Trudeau.

Pottery:

Baytown Plain, *var. unspecified*	7

Lithics:

Unutilized chert flakes/pieces	2

Organics:

Charcoal	13

most diagnostic of these artifacts, listed in table 20, are seven sherds of Baytown Plain. Although the variety is not specified, the ware characteristics are similar to the Mulberry Creek Cord Marked sherds from location VI (see fig. 120; tables 30–31). Together, they constitute the sole evidence for a third, and earlier, component at Trudeau. The only contextual evidence for this component of the Baytown culture is the surface described here, which fortunately, unlike the later occupations, was covered and protected by a thick layer of alluvial deposits (fig. 111).

The Baytown occupation surface is recorded as zone 1 in figure 111. An earlier surface (zone 2), which exhibited heavy organic content but no artifacts, turned up at a somewhat greater depth in B180 and B181. It

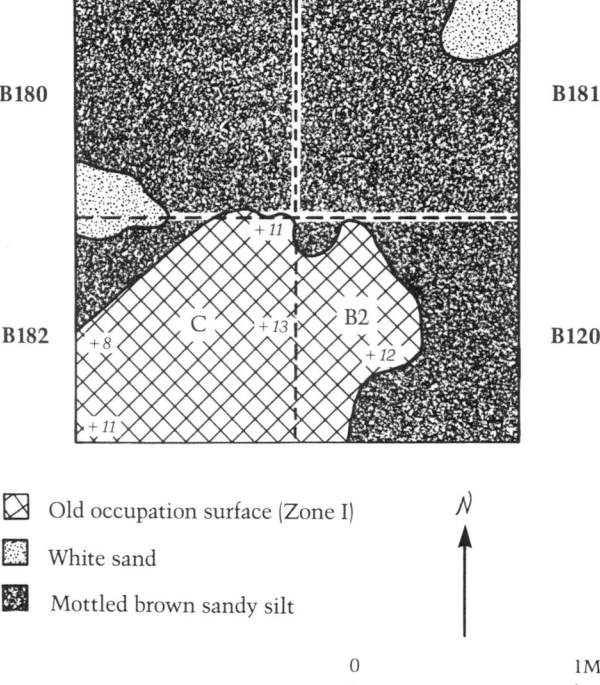

Figure 110. Old occupation surface at location III.2, Trudeau. View from the southeast, and plan of excavations.

Upon completion of the excavation of the disturbed burial pit, B120 was taken down farther to examine a deep radar signal. At a depth of 45 cm below the present ground surface an in situ burned occupation surface was uncovered (fig. 110). In order to expose a larger portion of this old surface, excavations were expanded to the north and west (figs. 106, 111), and three additional 1-m² units were opened up (B180–182). The plow zone was removed as level A, while the B level was an arbitrary unit varying between 20 and 25 cm. With the completion of the latter level all three squares were at a depth of 25 cm above datum. The burned occupation surface extended only into B182; its overall configuration is depicted in figure 110. The fire that burned the surface was probably natural in origin since there was no evidence of structural remains. Cultural artifacts, however, were found lying on this surface. The

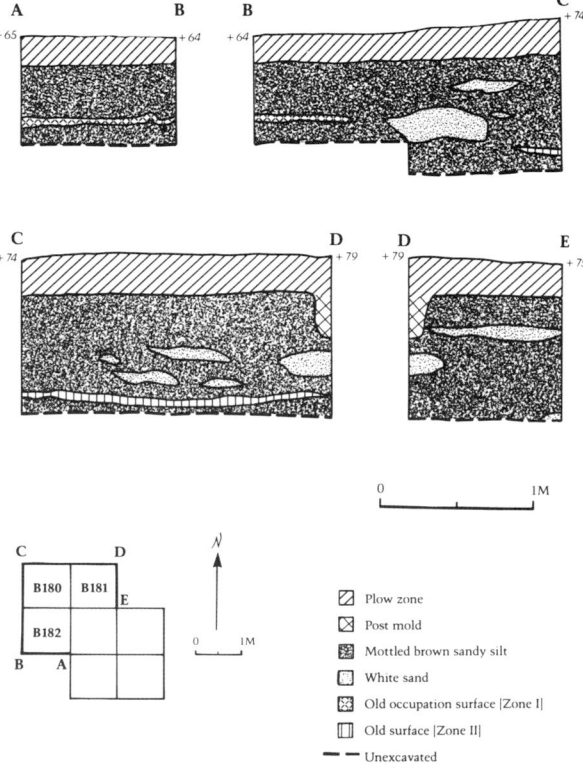

Figure 111. Stratification at location III.2, Trudeau.

Table 21. Aboriginal and European artifacts from the plow zone at location III.3, Trudeau.

ABORIGINAL		EUROPEAN	
Pottery:		*Earthenware:*	
		Faience	
Winterville Incised, *var. Tunica*	5	White	1
Barton Incised, *var. Trudeau*	2	Blue-and-white	1
Unclassified incised (Pocahontas)	4	Unclassified	1
Mississippi Plain, *var. Pocahontas*	52	Majolica	
		White	1
Owens Punctated, *var. unspecified*	1	Lead-glazed	
Mississippi Plain, *var. unspecified*	1	Type A	7
		Type B	16
Fatherland Incised, *var. Bayou Goula* (fig. 120d)	1	Type C	3
Fatherland Incised, *var. Nancy*	1	Type D	6
Fatherland Incised, *var. Snyders Bluff*	2	Type E	1
		Type F	3
Fatherland Incised, *var. Fatherland*	7	Type unspecified	2
Fatherland Incised, *var. unspecified*	16	Unglazed	4
Maddox Engraved, *var. unspecified*	1		
Unclassified incised (St. Catherine)	5	*Stoneware:*	
Chicot Red, *var. Grand Village*	1		
Addis Plain, *var. St. Catherine*	16	Bellarmine	2
		Grès (fig. 122i)	1
Leland Incised, *var. unspecified*	3		
Addis Plain, *var. Feliciana*	15	*Glass:*	
Addis Plain, *var. Skillikalia*	7		
Addis Plain, *var. unspecified*	192	Clear	2
		Olive green	18
Mazique Incised, *var. Kings Point*	1	Light blue-green	5
Mazique Incised, *var. unspecified*	1	Beads	
Pontchartrain Check Stamped, *var. Pontchartrain*	3	IIA7	2
Unclassified incised (Vicksburg)	1	IIIA1	2
Baytown Plain, *var. Vicksburg*	52		
		Iron:	
Baytown Plain, *var. Valley Park*	7		
Baytown Plain, *var. unspecified*	1	Wrought nails	
		Type unspecified	3
Daub:	67	Knife blade fragments	2
		Miscellaneous	137
Lithics:			
		Lead:	
Unutilized chert flakes/pieces/pebbles	150		
Ground quartzite	1	Miscellaneous	5
Hematite	2		
		Copper/brass:	
Organics:			
		Miscellaneous	2
Calcined mammal bones	44		
Charcoal	9	*Gun parts/munitions:*	
		Gunflint flakes	4

too was probably the result of a local fire, but in this case cultural remains were not found lying on the surface. Sand deposits associated with these surfaces probably were responsible for triggering the radar.

Location III.3 consisted of a 1- × -3-m trench (see fig. 106). Each of the 1-m² units was divided in half to fa-

cilitate correlation of archaeological discoveries with radar signals. Three levels were removed: the plow zone (A), a 10-cm arbitrary level (B), and a 15-cm arbitrary level (C). Artifacts were confined essentially to the plow zone (table 21). No features were observed, so no radar correlations were made.

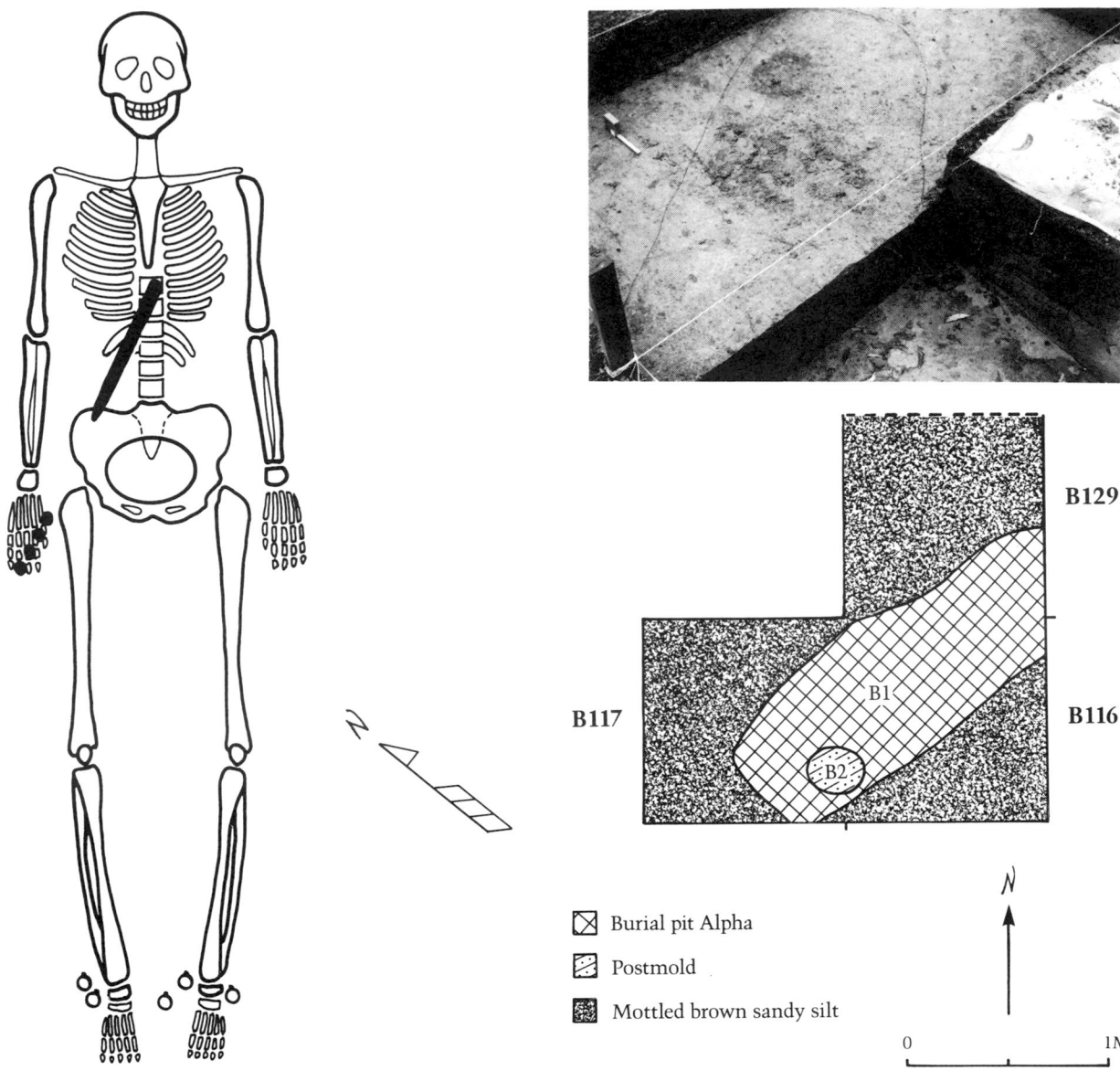

Figure 112. Burial Alpha at location III.4, Trudeau. View of burial pit from the northeast, and plan of excavations showing pit and burial.

Features were present, however, in location III.4 (see fig. 106). At the base of the plow zone (level A) in B127 two post molds were encountered. In B128 and B129 the plow zone was removed in two levels (A and B); at the base of the plow zone against the west wall of B129 a post mold appeared. In the southeastern corner of this same square a rather extensive dark gray stain was observed. Following the excavation of three 15-cm arbitrary levels, it became apparent that the stain was actually an undisturbed burial pit (designated burial Alpha). Two additional units (B116 and B117) were opened up to isolate this feature. At the base of the plow zone the burial pit once again stood out in sharp contrast to the surrounding soil (fig. 112). A large post mold, 25 cm in diameter, protruded into the southwestern end of this pit to a depth of 15 cm. Tables 22 and 23 present the artifactual contents of the plow zone and of the burial Alpha grave pit fill.

The grave turned out to be approximately 50 cm deep. Burial Alpha was in an extended supine position, with feet to the southwest and head to the northeast (fig. 112). The condition of the skeletal remains ranged from poor to moderately good. There seems to have been an object, perhaps a shroud, beneath the left chest and shoulder area, as the bones in this region were at a significantly higher elevation than those of the right side of the upper torso. As a result, pressure on the jaw broke it into three pieces; otherwise, the skull was relatively intact. All the teeth had erupted, but the degree of wear on the molars suggests that the burial was a young adult. Although the cranium exhibited rather gracile features, the pelvis was too narrow for a female. A height of 167 cm also seems to be more consistent with a male.

Table 22. Aboriginal and European artifacts from the plow zone at location III.4, Trudeau.

ABORIGINAL		EUROPEAN	
Pottery:		*Earthenware:*	
Winterville Incised, *var. Tunica*	4	Faience	
Mississippi Plain, *var. Pocahontas*	50	White	2
		Blue-and-white	4
Mississippi Plain, *var. Montfort*	8	Brown	2
Mississippi Plain, *var. unspecified*	2	Unclassified	1
Cracker Road Incised, *var. Cracker Road*	1	Lead-glazed	
		Type A	1
Fatherland Incised, *var. Bayou Goula*	1	Type B	8
Fatherland Incised, *var. Nancy*	1	Type C	9
Fatherland Incised, *var. Snyders Bluff*	1	Type D	5
Fatherland Incised, *var. Fatherland*	5	Type E	2
Fatherland Incised, *var. unspecified*	14	Type F	3
Maddox Engraved, *var. unspecified*	1	Type unspecified	3
Unclassified incised (St. Catherine)	5	Unglazed	4
Chicot Red, *var. Grand Village*	3		
Addis Plain, *var. St. Catherine*	28	*Stoneware:*	
Addis Plain, *var. Feliciana*	19	Bellarmine (fig. 122j)	2
Addis Plain, *var. Skillikalia*	17		
Addis Plain, *var. unspecified*	197	*Glass:*	
Anna Incised, *var. Australia* (fig. 120h)	1	Clear	1
Plaquemine Brushed, *var. Plaquemine*	1	Olive green	25
		Light blue-green	10
Coles Creek Incised, *var. Mott* (fig. 120l)	1	Bead	
Coles Creek Incised, *var. unspecified*	2	IIA7	1
Pontchartrain Check Stamped, *var. Pontchartrain*	2		
Baytown Plain, *var. Vicksburg*	44	*Iron:*	
Baytown Plain, *var. Valley Park*	8	Wrought nails	
Baytown Plain, *var. unspecified*	4	Type unspecified	3
		Miscellaneous	87
Daub:	44		
		Lead:	
Lithics:		Miscellaneous	3
Utilized chert flake	1		
Unutilized chert flakes/pieces/pebbles	147	*Copper:*	
Ground stone	4	Miscellaneous	1
Hematite	2		
Limonite	1	*Brass:*	
		Button (fig. 122l)	1
Organics:			
Calcined mammal bone	39	*Gun parts/munitions:*	
		Gunflint (fig. 122z)	1
		Gunflint flakes	3

Burial Alpha had five large Flushloop bells (2.3 cm in diameter) at the ankles: three around the left ankle, and two around the right. The bells had been attached by iron wire to thongs that were then wrapped around the ankles. Apparently these thongs were red, as a red pigment occurred on portions of the bone that came into contact with them. Fragments of vermilion were observed around the feet, lower legs, pelvis, hands, and head. A gray-and-white banded stain extended for approximately 10 cm around the entire skeleton, possibly indicating some sort of wrapping (bark?). At least four musket balls (18–19 mm in diameter) were placed in a

Table 23. Aboriginal and European artifacts from the fill of the grave pit above burial Alpha at location III.4, Trudeau.

ABORIGINAL

Pottery:

Mississippi Plain, *var. Pocahontas*	3
Fatherland Incised, *var. unspecified*	1
Addis Plain, *var. St. Catherine*	1
Addis Plain, *var. Feliciana*	1
Addis Plain, *var. unspecified*	7
Baytown Plain, *var. Vicksburg*	2
Daub:	6

Lithics:

Unutilized chert flakes/pieces/pebbles	5
Hematite	1

Organics:

Calcined mammal bone	19
Charcoal	2

EUROPEAN

Glass:

Bead	
IVB3	1

Iron:

Miscellaneous	2

Gun parts/munitions:

Lead shot	1

straight line running diagonally across the right hand. On the same line was a large case knife, which had been put on the individual's abdomen; it was 24 cm long, 3 cm wide, and had two rivets for holding a wooden handle. In accordance with a request from the Tunica-Biloxi tribe, we did not remove any of the above materials. Following analysis in the field, this burial was left in situ and reinterred.

Location III.5 was excavated to test radar signals—or the lack thereof. We obtained no signals whatsoever in the area designated B190 (see fig. 106), so this 1-m² unit served as a control unit. In B191–193, however, we expected to find a major change in soil strata at a depth of about 75 cm below ground surface. The archaeological findings correlated well with the radar: the signals recorded in B191–193 were caused by a complex zone of sand and gravel. The stratigraphy for location III.5 is illustrated in figures 113 and 114. Beneath the plow zone, which ranged between 8 and 24 cm thick, was a deposit of mottled gray and brown silt. This deposit was about 15 cm thick in B192, expanding to approx-

imately 40 cm thick in B190. Pockets of dark brown organic soil occurred throughout this layer, and an unusual dark gray silt with high organic content occurred beneath the brown silt. Although the dark gray silt layer maintained a constant thickness (15–20 cm) throughout the location III.5 units, it was barely visible in B193.

This portion of location III was excavated using a combination of natural and arbitrary levels. As at location II, we attempted to uncover strata as they were originally laid down, but this was not always possible. Cultural materials occurred most frequently in the plow zone, but some objects were recovered in underlying deposits (tables 24–25). The presence of a few sherds of pottery in the dark gray silt layer suggests it was indeed a cultural feature. Overall, the layers appeared to be undisturbed, but the discovery of pieces of recent glass in the B191/192C and B192F levels is a puzzle for which we have no solution. Large features were not encountered in location III.5, and only two post molds were observed: one at the base of the B level in B192 was 1i cm in diameter and attained a depth of 14 cm; one at the base of the plow zone in B190 was 10 cm in diameter and extended 6 cm into the B level. Otherwise, as predicted by the SIR survey, B190 displayed a notable lack of cultural or geological disturbance; in this, it was the "cleanest" of all the 1981 excavations.

To conclude, then, location III received the most extensive excavation during the 1981 season, and it accordingly provided the greatest range of archaeological information. In addition to a fine assemblage of artifacts from the historic mid-eighteenth-century Tunica occupation (see fig. 122), we found a modest representation of the Coles Creek component and the only in situ evidence of an even earlier Baytown context. Preservation of the Baytown context by Mississippi alluvial

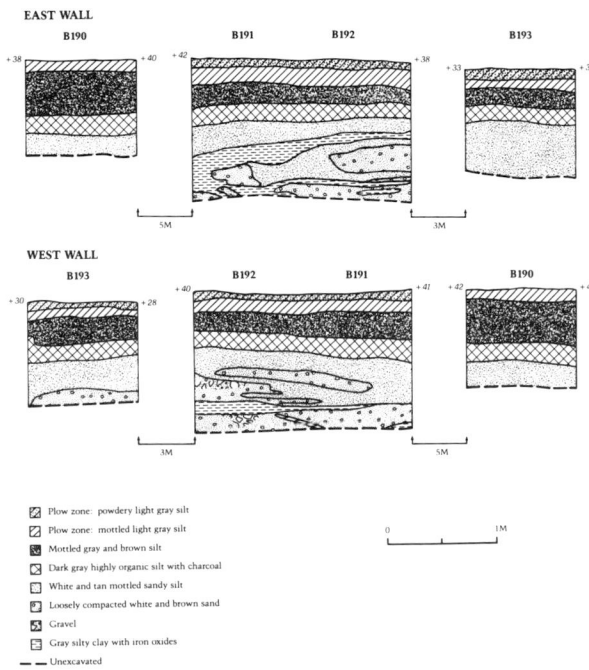

Figure 113. Stratification at location III.5, Trudeau.

Table 24. Aboriginal and European artifacts from the plow zone and underlying features at location III.5, Trudeau.

ABORIGINAL		Lithics:	
Pottery:		Unutilized chert flakes/pieces/pebbles	106
		Hematite	1
Unclassified incised (Pocahontas)	1		
Mississippi Plain, *var. Pocahontas*	36	*Organics:*	
Mississippi Plain, *var. Montfort*	1	Calcined mammal bone	4
Fatherland Incised, *var. Nancy*	1	EUROPEAN	
Fatherland Incised, *var. Fatherland*	3		
Fatherland Incised, *var. unspecified*	6	*Earthenware:*	
Chicot Red, *var. Grand Village*	4	Faience	
Addis Plain, *var. St. Catherine*	15	White	2
Leland Incised, *var. unspecified*	2	Blue-and-white	2
		Brown	3
Addis Plain, *var. Feliciana*	8	Lead-glazed	
Addis Plain, *var. Skillikalia*	9	Type B	9
Addis Plain, *var. unspecified*	171	Type C	8
		Type D	7
Coles Creek Incised, *var. Mott*	1	Type E	2
Coles Creek Incised, *var. unspecified*	1	Type F	1
Pontchartrain Check Stamped, *var. Pontchartrain*	1	Type unspecified	2
Baytown Plain, *var. Vicksburg*	36	Unglazed	10
		Kaolin pipe bowl	1
Baytown Plain, *var. Valley Park*	5		
		Glass:	
Daub:	19		
		Olive green	27
		Light blue-green	5
		Beads	
		IIA7	1
		IIIA1	1
		Iron:	
		Kettle fragment	1
		Wrought nail	
		Type unspecified	1
		Miscellaneous	82
		Copper:	
		Miscellaneous	2

Figure 114. South wall of excavation unit B191 at location III.5, Trudeau.

Table 25. Aboriginal artifacts from the prehistoric cultural stratum at location III.5, Trudeau.

Pottery:

Baytown Plain, *var. Vicksburg*	2

Lithics:

Unutilized chert pebbles	5

deposits attests to the nearby presence of the river after that occupation. By the time of the Coles Creek occupation, however, the river had moved away, and it did not return until recent times.

The only significant features dating to the historic period were a number of post molds, which unfortunately could not be connected into any meaningful patterns, and the two burials. Burial Alpha was the undisturbed interment of a young adult (probably male). It was typical in being a supine inhumation oriented with head to the northeast; it was unusual, however, in the relative paucity of grave goods. Burial Delta, on the other hand, must have been lavishly accompanied by grave furniture: even though it had been looted, many beads and other artifacts were left behind. Despite the disturbance, it could be determined that burial Delta also had been the supine inhumation of an adult oriented to the northeast.

The SIR survey did not identify either of the burial features. It did record the old Baytown occupation surface, but probably because it was composed of pockets of pure sand, in contrast to the other alluvial deposits. The radar also was successful in recognizing culturally undisturbed and geologically uniform subsurface conditions, so that it seems at least to have some capability for developing negative evidence. There is an indication that it may have responded to the numerous recent iron artifacts in the area, but positive correlations were not consistently replicated.

LOCATION IV

Location IV lay beneath the former tenant house, and because it had been protected by that structure it was known to have been undisturbed by the activities of Leonard Charrier. The 1980 SIR survey further excited our expectations of finding undisturbed features by recording large, deep anomalies that exhibited considerable detail in the printouts of the signals (Brain 1980, fig. 31). Other anomalies were also recorded in the overburden above the features, but they were interpreted as recent trash from the tenant house. Nevertheless, it was anticipated that they would provide a test of different classes of artifact signals.

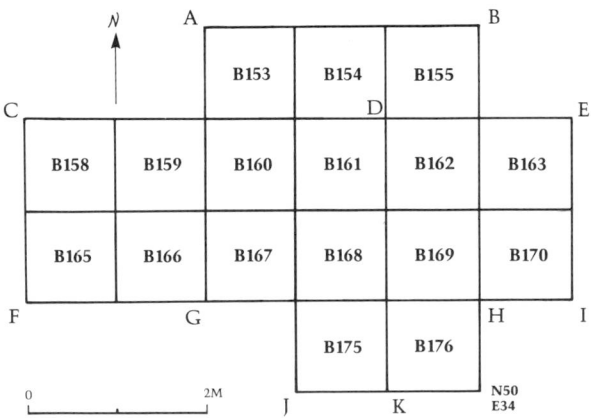

Figure 115. Plan of excavations at location IV, the Trudeau site.

a

b

Figure 116. Views of location IV excavations at Trudeau. a, general overview from the northeast; b, excavation techniques.

Because we hoped to find an undisturbed eighteenth-century occupation surface, the entire tenant house site was gridded at 1-m intervals. Ultimately, seventeen contiguous 1-m² units (with numerical designations between B153 and B176) were excavated, opening a horizontal area with maximum dimensions of 6 m east-west and 4 m north-south (figs. 115–116). The excavation levels were arbitrary, although they conformed fairly closely to natural layers.

The stratification at location IV is depicted in figure 117. Topsoil consisted of a thin lens of light gray-brown silty loam that contained varying quantities of recent tenant house trash (iron, glass, brick, mortar, and charcoal) as well as aboriginal artifacts (table 26). The recent debris was particularly abundant in the northern portion of the excavations. This layer was 5–20 cm thick, being thickest along the southern walls. Beneath the topsoil was an old plow zone that clearly predated the tenant house and probably was of nineteenth-century vintage. The plow zone showed up most clearly directly beneath the tenant house. As illustrated in the south wall sections (fig. 117), the area between I and H represents the ground east of the house; everything west of H was beneath the house. The plow zone in this area attained a maximum thickness of 15 cm.

Table 26. Aboriginal and European artifacts from the plow zone at location IV, Trudeau.

ABORIGINAL

Pottery:

Winterville Incised, *var. Tunica*	5
Barton Incised, *var. Trudeau* (fig. 120c)	1
Unclassified incised (Pocahontas)	2
Mississippi Plain, *var. Pocahontas*	18
Fatherland Incised, *var. Bayou Goula*	1
Fatherland Incised, *var. Nancy*	1
Maddox Engraved, *var. unspecified* (fig. 120g)	1
Unclassified incised (St. Catherine)	1
Addis Plain, *var. St. Catherine*	3
Addis Plain, *var. Feliciana*	2
Addis Plain, *var. Skillikalia*	1
Addis Plain, *var. unspecified*	40
Plaquemine Brushed, *var. Plaquemine* (fig. 120i)	3
Pontchartrain Check Stamped, *var. Pontchartrain*	1
Unclassified incised (Vicksburg)	1
Baytown Plain, *var. Vicksburg*	5
Baytown Plain, *var. Valley Park*	1
Baytown Plain, *var. unspecified*	2

Daub: 13

Lithics:

Unutilized chert flakes/pieces	66

Organics:

Conch shell bead (fig. 120r)	1

EUROPEAN

Earthenware:

Faience	
White	1
Blue-and-white	1
Lead-glazed	
Type B	4

Stoneware:

Bellarmine	1

Glass:

Olive green	9
Light blue-green	1

Gun parts/munitions:

Brass ferrule	1
Gunflint	1
Lead musket ball	1
Lead sprue	1

Table 27. Aboriginal and European artifacts from the midden zone at location IV, Trudeau.

ABORIGINAL

Pottery:

Mississippi Plain, *var. Pocahontas*	4
Unclassified incised/punctated (St. Catherine)	2
Addis Plain, *var. St. Catherine*	1
Addis Plain, *var. Skillikalia*	8
Addis Plain, *var. unspecified*	192
Plaquemine Brushed, *var. Plaquemine*	12
Avoyelles Punctated, *var. Dupree*	1
Coles Creek Incised, *var. Mott*	1
Pontchartrain Check Stamped, *var. Pontchartrain* (fig. 120j)	16
Baytown Plain, *var. Vicksburg*	18
Baytown Plain, *var. Valley Park*	10
Baytown Plain, *var. unspecified*	9

Daub: 15

Lithics:

Utilized chert flake	1
Unutilized chert flakes/pieces	57
Hematite	1
Limonite	4

Organics:

Calcined mammal bone	3
Garfish scale	1
Charcoal	8

EUROPEAN

Iron:

Wrought nail	
Type unspecified	1
Miscellaneous	5

A dark gray silt midden layer occurred beneath the old plow zone. This layer was thickest in the northern part of the excavations and thinned out to the south. In certain places it was as much as 45 cm thick. Underlying the midden was a series of culturally sterile layers of silt, sand, and clay. As revealed in the east wall sections (fig. 117), these soils achieved the highest complexity of interbedding in B169 (fig. 118).

A number of features appeared at the base of the A levels (fig. 119). Most of them related to the tenant house occupation. Feature B153B1 consisted of a very shallow spill of water-sorted beige and tan silt. This same soil constituted the drip line (B160B3) that formed along the eastern edge of the tenant house. This line can also be seen in the wall sections along the southern edge of B169 and the western edge of B153 (fig. 117).

NORTH WALLS

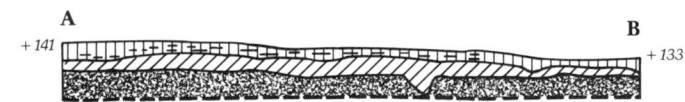

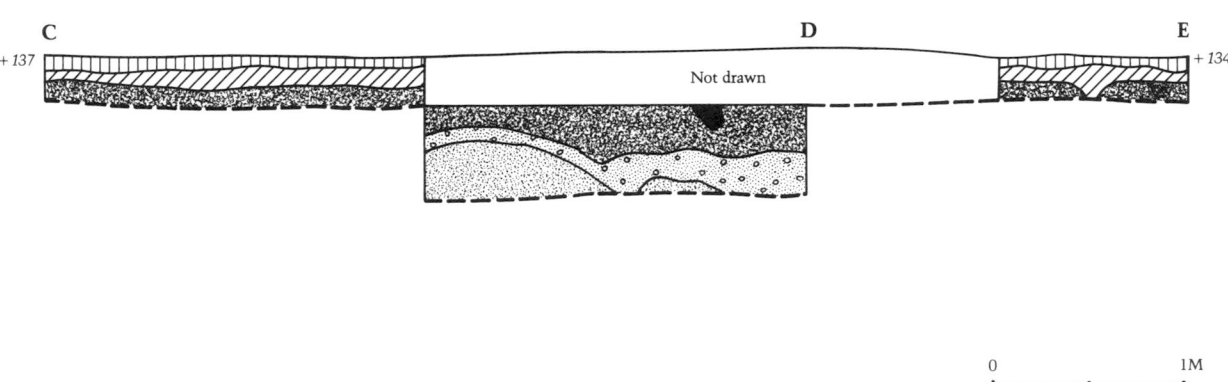

0   1M

SOUTH WALLS

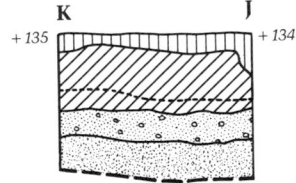

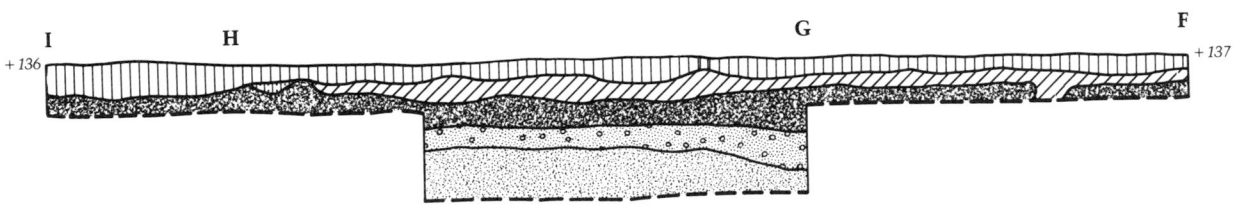

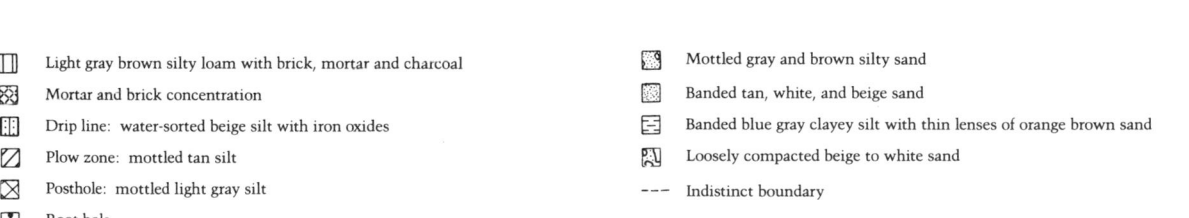

⊞ Light gray brown silty loam with brick, mortar and charcoal	▦	Mottled gray and brown silty sand
▨ Mortar and brick concentration	▦	Banded tan, white, and beige sand
⊞ Drip line: water-sorted beige silt with iron oxides	⊟	Banded blue gray clayey silt with thin lenses of orange brown sand
▨ Plow zone: mottled tan silt	▨	Loosely compacted beige to white sand
⊠ Posthole: mottled light gray silt	---	Indistinct boundary
▨ Root hole	▬ ▬	Unexcavated
▨ Midden: dark gray silt		

Figure 117. Stratification at location IV, Trudeau.

EAST WALLS

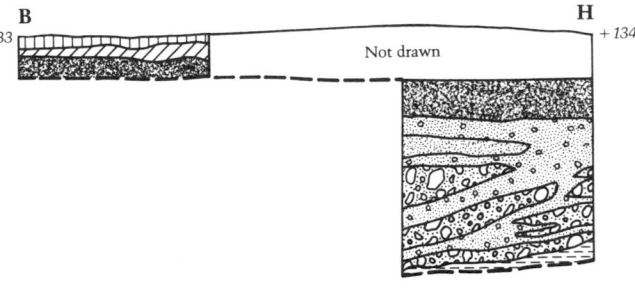

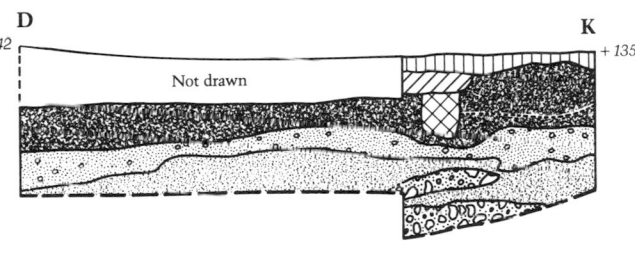

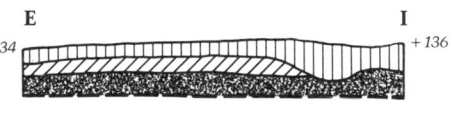

WEST WALLS

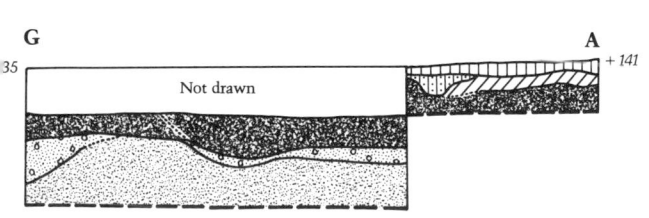

Figure 117 (continued).

Structural members of the house itself are marked by a rotted wooden post (B161B1); a very deep posthole, square in shape at its base (B168B1/C1/D1); and two square postholes (B1/C1) in B176 that were aligned with the drip line. The shallow amorphous stain (B162B2) of mottled sand and silt contained charcoal, mortar, and recent trash, and was clearly associated with the rotten post mentioned above. An unexcavated post mold (B1) in B155 also may have been of recent origin.

Three features appear to have been associated with the Tunica occupation. B160B1, a circular feature approximately 40 cm in diameter, appeared within the A level as a dark gray silt bearing a heavy concentration of calcined bone, daub, and charcoal, which suggests that it may have been a hearth. Only a small portion of this feature continued below the base of the A level. It was underlain by a thin lens of tan silt, which was followed by the midden zone—but even that produced some small bits of burned bone, a carbonized seed, and at least one sherd of Winterville Incised, *var. Tunica*. The crescent-shaped stain (B160B2) was also heavily laden with charcoal, bone, and daub, and contained a piece of burned faience. This feature was approximately 25 cm long at the base of the A level, but at the bottom of the B level it took on a more regular shape, circular and about 20 cm in diameter. It apparently was some sort of a pit. One post mold (B163B1) also may have related to the Tunica occupation, but it was observed only at the base of the B level (fig. 119). It, too, was 20 cm in diameter.

In all units but B176 the B levels were 10 cm thick. These levels were placed entirely within the dark gray silt midden, a cultural layer we hoped was of Tunica origin. The frequent occurrence of Pontchartrain Check Stamped and other Coles Creek pottery, however, thwarted our hopes (fig. 120j–l; table 27). The deposition clearly was the product of Coles Creek period peoples, and the few historic materials were undoubtedly intruded. This rich dark cultural layer yielded few material remains. The only structural features relating to the Coles Creek occupation were three small post molds: two found in the D level of B161, and one in the D level of B175.

Figure 118. East wall of excavation unit B169 at location IV, Trudeau.

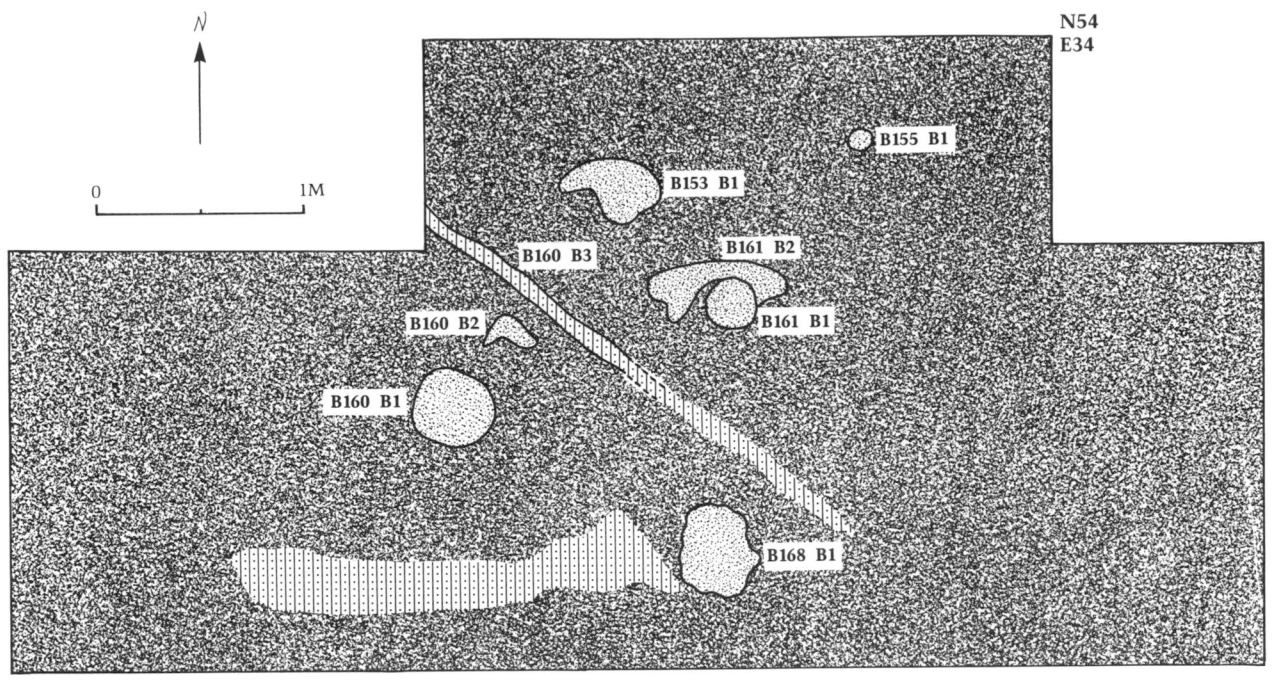

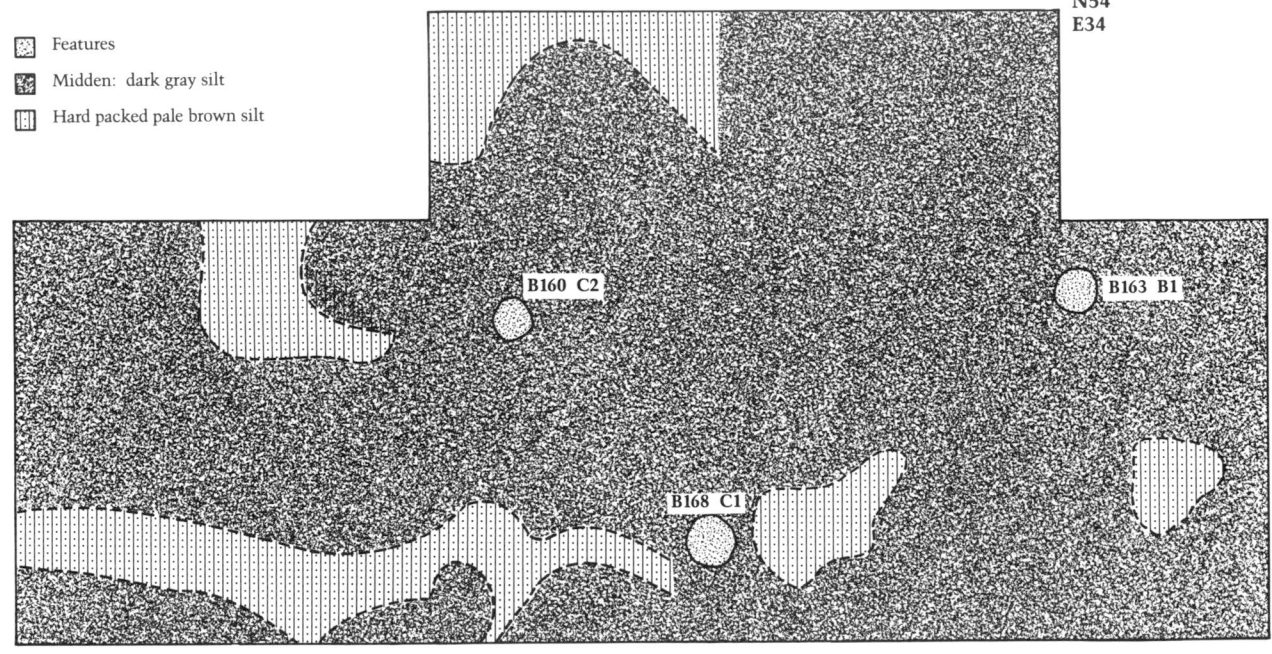

Figure 119. Plans of features at base of A and B levels at location IV, Trudeau.

Subsequent levels removed in location IV were 10 cm (C and D) and 25 cm (E) thick, but these excavations were confined solely to units B160, B161, B167, B168, and B169. The C levels consisted of half midden zone and half brown silty sand zone. The latter deposit was culturally sterile, as were all underlying deposits. We continued to excavate B168 and B169 below the E level, as the strongest radar readings were located in the area marked by these two units. The attempt was made to follow natural levels, but because the lenses of clay and

sand were so intricately interbedded, it was difficult to peel back the layers as they were originally laid down. These two units were terminated at the +15 cm level, or 1.2 m below the present ground surface. Units B175 and B176 were excavated somewhat differently, but once again a combination of arbitrary and natural levels was used.

The excavation of location IV yielded good information concerning the Coles Creek and tenant house occupations at the site. Aside from providing some ar-

Figure 120. Aboriginal artifacts from locations I–VI at Trudeau. a–b, Winterville Incised, *var. Tunica*; c, Barton Incised, *var. Trudeau*; d, Fatherland Incised, *var. Bayou Goula*; e, Fatherland Incised, *var. Fatherland*; f, Fatherland Incised, *var. Nancy*; g, Maddox Engraved, *var. unspecified*; h, Anna Incised, *var. Australia*; i, Plaquemine Brushed, *var. Plaquemine*; j, Pontchartrain Check Stamped, *var. Pontchartrain*; k, Mazique Incised, *var. Kings Point*; l, Coles Creek Incised, *var. Mott*; m, Mulberry Creek Cord Marked, *var. unspecified*; n, native gunflint of chert; o–p, Bayogoula Fishtailed, *var. Bayogoula* points; q, Mississippi Triangular, *var. unspecified* point; r, conch shell bead. (1:1)

tifactual data, however, the investigations proved disappointing as far as the Tunica are concerned. It is now clear that the tenant house protected not the Tunica but the Coles Creek occupation. The Tunica occupation surface in this area was almost entirely destroyed in the last century as a result of plowing, and there were no major subsurface Tunica features. The deep radar anomalies were determined to be geologic in origin, once again representing interbedded lenses of various kinds of sand. The suspected objects near the surface were found to be electronic "bugs": each was carefully investigated, and in no case was a definite correlation established.

LOCATION V

A 5-m-long trench in location V (fig. 121) was dug to obtain a cross section of a rather large cigar-shaped anomaly, which according to our SIR survey ran across the northeastern part of the plaza (see fig. 91). Its top was supposed to be situated 60 cm below the present ground surface, and for this reason we expected the

deposit to be natural in origin. However, a number of other anomalies detected at shallower depths were thought to be cultural.

Excavations were conducted using a combination of arbitrary and natural levels. Two levels (A and B) were used to get down to the base of the plow zone in squares B140 and B141, but in the remaining units the plow zone was removed as a single natural level (A). Most of the cultural material was found in the plow zone (table 28), and ten features appeared at the base of the plow zone (fig. 121). Only one of these could be correlated reasonably with the radar signals, and even then the identification was only tentative. Four of the features were aboriginal post molds (table 29), while three other post molds seem to have been recent. B140B1 was comprised of dark black midden soil bearing many fragments of bone and pottery. It was about 13 cm thick. The presence of plow zone soil beneath this feature (fig. 121, north wall) indicates this rich soil was a secondary deposit. It may have been backdirt from a nearby Charrier pit. Feature B140B2/B141B2 also appears to have

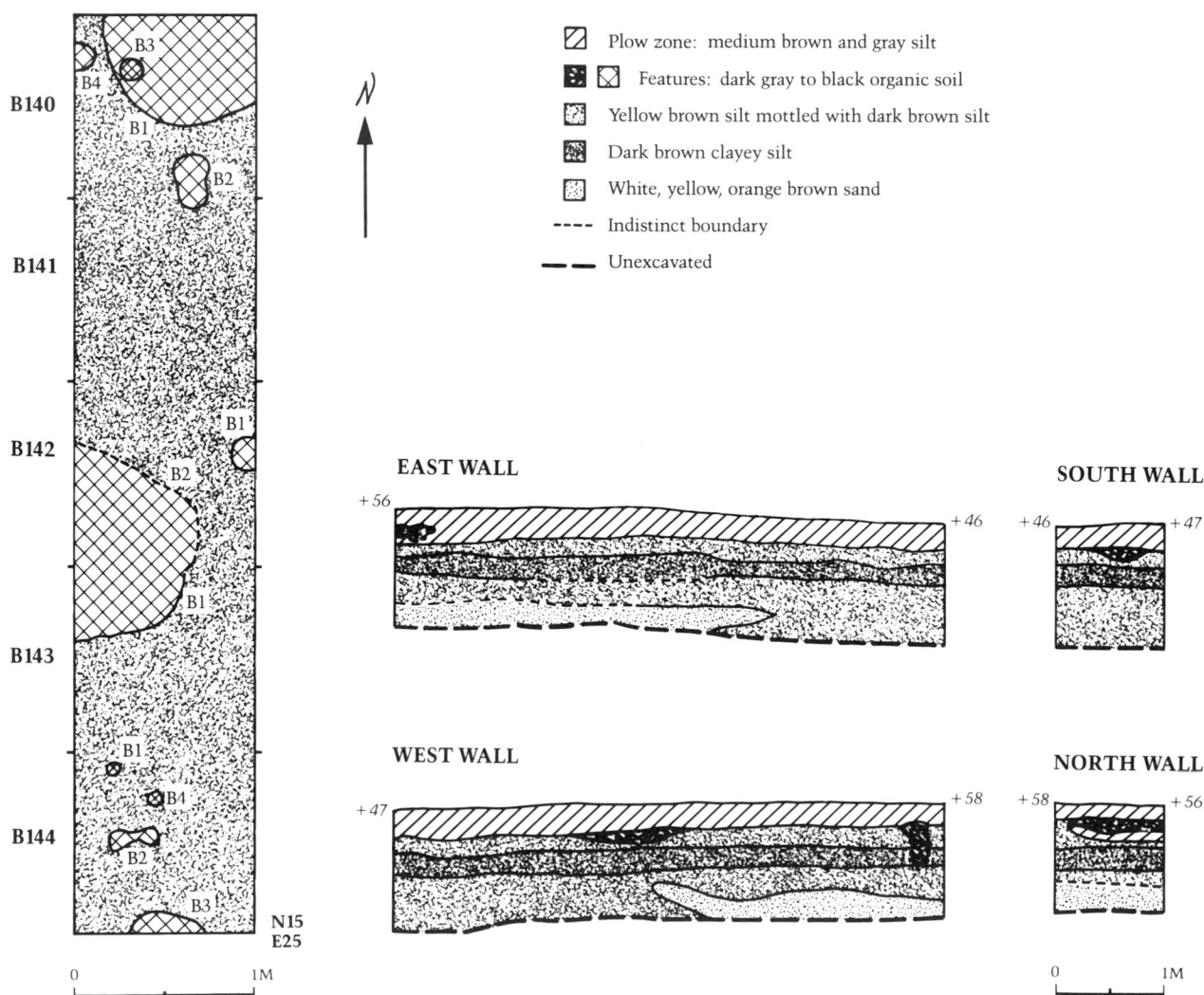

Figure 121. Plan of excavations, stratification, and features at location V, the Trudeau site.

Table 28. Aboriginal and European artifacts from the plow zone and underlying features at location V, Trudeau.

ABORIGINAL		EUROPEAN	
Pottery:		*Earthenware:*	
Winterville Incised, *var. Tunica*	4	Faience	
Barton Incised, *var. Trudeau*	2	White	4
Unclassified incised (Pocahontas)	7	Green-and-white	2
Mississippi Plain, *var. Pocahontas*	139	Brown	3
Mississippi Plain, *var. Montfort*	6	Lead-glazed	
Mississippi Plain, *var. unspecified*	1	Type A	5
		Type B	13
Fatherland Incised, *var. Bayou Goula*	1	Type C	5
Fatherland Incised, *var. Nancy*	2	Type D	5
Fatherland Incised, *var. Snyders Bluff*	2	Type E	3
		Type F	6
Unclassified engraved (Caddo)	1	Type unspecified	3
Fatherland Incised, *var. Fatherland*	11	Unglazed	6
Fatherland Incised, *var. unspecified*	29	Kaolin pipe fragments	2
Maddox Engraved, *var. unspecified*	4		
Unclassified incised (St. Catherine)	11	*Stoneware:*	
Addis Plain, *var. St. Catherine*	48	Westerwald	1
Leland Incised, *var. unspecified*	3	*Glass:*	
Addis Plain, *var. Feliciana*	28	Clear	3
Addis Plain, *var. Skillikalia*	15	Olive green	38
Addis Plain, *var. unspecified*	281	Light blue-green	13
		Beads	
Avoyelles Punctated, *var. Dupree*	1	IA3	1
Avoyelles Punctated, *var. unspecified*	2	IB2	1
		IIA1	1
Mazique Incised, *var. Kings Point*	3	IIA5	1
Pontchartrain Check Stamped, *var. Pontchartrain*	1	IIA6	3
Unclassified incised (Vicksburg)	1	IIA7	2
Baytown Plain, *var. Vicksburg*	42	IVB3	1
Baytown Plain, *var. Valley Park*	14	WID1	2
Daub:	51	*Iron:*	
Lithics:		Wrought nails	
		Type unspecified	9
Bayogoula Fishtailed, *var. Bayogoula* point (fig. 120o)	1	Miscellaneous	282
Utilized chert flakes/pieces	2	*Copper:*	
Unutilized chert flakes/pieces/pebbles	277	Miscellaneous	3
Ground stone	1	*Brass:*	
Hematite	2	Tinkling cone	1
Limonite	1	Miscellaneous	1
Organics:		*Gun parts/munitions:*	
Bone preserved by copper salts	1	Brass ferrule (fig. 122s)	1
Calcined mammal bone	173	Gunflints (fig. 122cc)	3
Garfish scales	25	Gunflint flakes	6
Charcoal	4	Lead musket ball	1
		Lead pistol balls or large shot (fig. 122y)	2

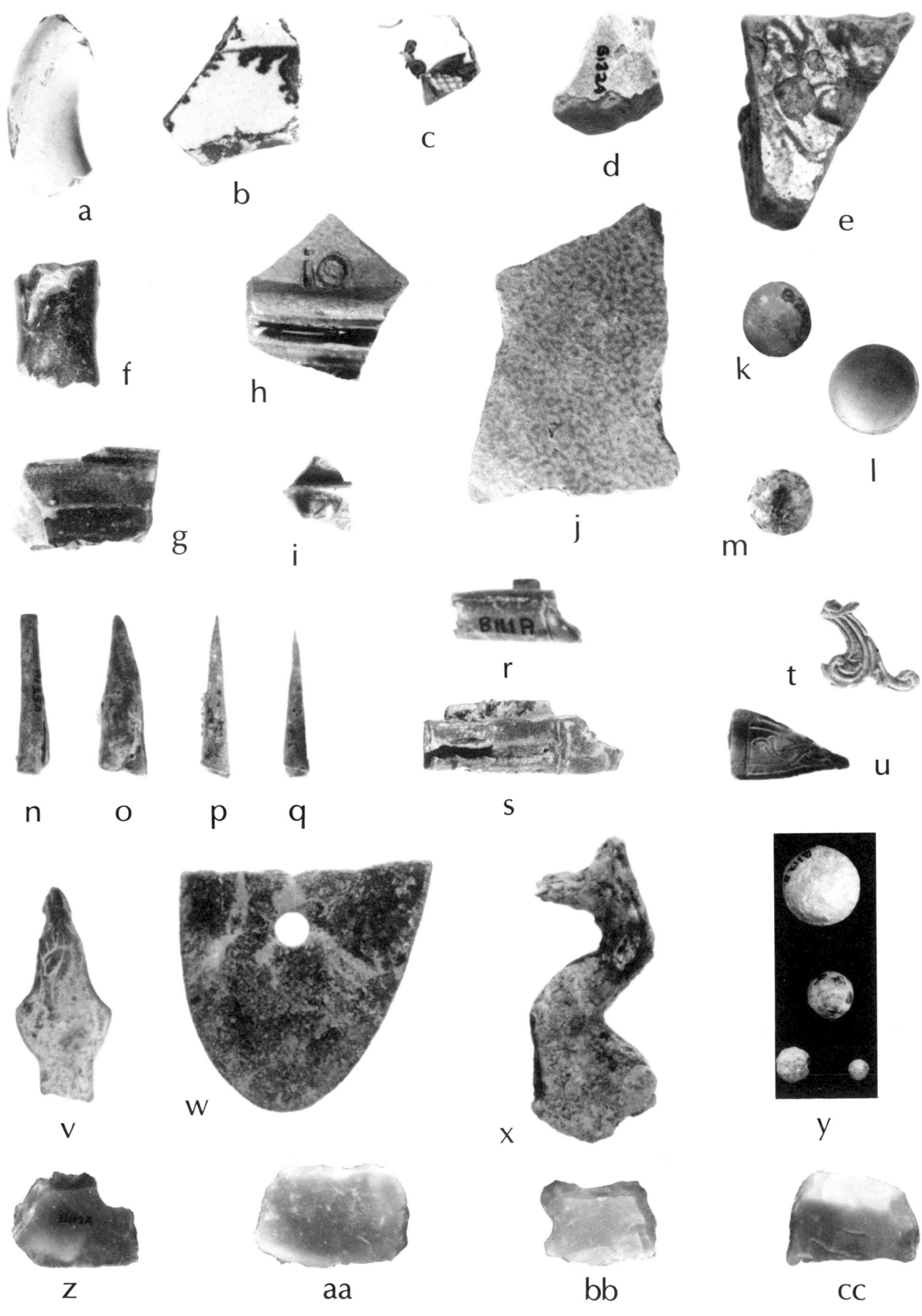

a

b

c

d

e

f

h

j

k

l

m

g

i

n   o   p   q

r

s

t

u

v

w

x

y

z

aa

bb

cc

Table 29. Metrical data on post molds at location V, Trudeau.

Provenience	Approx. Diameter (cm)	Top Elevation (cm)	Bottom Elevation (cm)	Total Length (cm)
B140B4	15	+28	−17	45
B142B1/C1	20	+31	+14	17
B144B1	10.5	+24	+19	5
B144B4/C1	8.5	+23	+5	18

been a recent spill. It contained the same soil as B140B1, but was considerably shallower (by approximately 2 cm). Within it was found a complete turtle carapace, which may have been removed from a burial. A posthole (B140B3) bearing plow zone soil as fill was intrusive within feature B140B1. Its diameter of 13 cm, about the size of a posthole digger, suggests it may have been one of a number of random postholes sunk by us in 1972.

The remaining features clearly were aboriginal. B142B2/B143B1 was either the lower portion of a pit or the remaining part of a midden that was situated deep enough to have survived the effects of plowing (fig. 121, west wall). It contained Coles Creek pottery and a Bayogoula point (fig. 120), suggesting a pre-Tunica date for the original deposition. An hour-glass-shaped stain (B2/C2) in unit B144 turned out to be a small pit. It was 21 cm long at the base of the plow zone and continued down to a depth of about 20 cm. The last feature (B144B3) clearly was a Tunica pit. It was 37 cm in diameter and had a maximum depth of 10 cm (fig. 121, south wall). A large sherd of Mississippi Plain, *var. Pocahontas* was found within it.

After the features had been excavated, the culturally sterile surrounding soil was removed in arbitrary levels until a depth of approximately 60 cm was reached. At this point, a thick layer of loosely compacted sand was encountered in the northern half of the trench (fig. 121). This layer correlated exactly in vertical and horizontal dimensions with the strong radar signal. To verify the correlation an additional 40 cm was excavated, but no other natural or cultural features were observed.

Location V produced important material evidence of the historic Tunica occupation (fig. 122; table 28). Natchezan pottery remains dominant, but the Mississippian types are unusually well represented and the Coles Creek are reduced to a mere showing. Nevertheless, the number and contents of features suggest that this was an important residential locus for both the Coles Creek and Tunica components.

LOCATION VI

Location VI was selected so that we might investigate a single major anomaly initially interpreted as the signal for a burial (Brain 1980, fig. 32). Our experience at other locations, however, had led us to revise our ex-

pectations, so that we anticipated a geological feature (probably another sand pocket) by the time excavations were begun. We originally intended to open up an area equivalent to that excavated in location IV. The investigations were terminated soon after they began, however, due to a request made by the Tunica-Biloxi tribe. As a result, only four 1-m² units were excavated (fig. 123). Despite the abbreviated investigation, these units proved to be quite informative. Of all the locations examined beneath the bluff, location VI was the only one to have a Tunica occupation surface still intact. Below the plow zone was a thick layer of dark brown to black midden that ranged between 20 and 30 cm thick. It contained two sizable trash pits and a post mold. A yellow-brown sandy silt formed the underlying sterile deposits.

All excavations in location VI were done by 10-cm arbitrary levels, but they matched the natural layers fairly closely. Level A was primarily the plow zone, whereas B and C were mainly midden. Level D cut well into the sandy silt layer, but we are confident that the artifacts came out of the midden (table 30).

As usual, most of the features showed up at the base of the plow zone (fig. 123). Unit B202C1/D1 was a large circular trash pit having a north-south diameter of 69 cm and a depth of about 25 cm. It contained a black greasy soil bearing a high density of charcoal and daub. Historic European artifacts and large fragments of Tunica pottery also were found within this feature (figs. 120, 122; table 31). Unit B202C2, another trash pit, consisted of dark brown silt. It too had large fragments of charcoal, bone, and pottery, but it was considerably less rich than B202C1/D1. It had an east-west dimension of 110 cm and a depth varying between 15 and 30 cm. The actual base is uncertain, as this feature graded imperceptibly into the surrounding midden.

The only other feature observed in this area was a post mold (B208E1; fig. 123, south wall), which appeared at the base of the D level, approximately 35 cm below the ground surface. It was 10 cm in diameter and continued down for 15 cm. Two potsherds, one of which is Winterville Incised, *var. Tunica*, were found within it. It is unusual to find a historic post mold buried so deep at Trudeau. This discovery suggests that the southeastern part of the site received the bulk of alluvial deposition in the last two centuries and therefore bears the highest potential for future investigations of the Tunica Indians.

Although the smallest excavation, location VI proved to be very important for establishing the eighteenth-century context. Primary midden and features were found, and they contained artifacts that were unusually well endowed with Tunica diagnostics. Unfortunately, the site's potential could not be fully realized because of the premature closing of the excavations. For this reason, too, the investigation of the radar signals could not be completed and the nature of the anomaly remains conjectural, although it is unlikely to indicate a burial.

◀ **Figure 122.** Eighteenth-century European artifacts from locations I–VI at Trudeau. a, white faience; b–c, blue-and-white faience; d, majolica; e–g, lead-glazed earthenware, Type B; h, Westerwald stoneware; i, Grès stoneware; j, Bellamine stoneware; k–l, brass buttons; m, brass Flushloop bell; n–q, copper and brass cones (tinklers or points); r–s, brass ferrules; t–u, brass side plate fragments; v–w, brass butt plate fragments; x, iron cock from flintlock; y, lead musket balls and shot; z–aa, spall gunflints; bb–cc, blade gunflints. (1:1)

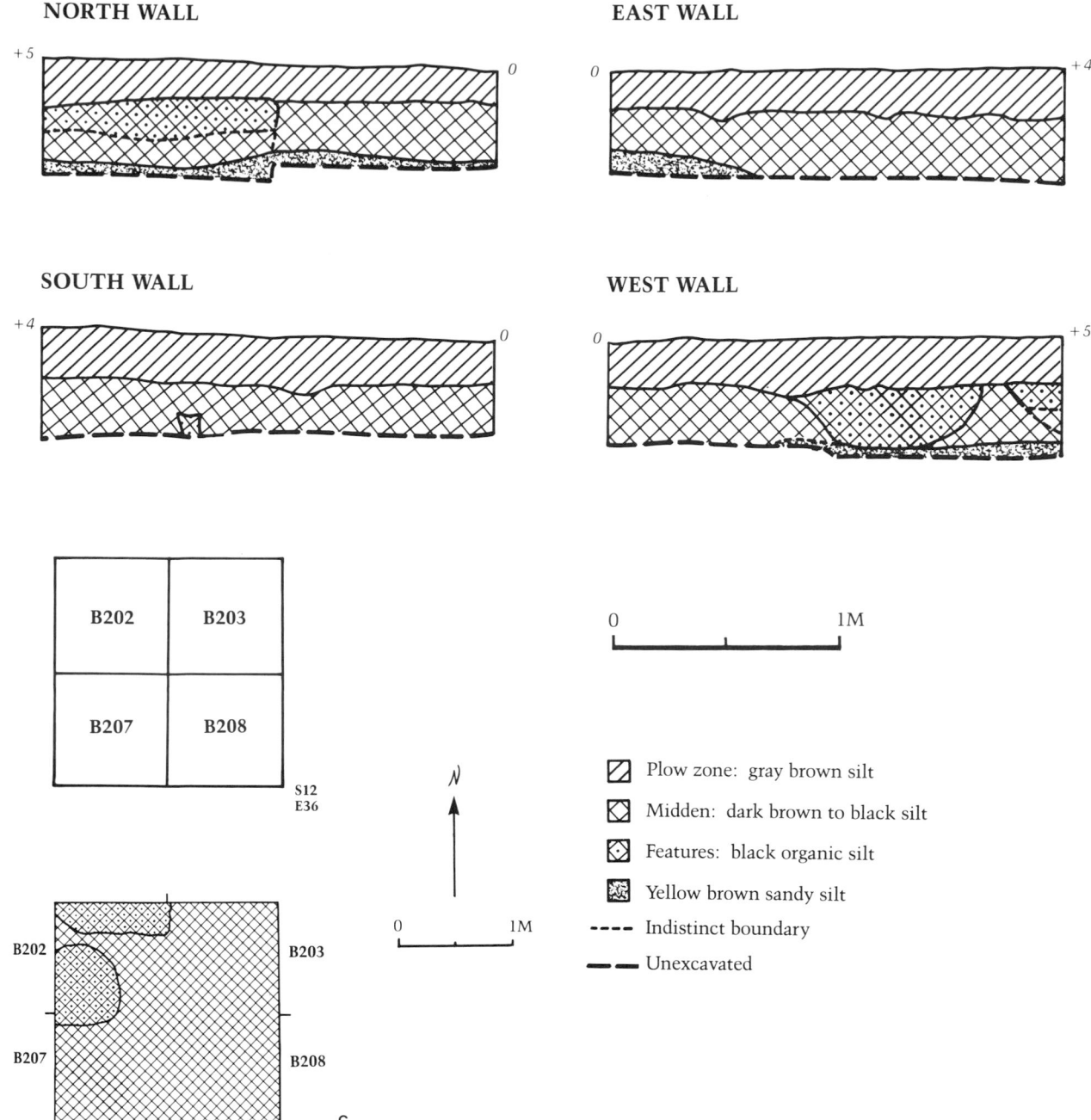

Figure 123. Plan of excavations, stratification, and features at location VI, the Trudeau site.

SUMMARY OF THE 1981 EXCAVATIONS

The 1981 excavations contributed substantially to our knowledge of the culture history of Trudeau and of patterns of site utilization through time, especially during the Tunica occupation. We also learned much about the site's subsurface conditions and its potential for future archaeological investigation.

Perhaps the most important culture-historical result was the unanticipated discovery of a third aboriginal occupation at the site. This occupation, the earliest so far documented, was a component of the Baytown culture (Phillips 1970, fig. 2); artifactual evidence is in-

sufficient to define a phase affiliation. The only intact in situ context confirmed was at location III, although diagnostic Mulberry Creek Cord Marked potsherds were found in later contexts at location VI (table 32). Because of the limited excavation, the nature of this occupation was not determined. The small piece of original ground surface that was uncovered did not display any cultural features and appeared quite natural in formation. Evidence of burning was found, but that need not have had a human origin. It can only be surmised that a small Baytown occupation was located nearby and that our excavations happened to nick the fringe of it.

Table 30. Aboriginal and European artifacts from the midden layer (including the plow zone) at location VI, Trudeau.

ABORIGINAL		EUROPEAN	
Pottery:		*Earthenware:*	
Winterville Incised, *var. Tunica* (fig. 120a–b)	1	Faience	
Unclassified incised (Pocahontas)	3	White	3
Tunican Mode	1	Brown	1
Mississippi Plain, *var. Pocahontas*	61	Majolica	
		White	2
Mississippi Plain, *var. Montfort*	1	Blue-and-white	2
Mississippi Plain, *var. unspecified*	1	Lead-glazed	
		Type A	3
Fatherland Incised, *var. Nancy*	2	Type B	6
Fatherland Incised, *var. Snyders Bluff*	2	Type C	6
Fatherland Incised, *var. Fatherland* (fig. 120e)	4	Type D	4
Fatherland Incised, *var. unspecified*	7	Unglazed	1
Maddox Engraved, *var. unspecified*	3		
Unclassified incised (St. Catherine)	2	*Glass:*	
Chicot Red, *var. Grand Village*	3		
Addis Plain, *var. St. Catherine*	14	Clear	2
		Olive green	16
Leland Incised, *var. unspecified*	1	Light blue-green	7
Addis Plain, *var. Feliciana*	5	Beads	
Addis Plain, *var. Skillikalia*	5	IIA7	1
Addis Plain, *var. unspecified*	111	IIIA1	1
Baytown Plain, *var. Vicksburg*	16	*Iron:*	
Baytown Plain, *var. Valley Park*	5		
		Wrought nails	
Mulberry Creek Cord Marked, *var. unspecified* (fig. 120m)	2	Type I	2
		Type unspecified	8
Baytown Plain, *var. unspecified*	2	Spring	1
		Miscellaneous	42
Daub:	21		
		Copper:	
Lithics:			
		Miscellaneous	1
Unutilized chert pebbles	570		
Hematite	1	*Brass:*	
Organics:		Button (fig. 122k)	1
		Tinkling cone	1
Calcined mammal bone	142		
Human bone	2	*Gun parts/munitions:*	
Charcoal	3		
		Pan from musket lock	1
		Gunflints (fig. 122aa)	2
		Lead splashes	5

Approximately half a millennium elapsed before Trudeau was reoccupied. During this interval, the Mississippi River apparently was in close proximity (Fisk 1944, pl. 22, sheet 13) and a thick blanket of alluvial deposits accumulated on the site. These deposits buried and protected the Baytown encampment and provided a fresh surface for the second known occupation during the Coles Creek period.

The second occupation was a late manifestation of the Coles Creek culture, perhaps a component of the nearby Greenhouse and early Spring Bayou phases (Belmont 1967). This occupation had been recognized during the previous investigations in 1972 and 1980 (Brain 1973, 1980). In fact, the distributions of Coles Creek artifacts found during the surface survey in 1980 (see fig. 79) conformed very closely to the proveniences of

Table 31. Aboriginal and European artifacts from features B202C1/D1, B202C2/D2, and B208E1 at location VI, Trudeau.

ABORIGINAL

Pottery:

Winterville Incised, *var. Tunica*	8
Barton Incised, *var. Trudeau*	2
Unclassified punctated (Pocahontas)	4
Mississippi Plain, *var. Pocahontas*	48
Mississippi Plain, *var. unspecified*[a]	2
Fatherland Incised, *var. Snyders Bluff*	1
Fatherland Incised, *var. Fatherland*	2
Addis Plain, *var. Feliciana*	2
Addis Plain, *var. Skillikalia*	4
Addis Plain, *var. unspecified*	32
Pontchartrain Check Stamped, *var. Pontchartrain*	1
Baytown Plain, *var. Vicksburg*	3
Mulberry Creek Cord Marked, *var. unspecified*	2
Baytown Plain, *var. unspecified*	1

Daub: 12

Lithics:

Unutilized chert flakes/pieces/pebbles	68

Organics:

Calcined human bone	3
Calcined mammal bone	156
Calcined bird bone	3
Calcined fish/turtle bone	12
Charcoal	1

EUROPEAN

Glass:

Clear	1
Olive green	2

Iron:

Miscellaneous	5

Brass:

Tinkling cones (fig. 122p–q)	2

[a]Unformed potter's clay.

Coles Creek pottery in the 1981 excavations (table 32). The only difference was the extension of the Coles Creek occupation toward the base of the bluff, an area that was obscured during the surface survey by the recent tenant house occupation. In fact, the best-preserved Coles Creek context was found beneath the tenant house (location IV). Significant numbers of diagnostic Coles Creek artifacts also were found at locations II, III, and V, but undisturbed contexts were rare. Even so, enough evidence survived to indicate the presence of a small village confined to this portion of the field. Locations I and VI were beyond the village limits, and the bluff top was not utilized at all.

Again Trudeau was abandoned for at least 500 years, during which time there was minimal alluviation and the Coles Creek village was left exposed to the ravages of the elements. When the site was reoccupied, the remains of the Coles Creek features were vulnerable to the new human activities and were almost completely destroyed.

The third, and final, aboriginal occupation of Trudeau was the most important. This was, of course, the mid-eighteenth-century Tunica village, considered the most important because it was the largest and left the most features. Evidence of it was found throughout the field at all six locations tested, and also on the bluff top. Unfortunately, however, subsequent agriculture and railroad construction have taken their toll. Centuries of plowing have destroyed the original Tunica occupation surface in the field, leaving only the deeper features: post molds, trash pits, burials. These confirm the basic village plan and associated mortuary aspect, but a considerable amount of information about structural details and activity patterning has been lost. The bluff top, where we discovered that the Tunica had an important structure, also had been cut through in order to make a railroad grade; only some debris from the burning of the structure survived on the south edge. Nevertheless, a few additional interpretations are possible based on the distributions of the remaining features and artifacts.

The bluff top structure was deemed of unusual importance because of its placement, large size, possibly new method of construction, and the quality of associated artifacts. Its size is suggested by the quantity and thickness of the daub fragments, the new construction techniques by both the saw blade and the hundreds of medium and large handwrought iron nails (table 33). While the latter could have had other uses, their large numbers and the fact that many were clinched indicate use for structural joining. Furthermore, they were found mixed in with the daub, and many had been reheated since manufacture, presumably by the fire. The other associated artifacts show a relatively large proportion of tin-glazed ceramics, especially compared with lead-glazed, and the only example of powder purple delft (table 34). Also significant is the predominance of light blue-green and clear glass over olive green (table 35), since the reverse is true elsewhere throughout the site. It generally is assumed that the olive green was not only the more common but the less prestigious glass-

Table 32. Proveniences of decorated aboriginal pottery found at Trudeau during the 1981 excavations.

	Bluff Top	I	II	III	IV	V	VI
Winterville Incised, *var. Tunica*	2	1	3	19	6	4	9
Barton Incised, *var. Trudeau*	1	1	3	13		2	2
Unclassified incised/punctated (Mississippian)	1	3	5	15	3	7	8
Cracker Road Incised, *var. Cracker Road*				1			
Fatherland Incised, *var. Bayou Goula*			1	4		1	
Fatherland Incised, *var. Nancy*			7	3	11	2	11
Fatherland Incised, *var. Snyders Bluff*	2	3	2	9		2	3
Unclassified engraved (Caddo)			2			2	
Fatherland Incised, *var. Fatherland*	6	10	18	24		10	6
Fatherland Incised, *var. unspecified*	3	9	25	70		29	6
Maddox Engraved, *var. unspecified*	4		1	5	1	3	3
Unclassified incised (St. Catherine)		4	10	34	3	11	2
Chicot Red, *var. Grand Village*		1	6	15		4	3
Owens Punctated, *var. Beland City*	1						
Leland Incised, *var. unspecified*				9		3	1
Anna Incised, *var. Australia*				1			
Plaquemine Brushed, *var. Plaquemine*			2	3	15		
Avoyelles Punctated, *var. Dupree*					1	1	
Harrison Bayou Incised, *var. Harrison Bayou*			1				
Avoyelles Punctated, *var. Kearney*			1				
Avoyelles Punctated, *var. unspecified*						2	
Coles Creek Incised, *var. Mott*			4	4	1		
Coles Creek Incised, *var. unspecified*			1	4			
Evansville Punctated, *var. unspecified*			1	1			
Mazique Incised, *var. Kings Point*		1	10	4		3	
Mazique Incised, *var. unspecified*			1	1			
Pontchartrain Check Stamped, *var. Pontchartrain*			24	9	15	2	1
Unclassified incised (Vicksburg)			1	2		1	
Mulberry Creek Cord Marked, *var. unspecified*							4

Table 33. Proveniences of handwrought iron nails found at Trudeau during the 1981 excavations.

	Bluff Top	I	II	III	IV	V	VI
Type I	102	3					2
Type II	27						
Type III	15						
Type IV	11					1	
Type V	1						
Type unspecified	51	5	8	25	1	10	8

Table 34. Proveniences of European ceramics found at Trudeau during the 1981 excavations.

	Bluff Top	I	II	III	IV	V	VI
Faience							
White	5	7	3	9	1	4	3
Blue-and-white	2	1	2	10	1		
Green-and-white						2	
Brown			2	13		2	
Unspecified				3	1		
Majolica							
White				1	4		2
Blue-and-white		2					1
Delft							
Powder purple	1						
Lead-glazed earthenware							
Type A		10	15	18		6	3
Type B		17	23	79	5	12	6
Type C	2	5	8	31		5	5
Type D	1	2	2	33		5	4
Type E		6	1	8		3	
Type F		6	3	13		8	
Stoneware							
Westerwald					1	1	1
Bellarmine			1	8			
Grès				1			
Unglazed		1					

Table 35. Proveniences of glassware found at Trudeau during the 1981 excavations.

	Bluff Top	I	II	III	IV	V	VI
Clear	10	5	1	7		3	3
Olive	9	37	62	122	11	40	17
Light blue-green	10	16	8	30	2	13	7

Table 36. Proveniences of glass beads found at Trudeau during the 1981 excavations.

	Bluff Top	Iᵃ	II	IIIᵇ	IV	V	VI
IA2			1				
IA3			1			1	
IB2						1	
IIA1		200		202		1	
IIA2				1			
IIA5				365		1	
IIA6			2	3	3		
IIA7			3	340		2	1
IIA10		2					
IIB2		3					
IIB10		3					
IIB13		2					
IIIA1				3			1
IVB1			1				
IVB2		1					
IVB3		2		1		1	
IVB4		9	1				
WIA1		4					
WID1		1	1			2	
WID4				4			
WIIA7				33			
Unclassified				1			

ᵃMostly from burial Beta.
ᵇMostly from burial Delta.

Table 37. Proveniences of copper and brass artifacts found at Trudeau during the 1981 excavations.

	Bluff Top	I	II	III	IV	V	VI
Copper							
Tinkling cones		1		1			
Wire				1			
Unidentified		9	1	13		2	1
Brass							
Buttons	1	9		1			1
Flushloop bells				9			
Flowerkey bell		1					
Saturn bell		1					
Tinkling cones		1				1	3
Unidentified		1	3	6		1	

ware. The olive green bottles contained rum, brandy, and wine; the light blue-green contained liquors and other exotic liquids (Brain 1979, pp. 92–93). The clear glass was mostly in the form of serving pieces, and fragments of at least one wine glass are counted among those from the bluff top. Curiously, no glass beads were found on the bluff (table 36). Their absence is less surprising, however, when one realizes how rare they actually are at the site outside of graves.

The graves are the most important and numerous features remaining in the field. Most of these have been looted, and at least one burial had even been removed

Table 38. Proveniences of gun parts and munitions found at Trudeau during the 1981 excavations.

	Bluff Top	I	II	III	IV	V	VI
Brass and iron furniture	1	2[a]	2		1	1	
Lock mechanisms	1		1				1
Lead balls	5	13	3	5	1	3	
Lead shot		148[b]		7			
Lead splashes and sprues		1	3	10	1		5
Gunflints	3	4[c]	1	4		4	2
Gunflint flakes	2		8	12		5	

[a]Does not include the many pieces of a Type C fusil associated with burial Beta.
[b]One hundred forty-three from burial Beta.
[c]Three from burial Beta.

Table 39. Description and measurements of lead balls found at Trudeau during the 1981 excavations.

Provenience	Description	Weight (g)	Diameter (mm)
B56B	Pistol ball	4	10.0
B59A	Musket ball	17.1	14.5
B75B2	Musket ball	17.8	15.5
B75B2	Musket ball	17.8	15.5
B75B3	Musket ball	12.4	15
B111A	Musket ball[a]	20.2	—
B112B	Musket ball	10.7	15
B114B	Musket ball[a]	16.9	—
B115A	Musket ball	15.2	15.5
B115B1	Musket ball[a]	2.2	—
B115B1	Musket ball	15.2	15
B115B1	Musket ball	17.6	14
B115B1	Musket ball	15.2	14
B115B1	Musket ball	13.6	15.5
B115B1	Musket ball	15.7	14
B115B1	Musket ball	15.5	14.5
B115B1	Musket ball	14.7	15
B115B1	Musket ball	17.1	15.5
B115B1	Musket ball	14.6	15.5
B115B1	Musket ball	15.2	15
B115B1	Musket ball	13.3	15
B115B1	Musket ball	14.3	15
B118B1	Musket ball[a]	14.7	—
B119B1	Musket ball	16.7	14
B120B1	Musket ball	14.3	15
B141A	Pistol ball	3.8	9
B142A	Musket ball	17.7	15
B143A	Pistol ball	1.3	7
B162A	Musket ball[a]	18.1	—
B182A	Musket ball	14.6	14

[a]Deformed.

by the Tunica themselves. Nevertheless, these disturbed graves contained the majority of the glass beads found in the 1981 excavations and most of the brass artifacts such as bells and buttons (table 37). Gun parts and munitions, which were common with male burials, had a relatively broad distribution across the site (table 38). Within categories, however, it is of some interest to note that gunflint flakes were most common in the village area, perhaps from the use of gunflints with strike-a-lights. Also, lead splashes and sprues occurred only in the field, suggesting that the manufacture of balls also was confined to the village. The balls themselves are listed in table 39. The musket balls fall entirely within the range of the larger trade gun calibers. Table 39 does not include the four lead balls with burial Alpha, however. These were measured in situ, and their diameters were found to be approximately 18–19 mm, a much larger caliber than those of the other balls found at the site. The pistol balls could have been used as large shot and do not necessarily indicate the presence of side arms, which were prestigious, but largely useless, weapons among the Indians.

The 1981 excavations at Trudeau contributed important information about the prehistoric occupations at the site and added many new details concerning the cultural provenience from which the Tunica Treasure had been wrested. Unfortunately, however, they also revealed that most of the eighteenth-century surfaces had been destroyed, except perhaps in the southeastern corner of the site. The most significant features left in the rest of the site are the graves, most of which have already been looted.

Attempts to use modern electronic methods, subsurface interface radar in particular, to discriminate subsurface features were a disappointment. We had hoped that it would be possible at least to distinguish burials from other features so that the burials could be avoided in future investigations. It is possible that such determination is within the capabilities of the radar, but at present neither it nor its operators are sophisticated enough to retrieve the information. The only reasonably certain result that the radar reported was negative: it seemed to be reliable in recognizing subsurface conditions characterized by minimal natural and cultural disturbance. In other words, it can indicate where not to dig.

Although we were disappointed in our hope that Trudeau might have great future potential, we were able to elaborate the context of the Tunica Treasure. More than just a collection of artifacts, it now has gained a secure provenience and archaeological pedigree. It is a valid datum from which to proceed.

Portage de la Croix

When the Tunica left the Yazoo region in 1706, they migrated down the Mississippi River (Haas 1950, p. 133) and settled in the vicinity of the Red River confluence. Contemporary historical documents record that they resided first with the Houma,* but the accommodation was short-lived and the Tunica soon chased their hosts away (some say with the shedding of much blood). The Tunica continued to live in the principal village of the Houma and remained masters of the land known as the Portage de la Croix for some twenty-five years.

The Portage de la Croix, the only major portage in the entire Lower Mississippi Valley, was a very important landmark in the early eighteenth century. Because of an unusually large meander at this point (fig. 124), travelers could substitute two leagues overland for ten winding leagues by water. At times of high water this passage could even be made afloat, through connecting bayous and the old oxbow cutoff now known as Lake

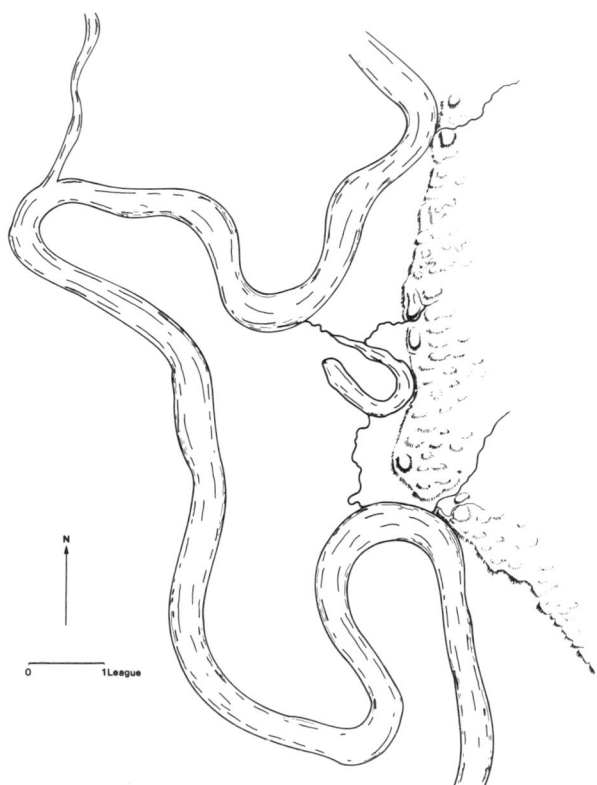

Figure 124. Reconstruction of the riverine-lacustrine system at the Portage de la Croix in the early eighteenth century.

Killarney (or Lac de la Croix). The lake's French name refers to a cross that Iberville erected at the southern end of the portage in 1699 to serve as a marker for subsequent travelers.

The principal Houma-Tunica village, often referred to as Grands Tonicas in contemporary documents after 1706, was described by many early French visitors. These descriptions tell of a fairly large village composed of at least 80 cabins, and perhaps as many as 140, arranged in a circle around an open plaza 100 to 200 paces wide. This village was situated on the flat crest of a hill near the Lac de la Croix. Distances given in the accounts, and numerous maps (e.g., figs. 20, 24), clearly locate the village in the vicinity of present Lake Killarney, presumably on the summit of one of the loess bluffs immediately to the east (fig. 125). Several likely bluff tops have been investigated, but none has yielded evidence of eighteenth-century occupation. Although we have not definitely established the provenience of Grands Tonicas,* we are certainly very close, for two small Tunica sites have been excavated. While neither their size nor their topographical situation fits the historical descriptions of the principal village, they do provide strong testimony that we are in the right neighborhood. These sites are Angola Farm and Bloodhound (29-J-2 and 29-J-19) (fig. 126).

ANGOLA FARM

The riverine and geomorphological conformation known in the eighteenth century as the Portage de la Croix now consists of a neck of rich alluvial bottomland embraced by a single large loop of the Mississippi River (fig. 126). The simplification of the meandering pattern of the river at this location reduced the amount of land enclosed on the east bank, but fortunately has not seriously damaged the area along the bluff margin that is believed to have been the focus of the early eighteenth-century settlement. Today, the entire neck—a natural prison surrounded by the Mississippi on three sides and the rugged Tunica Hills on the fourth—is occupied by the Louisiana State Penitentiary (Angola). The first historic site recognized was appropriately given the institution's familiar appellation, Angola Farm.

Previous Excavations

The Angola Farm site was discovered in 1934 and excavated by James A. Ford (1936, pp. 129–140), who described it as follows:

---

* If Swanton (1946, p. 139) is correct in believing that the Houma also originally came from the Yazoo region, the Tunica migration may have been a case of following the direction of their former neighbors.

* In fact, an intensive pedestrian survey conducted in 1975 around the entire Red River confluence and into the Tunica Hills failed to find any evidence of Tunica occupation other than the sites reported in these pages.

Figure 125. High, flat-topped bluff at edge of alluvial flood-plain northeast of Lake Killarney, West Feliciana Parish, Louisiana. It must have been a situation like this on which the principal village of the Tunica was located during the period 1706–1731.

In April, 1934, burials were discovered in plowing a broad talus fan spread out from the mouth of a small stream that flows out of the hundred-foot bluffs which border the eastern side of the Mississippi. The burials were located six hundred yards from the bluffs at a point where the fan had been carved by the Mississippi in former times. The old, filled-in stream channel was very apparent. A half mile to the south it opened up to form Lake Angola [Killarney].

Through the courtesy of Mr. R. L. Himes, Superintendent of the State Penitentiary, the writer was provided with a crew of men and was allowed to excavate the site for the Louisiana State University. The net result of eight days excavation was ten burials. Two had been disturbed by plowing. The remaining seven [sic] were the skeletons of adults, orientated in various directions, and extended on their backs approximately three feet beneath the present surface. Four males were accompanied by the metal parts of flintlock muskets. Masses of round lead balls with a few gunflints and a black substance which probably was powder lay over the stocks of two of the guns. Beads were found with almost every burial, and were clustered about the neck, chest and ankles. A number of small cones, crudely bent from sheet copper, lay at the ankles of one male [fig. 127]. Small turkey bells lay near the feet of two others. In the abdominal region of one male was a small metal pipe and the iron blade of a halberd [fig. 132]. Another had an iron axe blade. Three of the males had flat-bottomed, straight-sided copper kettles about fifteen inches in diameter placed above their shoulders. Two pottery vessels of native manufacture were near the skulls of two different burials.

The three other adults appeared to be females. Compared with the males, the burial furniture in their graves was scanty. Two of them had three native vessels each near their heads; the other had one. About the ankles of one of the females were a few porcelain beads.

An infant was buried in a wooden chest, nineteen inches deep, nineteen inches wide, and forty-three inches long. The wood had decayed. Nails, hinges, and a hasp

showed its outlines. The small skeleton lay on the bottom of the box. Over the pelvis was inverted a copper kettle similar to the ones that accompanied the adults. At the feet lay a crockery bottle of European manufacture, eight inches in diameter, and eleven inches tall. A few fragments of red ochre were found under the left side of the skull. (ibid., pp. 136–137)

The finds were important to our present research, but Ford's description and accompanying illustrations were incomplete (see also Quimby 1942a). Not only was some detail lacking, but individual grave lots were not clearly defined: for example, which pots, beads, kettles, and so forth, were found with which burials. We felt that enough had been learned during the intermediate period to warrant reanalysis of the collection.

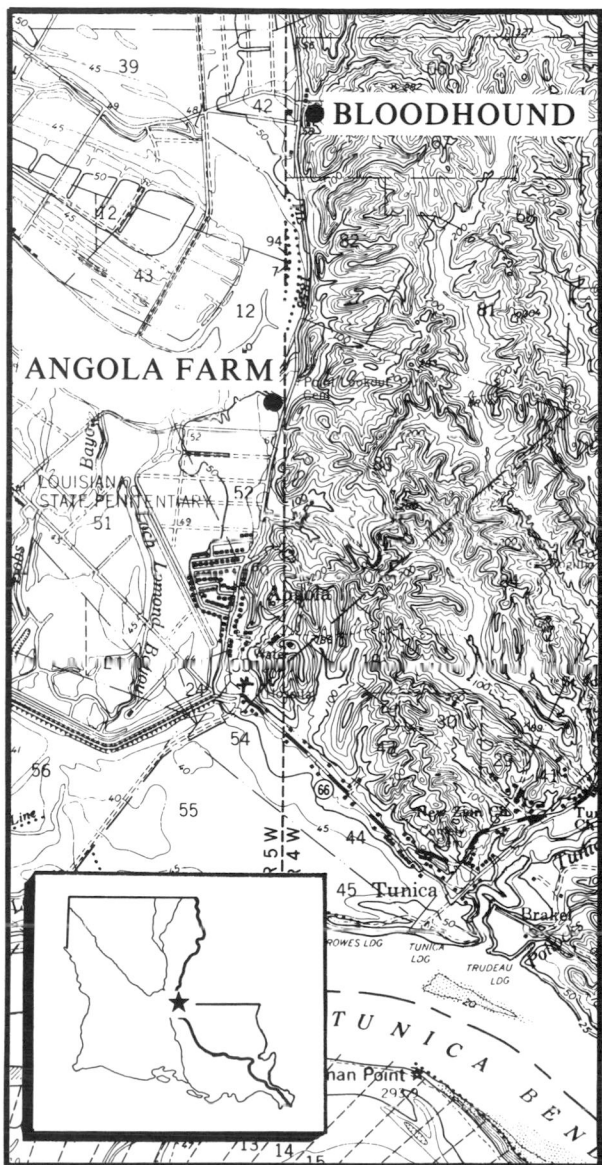

Figure 126. Locations of the Angola Farm (29-J-2) and Bloodhound (29-J-19) sites in West Feliciana Parish, Louisiana.

The 1973 Reanalysis

The artifacts and field notes from the Angola Farm excavations were borrowed from Louisiana State University in 1973.* Vincas Steponaitis successfully reconstructed most of the grave lots as an LMS research project that summer. The new data encouraged the comments and interpretations offered below on each of the burials.

Burial 1.   Apparently an adult male, burial 1 (fig. 127) is described as follows in the field notes:

B #1 is extended on back—head to S.E.—arms by sides. Flintlock gun lies by left side. Breech mechanism is over left hand—on this is what appears to have been a heavily loaded (large white) box full of round lead balls.

Ankles are both enclosed in cluster of small cones made from sheet copper. ? bell came from left ankle. Over abdomen is a mass of powdered red ochre intermingled with beads—white striped and very small blue.

On left side of head was a bell about 4" high. To right a brass kettle about 10" dia, 10" high. A native vessel with a scroll design lies S. of brass kettle. (Ford 1934)

The grave offerings are the most lavish found in any of the burials at the site. They include a complete fusil (LSU cat. no. 463) classified by Hamilton (1968, p. 3, fig. 2) as a Type B. The bore of this gun is .56 inches, or about 28 *calibre*, the largest of the standard French trade gun sizes. Type B is not independently dated, but the extensive use of iron furniture and other details of the musket would suggest a late seventeenth- to early eighteenth-century date of manufacture. The gun was accompanied by a large supply of balls and flints.

Other European metal items are the kettle, bells, and tinkling cones, or "bangles." The kettle (fig. 127b) was not studied but appears to be similar to a Type A (Brain 1979, p. 166) except that it is described as being made of sheet copper.† It is also unusual in that the rim is not iron reinforced and there are no lugs for the bail, which is simply inserted through two holes in the rim.

The bells include both cast brass and sheet brass types (fig. 127c–d). According to the LSU catalog, there were at least two of the latter. Both are examples of the Flush-loop variety (Brown 1979b, p. 201), and one may be the bell described in the field notes as being found at the left ankle. Ford does not mention this in his 1936 report and, as cited above, gives the impression that all the bells were found with two other burials. On the other hand, the LSU catalog lists "hawkbells" as being found only with burials 1 and 5. A single large cast brass bell of the "liberty" type was placed at the left side of the head. This type is probably a marker for the very early

eighteenth century and has been found at Bloodhound (see fig. 142) and at Wright's Bluff (22-M-15) on the Yazoo (Brown 1979a, p. 221, pl. 18).

The "bangles" are cones crudely made from sheet copper. There are 125 in the collection, only 3 of which are definitely labeled "B1." Ford's report describes but one burial (burial 1) with such items, which were clustered around the ankles. The LSU catalog, however, indicates that some of these items may have been found with burial 5.

The last and most numerous category of European artifacts accompanying burial 1 consists of the glass beads. However, it is not now possible to reconstruct the exact number and variety of beads that were present. The field notes quoted above (Ford 1934) describe an unspecified number of "white striped [probably one or more varieties of types IIB (IIB7?) or IVB] and very small

Table 40. Burial associations of glass beads found at the Angola Farm site (29-J-2) by James A. Ford during the 1934 excavations.

VARIETY[a]	BURIAL NUMBER				PERIODS
	1[b]	1/5[c]	5[d]	2[e]	
IIA1		ca. 2,244	5		I–VI
IIA3		1			II–VI
IIA4		35			III–VI
IIA5		1			I–VI
IIA6		22	1		I–VI
IIA7		ca. 7,706	13		I–V
IIA8		1			III–IV
IIA11[f]		11			
IIA13		8			II–III
IIA15		9			III–VI
IIA16[f]		7			
IIA17		5			III–IV
IIB2		6			III
IIB7	4				II–III
IIB9[f]		2			
IIB10		5			III
IIB11[f]		23			
IIB12[f]		1			
IVA2		4			I–VI
IVB1		53			II–III
IVB3		9			II–III
IVB4		2			II–III
WIA1		7			III–VI
WIC1		2		1	II–IV
WIE4		1			

[a] See Brain 1979, pp. 100–133 for variety descriptions and chronology.
[b] LSU catalog number 468.
[c] LSU catalog number 459.
[d] LSU catalog number 5241.
[e] LSU catalog number 446.
[f] New varieties: see appendix E.

* Special thanks are due to David Dye, then a graduate student at LSU, who aided considerably in assembling the collection and getting it to us.

† This is doubtful, for kettles of this form are invariably made of brass. Furthermore, while Ford described all four kettles from the site as being copper, the single example received for study (see fig. 131a) is indeed brass. They probably all were.

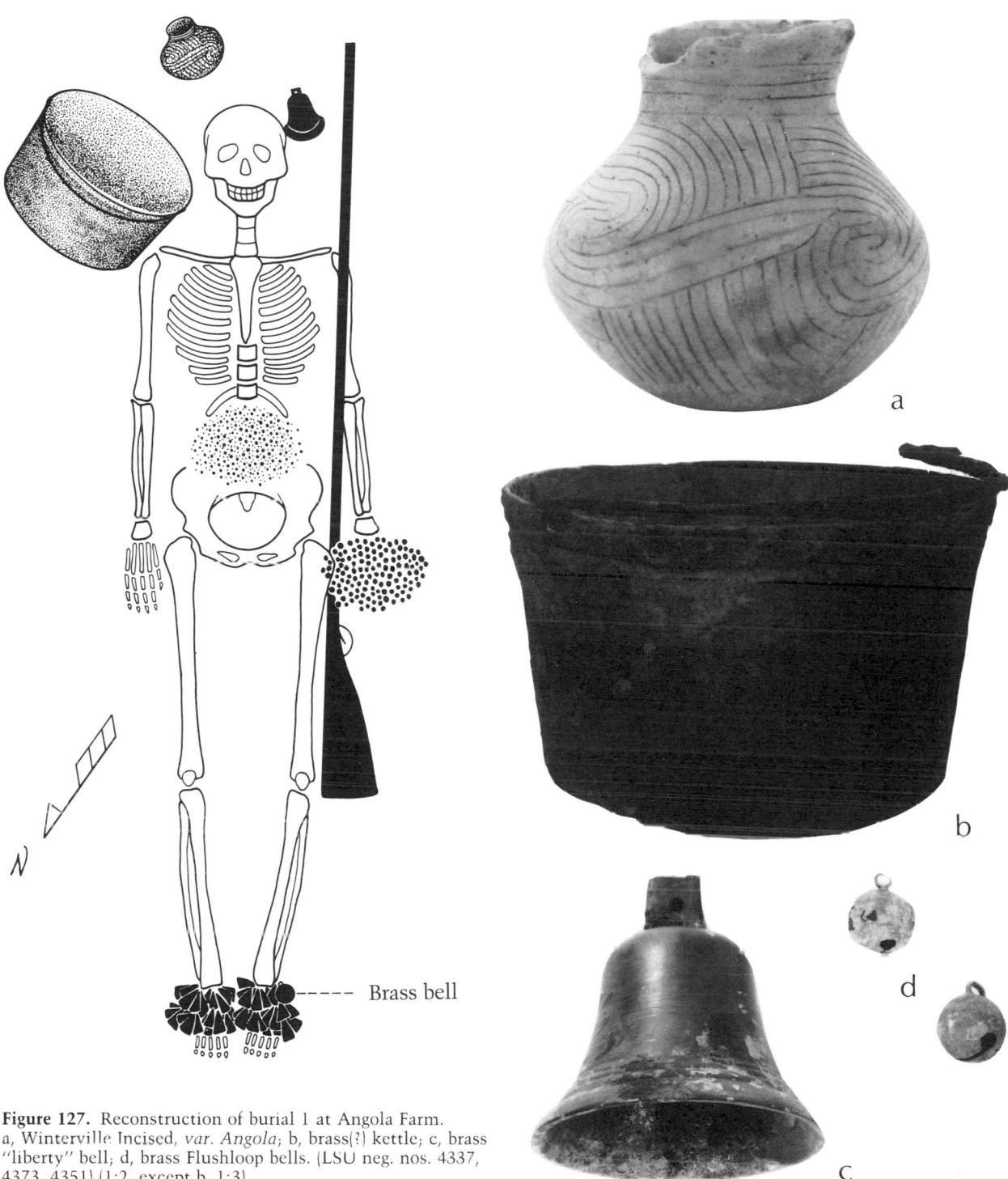

Figure 127. Reconstruction of burial 1 at Angola Farm.
a, Winterville Incised, *var. Angola*; b, brass(?) kettle; c, brass
"liberty" bell; d, brass Flushloop bells. (LSU neg. nos. 4337,
4373, 4351) (1:2, except b, 1:3)

blue [presumably IIA7]." The report (Ford 1936) is of no
help: in reference to the four male burials it says only
that "beads were found with almost every burial, and
were clustered about the neck, chest and ankles" (while
the field notes specify that in the case of burial 1 they
were found in the abdominal area); in the case of the
females, it mentions only that one had a few "porcelain" beads about the ankles. Further confusing the situation, the LSU catalog lists all the beads as having

come from just three burials—burials 1, 2, and 5—and
assigns all but 25 of the approximately 10,000 beads in
the collection to a single catalog number (459), which
in turn is shared by both burials 1 and 5! The classification of bead varieties according to catalog numbers
is presented in table 40. For present purposes, the collection is useful only as a general sample from the site.
From this perspective it is interesting to note that the
varieties present were most common in historical pe-

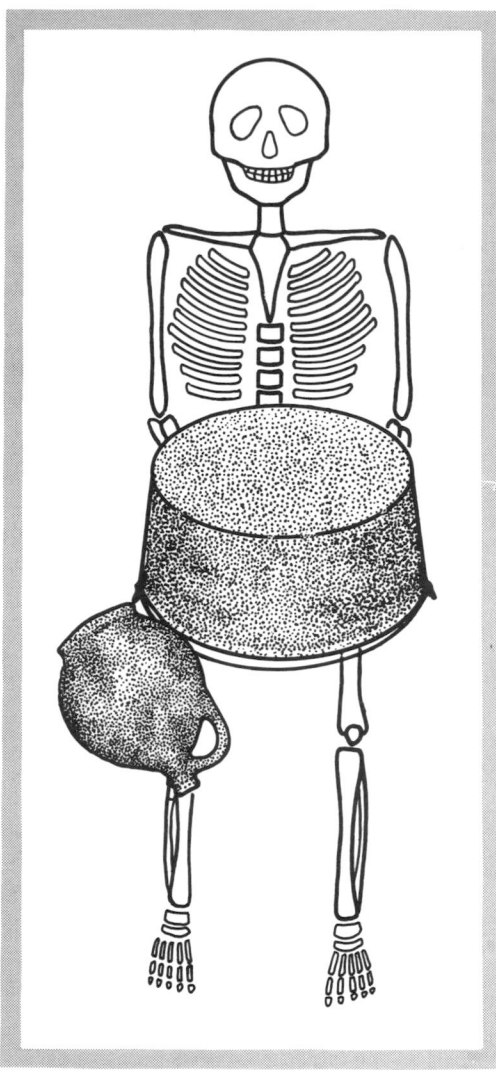

Figure 128. Reconstruction of burial 2 at Angola Farm. a, lead-glazed earthenware, Type A, Variety 1; b, brass kettle, Type A, Variety 1. (LSU neg. nos. 4374, 4373) (a, 1:3; b, 1:5)

riods II–IV (1700–1763) (Brain 1979, pp. 116–133), with a slight bias evident toward the earlier periods, II and III (1700–1729). This artifactual dating is consistent with the historical dating of the Angola Farm locale.

The only aboriginal artifacts associated with burial 1 were some "red ochre" (or vermilion), scattered in the abdominal area with the beads, and a pottery jar near the head. The latter (fig. 127a) is the type specimen of Winterville Incised, *var. Angola* (Phillips 1970, p. 173). Closely related to *var. Tunica*, it exhibits some distinctive decorative modes evocative of the Ouachita Caddoan ceramic tradition (e.g., see Moore 1909, figs. 10, 18, 23, 24, 129, 130, 141).

Burial 2. Burial 2 was an infant or small child who was buried in a wooden box, as described in the report. Also included in the box were an earthenware jug and

a kettle (fig. 128). The jug is a subvariety of Type A, Variety 1 lead-glazed coarse earthenware (Steponaitis 1979, p. 45). Another example was found with burial 1 at Bloodhound (see fig. 142). The squat form of both pieces would seem to be a good marker for the early eighteenth century since it was not found at Trudeau.* The kettle, which was not received for study, was a Type A, Variety 1 (Brain 1979, p. 166) and is described by Ford in his report as being "similar to the ones that accompanied the adults."

The only other items mentioned in the report are "a few fragments of red ochre," but the LSU catalog also lists seven shell beads, one glass bead (table 40), and eighteen lead balls.

* These jugs were probably made in the Saintonge region of France (Steponaitis 1979, p. 45; Cuisenier 1971, no. 11).

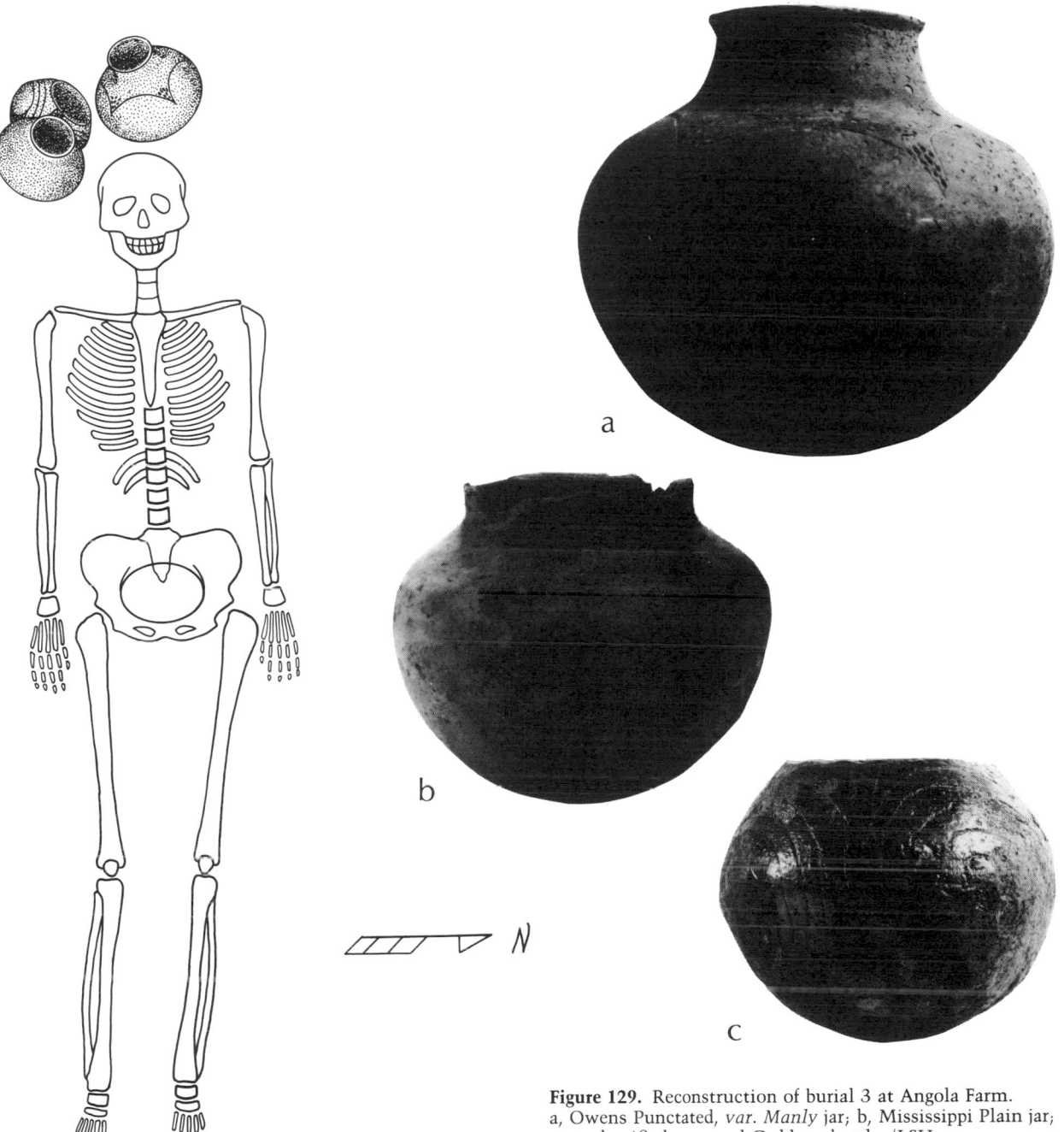

Figure 129. Reconstruction of burial 3 at Angola Farm. a, Owens Punctated, *var. Manly* jar; b, Mississippi Plain jar; c, unclassified engraved Caddoan bottle. (LSU neg. nos. 4336, 4349, 4335) (1:2)

Since this burial was that of an immature person, it would be interesting to know in which direction it was oriented. The child at Bloodhound Hill was laid to rest with the head to the west (see fig. 146), directly opposite the usual Tunica orientation. Unfortunately, because the information was not preserved here, we do not know whether the westerly direction is an exception to the rule or a more general pattern based on age distinction.

Burial 3. This burial is probably one of the adult females described in Ford's report, since the only certain accompaniments are three native pots (fig. 129). The pottery represents both the Mississippian and Caddoan ceramic traditions. There is one undecorated jar (LSU cat. no. 452) of Mississippi Plain (*var. Pocahontas?*), and one jar (LSU cat. no. 456) with shoulder decoration in the manner of Owens Punctated, *var. Manly* (formerly classified under Matthews Incised; see app. A.1). The latter originated in the northern part of the Lower Mississippi Valley (Phillips 1970, p. 128), and its presence at Angola Farm indicates the distant contacts of the Tunica within the valley. The third vessel (LSU cat. no. 455) is an unclassified example of Caddoan incised-engraved and red-slipped decoration on a bottle form (the neck was broken off in antiquity). The bottle provides evidence for the close Tunica contacts to the west, beyond the valley.

The glass beads mentioned in the report may have been associated with this burial, but the field notes and catalog are silent on this point.

Burial 4.   Although listed in the LSU catalog as a female, burial 4 was probably a male. Its major accompaniment was a flintlock gun, and in his report Ford specifically notes that all the guns were found with adult males (Ford 1936, p. 136) (one hopes that this observation was based on more than just logical assumption).

The gun (LSU cat. no. 462) is a Type A (Hamilton 1968, p. 3, fig. 1). The bore is unusually large (.69 inches), indicating the gun was not a light trade fusil. In fact,

.69 inches is approximately 17.5 mm, the standard French infantry bore of the time (Hamilton 1979, table 16). This gun, then, probably was military issue, or if a trade piece was assembled from military components. The furniture and lock are consistent with a late seventeenth- or early eighteenth-century dating.

Glass beads may have been associated with this burial, but the only other artifact listed in the LSU catalog and observable in the field photograph is an elongated (10 × 2.5 × 2.5 cm) chert cobble. This stone (LSU cat. no. 464) was located near the left shoulder, next to the stock of the gun (fig. 130). It is considerably abraded on one side near one end; the other end is slightly battered. No guess regarding its function in this world or the next is hazarded.

It is of considerable interest to note the difference in orientation between burials 3 and 4 in figure 130. Burial 4 is recorded in the field notes as lying with the head to the east, so burial 3 must be oriented approximately northeast. Whether this difference was accidental, or perhaps determined by sex, is presently unknown.

Burial 5.   According to Ford, burial 5 should have been another adult male since a gun was associated with it. However, the bones cataloged with the burial are those of a young child. Only one child, burial 2, was mentioned by Ford. Either a cataloging error was made (and these bones were perhaps left over from burial 2—the two lots are incomplete), or this was a multiple burial. The absence of adult male bones argues against the latter case.

The gun has been classified as Type C by Hamilton (1968, p. 7, figs. 4a, 5f). The brass furniture and small bore (only .50 inches) clearly identify it as a lightweight trade fusil. The only other major artifact unquestionably found with this burial was a kettle (fig. 131b)—the only one received for study—made of sheet brass (not copper, as described in the catalog and report). It is a typical example of Type A, Variety 1 (Brain 1979, p. 166).

Other objects apparently associated with burial 5 were ornamental. They included at least four varieties of glass beads (see table 40) and perhaps as many as four varieties of brass bells. The uncertainties of attribution are

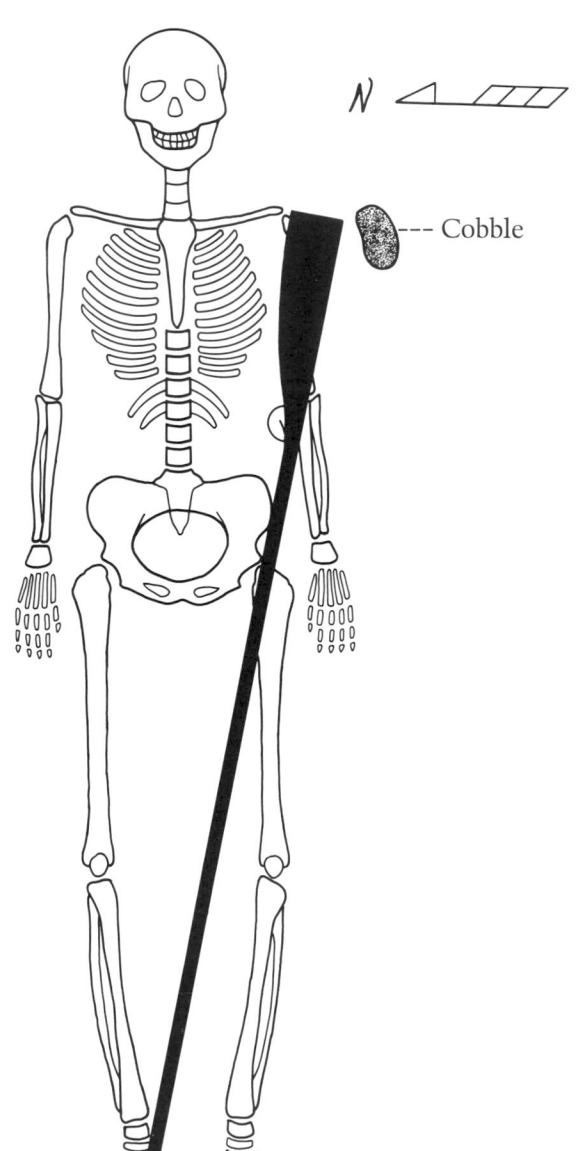

Cobble

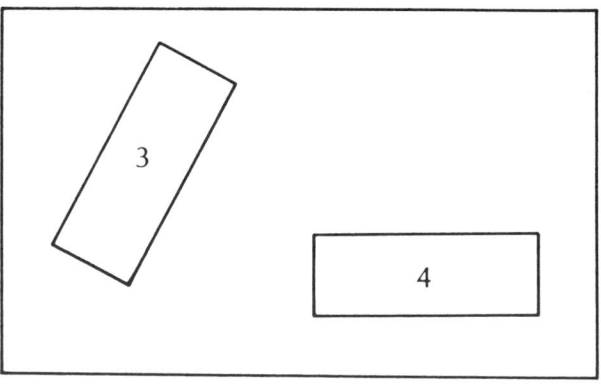

Figure 130. Reconstruction of burial 4 at Angola Farm, showing relative positions and orientations of burials 3 and 4 (inset).

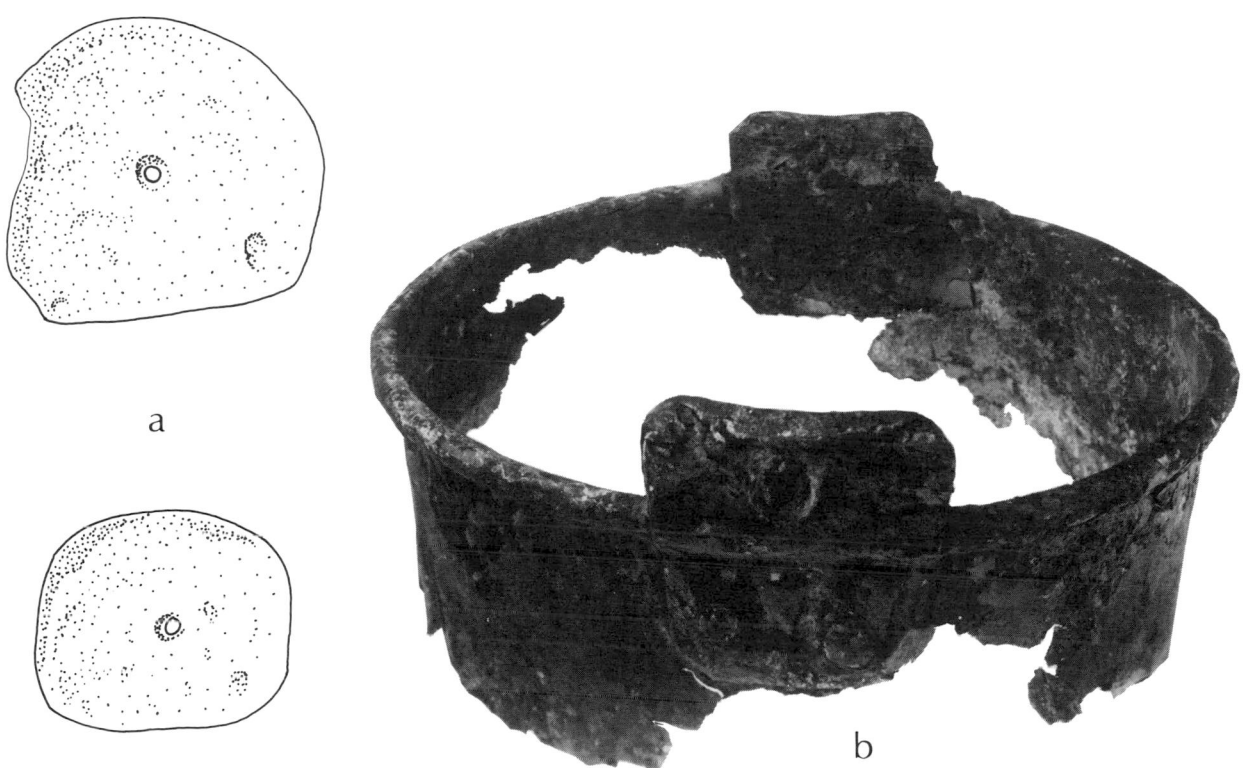

Figure 131. Some artifacts associated with burial 5 at Angola Farm. a, conch shell discs; b, brass kettle, Type A, Variety 1. (a, 1:1; b, 1:2)

discussed under burial 1. Two discs and seven beads of conch shell also were found (fig. 131a; see also Quimby 1942b, pl. 17.1 *A*). These ornaments of native manufacture were highly valued, and the beads, at least, continued in use during the Trudeau occupation. That discs and beads were found with a child burial at Bloodhound (see fig. 146b) advances the case for the presence of a child in this grave. Some vermilion and sheet copper bangles also may have been present.

Burial 6. This probably was one of the two burials plowed up in the discovery of the site (see Ford 1936). Apparently no bones or artifacts were preserved, as none is mentioned in the LSU catalog.

Burial 7. This burial must have been the fourth adult male reported by Ford. It was accompanied by a gun, which Hamilton did not analyze, and nineteen lead balls (presumably for the gun) that measured approximately 14 mm in diameter, although they were badly deteriorated. These probably were made for a 28-*calibre* fusil, a standard trade gun size (Hamilton 1979, table 16).

A number of iron (or steel) items accompanied this burial. In addition to unidentifiable fragments, they included seven handwrought nails, an oval strike-a-light, a folding knife, and a "halberd." The latter (fig. 132b), found in the abdominal area of the burial, is the most interesting artifact: it is actually a rare form of the spontoon type of tomahawk and seems to be early eighteenth-century French in origin (H. L. Peterson 1965, pp. 24–26; Russell 1967, p. 276). An identical example

was discovered in 1972 at Trudeau lying on the chest of an adult male (see fig. 69c).

Smaller European items included part of a pewter buckle (fig. 132a) and perhaps some glass beads, although none has been cataloged separately. A native bowl of Fatherland Incised, *var. Fatherland* (fig. 132c) was placed near the head of the burial.

Burial 8. Burial 8 was probably an adult female, since the only accompaniment listed in the catalog was "one urn, decorated." In his report, Ford mentioned that two of the females had three pots each near the head, while the third had only one. However, both burials 8 and 10 (the last putative female) also have only one pot cataloged. Whether this is due to error in the reporting or attrition in the collection is not now possible to determine.

The surviving pot is described by Ford (1936, p. 138) as having shell temper. If so, then the incised rectilinear decoration would require classification as a variety of Barton Incised (perhaps *var. Trudeau*). Steponaitis, however, did not see shell in the paste and classified the pot as Mazique Incised, *var. Manchac* (fig. 133a).

Burial 9. By process of elimination, we determined that this is the second burial disturbed in the discovery of the site. The only artifact listed in the LSU catalog, however, is an iron axe that Ford, in his report, seems to indicate was found with one of the four adult males he excavated. Thus, we are faced once again with the problem of whether to put our faith in the report or the catalog. We leave the puzzle unresolved.

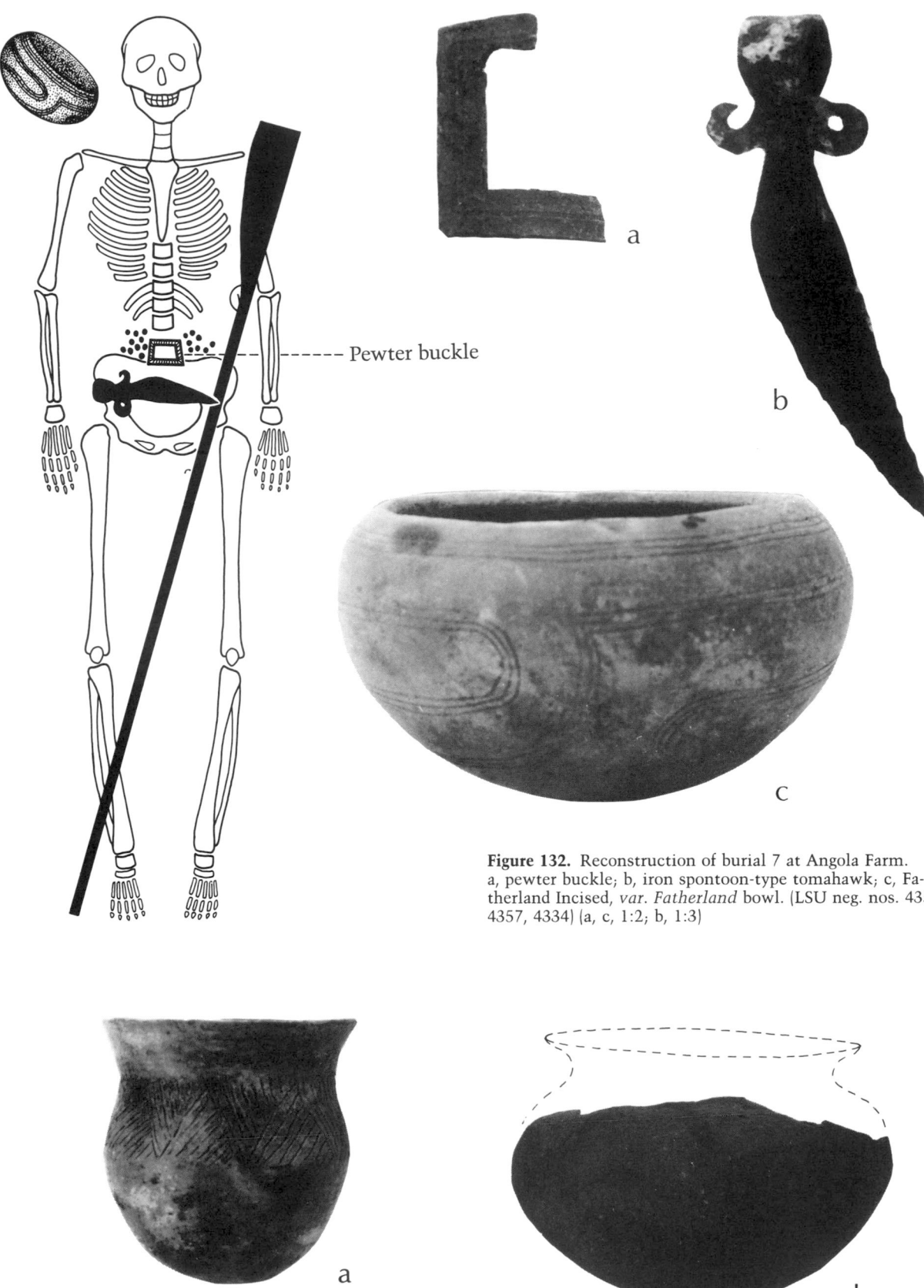

Pewter buckle

Figure 132. Reconstruction of burial 7 at Angola Farm. a, pewter buckle; b, iron spontoon-type tomahawk; c, Fatherland Incised, *var. Fatherland* bowl. (LSU neg. nos. 4358, 4357, 4334) (a, c, 1:2; b, 1:3)

Figure 133. Pottery from burials 8 and 10 at Angola Farm. a, Mazique Incised, *var. Manchac* jar from burial 8; b, Mississippi Plain, *var. Pocahontas* jar from burial 10. (LSU neg. nos. 4343, 4338) (1:4)

Burial 10. Presumed to be the third adult female mentioned in Ford's report, this burial was accompanied by at least one native pot (see discussion under burial 8 for possible additional pots with one of these two burials). Although damaged, this pot is a good example of the late jar form of Mississippi Plain, *var. Pocahontas* (fig. 133b).

Summary of the Burials. The burials at the Angola Farm site were interred during the early eighteenth century. To the extent that some of the more diagnostic artifacts may be dated, their deposition during the first three decades of the century would be perfectly consistent. This dating also accords well with the known historic occupation of the region by the Tunica. That the burials were those of the Tunica is thus presumed, but not proven beyond doubt.

A close similarity exists between these burials and those found nearby at Bloodhound Hill, all of which were individual supine inhumations. An eastern orientation was generally preferred, although considerable variation is evident. Males were more lavishly equipped than females, and a considerable variety of artifacts was found. The artifacts themselves are very similar, and many of the same types were present at both locations.

Figure 134. View of the 1934 Angola Farm excavations (right of center, middle background) from bluff top overlooking the floodplain and Lake Killarney. (LSU neg. no. 1234) ▶

The 1975 Survey

The precise location of Ford's excavations was determined from contemporary photographs (figs. 134–135) and from an on-site survey in 1975 (fig. 136). Measurements in Ford's field notes were found to be unreliable but corroborative. Ford estimated that the entire site covered about ten acres and included a village occupation as well as a cemetery. His excavations opened up an area of approximately 15 × 25 m (fig. 136), from which he removed the ten burials.

There is no indication in Ford's notes of structures or other features, but surface collections in the vicinity

Figure 135. View of the 1934 Angola Farm excavations from west-southwest. Note first bluffs rising in the background, and the old bank line beginning to slope down to Lake Killarney in the foreground. (LSU neg. no. 1140)

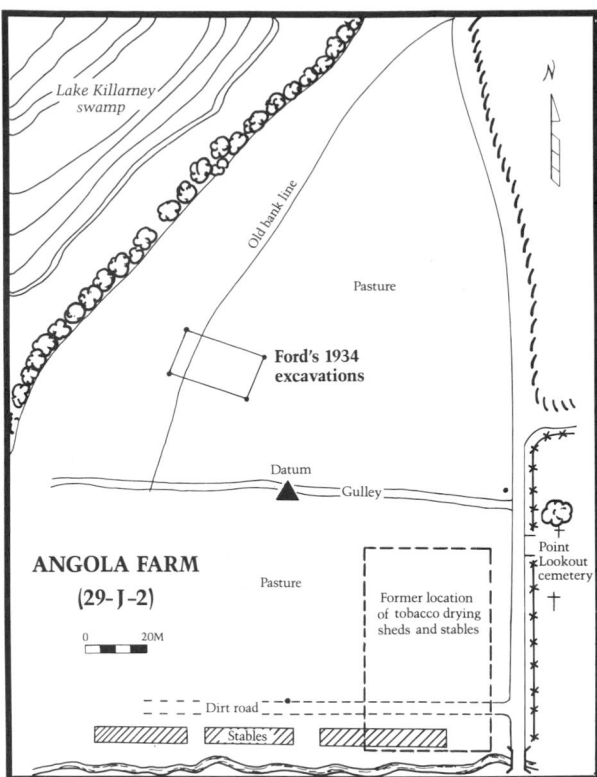

Figure 136. Sketch map of the Angola Farm site made during the 1975 survey. Locations of 1934 excavations and contemporary prison structures are indicated.

BLOODHOUND

Angola Farm was probably a Tunica site, but was only a small cemetery on the floodplain. We were looking for an important village believed to be located in the bluffs above, which appear to have been relatively untouched by man or nature since the eighteenth century. It is wild, heavily overgrown country, however, and brief attempts by the LMS in 1974 and 1975 to discover other archaeological contexts were thwarted by the rugged natural conditions. But then prison activities intervened once again. In the fall of 1976 two burials with an impressive array of grave goods were reported to have been unearthed by an inmate (the timing, if not the circumstances, of the discovery is in question, as noted below). Most of these finds were confiscated by the authorities and turned over to the state archaeologist, Alan Toth, who in turn brought them to our attention.

The prospect of forging another missing link to the chain of Tunica settlements through time and space—perhaps even discovering the great village—was sufficient encouragement to bring us to the field posthaste. The expedition was funded by a research grant from the National Geographic Society's Committee for Research and Exploration and was operated as a joint venture with the Louisiana Archaeological Survey and Antiquities Commission. The Lower Mississippi Survey crew consisted of Jeffrey P. Brain, field director, Vincas Steponaitis, Alan McMillan, Ian Brown, and Nancy Lambert-Brown. This core group was augmented by professional staff from the state archaeologist's office—most prominently Debbie Woodiel and George Castille—and by prison labor. The fieldwork was carried out in two stages, the first investigation during a five-week period in May/June 1977, the second a few months later during a fortnight in October.

The 1977 Excavations

The name of the Bloodhound site derived from its location at the headquarters of the "chase unit" of the penitentiary's security force (fig. 138). At the time, part of the site was occupied by kennels for the bloodhounds used to track the few escapees who dared venture into the wilds of the Tunica Hills, the only terrestrial border of this natural prison (see fig. 126). Bloodhound is located on the first terrace overlooking the valley floor, directly below the high bluff of the Tunica Hills proper. That this was an advantageous position for human occupation is attested by the eighteenth-century Tunica settlement, evidence of nineteenth-century plantation structures, and several different residential functions associated with prison operations during the last half century.

Physiographically, the site is composed of two parts: the terrace, and a sharp rise contiguous to the east that

did yield evidence of historic as well as earlier occupations (fig. 137; table 41). As listed in table 41, two locations (LSU cat. nos. 477, 481) were described specifically as being east and north of the excavations; it is therefore in the northeastern quadrant of the site, on the talus slope between the cemetery and the bluffs, that we might expect to find evidence of an early eighteenth-century village. (Note that the third specified collection, LSU cat. no. 478, has early Plaquemine pottery and no European artifacts; it is described as coming from an exposed midden 4 ft., 6 in. below the present surface on the west side of the site.) We did not confirm the presence of this early eighteenth-century village occupation during our 1975 survey, although there was good evidence for a late eighteenth-century/early nineteenth-century (presumably Anglo-American) settlement nearby. The location, which features a stream coming out of the bluffs, would have been a prime setting for a small settlement in the eighteenth century. It is probable that Angola Farm was not an isolated cemetery and that there was a small Tunica village or hamlet in the vicinity, as was found to be the case at the closely related Bloodhound site.

Figure 137. Aboriginal pottery from surface collections at Angola Farm. a–b, Winterville Incised, *var. Tunica;* c, Barton Incised, *var. Trudeau;* d, Cracker Road Incised, *var. Cracker Road;* e, Natchitoches Engraved, *var. Natchitoches;* f, L'Eau Noire Incised, *var. L'Eau Noire;* g, Fatherland Incised, *var. Fatherland;* h, Maddox Engraved, *var. unspecified;* i, Sanson Incised, *var. Sanson;* j, unclassified brushed-incised-punctated; k, Pontchartrain Check Stamped, *var. Pontchartrain;* l, Anna Incised, *var. Australia;* m, Anna Incised, *var. Anna;* n, Coles Creek Incised, *var. Hardy;* o, Medora Incised, *var. Medora;* p–r, Plaquemine Brushed, *var. Plaquemine.* (1:2)

a

b

c

d

e

f

g

h

i

j

k

l

m

n

o

p

q

r

Table 41. Aboriginal and European artifacts collected from locations other than the cemetery area during the 1934 excavations at Angola Farm.

	General Surface	LSU cat. no. 477	LSU cat. no. 481	LSU cat. no. 478
ABORIGINAL				
Pottery:				
Winterville Incised, *var. Tunica* (fig. 137a–b)	2	10		
Winterville Incised, *var. unspecified*			2	
Barton Incised, *var. Trudeau* (fig. 137c)	4	5		
Mississippi Plain, *var. Pocahontas*	16	6	15	
Cracker Road Incised, *var. Cracker Road* (fig. 137d)	1			
Natchitoches Engraved, *var. Natchitoches* (fig. 137e)	3			
Fatherland Incised, *var. Fatherland* (fig. 137g)	3	2		
Maddox Engraved, *var. unspecified* (fig. 137h)	2	2		
Addis Plain, *var. St. Catherine*	1		2	
Addis Plain, *var. Feliciana*	1	4		3
Leland Incised, *var. unspecified*	2	1	1	
Anna Incised, *var. Anna* (fig. 137m)		5		
Anna Incised, *var. Australia* (fig. 137l)	5	1		
L'Eau Noire Incised, *var. L'Eau Noire* (fig. 137f)		1		
Medora Incised, *var. Medora* (fig. 137o)	1			1
Sanson Incised, *var. Sanson* (fig. 137i)	1			
Plaquemine Brushed, *var. Plaquemine* (fig. 137p–r)	7	6	1	4
Avoyelles Punctated, *var. unspecified*	3			
Coles Creek Incised, *var. Hardy* (fig. 137n)			1	1
Mazique Incised, *var. unspecified*		1	1	1
Unclassified incised (Addis)	1	1	1	
Unclassified incised/red slipped (Addis)			1	
Unclassified brushed/punctated (Addis) (fig. 137j)	1	1		
Addis Plain, *var. Addis*	23	59	42	30
Pontchartrain Check Stamped, *var. Pontchartrain* (fig. 137k)	2	2	5	
Baytown Plain, *var. unspecified*	16	35	26	1
EUROPEAN				
Earthenware:				
Faience				
White	2	2		
Blue-and-white	1			
Brown		3[a]	2	
Lead-glazed				
Type A		3		
Type B		2	2	
Type D		3	4	
Type E		4	2	

[a]See Quimby 1966, figure 12.

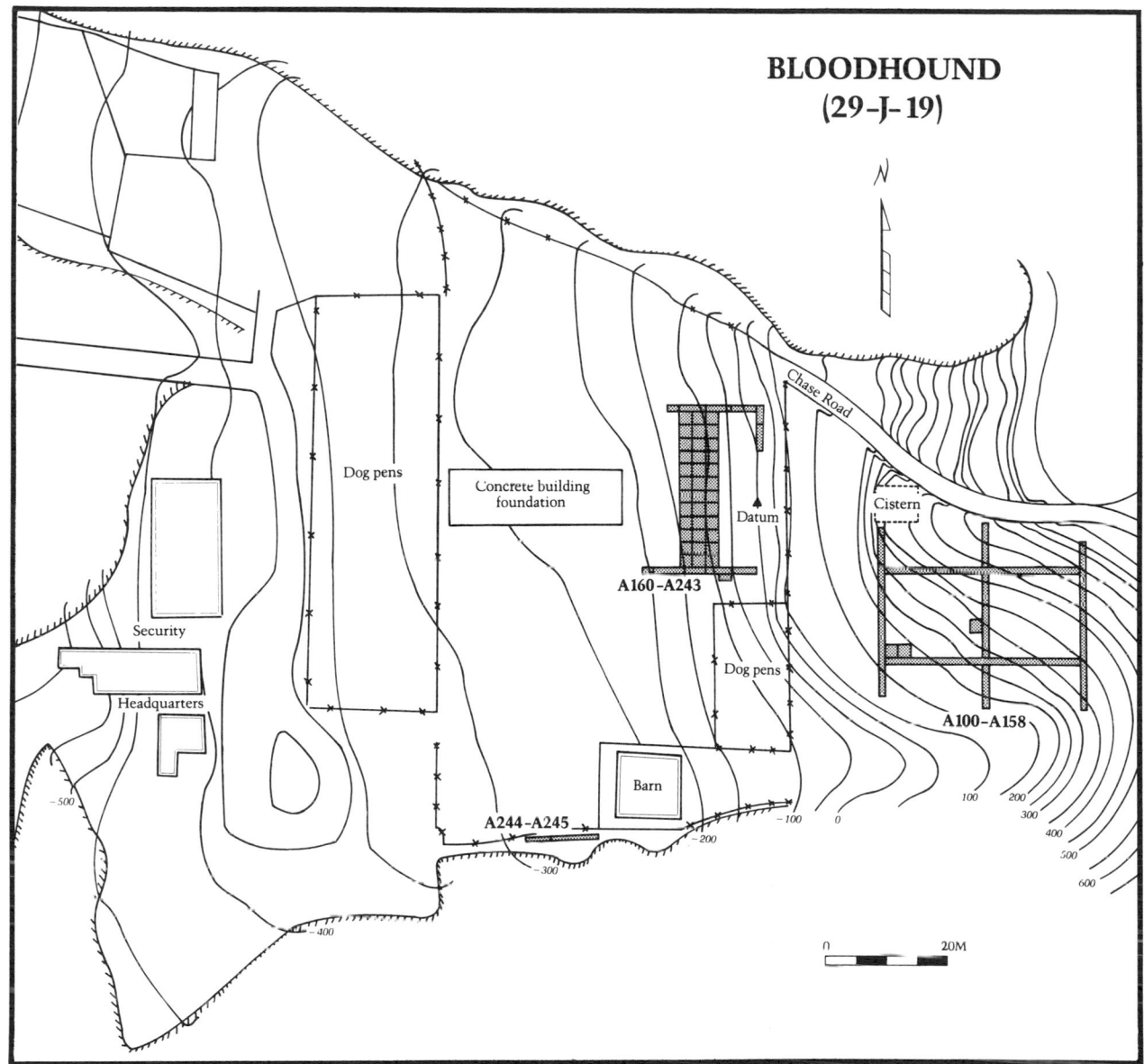

Figure 138. The Bloodhound site (29-J-19). Contour map and locations of excavations in 1977.

begins the long slope to the first loess ridge top above the 200-foot contour (fig. 139). The sharp rise, designated "Bloodhound Hill," was the locus of the burial discoveries; because we expected it to be a cemetery containing additional burials, our first attention was directed there. Exploratory work was carried out on the terrace at the end of the spring fieldwork, and the results were so encouraging that we returned there in the fall.

THE HILL

Our expectation that the Bloodhound Hill locus was an eighteenth-century Tunica cemetery and not just a case of isolated burials rested in large part upon Swanton's assertion, in reference to the Tunica, that "each cemetery was located on a hill" (Swanton 1946, p. 729). But also important was our strong belief that the principal Tunica village of the period 1706–1731 must have

been located in the immediate vicinity. Bloodhound Hill became a clue for pinpointing that village.

We were well aware that the Tunica did not place their cemeteries only on "hills in the open country" (Swanton 1911, p. 325). Evidence from the Haynes Bluff, Angola Farm, and Trudeau sites clearly demonstrates that other burial locations also were used by the Tunica in the eighteenth century. But a hillside cemetery certainly was possible and accorded well with secondary practice at both Haynes Bluff and Trudeau. It also coincided with the settlement patterning, which (we thought) placed the principal village on a nearby hilltop.

The overall slope of the hillside averaged twenty percent, but the surface topography was irregular and marked by sharp changes in relief (fig. 139a). Although the broken topography was due partly to recent construction and erosion, the location always must have been unsuitable for agricultural or habitational purposes. In-

a

b

Figure 139. Excavations at Bloodhound. a, exploratory trench, looking east up the hill; b, initial trench on the terrace, looking west down from the hill.

deed, our investigations revealed no signs of any aboriginal activity on the hill other than mortuary.

Recent human use of the hillside, however, reflected the variety of modern life, with a definite overlay of prison-specific activities. It was at once pasture, junk yard, access route into the hills, and firing range for target practice. There also was evidence of early twentieth-century houses associated with a large concrete

cistern. A road had been bulldozed up the north side of the hill in order to give the chase unit a more direct route into the interior. The road cut deeply into the ground, and profiling of the walls gave us our first confirmation of the mortuary nature of the site. This fortunate happenstance only partly made up for the fact that the extensive scatter of automobile and other machinery parts rendered useless our electronic subsurface detection gear.

The investigation of Bloodhound Hill was carried out in three stages, in an escalation of effort that may seem contrary to normal archaeological procedure but was dictated by circumstances. In stage one, the location first was intensively surveyed by the professional personnel. Although the electronic equipment (differential proton magnetometer and transmitter-receiver) was subverted by the surface scatter of metallic junk, visual inspection and profiling of the deeply cut chase road soon revealed burials 3 and 4 (numbers 1 and 2 were assigned to the burials said to have been found by the inmate the preceding year). Concurrently, three 2- × -2-m excavation units (A100–102) were placed in the vicinity where burials 1 and 2 were said to have been found (fig. 140). These excavations were without result. When further survey failed to produce any more aboriginal remains, we decided to avail ourselves of the unlimited labor supply at our disposal.

Stage two was carried out with a convict crew under the direction of the professional staff. In an attempt to find aboriginal features beneath the recent surface trash and disturbance, a series of exploratory trenches (A103–158 inclusive) 1 m wide and 26–30 m long was run across the hillside around and beyond where the earlier burials had been found (fig. 140). Following the surface contour, the trenches generally were dug out to a depth of approximately 20 cm before subsoil was reached. The floors were then troweled for features. Some small aboriginal pits of unknown purpose were located by this method, but no burials or other major features were found.

In the third stage of investigation we added a bulldozer to our repertoire. Since the hand clearing was so slow and unproductive, we decided that the last resort was to clear the modern surface layer from the entire hillside. With a "clean" environment the electronic instruments could be brought back for a final sweep of the site. Removing about 10 cm at a time, the bulldozer accordingly excavated up to 1 m of topsoil and associated junk from the surface of the site. One burial (burial 5) was exposed in this fashion, fortunately without damage. Electronic survey of the entire cleared area revealed two more burials (burials 6 and 7; figs. 140–141) but no additional aboriginal features.

Bloodhound Hill thus turned out to be a small cemetery, probably related to a minor satellite settlement. However, it does provide important information on early eighteenth-century mortuary customs and artifactual possessions.

Burial 1. "Burials 1 and 2" was the designation given to the initial discovery by the prison inmate, who claimed that the material turned over to the state archaeologist was recovered from two graves. Most of the artifacts,

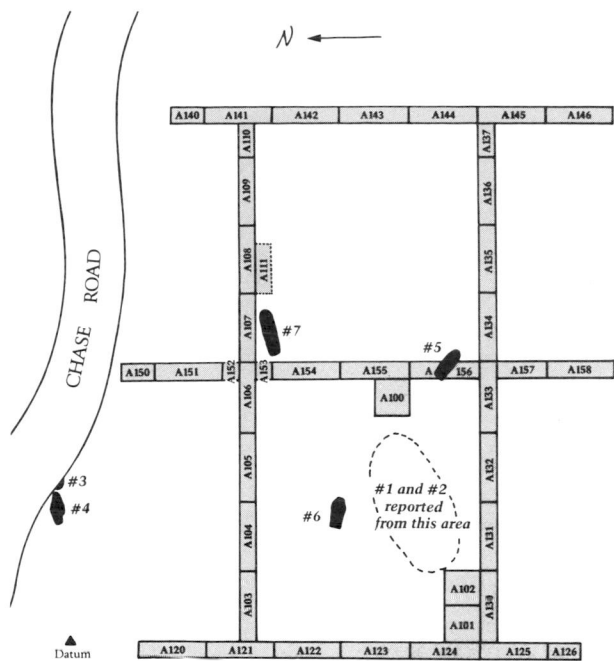

Figure 140. Plan of excavations on the hill and locations of burials at Bloodhound.

including all of the specifically identifiable ones, were reported to have been associated with burial 1 (fig. 142; table 42).

Burial 1 apparently was an adult male, presumably an extended supine inhumation with the head oriented to the east (fig. 142). The wealth of European items suggests an individual of some importance; furthermore, some of the artifacts are of unusual quality. Foremost among these is one of the flintlock muskets, a left-handed *fusil fin*. The handedness of this piece in-

---

Table 42. Aboriginal and European artifacts reportedly found with burial 1 at the Bloodhound site (29-J-19).

ABORIGINAL

Conch shell beads[a]	4

EUROPEAN

Earthenware jug	1
Glass mirror[a]	1
Glass beads[b]	—
Sword-rapier[a] (fig. 142b)	1
Brass kettles[c] (fig. 142a)	2
Brass-handled scissors	1
Brass bells[a] (fig. 142j–l)	7
Flintlock muskets[a] (fig. 142c–i)	2
Lead musket balls	2 or 3
Gunflints	2

[a]In possession of Louisiana state archaeologist.
[b]Some in possession of Louisiana state archaeologist.
[c]One in possession of Louisiana state archaeologist.

a

b

Figure 141. Burial excavations at Bloodhound. a, burial 5 (left background), burial 6 (right), burial 7 (left foreground); b, electronic retesting of burial 7 location with portable differential magnetometer.

dicates that it was a special order item, and consequently a better grade of gun than common trade fusils like the second gun that accompanied the burial (see app. G.2 for further discussion of these pieces by T. M. Hamilton, who dates both guns to "the opening of the eighteenth century at the latest").

Other important items are the seventeenth-century sword-rapier and the cast brass bells, which include the rare liberty bell form (Brown 1980, p. 93; this type appears to be a good marker for the early eighteenth century in the Lower Mississippi Valley) as well as a new

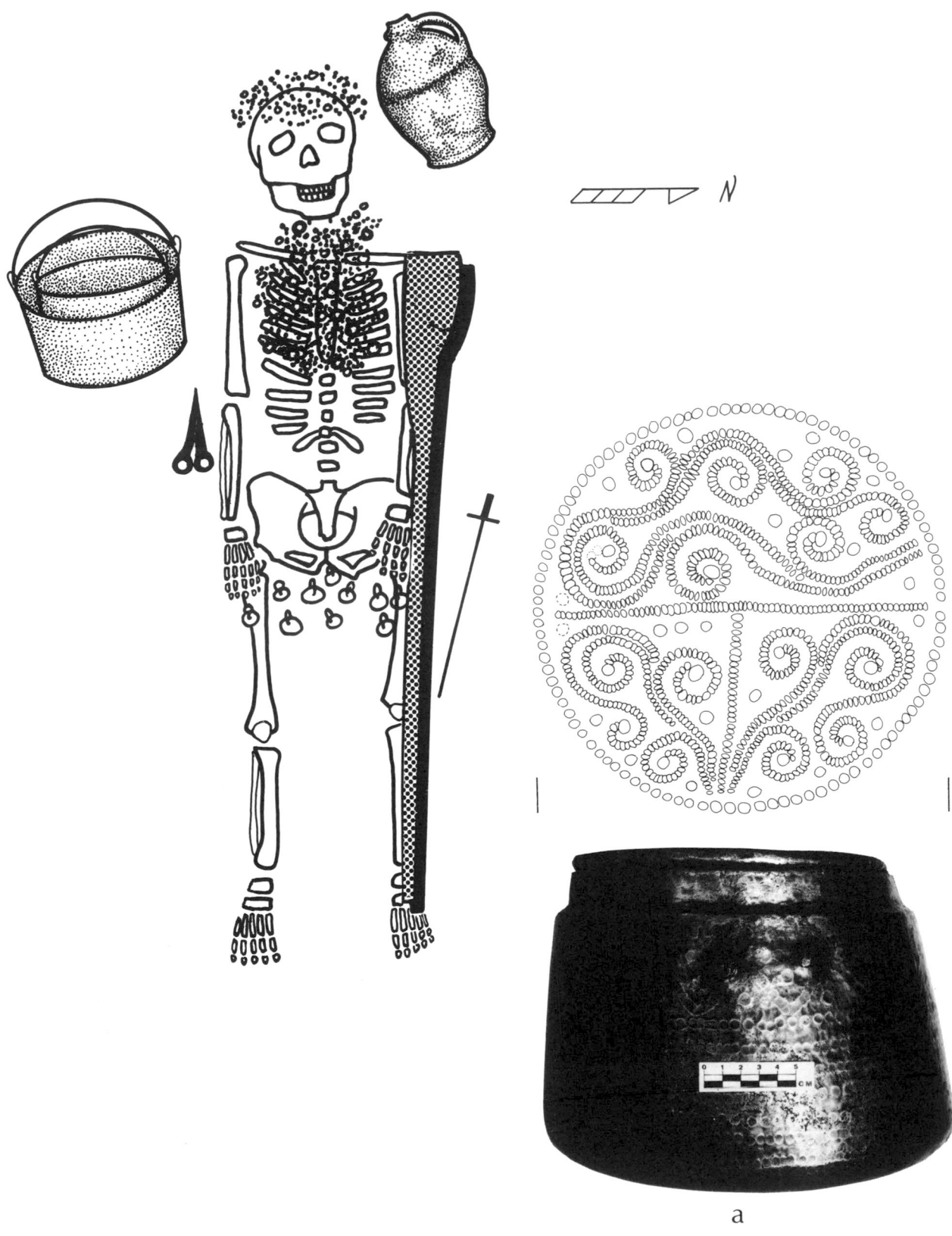

Figure 142. Reconstruction of burial 1 at Bloodhound (from a drawing by Alan Toth, who interviewed the finder). a, brass kettle, Type F, Variety 1; b, sword-rapier; c–f, brass hardware from Type C gun; g–h, brass hardware from left-handed Type C gun; i, flintlock from left-handed Type C gun; j, brass liberty bell; k–l, brass Angola bells; m, conch shell beads. (all 1:2, except a, 1:3)

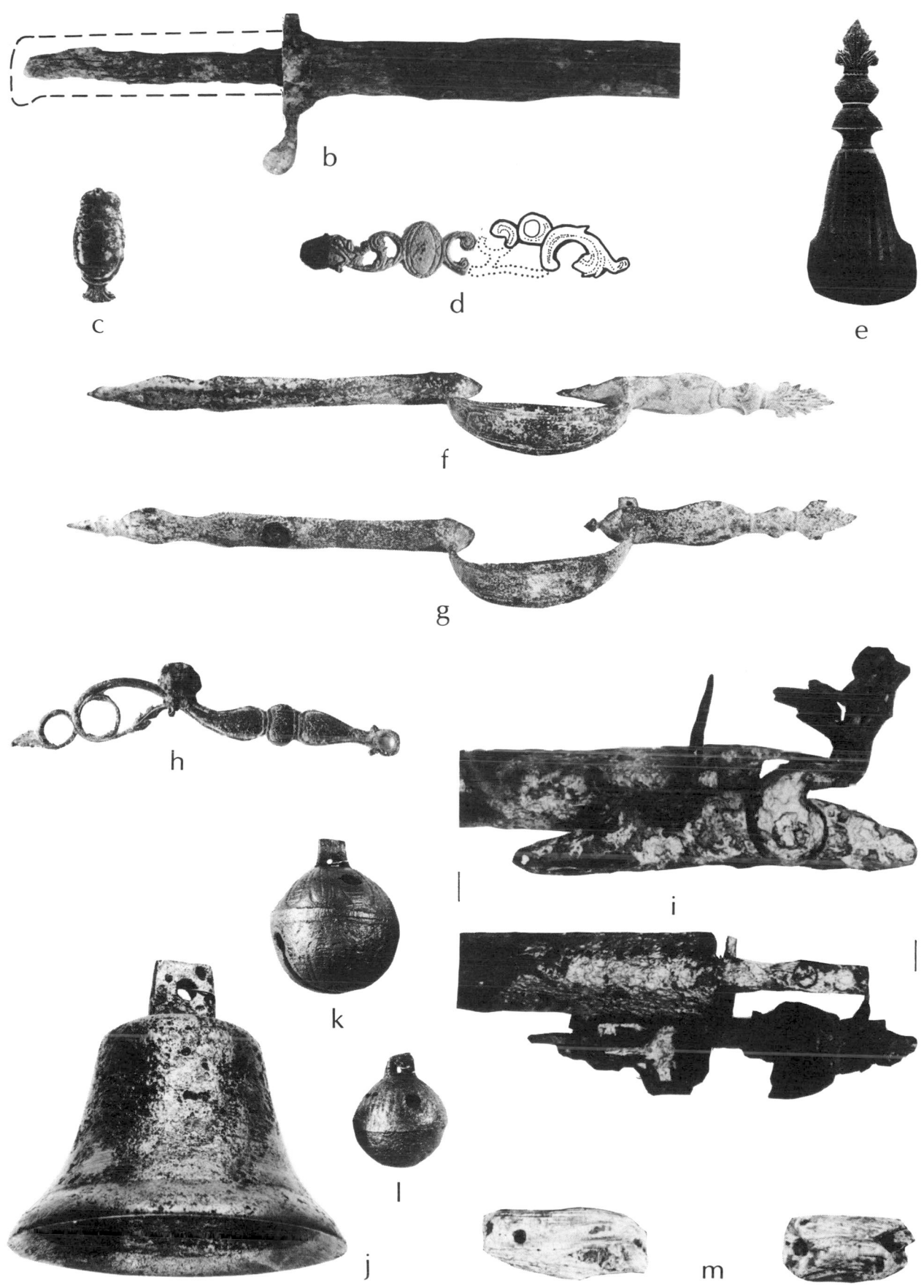

variety of the round Key type (Brown 1979b, pp. 197–198). Of the two metal kettles supposedly found, only one was turned over to the state archaeologist. It is made of sheet brass and is an example of Type F, Variety 1 with a complex style of hammered design presently known only from the Trudeau site (Brain 1979, pp. 178–179; note, however, that the kettles from Trudeau are made of copper). The pottery jug is a squat form of Type A, Variety 1 lead-glazed earthenware (Steponaitis 1979, p. 45).* Exactly the same form was found with burial 2 at the Angola Farm cemetery by Ford (1936, p. 137; Quimby 1966, fig. 13, lower right; see also fig. 128a and app. D, this vol., for illustration and further discussion).

The glass beads display a range of types generally characteristic of the early eighteenth century. Identifiable varieties include IIA1, IIA7, IIB5, IIB16, IVB1, WIA7, WIIA2, and WIIB2. How complete this sample might be is unknown, but it compares favorably with the list of varieties recovered from the entire 1977 excavations (cf. table 46). Clearly, the gentleman to whom they belonged had wide access to the total tribal inventory. Equally clearly, the glass beads did not completely replace the prized conch shell beads, an aboriginal mark of individual importance.

Burial 2.   Burial 2 is reported to have been another extended inhumation near (associated with?) burial 1. Unlike burial 1, however, it apparently had very few artifacts in accompaniment. Only one piece of galena and an unknown number of small white and "black" beads (probably IIA1 and IIA6) were recovered. The beads were described as being mainly seed beads in the chest area, which suggests they may have been strung into a necklace or sewn onto embroidery.

Burial 3.   The remains of burial 3 were discovered in the profile of the newly bulldozed chase road (see fig. 140), and further investigation revealed a pit some 30 cm deep containing European artifacts. The artifacts were mostly gun parts—two Type C brass butt plates (fig. 143), miscellaneous iron screws and other iron pieces, lead shot, and powder—but also included some pockets of vermilion and a few small white glass beads (IIA1). This select assemblage, plus the presence of a few fragments of large mammal (presumably human) bone in otherwise clean pit fill, provided us sufficient evidence to conclude that we had isolated the remnant of a burial. This conclusion was reinforced by the prison inmate's statement that he had found numerous artifacts in the road after it was cut. These artifacts were said to include more gun parts, cast brass bells at least two inches in diameter, a "gallon of beads" (?), and a native pottery vessel of type Mississippi Plain, *var. Pocahontas.*

Apparently the bulldozer had cut into this burial and, taking most of it, had spread the contents along the road. Judging from the remaining outline of the pit and the placement of the butt plates, the burial must have

---

* This jug was seen in private hands and photographed by LMS personnel in August 1975, a date that belies the official accounting given to the state archaeologist of the circumstances and chronology of the Bloodhound discovery.

Figure 143. Type C brass butt plates from burial 3 at Bloodhound. (1:2)

been oriented with the head more or less to the east. The presence of the two butt plates confirms that some individuals may have had more than one musket interred with them, as was reported for burial 1. Whether such conspicuous consumption at this relatively early stage of contact in the Lower Mississippi Valley is indicative of individual importance or unusual societal wealth remains unclear.

Burial 4.   Immediately to the southwest of burial 3 was burial 4. In fact, the burials were so close that 4 was discovered while 3 was being isolated. It could not be determined whether the contiguity was fortuitous or signified a life relationship of some sort.

Burial 4 was an extended supine inhumation of an adult female oriented with head to the east (figs. 140, 144). At interment she was attired in a European frock coat sporting wide (leather?) cuffs, each decorated with three large copper-covered wooden buttons. Another button found in the pelvic area may indicate that she was also wearing trousers. Thus, at least one member of society other than the chief wore articles of European clothing. This was probably true of many tribal members, including women, by the second or third decade of the eighteenth century (see Hanson 1982 for a comparative situation). Additional adornment consisted of one blue and hundreds of small white glass beads (IIA1) massed by the left side of the skull. As discussed under burial 5, these probably had been strung and woven into the hair, a common decorative practice among Indian women (Dumont de Montigny 1753, vol. 1, p. 137; Gayarré 1885, p. 291). A patch of vermilion on the right frontal bone may have been a cosmetic touch. A pair of native-made conch columella shell earpins, another distinctive female ornament, completed the remarkable ensemble. Other artifacts in the grave were a lump of lead ore, by the right shoulder, and a brass kettle containing a Natchezan pot, near the top of the skull. The kettle is a medium-size example of Type A, Variety 1 (Brain 1979, pp. 166–172), and the native bowl is a typical example of Fatherland Incised, *var. Fatherland* (fig. 144a).

Although none of the artifacts in this grave is distinctive enough to provide a fine chronology, all certainly are consistent with an early eighteenth-century date.

Burial 5.   All of the human skeletal remains at Bloodhound Hill were very poorly preserved, but this burial was in the worst condition and consisted of little more than faint stains in the ground. It could be determined that the burial was a pit inhumation of an extended supine individual with head oriented to the southeast (figs. 140, 145). Size and dentition suggested that it was an adolescent or very young adult. Sex was indicated as female by the presence of linear arrangements of hundreds of small glass beads around and beneath the skull. Apparently they had been strung and woven into the hair, a trait specifically mentioned by Dumont as being characteristic of Lower Mississippi Valley women and girls: "Their tresses are ordinarily interlaced by way of ornament with [strings of] blue, white, green, or black glass beads" (Dumont de Montigny 1753, vol. 1, p. 137). In this case the beads were turquoise blue (IIA7). Also present were one medium-size white bead (IIA1?) and a striped blue bead (IIB7).

Flecks of vermilion were observed mixed among the beads, and a patch of native red ochre was found near the chin. How these pigments were employed was not determined. The only other artifacts in this grave were two medium-size iron axes lying in the chest area (fig. 145a) and an unidentified piece of iron by the right arm.

Burial 6.   This was the most interesting burial found at Bloodhound Hill. Judging by dentition and general size, the individual was a child between five and eight years old at the time of death. The child must have been the offspring of someone important because it was accompanied by the greatest variety and quantity of artifacts (fig. 146), including several specific indicators of high rank.

The European artifacts featured an assortment of glass beads. Near the top of the head were six plain white beads (IIA1), one plain blue bead (IIA7), and six striped

Shell earpin

Lead

Cuff with copper-covered wooden buttons

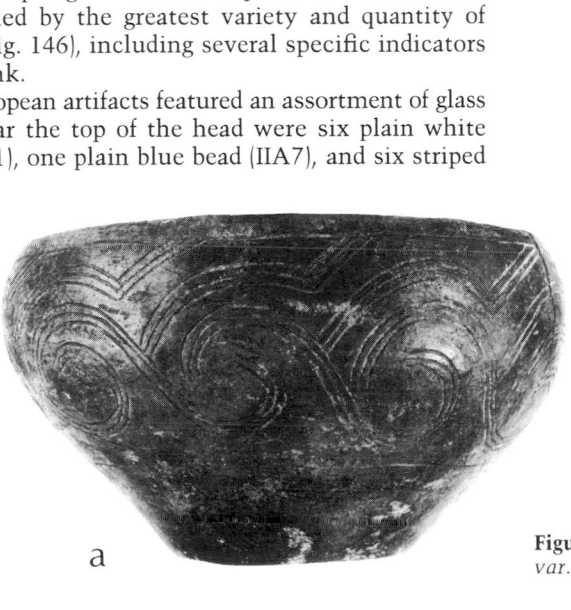

a

Figure 144. Burial 4 at Bloodhound. a, Fatherland Incised, *var. Fatherland* bowl. (1:3)

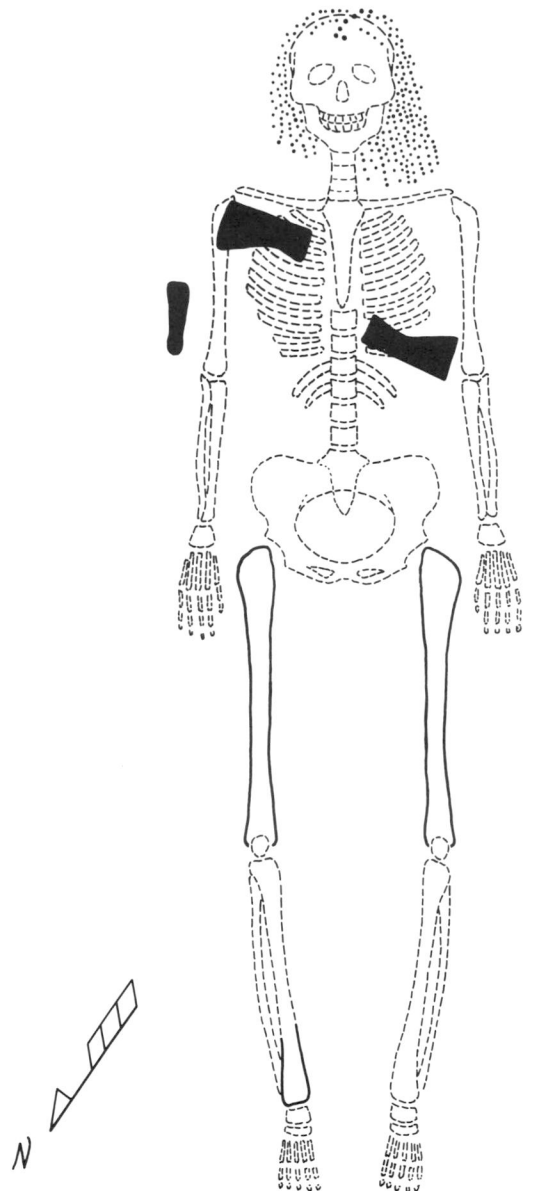

a

Figure 145. Burial 5 at Bloodhound. a, iron axe. (1:2)

At the right side of the head was a crushed pottery vessel of native Caddoan manufacture (fig. 146a), probably belonging to the upper Red River type Avery Engraved (Suhm and Jelks 1962, pp. 1–4). The only other aboriginal artifact was an elaborate necklace of conch shell discs and columella beads (fig. 146b). The significance of this type of necklace is unknown, but its value to the native Indian was observed by Cabeza de Vaca (Bandelier 1922, p. 75) and is suggested here by its continued use even in the presence of abundant European trade goods. The marine shell necklace must have been a native indication of high status (e.g., Essenpreis 1982, p. 126). Found within the necklace when it was disassembled in the laboratory was a copper crucifix (fig. 146c). It is recorded that Father Davion, the resident missionary among the Tunica, concentrated on baptizing the children of influential natives (Le Page du Pratz 1758, vol. 1, p. 123; Margry 1888, vol. 6, p. 247). Note that in the famous watercolor painted by DeBatz in 1732 (see fig. 208), the young son of the great Tunica chief Cahura-Joligo is identified as "Jacob," indicating that he had been baptized.

Another interesting aspect of burial 6 was its orientation. The Tunica generally seem to have buried their dead with the head to the east, but this burial is unusual in being oriented with the head to the west. Whether age, status, or religion had any bearing on this exception cannot be determined at the present time, but it is of interest to note that the one child inhumation found in mound C at the Fatherland site, the high-status burial place of the historic Natchez Indians, also was oriented with the head to the west (Neitzel 1983, p. 128; cf. Neitzel 1965, pp. 41–44).

blue beads (IIB7). Around the left wrist was a bracelet of large clear beads (IIA3). Most common of all were hundreds of small turquoise seed beads (IIA7) found scattered about the torso area. Although no patterns could be distinguished, it is probable that these small beads had been embroidered: "These same painted glass beads they also used in ornamenting their leather garments, and they composed with them fanciful embroideries" (Gayarré 1885, p. 291).

Other European items in the grave were two folding knives by the head, five copper wire bracelets around the left wrist, and at least nine small sheet brass bells of the Flushloop variety (Brown 1979b, p. 201) at each knee. The bells had been attached to leather bindings that were then tied around the legs, a popular form of personal adornment (Gayarré 1885, p. 291). A lead bale seal and an unidentified copper alloy object between the lower legs may have been incidental associations.

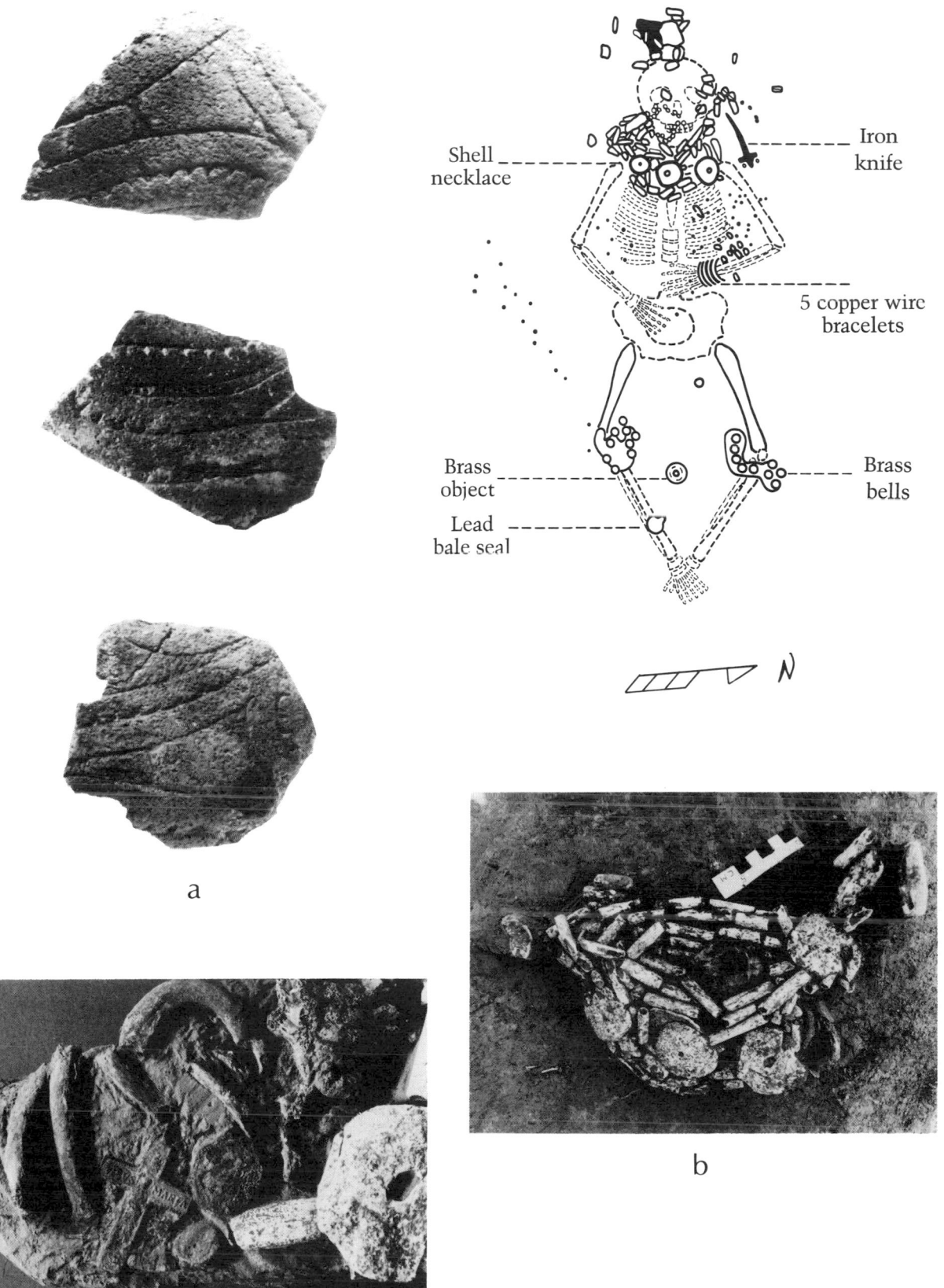

Shell
necklace

Iron
knife

5 copper wire
bracelets

Brass
object

Lead
bale seal

Brass
bells

N

a

b

c

Figure 146. Burial 6 at Bloodhound. a, potsherds from a vessel probably belonging to the Caddoan type Avery Engraved; b, shell bead and disc necklace; c, copper crucifix in situ beneath shell necklace. (a, 1:1; b, 1:4; c, 1:2)

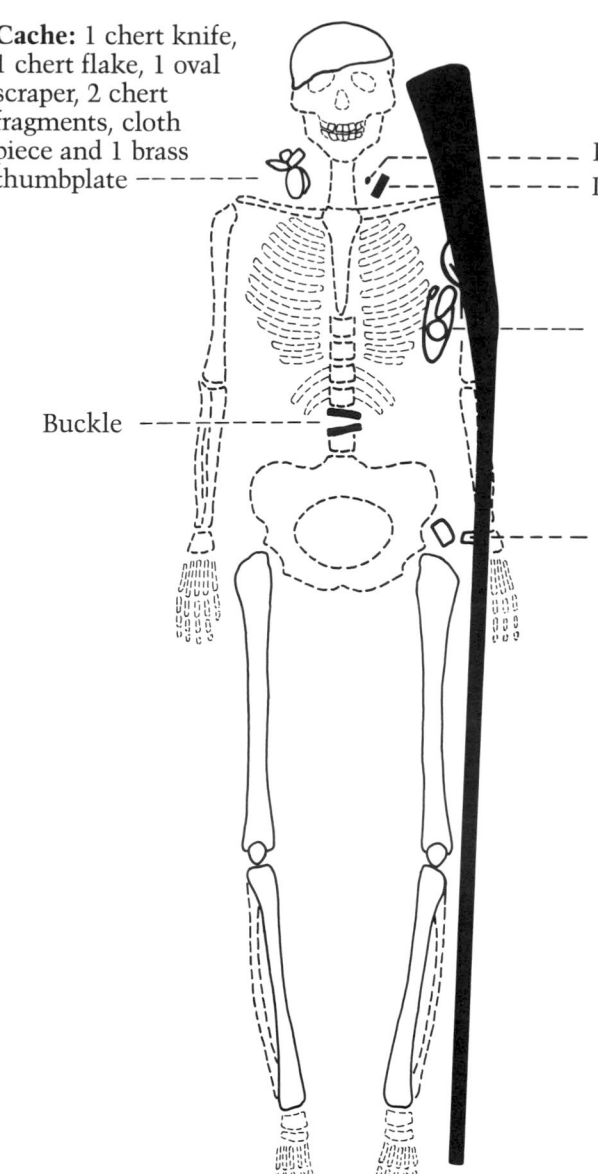

Cache: 1 chert knife, 1 chert flake, 1 oval scraper, 2 chert fragments, cloth piece and 1 brass thumbplate

Blue seed bead
Iron tube
Lock, gunpowder, escutcheon
Buckle
Thumbnail scraper

Figure 147. Burial 7 at Bloodhound.

N

Burial 7. Burial 7 was an extended supine inhumation of an adult male oriented with the head to the east (fig. 147). The condition of the skeletal remains again was very poor, with only scraps of long bones remaining. Even the skull was totally gone, leaving behind only a mold of the brain case. Age and sex determinations were based solely on the overall large size of the body (requiring a grave pit 215 cm in length) and the presumably masculine artifacts found in accompaniment.

The principal grave offering, and that which triggered our magnetometer (fig. 141b), was a flintlock musket of unidentified type (app. G.2). The fact that it was totally furnished in iron suggests that it was an early model. Before being placed in the grave the gun had been disassembled—i.e., the lock had been removed—and it and other miscellaneous gun parts were placed beside the trigger guard (fig. 147). Nearby were black powder and lead shot. Beneath the powder, a brass es-

cutcheon was found. It may not belong to the gun in the grave but may simply have been an incidental gun part acquired by the deceased, who seems to have had a special admiration for escutcheons: a second one was found in a cache of small artifacts near the head. Other artifacts in the cache, apparently contained in a cloth pouch suspended from the neck, were aboriginal chert tools. These included a knife, an oval scraper, and some small utilized pieces. Also near the chin area, and possibly suspended from the same string as the pouch, were a very small blue glass bead (IIA7) and a small iron tube that contained a fragment of bone. The remains of an iron buckle in the pelvic area may indicate that there had been a belt or even some article of European clothing. A snub-nosed end scraper of chert and a potsherd of type Fatherland Incised, *var. Fatherland* by the left hip may have been accidental inclusions in the grave.

Although this individual does not have the quantity and variety of grave goods found with the other burials at the site (with the possible exception of burial 2), it might not be accurate to consider him a poorer member of the society. He was, after all, interred with his gun, which, even if nonfunctioning, was a most valuable possession. Furthermore, if this gun is as early a model as is suspected, it may be that burial 7 was the earliest on the hill and comparatively well outfitted for the time.

Possible Additional Burials. Numerous other artifacts are reported to have been recovered from Bloodhound Hill. These artifacts presently are in private hands and are believed to have been taken from additional graves prior to the official notification to the state of the site's existence. The artifacts include gun parts (fig. 148a–q) and an iron harpoon point (fig. 148r). Nonmetallic artifacts probably also exist (see discussion of the earthenware jug under burial 1). The associations and number of burials from which these artifacts might have come are unknown.

Evidence for the previous existence of graves other than the putative burials 1 and 2 was uncovered in the course of our excavations. In excavation unit A108 (see

Table 43. Aboriginal and European artifacts found at locations other than the burials during the excavations on the hill at Bloodhound.

ABORIGINAL		EUROPEAN	
Pottery:		*Earthenware:*	
Winterville Incised, *var. Tunica*	5	Faience	
Barton Incised, *var. Trudeau*	7	White	1
Owens Punctated, *var. Redwood*	1	Unglazed (fig. 156n)	2
Mississippi Plain, *var. Pocahontas*	173		
		Glass:	
Mississippi Plain, *var. Montfort*	1		
		Olive green	1
Old Town Red, *var. unspecified*	2	Beads	
Unclassified incised (Mississippian)	3	IIA1	3
Mississippi Plain, *var. unspecified*	1	IIA6	1
		IIA13	2
Fatherland Incised, *var. Bayou Goula*	1	IIB5	1
Fatherland Incised, *var. Nancy*	1		
Fatherland Incised, *var. Snyders Bluff*	2	*Iron:*	
Unclassified incised/engraved (Caddo)	5	Kettle fragment	1
		Axe[a]	1
Fatherland Incised, *var. Fatherland* (fig. 148t)	9	Folding knife blades (fig. 148s)	2
Fatherland Incised, *var. unspecified*	4	Wrought nail	
Chicot Red, *var. Grand Village*	3	Type I (fig. 156d)	1
Addis Plain, *var. St. Catherine*	8		
		Copper:	
Leland Incised, *var. Russell*	1		
Leland Incised, *var. unspecified*	1	Miscellaneous	2
Addis Plain, *var. Skillikalia*	10		
		Brass:	
Plaquemine Brushed, *var. Plaquemine*	2		
Coleman Incised, *var. Coleman* (fig. 151i)	2	Kettle fragment	1
Mazique Incised, *var. Manchac* (fig. 151h)	1	Braid (fig. 148w–x)[b]	—
Unclassified incised (Addis)	3		
Addis Plain, *var. Addis*	12	*Gun parts/munitions:*	
Addis Plain, *var. unspecified*	90		
		Musket lock mainspring (fig. 155b)	1
Coles Creek Incised, *var. Mott*	1	Gunflint flake	1
Pontchartrain Check Stamped, *var. Pontchartrain*	2		
Baytown Plain, *var. unspecified*	11		
Lithics:			
Pipe drill (fig. 148u)	1		
Knife (fig. 148v)	1	[a] Possibly associated with burial 5.	
Utilized flakes	18	[b] Numerous fragments.	

fig. 140), just to the east of burial 7, a pit feature was discovered. Contained within the loose fill of the pit were fragments of metal braid, potsherds from a *Fatherland* bowl, and two stone tools: a chert knife and a chert pipe drill (fig. 148t–x). The remains of what appeared to be another disturbed grave were found in excavation unit A104. Although the pit feature (designated A73) was small, measuring only 0.75 × 1.5 m, it was oriented east-west and contained part of a broken

Mississippi Plain, *var. Pocahontas* pot in the east (head?) end, as well as a folding knife blade (fig. 148s) near the edge where the right arm of a supine burial would have been.

Several other features encountered during the excavations were much too disturbed to permit identification of their original configurations or functions. Material contents, however, included appropriate grave furniture such as pottery, glass beads, and gun parts (table 43).

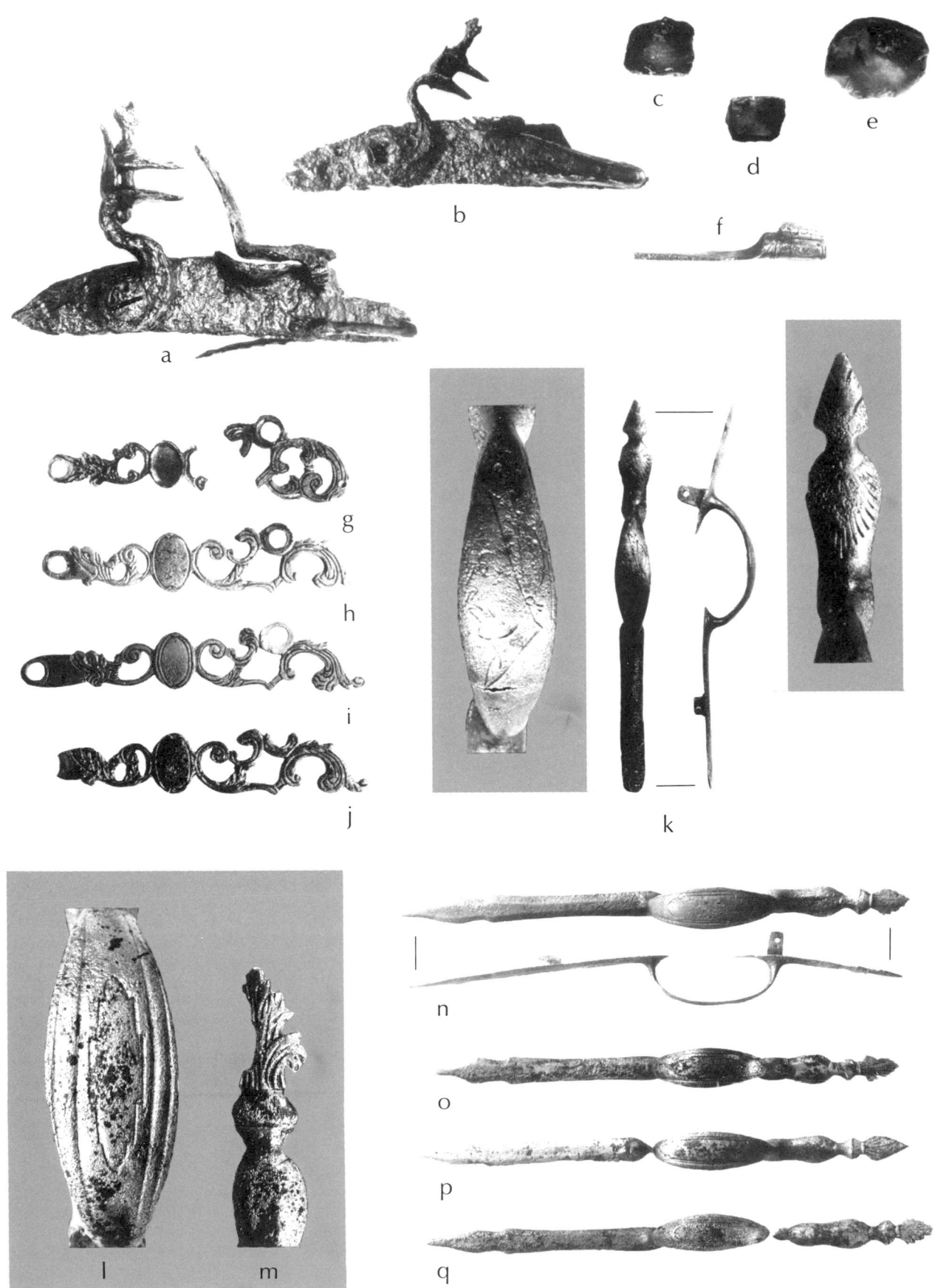

Figure 148. (continued).

Summary of the Burials.   The burials found at Blood-hound Hill were too far apart and original eighteenth-century ground surfaces were too disturbed for the firm establishment of horizontal and vertical relationships. Nevertheless, it can be reasonably argued that the in-terments at the cemetery represent a rough contem-poraneity: in archaeological terms a single component, which from historical sources may be dated to the first three decades of the eighteenth century. The dating of bead types and other diagnostic artifacts from the graves supports this assignment.

But even an interval of thirty years is not a suffi-ciently fine determination during this period of sporadic but increasing European contact. Burials only a few years apart could vary considerably in the type and amount of artifacts interred with them. Such slight temporal differences might well explain the variety observed. On the other hand, the range of age and sex characteristics represented by the limited number of individuals sug-gests that the cemetery was used by a small group within

a relatively short time. If this conclusion is correct, this group must have been well-to-do (or of high status, measured in economic terms) to be able to dispose of so many goods so quickly.

That this group was Tunica rests upon the proposi-tion that such a quantity and variety of European goods could only have been accumulated toward the end of the period, and certainly after 1706 when the Tunica arrived in the area and soon pushed out the Houma. Although no diagnostic aboriginal Tunica artifacts were found with the burials, the absence was compensated and the ethnic identification confirmed at the contig-uous habitation area on the terrace below the hill.

THE TERRACE

We never entertained the thought that we might be at the exact location of the Tunica's principal village during the first third of the eighteenth century because the Bloodhound site simply is not large enough to fit

Figure 148. Additional artifacts from the hill at Bloodhound. a–q, miscellaneous gun parts, mostly from Type C fusils; r, iron harpoon point; s, folding knife blade; t, Fatherland Incised, *var. Fatherland* potsherd; u, chert pipe drill; v, chert knife, w x, metal braid. (1:2, except details, s–x, 1:1)

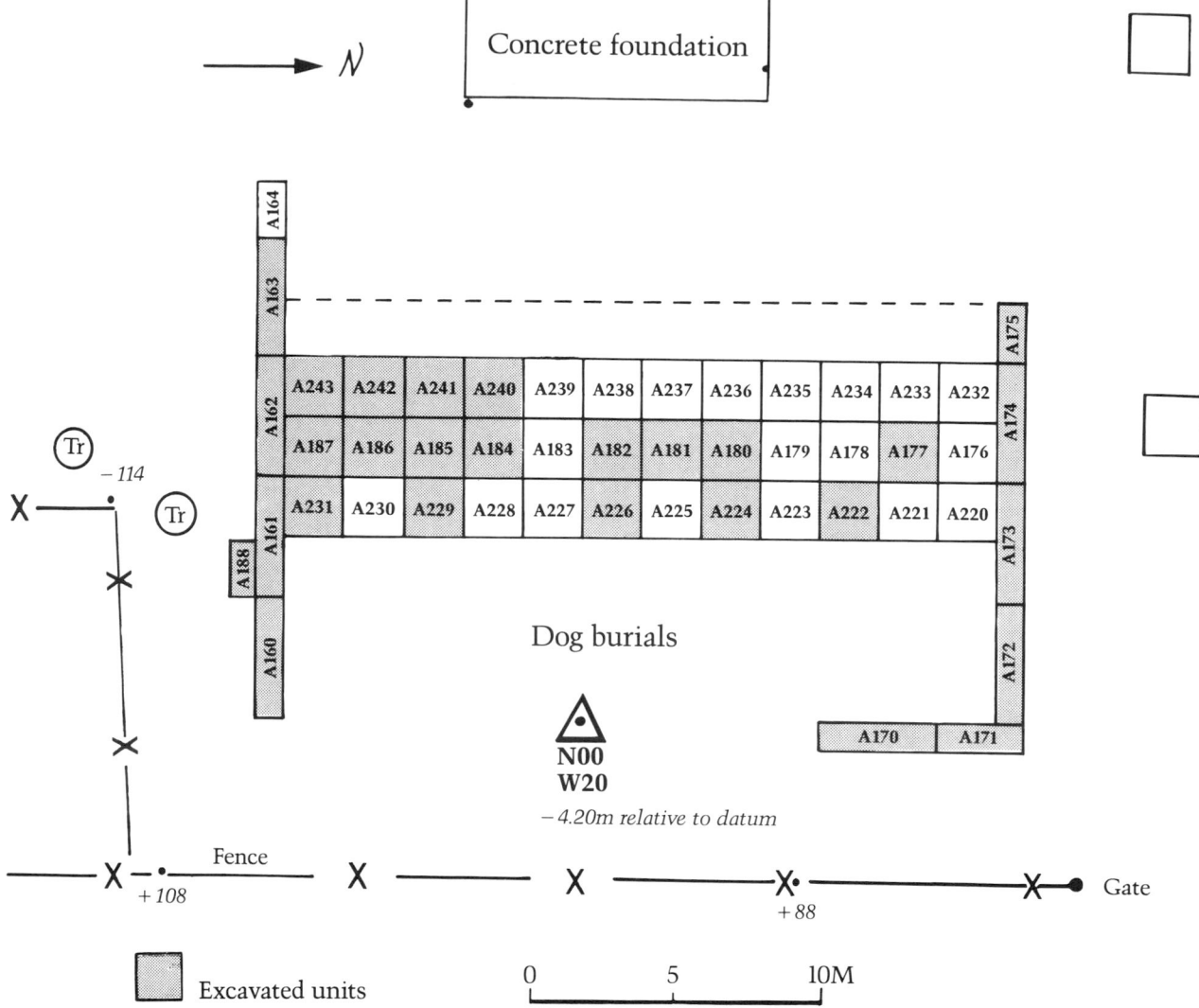

Figure 149. Plan of excavations on the terrace at Bloodhound.

the historical descriptions (see fig. 138). However, the documents' continual allusions to high ground and the placement of the village thereon were too insistent to be ignored: "*Le Village est au-delà du Lac sur un terrein assez élevé ... Il y a deux autres Villages de cette Nation, peu éloignés de celui-ci* (Charlevoix 1744, vol. 3, p. 433). Bloodhound may have been too small for the principal village, but the terrace would have been an attractive and well-situated location for a hamlet. Besides, an occupation near the cemetery was to be expected.

In 1977 the desirability of the terrace for human occupation was expressed by its use as the headquarters for the chase unit of the prison security division. In addition to the headquarters building and dog kennels, there were a first aid station, barn, chicken coop, two corrals, and other assorted structures. At an earlier period, approximately a half century ago, the terrace served as a residential area for prison personnel, and perhaps a dozen houses were scattered about. In more salubrious days, before the prison was built, the terrace supported several plantation structures. All of the current and past activities made instrument work on the terrace impossible: there was too much contemporary interference and long-term disturbance.

The site of the excavations thus was arbitrarily determined. Exploratory trenches were laid out on what appeared to be the best-preserved piece of unoccupied ground (fig. 149). That this same piece of ground also served as a shooting range (fig. 150) for the security division was more than a small distraction, and it was often necessary to abandon the trenches as target practice was carried out.

The initial trenches were laid out in the spring of 1977 according to a roughly H-shaped plan and were divided into smaller excavation units that were assigned numerical designations between A160 and A187. Control pits were dug in arbitrary levels until the local stratification was established, and then natural levels were used.

b

Figure 150. Terrace excavations at Bloodhound. a, excavation crew in October 1977, view from west to shooting range in background at the base of the hill; b–c, two views from the southwest; d, excavation units A240–243 from the south (the eighteenth-century midden layer is clearly visible in the walls; the square pits in the right foreground date to the prison era).

a

c

d

The stratification was simple. Generally throughout the excavations three soil zones were observed: topsoil 10–25 cm thick, consisting of humus over water-laid loess (talus from Bloodhound Hill) and containing a mixture of eighteenth-century and modern artifacts; a band of gray-black midden 5–60 cm thick, the original surface of which had been destroyed but which still preserved within it a number of aboriginal features and modern intrusions; and the loess subsoil of the terrace formation, into which ancient and modern features sometimes intruded. In the easternmost part of the excavations (excavation units A160, A170–173, A222,

A224) the midden layer was absent and subsoil was encountered immediately beneath a thin layer of topsoil. At some time in the recent past the edge of the hill apparently had been cut back some 10–15 m to the east. Posthole transects were run out across the rest of the terrace to the north, west, and south. Evidence of the black midden disappeared within a radius of 25 m from datum everywhere except in a narrow band along the southern edge of the terrace. Whether the limited extent of the midden layer indicated the actual extent of the historic occupation or the amount of recent disturbance was not determined.

In October 1977 a small crew from the LMS returned to Bloodhound to continue the excavations on the terrace (fig. 150). In an attempt to uncover some definitive architectural features and a stronger artifactual datum, the north-south trench was expanded (excavation units A220–243; fig. 149). A small trench (excavation units A244–245) was also placed near the southern edge of the terrace where posthole tests had revealed the strip of midden. This last excavation was purely exploratory and designed only to determine the age and character of the activity at that location.

Throughout the terrace excavations the basic stratification remained the same: disturbed topsoil, black midden layer, and subsoil. Although a few potsherds in-

dicating the presence of late Coles Creek–early Plaquemine components in the vicinity were found (fig. 151), it was determined that the Indian occupation that produced the in situ black midden dated to the early historic contact period. The terrace had then been abandoned for a period long enough to allow the accumulation of up to 10 cm of water-laid loess on the surface: talus from Bloodhound Hill. Subsequent occupations during the nineteenth century and continuing up to the time of the excavations in 1977 added another 10–20-cm accumulation of soil. In most places throughout the excavations, the upper layers—including the loess wash and even the original surface of the black midden— were thoroughly mixed by recent activities. These ac-

Figure 151. Prehistoric potsherds from Bloodhound and vicinity. a, Coles Creek Incised, *var. Mott*; b, Chevalier Stamped, *var. Perry*; c, Pontchartrain Check Stamped, *var. Pontchartrain*; d, Coles Creek Incised, *var. Hardy*; e, Mazique Incised, *var. Kings Point*; f, Anna Incised, *var. Anna*; g, Plaquemine Brushed, *var. Plaquemine*; h, Mazique Incised, *var. Manchac*; i, Coleman Incised, *var. Coleman*. (1:1)

Table 44. Aboriginal and European artifacts found during the excavations on the terrace at Bloodhound.

	Surface[a]	*Topsoil*	*Midden*
ABORIGINAL			
Pottery:			
Winterville Incised, *var. Tunica* (fig. 152b–h)	2	38	68
Winterville Incised, *var. Angola* (fig. 152a)	1		
Barton Incised, *var. Trudeau* (fig. 152k–m)		15	25
Barton Incised, *var. Portland* (fig. 152n–p)	1		2
Tunican Mode (fig. 152i–j)		4	3
Mississippi Plain, *var. Pocahontas*	15	342	544
Old Town Red, *var. Ballground*			1
Parkin Punctated, *var. Elise*		1	1
Winterville Incised, *var. Loubois*		4	9
Mississippi Plain, *var. Montfort*	5	8	43
Barton Incised, *var. unspecified*		1	5
Old Town Red, *var. unspecified*		2	3
Parkin Punctated, *var. unspecified*			2
Winterville Incised, *var. unspecified*		8	10
Unclassified incised (Mississippian)			1
Mississippi Plain, *var. unspecified*		2	
Cracker Road Incised, *var. Cracker Road* (fig. 153m)		1	3
Fatherland Incised, *var. Bayou Goula* (fig. 153h–i)	4	1	
Fatherland Incised, *var. Nancy* (fig. 153j)		1	
Fatherland Incised, *var. Snyders Bluff* (fig. 153f–g)		5	4
Unclassified incised/engraved (Caddo) (fig. 153o–p)			3
Fatherland Incised, *var. Fatherland* (fig. 153a–e)		7	9
Fatherland Incised, *var. unspecified* (fig. 153k–l)	1	4	17
Chicot Red, *var. Grand Village*	1	6	15
Addis Plain, *var. St. Catherine*	2	20	29
Leland Incised, *var. Russell* (fig. 153n)		3	10
Leland Incised, *var. unspecified*		1	3
Addis Plain, *var. Skillikalia*	1		9
Plaquemine Brushed, *var. Plaquemine*	1		2
Chevalier Stamped, *var. Perry* (fig. 151b)		2	5
Mazique Incised, *var. Manchac*			4
Unclassified incised (Addis)	2	5	6
Addis Plain, *var. Addis*	1	13	59
Addis Plain, *var. unspecified*	2	42	132
Pontchartrain Check Stamped, *var. Pontchartrain*			1
Coles Creek Incised, *var. Mott* (fig. 152a)	2	1	1
Baytown Plain, *var. Vicksburg*		1	
Baytown Plain, *var. Valley Park*		2	1
Baytown Plain, *var. unspecified*	2	1	
Earspool of Addis ware (fig. 154m)		1	

Table 44 continued

Table 44 (continued).

	Surface[a]	Topsoil	Midden
Lithics:			
Nodena Lanceolate, *var. Russell* point (fig. 154k)	1		
Native gunflint (fig. 155q)		1	
Triangular knife (fig. 154h)		1	
Knife blades (fig. 154e–g, i)	1	1	2
Chert celts (fig. 154b–d)	1	2	
Chert chopper (fig. 154a)		1	
Chert hammerstone		1	
Quartzite cobble (gamestone?) (fig. 154l)			1
Utilized chert cobbles		1	1
Utilized chert flakes		6	17
Galena crystal (fig. 154j)	1		

EUROPEAN

	Surface[a]	Topsoil	Midden
Earthenware:			
Faience			
White (fig. 156o–p)			4
Brown (fig. 156m)		1	
Glass:			
Clear (fig. 156s–t)			2
Olive green (fig. 156u–w)		3	6
Light blue-green (fig. 156q–r)			2
Emerald (fig. 156x)			3
Beads			
IIA1 (fig. 156y)		1	12
IIA4 (fig. 156z)		1	
IIA5			1
IIA6 (fig. 156aa)			11
IIA7 (fig. 156bb)			22
IIA13 (fig. 156cc)			1
IIA14 (fig. 156dd)			1
IIA15 (fig. 156ee)			2
IIB2 (fig. 156ff)		1	2
IIB3 (fig. 156gg)			1
IIB5 (fig. 156hh)			1
IIB7 (fig. 156ii)			2
IIB15 (fig. 156jj)			1
IIB16 (fig. 156kk)			1
IIB17 (fig. 156ll)			1
IVA2 (fig. 156mm)			4
IVB3 (fig. 156nn)			2
IVB6 (fig. 156oo)			1
WIIIA1 (fig. 156pp)			1
WIIIA2 (fig. 156qq)			1
Iron:			
Wrought nails			
Type I (fig. 156e)			1
Type unspecified		2	8
Case knife blade (fig. 156a)			1

Table 44 (continued).

	Surface[a]	Topsoil	Midden
Folding knife blades (fig. 156b–c)			2
C-bracelet (fig. 156f)	1		
Miscellaneous	1		27
Brass:			
Bell			
Flushloop (fig. 156i)			1
Tinkling cone (fig. 156h)			1
Scallop shell ornament (fig. 156j)		1	
Pendants (fig. 156k–l)	2		
C-bracelet (fig. 156g)			1
Wire ring			1
Miscellaneous	3	2	2
Gun parts/munitions:			
Musket flintlock (fig. 155f)			1
Brass musket side plate (fig. 155d)			1
Brass musket butt plate (fig. 155a)	1		
Brass musket trigger guard (fig. 155e)			1
Brass musket escutcheon (fig. 155c)	1		
Gunflints			
Musket (fig. 155i–p)	1	4	2
Pistol			2
Lead musket balls (fig. 155g)	8	2	5
Lead shot (fig. 155h)	21		
Lead miscellaneous			1
Miscellaneous:			
French chalcedony (for gunflints?)	1		1

[a]Away from excavated locations

Table 45. Nineteenth-century artifacts found during the excavations on the terrace at Bloodhound.

Number	Description	Dating	Provenience
2	Hand-painted pearlware, fine-line polychrome floral[a] (both pieces from same bowl)	Early nineteenth century (ca. 1800–1830)	A242 midden (there was considerable recent disturbance at this location)
1	Light green bottle glass	Nineteenth century	A242 midden
2	Dark olive green bottle glass (both from same bottle)	Early–mid nineteenth century	A226 topsoil
1	Annular decorated whiteware, white banded on yellow[b]	Late nineteenth century (post-1860)	Surface collection from gully on south side of terrace

[a]Price 1979, pp. 20–21.
[b]Ibid., p. 18.

---

tivities also were responsible for numerous intrusions through the midden layer and into subsoil. Fortunately, most of these intrusions could be identified by the artifactual content and/or the type of feature, and as a result they were excluded from the analysis of the Indian occupation.

The normal excavation procedure in a given unit was to strip the disturbed topsoil down to the black midden layer (or the overlying loess wash if present) and to search it for artifactual content. Eighteenth- and nineteenth-century artifacts were saved (tables 44–45); twentieth-century items—mostly building materials—

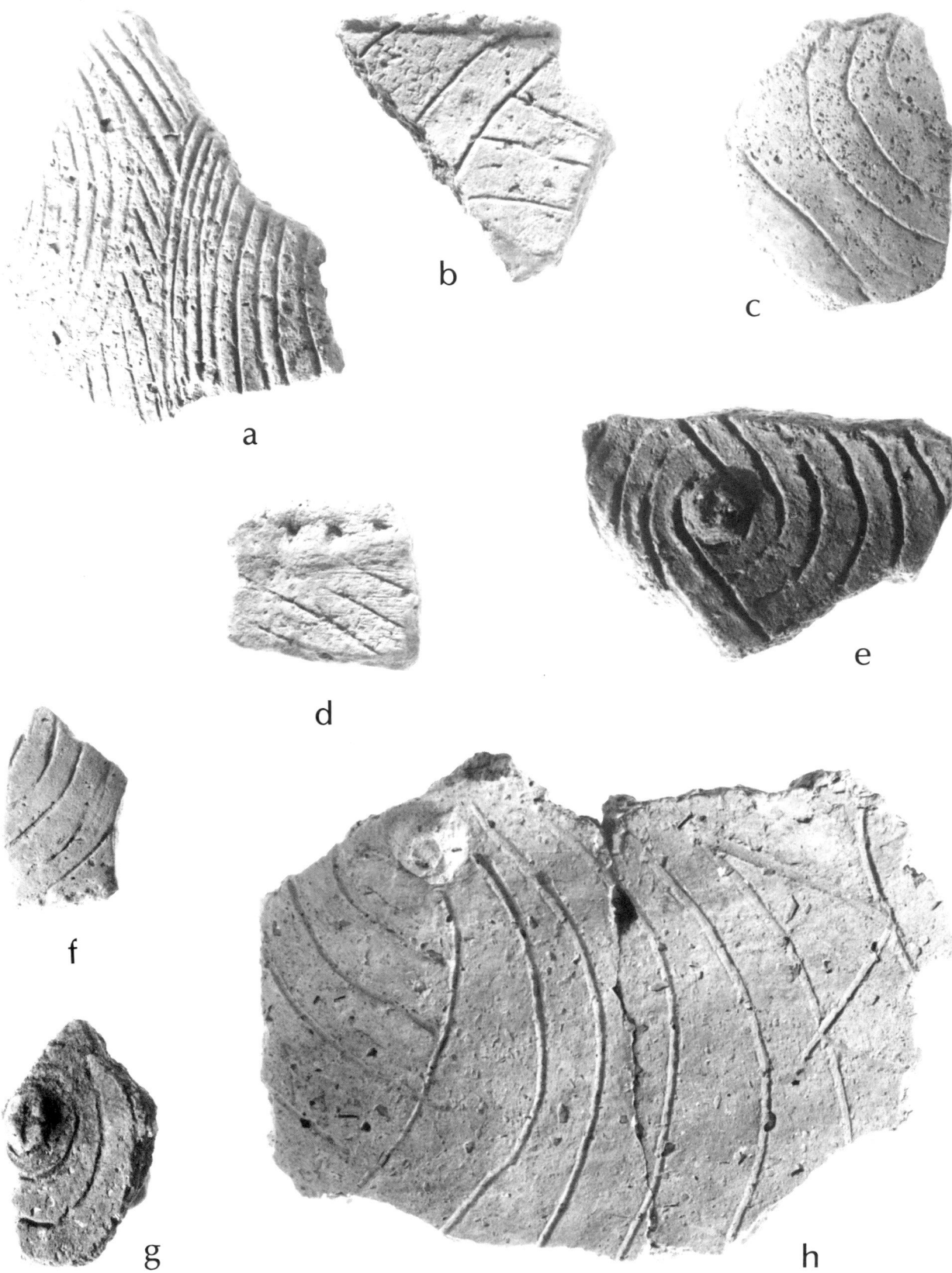

Figure 152. Eighteenth-century Tunica pottery found in the terrace excavations at Bloodhound. a, Winterville Incised, *var. Angola*; b–h, Winterville Incised, *var. Tunica*; i–j, Tunican Mode; k–m, Barton Incised, *var. Trudeau*; n–p, Barton Incised, *var. Portland*. (1:1)

i

j

k

l

m

n

o

p

Figure 152 (continued).

Figure 153. Eighteenth-century aboriginal pottery found in the terrace excavations at Bloodhound. a–e, Fatherland Incised, *var. Fatherland*; f–g, Fatherland Incised, *var. Snyders Bluff*; h–i, Fatherland Incised, *var. Bayou Goula*; j, Fatherland Incised, *var. Nancy*; k–l, Fatherland Incised, *var. unspecified* (k, from the Haynes Bluff site); m, Cracker Road Incised, *var. Cracker Road*; n, Leland Incised, *var. Russell*; o–p, unclassified Caddoan engraved pottery. (1:1)

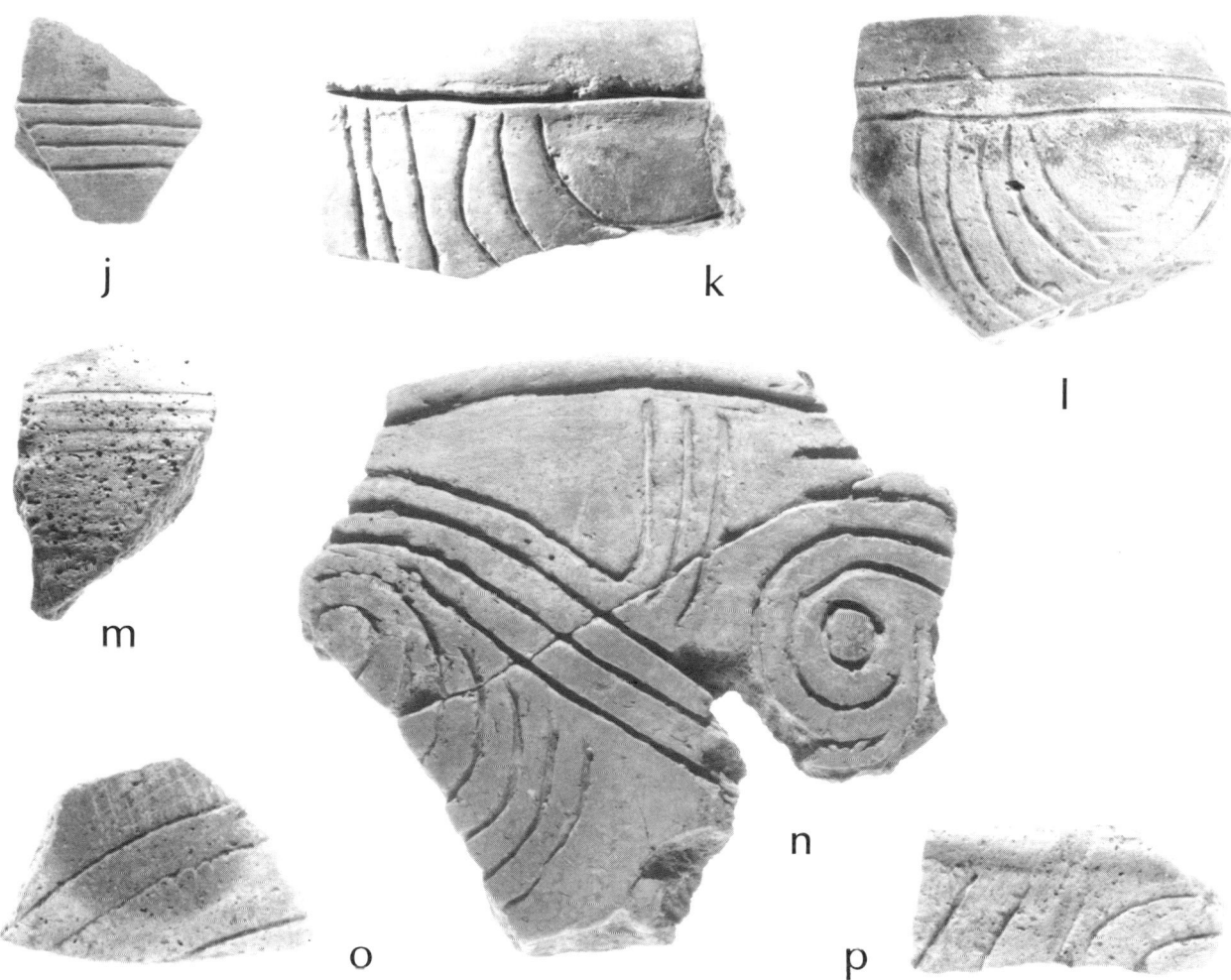

j k l

m

n

o p

Figure 153 (continued).

were discarded except for a type collection. The black midden layer, which rarely had observable internal stratification, was taken out as a single unit unless features were found. If the feature could be identified as recent, it was removed and the contents segregated. If the feature was aboriginal, it was isolated by the removal of the surrounding midden and then dissected. Generally, the midden layer was dry sifted through half-inch hardware cloth and the contents of the aboriginal features through quarter-inch hardware cloth or window screen.

The following discussion is restricted to the eighteenth-century cultural materials: the artifacts from the topsoil and midden layer (table 44) and the aboriginal features from the undisturbed portions of the midden. Since the site is considered a single-component occupation, the artifacts are described together as a group; specific features are then singled out for functional interpretation.

Artifacts. One of the objectives of the Bloodhound investigations was to secure a definitive artifactual datum for a Tunica site dating to the first decades of the eighteenth century. As noted at the end of the last sec-

tion, the ethnic identity of the burials could not be determined beyond doubt, but the excavations at the related terrace occupation provided abundant Tunica diagnostics.* There was, in addition, pottery attributable to other cultural traditions (and, therefore, presumably other ethnic groups), as well as a goodly representation of European artifacts from the late seventeenth and early eighteenth centuries.

As detailed in table 44, the diagnostic Tunica ceramics—Winterville Incised, *vars. Angola* and *Tunica,* and Barton Incised, *vars. Trudeau* and *Portland* (fig. 152)—predominate in the counts of decorated pottery. Also present are characteristic Tunica modes, such as nodes (fig. 152e, g–h) and the "Tunican Mode" punctated rim band (fig. 152d, i–j). Other Mississippian ceramics, not necessarily Tunica, are also present in small amounts. These include Parkin Punctated, *var. Elise,* Old Town Red, *var. Ballground,* Winterville Incised, *var. Loubois,* and unspecified varieties of these types.

---

* The absence of Tunica pottery in the known burials may have been due to sampling error, or possibly to the fact that the pottery was too coarse and common to be appropriate for use as grave furniture.

Mississippi Plain, *var. Montfort* is a late ware that has a close (but probably not exclusive) association with the Tunica.

To compare with other sites, *vars. Tunica* and *Portland* are found from Haynes Bluff to Trudeau, while *Trudeau* only appears at this time and continues on to Trudeau. On the other hand, *Elise, Ballground,* and *Loubois* are holdovers from the Yazoo region. In this assemblage, small changes as well as continuities are apparent in the Tunica ceramic tradition.

Ceramics from other cultural traditions include the Natchezan and Caddoan. In the case of the Natchezan examples, some certainly were made by the Natchez themselves: namely, Fatherland Incised, *vars. Fatherland, Nancy,* and *Snyders Bluff* (fig. 153a–g, j), and Old Town Red, *var. Grand Village.* Related types, Cracker Road Incised and Leland Incised (fig. 153m–n), are indigenous to the Haynes Bluff area and reflect northern influence in ware and decorative modes. These northern types are very rare in the Tunica ceramic assemblage by the time of the Trudeau occupation, but at this early eighteenth-century period the Haynes Bluff connection is still close. Another indication of this closeness is found in an unusual design treatment of Fatherland Incised that is replicated on sherds from Haynes Bluff and Bloodhound (fig. 153k–l) but is unknown from any other site at this writing.

Other connections also are evident. The southern end of the Natchezan tradition is represented by Fatherland Incised, *var. Bayou Goula* (fig. 153h–i), and from the west there are unclassified Caddoan types (fig. 153o–p). Caddoan pottery was present in small amounts at Haynes Bluff, but as an increasingly popular import it became an important part of the Tunica ceramic assemblage at Trudeau (Brain 1979, pp. 245–247). This trend emphasizes the long-established westward orientation of the Tunica.

Altogether, the ceramics from Bloodhound conform to expectations of an assemblage intermediate in time and space to those from other known Tunica occupations.

The inventory of aboriginal artifacts from Bloodhound includes a pottery earspool, a variety of chipped stone tools, and a shaped quartzite cobble (fig. 154). The cobble may have been a game stone, perhaps used in the games described by Gravier and Charlevoix as being played by the Houma and the Tunica (Swanton 1911, pp. 288, 313). The presence of so many traditional artifacts presumably being used for a range of utilitarian, ornamental, and possibly ceremonial functions suggests that even among the Tunica European replacements were not exactly a common commodity during the first third of the eighteenth century.

Nevertheless, there is a goodly representation of European artifacts from Bloodhound. In addition to the burial accompaniments, numerous European items were found in the general midden and features of the terrace occupation area. Most of the items are small and evi-

dently had been lost accidentally. Larger items had been damaged and apparently were disposed of purposely. European artifacts were plentiful enough, it seems, to allow some waste.

Gun parts and munitions form one of the larger categories of European goods. Muskets were an important trade item of the early contact period in Louisiana. As these guns broke and could not be fixed, parts were discarded (fig. 155). Curiously, there is no evidence that any of these, including the ornamental brass furniture, was reused. One might wonder, however, how the flintlock came to be bent at a right angle (fig. 155f)—not the usual wear and tear for a musket. Insofar as they can be identified, the parts came from Type C and Type D guns (Hamilton 1976, 1979).

Munitions from the terrace included sixteen lead musket balls and a quantity of shot (fig. 155g–h). The shot shows a range of sizes that apparently correspond to established eighteenth-century categories (Hamilton 1979, p. 208; Brain 1979, app. B). The balls range from 13 to 17 mm in diameter, and from 13 to 27.5 g in weight. However, the great majority of the balls (14 of the 16) are approximately 15 mm in diameter, indicating that they were probably made for 28-*calibre* guns, a common trade gun size. The one 13-mm ball would have fit a 32-*calibre* gun, another popular trade gun size, while the heavy 17-mm ball is within the range of the standard French infantry musket (Hamilton 1979, table 16).

The gunflints are predominantly of the spall type, but there are two of the blade type (fig. 155o–p). All but one are made of French blond flint; the exception is a native-made gunflint chipped from local chert (fig. 155q). Although carefully formed, the native gunflint was never used. Almost all the imported French flints, on the other hand, show heavy usage—in most cases far in excess of the patterns of wear to be expected in a flintlock. Clearly, the flints were too valuable to be discarded after they no longer fit a flintlock, and they were used with strike-a-lights or in other ways until they were reduced to unusable cores.

Utilitarian items of European origin include another favored trade object, the knife. Blades from both folding and case knives were found at Bloodhound (fig. 156a–c). All were too badly corroded for the recovery of identifying information, but in form were typical of eighteenth-century French products.

A few handwrought iron nails (fig. 156d–e) may have functioned as incidental tools or may have been part of a larger artifact. All are Type I, with the three-facet "rose" heads typical of Louisiana (Brain 1979, p. 156).

Functional categories of European artifacts in addition to tools include glass and ceramic containers. Bottles are represented by a number of fragments of blown glass, which range in color from dark olive green to light olive green to emerald green (fig. 156q–x; table 44). The dark olive green sherds are from the so-called wine or rum bottles of the period, but the pieces are

Figure 154. Stone artifacts and a pottery earspool found in the terrace excavations at Bloodhound. a, chert chopper; b–d, chert celts (note the decreasing quality of craftsmanship); e–i, chert knives (note the variety of forms—especially h, a triangular knife); j, galena crystal (covered with traces of vermilion); k, Nodena Lanceolate, *var. Russell* point; l, shaped quartzite cobble; m, earspool of Addis ware. (1:1)

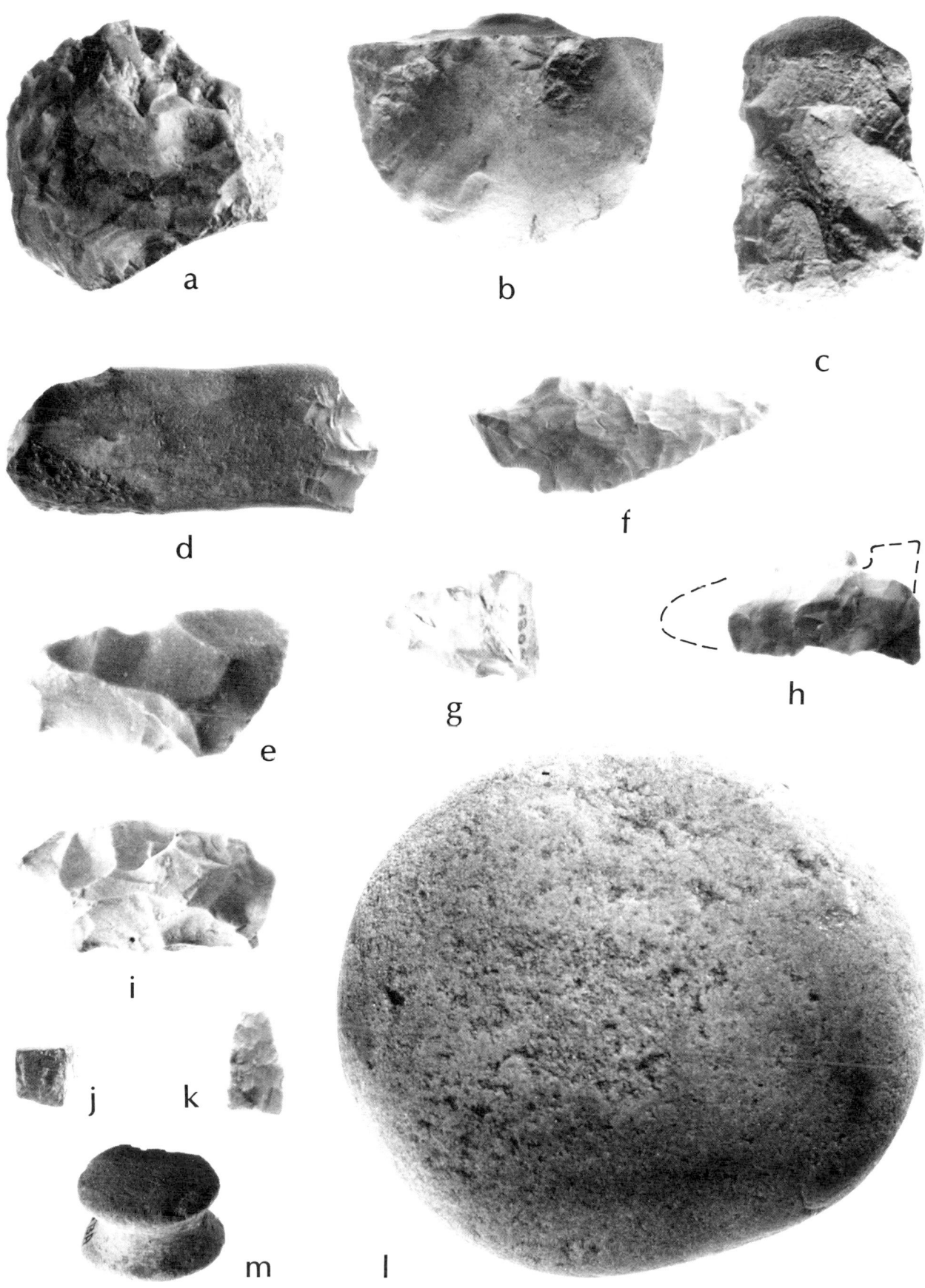

a

b

c

d

f

e

g

h

i

j

k

m

l

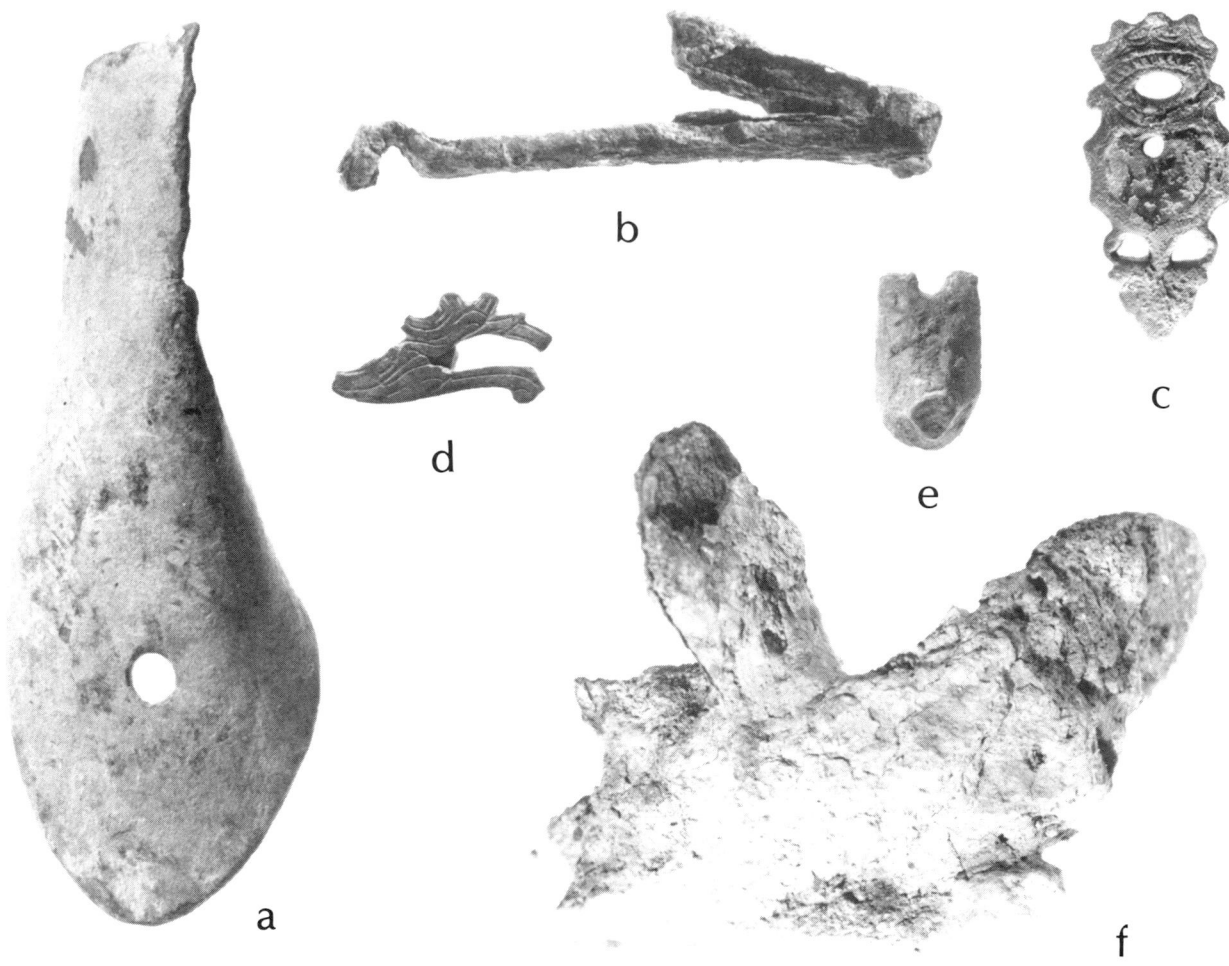

Figure 155. Gun parts and munitions found in the excavations at Bloodhound. a, brass butt plate, Type C or D; b, lock mainspring of steel; c, brass escutcheon, Type D; d, fragment of brass side plate, Type C; e, fragment of brass trigger guard; f, iron flintlock (bent, cock missing); g, lead musket balls; h, lead shot; i–n, spall gunflints; o–p, blade gunflints; q, native gunflint of chert. (1:1)

Table 46. Glass beads found during the excavations on the terrace at Bloodhound.

Variety[a]	Number	Periods[a]	Remarks
IIA1[b] (fig. 156y)	20	I–VI	18 medium oval, 2 small
IIA4 (fig. 156z)	1	III–VI	Medium
IIA5	1	I–VI	Small
IIA6[b] (fig. 156aa)	12	I–VI	
IIA7[b] (fig. 156bb)	75	I–V	62 small
IIA13 (fig. 156cc)	4	II–III	
IIA14 (fig. 156dd)	1		Light lime green
IIA15 (fig. 156ee)	2	III–VI	
IIB2 (fig. 156ff)	3	III	
IIB3 (fig. 156gg)	2	III–IV	1 red-striped
IIB5 (fig. 156hh)	1	III–IV	Red between blue stripes
IIB7[b] (fig. 156ii)	2	II–III	
IIB15[c] (fig. 156jj)	1		New variety
IIB16[c] (fig. 156kk)	2		New variety
IIB17[c] (fig. 156ll)	1		New variety
IVA2 (fig. 156mm)	4	I–VI	Cornaline d'Aleppo
IVB3 (fig. 156nn)	2	II–III	
IVB6 (fig. 156oo)	1	II–III	Red-blue-red compound stripes
WIIIA1 (fig. 156pp)	1	II–III	
WIIIA2 (fig. 156qq)	1		

[a]See Brain 1979, pp. 100–133 for variety descriptions and chronology.
[b]Also found with burials 3–7, but not quantified. Only one variety found with a burial (IIIA3, in burial 6) was not present on the terrace.
[c]New varieties: see appendix E.

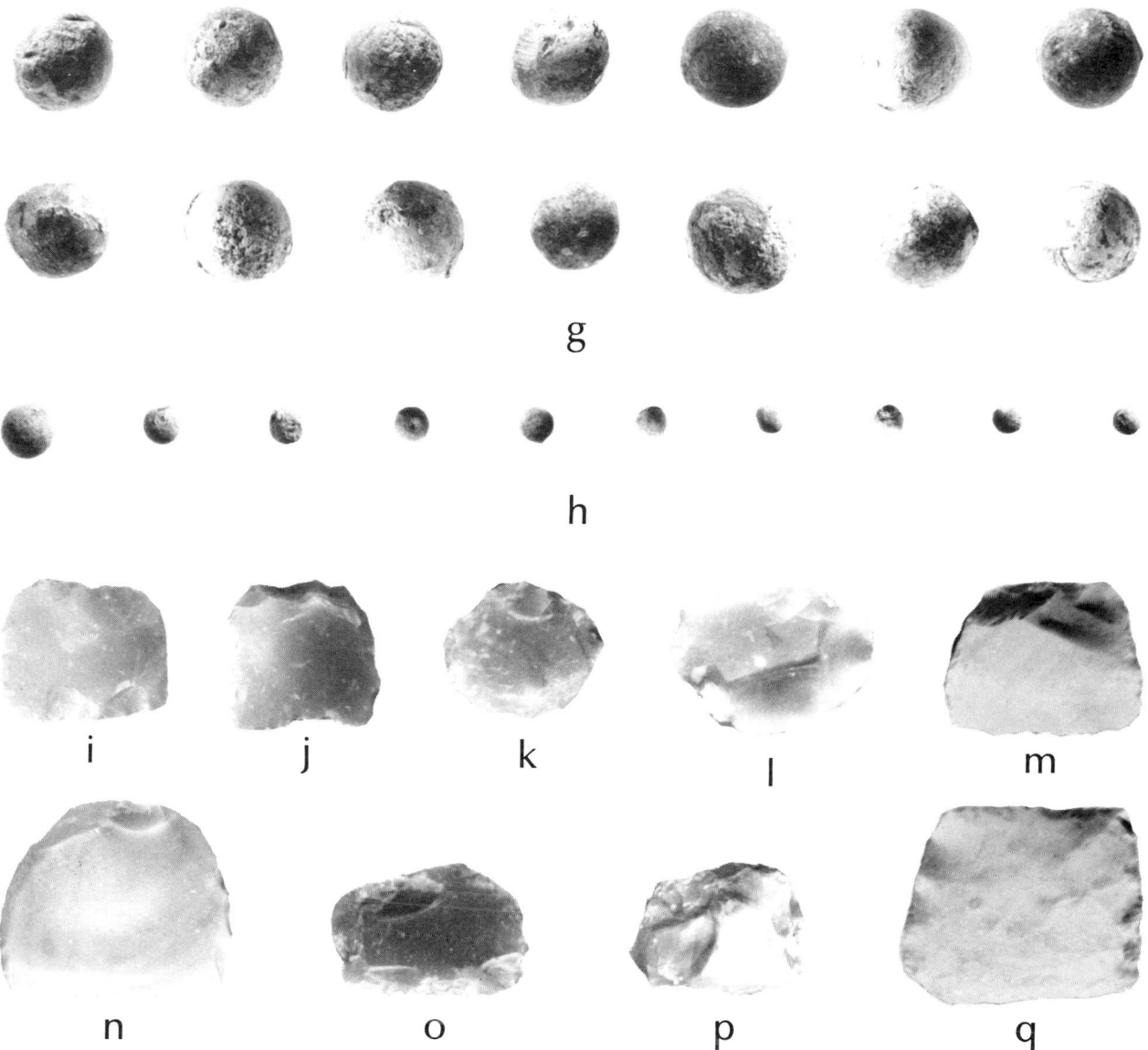

g

h

i   j   k   l   m

n   o   p   q

Figure 155 (continued).

too small to determine whether the bottles were French or English. The light olive green sherds are of poor quality glass: very thin and yet with more bubbles than usual for blown glass. They must have come from small, delicate bottles containing some inexpensive liquor, condiment, or medicine. The emerald green glass is unusual in its color, but that probably is only a variation of the more common light blue-green glass of the eighteenth century. In fact, a large basal fragment (fig. 156x) is from a bottle that belongs in form to a well-known light blue-green bottle type known as a *flacon* (Brain 1979, p. 92). The bottle was very large and contained an unknown liquid substance. Two pieces of clear glass without bubbles may have been from a wine glass or tumbler. Two sherds, one clear and one dark olive green, were used in a secondary role by the Indians: the first was chipped along one broken edge, and the second was

carefully flaked and shaped into an end scraper of the late protohistoric-historic snub-nosed type (fig. 156w).

Other than bottles, the only evidence of European-derived containers from the terrace excavations at Bloodhound are a few sherds of coarse earthenware. These include two pieces of white faience, one piece of brown faience (white tin-glazed interior, brown lead-glazed exterior), and one piece that was unglazed (fig. 156m–p). Insofar as can be determined, all came from simple, unadorned plates or shallow bowls. Clearly the accumulation of European ceramics exhibiting a variety of forms and decorations was not to occur among the Tunica until the Trudeau generation.

The third major category of European artifacts, after tools and containers, is composed of ornaments. In metal, these consist of an iron C-bracelet (fig. 156f), part of a brass C-bracelet, a cast brass scallop shell pierced for

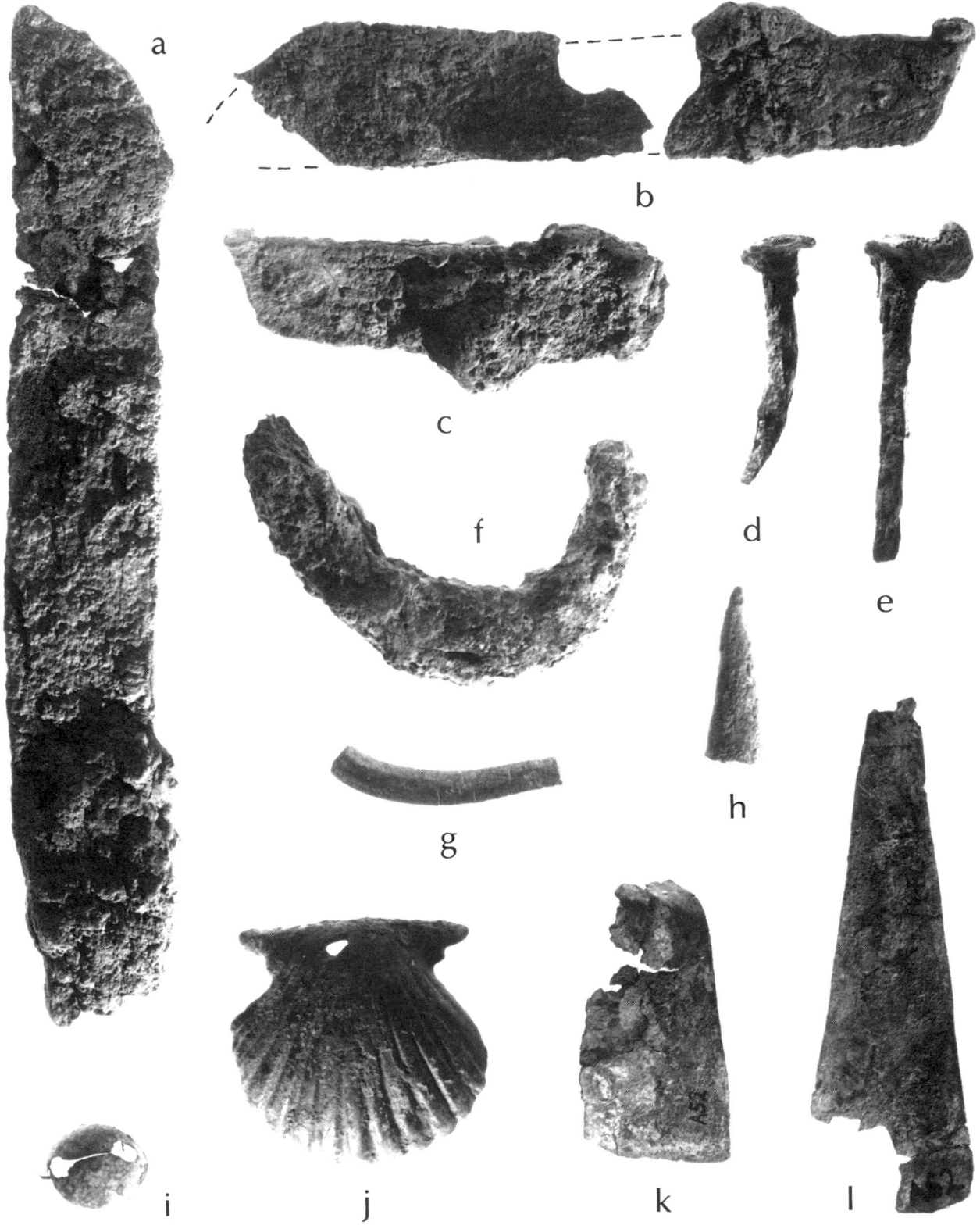

Figure 156. Metal, ceramic, and glass artifacts found in the excavations at Bloodhound. a, case knife; b–c, folding knife blades; d–e, handwrought iron nails, Type I; f, iron bracelet; g, cast brass bracelet; h, sheet brass tinkling cone; i, brass Flush-loop bell; j, cast brass scallop shell pendant; k–l, sheet copper pendants; m, brown faience; n, unglazed earthenware; o–p, white faience; q–r, light blue-green glass; s–t, clear glass; u–w, olive green glass (w, made into a snub-nosed end scraper); x, emerald green glass; y–qq, glass beads (IIA1, IIA4, IIA6, IIA7, IIA13, IIA14, IIA15, IIB2, IIB3, IIB5, IIB7, IIB15, IIB16, IIB17, IVA2, IVB3, IVB6, WIIIA1, WIIIA2). (1:1)

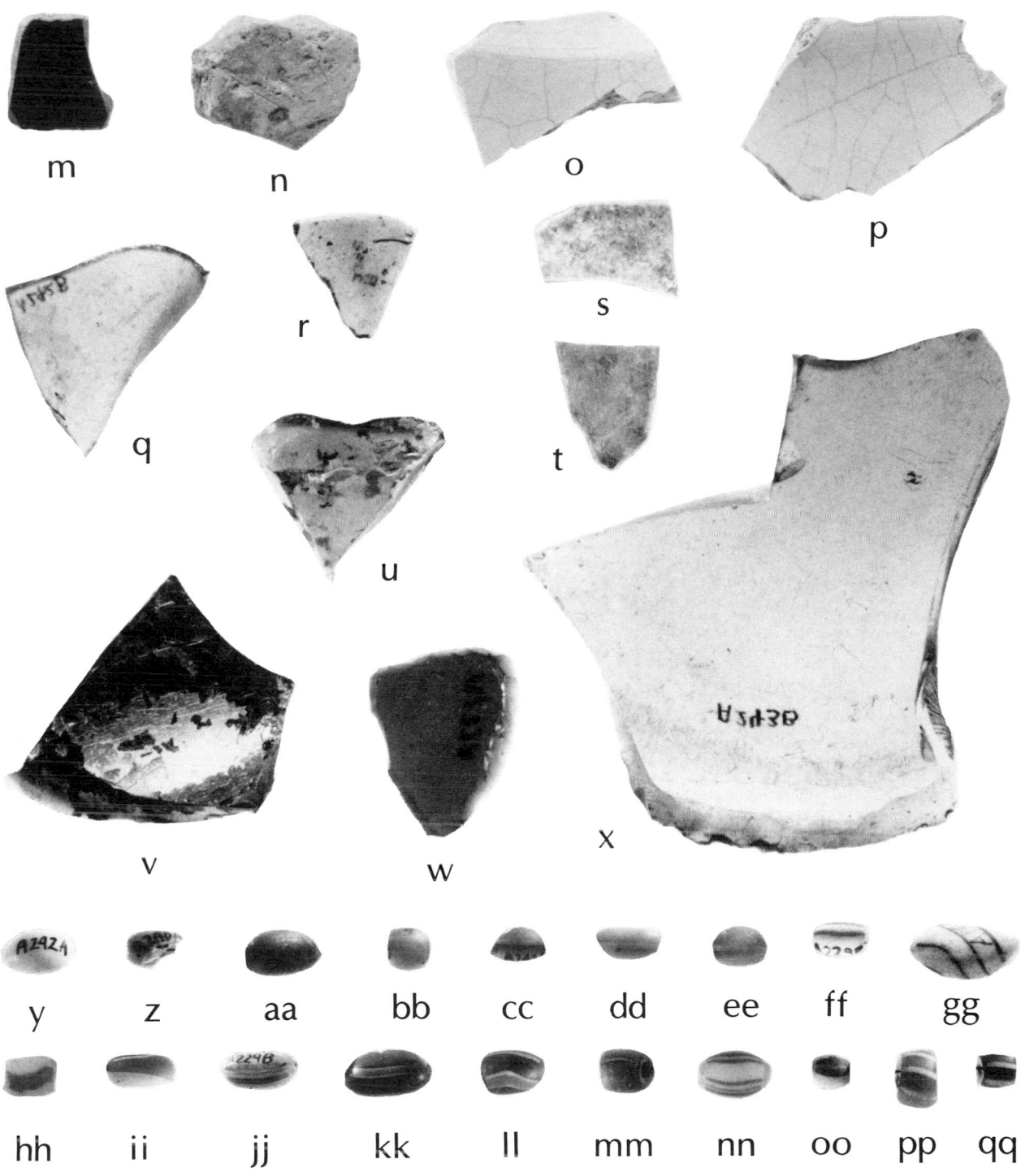

Figure 156 (continued).

suspension, and a brass Flushloop-type bell (fig. 156g, i–j). Metal ornaments made by the Indians from European-supplied raw materials, or from larger artifacts such as kettles, include two copper pendants and a brass tinkling cone (fig. 156h, k–l).

The most important class of European ornaments, however, consists of glass beads. Interestingly, although only a fraction of the number included with the burials was found in the terrace excavations, a much greater variety is represented. Only five common varieties accompanied burials 5–7, but at least twenty varieties were present in the occupational area (fig. 156y–qq; table 46). The reason for this discrepancy between life and death ornamentation is difficult to identify. It is

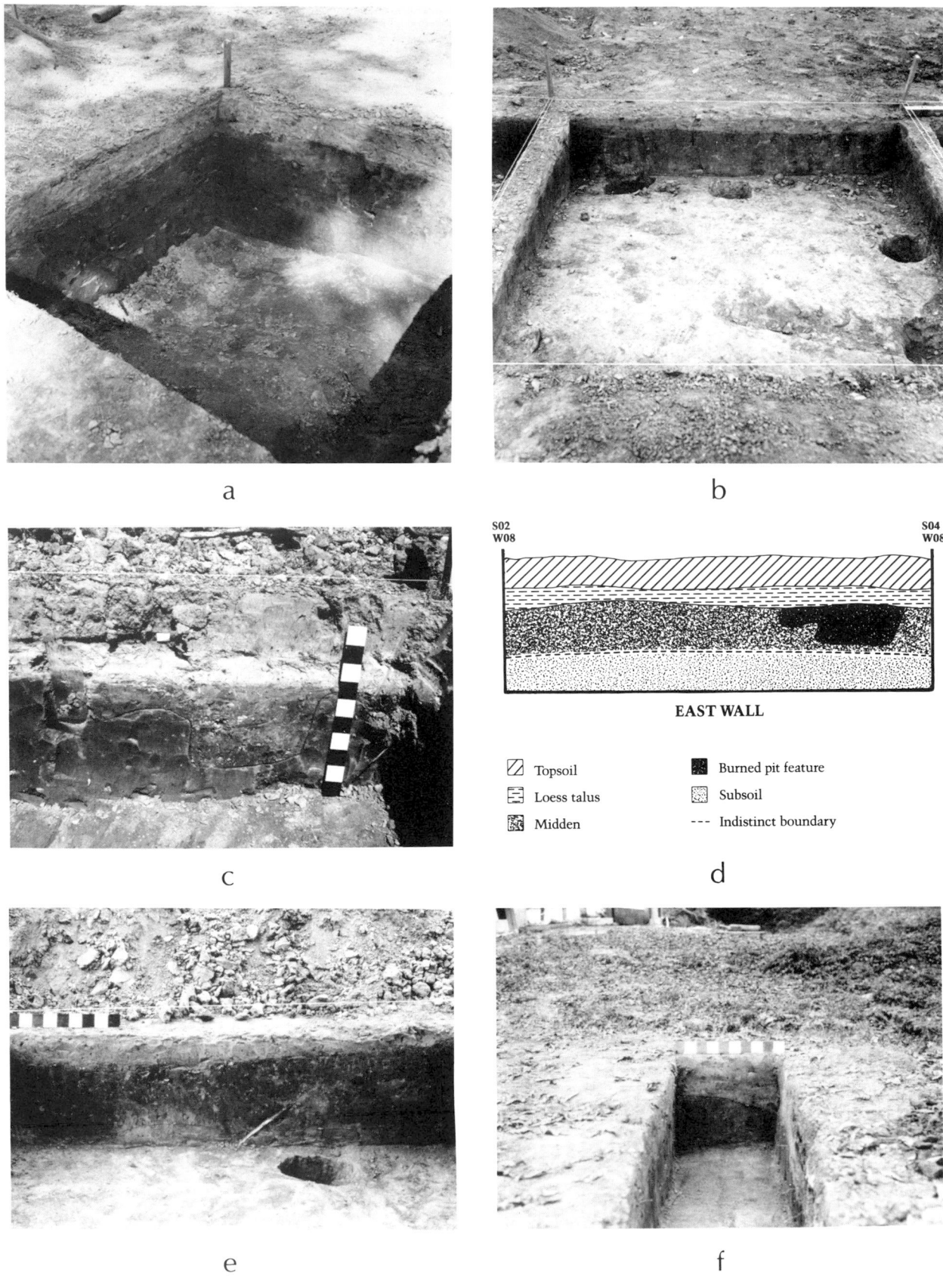

a

b

c

S02
W08   S04
                                                                 W08

EAST WALL

⧄	Topsoil	▨	Burned pit feature
⊟	Loess talus	▨	Subsoil
▨	Midden	- - -	Indistinct boundary

d

e

f

unlikely to be due to sampling error, since the difference is so great and the sample relatively large. There may be a time differential involved, the burials belonging to the earlier part of the occupation of Bloodhound before a wide variety of beads became available. This interpretation, however, is at variance with the conclusion offered in the summary of the burials, which suggests that the interments probably were made late in the occupation. It is supposed, then, that other unknown sociocultural factors were determinative when beads were selected as grave goods.

The varieties of beads found in the terrace excavations are of particular interest for chronological considerations. All are monochrome or striped beads, and the overwhelming majority (18 of the 20 varieties) are of drawn manufacture. An assemblage with these characteristics should date to the early eighteenth century in Louisiana, and indeed the probable peak popularities of varieties that may be dated from other evidence (table 46) are concentrated in periods II–III (1700–1729).

Altogether, the aboriginal and European artifacts from the cemetery and occupation areas of Bloodhound provide a solid datum: namely, the archaeological assemblage of an early eighteenth-century Tunica site.

Features. It has already been noted that the cultural layer at this location was composed of a matrix of "black" (really varying shades of dark gray) midden. Generally this midden was very mixed and devoid of observable horizontal stratification (fig. 157a). The relative homogeneity in composition and structure suggested that there had once been an in situ habitation site here, the surface of which was constantly being churned. The occupation appears to have been brief enough to prevent significant layering, an observation that is borne out by the artifactual evidence presented above. The churning, and thus blending, of the entire layer is best supported by potsherds from the same vessel of Addis Plain, *var. unspecified** that were found scattered about the site: in the topsoil in excavation units A173 and A240, in the undisturbed midden in A241, and as intrusions into subsoil in A187. The habitational nature of the occupation is confirmed by the types of artifacts found, the presence of quantities of daub and food remains (peach pits and animal bones, many of them burned) scattered throughout the layer, and the kinds of features contained within it. Although horizontal stratification was rare in the midden layer, vertical interruptions were

common. Aside from many modern intrusions, a number of aboriginal features were isolated.

The formal dimensions of the aboriginal features varied considerably in size and shape (figs. 157b–e). Only rarely, however, could functions be established firmly. Possible eighteenth-century postholes were numerous, but to our great disappointment did not form structural patterns (the only posthole alignments observed belonged to twentieth-century prison buildings). Aboriginal wall trenches were not found in the excavation despite all efforts to translate even the faintest stain into such a feature.

That the locus was residential rests upon the presence of pit features containing refuse: burned bone and other food remains, daub and charcoal, and a higher artifactual content than the surrounding sheet midden. An especially informative pit was found in excavation unit A243; its contents included burned dog bones and peach pits, an especially varied assortment of native and European artifacts, and burned dirt, charcoal, and daub. Most interesting were several mud dauber's nests, hymenopterous testimony to the former existence of a nearby structure. Judging from the concentration of features and material, this structure must have been in the vicinity of excavation units A229, A184–186, and A240–243.

The excavations on the southern edge of the terrace were very limited and did not uncover any specific features. They did reveal, however, that the narrow strip of sheet midden sloped down to the south (fig. 157f), thus establishing the antiquity of the gully that bounds the site on this side. Present in the eighteenth century, the gully, like its modern counterparts across the landscape, must have served as a convenient trash receptacle off to one side of the human occupation. The narrow strip of midden along the edge of the terrace was formed from trash that was not pushed into the gully.

SUMMARY OF THE 1977 EXCAVATIONS

Examined together, the evidence from the Bloodhound excavations on both the terrace and hill presents a picture of a small occupation of short duration. The burial data suggest a well-to-do group who could afford to furnish their dead with a quantity and variety of exotic imports. The habitational refuse identifies the group as Tunica (the diagnostic artifacts were the more common items and perhaps were not considered appropriate for placement with the burials). What we don't know, however, is how representative this sample is of the entire Tunica community during that period of great change. Bloodhound was only one of several small satellite villages occupied by the Tunica sometime (but probably not the entire time) between 1706 and 1731.

---

* This vessel is of unusual ware, obviously a very late variant of Addis Plain. The closest relationship is to the *Skillikalia* variety from the Haynes Bluff region. This establishes another link with the Yazoo.

◀ **Figure 157.** Stratification and features in the terrace excavations at Bloodhound. a, excavation unit A226 from the southeast, showing the midden layer that was much thicker (up to 60 cm) there than anywhere else but was not well endowed with artifactual materials or features; b, excavation unit A241 from the west, showing modern intrusions along the east wall and in the southwest corner, as well as aboriginal features that included a shallow trench (right foreground) and a small round pit in the south wall; c–d, photograph and drawing of east wall of excavation unit A184; e, north wall of excavation unit A243 and intrusive aboriginal pit feature; f, excavation unit A244 from the west, showing the original eighteenth-century ground surface sloping down to the south.

Lower Yazoo

The lower Yazoo region has been the focus of a considerable amount of archaeological attention (e.g., Phillips 1970; Williams and Brain 1983). During the protohistoric and early historic periods, most of the native inhabitants were found in locales on the banks of the Yazoo River itself. One of these locales, especially rich in archaeological remains, is situated along the bluff margin some 20–30 km from the mouth of the Yazoo. A number of historic Indian and European sites have been identified and quite a few have been excavated (Brown 1975, 1976, 1979a). Several relating to the Tunica and neighboring Indian groups are reported here: Haynes Bluff (22-M-5), Portland (22-M-12), Burroughs (22-M-10), and Russell (22-N-19).

HAYNES BLUFF

The French first found the Tunica—or Tonica, as they identified them—in 1699 on the lower reaches of the Yazoo River (Shea 1861).* The tribe was described as living on the bank of this river some three to seven leagues from the Mississippi. Although the exact location of the principal village had never been determined, a cluster of late prehistoric (and potentially historic) sites in the general locale was known, and the most important of these was Haynes Bluff (fig. 158).

Previous Investigations

The earliest known mention of Haynes Bluff as an archaeological site was recorded by B. L. C. Wailes, the noted Mississippi naturalist and man of letters, in his diary entry for 1 June 1853. He described it as

a group of mounds, seven in number, the principal one about 50 ft high, 75 ft square on the top and very steep sides. The other small ones rendered by long cultivation so depressed as to enclose a level space of five or six acres. Some of the small ones contain human bones and a quantity of fresh water bivalve shells from the Yazoo. (Wailes 1853)

The number of mounds is an important piece of information subsequently obscured by the "long cultivation." Unfortunately, we are given no clue as to where the missing mounds may have been located. The height of the principal mound is greatly overestimated, but otherwise the description is quite accurate. It is to be regretted that in this case Wailes's natural curiosity did not impel him to investigate further.

---

* La Salle was told about the Tunica when he passed by the Yazoo River in 1682, but he did not visit them (Margry 1879, vol. 1, p. 555; ibid., vol. 2, p. 189).

As so often in southeastern archaeology, C. B. Moore was the first to take official archaeological notice of Haynes Bluff, during his winter foray up the Yazoo River in 1908. He confirmed many of Wailes's observations and more accurately measured the height of the principal mound at about thirty feet. He noticed only three smaller elevations nearby, two of which were mound remnants, while the third was believed to be a natural knoll. Moore's excavations were brief and resulted in little he considered noteworthy. In the big mound,

fourteen trial-holes were put down, resulting in the discovery of a few fragments of bones of lower animals, mostly of the deer, and a bone which Prof. F. A. Lucas kindly has identified as being part of a tibia of a wild turkey. There were also some bits of earthenware, shell-tempered as a rule, a few having a fine black polish on each side. (Moore 1908, p. 570)

Moore's "trial-holes" were normally "designed to be 6 feet by 4 feet, by 4 feet deep" (ibid., p. 569). If the latter dimension was adhered to here, he barely scratched the surface of the principal feature. This was Moore's customary procedure, however, and was not without its rewards. Just below the surface of one of the smaller mounds he found "a skeleton having small glass beads at the neck" (ibid., p. 570). Thus, in addition to the late prehistoric (shell-tempered) material from the top of the big mound, a historic component was determined.

Eighteen years later, Calvin S. Brown of the Mississippi Geological Survey authored the first volume devoted to the archaeology of the state (Brown 1926). Brown referred to Moore's investigation of Haynes Bluff and then described a small collection of artifacts that was given to the Geological Survey by the landowner. These artifacts were "celts, circular stones, flint points, and trade beads" (ibid., p. 56); they are currently in the collection of the University of Mississippi. The trade beads could not be located, but the stone items include some late prehistoric pieces: specifically, greenstone celts, discoidal stones, and a Sunflower point, all of which are diagnostic of Mississippian culture in the region. Brown also illustrates a small hoe in the collection of the Davenport Academy of Sciences (Putnam Museum) that is identified as being from the large mound at Haynes Bluff (ibid., fig. 59). It too is a well-known type of Mississippian artifact, although it is generally found in the northern part of the Lower Valley; in fact, this example is the southernmost occurrence known at this writing.

A few years later, apparently in the winter of 1932, a Pennsylvanian by the name of Carl Clausen trenched several of the mounds (referred to as the Harris Mounds in recognition of the current owner). In 1935 his field report and many of the artifacts recovered were received at the Museum of Anthropology, University of Michigan, where they were cataloged under accession num-

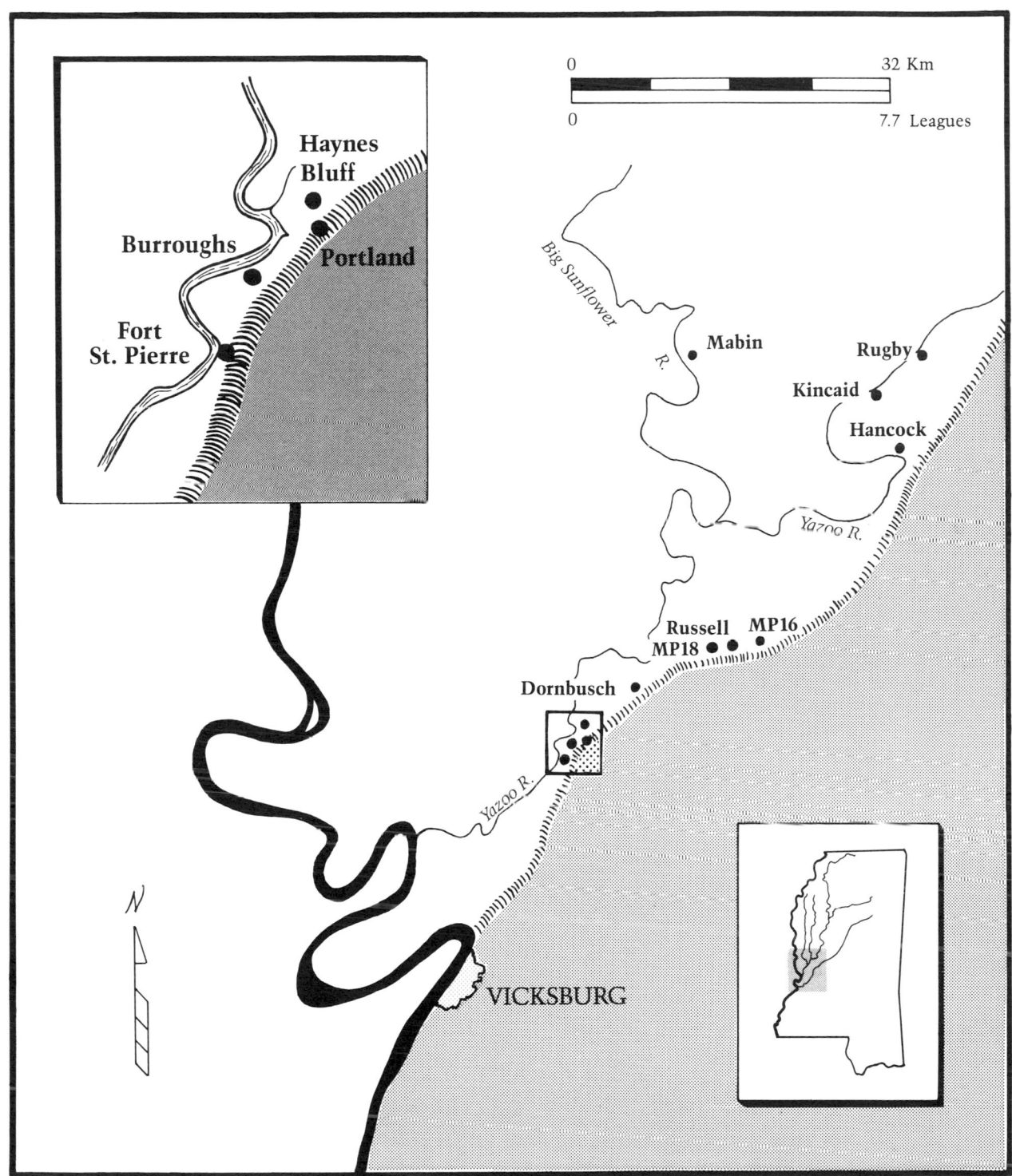

Figure 158. The lower Yazoo River bluffs and archaeological sites investigated in 1974.

bers 980 and 2160.* The report contains some very interesting details and, since it is unpublished, it is quoted here in its entirety:

* I am grateful to Vincas Steponaitis and John Belmont for bringing this collection and the following information to my attention.

This group comprises four mounds, one large and three smaller ones. Location: Northern end of Warren County, Mississippi, 13 miles north of Vicksburg, directly on highway to Yazoo City, and about one eighth of a mile from the eastern bank of the Yazoo River.

One of the smaller mounds nearest to the river was gone into first. After having determined the stratifi-

cation by test pits, a trench three feet deep and twenty feet wide was started on the western side of the mound, slicing to the depth of a foot, at the time.

Black mulch covered the entire surface to a depth of about eight inches. At the base of this black mulch was come upon a continuous layer of ashes and charcoal some two inches in depth with occasional pockets of hard burned clay.

Below this layer of charcoal and ashes was brown loose drift stratified with thin layers of shell and darker earth to a depth of eighteen inches. At this depth was come upon a second layer of charcoal and ashes, extending as in the case of the upper, over the entire bottom of the 20 foot trench.

In this eighteen inches of loose [loess] and shell and other kitchen midden debris, such as cracked bones and potsherd, three burials were encountered after trenching less than two hours.

Burial number one was a bundle burial with legs drawn up, hands crossed upon the chest and the head turned on the right side, facing east. Some two thousand trade beads of glass were found in a position to indicate that they had formed a series of bracelets about the subjects wrists. Two shell objects four inches long, of the variety known as "earplugs" were encountered, one on top of the skull and the other on the under side of it, in the region of the temples. The skeleton remains were too badly decomposed to ascertain the sex of the subject.

Burial number two was encountered at the same level as number one. The subject was stretched on its back. Beside the skull was found a large engraved vessel of the slender-necked bottle type, of approximately three quarts capacity, also one small shallow bowl with a very thin delicately flared rim decorated on the under side. Beneath the skull was found a clay pipe simply decorated and a small clay effigy of a bear. Skeleton remains extremely fragmentary.

Burial number three was at full length also. At or near the skull of this subject was come upon a very handsome large vessel with four handles at opposite sides, also one smaller vessel with a flared rim.

Some three feet beyond burial number one was come upon a very unusual and handsomely embossed bottle with extremely tall neck. This vessel was unassociated with any skeleton remains and appeared to have been buried alone. It lay on its side and contained a vertebrae of a fish, and no earth whatever, due to its slender neck.

The trench was continued to the summit of the mound without any further results. Two additional trenches were dug in the north and south side of the mound without encountering anything but kitchen midden refuse.

A pit, five feet square, was also dug at the apex of the mound to the level of the surrounding field. Nothing was encountered to a depth of eight feet.

In no case were the burials intrusive as far as the upper fire hearth was concerned. They all lay immediately upon the second hearth, slightly over two feet below the present surface of the mound, which had been greatly eroded by ploughing and rain.

Excavations by the same methods in a second mound (the most southerly of the group) disclosed nothing but one firepit in which was encountered an implement of antelope antler. Kitchen midden refuse was fairly abundant in this mound also.

Trenches at various points in the largest mound brought nothing but potsherd.

Potsherd from the deeper levels of the pit in mound number one were secured for comparison. (Clausen 1932)

Evidently, mounds C and D were excavated in addition to mound A (fig. 159). If these identifications are correct, then the burials were found in mound D. Burial 1 was in an unusual, flexed position. It may be interpreted as a female because of the earpins (Brain 1979, p. 252). Apparently the glass beads were mostly the IIA7 variety, but there also seem to have been examples of one of the drawn varieties of white beads with spiral decoration (e.g., IIB3, IIB13, or IVB4). The nearby, but unassociated, pottery bottle (fig. 160c) is probably a western variant of Leland Incised, as it displays formal

a

b

Figure 159. Clausen explorations at Haynes Bluff (22-M-5) in 1932. a, Mound A; b, excavations at one of the smaller mounds (either C or D). (Courtesy Museum of Anthropology, University of Michigan, Ann Arbor)

and decorative characteristics reminiscent of such Caddoan types as Keno Trailed (Suhm and Jelks 1962, pl. 44). The large vessel with burial 2 (fig. 160a) is typical of Ouachita River sites (e.g., Keno and Glendora), but cannot be classified to a specific type. The handled jar with burial 3 (fig. 160b) is an unspecified variety of the Mississippian type Winterville Incised that exhibits the Leflore Design Mode. This mixed bag of pottery pertaining to the late prehistoric–early historic occupation will be seen as typical of the site. Of considerable interest is the observation that the burials were not intrusive but lay beneath some two feet of mound overburden, which therefore had to have been added during the historic period.

Clausen clearly was most interested in the traditional search for "goodies" such as burials. In their absence, he conveys a minimum of detailed information. But the report does end with one detail that sounds a futuristic note: stratigraphic samples of potsherds were saved for comparative purposes. Whether or not anything was actually done with these sherds, the realization of their potential was a significant advance in archaeological methodology. Clausen's prescience was to be fulfilled almost immediately.

In the summer of 1932, James A. Ford initiated the modern era of archaeology at Haynes Bluff. Ford had visited the site at least as early as 1929, when he and Moreau B. Chambers made a brief survey and dug small "test holes" in mounds A and B (Ford 1929). Apparently, although they found only a few "shards" and "remains of skin, the hair still preserved in places, black and short," this experience was sufficient to inspire further investigation. Although Ford offered no new descriptive information, did not excavate, and illustrated only a few potsherds picked up from the surface of the site, he rigorously classified the latter and suggested ethnic attributions (Ford 1936, pp. 108–111). In fact, he identifies the site as the principal village of the combined Tunica-Yazoo-Koroa-Ofo settlement found by the French at the very end of the seventeenth century and awards it the distinction of being the type site for the Tunica ceramic complex (ibid., pp. 98–110). We shall see that his identification of the site was correct, but his ceramic complex is an amalgam of late prehistoric and early historic types, few of which can now be assigned with any confidence to Tunica craftsmanship. The problems confronting Ford, and which he was unable to control, were the long prehistoric occupation of the site, the late appearance of the Tunica on the scene, and the multiple ethnicities of the historic occupation. Although the Tunica loom large in the accounts of the latter, there is sufficient reason to believe that their sojourn at Haynes Bluff was relatively brief and, therefore, that their contributions to the archaeological assemblage from the site were modest—so modest that it is difficult to separate them even in well-defined contexts. Ford could not have realized the complexities of the problem, which are explored further in the following pages, and to him still goes the credit for making the first attempt to relate historic peoples and archaeological potsherds.

The Lower Mississippi Survey first visited Haynes Bluff in December of 1950, when Warren Eames, an

a

b

c

Figure 160. Aboriginal and European artifacts from the 1932 excavations at Haynes Bluff. a, unclassified Caddoan incised-engraved vessel from burial 2; b, Winterville Incised, *var. unspecified* jar with Leflore Design Mode from burial 3; c, Leland Incised, *var. unspecified* bottle from near burial 1, conch shell earpins, and glass beads directly associated with burial 1. (Clausen Collection, present location unknown; photographs courtesy Museum of Anthropology, University of Michigan, Ann Arbor) (1:3)

anthropology student at Harvard, carried out a one-day survey. The site appeared to be basically unchanged from the earlier descriptions, but more detailed observations were recorded (fig. 161). A collection of potsherds was picked up from the surface of mound B, which, Eames noted, resembled those illustrated by Ford (Eames 1950). Later visits secured additional samples from mounds A and D. The combined collections revealed a ceramic chronology that commenced with Coles Creek and continued to late Mississippian, the bulk of the evidence falling into the latter period (Phillips 1970, pp. 431–433). In unpublished notes, Phillips (1958) recorded his surprise at the lack of "Haynes Bluff rims," a marker for Ford's "Tunica complex," but also commented on the relative abundance of shell-tempered curvilinear incised and brushed wares. Both observations, we now know, connote a very late date for a Mississippian assemblage in the lower Yazoo. Eames did see a "decorated brass bell about 2 inches in diameter" that was in the possession of Mr. Harris, the former owner of the site, who also stated that glass beads were occasionally picked up (Eames 1950). But considering the "extraordinarily slender basis of archaeological information," Phillips (1970, pp. 430, 433) declined to contribute further to a discussion of Ford's hypothesis identifying Haynes Bluff as the location of the polyglot Tunica-Yazoo-Koroa-Ofo village of the early eighteenth century. In his cautious opinion, adequate proof of the identification was still wanting.

There the matter stood for more than fifteen years. Although Haynes Bluff was occasionally revisited by the LMS during the 1950s and early 1960s, no significant new data were recorded. Then a major change occurred in the site's status. In 1959 mound A nearly had been bulldozed away, but was saved when the Mississippi Department of Archives and History apprised the landowner that such action would be illegal under the statutes of the state's antiquities law (McPherson 1960, p. 33). The owner divested himself of the mound when he sold the site a few years later. The new owner was the International Paper Company, a major employer throughout the region. The management, unconcerned by the antiquities law, decided to make major changes in the local topography. The most serious damage occurred in 1967, when spur tracks were run to the paper mill being constructed just to the north of the site. One new railroad siding forced the relocation of Mississippi Route 3 and completely obliterated mound B (see fig. 164); another spur to the west artificially truncated the site on that side and reduced mound D to a barely observable rise.

Figure 161. Lower Mississippi Survey visit to Haynes Bluff in 1950. a, Mound A from the southeast (note error in caption of Phillips 1970, fig. 179), showing the prominent ramp ascending from the plaza to the left (LMS neg. no. 50/29); b, Mound A from the northeast, revealing the regularity of outline and flat summit plateau that demonstrate the unusually fine state of preservation of the mound, marred only by the natural sloughing into the creek on the northeastern corner (LMS neg. no. 50/30); c, sketch map of the site drawn by Philip Phillips (cf. Phillips 1970, fig. 178; also fig. 164, this vol.).

a

b

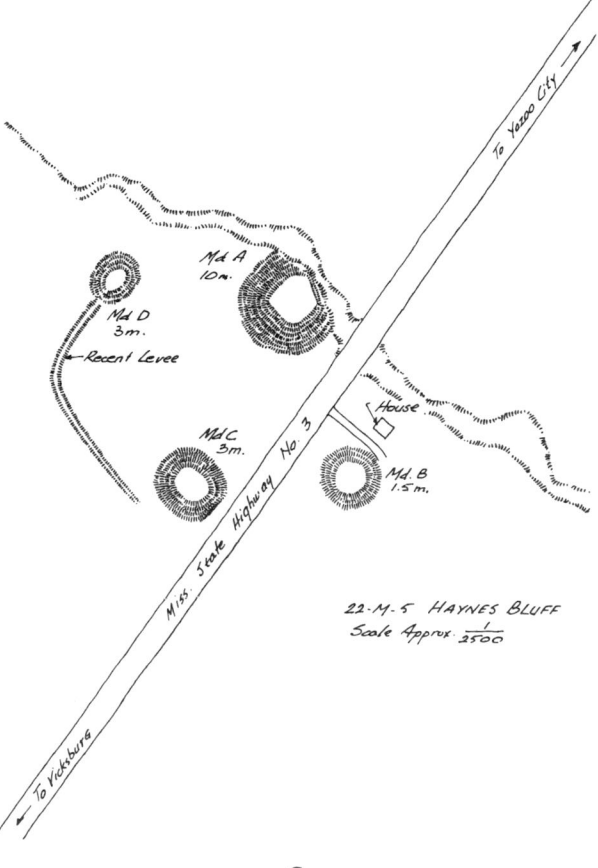

c

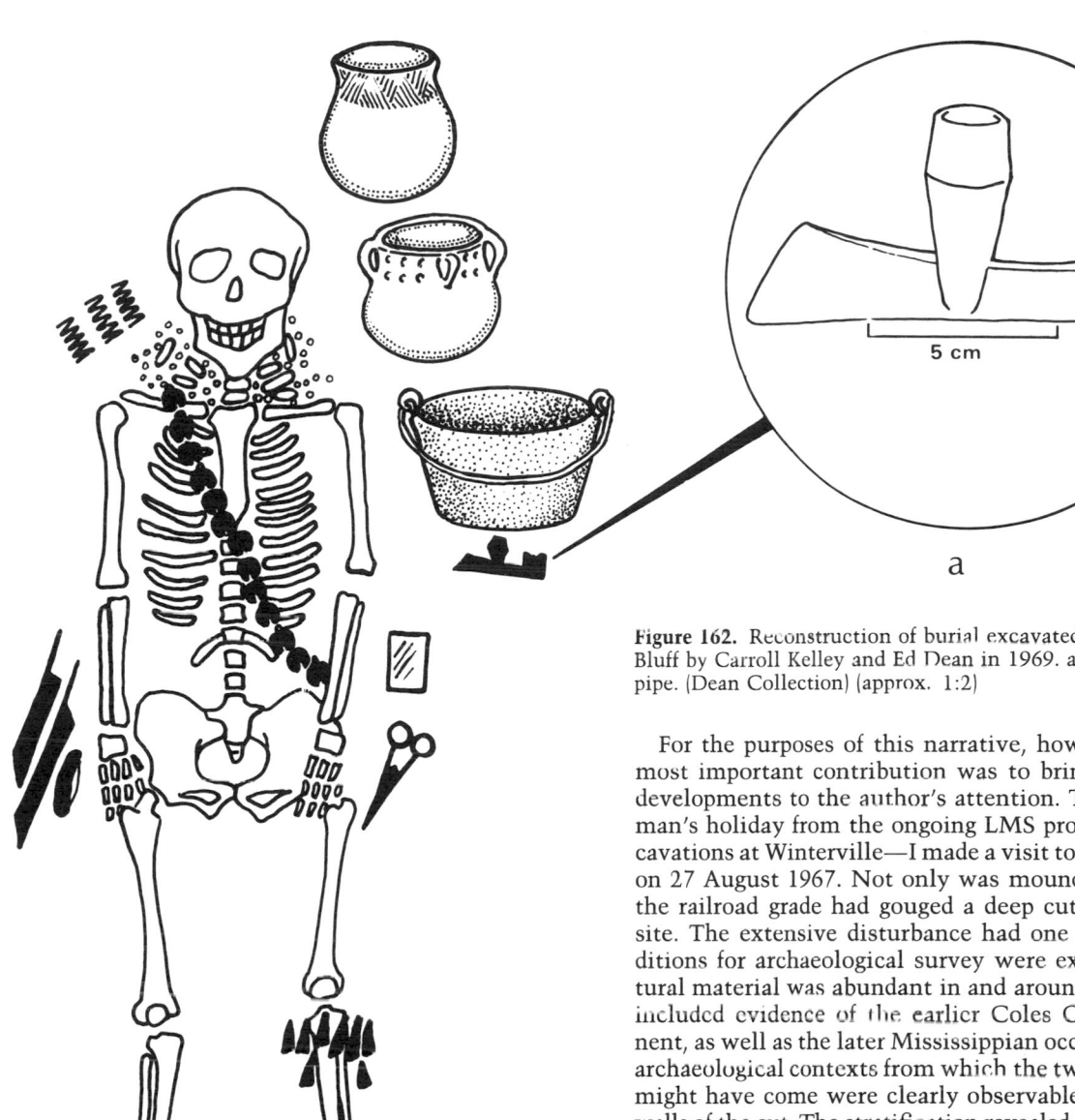

Figure 162. Reconstruction of burial excavated at Haynes Bluff by Carroll Kelley and Ed Dean in 1969. a, catlinite pipe. (Dean Collection) (approx. 1:2)

For the purposes of this narrative, however, Dean's most important contribution was to bring the recent developments to the author's attention. Taking a busman's holiday from the ongoing LMS project—the excavations at Winterville—I made a visit to Haynes Bluff on 27 August 1967. Not only was mound B gone, but the railroad grade had gouged a deep cut through the site. The extensive disturbance had one benefit: conditions for archaeological survey were excellent. Cultural material was abundant in and around the cut and included evidence of the earlier Coles Creek component, as well as the later Mississippian occupation. The archaeological contexts from which the two sets of data might have come were clearly observable in the fresh walls of the cut. The stratification revealed an old ground surface and occupation level up to 2 m below the modern ground surface at that location. Lying above the buried surface was a thick layer of loess talus, which was capped by another old ground surface and occupation level approximately 50 cm deep. That this surface could relate to the early eighteenth century was confirmed when several pieces of historic metal and some glass beads were pulled from it. Burials with European trade goods had been encountered when the cut was made and presumably were associated with this level.

In March 1969, Dean returned to Haynes Bluff with Carroll Kelley, another amateur archaeologist from Leland. Using Kelley's metal detector, the two men located a burial in an undisturbed area north of the mounds, between the railroad cut and old route 3 (see fig. 164). A reasonably accurate reconstruction of this burial is possible because Dean and Kelley proceeded carefully and kept thorough notes. As illustrated in figure 162, the burial was that of an adult, presumed by the collectors to have been a male, who had been interred in an extended supine position in a cypress bark-lined grave.

One ameliorating aspect of this disaster was the fact that the Illinois Central Railroad's foreman in charge of the construction was Ed Dean, then of Leland, Mississippi. Dean, an amateur archaeologist, had long been interested in the site. In fact, as discussed below, he had already conducted some minor excavations along the creek bank. He therefore knew the site well, and during the course of the construction he was able to salvage a considerable amount of data, especially in the vicinity of mound B, that otherwise would have been lost to us. Dean was sometimes assisted by Robert Morris, also of Leland.

Artifacts in accompaniment were numerous and manifested a considerable variety of aboriginal and European items.

The aboriginal artifacts included two pots, which were placed to the left of the head. Both were decorated jars, one Barton Incised, the other Parkin Punctated. The latter jar also had four strap handles around the rim. Both vessels were very late varieties of their respective types. Other aboriginal artifacts were seven conch shell beads and a catlinite pipe of the "smokestack" type. The shell beads, 8–9 cm long and about 1 cm in maximum diameter, were found around the neck of the skeleton intermingled with a few of the glass beads discussed below. The pipe was discovered beneath a brass kettle that had been placed next to the pots.

The kettle was the largest European artifact. It was described by the collectors as being approximately 50 cm in diameter and made of copper or brass. The large size suggests that brass was the more likely material, in which case the kettle may have been a Type A (Brain 1979, p. 166). It contained the bones of a small bird and most of the glass beads. Other metal artifacts included sixteen large cast brass bells, thirteen of which were strung across the torso from the right shoulder to the left hip, and three around the right ankle. Eight rolled copper tinklers were found at the left knee, and three coils of iron wire were probably in the vicinity of the head. Additional artifacts scattered about the torso were two cases knives, one folding knife, a pair of scissors, and a mirror.

Considering this array of artifacts, the number and variety of glass beads are surprisingly limited.* There were approximately fifty-five small white beads (probably varieties IIA1 or IVA1), one "Cornaline d'Aleppo" (IVA2), and two large clear oval beads (WIC__?). The small white beads were found in the kettle, the larger ones were strung around the neck with the shell beads.

---

* Another burial, hit by a bulldozer during the construction of the railroad spur in 1968, was accompanied by a large assortment of beads. Many were saved by the bulldozer operator, who later donated them to Cottonlandia Museum in Greenwood, Mississippi, which graciously loaned them to the author for analysis. Varieties identified were: IIA1, IIA2, IIA4, IIA6, IIA7, IIA8, IIA9, IIA15, IIB5, IIB10, IVA1, IVA2, WIIIA1, WIIIA2, and WIIIA3. All of these beads were typical of the early eighteenth century (Brain 1979, pp. 101–130). Whether this list includes all of the varieties present in the particular burial is unknown, due to the circumstances of discovery and preservation, but even as it stands it is an impressive representation.

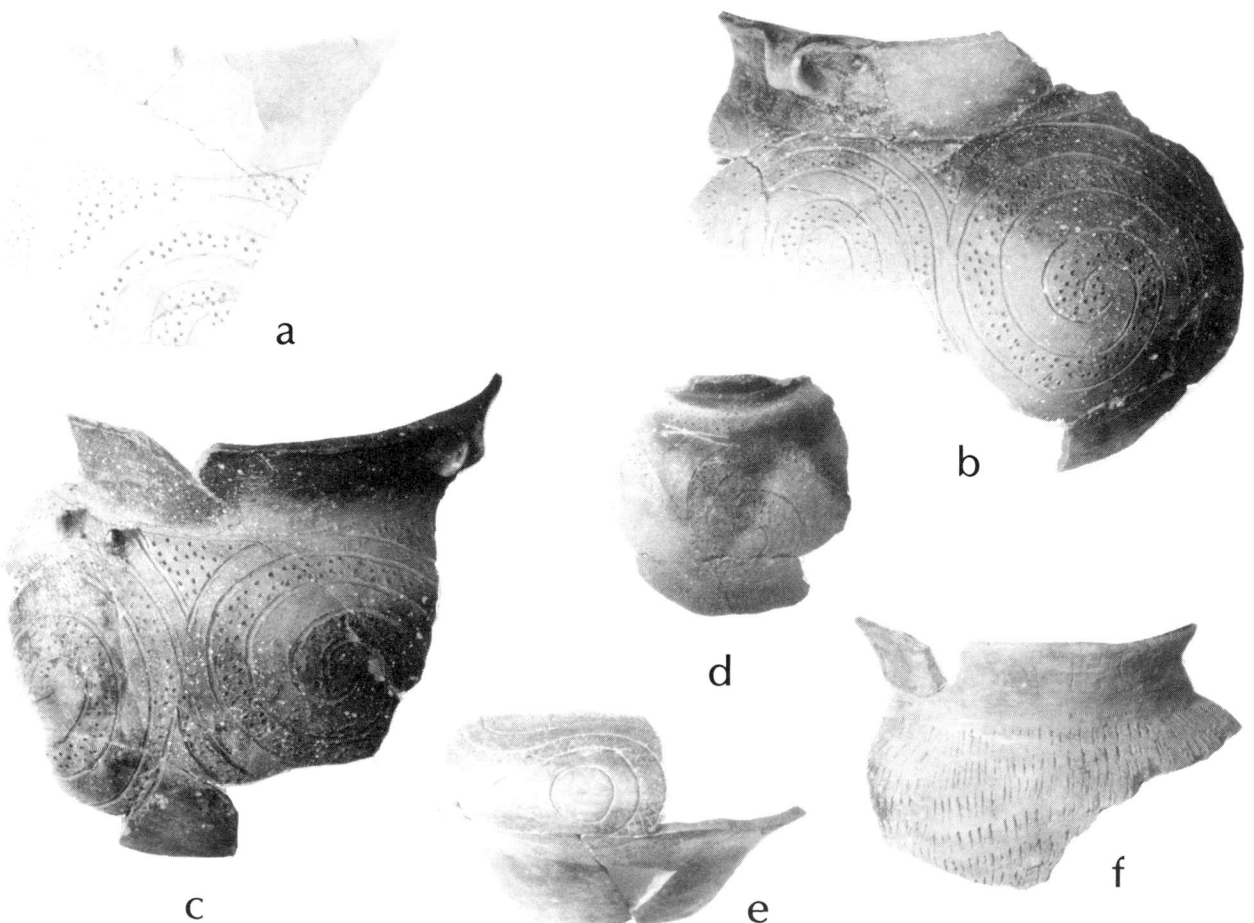

Figure 163. Pottery excavated from the midden area at Haynes Bluff by Ed Dean. a–d, Owens Punctated, *var. Menard*; e, Maddox Engraved, *var. Emerald*; f, Kinlock Simple Stamped, *var. Kinlock*. (Dean Collection) (approx. 1:3)

Table 47. Decorated pottery from the Haynes Bluff site (22-M-5) in the Dean Collection.

Winterville Incised, *var. Tunica*	2		Leland Incised, *var. Leland*	12
Barton Incised, *var. Portland*	5		Leland Incised, *var. unspecified*	1
Winterville Incised, *var. Loubois*	1		Barton Incised, *var. Estill*	5
Cracker Road Incised, *var. Cracker Road*	2		Parkin Punctated, *var. Hollandale*	1
			Parkin Punctated, *var. Transylvania*	4
Fatherland Incised, *var. Nancy*	3		Winterville Incised, *var. Winterville*	10
Fatherland Incised, *var. Snyders Bluff*	1			
Owens Punctated, *var. Manly*	5		Grace Brushed, *var. Grace*	9
Owens Punctated, *var. Menard* (fig. 163a–d)	30		Grace Brushed, *var. unspecified*	2
Winterville Incised, *var. Broutin*	1		Pouncey Pinched, *var. Patosi*	1
Winterville Incised, *var. Wailes*	4		Winterville Incised, *var. Blum*	1
			Barton Incised, *var. unspecified*	9
Grace Brushed, *var. Grand Gulf*	5		Winterville Incised, *var. unspecified*	2
Grace Brushed, *var. Warren*	14			
Kinlock Simple Stamped, *var. Kinlock* (fig. 163f)	1		Anna Incised, *var. Anna*	1
Leland Incised, *var. Bovina*	8		Carter Engraved, *var. Carter*	1
Nodena Red and White, *var. Ellison*	1		Leland Incised, *var. Bethlehem*	1
Nodena Red and White, *var. Nodena*	5		Hollyknowe Pinched, *var. Patmos*	1
			Plaquemine Brushed, *var. Plaquemine*	9
Fatherland Incised, *var. Fatherland*	1			
Fatherland Incised, *var. Stanton*	1		Coles Creek Incised, *var. Hardy*	1
Maddox Engraved, *var. Emerald* (fig. 163e)	2		Maziquc Incised, *var. Manchac*	3
Chicot Red, *var. Grand Village*	1		Coles Creek Incised, *var. Mott*	1
Chicot Red, *var. unspecified*	1			
Owens Punctated, *var. unspecified*	1		Coles Creek Incised, *var. unspecified*	1
			Coles Creek Incised, *var. Chase*	1
Leland Incised, *var. Blanchard*	13		Coles Creek Incised, *var. Wade*	1
Leland Incised, *var. Deep Bayou*	11		Coles Creek Incised, *var. Hunt*	1
Leland Incised, *var. Russell*	25		Coles Creek Incised, *var. Phillips*	1
Leland Incised, *var. Williams*	18		Larto Red, *var. Larto*	1
			Mulberry Creek Cord Marked, *var. Edwards*	1
Barton Incised, *var. Arcola*	41		Evansville Punctated, *var. unspecified*	1
Barton Incised, *var. Midnight*	1		Jaketown Simple Stamped, *var. Silver Lake*	1
Winterville Incised, *var. Belzoni*	19		Unclassified incised	1

In addition to the burial, Dean carried out controlled excavations on at least one other part of the site. Observing a thick layer of midden in the eroding south bank of the creek directly west of mound A, he dug in from the bank edge following the natural contours. The midden was very rich in organic and artifactual content. Being careful to keep potsherds together as discovered, he was able to reconstruct large portions of vessels (fig. 163). The roster of decorated pottery (table 47) included what were recognized as protohistoric varieties of such types as Barton Incised, Leland Incised, Maddox Engraved, Owens Punctated, Parkin Punctated, Kinlock Simple Stamped, Wallace Incised, and Winterville Incised, as well as many unclassified potsherds with painted, brushed, punctated, or incised decoration that were believed to be contemporary. Scattered throughout the midden in direct association with the aboriginal artifacts were small numbers of European artifacts, mostly beads and gun parts.

If this was a single deposit, it appears that Dean unearthed an archaeological context dating to the early historic period—probably, in fact, to the earliest European contact during the late seventeenth and early eighteenth centuries. The discovery of this context was more exciting than the burials themselves. The latter might have been intrusive into a prehistoric site, but the presence of the midden seemed to lend considerable support to Ford's hypothesis that Haynes Bluff was the location of the combined Tunica-Yazoo-Koroa-Ofo village at the time of initial French contact. When, in subsequent years, the program of Tunica research had been launched, the potential of Haynes Bluff was recalled, and it became increasingly important to resolve the question of the site's place in Tunica history.

The 1974 Excavations

The Lower Mississippi Survey returned to Haynes Bluff for a major program of excavation during the summer of 1974 (13 June–3 September). The expedition was funded by a research grant from the National Geographic Society and operated as a joint venture with the Mississippi Department of Archives and History (Brain 1975b, 1983b). The LMS team consisted of the field director, Jeffrey P. Brain, and six undergraduate and graduate students: Ian Brown, Winifred Creamer, Nora Groce, Nancy Lambert, Alan MacMillan, and Vincas Steponaitis. Additional local labor was hired as required. The Archives and History crew of six was led by Robert S. Neitzel and William C. Wright; in addition, Ian Brown was detailed to work with them most of the summer. At one point, the combined operation numbered a total of twenty-four individuals in the field.

The operations of the two crews were integrated and a common overall objective was shared: to establish the Indian and French presence in the region during the early historic contact period. The emphasis was to be placed upon the location and excavation of the principal French and Indian sites relating to this period. Archives and History was interested in finding the site of the French Fort St. Pierre, and the LMS was equally intent on pinning down the nearby Indian settlements. Both goals were achieved, but only the latter is reported here (see Brown 1975, 1979a for the description of the excavations at Fort St. Pierre).

In order to establish that Haynes Bluff was the focus of Tunica settlement on the Yazoo during the first years of the eighteenth century, three kinds of evidence were required: European artifacts diagnostic of the period, aboriginal artifacts with sufficient ethnic characteristics to identify the Tunica, and the close proximity of Fort St. Pierre. The latter was determined by the investigations of the Archives and History crew, who found the fort approximately "one league" south of Haynes Bluff (see fig. 158), the distance to the Indian village given by Charlevoix (1744, vol. 3, p. 413). The artifactual proof is presented below, but it may be noted in advance that appropriate European artifacts were found in native contexts that also contained Tunica diagnostics. (These are to be distinguished from Ford's "Tunica Complex," most of which preceded the appearance of the Tunica and thus had nothing to do with them.)

The Haynes Bluff site is located on the grounds of an International Paper Company mill. As already noted, the construction of this plant and its approaches in 1965–1968 destroyed much of the site, but spared mound A and some other features (fig. 164). It was in this remaining portion, in areas that did not appear to have suffered recent disturbance, that the excavations were placed. Four major locations were extensively tested. These were chosen according to the types of data they could be expected to produce that would contribute most directly to the primary objectives listed above. Each choice generally was determined by a combination of information derived from the prior work at the site and intuitive conclusions drawn from surface survey observations.

Specific placement of the excavations at each location was determined by electronic instrument survey, which pinpointed some of the types of features being sought, thus saving considerable effort in excavation. Four distinct kinds of electromagnetic investigation and seven different instruments were used during the survey. Fortunately, field conditions for this kind of survey were nearly ideal in 1974. Most of the site was maintained in grass which was mowed regularly by International Paper. Only mound A, which had a heavy cover of trees and brush, had to be cleared before the instruments could be used. The four techniques were magnetometry (both absolute and differential capabilities), resistivity, and two kinds of metal detection (one using a transmitter-receiver, the other a beta-frequency oscillator). Each of these produced different kinds of data in a given situation, and so some were more useful in a particular context than others—especially depending on the type of information sought. Usually, however, they complemented one another, and when used together they could make fine determinations about the nature of an anomaly not often possible with a single instrument (Steponaitis and Brain 1976).

The four locations excavated were mound A, the plateau north of where mound B had been situated (cf. figs. 161 and 164), mound C, and the creek bank (location D). All coordinates and measurements for the excavations were relative to a point arbitrarily set in the field southwest of mound A and relatively accessible to all locations. This primary site datum was marked by a capped steel pipe set in concrete. The cap was stamped "LMS 1974 DATUM."

MOUND A

Mound A was the most intensively investigated of the four locations at Haynes Bluff. Excavations were opened there on 24 June and continued until the last day of fieldwork, 31 August. The principal reason for the degree of attention was that the mound and its immediate surroundings appeared to be the best-preserved part of the site, so it was hoped that evidence of the latest occupations would be present there, if anywhere. Furthermore, previous surveys on the surface of the mound had indeed turned up native and European artifacts appropriate to the early historic contact period.

Both the summit plateau and the base of the mound were tested. Our primary objective was to locate and excavate historic aboriginal contexts, especially floors, structures, or burials. The electronic survey revealed several different kinds of anomalies that appeared promising for such features, and the excavations were placed so that a maximum number of the anomalies could be investigated. Since a second objective was to relate the historic occupation—which was expected to be a thin veneer at the site—to the prehistoric components, and thus complete the regional chronology, many of the excavations were to be continued beyond the identification of the anomaly. Excavations at the base of the mound would be dug all the way to subsoil, and at the summit down to prehistoric levels at least.

After being cleared, the mound summit plateau was found to be in a good state of preservation. It was flat

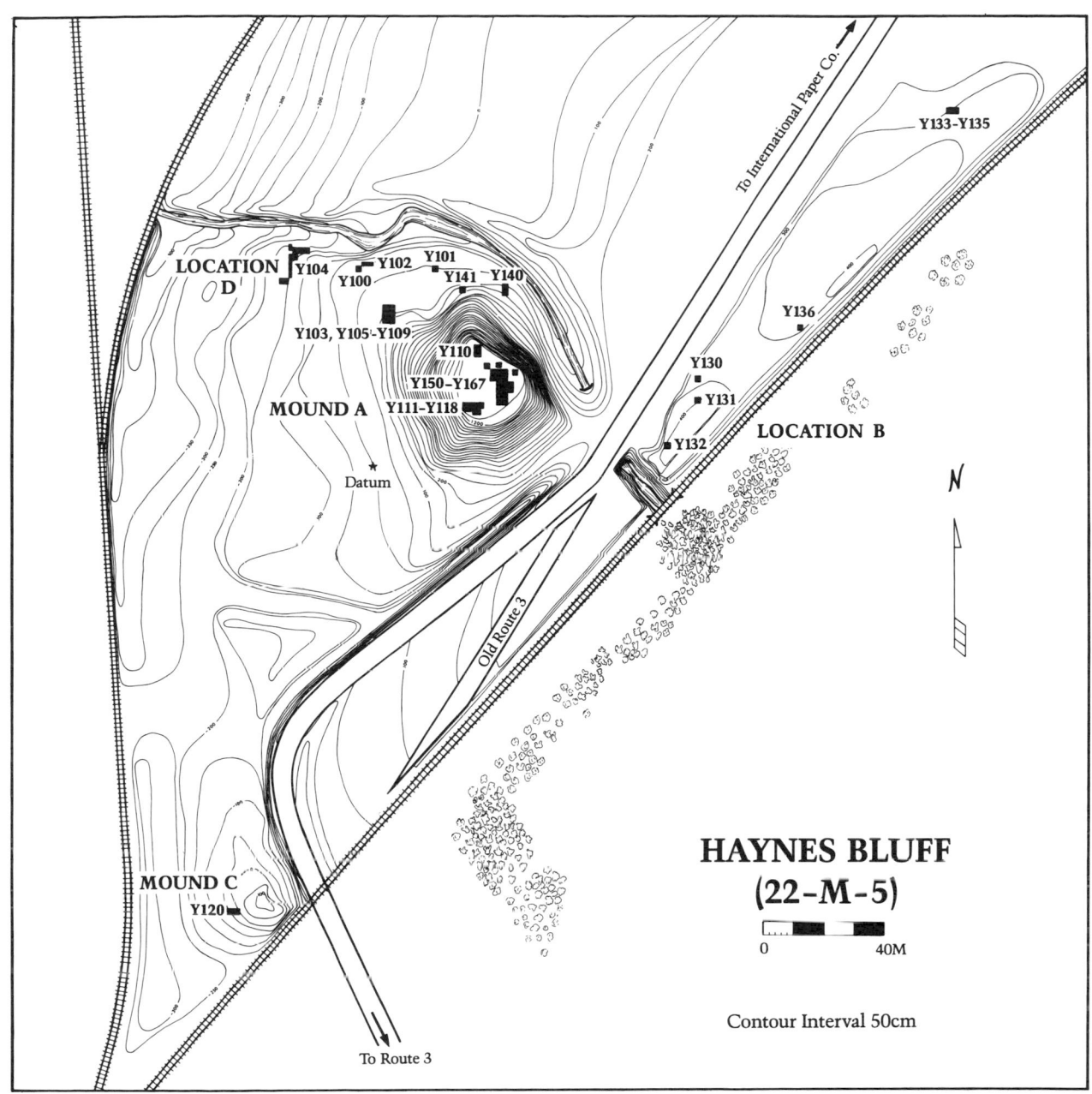

Figure 164. Map of the Haynes Bluff site, giving locations of the excavations by the Lower Mississippi Survey in 1974.

and regular, and only the northeastern corner was missing (due to undercutting by the creek on that side) (fig. 164). Although a few small potholes were evident, the depredations were unusually minor for such a prominent and well-known mound. It was, in fact, nearly pristine.

The instrument surveys detected a number of interesting anomalies. It appeared that the most important of these were two loci that gave strong indications of burials with large metal artifacts; a third locus was determined to have a high content of small metallic objects spread over a wide area. All three seemed to be good contexts for the historic occupation, and so they

were targeted for excavation. A fourth locus was chosen for a deep strata cut. It was placed as far away from the other three loci as possible so that the large amount of backdirt would not interfere with those investigations. The field catalog numbers assigned to the excavations were Y110, Y111–118, and Y150–167.

Excavation Unit Y110. Y110 was a 2-×-4-m excavation unit placed on the northern edge of the summit plateau between coordinates N36–40 and E33–35. Dug as the strata cut, it was taken down as far as safety permitted (more than 4m) and was stepped down from 2 × 4 m to 2 × 2 m, and finally to 1 × 2 m in horizontal

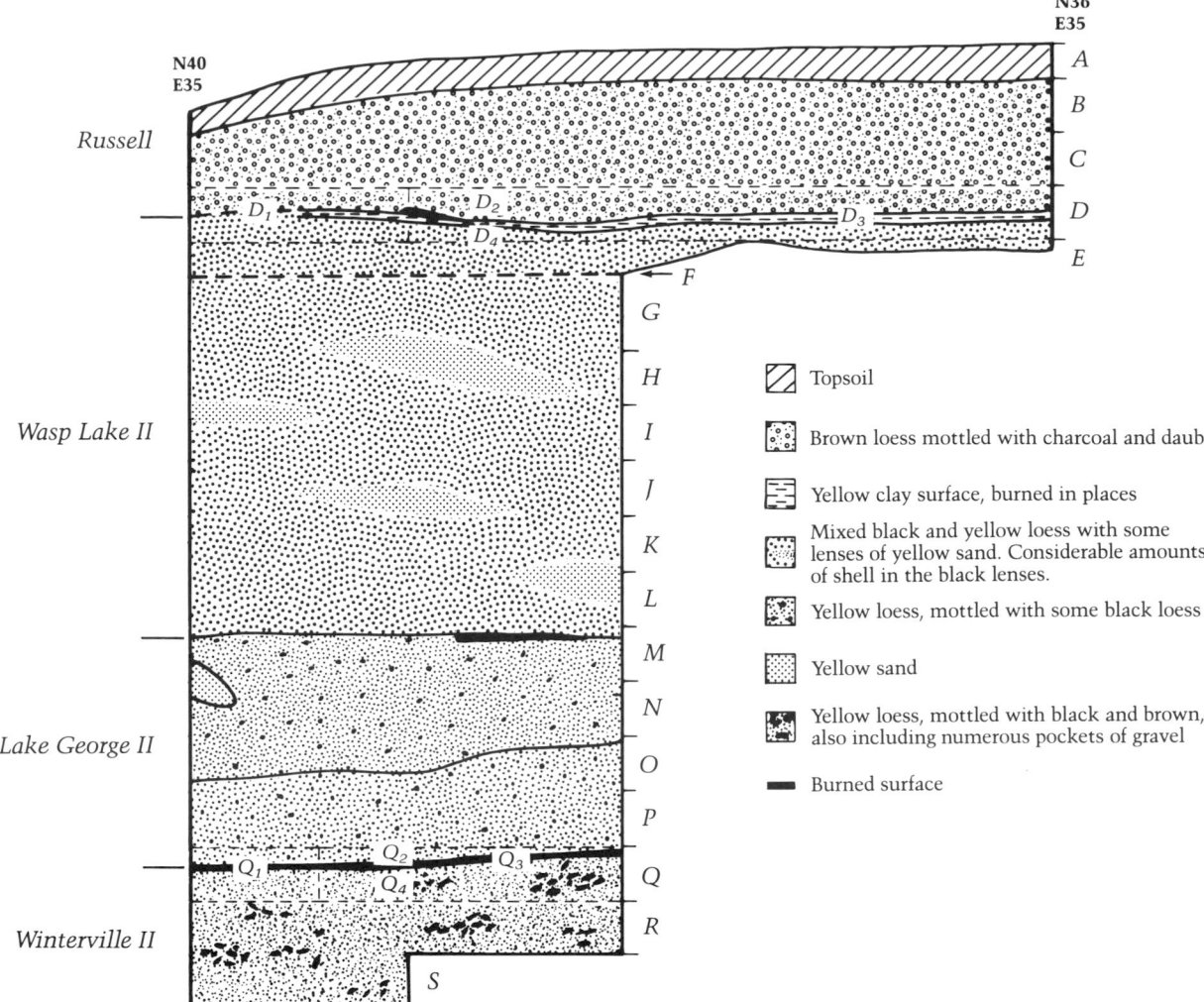

Figure 165. Stratification of mound A at Haynes Bluff as revealed in the east wall of excavation unit Y110.

dimensions (fig. 165). Levels were removed in arbitrary 25-cm increments, although they sometimes were subdivided when distinct breaks in the stratification were observed during excavation.

The stratification was relatively uncomplicated considering that this mound was a large-scale construction and a focus of human activity. Beneath 10–15 cm of humic topsoil was a layer of brown, loess-derived soil heavily mottled with flecks of charcoal and daub. At a depth of approximately 75 cm from the surface a yellow clay floor was encountered. This floor was 2–5 cm thick, hard packed, and burned in places. Associated with it were at least two postholes with diameters of 15 and 18 cm; their size indicated that a large structure had been present, but the limited scope of the excavations precluded inferences on its form and function. Under the floor was a mantle of mound fill some 175 cm thick. This fill was composed of a heterogeneous mix of yellow loess with lenses of sand and black midden. The pockets of midden contained a high proportion of mussel shell and cultural material. A second old mound surface was found at a depth of 270 cm. This surface,

too, showed evidence of burning, and it capped a mantle of yellow loess 50–60 cm thick that in turn lay directly over another mantle of mixed basket loads of loess, sand, and clay. Together, the two mantles comprised a full meter of loading. At 370 cm a third burned surface was uncovered, but no features were observed in association. Underneath it was more mound fill, this time composed of yellow loess mottled with black and brown stains and including numerous pockets of small pebbles. Although excavations were halted at 440 cm, an exploratory posthole was driven down another 130 cm and revealed that the loading continued at least that far. In summary, about one-half of the 10-m height of the mound was explored, and four major episodes of mound construction were revealed. The earlier three were capped by burned surfaces. It is probable that the last had been as well, since the topsoil contained a lot of daub, but the actual surface had disappeared.

The stratigraphic interpretation of the stratification described above is very enlightening. Although there is considerable admixture of earlier cultural materials that must be discounted for dating the construction, it is

Table 48. Aboriginal and European artifacts from excavation unit Y110 on mound A at Haynes Bluff (tabulated by mound stages and excavation levels).

	Topsoil (Y110A–B)	Stage IV (Y110C–D2)	Stage III (Y110D3–L)	Stage II (Y110M–Q2)	Stage I (Y110Q3–S)
ABORIGINAL					
Pottery:					
Winterville Incised, *var. Tunica*	1		2		
Barton Incised, *var. Davion*	1	1	1		
Barton Incised, *var. Charlevoix*	5	2	2		
Old Town Red, *var. Ballground*	4				
Parkin Punctated, *var. Elise*	3				
Winterville Incised, *var. Loubois*	1		1		
Cracker Road Incised, *var. unspecified*		1			
Fatherland Incised, *var. Nancy*		1			
Fatherland Incised, *var. Snyders Bluff*	1				
Mazique Incised, *var. North*	2	3	6		
Owens Punctated, *var. Manly*			1		
Winterville Incised, *var. Broutin*	1	2	5		
Winterville Incised, *var. Wailes*	1	1	4		
Grace Brushed, *var. Grand Gulf*		1			
Leland Incised, *var. Bovina*	1				
Fatherland Incised, *var. Fatherland*		1			
Fatherland Incised, *var. Stanton*		1			
Fatherland Incised, *var. unspecified*	2		4		
Maddox Engraved, *var. Emerald*	2				
Owens Punctated, *var. Poor Joe*				1	
Owens Punctated, *var. Widow Creek*		1			
Owens Punctated, *var. unspecified*		2			
Leland Incised, *var. Blanchard*		1			
Leland Incised, *var. Deep Bayou*	2	1	2		
Leland Incised, *var. Russell*	8	6	6		
Leland Incised, *var. Williams*	1		5		
Barton Incised, *var. Arcola*	2	2	7	2	
Winterville Incised, *var. Belzoni*	4	9	21	7	
Leland Incised, *var. Leland*		1	7		
Leland Incised, *var. Ferris*	1				
Leland Incised, *var. unspecified*	1	1	1		
Maddox Engraved, *var. Silver City*	2				
Coleman Incised, *var. Bass*			1		
Barton Incised, *var. Estill*	3	2	6		1
Parkin Punctated, *var. Hollandale*	6	3	4		
Parkin Punctated, *var. Transylvania*			5		
Winterville Incised, *var. Winterville*	2	3	8		1
Grace Brushed, *var. Grace*		2	3	2	
Grace Brushed, *var. unspecified*		1			

Table 48 continued.

Table 48 (continued).

	Topsoil (Y110A–B)	Stage IV (Y110C–D2)	Stage III (Y110D3–L)	Stage II (Y110M–Q2)	Stage I (Y110Q3–S)
Pouncey Pinched, *var. Patosi*	3				
Barton Incised, *var. unspecified*	4	5	14	3	
Winterville Incised, *var. unspecified*	5		8	5	
Unclassified incised (Yazoo)	2				
Anna Incised, *var. Anna*			1		
Carter Engraved, *var. Carter*		1	2		
Leland Incised, *var. Bethlehem*	2		5	1	
Powell Plain, *var. Powell*					1
Hollyknowe Pinched, *var. Patmos*				1	
Plaquemine Brushed, *var. Plaquemine*	2	2	5	1	
Coleman Incised, *var. Coleman*	1		1		
Coles Creek Incised, *var. Hardy*			1		
Evansville Punctated, *var. Sharkey*		1			
Mazique Incised, *var. Manchac*		1			
Unclassified incised (Addis)		2	1		
Coles Creek Incised, *var. Greenhouse*	1		4		1
Coles Creek Incised, *var. Mott*			3		
Evansville Punctated, *var. Rhinehart*			1		
Chevalier Stamped, *var. Chevalier*			1		
Coles Creek Incised, *var. Coles Creek*	3		4	1	
Coles Creek Incised, *var. unspecified*	3	1	15		
French Fork Incised, *var. Larkin*		1			
Mazique Incised, *var. unspecified*		1			
Coles Creek Incised, *var. Chase*		2	4		
Coles Creek Incised, *var. Stoner*	1	1	2		
Coles Creek Incised, *var. Wade*			4	1	
French Fork Incised, *var. Wilzone*				1	
French Fork Incised, *var. unspecified*			2		
Mulberry Creek Cord Marked, *var. Smith Creek*	1				
Chevalier Stamped, *var. Cornelia*	1	1	6		
Coles Creek Incised, *var. Hunt*	1		10		
Coles Creek Incised, *var. Phillips*		1	8		
Larto Red, *var. Larto*			5		
Mulberry Creek Cord Marked, *var. Edwards*			3		
Salomon Brushed, *var. Salomon*	3				
Evansville Punctated, *var. unspecified*	1				
Unclassified incised (Baytown)	1				
Lithics:					
Collins Side Notched, *var. Collins* point (fig. 175c)			1		
Collins Side Notched, *var. Claiborne* point				1	
Collins Side Notched, *var. Clifton* point			1		
Triangular knife			1		
Snub-nosed end scrapers (fig. 168s)	2				
Unclassified tools	3	1			

Table 48 (continued).

	Topsoil (Y110A–B)	Stage IV (Y110C–D2)	Stage III (Y110D3–L)	Stage II (Y110M–Q2)	Stage I (Y110Q3–S)
EUROPEAN					
Iron:					
Wrought nails					
Type I	2				
Type unspecified	2				
Miscellaneous	2				
Copper:					
Tinkling cone (fig. 168h)	1				
Miscellaneous	2				
Gun parts/munitions:					
Miscellaneous		1			

still quite evident that a long period of time is represented (table 48). In fact, the archaeological record of mound A extends back many centuries into prehistory, successfully meeting the objective of tying into the late prehistoric chronology. The earliest mantle uncovered was at least 2 m thick and may well have constituted the bulk of the remaining portion of the mound not investigated. According to the latest ceramic markers contained within it, this mantle appears to have been put in place late in the Winterville phase (see fig. 41). It may be presumed that a structure was erected on the summit of the mound at this time, although the only evidence of it found in the excavations was the indication that something had burned with a fire of such size and intensity that the surrounding mound surface was baked hard. Soon after the burning, another mantle was added, apparently during the latter part of the Lake George phase. Again, the presence of a structure may be inferred from the burned surface.

The next stage of mound construction was a thick mantle that was loaded on during the Wasp Lake phase. Although there is some artifactual evidence that the lower levels (I–L) were somewhat earlier than the upper ones (D4–H) (fig. 165; table 48), the stratification clearly reveals that the mantle was a one-time construction. The entire stratum therefore must be dated according to the later evidence, which is Wasp Lake II. After the structure that surmounted this stage had burned, a final mantle was added. Although relatively thin compared to the others, this last addition nevertheless represented a major construction effort. Its phase assignment is uncertain: although historic aboriginal and European artifacts were found throughout (in levels A–D2), in other excavations on the summit, as described below, they were confined to the topsoil except in the case of intrusions such as burials. It is possible that small intrusions, unnoticed during excavation, accounted for the pervasive distribution of the historic artifacts at this locus. In any event, this last construction could only have occurred during the brief interval spanned by the terminal Wasp Lake and Russell phases. The last occupation, of course, was Russell phase, and although the surface was gone the presence of a structure was attested by the charcoal and daub found scattered throughout the topsoil.

This excavation was successful, then, in establishing the basic stratigraphic record and tying together the prehistoric-to-historic continuum. The most exciting discovery was the considerable amount of mound construction carried on during the protohistoric, and possibly even historic, period. This supports the evidence from Clausen's excavations and constitutes the latest archaeologically documented mound construction in the Lower Mississippi Valley.

Excavation Units Y111–118. These excavations consisted of a series of contiguous 2-×-2-m and 1-×-2-m units placed near the southern edge of the summit plateau between coordinates N17–21 and E29–36. The purpose of the excavations was to explore the two loci indicated by the electronic surveys as possibly containing historic burials. Thus, in addition to the primary objective of gathering archaeological data on the historic occupation, the investigation was perceived as a test of the determinative capabilities of the instruments.

As predicted, two burials (designated YB-1 and YB-2) were encountered at the loci pinpointed by the electronic instruments. Burial YB-1 was found lying within coordinates N19–20 and E34–35 at an average depth of approximately 70 cm beneath the surface. The grave contained the skeleton of an adult male whose head was oriented to the northeast (fig. 166). His age at death was thirty-five to fifty years, and the remains showed no unusual pathology; dentition revealed caries, tooth loss, and resorption, and five major episodes of hyperplasia between the ages of one and a half and five and a half (Jerome C. Rose, personal communication, 1982). The body had been interred in a supine position, but the legs had been sharply flexed and widely spread (ac-

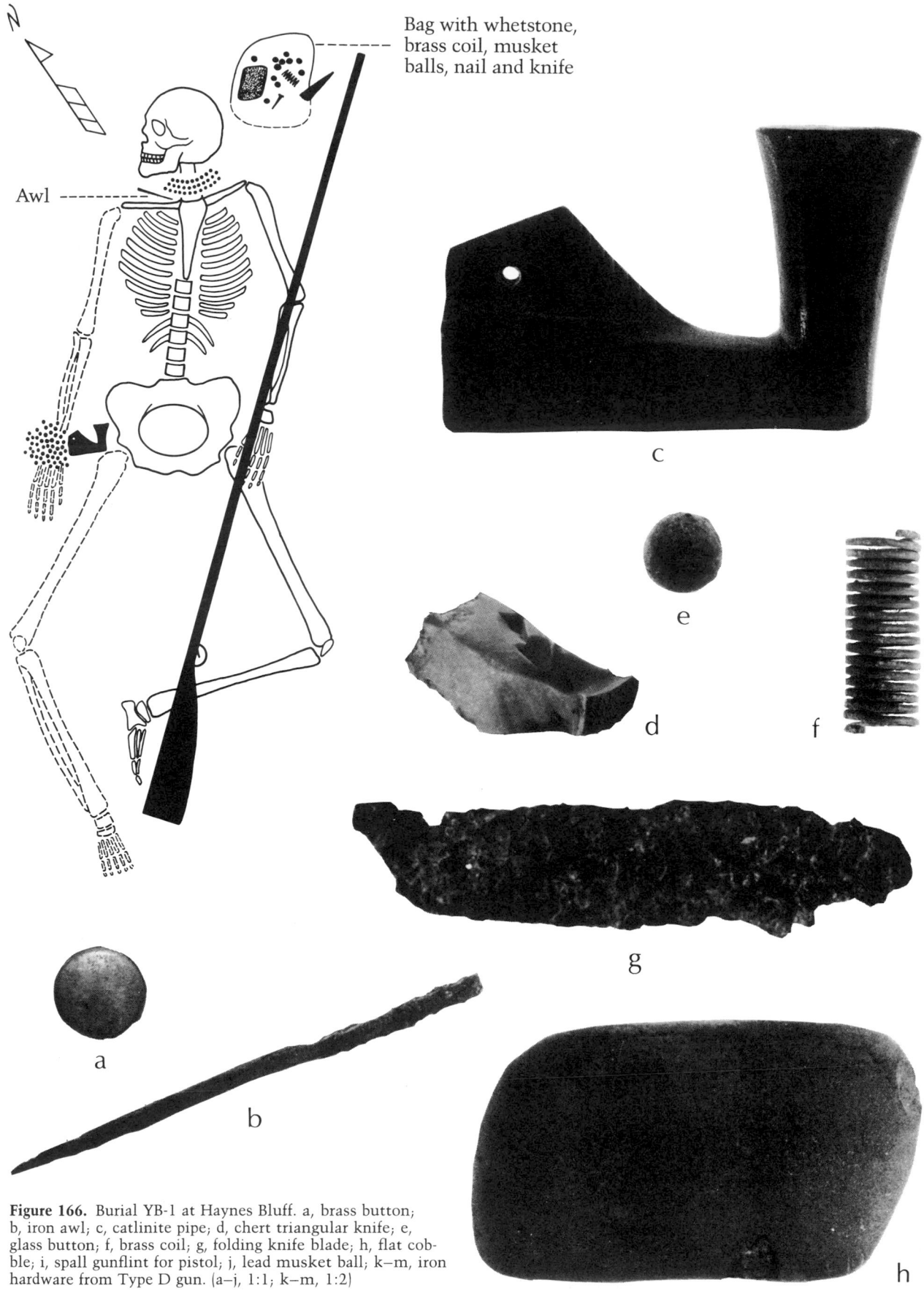

Figure 166. Burial YB-1 at Haynes Bluff. a, brass button; b, iron awl; c, catlinite pipe; d, chert triangular knife; e, glass button; f, brass coil; g, folding knife blade; h, flat cobble; i, spall gunflint for pistol; j, lead musket ball; k–m, iron hardware from Type D gun. (a–j, 1:1; k–m, 1:2)

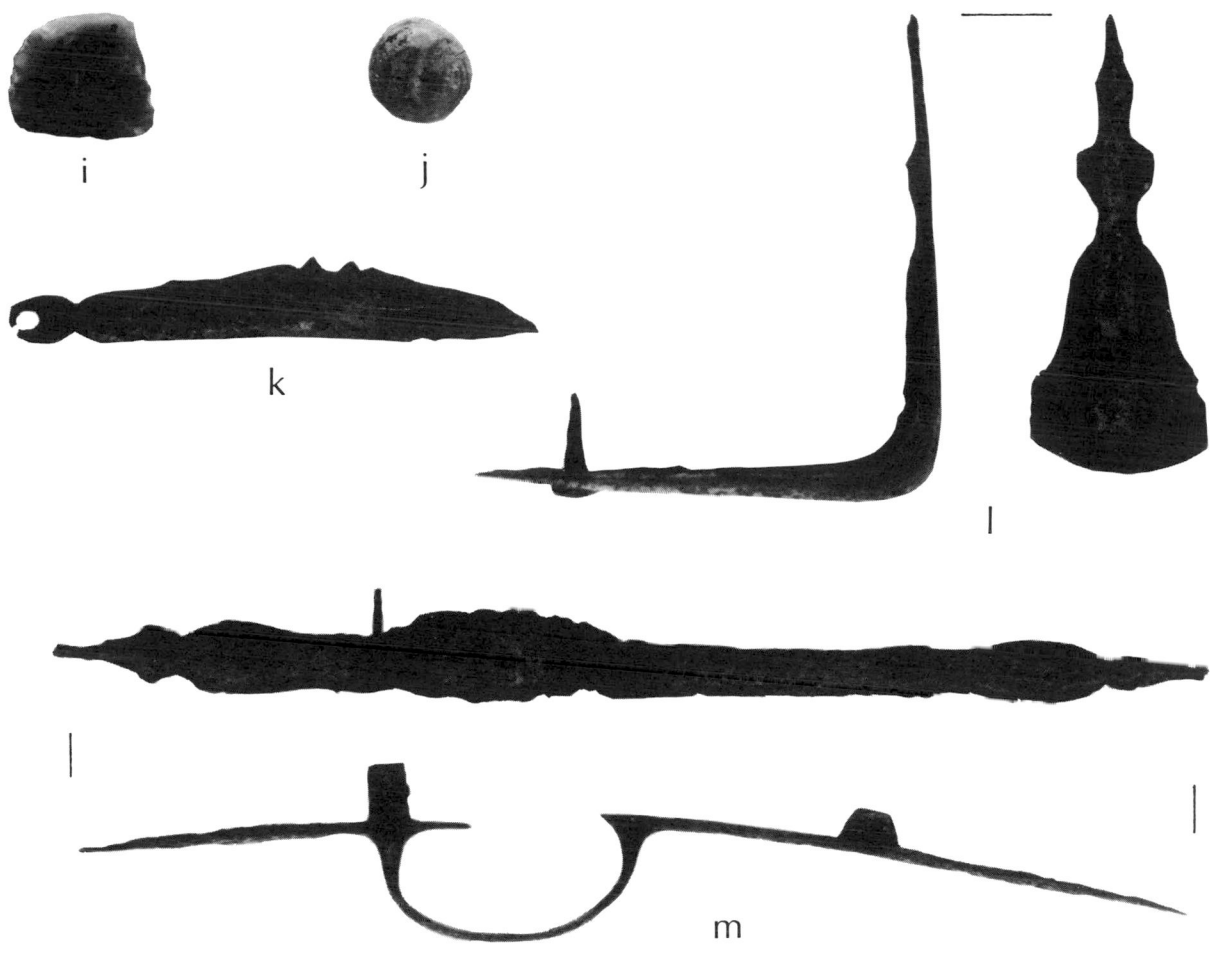

i

j

k

l

l

l

m

Figure 166 (continued).

counting for the small size and oval shape of the grave pit). The burial had been badly disturbed sometime in the distant past, probably by natural agency: much of the right side of the skeleton was missing, and the cranium and mandible had been dislocated.

The artifacts found with burial YB-1 are listed in table 49, and some are illustrated in figure 166. In nature and quantity they are consistent with an early contact situation. The most datable object, the fusil, is believed by Hamilton to date before 1710 (app. G.2). The most interesting aboriginal artifact is the catlinite pipe, which is interpreted as indicative of chiefly status. All of the objects—except the fusil, beads, iron awl, and pipe—were found in a leather ditty bag with a metal-braid rim that had been placed at the left side of the head. The pipe and seventy-nine of the beads were at the right side of the pelvis, where they may have been associated with the missing right hand. The remaining 211 beads had been strung in three strands around the neck.

Burial YB-2 (fig. 167) was located between coordinates N19–21 and E29.5–31 and lay at a depth of 110–140 cm. The grave contained the skeleton of a single individual with the head oriented to the southeast. Again,

the interment was the supine inhumation of a young adult male (20–30 years of age) whose skeleton appeared normal and exhibited no unusual pathologies. He did, however, have severe dental caries and five minor episodes of hyperplasia between the ages of two and four (Jerome C. Rose, personal communication, 1982).

The associated artifacts (table 49) are of considerable interest. They include both a musket and a pistol; the musket is a Type C fusil, and both firearms have a mix of brass and iron hardware that along with other details indicates a date of around 1700 for their manufacture (app. G.2). Lying across the left side of the chest was a hafted, lightweight axe-tomahawk (fig. 167; this is very similar to, and may be an early version of, the so-called Missouri war hatchet described by H. L. Peterson [1965, pp. 22–23]). A small pouch on the right side of the chest contained hundreds of small white (IIA1/IVA1) and small to large blue (IIA6, IIA7) glass beads, a circular glass mirror, an iron strike-a-light, a French gunspall, two native gunflints, two small snub-nosed end scrapers that could have been used as gunflints, a polished biconical stone, a galena crystal, a small quantity of vermilion, and some unidentified fragments of iron. Near the head

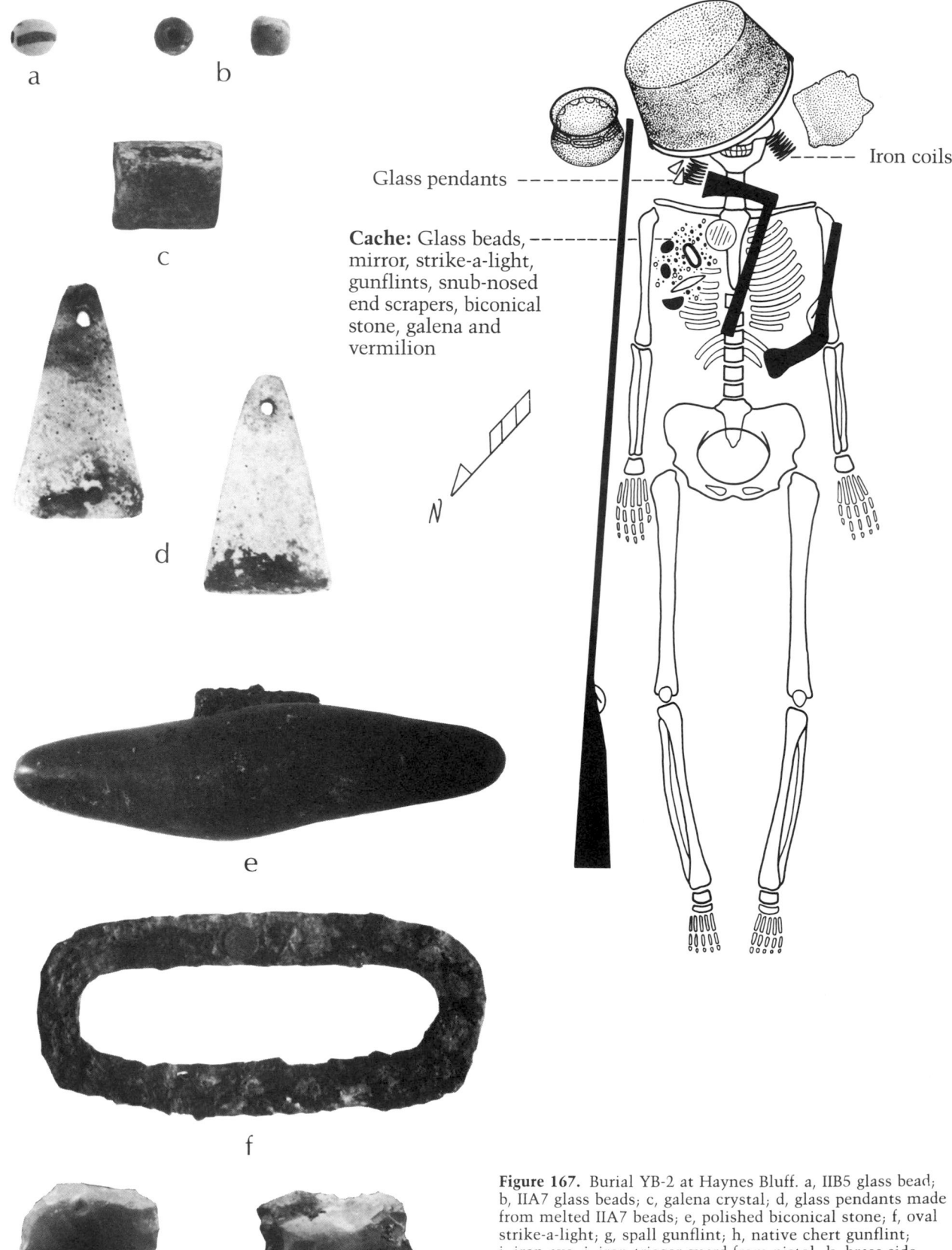

Glass pendants

Cache: Glass beads, mirror, strike-a-light, gunflints, snub-nosed end scrapers, biconical stone, galena and vermilion

Iron coils

N

a

b

c

d

e

f

g

h

Figure 167. Burial YB-2 at Haynes Bluff. a, IIB5 glass bead; b, IIA7 glass beads; c, galena crystal; d, glass pendants made from melted IIA7 beads; e, polished biconical stone; f, oval strike-a-light; g, spall gunflint; h, native chert gunflint; i, iron axe; j, iron trigger guard from pistol; k, brass side plate from pistol; l, flintlock from pistol; m, butt cap from pistol; n, barrel from pistol; o, barrel from Type C gun. (a–h, 1:1; i–o, 1:2)

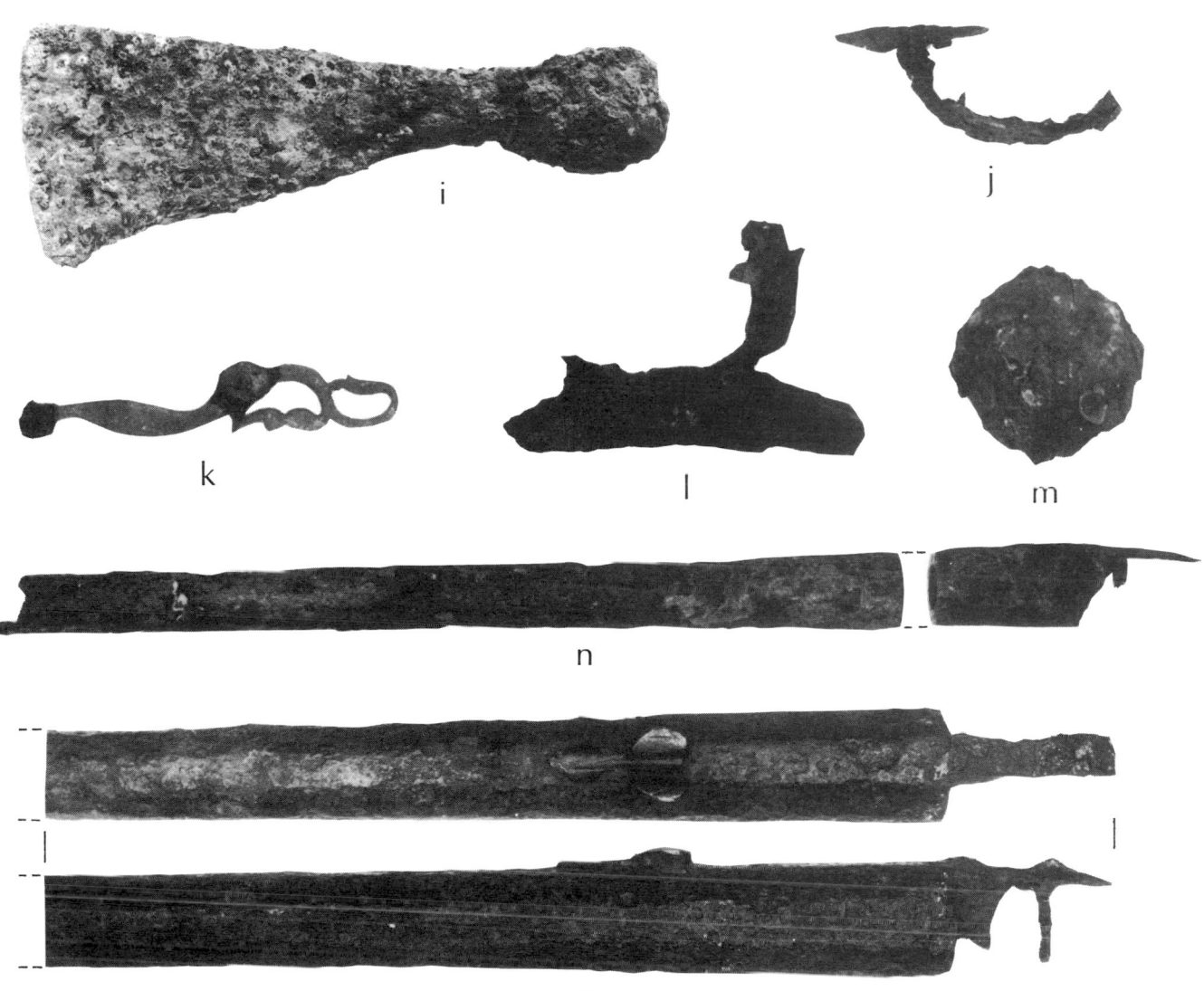

Figure 167 (continued).

were two pieces of aboriginal pottery: a Winterville Incised, *var. unspecified** jar on the right, and a partial
vessel of Winterville Incised, *var. Wailes* on the left. A
large (diameter 46 cm) brass kettle was inverted over
the crown of the head in order to protect a miter-shaped
leather headdress that had been tied to the head by a
cloth band embroidered with many hundreds of small
blue and white glass beads (cf. Swanton 1931, p. 102).
On each side of the neck was an iron coil which may
have been a ring for a hair braid. This functional interpretation is strengthened by the fact that two native-
made triangular glass pendants were found associated
with the right coil; among some peoples these pendants
were often tied in the hair (Howard 1972). Also with
the right coil were one IIB5 and two IIA1 glass beads,
and two small pieces of brass wire.

* Mississippi jar with Leflore Design Mode around the shoulder. This combination has recently been classified as Winterville Incised, *var. Chickasaw* (Atkinson 1986).

The status, dating, and ethnic affiliation of these burials become more speculative with each consideration.
Clearly, these two individuals were important members
of their social group(s), as attested by the mound-top
burial and the kind and quantity of grave goods. Especially noteworthy are the catlinite pipe with YB-1 and
the glass pendants with YB-2, both highly valued artifacts of native manufacture thought to have signified
high social status among many groups of Indians (e.g.,
Le Page du Pratz 1758, vol. 1, p. 206; Howard 1972;
Jolly 1973; Salter 1977; Mainfort 1979).

The dating of the burials is not quite as certain. All
of the artifacts are consistent with an early eighteenth-
century French contact situation, but the crucial question is how early. The firearms would seem to date
within a few years of the turn of the century, but of
course there may have been a considerable time lapse
before they were given into the hands of the Indians
(also, the absence of locks on both fusils might indicate
that the guns were outdated relics at the time of dep-

Table 49. Aboriginal and European artifacts associated with burials YB-1 and YB-2 at the summit of mound A, Haynes Bluff.

Burial YB-1		Burial YB-2	
ABORIGINAL		*ABORIGINAL*	
Lithics:		*Pottery:*	
Catlinite pipe	1	Winterville Incised, *var. Wailes*	1
Triangular knife	1	Winterville Incised, *var. unspecified*	1
Flat, rectangular chert cobble	1		
		Lithics:	
EUROPEAN		Native gunflints	2
		Snub-nosed end scrapers[b]	2
Glass:		Polished biconical stone	1
		Galena crystal	1
Beads			
IIA1/IVA1	290	*EUROPEAN*	
Button	1		
		Glass:	
Iron:			
		Circular mirror	1
Wrought nails		Beads	
Type unspecified	5	IIA1/IVA1	1,128
Folding knife blade	1	IIA6	1
Awl	1	IIA7	1,460
Strike-a-light	1	IIB5	1
Springs	9	Triangular pendants[c]	2
Miscellaneous[a]	—		
		Iron:	
Pewter:			
		Axe	1
Button (pewter-sheathed bone)	1	Strike-a-light	1
		Coils	2
Brass:			
		Brass:	
Spring	1		
Button	1	Kettle	
Braid[a]	—	Type A, Variety 1	1
		Wire	2
Guns/munitions:			
		Guns/munitions:	
Fusil			
Type D (iron hardware, no lock)	1	Fusil	
Spall gunflints		Type C (brass/iron hardware, no lock)	1
Musket	3	Pistol (brass/iron hardware)	1
Pistol	1	Spall gunflint	
Lead musket balls	27	Musket	1
Lead lumps	8		
Gunpowder[a]	—	*Miscellaneous:*	
		Vermilion[a]	—

[a]Numerous fragments.   [b]For use as gunflints?   [c]Native-made from IIA7 glass beads.

Table 50. Aboriginal and European artifacts from excavation units Y111–115 on mound A at Haynes Bluff (tabulated by mound stages).

	A	B	C	D	E	F	G	H	I
ABORIGINAL									
Pottery:									
Winterville Incised, *var. Tunica*	17	18	5	1	1		1		
Barton Incised, *var. Davion*	4		3						
Barton Incised, *var. Portland*	3	1							
Owens Punctated, *var. Redwood*	1	1							
Barton Incised, *var. Charlevoix*	8	14	7			4			
Old Town Red, *var. Ballground*	3	1							
Parkin Punctated, *var. Elise*	4	4	2						
Winterville Incised, *var. Loubois*	10	4				1			
Cracker Road Incised, *var. Cracker Road*	2	1							
Cracker Road Incised, *var. unspecified*								1	1
Fatherland Incised, *var. Nancy*	1								
Mazique Incised, *var. North*	7							1	
Winterville Incised, *var. Broutin*	9	4	3	1					
Winterville Incised, *var. Wailes*	1	5	4	1				1	1
Grace Brushed, *var. Grand Gulf*	1		2						
Fatherland Incised, *var. Fatherland*	1								
Fatherland Incised, *var. unspecified*									1
Maddox Engraved, *var. Emerald*	2	1							1
Chicot Red, *var. Grand Village*	1								
Owens Punctated, *var. Widow Creek*			1						
Owens Punctated, *var. unspecified*			1						
Winterville Incised, *var. Ranch*		8	1	1			4	2	
Leland Incised, *var. Deep Bayou*	1		1	1					
Leland Incised, *var. Russell*	12	9	2	1			2		2
Leland Incised, *var. Williams*	3	3	2					3	1
Barton Incised, *var. Arcola*	4	10	9	3	2		1		
Barton Incised, *var. Midnight*	1	1	2		1				
Winterville Incised, *var. Belzoni*	9	15	7			1	4	2	
Leland Incised, *var. Leland*	4	2	4			1	2	2	1
Leland Incised, *var. unspecified*	1		1						
Maddox Engraved, *var. Silver City*	1								
Coleman Incised, *var. Bass*	3				1				
Barton Incised, *var. Estill*	4	3	1				1	1	1
Parkin Punctated, *var. Hollandale*	2	8	2					1	
Parkin Punctated, *var. Transylvania*	4		3						1
Parkin Punctated, *var. unspecified*									1
Winterville Incised, *var. Winterville*	5	5	3	2			4	1	

Table 50 continued

Table 50 (continued).

	A	B	C	D	E	F	G	H	I
Grace Brushed, *var. Grace*	2	4	3		1		1	1	
Grace Brushed, *var. unspecified*			1			1			
Pouncey Pinched, *var. Patosi*	1								
Barton Incised, *var. unspecified*	14	14	6		1		3	3	
Winterville Incised, *var. unspecified*	2	2							1
Unclassified incised (Yazoo)		1	1						
Anna Incised, *var. Anna*	2	1							
Carter Engraved, *var. Carter*		1	1						
Cahokia Cord Marked, *var. Montrose*	1		1						
Hollyknowe Pinched, *var. Patmos*	1								
Plaquemine Brushed, *var. Plaquemine*	4	7	4				1	2	1
Avoyelles Punctated, *var. Dupree*			3						
Avoyelles Punctated, *var. Tatum*	1								
Beldeau Incised, *var. Bell Bayou*	1								
Coleman Incised, *var. Coleman*	3	2	1						
Coles Creek Incised, *var. Hardy*	2								
Evansville Punctated, *var. Sharkey*		2					1		
Mazique Incised, *var. Manchac*		2	2						
Unclassified incised (Addis)			1		1				
Coles Creek Incised, *var. Greenhouse*					1				
Coles Creek Incised, *var. Mott*	3								
Chevalier Stamped, *var. Chevalier*	1								
Coles Creek Incised, *var. Coles Creek*	1	2							
Coles Creek Incised, *var. unspecified*	2	1	3						
Mazique Incised, *var. unspecified*	1	1							
Coles Creek Incised, *var. Stoner*	1								
Coles Creek Incised, *var. Wade*	1	1	1						
French Fork Incised, *var. unspecified*	2								
Alligator Incised, *var. Oxbow*	1								
Coles Creek Incised, *var. Hunt*	2								
Coles Creek Incised, *var. Phillips*		1							
Mulberry Creek Cord Marked, *var. Edwards*	1								
Evansville Punctated, *var. unspecified*		1							
Marksville Stamped, *var. Mabin*		1							
Unclassified incised (Baytown)	1								
Lithics:									
Edwards Stemmed, *var. Sunflower* point		1							
Triangular knife					1				
Snub-nosed end scraper	1								
Unclassified tool					1				

Table 50 (continued).

	A	B	C	D	E	F	G	H	I
EUROPEAN									
Glass:									
Olive green	2								
Iron:									
Wrought nails									
Type I	1								
Type III	2								
Type IV	1								
Type V	1								
Type unspecified	1								
Copper:									
Wire	1								

osition, although more likely the locks were simply too valuable during the first few decades of contact to have been buried). The only other temporally sensitive artifact was the brass button with YB-1, which is of a type that may not have been introduced to Louisiana until 1716 (Chartrand 1973; Brown 1975, p. 172; Brain 1979, p. 189). If this terminus post quem holds for both burials, then they postdate the Tunica occupation.

The absence of aboriginal diagnostics makes it imprudent to even hazard a guess as to the ethnicity of YB-1. A very uncertain ethnic identification of YB-2 is based on the pottery vessels, which exhibit Winterville Incised decoration of distinctive northern derivation: in addition to *Wailes*, the *var. unspecified* jar displays the Leflore Design Mode (usually found on Leland Incised). These decorative modes are found together at the Leflore site (18-P-3), which may have been a village of the historic Chakchiuma (see fig. 203). The Chakchiuma are known to have visited and even lived among the lower Yazoo tribes around Haynes Bluff (Swanton 1911, p. 294); there is even some evidence that they may have been the last native inhabitants of Haynes Bluff, being located there as late as 1736 (see fig. 21). Burial YB-2, then, may have been Chakchiuma (or possibly Ofo; in either case, the artifactual evidence points in that general direction). This identification is further supported by the glass pendants, a very distinctive northern artifact type (Ubelaker and Bass 1970; Brown 1972; Perino 1975; Walthall and Benchley 1987, p. 44.), the nearest example of which was found at the French site (19-P-10) just south of Leflore (Smith 1981).

After the burials were removed, excavation unit Y115 was continued as a strata cut in an effort to ascertain details of stratification that could be aligned with those found in excavation unit Y110. The effort was unsuccessful, however, in that only the gross distinction of mound fill was observed between the topsoil and a depth of 225 cm below the surface, at which point excavations were terminated. Although it could not be established whether these 2 m of loading constituted more than one mantle, the cultural stratigraphy confirmed that they dated to the late Wasp Lake phase (table 50). Here, too, was evidence for major mound construction during the protohistoric period.

Excavation Units Y150–167. These excavations were laid out to investigate the series of electronic signals that were interpreted as indicating many small bits of metal (apparently iron) at shallow depth. It was soon determined that the small bits of metal were numerous handwrought iron nails that were scattered throughout the topsoil. Seizing the opportunity to gather more information about the historic eighteenth-century occupation, we opened up an extensive area on the eastern side of the summit plateau (see fig. 164). Ultimately, eighteen units (seventeen 2-m squares and one 2-×-4-m rectangle) were excavated between coordinates N20–34 and E36–48. In all, 10–25 cm of topsoil were removed and carefully sifted for cultural content; then the surface of the last mantle was troweled for postholes and other intrusive features. Unfortunately, no patterns of postholes or other major features were observed, so that the information gained was confined to the artifacts retrieved from the topsoil (table 51).

The most striking thing about this assemblage of artifacts is the relatively large number of European materials. There are, in fact, more of these artifacts from the summit of mound A, even excluding the burials, than from any other known location on the site. Not only quantity but also quality is represented: all of the most prestigious items, for example, brass ornaments and faience (fig. 168i–k), are restricted to the summit

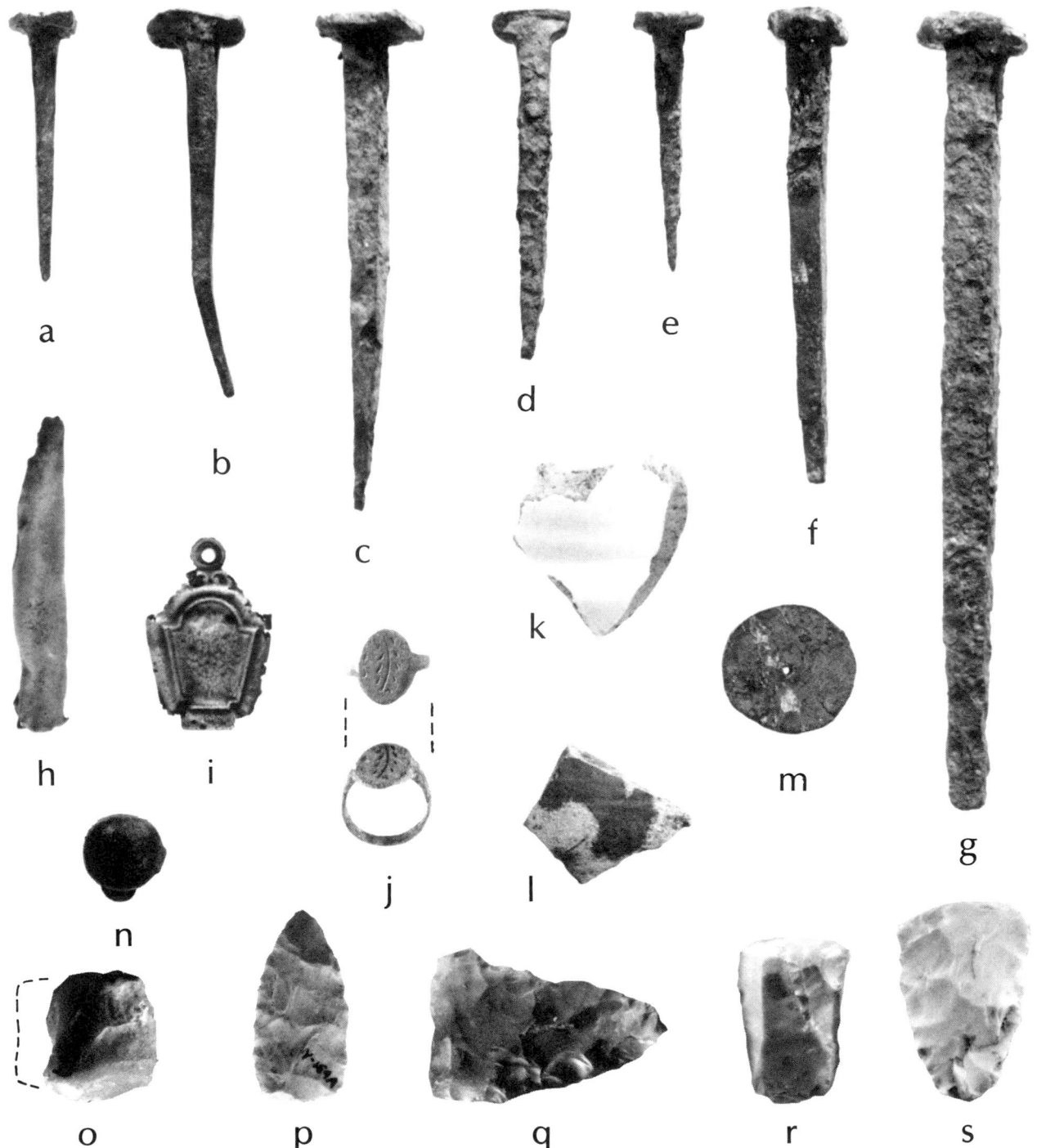

Figure 168. Eighteenth-century European and aboriginal artifacts from mound A at Haynes Bluff. a–c, handwrought iron nails, Type I; d, handwrought iron nails, Type II; e, handwrought iron nails, Type III; f, handwrought iron nails, Type IV; g, handwrought iron nails, Type V; h, sheet copper tinkler; i, pendant of stamped sheet brass; j, brass finger ring; k, white faience; l, lead-glazed earthenware, Type C; m, lead button(?); n, lead musket ball; o, spall gunflint; p, Nodena Lanceolate, *var. Russell* point; g, chert triangular knife; r–s, chert snub-nosed end scrapers. (1:1)

Table 51. Aboriginal and European artifacts from the topsoil in excavation units Y150–167 on mound A at Haynes Bluff.

ABORIGINAL

Pottery:

Winterville Incised, *var. Tunica*	16
Barton Incised, *var. Davion*	7
Barton Incised, *var. Portland*	3
Barton Incised, *var. Charlevoix*	27
Old Town Red, *var. Ballground*	15
Parkin Punctated, *var. Elise*	4
Winterville Incised, *var. Loubois*	20
Cracker Road Incised, *var. Cracker Road*	5
Cracker Road Incised, *var. unspecified*	1
Fatherland Incised, *var. Bayou Goula*	1
Mazique Incised, *var. North*	5
Unclassified incised/engraved (Caddo)	1
Winterville Incised, *var. Broutin*	11
Winterville Incised, *var. Wailes*	5
Grace Brushed, *var. Grand Gulf*	4
Fatherland Incised, *var. Fatherland*	3
Fatherland Incised, *var. Stanton*	1
Fatherland Incised, *var. unspecified*	2
Chicot Red, *var. unspecified*	1
Owens Punctated, *var. unspecified*	1
Leland Incised, *var. Blanchard*	1
Leland Incised, *var. Deep Bayou*	4
Leland Incised, *var. Russell*	27
Leland Incised, *var. Williams*	6
Barton Incised, *var. Arcola*	7
Winterville Incised, *var. Belzoni*	9
Leland Incised, *var. Leland*	6
Leland Incised, *var. unspecified*	2
Maddox Engraved, *var. Silver City*	1
Barton Incised, *var. Estill*	5
Parkin Punctated, *var. Hollandale*	1
Parkin Punctated, *var. Transylvania*	1
Winterville Incised, *var. Winterville*	5

Grace Brushed, *var. Grace*	4
Grace Brushed, *var. unspecified*	6
Barton Incised, *var. unspecified*	17
Winterville Incised, *var. unspecified*	8
Unclassified incised (Yazoo)	1
Anna Incised, *var. Anna*	1
Plaquemine Brushed, *var. Plaquemine*	7
Avoyelles Punctated, *var. Dupree*	1
Coleman Incised, *var. Coleman*	2
Coles Creek Incised, *var. Hardy*	1
Evansville Punctated, *var. Sharkey*	4
Mazique Incised, *var. Manchac*	1
Unclassified incised (Addis)	1
Beldeau Incised, *var. Beldeau*	1
Coles Creek Incised, *var. Blakely*	2
Coles Creek Incised, *var. Mott*	3
Coles Creek Incised, *var. Coles Creek*	4
Coles Creek Incised, *var. unspecified*	3
Coles Creek Incised, *var. Wade*	1
Larto Red, *var. Larto*	4
Yates Net Impressed, *var. Yates*	1
Marksville Stamped, *var. Manny*	1
Unclassified incised (Baytown)	2

Daub: 1,340

Lithics:

Nodena Lanceolate, *var. Russell* point (fig. 168p)	1
Mississippi Triangular, *var. Madison* point	1
Triangular knife (fig. 168q)	1
Snub-nosed end scrapers	3
Oval scraper	1
Unclassified tool	1
Utilized flakes	11

Organics:

Human skull fragment	1
Unclassified bone	94

Table 51 continued

Table 51 (continued).

EUROPEAN			*Copper:*	
			Miscellaneous	2
Earthenware:				
Faience			*Brass:*	
White (fig. 168k)		7[a]	Pendant (fig. 168i)	1
Glass:			Ring (fig. 168j)	1
Olive green		7		
Iron:			*Lead:*	
Wrought nails			Button(?) (fig. 168m)	1
Type I (fig. 168a–c)		88		
Type II (fig. 168d)		2	*Gun parts/munitions:*	
Type III (fig. 168e)		4	Spall gunflint (fig. 168o)	1
Type IV		3	Lead musket ball (fig. 168n)	1
Type V (fig. 168g)		4		
Type unspecified		11		
Miscellaneous		2		

[a] All from three contiguous excavation units, probably same vessel.

area, as are all but one piece of glass. Perhaps most intriguing are the large number and variety of hand-wrought iron nails, which had originally triggered the electronic instruments. Nails, of course, could have had many functions for the Indians, since they would have been quite useful as awls, punches, styli, scarifiers, and even implements of torture (heated and applied to the bare skin of victims). The large number and broad distribution, however, suggest a more traditional European function—that is, for construction. The nails were not found in a distinctive architectural pattern, but the former presence of a structure was confirmed by the large amount of daub in the topsoil. The burning of such a structure is further indicated by the fact that most, if not all, of the nails had been subjected to intense heat, while many of the faience and glass sherds also show evidence of burning. Clearly, the conflagration of a structure, perhaps built partly with the aid of nails, terminated the last mound-top occupation. A parallel situation was found to exist at Trudeau (see discussion in part 3).

The aboriginal artifacts are also of considerable interest. Although Tunica markers are present, the predominant ceramic group is the Montfort set. Together with the Holly Bluff 2 subset, the indigenous lower Yazoo pottery tradition is obviously the strongest element in the assemblage. Perhaps the Yazoo Indians were the keepers of the temple, as well as "masters of the soil" (French 1846, p. 83). Or perhaps the Tunica were not in residence long enough to leave as substantial a record of their presence.

In summary, excavations at this locus revealed the remains of a burned structure which contained some of the choicest European artifacts discovered at the site. It is tempting to identify the structure with the Tunica temple that Charlevoix records as having been burned by Father Davion (Charlevoix 1744, vol. 3, p. 433; French 1851, p. 174). Swanton (1911, p. 310) discounts this story, however, even if it refers to the same venue. Furthermore, the evidence of the aboriginal pottery suggests that the structure continued to be used by the Yazoo after the Tunica had left. Whenever the event occurred, the structure had burned by the time burial YB-2 (and perhaps YB-1, as well) was interred, for the grave pit fill contained a considerable amount of the daub and charcoal debris.

The base of mound A was tested at several loci in order to investigate different kinds of electronic anomalies detected by the instruments. At the same time, it was hoped that the stratigraphies could be correlated with those revealed in the mound summit explorations and that the entire history of mound A could be reconstructed. The field catalog numbers assigned to these excavations were Y100–102, Y103, Y105–109, Y140–141 (see fig. 164).

Excavation Units Y100–102. These units were small tests placed to the north-northwest of mound A. Their precise placement was determined by the anomalies that were selected for investigation.

Y100 was a 2-×-2-m unit laid out between coordinates N64–66 and W4–6, the approximate center of a large generalized anomaly of unknown character. Y102 was a 1-×-4-m extension to the northeast (coordinates N66–67/W0–4), designed to determine the limits of the anomaly. Both units were excavated down to subsoil using arbitrary 25-cm levels. The stratification of both was found to be similar (fig. 169): beneath 15–30 cm of topsoil was 70–85 cm of mottled, loess-based loading, which in turn overlay two zones of midden, each approximately 25 cm thick. Between the two midden zones was a lens of water-laid loess, and over much of the

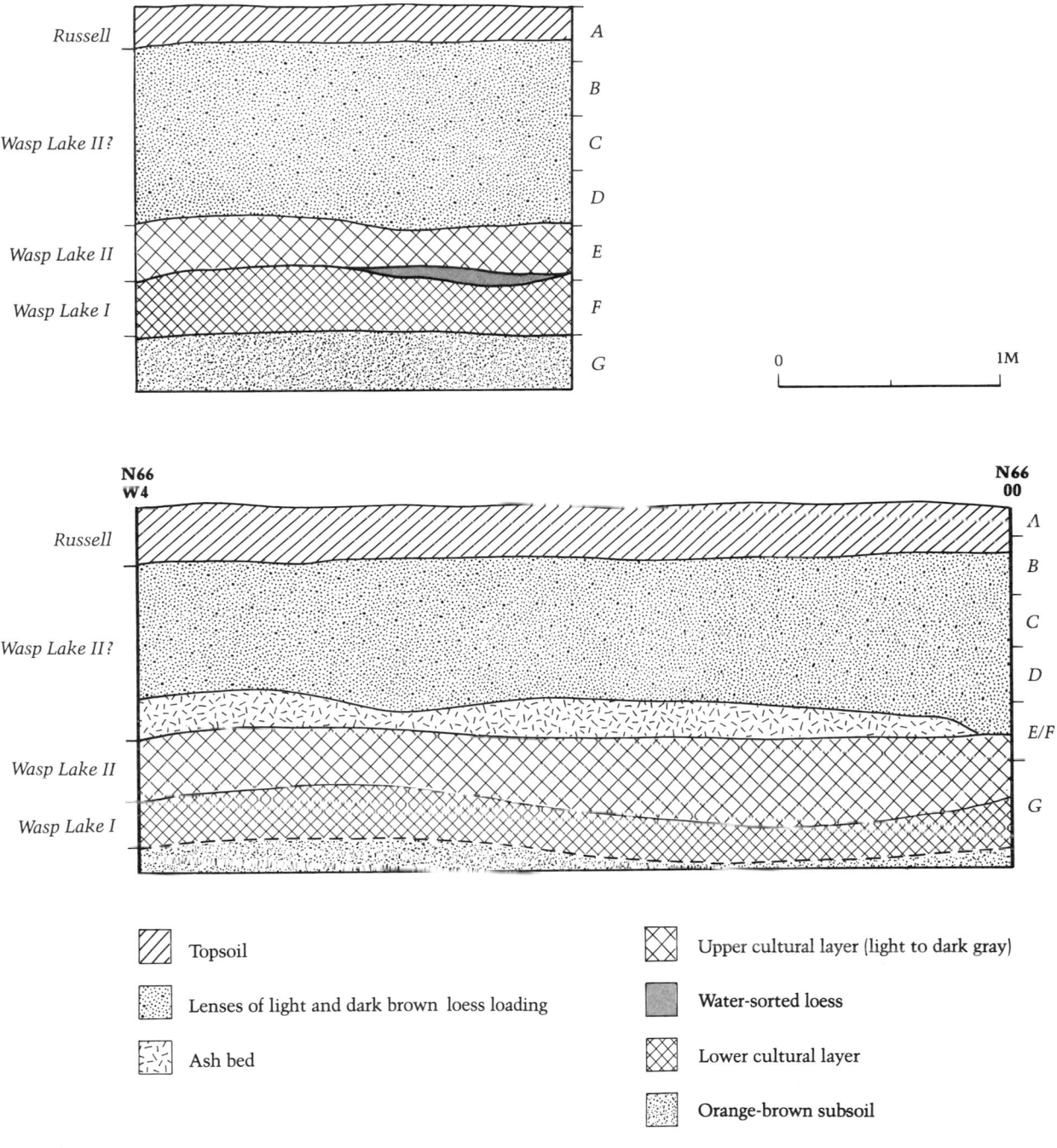

Figure 169. Stratification in excavation units Y100 and Y102, Haynes Bluff. a, west wall of Y100; b, south wall of Y102.

upper zone was a bed of ash, daub, and charcoal. No distinctive cultural features were observed, and no explanation was found for the anomaly (although it is possible that the bed of burned matter was sufficient to unsettle the instruments). The cultural stratigraphy (table 52) reveals that the first midden was laid down during successive phases through early Wasp Lake. Apparently there was then a break long enough for a lens of loess wash—perhaps talus from the mound—to accumulate before a second midden was deposited during the Wasp Lake II subphase. Considering the heteroge-

neous cultural content of this upper midden and the lack of internal features, it may have been redeposited —that is, brought in as fill like the levels above it. Between these major strata in Y102 is the ash bed, which is probably to be correlated with the burned level D in excavation unit Y110 at the summit (see fig. 165). The interval of time represented by this event does not seem to have been long, and a major episode of landfill soon ensued. As was the case in Y110, the dating of this last major loading is debatable: no European artifacts were found in it, but there are some very late aboriginal ce-

Table 52. Aboriginal and European artifacts from excavation units Y100 and Y102 at Haynes Bluff (tabulated according to strata).

	Topsoil	Loading	Upper Midden	Lower Midden
ABORIGINAL				
Pottery:				
Winterville Incised, *var. Tunica*	2		2	
Barton Incised, *var. Davion*	2	1	3	
Barton Incised, *var. Portland*	4			
Owens Punctated, *var. Redwood*		1		
Barton Incised, *var. Charlevoix*	14	3	4	
Old Town Red, *var. Ballground*	4	1		
Parkin Punctated, *var. Elise*	2	1		
Winterville Incised, *var. Loubois*	9	1		
Cracker Road Incised, *var. Cracker Road*	3			
Cracker Road Incised, *var. unspecified*	1	1		
Mazique Incised, *var. North*	2	2	5	1
Fatherland Incised, *var. Nancy*	1	1		
Owens Punctated, *var. Manly*	1			
Winterville Incised, *var. Broutin*	9	1	9	1
Winterville Incised, *var. Wailes*	5	1	2	
Old Town Red, *var. unspecified*	1	1		
Grace Brushed, *var. Grand Gulf*	3	2	2	
Grace Brushed, *var. Warren*	3	1		
Leland Incised, *var. Bovina*			1	
Leland Incised, *var. Leflore*	1			
Fatherland Incised, *var. Fatherland*	2		1	2
Fatherland Incised, *var. unspecified*	2			
Maddox Engraved, *var. Emerald*	1	2		1
Chicot Red, *var. Grand Village*	1			
Chicot Red, *var. unspecified*			3	
Owens Punctated, *var. Widow Creek*			1	
Owens Punctated, *var. unspecified*	1	1	1	
Winterville Incised, *var. Ranch*			4	
Leland Incised, *var. Blanchard*		1		
Leland Incised, *var. Deep Bayou*	4	2	2	
Leland Incised, *var. Russell*	21	6	4	
Leland Incised, *var. Williams*	18	9	4	1
Barton Incised, *var. Arcola*	40	9		
Barton Incised, *var. Midnight*	9	4		
Winterville Incised, *var. Belzoni*	19	10	23	2
Leland Incised, *var. Leland*	15	3	1	1
Leland Incised, *var. unspecified*	3		2	
Maddox Engraved, *var. Silver City*	2			1
Coleman Incised, *var. Bass*	1			

Table 52 (continued).

	Topsoil	Loading	Upper Midden	Lower Midden
Barton Incised, *var. Estill*	9	5	1	
Parkin Punctated, *var. Hollandale*	2	5	4	2
Parkin Punctated, *var. Transylvania*	7	3	2	1
Parkin Punctated, *var. unspecified*		1	1	3
Winterville Incised, *var. Winterville*	10	8	14	2
Grace Brushed, *var. Grace*	16	4	8	
Grace Brushed, *var. unspecified*	1	2	3	2
Pouncey Pinched, *var. Patosi*	5		1	1
Winterville Incised, *var. Blum*			1	
Barton Incised, *var. unspecified*	48	17	7	3
Winterville Incised, *var. unspecified*	6	2	1	
Unclassified incised (Yazoo)		2	1	
Anna Incised, *var. Anna*	3	1		
Carter Engraved, *var. Carter*	4	2	2	
Leland Incised, *var. Bethlehem*	2	1		
Hollyknowe Pinched, *var. Patmos*	4			
Plaquemine Brushed, *var. Plaquemine*	7	17	12	1
Avoyelles Punctated, *var. Dupree*	1			
Evansville Punctated, *var. Sharkey*		1	1	2
Mazique Incised, *var. Manchac*		1	2	
Coles Creek Incised, *var. Blakely*	1			
Coles Creek Incised, *var. Greenhouse*	2			
Mazique Incised, *var. Kings Point*		1		
Chevalier Stamped, *var. Chevalier*	1			
Coles Creek Incised, *var. Coles Creek*			1	2
Coles Creek Incised, *var. unspecified*	2	2	1	1
Unclassified incised (Valley Park)	2			
Coles Creek Incised, *var. Chase*	1			
Coles Creek Incised, *var. Stoner*		1		
Coles Creek Incised, *var. Wade*	1			
Mulberry Creek Cord Marked, *var. Smith Creek*	1		1	
Alligator Incised, *var. Oxbow*	1	1	2	
Chevalier Stamped, *var. Cornelia*			1	
Coles Creek Incised, *var. Hunt*	1	1		
Coles Creek Incised, *var. Phillips*	1		2	
Larto Red, *var. Larto*	1		1	1
Mulberry Creek Cord Marked, *var. Edwards*	4	1		1
Unclassified incised (Baytown)			1	
Daub:	312	258	161	15
Lithics:				
Edwards Stemmed, *var. Enola* point			1	
Unclassified projectile point	1			
Unspecialized scrapers	2			
Unclassified bifaces			1	1
Hammerstones		1		1
Utilized flakes	4		4	1

Table 52 continued

Table 52 (continued).

	Topsoil	Loading	Upper Midden	Lower Midden
Organics:				
Mammal bone	104			
Bird bone	3			
Fish bone	21			
Turtle bone/shell	7			
Unclassified bone	17	329	429	343
Bone awls		1		1
Bone earpin (fig. 175a)		1		
EUROPEAN				
Earthenware:				
Lead-glazed				
Type C (fig. 168l)	1			
Glass:				
Bead				
IVB1 (fig. 175j)	1			
Iron:				
Wrought nail				
Type unspecified	1			
Miscellaneous	3			
Copper:				
Miscellaneous	1			
Lead:				
Miscellaneous	1			

ramic markers. The question is of little practical importance, however, for it is really only a matter of a few years between the terminal Wasp Lake phase and the very early Russell phase. The topsoil, of course, represents the remains of the full Russell phase context.

Excavation unit Y101 was located between coordinates N64–66 and E14–16. This 2-×-2-m unit was placed directly over a very strong anomaly interpreted as a large piece of iron, perhaps indicating a burial. The excavation was carried out in seven 25-cm levels and revealed a stratification somewhat different than that found in Y100 and Y102 (fig. 170). Beneath the topsoil was approximately 50 cm of water-laid loess, followed by 25 cm of midden. Below that was 40 cm of interbedded midden and gray clay loading, and finally a layer of midden 20 cm thick. Subsoil was reached at a depth of approximately 160 cm from the surface. The cultural content of these strata is presented in table 53. It is

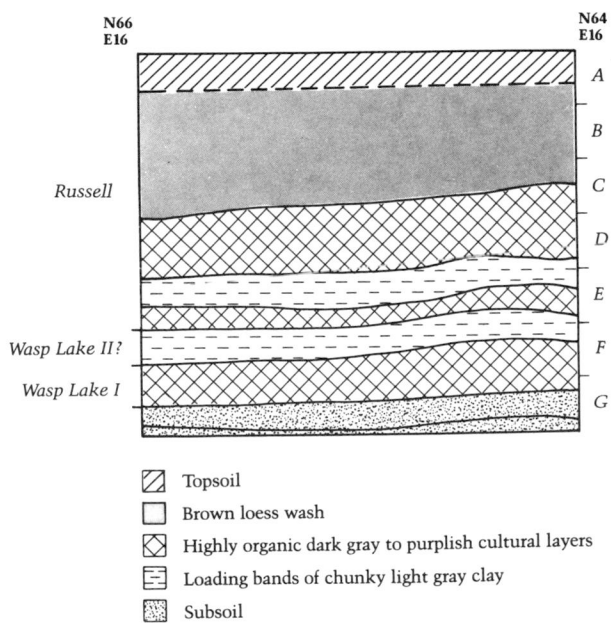

Figure 170. Stratification of excavation unit Y101, Haynes Bluff, as revealed in the east wall.

Table 53. Aboriginal and European artifacts from excavation unit Y101 at Haynes Bluff (tabulated by level).

	A	B	C	D	E	F	G
ABORIGINAL							
Pottery:							
Winterville Incised, *var. Tunica*	1	2	3	4	2	1	
Winterville Incised, *var. Angola*			1				
Barton Incised, *var. Davion*		1					
Barton Incised, *var. Portland*			2	1			
Barton Incised, *var. Charlevoix*	1	3	2		2	2	
Old Town Red, *var. Ballground*	3		8				
Winterville Incised, *var. Loubois*	1	1					
Cracker Road Incised, *var. Cracker Road*	2		1	1	1		
Cracker Road Incised, *var. unspecified*		1				1	
Old Town Red, *var. St. Pierre*				1			
Fatherland Incised, *var. Nancy*	1						
Fatherland Incised, *var. Snyders Bluff*				1	1		
Winterville Incised, *var. Broutin*	3	1			1	1	1
Winterville Incised, *var. Wailes*	3		1	1			
Old Town Red, *var. unspecified*	1	3					
Grace Brushed, *var. Warren*	1	1					
Leland Incised, *var. Bovina*					2	2	
Nodena Red and White, *var. Ellison*						1	
Fatherland Incised, *var. Fatherland*			1			1	
Fatherland Incised, *var. unspecified*		1		1			
Maddox Engraved, *var. Emerald*	2						
Chicot Red, *var. Grand Village*		1					
Leland Incised, *var. Russell*	4	5	5		7	7	
Leland Incised, *var. Williams*	4	2	3	2		1	
Owens Punctated, *var. Beland City*					1	1	
Barton Incised, *var. Arcola*	8	5	5	1	7	4	1
Barton Incised, *var. Midnight*	2			1	1	1	
Winterville Incised, *var. Belzoni*	5	3	6	2	1		
Leland Incised, *var. Leland*	2		1		1	2	
Leland Incised, *var. unspecified*	1	1					
Coleman Incised, *var. Bass*			1				
Barton Incised, *var. Estill*	1		2	2			
Parkin Punctated, *var. Hollandale*	4	2		2		1	
Parkin Punctated, *var. unspecified*	1						
Winterville Incised, *var. Winterville*	1	1	7	2		2	
Grace Brushed, *var. Grace*	2	1	3	1			
Grace Brushed, *var. unspecified*					1		
Pouncey Pinched, *var. Patosi*						4	
Barton Incised, *var. unspecified*	6	6	5	3	7	4	
Winterville Incised, *var. unspecified*	1			1	1		

Table 53 continued

Table 53 (continued).

	A	B	C	D	E	F	G
Anna Incised, *var. Anna*	1						
Carter Engraved, *var. Carter*	1						
Leland Incised, *var. Bethlehem*	1		1			1	
Plaquemine Brushed, *var. Plaquemine*	3	1	2		1		
Coles Creek Incised, *var. Hardy*		1					
Evansville Punctated, *var. Sharkey*	1						
Unclassified incised (Addis)					1		
Coles Creek Incised, *var. Greenhouse*			2				
Coles Creek Incised, *var. Mott*						1	
Coles Creek Incised, *var. Coles Creek*	1						
Coles Creek Incised, *var. unspecified*	2						
Mazique Incised, *var. unspecified*				1			
Coles Creek Incised, *var. Chase*	1						
Coles Creek Incised, *var. Wade*			1			1	
French Fork Incised, *var. unspecified*	1	1					
Mulberry Creek Cord Marked, *var. Smith Creek*					1		
Coles Creek Incised, *var. Phillips*		1					
Larto Red, *var. Larto*			1				
Mulberry Creek Cord Marked, *var. Edwards*		1					
Evansville Punctated, *var. unspecified*		1					
Unclassified incised (Baytown)			1				
Daub:	58	80	85	32	37	11	5
Lithics:							
Unclassified point						1	
Snub-nosed end scraper			1				
Utilized chert flakes	5			1			
Organics:							
Human skull fragment					1		
Unclassified bone	27	56	45		22	69	14
EUROPEAN							
Iron:							
Wrought nails							
Type unspecified	2						
Hoop			1				

clear that the earliest occupation dates to the Wasp Lake phase, at the conclusion of which a series of midden and sterile clay loadings was brought in during the early Russell phase. The uppermost midden testifies to the significant Russell phase occupation that followed. Lying directly on the surface of that midden was a large (diameter approx. 50 cm) iron barrel hoop that explained the metallic anomaly detected by the instruments. The last 60–75 cm between the upper midden and the surface was wash from mound A that accumulated during the centuries since the site was abandoned.

The excavation of Y100–102 documented the intensity of the protohistoric-historic occupation at this location. Of considerable interest is the evidence for earthen construction during this time, confirming the data from the summit of mound A.

Excavation Units Y103, Y105–109. These excavations were placed at the very bottom of the mound on its northwestern side (see fig. 164). The first unit, Y103, was dug to investigate a magnetometer signal described in the instrument log as a "wide, non-metallic" anomaly. This turned out to be a series of superimposed burned occupation surfaces. In order to reveal more of this dramatic stratification and (we hoped) isolate in situ contexts for fine-tuned stratigraphic interpretation, we opened up five more contiguous 2-×-2-m units (fig. 171a). The coordinates of the six units together were N47–53 and E3–7.

Beneath approximately 15 cm of topsoil was a complex zone of brown loess interbedded with layers of burned soil and daub. Because of the mound slope, this zone ranged from only 20 cm thick in the northwest corner of Y105 to nearly a meter thick in the southeast corner of Y107; accordingly, the internal stratification was most compressed in the northwestern part of the excavations and most detailed in the southeastern. Thus in Y107 the following sequence of layers could be observed below the topsoil: brown loess flecked with charcoal and daub that apparently was washed from the mound; two old occupation levels, each consisting of in situ deposits of daub lying on burned surfaces; and another layer of brown loess. All of this overlay yet a third burned occupation level consisting of a layer of daub averaging 10 cm thick on a hard baked surface. A number of wall-trench and posthole features found in it were intrusive from the first and second levels. This third level was found in all six excavation units (fig. 171b) and was on a common horizontal plane (elevation +55 cm in reference to the main site datum at N00/E00). Clearly, it was primarily responsible for the anomaly detected by the magnetometer. Further exploration below this level in Y109 revealed a thick midden which was interrupted by a fourth burned surface after 95 cm and replaced by gravel subsoil at a depth of 145 cm (elevation −90).

The cultural stratigraphy of these excavation units is presented in table 54. Unfortunately, the cultural content of the lowermost strata was not determined due to the limited scope of the exploratory test. The earliest layer consisted of the midden capped by the extensive ("third") burned level. This dated to the Lake George phase, and the burning occurred during subphase II and correlates with level M in excavation unit Y110. No wall trenches or post molds were found to be associated definitely with the surface at this locus, and it may be that the great amount of daub was rubble from a structure on the contemporary mound summit. The smaller size of the mound at that time is indicated by the relative flatness of this burned surface, with no hint of incline apparent within the limits of the excavations even at the closest approach to the mound. The subsequent enlargement of the mound, however, encroached upon this locus, as was revealed by the sloping strata of mound fill and burned surfaces. Of considerable interest, but unknown function, are the wall trench structures originating from these surfaces; their forty-five degree angle to the cardinal points would seem to confirm the northeast-southwest orientation of mound

a

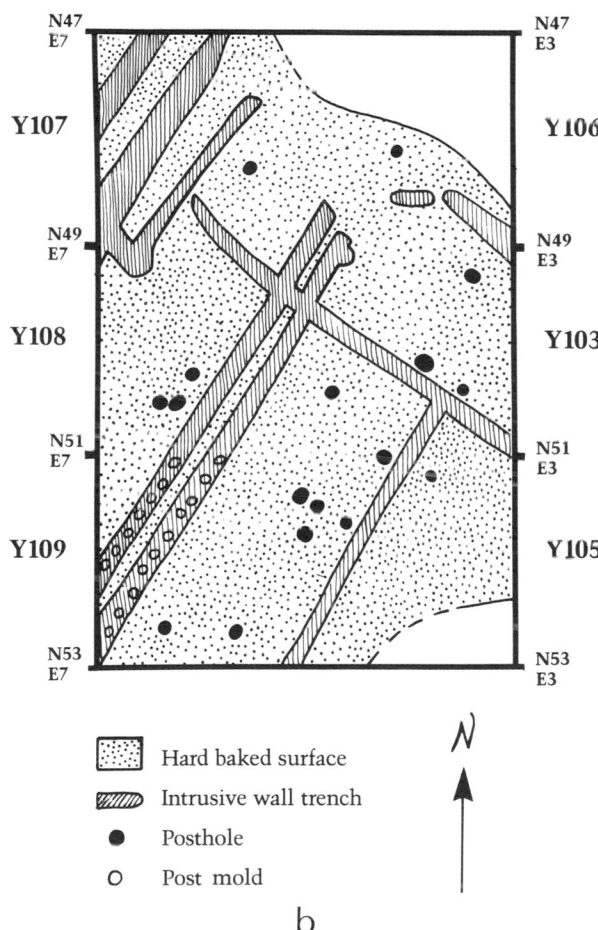

b

Hard baked surface

Intrusive wall trench

● Posthole

○ Post mold

N

Figure 171. Excavation units Y103 and Y105–109, Haynes Bluff. a, general view from the north, mound A sloping up to the left; b, plan of third burned level and intrusive features.

A. The surfaces dated to Wasp Lake II and presumably correlate with the upper levels in Y110. Finally, the covering layer of mound wash and topsoil preserved artifactual evidence of the Russell phase.

Table 54. Aboriginal and European artifacts from excavation units Y103 and Y105–109 at Haynes Bluff (tabulated according to strata).

	Topsoil	Mound Wash	Burned Structure	Midden
ABORIGINAL				
Pottery:				
Winterville Incised, *var. Tunica*	4	1		
Barton Incised, *var. Davion*	1			
Barton Incised, *var. Portland*	5			
Owens Punctated, *var. Redwood*	1			
Barton Incised, *var. Charlevoix*	5	4		
Old Town Red, *var. Ballground*	2			
Parkin Punctated, *var. Elise*	2	2		
Winterville Incised, *var. Loubois*	7	1		
Cracker Road Incised, *var. Cracker Road*	1			
Cracker Road Incised, *var. unspecified*	1			
Mazique Incised, *var. North*	4	3		
Owens Punctated, *var. Menard*	2			
Winterville Incised, *var. Broutin*	13	4		
Winterville Incised, *var. Wailes*	9	4		
Old Town Red, *var. unspecified*	2			
Grace Brushed, *var. Grand Gulf*	1	1		
Grace Brushed, *var. Warren*	1	1		
Kinlock Simple Stamped, *var. Kinlock*	1			
Fatherland Incised, *var. Fatherland*	2	2		
Fatherland Incised, *var. unspecified*	2			
Maddox Engraved, *var. Emerald*	2	4		
Chicot Red, *var. Grand Village*	1			
Owens Punctated, *var. unspecified*	1	1		
Winterville Incised, *var. Ranch*			1	
Leland Incised, *var. Deep Bayou*	2	1		
Leland Incised, *var. Russell*	23	10		
Leland Incised, *var. Williams*	11	3		
Barton Incised, *var. Arcola*	28	25	1	
Barton Incised, *var. Midnight*	1	2	1	
Winterville Incised, *var. Belzoni*	29	7	2	1
Leland Incised, *var. Leland*	11	5		
Leland Incised, *var. Ferris*	2			
Leland Incised, *var. unspecified*	1			
Maddox Engraved, *var. Silver City*	3	3		
Coleman Incised, *var. Bass*	1			
Barton Incised, *var. Estill*	5	2		
Parkin Punctated, *var. Hollandale*	10	7	2	
Parkin Punctated, *var. Transylvania*	9	4		
Winterville Incised, *var. Winterville*	22	6		

Table 54 (continued).

	Topsoil	Mound Wash	Burned Structure	Midden
Grace Brushed, *var. Grace*	7	6		
Pouncey Pinched, *var. Patosi*		2	1	1
Winterville Incised, *var. Blum*	1			
Barton Incised, *var. unspecified*	35	15		
Winterville Incised, *var. unspecified*	3	2		
Unclassified incised (Mississippi)	1			
Anna Incised, *var. Anna*	4			
Carter Engraved, *var. Carter*	1			
L'Eau Noire Incised, *var. L'Eau Noire*		1		
Hollyknowe Pinched, *var. Patmos*		1		
Plaquemine Brushed, *var. Plaquemine*	6	2		
Coles Creek Incised, *var. Hardy*	1			
Evansville Punctated, *var. Sharkey*		1	1	
Mazique Incised, *var. Manchac*	1	1		
Unclassified incised (Addis)	5	1		
Coles Creek Incised, *var. Greenhouse*	1	3		
Coles Creek Incised, *var. Mott*	1	1		
Evansville Punctated, *var. Rhinehart*		1		
Chevalier Stamped, *var. Chevalier*		2		
Coles Creek Incised, *var. Coles Creek*	5			
Coles Creek Incised, *var. unspecified*	5	3		
Unclassified incised (Valley Park)	2			
Coles Creek Incised, *var. Stoner*		1		
Coles Creek Incised, *var. Wade*	5			
French Fork Incised, *var. unspecified*	1			
Larto Red, *var. Silver Creek*		1		
Mulberry Creek Cord Marked, *var. Smith Creek*	2			
Chevalier Stamped, *var. Cornelia*	1			
Coles Creek Incised, *var. Hunt*	3	1		
Coles Creek Incised, *var. Phillips*	4			
Larto Red, *var. Larto*	4	1		
Mulberry Creek Cord Marked, *var. Edwards*		1		
Salomon Brushed, *var. Salomon*	1			
Jaketown Simple Stamped, *var. Silver Lake*	1			
Daub:[a]	—	—	—	
Lithics:				
Native gunflint	1			
Unclassified tool	1			
Utilized flakes	4	4		
Organics:				
Mammal bone	158	239	10	2
Bird bone		7		
Fish bone	73	149	10	
Turtle bone/shell	23	29		
Shell earpin (fig. 175b)	1			

Table 54 continued

Table 54 (continued).

	Topsoil	Mound Wash	Burned Structure	Midden
EUROPEAN				
Earthenware:				
Unclassified[b]	1			
Glass:				
Light blue-green	1			
Iron:				
Wrought nail				
Type IV (fig. 168f)	1			
Miscellaneous	2			
Copper:				
Miscellaneous	1			

[a]Large quantities.
[b]Slipped, but unglazed.

In summary, the excavations at this locus confirmed the stratigraphic sequence unearthed at the mound summit and provided important details about mound construction and structural features. Under certain circumstances, the remote sensing of the structural features was found to have a distinctive electronic signature.

Excavation Units Y140–141. When an intensive surface survey of the site was conducted during the opening days of the investigation, the creek north of the mound was found to be a source of much information. An active erosional feature, its bed contained a wealth of artifactual materials; being deeply entrenched, its walls provided natural deep strata cuts which were profiled at intervals. Of special interest was the section where the creek cut into the north side of the mound. Here, a thick black cultural layer was observed at a depth of more than 2 m below the top of the bank. Although this black layer produced some pottery that appeared to be very late, it was overlain by some water-deposited loess, followed by at least 2 m of what appeared to be mound fill. In order to investigate this stratification more fully and relate it to the construction of mound A, we established excavation units Y140 and Y141.

Excavation unit Y140 was placed halfway between the creek bank and the eroded base of mound A. Its coordinates were N56–60 and E42–44. The 2-×-4-m dimensions were maintained only through level B; from then on, just the southern half of the unit was excavated down to subsoil. After a wedge-shaped level A had created a horizontal working surface, all subsequent levels were taken out in 25-cm segments. The final excavation was more than 3 m deep (fig. 172).

Despite the depth of the deposits, the stratification was relatively uncomplicated. Beneath 15–20 cm of topsoil was a zone approximately 1 m thick consisting

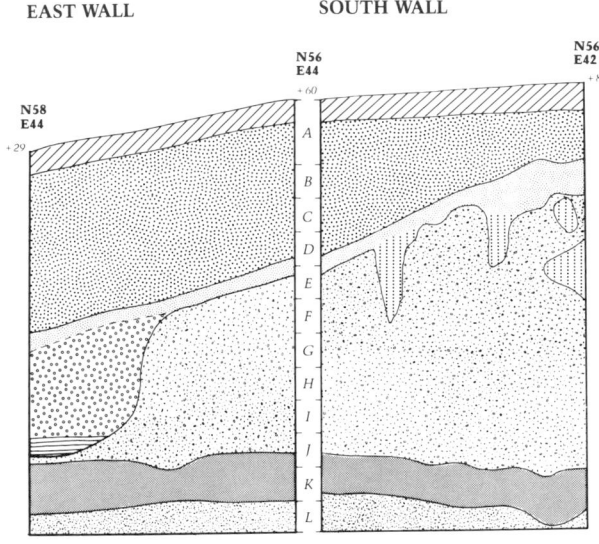

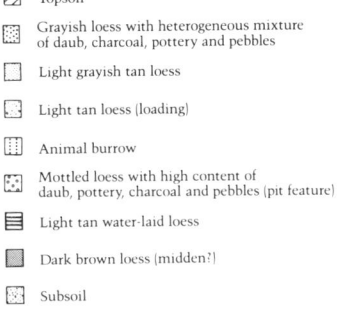

Topsoil

Grayish loess with heterogeneous mixture of daub, charcoal, pottery and pebbles

Light grayish tan loess

Light tan loess (loading)

Animal burrow

Mottled loess with high content of daub, pottery, charcoal and pebbles (pit feature)

Light tan water-laid loess

Dark brown loess (midden?)

Subsoil

Figure 172. Stratification in excavation unit Y140, Haynes Bluff. a, east wall; b, south wall.

Table 55. Aboriginal and European artifacts from excavation unit Y140 at Haynes Bluff (tabulated according to strata).

	Topsoil	Old Surface	Pit Feature	Midden
ABORIGINAL				
Pottery:				
Winterville Incised, *var. Tunica*	7			
Barton Incised, *var. Portland*	1	1		
Barton Incised, *var. Charlevoix*	1			
Old Town Red, *var. Ballground*	1			
Parkin Punctated, *var. Elise*	1	1		
Winterville Incised, *var. Loubois*	1			
Cracker Road Incised, *var. Cracker Road*	1			
Mazique Incised, *var. North*	4			
Unclassified incised/engraved (Caddo)		2		
Winterville Incised, *var. Broutin*	2	3		
Winterville Incised, *var. Wailes*	2	2		
Old Town Red, *var. unspecified*		1		
Grace Brushed, *var. Warren*	1			
Fatherland Incised, *var. unspecified*			1	
Chicot Red, *var. unspecified*		1		
Owens Punctated, *var. unspecified*	1			
Leland Incised, *var. Russell*	7	1		
Leland Incised, *var. Williams*	2	1		
Barton Incised, *var. Arcola*	5	3	3	
Winterville Incised, *var. Belzoni*	5	4	1	
Leland Incised, *var. Leland*	3			
Leland Incised, *var. unspecified*	2			
Coleman Incised, *var. Bass*	2			
Barton Incised, *var. Estill*	1			
Parkin Punctated, *var. Hollandale*	3	1	2	
Parkin Punctated, *var. Transylvania*	1	4	1	
Winterville Incised, *var. Winterville*	2	15		
Grace Brushed, *var. Grace*	3	3		
Grace Brushed, *var. unspecified*		1		
Pouncey Pinched, *var. Patosi*	2			
Barton Incised, *var. unspecified*	9	10	2	1
Winterville Incised, *var. unspecified*	1	1	1	
Carter Engraved, *var. Carter*		1		1
Leland Incised, *var. Bethlehem*		1		
Cahokia Cord Marked, *var. Montrose*	2			
Plaquemine Brushed, *var. Plaquemine*	6	3		
Avoyelles Punctated, *var. Dupree*	1			
Chevalier Stamped, *var. Perry*		1		
Coles Creek Incised, *var. Hardy*	1			
Mazique Incised, *var. Manchac*	2			

Table 55 continued

Table 55 (continued).

	Topsoil	Old Surface	Pit Feature	Midden
Coles Creek Incised, *var. Coles Creek*		1		
Coles Creek Incised, *var. unspecified*	1	1		
Alligator Incised, *var. Oxbow*		1		
Coles Creek Incised, *var. Hunt*	2	2		
Coles Creek Incised, *var. Phillips*		1		
Mulberry Creek Cord Marked, *var. Edwards*	1			
Daub:	112	196	47	
Organics:				
Mammal bone	26	45	2	2
Bird bone				1
Fish bone	1	10	3	
Turtle bone/shell	1	1	8	
EUROPEAN				
Glass:				
Olive green	2			
Gun parts/munitions:				
Iron tumbler from musket lock	1			
Brass trigger guard	1			

of a heterogeneous mix of loess, pebbles, charcoal, daub, pottery, and other cultural materials. Next, an old mound surface was encountered: a grayish, loess-based soil which sloped down to the northeast from the southwestern corner of the excavation. This surface capped a mantle of tan loess mound fill, which was up to 2 m thick. The mantle had been loaded on an old ground surface of brown loess with some midden contamination. Subsoil was composed of the same brown loess.

The cultural stratigraphy (table 55) reveals that the old ground surface was occupied during the Winterville phase. It could not be determined exactly when the great mantle was loaded on, because it was devoid of cultural content. It was in place by the Lake George phase, however, when a pit bisected by the northeastern corner of the excavation was filled. The surface of the mantle was in use at least until Wasp Lake II times and probably correlates with the burned surface found in unit Y110D. The thick zone of heterogeneous composition is eroded material from this damaged side of the mound, and it contains evidence of the Russell phase occupation at the summit.

Y141 was a 2-×-2-m excavation unit placed on the northern edge of the mound, just west of the badly eroded section tested by Y140. Its coordinates were N57–59 and E28–30, and it was excavated to a maximum depth of 1 m from the highest point of the mound surface. Despite the small dimensions of the excavation, Y141 replicated the late stages of mound construction found elsewhere. Underlying the topsoil was the

same mantle of tan loess mound fill encountered in Y140. This time, however, it included pockets of the dark brown midden also found in the stage III mantle in Y110 (see fig. 165). Once again, this mantle dates to the late Wasp Lake phase, although the cultural content of the midden pockets was redeposited from a Baytown context (table 56).

Excavation units Y140 and Y141 confirmed that much of mound A was a very late construction indeed. Even where part of the mound had been eroded, the earliest possible construction stage was Lake George phase. Most of the evidence pointed to the Wasp Lake phase, and even then to the late subphase II.

In summary, the mound A excavations determined that there was continuity in site occupation from late prehistoric to historic times. The most startling (although not entirely unanticipated) discovery was the demonstration of major mound construction during the protohistoric period, and an indication that some may have occurred during the historic period as well. The Russell phase occupation was found to be substantially represented, especially at the mound summit. Although the only discrete historic contexts were the burials, it is clear that the entire mound top was a focal point of activity during the Russell phase.

Table 56. Aboriginal and European artifacts from excavation unit Y141 at Haynes Bluff (tabulated according to strata).

	Topsoil	Mound Fill	Midden Pockets in Mound Fill
ABORIGINAL			
Pottery:			
Winterville Incised, *var. Tunica*	1		
Barton Incised, *var. Charlevoix*		1	
Parkin Punctated, *var. Elise*	1		
Winterville Incised, *var. Loubois*	1		
Winterville Incised, *var. Broutin*		2	
Leland Incised, *var. Russell*	4		
Leland Incised, *var. Williams*	1		
Barton Incised, *var. Arcola*	2		
Barton Incised, *var. Midnight*	1		
Winterville Incised, *var. Belzoni*	2		
Barton Incised, *var. unspecified*	1		
Winterville Incised, *var. unspecified*	1		
Leland Incised, *var. Bethlehem*	1		
Plaquemine Brushed, *var. Plaquemine*	2		
Coles Creek Incised, *var. Greenhouse*	2		
French Fork Incised, *var. McNutt*	1		
Coles Creek Incised, *var. Coles Creek*	1		
Coles Creek Incised, *var. Stoner*			1
Coles Creek Incised, *var. Wade*	1		
French Fork Incised, *var. Wilzone*			1
French Fork Incised, *var. unspecified*	1		
Mulberry Creek Cord Marked, *var. Smith Creek*	1		
Alligator Incised, *var. Oxbow*	3		
Coles Creek Incised, *var. Hunt*	3		
Coles Creek Incised, *var. Phillips*			2
Larto Red, *var. Larto*	4		2
Evansville Punctated, *var. unspecified*	1		
Unclassified incised (Baytown)			1
Daub:	4		1
Lithics:			
Utilized flake	1		
Organics:			
Mammal bone	30	18	11
Bird bone	3	2	
Fish bone	14	2	7
Turtle bone/shell	2		5
EUROPEAN			
Iron:			
Wrought nail			
Type I	1		

LOCATION B

Mound B had been completely destroyed by the rail-road spur line in 1968. North of the mound, however, between the spur line and old route 3, was the remnant of a natural raised terrace that resembled a narrow plateau (see fig. 164). In 1969, as described above, Ed Dean and Carroll Kelley had excavated a historic burial from this location. Thus, it seemed that this remnant of the site might be relatively untouched and still contain some pristine contexts. Although we entertained hopes of emulating Dean's and Kelley's discoveries, we were most interested in finding house sites, middens, and other such domestic activity areas. Since no features were observable, an electronic survey was conducted. A number of subsurface anomalies (mostly metallic) were detected, and the most promising of these were

selected for excavation. Three loci were tested with seven excavation units (Y130–136) during the period 29 July–13 August.

The first locus to be investigated was a knoll on the southwestern end of the plateau. Three 2-×-2-m excavation units (Y130–132; respective coordinates N28–30/E106–108, N21–23/E106–108, N6–8/E96–98) were placed over three distinct instrument readings that were interpreted as indicating metal objects. Unfortunately, it was soon discovered that the locus had been disturbed during the construction and operation of the paper mill and that the instruments were detecting recent trash: in all cases, beer cans at shallow depth. All of the cultural materials, ancient as well as recent, were recovered from the mixed topsoil, which was approximately 20 cm thick. The aboriginal pottery shows a strong late (i.e., post-Tunica) Russell phase component (table 57), but because of the disturbance it is uncertain whether the occupation was in situ.

Excavation units Y133–135 were placed on the northeastern slope of the plateau. They consisted of one 2-×-2-m unit, which was expanded with two 1-×-2-m units, all within coordinates N117.5–119.5 and E193–197. Again, exact placement of the excavations was determined by two anomalies detected by the instruments, and, again, these turned out to be recent trash. However, the topsoil also contained late Russell phase pottery (table 58). There were no aboriginal features, and subsoil was encountered at a maximum depth of 20 cm.

The last excavation unit, Y136, was located near the middle of the plateau on the eastern edge (coordinates N46–48 and E140–142) and also was excavated to investigate an instrument anomaly. But this time no reason for the anomaly was discovered, even though the excavations were carried down to a meter beneath the surface. This part of the plateau seemed to be less disturbed than the other loci tested, but still the aboriginal materials (table 59) were restricted to the topsoil, and no features were observed within it or intruded into the immediately underlying subsoil.

In summary, the location B excavations were something of a disappointment: no undisturbed aboriginal contexts were isolated. Artifactual evidence of the lat-

Table 57. Aboriginal artifacts from excavation units Y130–132 at Haynes Bluff.

Pottery:

Barton Incised, *var. Charlevoix*	1
Old Town Red, *var. Ballground*	1
Winterville Incised, *var. Loubois*	2
Cracker Road Incised, *var. Cracker Road*	1
Fatherland Incised, *var. Nancy*	1
Fatherland Incised, *var. Snyders Bluff*	1
Owens Punctated, *var. Manly*	1
Winterville Incised, *var. Broutin*	1
Grace Brushed, *var. Grand Gulf*	1
Fatherland Incised, *var. unspecified*	2
Maddox Engraved, *var. Emerald*	1
Leland Incised, *var. Williams*	2
Barton Incised, *var. Arcola*	2
Winterville Incised, *var. Belzoni*	2
Leland Incised, *var. Leland*	1
Leland Incised, *var. unspecified*	1
Winterville Incised, *var. Winterville*	1
Barton Incised, *var. unspecified*	6
Plaquemine Brushed, *var. Plaquemine*	1
Coles Creek Incised, *var. Mott*	1

Daub: 4

Lithics:

Utilized flakes	3

Organics:

Mammal bone	1

Table 58. Aboriginal artifacts from excavation units Y133–135 at Haynes Bluff.

Pottery:

Old Town Red, *var. St. Pierre*	4
Leland Incised, *var. Russell*	3
Grace Brushed, *var. unspecified*	1
Barton Incised, *var. unspecified*	2

Organics:

Mammal bone	1
Fish bone	1

Table 59. Aboriginal artifacts from excavation unit Y136 at Haynes Bluff.

Pottery:

Barton Incised, *var. Davion*	1
Barton Incised, *var. Charlevoix*	1
Old Town Red, *var. Ballground*	2
Unclassified incised/engraved (Caddo)	1
Winterville Incised, *var. Wailes*	1
Leland Incised, *var. Russell*	4
Leland Incised, *var. Williams*	1
Barton Incised, *var. Arcola*	1
Winterville Incised, *var. Belzoni*	1
Leland Incised, *var. Leland*	1
Leland Incised, *var. unspecified*	1
Grace Brushed, *var. unspecified*	2
Barton Incised, *var. unspecified*	2
Coles Creek Incised, *var. Coles Creek*	2
Unclassified incised (Baytown)	2

Daub: 13

Organics:

Mammal bone	2
Fish bone	4

est phases of occupation was recovered, but this part of the site had sustained too much damage for us to consider pursuing an intensive effort. Dean and Kelley had been lucky, and it is probable that the burial they found was the only one at this location to have escaped destruction during the cutting of the railroad spur.

MOUND C

In 1974, mound C was the only major aboriginal earthwork other than mound A to have survived. Survival, however, is to be understood only in the sense that it was still noticeable. It had been plowed over for many years, so that both shape and height were lost, and its eastern and southern edges had been cut away by old route 3, the railroad spur, and the new main entrance road to the mill (see fig. 164). Furthermore, it had probably been subjected to excavations by Clausen and perhaps numerous unknown despoilers. It hardly seemed a promising object for our attention, but it could not be ignored. When the instrument survey detected a metallic object on the mound's southwestern flank, we took the opportunity to investigate both the anomaly and the mound. A 2-×-4-m excavation unit, Y120, was placed over the anomaly between coordinates S146–148 and W44–48. The excavation was carried out during the second week in August.

The anomaly was quickly disposed of (a tin can at grass roots level), and the mound test took little longer. The stratification was simple: first there was a zone of brown loess 20–50 cm thick; then about 20 cm of dark brown midden; and finally a yellow loess subsoil. The latter had a high pebble content and appeared to be of colluvial origin. The interpretation was equally straightforward: an occupation on the bluff talus was superseded by mound construction. The mound had been truncated, and we were unable to ascertain whether there had been more than one stage of construction. The cultural stratigraphy, however, does not leave much time for more than one episode: the pre-mound occupation lasted into the Wasp Lake phase, and the mound was raised either in the late Wasp Lake II subphase or the Russell phase (table 60). Once again, the lateness of the mound construction activities at the site was conclusively demonstrated.

LOCATION D

This location is named after mound D, which, according to local informants, was bulldozed away in 1965. Since the mound was gone, the excavations were not concerned with it but were directed to the nearby creek bank. The objective was to relocate the rich midden mined by Ed Dean some years before. The artifacts he had recovered included many from the protohistoric and early historic periods, and it was our hope that intact middens and other occupational features dating to these periods might still be found in the vicinity.

We were successful in relocating Dean's pit, and a 1-×-11-m trench (Y104A–E) was established which bisected it and also included two anomalies that the instruments had detected to the south (fig. 173). The excavations subsequently were expanded on the north-

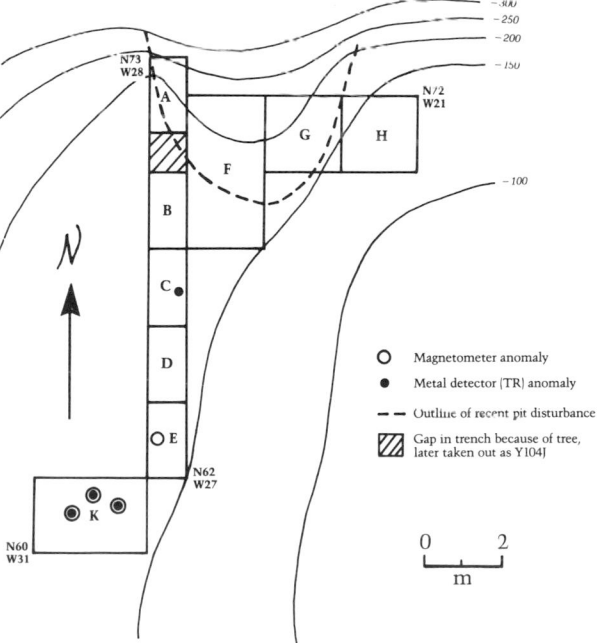

Figure 173. Plan of excavations and landforms at location D, Haynes Bluff.

Table 60. Aboriginal artifacts from excavation unit Y120 on mound C at Haynes Bluff (tabulated according to strata).

	Mound Fill	Mixed Mound Fill/Midden	Midden
Pottery:			
Owens Punctated, *var. Redwood*	1		
Barton Incised, *var. Charlevoix*	1		
Old Town Red, *var. Ballground*		1	
Parkin Punctated, *var. Elise*	1		
Winterville Incised, *var. Loubois*	1		
Cracker Road Incised, *var. Cracker Road*	1		
Mazique Incised, *var. North*	4	2	
Winterville Incised, *var. Broutin*	3		
Winterville Incised, *var. Wailes*	1		
Grace Brushed, *var. Grace*			1
Maddox Engraved, *var. Emerald*	1		
Chicot Red, *var. unspecified*			1
Owens Punctated, *var. Widow Creek*	1		
Leland Incised, *var. Deep Bayou*	2		
Leland Incised, *var. Russell*	1		1
Leland Incised, *var. Williams*	2		
Barton Incised, *var. Arcola*	1		
Winterville Incised, *var. Belzoni*	3		
Leland Incised, *var. Leland*	2		1
Leland Incised, *var. Ferris*	1		
Barton Incised, *var. Estill*	1	1	
Parkin Punctated, *var. Hollandale*	1		
Parkin Punctated, *var. Transylvania*	2		
Winterville Incised, *var. Winterville*	8		
Grace Brushed, *var. Grace*	1	1	1
Grace Brushed, *var. unspecified*	1		
Pouncey Pinched, *var. Patosi*	4		
Barton Incised, *var. unspecified*	5	1	
Winterville Incised, *var. unspecified*	1		
Anna Incised, *var. Anna*	3	1	
Carter Engraved, *var. Carter*	1	1	
L'Eau Noire Incised, *var. L'Eau Noire*	2		
Hollyknowe Pinched, *var. Patmos*	2		1
Plaquemine Brushed, *var. Plaquemine*	16	4	1
Coleman Incised, *var. Coleman*		1	
Evansville Punctated, *var. Sharkey*	2	1	
Harrison Bayou Incised, *var. Harrison Bayou*	1		
Mazique Incised, *var. Manchac*	1		
Unclassified incised (Addis)	2		
Coles Creek Incised, *var. Greenhouse*	1		
Coles Creek Incised, *var. Mott*	1		

Table 60 (continued).

	Mound Fill	Mixed Mound Fill/Midden	Midden
Coles Creek Incised, *var. Coles Creek*	1		
Coles Creek Incised, *var. unspecified*	1		
Mazique Incised, *var. unspecified*	1		
Marksville Stamped, *var. Manny*			1
Daub:	11	2	
Organics:			
Mammal bone	27	14	
Fish bone	47	14	
Turtle bone/shell	3		

Table 61. Aboriginal artifacts from excavation unit Y104E at Haynes Bluff (tabulated according to strata and levels).

	Topsoil (Y104E1)	Midden (Y104E2–3)		Topsoil (Y104E1)	Midden (Y104E2–3)
Pottery:			Barton Incised, *var. Estill*	1	
			Parkin Punctated, *var. Hollandale*	1	2
Barton Incised, *var. Portland*	4		Parkin Punctated, *var. Transylvania*	2	
			Parkin Punctated, *var. unspecified*	1	
Barton Incised, *var. Charlevoix*	2		Winterville Incised, *var. Winterville*	6	2
Parkin Punctated, *var. Elise*	2				
Winterville Incised, *var. Loubois*	5		Grace Brushed, *var. Grace*	8	1
			Grace Brushed, *var. unspecified*		1
Winterville Incised, *var. Broutin*	4		Barton Incised, *var. unspecified*	10	1
Winterville Incised, *var. Wailes*	4	2	Winterville Incised, *var. unspecified*	5	1
			Unclassified incised (Yazoo)	1	
Grace Brushed, *var. Grand Gulf*	1				
			Mazique Incised, *var. Manchac*	1	1
Nodena Red and White, *var. Dumond*	1		Unclassified incised (Addis)	1	
Maddox Engraved, *var. Emerald*	3		Coles Creek Incised, *var. Coles Creek*		1
Winterville Incised, *var. Ranch*	1				
			Coles Creek Incised, *var. Hunt*	1	
Leland Incised, *var. Deep Bayou*	1				
Leland Incised, *var. Russell*	5	1	*Daub:*	29	19
Leland Incised, *var. Williams*	3	1	*Lithics:*		
Barton Incised, *var. Arcola*	3				
Barton Incised, *var. Midnight*	4		Unclassified tool	1	
Winterville Incised, *var. Belzoni*	5	2	Utilized flakes	2	1
Leland Incised, *var. Leland*	2		*Organics:*		
Maddox Engraved, *var. Silver City*		1			
			Mammal bone	15	19
			Fish bone	11	57
			Turtle bone/shell	3	5

Table 62. Aboriginal artifacts from the topsoil and midden layer in excavation units Y104C, Y104D, and Y104K at Haynes Bluff.

Pottery:

Winterville Incised, *var. Tunica*	4
Barton Incised, *var. Portland*	1
Barton Incised, *var. Charlevoix*	11
Old Town Red, *var. Ballground*	1
Parkin Punctated, *var. Elise*	1
Winterville Incised, *var. Loubois*	17
Cracker Road Incised, *var. unspecified*	2
Mazique Incised, *var. North*	4
Unclassified incised/engraved (Caddo)	1
Winterville Incised, *var. Broutin*	13
Winterville Incised, *var. Wailes*	14
Old Town Red, *var. unspecified*	3
Grace Brushed, *var. Grand Gulf*	4
Grace Brushed, *var. Warren*	8
Fatherland Incised, *var. Fatherland*	1
Fatherland Incised, *var. Stanton*	3
Fatherland Incised, *var. unspecified*	2
Maddox Engraved, *var. Emerald*	3
Chicot Red, *var. Grand Village*	2
Owens Punctated, *var. unspecified*	9
Winterville Incised, *var. Ranch*	1
Leland Incised, *var. Deep Bayou*	2
Leland Incised, *var. Russell*	22
Leland Incised, *var. Williams*	52
Barton Incised, *var. Arcola*	46
Barton Incised, *var. Midnight*	17
Winterville Incised, *var. Belzoni*	56
Leland Incised, *var. Leland*	17
Leland Incised, *var. Ferris*	1
Leland Incised, *var. unspecified*	1
Maddox Engraved, *var. Silver City*	3

Barton Incised, *var. Estill*	8
Parkin Punctated, *var. Hollandale*	7
Parkin Punctated, *var. Transylvania*	4
Parkin Punctated, *var. unspecified*	1
Winterville Incised, *var. Winterville*	41
Grace Brushed, *var. Grace*	23
Pouncey Pinched, *var. Patosi*	5
Barton Incised, *var. unspecified*	93
Winterville Incised, *var. unspecified*	19
Unclassified incised (Yazoo)	6
Anna Incised, *var. Anna*	1
Carter Engraved, *var. Carter*	1
Plaquemine Brushed, *var. Plaquemine*	6
Coleman Incised, *var. Coleman*	3
Coles Creek Incised, *var. Hardy*	1
Evansville Punctated, *var. Sharkey*	1
Mazique Incised, *var. Manchac*	1
Unclassified incised (Addis)	4
Coles Creek Incised, *var. Greenhouse*	2
Coles Creek Incised, *var. Mott*	1
Mazique Incised, *var. Kings Point*	2
Coles Creek Incised, *var. unspecified*	2
Mazique Incised, *var. unspecified*	1
Unclassified incised (Valley Park)	2
Coles Creek Incised, *var. Phillips*	1

Daub:	183

Lithics:

Native gunflint (fig. 175h)	1
Snub-nosed end scraper	1
Unclassified tools	4
Utilized flakes	21

Organics:

Unclassified bone[a]	—

[a]Large quantity.

eastern side of the trench (Y104F–H) and to the southwest (Y104K). The description of the excavations, which were carried out concurrently between 25 July and 23 August, will be consolidated and presented in two parts in order to simplify the complexities of the archaeological procedure* and discriminate the significant results.

* It will be noted that all the excavations at this location were given one number (the ultimate extent of the excavations not having been anticipated); individual units were then differentiated by letters, while levels were given numbers: thus, the first level in trench segment A was designated Y104A1, and so forth.

Excavation Units Y104C–E, Y104K. The southern part of the original trench was investigated first in order to establish the basic stratification at this location and to examine the anomalies detected during the electronic survey. Unit K was added later to explore additional electronic anomalies. The remote-sensing tests were disappointing: the anomalies in units C and E were never satisfactorily explained, while those in unit K were found to have been caused by a long strand of barbed wire. The primary objective was realized, however, and because the simple stratification was similar throughout all of the units they may be discussed together as one.

Beneath approximately 20 cm of topsoil was a rich brown midden mottled with charcoal and daub. This layer was 40 cm thick and quite homogeneous in appearance. There was no evidence of microstrata or features, except for a large trash pit at the intersection of units C and D that had been intruded down through the midden from an origin now obliterated by the disturbance in the topsoil. A light brown loess devoid of cultural materials was encountered throughout the trench at a total depth of about 65 cm from the surface. It was presumed that this was subsoil, although a posthole probe sunk more than a meter deeper in unit E encountered at a depth of 175 cm a dark brown soil that had the appearance of midden but again lacked cultural content. If the latter soil was a midden, it may correlate with the deep midden found at location A. The correlation seems unlikely, however, for the location A midden had been buried by constructional fill and/or wash from mound A and it is improbable that the more modest mound D had a similar impact.

The only definite evidence of human occupation, then, was confined to the first 65 cm below the surface. The midden layer was undifferentiated except where it faded into the topsoil or was intruded into by the trashpit. That there may have been some internal stratigraphy, however, is indicated by the cultural contents of the metrical levels in unit E, which show a transition from early to late Wasp Lake phase (table 61). That there was a longer occupation in the vicinity is demonstrated by the evidence from the rest of this part of the excavations (table 62). Clearly, however, the principal components were late prehistoric-protohistoric, and the final formation of the midden (including the trash pit and whatever features might have been in the topsoil) occurred during the late Wasp Lake phase. Only a single indication of the Russell phase was found: a native-made gunflint of chert (fig. 175h), which was recovered from the topsoil. While the presence of the rich midden attests to domestic activity, the lack of structural features and the relatively small amount of daub would seem to rule out a residence at this precise locus. Nevertheless, a Wasp Lake II context had been defined, and it provides the base with which the data from the northern part of the excavations may be correlated.

Excavation Units Y104A–B, Y104F–H, Y104J, Y104Z.

As already noted above, the northern segments of trench Y104A–E cut into the pit previously dug by Ed Dean (fig. 173). The excavation of units A and B revealed that Dean had penetrated into just the upper levels of a large trash pit. In order to salvage the rest, units F–H were added to the east. Unit J was a 1-m² block between units A and B that previously had been skipped because it supported a locust tree; unit Z was a free-standing balk between units B and F that was left as a visual record of the internal stratification of the trash pit, and then was removed stratum by stratum according to the smallest significant demarcations that could be observed (see fig. 177). Because of these circumstances—the disturbance, the patchwork of excavation units, and the complicated soil structures—a complex set of archaeological data was developed. Analysis, however, has greatly reduced the apparent archae-

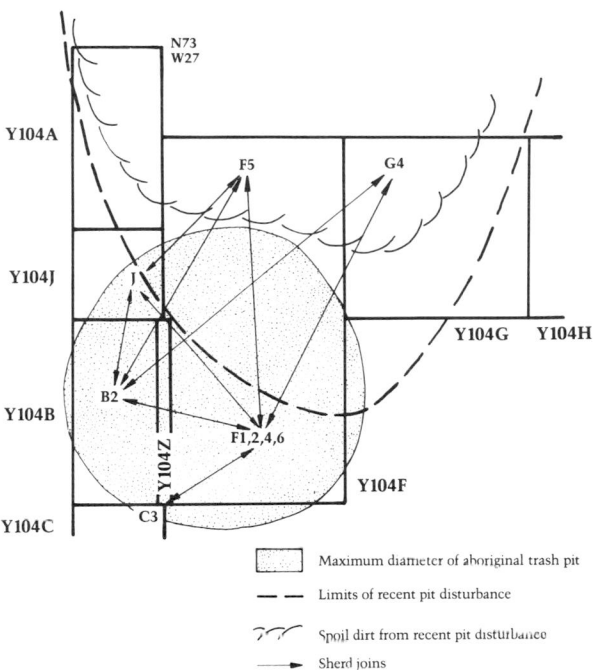

Figure 174. Detail of excavations at location D, Haynes Bluff, showing the position of the aboriginal trash pit and distributions of sherds from the same vessels (see table 67).

ological complexity, and the simplified discussion that follows is perfectly adequate for interpretive purposes.

Dean's pit was a large irregular depression that had been scooped out of the edge of the creek bank to a maximum depth of about 1 m (fig. 173). This pit and its associated spoil were cleaned out (levels Y104A1–3, F2, F3, F5, G2, G4, G5) (table 63), and the surrounding topsoil was stripped off (levels Y104B1, F1, G1, H1) (table 64). The large aboriginal trash pit that Dean had partially destroyed was exposed and isolated in units B, F, and J (fig. 174). The contents were then removed in several sections (levels Y104B2, F4, F6, J, Z1–8). The final, roughly circular pit was found to be approximately 3 m in diameter and more than 1 m deep; the full depth remained undetermined because the original surface was lost in the topsoil. The pit had intruded into the natural loess subsoil. The only other aboriginal feature discovered was a layer of brown midden that began in the eastern part of excavation unit Y104G and continued in Y104H. This midden lay directly beneath the topsoil and was 60–75 cm thick. In appearance, it was similar to the layer of midden found in Y104C–E: brown, mottled with charcoal and daub, but otherwise homogeneous and lacking in internal details.

The cultural content of this location at Haynes Bluff was quite extraordinary. As already noted, Dean's discoveries here had been a major impetus to our investigations, and we were not disappointed in our expectations. More cultural materials were recovered from Y104 than from the rest of our excavations combined (figs. 175–176). The most prolific single feature, of course, was the large trash pit, the contents of which are pre-

Table 63. Aboriginal artifacts from the disturbed area in excavation units Y104A1–3, Y104F2–3, Y104F5, Y104G2, and Y104G4–5 at Haynes Bluff.

Pottery:

Winterville Incised, *var. Tunica*	7
Barton Incised, *var. Davion*	4
Barton Incised, *var. Portland*	1
Owens Punctated, *var. Redwood*	1
Barton Incised, *var. Charlevoix*	10
Old Town Red, *var. Ballground*	9
Parkin Punctated, *var. Elise*	1
Winterville Incised, *var. Loubois*	10
Cracker Road Incised, *var. Cracker Road*	1
Cracker Road Incised, *var. unspecified*	3
Mazique Incised, *var. North*	3
Owens Punctated, *var. Manly*	1
Owens Punctated, *var. Menard*	13
Winterville Incised, *var. Broutin*	16
Winterville Incised, *var. Wailes*	11
Old Town Red, *var. unspecified*	3
Grace Brushed, *var. Grand Gulf*	10
Grace Brushed, *var. Warren*	6
Leland Incised, *var. Bovina*	8
Nodena Red and White, *var. Nodena*	1
Fatherland Incised, *var. Fatherland*	5
Fatherland Incised, *var. unspecified*	5
Maddox Engraved, *var. Emerald*	4
Chicot Red, *var. Grand Village*	3
Owens Punctated, *var. Owens*	1
Owens Punctated, *var. unspecified*	5
Winterville Incised, *var. Ranch*	1
Leland Incised, *var. Blanchard*	6
Leland Incised, *var. Deep Bayou*	4
Leland Incised, *var. Russell*	52
Leland Incised, *var. Williams*	18
Owens Punctated, *var. Beland City*[a]	2
Barton Incised, *var. Arcola*	67
Barton Incised, *var. Midnight*	9
Winterville Incised, *var. Belzoni*	40
Leland Incised, *var. Leland*	19
Leland Incised, *var. unspecified*	2
Maddox Engraved, *var. Silver City*	8
Coleman Incised, *var. Bass*	1

Barton Incised, *var. Estill*	12
Parkin Punctated, *var. Hollandale*	15
Parkin Punctated, *var. Transylvania*	4
Parkin Punctated, *var. unspecified*	3
Winterville Incised, *var. Winterville*	36
Grace Brushed, *var. Grace*	21
Grace Brushed, *var. unspecified*	1
Pouncey Pinched, *var. Patosi*	7
Barton Incised, *var. unspecified*	96
Winterville Incised, *var. unspecified*	19
Unclassified incised (Yazoo)	3
Carter Engraved, *var. Carter*	4
Leland Incised, *var. Bethlehem*	1
Plaquemine Brushed, *var. Plaquemine*	2
Coleman Incised, *var. Coleman*	1
Mazique Incised, *var. Manchac*	2
Unclassified incised (Addis)	1
Coles Creek Incised, *var. Mott*	1
Coles Creek Incised, *var. Coles Creek*	2
Coles Creek Incised, *var. unspecified*	3
Coles Creek Incised, *var. Stoner*	1
Coles Creek Incised, *var. Wade*	1
Chevalier Stamped, *var. Cornelia*	1
Coles Creek Incised, *var. Hunt*	1
Larto Red, *var. Larto*	2
Evansville Punctated, *var. unspecified*	2
Unclassified incised (Baytown)	1

Daub:	337

Lithics:

Edwards Stemmed, *var. Sunflower* point (fig. 175d)	1
Snub-nosed end scraper	1
Utilized flakes	17

Organics:

Unclassified bone[b]	—

[a]One sherd red-slipped.
[b]Large quantity.

Table 64. Aboriginal and European artifacts from the topsoil in excavation units Y104B1, Y104F1, Y104G1, and Y104H1 at Haynes Bluff.

ABORIGINAL

Pottery:

Winterville Incised, *var. Tunica*	5
Barton Incised, *var. Davion*	4
Barton Incised, *var. Portland*	6
Barton Incised, *var. Charlevoix*	15
Old Town Red, *var. Ballground*	5
Parkin Punctated, *var. Elise*	1
Winterville Incised, *var. Loubois*	16
Cracker Road Incised, *var. Cracker Road*	1
Cracker Road Incised, *var. unspecified*	1
Mazique Incised, *var. North*	1
Owens Punctated, *var. Manly*	1
Owens Punctated, *var. Menard*	2
Winterville Incised, *var. Broutin*	11
Winterville Incised, *var. Wailes*	14
Old Town Red, *var. unspecified*	14
Grace Brushed, *var. Grand Gulf*	4
Leland Incised, *var. Bovina*	4
Fatherland Incised, *var. Fatherland*	2
Fatherland Incised, *var. Stanton*	3
Maddox Engraved, *var. Emerald*	2
Chicot Red, *var. Grand Village*	3
Owens Punctated, *var. Poor Joe*	1
Owens Punctated, *var. unspecified*	9
Winterville Incised, *var. Ranch*	2
Leland Incised, *var. Blanchard*	1
Leland Incised, *var. Deep Bayou*	6
Leland Incised, *var. Russell*	47
Leland Incised, *var. Williams*	12
Barton Incised, *var. Arcola*	57
Barton Incised, *var. Midnight*	11
Winterville Incised, *var. Belzoni*	71
Leland Incised, *var. Leland*	23
Leland Incised, *var. unspecified*	2
Maddox Engraved, *var. Silver City*	5
Coleman Incised, *var. Bass*	3
Barton Incised, *var. Estill*	7
Parkin Punctated, *var. Hollandale*	8
Parkin Punctated, *var. Transylvania*	4
Parkin Punctated, *var. unspecified*	3
Winterville Incised, *var. Winterville*	46

Grace Brushed, *var. Grace*	31
Grace Brushed, *var. unspecified*	3
Pouncey Pinched, *var. Patosi*	8
Barton Incised, *var. unspecified*	94
Winterville Incised, *var. unspecified*	19
Unclassified incised (Yazoo)	3
Anna Incised, *var. Anna*	1
Carter Engraved, *var. Carter*	1
Hollyknowe Pinched, *var. Patmos*	1
Plaquemine Brushed, *var. Plaquemine*	6
Coleman Incised, *var. Coleman*	2
Evansville Punctated, *var. Sharkey*	1
Mazique Incised, *var. Manchac*	2
Unclassified incised (Addis)	5
Coles Creek Incised, *var. Greenhouse*	1
Coles Creek Incised, *var. unspecified*	2
Mazique Incised, *var. unspecified*	1
Coles Creek Incised, *var. Stoner*	2
Alligator Incised, *var. Oxbow*	1
Chevalier Stamped, *var. Cornelia*	1
Larto Red, *var. Larto*	2
Mulberry Creek Cord Marked, *var. Edwards*	2
Evansville Punctated, *var. unspecified*	2

Daub:	324

Lithics:

Mississippi Triangular, *var. Madison* points (fig. 175e, g)	2
Mississippi Triangular, *var. unspecified* point	1
Snub-nosed end scraper	1
Unclassified tools	2
Utilized flakes	23

Organics:

Mammal bone	293
Fish bone	240
Turtle bone/shell	60

EUROPEAN

Earthenware:

Lead-glazed Type B(?)	1

Iron:

Miscellaneous	3

Table 65. Aboriginal and European artifacts from the trash pit in excavation units Y104B2, Y104F4, Y104F6, Y104J, and Y104Z1–8 at Haynes Bluff.

ABORIGINAL

Pottery:

Winterville Incised, *var. Tunica*	6
Barton Incised, *var. Davion*	4
Barton Incised, *var. Portland*	6
Barton Incised, *var. Charlevoix*	27
Old Town Red, *var. Ballground*	8
Parkin Punctated, *var. Elise*	6
Winterville Incised, *var. Loubois*	9
Cracker Road Incised, *var. Cracker Road*	9
Cracker Road Incised, *var. unspecified*	27
Fatherland Incised, *var. Bayou Goula*	2
Mazique Incised, *var. North*	3
Unclassified incised/engraved (Caddo)	1
Owens Punctated, *var. Manly*	6
Owens Punctated, *var. Menard*	19
Winterville Incised, *var. Broutin*	17
Winterville Incised, *var. Wailes*	28
Old Town Red, *var. unspecified*	10
Grace Brushed, *var. Grand Gulf*	23
Grace Brushed, *var. Warren*	37
Kinlock Simple Stamped, *var. Kinlock*	1
Vernon Paul Appliqué, *var. Vernon Paul*	2
Leland Incised, *var. Bovina*	22
Fatherland Incised, *var. Fatherland*	4
Fatherland Incised, *var. Stanton*	4
Fatherland Incised, *var. unspecified*	13
Maddox Engraved, *var. Emerald*	1
Chicot Red, *var. Grand Village*	1
Owens Punctated, *var. Owens*	23
Owens Punctated, *var. unspecified*	11
Leland Incised, *var. Blanchard*	17
Leland Incised, *var. Deep Bayou*	8
Leland Incised, *var. Russell*	144
Leland Incised, *var. Williams*	66
Barton Incised, *var. Arcola*	209
Barton Incised, *var. Midnight*	8
Winterville Incised, *var. Belzoni*	121
Leland Incised, *var. Leland*	41
Leland Incised, *var. Ferris*	5
Leland Incised, *var. unspecified*	13
Maddox Engraved, *var. Silver City*	9
Coleman Incised, *var. Bass*	2

Barton Incised, *var. Estill*	19
Parkin Punctated, *var. Hollandale*	13
Parkin Punctated, *var. Transylvania*	1
Parkin Punctated, *var. unspecified*	7
Winterville Incised, *var. Winterville*	92
Grace Brushed, *var. Grace*	61
Grace Brushed, *var. unspecified*	3
Pouncey Pinched, *var. Patosi*	35
Winterville Incised, *var. Blum*	2
Barton Incised, *var. unspecified*	236
Winterville Incised, *var. unspecified*	28
Unclassified incised (Yazoo)	9
Anna Incised, *var. Anna*	1
Carter Engraved, *var. Carter*	5
L'Eau Noire Incised, *var. L'Eau Noire*	1
Leland Incised, *var. Bethlehem*	1
Plaquemine Brushed, *var. Plaquemine*	9
Coleman Incised, *var. Coleman*	4
Evansville Punctated, *var. Sharkey*	2
Harrison Bayou Incised, *var. Harrison Bayou*	2
Mazique Incised, *var. Manchac*	1
Unclassified incised (Addis)	5
Coles Creek Incised, *var. Mott*	1
French Fork Incised, *var. McNutt*	1
Chevalier Stamped, *var. Chevalier*	1
Coles Creek Incised, *var. Coles Creek*	3
Coles Creek Incised, *var. Campbellsville*	1
Coles Creek Incised, *var. unspecified*	4
Mazique Incised, *var. unspecified*	1
Unclassified incised (Valley Park)	1
Coles Creek Incised, *var. Stoner*	2
Coles Creek Incised, *var. Wade*	1
Mulberry Creek Cord Marked, *var. Smith Creek*	2
Chevalier Stamped, *var. Cornelia*	1
Coles Creek Incised, *var. Hunt*	1
Mulberry Creek Cord Marked, *var. Edwards*	2
Evansville Punctated, *var. unspecified*	4
Indian Bay Stamped, *var. Shaw*	1

Daub:	ca. 600

Lithics:

Alba Stemmed, *var. Catahoula* point	1
Unclassified projectile point	1
Triangular knife	1

Table 65 (continued).

Snub-nosed end scraper	1	*EUROPEAN*	
Pebble celts	4	*Iron:*	
Polished celt	1		
Unclassified tools	4	Miscellaneous	2
Utilized flakes	29	*Gun parts/munitions:*	
Organics:			
		Brass butt plate tang (fig. 175l)	1
Human cranium	1		
Unclassified bone[a]	—	[a]Large quantity.	

sented in tables 65 and 66. Table 65 lists the entire contents, which show a strong representation of Lake George and Wasp Lake phase artifacts as well as a scattering of both earlier and historic materials. The cultural stratigraphy derived from the microstratification of Y104Z, presented in table 66, would seem to confirm that the pit was a Lake George–Wasp Lake feature; at first glance, in fact, there appears to be a nice stratigraphic progression from late Lake George at the bottom to late Wasp Lake at the top (fig. 177). That this neat progression is a spurious coincidence (presumably resulting from a limited sample), however, may be determined from the fact that the entire pit appeared to have been filled during a brief interval: the side and bottom contours were still sharply defined, the surfaces of the individual deposits were quite unweathered, and sherds from different deposits had come from the same vessels (table 67).

A clue to the true chronological positioning of the pit is offered by the sherd of Parkin Punctated, *var. Elise* from level Z6. A single sherd is not sufficient evidence for such important matters of interpretation, but level 6 was a very distinctive ash lens that was also found in unit F and excavated separately as F6 because it was so distinguishable. The correlation is important because F6 contained not only late Wasp Lake phase diagnostics, but also Russell phase markers. Therefore, since the F6/Z6 deposit was near the bottom of the pit,

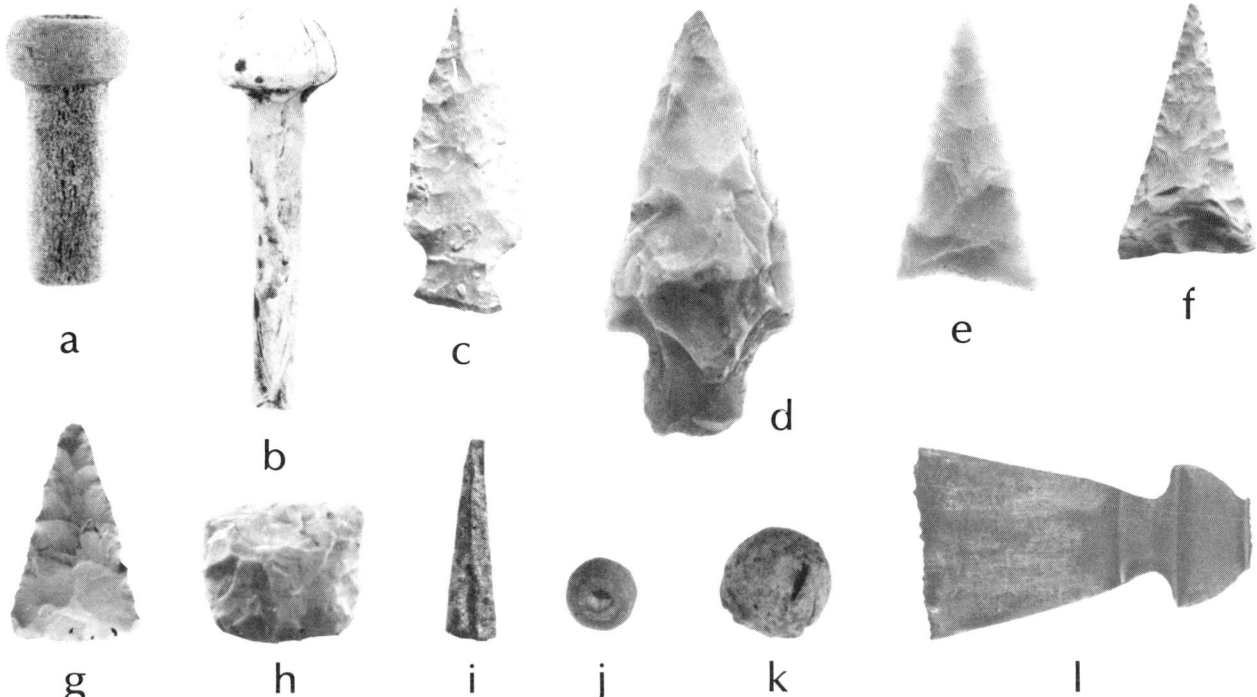

Figure 175. Miscellaneous aboriginal and European artifacts from Haynes Bluff. a, bone earpin; b, shell earpin; c, Collins Side Notched, *var. Collins* point; d, Edwards Stemmed, *var. Sunflower* point; e–g, Mississippi Triangular, *var. Madison* points (g, tending toward Nodena Lanceolate, *var. Russell*); h, native gunflint; i, sheet brass tinkler; j, glass bead (IVB1); k, lead musket ball (26 *calibre*); l, fragment of tang from brass butt plate, Type C (cf. fig. 143). (1:1)

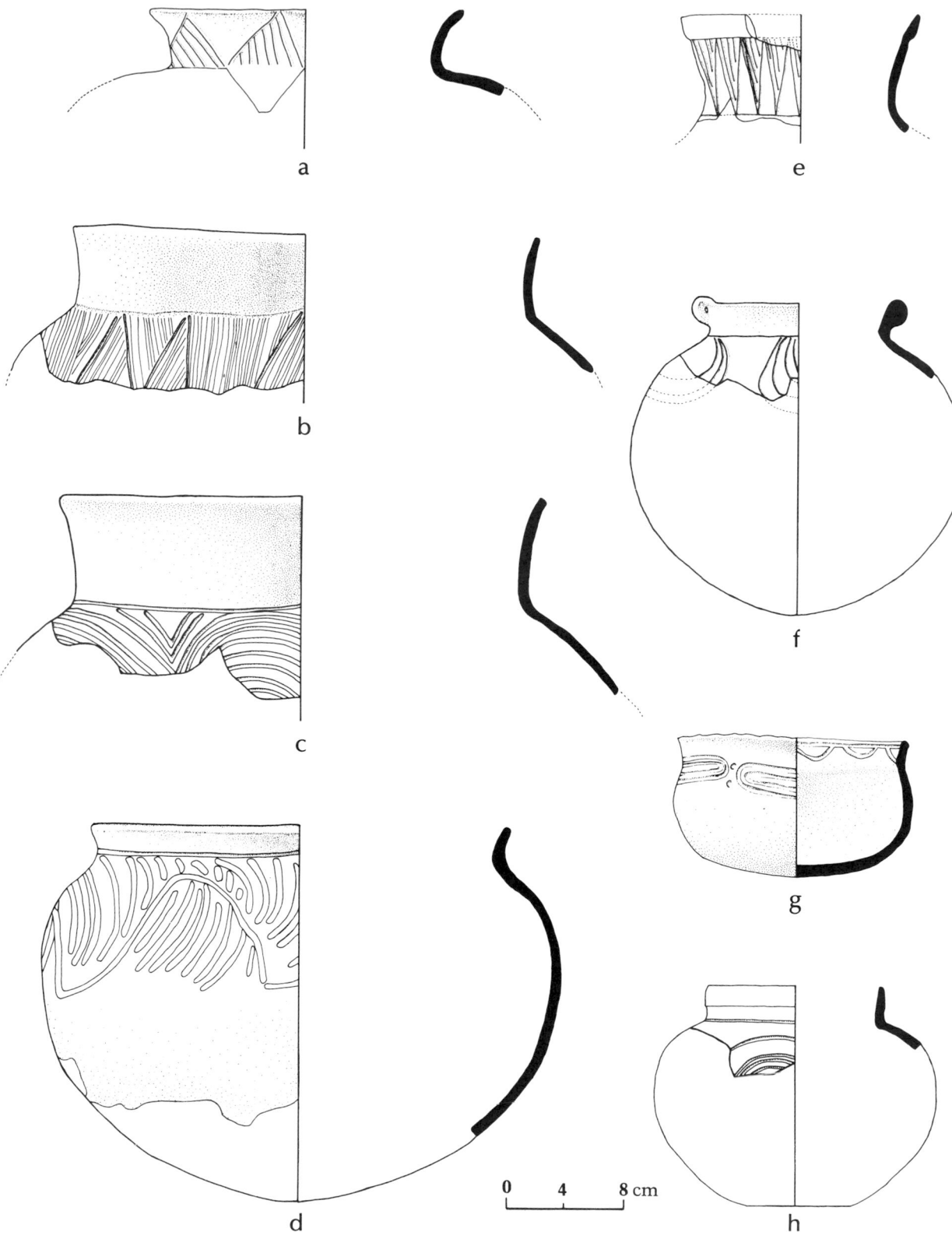

0   4   8 cm

Figure 176. Reconstructions of aboriginal pottery vessels from Haynes Bluff. a, e, Barton Incised, *var. Portland*; b, Grace Brushed, *var. Warren*; c, Winterville Incised, *var. Belzoni*; d, Winterville Incised, *var. Wailes*; f, Winterville Incised, *var. unspecified*; g, Winterville Incised, *var. unspecified* (Leflore Design Mode); h, Leland Incised, *var. Leland*; i, Leland Incised, *var. Ferris*; j, p, Leland Incised, *var. Blanchard*; k, Leland Incised, *var. unspecified*; l, Leland Incised, *var. Deep Bayou*; m–o, Mississippi Plain, *var. Yazoo*; q, Addis Plain, *var. Holly Bluff*. (1:4)

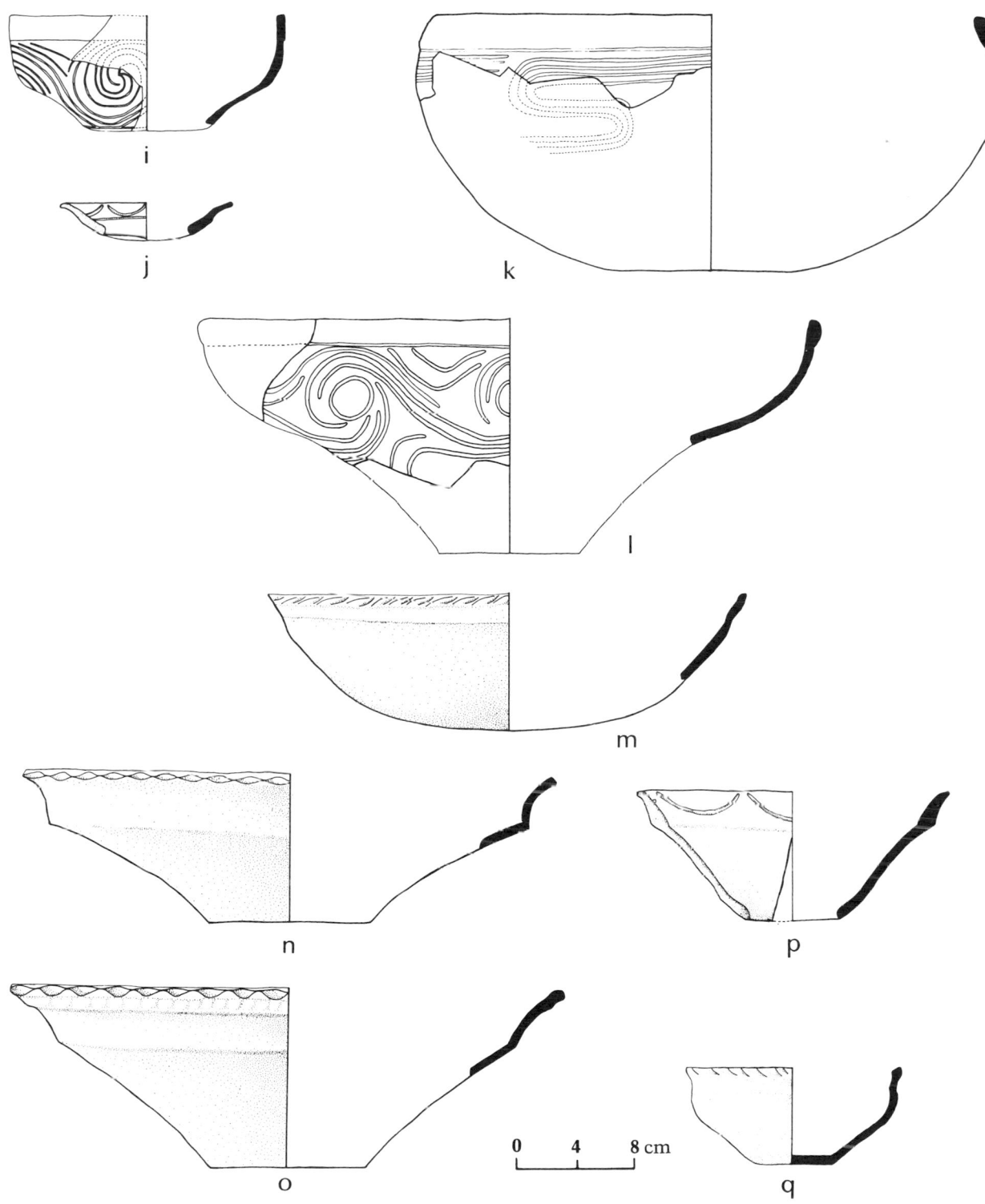

Figure 176 (continued).

and since sherds from this deposit join with sherds from other parts of the pit (demonstrating the close relationship of this deposit to the entire fill), it may be argued that the final pit feature was dug out and refilled during the Russell phase. As noted above, Dean also found gun parts and beads in the area that we now identify as having been part of the trash pit. If the pit was indeed a feature of the Russell phase, it must be correlated with the midden to the east in units G and H rather than with that to the south (units C–E) because the former continued into the Russell phase (table 68) and the latter apparently did not.

Table 66. Aboriginal artifacts from excavation unit Y104Z at Haynes Bluff (tabulated according to strata).

	Z1	Z2	Z3	Z4	Z5[a]	Z6	Z7	Z8
Pottery:								
Barton Incised, *var. Charlevoix*		1						
Parkin Punctated, *var. Elise*						1		
Winterville Incised, *var. Loubois*	3							
Winterville Incised, *var. Broutin*	3							
Winterville Incised, *var. Wailes*	1			1				
Grace Brushed, *var. Grand Gulf*			3	3				
Grace Brushed, *var. Warren*			4					
Leland Incised, *var. Bovina*		2						
Fatherland Incised, *var. Fatherland*	1							
Owens Punctated, *var. Owens*							1	
Owens Punctated, *var. unspecified*		1						
Leland Incised, *var. Blanchard*		1						
Leland Incised, *var. Russell*		2	5	1			1	1
Leland Incised, *var. Williams*	1							
Barton Incised, *var. Arcola*	1	1	7	2		2	1	
Winterville Incised, *var. Belzoni*	1	2	6	2		1		
Leland Incised, *var. Leland*		2	2					
Leland Incised, *var. unspecified*	1	1	1					
Maddox Engraved, *var. Silver City*		1						
Barton Incised, *var. Estill*		1						
Parkin Punctated, *var. Hollandale*	2	1						
Parkin Punctated, *var. Transylvania*		1						
Winterville Incised, *var. Winterville*		2		1		2		
Grace Brushed, *var. Grace*		1						
Grace Brushed, *var. unspecified*			2					
Pouncey Pinched, *var. Patosi*		1		1		1		
Barton Incised, *var. unspecified*		4		5		3	1	
Winterville Incised, *var. unspecified*				1				
Unclassified incised (Yazoo)							1	
Plaquemine Brushed, *var. Plaquemine*		1						
Evansville Punctated, *var. Sharkey*			1					
Mazique Incised, *var. Manchac*			1					
Unclassified incised (Addis)		1						
Daub:	11	13	5	4		4	9	1
Lithics:								
Unclassified tool			1					
Utilized flakes	3	2	1			2		
Organics:								
Mammal bone		5	104	52		12	34	
Bird bone			2			5	7	
Fish bone	2	2	256	125		134	26	
Turtle bone/shell		1	5			1	3	

[a]No data.

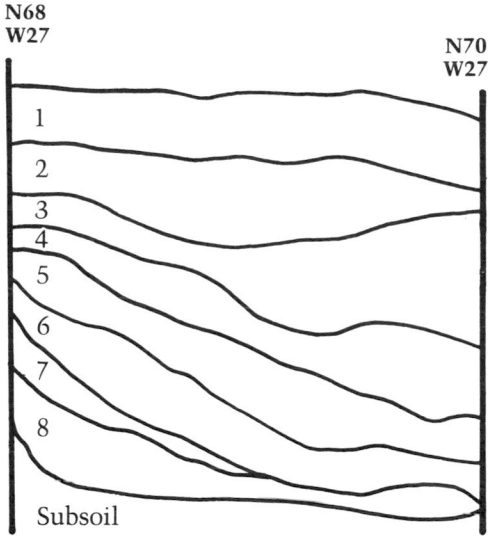

Figure 177. Stratification of excavation unit Y104Z (balk between Y104B and Y104F) at Haynes Bluff.

Table 67. Distribution of sherds from partial vessels found in the trash pit in excavation unit Y104 at Haynes Bluff (see fig. 174).

Type of Vessel	Provenience
Barton Incised, *var. Arcola*	F1,2,4,6; Z3
Barton Incised, *var. Midnight*	B2; F4,6; G4
Barton Incised, *var. Portland*	F4; J[a]
Cracker Road Incised, *var. unspecified*	B2; F4,6
Grace Brushed, *var. Warren*	B2; F4,6; J; Z3
Grace Brushed, *var. Warren* (fig. 176b)	C3; F6
Leland Incised, *var. unspecified* (fig. 176k)	B2; F1,4,6; Z3
Owens Punctated, *var. Owens*	B2; F4,5,6; J; Z7
Winterville Incised, *var. Belzoni* (fig. 176c)	F4,6; Z2

[a] Also present in the Dean Collection.

In summary, these excavations confirmed the residential nature of the aboriginal activities at location D. Although again no structures were identified, the trash pit and the character of the associated midden were sufficient evidence of occupation. These features also provided proof that the occupation along this part of the creek bank, at least, continued into the earliest part of the historic contact period—that is, the early Russell phase. The success of this occupation is amply attested by the rich contents of both the general midden and the trash pit. The latter, especially, was unusually well endowed with a concentration of artifacts and food remains. There was a variety of animal bones, but deer and fish predominated. The adequacy of this diet was clearly demonstrated by the waste: many of the bones were still articulated, indicating the disposal of large parts of the carcass. Speculation on the significance of a young adult (age 20–30 years) human female cranium found at the bottom of the pit will not be hazarded; the skull is of great intrinsic interest, however, for it displays extreme occipital-frontal deformation, a trait said to have been practiced by the Tunica (Shea 1861, p. 134) but never before demonstrated archaeologically. Of course, the skull need not have belonged to a Tunica, for head deformation also was practiced by many other Indian groups (e.g., Swanton 1911, pp. 54–55, 89–90, 262, 350), but if it did it is of great interest to note that otherwise the trait has not been observed archaeologically either at Haynes Bluff or the later sites in the Red River region (nor is it illustrated in the DeBatz watercolor of three prominent Tunica [see fig. 208]).

SUMMARY OF THE 1974 EXCAVATIONS

The most significant findings derived from the excavations at Haynes Bluff were the lateness and nature of the occupation. The most interesting discovery was the considerable amount of mound construction that was done during the protohistoric period and perhaps even during the historic. Clearly, these people were among the last of the mound builders, and whether such construction was actually carried out during the Russell phase or not, it certainly occurred within the memories of the historic peoples. The evidence of activities on the summit of mound A demonstrates that the tradition of mound usage was still very much alive. The individuals buried at the summit attest to the fact that social and sexual distinctions were maintained: they were high status males who were well equipped with mortuary artifacts.[*] These included a relatively large number and variety of European artifacts dating to the early historic contact period. The Russell phase occupation was a flourishing settlement, rich in artifacts and foodstuffs.

In addition to confirming the Russell phase occupation, the excavations demonstrated in situ continuities into the protohistoric and prehistoric past. But the record shows change as well as continuity, the most pertinent consisting of introductions from outside sources. These include obvious Tunica diagnostics. As regards the theme of this study, however, it is not possible to distinguish a single definite Tunica context (burial, midden, structure, or the like), although Tunica presence can be demonstrated. Apparently there was too much other ethnic interference in the archaeological record (or else we were unlucky in our sampling). It may be expected that the primary center of the amalgamated Yazoo region tribes would reflect exactly this condition. In order to isolate a Tunica component, therefore, it was necessary to move away from Haynes Bluff to smaller outlying sites, which presumably would be of purer ethnic composition.

---

[*] Compare the burials found by Clausen in one of the smaller mounds (see fig. 160). The Kelley-Dean burial, which was well accompanied, might be the exception that proves the rule.

Table 68. Aboriginal and European artifacts from the midden layer in excavation units Y104G3 and Y104H2–4 at Haynes Bluff.

ABORIGINAL

Pottery:

Winterville Incised, *var. Tunica*	2
Barton Incised, *var. Davion*	2
Barton Incised, *var. Portland*	1
Barton Incised, *var. Charlevoix*	11
Old Town Red, *var. Ballground*	1
Parkin Punctated, *var. Elise*	1
Winterville Incised, *var. Loubois*	5
Cracker Road Incised, *var. Cracker Road*	3
Cracker Road Incised, *var. unspecified*	2
Fatherland Incised, *var. Snyders Bluff*	1
Mazique Incised, *var. North*	1
Owens Punctated, *var. Menard*	1
Winterville Incised, *var. Broutin*	8
Winterville Incised, *var. Wailes*	5
Old Town Red, *var. unspecified*	1
Grace Brushed, *var. Grand Gulf*	1
Nodena Red and White, *var. Nodena*	1
Fatherland Incised, *var. Fatherland*	5
Fatherland Incised, *var. unspecified*	1
Maddox Engraved, *var. Emerald*	1
Owens Punctated, *var. unspecified*	4
Winterville Incised, *var. Ranch*	1
Leland Incised, *var. Deep Bayou*	2
Leland Incised, *var. Russell*	32
Leland Incised, *var. Williams*	13
Barton Incised, *var. Arcola*	26
Barton Incised, *var. Midnight*	4
Winterville Incised, *var. Belzoni*	36
Leland Incised, *var. Leland*	8
Leland Incised, *var. unspecified*	3
Maddox Engraved, *var. Silver City*	4
Coleman Incised, *var. Bass*	2
Barton Incised, *var. Estill*	1
Parkin Punctated, *var. Hollandale*	17
Parkin Punctated, *var. Transylvania*	1
Parkin Punctated, *var. unspecified*	3
Winterville Incised, *var. Winterville*	34
Grace Brushed, *var. Grace*	15
Grace Brushed, *var. unspecified*	1

Pouncey Pinched, *var. Patosi*	5
Winterville Incised, *var. Blum*	1
Barton Incised, *var. unspecified*	53
Winterville Incised, *var. unspecified*	9
Unclassified incised (Yazoo)	2
L'Eau Noire Incised, *var. L'Eau Noire*	1
Leland Incised, *var. Bethlehem*	2
Hollyknowe Pinched, *var. Patmos*	2
Plaquemine Brushed, *var. Plaquemine*	1
Coleman Incised, *var. Coleman*	3
Unclassified incised (Addis)	1
Coles Creek Incised, *var. Mott*	1
Coles Creek Incised, *var. unspecified*	5
Mazique Incised, *var. Mazique*	1
Coles Creek Incised, *var. Stoner*	1
Coles Creek Incised, *var. Hunt*	1
Coles Creek Incised, *var. Phillips*	1
Larto Red, *var. Larto*	1
Unclassified incised (Baytown)	1
Lake Borgne Incised, *var. Tenhut*	1

Daub: 269

Lithics:

Mississippi Triangular, *var. Madison* point (fig. 175f)	1
Pipe drill	1
Snub-nosed end scraper	1
Utilized flakes	9

Organics:

Mammal bone	237
Bird bone	8
Fish bone	821
Turtle bone/shell	31

EUROPEAN

Glass:

Olive green	1

Iron:

Miscellaneous	1

Gun parts/munitions:

Lead musket ball (15mm/26 *calibre*) (fig. 175k)	1

PORTLAND

In an effort to find outlying settlements pertaining to the early historic contact period, we intensively surveyed the loess bluffs overlooking Haynes Bluff and St. Pierre. Special attention was directed to this topography because of reports that local collectors using metal detectors had turned up numerous French artifacts there during the previous two years. Several promising locations were discovered despite the adverse natural conditions caused by dense vegetation and heavy erosion. These locations were surveyed further with electronic instruments, and many anomalies were detected. Some of the local amateur archaeologists verified two of the locations as the proveniences of many of their finds, which included at least eight "Colonies Francoises 1722" coins, a 1692 German coin (fig. 178), an English coin dated 1588(!), and a French trade axe, as well as an Indian burial with an early contact period musket and many other miscellaneous items.* The general locale, designated the Portland site (22-M-12), is situated less than 0.5 km south of Haynes Bluff (see fig. 158). Test excavations were carried out at the site during the period 2–20 July by the Archives and History crew with assistance and supervision from the LMS (Brown 1975, 1976, 1979a). The following description of the excavations and significant findings is excerpted from Brown 1979a (pp. 207–214).

Six 2 meter squares were excavated at the Portland Site [fig. 179], four of which (Y500–Y503) were placed over a series of trash pits. It was originally supposed that there was just one single large pit, but excavation revealed four additional pits. The habitation area, represented by a thin sheet midden, is situated to the south and southwest of the pits and was discovered by means of a post hole survey. A single 2 meter square (Y504) excavated in the above area was unproductive. Only 20 potsherds were found out of a total of 2,146 retrieved at the site. Four-fifths of the assemblage within this square is either Addis Plain, var. Addis or Mississippi Plain, var. Yazoo.

Figure 178. A 1692 silver *kreutzer* from Maintz (*sic*) found at the Portland site by Jackie Sarrett of Jackson, Mississippi. (Sarrett Collection) (1:1)

---

* Such scattered burials in the bluffs are not uncommon, as exampled by another burial pothunted two years later (Brown 1979a, pp. 214–224). Although these burials could have been associated with nearby hamlets, they also might have been isolated occurrences following the mortuary practice—"In the woods" and "on a hill"—reported by Swanton (1946, p. 729).

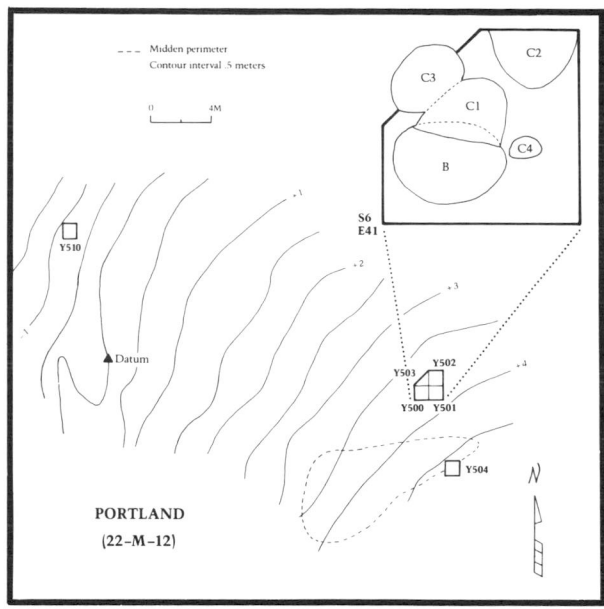

Figure 179. Plan of the 1974 excavations at the Portland site (22-M-12) and detail of features Y506B and Y506C1–4 in excavation units Y500–503 (adapted from Brown 1979a, figs. 22–23).

An additional test square (Y510) was excavated to the northwest of the main excavations, in the area in which "Colonies Francoises" coins are reported to have been found. Ninety-two potsherds were discovered most of which occur in the second level. Historic artifacts include a piece of green lead-glazed earthenware, a musket ball, and five glass beads.

Squares Y500 through Y503 were excavated by arbitrary levels, in each case being taken down to the +3.61 meter level above datum. This level extends no deeper than 50 cm below ground surface. Y501 required the removal of two arbitrary units to get down to this level, but only one level was removed in the other squares. At this depth, a large oval feature [designated Y506], over 4 meters in length and 2.5 meters at the widest point, stood out from the surrounding subsoil. This was at first thought to be a burial pit, as some human bone was discovered, but the large quantity of various animal bones and small potsherds indicated it to be a large trash pit. Further excavation revealed a series of five trash pits, some of which overlap [fig. 179].

Y506B is the largest of these pits, 2.25 meters long and approximately 1.7 meters wide. The original width cannot be determined as the southern portion of pit Y506C1 had been dug into Y506B. As with many of the pits excavated at the Fatherland Site, Y506B is bathtub-shaped (Neitzel–personal communication). It has a maximum depth of 26 cm. A large fragment of a Winterville Incised, var. Tunica jar [fig. 180d] was found within this pit, it being quite similar to material found at the historic Tunica site of Trudeau (29-J-1).

It was hoped that a chronological ordering of artifacts would be attained through the analysis and comparison of trash pits Y506B and Y506C, as the latter is known to have been dug at a somewhat later date. Pot

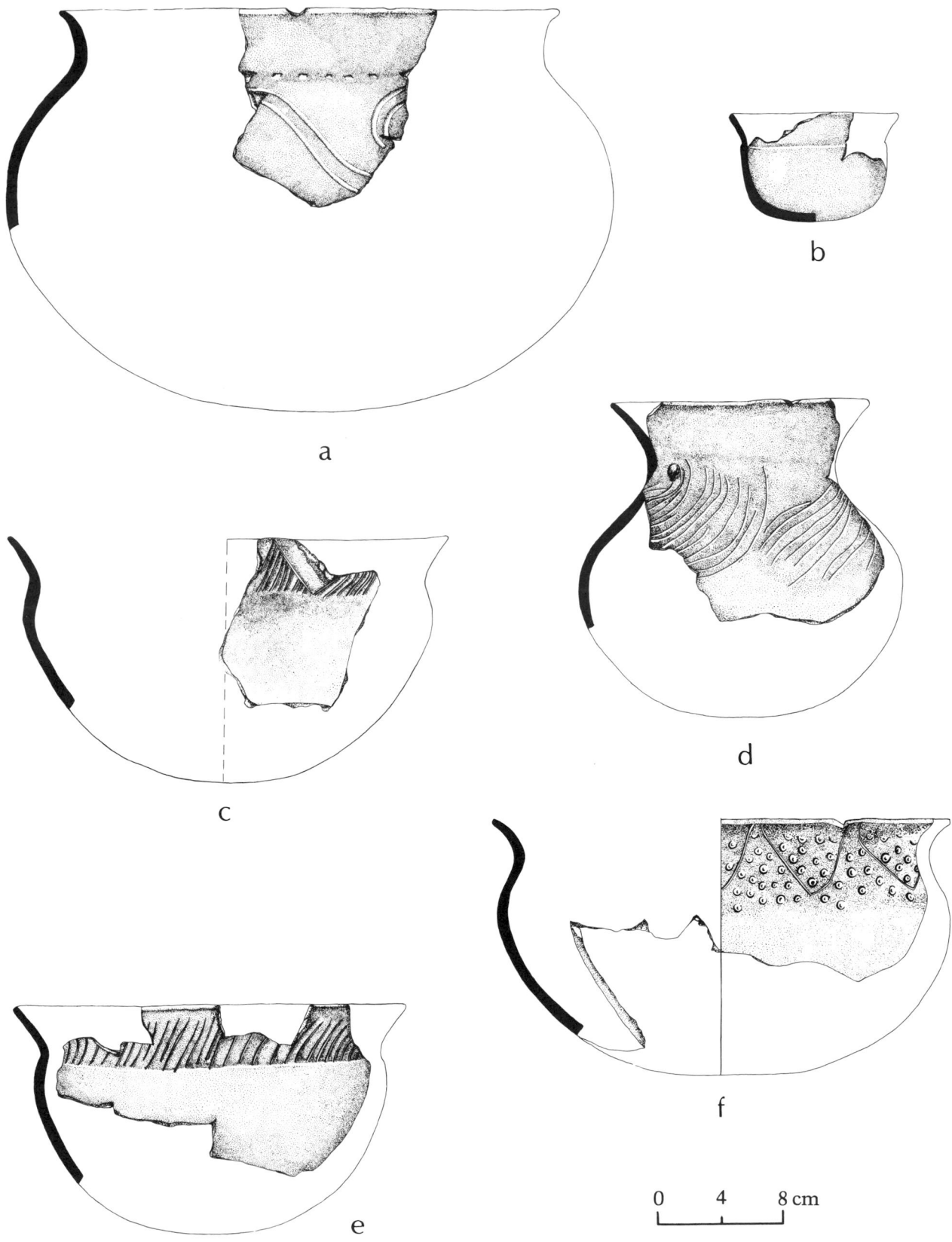

Figure 180. Reconstructions of aboriginal pottery vessels from Portland. a, Leland Incised, *var. Williams*; b, Mississippi Plain, *var. unspecified*; c, Barton Incised, *var. Portland*; d, Winterville Incised, *var. Tunica*; e, Barton Incised, *var. Davion*; f, Owens Punctated, *var. Redwood*. The diagnostic Tunica markers are c–f, comprising the Yazoo 8 subset and *var. Tunica*. (1:4)

Table 69. Aboriginal and European artifacts found at the Portland site (22-M-12) during the 1974 excavations (compiled from Brown 1976, 1979a).

ABORIGINAL		EUROPEAN	
Pottery:		*Earthenware:*	
Winterville Incised, *var. Tunica* (fig. 180d)	18	Faience	
Barton Incised, *var. Davion* (fig. 180e)	30	Blue-and-white	1
Barton Incised, *var. Portland* (fig. 180c)	28	Lead-glazed	
Owens Punctated, *var. Redwood* (fig. 180f)	11	Type A(?)	1
		Kaolin pipestem	4
Barton Incised, *var. Charlevoix*	11		
Old Town Red, *var. Ballground*	24	*Glass:*	
Parkin Punctated, *var. Elise*[a]	—		
Winterville Incised, *var. Loubois*[b]	—	Clear, olive green, light blue-green, and amber	25
		Beads	
Cracker Road Incised, *var. Cracker Road*	22	IIA1	44
		IIA4	1
Winterville Incised, *var. Wailes*[c]	1	IIA6	16
		IIA7	1
Grace Brushed, *var. Warren*	1	IIA8	6
		IIA13	3
Leland Incised, *var. Bovina*	9	IIB2	1
		IIB15	2
Fatherland Incised, *var. Fatherland*	14	IIB16	1
		IVB1	1
Owens Punctated, *var. Widow Creek*	6	IVB3	2
		IVB9	1
Leland Incised, *var. Blanchard*	9	IVB10	1
Leland Incised, *var. Russell*	15	IVB11	1
Leland Incised, *var. Williams* (fig. 180a)	30	WIIA3	1
		WIIA11	1
Barton Incised, *var. Arcola*	9	WIIB2	3
Barton Incised, *var. Midnight*	2	WIIB3	1
Winterville Incised, *var. Belzoni*	2	WIIIA4	1
Leland Incised, *var. Leland*	8	*Iron:*	
Parkin Punctated, *var. Hollandale*[a]	4	Folding knife	1
Winterville Incised, *var. Winterville*[b]	8	Axe	1
		Buckle	1
Grace Brushed, *var. Grace*	7		
		Brass:	
Plaquemine Brushed, *var. Plaquemine*	7		
		C-bracelet	1
Coles Creek Incised, *var. Mott*	2	Crucifix corpora	1
Avoyelles Punctated, *var. Avoyelles*	1	*Gun parts/munitions:*	
Coles Creek Incised, *var. Coles Creek*	2		
		Brass butt plate	1
Lithics:		Brass ferrules	2
		Spall gunflints	3
Mississippi Triangular, *var. Madison* points	5	Blade gunflints	5
Native gunflints	3	Lead musket balls	5
Knife	1	Lead shot	2
Drill	1		
Snub-nosed end scrapers	4		
Unspecialized scraper	1		
Unclassified tools	6		
Cores	2		
Hammerstone	1		
Utilized flakes	3		

[a] At least one *Elise* was seen in the collection.
[b] *Loubois* presumably was counted within *Winterville*.
[c] Listed as Wallace Incised.

hunters unfortunately succeeded in tearing up a large portion of these pits, thereby preventing such a study. The loose dirt from their destruction was sifted and labeled Y506C, but it was later learned that Y506C consists of three additional pits, only one of which (Y506C1) overlaps with Y506B. The artifacts, therefore, cannot be arranged chronologically through stratigraphic means. A large portion of an Owens Punctated, var. Redwood bowl [fig. 180f] was found in Y506C1.

The remaining three trash pits are of a smaller size than the first two pits. Y506C2 was only partially excavated, because of time limitations. It is 1.8 meters wide and, had it been symmetrical, 2.4 meters long. Its maximum depth, below the arbitrary +3.61 meter level, is 15 cm. A partial Leland Incised, var. Williams bowl [fig. 180a] was reconstructed out of the remains left by the pot hunters. Y506C3 is somewhat smaller, but has a shape similar to Y506C2. Its long axis runs northeast-southwest, instead of north-south. Its length and width are 1.9 meters and 1.25 meters respectively, and its maximum depth is 26 cm. The discovery of a historic trade axe within this trash pit supports the local amateurs' claim that axes were unearthed by them in this region. Y506C4, the remaining pit, is a peculiar feature. It does not overlap with any of the other pits. It is small and round, having a length of 60 cm and a width of 45 cm, its long axis oriented east-west. Its maximum depth is similar to Y506C2 at 14 cm. Unlike the other pits, Y506C4 is culturally sterile.

In sum, the excavations at Portland uncovered a series of five pits containing variable amounts, but essentially similar types of artifacts. Some of the pits overlap with earlier ones, but little time probably passed between when the various pits were used. The associated house remains are probably located to the south and southeast of the trash pits, as revealed in a thin veneer of cultural material which appeared in a posthole survey.

Brown concluded that the remains probably pertained to a small Indian settlement—a single homestead or hamlet. Such a settlement was consistent with the relatively dispersed pattern described in the early French accounts (e.g., Shea 1861, pp. 80–81, 132–136). The artifactual assemblage that was recovered had a relatively high amount of European artifacts (table 69), and, in fact, is a fine sample for the early contact period. Most important of all were the native artifacts, which included the purest complex of Tunica pottery yet isolated in the region (fig. 180). It seems safe to accept Brown's overall conclusion that the site features represented "the remains of a single Tunica occupation dating to the 'missionary' period (1698–1706)" (Brown 1979a, p. 207).

BURROUGHS

The Burroughs site (22-M-10) is approximately 2 km southwest of Haynes Bluff (see fig. 158), and is situated on the bluff talus just a few hundred meters from the left bank of the Yazoo River. Some 100 m west of Mississippi Route 3, and bisected by an Illinois Central

Railroad spur line (the same line that continues to Haynes Bluff), a midden area is found on both sides of an unnamed stream (fig. 181). Between the midden and the road, in the yard of a modern residence—the Burroughs's homestead—are two mound-like features that have been the focus of attention for years but were determined by our investigations to be natural limestone outcroppings.

The site may have been visited on 1 June 1853 by B. L. C. Wailes, who refers to a small mound group in this vicinity (Wailes 1853), but the first visitor to record its archaeological potential was C. B. Moore (1908, p. 569). He dismissed the mounds but noted the midden area, from the surface of which he picked up a grooved stone plummet of a type common in the Coles Creek culture (Williams and Brain 1983, pp. 262–263). These credentials would not have been sufficient to have elicited our further attentions had not fate intervened in the agency of the Illinois Central Railroad.

In 1964 the railroad spur line to the International Paper Company plant at Haynes Bluff was being constructed across the site, and in the process burials were encountered. The discovery was duly reported in the Vicksburg newspapers on 19 July. By fortunate coincidence, the LMS, under the direction of Stephen Williams, happened to be surveying the Tensas Basin across the river that summer. The nineteenth was a Sunday, and so, after reading about the discovery, most of the crew members decided to take a busman's holiday and check it out. They found that a bulldozer clearing the right-of-way had uncovered and partially disturbed the burials of three individuals. These had already been further damaged by pothunters before our right-minded colleagues could reach the scene. Enough remained, however, to be worth a salvage effort. Work commenced that day, and a small crew returned on the twentieth and twenty-first to remove the burials and to map and test the site.

The three burials were single interments of adults, sex unknown. Each was laid in an extended supine position; burial 1 was oriented with the head to the southwest, burials 2 and 3 to the northeast (fig. 181). Fragments of at least three vessels—a Leland Incised, var. unspecified bowl and two Winterville Incised jars, one var. unspecified, the other var. Tunica (fig. 182a–b)—were found with burial 1. Nothing was found with burial 2, the upper half of which had been almost entirely destroyed. Burial 3 contained part of a Mississippi Plain, var. Yazoo bowl, and a large lump of solidified vermilion had been placed on the lower thorax. Although this is almost certainly not a complete listing of the artifacts that had accompanied the burials originally, it is nevertheless quite informative. From the evidence, it may be argued that burial 1 was of Tunica affiliation and that burial 3 was laid to rest after European contact. The parallel alignment and close association of all three burials indicate that they should be treated as a group. Thus, it does not seem unreasonable to conclude that together they represent a small burial component of the early historic Tunica.

It was therefore mandatory that Burroughs be accorded more attention when we returned to the area in

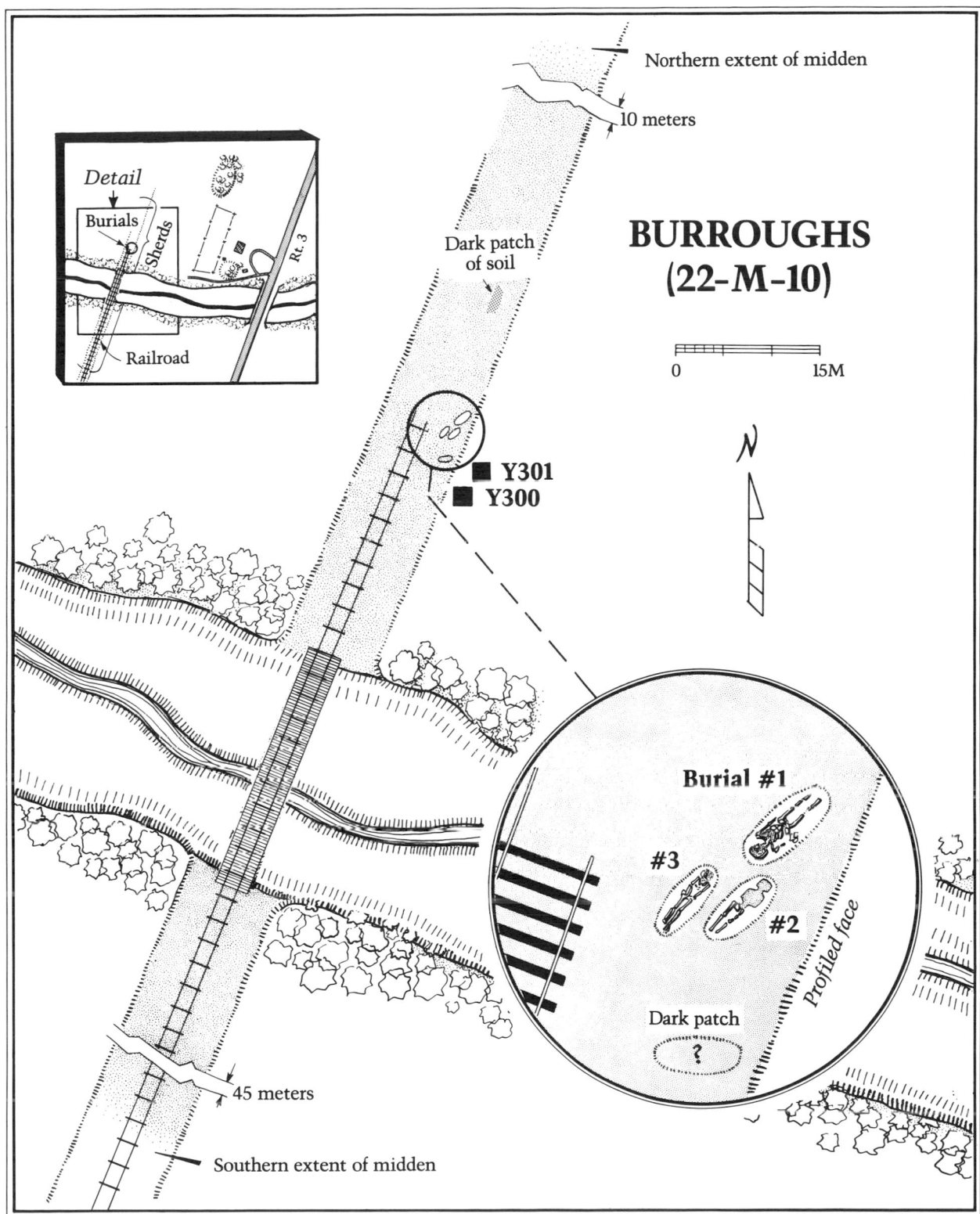

Figure 181. Map of the Burroughs site (22-M-10), giving locations of the 1964 and 1974 excavations by the Lower Mississippi Survey.

1974, this time with a specific focus on the Tunica. Preliminary pedestrian and electronic surveys were conducted early in August, and the results were encouraging. Artifactual materials from the surface of the midden area (table 70) included some very late materials, as well as evidence of the earlier components reported by Moore and found by the LMS during the brief 1964 tests around the burials. The electronic survey detected anomalies in the vicinity of the burial area. It was hoped that additional, undisturbed burials could be found, or, even better, an associated occupation area; at the least, we were determined to establish the archaeological context for the three known burials. Accordingly, two 2-×-2-m excavation units (Y300–301) were staked out over the most promising anomalies closest to the earlier burials, but in the field undisturbed by the railroad cut. Unfortunately, the anomalies turned out to be caused by modern trash, and no further evidence of aboriginal burials was recovered. The excavations were continued, however, in the hope of achieving our other objectives. A small crew was detailed to this work during the period of 15–23 August.

The stratification of excavation units Y300 and Y301 was parallel to a depth of 75 cm, at which point Y301 was discontinued due to a paucity of cultural materials. Y300 was carried down another meter, where subsoil was reached. The combined stratification revealed a very mixed and densely packed topsoil, the character of which was probably due to centuries of flooding,

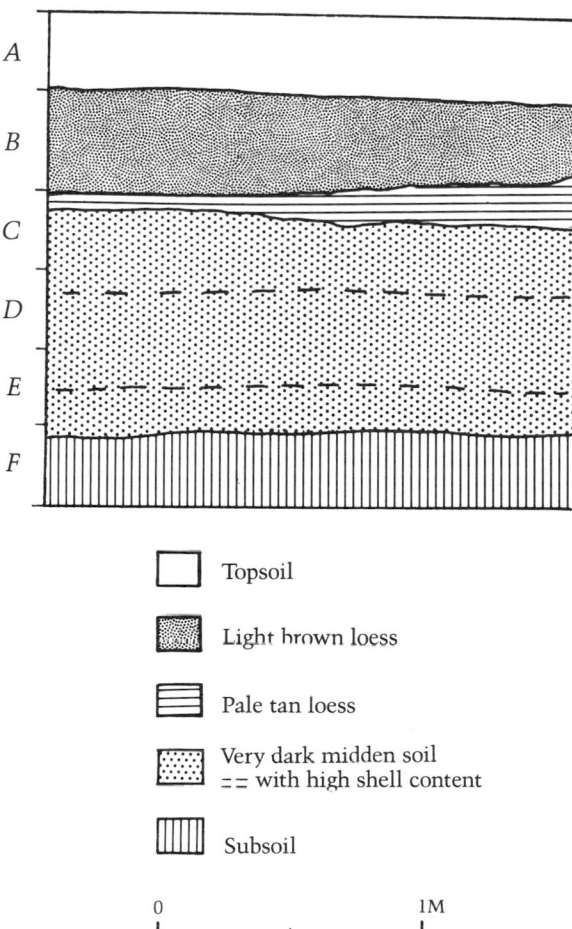

Figure 183. Stratification of excavation unit Y300, Burroughs, as revealed in the north wall.

Legend:
- ☐ Topsoil
- ▨ Light brown loess
- ▤ Pale tan loess
- ▦ Very dark midden soil == with high shell content
- ▥ Subsoil

0 ——————— 1M

Table 70. Aboriginal artifacts collected from the surface of the Burroughs site (22-M-10) in 1974.

Pottery:

Fatherland Incised, *var. unspecified*	1
Barton Incised, *var. Arcola*	1
Unclassified incised (Addis)	1
Chevalier Stamped, *var. Chevalier*	2
Coles Creek Incised, *var. Coles Creek*	1
Mazique Incised, *var. unspecified* (fig. 182g)	1
Coles Creek Incised, *var. Stoner*	1
French Fork Incised, *var. Wilzone*	1
Indian Bay Stamped, *var. unspecified*	1
Marksville Stamped, *var. Manny*	2

Lithics:

Utilized flake	1

Organics:

Fish bone	2

---

plowing, and more recent use as a cow pasture. Below the topsoil was evidence of both colluviation and alluviation, until finally at a depth of about 75–80 cm from the surface a dark black midden was encountered (fig. 183). This midden, which contained a high concentration of mussel shell, was found to a depth of more than 160 cm. Excavations were continued to −185 cm, which was well into sandy subsoil.

The cultural materials recovered from these excavations confirm the evidence from the earlier investigations that the site had a long history of occupation, extending from Marksville to late Mississippian (tables 71–72). The earliest contexts apparently had been destroyed by subsequent occupations, for the lowest cultural stratum, the black midden, was obviously a feature of the Coles Creek component (fig. 182d–g). Even this zone was subjected to later disturbance, as manifested by a few of the potsherds from these levels. A hiatus in site occupation, at least at this location, is suggested by the water-laid strata and the absence of artifactual diagnostics for the interval between late Coles Creek

---

Figure 182. Aboriginal pottery from Burroughs. a–b, Winterville Incised, *var. Tunica* (from vessel found with burial 1); c, Winterville Incised, *var. unspecified* (found with burial 1); d, Chevalier Stamped, *var. Chevalier*; e, Coles Creek Incised, *var. Mott*; f, French Fork Incised, *var. McNutt*; g, Mazique Incised, *var. unspecified*. (1:1, except c, 1:2)

Table 71. Aboriginal artifacts from excavation unit Y300 at Burroughs (tabulated by level).

	A	B	C	D	E	F
Pottery:						
Old Town Red, *var. unspecified*		1				
Leland Incised, *var. Bovina*		1				
Chicot Red, *var. Grand Village*					1	
Leland Incised, *var. Deep Bayou*				2		
Leland Incised, *var. Williams*		1				
Barton Incised, *var. unspecified*			2			
Winterville Incised, *var. unspecified*			1			
Carter Engraved, *var. unspecified*			1			
Mazique Incised, *var. Manchac*			1	1		
Coles Creek Incised, *var. Mott*						1
French Fork Incised, *var. McNutt*						1
Mazique Incised, *var. Kings Point*			1			
Chevalier Stamped, *var. Chevalier*				1		
Coles Creek Incised, *var. Coles Creek*						1
Coles Creek Incised, *var. unspecified*		1		1		1
Mazique Incised, *var. unspecified*			6		1	1
Coles Creek Incised, *var. Stoner*			1			
Larto Red, *var. Larto*		1				
Mulberry Creek Cord Marked, *var. unspecified*						1
Marksville Stamped, *var. Manny*			1			
Marksville Incised, *var. unspecified*[a]					1	
Unclassified incised (Baytown)				1		
Daub:	1			3	1	
Lithics:						
Unclassified biface					1	
Organics:						
Mammal bone		1	30	42	19	18
Fish bone				1	7	
Turtle bone/shell				3	12	2

[a]Red-slipped.

and the Wasp Lake phase. The actual context for the latter seems to have been lost in the plow zone. Furthermore, the extensive surface disturbance caused by the railroad construction ensured that nothing remained of any historic Indian occupation that may have existed at the site. Thus, although it is unlikely that the burials excavated in 1964 were isolated intrusions, we were unable to associate them with an occupational context.

Finally, it is interesting that, aside from the plummet found by C. B. Moore, the site's lithic material is noteworthy only in its near absence (a broken biface from Y300E was the only such artifact found, and even utilized flakes were not present). This absence is in stark contrast to the abundance of stone artifacts and debitage found at the Russell site and constitutes a basic difference between the two sites that may be of some significance for ethnic identifications.

Table 72. Aboriginal artifacts from excavation unit Y301 at Burroughs (tabulated by level).

	A	B	C
Pottery:			
Leland Incised, *var. unspecified*		1	
Barton Incised, *var. unspecified*	1		
Mississippi Plain, *var. Yazoo*			1
Coles Creek Incised, *var. unspecified*		1	
Organics:			
Mammal bone	1	1	

Table 73. Aboriginal and European artifacts from the Russell site (22-N-19) in the Russell Collection (inventoried in 1961).

ABORIGINAL

Pottery:

Cracker Road Incised, *var. unspecified*[a]	1
Fortune Noded, *var. unspecified* (fig. 184a)	1
Winterville Incised, *var. Broutin*[a]	3
Winterville Incised, *var. Wailes*[a]	7
Barton Incised, *var. unspecified*[a]	1
Unclassified incised (Yazoo)[a]	2
Mississippi Plain, *var. Yazoo*[b] (fig. 184d–h)	13
Leland Incised, *var. Russell* (fig. 184c)	2
Chicot Red, *var. unspecified*[a] (fig. 184b)	4
Addis Plain, *var. Holly Bluff*	2
Elbow pipe of Yazoo ware[a]	1

Lithics:[b]

Mississippi Triangular, *var. Madison* points[a]	3
Nodena Lanceolate, *var. Nodena* point	1
Nodena Lanceolate, *var. Russell* points[a]	9
Triangular knives	2
Pipe drills[a] (fig. 187s–u)	5
Expanded base drills	2
Unspecified scrapers[c]	10
Chipped celts	3
Pebble celts[a]	5
Polished celts	4
Polished spud[a]	1
Discoidal stones[a]	5
Hammerstones	17
Quartz crystal	1
Crinoid stem beads	11
Jasper bead[a]	1

Organics:

Bone awl	1
Conch shell gorget[a]	1
Conch shell knobbed earpins[a]	2
Conch shell beads[a]	4

EUROPEAN

Glass:

Beads[a]	
IIA1/IVA1	105
IIA6(?)	10
IIA7	140
IIB1	7
IIB3	1
IVB1	3
WIIA2	4

Iron:

Axes[a]	3
Folding knife blade	1
C-bracelets[a]	3

Copper/brass:

Type A, Variety 1 kettle fragment[a]	1
Bells[a]	
Key type, variety unspecified	3
Sheet metal rolled beads	2
Tinkling cones[a]	2
Semicircular gorget[a]	1
Miscellaneous fragments	5

Gun parts/munitions:

Steatite bullet mold[a]	1

[a]Some (if not all) of the objects in this category are now in the collections of the Mississippi Department of Archives and History at Jackson (see Williams and Brain 1983, fig. 11.23 for additional illustrations).

[b]List does not include at least 158 Paleo-Indian and Meso-Indian projectile points, including fluted, Dalton, Cache River, Big Sandy, Kirk, Morrow Mountain, Guilford, Savannah River, Carrolton, and Gary types (see Williams and Brain 1983, fig. 11.3). Although in the Russell Collection, these points were not found at the Russell site, but at another unidentified site nearby.

[c]Includes snub-nosed end scrapers.

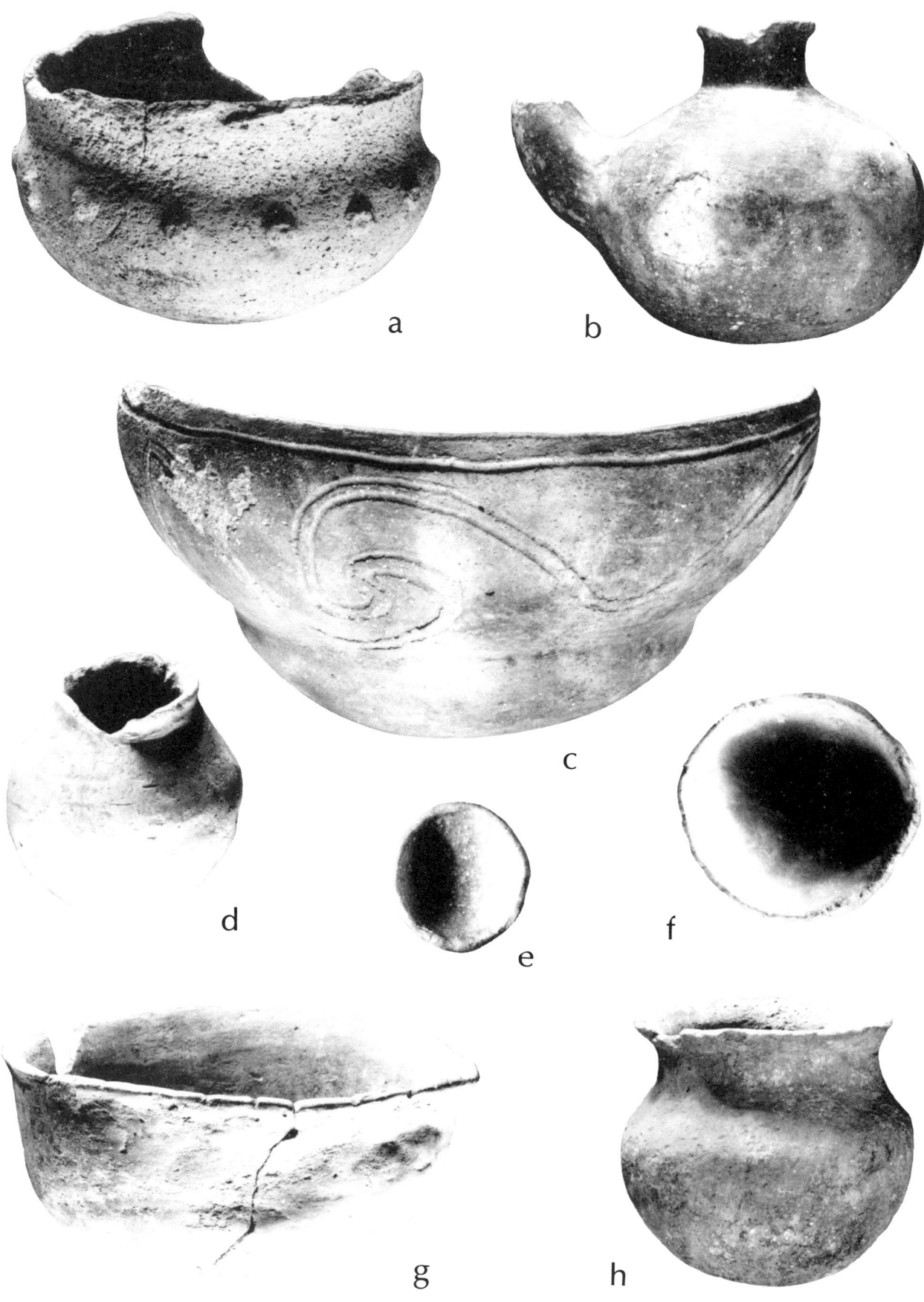

RUSSELL

"Russell" was originally just a name and a collection without a site. A rather fine collection of native and European artifacts dating from the early historic period was known to have come from land owned by the Russell family, but the exact provenience had not been ascertained. The Russell plantation is located some 3.5 km east-northeast of the small village of Eldorado and 13 km northeast of Haynes Bluff (see fig. 158). The archaeological importance of the general locale had been recognized since the time of Calvin Brown (1926, p. 57). James A. Ford recorded a site at "Russell Place" in 1939, but his description offers no clue to its cultural or temporal assignment (Ford 1939). In 1949 Ford returned to

the site with Philip Phillips.* Phillips noted that they were shown a collection of artifacts from the site that included late Mississippian pottery and historic European trade materials; he designated the site 22-N-19 and suggested that it deserved further investigation (Phillips 1949). Meanwhile, he appropriated the site's

---

* This visit was probably responsible for the small collection of artifacts that ultimately ended up at the Museum of Anthropology, University of Michigan (acc. no. 1826, cat. no. 32449). This collection includes a Nodena Lanceolate, *var. Nodena* point and eight decorated potsherds, the most diagnostic of which are late varieties of Barton Incised, Leland Incised, and Old Town Red (Vincas Steponaitis, personal communication, 1978).

Figure 185. Aboriginal pottery from the Russell site, donated to the Lower Mississippi Survey in 1968. a, Cracker Road Incised, *var. Cracker Road*; b, Owens Punctated, *var. Redwood*; c, Carson Red on Buff, *var. Olmond*; d, Winterville Incised, *var. Wailes*; e, Fatherland Incised, *var. Fatherland*; f, Barton Incised, *var. Portland*. (1:1)

Figure 184. Aboriginal pottery vessels from the Russell site (22-N-19). a, Fortune Noded, *var. unspecified*; b, Old Town Red, *var. unspecified*; c, Leland Incised, *var. Russell*; d–h, Mississippi Plain, *var. unspecified*. Vessels a–b and d–g would not be out of place in the lower Arkansas region; c is an indigenous lower Yazoo variety; and h is a typical Tunica form. (Russell Collection, Mississippi Department of Archives and History, Jackson) (1:2)

Table 74. Aboriginal artifacts from the Russell site donated to the Lower Mississippi Survey in 1968.

Pottery:

Barton Incised, *var. Portland* (fig. 185f)	4
Owens Punctated, *var. Redwood* (fig. 185b)	2
Cracker Road Incised, *var. Cracker Road* (fig. 185a)	1
Cracker Road Incised, *var. unspecified*	1
Winterville Incised, *var. Wailes* (fig. 185d)	2
Old Town Red, *var. unspecified*	7
Nodena Red and White, *var. Nodena*	1
Carson Red on Buff, *var. Olmond* (fig. 185c)	1
Fatherland Incised, *var. Fatherland* (fig. 185e)	1
Fatherland Incised, *var. unspecified*	1
Chicot Red, *var. Grand Village*	2
Leland Incised, *var. Blanchard*	2
Leland Incised, *var. Russell*	2
Barton Incised, *var. unspecified*	2
Unclassified incised (Addis)	3
French Fork Incised, *var. McNutt*	1

Lithics:

Nodena Lanceolate, *var. Russell* points	3
Unclassified projectile points	2
Oval scraper	1
Unspecialized scrapers	6
Unclassified bifaces	5

Table 75. Aboriginal artifacts collected from the surface of the Russell site in 1974.

Pottery:

Barton Incised, *var. Davion*	1
Owens Punctated, *var. Menard*	1
Winterville Incised, *var. Wailes*	1
Old Town Red, *var. unspecified*	1
Barton Incised, *var. unspecified*	3

Lithics:

Edwards Stemmed, *var. Sunflower* point	1
Unspecialized scraper	1
Utilized flake	1

Organics:

Fish bone	1

name for the last aboriginal phase of occupation in the region (Phillips 1970, pp. 14, 434). In 1961 Stephen Williams visited Mr. and Mrs. Lee V. Russell, who graciously permitted him to inventory and photograph their entire collection (fig. 184; table 73) (see Williams 1962, pp. 55–56, for a brief discussion, and Williams and Brain 1983, fig. 11.23, for a sampling of the historic artifacts). I became interested in the site in 1968 when a small collection of artifacts was donated to the LMS by Ed Dean (fig. 185; table 74). My interest coincided with the revelations at Haynes Bluff, and these, together with the Burroughs finds, seemed to indicate that there were now several possibilities for pinning down the early historic occupation of the lower Yazoo Bluffs region.

In the case of Russell, we had a good set of artifactual data but no provenience information to go with it. We knew that the Russell collection had been gathered together by Lee V. Russell, Jr., apparently in the 1940s between Ford's first and second visits (much of the collection was given to the University of Mississippi Museum in Oxford [see table 73], but a few items from the site are on deposit at the Old Capitol Museum in Jackson). The historic artifacts had been found with burials on the Russell plantation. The younger Russell died even before Williams's visit, and Mr. Russell, Sr., had

also died by the time we arrived in 1974. Mrs. Russell, however, recalled that her son had made most of his finds in the pasture north of the house and along the creek bank to the west: the burials, she indicated, had been found in the east bank of the creek south of Mississippi Route 3 (fig. 186). Robert Selby, a neighbor to the west who had helped remove the burials, confirmed this location. Unfortunately, Selby had been very young

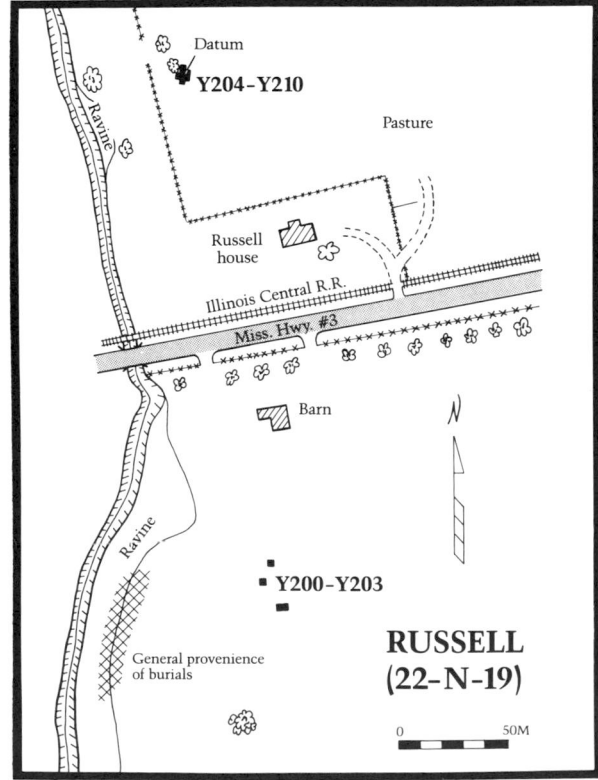

Figure 186. Map of the Russell site, giving locations of the 1974 excavations by the Lower Mississippi Survey.

Table 76. Aboriginal and European artifacts from excavation units Y200–203 at the Russell site.

ABORIGINAL		
Pottery:		
Winterville Incised, *var. Tunica*	1	
Winterville Incised, *var. Loubois*	1	
Cracker Road Incised, *var. unspecified*	1	
Mazique Incised, *var. North*	1	
Owens Punctated, *var. Manly*	1	
Winterville Incised, *var. Wailes*	3	
Old Town Red, *var. unspecified*	6	
Kinlock Simple Stamped, *var. Kinlock*	1	
Fatherland Incised, *var. unspecified*	1	
Leland Incised, *var. Russell*	1	
Leland Incised, *var. unspecified*	1	
Parkin Punctated, *var. Transylvania*	2	
Barton Incised, *var. unspecified*	4	
Winterville Incised, *var. unspecified*	5	
Unclassified incised (Yazoo)	2	
Evansville Punctated, *var. Sharkey*	1	
Harrison Bayou Incised, *var. Harrison Bayou*	1	
Mazique Incised, *var. Manchac*	1	
Unclassified incised (Addis)	1	

Coles Creek Incised, *var. Greenhouse*	1	
Coles Creek Incised, *var. Mott*	5	
French Fork Incised, *var. McNutt*	1	
Coles Creek Incised, *var. Campbellsville*	1	
Coles Creek Incised, *var. unspecified*	1	
Unclassified incised (Valley Park)	5	
Unclassified incised (Baytown)	1	
Daub:	48	
Lithics:		
Nodena Lanceolate, *var. Russell* points (fig. 187a–b)	3	
Unclassified projectile point	1	
Triangular knives (fig. 187g, j–l)	10	
Snub-nosed end scrapers (fig. 187m)	4	
Oval scrapers	4	
Unspecialized scrapers	4	
Unclassified bifaces	11	
Utilized flakes	99	
Organics:		
Unclassified bone	7	
EUROPEAN		
Gun parts/munitions:		
Lead musket ball (32 *calibre*)	1	

at the time, and he was unable to recollect any details about the graves and artifact associations.

The objectives of our investigations in 1974 were to verify the provenience of the burials and then to establish their archaeological context. Initial survey of the site was carried out in early August. Surface collections were sparse but encouraging: despite poor conditions of ground visibility, a small number of protohistoric-historic potsherds (table 75) were found along the creek bank and in the pasture. In order to offset the visibility problem, an electronic subsurface survey also was conducted at these locations. Several anomalies were discovered on the south side of the site not far from the reputed provenience of the burials. The locus also exhibited an unusually abundant scatter of lithic debitage. The possible existence of a workshop/habitation situation, as well as burials, was sufficient to warrant further testing, so four 2- × -2-m excavation units (Y200–203) were placed for maximum exposure of both the anomalies and the debitage. Seven more 2- × -2-m units (Y204–210) subsequently were excavated on the northern side of the site, at a location in the pasture that had yielded several of the more diagnostic potsherds listed in table 75. All of the excavations were carried out during the two-week period of 13–27 August.

Each of the Y200–203 excavations revealed exactly the same stratification: beneath 20 cm of well-mixed topsoil were 7 cm of dark brown midden soil, followed by subsoil at 27–28 cm below the surface. The midden layer appeared to be a primary deposit but was featureless. The cultural content (table 76) reveals the presence of at least two components: middle/late Coles Creek and protohistoric/historic. The latter component was clearly the most significant, but its character was not ascertained beyond a generalized occupation. No burials were discovered, and in every instance the electronic survey anomalies were found to be modern trash in the topsoil.

Excavation units Y204–210 were clustered between the bases of several huge old pecan trees. We reasoned that if an intact eighteenth-century ground surface and associated features were to be found anywhere, it would be under the protection of these ancient giants. But in fact, no clearly defined cultural strata whatsoever were observed: rather, humic topsoil, 10–20 cm thick, lay directly on a loess-based subsoil. Our efforts were rewarded, however, by the fact that the topsoil contained a relatively large number of artifacts that seem to be confined to a late protohistoric-historic component (table 77).

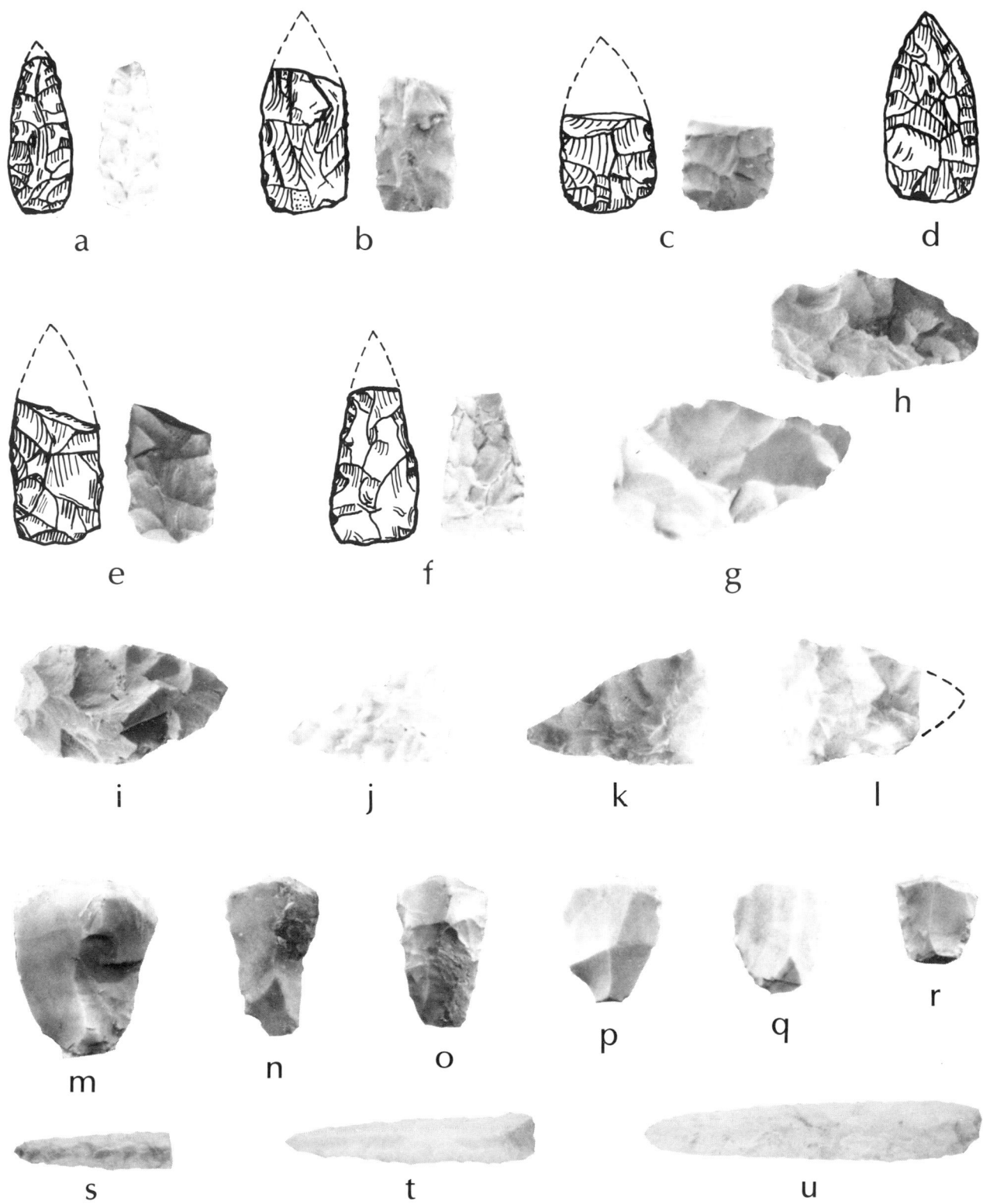

Figure 187. Oliver lithic complex from the Russell site. a–f, Nodena Lanceolate, *var. Russell* points; g–l, triangular knives; m–r, snub-nosed end scrapers; s–u, pipe drills. (1:1)

In summary, it must be acknowledged that the primary objectives of our investigations at Russell were not achieved. The exact provenience and archaeological context of the historic burials were not definitely es-

Table 77. Aboriginal artifacts from excavation units Y204–210 at the Russell site.

Pottery:

Owens Punctated, *var. Menard*	1
Winterville Incised, *var. Broutin*	4
Winterville Incised, *var. Wailes*	4
Old Town Red, *var. unspecified*	10
Fatherland Incised, *var. unspecified*	1
Chicot Red, *var. Grand Village*	1
Leland Incised, *var. Russell*	1
Barton Incised, *var. unspecified*	11
Winterville Incised, *var. unspecified*	3
Unclassified incised (Yazoo)	3
Unclassified incised (Addis)	1

Daub: 2

Lithics:

Nodena Lanceolate, *var. Russell* points (fig. 187e–f)	3
Unclassified projectile points	5
Triangular knives (fig. 187h–i)	11
Snub-nosed end scrapers (fig. 187n–r)	7
Oval scraper	1
Unspecialized scrapers	6
Unclassified bifaces	9
Unclassified unifaces	5
Utilized flakes	40

Organics·

Unclassified bone 2

---

tablished.* Nevertheless, a general site context dating to the protohistoric-historic period was verified. Moreover, the rosters of aboriginal artifact types from both the burials and the excavations were closely similar (cf. tables 73, 76, 77), and the complex of pottery and lithics was quite different from the assemblages found at other Russell phase sites. The predominance of Old Town Red and the Yazoo 7 subset, as well as the presence of such distinctive stone tools as the Nodena Lanceolate, *var. Russell* points, triangular knives, snub-nosed end scrapers, and pipe drills (fig. 187), indicate a very late

* A further dimension to this problem was introduced in August 1976, when Ian Brown and Nancy Lambert learned from Anne Mayeaux Hines that a small mound had once existed north of the highway and west of the creek. This may have been one of the mounds referred to by Calvin Brown (1926, p. 57). Mrs. Hines stated that the mound had contained historic burials, and she had in her possession an Old Town Red teapot that had been found in it by her great-great-grandfather, Arnold Russell, in 1825! The mound had been destroyed long since (at least prior to LMS visitation), and a survey of the locus by Lambert and Brown was fruitless.

protohistoric-historic introduction from the north. Although many of these traits are distributed over a fairly large area upriver (Phillips, Ford, and Griffin 1951, p. 136; Chapman and Anderson 1955; Williams 1980), the closest parallels can be found with the Menard site (17-K-1), which has been identified as a historic village of the Quapaw (Ford 1961). It may be that Russell can be identified with the Ofo, whose nearest linguistic (and cultural?) relatives were the Quapaw. The Ofo are presumed to have been late prehistoric-historic immigrants to the Yazoo (Swanton 1946, pp. 165–166), and it would seem that their ethnic distinctiveness is also reflected in the archaeology.

The Lower Yazoo was clearly a place of refuge for many different remnant groups during the late protohistoric–early historic periods (fig. 188). The diversity of ethnicities was recorded historically and confirmed linguistically and, fortunately, is apparent in the archaeological evidence. It is revealed especially in the mixed assemblage from Haynes Bluff, the principal site in the region at the time. It has been possible to identify the Tunica presence at Haynes Bluff and to isolate it at neighboring sites such as Portland and Burroughs. The artifactual evidence from these sites contrasts sharply with that from certain other sites that are presumed to have components of other ethnic groups (e.g., Russell, and sites farther up the Yazoo River). Of course, no assemblage was "pure," since these peoples must have been in constant contact with each other and also with surrounding groups outside the region. Nevertheless, sufficient archaeological differentiation exists to enable us to continue our search for the Tunica into the prehistoric past.

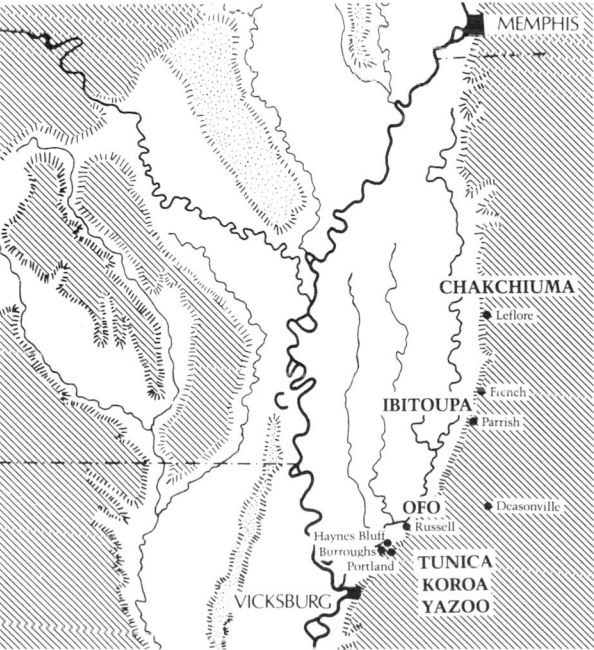

Figure 188. Late protohistoric–early historic archaeological sites and possible ethnic identifications.

Upper Sunflower

In 1541, De Soto reached the east bank of the Mississippi River within the territorial boundaries of a native province recorded in the narratives of the expedition as "Quizquiz" or "Quizqui" (Bourne 1904, vol. 1, pp. 110–111; ibid., vol. 2, pp. 25, 137). It has been theorized that Quizquiz was contained within the modern geographic subdivision identified as the upper Sunflower region and that the river was discovered and crossed in the vicinity of Friars Point, Coahoma County, Mississippi (Brain, Toth, and Rodriguez-Buckingham 1974, pp. 255–262). It also has been argued that the people of Quizquiz were ancestors of the Tunica (ibid.). These hypotheses are further substantiated below, at least to the extent that protohistoric archaeological remains from the upper Sunflower region include cultural materials antecedent to, and prototypical of, the historical Tunica (and possibly also other groups, as discussed below).

QUIZQUIZ

The use of the ethnohistoric nomenclature "Quizquiz" is intended to celebrate the dawning of history in the Mississippi Valley and to emphasize that archaeological identifications of the provinces described in the documents have not been fully secured. There is, however, a body of archaeological data available, and it is the purpose of this section to mesh these data with the historic documentation in order to establish a base for the consideration of Tunica origins.

Archaeological Investigations

As the focus of intensive aboriginal occupation, the northern Yazoo Basin has long attracted professional archaeological attention (Thomas 1894, pp. 253–258; Peabody 1904; Phillips, Ford, and Griffin 1951, pp. 253–265; Beaudoin 1951, 1952; Johnson n.d.; Tesar and Fichtner 1974; Tesar 1976; Brown 1978a; Connaway 1984). Belmont (1961) and Phillips (1970, pp. 939–942) attempted the first integration of the data, and they formulated a series of tentative culture phases which included several dated to the late prehistoric through historic periods. The most germane of these for our purposes were three phases centered on Coahoma County in the upper Sunflower region (Fisk 1944, p. 27; Phillips 1970, p. 437): the late prehistoric-protohistoric Hushpuckena and Parchman phases, and the historic Oliver phase. Three other neighboring phases recognized by Phillips were Quitman, which slightly predates our considerations, and Kent and Walls, which were primarily located in the St. Francis Basin (Phillips 1970, fig. 447).

The Hushpuckena and Oliver phases were defined by Belmont on the basis of Peabody's work at the Oliver site in 1901–1902 (Peabody 1904). Reanalyzing the large collection of artifacts and supporting data, Belmont concluded that Hushpuckena and Oliver were discrete sequential phases dating to the prehistoric and historic periods, respectively. Furthermore, he felt that although these were phases of the Mississippian cultural tradition there was sufficient difference between them in artifactual content and burial practice to hypothesize a break that presumably reflected a temporal hiatus—and possibly ethnic discontinuities as well (Belmont 1961, pp. 111, 130–132, 173). In other words, Belmont did not believe that the evidence from Oliver indicated a single sociocultural continuum and, in fact, thought that part of the regional record might even be missing.

In his masterful synthesis, Phillips (1970, p. 941) glossed over the separation between Hushpuckena and Oliver, "not because of any distrust of Belmont's reconstruction," but because the distinctions were too finely drawn to register among the criteria he used for interregional comparison. Phillips did contribute an important missing piece, however: to the north of Hushpuckena-Oliver, in northern Coahoma and southern Tunica counties, he established the Parchman phase. Although he did not express great confidence in his formulation, Phillips considered the chronological clues sufficient to confine it to the prehistoric period—well before Oliver, and perhaps even antedating the late prehistoric-protohistoric Kent and Walls phases in northern Tunica and southern De Soto counties.

Thus, when in 1973 we deliberated the problem of the route of the De Soto expedition in the Lower Mississippi Valley, there were five late prehistoric-historic phases in the northern Yazoo Basin that had to be fitted into the equation—more than the De Soto problem required. Looking over the ceramic evidence, and relying on the presence or absence of diagnostic markers rather than on percentages, we suggested a simplification of Phillips's scheme (Brain, Toth, and Rodriguez-Buckingham 1974, p. 282): Parchman was moved up in time to correlate with the late prehistoric–early protohistoric Hushpuckena phase, and together the two phases were seen as the archaeological manifestation contemporary with the province of Quizquiz. Kent and Walls were identified with the provinces of Casqui and Pacaha encountered by the entrada upstream from Quizquiz. The Oliver phase was removed from the lists by virtue of its much later dating in the early French contact period (ibid., p. 283; Brain 1975a).

This solution seemed to fit the facts better, but that it was still quite unsophisticated became apparent when the current study required that the archaeological evidence be examined for details of possible ethnic connection and succession, not simply for artifactual chronology. The emphasis in the earlier analysis was on the recognition of horizon markers, mostly pottery, that were believed to identify the mid-sixteenth century. These were found, and their presence at a number of sites in the Hushpuckena-Parchman phase of the northern Yazoo established a degree of contemporaneity satisfactory for the problem under consideration. The most reliable of these markers are fancy decorated vessels that had a broad distribution in northeastern Arkansas and northwestern Mississippi and were commonly used as mortuary furniture. As exotic trade wares, they provide excellent chronological control for correlations between sites and regions; but because they were widely traded items, it would be risky to assume consistent ethnic associations in each archaeological context. In fact, it is suspected that many, if not most, of the examples from the northern Yazoo are imports. Furthermore, most have been pothunted, so their precise archaeological contexts are largely unknown. Thus, since both proveniences (in-ground, as well as ultimate origin) are uncertain, the utility of these data for ethnic interpretations is practically nil. Except for a few cases of professional excavation noted below, the bulk of this spectacular evidence must be set aside. Instead, ethnic identifications are sought in the nonmortuary artifacts, especially the common utilitarian pottery which may be expected to exhibit more local idiosyncrasies.

The basic late prehistoric Mississippian decorative idea for the coarse utilitarian pottery relied on the techniques of punctation and incision, although other techniques (e.g., painting or brushing) were occasionally used. Incised designs were either rectilinear or curvilinear, the former being classified under the type Barton Incised and the latter under Winterville Incised. Simple punctation is typed as Parkin Punctated, and designs composed of both punctations and incisions are classified under Owens Punctated. Most late Yazoo decorated wares may be included in these types (e.g., fig. 189a–c), and they form a general background commonly shared by many groups in different regions. Varieties of these types distinguish subtle regional variations

in technique or design which are usually singled out because they are believed to have spatial or temporal significance that would be useful for culture-historical reconstruction. Sets or subsets of closely related varieties* exhibiting a similar ware and decorative intent form associations that are expected to reflect group behavior at a higher level of integration and interpretation. That is, they are designed to isolate the basic differences and unique characteristics of a pottery complex in a given spatial-temporal context, and in the present study are the building blocks for ethnic identification. The predominant utilitarian pottery in the Yazoo during the late prehistoric period is the Yazoo set, of which nine subsets have been distinguished (see fig. 41).

The primary difficulty in the development of the following discussion is that the data are not sufficiently comprehensive. Subsurface archaeology keyed to this program has not yet been accomplished, and although some earlier excavations do provide useful information, most of the evidence is derived from surface survey. The bulk of the survey data was collected during the fieldwork of Phillips, Ford, and Griffin (1951). Their collections have since been divided and high-graded, however, so that they are now valid only for establishing the presence of diagnostic artifactual markers. They have been useful in this respect, and their validity has been reinforced by the only new research carried out under the auspices of the current project (Brown 1978a). But because of the problems enumerated above, it must be understood that the following reconstruction is only hypothetical, the first tentative exposition of Tunica origins until more and better data are accumulated.

* (Sub)sets are abstractions of varieties, not of types, and the component varieties may have an existence in time and space beyond that defined for the set or subset (see Williams and Brain 1983, pp. 89–90).

Figure 189. Miscellaneous pottery from the Oliver site (16-N-6). a, Barton Incised; b, Parkin Punctated; c, Winterville Incised; d, Leland Incised; e, unclassified Caddoan Engraved. Types a–c form the core of the Yazoo set; d and e are southern and western trade wares. (1:2)

Tunica Origins

The archaeological record of the Yazoo Basin has been set forth in considerable detail by Phillips (1970) and Williams and Brain (1983). During the closing centuries of prehistory, new influences were seen to be having an impact on native cultural traditions. These influences primarily seem to have originated farther up the valley, and they were ascribed to that late prehistoric cultural phenomenon known as Mississippian. Lumping together under this general rubric the nuances observed in the archaeological patternings (Brain 1978a, n.d.; Williams and Brain 1983) does little to define or explicate the dynamics of the situation. Therefore, let it be noted at the outset that the entire Yazoo Basin had been "Mississippianized" by the middle of the fourteenth century, when the following discussion begins; use of the term will be avoided hereafter. The emphasis instead will be on the delineation and interaction of regional phases, with specific focus on the question of Tunica origins. The interpretations are based upon analysis of the stratigraphic data presented in the last section, as it was the excavation of the artifactual materials at Haynes Bluff and neighboring sites which established a datum that could be used for a direct historical approach to Tunica origins. The thread of Tunica continuity can be traced from the lower Yazoo to the upper Sunflower regions and into the prehistoric past. Because this requires the broader perspectives of both greater temporal depth and a larger geographic context, the deliberations will include the last four centuries of aboriginal occupation and the contiguous regions of the valley in Mississippi, Arkansas, and Louisiana.

HUSHPUCKENA I

In the fourteenth century, the central portion of the Lower Mississippi Valley was teeming with activity as florescent developments crowded every major physiographic province. The Foster phase followed the Anna phase in the Natchez Bluffs (Brain, Brown, and Steponaitis n.d.), and the closely related Fitzhugh phase dominated the bottoms across the river in the Tensas Basin (Hally 1972, pp. 343–477). The Lake George phase included all of the lower Yazoo Basin (Williams and Brain 1983) and by the turn of the century had entered subphase II, which was probably coeval with Lakeport (Rolingson 1971) and a late manifestation of the tentative Bellaire phase (Phillips 1970, pp. 944–945; Jeter 1982c) in the Bayou Macon-Bartholomew drainages of southeastern Arkansas. Also by A.D. 1400, early occupations of the Parkin, Nodena, Walls, and Kent phases (Phillips 1970, pp. 930–939; Morse 1982, p. 33; Morse and Morse 1983, pp. 271–301) filled the St. Francis Basin in northeastern Arkansas. Contemporary with these latter occupations and Lake George II, and intermediate to them in the upper Sunflower region of the northern Yazoo Basin, was the early Hushpuckena phase (subphase I).

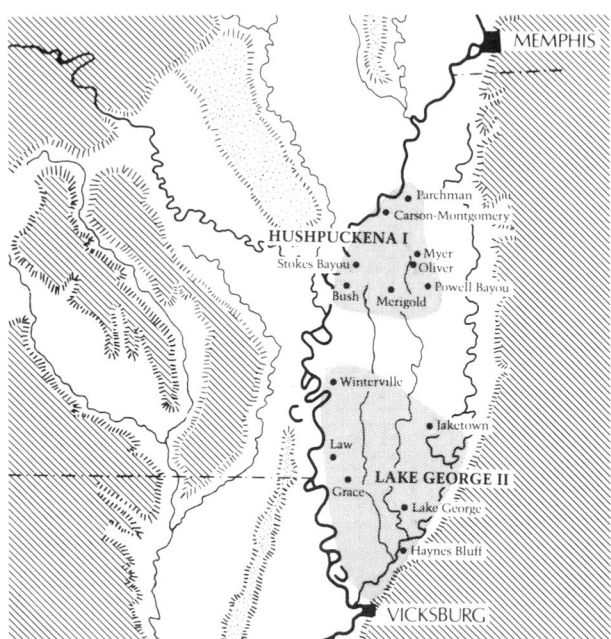

Figure 190. Cultural phases in the Yazoo Basin circa A.D. 1400.

The Hushpuckena phase was located opposite the mouth of the Arkansas River between the Mississippi and the east bank of the Sunflower River; it is almost exactly coterminous with modern Coahoma County and the northern half of Bolivar County (fig. 190). Principal components of the Hushpuckena I subphase are found at Parchman (15-N-5), Carson-Montgomery (15-N-6), Stokes Bayou (16-M-6), Oliver (16-N-6), Myer (16-N-10), Bush (17-M-11), Merigold (17-N-1), and Powell Bayou (17-0-9). Phillips (1970, p. 942) included several more sites in his Hushpuckena-Oliver phase, and even went as far south as Failing (19-N-5). According to the criteria used here, however, it is difficult to assign these components, and so a no-man's-land is shown in figure 190 north of the definite frontier of the Lake George phase.

The diagnostic pottery markers for Hushpuckena I are incorporated in the Yazoo 5 subset (fig. 191): all of the varieties seem to be native to the region and are most prominent there at this period. They do also occur as a minority element in the pottery assemblages of some Lake George II contexts to the south, but as obvious imports (Williams and Brain 1983, p. 341). Accompanying this subset are the pan-regional painted types, Avenue Polychrome and Nodena Red and White. These types were widely traded and so were not distinctive of the Yazoo; therefore, it is the Yazoo 5 subset that has diagnostic value for present purposes. This is a significant finding, for Yazoo 5 is a direct outgrowth of the indigenous Yazoo pottery tradition, and, in turn,

Figure 191. Yazoo 5 and associated painted pottery from the Carson-Montgomery (15-N-6), Stokes Bayou (16-M-6), and Myer (16-N-10) sites. a–e, Owens Punctated, *var. Owens;* f–g, Owens Punctated, var. *Poor Joe;* h–l, Owens Punctated, *var. Widow Creek;* m–o, Winterville Incised, *var. Ranch;* p–q, Nodena Red and White, *var. Nodena;* r, Avenue Polychrome, *var. Avenue.* (1:1)

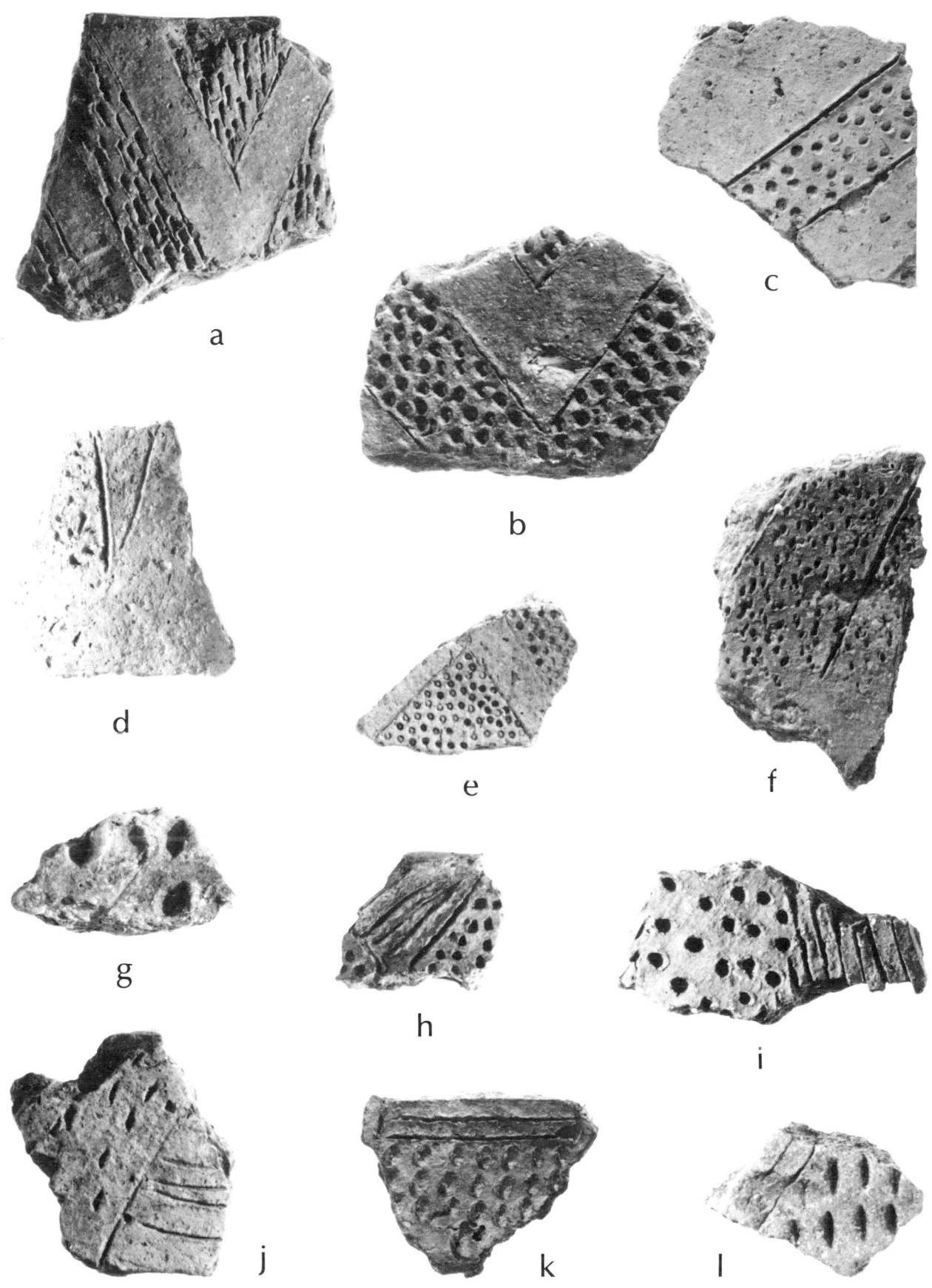

Figure 191 (continued).

it will be found to be the basis from which subsequent ceramic developments were to spring.

The Yazoo 5 subset strongly favors punctations and incisions arranged in relatively complex designs on the exterior upper body surface of coarsely shell-tempered, medium-size jars. These defining characteristics of Yazoo 5 certainly originated within the early Hushpuckena phase and serve to distinguish it. While the subset is also found in contexts of the late Lake George phase to the south, it appears there as a minor addition to the Lake George complex (Williams and Brain 1983, p. 341), and at this point there is no evidence to suggest more than a close interaction between the peoples in the upper and lower Yazoo. Whoever they were, they seem to have remained largely in place, and the movements from north to south that were to characterize the next centuries apparently had not yet begun.*

---

* It should be noted, however, that the construction of an encircling palisade and ditch at Lake George, followed by the abandonment in the fifteenth century of both this site and Winterville—the preeminent Lake George phase centers—might have been reactions to new pressures that were just beginning to be felt.

HUSHPUCKENA II

The years from 1450 to 1541 were a time of climax for the Lower Mississippi Valley—a climax in the sense that they saw the last florescence of many of the great regional developments rooted deep in prehistory. The period was concluded by the first arrival of European explorers and was followed by a dramatic time of upheaval and change, but it began on a note of continuity so strong that the regional succession is apparent only in minor differences in the archaeological record. Nevertheless, many of these differences would seem to be significant for the present study.

In the Natchez region, the Emerald phase (Brain, Brown, and Steponaitis n.d.) continued the indigenous Lower Valley cultural tradition, while across the river the Mississippian-influenced Transylvania phase (Hally 1972, pp. 478–550; Hally dated the phase after 1550 [pp. 602, 606, 625], but present evidence would seem to force it back a century) replaced Fitzhugh in the Tensas Basin of northeastern Louisiana (fig. 192). Transylvania was closely related to the Kinnaird phase in the Boeuf Basin (Kidder 1986), the early Wasp Lake phase in the lower Yazoo (Brain 1978a; Williams and Brain 1983), and the Wilmot phase in southeastern Arkansas (Wesolowski 1974; Rolingson 1976). Farther up Bayou Bartholomew, the Hog Lake "complex" (Jeter, Kelley, and Kelley 1979;

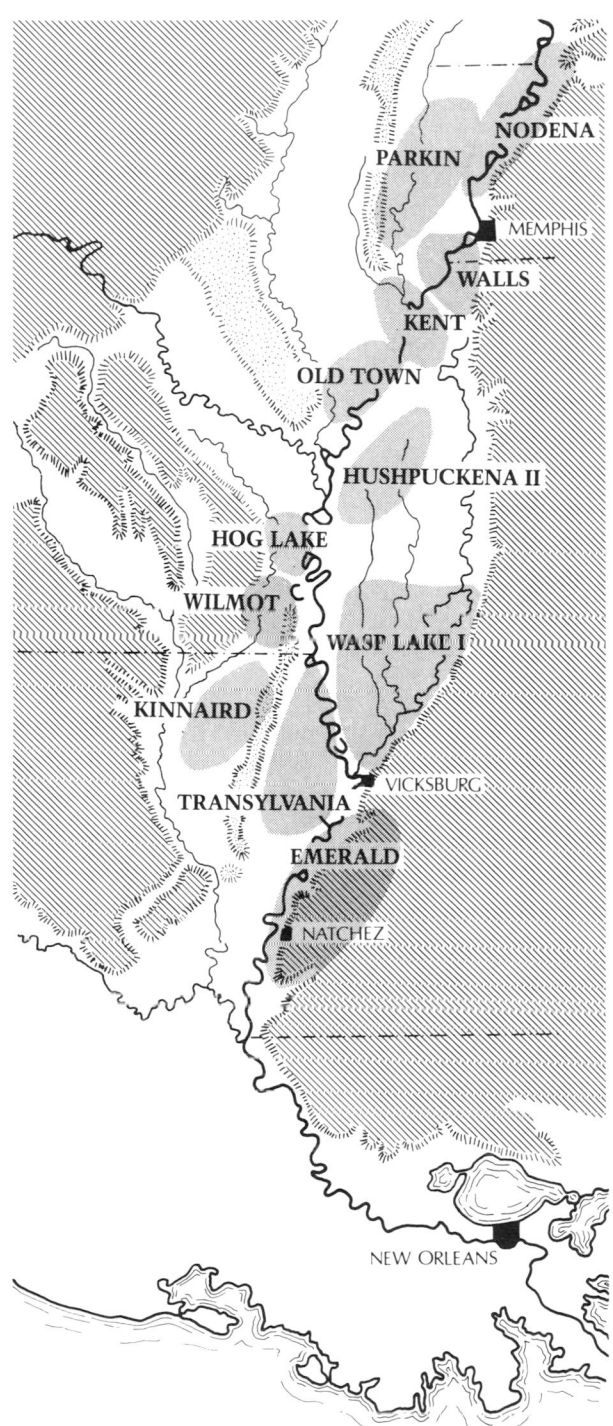

Figure 192. Cultural phases in the Lower Mississippi Valley circa A.D. 1500.

Jeter 1986) manifests close ceramic connections with Wilmot, Transylvania, and Wasp Lake (Jeter 1982a), but is even more closely related to the Hushpuckena phase directly to the north and east. In northeastern Arkansas, the classic late prehistoric phases of Old Town, Kent, Walls, Parkin, and Nodena were in full flower (Morse 1981; Morse 1982; Morse and Morse 1983; House 1984)

and also influencing Hushpuckena. Together, these are the archaeological manifestations of those vital provinces encountered by De Soto and his army at the conclusion of the period.

Hushpuckena II is characterized by the Yazoo 7 subset and the closely associated painted type, Old Town Red (fig. 193). Presumably, Barton Incised and Parkin Punctated also were present. Again, this complex falls within the general Mississippian pottery tradition, as revealed by the reliance on incised, punctated, and painted decoration. The incising and punctating of Yazoo 7 may be traced back directly to the precedent Yazoo 5, and together they represent an indigenous sequential development (which is not to say that Yazoo 7 necessarily replaced Yazoo 5 completely at this time). The emphasis on curvilinear designs and wide-line incising, however, distinguishes Yazoo 7, and in turn relates it to the Hog Lake and later Quapaw pottery complexes described below. It should be noted, however, that while there is a certain relationship, the complexity of the situation that follows cautions against easy ethnic identifications (cf. Lemley and Dickinson 1937).

The Hushpuckena II subphase occupied approximately the same territory as Hushpuckena I, although there seems to have been some readjustment of the southern boundary (fig. 194). There is also considerable evidence of a close association with the lower Arkansas and the sites of the Hog Lake complex, as noted above. The relationship with the lower Yazoo seems to have shifted as well: the northern frontier of the Wasp Lake phase withdrew to the south during subphase I, widening the gulf between the northern and southern regions. Apparently, however, the geographic distance did not diminish the impact of the Hushpuckena phase upon the lower Yazoo, and, in fact, the influence seems to have intensified during this period: Hushpuckena ideas and artifacts continued to diffuse southward and, by the sixteenth century at least, were probably carried by migrating peoples. The Russell site (22-N-19) has a relatively pure component and almost certainly represents a site unit intrusion. The same may also be true for the nearby Deasonville site (21-P-1), which displays a full roster of Yazoo 7 varieties, as well as a distinctive local variety of Nodena Red and White (Collins 1932a, pls. 3, 5–7). On the west side of the river, LMS collections from Transylvania (22-L-3) and Jordan (22-I-1) have a good showing of Yazoo 7 but contain no painted wares. Both sites also have the late varieties of Grace Brushed that are indigenous to the Ouachita-Boeuf regions and form the core of the Yazoo 6 subset in the lower Yazoo. Clearly, this part of northeastern Louisiana was in close interaction with neighboring regions. The nature of the relationships that brought influences from the north and west and transmitted some to the east has not been determined, but again the movements of peoples are suspected. Certainly that is the explanation for the southernmost extension of the Yazoo 7 subset to the Beasley site (24-L-14) (Williams 1967), where another strong component, complete with Old Town Red, also must represent a site unit intrusion from the vicinity of the Arkansas River.

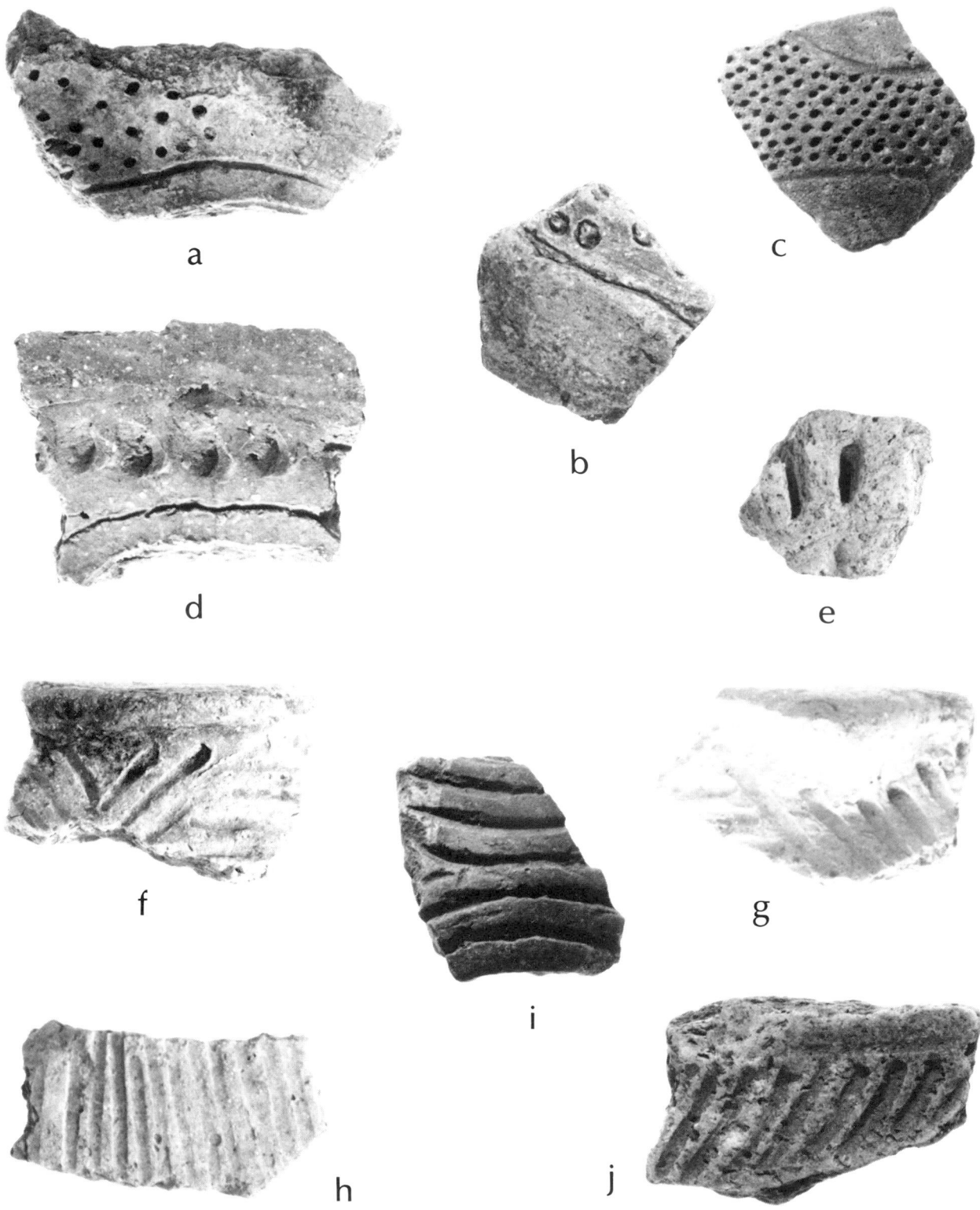

Figure 193. Yazoo 7 and associated painted pottery from the Stokes Bayou, Oliver, and Myer sites. a–c, Owens Punctated, *var. Menard*; d–e, Owens Punctated, *var. Manly*; f–j, Winterville Incised, *var. Broutin*; k–q, Winterville Incised, *var. Wailes*; r, Avenue Polychrome, *var. Avenue*; s, Old Town Red, *var. unspecified.* (1:1)

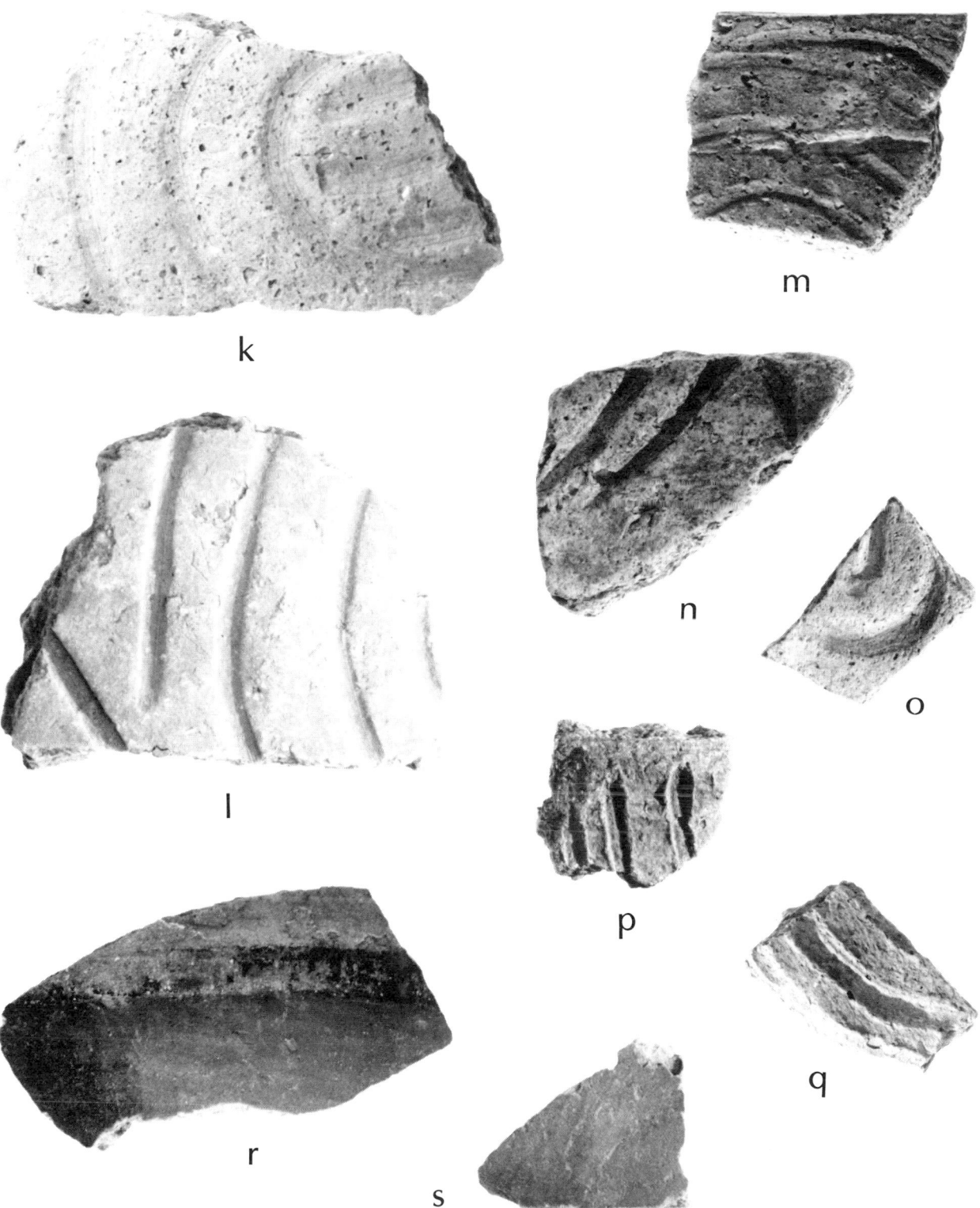

Figure 193 (continued).

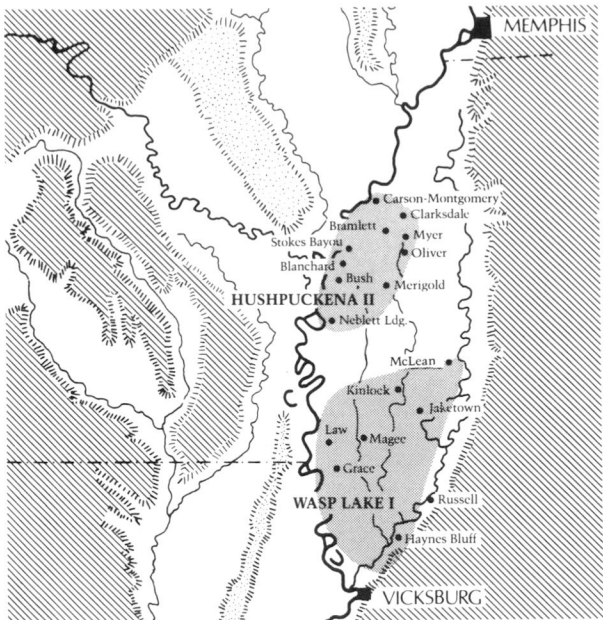

Figure 194. Cultural phases in the Yazoo Basin circa A.D. 1500.

PARCHMAN

The protohistoric period in the Lower Mississippi Valley was a time of profound change, overshadowed only by the even more dramatic events that occurred during the final, historic period.* Continuities from the Hushpuckena phase are apparent, but substantial shifts in archaeological patterns indicate that major movements of peoples were occurring, especially from 1550 to 1650 (e.g., Brain 1978a, 1978b). The changing demography is especially evident in respect to the Parchman phase and its neighbors (fig. 195). For example, the early Quapaw phase on the lower Arkansas River may represent the dissolution and displacement of the Old Town, Kent, and perhaps Walls phases (Morse and Morse 1983; Hoffman 1986), the remnant populations of which moved to the Arkansas and mixed with local peoples. To the north, the Armorel phase incorporated the descendants of the Nodena and Parkin phases, and perhaps peoples from even farther afield, as attested by many new traits, especially from the north and east (Williams 1980). Armorel phase sites also have produced evidence of the ultimate foreign influence: sixteenth-century European artifacts presumably introduced by the De Soto expedition (Williams 1980; Brain, Toth, and Rodriguez-Buckingham 1974; Brain 1975a, 1984; Klinger 1977; Morse 1981; House 1982; Hathcock 1983). Thus, the advent of the protohistoric period was marked by the

harbinger of change and by movements of peoples that were to continue through the historic period, particularly in this part of the valley.

Far to the south, however, the Emerald phase held on in the Natchez Bluffs, while the Canebrake and Jordan phases (Moore 1913, pp. 49–54; Belmont 1981; Kidder and Williams 1984; Kidder 1986, 1987) dominated northeastern Louisiana. Continuity also was strongly evident in southeastern Arkansas as Hog Lake was fol-

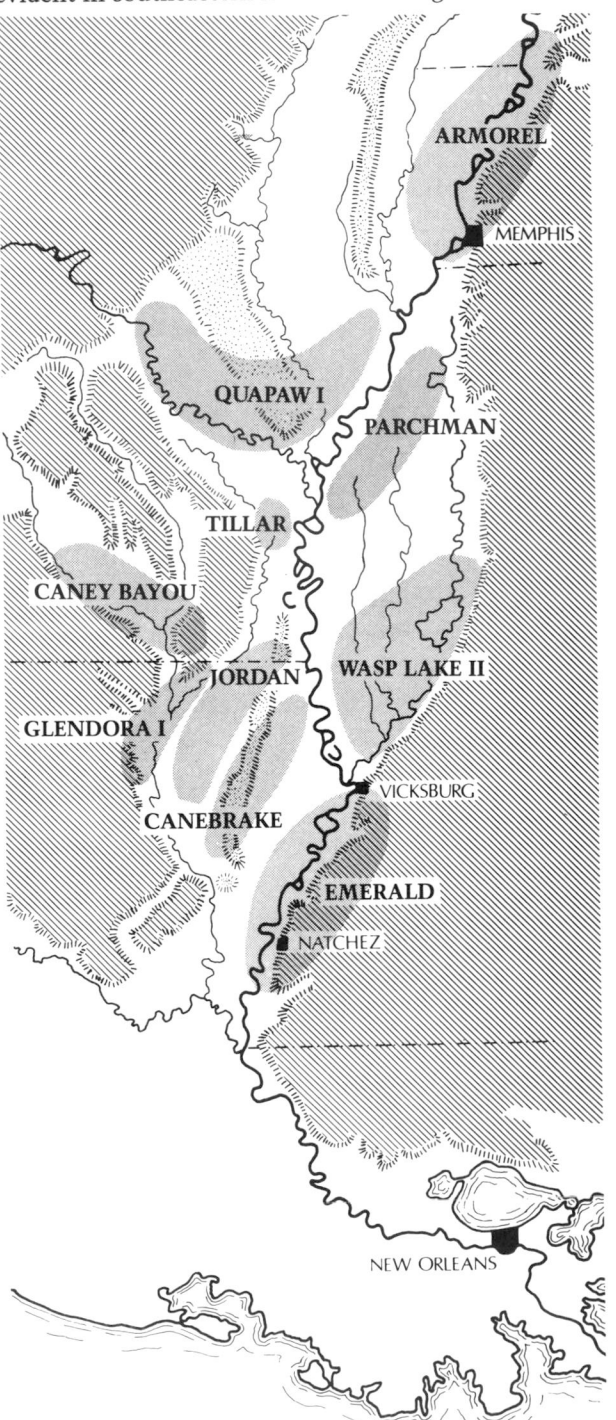

Figure 195. Cultural phases in the Lower Mississippi Valley circa A.D. 1600.

---

* The protohistoric period in the Lower Mississippi Valley may be given very precise chronological boundaries, dating from the De Soto entrada of 1541–1543 to the Marquette-Jolliet expedition of 1673. The Parchman site itself has produced a radiocarbon date of 1610 ±95 (Connaway 1985; see also Connaway 1981, pp. 49, 83, and 1984, p. 162 for more dates from other Parchman phase sites). This was a period of possible European influence, an influence that was transmitted indirectly, as no direct contacts are recorded.

lowed by the closely related Tillar complex (Jeter 1982a, p. 108; Jeter 1982b, 1986; although Jeter considers these two complexes to be roughly contemporary, it would seem more likely that they overlap since Hog Lake had a clear priority and Tillar lasted well into the seventeenth century).

In the Yazoo, the Wasp Lake phase still held sway in the southern part of the basin. Although there is considerable evidence of close interaction with the Emerald phase to the south, the Jordan phase to the west, and undefined peoples to the east, the strongest influence seems to have emanated from the Parchman phase to the north. Parchman had replaced the Hushpuckena phase in the upper Sunflower region (fig. 196; cf. Phillips 1970, fig. 447), and, like its predecessor, Parchman also had close ties with eastern Arkansas, especially as revealed in the Tillar ceramic complex.

The Parchman phase is defined ceramically by the presence of the Yazoo 8 subset and associated Winterville Incised, *var. Tunica* and Tunican Mode of punctation (fig. 197i). Together, these decorated markers form the Tunica pottery complex as it has been recognized on the lower Yazoo (see fig. 180). This ceramic identification is obviously crucial evidence for the whole question of Tunica origins. That such origins must be sought here in the Parchman phase during the protohistoric period is argued by the fact that it is only here that prototypes are found demonstrating a developmental sequence (see especially examples of the diagnostic Tunican Mode in fig. 197j–m, v–y, gg–ii). Similar decorative ideas are found in eastern Arkansas, but the actual expression is aberrant. The Tillar complex, for example, is certainly closely related to the Tunica complex, but it is inconceivable on stylistic grounds that Tillar could have been ancestral to Tunica. Tillar is most logically interpreted as a roughly contemporary, collateral development—the product of a kindred people sharing concepts of ceramic decoration. In subsequent pages, this larger communion will be referred to as "Tunican." It is assumed that Tunicans shared language and other customs but were divided into smaller political units such as the Tunica proper.

The origins of the Tunica pottery complex before its developmental phase in the upper Yazoo are uncertain, but they appear to have been outside the region since the Tunica presence is intrusive in the archaeological record here. This is not to assert that there was a major break in the sequence, but rather a definable difference in artifactual contents that are believed to have ethnic significance. Ceramically, the Tunica complex developed straight out of the local Mississippian tradition, specifically the Yazoo 5 subset which was characteristic of this part of the valley a century earlier. Thus, the Tunica could not have come from far away; in fact, they probably just moved across the river. Those decorative elements that most distinguish the Tunica complex from other Yazoo subsets have their closest parallels in the Ouachita River–Bayou Bartholomew drainages. The hypothesis to be tested is that Yazoo 8 started to develop in southeastern Arkansas out of Yazoo 5 under influence from Hog Lake or some other unknown complex. The process was completed in the Yazoo when Tunica forebears crossed the river, leaving behind those

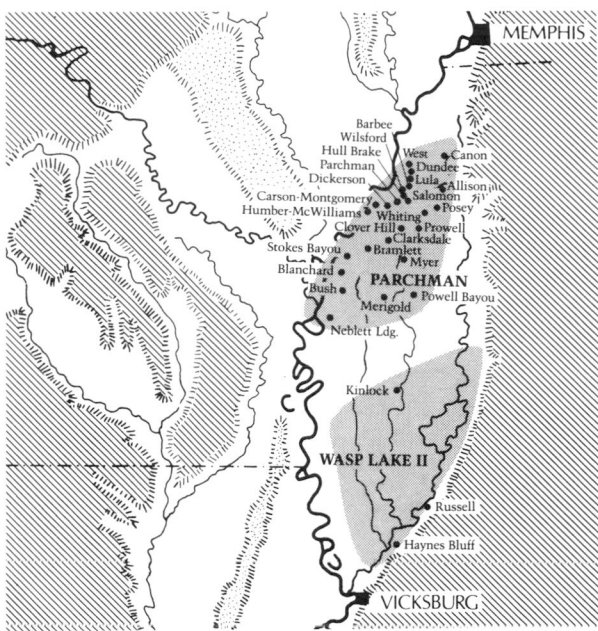

Figure 196. Cultural phases in the Yazoo Basin circa A.D. 1600.

who went on to produce the Tillar complex. Whatever the merits of the foregoing scenario, the new Tunica presence—as marked by the appearance of the Yazoo 8 subset and associated pottery—permeated the upper Sunflower locale by the advent of the De Soto entrada. The coincidence of these events requires the recognition of a new phase: Parchman.

The Parchman phase occupied approximately the same territory as the Hushpuckena phase, although the center of gravity shifted somewhat to the north (cf. figs. 194, 196). As already noted, Oliver (16-N-6) seems to have been abandoned at about this time, but strong components of the Tunica complex are found around Clarksdale. The Clarksdale site (16-N-26) itself has been hypothetically identified as the first town of Quizquiz encountered by De Soto (Brain, Toth, and Rodriguez-Buckingham 1974), but since the site has been obliterated by the modern town this identification must remain conjectural. Nevertheless, that first town must have been in the immediate vicinity, and it is most logical that the town on the bank of the river near which the army camped would have been the Carson-Montgomery site (15-N-6) (ibid.). This was the core area of the Parchman phase, and Carson-Montgomery is the best remaining type site (Connaway 1984, pp. 175–179). The nearby Humber-McWilliams site (Tesar 1976; Tesar and Fichtner 1974) may also be a component.

Analysis during the fall of 1978 of more than 1,500 potsherds in the Pellegrin (owners of the Carson-Montgomery site) and Jaeger collections revealed an assemblage of broad late prehistoric dimensions. In addition to Tunican diagnostics and other more general late Mississippian markers, there were Leland Incised and Fatherland Incised from the south, Chickachae Combed from the east (see also Penman 1983, p. 289), and four sherds of (Etowah?) Complicated Stamped from even farther to the east. Clearly, Carson-Montgomery had far-flung

Figure 197. Yazoo 8 and associated pottery from the Carson-Montgomery, Stokes Bayou, and Myer sites. a, n–o, z–aa, Barton Incised, *var. Davion*; b–c, p–s, bb, Barton Incised, *var. Portland* (q–r, prototypical; s, reverse design); d–e, t, cc, Owens Punctated, *var. Redwood*; f–i, u, dd–ff, Winterville Incised, *var. Tunica* (i, with Tunican Mode); j–m, v–y, gg–ii, Tunican Mode on incised and plain types (l–m, w–x, and gg–hh are prototypical, and w exhibits *Redwood*-like punctations) (a–m, Carson-Montgomery; n–y, Stokes Bayou; z–ii, Myer). (1:1)

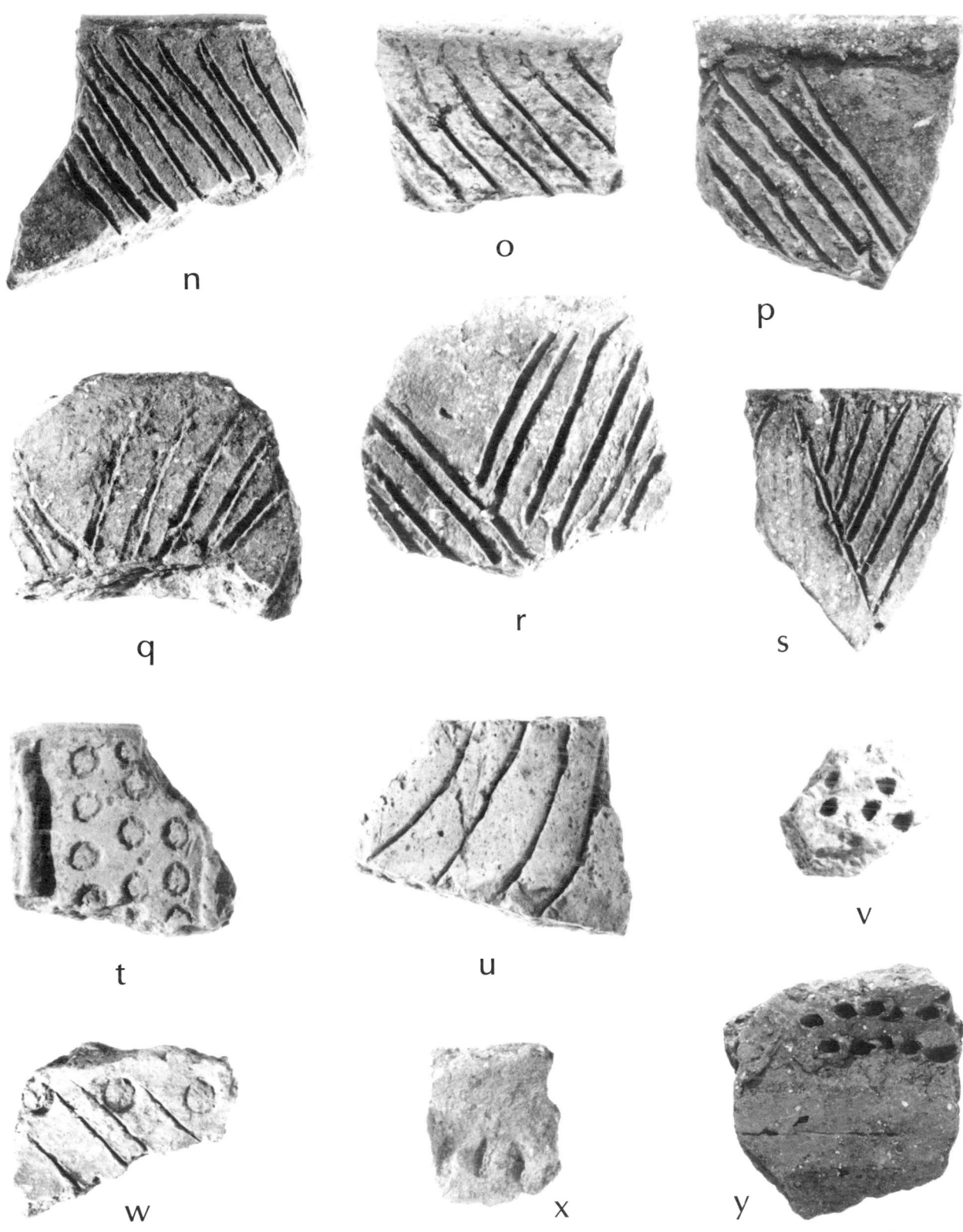

Figure 197 (continued).

z

cc

aa

bb

dd

ee

ff

gg

hh

ii

Figure 197 (continued).

connections.* That this locale was a strategic cross-roads is attested by the early historic record of important land and water communication routes in the immediate vicinity (e.g., Myer 1928, pl. 15; Faye 1942, pp. 924–925). This geographic significance and the supporting evidence for long-distance contact coincide well with our perception of Tunica dynamics. In other words, on locational grounds alone this particular region would seem to be an especially appropriate one to search for Tunica origins. It is gratifying that, as discussed above, the artifactual diagnostics would seem to confirm this expectation.

In summary, our penetration into the prehistoric past of the Yazoo Basin has been successfully consummated: the protohistoric morass has been bridged, and Tunica origins founded in sixteenth-century Quizquiz. It is no coincidence that this province lay just south of the modern town of Tunica, Mississippi. The ancient Tunica were not, however, to remain long in this location, and by the end of the phase they had moved (probably via the Sunflower River) to the lower Yazoo.

OLIVER

The changes foreshadowed during the protohistoric period in the valley reached a dramatic conclusion during the fully historic period. This period began with the first tentative exploration by Marquette and Jolliet in 1673, which was soon followed by the La Salle expeditions which firmly established a continuing French presence in Louisiana. What these explorers found was a far remove from the vibrant province of Quizquiz and its neighbors. Along the river lived only the Quapaw, around the Arkansas-Mississippi confluence, the Tunica and other remnant groups on the lower Yazoo, and below them the Taensa and Natchez (fig. 198). It is the Quapaw that concern us here, since they were the only known tribal unit in the vicinity of the upper Sunflower during this period.

When Belmont (1961) defined the Oliver phase, he naturally speculated on the ethnicity of the peoples responsible for it. While it was known that some Quapaw lived on the east side of the Mississippi (Phillips 1970, p. 944; see Phillips, Ford, and Griffin 1951, pp. 392–421 for a review of documentary source materials for the Quapaw and a discussion of settlement patterns), Belmont shied away from placing them at his type site. As mentioned above, the Oliver site (16-N-6) seems to have been reoccupied at this time, and the distinguishing artifactual characteristics would certainly seem to indicate at least "a close relationship with the Quapaw" (Belmont 1961, p. 171). The ceramic assemblage includes Wallace Incised, Old Town Red, and other diagnostics of the Quapaw complex (Ford 1961; Phillips 1970, p. 943; Hoffman 1975–1977, p. 34; Hoffman 1986; House 1983). These Oliver-Quapaw ceramics are very similar to the Yazoo 7 subset and associated pottery, and are probably derived from them.

* A condition that is perhaps rooted in the Cahokia horizon, for there is also an early Mississippian assemblage that includes Cahokia Cord Marked and Kimmswick Fabric Impressed, and the nearby Craig site (15-N-11) also has Cahokia Cord Marked, Powell Plain, and Ramey Incised.

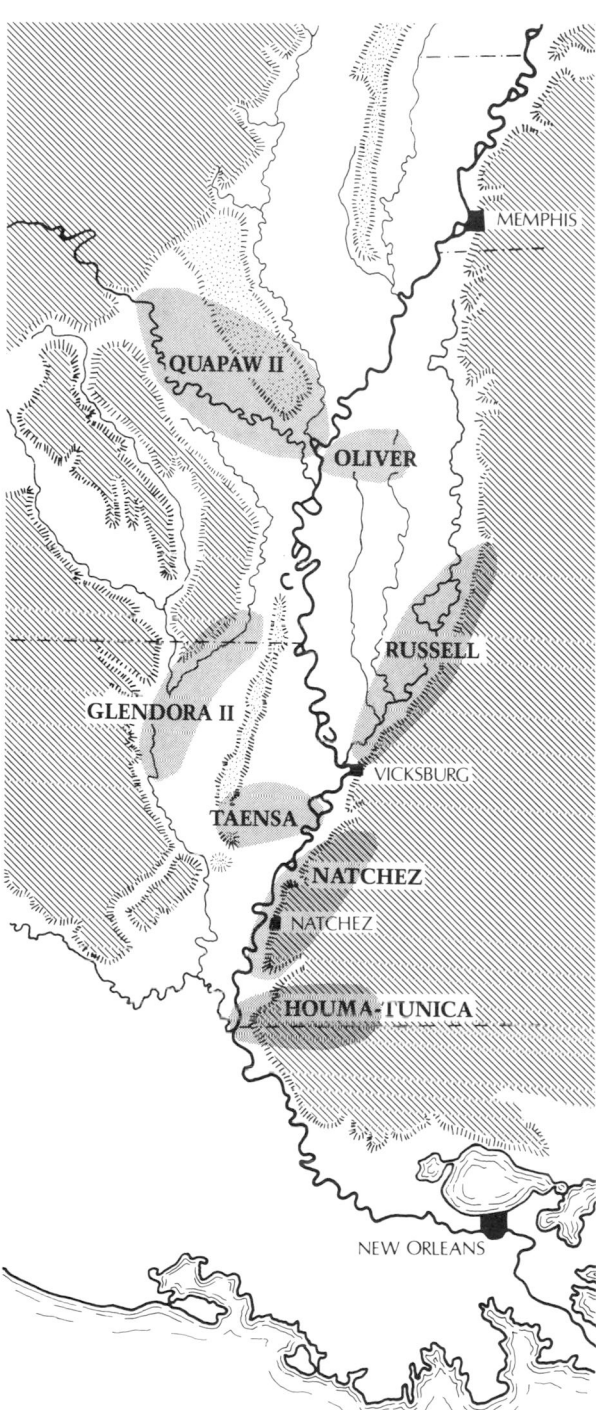

Figure 198. Cultural phases in the Lower Mississippi Valley circa A.D. 1700.

Quite unlike the ceramic continuity, however, is another characteristic of the Quapaw and Oliver phases: the sudden appearance in the archaeological record of the Oliver lithic complex, consisting of Nodena Lanceolate points, triangular knives, pipe drills, and snub-nosed end scrapers (fig. 199; app. B). This complex appears to be a horizon marker for a larger part of the mid-South during the late protohistoric and historic periods.

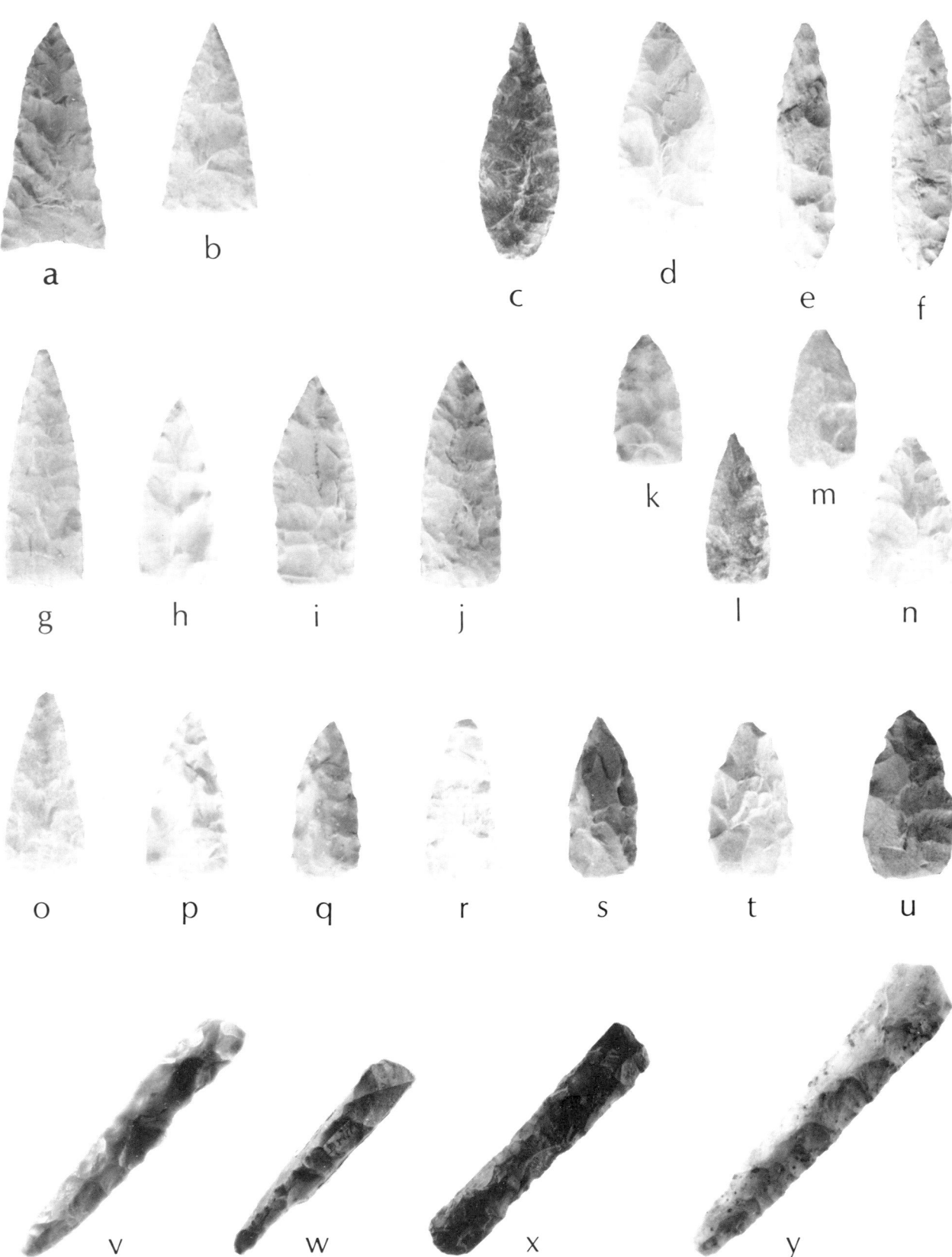

Figure 199. Chipped stone artifacts from the Oliver site. a–b, Mississippi Triangular, *var. Madison* points; c–f, Nodena Lanceolate, *var. Nodena* points; g–j, Nodena Lanceolate, *var. unspecified* points (intermediate between *vars. Nodena* and *Russell*); k–u, Nodena Lanceolate, *var. Russell* points; v–y, pipe drills; z–ii, triangular knives; jj–rr, snub-nosed end scrapers. (see Peabody 1904, pls. 8–9 for additional illustrations) (Peabody Museum of Archaeology and Ethnology, Harvard University, Charles Peabody Collection) (1:1)

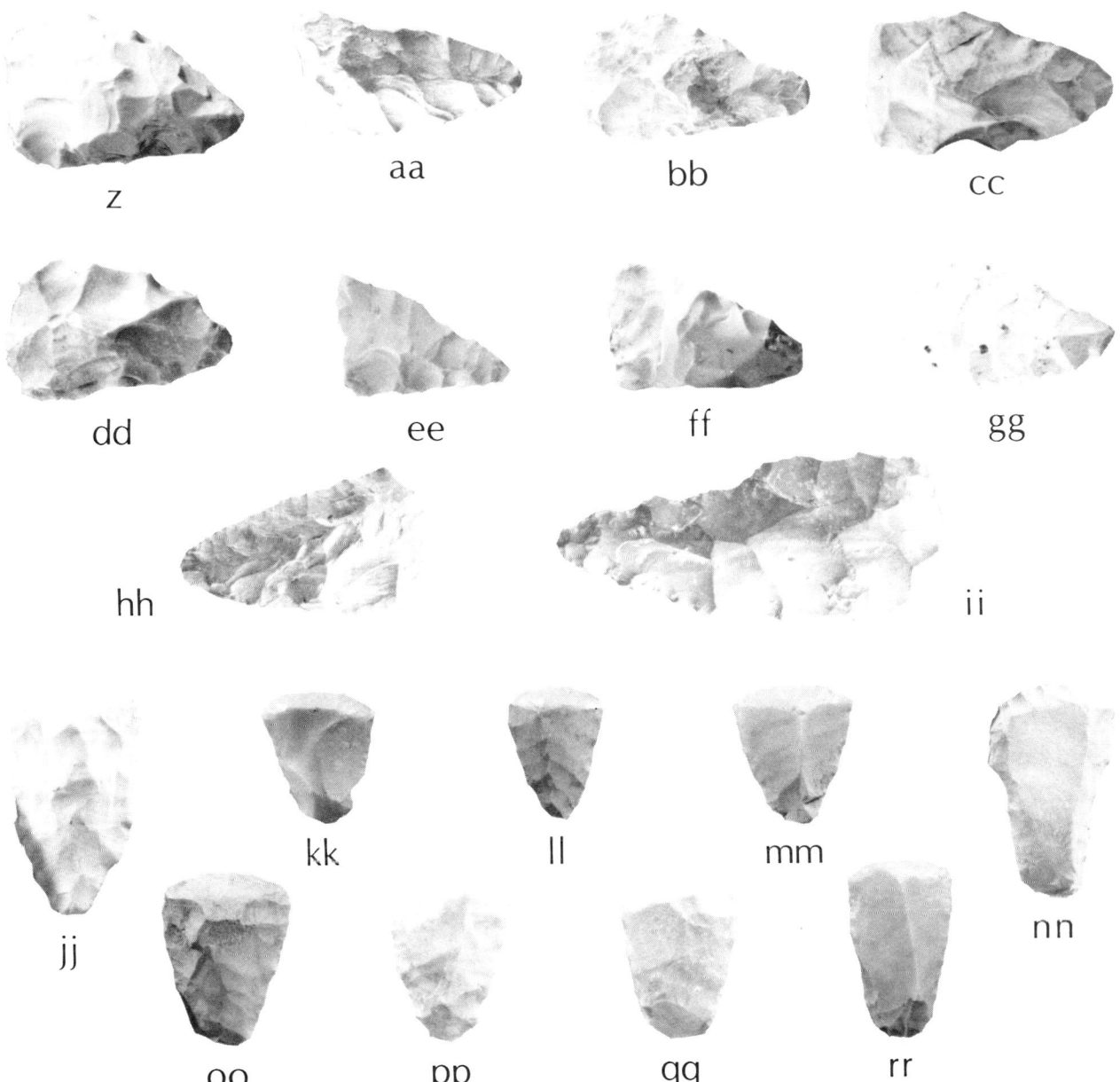

Figure 199 (continued).

As plotted in figure 200, the northern Yazoo is on the southern frontier of its distribution (its occurrences at One Cypress Point [Hemmings 1982, pp. 178–182], Russell, and Beasley being detached intrusions into the linguistically related Ofo and closely allied Taensa). In addition to Oliver (Belmont 1961, pp. 156–161), essentially the same complex has been found at Quapaw phase sites on the lower Arkansas River (Ford 1961, p. 157), at Armorel phase sites in the St. Francis Basin (Chapman and Anderson 1955, pp. 15–20, figs. 2–3; Davis 1966, pp. 27–29; Perino 1966, pp. 33–37; Morse 1973, fig. 9; Williams 1980; Morse 1981, fig. 9), and at Caborn-Welborn phase sites on the lower Ohio River (Green and Munson 1978, pp. 302–303). A closely similar complex is found at late protohistoric-historic Oneota sites farther to the west and north (Berry and Chapman 1942; Chapman 1959, figs. 7–9, 35; Wedel 1959, figs. 4, 7, 8; Henning 1970, p. 4). This distribution seems to conform remarkably closely to the area occupied by Siouan tribes that spoke dialects of the Dhegiha language (fig. 200). Although it is quite risky to claim too strong a connection between linguistic evidence and archaeological material cultures, the coincidence in this case is too close to be ignored. It should be noted, however, that an even more convincing correlation is with the sudden European stimulation of the deer skin trade at this time: the Oliver lithic complex would have been most appropriate for the procurement and processing of skins, and it is known that the earliest (seventeenth-century) trade route from Charleston terminated at the Mississippi in the northern Yazoo-Memphis area (see fig. 6). These correlations are not mutually exclusive.

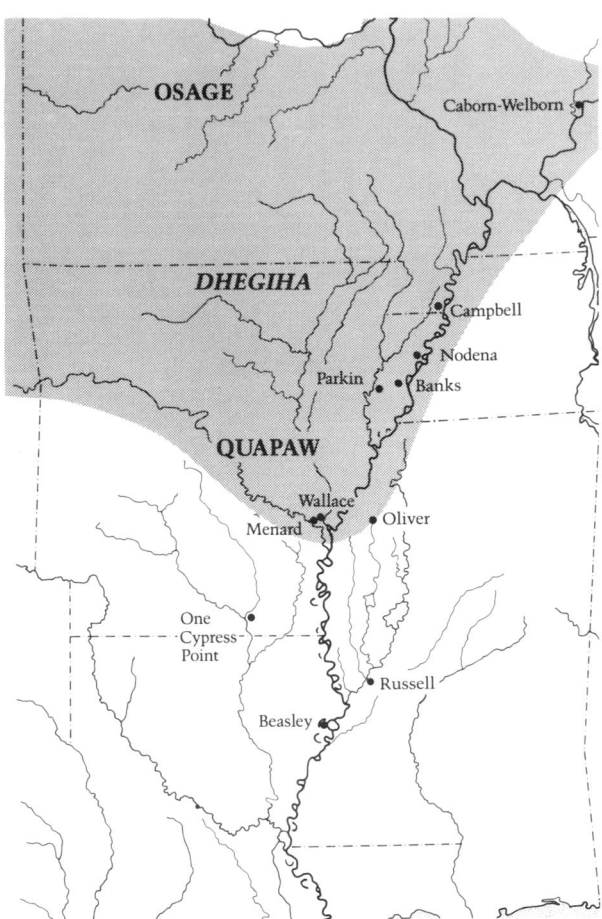

Figure 200. Distribution of the Oliver lithic complex and the territory occupied by Dhegiha-speaking peoples in the Lower Mississippi Valley.

The Oliver lithic complex was not part of the Tunican tool inventory, and the Tunica proper were not very active in the deer skin trade.

Thus, to return to the question of who the people of the Oliver phase might have been, a seeming paradox must be resolved. These were people who shared a widely distributed lithic technology but who participated in only a very local ceramic tradition. The latter had deep roots in the region, while the lithic complex just as clearly was intrusive. Were these new people or old? Perhaps they were both: one of those hybrid groups that became so typical of the period. The Quapaw were just such a group, and it has been demonstrated that they had essentially the same mixed pedigree in the archaeological manifestation of artifactual remains. Therefore, it is reasonable to argue that the Oliver people were indeed Quapaw. But whoever they were, the important point is that they were distinctively non-Tunican. Intruders into the region, they were strong enough to force the Tunica out by the end of the Parchman phase (Baird 1980, pp. 6–8; Bizzell 1981, p. 72; Dickinson 1984, pp. 201–202). They apparently were not sufficiently viable, however, to survive more than a decade into the eighteenth century, by which time the Oliver site and its vicinity were abandoned.

Tunica Neighbors

Based on the above interpretations, we conclude this section with a roster of ethnic identities, movements, and archaeological correlations that helps define the Tunica more clearly during the protohistoric and early historic periods. The following brief discussions of recorded Lower Mississippi Valley tribal groups are arranged according to language families on the assumption that linguistic differences are a basic (although not infallible) correlate to ethnic differentiation. Many of the groups discussed here shared features of cultural accoutrements and behavior patterns—at least, general similarities were often noted in contemporary French accounts. That these similarities should also extend to the remains recovered archaeologically is to be expected. Nevertheless, there are distinctions in the archaeological data that may be supposed to have ethnic significance, and on the basis of this supposition some correlations may be offered.

NATCHEZAN

Natchez. The Natchez are of considerable interest, since they are the only major tribe in the Lower Valley that remained in situ from the sixteenth century until they were finally dispersed by the French in 1730–1731 (Brain 1978a, 1982). Their ancestors are certainly to be identified with the great province of Quigualtam (fig. 201) described in the De Soto narratives and located in the vicinity of modern Natchez, Mississippi (ibid., 1984, 1985). The Natchez are easily recognized from their distinctive ceramic complex, which features the St. Catherine 1 subset and Mazique Incised, *var. North* (Quimby 1942b, 1953; Neitzel 1965, 1983; Brown 1983, 1984, 1985; Brain, Brown, and Steponaitis n.d.).

Taensa. These linguistic relatives of the Natchez probably lived on the banks of Lake St. Joseph in Tensas Parish, Louisiana (fig. 203). The Beasley site has been tentatively identified as the location of a Taensa village (Williams 1967). As might be expected, considering the site's intermediate geographic position, aboriginal pottery from Beasley displays modes from both the Natchezan and Mississippian traditions (St. Catherine subsets 1 and 2, Cracker Road, *var. Cracker Road,* and various unspecified Mississippi Plain and decorated wares). The Oliver lithic complex is also well represented at the site and, as the southernmost known provenience of the complex, may reflect the close alliance of the Taensa with the Quapaw (Margry 1879, vol. 1, pp. 556, 568, 599–600; ibid., vol. 2, p. 209).

It should be emphasized, however, that the Taensa probably had deep roots in this part of the valley and were not recent intruders like the Quapaw. The reasonable argument has been advanced that their ancestors were in place at least as early as De Soto: "Conchayon," the name of a Taensa town recorded by Iberville in 1700, is similar phonetically to "Guachoya," where De Soto died (Swanton 1911, p. 258; Gibson 1968, p. 212; Gibson 1977, p. 37). Furthermore, the 1682 relation of Nicolas de la Salle describes the presence in the cabin of the Taensa chief of *"une vieille espée à l'Espagnole et trois vieux fusils"* (Margry 1879, vol. 1, p. 566). Although this evidence is only circumstantial, it is supported by the available archaeological and geographical data (Brain 1985).

Avoyel. Very little is known about this Red River tribe. They probably were related to the Natchez and Taensa, but unlike them they had close associations with the Tunica. The Avoyel and Tunica were trading partners and military allies during the eighteenth century, and the two tribes finally merged after the Tunica had settled in Marksville. It may be expected that in characteristics of material culture, the Avoyel were similar to the Natchez (McWilliams 1953, p. 147). Their name, however, suggests a distinction that should be looked for archaeologically: "Nation of Stones" or "Flint People" is an appellation that stands out in the rockless Mississippi Valley. More specifically, the Tunica referred to them as "Flint-arrow-point People" (Swanton 1911, pp. 24, 274), an even more outstanding designation among the native Lower Valley tribes, who generally did not put stone points on their arrows during this period. Thus it may be that the Avoyel, like their relatives the Taensa, had the Oliver lithic complex—or at least were influenced by it.

SIOUAN
Quapaw. The Quapaw were found by the French near the confluence of the Arkansas and Mississippi rivers. They were one of the more important late Mississippian groups in the Lower Mississippi Valley, and because their origins are somewhat obscure they require extended discussion.

According to their own legends, the traditional home of the Quapaw was on the Ohio River in the vicinity of the mouth of the Wabash River (Nuttal 1821, p. 82; Shea 1861, p. 120; Hodge 1910, pp. 333–334; Dixon 1913, p. 564; Swanton 1946, p. 176; Baird 1980, p. 5; Bizzell 1981, p. 72; Hathcock 1983, pp. 15–18). This tradition agrees well with the linguistic evidence and with the distribution of the Oliver lithic complex (fig. 200). A definite cultural link was established between the lower Ohio and lower Arkansas rivers during the very late protohistoric period. But did this connection involve the movement of peoples from the Ohio to the Arkansas? Very conceivably. Although the stone tools could have been diffused at a more general level of interaction, their presence in the same distinctive complex in both regions indicates an intimacy in a basic technological pattern—an intimacy also expressed linguistically. Recent work at Quapaw sites along the lower Arkansas, however, has demonstrated the same kind of ceramic continuity that is found east of the Mississippi, prompting some scholars to question the traditional view of Quapaw origins (Phillips, Ford, and Griffin 1951, p. 420; Phillips 1970, pp. 943–944; Hoffman 1975–1977, pp. 32–35; Hoffman 1985, 1986; House 1983).

It has been argued that a conceptual distinction must be made between the archaeological Quapaw phase—defined by the painted varieties of the Bell set and such utilitarian types as Wallace Incised, as well as the Oliver lithic complex—and the historic Quapaw tribe because of the problems in correlation (House and McKelway

1982; Hoffman 1985, 1986). While such caution is warranted, it is contrary to the identification attempted in these pages. The relationship is probably similar to that between the historic Tunica and their protohistoric ancestors.

The nagging problem of "Pacaha" is crucial to the whole question. Pacaha, also called "Capaha," was one of the native provinces identified by the De Soto expedition on the west bank of the Mississippi River. Because of the phonetic similarity, it has long been suggested that the Pacaha or Capaha were ancestral Quapaw (Hodge 1910, p. 333; Swanton 1911, p. 186; Brain, Toth, and Rodriguez-Buckingham 1974, pp. 276–277; but cf. Swanton 1939, pp. 51–52; Swanton 1946, pp. 53, 176; Phillips, Ford, and Griffin 1951, p. 420). In fact, one of the earliest French recorders, La Metairie, specifically refers to the "Kapaha" on the Arkansas (French 1875, p. 21). Their name is usually shortened to "Kappa" or "Cappa" by other French writers (Hodge 1910, p. 336), by whom they are universally identified as the Quapaw (e.g., French 1875, p. 21; Swanton 1942, p. 9). We now know that sixteenth-century Pacaha must have been located in the St. Francis Basin of northeastern Arkansas (Brain, Toth, and Rodriguez-Buckingham 1974, pp. 271–276; Morse and Morse 1983, p. 311; Brain 1984), and probably in the vicinity where the Armorel phase developed (see figs. 195, 201). One of the characteristics of the Armorel phase is the Oliver lithic complex (Williams 1980), and one of the intriguing observations about Pacaha was that it was obviously intrusive into the region and was actively encroaching upon the territory of its southern neighbor (Varner and Varner 1951, p. 435). A reasonable conclusion would be that Pacaha represented some part of the ancestral Quapaw in the process of moving to the lower Arkansas (figs. 201–203). Whether or not the origin of this movement can be traced ultimately to the Ohio* is unimportant for this study, but it seems likely that the immediate genesis was a result of the collapse of the great late prehistoric phases of northeastern Arkansas (Griffin 1960, p. 852; Ford 1961, p. 182; Morse and Morse 1983, pp. 300–301, 320). Whoever these people were, they preserved their language and stone technology but proved adaptable in accepting new ceramic arts (cf. Penman 1983).

A solution to the Quapaw problem might be found in Belmont's (1961, p. 132) suggestion that a successful invasion of Dhegiha speakers took the form of conquest and incorporation, in the course of which most of the indigenous warriors were killed or dispersed and the women and children adopted. This solution conveniently explains the continuity in female crafts at the same time that there was a radical change in male manufactures in the local archaeological record. The conqueror's language prevailed, and the resulting mélange

---

* Another tantalizing clue is found in the observation of Phillips, Ford, and Griffin (1951, p. 419) that the bastioned palisade protecting the first village of Pacaha (Bourne 1904, vol. 1, p. 123; ibid., vol. 2, pp. 28, 139; Varner and Varner 1951, p. 436) is most reminiscent of the type found at the great Angel site on the Ohio River just above the Wabash (Black 1967, fig. 546; Green and Munson 1978, p. 311).

Figure 201. Approximate locations of the native provinces identified in the De Soto narratives (cf. figs. 192, 195).

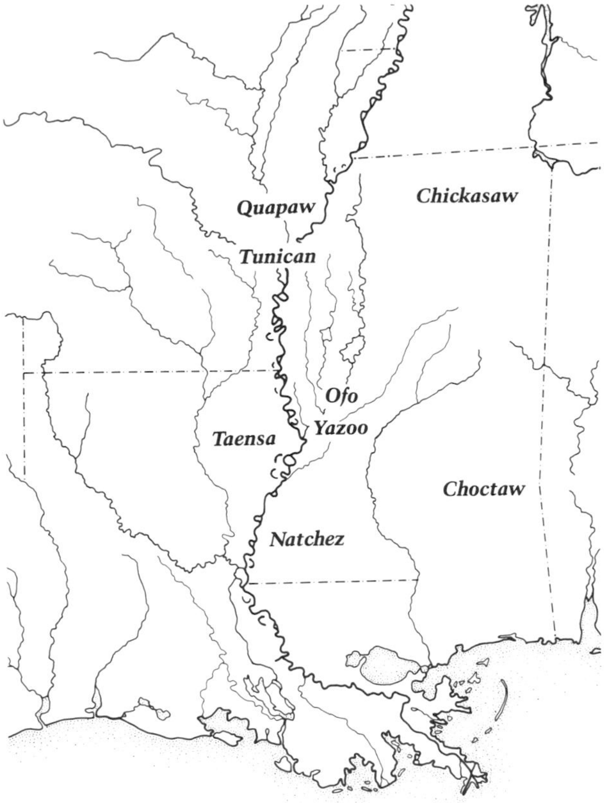

Figure 202. Approximate locations of ancestral tribes circa A.D. 1600–1650.

Figure 204. Locations of historic tribes circa A.D. 1750.

Figure 205. Locations of historic tribes circa A.D. 1800.

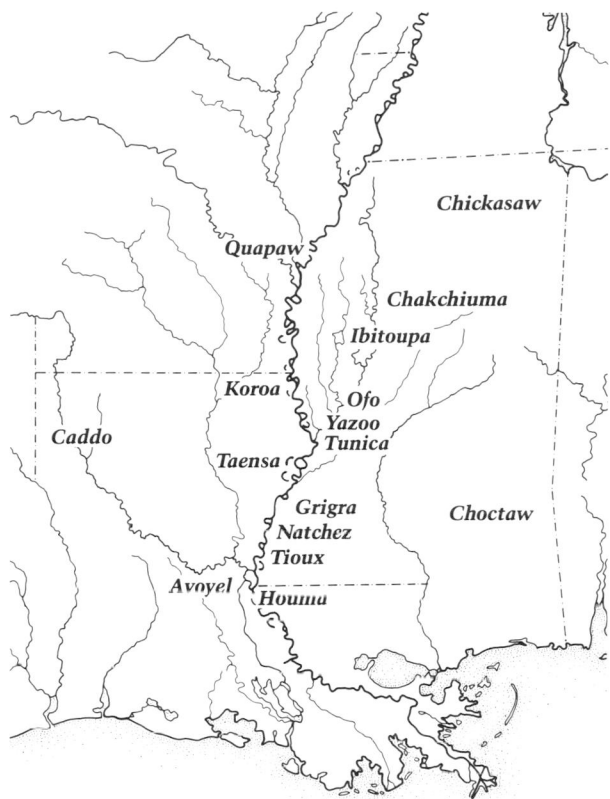

Figure 203. Locations of historic tribes circa A.D. 1700.

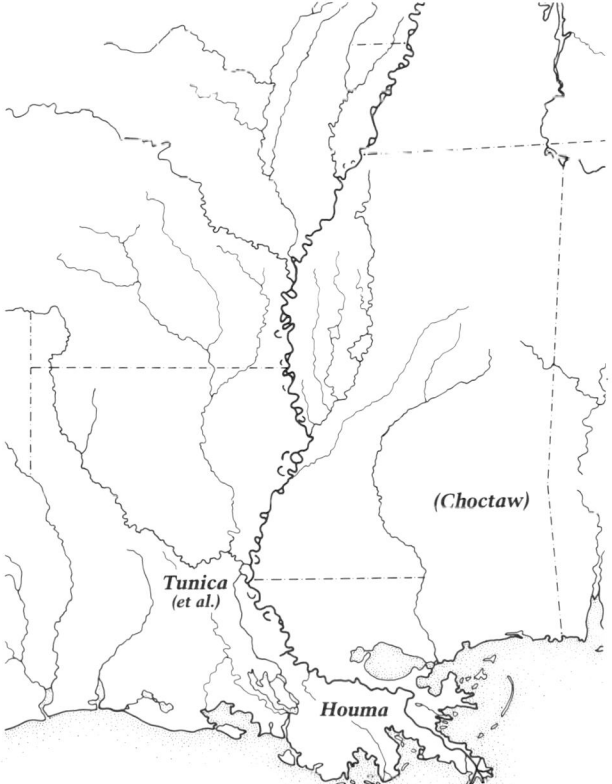

Figure 206. Locations of remnant tribal groups circa A.D. 1850.

of peoples became the historic Quapaw. Although we will probably never know the accuracy of this model, it is supported by the observations that Dhegiha speakers in general "appear to have adapted easily to the cultural practices of those peoples indigenous to the area in which they settled" (Henning 1970, p. 148) and that the Quapaw in particular mixed easily with other groups (e.g., Charlevoix 1744, vol. 3, p. 410; Le Page du Pratz 1758, vol. 2, pp. 243–244; Bossu 1777, p. 144; Nuttal 1821, p. 84; Dickinson and Dellinger 1940, p. 95; Phillips 1970, p. 943; Dickinson 1982, p. 154; Dickinson 1984, p. 203; Hoffman 1985, 1986; Jeter 1986).

Ofo. The Ofo (also "Offagoula," "Ounspik," "Ushpie," and variations of these) were first recorded by the French on the Yazoo River (fig. 203). Siouan speakers, they represented another remnant group in the mixed ethnic population of that refuge. If the Ofo are correctly identified with the archaeological remains found at the Russell site, then it seems clear that Griffin's (1960, p. 852) hypothesis that they might have migrated from northwestern Mississippi near the mouth of the Arkansas would seem to have considerable validity, as has been argued above. Further strengthening the connection is Swanton's (1946, pp. 165–166) belief that the Mosopolea were related to the Ofo: found in the same general Arkansas-Mississippi area at the end of the seventeenth century, the Mosopolea might have been a splinter group left behind when the Ofo moved south. Swanton also notes that the Mosopolea apparently had roots in or near southern Ohio, which correlates well with the possible origins of those other famous Siouan speakers, the Quapaw. Linguistically, however, the Ofo were more closely related to the eastern Siouan dialects than to the Dhegiha of the Quapaw (Dorsey and Swanton 1912). Voegelin (1941) believes that the Ofo, together with the Biloxi and Tutelo, represent a separate dispersal from the Ohio Valley.

The Ofo are probably to be recognized in the Yazoo 7 subset, and perhaps also in Holly Bluff 3. The decorative modes of Yazoo 7 and the associated Old Town Red slipped ware were clearly derived from upriver, where they were common in eastern Arkansas and northwestern Mississippi in the protohistoric and early historic periods. Holly Bluff 3 is an elaboration of the local fine ware tradition that, based on the restricted geographic distribution, may have been developed by the Ofo after their arrival in the lower Yazoo region. Most distinctively of all, the Ofo seem to have brought with them the Oliver lithic complex, a tool kit generally not found in the southern half of the Lower Valley.

Biloxi. The Biloxi are mentioned here only because of their intimate association with the Tunica. By the time this association had occurred, however, native artifactual diagnostics had disappeared from the archaeological record. It might be difficult to identify the Biloxi archaeologically even for the eighteenth century since this tribe lived in so many places with so many different peoples. It would be a marvel if they could be distinguished, although they should be identifiable along the Gulf Coast at initial French contact.

CADDOAN

No distinct tribes are listed here because of the difficulty in establishing Caddoan ethnicities and archaeological correlates. The Tunica were known to have had frequent contacts with tribes on the Ouachita and Red rivers, and eighteenth-century Tunica pottery assemblages always included a minority representation of types from those regions. Most popular were engraved wares, especially the type Natchitoches Engraved (Brain 1979, p. 245).

MUSKHOGEAN

Chickasaw. Although not a Lower Mississippi Valley tribe, this long-standing foe of the Tunica cannot be ignored. Archaeologically, the Chickasaw are distinguished by pottery tempered with fossilized shell and/or sand, and rare decoration consisting of simple incising, brushing, or cord marking (Jennings 1941; Stubbs 1984).

Choctaw. The Choctaw of southeastern Mississippi were the largest tribe in the vicinity of the Lower Mississippi Valley. Although not resident in the valley, they had a strong impact on it because of their proximity and size. Curiously, however, they have yet to be well identified archaeologically. It had long been held that the pottery type Chickachae Combed was a reliable diagnostic (Collins 1927c; Ford 1936, p. 42; Haag 1953; Phillips 1970, p. 65; Penman 1977, 1978). However, recent research apparently has revealed that the reliability is restricted to the late eighteenth–early nineteenth centuries (Williams 1981a; Penman 1983; Galloway 1984; Blitz 1985, pp. 47–55). Early eighteenth-century pottery may be related to the Fatherland Incised type of the Natchez, but distinctive varieties have yet to be recognized.

Chakchiuma. Assuming that they remained somewhat in place, this tribe may have been descendant from the "Saquechuma" or "Sacchuma" of the De Soto narratives (Bourne 1904, vol. 1, p. 101; ibid., vol. 2, p. 132). In the sixteenth century, they were located near the Chickasaw but were rebellious against their authority. It has been suggested that they lived south of the Chickasaw (Atkinson 1979), but southwest seems more likely, and in the late seventeenth and early eighteenth centuries they were definitely placed on the Yazoo River (Swanton 1946, pp. 105–107). At that time their principal village was probably the Leflore site north of Greenwood, Mississippi (fig. 203). They also had an association with the lower reaches of the Yazoo River, however, and seem to have sought temporary refuge among the Tunica during the first year or two of the eighteenth century (ibid.). In 1736 they are recorded as being again in the vicinity of Haynes Bluff (see fig. 21).

The Chakchiuma may be identified by the Montfort set. Protohistoric–early historic pottery vessels from the Leflore site exhibit the distinctive Leflore Design Mode, which also might be a diagnostic for the Chakchiuma.

Houma. Found by the French in the Portage de la Croix region, the Houma were probably recent emigrants from the Yazoo and may have been related to the Chakchiuma (Swanton 1911, p. 29). If the relationship is valid, then the Houma appear to have been pioneers on the trail subsequently followed by the Tunica. The Tunica, however, seem to have turned on their hosts and were guilty of pushing them farther downriver within a few years. Houma artifactual diagnostics have not yet been isolated (Guevin 1985), but if the Houma were related to the Chakchiuma they may also be identified by the Montfort set.

Ibitoupa. The Ibitoupa were a little-known tribe that Swanton (1946, p. 140) identified as living between Abyache (Abiaca) and Chicopa creeks on the banks of the Yazoo River (see fig. 27). Locations with historic artifacts in this vicinity include the French and Parrish sites (see fig. 188), both of which have early French contact materials (Potts 1975; Brown 1978b; Gordon and Parrish collections, Cottonlandia Museum, Greenwood, Mississippi). Aboriginal diagnostics, however, remain unidentified.

Yazoo. This small tribe may have been native to the region and river that still bear its name (Swanton 1911, p. 332; Williams and Brain 1983, p. 384). Their linguistic affiliation is uncertain: Swanton (1911, p. 9) grouped them with Tunican, but in 1702 Father Gravier specifically noted that they spoke a different language from the Tunica (Shea 1861, p. 133), so it is more likely that they were Muskhogean speakers.

If the Yazoo were indeed the most indigenous of the historic tribes in the region, and thus the heirs of the long prehistoric-protohistoric continuity (see figs. 190, 194, 196), then they are certainly to be identified in the Holly Bluff set, especially in subsets 1 and 2. This series is ubiquitous throughout the lower Yazoo from the Lake George to Russell phases. The associated utilitarian wares would have been Yazoo 3, 4, and perhaps 5 during the late prehistoric and protohistoric periods, and possibly the Montfort set during the historic. These all manifest the late Mississippian predilection for incising and punctating, and share the same simple curvilinear and rectilinear design modes. The addition of sand to the paste of the Montfort set is an eastern trait that is consistent with the known relationship of the Yazoo with peoples in that direction (Swanton 1911, p. 9; Swanton 1946, p. 212). The distribution of the *Montfort* variety, however, coincides most closely with the historic distributions of the Chakchiuma-Houma or the ephemeral Tioux.

Although Rowland (1931) speculated that the Deasonville site (Collins 1932a) might be identified with the Yazoo, it is now clear that they must have lived in the vicinity of Haynes Bluff, where they were close neighbors of the Tunica during the latter's stay in the region. Apparently, the Yazoo were driven out of the valley by the Quapaw after the 1729 uprising against the French.

TUNICAN

Grigra. Possibly a Tunican group (Swanton 1911, p. 336) who had been adopted by the Natchez, the Grigra are believed to have lived in the northern part of the Natchez district (fig. 203) and might be identified archaeologically by sites in the vicinity of Coles Creek (Brown 1983, 1984, 1985; Brain, Brown, and Steponaitis n.d.). A distinctive stepped motif (Brown 1985, fig. 37h–1) may be a diagnostic design mode of their pottery.

Tioux. This small tribe lived among the Natchez in the early eighteenth century (fig. 203). They were probably a branch of the Koroa and may have been found archaeologically at the International Paper site near the Grand Village of the Natchez (Brain, Brown, and Steponaitis n.d.).

Koroa. The Koroa, another historic Tunican tribe, were probably the same group referred to as the Tioux (see Brain 1982). Although apparently quite independent of the Tunica proper, they seem to have behaved in much the same fashion, at least to the extent that they display similar patterns of movement and were often closely associated.

The first possible mention of the Koroa might be in the De Soto narratives, which record "Coligoa," "Coligua," or "Colima" as being a near neighbor of Tanico (Bourne 1904, vol. 1, p. 133; ibid., vol. 2, pp. 31, 146–147; Varner and Varner 1951, p. 453). Swanton (1939, p. 52) and Dickinson (1977, p. 2; 1980, p. 4) theorize that the nomenclature may have been derived from the way the Spaniards heard Koroa pronounced by Muskhogean Indians, who would have substituted an *l* for the *r* missing in their language. Whatever the merits of this theory, the historic Koroa of the late seventeenth and early eighteenth centuries not only seem to have been Tunican but were close neighbors of the Tunica proper, and like them may have been pushed south from their sixteenth-century home (figs. 202–203) (see Bizzell 1981, p. 72; Dickinson 1984, pp. 201–202).

In fact, the Koroa seem to have had an even greater proclivity for movement than the Tunica. The record is somewhat unclear, however, since they appear to have been identified by more names than can be accounted for by the usual orthographic vagaries. It may be that at various times in their history they were constituted of one or more relatively autonomous groups. This might explain much of their apparent wanderlust, for they are recorded in quick succession and sometimes contemporaneously as being in southeastern Arkansas/northeastern Louisiana, on the Yazoo with the Tunica, and among the Natchez. And if the tribe included the Tioux, they appeared not only among the Natchez—for possible archaeological evidence of such a group among the Natchez see Brown (1983, 1984, 1985) and Brain, Brown, and Steponaitis (n.d.)—but also with the Tunica in the Portage de la Croix region (see fig. 30).

In response to this ethnic chimera, a possible reconstruction is proposed as follows: The Koroa were another Tunican remnant who ranged the west side of the Mississippi but also established permanent settlements on the Yazoo and at the Natchez. The Yazoo Koroa remained in place until they were chased out after the 1729 massacre, when they may have joined the Choctaw. The Koroa-Tioux left Natchez in 1727, were briefly recorded in the vicinity of the Tunica around the year 1732, and then they, too, became lost to history.

The Koroa may be represented by the Yazoo 6 and 9 subsets. The eclectic decorative modes display closest connections with the west and south, a distribution which certainly agrees with the known peripatetic history of this tribe. They might be identified archaeologically with some of the late sites on a latitude crosscutting the mid-Ouachita River, lower Bayou Bartholomew, and upper Boeuf River (Moore 1909, pp. 27–80, 120–151; Webb and Gregory 1978, p. 29; Rolingson and Schambach 1981, p. 106; Jeter 1982b; Kidder 1987). A working hypothesis would place the late seventeenth-century Koroa in southeastern Arkansas/northeastern Louisiana, in an area centering on southern Ashley County and Moorehouse Parish (Kniffen 1935; Faye 1942, p. 930; Dickinson 1977, 1980; see also Delisle 1701, 1703, 1718). The Jordan site in the Boeuf Basin exhibits a particularly good representation of Yazoo 6 and 9 pottery (Kidder 1987), while a compound vessel from the Glendora site on the Ouachita River is composed of a Cracker Road Incised pot surmounted by a bottle with Tunican decoration (Moore 1909, fig. 72). The close relationship between a probable Koroa marker—Cracker Road—and the general Tunican style could not be made more explicit.

The Tunica proper, of course, are clearly recognized by the Yazoo 8 and Pocahontas sets. Again, the closest relationships and obvious antecedents are found to the north and west. Prototypical as well as typical examples of Yazoo 8 varieties, Winterville Incised, *var. Tunica*, and the Tunican Mode are all present in a tight cluster of sites in northwestern Mississippi identified with De Soto's province of Quizquiz, the probable ancestral home of the Tunica (see fig. 196).

Summary

The origins, subsequent movements, and demographic changes of the Tunica during the late prehistoric through historic periods in the Lower Mississippi Valley may now be delineated in some detail (figs. 201–206). It must be emphasized that the use of the appellation "Tunica" is appropriate only for the group found by the French on the banks of the lower Yazoo River at the end of the seventeenth century and their descendants. It is assumed that this group was a remnant of a much larger polity, or polities, which according to oral tradition and archaeological evidence had their original home elsewhere.

It has been argued in these pages that these "proto-Tunica" lived in the northern Yazoo Basin—specifically, the upper Sunflower region—and a contiguous portion of eastern Arkansas at the time the De Soto entrada forced its way through the Mississippi Valley, and that they may be identified with the province of Quizquiz (and probably also Aquixo on the west side of the river) mentioned in the narratives of that expedition. The proto-Tunica were recent intruders into the Yazoo Basin, having begun to move across the river from eastern Arkansas, perhaps under pressure from the ancestral Quapaw (Bizzell 1981, p. 72).* The proto-Tunica, in turn, pushed out other peoples, one group of whom settled on the lower Yazoo River and became known as the Ofo. The Quapaw pressure continued and at least one group, who became the historical Tunica, also was forced out of the upper Sunflower region by the mid-seventeenth century. They, too, settled on the lower Yazoo River, where they were found by the French. Tunica occupation has been identified at the Haynes Bluff site and nearby locations.

When the Tunica left the Yazoo Basin in 1706, they migrated to the vicinity of the Red River confluence. There they may be recognized archaeologically at a number of locales until 1764. An archaeological hiatus then ensues, because the late eighteenth-century village at Pointe Coupée has been lost to the encroachment of the Mississippi River. By 1800 the Tunica had moved to Marksville, at which location their archaeology picks up again, but without the ethnic artifactual diagnostics that had identified them before. Nevertheless, distinctive configurations of artifacts were retained, and they contribute much to our understanding of nineteenth-century Tunica lifeways.

Thus, in the foregoing pages we have archaeologically identified and explored a series of stages in the Tunica continuum. These stages are treated as synchronic episodes because, as relatively brief archaeological components, they present little opportunity to measure internal changes in situ. Instead, they provide the data for reconstructing past lifeways at each individual stage, and it is in the comparison of these stages that the broad trends of cultural continuity and change may be measured. These reconstructions and comparisons are the subject of part 3.

---

* Other Tunicans probably were to be found as far west as Little Rock and Hot Springs (the Tanico of the narratives), but they were split off by the Quapaw settlement on the lower Arkansas. These western Tunica may have been the ancestors of the Koroa (Dickinson 1984, pp. 201–202).

Part Three: Ethnohistorical Reconstruction

In part 1 of this volume, the Tunica were defined historically: that is, an Indian tribal group identified as Tunica in the historical documentation was placed at various locations through time. Partly because of the superficial nature of most of the descriptions, however, and partly because of a seemingly ephemeral attachment to any particular piece of land during the early contact period, the ancient Tunica were little more than historical ghosts at the beginning of this project. The presence of the modern Tunica attested to the existence of their forebears, but the latter remained intangible. The historical Tunica gained corporeal reality in part 2, as archaeological investigations confirmed historical documentation and added considerable new evidence for both material and behavioral identification. The historical and archaeological concordance is close enough to allow us to state confidently that we now can follow a single ethnic group through time.

Considered together, these historical and archaeological data sets provide the substance for reconstructing the Tunica past. Using the approach of ethnohistoric archaeology, we are able to integrate all the known data in order to extract a detailed synopsis of Tunica lifeways at each of the locations they inhabited during the six periods described in the historical and archaeological sections above. Because these reconstructions form a series of related episodes, they may be compared diachronically not only to reveal the amount of change that has occurred between them, but also to discriminate important, dynamic trends in the continuum. Furthermore, they may be analyzed for those significant and recurrent processes of change that may have been occurring during each period and throughout the sequence (cf. Quimby 1957, p. 161). The ultimate objective, of course, is to isolate the particular attributes and processes that enabled the Tunica to survive as an ethnic group, especially during the critical eighteenth century.

Change and Continuity in Tunica Lifeways

In this section, the lifeways of the Tunica are reconstructed for each of the locations known to have been inhabited by the tribe since first European contact. As might be expected, the quality and quantity of information available for each of the Tunica locations vary considerably. In some cases, the archaeological data are stronger, in others the historical; in some cases, we know more about mortuary practices, in others about settlement patterns; in some cases, it is possible to identify actual Tunica personages, in others the identification of the entire group is in doubt. Through the establishment of the continuum, however, and the inferences made possible thereby, many of the lacunae may be filled satisfactorily and a reasonably complete picture of the Tunica past emerges.

UPPER SUNFLOWER

The upper Sunflower locale of the northern Yazoo Basin was hypothesized in part 1 to have been the provenience of the sixteenth-century province of Quizquiz encountered by the De Soto entrada. Whatever the merit of that hypothesis, the general location has been positively identified as the ancestral hearth of the Tunica.

The oral traditions of the Tunica contain an origin myth that refers to their emergence from a mountain (Haas 1950, pp. 19, 141). It was speculated in part 1 that this reference could be to a homeland in the mountains of central Arkansas, a region with which there is good reason to associate Tunican ancestors. However, the symbolic equivalence of mountains and man-made mounds among some southeastern groups (Knight 1985b, p. 2) suggests an alternative interpretation: that is, an origin in the mound-building tradition of the Mississippian cultures. In any event, the two interpretations are not incompatible if the geographical and cultural parameters are merged.

The ancestors of the Tunica were part of that late prehistoric florescence identified by archaeologists as the Mississippian cultural tradition. It is probable that Tunican peoples had long occupied an area in central and eastern Arkansas, where they spoke their own unique language, and had been drawn into the developing Mississippian sphere during the last centuries of the prehistoric era. Many studies describe the great Mississippian achievements in the area during this period, and we have come to some general understanding of the high developments and quality of life (Phillips, Ford, and Griffin 1951; Phillips 1970; Morse and Morse 1983; Williams and Brain 1983).

It is not necessary to rely only on archaeological reconstructions of Mississippian culture, however, since if the hypothesis is correct ancestors of the Tunica were visited by De Soto (Phillips, Ford, and Griffin 1951, p. 421; Brain, Toth, and Rodriguez-Buckingham 1974, p. 262; cf. Springer and Witkowski 1982, p. 82). The narratives of that expedition have preserved revealing descriptive detail of those forebears. Even if the hypothesis is incorrect, the peoples encountered would have been near neighbors with similar customs, and it is therefore warranted to quote the chronicles verbatim.

We begin with a description of the incident by the anonymous Gentleman of Elvas:

[De Soto] *arrived at a town of Quizquiz without being descried, and seized all the people before they could come out of their houses. Among them was the mother of the Cacique; and the Governor [De Soto] sent word to him, by one of the captives, to come and receive her, with the rest he had taken. The answer he returned was, that if his lordship would order them to be loosed and sent, he would come to visit and do him service.*

The Governor, since his men arrived weary, and likewise weak, for want of maize, and the horses were also lean, determined to yield to the requirement and try to have peace; so the mother and the rest were ordered to be set free, and with words of kindness were dismissed. The next day, while he was hoping to see the Chief, many Indians came, with bows and arrows, to set upon the Christians, when he commanded that all the armed horsemen should be mounted and in readiness. Finding them prepared, the Indians stopped at the distance of a crossbow-shot from where the Governor was, near a river-bank, where, after remaining quietly half an hour, six chiefs arrived at the camp, stating that they had come to find out what people it might be; for that they had knowledge from their ancestors that they were to be subdued by a white race; they consequently desired to return to the Cacique, to tell him that he should come presently to obey and serve the Governor. After presenting six or seven skins and shawls brought with them, they took their leave, and returned with the others who were waiting for them by the shore. The Cacique came not, nor sent another message.

There was little maize in the place, and the Governor moved to another town, half a league from the great river, where it was found in sufficiency. He went to look at the river, and saw that near it there was much timber of which piraguas might be made, and a good situation in which the camp might be placed. He directly moved, built houses, and settled on a plain a crossbow-shot from the water, bringing together there all the maize of the towns behind, that at once they might go to work and cut down trees for sawing out planks to build barges. The Indians soon came from up the stream, jumped on shore, and told the Governor that they were the vassals of a great lord, named Aquixo, who was the suzerain of many towns and people on the other shore; and they made known from him, that he would come the day after, with all his people, to hear what his lordship would command him.

The next day the Cacique arrived, with two hundred canoes filled with men, having weapons. They were painted with ochre, wearing great bunches of white and other plumes of many colours, having feathered shields in their hands, with which they sheltered the oarsmen on either side, the warriors standing erect from bow to stern, holding bows and arrows. The barge in which the Cacique came had an awning at the poop, under which he sate; and the like had the barges of the other chiefs: and there, from under the canopy, where the chief man was, the course was directed and orders issued to the rest. All came down together, and arrived within a stone's cast of the ravine, whence the Cacique said to the Governor, who was walking along the river- bank, with others who bore him company, that he had come to visit, serve, and obey him; for he had heard that he was the greatest of lords, the most powerful on all the earth, and that he must see what he would have him do. The Governor expressed his pleasure, and be- sought him to land, that they might the better confer; but the Chief gave no reply, ordering three barges to draw near, wherein was great quantity of fish, and loaves like bricks, made of the pulp of ameixas, *which Soto receiving, gave him thanks and again entreated him to land.*

Making the gift had been a pretext, to discover if any harm might be done; but, finding the Governor and his people on their guard, the Cacique began to draw off from the shore, when the crossbow-men who were in readiness, with loud cries shot at the Indians, and struck down five or six of them. They retired with great order, not one leaving the oar, even though the one next to him might have fallen, and covering themselves, they withdrew. Afterwards they came many times and landed; when approached, they would go back to their barges. These were fine-looking men, very large and well formed; and what with the awnings, the plumes, and the shields, the pennons, and the number of people in the fleet, it appeared like a famous armada of galleys. (Bourne 1904, vol. 1, pp. 111–114)

Another chronicler was Luys Hernandez de Biedma, the king's factor, who recorded the incident as follows:

One mid-day we came upon a town called Quizquiz, and so suddenly to the inhabitants, that they were without any notice of us, the men being away at work in the maize-fields. We took more than three hundred women, and the few skins and shawls they had in their houses. There we first found a little walnut of the coun- try, which is much better than that here in Spain. The town was near the banks of the River Espiritu Santo. They told us that it was, with many towns about there, tributary to a lord of Pacaha, famed throughout all the land. When the men heard that we had taken their women, they came to us peacefully, requesting the Governor to restore them. He did so, and asked them for canoes in which to pass that great river. These they promised, but never gave; on the contrary, they col- lected to give us battle, coming in sight of the town where we were; but in the end, not venturing to make an attack, they turned and retired.

We left that place and went to encamp by the riv- erside, to put ourselves in order for crossing. On the other shore we saw numbers of people collected to oppose our landing, who had many canoes. We set about building four large piraguas, each capable of taking sixty or seventy men and five or six horses. We were engaged in the work twenty-seven or twenty-eight days. During this time, the Indians every day, at three o'clock in the afternoon, would get into two hundred and fifty very large canoes they had, well shielded, and come near the shore on which we were; with loud cries they would exhaust their arrows upon us, and then re- turn to the other bank. (Bourne 1904, vol. 2, pp. 25–26)

Rodrigo Ranjel, De Soto's personal secretary, noted only that the army

came to the first village of Quizqui, which they took by assault and captured much people and clothes; but the Governor promptly restored them to liberty and had everything restored to them for fear of war, al- though that was not enough to make friends of these Indians. A league beyond this village they came upon another with abundance of corn, and soon again after another league, upon another likewise amply provi- sioned. There they saw the great river. Saturday, May 21, the force went along to a plain between the river and a small village, and set up quarters and began to build four barges to cross over to the other side. Many of these conquerors said this river was larger than the Danube.

On the other side of the river, about seven thousand Indians had got together, with about two hundred ca- noes, to defend the passage. All of them had shields made of canes joined, so strong and so closely inter- woven with such thread that a cross-bow could hardly pierce them. The arrows came raining down so that the air was full of them, and their yells were something fearful. But when they saw that the work on the barges did not relax on their account, they said that Pacaha, whose men they were, ordered them to withdraw, and so they left the passage free. (Bourne 1904, vol. 2, pp. 137–138)

The most extensive and interesting account, al- though most suspect in the reliability of its historical data, is that preserved by Garcilaso de la Vega, whose informants professed to recall numerous details of that memorable encounter with the peoples of Quizquiz (here referred to as "Chisca"):

Because of their continuous war with the people of Chicaza, and because of the wilderness lying between the two provinces, the Indians of Chisca knew nothing of the coming of the Spaniards to their land and as a result were not on the lookout. So when our men caught sight of the town, they charged upon it without order, and in addition to capturing males and females of all ages, pillaged everything that they found within the place just as if it had belonged to the province of Chic- aza where they had been so maltreated.

Off to one side of the town was the dwelling place of the Curaca [cacique]. It was situated on a high mound which now served as a fortress. Only by means of two stairways could one ascend to this house. Here many Indians gathered while others sought refuge in a very wild forest lying between the town and the Great River. The lord of the province, who like his land was called Chisca, was now old and sick in bed; but on hearing the noise and confusion in his village, he arose and came from his bedchamber. Then beholding the pillage and the seizure of his vassals, he grasped a battle-ax and began to descend the stairs with the greatest fury, in the meantime vowing loudly and fiercely to slay anyone who came into his land without permission. Thus this wretched creature threatened when he had neither the person nor the strength to kill a cat, for besides being ill, he was very old and shriveled. Indeed among all the Indians that these Spaniards saw in Florida, they found none other of such wretched appearance. But the memory of the valiant deeds and triumphs of his bellicose youth, and the fact that he held sway over a province so large and good as his, gave him the strength to utter those fierce threats and even fiercer ones.

The Cacique's wives and servants now seized him, and with tears and entreaties and enlargements upon his poor health, persuaded him from descending. Then those Indians who came up from the town warned him that the strangers who had arrived were such as he had never seen or heard of before, and that in addition to being extremely numerous, they had brought with them some very large and swift animals. And they said that if he had determined to fight these people, he should consider first the lack of preparation of his own men, and that to avenge his injury he should summon the inhabitants of the district and await a better opportunity. Meanwhile, he would be wise to feign the most friendly appearance and adjust himself to such occasions as were offered, either of forbearance and suffering or of vengeance and wrath, and he should not inconsiderately attempt any rash act because of the great injury it would bring upon both himself and his vassals.

With these and similar reasonings the wives, servants and vassals of the Curaca detained him from closing with the Christians, but he was so enraged that when the Governor (on learning that he was in the chieftain's house) sent a message of peace and friendship, he refused to listen, remarking that he had no desire to hear the words of a man who had offended him but wished rather to wage upon that man a war of fire and blood, and that he thus was declaring such a war at once lest the fact be overlooked that he planned soon to annihilate all of the Spaniards. . . .

Exhausted by all the inclemencies of the past winter, disgusted with fighting, and burdened with many wounded and sick (both men and horses), the General and his captains and soldiers had come to this place with a desire for peace and not war. And since this desire was mingled with fear because of their having sacked the town and angered the Curaca, they sent to Chisca many additional messages, filled with all the suave words they were permitted to utter. For they

perceived that in addition to the obstacles they brought with them, almost four thousand armed warriors had gathered around the Cacique within less than three hours after their arrival in this town; and they were afraid that since these men had assembled in such a brief time, many more would come later. Again, they perceived that the site of the town, both inside and outside, was very favorable to the Indians and unfavorable to themselves, and that because of the many streams and forests lying throughout that region, they would be unable to use their horses to the extent necessary for an offensive. But what caused them greater reflection, and they came by it through much experience, was the realization that they did not thrive on battles and instead were being consumed by them, for the Indians from day to day were killing both their men and horses. All of these things, therefore, moved them to seek peace with great earnestness.

But among the Indians, on the other hand, there were many who (after having met to discuss the messages of our men) wanted war, for they were offended by the seizure of their wives, children and other kinsmen, and by the pillage of their possessions. Being men of a bellicose nature, they felt that the speediest way to reimburse themselves for their losses was through arms, and that any other means would necessitate too much time. Desiring to start the conflict at once, they rejected the peace offers without giving any reason except that of their loss. Other Indians who had lost nothing they cared about regaining, but who, because of the natural inclination of their race for war, wanted to prove their strength and courage, also rejected the overtures of peace. Holding out for consideration the fact that this was a question involving their honor, they declared that it would be wise to learn by experience just what such strange and unknown people were like in arms, and what were the limits of their courage and strength, while at the same time letting these people know something of their own force and valor so that they and others would be warned against coming to their land in the future. There were still other more prudent and pacific Indians, however, who maintained that they should accept the Spaniards' proffer of peace and friendship; first, because by this means they were more certain of recovering their captured wives and children and their stolen goods than they would be by enmity and war, and then because they thus would be assured of avoiding the sight of damage that still might be done (such for instance as the burning of their towns and the desolation of their fields at a time when the grain was near ripening). And, they continued, there was no cause to discover by experience how valiant these people were since reason clearly told them that men who had passed through as much enemy territory as had these men before arriving at Chisca could not but be most valiant. Peace and concord with them were therefore better than war, for in addition to the ills already set forth, war would bring about the death of many of those present as well as that of their brothers, relatives and friends; and it would in itself give vengeance to their enemies among the neighboring Indians. For the reasons expressed, they concluded, it would be better to accept the friendship of the Spaniards and see how they fared with it, since in the event that it was not to their advantage, they could very easily and with more odds than they now held, take up arms again and succeed in their present aspirations.

This last counsel won over the others, and the Curaca bowed before it, reserving his anger for a time when he might be offered a better occasion to express it. Hence he answered the Governor's messengers by saying that first of all they should state what it was the Castilians desired. These men thereupon replied that since they were merely passing through this land and could not stop long, their Governor asked no more of the Indians than that they disoccupy their town for his camp and provide his men with what little food they might need. At that the Curaca responded that he was content to concede the peace and friendship requested, to disoccupy his town, and to supply food, but that he would do so only with the understanding that the Spaniards were to release his vassals at once and restore to them their possessions, not omitting so much as a single earthenware pot (these are his words), and that they were not to ascend to his house to see him. Under these conditions, he said, he would receive the Spaniards peacefully; otherwise, he was challenging them to fight at once.

Our men accepted the Cacique's stipulations because they had brought sufficient servants and had no need for these new captives, and again because the property they had seized consisted of no more than a miserable lot of chamois and a few robes. So all was restored according to the Curaca's specification, not so much as one earthenware pot being omitted. The Indians thereupon disoccupied the town and left the food they had in their houses for the Castilians, who because of their sick and their need to refresh themselves stopped six days in this town called Chisca. On the last of these days, the Governor, with the Cacique's consent, paid him a visit and thanked him for his friendship and hospitality. Then on the ensuing day, he set out once again upon his journey and exploration. (Varner and Varner 1951, pp. 423–427)

Despite problems of reliability, the De Soto chronicles are a unique corpus that preserves a fascinating glimpse of a time when the native peoples had attained a high point in their cultural development and were as yet untouched by European influence. When the descriptive detail pertaining to these pristine conditions in the province of Quizquiz is integrated with the archaeological data from the upper Sunflower region, a substantial account of proto-Tunica lifeways in the mid-sixteenth century may be reconstructed.

Sixteenth-century Quizquiz was populous and highly organized, both politically and socially. It comprised many towns and villages occupied by thousands of people. The Quizquizians commanded a fleet of large canoes, each manned by up to eighty rowers and warriors. These canoes maneuvered together on the water and worked in concert with fleets from other allied groups. In fact, it was interpreted by the chroniclers that Quizquiz was subject to yet another power, identified as Pacaha, or Capaha. So a political hierarchy appears to have existed that extended beyond the domains of Quizquiz. The many towns of Quizquiz must also have been ranked in a hierarchical relationship, which is probably

Figure 207. Hypothetical reconstruction of the Clarksdale site (16-N-26) at the time of the De Soto entrada. (Original painting by Fred Beasley, courtesy Carnegie Public Library of Clarksdale and Coahoma County, Mississippi)

reflected in the amount of earthen construction in each settlement. There are many late prehistoric mound sites that may be related to the Parchman phase (see fig. 196), the putative archaeological correlate to historical Quizquiz, and many of these were very large (fig. 207). Other sites, such as Humber-McWilliams (Tesar 1976; Tesar and Fichtner 1974), may not have many earthworks, but they do exhibit the remains of the large populations that supported the activities at the nearby mound centers. Both the mounds and the cemeteries attest to the complex social, political, and religious development of Quizquiz. But they tell us little about the nature of those developments beyond the fact that they must have been as spectacular as was recorded in the De Soto narratives. Those accounts describe the chiefdoms, the organization, and the power to marshal the peoples—whether it was to build the public works or to confront De Soto.

We know, too, from the narratives that the people of Quizquiz had an abundance of food. Specifically mentioned were corn, fish, persimmons, and pecans. Situated in the lush Yazoo Basin, Quizquiz had access to an indulgent and rich environment: the alluvial bottomlands of the region supported a great diversity of terrestrial, aquatic, and avian biota (Williams and Brain 1983, pp. 8–9). All the necessities of sustenance were easily procured from the natural abundance, and when imported cultigens were propagated in the incomparably fertile ground the yields were considerable. The surpluses still available in the early spring of 1541 were a godsend to the entrada, but even more a testimonial to the subsistence economy of Quizquiz. Subsistence strategies may have developed to the point that the men rather than the women were responsible for the cultivation of the fields, since the men were said to have been so occupied when the Spaniards arrived.

Disappointingly little is revealed in the narratives about other aspects of Quizquizian life. All the accounts recall that skins, shawls, or articles of clothing were taken in the initial assault, but this notation is merely an indication of the army's dire need for such vestments and the local ability to provide them. The only other reference to domestic material culture is to pottery (Varner and Varner 1951, p. 427). The Spaniards had no use for pottery, however, and Garcilaso's passing comment is contemptuous. Ironically, pottery is the most abundant artifactual material retrieved archaeologically, and hence it has become very important in our study. We now have a fairly complete inventory of local pottery, and it has served us well in tracing relationships, especially to the historical Tunica.

The only other items of material culture to receive much attention from the Spaniards were those that threatened them: bows and arrows, other weapons, and canoes. Examples of all of these have been found archaeologically, but the descriptions of their use against De Soto give them life.

There is also archaeological evidence of the De Soto entrada itself in the upper Sunflower region. Interestingly, the most diagnostic artifact found to date is not of a martial nature: it is the little brass bell named the "Clarksdale bell" (Brain 1975a, 1985). These have been found in at least one major mound site in what otherwise would have been purely aboriginal prehistoric contexts. Another possible De Soto item, a distinctive type of halberd, has also been found in the vicinity, and other probable artifacts of the expedition have been reported across the river in northeastern Arkansas (Moore 1911, p. 415; Davis 1966, p. 11; Brain 1975a; Klinger 1977, pp. 77–78; John House, personal communication, 1979, 1980; Hathcock 1983, pp. 158, 162).

This leads us to consider why and how De Soto came to Quizquiz. The answer remains a matter of debate, but it is important to note that the upper Sunflower region was a major crossroads of trade and travel throughout the prehistoric and early historic periods. At times of large-scale interregional contact in prehistory—identified with the Poverty Point, Marksville, and Mississippian cultures (Williams and Brain 1983, chs. 11–12)—significant components of contemporary cultural phases were present. The reason may have been strategic. The location on the bank of the Mississippi River fostered interregional communication, of course, but even more important was the local coincidence of riverine and terrestrial routes of communication. The headwaters of the Sunflower River presently rise within a few kilometers of the Mississippi, to which, probably, the Sunflower originally was often connected as a distributary. In any event, it provided direct access to the populous interior of the Yazoo Basin, and via the nearby Coldwater River there was a connection to the Yazoo River.* In addition to its place in riverine communication, this location was also the terminus of a major east-west land trail that was known in the early nineteenth century as "Charlie's Trace" and clearly was of considerable antiquity (Myer 1928, pl. 15). De Soto did not arrive at Quizquiz by accident: he followed the trail to this strategic location.

In summary, sixteenth-century Quizquiz was characterized by a population that could field thousands of warriors, by large permanent towns with monumental earthworks, by ranked social structure, and by a chiefdom level of political organization that was federated under a paramount chief. Many of these developmental features were shared by other southeastern peoples. What stands out about Quizquiz is the exceptionally large population described in the accounts and confirmed archaeologically; this implies ever more complex sociocultural elaborations, such as those described in the De Soto chronicles. All of these developments were a benefice of the rich environment, but many other locations in the Yazoo would have been satisfactory for meeting the needs of subsistence. The demographic concentration at this particular locale, however, was determined by the coincidence of geographic features that facilitated interregional contact. These geographic correlations are important to our consideration of the Tunica.

To continue our story, we must first pass through a very dark time for which we have no historical documentation and little archaeological information, and

---

* It is no coincidence that it was precisely here that in 1862 the Union forces attempted to dig the "Yazoo Pass" from the Mississippi to the Coldwater in order to take Vicksburg from the rear.

during which we cannot speak directly of the Tunica at all. It was, however, a time of great changes, and so it cannot be ignored.

Interregnum

Although the Mississippi Valley was brought into the historic record with the De Soto entrada of 1541–1543, there subsequently were no known European contacts until Marquette and Jolliet ventured down the river more than a century later. Consequently, no historical documentation exists for the interval. This time of historical limbo is referred to here as the protohistoric period. It is a matter of great regret that we do not have historical insight into events during this period, for clearly they were cataclysmic. It is impossible for us, in our relatively protected world, to imagine the magnitude of the changes that occurred. In fact, the changes that will be described in later periods are minor compared to what must have been imposed during this "dark age." In trying to comprehend it, we have only some hypotheses that are beginning to be substantiated in the archaeological record.

We may begin with the De Soto entrada itself. This was surely a traumatic event. The conquistadores were loose in an alien land, and they were ruthless in their search for wealth and struggle for survival: native polities were disrupted, peoples killed or enslaved, and food reserves stolen, not to mention other unrecorded atrocities. The depredations, of course, were quite variable in their effects. Some peoples were completely untouched except by the wonder of it all, others received a glancing blow from which they may have recovered immediately, while a few were devastated. According to the narratives, Quizquiz apparently was little affected by force of arms from the entrada because the Spaniards were quite exhausted by this point. The Quizquizians did lose important food stores, however, and the army remained in the vicinity for a month while building barges in which to cross the river. These are two very important facts that merit further consideration.

Remaining in place for a month, the marauding army must have cleaned out all available food reserves (Bourne 1904, vol. 1, pp. 112). This was not just a case of passing through a province and taking what could be carried in the belly, but of living off the land for an extended period and provisioning for the continuation of the expedition across the river. Since there is no record in the narratives of established intercourse with the natives of Quizquiz during the stay, it may be assumed that the foodstuffs were simply stolen. Although no major conflicts are recorded in the chronicles, and it would seem that few lives were lost thereby, the loss of food reserves must have been a disaster for the large populations. Yet in the rich environment of the Mississippi Valley they might have survived this one disaster.

An even more ominous threat, considering the length of the entrada's stay in this venue, could have been the transmission of European diseases—that scourge of the intruders that was to have more effect on Indian populations than any purposeful introduction, as will be discussed below. Yet it is to be doubted that the De Soto entrada was a great culprit in this respect. The army was small, already two years into its march, and not known to have harbored many children, those great incubators of pathogens. Furthermore, as already noted, there does not seem to have been much intercourse with the natives of Quizquiz, intimate or otherwise. But the threat of disease was to come, and combined with the disruptions already described, it suggests a dire scenario.

De Soto may not have embodied the four horsemen of the apocalypse, but certainly he was their harbinger. During that dark age, they finally struck. It may be presumed that the first to arrive was epidemic disease. From the early European colonial settlements on the Atlantic and Gulf coasts, which had sufficient incubating populations, there must have been a rapid spread of pathogens among native populations in contact with those settlements. In turn, the native routes of communication became deadly avenues, and that great central artery, the Mississippi River, would have been one of the worst of all. Along the Mississippi communication was rapid, constant, and far-reaching, all factors that would contribute to epidemic conditions, and the large nucleated populations would have been especially susceptible and could even have hosted endemic conditions (Phillips, Ford, and Griffin 1951, pp. 419–421; Milner 1980; Ramenofsky 1982; Dobyns 1983, pp. 306–308; Smith 1984).

The results of disease alone would have been disastrous, but then the other horsemen claimed their toll. Famine was an immediate consequence. Depending on the time of year a disease struck, crops were not planted, tended, or harvested, the hunt was abandoned, the gathering of wild foods neglected: in short, the normal subsistence activities were fundamentally disrupted. Cumulative disruptions of this sort could only have been devastating to the remaining populations. But even they were not spared, for warfare now assumed a new dimension as the survivors struggled for their very existence.

The disintegration of populations brought about the collapse of social and political structures that had been developed to control those populations. It may be expected, of course, that the controlling segments of the populations suffered the same fate as their subjects, so that the hierarchy did not "collapse" but was annihilated. Whatever happened, the relatively well developed polities encountered by De Soto ceased to exist and a period of reorganization ensued. This period saw remnant groups migrating and coalescing in response to these stresses (Brain 1978a; Dobyns 1983, p. 311). When the French arrived at the end of the seventeenth century, they witnessed but the very last pitiful expressions of this sequence.

In summary, this very dark age, the protohistoric period, was catastrophic for the Indian polities and populations of De Soto's experience. Those earlier polities collapsed completely, and demographic changes occurred that included not only depopulations as great as seventy to eighty percent but also the migration and amalgamation of the survivors into new groups. The Tunica were just such a group when the Europeans returned to the scene.

LOWER YAZOO

The protohistoric period ended in the Lower Mississippi Valley with the French explorations in the last decades of the seventeenth century. Marquette and Jolliet were the earliest of these explorers known to have penetrated the valley, but they descended only as far as the Arkansas River before turning back upriver. It was La Salle, in 1682, who first traveled the Mississippi all the way to the Gulf of Mexico and placed the entire valley under the flag of France. La Salle did not visit the Yazoo, however, and so this region remained terra incognita until the closing years of the century, when permanent French presence was established.

The first recorded contact with the Tunica was in 1699 when the tribe was visited by missionary fathers and their escort from the Séminaire de Québec. The renewed European contact, now direct and sustained, brought even more dread disease to these poor survivors. The effects were noted almost from the first French visitation (Shea 1861, pp. 72, 81, 150). According to these accounts, populations dropped from the thousands to a few hundred within a brief period, after which there was a leveling off in deaths from disease. There were to be continuing epidemics, but the subsequent impact of European influence was to be more cultural than biological.

The Tunica of 1699 were far removed from their ancestors in sociocultural development as well as geography. But they were still aboriginal, untouched by significant European cultural influence (although they had undoubtedly been exposed to some before the first official contact). Much of the following ethnohistorical detail concerning the aboriginal Tunica is from the reports of J.-B. La Source and Father Jacques Gravier (Shea 1861, pp. 80–81, 132–136). La Source accompanied the Seminarians on their initial trip to select missions in 1698–1699, while Gravier visited the Tunica in November 1700. Thus both men were on the scene at the very beginning of French contact, and fortunately both were keen and seemingly reliable observers. They recorded practically all we know historically about aboriginal Tunica customs before they were changed irrevocably by prolonged European contact.

The population of the lower Yazoo River region in 1699 was estimated by the missionary fathers at approximately 2,000 "souls" (Shea 1861, p. 76), of whom the Tunica probably comprised somewhat more than half, while the rest were divided among at least three or four other smaller tribes (the Yazoo, Ofo, Koroa, and/or Tioux). These peoples seem to have been dispersed in little hamlets, but the Tunica at least had a principal village that was the residence of their civil chief and locus of the tribal temple. This village has been identified with the archaeological site of Haynes Bluff. The preeminence of Haynes Bluff is attested by the presence of four mounds, one of which is some 10 m in height. This mound probably supported the tribal temple, which La Source states was placed on a "little hill" (Shea 1861, p. 81). Archaeological excavations at the summit revealed the remains of a structure, although its function could not be determined. This temple mound pattern had roots deep in the prehistoric past, and the Tunica seem to have been among the last to preserve the custom. They may even have been the last of the mound builders (as well as users), for archaeological evidence reveals that the final mantle was added to the temple mound either just before or immediately after European contact, a period which coincides with the Tunica occupation of the site. The overall site plan of Haynes Bluff also reflects the ancient configuration of a ceremonial center with the four mounds arranged around an open plaza. Such sites had small residential populations, and most people lived in scattered settlements in the vicinity: a pattern described for the Tunica and their neighbors in the historical documents and confirmed archaeologically. This pattern might be described as nucleated: that is, clustered around a tribal center rather than being either concentrated or completely dispersed. Such a pattern would have allowed the coexistence of different ethnic groups.

Little of the nonmaterial culture of the Tunica was preserved in the records of the early observers. The lack of ethnohistorical detail is probably due at least partly to the fact that the Tunica appeared to differ hardly at all from the other Lower Valley tribes and thus did not provoke special observation. Father Gravier, however, considered the Tunica "very docile" (Shea 1861, p. 133), by which he meant that they appeared to have few offensive habits and therefore were appropriate subjects for proper religious instruction. True, some polygyny was practiced and divorce was easily achieved, but the women at least were modest and not so "loose or bold" (ibid.) as among the Natchez and Taensa.

For those who cared to listen, the Tunica also could be heard to speak a very different language from their neighbors. It was the only one in the Lower Mississippi Valley to have the *r* phoneme (Le Page du Pratz 1758, vol. 2, p. 221), and one of the very few American Indian languages to have sex gender distinctions in its grammar (Gatschet 1889; Swanton 1919, 1921; Haas 1940, 1953, 1971, 1973; Gursky 1969). Father Davion found the language especially difficult to learn, but he was old and obviously no linguist. There is some question whether any of the other small Yazoo tribes spoke the Tunica language. Gravier, who got his information directly from Davion, reported that the Yazoo and Ofo each spoke different languages. Another missionary report confirmed this trilingual situation and added that the Koroa spoke the same language as the Yazoo, but the Tioux and unnamed others were Tunica speakers (Delanglez 1935, pp. 446–447). On the basis of the *r* in their names, Swanton (1911, p. 9) included the Koroa (and therefore also the Yazoo) and Grigra with the Tioux and Tunica. The Koroa were probably closely related to the Tunica and there is evidence that they are the same people as the Tioux, but the case for the Yazoo and Grigra is purely circumstantial. Only for the Tunica do we have actual linguistic data, and thus they stand alone.

In matters of political and social structure, the record is even more incomplete. There are references to more than one chief (e.g., McWilliams 1981, pp. 144–145; Cain, Koenig, and Conrad 1971, pp. 48–49), and at a later period it is known that the Tunica, like many other southeastern tribes, recognized dual chiefs: one for war and another for civil affairs. The latter was paramount, and on occasion a strong individual even seems to have usurped both roles. The rule governing the transmission of political authority is not stated, but again later evidence indicates that the matriline predisposed selection. Whether the Tunica actually had matrilineal clans or other such social divisions is uncertain; a strict class system like that of the Natchez seems to have been lacking, but ranked social stratification is evident.

In their religious beliefs and practices, the Tunica were most uncommunicative: Gravier noted that "they are so close-mouthed as to all the mysteries of their religion that the missionary [Davion] could not discover anything about it" (Shea 1861, p. 134). Nevertheless, the curious father was able to extract that "they acknowledge nine gods, the sun, thunder, fire, the god of the east, the north, south and west, of heaven and earth" (ibid., p. 133). This polytheistic roster is unexceptional in composition and in the apparent preeminence of the sun. However, latter-day recovery of myth fragments has suggested several interesting features: namely, that the solar deity was feminine, and that fire may not have been symbolic of the sun, as was the case in other southeastern belief systems, but may itself have been deified (Haas 1942).*

The Tunica maintained their fire in a temple (presumably on the large mound at Haynes Bluff) that was the focus of religious activities and contained earthen effigies of a woman and a frog, the former probably symbolic of the sun, the latter perhaps representing the underworld. (The frog was also prominent in some other southeastern religious ideologies [e.g., Rowland and Sanders 1932, vol. 3, p. 530].) Pénicaut reported that Father Davion in his "zeal" (or, more likely, frustration at his lack of success) stole into the temple one night and smashed those idols he could, carrying off the rest (McWilliams 1953, p. 77). He escaped with his life because of the high regard in which the Tunica held him. Almost twenty years later, after Davion had finally forsaken his mission, Charlevoix reported the story that Davion had actually destroyed the temple itself by setting it on fire and that because of their "indifference with respect to religion" the Tunica did not bother to rebuild it (Charlevoix 1744, vol. 3, p. 433). In this case, Charlevoix's information is as suspect as is his observation on the lack of religiosity among the Tunica (a sour comment clearly based on the Tunica's rejection of Davion's best efforts to persuade them to embrace the only true religion), and it is probable that Pénicaut's version is more nearly correct. Nevertheless, it is worth noting that the remains of the structure found on the summit of mound A at Haynes Bluff in the 1974 excavations revealed that the building had been burned. Furthermore, artifacts found in the ruins indicated that the structure dated to the early historic contact period. In any event, although they did tolerate Davion and some of his baptizing, religious instruction, and even more zealous behavior, the Tunica probably did not significantly change their real beliefs.

Tunica conservatism is certainly expressed in mortuary patterns, which the tribe did not appear to alter at this time or for many generations to come. La Source stated that "they inter their dead and the relations come to weep with those of the house, and in the evening they weep over the grave of the departed and make a fire there and pass their hands over it, crying out and weeping" (Shea 1861, p. 81). Archaeological evidence from probable Tunica burials at the Burroughs site, and possibly also Haynes Bluff, confirms that inhumation was practiced. The bodies were placed in graves, often lined with bark, in an extended supine position with the head generally oriented in an easterly direction. No evidence of fire was noted, although funeral fires were to be an enduring tradition. Graves were often placed in residential areas, near or even inside the house of the deceased—a pattern different from that displayed by the Natchez and other indigenous Lower Valley tribes but shared by Mississippian peoples to the north and elsewhere in the Southeast (Nairne 1708; Adair 1775, pp. 181–182; Bushnell 1920, pp. 106–110). The burials were almost always accompanied by an assortment of grave furniture, usually personal ornamental and utilitarian items. At this early stage of contact the majority of European goods are found with burials, as were the more highly prized aboriginal artifacts. Gravier specifically noted that the Tunica carried all their personal possessions with them in life, and apparently the same was true in death.

In appearance, the Tunica looked like their neighbors. Gravier reported that the heads of infants of both sexes were compressed in the cradle to produce artificial flattening, but archaeological evidence has failed so far to support this observation, and it is not depicted in the DeBatz watercolor sketch of prominent Tunica (see fig. 208). A cranium found in a trash pit at Haynes Bluff exhibited frontal-occipital deformation, but the context precluded ethnic identification. If the individual was Tunica, it must be inferred that the custom was rare even in Gravier's time and was soon dropped altogether, for it has not been found in contemporary or later Tunica burials.

Whatever the shape of their skulls, both men and women let their hair grow long, and women arranged it in a heavy plait hanging down the back to the waist or coiled in a crown around the head. The hair was not oiled or greased. Tattooing was practiced by both men and women, and the latter cosmetically blackened their teeth. Neither trait is preserved archaeologically, but there is no reason to doubt their existence, as they were common practices among many Tunica neighbors; the tattooing, at least, is depicted in figure 208. Also like other Lower Mississippi Valley tribes, the Tunica wore the very minimum cover. For women this consisted of a short fringed skirt usually made of mulberry cloth, and for men a deerskin loincloth. Preadolescent children went naked. In cold weather, both sexes wore mantles of mulberry cloth, turkey feathers, or muskrat skins (e.g., Bushnell 1927, pl. 6). Ornaments included marine shell gorgets, beads, and earpins (of which the latter, at least, seem to have been worn exclusively by the women).

---

* Perhaps this was why a Natchez tradition—otherwise quite inexplicable considering the inherent enmity of the two peoples—dictated that in the event of their temple fire being inadvertently extinguished it was necessary to relight it from that of the Tunica (Thwaites 1900, vol. 67, pp. 310, 311).

The Tunica inventory of utilitarian artifacts was similar to that of other Lower Valley tribes, although in specific subartifactual attributes, such as pottery technology and decoration and the forms of some lithic tools, a distinctive pattern derived from their Mississippian heritage may be recognized. Gravier specifically noted "earthenpots quite well made, especially little glazed ["*vernies*," i.e., polished; glazing was not known in aboriginal southeastern pottery manufacture] pitchers, as neat as you would see in France" (Shea 1861, p. 135). We know from archaeological evidence that Tunica pottery was tempered with crushed live mussel shell, unlike the pottery of the indigenous traditions of the Chickasaw, Choctaw, Natchez, Caddo, and others. It also displays different forms and decorations. More than any other artifactual trait, their pottery distinguishes the Tunica from their neighbors, as was demonstrated in part 2. They also probably used triangular stone arrow points, unlike the Natchez and most other peoples to the south, although they do not seem to have had the Oliver lithic complex which was found among their neighbors to the north. Since elements of this complex are believed to have been designed for dressing skins, their absence among the Tunica would seem to indicate a low priority for this activity. Nevertheless, Gravier noted that "they dress [deer and buffalo skins] the best of all Indians that I have seen" (ibid.). It is difficult to be certain about the stone tools because they were replaced by metal tools and firearms so rapidly after the coming of the French. As early as 1700, Gravier wrote about kettles, hatchets, and guns as common Tunica possessions (ibid.). Archaeological evidence of European tools and ornaments may not be abundant on lower Yazoo sites of the period, but it is frequently present.

The only possible archaeological example of Tunica architecture of the period was the burned structure found on the summit of mound A at Haynes Bluff; however, the remains were not sufficiently preserved to reveal details of size, form, or function. What such a building might have looked like may be inferred from Gravier's description of a typical house:

Their cabins are round and vaulted. They are lathed with canes and plastered with mud from bottom to top, within and without with a good covering of straw. There is no light except by the door, and no matter how little fire there is (the smoke of which has no escape but the door) it is as hot as a vapour bath. At night a lighted torch of dried canes serves as a candle and keeps all the cabin warm. (Shea 1861, p. 135)

La Source added that "their houses are made of palisades and earth, and are very large" (Shea 1861, p. 80). The construction technique that both sources described is the standard wattle-and-daub building method common in late prehistory and especially identified with the Mississippian culture, in contexts of which it has often been confirmed archaeologically (e.g., Williams and Brain 1983). The unusual feature is the round plan mentioned by Gravier, since prehistoric Mississippian houses were generally square or rectangular. This alternative floor plan may be distinctive of the Tunica

and should be a focus of future archaeological investigations. Near such houses should be fire hearths—for La Source noted that cooking was done outside—and postholes for the granaries, which Gravier described as being

near their cabins, made like dovecotes, built on four large posts 15 or 16 feet high, well put together and well polished, so that the mice cannot climb up. (Shea 1861, p. 135)

In these granaries the Tunica protected their corn and squash, judged by Gravier to be better than those of the Illinois with whom he had spent some time. Both he and La Source observed that Tunica corn grew fifteen to twenty feet high (Shea 1861, pp. 81, 132). Sunflowers, grown for their seeds, matched the corn in height. Beans were not mentioned, but they may be presumed to have been present. These domesticates were the staples of the Tunica diet, and in this repect the Tunica did not differ from their neighbors. But it may be that their agricultural practice, if not products, did differ. La Source, emphasizing the vegetarian nature of their diet, wrote that the men were "employed solely on their fields, they do not hunt" (ibid., p. 81), while Gravier was even more explicit: "The men do here what peasants do in France; they cultivate and dig the earth, plant and harvest the crops" (ibid., p. 134). These statements recall the intriguing passage in the De Soto narrative that referred to the men being away tending the fields (Bourne 1904, vol. 2, p. 25). It may be that these people, almost alone among eastern tribes, had made the transition to an agricultural strategy wherein the men performed the primary function of working the fields.

Like other southeastern tribes, however, the Tunica also helped themselves to the great variety of natural vegetable and animal resources that were especially abundant in the lush Mississippi Valley environment. These were maximized along the lower Yazoo in the rich ecotone between the loess uplands and alluvial bottomlands. As had been reported for Quizquiz, persimmons (*piakimina*) seem to have been one of the most important wild products; they could be dried, pounded into flour, and baked into a long-lasting bread. Also collected—and adding variety to the menu—were berries, roots, herbs, seeds, nuts, and fruits (especially peaches and plums when they became available). Nor was hunting neglected, despite La Source's statement. Archaeological evidence confirms the importance of deer and bear in the diet, and many smaller mammals, fish, and birds also were eaten. Bison were rare in the Yazoo region, but they were hunted during expeditions west of the Mississippi.

Those western expeditions bring us to a larger consideration of Tunica economy—that is, to matters beyond subsistence. From the very first French contact, the Tunica were specifically mentioned as being actively involved in the production and trade of salt (Margry 1879, vol. 3, p. 423; Swanton 1946, pp. 197–198, 301, 738, 819). At that time, the Tunica were probably exploiting salt springs along the upper Ouachita River in Arkansas (and it is then that they could have taken buffalo that came to the salt licks). It is unclear whether there was a western branch of Tunicans who maintained permanent residence on the Ouachita or whether these peoples were seasonal immigrants from the Yazoo. The latter condition eventually prevailed, but it is possible that at first contact a western group of Tunicans was still in existence. Whatever might have been the case, the prehistoric Tunicans clearly were involved in the collection and trade of salt (witness the Tanico in the "province of salt" described in the De Soto chronicles), and the Yazoo Tunica maintained a certain control, if not monopoly, of this basic commodity well into the historic period. This successful entrepreneurship may have given the Tunica an advantage over other Indians in their initial dealings with the French, and it was probably an important factor in their ultimate survival. At the very least, the salt trade gave the Tunica a competitive edge in the new economic relationships that the European presence engendered.

The Tunica were in an awkward position, however. From the beginning of the establishment of Louisiana, they kept faith with the French and supplied the struggling colony with foodstuffs, as well as salt. But the French were not the only Europeans on the scene. English traders were already resident among the Chickasaw and in contact with the Yazoo tribes when the first French missionaries arrived. At the far end of their trading routes from Charleston, the English were primarily interested in developing the high value items of the "skin" trade: that is, deer skins and human slaves (Nairne 1708; Delanglez 1935, p. 447; Cain, Koenig, and Conrad 1971, p. 48; McWilliams 1981, pp. 110, 119, 133; see also de Villiers 1922; Kernion 1926, p. 32; Knight and Adams 1981, p. 35). The historical documents make it clear that the Tunica were never very active in either market, and archaeology at least confirms their disinterest in deer skin procurement and processing by the notable lack of the Oliver lithic complex in their tool assemblage. Whether from disinclination or allegiance to the French, the Tunica generally refused to trade with the English, although the prohibition was lifted occasionally (e.g., Cain, Koenig, and Conrad 1971, p. 48). Even so, their residence on the Yazoo put them in a vulnerable position: they were caught squarely between the most distant outposts of the two European powers.

After some years of conflict, the English were finally successful in expelling the uncooperative Tunica from the Yazoo. The climactic event apparently was the capture of an English slave trader by the Tunica (Cain, Koenig, and Conrad 1971, p. 54). Although eventually released, the trader incited the Chickasaw and allied tribes to take revenge. Before this could come to pass, the Tunica prudently decided to leave the Yazoo and moved farther south to be closer to the principal French settlements, with which they had already established a satisfactory trading relationship. This theme will be continued in the next section, but let us note here that the success of this relationship was fundamental to Tunica survival at this stage. Their entrepreneurial value ensured a welcoming haven, for the French were not as concerned with the skin trade as they were with the very survival of the colony.

In summary, the Tunica at this first stage of permanent European contact were a small, well-organized,

peaceable group who lived a sedentary life much dependent upon corn agriculture. In these respects, they seem to have been little different from their neighbors (except, perhaps, for the change in the sexual division of labor regarding subsistence). But the Tunica clearly were intruders into the region, and they possessed some distinctive artifactual and behavioral traits. One of the latter was an entrepreneurial inclination that was deeply rooted in the prehistorically developed salt trade. This involvement had led the tribe to settle on the lower Yazoo, the most important eastern tributary of the Mississippi south of the Ohio, where they were still within easy access of the salt resources on the upper Ouachita River. The Yazoo location, however, placed the Tunica at one of the most sensitive frontiers between the developing English and French interests. The French, recognizing the importance of the region (as well as the potential of such a settled, "docile" tribe) placed a missionary in their midst. Father Davion was a failure in his primary role of proselytizing the faith, but he was inordinately successful in attaching the Tunica forever to the French cause. As good entrepreneurs, they obviously recognized the potential of Davion's presence for secular affairs. This allegiance must be the principal explanation for their otherwise curious rejection of an equally profitable entrepreneurial venture: participation in the newly developed skin trade with the English. This decision doomed their attachment to the Yazoo, from which they were successfully removed by the English in 1706.

PORTAGE DE LA CROIX

The direction of the Tunica move in 1706 was south toward the nascent French colony. Significantly, the tribe chose to settle at yet another confluence of the Mississippi and a major tributary, this time the Red River. In the early eighteenth century, the Mississippi meandered in a great double loop that not only captured the Red River but nearly came back upon itself (see fig. 24 et seq.). The intervening narrow neck of land was a well-known portage, the southern end of which Iberville marked with a cross—and so the French referred to it as the Portage de la Croix.

This new location was doubly attractive to a people with entrepreneurial inclinations. They could both control access to the Red River, the most important western tributary south of the Arkansas River, and control travelers on the Mississippi who chose to use the portage. In this position, the Tunica were able to monitor traffic along both the Mississippi and Red rivers, could continue their aboriginal trade in salt and other resources of central Louisiana and beyond, and were well placed to take advantage of the eventual development of the French colony in the Lower Mississippi Valley during the second decade of the eighteenth century. Under the circumstances, the Tunica flourished at this location, especially as they also had the advantage of a hospitable environment characterized by exceptional biotic diversity (Albrecht 1945; Delcourt and Delcourt 1974, 1975, 1977; Dunn 1983).

Allowing for the particulars of geographical and ecological differences, the Tunica settlement pattern during this period seems to have been similar to that recorded in the lower Yazoo region, although it may have been slightly more concentrated. The principal village, referred to as Grand Tonicas (Thwaites 1900, vol. 67, p. 304), or simply Tonicas, was surrounded by satellite settlements called Petits Tonicas that were strategically placed at the southern and northern ends of the portage and near the Red River and Mississippi River confluence (see figs. 24–26).

The principal village, which was taken from the Houma, was apparently situated midway along the portage and overlooked it from a bluff top. This location has not yet been identified archaeologically, but historical accounts describe the village as a circular settlement on the top of the bluff, two or three houses deep around a plaza one hundred paces in diameter. Charlevoix reported that some of the houses were square and some were round (Charlevoix 1744, vol. 3, p. 433). Gravier had described Tunica houses on the Yazoo as being round, but the Dumont de Montigny sketch of a Tunica village of this period depicts square houses, although this may be only artistic convention (see cover illustration). Some structures must have remained from the Houma occupation and might have been simply reinhabited, which could explain a difference in architectural styles. While the shape of Houma houses has not yet been identified, a clue might be found in Charlevoix's observation (ibid.) that the house of the Tunica chief, Cahura-Joligo, was square. Rather than meaning that Tunica houses were square, however, this might indicate that the square houses were of Houma origin, for there is reason to suspect that the same structure served first as the Houma temple and then as the Tunica chief's house.

Gravier described the temple of the Houma as having a

vestibule which is adorned with the most agreeable grotesques and the best made almost that one could see. They are four satyrs, two of whom are en bosse, all four standing out from the wall, having around the head, hands and feet in bands, bracelets, garters, baldrics and belts, snakes, mice and dogs. The colors are black, white, red and yellow, and so well applied and without confusion, that it is a spectacle that surprises agreeably. (Shea 1861, p. 144)

In 1721, Charlevoix seems to have been referring to the same features in the Tunica chief's house (albeit with a studied lack of enthusiasm), which he describes as "quite ornamented for the house of a savage, with figures in relief that are not as bad as you might expect" (Charlevoix 1744, vol. 3, p. 433). If these structures were indeed the same, it would seem that Cahura-Joligo moved into the Houma temple. In that case, the reuse should not be interpreted simply as evidence of disregard for native religion and adoption of Christianity, but more likely as the abrogation of a previous native precinct and the establishment of Tunica domination in their new land.

In matters of religion it may be presumed that the Tunica maintained their traditional beliefs essentially unaltered during this period. Although La Harpe felt

that they had abandoned the "greater part of their idolatry," he noted that they still kept the sacred images of a frog and a woman (Margry 1888, vol. 6, p. 247). Archaeological evidence would seem to support a lack of significant Christian impact: a crucifix was found with burial 6 at Bloodhound, for example, but it was concealed under an elaborate marine shell necklace of native manufacture. That the crucifix was present at all certainly attests to Davion's efforts, and perhaps a certain ambivalence on the part of the Indians, but the lack of prominent display reveals the Tunica's true feelings.

By 1710 Father Davion had abandoned his permanent mission among the Tunica (Rowland and Sanders 1932, vol. 3, p. 153), and although he returned to visit many times during the subsequent decade, his failure to convert the tribe was evident to the good father, as well as most commentators (e.g., Charlevoix 1744, vol. 3, p. 431; Dumont de Montigny 1753, vol. 1, p. 166; Le Page du Pratz 1758, vol. 1, p. 123; Thwaites 1900, vol. 67, p. 308; cf. Margry 1888, vol. 6, p. 247).* Although he did baptize a number of children and the dying, it must be presumed that neither group had much say in the matter. His most notable success was the baptism of Cahura-Joligo, although the perceptive Father Poisson considered the chief a Christian in name only (Thwaites 1900, vol. 67, p. 308). Nevertheless, as shall be seen in the next section, Davion did sow a few proselytical seeds that eventually bore some fruit.

Charlevoix recorded in 1721 that the Tunica did not have a temple, which he attributed to a weakness in Tunica convictions rather than to Davion's efforts, but he apparently was not as observant as usual or else was too much influenced by what he wished to see. Charlevoix may have been misled by Father François Le Maire, who reported in 1714 that "the Houmas and the Tounikas in changing their locations ceased to dream of rebuilding their temples which they had in their old villages"; on the other hand, in 1717 he referred to a "small idol taken from the temple of the Tounikas" (Le Maire n.d.). Le Maire also claimed a "good number" of Christian converts among the Tunica, but since his information was secondhand—he never visited the Mississippi tribes—his pronouncements are clearly suspect, especially in these matters of religion. The Dumont de Montigny sketch of the Tunica village made only a few years after Charlevoix's record depicts a temple as the focus of the village (see cover illustration). Furthermore, Father Poisson remarked, at approximately the same time, that if the eternal fire of the Natchez were ever extinguished it must be relit from the Tunica fire—an indication that the latter was still burning (Thwaites 1900, vol. 67, pp. 310, 311).

---

* It has been suggested that the overall failure of the missionary effort in the Lower Mississippi Valley was due to a lack of economic support (McDermott 1949, pp. 72–73). Although this indeed may have been a contributing factor, the notable lack of success by individual missionaries must owe more to the intransigence of the various native peoples regarding religious matters and to the lack of secular incentives. It also might be noted that Davion appears to have been rather well equipped with the essentials of a religious and civilized life, according to the inventory of his personal effects (ibid., pp. 66–68). It is difficult to see what more he might have needed to make his mission a success.

It may be doubted, therefore, that there was much real change in Tunica religious practice at this time, even if there was some token concession to Davion's efforts (Le Page du Pratz 1758, vol. 1, p. 123; Margry 1888, vol. 6, p. 247). Certainly mortuary customs, the most reliable archaeological indicator, remained basically unchanged, and although European items were now at least as numerous as native artifacts in the graves, it may be questioned whether they represent a significantly altered ideology.

Even though Davion had finally abandoned the Tunica by 1720, these friendly allies were not denied a continuing French presence. In addition to the visitors of record, who can reflect only a tiny fraction of the numerous voyageurs, explorers, colonists, soldiers, and other travelers who would have stopped among the Tunica during this period, there is evidence of a permanent French establishment *aux Tonicas*. As early as 1712, "a few French stragglers settled among the Tunica" (Butler 1924, p. 93). By 1722, there were twenty-one French men, women, and children, and the following year Diron d'Artaguiette noted the presence of fifteen French "places" (Mereness 1916, p. 44). By 1726, those fifteen families numbered forty-eight persons, a considerable French presence which was confirmed by Poisson in 1727 (Thwaites 1900, vol. 67, p. 310; see also Le Page du Pratz 1758, vol. 1, p. 137; Rowland, Sanders, and Galloway 1984, vol. 4, p. 77). Two of these Frenchmen are even named in official documents in 1727 and 1728 (Louisiana Historical Quarterly 1921, pp. 220, 506). Dumont de Montigny's sketch of the Tunica village a few years later graphically depicts the situation, showing French houses nearby, as well as the temporary fort of Loubois (see cover illustration). Other contemporary French maps also place several French habitations in the vicinity of the Portage de la Croix (Broutin 1731; Gonichon 1731; DeBatz ca. 1732). Although the French settlement among the Tunica never attained the proportions of their Natchez settlement, it was sufficient to keep the Tunica firmly attached to the French cause (and at the same time it was small enough not to pose a threat?). This attachment was most beneficial to the Tunica, as has been described and as is revealed archaeologically in the relative wealth of European artifacts that they possessed.

Much of the Tunica success during this critical, dynamic period was certainly due to the fact that they were blessed with a strong but accommodating personality as chief. It was really Cahura-Joligo who firmly attached the Tunica to the French. His commitment and admiration extended to adopting French clothing and learning some of the language. The French, in turn, bestowed medals and titles upon him and relied on his military and economic assistance. Although the Tunica officially recognized the traditional two chiefs, one for war and the other for civil affairs (Margry 1888, vol. 6, p. 247), Cahura-Joligo often assumed both roles during this period.[*] His greatest role, however, was economic.

Charlevoix noted in 1721 that Cahura-Joligo "trades with the French . . . and he understands his trade very well. He has learned of us to hoard up money, and he is reckoned very rich" (Charlevoix 1744, vol. 3, p. 433). While Charlevoix may be forgiven a certain ethnocentric viewpoint, his perception would seem to be valid. Under the leadership of Cahura-Joligo, the Tunica demonstrated good business sense. In 1713 they "sang the calumet" to the British trader Price Hughes on his tour through the Lower Mississippi Valley (McWilliams 1953, p. 161). It may be surmised that they were hospitable to Hughes more to keep the French from taking them for granted than from any real interest in trading with the English, as this was before the French had made a concerted effort to establish economic hegemony in the valley. Hughes was to be the catalyst, however, that brought the French to make such an effort.

The Tunica quickly fell into line. In addition to their role in the salt trade, they are mentioned as being prominent in supplying the French with horses, fowl, corn, and other products (Charlevoix 1744, vol. 3, p. 433; Margry 1888, vol. 6, pp. 246, 249; Mereness 1916, pp. 44–45; Rowland and Sanders 1932, vol. 3, p. 423; Menier, Taillemite, and de Forges 1976, p. 122). They still were not major participants in the deerskin trade, however, for in 1726 Bienville noted that "only one thousand deerskins can be obtained from them" (Rowland and Sanders 1932, vol. 3, p. 530). The value of the Tunica was to the basic requirements of the colony itself, not to the world market. In this role they succeeded remarkably well.

Whatever the success of the Tunica in trading with their French—and also Indian—neighbors, their accumulation of European material goods did not rest on that alone. Although Bienville estimated that the Tunica could muster only 120 warriors in 1726 (Rowland and Sanders 1932, vol. 3, p. 530), as consistent allies of France they were recipients of annual presents and other unscheduled gifts (e.g., Charlevoix 1744, vol. 3, p. 433; Rowland and Sanders 1929, vol. 2, p. 340; Rowland, Sanders, and Galloway 1984, vol. 4, p. 77). There were also remunerations for specific military ventures (see Merveilleux n.d. for the goods that the Indian allies were able to extort from the French for their services in dire circumstances). In 1712 a Tunica contingent accompanied St. Denis on his trip up the Red River to establish the Natchitoches post (McWilliams 1953, p. 149). In 1715–1716, the Tunica helped the French in the first war against the Natchez (ibid., pp. 174–182 [note that Pénicaut mistakenly dates this event to 1714]; Rowland and Sanders 1932, vol. 3, pp. 203–215), for which Cahura-Joligo received a commission as "Brigadier of the Red Armies." Again, in 1723, the Tunica joined the second punitive expedition against the Natchez, during which Cahura-Joligo was grievously wounded (Dumont de Montigny 1753, vol. 2, pp. 99–110; Le Page du Pratz 1758, vol. 1, p. 210; Rowland and Sanders 1929, vol. 2, p. 374). In 1726 Bienville described

---

[*] Another apparent deviation from the expected pattern among southeastern Indians is indicated in an observation by La Harpe that could be interpreted as meaning that Cahura-Joligo's son, who died in adolescence, would have been his successor (Margry 1888, vol. 6, p. 247). The word La Harpe used is *héritier*, which does not necessarily have a political connotation, but the context suggests this meaning. Patrilineal succession was not the norm, although conceivably the prosperity of Cahura-Joligo's leadership might have encouraged the Tunica to waive the rules.

them as "formerly a very warlike nation," a prematurely negative assessment of their military abilities, as shall be demonstrated. In 1730 the Tunica participated in the final Natchez war, which resulted in the removal of that unfortunate people from their ancestral homeland (Le Page du Pratz 1758, vol. 3, pp. 283–293).

Despite their official steadfastness, however, the Tunica were sometimes suspect, as in 1716 when Bienville deemed it necessary to build his encampment in a defensible position some distance from the village of his erstwhile allies (Swanton 1911, pp. 197–198). In 1723 the Tunica felt compelled to prove their loyalty by killing three Natchez, "although they were allied" to that nation at the time (Rowland and Sanders 1932, vol. 3, p. 369). When the final showdown occurred between the Natchez and the French, the Natchez did not even consider including the Tunica in their conspiracy, because they were "too much wedded to the French" (Le Page du Pratz 1758, vol. 2, p. 220; vol. 3, p. 250; see also Charlevoix 1744, vol. 2, pp. 464–465, 470). This attachment, and the Natchez perception of it, was to prove disastrous to the Tunica.

The unsettled situation blew apart in November 1729. The Natchez finally tired of their relationship with the French and massacred the French colony almost to a man. Many women and children also were killed, as well as a contingent of six Tunica warriors (Rowland 1925, p. 232). The substantial French presence in the Natchez region, the "pearl of Louisiana," was forever destroyed. The French could not afford to allow this outrage to go unpunished, and in 1730 they attacked the Natchez and drove them from their villages. The following year, most of the Natchez were captured and enslaved, and this ancient nation ceased to exist. It was a Pyrrhic victory for the French, but the magnitude of their loss was not yet fully realized. The Tunica, however, were the first to suffer. As allies, the Tunica had joined the French in the first attack, although they apparently were not part of the final expedition. In retaliation for their participation, however, the few remaining Natchez sought revenge.

In June 1731 the Tunica suffered the greatest disaster in their recorded history. Misjudging the resentment of the Natchez, Cahura-Joligo welcomed a band of survivors into his village. One may wonder at the naiveté of this great chief, who had to this point so successfully guided his nation through the early decades of contact and conflict. But perhaps past accommodations with the Natchez were recalled, as well as the fact that the loss of Tunica warriors in the Natchez massacre of 1729 more than offset the relatively minor Tunica participation in Natchez destruction. Or perhaps Cahura-Joligo was just getting old: he had been chief for at least fifteen years, according to the historical records, and there is reason to believe that he may even have brought his people from the lower Yazoo twenty-five years earlier. In any case, his new accommodation with what appeared to be a few pitiful Natchez was a catastrophe.

The reports of what actually happened that June night conflict somewhat in their details (Charlevoix 1744, vol. 2, pp. 497–498; Le Page du Pratz 1758, vol. 3, pp. 301–302; Menier, Taillemite, and de Forges 1976, p. 193; Rowland, Sanders, and Galloway 1984, vol. 4,

pp. 77, 79, 102–103), but a general scenario may be reconstructed. There was a feast and a dance, and then in the early morning hours after the Tunica had retired the Natchez attacked. They killed Cahura-Joligo (although not before he slew several Natchez) and took possession of the village. The Tunica war chief rallied his warriors, and after a few days of prolonged battle they regained the village and forced the Natchez out. Both sides lost at least twenty killed and as many wounded and captured. This may not seem like a great loss, but it reduced Tunica fighting strength by half, and Cahura-Joligo was dead. Furthermore, since their village had been the scene of the battle, it was destroyed (Juzan 1731a). The tribe had lost everything else as well: food, munitions, arms—in short, "all they had been provided with" (Rowland, Sanders, and Galloway 1984, vol 4, p. 79). It was indeed a disaster for the Tunica, and so it was bemoaned in the various French accounts. Under these new circumstances of confrontation and the destruction of their village, the Tunica opted to move once again.

Before moving on with them, let us briefly summarize the changes that had occurred among the Tunica after three decades of French contact. They had moved from the fringe of French influence toward its core. They had integrated economically and militarily with the French colony. They had a chief who was comfortable in European clothes, was given a military commission, and even spoke a little French. He and many of his people were nominal Christians: children had been baptized, and some of the ritual formalities were carried out by a few women, but most of the adult males—although they liked ringing the bell for services—demurred, saying "the rules were too hard" (probably meaning they were not about to give up their plurality of wives [Margry 1888, vol. 6, p. 247]). The Tunica avidly accepted European technology yet retained many aboriginal artifacts that had traditional significance. Burial 4 at Bloodhound, a woman, was dressed in a frock coat and perhaps trousers (demonstrating that other members of society besides Cahura-Joligo wore European clothing), but she also had shell earpins. Burial 5 had iron axes and glass beads, but the latter were woven into the hair in the aboriginal fashion. Burial 6, a child, was well endowed with imported artifacts which included a crucifix, but it was concealed beneath an elaborate shell necklace. The Tunica had changed, but they still maintained many customs and artifacts that were traditional.

TUNICA BAYOU

The Tunica response to the recent disaster was to move once again, a repeated pattern in the face of adversity. This time the move was only a few kilometers south, to the bayou that has ever since borne their name. The new location brought them even closer to their French friends, whom they needed now more than ever, and yet left them within easy reach of the Portage de la Croix and the Mississippi and Red rivers.

Greatly reduced in numbers, the Tunica concentrated in a single village: the Trudeau site and its environs (Claiborne 1880, p. 67). Apparently there also were a few camps along the east bank of the Mississippi that kept track of river traffic, since Trudeau at the time was at least 1 km from the river. Archaeological investigations at Trudeau revealed that a traditional site plan was maintained in which houses were arranged around a central plaza (see fig. 84 and cover illustration). However, the village also incorporated a cut-off bluff remnant, the mound shape of which evoked earlier practice and was apparently utilized in the same fashion. A structure was placed on its summit, and some of the finest artifacts were found there.

The Trudeau site, of course, was the provenience of the Tunica Treasure, the most extraordinary collection of European artifacts from the colonial period to have been found in the entire Lower Mississippi Valley. Obviously, the Tunica had quickly recouped the losses they had suffered at the hands of the Natchez. The question is how the Tunica were able to accumulate so much material wealth, especially now that they had been reduced to such small numbers (at most, a couple hundred people). Much of the answer must be found in the fact that they remained one of the only viable tribes in the Lower Mississippi Valley and still had some economic and military usefulness to the French. It is the military function that is especially mentioned in the records of the period, as is discussed further below.

It is important to realize that this stage of contact was not simply a case of domination and submission. The Tunica were changing, and in many respects they were acculturating to French requirements and lifeways. But neither at this time nor previously was this relationship forced, for the Tunica generally seem to have been accommodating. They never had a serious confrontation with the French, although occasionally there were problems that required correction. Overall, however, the Tunica were too important to the French, and the relationship first established by Davion had developed under Cahura-Joligo into a beneficial symbiosis. The Tunica and the French needed each other, and in the Tunica case, at least, the relationship resulted in a fine florescence during the middle decades of the eighteenth century. This florescence was indeed expressed by the relative wealth of European goods in their possession, but it is significant that at the same time the Tunica maintained a continuing regard for native artifacts, technologies, and ideologies. As much as the Tunica were influenced by the French and their goods, they remained a people—a people in transition, to be sure, but with much of their own culture and traditions intact.

The artifacts of the Tunica Treasure were removed from graves located within the village compound at Trudeau. Those graves and their contents tell us much about the Tunica in the mid-eighteenth century. Although most of the burials were exhumed under unprofessional circumstances, we do have some reliable data (Brain 1979). The burials continued to be supine inhumations with the heads generally oriented in an easterly direction.* They had more European materials

than before, but these were arranged as native custom dictated. Furthermore, there were still many aboriginal artifacts, and these were not heirloom pieces. The ceramic arts, at least, were still practiced, and shell ornaments continued to be made, as well as some lithic tools. The proof of these traditions is not just in the graves, where their symbolic usage could be expected to endure, but also in the middens. The large trash pit excavated in 1972 (see fig. 63) contained a vast array of items representing most of the types and classes of artifacts found with the burials (see table 6). The metal artifacts are of special interest since many were still usable, and even large broken items were simply discarded instead of being recycled. Clearly, the Tunica of Trudeau could afford to be as profligate with their material wealth in life as in death.

The same trash pit gave further evidence attesting to the high quality of Tunica life. The tribe ate very well, for prominent in the faunal remains were the bones of

Figure 208. Watercolor sketch of Tunica Indians rendered by Alexandre DeBatz in June 1732. Depicted are Bride-les-Boeufs, a chief (probably the war chief) of the Tunica during their occupation of Trudeau, and the wife and son of the great chief Cahura-Joligo, who had been massacred by the Natchez the preceding June. The background may represent the landscape of Trudeau. (Courtesy Peabody Museum of Archaeology and Ethnology, Harvard University, David I. Bushnell Collection)

---

* An interesting departure from normal practice is the case of burial Beta, which was excavated in 1981. The original interment had been made in the traditional manner, but then

the body had been carefully disinterred, apparently within living memory. We have no idea why this grave was disturbed, but the important fact is that it must have been done by the Tunica themselves.

large mammals such as bear and bison, as well as deer (see app. H). The nearby loess uplands (called the Tunica Hills) and the Louisiana lowlands across the river were rich hunting grounds, and the small Tunica population could obviously afford to be selective in its choice of foods. Domesticated chickens were also part of the diet, as were the occasional wild bird and fish. Corn was certainly grown and consumed, as attested by the recovery of carbonized cobs and kernels in the excavations and the historic references to surpluses that were sold to the French. Cucurbit seeds were found in containers associated with many of the burials (Brain 1979, p. 254), and wild fruits, nuts, and vegetables also were gathered. The Tunica even drank well—perhaps too well. The numerous bottles and drinking vessels evidence a steady access to spiritous liquors. Indeed, in 1758 the Chevalier de Kerlérec specifically decried "the drink that has been so liberally lavished upon them for more than twenty years" (Rowland, Sanders, and Galloway 1984, vol. 5, p. 212) and attributed their declining population to its effects. All in all, however, it was obviously a bountiful life for the mid-eighteenth-century Tunica. They were well fed and relatively secure economically and politically.

The political structure of the Tunica seems to have reverted to the more usual division of powers after the death of Cahura-Joligo. His strong personality apparently dominated the chieftaincy throughout the preceding decades, but during the Trudeau period a plethora of chiefs is mentioned. In his famous 1732 watercolor, DeBatz referred to Bride-les-Boeufs as chief of the Tunica and stated that "*il remply la place de son predecesseur que les Natchez tuerrent au mois de juin dernier*" (fig. 208). Nevertheless, it is more likely that he was a war chief, and perhaps the real meaning of DeBatz's phrasing is that he was the one who rallied the Tunica after Cahura-Joligo had been killed. The year before, Bride-les-Boeufs was mentioned by Juzan (1731b), but only as one of the Tunica "*considerés*" (men of distinction). He seems to have remained influential for the next thirty years and is referred to as a chief in 1764 (Brasseaux 1979, p. 122). Juzan also lists six more *considerés* without specifically naming any one of them as chief, although the prominence in the manuscript of a certain Dominique suggests that he was preeminent at the time.* Two other *considerés*, Atanache (Lattanash) and Carodet, are mentioned as chiefs in later years (ibid.; Rowland and Sanders 1927, vol. 1, p. 406). In fact, Lattanash was even longer lived than Bride-les-Boeufs and was recognized as principal chief as late as 1771 (Rea 1970a, p. 14). Thus it would seem that while one chief may have been recognized before all others

during the middle decades of the eighteenth century, his power was shared (Rowland and Sanders 1927, vol. 1, pp. 281–282; Rowland and Sanders 1932, vol. 3, p. 735; Swanton 1911, p. 314; Bridges and Delanglez 1964, p. 260).

Evidence of chiefly status was found among the burials at Trudeau (Brain 1979, p. 279). If the associations are valid, one multiple interment in particular clearly indicated that one or more of the deceased had occupied a position of prominence; many other burials had been only slightly less well endowed with status items. Furthermore, at least five catlinite pipes, symbols of chieftaincy, have been found at Trudeau.

In matters of religion the Tunica seem to have maintained traditional practices, as evidenced by their temple and mortuary patterns. These were private matters not discussed in the historical documents of the period. Significantly, the only overt references to religion are to the fact that the Tunica continued to practice some of the formalities of Christianity (Bridges and Delanglez 1964, p. 260). Many used their baptismal names (e.g., Jacob and Dominique), and when Father Davion's generations came of age and had children of their own they had them christened: in 1740 alone, twenty-seven children were baptized with the "consent and demand" of their parents, who included Jean Louis, the Christian name of the chief Carodet (DeVille 1974, pp. 48–49). Davion may have rested more peacefully knowing that his efforts had not been totally in vain. On the other hand, it must be noted that in all the Tunica Treasure there are only four crucifixes and a small handful of rosary beads, and no other specifically Christian artifacts. The mortuary practices reveal the preservation of native customs, and it may be inferred that there was an overwhelming continuity in traditional religion and ideology overlaid with only a thin veneer of Christianity.

The overt display of Christianity by the Tunica, however handled privately, was probably intended primarily as a mechanism for dealing with their patrons and may have been necessitated by the growing French presence within their midst. The French apparently maintained a post among the Tunica throughout the period, with a few possible hiatuses (Juzan 1731b; Rowland and Sanders 1932, vol. 3, pp. 590, 706; Parkhurst 1945, pp. 683–684; Menier, Taillemite, and de Forges 1976, pp. 194–196, 202, 233, 293, 432; Rowland, Sanders, and Galloway 1984, vol. 5, pp. 43–44, 88, 142, 145). This presence obviously contributed to the Tunica adoption of French customs as well as material culture.

The Tunica retained a significant economic position in the colony during this period, but their real importance to the French was military. Despite official reports to Paris of the destruction of the Natchez, the colonial records reveal that attacks from remnant guerrilla bands continued well into the 1740s, and the threat remained for many years thereafter. Furthermore, many Natchez had found refuge among the Chickasaw, and this was part of the cause for renewed conflict. The Chickasaw wars in the 1730s were another disaster for the French and ultimately destroyed their credibility for the control, if not possession, of the Lower Mississippi Valley. The Tunica played no direct role in that

---

* Most telling of all is the report that a deputation of Natchitoches Indians was to arrive shortly and sing the calumet to Dominique and Jacob. The reference to Jacob is especially interesting since he was the surviving son of Cahura-Joligo. He, too, is depicted in the DeBatz watercolor, drawn some months later, and he clearly was preadolescent. Perhaps Cahura-Joligo's wish that his son succeed him left matters of leadership temporarily in a state of flux. Jacob, however, is not heard of again after this time, and it may be presumed that ability, rather than inheritance, was reasserted as the primary criterion for leadership.

debacle (Bridges and Delanglez 1964, pp. 292–293), but they were important in helping to counter Natchez incursions in and around the Natchez ancestral home. The rewards for this and other services apparently were considerable. Thus, at least in part, the accumulation of the Tunica Treasure may be explained.

The Tunica had become mercenaries, more politely known as native auxiliaries. Kerlérec noted in 1758 that although reduced to only about sixty warriors, "this nation . . . is very brave and has always served the French well" (Rowland, Sanders, and Galloway 1984, vol. 5, p. 212). Indeed, Tunica warriors served in many police actions during the 1730s to 1750s (e.g., Juzan 1731b; Rowland and Sanders 1927, vol. 1, pp. 208, 215, 282–283; Rowland and Sanders 1932, vol. 3, pp. 552, 623, 635, 708, 730, 756; Feiler 1962, p. 30; Barron 1975, pp. 40–41, 60, 66, 148, 248; Menier, Taillemite, and de Forges 1976, pp. 214, 225–226, 247–249, 289, 299, 308, 404, 417–418, 420; Rowland, Sanders, and Galloway 1984, vol. 4, pp. 112, 188, 338; vol. 5, pp. 24, 34, 43–44, 48, 88, 145, 212). Curiously, a martial life is not especially indicated in the mortuary evidence revealed archaeologically. No trophies and remarkably few firearms were found at Trudeau. It could be argued that under the circumstances weapons were required in the hands of the living, but given the overall display of material wealth it is unlikely that firearms were in short supply. It is possible that while the Tunica were sometime mercenaries of the French, their own perception of themselves was somewhat different.

Nevertheless, the effectiveness of the Tunica in military affairs was recognized at the highest levels, not only by Kerlérec, but also by governors Perier, Bienville, and Vaudreuil. In 1733, Perier considered the Tunica "the best nation, although small, that the king has in his service" (Rowland and Sanders 1927, vol. 1, p. 167), and Bienville remarked that "this brave nation has given us enough proof of its devotion to make it unnecessary for us to be convinced that it will spare nothing to keep the promise that it has given me" (Rowland and Sanders 1932, vol. 3, p. 623). In 1751, Vaudreuil expressed his satisfaction with "the Indians with whom we have reason to be pleased" (Rowland, Sanders, and Galloway 1984, vol. 5, p. 88).

In fact, however, Tunica loyalties were sometimes questioned during this period, as they had been before. Despite the protestations given above, the histories reveal the nagging suspicion that *"les sauvages,"* even the Tunica, could not always be fully trusted. In 1736 the Tunica were implicated in a plot proposed by the Chakchiuma: namely, peace (which was a euphemism for economic relations) with the Chickasaw and English. The Tunica role was to seduce the Red River tribes into joining this grand alliance (Menier, Taillemite, and de Forges 1976, pp. 302, 313; Rowland, Sanders, and Galloway 1984, vol. 4, p. 157; there is some confusion here about the dating). Apparently, the first chief of the Tunica, with several other men of distinction, entered into this "chimerical project" (Rowland and Sanders 1927, vol. 1, p. 281). However, Bienville was able to bribe two war chiefs with presents while the first chief was absent on his mission to the Red River. When the latter returned, he was made to see his folly,

and the Tunica resumed their pro-French stance. They demonstrated their loyalty by attacking the Chakchiuma and burning their village (which coincidentally was at the former Tunica home on the Yazoo River, the Haynes Bluff site; see fig. 21). In the process, they captured a great deal of booty which further contributed to their material wealth.

In 1737 there was another incident. While not as threatening to the colony as a whole, it nevertheless was a serious matter. "Several riotous men" murdered a Frenchman (Rowland and Sanders 1932, vol. 3, p. 706; Menier, Taillemite, and de Forges 1976, p. 289). This time heads rolled—at least one (Rowland and Sanders 1932, pp. 735; Menier, Taillemite, and de Forges 1976, p. 322), and perhaps two, said to be chiefs (Swanton 1911, p. 314). In reference to this incident, an anonymous French officer in 1739 recorded in his journal that the Tunica had "much degenerated in the qualities which they had originally possessed for war" (ibid.). If this observation was based on the declining numbers of Tunica warriors, it was accurate. But it did not reflect their real contribution to French enterprises before and after this date, nor the proof of their "qualities" at the conclusion of French sovereignty.

In March 1764, the Tunica and some other Indians ambushed the first English convoy to attempt an ascent of the Mississippi after the Peace of Paris had given them the right (Rea 1973a). The attack was successful in forcing the convoy to retire downriver. The English, of course, blamed the French for this violent effrontery, and the French officially berated the Tunica for ignoring the orders they had been given to welcome the newcomers (Alvord and Carter 1915, pp. 180, 191; Brasseaux 1979, p. 123). It is doubtful, however, that the Tunica and their friends acted on their own initiative in this affair. They had been used as French policemen on the river for decades, and unofficially this was but one more action—a final display of bravado. The Tunica must have been receptive to the idea, for they had already suffered much at the hands of the English and their allies, the Natchez and Chickasaw, and they surely feared the coming of the English presence itself. There was a momentary suspicion on the part of the English that the attack was linked to Pontiac's Rebellion, but it was really just a local affair. The Tunica's given reasons for their action were that they did not wish to give up a slave that had fled to their protection (Dorsey and Swanton 1912, p. 12), and that the English had "bad hearts" and "corrupted the ways among all the tribes" (Alvord and Carter 1915, p. 180; Rea 1973a, p. 186; Brasseaux 1979, p. 123). The Tunica contritely apologized to the English at the behest of French officials and were not punished despite strong recommendations from the humiliated British soldiery (Alvord and Carter 1916, p. 232). Thus they came briefly under English rule.

At this point—the conclusion of French sovereignty —the Tunica had survived sixty-five years of Euroamerican contact and conflict. They had been much influenced by French customs and material culture and had become important economic and military partners with the Louisiana Colony. Nevertheless, they still maintained many traditional patterns, especially in settlement, diet, sociopolitical structure, language, and ideology. The Tunica had undergone a considerable amount of culture change, but they were still only semi-acculturated (Brain 1979, p. 282).

POINTE COUPÉE

After making peace with the English, the Tunica settled at a new location on the east bank of the Mississippi River about 20 km south of Trudeau and at the northern edge of the French settlement of Pointe Coupée. Although technically under English rule, the Tunica chose to improve their situation by moving as close as possible to their French allies while still maintaining their tribal integrity. The Tunica remained at Pointe Coupée for about twenty-five years—that is, for some ten years after the Spanish wrested control of the east bank from the English in 1779. Thus, during this period they directly experienced both English and Spanish sovereignty.

Unfortunately, the Pointe Coupée village site of the Tunica has since been destroyed by the Mississippi River, so there are no archaeological data for this occupation.* Equally regrettably, there is a general lack of historical knowledge for this period in the Lower Mississippi Valley. The English tenure was brief and never fully consolidated. Ironically, when after striving for nearly a century to take control of the Mississippi River they had finally gained its bank, the English were still thwarted by the Spanish, whose possession of New Orleans gave them a stranglehold on the river. Therefore, the English never realized the expected potential of their new dominion, especially as troubles in the Atlantic seaboard colonies soon distracted their attention. Although there was a major influx of English and Anglo-American settlers, these did not include men of letters with an interest in the natural and aboriginal phenomena comparable to that of their French predecessors. Only the official government records are applicable for our purposes, and the few useful documents consist mainly of cartographic surveys, land grants, and the reports of Indian agents (Rea 1970b; see also Rea 1973b for a historical overview of the English period).

The Spanish Dominion also is not well documented. Reluctant in their possession of the vast new territory, the Spanish were never more than an administrative presence. Thus the historical legacy of the Spanish for this period is also limited to official documents principally concerned with the running of the colony (De la Peña y Camara et al. 1968). Some secondary works on the Spanish regime provide additional perspective, but very little information relating to the Indians (e.g., Caughey 1934; Kinnaird 1946a, 1946b, 1949; McDermott 1974). Nevertheless, a few facts about the Tu-

nica survive and some surmises about their lifeways during this period may be made.

The Tunica village at Pointe Coupée was estimated to consist of about thirty "huts" in 1766 (Alvord and Carter 1916, p. 446), although by the end of the English administration it seems to have been somewhat smaller (Hutchins 1784, p. 44). The Durnford 1770 map (see fig. 37) depicts a linear site plan—two rows of at least a dozen houses—which if accurate indicates a significant change from aboriginal patterns. Another interesting feature on the map is what appears to be a large communal cornfield near the village. Additional documentation records a peach orchard (Rea 1970a, p. 20) and detached encampments of hunting parties (Alvord and Carter 1916, p. 446).

Hunting was not only a major part of subsistence but by this time had become the principal contribution of the Tunica to the colonial economy. Governor d'Abbadie wrote that "it is not possible for us to do away entirely with powder and ball as gifts to the savages who no longer make their living except by hunting with the gun and contribute by that means to our own subsistence and to a part of the commerce of this colony" (Alvord and Carter 1915, p. 312). Tunica hunters could also be hired (Romans 1961, p. 71). During his 1771 journey up the Mississippi, Jean-Bernard Bossu was "obliged to hire two savages of the Tonikas nation to hunt during the course of our trip. They obtained for us an abundance of food while we were going up the river" (Dickinson 1982, p. 36). One of those hunters demonstrated his marksmanship by shooting a rattlesnake that was crossing the river; for this feat he was honored with the title Chevalier of the Rattlesnake, and the figure of a serpent was tattooed around his body "with its head falling on a place which ladies will permit me to let them guess" (ibid.).

Overall, the Tunica of Pointe Coupée displayed the characteristics of a semi-acculturated people. They still practiced tattooing but were likely to wear articles of European clothing. The principal men possessed complete suits of clothes which they donned on public occasions, although Bossu observed that one Tunica notable would wear everything except the breeches (Dickinson 1982, p. 99; perhaps, like the Chevalier of the Rattlesnake, he had something to show off). They continued to have their children baptized (Baudier 1939; Gregory 1978, p. 156), but there is no evidence that they took Christianity more seriously than they had before. They certainly conducted themselves with sophisticated decorum in the colonial councils of state, but they still performed the "barbarous and ancient exhibitions of the Indians, cutting themselves with the teeth or bones of fish till the blood ran in streams, to show their warlike disposition" (Bjork 1926, p. 401). Despite these displays, Governor d'Abbadie contrasted their gentleness with the drunken behavior of the Pacana, who had accompanied them from Mobile (Alvord and Carter 1915, p. 182). The Tunica were not immune to this vice either, and Pittman at the beginning of the period and Hutchins at the end noted the decline in population caused by the "immoderate use of spirituous liquors" (Pittman 1770, p. 35; Hutchins 1784, p. 44). This was a peril that native medicine could not treat, although

---

* An example of what such a late eighteenth-century Indian occupation might look like archaeologically may be revealed at a contemporary village site on the Red River in Rapides Parish. This site (16RA335) apparently was occupied by a band of Apalache (and perhaps a few Taensa and Pacana). Preliminary investigations have shown that aboriginal artifacts are common at this site, especially pottery that can be recognized as being derived from ethnically distinctive traditions east of the Mississippi (Hunter 1987).

a Tunica medicine man was famous for his cures of lesser ills (Dickinson 1982, p. 71).

The principal chief during the period of English sovereignty was the aged Lattanash. He apparently shared power with others at first, for in 1764 Bride-les-Boeufs and Perruquier are mentioned as important subchiefs (Alvord and Carter 1915, pp. 191, 235). Bride-les-Boeufs, although also elderly by this time, probably continued in the position of war chief; while Perruquier, who actually was an Ofo, was accepted as a spokesman for the Tunica-Ofo alliance. By the early 1770s, Lattanash was the only chief mentioned (Bjork 1926; Rea 1970a), and it is probable that from this point on the declining population generally required only a simple chieftaincy.

While the economic and military roles of the Tunica were much reduced in importance during this period, the tribe was still the "leading nation" in this part of the valley (Rowland 1911, p. 267), so the English and Spanish vied for their loyalty with presents. Medals, flags, and other regalia were also bestowed upon the chiefs according to established rules of protocol (Ewers 1974). The Tunica accepted favors from both sides and generally got away with it, once again demonstrating their ingenious adaptability. In fact, they apparently did quite well. The records reveal that the Spanish were more generous with their gifts and bribes (Kinnaird 1946a, p. 209; Moore 1974, p. 80), and in 1772 the English Indian agent complained that the presents at his disposal "amounted to less for all the tribes than the Spanish provided for the Tonicas alone" (Rea 1970a, p. 26). In 1769 the value of the annual Spanish gift to the Tunica was more than 121 pesos, a sum larger than that given to any other tribe south of the Arkansas and east of the Caddo (Kinnaird 1949, p. 154). The English sniffed that the Tunica and their neighbors were simply "importunate beggers" (Rea 1970a, p. 34), but they did not wish to lose their allegiance and sufficiently increased their allotments to induce the Tunica to stay on the east bank (Bjork 1926; Rea 1970a; Fortier 1972, p. 42).

The Anglo-Spanish rivalry for the loyalty of the tribes was more a matter of national pride than military necessity. Although at the beginning of the period both sides had envisioned using the Indians to guard the respective banks of the river, the plan was soon cast aside. The tribes were simply too small, weak, and vacillating for the purpose (Berry 1917). The Tunica were even ordered by the English to abstain from any possible future conflict between England and Spain (Bjork 1926, p. 406). Yet, as already noted, on at least one occasion the Tunica demonstrated their "warlike disposition" to Spanish officials (ibid., p. 401), and it is probable that they were among the 160 Indians who accompanied Governor Bernardo de Galvez in the capture of Baton Rouge in 1779 (BIA 1980, AR, p. 6). If so, this was the last recorded military venture of the Tunica as a tribe.

The Tunica were content under Spanish rule. Their temporary allegiance to the English had been a political necessity, but even then the Tunica had demonstrated an affinity for their French and Spanish neighbors across the river. When both banks of the Mississippi, indeed all Louisiana, came under the flag of Spain, the Tunica were relieved of the delicate business of diplomacy. Furthermore, under English rule settlers had been en-croaching upon tribal lands and officialdom was unsuccessful in putting a stop to it (Rea 1970a, p. 20). In November 1779, however, after the defeat of the English, Galvez ordered "all officers and soldiers and inhabitants under His Catholic Majesty to respect and protect the rights of the tribe of Thonicas" (Downs 1979, p. 75). This order was not a mere formality but a sincere attempt to protect Indians in their holdings. Christianized Indians, as the Tunica now officially were presumed to be, even had the legal right to hold land on a basis of equality with white settlers (Arena 1974). Nevertheless, pressures from the influx of Anglo-American settlers encouraged during the English and Spanish regimes probably continued to irritate the Tunica, and the tribe finally left Pointe Coupée sometime in the late 1780s or early 1790s.

In summary, although the evidence is circumstantial, it is reasonable to conclude that further adaptations in Tunica lifeways took place during this last sojourn on the Mississippi. There appear to have been major modifications in their settlement pattern, and it may be expected that material culture and behavioral correlates continued to be updated. The move to Marksville occurred during the time of Spanish sovereignty. That beneficent rule was soon to be replaced, however, and acculturative pressures were to increase.

MARKSVILLE

The choice of Marksville Prairie for resettlement was logical in the context of Tunica history. Finally abandoning their ancestral abode on the Mississippi, and thwarted in their age-old progress downriver by intensive Euroamerican settlement from Pointe Coupée southward, the Tunica found on the Red River an open way to the west and a familiar avenue of trade and contact. Marksville Prairie was the first significant habitable land up the Red River from the Mississippi confluence and was a gateway controlling access. Once again, the Tunica demonstrated their proclivity for inhabiting strategic locations.

Marksville was dismissed as being of little economic importance by the early nineteenth century (e.g., Berquin-Duvallon 1803, p. 58) and the development of alternate forms of communication soon diminished its strategic value, but its salubrious environment has apparently encouraged continuous Tunica habitation to the present day. The prairie is a relict Pleistocene feature that protrudes some 15 m above the younger alluvial floodplain surrounding it. The location offered good agricultural land and certain biota not found in the already well-endowed bottomlands below. Subsistence strategies, therefore, could draw upon several different and very productive environments: prairie, bottomland, riverine, and intervening ecotones (Toth 1974, pp. 4–8). It was the ideal home for the Tunica (Saucier 1956, pp. 28–29).

With the occupation at Marksville, we enter the nineteenth and twentieth centuries. Unlike their relatively brief sojourns discussed in the foregoing pages, at Marksville the Tunica—or at least a Tunica core—have remained in place for about two centuries. These, of course, have been centuries of terrific change within the larger American, not to mention world, context. It may be argued that while these changes have been reflected on Marksville Prairie, they have rarely intruded with the same force that gave them birth elsewhere. Therefore, despite its geographic and environmental advantages, Marksville is best characterized as a placid backwater during the nineteenth and twentieth centuries. A period of two centuries is too long a comparative unit for this study, however, and in fact significant changes in Tunica lifeways may be demonstrated throughout these years. For purposes of discussion the period will be divided into three intervals: the early nineteenth century, the hundred years from the 1840s to the 1940s, and the modern era. The first interval is the best known historically and archaeologically; the second interval is poorly documented until the rise of anthropological interest around the turn of the century; and the third interval speaks for itself.

The Early Nineteenth Century

When the United States gained sovereignty over the Louisiana Territory there followed an initial flurry of censuses, reports, and other documents regarding the native inhabitants. Attention soon focused on those largely unknown and potentially threatening tribes that roamed the interior vastness above the thirty-fifth degree of latitude, however, and remnant tribes in the settled regions to the south were literally forgotten if they were small enough and presented no problems. Such was the fate of the Tunica. But official and historical limbo was to be a mixed blessing for the tribe and a dire complication for this study.

The only official federal record of the Tunica until 1938 is the brief description in 1806 by the Indian agent John Sibley (1832, p. 725):

These people formerly lived on the Bayou Tunica, above Pointe Coupee, on the Mississippi, East Side, live now at Avoyelles [Marksville]; do not, at present, exceed twenty-five men. Their native language is peculiar to themselves, but speak Mobilian; are employed occasionally by the inhabitants as boatmen, &c.; in amity with all other people, and gradually diminishing in number.

Despite its brevity, this account provides some basic facts and a point of departure for discussing the early nineteenth-century Tunica. The salient points are that the population seems to have remained quite stable since Pointe Coupée, their language was still spoken, they were available as hirelings (it would be good to know what the "&c." included), and lived in peace with their neighbors. Insofar as it goes, this sketch describes the Tunica of an earlier generation. Although they had relocated, there were no major changes in at least these basic demographic, linguistic, economic, and political aspects of their lifeways. Other continuities may also be assumed.

At almost exactly the same time that Sibley was taking his census, a French traveler, C. C. Robin, encoun-

tered an unidentified group of Indians on the Black River not far from Marksville (Landry 1966, pp. 128–130). Although we do not know that these people were Tunica, it is probable that Robin's account accurately reflects some details of Tunica lifeways at this time and place. Robin visited what was apparently a temporary camp; it was spring, and the men were away hunting deer and bear for skins, tallow, and oil that they could trade at the Rapides and Avoyelles (Marksville) posts. About a dozen families were living in tiny, oval, palmetto-thatched huts which were used only for sleeping. They had brought with them chickens and dogs, as well as pots of iron, copper, wood, and clay. Robin made the interesting observation that the clay pots were made by the Indians and that ground-up shells were kneaded into the clay before the pots were fired. Whoever these people were, they still practiced some traditional ceramic arts (see also Williams 1981a; Penman 1983); let it be remembered that the tempering of pottery with pulverized mussel shell was a distinctive characteristic of the earlier Tunica in the Lower Mississippi Valley. Robin also indicated that the Indians were not agriculturalists, or at most grew only a little corn in temporary plots. This was undoubtedly true at hunting camps, but it may be expected that at the principal village (such as Marksville) agriculture was more important, the fields perhaps being maintained communally. Finally, Robin noted the Indian desire for liquor and ornaments. Although his observations may not apply specifically to the Tunica, they describe a level of acculturation probably shared by all Indian groups in the region.

In a later section of his account, Robin displays an insight that is remarkably anthropological and in sympathy with the concerns of this study. Referring to the fact that "many writers have remarked on the change in customs brought about by their contact with Europeans" (Landry 1966, p. 152), he offers some general perceptions that could have applied to the contemporary Tunica:

With the arrival of fire-arms, far more efficient than arrows, it was possible for a single individual or at best a few hunters to engage in hunting. Thus every hunting affair ceased to be a public occasion, and the great celebrations became less frequent, and no longer involved the same ceremoniousness. The dances and games became obsolescent. Public affairs among the Indians deteriorated. They lived more in single families and small aggregations. They no longer needed to associate themselves into great nations except in time of war, against those who interfered with their hunting. War was thus almost the only bond left to them, but those peoples who were neighbors of the European settlers, no longer fearing destruction by enemy warriors, have almost ceased to exist as nations. They have gradually become dispersed in small bands and families, whose relationship to each other is only casual. At the same time, the use of fire-arms made them dependent upon the Europeans for guns, powder and lead, as well as for iron tools like hatchets and knives, which were far superior to those they had before. These they obtained in exchange for skins which they had formerly used as clothing, but now they accustomed themselves

Figure 209. Paintings of Louisiana Indians in the 1840s. *Top,* "Choctaw Settlement near the Chefuncte," by Francois Bernard (dated 1846 by Bushnell 1919, p. 64). A Tunica village of the period would have revealed a comparable scene, even to details of architecture, dress, and activities. (Courtesy Peabody Museum of Archaeology and Ethnology, Harvard University, David I. Bushnell Collection); *bottom,* "Louisiana Indians walking along a Bayou," by Alfred Boisseau (1847). Although the tribe is not identified, contemporary Tunica would have had similar dress and artifacts. Note that the boy is carrying a blowgun and darts. (Courtesy New Orleans Museum of Art: gift of Mr. William E. Groves)

to replacing these with blankets and coarse cloth which were much more convenient. Thus, little by little, they got out of the habit of using skins as clothing. This is the sort of influence that Europeans have had on the Indians. (ibid., p. 153)

In 1813, William Darby noted that "the Tonicas have adopted the manners and customs of the French. One or two white families reside amongst them, and it would puzzle Montesquieu himself to determine which of the parties has been the most influenced by the other" (Darby 1818, p. 70). A harsher and obviously less knowledgeable official view in 1826, however, claimed that the Tunica were not only Indians but "savages," because they "were not using the land as Providence had decided; for farming"; they were, furthermore, "not reclaimed from their savage mode of life," nor "of the chosen," because they had not "subdued their original propensities and evidenced a determination to live and cultivate the ground as white men do" (BIA 1980, HR, p. 8). These two perceptions express the equivocal position of the Tunica in the early nineteenth century.

Only slightly later, in the 1840s, an account of Chickasaw neighbors provides a description that could probably apply equally well to the Tunica in many particulars:

They live in simple huts, ten or twelve feet square, constructed of pine poles and covered with bark. They subsist principally on the flesh of deer, the coon, and opossum, all of which are plenty in these woods. Sometimes they exchange venison for a little corn and whisky with the planters on the bayous. Their usual dress is buckskin breeches and calico hunting shirts of fantastic colors, buttoned from belt to chin. They wear brass rings on their wrists, and in their ears and noses. The dress of the squaws is very similar. They are fond of dogs and horses—owning many of the latter, of a small, tough breed—and are skillful riders. (Northup 1968, p. 71)

Contemporary visual portrayals add further details about the life of Louisiana Indians (fig. 209).

There are indications that the Tunica lived in more than one village in Avoyelles Parish during the early years of the nineteenth century. In addition to Marksville, there appears to have been a settlement on Bayou Rouge a few kilometers to the south. If the population was initially divided between two permanent villages it would explain the apparent plurality of chiefs mentioned in the records at the time (see table 80), as each village would have had its own headman. However, the tribe soon consolidated at Marksville, and by the 1840s there was only one chief: the tragic Melancon, who was killed defending the tribal lands from white encroachment (BIA 1980, HR, p. 9).

The early nineteenth-century burials from the Pierite site confirm some of the lifeways described above and provide details on others. The first impression of the Pierite burials is that they represent a relatively well-to-do population. Most of the graves were furnished with a variety of artifacts, many of which were of high quality. It was inferred that at least two burials were those of chiefs and therefore should not be considered representative of the population as a whole. Neverthe-

less, they do reflect a society that was prosperous at least in part. The precise reason for the prosperity was not indicated, but the replication of well-furnished graves demonstrates that it was an enduring condition.

The artifacts with the burials not only were numerous and of high quality, they also were exclusively Euroamerican in origin. Although native artifacts may still have been made of wood and clay for various functions in the living society, they apparently were not deemed appropriate for use in the afterlife. They certainly would not have been missed, since the complement of Euroamerican artifacts was sufficient for all personal requirements. Most of these items appear to have been used in the manner for which they were intended. Thus we may infer from the guns, knives, and harpoons that hunting and fishing were important pursuits, and the hoes indicate that farming was not neglected. Axes and large adzes suggest carpentry and heavy construction: Tunica houses at Marksville may have been more solidly built than those of their neighbors. The stirrups and bridles demonstrate the Tunica's continued involvement with horses. On the other hand, paisley shirts, beadwork, and silver ornaments were distinctively native transformations into more congenial items of dress that signified Indian—if not always more ethnically specific—identity. There is sufficient evidence that the Tunica were active in such remanufacture of Euroamerican goods (Gregory 1978, pp. 160–161).

One category of artifacts, though, is conspicuously absent: there is not a single artifact from all the Pierite graves that might be interpreted as having Christian significance. The silver ornaments indicate sociopolitical status, and neither they nor any of the other items have any overt religious meaning. While Christian regalia were rare enough at earlier eighteenth-century sites and consisted of only a few crucifixes and rosary beads, their absence is surprising at this later time, when at least nominal profession of the faith could be expected. Clearly, the secularization of the prevailing American society allowed the Tunica considerable freedom in following and expressing their beliefs. The very graves themselves are expressive in this matter, for the presence and configurations of the artifacts are non-Christian traits that may be traced far back into the Tunica past.

The above evidence describes a native people who were at an advanced stage of acculturation. They had been submerged into the prevailing American economic and political systems, but they still clung to some traditional ways of doing things. In many respects they were relatively free and prosperous—or, as superficially summed up by a mid-nineteenth-century romantic, again in reference to Chickasaw neighbors: "They worshipped the Great Spirit, loved whiskey, and were happy" (Northup 1968, p. 72).

The Intervening Century

As the nineteenth century progressed, things did not go as well for the Tunica. The death of Chief Melancon in 1841 and subsequent litigation seem to have been traumatic events. The Tunica received no justice from

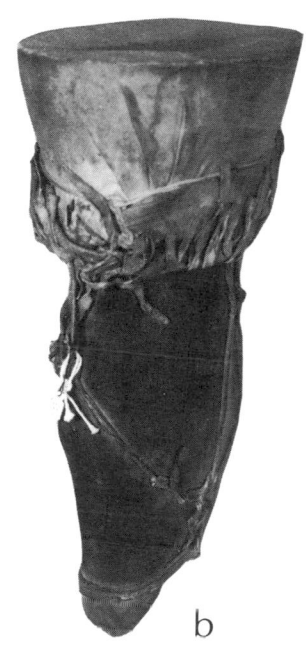

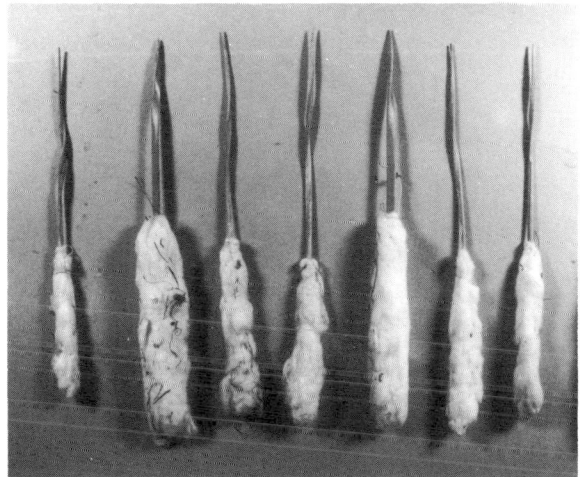

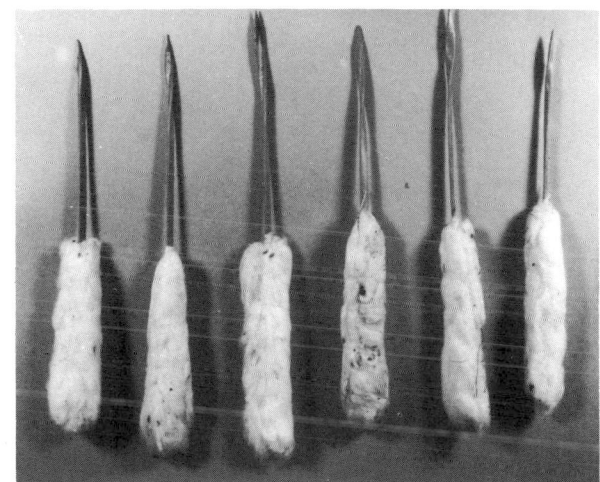

Figure 210. Early twentieth-century Tunica artifacts. a, shirt of red cotton decorated with white and yellow appliqués and edgings (length 81.3 cm); b, hand-held drum made from a cypress knee and used in dances (height 30.5 cm); c, blowgun darts with twisted cane points and cotton wadding (lengths 20–25.4 cm); d, pair of wooden figures and their case (heights of figures 14.6 and 15.3 cm, height of case 17.8 cm). (Courtesy Jonathan Holstein, Frank G. Speck Collection)

an officialdom that considered them still to be "savages" without full rights before the law. In many respects, they entered a century of decline from which they are just recovering. The chieftaincy apparently went underground, and the tribe's economic position became ever more precarious. They continued subsistence farming, hunting, and fishing and augmented their income with cash crops of cotton, vegetables, chickens, and pecans, as well as wage work. They were no longer prosperous, but they survived.

In the 1870s Volsin Chiki, who later became chief and an informant for both Albert Gatschet and John Swanton, was instrumental in reuniting the tribe and restoring its pride. According to oral history, he refurbished the cemeteries and rejuvenated the ceremonies (Downs 1979, p. 79). In 1899 a Professor Chambers reported, in a manner suggesting that it was a curiosity, that the Tunica were "leading an agricultural life and still maintaining a tribal organization" (Chambers 1900). Their continued survival was certainly due in large part to the fact that they retained their land and tribal organization. They succeeded in keeping their land because they held it in common: the chief parceled it out to individual families, and periodic redistributions adjusted for demographic changes. Certain areas were set apart for public dance and ceremonial grounds, others for family cemeteries. Hunting rights were also communal. This communal attitude was a cohesive factor that preserved the tribe and its institutions. To it we owe the continuance until recent times of a viable chieftaincy, traditional ceremonies such as the green corn or busk, a corpus of mythology and religious beliefs, and language. Mortuary practices also seem to have remained basically unchanged: Gatschet and Swanton reported that burials were oriented with heads to the east and that a fire was placed at the head during a period of vigil and fasting (Swanton 1946, p. 729). Together, these customs formed the core of Tunica ethnic distinction.

During this interval the Tunica continued to intermarry with other Indians, and with non-Indians as well. They had already absorbed the Ofo and Avoyel tribes and part of the Biloxi, and they also incorporated Choctaw and probably many other Indian bloodlines. Blacks and whites were also accepted, to the point that in 1938 the people were pronounced "too mixed to be considered Indians from a government standpoint" (BIA 1980, HR, p. 13). This judgment was faulty, of course, for the people considered themselves not only Indians but Tunica, and they had the institutions to prove it.

In matters of dress and housing, however, the Tunica were now indistinguishable from their non-Indian neighbors. Photographs of Tunica people taken about 1910 show them wearing clothing and living in houses comparable to what would have been found in any contemporary rural Louisiana community of the poor (Swanton 1911, pls. 16–18; Swanton 1946, pl. 49). But Indian dress had not been totally discarded (fig. 210a) (Swanton 1946, pl. 50) and was worn on ceremonial occasions.

Some native crafts also persisted but were becoming more pan-Indian. Racquet-ball sticks were still made and used, as were drums and blow guns (fig. 210b–c).

Of particular interest are a pair of cased wooden figures similar to eastern Sioux "tree-dweller" dolls (fig. 210d). Their significance is not known, but it is probable that they had traditional value: the horns on the two figures may indicate horned owls. Although they may have had negative connotations, owls and the transfiguration of humans into owls were popular themes in Tunica myths (Swanton 1911, p. 320; Haas 1950, p. 81).

A nadir of Tunica fortunes was reached during the national economic depression of the 1930s. By that time they had been effectively assimilated into the dominant American culture, but because of their Indian heritage they were relegated to the lower social echelons. They were disadvantaged economically, politically, and educationally. As a result, many tribal members left Marksville to improve their prospects. Most went to Texas, where a large number of Tunica still live today.

The Modern Era

The modern era may be said to have begun in the 1940s. It was during this decade that the Tunica lost some important parts of their heritage: Sesostrie Youchigant, the last fluent speaker of the language, died, and the last known corn festival was held. At the same time, the Tunica had formally launched their campaign for federal recognition as a tribe, and economic and educational opportunities improved. All together, these changes tended to hasten the removal of the Tunica from their past and attach them more firmly to the present.

Although Gatschet, Swanton, and Haas preserved the Tunica language, it is now only an anthropological curiosity and serves no sociological function. A few members of the tribe still know some words and phrases, but the language is no longer the tongue that binds. In fact, the language had actually been dead since early in the century, for Youchigant had no one to converse with during the last thirty-five years of his life.

When the traditionalists such as Youchigant died, they took more than language with them. The corn festival was formerly the principal annual ceremony. It is still remembered by a few older members of the tribe, and there has been talk of reviving it, but the function it once served clearly is required no longer. There are other ceremonies now, and the most important of these revolve around the tribal organization and plans for the future.

The last chief, Joseph Alcide Pierite, Sr. (fig. 211), died in 1976. He had been a farmer, fishing guide, tanner, carver, and professional stickball player, as well as an activist in gaining tribal recognition. His burial reflected this mixture of old and new. He was interred in the family plot next to his home on the Marksville reservation. The grave was a crypt above ground in the Louisiana French fashion, but it was oriented in the traditional manner, and an electric light was to shine over it. Within the coffin were placed a peace pipe and a beaded eagle feather, artifacts that have significance in the modern pan-Indian movement.

Even before the death of Chief Joe, however, the ancient office of chief had been abolished and replaced with a chairman and council when the tribe incorpo-

Figure 211. Joseph Alcide Pierite, Sr., last chief of the Tunica. (LMS photograph 1971)

rated as the "Tunica-Biloxi Indian Tribe of Louisiana" in 1974. This step was taken to meet the criteria for state and federal recognition. The state accorded formal recognition as an Indian tribe in 1975, and the federal government finally followed suit in 1981. The Tunica had proven that they had been continuously identified from early historical times as a distinct Indian group and had maintained sufficient political, ethnic, and cultural integrity as specified in regulations promulgated by the Bureau of Indian Affairs in 1978. They could, in fact, proclaim: "We have proved that we are who we say" (Butler 1978).

At this writing, the Tunica may be recognized as fully assimilated into the contemporary world. They are not only functioning within the larger society but are operating to their advantage the rules of that society. They remain Tunica, and they are an effective force in a country that has come to recognize its ethnic heterogeneity in place of the old concept of "melting pot." There is a growing pride in being Indian, a pride that may be expressed in the artifacts and solidarity of the pan-Indian movement rather than in traditional crafts and beliefs, but is sincere nonetheless. It may be predicted that the Tunica will move confidently into a new era in which their rights and prospects will not be compromised by—and may even be enhanced by—their Indian identity.

Table 78. Schematic representation of Euroamerican and Tunica interaction through time.

Periods	Euroamerican Influence	Tunica Reaction	Remarks
VI	Modern American expiation	Active response	The Tunica become involved in the pan-Indian movement and in legal maneuvering to recoup their economic position and, ultimately, sociopolitical prominence.
	Anglo-American control	Passive acceptance	Despite some difficulties, the Tunica become assimilated into the dominant culture.
V	English and Spanish sovereignty	Migration and vacillation	After repulsing the first English expedition up the Mississippi River, the Tunica are uncertain where their loyalties and advantages lie; material and sociopolitical acculturation are accelerated.
IV	French decline	Migration and integration	After massacre by the Natchez, the Tunica move even closer to the French and become more intimately involved with the economic and military welfare of the French colony.
III	French colonization	Accommodation	Major acculturation begins as colonists, soldiers, and administrators interact with the Tunica at many levels.
II	English pressure	Migration	To avoid overt conflict, the Tunica move closer to the French sphere of influence.
	French exploration	Friendly reception	Direct prolonged contact begins, as explorers are followed by missionaries and traders; the impact is mostly technological, and economic relationships are established.
I	Epidemic disease	Demographic and sociopolitical collapse; migration and amalgamation	Indirect introduction of pathogens leaves only remnant populations and causes drastic demographic, sociopolitical, and cultural change.
	De Soto entrada	Militant resistance	Violent confrontations occur, but probably no immediate significant culture change.

SUMMARY

Culture change along the Tunica continuum took many forms because it was the result of many influences at different times and in different places (figs. 212–221; table 78). The first direct contact with Europeans in the sixteenth century must have been quite unsettling, but it resulted in minimal immediate change. The biological stress of introduced disease during the subsequent century of indirect contact, on the other hand, obviously forced a period of extensive changes in demography, society, polity, and to a lesser extent material culture. The changes were fundamental, but because they were due to indirect causes of a noncultural nature they do not represent acculturation as defined here. If anything, it was a time of deculturation during which many lifeways and institutions were simplified (Smith 1984).

It was during the period of direct contact with the French and other nationalities in the eighteenth and early nineteenth centuries that the most intense acculturation was experienced, especially in material culture and external economic and political relationships. Although this was a time of exploitation of the Indians by the various Euroamerican parties, the Tunica maintained a relatively successful partnership with the French. They were not equal partners, but they managed to survive and even experienced a period of relative florescence.

The nineteenth century brought a new set of problems that the Tunica in effect resolved by going underground with many of their institutions so that their Indianness was less visible. Again they survived, but only at the cost of becoming fully acculturated and then assimilated into the lower echelons of the dominant American society. They did maintain some aboriginal continuities, however, particularly in the sociopolitical and ideological realms.

In the twentieth century, Tunica participation in the moral and legal ethos of the dominant society has allowed them to reassert their ethnicity and once again gain some control over their destiny. As optimistically expressed by the late Chief Joseph Alcide Pierite, Sr.: "We have a promise from the sun. As long as there is the sun, there will be Indian people here" (Gregory 1985, p. 109).

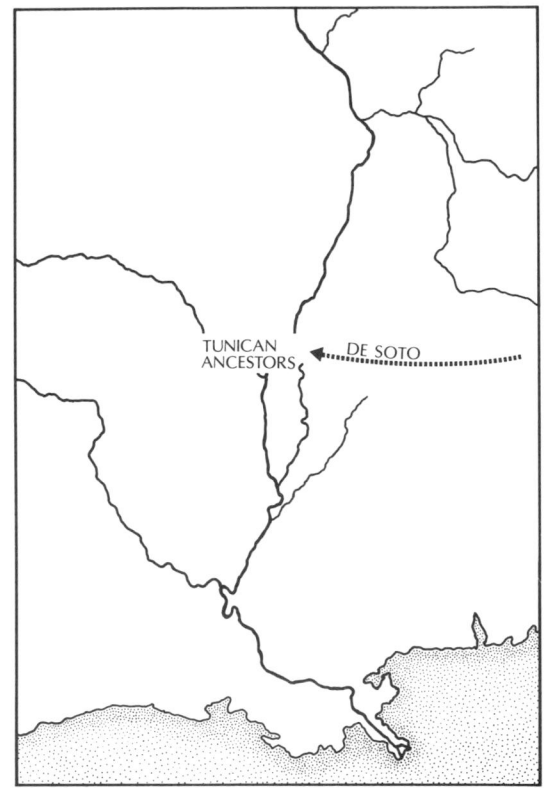

Figure 212. The De Soto entrada encounters Tunican ancestors in the upper Sunflower region, A.D. 1541.

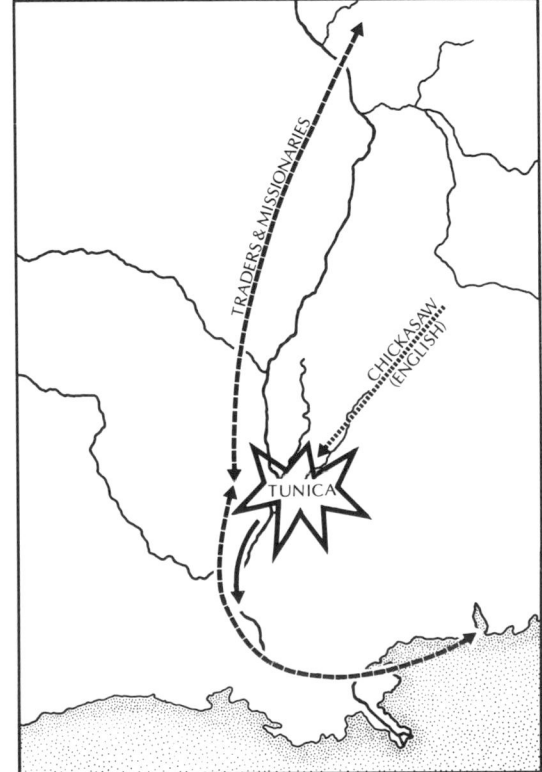

Figure 215. Period of French missionary effort and intense pressure from English traders and their Chickasaw allies, A.D. 1700–1715.

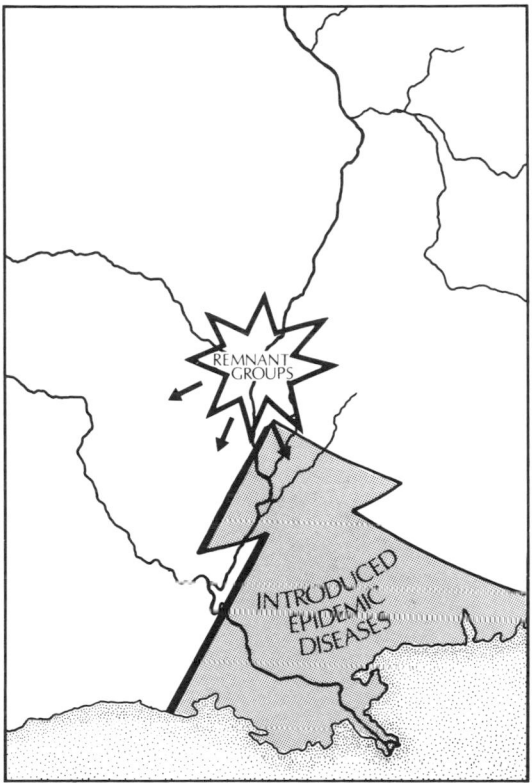

Figure 213. Epidemic diseases are introduced into the Lower Mississippi Valley, destroying the large populations encountered by De Soto, A.D. 1550–1650.

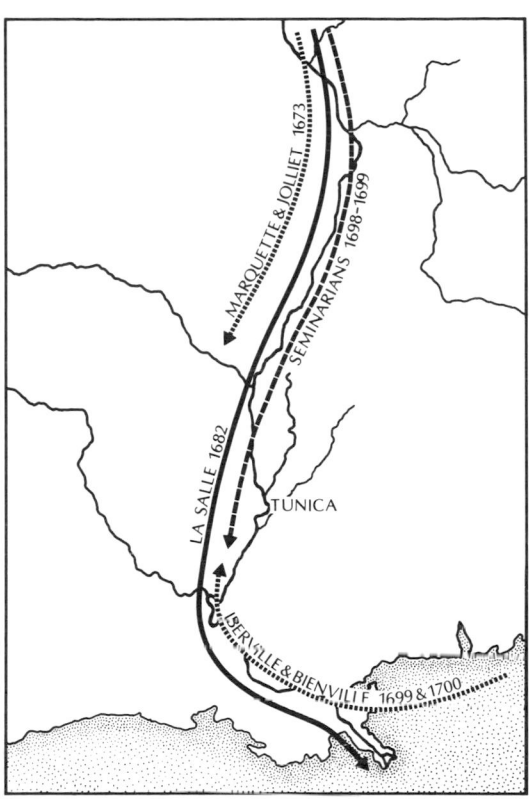

Figure 214. French exploration of the Lower Mississippi Valley begins in the last part of the seventeenth century and concludes with the establishment of the Louisiana Colony, A.D. 1673–1700.

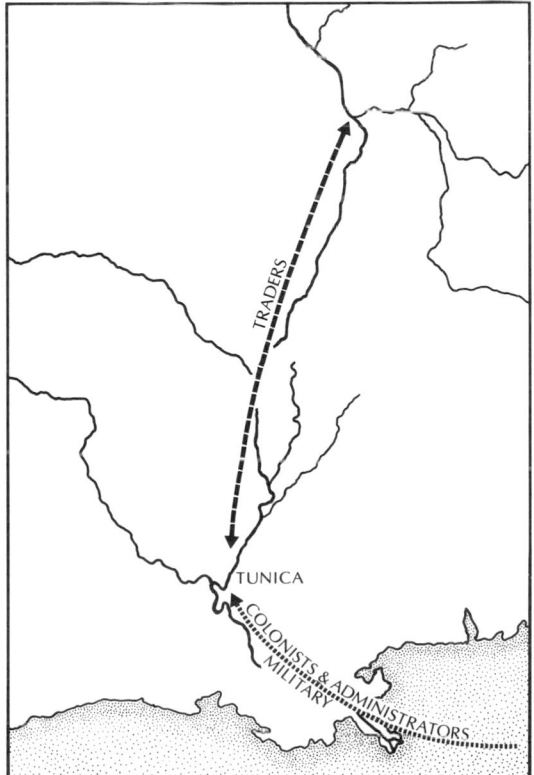

Figure 216. French colonization reaches its peak, A.D. 1715–1730.

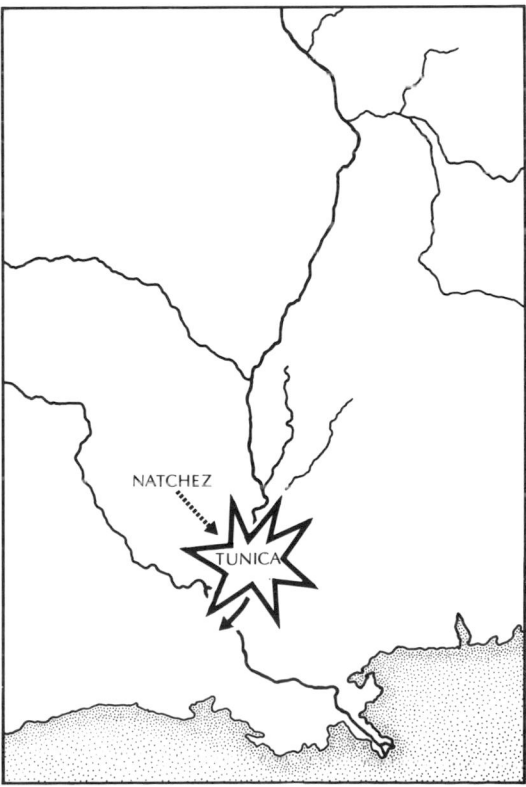

Figure 217. Massacre of the Tunica by vengeful Natchez, A.D. 1731.

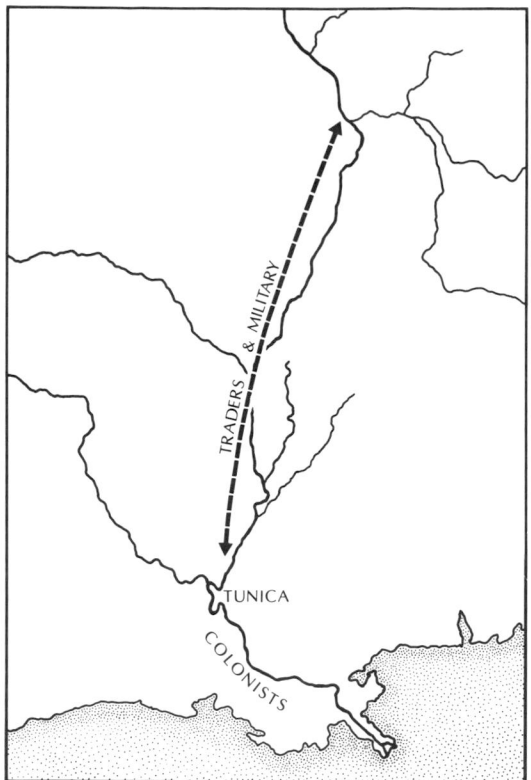

Figure 218. Chickasaw wars and French decline, A.D. 1731–1764.

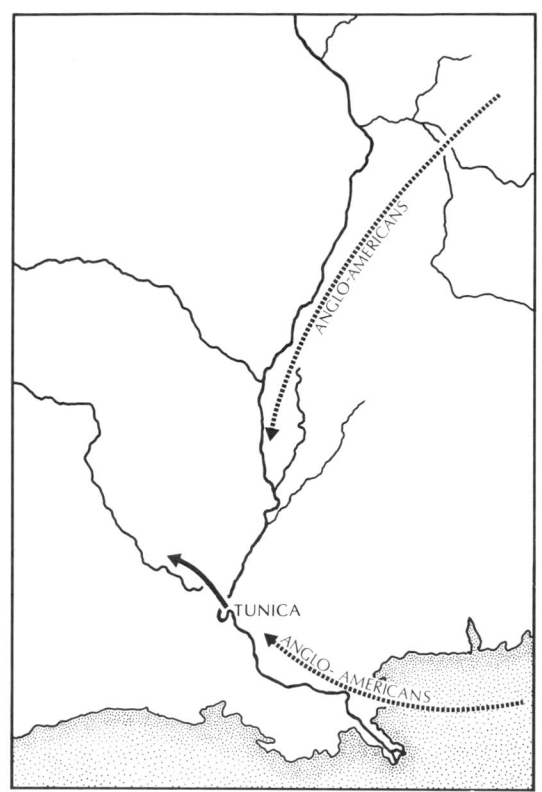

Figure 220. The period of English and Spanish sovereignties, A.D. 1765–1803.

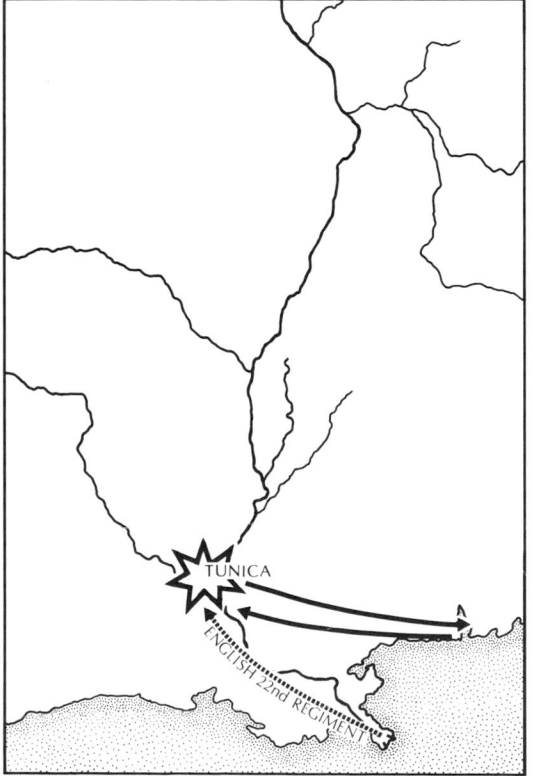

Figure 219. Ambush of the Loftus expedition, A.D. 1764.

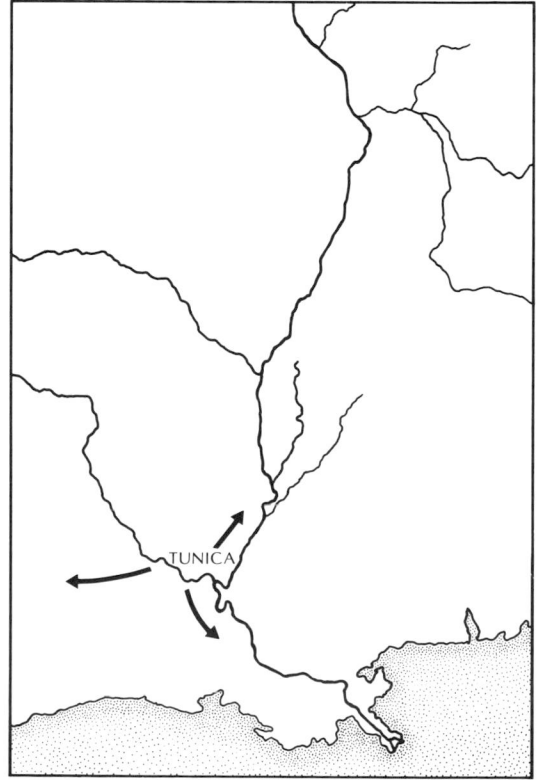

Figure 221. American dominion, A.D. 1803–present.

A Dynamic Perspective of Tunica Change

The description of the overall design of the culture of an ethnic group through time, as it changes, expands, retracts, incorporates new elements, readjusts, and proceeds, is a formidable task.

Dark 1957, p. 250

In the foregoing pages, stages in the Tunica continuum have been reconstructed using the approach and data of ethnohistoric archaeology. Those reconstructions were described as synchronic episodes in order to provide a holistic view of Tunica lifeways at each stage. A comparison of these stages now provides the basis for an analysis of the dynamics of change. Because we have a direct continuum, change can be perceived as it happens, not as interpolations between isolated episodes.

One of the clearest conclusions to be reached from the study of the Tunica continuum is that change did not occur at a constant rate. Contact situations are very complex, and the complexity is compounded through time. The contacted societies are composed of individuals who differ in age, sex, and perhaps status, and who therefore have different agendas. The Euroamericans who contacted them were generally a more homogeneous lot in age and sex, but were also motivated by many different concerns. Therefore, change occurred at variable rates of intensity through time. Because of these temporal and cultural variables, it is now desirable to adopt a diachronic and multidimensional perspective that analyzes change within separate categories of Tunica lifeways and institutions.

DEMOGRAPHY

The most fundamental consideration, of course, is people: genetic succession provides the nexus for the measure of culture change. It is now possible to trace Tunica demographics from late prehistory to the present with considerable precision (table 79). The most obvious pattern has been a steady decline in population until this century. It is, of course, a "main line" that has been followed: splinter groups have been ignored, and it must be recognized that in the present era the majority of Tunica do not live in Avoyelles Parish, much less on tribal land. It is also true that the Tunica in Avoyelles Parish have often lived with other peoples, Indian and Euroamerican alike, during the past three centuries of historical record. Nevertheless, despite the inevitable admixture, there has been an underlying perception of ethnicity that has been identified to this day as Tunica.

A conservative population estimate for the proto-Tunica province of Quizquiz would be 5,000 people. Biedma recorded that more than 300 women were captured in the first town surprised by the Spaniards; many

others presumably escaped, and the men were said to be away in the fields. Garcilaso de la Vega was informed that almost 4,000 armed warriors assembled in less than three hours after the arrival of De Soto. Garcilaso must always be considered suspect in matters statistical, but in this case he may not have exaggerated unduly: witness the usually reliable Ranjel's figure of 7,000 for the combined Pacaha alliance. Therefore, a population of at least 5,000 seems a reasonable interpolation and is supported by the archaeological evidence. The Parchman phase in the upper Sunflower region is characterized by numerous large mound centers (see fig. 196), of which the Spaniards apparently visited only two or three. Furthermore, at least one known village/cemetery area (Humber-McWilliams), occupied in some part during this phase, is found along a natural levee for approximately 3 km and contained thousands of graves (Tesar 1976).

The next 130 years brought drastic changes to the upper Sunflower region. The great populations disappeared and were replaced by smaller numbers of Quapaw-related peoples. It is probable that the general population loss was not so much the result of violent displacement as the work of the unseen killer, introduced infectious disease. In fact, such a scourge was at work among the Tunica on the lower Yazoo when French contact was first established in 1699. La Source noted that they "were dying in great numbers" from a smallpox epidemic (Shea 1861, pp. 80–81). An idea of how great those numbers might have been even after earlier ravages is given by Iberville in 1699 during a visit to the Bayogoula: "Smallpox which continues to ravage the population has exterminated one-fourth of the village" (Brasseaux 1979, p. 50).

La Source counted 260 cabins for the Tunica and their neighbors, the Yazoo and Ofo, which his companion de Montigny estimated were occupied by 2,000 people. Some years later, Bienville recalled that the Tunica (and allied tribes?) could muster more than 500 warriors at this time, a figure that seems rather excessive although it will be seen that the Tunica were consistently able to produce a rather higher number of warriors in proportion to the general population than is usually credited to Lower Mississippi Valley tribes (Swanton 1911, p. 43).

In November 1700, Gravier recorded only fifty to sixty cabins for the Tunica (100 including the allied tribes). If his estimate is correct, it confirms the observations in 1702 of Father Louis-Marc Bergier, who called the Tunica "much diminished" (Bergier 1702), and of Iber-

Table 79. Estimates of Tunica population derived from historical sources.[a]

Date	Population	Ethnohistoric Data	Reference
1541	5,000	More than 300 women (in first Quizquiz town)	Biedma (Bourne 1904, vol. 2, p. 25)
		Almost 4,000 armed warriors	Garcilaso de la Vega (Varner and Varner 1951, p. 425)
1699	1,200	2,000 souls (including Yazoo and Ofo)	de Montigny (Shea 1861, p. 76)
		260 cabins (including Yazoo and Ofo)	La Source (Shea 1861, p. 80)
		More than 500 warriors	Bienville (Rowland and Sanders 1932, vol. 3, p. 530)
1700		50–60 cabins	Gravier (Shea 1861, p. 133)
1702	1,000	300 families (probably including Yazoo, Ofo, Koroa)	Iberville (Margry 1881, vol. 4, p. 602)
1719	500	460 inhabitants	La Harpe (Margry 1888, vol. 6, p. 247)
1723		200 warriors	Diron d'Artaguiette (Mereness 1916, p. 44)
1725		120 men	Bienville (Rowland and Sanders 1932, vol. 3, p. 530)
1731			
13 January	375	150 warriors	Barthellon (1731)
24 June	180	More than 60 men	Diron d'Artaguiette (Rowland, Sanders, and Galloway 1984, vol. 4, p. 77)
1737	150	50 warriors	Bienville (Rowland and Sanders 1932, vol. 3, p. 706)
1739		90–100 warriors	Anonymous officer with de Nouaille (Claiborne 1880, p. 67)
1748		At least 60 warriors	Vaudreuil (Rowland, Sanders, and Galloway 1984, vol. 4, p. 338)
1758		60 warriors	Kerlérec (de Villiers 1907, p. 75)
1764	80	80 people, 30 warriors	d'Abbadie (Brasseaux 1979, pp. 114, 122)
1765		About 30 warriors	Pittman (1770, p. 35)
1766		About 30 men	Gordon (Mereness 1916, p. 483)
		About 30 huts	Morgan (Alvord and Carter 1916, p. 446)
1771		Some 35 families	Thomas (Rea 1970a, p. 13)
1783	60	About 20 warriors	Hutchins (1784, p. 44)
1802		50–60 people	Berquin-Duvallon (1803, p. 189; see also Davis 1806)
1803		50–60 people	Jefferson (Swanton 1911, p. 42)
1805		25 men	Sibley (1832, p. 725)
1806		50–60 people	Dunbar (Rowland 1930, p. 209)
1813	40	40–50 people	Darby (1818, p. 70)
1815		140 people (presumably should read 40)	Warden (1819, p. 530)
1822	30	30 people	Morse (Swanton 1911, p. 42)
1886		About 25 (people)	Powell (1891, p. 125)
1908	50	50 mixed bloods	Swanton (1911, p. 45)
1946	30	30 (people)	Swanton (1946, p. 198)
1980	15	Approximately 15 residents	Bureau of Indian Affairs (BIA 1980, AR, p. 2)

[a]Figures after 1800 are for the Marksville community only; overall tribal membership in 1980 was officially listed as 200, with some unofficial estimates as high as 600.

ville, who reckoned 300 families for all the Yazoo tribes combined.

The decline apparently continued after the Tunica moved downriver to the Portage de la Croix. By the time of the next census, in 1719, La Harpe counted only 460 people. In 1722, Charlevoix stated merely that "the village is . . . moderately peopled" (Charlevoix 1744, vol. 3, p. 433). Yet, in 1723, Diron d'Artaguiette, on an official fact-finding tour, estimated that the Tunica could field 200 warriors, again a high proportion of the pop-

ulation if La Harpe was accurate. Bienville's count reduced the number of men to 120 in 1725, which seems a more realistic figure, but in early 1731 Abbé Barthellon raised it to 150. Although there are discrepancies between these figures, they were approximations made by reliable sources, and the differences are easily attributable to seasonal fluctuations in the male patterns of hunting, warring, or trading. Overall, the estimates indicate a relative stability of the population during this period. But this was to change.

On the fourteenth of June in 1731, one of the great catastrophes in Tunica history occurred. In reprisal for their aid to the French during the Natchez rebellion of 1729–1731, the Tunica were massacred by a renegade band of Natchez and their allies. Although recorded losses were only some forty men killed or wounded (Charlevoix 1744, vol. 2, p. 498; Rowland, Sanders, and Galloway 1984, vol. 4, p. 103), a greater tragedy is indicated. In his report soon after the event, Diron d'Artaguiette referred to only "more than sixty men" (Rowland, Sanders, and Galloway 1984, vol. 4, p. 77), a reduction by half of the Tunica's fighting strength earlier in the year.

Then a period of stability set in again, and for the next two decades the Tunica seem to have been able to continue to field about sixty men. The only significant exception to this figure was a record of ninety to a hundred warriors made in 1739 by a French officer whose anonymity prevents an evaluation of reliability and so may be disregarded. The last official visitor during this period, Kerlérec, cited the excessive use of spirituous liquors as a major villain contributing to the low population, but it is probable that the Tunica were not exceptional in this regard.

When France gave up Louisiana in 1763, her "most consistent and loyal" native friends demonstrated their loyalty one last time. The Tunica and their Indian allies ambushed the first English convoy to ascend the river in 1764. Fearing reprisals, the Tunica fled to Mobile, but they shortly returned to the Mississippi and eventually settled near Pointe Coupée. Numerous censuses, however, reveal that the population had again been halved

(table 79). Since there do not appear to have been any military casualties during the ambush, it can only be theorized that the losses occurred during the subsequent perambulation, although there is no evidence to suggest what might have caused them. In any event, the population seems to have remained relatively constant during the stay at Pointe Coupée.

The population continued to be quite stable after the move to Marksville, but then declined as the nineteenth century progressed. The figures in table 79 might be somewhat deceiving, however, for they reflect only the Marksville village and it is known that there were other Tunica settlements in the vicinity before they amalgamated in mid-century. Since 1900 the population has increased markedly, although it has been much mixed with non-Indian, as well as Indian, neighbors, and the number of family lines has decreased (BIA 1980, AR, p. 2). There has been attrition throughout the twentieth century, as many tribal members have moved away on their own initiative, and during the depression days of the 1930s there was substantial emigration to Texas.

At the time of federal recognition in 1981, the Tunica tribal role listed two hundred persons, ninety-one of whom lived in Louisiana (fifteen on tribal land, the majority of the rest in Avoyelles and Rapides parishes), ninety in Texas, fifteen in Illinois, two in California, one in Florida, and one in Washington, D.C. It is interesting to note that the tribal membership requirement is now simply Tunica declaration and "1/4 degree Indian blood (of any kind)" (BIA 1980, AR, p. 26).

In summary, Tunica population underwent a predictable decline and dilution through the centuries. But

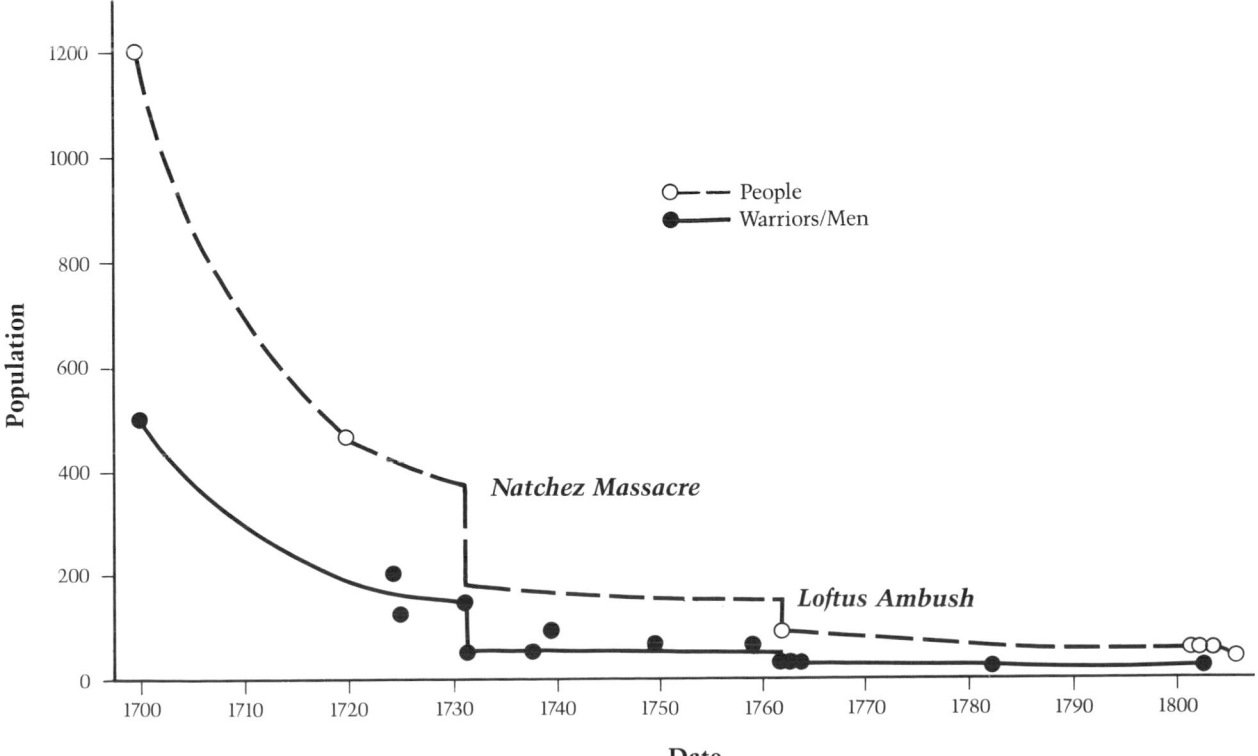

Figure 222. Tunica population decline during the eighteenth century.

more revealing is a characteristic demographic pattern. Although for his population estimates of the Tunica in 1698, Swanton (1911, p. 43) arrived at a ratio of 1 warrior for every 3.5 people, and 2.5 warriors to each cabin, the data presented here would seem to indicate a ratio of 1 warrior for every 2.5 people, or 1 warrior equals 1 family equals 1 cabin. The 1:2.5 ratio is supported by the archaeological data from Trudeau. Since the site was occupied for a period of time approximately equivalent to the average life expectancy, the total number of burials should equal the entire population for that generation. While the exact number of burials at Trudeau is not known, a reasonable estimate may be arrived at. The Tunica Treasure apparently was retrieved from the graves of at least 113 individuals (Brain 1979, pp. 275–276). Leonard J. Charrier (1984) has stated that he unearthed approximately 130 to 150 burials at Trudeau, but the evidence suggests that this figure is too high, although many of the graves contained multiple interments. Three burials were reported by Captain Hall and C. B. Moore, and when the railroad grade was cut through the bluff other interments apparently were revealed. Numerous unreported burials also must have been destroyed during two centuries of farming. Yet in the course of our limited investigations, three more previously undisturbed burials were confirmed, indicating that many more surely are still present at the site. Thus, an average population of 150 during the occupation of Trudeau is quite reasonable and agrees well with the population curve in figure 222 and the estimates of warriors presented in table 79. The high ratio of men may reflect the martial emphasis of the Tunica during this period, but the ratio is not incompatible with earlier censuses or even those of the present day (BIA 1980, DR, p. 4).

LANGUAGE

Although all Indians may have looked much alike to Euroamerican eyes, the Tunica at least had the distinction of sounding different to the discriminating ear. The first French contact was made by missionaries whose foremost consideration was to effect communication in order to be able to spread the word of God. It was noticed from the beginning that the Tunica, and perhaps some of their neighbors, spoke a language different from all other languages in the Lower Mississippi Valley. In fact, the Tunica language was unrelated to any other known linguistic group below the level of a general Gulf stock (Haas 1973). The linguistic position of the Tunica poses a problem. The remnant Tunica were a population isolate; that they spoke a language isolate confirms the magnitude of the disaster that overtook their ancestors and destroys any hope of determining their origins through linguistic connections.

That the Tunica maintained their language through the cataclysmic events of the protohistoric period, the subsequent centuries of travail and acculturative pressure, and up into the modern era, represents a fundamental continuity. Considering the small size of the population and the many changes that occurred within it, this continuity expresses more clearly than any other cultural factor a commitment to ethnic identity. Today,

however, the language is dead. Although a few words and phrases might be remembered, the living languages of everyday communication are the local French patois (among the older generation) and English.

RELIGION, IDEOLOGY, AND CEREMONY

Religion and ideology tend to be especially resistant to change, and Tunica beliefs were no exception. Even though the Tunica were exposed to the most intensive missionary effort in the southern part of the Lower Mississippi Valley during the early French contact period, they were not easy converts to Christianity. After two decades of intermittent endeavor, Father Davion—a sincere, sometimes overly eager, if incompetent proselytizer of the Faith—acknowledged his failure, gave in to his frustration, and abandoned his mission.

Davion was old and did not live to see his efforts bear fruit. Although the Tunica resisted Christianity and largely maintained their traditional religious beliefs, they turned the other cheek when Davion defaced their temple, and they even allowed some of their children to be baptized. There is a touching (and perhaps apocryphal) story that Cahura-Joligo's dying son exhorted his father to attend services and abandon idolatry (Le Page du Pratz 1758, vol. 1, p. 123; Margry 1888, vol. 6, p. 247). Apparently Cahura-Joligo did undergo baptism (Dumont de Montigny 1753, vol. 1, p. 166; Thwaites 1900, vol. 67, p. 308), but Father Poisson considered him a Christian in name only (although even Poisson does not record his baptismal name). Nevertheless, Poisson felt that the Tunica were well disposed toward Christianity (Twaites 1900, vol. 67, p. 312).* Indeed, another son of Cahura-Joligo was also baptized, and given the name Jacob (see fig. 208). During the Trudeau occupation other Tunica were identified by Christian names as well. Although all need not have been baptismal names, some definitely were, and Davion would have been immensely gratified to know that as his generation of infants became parents they sought baptism for their own children (DeVille 1974, pp. 48–49). That at least one of these parents was a subchief indicates that Davion's seedlings had taken root and grown strong in a new generation.

Religious conversion at this time, however, was only superficial at best. The lack of success of the proselytizing efforts may be inferred from the fact that so few symbols of Christianity have been found at Tunica sites of the eighteenth and nineteenth centuries. From among hundreds of burials only a few crucifixes and rosary beads have been found, and not a single example of a native-made religious article showing Christian influence. Clearly, Poisson's observation was wishful thinking, and Davion's experience not simply a matter of ineptitude. While individual Tunica may have adopted the outward forms of Christianity, and perhaps even

---

* In 1727 there was even official recommendation for the establishment of a real parish *aux Tonicas*, but only two years later there was a call for more missionaries (Menier, Taillemite, and de Forges 1976, pp. 163, 173).

some articles of faith, a core of traditional beliefs was retained by the society at large. Nowhere is this better illustrated than in burial 6 at Bloodhound. It contained a crucifix—indicating that the individual had been baptized—which was concealed beneath an elaborate shell necklace that was the real symbol of native values. (It is tempting to suppose that this child, obviously the scion of someone important, was that baptized son of Cahura-Joligo who died prematurely.)

The strength of aboriginal beliefs is also revealed by Tunica commitment to the mound concept. Their putative ancestors, the Quizquiz, lived among many mounds. The survivors who became the Tunica adopted the most important mound site on the lower Yazoo River and worshipped in a temple on the summit of the largest mound. They may even have enlarged that mound, the latest known example of mound construction in the Lower Mississippi Valley. At Trudeau they apparently used a mound-like bluff remnant in the same manner as a mound, the latest known example of "mound" usage in the valley. Even their final settlement at Marksville is not without the image: as remembered in their folklore, Tunica women were believed to have built the mounds at the nearby Marksville site (Haas 1950, pp. 137, 141),* although those mounds predated the Tunica by two millennia.

Other elements of the traditional Tunica belief system have persisted to very recent times as well, and some seem to be present today. In fact, there is even evidence of a reactionary return to a kind of general Indian consciousness in ceremonial behavior. This may be attributed to the success of the pan-Indian movement. An interesting example is provided by the case of the calumet pipe. A late introduction into the Mississippi Valley, these pipes were symbolic of an important ideological and ceremonial behavior. Curiously, the Tunica are mentioned only once in the historical descriptions of the calumet ceremony (Rowland, Sanders, and Galloway 1984, vol. 4, p. 113), yet archaeologically more of the distinctive catlinite pipe bowls have been found at sites related to the Tunica than to any other ethnic group. Trudeau alone has produced at least five, the largest single assemblage from any site in the valley. If the calumet ceremony was indeed a necessary formality when two peoples met, the number of pipes among the Tunica would seem to attest to an intensive program of interaction which would fit their entrepreneurial role. No pipes are known from nineteenth-century sites, but by then calumet ceremonialism seems no longer to have been practiced in the Southeast. It persisted on the Plains, however, and the pipes—endowed with a new pan-Indian symbolism—have been reintroduced in this century. The last chief of the Tunica, Joseph A. Pierite, Sr., took one with him to his grave. The symbolic value of such pipes may thus extend to the supernatural world. Tunica cemeteries are said to be noisy places on rainy, cloudy days when "they"

are talking and fussing at one another (Hiram F. Gregory, personal communication, 1984). A pipe might be considered a necessity in such circumstances. The real point is that, contrary to Christian doctrine, traditional belief holds that both artifacts and spirits belong with the bones.

There has been considerable continuity, therefore, in mortuary ceremonialism. Throughout the identifiable Tunica past the dead have been interred among the living, either in or near residential areas. Furthermore, the bodies generally have been oriented with the head in an easterly direction, a fire has marked the grave, and, as noted above, burial goods have been consistently included. It is in the latter that we find some important changes. Burials early in the contact period are distinguished by a limited number of types of introduced European artifacts that because of their exotic character gained symbolic value and were quickly removed from the realm of the profane to that of the sacred. As time progressed, however, the contact became more intensive and the artifacts more common. The Tunica of the eighteenth and nineteenth centuries were increasingly well endowed with a diversity and quantity of Euroamerican artifacts; and their graves were liberally furnished with commonplace items of every description. Modern mortuary practices recall earlier customs, but with important changes. When the late Chief Joseph A. Pierite, Sr., was interred, his grave may have been above ground in the local French fashion, but it was near his house, and tradition required that a light (in this case electric) be maintained over it. Chief Joe was also accompanied by artifacts that, like the calumet pipe, were of symbolic value in pan-Indian ideology and ceremonialism.

SOCIAL STRUCTURE

Clearly, there have been many changes in Tunica social structure through time. These changes were caused by demographic losses and shifts, as well as adjustments to Euroamerican patterns.

According to the ethnohistorical and archaeological data, Tunican ancestors belonged to socially ranked societies. The existence of distinct social classes may be inferred from the De Soto narratives, and social differentiation is apparent in the placement and furnishing of the graves. Hierarchies of sites distinguished according to size and number or type of mound features presumably also denote a society of classes and ascribed status.

The great loss of population during the protohistoric period destroyed those societies, and the remnant groups were structured much more simply. Nevertheless, the Tunica apparently still recognized social differentiations. Mortuary data, especially from Angola Farm, Bloodhound, Trudeau, and Pierite, confirm these distinctions if one accepts the assumption that patterning in death replicates patterning in life. It could be argued that the differences in grave accompaniments are only economic indicators reflecting unequal distribution of wealth in an otherwise egalitarian society. Such was not the case, however, for contemporary documents

---

* Here we could have a fascinating sociological insight: Could it be, at least according to the Tunica, that the women customarily built the mounds? Such a sexual division of labor might put a different perspective on the analysis of the great prehistoric public works projects.

Table 80. Documented Tunica chiefs.

Name	Date	Reference	Remarks
Quizquiz	fl. 1541	Bourne 1904, vol. 1, pp. 111–112; Varner and Varner 1951, p. 423	This cacique was the head chief of the first village of Quizquiz—and perhaps of the whole province, according to Garcilaso.
Paul	d. 1699	Shea 1861, pp. 78, 81	A chief baptized on his deathbed by de Montigny.
Cahura-Joligo	[1719]–1731	Le Page du Pratz 1758, vol. 2, pp. 220–221; Charlevoix 1744, vol. 3, p. 433; Margry 1888, vol. 6, p. 247	Head chief and staunch ally of the French, first specifically mentioned in 1719 but probably already in power for some time, he was assassinated by the Natchez in 1731.
Dominique	fl. 1731	Brain 1979, pp. 311–313; Rowland, Sanders, and Galloway 1984, vol. 4, pp. 112–113	Listed first among the Tunica *considerés* and principal in the calumet ceremony, Dominique may have been acting chief after the death of Cahura-Joligo.
Bride-les-Boeufs	fl. 1731–1764	Alvord and Carter 1915, pp. 191, 235; Brain 1979, p. 312, cover illustration; Rowland, Sanders, and Galloway 1984, vol. 4, p. 112	Apparently one of the chiefs (war chief?) during the occupation of Trudeau, and still recognized as a principal leader as late as Pointe Coupée. DeBatz was mistaken in considering him the successor of Cahura-Joligo.
Lattanash	fl. [1731]–1778	Alvord and Carter 1915, p. 191; Bjork 1926, p. 409; Rea 1970a, p. 14; Brain 1979, p. 312; Rowland, Sanders, and Galloway 1984, vol. 4, p. 112	Also known as Atanaché, a *consideré*, in the Juzan manuscript of 1731 (Juzan 1731b), Lattanash seems to have been recognized as head chief by 1771 and to have remained in that position at least until 1778, although he may have shared power with Falaza after about 1775.
Carodet	fl. 1739–1740	Rowland and Sanders 1927, vol. 1, p. 406; DeVille 1974, pp. 48–49; Rowland, Sanders, and Galloway 1984, vol. 4, p. 112	A *consideré* in 1731, Carodet is referred to as a chief (almost certainly a sub-chief) in 1739 and 1740.
Falaza	fl. 1775–ca. 1790	British West Florida Records 1775; BIA 1980, AR, p. 7; ibid., HR, p. 9	Falaza apparently began to replace Lattanash (his uncle?) by 1775, when he was identified as a principal chief; he is remembered as the chief during the move to Marksville (ca. 1790).
Panroy[a]	fl. 1779–1794 [–1826?]	BIA 1980, AR, pp. 5, 8; ibid., HR, pp. 5, 7	Cited as an important friend by the Spanish in 1779, Panroy was not definitely identified as a "head man" until 1826, although it is not clear that he was then still alive.
Tanaroyat[a]	fl. 1791	BIA 1980, HR, p. 4	Identified as a leader, probably the chief.
Thomas	fl. 1793	BIA 1980, AR, p. 7; ibid., HR, p. 9	Identified as a chief, his place in the succession is uncertain.
Valentine	fl. 1812	BIA 1980, AR, p. 7; ibid., HR, p. 9	Definitely a chief, but his place in succession and dates are uncertain.
Jean Baptiste[a]	fl. 1826	BIA 1980, AR, p. 8	Identified as the chief.
Melancon	d. 1841	BIA 1980, AR, p. 12	Chief, killed in land dispute.
Zenon La Joie	fl. 1867	BIA 1980, AR, p. 12; ibid., HR, p. 10	Son of Melancon, apparently recognized as chief of underground government.
Volsin Chiki	[1896]–1911	Swanton 1911, p. 319; Downs 1979, p. 79; BIA 1980, AR, pp. 3, 15–16	A man of considerable "medicine," he restored tribal confidence in the 1870s and had assumed the chieftaincy by 1896.
Sesostrie Youchigant	1911–1921	Downs 1979, p. 83; BIA 1980, AR, p. 16	Nephew of Volsin Chiki, recognized as chief by the adult male population.
Ernest Pierite	1921–1932	BIA 1980, AR, pp. 16, 20	Elected chief when Youchigant resigned.

Table 80 (continued).

Name	Date	Reference	Remarks
Eli Barbry	1932–1947	Downs 1979, pp. 83–85; BIA 1980, AR, pp. 16, 20	Half brother of Youchigant, elected subchief in 1921, assumed chieftaincy in 1932 when Ernest Pierite died, formally elected chief in 1936.
Horace Pierite, Sr.	1947–1955	Downs 1979, p. 85; BIA 1980, AR, p. 20	Elected subchief in 1936 and chief when Barbry resigned in 1947.
Joseph Alcide Pierite, Sr.	1955–1974[b]	Downs 1979, p. 85; BIA 1980, AR, p. 21	Elected subchief in 1947 and succeeded as chief in 1955 (without a new election being held) when Horace Pierite died.

[a] Possibly chiefs of the Bayou Rouge settlement.
[b] After 1974, the office of chief was replaced by an elected chairman and council.

---

refer to chiefs, subchiefs, *considerés*, and warriors, a hierarchy that must be considered social as well as political.

During the nineteenth century the reduced population must have deemphasized social distinctions, but as interracial marriage occurred bloodlines became more important. Even today, as the values of the dominant American society have been absorbed by the Tunica, these subtle genetic distinctions continue to have some social significance.

POLITICAL ORGANIZATION AND SUCCESSION

The Tunica have displayed a persistent political organization throughout their history, and it has even been stated that "the traditional Tunica culture had a formalized chieftainship which was more highly organized and centralized than most American Indian cultures" (BIA 1980, AR, p. 3). While the latter claim might be somewhat exaggerated, the office of chief can be documented from the moment of first contact until the present era (table 80). Although the Tunica have maintained a chieftaincy, it would be misleading to characterize their political system as a chiefdom in the classic anthropological sense (Service 1962, p. 143) since at least the early eighteenth century. Clearly, the smaller population size required the less formalized structure of tribal organization, and there was none of the pomp and circumstance described for the Natchez chiefs. Nevertheless, the important point is that a political organization was maintained. The character of the office and the rules of succession seem to have changed over the years, however.

The great Cahura-Joligo, who played such an important role during the critical decades at the beginning of the eighteenth century, seems to have been a dominant chief. He was supported by a war chief, as was usual in the Southeast, but one who was greatly overshadowed by Cahura-Joligo and whose role often seems to have been assumed by the latter. It was the war chief, however, who saved the Tunica after the massacre of 1731 when Cahura-Joligo was killed. This war chief may have been Bride-les-Boeufs, who was identified as chief by DeBatz the following year (see fig. 208), although the Juzan manuscript dated December 1731 (Juzan 1731b) lists Bride-les-Boeufs as but one of seven Tunica *considerés*, or honored men, of whom another, Dominique, seems to have been the most important (Brain 1979, app. C.2; Rowland, Sanders, and Galloway 1984, vol. 4, pp. 111–114). Yet another individual, Carodet, is referred to as "one of their chiefs" in 1739 (Rowland and Sanders 1927, vol. 1, p. 406), and it is reported that in the same year, "their two principal chiefs" lost their heads (Swanton 1911, p. 314). The previous year, Father Vitry also referred to a plurality of Tunica chiefs (Bridges and Delanglez 1964, p. 260), and it may be surmised that during this period a corporate leadership of two or more individuals prevailed. The pattern still existed in 1764, when two Tunica chiefs are identified: Bride-les-Boeufs, again, and Lattanash, who also was listed as a *considéré* by Juzan in 1731 (obviously neither achieved the highest chiefly rank until after 1739, when the two reigning principal chiefs were executed). An Ofo chief, Perruquier, is also frequently mentioned as a leader in Tunica affairs during the 1760s and 1770s (e.g., Alvord and Carter 1915, pp. 235, 285–286). By 1771, however, Lattanash seems to have assumed the chieftaincy alone (Rea 1970a, p. 14; Bjork 1926, pp. 409–410).

Probably sometime between 1786 and 1791 the Tunica moved to Avoyelles Parish. Their traditions recall that this event occurred under the leadership of one Falaza (BIA 1980, AR, p. 7; ibid., HR, p. 9), whose name appears on a land grant by the Tunica to John Thomas in 1775 (British West Florida Records 1775). This document identifies Falaza as the "Principal Chief Mingo" and lists a certain Camiere as "second chief." The record subsequently becomes quite confused, and at least six men seem to be identified as chiefs during the period 1791–1841, but the dates and order of succession are uncertain. The confusion may be due in part to the fact that initially there were two or more separate Tunica settlements in Avoyelles Parish. The principal village was Marksville, of course, but there was another settlement a few kilometers to the south on Bayou Rouge, and each of these may have required a headman. A third settlement, somewhere on the Red River, may have been briefly led by a Don Luis (BIA 1980, AR, p. 7), the Spanish honorific indicating a pre-1803 date for his leadership. In Marksville at least two individuals of chiefly status were buried at the Pierite site, probably during this period.

A critical event in Tunica history occurred in 1841 when Melancon, the chief at Marksville, was shot and killed in a land dispute. That tragedy and a subsequent lawsuit seem to have been sufficient to intimidate the Tunica, and tribal organization went underground for the next twenty to thirty years (Downs 1979, p. 79). Even then, however, a chief apparently was secretly recognized: Melancon's son, Zenon La Joie (BIA 1980, HR, p. 10).

Tribal confidence was restored in the 1870s by Volsin Chiki, a man of considerable "medicine," who "reunited the tribe, restored the cemeteries, and rejuvenated the ceremonies" (Downs 1979, p. 79). Volsin was recognized as chief by 1896, if not before, and under him the office was consolidated. He resigned in 1911 and was succeeded by his nephew, Sesostrie Youchigant. From this point on, chiefs were formally elected, although the choice was always very limited because of the small resident population. The chieftaincy was shared between two rival factions represented by the Pierite and Barbry lines until 1976, when Joseph Alcide Pierite, Sr., died.

In 1974 an incorporated government was instituted that replaced the office of chief with an elected chairman and council. That same year Joe Pierite, Jr., was elected the first chairman. The factionalism continued, however, and in 1979 he relinquished the chairmanship to Earl Barbry, Sr., who continues to head the government at this writing.

The traditional rules of succession prior to the electoral procedures instituted in this century are unclear. It is probable that the usual Lower Mississippi Valley pattern of transmission through the female line was followed when possible, although the declining population must have limited the choices. Lattanash referred to his nephew as his successor, but unfortunately he did not further identify him or their exact relationship (Bjork 1926, p. 410). There is also some indication that Melancon might have been the nephew of an earlier chief named Valentine (BIA 1980, AR, p. 7). But only in the case of the last pre-election transfer is this relationship clearly stated: Sesostrie Youchigant was Volsin Chiki's sister's son. Direct succession in the paternal line does seem to have been avoided, except perhaps in difficult times. For example, while Jacob did not actually follow his famous father, Cahura-Joligo, he may have served temporarily as a symbolic rallying point (Rowland, Sanders, and Galloway 1984, vol. 4, pp. 112–113; see also fig. 208, this vol.), and Zenon La Joie may have served surreptitiously as chief after the violent death of his father. It would also seem likely that brothers could succeed without violating the rules, especially if no other suitable candidate was available. The only known case of brother succession in the Tunica sequence is Sesostrie Youchigant and his half brother Eli Barbry, but the latter did not succeed directly and was elected.

SETTLEMENT PATTERNS, SITE PLANS, AND ARCHITECTURE

Tunica residential patterns seem to have changed somewhat through time, as might be expected considering the changes that occurred in demography, location, and lifeways. Nevertheless, there also were significant continuities. Much has already been made of the Tunica predilection for settling at strategic points in lines of communication. Especially favored were major riverine junctions; in fact, the tribe settled near the three most important confluences of the Mississippi River and its tributaries during their known perambulations in the Lower Valley. They were first found opposite the mouth of the Arkansas and at the Mississippi terminus of a major land route; next on the lower Yazoo River, the largest tributary of the Mississippi south of the Ohio River on the left bank; then at the confluence of the Red and Mississippi rivers, where there was also an important portage; and finally commanding the Red River as it rose to the west. Since there were many other equally habitable spots, especially as the depopulations of the protohistoric period opened up vast areas for occupation, the selection of these specific locations must have been determined by their strategic value.

The emphasis on a primary village has also remained constant. Even Quizquiz, with its many mound sites, probably recognized one center above all others (perhaps Clarksdale or Carson-Montgomery). On the lower Yazoo, the Haynes Bluff mounds were clearly the central seat of the tribe, although the site may have been shared with other peoples and the population was largely dispersed in surrounding hamlets. In the Portage de la Croix location essentially the same pattern prevailed, although the principal village was located on a bluff. At Trudeau the reduced population was probably more concentrated, and a small bluff remnant substituted for a mound, clearly revealing that the concept, if not the man-made feature, was still present. At Pointe Coupée, however, there seem to have been changes. The small population appears to have lived in a single village, which according to Durnford's map (see fig. 37) was arranged in a linear site plan more like contemporary Euroamerican settlements than the arrangement of mounds and/or houses around an open plaza found in all earlier Tunica villages.

Another innovation in village structuring also appears at this time. Fences are mentioned in a contemporary document (British West Florida Records 1775) and may even be indicated around the cornfield on the Durnford map. These fences were designed to keep cattle out of the fields, a precaution unnecessary in preceding Tunica villages and again more like Euroamerican patterns. The adoption of fences may also have been occasioned by encroaching Euroamerican settlements and the necessity to delimit territorial boundaries. This was an increasing source of trouble, and it was a boundary fence that led to a major land dispute and the tragic death of Chief Melancon in 1841 after the Tunica had moved to Marksville.

Other than the disputed fence, we know little about Tunica settlements and site plans during the nineteenth century. It can only be noted that Marksville was recognized as the principal village, although initially there were other small settlements nearby. Tunica residential patterns in the twentieth century are indistinguishable from other regional patterns, but Marksville still remains the tribal center.

Tunica architecture has undergone considerable change. In the upper Sunflower region, Tunican ancestors of the Parchman phase built square wattle-and-daub structures with thatched roofs typical of the late Mississippian culture (Connaway 1984, p. 93). At the Wilsford site some of these structures may have been raised on piles and apparently were of exceptionally large dimensions (ibid., pp. 40–49). By the time of the lower Yazoo settlement, however, the houses and public buildings were of a more modest size, the average "cabin" being sufficient for a single family. Gravier described these cabins as being round. Archaeologically, however, only rectilinear patterns of wall trenches and post molds were found at Haynes Bluff. These might have been of Tunica origin, but the identification was not established beyond doubt. An interesting technological feature of the structure on the summit of mound A is the apparent use of iron nails in its construction, as is discussed below in the section on artifacts and technology.

At the principal village of Portage de la Croix the houses were described as being partly square and partly round (Charlevoix 1744, vol. 3, p. 433), apparently meaning that both round and square structures were present. The Dumont de Montigny watercolor sketch of an approximately contemporary Tunica village, however, depicts only rectangular buildings. A few wall trenches and arrangements of post molds at the Trudeau site indicate that the houses there were square or rectangular, while the remains of a burned structure on the bluff top give ample evidence that traditional daub construction continued, although (as at Haynes Bluff) the above-mentioned technological innovation distinguishes this important building from the residences in the field below.

Unfortunately, the archaeology of Tunica architecture stops after Trudeau. There is no information about the houses at Pointe Coupée nor about the permanent structures at Marksville during the nineteenth century. Robin's descriptions apply to the temporary structures erected at hunting camps (Landry 1966, p. 129). A later survey map identifies the Indian village with tipi-like symbols (see fig. 40), a cartographic detail that owes more to convention than authenticity. By the early twentieth century, and probably throughout the later nineteenth century, the Tunica lived in houses indistinguishable from those of their poorer non-Indian neighbors (Swanton 1911, pl. 16b; Swanton 1946, pl. 50), and this pattern continued until recently (Saucier 1956, p. 29). After federal recognition, however, funds became available for better housing, and a tract of modern brick ranch houses has been built on tribal land.

Thus, Tunica architecture during the last three centuries is characterized by modest structures: single-family dwellings and similar but slightly larger public buildings. As Tunica fortunes and circumstances changed, construction evolved from aboriginal wattle-and-daub cabins to simple plank houses to state-of-the-art masonry residences.

SUBSISTENCE AND ECONOMY

Tunica survival was obviously based on an ability to gain the necessities of life, and the Tunica were successful in extracting these from both the natural and social environments. Their ability to find sufficient food and sustenance was almost inevitable in the rich environment of the Lower Mississippi Valley, and it is reviewed briefly only to put the study into biogeographical context. It is the success of Tunica economic interaction with other communities, including the Euroamericans, that is of particular interest to this study.

The diversity and richness of the natural environment of the Mississippi Valley is well known and need not be elaborated here (see Phillips, Ford, and Griffin 1951, pp. 15–36; Williams and Brain 1983, pp. 8–9). It is sufficient to note that it was an environment wherein most necessities for sustenance were available and could be extracted with relative ease within uncountable locales; those under consideration here were no exception.

During the protohistoric and early historic periods, before Euroamerican populations began to expand, there was considerable opportunity for the native peoples to be selective and choose the most productive econiches. The Tunica moved from the alluvial bottomlands of the upper Sunflower region to the bluff-edge ecotone of the lower Yazoo and Portage de la Croix/Tunica Bayou to the Marksville Prairie. These were all very different topographies with very different, although exceptionally rich, resources. The selection of these locales clearly demonstrates the ecological adaptability of the Tunica.

This adaptability allowed settlement locations to be determined by the more important considerations of cultural geography. Each of the locales chosen by the Tunica had strategic value for the purposes of communication, travel, and trade. In addition to the Mississippi River, the upper Sunflower region had direct access to the Arkansas River and the interior of the Yazoo Basin, and it lay athwart a major east-west land trail (known later as Charlie's Trace) which not so coincidentally had brought De Soto to the region. The lower Yazoo may have been a refuge for protohistoric tribes, but again it is no coincidence that the Tunica chose to settle near the confluence of the most important eastern tributary of the Mississippi south of the Ohio River. The relocation to the Portage de la Croix and Tunica Bayou locales allowed the Tunica to assume control of the Red River confluence. Finally, Marksville Prairie, the first habitable land to be found in ascending the Red River, also controlled access to that river and western connections.

The consistent selection of settlements at the most strategic natural points of communication was obviously purposeful. The Tunica were a small tribe and had no grand political ambitions. They were motivated instead by economic considerations beyond subsistence. Given their entrepreneurial inclination, their choice of settlement was determined by the potential of a locale for trade. Of course there were many other factors involved, but this appears to have been the overriding one.

The Tunica had been much involved in the aboriginal salt trade. The manufacture and distribution of this basic necessity gained them access to other territories and peoples, an experience that served them well in their interactions with the Euroamericans when they arrived on the scene. The French colonists also required salt—and other commodities as well, such as livestock and foodstuffs. The western connections already established in the salt trade gave the Tunica an advantage in procuring horses and cattle for the colony. The Tunica also traded on their friendship and their services as warriors, hunters, and guides. Thus the success of their interaction with the French was based on a series of symbiotic client-patron relationships that made the Tunica indispensable and for which they were well rewarded.

When the French were forced out of Louisiana in 1763, the Tunica role changed dramatically vis-à-vis their Euroamerican neighbors, and they became the increasingly subordinate partner in an unequal acculturation situation. Nevertheless, the Tunica maintained a degree of affluence well into the nineteenth century by continuing their role as intermediaries between different ethnic groups in one of the last real frontier situations in the eastern United States. When that frontier finally dissolved, the Tunica were perceived as an unnecessary nuisance, and their economic position worsened steadily from that time on.

But let us return, in summary, to the decisive eighteenth century. The changes in native cultures so often attributed to generalized Euroamerican influence may be seen in the case of the Tunica to reflect an adaptability of traditional economic strategies that resulted in a beneficial symbiosis. Why this was so successful for the Tunica will be considered in a later section, but it is suggested that a steady economic relationship signified a deeper relationship to the Tunica—that is, a commitment of friendship and alliance. Because of this ethic, the Tunica—consciously or unconsciously—played their entrepreneurial role according to European rules. (This is not to say that they understood and participated in a market economy, but that they played the game of barter and exchange well.) It is significant that there is no record of theft or massacre of Euroamerican traders by the Tunica, unlike their neighbors the Natchez or Koroa. Instead, there was Cahura-Joligo, who was especially cited by the French as a friend who understood his trade very well.

The commitment of the Tunica to an entrepreneurial way of life may be inferred from their settlement pattern, is documented by their Euroamerican partners, and is expressed most fundamentally in their own language. The Tunica had a word, _lápu_, which used as a verb means "to trade" and as an adjective, "good" (Haas 1953, p. 229). There is also the adverb _lápuya_, meaning "well, properly." And there is the noun _láspi_, "money," which Haas (ibid., p. 230) thought might be a corruption of the French _espèces_ but conceivably is a combinative of both the Tunica and French words.

ARTIFACTS AND TECHNOLOGY

As measured and interpreted archaeologically, it is in the category of artifacts and technology that the most abundant and particularistic evidence of culture change

exists. Quimby and Spoehr (1951, p. 107) noted that "a complete inventory of a primitive people's material culture from the time of initial contact with the West to the time of assimilation would provide an enlightening record of acculturation." That changes in material culture do not mirror precisely the overall acculturation of a people is a truism that has become clichéd. Nevertheless, a record of artifactual and technological changes within an ethnic continuum does provide an important guide to the degree and direction of change. A contribution to the interpretation of dynamics and processes is also possible if the component contexts are adequately controlled. Only then may the spectra of natural and social forces that existed when various artifacts and technologies were offered, acquired, used, and disposed be identified. In short, all changes must be considered in context.

There are many problems in interpreting culture change from archaeological remains. Social, economic, political, and ideological factors in both the donor and recipient cultures determined the transmission and adoption of various artifacts (Brown 1979a, 1979c, 1979d; Fitzhugh 1985, p. 6). Once an object has passed a cultural boundary there may be many changes in its function or value. We cannot be aware of all these factors and their relative importance at any one point in time, but we must be sensitive to the fact that the historical documentation may provide some clues. A further problem with archaeological data is the delay between the acceptance of an item and its deposition (i.e., archaeological manifestation). Within the perspective adopted here, however, the discrepancy does not appear to be a significant problem as long as the probability of some temporal slippage is recognized. The long Tunica continuum provides a single scale for the identification and measurement of culture change.

In the first volume of this set, a system for measuring the degree of culture change represented by the Tunica Treasure was proposed (Brain 1979, pp. 270–274). It was emphasized that this was a crude sort of measurement and had no meaning out of context, although it has since been used successfully in other case studies (e.g., Kilmarx 1985). The system is not used here, however, partly because it would be too cumbersome for the entire study, partly because the data are not sufficient to apply it in some cases, but mostly because the continuum developed in the foregoing pages makes such an artificial measurement unnecessary. Furthermore, of greater importance than the intrinsic value of the artifacts in measuring culture change is their extrinsic significance in identifying the dynamics and processes of change. Cultural dynamics and processual patterns may be derived from the contexts of the artifacts and their configurations described in the series of synchronic stages presented in the foregoing pages. It is the objective in this section to identify the significant patterns that relate those stages.

The overall pattern, of course, is the replacement of aboriginal artifacts and technologies with European ones. That this was a continuous process that proceeded equally in all artifactual and technological classes, however, would be a mistaken assumption. It will be found that change occurred at differential rates within and between classes, and these differences reflect the real acculturative experiences. The ultimate interpretation of processes will depend in large part on these unequal rates of change and their manifestations in a given context.

Tunica ancestors experienced no significant change in material culture as a result of the first European contact. The few trinkets and other items left behind by De Soto and his army probably were quickly removed to the ceremonial realm. Significant material culture change began with the establishment of a direct and continuing French presence at the turn of the seventeenth century. The period of early French contact on the lower Yazoo was characterized by the addition and substitution of some elements of European material culture. As the century progressed, changes became more extensive and the acculturative pressures increased. Nevertheless, some continuities are also to be found, and they are as important as the changes in understanding the dynamics of a situation. These trends of change and continuity will be discussed under general topics basic to Tunica lifeways: tools and weapons, ornaments and clothing, and containers. Unfortunately, none of these topics can be dealt with here to the extent that it deserves and that the data in part 2 would allow, but a few examples will be illustrative.

Tools and Weapons

In general, metal tools, weapons, and other hardware were readily accepted and quickly replaced aboriginal counterparts wherever they were introduced. However, this replacement in itself brought about little real acculturative change. The objects were new and more efficient, perhaps, but the functions remained the same. An axe was an axe, whether of stone or metal. Even guns, while they may have been relatively sophisticated artifacts, were but another technology for throwing a missile that could bring down man or beast. Once accepted, however, these tools and weapons became a necessity to the maintenance of basic lifeways right up to the modern era.

As a result of the acceptance of metal tools, stone artifacts rapidly disappeared from the cultural inventory of the Tunica: within a lifetime, the Tunica leapt from the Stone Age to the Iron Age. Some stone tools were still being used in the Portage de la Croix sites, however, and even appeared as late as Trudeau. They mostly are simple bifaces and incidental tools, although a few arrow points are still to be found. It seems that stoneworking was remembered well enough that tools could be supplied when European counterparts were scarce. Native-made gunflints were one of the most important items.

Guns were particularly significant artifacts and were avidly sought by the Indians. The Tunica were no exception, and they were well supplied. Yet, in context, archaeology reveals some significant patterns. Nearly every adult male from the lower Yazoo, Portage de la Croix, and Marksville was buried with a gun, but these weapons were often inoperative because the locks were broken or missing. It is probable that working locks were too valuable to be deposited with the dead and

were recycled to maintain the guns in the hands of the living. At Trudeau, on the other hand, where it seems that most of the guns had their locks, there were only a couple of dozen guns from over a hundred burials. This would seem to be an exceptionally small number at a time when the Tunica were at the height of their economic and military partnership with the French. It may have been that all the guns at Trudeau had locks because of the exceptional access to French goods at this time, and that relatively few guns were placed with the dead because they were constantly needed in the hands of the living warriors. If the martial importance of the Tunica during the Trudeau occupation were not known historically, the archaeological data would indicate a large disconformity in the overall pattern.

A contrasting example of the larger technological significance that a seemingly insignificant artifact might have in documenting culture change when analyzed in archaeological context is found in the case of handwrought iron nails. As noted in the section on architecture, the majority of the nails described in appendix F.1 were recovered archaeologically from two restricted proveniences: the summit of mound A at Haynes Bluff and the bluff top at Trudeau. These locations are believed to have been the most important at both sites, being the focal points of ceremonial and, perhaps, sociopolitical activities. Therefore, the large number of nails from these locations and the fact that so many were so well preserved (that is, not oxidized) attracted our attention.

Technical analyses revealed that the uncorroded nails had been protected by "firescale" prior to deposition (Waldbaum 1982; LaViolette 1982). In other words, many of the nails had been subjected to prolonged heat sometime after manufacture and before reaching the archaeological context. The ways in which such heat treatment may have occurred are, of course, myriad. The most likely explanations, however, are two, and the choice between them depends primarily upon whether the nails had been heated accidentally or purposely. Purposeful heating might have occurred if the nails were used as instruments of torture. Although such activities are not recorded for the Tunica, their close associates the Koroa are infamous for their treatment of war captives, as described by Pénicaut:

The poor wretch is fastened up this way [spread-eagled on a frame] *entirely naked, and the whole village gathers around him. In that place they have a fire burning in which they have put pieces of iron to get red hot— old gun barrels, spades, or axeheads, and other such things. When these get red hot, they rub his back with them, his arms, thighs, and legs.* (McWilliams 1953, pp. 99–100)

The "other such things" might well have included nails, as reported by Le Page du Pratz (1758, vol. 2, p. 431; see also Brown 1979d, pp. 153–154), but the archaeological evidence does not seem very supportive in this case. The interpretation has nothing to do with a reluctance to attribute such grim pastimes to the Tunica, who were probably no better or worse than their neighbors in this respect. The problem is that these nails are too numerous and are more corroded than not, while many have an obviously used look, having been hammered and broken, and approximately one-third of them were clinched. If the nails had indeed been employed in their intended architectural function—and most of them clearly are structural types—it is possible that they had been salvaged from some nearby colonial structure. But another interpretation is suggested by the archaeological contexts.

At both the summit of mound A at Haynes Bluff and the bluff top at Trudeau, the remains of burned structures were evident. Hard-fired daub and charcoal were abundant, and in both locations it was among this debris that the nails were indiscriminately scattered. The remains appeared to be from structures fired in situ (the differential heating of the nails in various parts of the conflagration accounting for differences in firescale, and thus corrosion, of individual specimens). While it is possible that these buildings could have been colonial constructions, the evidence indicates otherwise. The remains are similar to what might be expected from the burning of a structure built in the most common construction method in eighteenth-century French Louisiana, known as *poteaux en terre bousillée* (C. E. Peterson 1965, p. 27; Kniffen and Glassie 1966, p. 47), but they also are virtually indistinguishable from native construction techniques.* Indistinguishable, that is, except for the nails. If the latter are ignored for the moment, the case for native construction grows stronger. The artifactual content of both structures is much more like that to be expected from an Indian structure than a colonial one. Furthermore, comparisons with artifacts from other locations at each site demonstrate contemporaneity, so it is most reasonable to argue that structure usage coincided with the main site occupation. Finally, the replication of similar constructions at similar locales reveals a persistence that parallels the ethnic continuity.

The conclusion that we have reached with the above reasoning is that the nails at these locations were associated with a native structure and that they seem to have been used in their intended function, presumably by the Indians themselves. Prehistoric Indian construction used wattles between the posts and withes to join the timbers. Daub fragments from the bluff top at Trudeau did not reveal any evidence of wattles or withes, although the surface smoothing and molds of the posts (which were left in the round in the native style and not squared like the French *poteaux*) were well preserved. There was no indication of how the structural members were joined. The solution, and the answer to the whole question of the nails, might be found in a clue from Haynes Bluff. Daub from this site manifests many marks of wattles and withes, and a small piece displaying crossbinding (at a juncture?) also seems to have preserved the impression of a faceted head from a

* Indeed, in the opinion of this writer rather too much has been made of the hypothesis that the French learned the idea in the West Indies before coming to the mainland (Kniffen and Glassie 1966, p. 47), for the setting of posts in the ground and daubing between them was the most common Indian method of making walls throughout the Southeast during late prehistory and into the historic period (e.g., Le Page du Pratz 1758, vol. 3, pp. 16–17).

handwrought iron nail. Haynes Bluff, then, may represent an early stage in the transition from aboriginal techniques of joinder to the newly introduced technology. By the mid-eighteenth century the Tunica relied upon nails exclusively, although the basic materials and construction (and probably appearance) of the architecture remained unchanged. To what extent this technology was restricted to public buildings is still unknown, but it may be that residences and other lesser structures were not commonly put together with nails until a much later period.

Ornaments and Clothing

Ornamental items comprised a second major class of sought-after European artifacts, but compared with tools and weapons, they had a very different pattern of acceptance and influence in the trajectory of change. Once again, the European artifacts were designed to replace aboriginal counterparts and become indispensable. In actuality, however, they were not so much substitutive as additive. Glass beads were a favorite item, but even as late as Trudeau they did not completely replace the aboriginal shell beads, and although vermilion may have been preferred, ochre continued in use. Some new ornaments were added, such as metal bells, medals, arm bands, and earbobs. But the only real change overall was of degree: people were better ornamented, noisier, and flashier.

Possibly a greater indication of change was the transformation of utilitarian European artifacts and raw materials into ornaments. Brass and copper kettles were cut up into janglers, tinklers, gorgets, and other ornaments. Metalworking, albeit primitive, and the adoption of new forms indicate some acculturative change. Yet the adaptation of the strainer from an *écumoire* as a gorget at Trudeau (Brain 1979, p. 186) was a simple substitution. Far more culture change would have been indicated if it could have been demonstrated that the *écumoire* had been used as originally intended and represented the adoption of new ways of preparing food. Nevertheless, this particular item was to have a curious acculturative impact: when the Tunica made yet another gorget, this time from a kettle and in semilunar form in imitation of European gorget styles, they punched holes in it, apparently emulating the *écumoire* gorget (ibid., p. 196). This second gorget illustrates a greater degree of acculturative change.

Native shell ornaments were gone by the nineteenth century. Glass beads were still present, but most important were silver brooches, pins, gorgets, arm bands, and headbands. Many of these items were handmade, again transformed from other artifacts, often coins. Many others, however, were mass-produced by Euroamerican silversmiths. All conformed to a few styles and limited number of forms that were widely distributed among many other Indian groups. These early pan-Indian traits were really artifacts of the Euroamerican and major evidence of acculturative change.

Clothing is certainly one of the most visible indications of acculturation. Cahura-Joligo was described in 1722 by Charlevoix (1744, vol. 3, p. 433) as "dressed all in the French fashion," and items of European clothing and adornment were found in the graves at Angola and Bloodhound. Yet Bride-les-Boeufs and Cahura-Joligo's wife and son chose to be depicted by DeBatz in native attire (of course, this could have been at the request of the artist). The evidence from Trudeau does include European costumery, but also a goodly representation of aboriginal items. In 1771, Bossu described a Tunica man who had a complete suit of European clothes but preferred to carry his trousers (Dickinson 1982, p. 99).

By the nineteenth century the Tunica, like other southeastern Indians, had adopted a distinctive style of dress that adapted Euroamerican materials and forms. A paisley shirt set off with silver ornaments unmistakably proclaimed the wearer to be Indian. Even today, variations of this clothing may be found, as well as even more quintessential pan-Indian exemplars such as feather warbonnets and turquoise-and-silver jewelry. All of these have been endowed with a symbolic value beyond the merely ornamental or functional.

Containers

Nearly as important in the Indian trade as hardware and ornaments were containers, especially kettles of brass or copper. The durability and light weight of these kettles endowed them with a functional versatility that included carrying, cooking, and storing. When broken beyond repair they also became an important source of raw material: arrow points, ornaments, and other items were made from cut-up kettles. Finally, these kettles often served a mortuary function, not only as burial accompaniments, but often as a protective covering for the head of the deceased.

Kettles of iron were rarer in the Indian trade. More durable, they were also heavier and bulkier, and hence more difficult to transport. They were most common among sedentary Indians near major Euroamerican ports. The large number of iron kettles at Trudeau was undoubtedly due to the tribe's easy accessibility by river transport.

Nonmetallic containers were also important introductions. Wooden chests, often with locks, seem to have been desired for storage of valuables (e.g., Charlevoix 1744, vol. 3, p. 433), and they were used as coffins for infants. Far more common, however, were glass and ceramic containers. Many of these were originally intended only for the transport of liquid or viscous substances, but they continued in use as storage or serving vessels. Many more had always been intended as tableware and seem to have been accepted as such by the Tunica. At the time of the Trudeau occupation, glass and ceramic containers of European origin outnumbered native pottery vessels by almost two to one. In the nineteenth century, native pottery totally disappeared and was replaced by European and American ceramics.

It is of great interest, however, to note the strong continuity manifested by native pottery. One of the long-held tenets of acculturation studies was that pottery was quickly replaced. But one of the surprises of the Tunica Treasure was the number of native pots, even when the Tunica had access to a variety of imported ceramics. That these pots were not simply heir-looms but were continuing in production is demonstrated by the copying of introduced forms. That the native pottery was still a valuable component of material culture is indicated by its inclusion in grave offerings. It is unfortunate that we do not have better information on grave lots from Trudeau. It could be that most of the native pots were found with women, which might indicate a certain conservatism in female crafts. On the other hand, the continuing production might simply reflect a need for more containers than the French could supply. Such a need might also explain the presence of so many pottery vessels from other native groups such as the Natchez and Caddo. Whatever the case, pottery manufacture continued, with changes, at least through Trudeau and probably into the early occupation at Marksville.

The fact that the Tunica chose to replace some parts of their material culture inventory (e.g., tools and weapons) sooner than others (e.g., shell ornaments and pottery), when they were presented with an equal quantity of replacements, is contrary to generally accepted statements that all aspects of aboriginal material culture were quickly abandoned in the face of more advanced and durable European goods. That Tunica material culture changed extensively is obvious, but that it changed unequally through time is also obvious. There were many replacements and additions, but there were also significant adaptations and continuities.

The dynamics reflected by such a pattern indicate a positive acculturative experience. Traditional views of the process have tended to emphasize the decline and disintegration of native material culture as it was overwhelmed by a flood of introduced goods and technologies. Of course there were significant changes in Tunica material culture once direct and continuing Euroamerican contact was established. The early changes may have been subtle and gradual, but they soon became more intensive and extensive. Many undoubtedly were negative, but they did not simply overcome Tunica artifactual traditions and technologies. New elements were actively incorporated and adapted, and traditional categories of artifacts and technologies were reoriented. Pottery making continued for a long time, while incorporating new forms, and lithic skills turned from the production of arrow points to gunflints.

The Tunica demonstrated the ability to select from Euroamerican material culture elements that were useful to them and to integrate them successfully into their existing lifeways. To paraphrase Gibson (1980, p. 24), the adoption of Euroamerican trade objects did not imply adoption of Euroamerican technologies or material culture systems as a whole. The Tunica adopted certain elements of Euroamerican culture, but adapted and reinterpreted those elements and incorporated them into their own technological system. Because they were used in a traditional Tunica context, the introduced objects were not simply bits of transplanted Euroamerican technology but Tunica artifacts that happened to have come from abroad.

It must be recognized, however, that material culture was the essential lure in Euroamerican-Indian interaction. Introduced artifacts became a necessity to the Indians. Even more than the items themselves, this necessity brought about the real acculturative change because it generated changes in other cultural categories. The Tunica had to concentrate on procuring items or raw materials that the Euroamericans desired and would accept in exchange; they had to provide military service, often against peoples for whom they held no special grievance; and they had to accept a missionary who continually assailed their most sacred beliefs. The adoption of new artifacts and technologies required considerable adaptations beyond the realm of material culture.

SUMMARY

In the various social and cultural categories discussed above there have been changes, but even within categories, change was neither continuous nor comprehensive. From the first, rapid replacements occurred in such material categories as weapons, tools, and dress. Food-ways, settlement patterns, ideology, sociopolitical structure, and language all demonstrated great tenacity, although they also eventually underwent varying degrees of change and only a few remnants of the ancient customs survive today. Altogether, then, acculturation has occurred to the point that the Tunica now are as assimilated a segment of modern American society as any other group that similarly has maintained sufficient continuities to be regarded as ethnically distinct.

Despite the changes, then, an ethnic continuum is demonstrated: a continuum that has been biologically self-perpetuating, has shared fundamental cultural values, has constituted a field of communication and interaction, and has had a membership that identifies itself—and has been identified by others—as constituting a group distinguishable from other groups (Barth 1969, pp. 10–11; but note that in the case of the Tunica there have been enduring qualities). The dynamics of this changing situation have been exposed in the foregoing pages insofar as the data have allowed us to reconstruct them. In the next section, we shall attempt to go one step further and identify some of the processes that may have been responsible for Tunica survival.

A Consideration of the Processes of Tunica Continuity

Having distinguished the above patterns of change, we now turn to the interpretation of possible processes. Those that demand our attention are not the external causative factors that may have initiated a particular sequence of change, but rather those internal decisions that helped the Tunica to acculturate and survive (Bohannon 1967, p. xvii). The culmination of this study, therefore, is not an exploration of causes, but of reactions to those causes, of choices made at crucial times of stress.

It is probable that the processes of change were not recognized, or at least not clearly articulated, by the Tunica as they were occurring. Nor are we in much better position to determine those processes, despite the advantage of hindsight and the evidence from an unusually detailed ethnohistorical and archaeological record. Obviously, through time many different causative factors provoked varying responses from the Tunica and contributed to the changing patterns of their lifeways. Many of these causes and reactions have already been explored above. What we seek now, however, is a broader perspective and more fundamental interpretation of the dynamics of change. Specifically, we seek replications in the patterns of change that disclose consistencies in Tunica responses to stressful circumstances. Here we enter a structural phase of interpretation, for the goal is to discover if there were underlying principles (Deetz's "deeper organizing principles" or "internal dynamics" [Deetz 1983, pp. 28–29]) that guided the decision-making process and enabled the Tunica to survive Euroamerican contact and acculturation.

The principal period of acculturation was the eighteenth and nineteenth centuries; it was also, however, a period of florescence for the Tunica. It would seem that in this case acculturation was by no means an entirely negative experience. The Tunica found a viable niche in the new world that the Euroamericans fashioned in their land. Changes did occur, but they were adapted relatively comfortably within a traditional sociocultural framework. It was their ability to make internal systemic adjustments that consistently enabled the Tunica to adapt and cope with a destabilized external sociocultural environment and to maintain their continuity while so many others failed. It is this ability that we seek to explicate.

Much has already been made of the contrast between Tunica and Natchez reactions to the intrusion of the Euroamericans in the eighteenth century (Brain 1979, 1983a). The Tunica and the Natchez were neighbors at the time of early French contact and both were subject to many of the same stresses, yet the Tunica survived and the Natchez did not. While this may seem no more than fortuitous, there are reasons to think it was not. The Tunica and the Natchez were two very different peoples, completely unrelated ethnically, linguistically, traditionally, and historically, and they reacted very differently to Euroamerican contact. The Tunica were able to adapt to the French and their requirements; the Natchez were not. The Tunica traded, provided military assistance, and accepted a missionary; the Natchez were unreceptive to all of these relationships, and when they refused to grow and trade enough of their fine tobacco to satisfy the French, the latter moved in to grow their own. It was, as usual in the annals of Euroamerican-Indian conflict, the growing foreign population and its desire for land that led to the final disastrous confrontation and destruction of the Natchez.* It could be argued that the Tunica were not subjected to this classic situation and that their survival was therefore simply a matter of luck. The greater truth probably is that they chose to avoid confrontational situations, and by exercising their alternatives were able to maintain both their independence and continuity.

The structural elements underlying these comparisons are simply stated. The Tunica were an adaptable, open society; the Natchez a rigidly structured, closed one. This characterization is superficial, to be sure, but it reveals a crucial difference in the response to sudden overwhelming external pressures. On the one hand, the traditional internal ideology and cultural strategies of the Tunica allowed survival, given the opportunity for adjustments to be made, while those of the Natchez could not cope with the emergency. These attitudes are essential elements of ethnicity and critical correlates for continuity.

The most important Tunica asset, then, was adaptability, a sociocultural flexibility that allowed the development of a successful strategy of accommodation. This advantage may have been developed in many ways, but there appear to have been two particular adaptive processes that may be presented as hypotheses:

1. The "Gypsy Hypothesis" (Craig and Peebles 1974). As suggested by Craig and Peebles, a people forced into frequent movement from place to place, each with differing sociocultural and natural environments, may adopt an unusually adaptable mode of life, or at least not resist necessary change. Although it is an obvious vehicle for change, such a migratory disposition also reveals a deeper structural continuity if it becomes a consistent reaction. During the eigh-

* One of the clichés in the European colonization of North America must be exposed here: namely, that the beneficent French got along better with the Indians than the more tyrannical English. It is true that the French in Canada, few in numbers, adopted a trading relationship with the Indians that contrasted with the territorial demands of the many English colonists in the Northeast. In Louisiana, the roles were reversed: it was the French who were moving in as a large colonial presence, and the English who were distant traders.

teenth century, the Tunica repeatedly chose to migrate and avoid the stark dichotomy of resistance or incorporation, either of which would have resulted in ethnic annihilation. In the nineteenth century, confronted by a local community that did not accord them a prominent place, the Tunica survived again by turning inward. Throughout, they survived, sometimes even prospered, and maintained a core of ethnic continuity. But proving that some peoples can move, adapt, and survive, even survive well, does not explain how and why they have this ability when others do not.

2. The Entrepreneur Hypothesis. Although not a complete explanation, the entrepreneurial role of the Tunica in the Lower Mississippi Valley during protohistoric and historic times may have been an important factor in their survival. There is ample evidence in the documents of the early historic contact period that the Tunica were traders of important commodities—such as salt, foodstuffs, and horses—to their Indian and Euroamerican neighbors. To be successful, entrepreneurs have to be widely adaptable. Although headquartered on the Mississippi, the Tunica gathered their resources from the far western Caddo country, apparently living among many different peoples while doing so. In the distribution of the commodities that they controlled, they came into contact with yet other peoples, first Indian and then the French intruders. When adverse conditions dictated, they seem to have found it possible to move from one location to another and still maintain their successful trading position. This is the true test of accomplished entrepreneurs.

The proof of the entrepreneur hypothesis archaeologically would be the identification of an unusual abundance of the controlled trade items. Such proof is extremely difficult, if not impossible, to gather in the case of salt and foodstuffs. Equally difficult is the case of horses, if they were not used (or eaten) but simply traded. Therefore, other indications of trading activity must be sought.

Evidence in support of such a hypothesis would be a particular and distinctive settlement pattern. Specifically, it is expected that settlement locations would tend to cluster at major junctions of communication routes, thus ensuring control of, and access to, the trade network. In the case of the Tunica, it has been demonstrated that in the course of their several moves they consistently chose to settle at the major riverine confluences: namely, the Arkansas, the Yazoo, and the Red, the three most important tributaries south of the Ohio River. Whatever part land routes might have played, at the very least the Tunica certainly were in command of important segments of riverine communication.

Additional evidence would be provided artifactually if the sequence of occupations reveals a progressive increase in quantity and variety of material goods, with entrepreneurial success demonstrated especially by an unusual wealth of imported (both Euroamerican and aboriginal) artifacts. It should be emphasized that this evidence is only circumstantial, since the standard of measure used may not have been the actual source of affluence, but rather its reward. Nevertheless, the prediction is testable and, again, supported by the archaeology, at least during the best-known part of the occupational sequence from the Yazoo to Trudeau. Clearly, the Tunica had exceptional access to Euroamerican resources, which attests to their entrepreneurial success.* They seem to have been an exception to the general observation that

Indians who constantly engaged in trade never got rich at it even under the most favorable circumstances . . . They failed to acquire property because they did not accept the European trait of capital accumulation. (Jennings 1976, pp. 102–103)

In the case of the Tunica, ethnohistorical (Charlevoix 1744, vol. 3, p. 433) and archaeological evidence indicates otherwise.

The important adaptive processes, then, were a migratory disposition and an entrepreneurial ability that fostered interaction and minimized conflict. By being selectively accommodating rather than resistant, the Tunica revealed creativity and sophistication as they adjusted to the new economic, political, and social orders. Of course, there was a bit of luck involved too, but fortune really was manifested in the form of a small population which made itself useful: the Tunica survived because they were never a serious threat to the French and often a significant asset. Most of all, they survived because they learned, if not to be French, at least to play by French rules. Altogether, the salient characteristics of the adaptive processes among the Tunica were a predisposition for change already built into their sociocultural system, the ability to change large segments of this system to integrate with Euroamerican rules of behavior, a reasonable degree of internal control that enabled the realization of most of the goals of adaptation, and the alteration of traditional lifeways to create an acceptable sociocultural balance. In these respects, the Tunica exhibited the qualities of what has been called a "persistent cultural system":

A cumulative cultural phenomenon, an open-ended system that defines a course of action for the people believing in it. Such peoples are able to maintain continuity in their experience and their conception of themselves in a wide variety of sociocultural environments. (Spicer 1971, p. 799)

Developments during the last two centuries greatly altered these earlier patterns. But the strength of Tunica adaptability manifested during the pivotal years of the early contact period must have endured and been a prime reason for Tunica survival to the present day. In pro-

---

* Even if much of Tunica wealth manifested at Trudeau was the result of payment for services rather than goods, the overall relationship with the Euroamericans was but an expanded entrepreneurial trade which included both goods and services.

gressive, albeit unequal, stages they gave up their dominance, their sovereignty, and eventually most of their culture, but they retained their ethnicity. Confronted by forces, motivations, and events often beyond their comprehension, much less control, the tribe nevertheless managed to make choices at critical times—choices that may not have been the best ones but that at least ensured their survival. These choices reveal a common theme, a guiding ethic, that may be identified as corporate adaptability. Let it be emphasized that such an ethic refers to group behavior. Individuals made bad choices and suffered the consequences, but such occurrences are beyond the normal scope of most archaeological studies, and this one is no exception. The survivors in the continuum, however, maintained a group cohesiveness that contributed to tribal survival for a significant part of Tunica history. Some individuals, such as Cahura-Joligo, could be important catalysts to events, but ultimately Tunica survival was a corporate affair.

Concluding Remarks

In the introduction to this volume, much was said about what archaeology could and should do. Whether its paradigms are those of science, history, or anthropology, or an even broader humanistic discipline, is really quite immaterial, for by its very nature it should lend itself to profitable studies in all those domains. Archaeological research should be free of artificial constraints in explorations of the past (Cohen 1953, pp. 341–366; Eisley 1973, pp. 102–108; Deetz 1983; Trigger 1984; see further discussion by Bamforth and Spaulding 1982). We are, in the final analysis, dealing with people without whom the science, history, and anthropology do not exist. Archaeology is not a game to be played only in ivory towers: games of skeletal culture histories that stand alone, or of nonreplicative predictive statements, or of general laws that are so general as to have little explanatory value. And whatever theoretical stances we take and approaches we use, it is mandatory that we recognize the limitations as well as the possibilities of our data for interpreting the human experience (Chapple 1977, p. 139; Chang 1978, p. 25; Coe 1978, p. 84; Adams 1979).

The approach taken in the foregoing pages has been an eclectic one, although admittedly it has been weighted toward humanistic historicism. The rationale for this approach has been set forth, but it bears repeating that it was determined by the objectives of confirming the continuity of the Tunica past and inferring some of the reasons for that continuity. With our help, the Tunica can indeed now proudly proclaim that "We have proved that we are who we say." This is no small accomplishment.

There is no question that other approaches, other theoretical positions and methodologies, could have been applied with equal profitability. But the fact remains that we now know more about the Tunica than we did before, and if future studies explore this people in yet another way, then we can anticipate further understanding. It is my hope that such studies will occur, but also that they will never lose sight of the object of study. The Tunica, or any other people, should be studied for who they are, and not as an experiment in some theoretical debate. Our subjects are human, and they deserve appropriate humanistic investigations into their past. Otherwise, we are guilty, as many Indians assume we are, of mere "ghoulish academic voyeurism" (Gregory 1981, p. 130). The Tunica understand the need to explore their past, and they respect responsible archaeology. There is no more appropriate way to close this book than with a paraphrase of the words of Antoine Simone Le Page du Pratz (1758, vol. 2, p. 405), that unusually sensitive eighteenth-century friend of the Indians:

If those who have occasion to study them will but have sentiments of humanity, they will in them meet with men.

Appendices: Artifact Classification and Description

Appendices A through C describe the artifacts of aboriginal manufacture and D through F those of European origin. The collection is arranged according to material categories: aboriginal pottery, stone, bone, and shell; European ceramics, glass, and metal. Within each category, the artifacts are presented in a framework of typologies or other descriptive formats established in previous volumes (Phillips 1970; Brain 1979; Williams and Brain 1983; Brain, Brown, and Steponaitis n.d.). The presentation here is somewhat simplified, so the cited works should be consulted for additional discussion, background information, and other details concerning each artifact taxon. These appendices are limited to collections made by the LMS at those sites excavated during the course of the present project: Haynes Bluff (22-M-5), Burroughs (22-M-10), Russell (22-N-19), Bloodhound (29-J-19), and Trudeau (29-J-1).

Appendix G treats as a whole European artifacts of several material categories that are best considered together as a single technological system: guns, gun parts, and munitions. These artifacts were found at Haynes Bluff, Russell, Bloodhound, and Trudeau.

Appendix H presents the faunal analysis of a trash pit excavated at Trudeau.

Appendix A: Aboriginal Pottery

The pottery is classified using the concepts of types-varieties, sets, and modes. First the collection is described using the type-variety system, and then sets are used to organize the data for comparative purposes. Modes are used throughout as the defining characteristics of both varieties and sets, and some modes are acknowledged independently: e.g., the Tunican Mode, Haynes Bluff Rim Mode, Leflore Design Mode, and so forth.

1. Types and Varieties

The following classification uses the type-variety system as set forth by Phillips (1970) and modified by Brain (Williams and Brain 1983). Previously established varieties are presented in an abbreviated format that gives the particulars of the present sample, diagnostic modes, set assignment, and most pertinent references. New varieties are accorded a more extensive treatment, especially regarding background information and relationships. New varieties of plainware are presented first; for already published varieties see Phillips (1970), Brain (1979), and Williams and Brain (1983). The succeeding list is arranged alphabetically according to decorated types. Most of the sherds illustrated in this appendix are from Haynes Bluff.

Addis Plain, *var. Feliciana*

Description: This late variety of Addis Plain appears to be restricted to the historic period and so far has been found only at Trudeau. It is distinguished by the addition of pulverized bone to the paste. The use of this tempering agent demonstrates close connections with the Caddoan area, where the trait is common.

Diagnostic modes: Fine- to medium-textured, mixed-clay-tempered pottery to which pulverized bone has been added.

References: None, but see Suhm and Jelks 1962 for numerous examples of bone tempering.

Proveniences: Trudeau.

Addis Plain, *var. Skillikalia*

Description: This variety of Addis is distinguished by its high sand content. Apparently, sand was purposely added to the basic mixed-clay paste as an additional tempering agent. The use of sand tempering is a late protohistoric-historic mode that also occurs in Mississippi Plain, *var. Montfort* and is characteristic of contemporary Chickasaw and Choctaw wares to the east.

Diagnostic modes: Medium-textured, mixed-clay-tempered pottery with high sand content.

References: None, but see Phillips 1970, p. 54 for a general discussion of sand tempering.

Proveniences: Haynes Bluff, Bloodhound, Trudeau.

Mississippi Plain, *var. Montfort*

Description: This late (protohistoric-historic) variety of Mississippi Plain is distinguished primarily by the noticeable sand content of the paste. This must have been a purposeful addition, and it correlates with the sand-tempered Chickasaw and Choctaw wares to the east. A secondary characteristic is that *Montfort* is usually highly oxidized, which distinguishes it from the gray reduced ware of *var. Yazoo*.

Diagnostic modes: Coarse-textured, shell-tempered pottery with high sand content.

References: Brain, Brown, and Steponaitis n.d.

Proveniences: Haynes Bluff, Russell, Bloodhound, Trudeau.

Alligator Incised, *var. Oxbow*

Illustrations in text: None.

Sample: 10 sherds.

Description: As described in the references.

Diagnostic modes: Very careless incisions, usually haphazardly arranged on the exterior surface of coarse-textured, clay-grit-tempered pottery.

Set: Reed 1.

References: Phillips 1970, pp. 39–40; Williams and Brain 1983, p. 118.

Proveniences: Haynes Bluff (Y100A,B,E; 104F1; 115A; 140C; 141B1).

Anna Incised, *var. Anna*

Illustrations in text: Figures 137m, 151f.

Sample: 23 sherds.

Description: As described by Phillips and modified by Williams and Brain.

Diagnostic modes: Incised lines arranged in curvilinear or rectilinear patterns on the interior surface of medium-textured, mixed-clay- and sometimes shell-tempered pottery.

Set: Greenville.

References: Phillips 1970, p. 102; Williams and Brain 1983, p. 120.

Proveniences: Haynes Bluff (Y100D1; 101A; 102B; 103A; 104F1,4,K1; 107A; 108A; 110D3; 111A,C; 112A; 120A,B2; 155A; surface), Trudeau (V710/711).

Anna Incised, *var. Australia*

Illustrations in text: Figures 74e, 120h, 137l.

Sample: 2 sherds.

Description: As described in the references. This variety definitely has a valid existence in the southern part of the Lower Valley (cf. Williams and Brain 1983, pp. 118–120).

Diagnostic modes: Multiple parallel incisions on the interior rim surface of medium-textured, mixed-clay-tempered pottery.

Set: Addis(?).

References: Phillips 1970, p. 102; Brain, Brown, and Steponaitis n.d.

Proveniences: Trudeau (B127B1; surface).

Avoyelles Punctated, *var. Dupree*

Illustrations in text: None.

Sample: 9 sherds.

Description: As described in the references.

Diagnostic modes: Careless wet-paste incisions and punctations arranged in rectilinear patterns, consisting of alternating plain and decorated zones, on the exterior rim or upper body surface of medium-textured, mixed-clay-tempered pottery.

Set: Addis 1.

References: Phillips 1970, p. 42; Williams and Brain 1983, pp. 120, 121.

Proveniences: Haynes Bluff (Y102B; 104F1; 111D; 115C; 140B2; 153A), Trudeau (B140B1; 160B).

Avoyelles Punctated, *var. Tatum*

Illustrations in text: None.

Sample: 1 sherd.

Description: As described in the references.

Diagnostic modes: Careless wet-paste incisions and punctations arranged in rectilinear patterns, consisting of alternating zones of incising and punctating, on the exterior rim or upper body surface of medium-textured, mixed-clay-tempered pottery.

Set: Addis 1.

References: Williams and Brain 1983, p. 124; Brain, Brown, and Steponaitis n.d.

Proveniences: Haynes Bluff (Y114A).

Barton Incised, *var. Arcola*

Illustrations in text: None.

Sample: 696 sherds.

Description: As described by Phillips and modified by Williams and Brain. This sample divides into two sub-varieties: sloppy, widely spaced incisions on large vessels, and fairly neat, closely spaced incisions on smaller vessels. No significant stratigraphic differences were observed between these groups at Haynes Bluff, so the division was not formalized with the separation of a new variety.

Diagnostic modes: Narrow, wet-paste incisions arranged in simple rectilinear patterns (line-filled triangles or alternating hatched areas) on the exterior body surface of medium- to coarse-textured, shell-tempered pottery.

Set: Yazoo 4.

References: Phillips 1970, p. 45; Williams and Brain 1983, p. 127.

Proveniences: Haynes Bluff (Y100A,D1; 101A,B,C,D,E, F,G; 102A2,B,C,D; 103A,B,C; 104A1,2,3,B1,2,C1,2,3, 4,D1,2,E1,F1,2,3,4,5,6,G1,2,3,H1,2,3,4,J,K1,Z1,2,3,4,6,7; 105A; 106A,B1,2; 107A,B,C1,7; 108A,B; 109A,B,E3; 110A, B,D2,D4,E,G,H,N,P; 111B,C,D,X; 112A,B; 113A,B,C; 114A,B; 115B,C,D1,2,E1,F2,G; 118A,B; 120A; 130A; 136A; 140B1,2,F,H/L,I2; 141A; 152A; 157A; 158A; 160A; 166A; surface), Burroughs (surface).

Barton Incised, *var. Charlevoix*

Illustrations in text: None.*

Sample: 196 sherds.

Description: As described in the reference, except that a broader range of design motifs and placement is probably included. *Charlevoix* is a member of the historic period *Montfort* set, which also includes Old Town Red, *var. Ballground*, Parkin Punctated, *var. Elise*, and Winterville Incised, *var. Loubois*.

* Photographically indistinguishable from other varieties of Barton Incised.

Diagnostic modes: Wet-paste incisions arranged in simple rectilinear patterns on the exterior surface of coarse-textured, sand-shell-tempered pottery.

Set: Montfort.

References: Brown 1979a, pp. 607–609.

Proveniences: Haynes Bluff (Y100A,E; 101A,B,C,E,F; 102A1,B,C,D2; 103C; 104A2,B1,2,C1,D1,E1,F1,3,4,5,6, G1,2,3,H1,2,3,J,K1,Z2; 106A; 107C1,D3; 109A; 110A, B,C,D4,G; 111B,C,D,X; 112A,B; 113A,B; 114A; 115A, B,C,F1; 117A; 120A; 132A; 136A; 140B2; 141C1; 150A; 151A; 152A; 154A; 155A1; 156A1; 157A; 158A; 159A; 160A; 161A; 162A; 163A; 165A; surface).

Barton Incised, *var. Davion*

Illustrations in text: Figures 180e; 197a, n–o, z–aa.

Sample: 43 sherds.

Description: As described in the reference, this variety distinguishes a simple design motif that is restricted to one part of the vessel.

Diagnostic modes: Narrow, wet-paste incisions arranged as a band of parallel oblique lines around the necks of jars or bowls of coarse-textured, shell-tempered pottery.

Set: Yazoo 8.

References: Brown 1979a, pp. 609–612.

Proveniences: Haynes Bluff (Y100A,B,E; 101B; 104B1, 2,F3,4,5,6,G1,2,H1,2,3; 105F; 106A; 110B,E; 111B,D; 112A; 113A; 115A,C,D2; 118A; 136A; 150A; 153A; 154A; 155A1; 156A1; 158A; 167A), Russell (surface).

Barton Incised, *var. Estill*

Illustrations in text: None.

Sample: 113 sherds.

Description: As described in the references.

Diagnostic modes: Usually rather careless wet-paste incising arranged in line-filled triangles on the exterior rims and extending onto the upper shoulder area of medium- to coarse-textured, shell-tempered pottery.

Set: Yazoo 3.

References: Phillips 1970, pp. 45–46; Williams and Brain 1983, p. 127.

Proveniences: Haynes Bluff (Y100A,B,C1,D1,E; 101A, C,D; 102A1,2,B,C, 103A; 104A1,2,B1,2,C1,D1,2,E1,F1, 2,3,4,6,G1,2,4,H4,J,K1,Z2,3; 106A; 107B,D3; 108A; 109A; 110A,B,D2,4,E,G,I,J,L,P,R; 111C; 115G,H,I; 120A, B2; 140B2; surface).

Barton Incised, *var. Midnight*

Illustrations in text: None.

Sample: 87 sherds.

Description: As described by Williams and Brain.

Diagnostic modes: Careful, close-spaced incising, arranged as hatchure on the exterior rim and upper body surfaces of medium-textured, shell-tempered pottery.

Set: Yazoo 4.

References: Williams and Brain 1983, p. 132.

Proveniences: Haynes Bluff (Y100A; 101A,D,E,F; 102A2, B,C; 104A2,B1,2,C1,2,3,D1,E1,F1,2,4,5,6,G1,2,3,4,H1,2, J,K1; 105C; 106A; 107B; 113A,B; 115C,E1,F2; 141B; surface).

Barton Incised, *var. Portland*

Illustrations in text: Figures 64j; 152n–p; 176a,e; 180c; 185f; 197b–c, p–s, bb.

Sample: 66 sherds, 1 partial vessel.

Description: As described in the reference, this is another variety that distinguishes a specific design motif and placement.

Diagnostic modes: Narrow, wet-paste incisions arranged in alternating blank and line-filled triangles on the exterior rim/neck surface of jars of coarse-textured, shell-tempered pottery.

Set: Yazoo 8.

References: Brown 1979a, pp. 613–616.

Proveniences: Haynes Bluff (Y100A; 101C,D; 102B; 103A; 104B1,2,D1,E1,F1,4,G1,4,H1,3,J; 106A; 107A; 109A; 111C; 112A; 113A; 115A,E2,F2; 118B; 140B2,F; 154A; 155A; 158A; surface), Bloodhound (A181B; 185B), Trudeau (V710/711).

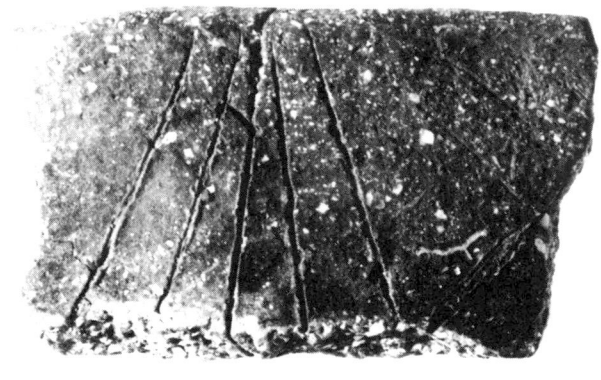

Barton Incised, *var. Trudeau*

Illustrations in text: Figures 64f–i, 120c, 137c, 152k–m.

Sample: 158 sherds.

Description: As described in the reference, this variety includes all Barton Incised found at Trudeau—and by extension at other sites in the Tunica Hills region. The problem is that at this distance from its place of origin the type is considerably extended and the component varieties established for the Yazoo begin to lose definition (see Phillips 1970, pp. 43–45 for a discussion of this general problem). Although perfectly good examples of the prime Tunica markers *vars. Davion* (Brain 1979, p. 239) and *Portland* exist, especially at earlier sites such as Bloodhound, they are rare and generally have completely disappeared by the time of Trudeau.

New design modes are present, and technique is quite variable. The only real coherence is typological: rectilinear incising on Mississippi Plain pottery.

Diagnostic modes: Wet-paste incisions arranged in rectilinear patterns on the exterior surface of coarse-textured, shell-tempered pottery.

Set: Pocahontas.

References : Brain 1979, pp. 238–240.

Proveniences: Bloodhound (A75B; 100B; 108A; 111B; 161A,B; 163A; 177A; 182B; 186B; 187B; 188; 229A,B; 231A; 240A; 241A,B; 242B; 243A,B), Trudeau (V702A,B; 705B,C; 707A,B; 709A,C3; 710/711; B104A; 108A; 110A; 115B1; 118A; 119A; 121A; 123A1; 125A2; 140A; 144A; 160A; 180A; 185B; 186A; 187A; 202C1; surface).

Beldeau Incised, *var. Beldeau*

Illustrations in text: None.

Sample: 1 sherd.

Description: As described by Phillips, modified by Williams and Brain.

Diagnostic modes: Neat incisions and punctations arranged in a rectilinear crosshatched pattern on the exterior rim or upper body surface of fine-textured, clay-tempered pottery.

Set: Vicksburg.

References: Phillips 1970, p. 58; Williams and Brain 1983, p. 133.

Proveniences: Haynes Bluff (Y151A).

Beldeau Incised, *var. Bell Bayou*

Illustrations in text: None.

Sample: 2 sherds.

Description: As described in the references.

Diagnostic modes: Careless wet-paste incising and punctating arranged in a rectilinear crosshatched pattern on the exterior rim surface of medium-textured, mixed-clay-tempered pottery.

Set: Addis 1.

References: Williams and Brain 1983, pp. 133–134; Brain, Brown, and Steponaitis n.d.

Proveniences: Haynes Bluff (Y113A), Trudeau (surface).

Cahokia Cord Marked, *var. Montrose*

Illustrations in text: None.

Sample: 4 sherds.

Description: As described by Williams and Brain.

Diagnostic modes: Cord marking on the exterior of thin, medium-textured, shell-tempered pottery.

Set: Coker.

References: Williams and Brain 1983, pp. 135–136.

Proveniences: Haynes Bluff (Y111B,D; 140B1).

Carter Engraved, *var. Carter*

Illustrations in text: None.

Sample: 32 sherds.

Description: As described in the references.

Diagnostic modes: Engraved lines arranged in curvilinear patterns on the exterior rims of medium-textured, mixed-clay- and sometimes shell-tempered pottery.

Set: Greenville.

References :   Phillips 1970, p. 103; Williams and Brain 1983, p. 136.

Proveniences: Haynes Bluff (Y100A,D1,E; 101A; 102A1,B,F; 103A; 104B2,C3,F1,5,G2; 110D2,H,I; 112B; 113C; 120A,B2; 140E,J; surface), Trudeau (V710/711).

Chevalier Stamped, *var. Chevalier*

Illustrations in text: Figure 182d.

Sample: 9 sherds.

Description: As described in the references.

Diagnostic modes: Rocker stamping applied in parallel vertical rows on the exterior upper body surface of medium-textured, clay-tufa-tempered pottery.

Set: Valley Park

References: Phillips 1970, p. 65; Williams and Brain 1983, pp. 140–141.

Proveniences: Haynes Bluff (Y102A2; 104B2; 105B; 106B3; 110G; 111B), Burroughs (Y300D; surface).

Chevalier Stamped, *var. Cornelia*

Illustrations in text: None.

Sample: 13 sherds.

Description: As described in the references.

Diagnostic modes: Crude rocker stamping carelessly applied in wide-spaced vertical rows to the exterior surface of coarse-textured, clay-grit-tempered pottery.

Set: Reed 2.

References: Williams and Brain 1983, p. 141; Brain, Brown, and Steponaitis n.d.

Proveniences: Haynes Bluff (Y102E; 104F1,G2,J; 107A; 110A,C,E,G,J).

Chevalier Stamped, *var. Perry*

Illustrations in text: Figure 151b.

Sample: 10 sherds.

Description: As described in the references.

Diagnostic modes: Careless rocker stamping applied in vertical rows to the exterior rim surface of medium-textured, mixed-clay-tempered pottery.

Set: Addis 1.

References: Williams and Brain 1983, pp. 142–143; Brain, Brown, and Steponaitis n.d.

Proveniences: Haynes Bluff (Y111X; 117A; 140E), Bloodhound (A182B; 184B; 226C; 229A; 241A; 242B).

Chickachae Combed, *var. Chickachae*

Illustrations in text: None.

Sample: 1 sherd.

Description: As described in the references. Presumed to be intrusive from the Choctaw area, this type appears to be a good marker for the protohistoric and historic periods.

Diagnostic modes: Multiple combed lines arranged in simple curvilinear and less frequently rectilinear patterns on the exterior surface of mixed-sand-tempered pottery.

Set: None.

References: Brain 1969, pp. 215–216; Phillips 1970, pp. 65–66.

Proveniences: Trudeau (V702A).

Chicot Red, *var. Grand Village*

Illustrations in text: Figure 62e.

Sample: 94 sherds, 1 partial vessel.*

Description: As described by Brain, Brown, and Steponaitis.

Diagnostic modes: Red slip on the interior and/or exterior surfaces of simple bowls or bottles made of fine- to medium-textured, mixed-shell-tempered pottery.

* Vessel found with looted burial V705C at Trudeau.

Set: St. Catherine 1.

References: Brain, Brown, and Steponaitis n.d.

Proveniences: Haynes Bluff (100A; 101B; 104A2,B1, F1,2,4,5,G1,K1; 105A; 112A; surface), Burroughs (Y300E), Russell (Y207A), Bloodhound (A111A; 161A; 174B1; 182B; 186C; 187B; 226B; 241A; 242B; 243A,B; surface), Trudeau (V702A,B,C4; 705B,C; 707A; 710/711; 723A; B100A; 105B; 111A; 112B; 113A; 114B; 117A; 119A; 125A2; 128A; 129B; 139A; 140A; 141B; 142A; 144A; 180A; 181A; 182A; 186A,B; 190B; 191A; 192B; 193B; 202B; 203A; 207A; surface).

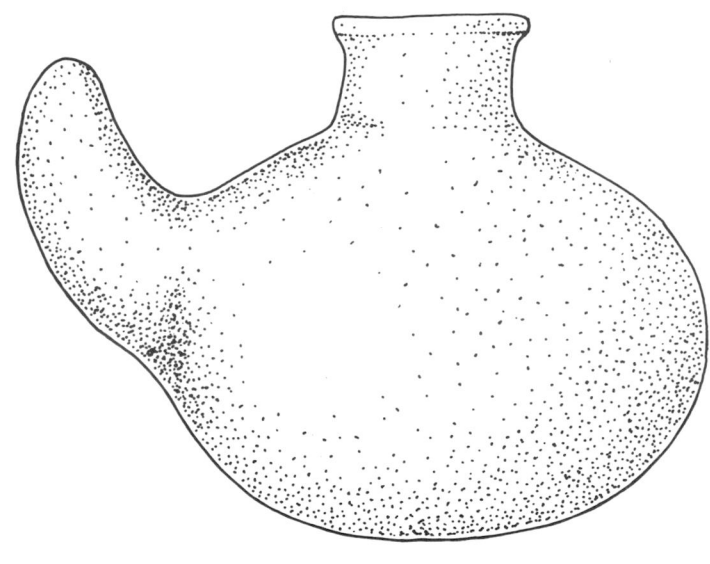

Coleman Incised, *var. Coleman*

Illustrations in text: Figure 151i.

Sample: 27 sherds.

Description: As described in the references.

Diagnostic modes: Careless incisions made with a pointed instrument and arranged in curvilinear patterns on the exterior surface of medium-textured, mixed-clay-tempered pottery.

Set: Addis 1.

References: Phillips 1970, p. 69; Williams and Brain 1983, p. 145; Brain, Brown, and Steponaitis n.d.

Proveniences: Haynes Bluff (Y104A2,B1,C1,F1,4,H3,4, J,K1; 110B,I; 111A,B; 112B; 113C; 115A; 120B2; 151A; 160A; surface), Bloodhound (A111A).

Coleman Incised, *var. Bass*

Illustrations in text: None.

Sample: 18 sherds.

Description: As described by Brain, Brown, and Steponaitis.

Diagnostic modes: Carelessly executed broad incisions arranged in curvilinear patterns on the exterior surface of medium-textured, mixed-clay-tempered pottery.

Set: Not assigned (Addis).

References: Brain, Brown, and Steponaitis n.d.

Proveniences: Haynes Bluff (Y100A; 101C; 104B1, F1,4,5,G1,H4; 106A; 110E; 111B; 113A; 114A; 115E1; 140B1,2).

Coles Creek Incised, *var. Coles Creek*

Illustrations in text: None.

Sample: 37 sherds.

Description: As described in the references.

Diagnostic modes: Multiple closely spaced, broad, overhanging lines incised horizontally around the rims of medium-textured, clay-tufa-tempered pottery.

Set: Valley Park.

References: Phillips 1970, p. 70; Williams and Brain 1983, p. 146; Brain, Brown, and Steponaitis n.d.

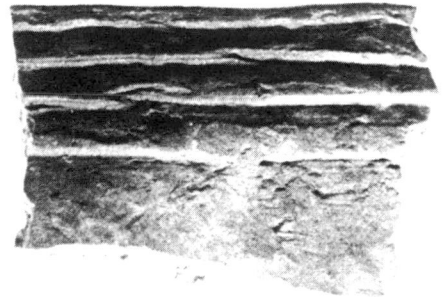

Proveniences: Haynes Bluff (Y100F; 101A; 102E; 103A; 104A2,B2,E3,F4; 108A; 109A; 110B,D4,H,J,N; 111B; 113B; 120A; 136A,B; 140E; 141B; 150A; 160A; 166A), Burroughs (Y300F; surface).

Coles Creek Incised, *var. Blakely*

Illustrations in text: None.

Sample: 3 sherds.

Description: As described in the references.

Diagnostic modes: Multiple widely spaced horizontal lines neatly incised around the rims of fine-textured, clay-tempered pottery.

Set: Vicksburg.

References: Phillips 1970, pp. 70–71; Williams and Brain 1983, p. 146; Brain, Brown, and Steponaitis n.d.

Proveniences: Haynes Bluff (Y100A; 150A; 157A).

Coles Creek Incised, *var. Campbellsville*

Illustrations in text: None.

Sample: 2 sherds.

Description: As described in the references.

Diagnostic modes: Wide-spaced overhanging lines incised horizontally on the rim, accompanied by two lines incised in the lip, of medium-textured, clay-tufa-tempered pottery.

Set: Valley Park.

References: Phillips 1970, p. 71; Williams and Brain 1983, p. 147.

Provenience: Haynes Bluff (Y104F4), Russell (Y201A).

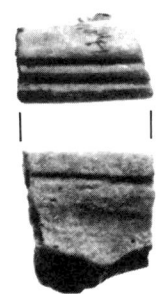

Coles Creek Incised, *var. Chase*

Illustrations in text: None.

Sample: 8 sherds.

Description: As described in the references.

Diagnostic modes: Two or three well-made and very closely spaced horizontal lines incised on the exterior rim strap of medium-textured, clay-grit-tempered pottery.

Set: Sharfit.

References: Phillips 1970, pp. 71–72; Williams and Brain 1983, pp. 147–148.

Proveniences: Haynes Bluff (Y100A; 101A; 110C,D4, G,J,L).

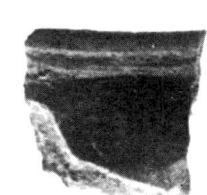

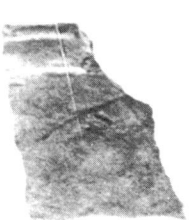

Coles Creek Incised, *var. Greenhouse*

Illustrations in text: None.

Sample: 24 sherds.

Description: As described in the references.

Diagnostic modes: Two or three widely spaced horizontal lines neatly incised around the exterior rim surface of fine-textured, clay-tempered pottery.

Set: Vicksburg.

References: Phillips 1970, pp. 72–73; Williams and Brain 1983, pp. 148–151; Brain, Brown, and Steponaitis n.d.

Proveniences: Haynes Bluff (Y100A; 101C; 102B; 103B; 104D2,F1,K1; 106A,B3; 107D3; 110B,J,K,L,R; 115E1,F2; 120A; 141B), Russell (Y200A).

Coles Creek Incised, *var. Hardy*

Illustrations in text: Figures 137n, 151d.

Sample: 9 sherds.

Description: As described in the references.

Diagnostic modes: Multiple horizontal lines rather crudely incised around the exterior rim surface of medium-textured, mixed-clay-tempered pottery.

Set: Addis 1.

References: Phillips 1970, pp. 73–74; Williams and Brain 1983, p. 151; Brain, Brown, and Steponaitis n.d.

Proveniences: Haynes Bluff (Y101B; 104D2; 109A; 110G; 113A; 140B2; 158A; surface).

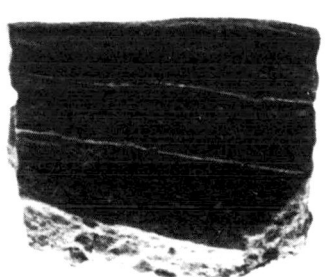

Coles Creek Incised, *var. Hunt*

Illustrations in text: None.

Sample: 31 sherds.

Description: As described in the references.

Diagnostic modes: Two or three crudely incised horizontal lines placed just below the lip on the exterior rim surface of coarse-textured, clay-grit-tempered pottery.

Set: Reed 2.

References: Phillips 1970, pp. 74–75; Williams and Brain 1983, p. 151.

Proveniences: Haynes Bluff (Y102B,C; 103A; 104E1, F4,G2,H3; 107A; 108B; 109A; 110B,E,G,I,J,K,L; 112A; 140B2,C,D; 141B; surface).

Coles Creek Incised, *var. Mott*

Illustrations in text: Figures 120l, 151a, 182e.

Sample: 41 sherds.

Description: As described in the references.

Diagnostic modes: Multiple close-spaced lines, usually neatly incised horizontally around the exterior rim surface of fine-textured, clay-tempered pottery.

Set: Vicksburg.

References: Phillips 1970, pp. 75–76; Williams and Brain 1983, pp. 151–154; Brain, Brown, and Steponaitis n.d.

Proveniences: Haynes Bluff (Y101F; 103A; 104A2, D2,F4,H3; 107C6; 110E,G,L; 112A; 114A; 120A; 130B; 151A; 158A; 160A; surface), Burroughs (Y300F), Russell (Y200A; 201A; 202A; 203B), Bloodhound (A108A; 161A; 226B; surface), Trudeau (V710/711; B111A; 114A; 117A; 119A; 160B; 182A; 193B).

Coles Creek Incised, *var. Phillips*

Illustrations in text: None.

Sample: 25 sherds.

Description: As described in the references.

Diagnostic modes: A single crudely incised horizontal line placed just below the lip on the exterior rim surface of coarse-textured, clay-grit-tempered pottery.

Set: Reed 2.

References: Williams and Brain 1983, pp. 154–156; Brain, Brown, and Steponaitis n.d.

Proveniences: Haynes Bluff (Y101B; 102A2,E; 104D1, H2; 105A; 108A; 110C,D4,E,G,J; 113B; 140E; 141C3; surface).

Coles Creek Incised, *var. Stoner*

Illustrations in text: None.

Sample: 16 sherds.

Description: As described in the references.

Diagnostic modes: A single overhanging horizontal line incised on the exterior rim surface well below the lip of medium-textured, clay-grit-tempered pottery.

Set: Sharfit.

References: Phillips 1970, p. 76; Williams and Brain 1983, p. 156; Brain, Brown, and Steponaitis n.d.

Proveniences: Haynes Bluff (Y102C; 104A2,B2,F1,4, G1,H3; 106B2; 110B,C,G,I; 113A; 141C3), Burroughs (Y300C; surface).

Coles Creek Incised, *var. Wado*

Illustrations in text: None.

Sample: 22 sherds.

Description: As described in the references.

Diagnostic modes: Two overhanging horizontal lines incised on the exterior rim surface just below the lip (and sometimes a line incised in the lip) of medium-textured, clay-grit-tempered pottery.

Set: Sharfit.

References: Phillips 1970, p. 76; Williams and Brain 1983, p. 156; Brain, Brown, and Steponaitis n.d.

Proveniences: Haynes Bluff (Y101C,F; 102A2,B; 103A; 104F2,J; 106A; 107A; 108A; 110E,F1,H,L,N; 111C,D; 115A; 141B; 159A; surface).

Cracker Road Incised, *var. Cracker Road*

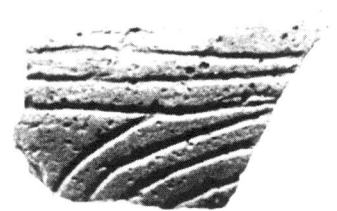

Illustrations in text: Figures 62a, 64aa, 67o, 137d, 153m, 185a.

Sample: 47 sherds, 1 partial vessel.*

Description: As described by Brown, this is a fully shell-tempered counterpart to Fatherland Incised. It is a development of the lower Yazoo Bluffs and contiguous regions during the historic period.

Diagnostic modes: Multiple parallel lines rather carelessly incised with a pointed instrument and arranged in curvilinear (meander, scroll, or sunburst) patterns on the exterior surfaces of bowls or bottles of medium-textured, shell-tempered pottery.

Set: Yazoo 9.

References: Brown 1979a, pp. 647–751.

Proveniences: Haynes Bluff (Y100A; 101A,C,D,E; 102B; 103A; 104A2,B2,F1,4,6,G3,H2,3,J; 111A; 113B; 115A,D2; 117A; 120A; 130A; 140B2; 151A; 158A; 162A; surface), Bloodhound (A182B; 187A; 240B), Trudeau (V705C; 710/711; B128B; surface).

* Vessel found with looted burial V705C at Trudeau.

Evansville Punctated, *var. Rhinehart*

Illustrations in text: None.

Sample: 3 sherds.

Description: As described in the references, except that the ware is coarser than usual. Only the circular punctations are present on these sherds; an incised overhanging line just beneath the lip borders the punctated zone.

Diagnostic modes: Punctations arranged in a band on the exterior rim surface of fine- to medium-textured, clay-tempered pottery.

Set: Vicksburg.

References: Phillips 1970, pp. 80–81; Williams and Brain 1983, p. 158.

Proveniences: Haynes Bluff (Y108B; 110G), Trudeau (V704B).

Evansville Punctated, *var. Sharkey*

Illustrations in text: None.

Sample: 24 sherds.

Description: As described in the references.

Diagnostic modes: Careless punctating on the exterior upper body surface of medium-textured, mixed-clay-tempered pottery.

Set: Addis 1.

References: Phillips 1970, pp. 78–79; Williams and Brain 1983, pp. 158–160; Brain, Brown, and Steponaitis n.d.

Proveniences: Haynes Bluff (Y100F; 101A; 102C,E,G2; 103C; 104F1,4,K1,Z3; 105C; 110C; 111C; 112B; 115G; 120A,B2; 151A; 159A; 162A; 164A), Russell (Y200A), Trudeau (V706A).

Fatherland Incised, *var. Fatherland*

Illustrations in text: Figures 64k–p, 75c-e, 97w, 120e, 132c, 137g, 144a, 148t, 153a–e, 185e.

Sample: 289 sherds, 2 partial vessels, 1 whole vessel.*

Description: As described by Brain, Brown, and Steponaitis, except that many of the examples from Trudeau are on *var. Feliciana* ware.

Diagnostic modes: Two or three narrow (approx. 1 mm or less) parallel incisions arranged in curvilinear meander or scroll patterns on the exterior of bowls or bottles of fine- to medium-textured, mixed-shell-tempered pottery.

Set: St. Catherine 1.

References: Phillips 1970, pp. 106–107; Williams and Brain 1983, pp. 175–177 (included within Leland Incised); Brain, Brown, and Steponaitis n.d.

Proveniences: Haynes Bluff (Y100F; 101C,F; 102B,F; 104A1,2,B2,D2,F1,2,4,G2,3,H1,2,3,Z1; 107C7,D3; 109A; 110D1; 113A; 153A; 155A2; surface), Bloodhound (burial 4,7; A75A,B; 108A,B; 111A,B; 162A; 174A; 181B; 182B; 231B; 240A; 241B; 243A,B), Trudeau (V702A,B; 703A,B; 707A; 710/711; 723B; 727A; 729A; 730A, B56B; 75B1; 102A; 104A,B1; 105A; 109A; 110A; 111A; 112B; 114A,B; 115B1; 118A; 119A; 121A,B1; 123A1,2; 124A2; 125A2; 128A; 129A; 130A; 134A; 135A; 137A; 138A; 139A; 140B; 141A; 142A; 143A; 144A; 181A,B1; 182A; 190A; 191B; 193B; 202A,D2; 203A; 207B; surface).

* Whole vessel found with burial 4 at Bloodhound.

Fatherland Incised, *var. Bayou Goula*

Illustrations in text: Figures 64w–y, 120d, 153h–i.

Sample: 34 sherds.

Description: As described in the references.

Diagnostic modes: Five or more closely spaced narrow incisions forming curvilinear scroll patterns on the exterior of bowls of fine- to medium-textured, mixed-shell-tempered pottery.

Set: St. Catherine 2.

References: Phillips 1970, pp. 104–105; Brain, Brown, and Steponaitis n.d.

Proveniences: Haynes Bluff (Y104B2,F6; 150A), Bloodhound (A111B; 243A; surface), Trudeau (V710/711; B109A; 117A; 118A,B1; 125A2; 144B3; 166A).

Fatherland Incised, *var. Nancy*

Illustrations in text: Figures 64t–v, 120f, 153j.

Sample: 70 sherds.

Description: As described in the reference, this variety is distinguished by the number of lines used to make up the designs. In terms of design, it falls squarely between *vars. Fatherland* and *Bayou Goula*, but chronologically it appears to be the latest of all.

Diagnostic modes: Four narrow parallel incisions arranged in curvilinear meander or scroll patterns on the exterior surface of bowls or bottles of medium-textured, mixed-shell-tempered pottery.

Set: St. Catherine 2.

References: Brain, Brown, and Steponaitis n.d.

Proveniences: Haynes Bluff (Y100A; 101A; 102C; 110D2; 113A; 132A; surface), Bloodhound (A75A; 240A), Trudeau (V702C4; 705C; 706B; 707A,C; 708B,C1; 710/711; B102A; 105B; 108A; 110A; 112A; 113B; 114B; 117A; 124A1; 140A; 143A; 159A; 193A; 202B; 207B; surface).

Fatherland Incised, *var. Snyders Bluff*

Illustrations in text: Figures 64q–s, 153f–g.

Sample: 67 sherds, 2 partial vessels.*

Description: As described in the reference, this variety is similar to the established *var. Fatherland*, but has the additional mode of red slipping. It is believed that the appearance of this mode in the type is a marker for the historic period.

Diagnostic modes: Narrow parallel incisions arranged in curvilinear patterns, plus overall red slipping on fine- to medium-textured, mixed-shell-tempered pottery.

Set: St. Catherine 2.

References: Brown 1979a, pp. 663–666.

Proveniences: Haynes Bluff (Y101D,E; 104G3; 110A; 130A; surface), Bloodhound (A111B; 161A; 175C; 181B; 226A; 242B; 243A), Trudeau (V704B; 705C; 708A; 710/711; 723A, B114A,B; 118A; 119A; 121A; 123A2; 124A2; 127A; 132A; 134A; 139A; 140B; 141B; 186A; 202B,C1; 208B; surface).

* Both vessels from pit feature V710/711 at Trudeau.

Fatherland Incised, *var. Stanton*

Illustrations in text: None.

Sample: 12 sherds.

Description: As described in Brain, Brown, and Steponaitis.

Diagnostic modes: Narrow incisions arranged in relatively open-spaced curvilinear designs on the exterior of vessels of usually fine- to medium-textured, mixed-shell-tempered pottery.

Set: St. Catherine 1.

References: Brain, Brown, and Steponaitis n.d.

Proveniences: Haynes Bluff (Y104C3,D,F1,4,J; 110D2; 150A).

French Fork Incised, *var. Larkin*

Illustrations in text: None.

Sample: 1 sherd.

Description: As described in the references.

Diagnostic modes: Punctations and incisions arranged in generally curvilinear patterns on the exterior rim or upper body surface of medium-textured, clay-tufa-tempered pottery.

Set: Valley Park.

References: Phillips 1970, p. 85; Williams and Brain 1983, p. 162; Brain, Brown, and Steponaitis n.d.

Proveniences: Haynes Bluff (Y110C).

French Fork Incised, *var. McNutt*

Illustrations in text: Figure 182f.

Sample: 4 sherds.

Description: As described in the references.

Diagnostic modes: Incisions, often close-spaced and zoned, arranged in curvilinear patterns on the exterior rim or upper body surface of fine-textured, clay-tempered pottery.

Set: Vicksburg.

References: Phillips 1970, p. 86; Williams and Brain 1983, pp. 162–163; Brain, Brown, and Steponaitis n.d.

Proveniences: Haynes Bluff (Y104F4; 141B), Burroughs (Y300F), Russell (Y200A).

French Fork Incised, *var. Wilzone*

Illustrations in text: None.

Sample: 3 sherds.

Description: As described in the references.

Diagnostic modes: Rocker stamping and incising, usually arranged in curvilinear patterns on the exterior body surface of medium-textured, clay-grit-tempered pottery.

Set: Sharfit.

References: Phillips 1970, pp. 86–87; Williams and Brain 1983, p. 163.

Proveniences: Haynes Bluff (Y110M; 141C3), Burroughs (surface).

Grace Brushed, *var. Grace*

Illustrations in text: None.

Sample: 257 sherds.

Description: As described in the references. The apparent longevity of this variety at Haynes Bluff is probably due to the unusually extended popularity of brushing as a decorative technique in the region, and it required the establishment of two later varieties, *Grand Gulf* and *Warren*. Many of the small sherds counted here may be fragments from vessels of the latter varieties.

Diagnostic modes: Overall brushing, apparently often arranged in rectilinear patterns, on the exterior surface of coarse-textured, shell-tempered pottery.

Set: Yazoo 2.

References: Phillips 1970, p. 153 (listed as a variety of Plaquemine Brushed); Williams and Brain 1983, p. 165; Brain, Brown, and Steponaitis n.d.

Proveniences: Haynes Bluff (Y100A,D1,E; 101A,B,C,D; 102A1,2,B,C,E; 103A; 104A1,2,B1,2,C1,2,3,D1,2,E1,2, F1,2,3,4,5,6,G1,2,3,4,H1,2,3,4,J,K1,Z2,3; 106B1,3; 107A, C1; 108A,B,C; 110D1,2,E,F,H,M,O; 111C,D; 112A,B; 113B; 115A,B,E1,G,H,I; 116A; 120A,B1,2; 140B2,E,G; 151A; 157A; 159A; surface).

Grace Brushed, *var. Grand Gulf*

Illustrations in text: None.

Sample: 69 sherds.

Description: New variety.

Background.   The popularity of brushing as a decorative technique apparently increased during the protohistoric period in the lower Yazoo Bluffs. One late variation on the basic theme was to brush with curved strokes rather than straight ones. Sometimes these strokes are long, gentle arcs, and at other times they are tightly curved semilunes and even semicircles. In both cases, the decorative patterns are more complex than is the case for *var. Grace.* The arcs bear a resemblance to guilloche designs from the Transylvania site (22-L-3), which in turn are related to such late Caddoan types as Cowhide Stamped and Keno Trailed. The tightly curved arcs may be imbricated in a fashion similar to Winterville Incised, *var. Ranch,* while the semicircles are arranged to give the same general decorative effect as some complicated stamped wares far to the east. Although no special significance is attached to these similarities, it is clear that some of the design modes found in *Grand Gulf* are derived from a number of different, but widespread, decorative ideas.

Sorting criteria.   Brushing in curved arcs which are used in a variety of designs on the rims and bodies of jars of Mississippi Plain, *var. Yazoo.*

Distribution.   So far known only from Haynes Bluff.

Chronological position: Protohistoric.

Documentation.   None, but see discussions of types cited above.

Diagnostic modes: Brushing arranged in curvilinear patterns on the exterior surface of coarse-textured, shell-tempered pottery.

Set: Yazoo 6.

References: None.

Proveniences: Haynes Bluff (Y100A,B,E; 102A2,C; 104A1,2,B1,2,E1,F2,3,4,5,G1,2,5,H2,J,K1,Z3,4; 107C7; 108A; 110D2; 111D; 113A; 115C; 117A; 120B1; 130A; 153A; 158A; 159A).

Grace Brushed, *var. Warren*

Illustrations in text: Figure 176b.

Sample: 64 sherds, 1 partial vessel.*

Description: New variety.

   Background.   The resurgence of brushing during the late protohistoric period in the lower Yazoo region combined with at least one other technique: incising. Considering the broad exchange of decorative modes that occurred at this time, and which tends to blur typological distinctions, such a development was almost inevitable. In this case, incisions were made after straight brushing. Both the incising and brushing were applied vertically, but rarely parallel to each other: that is, the incisions are generally diagonal, cutting across the grain of the brushing. The incisions are often placed at oblique angles to each other, forming simple triangular patterns of zoned brushing.

   Sorting criteria. Rather careless, straight-line brushing and over-incising. The incisions may be arranged in a pattern of alternating triangles filled with brushing. The ware is Mississippi Plain, *var. Yazoo,* and the only known vessel shape is the jar. The decoration is placed on the rim and upper part of the body.

   Distribution.   Lower Yazoo Bluffs: Haynes Bluff, Portland, and St. Pierre.

   Chronological position.   Protohistoric.

   Documentation.   Brown 1979a, pp. 668–669.

Diagnostic modes: Brushing and incising arranged in simple rectilinear patterns on the exterior surface of coarse-textured, shell-tempered pottery.

Set: Yazoo 6.

References: None.

Proveniences: Haynes Bluff (Y100A; 101A,B; 102C; 104A2,B2,C3,F2,4,5,6,J,K1,Z3; 106A,B1; 140B1).

* Vessel from pit feature in excavation unit Y104 at Haynes Bluff.

Harrison Bayou Incised, *var. Harrison Bayou*

Illustrations in text: Figure 74f.

Sample: 5 sherds.

Description: As described in the references.

Diagnostic modes: Carelessly incised lines arranged in a rectilinear crosshatched pattern on the exterior rims of medium-textured, mixed-clay-tempered pottery.

Set: Addis 1.

References: Phillips 1970, pp. 87–88; Williams and Brain 1983, p. 165.

Proveniences: Haynes Bluff (Y104B2,F4; 120A), Russell (Y200A), Trudeau (surface).

Hollyknowe Pinched, *var. Patmos*

Illustrations in text: None.

Sample: 15 sherds.

Description: As described by Williams and Brain.

Diagnostic modes: Pinching, usually ridged and arranged in overall rectilinear patterns on the exterior rims (or upper body surface) of medium-textured, mixed-clay-tempered pottery.

Set: Addis 2.

References: Phillips 1970, p. 90; Williams and Brain 1983, p. 167.

Proveniences: Haynes Bluff (Y100A; 102B; 104F1,H3; 106B3; 110P; 111B; 115E2; 120A,B1).

Indian Bay Stamped, *var. Shaw*

Illustrations in text: None.

Sample: 1 sherd.

Description: As described by Phillips.

Diagnostic modes: Rocker stamping on the exterior surface of coarse-textured, clay-grit-tempered pottery.

Set: Satartia(?).

References: Phillips 1970, p. 93, Williams and Brain 1983, p. 167.

Proveniences: Haynes Bluff (Y104F4).

Jaketown Simple Stamped, *var. Silver Lake*

Illustrations in text: None.

Sample: 2 sherds.

Description: As described by Phillips.

Diagnostic modes: Simple stamping on the exterior surface of medium- to coarse-textured, clay-grit-tempered pottery.

Set: Satartia.

References: Phillips 1970, p. 94.

Proveniences: Haynes Bluff (Y108A; surface).

Kinlock Simple Stamped, *var. Kinlock*

Illustrations in text: Figure 163f.

Sample: 3 sherds.

Description: As described by Phillips.

Diagnostic modes: Short parallel lines arranged in horizontal bands on the exterior surface of coarse-textured, shell-tempered pottery.

Set: Yazoo 6.

References: Phillips 1970, p. 97.

Proveniences: Haynes Bluff (Y104F4; 109A), Russell (Y201A).

Lake Borgne Incised, *var. Tenhut*

Illustrations in text: None.

Sample: 1 sherd.

Description: As described by Phillips.

Diagnostic modes: Punctated incising on the exterior surface of poor quality, "untempered" pottery.

Set: Not assigned (Tchefuncte).

References: Phillips 1970, p. 98.

Proveniences: Haynes Bluff (Y104H2).

Larto Red, *var. Larto*

Illustrations in text: None.

Sample: 34 sherds.

Description: As described in the references.

Diagnostic modes: Overall red slipping applied to the interior surface, exterior surface, or both, of medium- to coarse-textured, clay-grit-tempered pottery.

Set: Reed 1.

References: Phillips 1970, p. 99; Williams and Brain 1983, p. 169.

Proveniences: Haynes Bluff (Y100E; 101C; 102B,G1; 104A2,B1,G1,H3; 105A; 106B3; 109A; 110G,J,L; 111D; 141B,C3; 151A; 152A; 155A1; 156A1; surface), Burroughs (Y300B), Trudeau (V710/711).

Larto Red, *var. Silver Creek*

Illustrations in text: None.

Sample: 1 sherd.

Description: As described in the references.

Diagnostic modes: A single horizontal incision on the exterior rim below the lip, and overall red slipping on both the interior and exterior surfaces of medium-textured, clay-grit-tempered pottery.

Set: Sharfit.

References: Phillips 1970, p. 100; Williams and Brain 1983, pp. 169–170.

Proveniences: Haynes Bluff (Y108B).

L'Eau Noire Incised, *var. L'Eau Noire*

Illustrations in text: Figure 137f.

Sample: 6 sherds.

Description: As described by Williams and Brain.

Diagnostic modes: Dry-paste incision and "excision" arranged in distinctive interlocked rectilinear patterns on the exterior of medium-textured, mixed-clay- and sometimes shell-tempered pottery.

Set: Greenville.

References : Phillips 1970, p. 101; Williams and Brain 1983, p. 171.

Proveniences: Haynes Bluff (Y104F4,H2; 108B; 120A), Trudeau (V710/711).

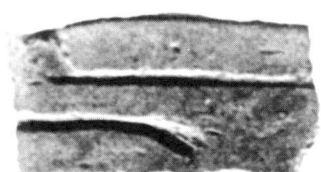

Leland Incised, *var. Leland*

Illustrations in text: Figure 176h.

Sample: 219 sherds.

Description: As described in the references.

Diagnostic modes: Trailed incisions,* usually well executed and "polished over," arranged in curvilinear patterns on the exterior surface of fine-textured, mixed-shell-tempered pottery.

Set: Holly Bluff 1.

References: Phillips 1970, p. 104; Williams and Brain 1983, pp. 171–174.

Proveniences: Haynes Bluff (Y100A,E; 101A,C,E,F; 102A1,2,B,C,D,G2; 103A; 104A1,2,B2,C3,D1,E1,F1,3,4, 5,6,G1,2,3,4,H1,2,3,4,J,K1,Z2,3; 106A; 107A,B,C2,D3; 108A,B,C; 109A; 110D1,3,G,J,O; 111C; 112A; 113A,B; 114A; 115C,D2,F1,2,G,H,I; 116A; 118B; 120A,B; 130A; 136A; 140B2; 150A; 153A; 157A; 158A; 160A; 161A; surface).

* Trailed incisions may be defined as neat, relatively broad incisions in a leather-hard surface, often polished over to remove burred edges.

Leland Incised, *var. Bethlehem*

Illustrations in text: None.

Sample: 19 sherds.

Description: As described by Williams and Brain.

Diagnostic modes: Trailed incisions arranged in curvilinear patterns on the exterior surface of medium-textured, mixed-clay and sometimes shell-tempered pottery.

Set: Greenville.

References: Williams and Brain 1983, pp. 174–175.

Proveniences: Haynes Bluff (Y101A,D,F; 102A1,B,C; 104A3,F4,H2,3; 110H,I,K,N; 140C; 141A; surface).

Leland Incised, *var. Blanchard*

Illustrations in text: Figure 176j, p.

Sample: 41 sherds

Description: As described in the references.

Diagnostic modes: Single trailed incisions drawn in a series of arches or festoons on the interior rim surface of fine- to medium-textured, mixed-shell-tempered pottery.

Set: Holly Bluff 2.

References: Phillips 1970, p. 105; Williams and Brain 1983, p. 175.

Proveniences: Haynes Bluff (Y100B; 104B2,F1,2,3,4, 5,6,J,Z2; 110C; 158A; surface).

Leland Incised, *var. Bovina*

Illustrations in text: None.

Sample: 50 sherds.

Description: New variety.

Background. Leland Incised is one of only two unpainted types that can have interior decoration, as well as exterior. While most of the varieties are exterior, *var. Blanchard* is decorated only on the interior. *Bovina* cements the alliance by having decoration on both the interior and exterior surfaces. No precedence appears to be given to one field over the other: the entire interior may be decorated as much as the exterior (some Leland varieties, such as the new *var. Leflore*, may exhibit a single line or simple festoon on the interior of the rim, but these are just extended lip treatments).

Sorting criteria. Generally neat, polished-over incising in leather-hard surface. Designs are composed of parallel lines probably forming festoons, whorls, scrolls, and other motifs. The ware is Addis Plain, *var. Holly Bluff*, and the only vessel form is the simple bowl.

Distribution. Lower Yazoo Bluffs region: in addition to Haynes Bluff, also reported from the Portland and St. Pierre sites.

Chronological position. Protohistoric.

Documentation. Brown 1979a, pp. 679–680.

Diagnostic modes: Trailed incisions arranged in curvilinear patterns on both the interior and exterior surfaces of bowls of medium-textured, mixed-shell-tempered pottery.

Set: Holly Bluff 3.

References: Phillips 1970, pp. 104–107.

Proveniences: Haynes Bluff (Y101E,F; 102E; 104A1, 2,B2,F1,2,4,5,G1,J,Z2; 110B; surface), Burroughs (Y300B).

Leland Incised, *var. Deep Bayou*

Illustrations in text: Figure 176l.

Sample: 64 sherds.

Description: As described by Phillips and by Williams and Brain.

Diagnostic modes: Exceptionally wide (3–5 mm) trailed incisions arranged in simple curvilinear patterns on the exterior body surfaces of bowls of medium-textured, mixed-shell-tempered pottery.

Set: Holly Bluff 2.

References: Phillips 1970, p. 106; Williams and Brain 1983, p. 175; Brain, Brown, and Steponaitis n.d.

Proveniences: Haynes Bluff (Y100A,E; 102B,C; 103B; 104A2,B1,D1,E1,F1,2,4,5,6,G1,3,4,H1,4,K1; 105A; 108A; 110B,C,D4,E; 111D; 114A; 115D1,F2; 118B; 120A; 156A1; 158A; 159A; 167A; surface), Burroughs (Y300D).

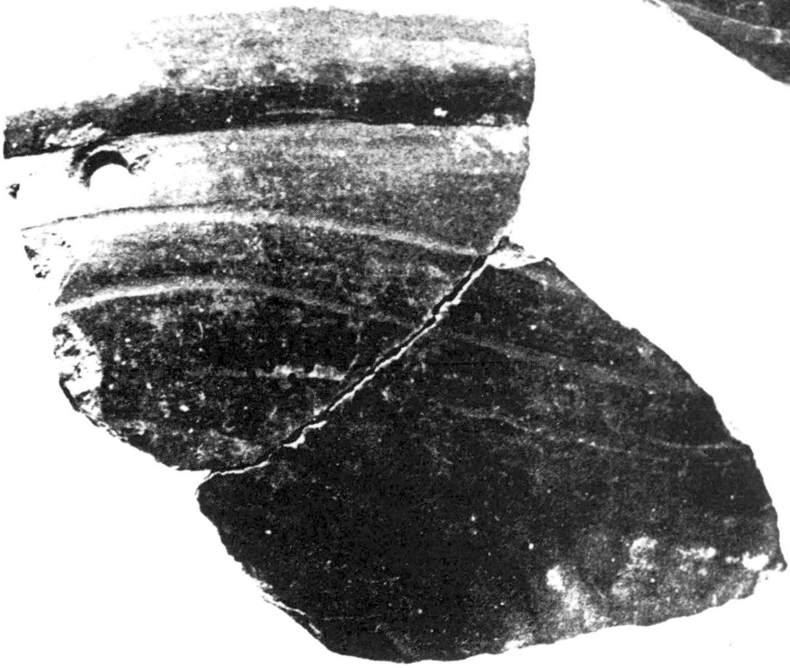

Leland Incised, *var. Ferris*

Illustrations in text: Figure 176i.

Sample: 5 sherds, 1 partial vessel.

Description: As described by Phillips and by Williams and Brain.

Diagnostic modes: Multiple parallel trailed incisions arranged in curvilinear patterns on the exterior of fine-textured, mixed-shell-tempered pottery.

Set: Holly Bluff 1.

References: Phillips 1970, pp. 106–107; Williams and Brain 1983, p. 177; Brain, Brown, and Steponaitis n.d.

Proveniences: Haynes Bluff (Y103A; 104D1; 108A; 110B; 120A).

Leland Incised, *var. Leflore*

Illustrations in text: None.

Sample: 1 sherd.

Description: New variety.

Background. While minimally represented at Haynes Bluff, this variety has been discussed informally by Yazoo archaeologists for some time, and this is as good an opportunity as any to establish it formally. *Leflore* was first recognized as a significant member of the ceramic assemblage from historic period burials at the Jack Leflore site (18-P-3), possibly a village of the Chakchiuma. The design motif that characterizes *Leflore* was found by Jennings (1941, pl. 4c) at a Chickasaw site and also occurs on one of the mortuary vessels found with burial YB-2 during our excavations at Haynes Bluff (see fig. 167). The closest associations, however, are with designs on Creek pottery (e.g., Burke 1936, pl. I; see also Atkinson 1979 for possible Chakchiuma-Creek relationships). While this distinctive motif appears to crosscut types and even culture areas, and thus is a design mode horizon marker, its most typical expression in the Yazoo is clearly as a late variety of Leland Incised.

Sorting criteria. Broad trailed incisions similar to *Deep Bayou* but used to draw a distinctive closed design composed of a narrow, zoned horizontal band within which are ovals, usually separated by a pair of dots. The band is placed below the rim of the exterior surface of simple bowls. Festoons may decorate the inner rim surface. Ware is equivalent to the coarser range of Addis Plain, *var. Holly Bluff*.

Distribution. Yazoo Bluffs.

Chronological position. Protohistoric and early historic.

Documentation. Brown 1978b.

Diagnostic modes: Broad trailed incisions arranged in a closely drawn band of curvilinear motifs on the exterior surface of medium-textured, mixed-shell-tempered pottery.

Set: Holly Bluff 3.

References: None.

Proveniences: Haynes Bluff (Y102B).

Leland Incised, *var. Russell*

Illustrations in text: Figures 64ee, 153n, 184c.

Sample: 557 sherds.

Description: As described by Williams and Brain.

Diagnostic modes: Carelessly executed trailed incisions arranged in simple curvilinear patterns on the exterior surface of medium-textured, mixed-shell-tempered pottery.

Set: Holly Bluff 2.

References: Williams and Brain 1983, pp. 177–179; Brain, Brown, and Steponaitis n.d.

Proveniences: Haynes Bluff (Y100A,B,D1; 101A,B,C, E,F; 102A1,B,C,E; 103A,C; 104A1,2,3,B1,2,C1,2,D1,E1,3, F1,2,3,4,5,6,G1,2,3,4,H1,2,3,J,K1,Z2,3,4,7,8; 105A; 106A, B1,2,3; 107A,C1,D1,3; 108A,B; 109A; 110A,B,C,D1,2,4, E,G; 111A,B,C,D,X; 112A,B; 113A; 114A,B; 115A,B,C, D1,2,F2,G,I; 116A; 117A; 118A; 120A,B1; 133A; 135A, B; 136A; 140B1,2,E; 141A,B; 150A; 151A; 152A; 153A; 155A1; 156A1; 157A; 158A; 159A; 161A; surface), Russell (Y202A; 210A), Bloodhound (A108B; 174A; 181B; 187A; 226A; 231B; 241B; 242A,B; 243A).

Leland Incised, *var. Williams*

Illustrations in text: Figure 180a.

Sample: 293 sherds.

Description: As described by Williams and Brain.

Diagnostic modes: Medium-wide trailed incisions arranged in simple curvilinear patterns on the exterior surface of medium-textured, mixed-shell-tempered pottery (intermediate to Addis Plain and Mississippi Plain).

Set: Holly Bluff 2.

References: Williams and Brain 1983, p. 179; see also Phillips's discussion of *Dabney* and *Deep Bayou* (1970, pp. 105–106).

Proveniences: Haynes Bluff (Y100A,B,C3,E,F; 101A,B, C,D,F; 102A1,B,C,D,E,F; 103A; 104A1,2,3,B1,2,C1,2,3, D1,2,F1,3,F1,2,3,4,5,6,G1,2,3,4,5,H2,3,I,K1,Z1; 105A; 106A; 107A,C7; 108A; 109A; 110A,D3,4,E,G; 111D,X; 112A; 113B, 114A,B; 115A,C,D2,F2,H,I; 116A; 120A; 131A; 136B; 140B1,2; 141B; 152A; 154A; 156A1; 160A; surface), Burroughs (Y300B).

Maddox Engraved, *var. Emerald*

Illustrations in text: Figure 163e.

Sample: 36 sherds.

Description: As described by Phillips for both *Baptiste* and *Emerald*, and as described in Brain, Brown, and Steponaitis.

Diagnostic modes: Incising and engraving arranged in zones of complicated patterns on the exterior surface of fine-textured, mixed-shell-tempered pottery.

Set: St. Catherine 1.

References: Phillips 1970, pp. 108–109; Brain, Brown, and Steponaitis n.d.

Proveniences: Haynes Bluff (Y100D1,F; 101A; 102B,C; 103A; 104C1,D1,E1,F2,4,5,G1,2,H2,K1; 106A; 107B,C6, 7,D3; 110B; 111C; 114A; 115A,I; 120A; 130A; surface).

Maddox Engraved, *var. Silver City*

Illustrations in text: None.

Sample: 49 sherds.

Description: As described by Phillips and by Williams and Brain.

Diagnostic modes: Trailed incising and engraving— the incisions drawing curvilinear patterns, zones of which are filled with engraved cross-hatching—on the exterior surface of fine-textured, mixed-shell-tempered pottery.

Set: Holly Bluff 1.

References: Phillips 1970, p. 109; Williams and Brain 1983, pp. 179–180; Brain, Brown, and Steponaitis n.d.

Proveniences: Haynes Bluff (Y100F; 102B; 104A2,B1,2, C1,E2,F4,5,6,G1,2,4,H1,2,3,4,K1,Z2; 107B,C1; 108A; 109A; 110B; 111B; 115F2; 160A; surface).

Marksville Incised, *var. Yokena*

Illustrations in text: None.

Sample: 2 sherds.

Description: As described by Phillips.

Diagnostic modes: Wide U-shaped incisions on the exterior surface of medium-textured, clay-grit-tempered pottery.

Set: Satartia.

References: Phillips 1970, pp. 117–119; Williams and Brain 1983, p. 181.

Proveniences: Haynes Bluff (surface).

Marksville Stamped, *var. Mabin*

Illustrations in text: None.

Sample: 1 sherd.

Description: As described in the references. Like the example from Lake George, this sherd is carelessly decorated on a poor quality ware.

Diagnostic modes: Nonrocker dentate stamping zoned by U-shaped incisions arranged in simple patterns on the exterior surface of lumpy, clay-grit-tempered pottery.

Set: Not assigned (Marksville).

References: Phillips 1970, pp. 122–123; Williams and Brain 1983, p. 182.

Proveniences: Haynes Bluff (Y113B).

Marksville Stamped, *var. Manny*

Illustrations in text: None.

Sample: 5 sherds.

Description: As described in the references.

Diagnostic modes: Dentate rocker stamping zoned by broad U-shaped incisions arranged in curvilinear patterns on the exterior surface of medium- to coarse-textured, clay-grit-tempered pottery.

Set: Satartia.

References: Phillips 1970, pp. 123–125; Williams and Brain 1983, p. 182.

Proveniences: Haynes Bluff (Y120B1; 151A), Burroughs (Y300C; surface).

Mazique Incised, *var. Mazique*

Illustrations in text: None.

Sample: 1 sherd.

Description: As described in the references, except that the incisions in this example were not cut at an angle.

Diagnostic modes: Closely spaced incisions, usually made with a square-ended implement held at an oblique angle, arranged in rectilinear patterns on the exterior rim surface of medium-textured, clay-tufa-tempered pottery.

Set: Valley Park.

References: Phillips 1970, p. 129; Williams and Brain 1983, p. 184; Brain, Brown, and Steponaitis n.d.

Proveniences: Haynes Bluff (Y104H2).

Mazique Incised, *var. Kings Point*

Illustrations in text: Figures 74b, 120k, 151e.

Sample: 30 sherds.

Description: As described in the references.

Diagnostic modes: Neat incisions arranged in rectilinear patterns on the exterior rim surface of fine-textured, clay-tempered pottery.

Set: Vicksburg.

References: Phillips 1970, p. 129; Williams and Brain 1983, pp. 184–186; Brain, Brown, and Steponaitis n.d.

Proveniences: Haynes Bluff (Y102C; 104K1; surface), Burroughs (Y300C), Trudeau (B104A; 105A; 106A; 107A; 109A; 110A; 111A; 113B; 114B; 123A1; 135A; 140A; 142A,B2; 181A; 187A; surface).

Mazique Incised, *var. Manchac*

Illustrations in text: Figures 74g, 133a, 151h.

Sample: 44 sherds.

Description: As described in the references.

Diagnostic modes: Carelessly incised lines arranged in rectilinear patterns on the exterior rims of medium-textured, mixed-clay-tempered pottery.

Set: Addis 1.

References: Phillips 1970, pp. 129–130; Williams and Brain 1983, p. 186; Brain, Brown, and Steponaitis n.d.

Proveniences: Haynes Bluff (Y100C6,E; 102F; 104A2, B1,E1,2,F1,5,K1,Z3; 107A,D3; 110D1; 112B; 113B,C; 115C; 120A; 140B2; 164A; surface), Burroughs (Y300C, D), Russell (Y200A), Bloodhound (A174B2; 186C; 226B, D; surface), Trudeau (V702C4; 707A; 710/712; surface).

Mazique Incised, *var. North*

Illustrations in text: None.

Sample: 74 sherds.

Description: As described by Brain, Brown, and Steponaitis.

Diagnostic modes: Very carelessly executed incisions arranged in rectilinear patterns on the exterior rims of coarse-textured, mixed-clay-tempered pottery.

Set: Not assigned (Addis).

References: Brain, Brown, and Steponaitis n.d.

Proveniences: Haynes Bluff (Y100B,C2,E,F; 102B,F; 103A,B; 104A1,B2,F4,5,6,G1,H2,K1; 106A; 107A,B,C1; 109A; 110A,B,C,E,H,J,K; 111X; 112A; 114A; 115A, E2,F2,H; 118A; 120A,B2; 140B1,2, 150A, 152A, 154A, 155A1; 158A; 159A; surface), Russell (Y200A).

Mulberry Creek Cord Marked, *var. Edwards*

Illustrations in text: None.

Sample: 18 sherds.

Description: As described in the references.

Diagnostic modes: Careless cord marking applied with a cord-wrapped paddle to the exterior surface of coarse-textured, clay-grit-tempered pottery.

Set: Reed 1.

References: Phillips 1970, p. 137; Williams and Brain 1983, pp. 188–189.

Proveniences: Haynes Bluff (Y100D1; 101B; 102A2,B, G2; 104B1,F1,4; 106B1; 110E,J,L; 111A; 140B2; surface).

Mulberry Creek Cord Marked, *var. Smith Creek*

Illustrations in text: None.

Sample: 9 sherds.

Description: As described in the references.

Diagnostic modes: Relatively neat cord marking, usually crisscrossed, applied with a cord-wrapped paddle to the exterior surface of medium-textured, clay-grit-tempered pottery.

Set: Sharfit.

References: Phillips 1970, pp. 138–139; Williams and Brain 1983, pp. 189–190.

Proveniences: Haynes Bluff (Y101E; 102B,F; 103A; 104B2,F6; 105A; 110B; 141B).

Natchitoches Engraved, *var. Natchitoches*

Illustrations in text: Figures 62d, 75f, 137e.

Sample: 6 sherds, 1 partial vessel.*

Description: As described in the reference. This distinctive import from the Caddoan area seems to be an important marker for the historic period.

Diagnostic modes: Fine engraving, supplemented by ticking, incising, and excising, arranged in complex curvilinear patterns on the exterior surface of fine- to medium-textured; shell-tempered pottery. A red slip is often added.

Set: None (Caddoan).

References: Brain 1979, p. 245.

Proveniences: Trudeau (V702A,B; 705A,B,C; 710/711; surface).

* Vessel found with looted burial V705C at Trudeau.

Nodena Red and White, *var. Nodena*

Illustrations in text: Figure 191p–q.

Sample: 8 sherds.

Description: As described by Phillips.

Diagnostic modes: Red and white painting on the exterior surface of fine-textured, shell-tempered pottery.

Set: Bell.

References: Phillips 1970, p. 142; Williams and Brain 1983, p. 190; Brain, Brown, and Steponaitis n.d.

Proveniences: Haynes Bluff (Y104G4,H2; surface).

Nodena Red and White, *var. Dumond*

Illustrations in text: None.

Sample: 1 sherd.

Description: As described by Phillips.

Diagnostic modes: Designs painted in red and white against a buff background on the exterior surface of fine-textured, shell-tempered pottery equivalent to Bell Plain.

Set: Bell.

References: Phillips 1970, p. 143.

Proveniences: Haynes Bluff (Y104E1).

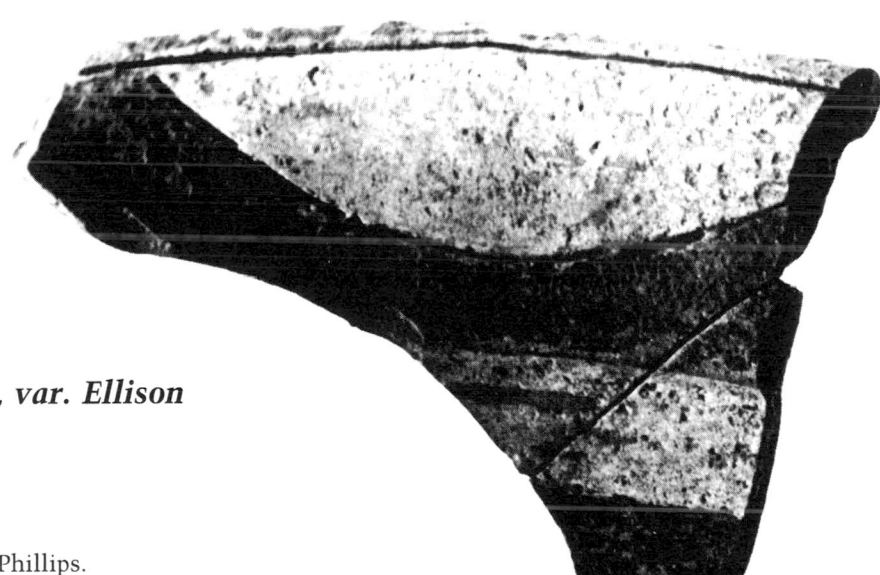

Nodena Red and White, *var. Ellison*

Illustrations in text: None.

Sample: 2 sherds.

Description: As described by Phillips.

Diagnostic modes: Red and white painting, often zoned with incised lines, on the interior and exterior surfaces of fine-textured, shell-tempered pottery.

Set: Holly Bluff 3.

References: Phillips 1970, pp. 143–144.

Proveniences: Haynes Bluff (Y101F; surface).

Old Town Red, *var. Ballground*

Illustrations in text: None.

Sample: 72 sherds.

Description: As described in the reference, this red-slipped ware is distinguished by the addition of sand to the shell-tempered paste. This makes it another member of the important Montfort set, which also includes Barton Incised, *var. Charlevoix*, Parkin Punctated, *var. Elise*, and Winterville Incised, *var. Loubois*.

Diagnostic modes: Generally poor quality red slip on the exterior and/or interior surfaces of coarse-textured, sand-shell-tempered pottery.

Set: Montfort.

References: Brown 1979a, pp. 702–704.

Proveniences: Haynes Bluff (Y100A,B; 101A,C; 102B; 104A2,3,F1,2,3,4,5,G1,2,4,H3,J,K1; 109A; 110A,B; 111A; 115A; 116A; 120B2; 130A; 136A; 140A; 150A; 151A; 152A; 153A; 154A; 155A1; 160A; 161A; 162A; 164A; 165A; surface), Bloodhound (A182B).

Old Town Red, *var. St. Pierre*

Illustrations in text: None.

Sample: 5 sherds.

Description: As described by Brown. This may be one of the latest of all pottery varieties from the lower Yazoo Bluffs.

Diagnostic modes: Thick pink slip on the exterior of coarse-textured, shell-tempered pottery.

Set: Yazoo 9.

References: Brown 1979a, pp. 704–707.

Proveniences: Haynes Bluff (Y101D; 133B).*

* A Fatherland Incised, *var. Snyders Bluff* sherd from Trudeau also exhibits this peculiar pink slip mode.

Owens Punctated, *var. Owens*

Illustrations in text: Figure 191a–e.

Sample: 24 sherds (all from the same vessel).

Description: As described by Phillips, except that this vessel appears to be the standard Mississippi jar form.

Diagnostic modes: Zoned, incised, and punctated treatment consisting of alternating punctate-filled and plain bands or triangles arranged in simple rectilinear patterns on the exterior surface of coarse-textured, shell-tempered pottery.

Set: Yazoo 5.

References: Phillips 1970, pp. 149.

Proveniences: Haynes Bluff (Y104B2,F4,5,6,J,Z7).

Owens Punctated, *var. Beland City*

Illustrations in text: Figures 64bb–cc, 97v.

Sample: 7 sherds.

Description: As described by Williams and Brain, except that three of these sherds (1 from Haynes Bluff, 2 from Trudeau) are also red-slipped, indicating that they must be quite late, and if additional examples are found in historic contexts a new variety should be considered.

Diagnostic modes: Relatively well executed punctation and incision arranged in zones, usually featuring curvilinear patterns, on the exterior of fine-textured, mixed-shell-tempered pottery.

Set: Holly Bluff 2.

References: Williams and Brain 1983, p. 193; see also Phillips 1970, pp. 149 (included within Owens Punctated).

Proveniences: Haynes Bluff (Y101E,F; 104A2), Trudeau (V710/711; B56B).

Owens Punctated, *var. Manly*

Illustrations in text: Figures 129a, 193d–c.

Sample: 17 sherds.

Description: This is not a new variety, but because there have been major typological changes an extended discussion is in order.

Background. This category was originally recognized as Manly Punctated by Phillips, Ford, and Griffin (1951). Phillips (1970) made it a variety of the northern type Matthews Incised; at the same time, he set up a southern counterpart, Pocahontas Punctated, *var. Pocahontas*, based upon the single vessel found at Angola Farm by Ford (see fig. 129a). Phillips felt that the geographical separation required typological separation. The appearance of this material at Haynes Bluff, however, bridges the geographic gap and supports the belief that his *Manly* and *Pocahontas* are the same thing, the unusually extensive geographical distribution of which may be due to the agency of the Tunica. In terms of nomenclature, the most economic solution is to eliminate the newer Pocahontas Punctated and its *var. Pocahontas*, which would also remove the semantic confusion caused by the fact that a *var. Pocahontas* of Mississippi Plain is now well established. But, as originally recognized, *Manly* clearly belongs to a punctated-incised type, not an incised type, varieties of which may have the additional mode of punctation. Reassignment to Owens Punctated seems to make good decorative and geographical sense.

Sorting criteria. A single arcaded line carelessly incised on the shoulders of jars and bordered on the upper side by punctations that are most numerous in the spandrels of the arcs. The ware is equivalent to the late varieties of Mississippi Plain.

Distribution. Upper regions of the Lower Valley south to the lower Yazoo, with at least one vessel carried as far as the Tunica Hills.

Chronological position. Wasp Lake and Russell phases.

Documentation. Phillips, Ford, and Griffin 1951, p. 147; Phillips 1970, pp. 128, 154.

Diagnostic modes: Careless incising bordered by punctations on one side and arranged in a simple curvilinear pattern on the exterior body surface of coarse-textured, shell-tempered pottery.

Set: Yazoo 7.

References: As above.

Proveniences: Haynes Bluff (Y100A; 104B2,F3,4,G1; 110D4; 130A; surface), Russell (Y200A).

Owens Punctated, *var. Menard*

Illustrations in text: Figures 163a–d, 193a–c.

Sample: 77 sherds.

Description: As described by Phillips and modified by Williams and Brain.

Diagnostic modes: Rather careless punctating and incising arranged in zoned curvilinear patterns on the exterior body surface of coarse-textured, shell-tempered pottery.

Set: Yazoo 7.*

References: Phillips 1970, pp. 149–150; Williams and Brain 1983, pp. 193–194; Brain, Brown, and Steponaitis n.d.

Proveniences: Haynes Bluff (104A1,2,B2,F1,2,4,5,G4, H2,J; 107A; surface), Russell (Y206A; surface).

* Note that this represents a reassignment from Yazoo 5, where the variety was placed by Williams and Brain (1983, pp. 194, 324) on the basis of less complete data.

Owens Punctated, *var. Poor Joe*

Illustrations in text: Figure 191f–g.

Sample: 2 sherds.

Description: As described by Williams and Brain.

Diagnostic modes: Careless overall punctating and occasional incised lines, which do not seem to attempt any distinctive patterning, on the exterior body surface of coarse-textured, shell-tempered pottery.

Set: Yazoo 5.

References: Williams and Brain 1983, pp. 194–195; Brain, Brown, and Steponaitis n.d.

Proveniences: Haynes Bluff (Y104B1; 110P).

Owens Punctated, *var. Redwood*

Illustrations in text: Figures 180f; 185b; 197d–e, t, cc.

Sample: 8 sherds.

Description: As described in the reference, this new variety is probably one of the latest examples of the type. It is distinctive in design mode and also technique, which requires the use of at least two implements. There is a close relationship to *var. Manly* and to Winterville Incised, *var. Tunica*.

Diagnostic modes: Careless narrow incisions (made with a pointed stick) zoning large circular punctations (made with the end of a cane) arranged in a band of alternating triangles on the exterior neck surface of coarse-textured, shell-tempered pottery.

Set: Yazoo 8.

References: Brown 1979a, pp. 711–715.

Proveniences: Haynes Bluff (Y102C; 104A1; 106A; 113C; 115A,B; 120A), Bloodhound (A106B).

Owens Punctated, *var. Widow Creek*

Illustrations in text: Figure 191h–l.

Sample: 3 sherds.

Description: As described by Williams and Brain. This sample exhibits a considerable amount of variation in technique.

Diagnostic modes: Contrasting zones of incisions and punctations arranged in usually rectilinear patterns on the exterior surface of coarse-textured, shell-tempered pottery.

Set: Yazoo 5.

References: Williams and Brain 1983, pp. 195–196; see also Phillips 1970, pp. 45–46 (partially included within Barton Incised, *vars. Arcola* and *Estill*).

Proveniences: Haynes Bluff (Y102E; 110C; 120A).

Parkin Punctated, *var. Elise*

Illustrations in text: None.*

Sample: 46 sherds.

Description: New variety.
Background.   *Elise* is a rare example of a successful effort to sort out from this widespread type a narrowly defined variety with useful spatial-temporal parameters. The defining mode in this case is the addition of small amounts of sand to the shell-tempered ware, a mode which cross cuts types during the historic period (see Barton Incised, *var. Charlevoix*, Old Town Red, *var. Ballground*, and Winterville Incised, *var. Loubois*).
Sorting criteria.   Punctating, generally with a pointed stick or fingernail, on ware tempered with shell and sparse amounts of sand equivalent to Mississippi Plain, *var. Montfort*.
Distribution.   Lower Yazoo Bluffs and Tunica Hills regions.
Chronological position.   Late protohistoric and historic.
Documentation.   None.

Diagnostic modes: Random overall punctation on the exterior surface of coarse-textured, sand-shell-tempered pottery.

Set: Montfort.

References: Phillips 1970, pp. 150–152 (included within Parkin Punctated).

Proveniences: Haynes Bluff (Y100A,E; 104D1,3,E1,F1, 2,4,Z6; 107C1; 109A; 110A,B; 111B,C,D; 113B,C; 114A,B; 115A,B,E2; 117A; 120A; 140D; 141B; 150A; 153A; 154A; surface), Bloodhound (A181B; 243A).

* Photographically indistinguishable from other varieties of Parkin Punctated.

Parkin Punctated, *var. Hollandale*

Illustrations in text: None.

Sample: 146 sherds.

Description: As described in the references, this variety needs more precise definition. Presently, it includes all random punctation on ware equivalent to *var. Yazoo*. Considering the popularity of punctated decoration in late prehistory, some further refinement of this group is necessary if it is to have diagnostic value. As constituted, *Hollandale* has too ubiquitous a distribution to be useful, but at the same time it has resisted all efforts to sort it into more meaningful groups.

Diagnostic modes: Random overall punctation on the exterior upper body surface of coarse-textured, shell-tempered pottery.

Set: Yazoo 3.

References: Phillips 1970, p. 152; Williams and Brain 1983, p. 196.

Proveniences: Haynes Bluff (Y100A,B,E,F; 101A,B,D,F; 102B,C,D,E,F; 103A,C; 104A1,2,B1,2,D1,E1,2,3,F1,2,3,4, 5,6,G1,2,3,H1,2,3,4,J,K1,Z1,2; 105A; 106B3; 107A,B; 108A,B; 109D2,E3; 110A,B,C,D1,E,I,J,P; 111C,D; 113A, C; 114A,B; 115F2,H; 117A; 118B; 120A; 140B2,F,I2; 158A; surface).

Parkin Punctated, *var. Transylvania*

Illustrations in text: None.

Sample: 72 sherds.

Description: As described by Phillips and by Williams and Brain.

Diagnostic modes: Punctations arranged in linear (usually curvilinear) patterns on the exterior upper body (rim and shoulder) surface of coarse-textured, shell-tempered pottery.

Set: Yazoo 3.

References: Phillips 1970, p. 152; Williams and Brain 1983, p. 196; Brain, Brown, and Steponaitis n.d.

Proveniences: Haynes Bluff (Y100A,B,C4,D1,E,F; 102B, E; 103A; 104A2,C1,D1,E1,F1,2,G1,2,3,K1,Z2; 105A; 106A; 107B,C2,6,D3; 108A; 110E,G,J; 111A,B,D; 112A; 115I; 120A; 140B2,E,F,G,H/L; 153A; surface), Russell (Y200A,B).

Plaquemine Brushed, *var. Plaquemine*

Illustrations in text: Figures 74h–i, 120i, 137p–r, 151g.

Sample: 200 sherds.

Description: As described in the references.

Diagnostic modes: Brushing, usually with an attempt at rectilinear patterning, on the exterior surface of medium-textured, mixed-clay-tempered pottery.

Set: Addis 2.

References: Phillips 1970, p. 153; Williams and Brain 1983, pp. 196–200; Brain, Brown, and Steponaitis n.d.

Proveniences: Haynes Bluff (Y100A,B,C1,2,6,D1,E,F; 101A,B,C,E; 102B,C,E,F; 103A; 104B1,2,C2,D1,F1,4,5, G3,4,H1,K1,Z2; 105A; 106B3; 107D3; 108A; 109A; 110A,B,C,D1,4,E,J,L,Q2; 111A,C,D,X; 112B; 113B,C; 114A,B; 115B,F2,G,H,I; 120A,B1,2; 130B; 140B1,2,C,E,G; 141B; 151A; 153A; 154A; 156A2; surface), Bloodhound (A51; 111A; 174B1,2; surface), Trudeau (V702C4; 705C; 710/711; B110A; 129A; 154A,B; 155A; 161A,B; 162B; 163B; 167B; 168B; 169B; 170B; 181A; 185A; surface).

Pontchartrain Check Stamped, *var. Pontchartrain*

Illustrations in text: Figures 74c–d, 120j, 137k, 151c.

Sample: 93 sherds.

Description: As described by Phillips.

Diagnostic modes: Stamping in a rectilinear pattern on the exterior surface of fine-textured, clay-tempered pottery.

Set: Vicksburg.

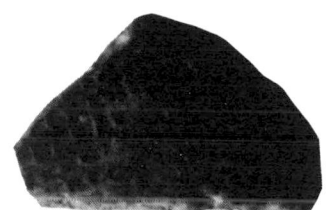

References: Phillips 1970, p. 154.

Proveniences: Bloodhound (A111A; 174B1), Trudeau (V702B; 704B; 705B; 706B; 710/711; B101A; 102A; 104A,B; 106A; 107A; 108A; 110A; 113A,B; 114A,B; 120B1; 121B1; 123A1; 124A2; 125A2; 128A; 129A; 143B1; 153B; 154A; 155B; 158B; 159B; 160C; 167B,C; 168C; 169B,C; 170B; 186A; 193B; 202C1; surface).

Pouncey Pinched, *var. Patosi*

Illustrations in text: None.

Sample: 90 sherds.

Description: As described in the references.

Diagnostic modes: Pinches, made by squeezing the clay surface between finger and thumbnail, aligned into rows which often form ridges, and arranged in simple rectilinear patterns on the exterior surface of coarse-textured, shell-tempered pottery.

Set: Yazoo 2.

References: Phillips 1970, p. 155; Williams and Brain 1983, p. 200.

Proveniences: Haynes Bluff (Y100F; 101F; 102A1,B,F; 103D; 104A2,3,B1,2,3,C1,D2,F1,2,4,5,6,G1,3,H1,2,3,K1, Z2,3,4,6; 106B3; 108C; 109E1; 110A,B; 112A; 115E2; 120A; 140B1; surface).

Powell Plain, *var. Powell*

Illustrations in text: None.

Sample: 1 sherd.

Description: As described by Williams and Brain.

Diagnostic modes: Black slipping on the exterior of medium-textured, shell-tempered pottery.

Set: Powell.

References: Williams and Brain 1983, pp. 200–202.

Proveniences: Haynes Bluff (Y110R).

Salomon Brushed, *var. Salomon*

Illustrations in text: None.

Sample: 5 sherds.

Description: As described in the references.

Diagnostic modes: Careless overall brushing on the exterior surface of coarse-textured, clay-grit-tempered pottery.

Set: Reed 1.

References: Phillips 1970, pp. 158–159; Williams and Brain 1983, pp. 203–204.

Proveniences: Haynes Bluff (Y108A; 110A,B; 156A2).

Vernon Paul Appliqué, *var. Vernon Paul*

Illustrations in text: None.

Sample: 2 sherds (same vessel).

Description: As described in the references.

Diagnostic modes: Parallel vertical ridges made by applying fillets of clay to the exterior surface of coarse-textured, shell-tempered pottery.

Set: Yazoo 6(?).

References: Phillips, Ford, and Griffin 1951, p. 120; Phillips 1970, pp. 167–168.

Proveniences: Haynes Bluff (Y104F4,6).

Winterville Incised, *var. Winterville*

Illustrations in text: None.

Sample: 435 sherds.

Description: As described by Phillips and by Williams and Brain. This variety describes curvilinear incisions made with a pointed instrument so that the lines are at least as deep as they are broad.

Diagnostic modes: Narrow wet-paste incisions arranged in simple curvilinear patterns on the exterior rim or upper body surface of coarse-textured, shell-tempered pottery.

Set: Yazoo 3.

References: Phillips 1970, p. 173; Williams and Brain 1983, pp. 205–206; Brain, Brown, and Steponaitis n.d.

Proveniences: Haynes Bluff (Y100A,C6,D1,E,F; 101A,B, C,D,F; 102A1,B,C,E,F,G2; 103A; 104A1,2,3,B1,2,C1,2, 3,D1,E1,2,3,F1,2,3,4,5,6,G1,2,3,4,H1,2,3,4,J,K1,Z2,3,4,6; 105A; 106A,B1,3; 107A,B; 108A,B; 109A; 110A,D1,2, 4,E,G,I,L,R; 111A,B,C,D,X; 112A,B; 114B; 115A,C,D1, 2,F2,G,H; 117A; 120A; 130A; 135A; 140A,B2,D,E,F,G; 152A; 153A; 158A; 164A; 166A; surface).

Winterville Incised, *var. Angola*

Illustrations in text: Figures 127a, 152a.

Sample: 3 sherds.

Description: As described by Phillips, this variety is similar to *Winterville*. It is even more similar to *Tunica*, differing primarily in the greater complexity of the design, the closest parallels to which are found on Keno Trailed vessels from the mid-Ouachita region, especially the Glendora site (e.g., Moore 1909, fig. 10; see Schambach and Miller 1984, p. 123: their *Glendora* variety). A "Rosetta" pot from the Kinkead-Mainard site (Hoffman 1975–1977, figs. 9, 35a) provides a transitional example of decorative styles. Classified as Keno Trailed, it also exhibits the *Angola* design and Tunican Mode. Since it is primarily distinguished on the basis of a design mode, *Angola* is very difficult to recognize from sherds. Therefore, unless whole or partial vessels are present, it is expected that *Angola* would generally be submerged in the sample for *Tunica*. If it had not already been established by Phillips, *Angola* would simply have been treated as a design mode of *Tunica*.

Diagnostic modes: Narrow wet-paste incisions arranged in complex curvilinear patterns on the exterior surface of coarse-textured, shell-tempered pottery.

Set: Pocahontas.

References: Phillips 1970, p. 173.

Proveniences: Haynes Bluff (Y101C; surface), Bloodhound (surface).*

---

* Note that a complete vessel was found with burial 1 at Angola Farm (see fig. 127a). The presence of *Angola* at Tillar complex sites on Bayou Bartholomew (Marvin Jeter, personal communication, 1980) and at Keno-Glendora, as well as at Haynes Bluff and Bloodhound-Angola Farm, might suggest that this variety should be interpreted as a Koroa-Tioux marker, but in any case it is safely Tunican.

Winterville Incised, *var. Belzoni*

Illustrations in text: Figure 176c.

Sample: 572 sherds, 1 partial vessel.

Description: As described by Phillips and by Williams and Brain, except that the definition is restricted to incisions that are approximately 2–3 mm in width and are about as deep as they are broad. These incisions are placed at least as far apart as twice their widths, the spacing averaging 5–8 mm.

Diagnostic modes: Careless wide-line incisions, arranged in open curvilinear patterns on the exterior body surface of medium- to coarse-textured, shell-tempered pottery.

Set: Yazoo 4.

References: Phillips 1970, pp. 173–174; Williams and Brain 1983, p. 208; Brain, Brown, and Steponaitis n.d.

Proveniences: Haynes Bluff (Y100A,C6,D1,E,F; 101A, B,C,D,E; 102A1,2,B,C,D,F; 103A,C; 104A2,3,B1,2,C1,2, 3,D1,E1,3,F1,2,3,4,5,6,G1,2,3,4,H1,2,3,4,J,K1,Z1,2,3, 4,6; 105A; 106A,C6; 107A,B,C1,6; 108A; 109A,B,C,D1, E1; 110A,B,C,D1,2,4,E,G,H,I,J,L,O,P; 111A,C,D; 112A,B; 113A,B,C; 114A,B; 115A,B,C,F1,2,G,H; 116A; 118B; 120A; 130A; 131A; 135A; 136A; 140B1,2,E,F,G,H/L; 141B; 151A; 155A; 160A; 161A; 166A; surface).

Winterville Incised, *var. Blum*

Illustrations in text: None.

Sample: 7 sherds.

Description: As described in the references.

Diagnostic modes: Rather crude incisions arranged in simple patterns, basically curvilinear, on the interior surface of coarse, shell-tempered pottery.

Set: Yazoo 2.

References: Phillips 1970, p. 174; Williams and Brain 1983, p. 208.

Proveniences: Haynes Bluff (Y100E; 104F4,G3; 108A, surface).

Winterville Incised, *var. Broutin*

Illustrations in text: Figure 193f–j.

Sample: 176 sherds.

Description: New variety.
   Background.   The close spacing of incisions is a decorative mode that assumes increasing popularity during the protohistoric period. Among the curvilinear types the tendency is evident in Rhodes Incised and the closely related Winterville Incised, *var. Tunica*. Those categories are defined by narrow incisions, however, and it is the purpose of this new variety to recognize a broad-line counterpart. The result might be perceived only as a close-spaced *Belzoni*, but the significance is more than decorative, for *Broutin* appears to have rather different temporal and spatial boundaries. It is common at the Hushpuckena phase sites in the upper Sunflower region, and in the lower Yazoo Bluffs it is found at Haynes Bluff, Jack Leflore (18-P-3), and Deasonville (21-P-1).
   Sorting criteria.   Broad parallel incisions spaced no farther apart than the width of the lines. The most characteristic design is a whorl squashed into a distinctive oblong form. Ware is coarsely shell-tempered, and jars are the only known vessel form.

Distribution. Yazoo Basin, with unknown eastward extension into the hills and west across the Mississippi to the Boeuf Basin.

Chronological position. Protohistoric, perhaps extending into the historic.

Documentation. Collins 1932a, pls. 5a, c, 7a; Belmont 1961, p. 108 (his "variety C"); Brown 1978b.

Diagnostic modes: Careless wide-line incisions, closely spaced and arranged in curvilinear patterns on the exterior body surface of coarse-textured, shell-tempered pottery.

Set: Yazoo 7.

References: Phillips 1970, pp. 173–174 (included under the discussion of *var. Belzoni*).

Proveniences: Haynes Bluff (Y100A,E; 101A,B,E,F,G; 102A1,B,C,F,G2; 103A; 104A1,B1,2,C1,2,3,D1,E1,F1,2, 3,4,5,6,G1,2,H1,2,3,J,K1,Z1; 105A; 106B1; 107A,C1; 108A; 109A,B; 110B,C,D4,E,G,I,L,O; 111B,C,D; 112A,B; 113A,C; 114B; 115A,C,D1,E2,F2; 117A; 120A; 130A; 140B2,D,F,G; 141C1,2; 151A; 155A1; 156A; 158A; 159A; 160A; 164A; surface), Russell (204A; 206A; 207A).

Winterville Incised, *var. Loubois*

Illustrations in text: None.*

Sample: 136 sherds.

Description: New variety.

Background. In his dissertation on the Yazoo Bluffs region, Brown (1979a, p. 725) notes that "there are two sherds . . . from St. Pierre which are similar to *Belzoni* yet occur on Mississippi Plain, *var. Montfort* paste. They certainly date to the Russell phase and may in the future be worthy of a varietal status of their own." With the large sample from Haynes Bluff, this status is confirmed. *Loubois* thus takes its place with the other members of the Montfort set (Barton Incised, *var. Charlevoix*, Old Town Red, *var. Ballground*, Parkin Punctated, *var. Elise*) as an important marker for the historic period.

Sorting criteria. Curvilinear incising on sandy, shell-tempered ware. The width and execution of the lines

are similar to *var. Belzoni* but may tend toward *var. Winterville* on one end of the range and *var. Wailes* on the other.

Distribution. Lower Yazoo Bluffs and Tunica Hills regions.

Chronological position. Late protohistoric and historic.

Documentation. Brown 1979a, p. 725.

Diagnostic modes: Wet-paste incisions arranged in simple curvilinear patterns on the exterior surface of coarse-textured, sand-shell-tempered pottery.

Set: Montfort.

References: None.

Proveniences: Haynes Bluff (Y100A; 101A,B; 102A1, 2,B,C; 103A; 104A2,B1,2,C1,2,3,D1,2,E1,F1,2,3,4,G1,2, H1,2,3,4,J,K1,Z1; 105A; 107A,C6; 109A; 110B,E; 111A, B,X; 112A,B; 113A; 114A,B; 115B,F1; 120A; 130A; 132A; 140B2; 141A; 150A; 151A; 152A; 153A; 155A1; 157A; 159A; 160A; 161A; 165A; 166A; surface), Russell (Y203B), Bloodhound (A181B; 182B; 186B; 240A; 242A,B; 243A), Trudeau (surface).

---

* Photographically indistinguishable from other varieties of Winterville Incised.

Winterville Incised, *var. Ranch*

Illustrations in text: Figure 191m–o.

Sample: 30 sherds.

Description: As described by Williams and Brain. In technique, this variety is similar to *vars. Winterville* and *Tunica*. It differs from the latter in being restricted to the upper part of the vessel, and from both in design mode. Chronologically, *Ranch* falls exactly between *Winterville* and *Tunica*.

Diagnostic modes: Careless incising arranged in imbricated patterns on the exterior rim and upper body surface of medium- to coarse-textured, shell-tempered pottery.

Set: Yazoo 5.

References: Phillips 1970, p. 173 (included in his description of *var. Winterville*; see fig. 65a, d, h); Williams and Brain 1983, p. 208.

Proveniences: Haynes Bluff (Y100E; 102F; 104B1, E1,F1,G2,3,K1; 109D; 111C; 115C,D1,F2,G,H; 116A; 158A).

Winterville Incised, *var. Tunica*

Illustrations in text: Figures 60a; 62b; 64a–e; 75a–b; 120a–b; 137a–b; 152b–h; 180d; 182a–b; 197f–i, u, dd–ff.

Sample: 392 sherds, 1 partial vessel.*

Description: As described in the reference, this variety distinguishes narrow, wet-paste, curvilinear incisions on the bodies of jars. Two subvarieties have been recognized: in the first, the decoration is placed on the upper body surface of subglobular jars with short, flaring rims; in the second, the decoration is more tightly drawn (approaching *var. Broutin* in design) and is placed over

* Vessel found with looted burial V705C at Trudeau. Part of another vessel was found with burial 1 at Burroughs during the 1964 excavations (see fig. 182a–b).

the entire body of smaller globular jars that have tall vertical rims. Both forms occur together, at least from Haynes Bluff to Trudeau, and therefore have not been separated at the variety level.

Tunica is part of a broad protohistoric horizon of curvilinear incising that includes such types as Rhodes Incised to the north and Foster Trailed-Incised (and probably some incised versions of Emory Punctated) to the west. All of these exhibit simple curvilinear designs, usually rather carelessly executed. The primary design known for *Tunica* is the whorl or volute; this design is common in Rhodes, but rarer in Foster, which favors concentric circles. Also, as the name indicates, Foster tends to be trailed rather than incised. A band of punctations around the rim, the Tunican Mode (see figs. 152i–j, 197i) is characteristic of *Tunica* and is a trait shared with the western types. The ware is coarsely shell-tempered in the later, more highly oxidized, and less well made range of Mississippi Plain that is identified as *var. Pocahontas* in the Tunica Hills region.

Diagnostic modes: Narrow, generally careless, wet-paste incisions, usually closely drawn and arranged in simple curvilinear patterns which feature, almost exclusively, variations of the whorl motif on the exterior body surface of coarse-textured, shell-tempered pottery.

Set: Pocahontas.

References: Brain 1979, pp. 234–237.

Proveniences: Haynes Bluff (Y100A,E,F; 101A,B,C,D, E,F; 102A2,B,F; 104A1,2,C1,D1,F1,2,4,5,G2,H1,2,3,K1; 105A; 106A; 107A; 108A,B; 110A,D4; 111A,B,C,D,X; 112A,B; 113B; 114A,B; 115A,B,C,D1,E1,F2,G; 117A; 118A,B; 140B1,2; 141A; 151A; 153A; 154A; 155A1; 156A1; 158A; 162A; 163A; 166A; surface), Russell (Y203A), Bloodhound (A73; 108B; 111A; 161A; 162A; 181B; 182B; 186B; 187B; 226B1,C; 229B,C; 231B,C; 240A; 241B; 242A,B; 243A,B; surface), Trudeau (V702A,B,C4; 703A; 705C; 708C5; 709C3; 710/711; B93A,B; 101A; 111A; 112A; 115A; 118A; 119A; 121A; 123A2; 124A1, 2; 127A; 128A; 129B; 141A; 142A; 143A; 159A; 160A, B1; 182A; 185B; 186A; 187A; 202C1,2,D1,2; 208A,E1; surface).

Winterville Incised, *var. Wailes*

Illustrations in text: Figures 176d, 185d, 193k–q.

Sample: 148 sherds, 1 partial vessel.*

Description: New variety.

Background. The type Wallace Incised is a distinctive marker for the protohistoric-historic Quapaw phase around the mouth of the Arkansas River. It is abundant at the Menard, Wallace, and related sites on the lower Arkansas, and is also found at Oliver (16-N-6) in the northern Yazoo Basin. Phillips did not recognize any from the "southern Yazoo Basin area." Nevertheless, a large number of sherds from the lower Yazoo and a large fragment of a vessel from a grave at Haynes Bluff are technically identical to the published description of Wallace Incised. The most prominent difference is that in this sample the designs are curvilinear and placed on the body, while *Wallace,* the only variety of Wallace Incised, features rectilinear designs on the rim. For this reason, Phillips notes that Wallace Incised is closely related to Barton Incised. In fact, *Wallace* might best be considered simply as a late, wide-line variety of Barton. The curvilinear version would thus, by default, fall into Winterville Incised, where there is a close relationship with *var. Belzoni.* The actual dismemberment of Wallace Incised is not effected here, and the suggestion is made only by way of explanation for the creation of yet another variety of Winterville Incised. John Belmont foreshadowed all of this in describing what he referred to as "proto-Wallace" (under the nomenclature of Barton Incised, *var. Wallace*) at the Oliver site.

* Vessel found with burial YB-2 at Haynes Bluff.

Sorting criteria. Incision by means of a flat-ended instrument forming broad, shallow lines at least 4 mm wide and approximately 1 mm deep. Interior striations sometimes give a superficial impression of brushing but are presumably caused by irregularities in the edge of the tool. Designs are simple curvilinear motifs of multiple parallel lines, which are placed at least as far apart as (and usually farther than) the width of the individual lines. Ware is coarse shell tempered, and vessel forms seem to fall within the range of late jar shapes in the region (note that the partial vessel is a lower Yazoo jar form, not at all like the distinctive lower Arkansas jars on which *Wallace* is found).

Distribution. Yazoo Basin from Haynes Bluff to the upper Sunflower, and west to the Ouachita River.

Chronological position. Protohistoric and historic.

Documentation. Belmont 1961, p. 98–101; Phillips 1970, p. 168–169.

Diagnostic modes: Very wide, but shallow, incisions arranged in curvilinear patterns on the exterior body surfaces of medium to large jars of coarse, shell-tempered pottery.

Set: Yazoo 7.

References: None, but see Phillips, Ford, and Griffin 1951, pp. 134–136; Ford 1961; Belmont 1961; Phillips 1970, pp. 168–169, 173–174.

Proveniences: Haynes Bluff (Y100A,D1; 101A,C,D; 102A1,B,E,F; 103A,C; 104A1,2,B1,2,C1,2,3,D1,E1,2,3, F1,2,3,4,5,G1,2,H1,2,3,J,K1,Z1,4; 105A; 106A,B1; 107A, C1; 108A; 109A; 110A,C,D4,E,J,K; 111C; 113B; 114A,B; 115C,D1,2,E2,H,I; 116A; 117A; 118A; 120A; 136A; 140B2,C,F; 151A; 152A; 160A; YB-2; surface), Russell (Y202A; 203A; 204A; 206A; surface).

Yates Net Impressed, *var. Yates*

Illustrations in text: None.

Sample: 1 sherd.

Description: As described by Phillips.

Diagnostic modes: Impressions made by a fine netting on the exterior surface of coarse-textured, clay-grit-tempered pottery.

Set: Reed 1.

References: Phillips 1970, p. 176.

Proveniences: Haynes Bluff (Y150A).

Unclassified Incised

Among the decorated pottery from Haynes Bluff, 102 incised sherds could not be classified, either because they are too small or because the decoration is unusual. Among the latter are five sherds that feature a rectilinear trailed motif on the exterior rim surface of *Yazoo* bowls. Another unique sherd with *Yazoo* paste has a curvilinear design incorporating crosshatched zones: a crude version of Maddox Incised. Six sherds exhibiting definite Caddoan influence are too small to be classified but exhibit decorative modes shared by several late prehistoric types in the Ouachita and Red River regions.

At Bloodhound, a vessel of Caddoan manufacture was found with burial 6 (see fig. 146a). It is most similar to the Red River type Avery Engraved (Suhm and Jelks 1962, pp. 1–4). Three other unclassified incised/engraved sherds were found in the village midden on the terrace (see fig. 153o–p).

Caddoan ceramics are most common at Trudeau. In addition to Natchitoches Engraved, *var. Natchitoches* (q.v.), two partial vessels and thirteen sherds of unclassified engraved/incised pottery of Caddoan origin have been recovered from the site (V705C; 710/711; B101B2; 109A; 141B; surface) (see figs. 62c, f; 64dd).

2. Sets

The pottery sets described below are groups of varieties that are stylistically related. It is hypothesized that the sets have ethnic significance (see pp. 52, 283–287). Because the earlier sets have been described elsewhere (Williams and Brain 1983, pp. 313–324), and because they are not important to the focus of this study, only new ones relating to the late prehistoric through historic periods are presented here, commencing with those that ended the prehistoric record at Lake George: Yazoo 5 and Holly Bluff 2. These two subsets, representing respectively the coarser and finer ware traditions, require slight revisions from the perspective of new data.

Yazoo 5

As described in Williams and Brain (1983, p. 324), this subset is characterized by coarsely shell-tempered jars on the exterior upper body surface of which are relatively complex incised, and often punctated, designs. The only revision required is the substitution of Owens Punctated, *var. Owens*, which was not present at Lake George, for Owens Punctated, *var. Menard*, which clearly is a later expression lasting up into the historic period (see Yazoo 7). The assignment of *Menard* to this subset at Lake George was the result of not recognizing that the occupation of that site lasted into the early Wasp Lake phase; thus, the early markers for that phase were telescoped into the late Lake George phase.

The decorative ideas that characterize Yazoo 5 would seem to have had an origin in the northern Yazoo (see fig. 191). The ware, however, is typical of the Lower Yazoo and there is no reason to suspect that the actual pots were made anywhere else. It seems most reasonable, therefore, to conclude that the introduction was a case of diffusion of decorative ideas. Whatever happened was a prehistoric event, so no ethnic identifications are attempted, but a certain relationship with Yazoo 7 should not be overlooked.

Yazoo 6

This grouping is more an act of faith than a tightly defined unit consistent with the concept of subset. Again, jars are the only known vessel form, and the decorative intent is to provide visual relief over the exterior surface, but now the decorative techniques are very eclectic, even novel: brushing and stamping, in addition to some incising and even appliquéing, if *Vernon Paul* is accepted as a full member. This technical heterogeneity is reflected in the known distributions of the component varieties beyond Haynes Bluff. Generally, brushing seems to have been more common to the west and is particularly noted as a characteristic treatment along the Lower Ouachita and Boeuf rivers in Louisiana and Arkansas (Hoffman 1975–1977, p. 18; Rolingson and Schambach 1981, pp. 144–146; Kidder 1986, pp. 281–288). The contemporary Caddo type Karnack Brushed-Incised (Suhm and Jelks 1962, pp. 85, 86; Schambach and Miller 1984, p. 123) is a probable cognate for *Warren*, and the curvilinear brushing of *Grand Gulf* is sometimes present on the type Cowhide Stamped (Suhm and Jelks 1962, pp. 29, 30; Hally 1972, pp. 499–500; Rolingson and Schambach 1981, p. 156). So, too, the simple stamping of *Kinlock* is found to be a common technique in the more complex designs of Cowhide Stamped. Even *Vernon Paul*, the membership of which is only tentative due to the small sample and presumed far northerly origins, is most closely related to the Caddo area, where several types display the technique, especially the late prehistoric Cass Appliquéd (Suhm and Jelks 1962, pp. 25, 26).

In sum, this putative subset is characterized by its apparent Caddo affiliations in the use of relatively exotic techniques. There is no question, however, that the varieties are locally manufactured, for they exhibit familiar modes of ware and decorative intent. A tentative ethnic identification with the Koroa may be suggested.

Yazoo 7

This subset is important as a continuation of the northern influence initiated with Yazoo 5. Again, the emphasis is on incising, often accompanied by punctating. The lines are broader, however, while the designs are entirely curvilinear and restricted to the exterior body surface (see fig. 193). Jars are the favored vessel form, but these may become so widely flaring that they approach a bowl form with complex silhouette (the "German Helmet" bowl); simple bowls may also be present but have not been definitely identified.

Also associated with this subset, but not assigned to it because of the different decorative intent and unrefined typological status, is an *unspecified* variety of Old Town Red. The simultaneous appearance of red slipping and incised/punctated decorative modes similar to Wallace Incised and related types of the lower Arkansas River suggests a close affinity with the protohistoric Quapaw phase ceramic complex (Dickinson and Dellinger 1940; Ford 1961; Phillips 1970, p. 943; Hoffman 1975–1977, p. 34). A relatively pure assemblage of Ya-zoo 7 is found at Deasonville (Collins 1932a), as well as a number of other sites in the lower Yazoo. Related complexes, but different again in the combination of formal and decorative modes from both the Quapaw and Yazoo 7 assemblages, are the Hog Lake and Tillar complexes of southeastern Arkansas (Lemley and Dickinson 1937; White 1970; Jeter, Kelley, and Kelley 1979; Jeter 1982a, 1982b). Clearly, a horizon featuring combinations of curvilinear wide-line incising and punctating is an important ceramic marker for the protohistoric period in this part of the Lower Mississippi Valley.

Because of the strong northern connection and similarity to the protohistoric and historic complexes of eastern Arkansas, it is speculated that Yazoo 7 may identify the Ofo.

Yazoo 8

The Yazoo 8 subset is characterized by incisions (and punctations) arranged in simple rectilinear patterns on the exterior rim surface of widely flaring jars or complex bowls.

This subset is extremely important to this study as it seems to mark—together with Winterville Incised, *var. Tunica*—the appearance of the Tunica. Much like Yazoo 7, the closest ties are to the north (see fig. 197), whence the component varieties were introduced into the lower Yazoo.

Yazoo 9

Unlike the other subsets discussed above, Yazoo 9 reflects influence from southern ceramic developments. Specifically, this subset is Natchez-like, and, in fact, is partly parallel to the St. Catherine 2 subset. Both are markers for the fully historic period.

Yazoo 9 is characterized by decoration similar to Fatherland Incised on small jars of Yazoo ware (Cracker Road, *var. Cracker Road*). These vessels may also be red-slipped (Cracker Road, *var. Souel*—not yet identified at Haynes Bluff, but present at other historic sites in the vicinity; see Brown 1979a, pp. 651–654), and red slipping may occur as the only decorative mode (Old Town Red, *var. St. Pierre*). It might be argued that red slipping was not an indigenous Natchezan trait and that it was introduced into the Natchez ceramic complex only in the protohistoric period. Nevertheless, by the historic period it had been accepted as an important mode of decoration by the Natchez as well as other Lower Valley groups.

Ethnic identity might be with the Koroa, a Tunican tribe known to have had very close relationships with the Natchez and who could be expected to have explored Natchezan ideas most intimately. A compound vessel from Glendora, a possible Koroa site in northeastern Louisiana, is of particular interest for establishing the ethnicity of this set. The vessel (Moore 1909, fig. 72) is composed of two conjoined pots: one apparently Cracker Road Incised pot which is surmounted by another exhibiting a typical mid-Ouachita form but decorated in the manner of Winterville Incised, var. *Tunica*. The relationship could not be more manifest.

The prevalence of Cracker Road Incised at Beasley (24-L-14), the putative historic village of the Taensa (Williams 1967), might be due more to proximity than to an alternative ethnic identity. Whatever the ultimate ethnicity, however, there seems little doubt that Yazoo 9 was an indigenous production of the Yazoo Bluffs and contiguous regions.

Montfort

The Montfort set is one of the most interesting of the ceramic developments found at Haynes Bluff. The decorative intent reveals the same overall incising, punctating, and painting on the exterior surfaces of standard jar forms that is characteristic of other late Mississippian complexes. But there is a basic change in ware: the paste is very sandy. Apparently, large quantities of sand were introduced into the clay along with live shell. The technical reasons for including this additional tempering agent are unknown, but whatever the reasons the trait is significant from a historical perspective. The combination of both sand and shell tempering is diagnostic of the latest aboriginal phases in the hill country far to the east. These sandy shell wares are related to the historic Choctaw and/or Chakchiuma, and possibly Chickasaw* (Atkinson and Blakeman 1975, p. 12; Penman 1977, p. 286; Atkinson 1979; Marshall 1985, n.d.; Stubbs 1983; Jennings 1941).

To date, the distribution of Montfort is known only from the eastern fringe of the Lower Mississippi Valley, and even then it is restricted to the stretch from the lower Yazoo Bluffs to the Tunica Hills. This distribution would suggest a close association with the historic Tunica, and certainly temporally, too, the closest coincidence is with the Yazoo 8-Pocahontas complex. There is more than a suspicion, however, that Montfort is simply the latest development out of the long Yazoo tradition, and, in fact, may represent the historic Yazoo themselves, or possibly their cohabitants, the Tioux (-Koroa).

Pocahontas

This set could as easily have been established as yet another Yazoo subset, except that the type material has already been discussed in print under this rubric (Brain 1979, pp. 224–239). Moreover, historical significance and spatial considerations make it appropriate for this set to be distinguished nomenclaturally.

The Pocahontas set is defined by narrow, wet-paste incising on the exterior body surface of coarsely shell-tempered jars. The Tunican Mode, a punctated fillet around the rim, is characteristic.

Together with the Yazoo 8 subset, Pocahontas is a marker for the Tunica. As in the case of Yazoo 8, a northerly origin can be demonstrated (see fig. 197), but a strong western connection is also evident. The latter

* The latter connection is also established with the Leflore Design Mode.

is apparent in the similarity of *Tunica* and *Angola* to the Caddo types Foster Trailed-Incised and Keno Trailed, respectively (Webb 1959, pp. 131–136). Yet although the decorative modes show Caddoan influence, the traditional Mississippian ware attributes of paste, body form, and rim profile make it clear that the origins of *Tunica*, and probably also *Angola*, lie within the Lower Mississippi Valley; therefore, these are properly classified within the local type Winterville Incised. While they do not dispute the classification, Schambach and Miller (1984, pp. 121–122) demonstrate the close similarity of *Tunica* to their late *Shaw* variety of Foster. They suggest that *Shaw* was ancestral to Emory Punctated, which in turn spread down the Red River to become *Tunica* at Trudeau. While agreeing with the relationships, I would argue a different genesis and sequence of events: namely, that *Tunica* developed in northwestern Mississippi, drawing decorative inspiration from *Shaw* directly, and then was taken first to the Yazoo and finally to Trudeau (where it is the dominant decorated variety), whence it was taken up the Red River to Los Adaes (Gregory 1980, p. 39; Gregory 1982, pp. 67–73) and Gilbert (Jelks 1967, pp. 136–139). In the process, it completely surrounded the distribution of Foster. As for Emory Punctated, it is characteristically found on a Mississippi jar form—similar to those of var. *Tunica*—that is not common in Caddoan ceramics, and "stylistically Emory resembles vessels from the Middle Mississippi Valley" (Gregory 1980, p. 45). Heavy mineral analysis of sherds of Emory Punctated from Los Adaes and of *Tunica* from Trudeau distantly related the two groups, but also revealed significant differences and failed to establish a common or precise origin (Maher 1983, pp. 108–143). This lack of mineralogical identity argues against the possibility that *Tunica* was an imported type at Trudeau but does not deny stylistic sharing with peoples up the Red River. In any event, whether or not *Tunica* was actually made by the Tunica, it appears to be a prime Tunica diagnostic, being found almost exclusively at Tunica and Tunica-related sites along the east bank of the Mississippi from Quizquiz to Trudeau.

Angola, on the other hand, probably developed in southeastern Arkansas, or possibly northeastern Louisiana, on the eastern marches of Keno Trailed, and in its subsequent history it seems to have stayed along the Mississippi. Whatever its origin, *Angola* is closely related to *Tunica*, being distinguished only by design mode, and together they attest to the close Tunican relationship with the eastern Caddo. The presence of *Angola* along Bayou Bartholomew, as well as in the Yazoo and Tunica Hills regions, suggests that it could be a marker for the Koroa-Tioux rather than the Tunica proper, but in any case it certainly is a Tunican diagnostic.

Holly Bluff 2

This subset remains unchanged from the formulation presented in Williams and Brain (1983, pp. 320–321), except for the removal of *Fatherland* (see St. Catherine 1). Holly Bluff 2 then becomes totally a phenomenon of the Yazoo.

The decoration consists of simple curvilinear motifs which generally were drawn with an unusual lack of care. The ware is also somewhat coarser. Bowls are the only known vessel forms.

Holly Bluff 2 is primarily a marker for the Wasp Lake phase, but apparently it first appears late in the Lake George phase and continues into the Russell phase.* This subset thus becomes the strongest evidence for in situ late prehistoric to historic continuity, and as such it may identify those reputed regional heirs, the Yazoo.

Holly Bluff 3

Holly Bluff 3 is characterized by very distinctive decorations which minimize classificatory ambiguities. The designs are generally more complex than in Holly Bluff 2, and are found on the interior, as well as exterior, of bowls, which are the only vessel form. The ware is noticeably shell tempered and varies from the coarser textures of Holly Bluff 2 to the finer fabric of Holly Bluff 1.

This subset was clearly the superior local product in (and so far restricted to) the lower Yazoo Bluffs during the Wasp Lake phase. It may have lasted into the very early historic period, but certainly was passé by the eighteenth century.

St. Catherine 1

This subset recognizes foreign influence and probably is composed mostly of introduced vessels, although in some cases the decorative modes may have been copied and transferred to local wares. The distinctive designs feature complex curvilinear motifs drawn by usually well executed, fine-line incising. Engraved cross-hatching between the lines may also be present. Overall red slipping is an alternative decoration. Bowls (often of complex shape), beakers, and bottles are the usual vessel forms.

* Even *Beland City*, which would be expected to have the briefest longevity, occurs with zoned red slipping, an additional decorative mode that can be considered exclusive to the historic period in the lower Yazoo.

St. Catherine 1 is clearly derived from the Natchezan ceramic tradition, where it is an important marker for the protohistoric and historic periods. Its appearance in the Yazoo as trade ware would seem to be contemporary.

St. Catherine 2

This subset exhibits a decorative elaboration of St. Catherine 1: designs have more lines, and zoned red slipping appears. On the other hand, vessel forms display less variation and seem to be restricted to simple bowls and bottles.

There is some indication that St. Catherine 2 represents the spread of Natchezan decorative ideas into neighboring ceramic traditions. Such a diffusion might account for the elaborations in decoration, as well as the simplification of vessel forms. Whatever its genesis and ultimate ethnic affiliation, St. Catherine 2 is one of the best aboriginal markers for the historic period.

Bell

The Bell set describes a group of exotic painted vessels from the north.* The designs are painted in red or white (and sometimes black, although not yet found at Haynes Bluff), and may be rectilinear or curvilinear, geometric or symbolic. Decoration generally covers the entire surface, including the interiors of bowls and some bottles. The most common vessel form is the long-necked bottle. The ware is usually fine textured, thin, and exceptionally well made.

This set represents a group of fine trade ware which was distributed widely throughout the Lower Mississippi Valley. Because of this broad distribution, no ethnic affiliations are suggested, although eventually centers of production (probably in northeastern Arkansas) may be identified. The broad distribution, however, does make the set useful as a cross-cultural horizon marker for the protohistoric period in the valley.

* Eventually, it may prove desirable to include Walls Engraved in this set.

3. Miscellaneous Artifacts

Aboriginal artifacts of baked clay other than pottery vessels are rare in the collections. From Haynes Bluff there are only two items of note: part of a perforated disc of Addis Plain ware (Y104C1), and a crude earplug of Mississippi Plain ware (Y104J). The latter is of special interest since it adds another material category (in addition to bone and shell) to this important form of or-

namentation. An earspool of Addis Plain ware was found at Bloodhound (A173A) (see fig. 154m); it probably dates to the late Coles Creek occupation. Two pipe fragments, one imitating the form of a kaolin pipe bowl, came from the bluff top at Trudeau (B56B; 93B), while two more were found in the village area (see figs. 64gg, 75g).

Appendix B: Stone Artifacts

Stone artifacts are not common in the Lower Mississippi Valley during the later stages of aboriginal occupation, and even projectile points become rare.* An important exception to this general trend, however, occurred during the protohistoric and historic periods when a complex of stone tools was introduced into the northern part of the valley. Diagnostic tools in this complex are Nodena Lanceolate projectile points, triangular knives, pipe drills, and snub-nosed end scrapers. Other bifaces and unifaces may be present, and sites that have this complex also exhibit a considerable amount of debitage, attesting to local manufacture. This complex (referred to as the "Oliver lithic complex") marks the adoption of an important new technological pattern and is a horizon marker for the protohistoric and historic periods. However, it is not found everywhere throughout the valley, and not at all in the southern regions; it would seem to be identified with some of the late population movements (as discussed earlier in the appropriate sections). There are stone artifacts from the southern part of the valley, but these generally date to earlier periods.

PROJECTILE POINTS

Following Williams and Brain (1983, p. 221), the projectile points are presented using the type-variety system of classification. Types are distinguished by formal criteria, especially of the haft area, while varieties reflect other formal and technical qualities.

The format differs in presentation from Williams and Brain in that background information pertaining to the formulation of the type has been omitted (for which see the references) and provenience data have been added.

Alba Stemmed, *var. Catahoula*
Illustrations in text: None.

Sample: 1.

Description: The assignment of this point as a variety of the late Coles Creek type Alba Stemmed is based on obvious formal congruity and on the observation by Webb and Gregory in 1956 that it is a "variant of the previously established Alba type" (Baker and Webb 1976, p. 226). As described in the references, the *Catahoula* differs from the other varieties of the Alba primarily in

---

the greater prominence of the barbs, which make the point nearly as wide as it is long. The specimen described here has a reconstructed length of approximately 35 mm and a width of approximately 25 mm.

References: Bell 1960; Baker and Webb 1976; Patterson 1976.

Proveniences: Haynes Bluff (Y104F4).

Alba Stemmed, *var. Scallorn*
Illustrations in text: None.

Sample: 1.

Description: As described in the references. These are small barbed points with expanded bases.

References: Brain 1969, pp. 229–230; Williams and Brain 1983, p. 222.

Proveniences: Trudeau (surface).

Bayogoula Fishtailed, *var. Bayogoula*
Illustrations in text: Figure 120o–p.

Sample: 2.

Description: As described in the references. These are very distinctive late prehistoric points indigenous to the southern part of the Lower Mississippi Valley. Although originally thought to be diagnostic of the "Natchezan culture type" (Quimby 1942b, pl. 16), they are now known to be a marker for the early (i.e., prehistoric) phases of Plaquemine culture. The presence of these two examples at Trudeau has nothing to do with the historic Tunica occupation.

References: Williams and Brain 1983, p. 222; Brain, Brown, and Steponaitis n.d.

Proveniences: Trudeau (B104A; 142B2).

Collins Side Notched, *var. Collins*
Illustrations in text: Figure 175c.

Sample: 1.

Description: These well-made points are the earliest known arrowheads in the valley, dating to the Baytown period. This specimen exhibits the characteristic needle

---

* The early Spanish and French chroniclers observed this fact and recorded with some amazement the effectiveness of cane arrows, the tips of which had merely been pointed and fire hardened or fixed with a bit of bone, antler, or fish scale (Garcilaso de la Vega 1723, pp. 96–97, 249; Le Page du Pratz 1758, vol. 2, pp. 156, 167).

nose and meets other formal and technical criteria. It is 40 mm long, the average for the *Collins*, and its width at the shoulders is 15 mm, which is within the restricted 13–15 mm range diagnostic of the variety.

References: Williams and Brain 1983, pp. 223–224.

Proveniences: Haynes Bluff (Y110J).

Collins Side Notched, *var. Claiborne*
Illustrations in text: None.

Sample: 1.

Description: Similar to *var. Collins*, but not as well made and proportionally shorter. This example is 13 mm wide at the shoulders and has a reconstructed length of approximately 28 mm.

References: Williams and Brain 1983, p. 224.

Proveniences: Haynes Bluff (Y110M).

Collins Side Notched, *var. Clifton*
Illustrations in text: None.

Sample: 1.

Description: This variety includes the smallest and least well made examples of the type. They are relatively narrow points. This specimen has a reconstructed length of approximately 35 mm and a maximum width of 11 mm.

References: Williams and Brain 1983, p. 225.

Proveniences: Haynes Bluff (Y110M).

Edwards Stemmed, *var. Enola*
Illustrations in text: None.

Sample: 1.

Description: As described in the reference, this is a crudely made point, relatively long in relation to its width and having a fully chipped rectangular stem. It does exhibit some secondary pressure retouching along both blade edges, which is unusual for the type. Reconstructed length is approximately 58 mm; width at shoulders is 21 mm.

References: Williams and Brain 1983, p. 227.

Proveniences: Haynes Bluff (Y102E).

Edwards Stemmed, *var. Sunflower*
Illustrations in text: Figure 175d.

Sample: 3.

Description: These late prehistoric points are distinctive in that generally the base of the stem is unfinished and the shoulders are asymmetrical. Workmanship is crude percussion flaking, occasionally with some retouching around the tip. These examples are all 25 mm wide, but approximately 50 and 55 mm long.

References: Williams and Brain 1983, p. 227.

Proveniences: Haynes Bluff (Y104A3; 114B), Russell (surface).

Mississippi Triangular, *var. Madison*
Illustrations in text: Figures 75i, 175e–g, 199a–b.

Sample: 7.

Description: These points are characteristic of the late prehistoric Mississippian culture. They are triangular in outline, with straight or incurvate sides. All of these points are similar in width at the base (19–20 mm), but they range from 34 to 44 mm in reconstructed lengths. An *unspecified* example of the type from Haynes Bluff exhibits a slightly excurvate base reminiscent of the Nodena Lanceolate, *var. Russell* points; although the sharply defined shoulders place it firmly in this type, it may be one of the latest examples. Another point is abnormally thick and made of a foreign dark gray chert. A fragment of a Mississippi Triangular point from location I at Trudeau (B130A) is also classified as *var. unspecified* because of its unusual proportions and material (see fig. 120q).

References: Williams and Brain 1983, pp. 234–236.

Proveniences: Haynes Bluff (Y104B1,F1,H1,2; 151A), Trudeau (surface).

Nodena Lanceolate, *var. Russell*
Illustrations in text: Figures 75h, 154k, 168p, 187a–f, 199k–u.

Sample: 12.

Description: Although cruder and foreshortened, these points are obviously closely related to the Nodena type. The relationship has been noted before (Chapman and Anderson 1955, p. 17: their "Triangular B" point; Belmont 1961, pp. 163–164: his "Oliver" point; Ford 1961, p. 157) and is expressed typologically here. The *Russell* is a late variety of Nodena, being diagnostic of the protohistoric and early historic periods. It is one of the distinctive items in the Oliver lithic complex—which also includes triangular knives, pipe drills, and snub-nosed end scrapers—that is found from the Yazoo to the Ohio rivers. While it may be idle at this stage of our knowledge to speculate on origins, it can be noted that the "Banks" point (Perino 1966, p. 35; Morse 1973, fig. 9c) is formally and technically intermediate to the classic *var. Nodena*, which is presumed to be prototypical, and to the *var. Russell* described here.

The *Russell* is a small- to medium-size point with excurvate outline and rounded base.* Workmanship is indifferent, and edges often do not show evidence of retouching. The variety of cherts present in this sample indicates sources outside of the valley. Two were heat treated before flaking. Lengths range from approximately 30 to 40 mm, widths from 11 to 19 mm.

References: Chapman and Anderson 1955; Belmont 1961; Ford 1961; Perino 1966; Morse 1973.

Proveniences: Haynes Bluff (Y154A), Russell (Y201A; 203B; 204A; 205A; 210A; surface), Bloodhound (surface).

TRIANGULAR KNIVES

Triangular knives are one of the tools in the Oliver lithic complex. Characteristically, they are roughly in the shape of a scalene triangle, although sometimes they may be more ovoid (see fig. 199z–ii). They are crudely flaked by percussion and rarely show any retouch along the edges. Shallow notches may be present in the edge on one or both sides of the wider angles. The smallest angle, or "point," is often unfinished and presumably was not meant to be used. Lengths range from 30 to 45 mm.

Only five examples of this distinctive tool were found in the latest contexts at Haynes Bluff (Y104J; 110G; 115E; 150A; YB-1) (see figs. 166d, 168q), whereas twenty-one more were excavated at Russell (Y200A; 201A; 202A; 203B; 204A; 205A; 206A; 207A; 210A) (see fig. 187g–l). A single specimen came from Bloodhound (A240A) (see fig. 154h), and an exceptionally crude one was found in feature V710/711 at Trudeau (see fig. 64ii).

PIPE DRILLS

Although this type of drill is an important member of the Oliver lithic complex (see fig. 199v–y), it is unaccountably rare in our excavations: only one broken example was found at Haynes Bluff (Y104H3) and another at Bloodhound (see fig. 148u), but none turned up at Russell, which is the prime site for the complex in the lower Yazoo region. Perfectly good examples, however, are known to exist in the Russell collection at the University of Mississippi (see fig. 187s–u; table 73). These drills are slender and do not have an expanded proximal end (see Williams and Brain 1983, p. 251). Known examples range from 40 to 80 mm in length.

* Two reworked Nodena points from Trudeau (V702C4; surface) have concave bases and so are classified as *var. unspecified* (see fig. 60l).

SNUB-NOSED END SCRAPERS

The snub-nosed end scraper is the fourth diagnostic tool of the Oliver lithic complex. Characteristically, it is a small, generally oval uniface, the broader end of which has been chipped to a steeply beveled edge (see fig. 199jj–rr). Although usually small, averaging about the size of a thumbnail (and often so termed in the literature), some occasionally may be found that are larger (e.g., see fig. 187m).

Of the twenty-five excavated examples in the Yazoo, slightly more came from Haynes Bluff (Y101C; 104A1,F1,4,H2,K1; 110A; 118A; 152A; 159A; YB-2) (see fig. 168r–s) than from Russell (Y200B; 203B; 204A; 205A; 206A; 207A; 210A) (see fig. 187m–r), but considering the difference in the sizes of the excavations it is obvious that the artifact is far more common at Russell. A single occurrence is recorded for Bloodhound, where it was found next to burial 7.

OVAL SCRAPERS

This late prehistoric artifact (Brain 1969, pp. 225–226; Williams and Brain 1983, pp. 239–242) seems to have continued in use into the historic period. The scrapers are roughly percussion-flaked, ovoid bifaces that have a sinuous working edge around the entire perimeter. These examples average approximately 30 mm in diameter. One was found at Haynes Bluff (Y160A), and six at Russell (Y200A; 202A; 203A; 210A; surface). At Bloodhound, one was found with burial 7 and another in the village midden (A240A).

UNSPECIALIZED SCRAPERS

This catchall group is formally, functionally, and chronologically undiagnostic (Williams and Brain 1983, p. 244). It really describes an amorphous, general-purpose biface that has been crudely shaped by careless percussion flaking. The working edge thus created around most of the circumference is irregular but sharp, and perfectly effective for a primary function of scraping. Only one of these was found at Haynes Bluff (Y100A), while seventeen came from Russell (Y201A; 202A; 203A; 204A; 205A; 206A; 209A).

NATIVE GUNFLINTS

This is one of the few tool types in which a European idea was successfully replicated within the aboriginal technological tradition. Of course, the gunflint was the only important European artifact made of stone and therefore was the only one in this category to be reproduced. While manufacturing techniques differed, a serviceable substitute was roughly chipped from a chert flake.

There are four examples of native gunflints from Haynes Bluff (Y104K1; 105A; YB-2) (see figs. 167h, 175h), at least two of which show usage. All measure 20 mm from front to back, but 22 to 27 mm from side to side, dimensions that fall into the small range of European standards. Another specimen (see fig. 155q) was found in the village midden at Bloodhound (A240A). Three examples (see fig. 120n) were recovered from excavations at Trudeau (V710/711; B102A; 135A).

PEBBLE CELTS

The pebble celt is another distinctive late prehistoric artifact (Williams and Brain 1983, p. 252) that seems to have survived at least into the protohistoric period. These tools are roughly shaped by percussion flaking from pebbles of appropriate size and shape. The proximal end is unfinished and often not even shaped, while the working end is ground smooth bifacially to create a narrow bit with a strong sharp edge.

There are five pebble celts from Haynes Bluff, primarily from a single feature (Y104B2,F4,6,J; surface). Two whole specimens are 55 and 60 mm long. Four are made of chert, while a fifth is of petrified wood (a resource occasionally used only for this tool type). Two more celts are known from Trudeau, where they were collected from the surface (see figs. 67r, 75j). One is 65 mm in length, the other is incomplete.

POLISHED CELTS

A single ground and polished greenstone celt was found at Haynes Bluff (Y104B2). It is ovoid in shape and unusually small, measuring only 20 mm in maximum width near the bit and 40 mm in length.

CATLINITE PIPES

One pipe made of catlinite was found with burial YB-1 at the summit of mound A at Haynes Bluff. It is a simple example of the "smokestack" form (see fig. 166c), which was the most common type found at early historic sites in the Lower Mississippi Valley (Brain 1979, p. 248).

A fragment of flat catlinite decorated with drilled holes around the edge was found at Trudeau (V707A). It was probably part of the "prow" of a smokestack pipe. After being broken it apparently was used as a whetstone or sharpener, as it displays many scratches and grooves (see fig. 60b).

MISCELLANEOUS

A large number of unclassified projectile points and other chipped stone tools are present in the collections. Most of these are unclassified because they are undiagnostic fragments of larger artifacts (such as the distal ends of points). Most are bifaces, but a few unifaces were also found at Russell.

Artifacts from Haynes Bluff that may not have been manufactured, but nevertheless were used, include two hammerstones (Y100C2,F). Of unknown function were a flat cobble with burial YB-1 (see fig. 166g) and a polished stone and small galena crystal with burial YB-2 (see fig. 167c,e).

Another galena crystal was a surface find at Bloodhound (see fig. 154j), and a lump of the same material was found with burial 4. A small amount of ochre accompanied burial 5. Unclassified chert bifaces, including some in the forms of celts or adzes (see fig. 154b–d), knife blades (see figs. 148v, 154c–i), and a chopper (see fig. 154a) were also found at Bloodhound. Two shaped quartzite cobbles may have been game stones (see fig. 154l).

Stone artifacts were very rare at Trudeau. Miscellaneous items included a few point fragments (see fig. 64hh), an adze (see fig. 64kk), knives (see fig. 64ii–jj), a quartz scraper, and some abraded sandstone from the general excavations, and a crude chopper-scraper and three small pieces of red ochre from burial V705C (see fig. 62i). Hematite fragments, probably contained naturally in the soil, were frequently encountered in the excavations.

Appendix C: Bone and Shell Artifacts

Bone artifacts from Haynes Bluff (Y100D1,F; 110K) include a distinctive type of knobbed earpin (see fig. 175a), a long bone awl made from a turkey tibiotarsus, and one small splinter awl (see Williams and Brain 1983, pp. 275, 278). At Trudeau, a bear canine and an antler flaker were found in trash pit V710/711 (see fig. 64mm–nn).

With one exception, shell artifacts are restricted to ornamental items: marine conch earpins, discs, and beads (see Brain 1979, p. 252 for a discussion of these artifacts). One earpin was found in the general excavations at Haynes Bluff (Y105A) (see fig. 175b). A pair of earpins accompanied burial 4 at Bloodhound, and a single example was recovered from the disturbed burial V715 at Trudeau (see fig. 67m), where four fragments were also found in looted burial V705C (see fig. 62m). A necklace of shell discs and beads was found with burial 6 at Bloodhound (see fig. 146b), and another necklace was reported with burial 1 (see fig. 142m). A single large bead was found on the surface at Trudeau (see fig. 120r), and a mussel shell spoon was recovered from trash pit V710/711 (see fig. 64ll).

Appendix D: European Ceramics

The European ceramics are divided into two basic groups: earthenware and stoneware. These groups are further subdivided: the earthenware into tin-glazed, lead-glazed, and unglazed classes; and the stoneware into salt-glazed and unglazed classes. Types of these classes are described below (for a fuller discussion of the typology, see Brain 1979, pp. 34–84).

A third ceramic group discussed in this appendix is not European in origin, although its presence is due of course to European contact. This group is composed of oriental porcelains.

TIN-GLAZED EARTHENWARES

Most of the tin-glazed earthenwares in the collections are assumed to be faience, although some of the smaller white and blue-and-white sherds are so undiagnostic that they could be delft or majolica. Only certain examples of the latter are so identified.

White Faience

Plain white faience is the most common tin-glazed earthenware at early historic French contact sites. Examples characteristically have a soft, pinkish buff paste and a poor quality glaze that often has an "orange peel" appearance.

At Haynes Bluff, this was the only kind of tin-glazed earthenware found. Seven sherds, all probably from the same small deep bowl (see fig. 168k), were recovered from the excavations at the summit of mound A (Y151A; 152A; 154A). At Bloodhound, six sherds were found on the hill (A110A) and terrace (A181B; 185B) (see fig. 156o–p). Trudeau, however, produced ninety-five sherds from the surface and excavations (V702A; 705C; 706A; 707C; 710/711; 727A; B59A,B; 101A; 111A; 117A; 118B1; 119A; 121B1; 125A2; 127A; 130A; 132A; 136A; 137A; 139A; 140B; 141A; 142A; 143A; 168A; 186A; 192A; 193A; 202A; 208A,B; surface). Vessel forms include bowls and pitchers (see figs. 97r, 122a).

Blue-and-White Faience

This is white faience decorated with designs painted in blue (sometimes highlighted with black or purple). Among the sites investigated, only Trudeau produced examples (see figs. 60d; 65a; 76a–b; 97s, u; 122b–c). Thirty-two sherds were found (V702A; 709A; 710/711; B59A; 75B; 118A; 121A; 125A2; 127A,B1; 130A; 160A; 187A; 190A; 191B; surface), and part of a small vessel was recovered from looted burial V705C (see fig. 62q). The latter appears to be a *salière*; other vessel forms are bowls and plates.

Polychrome Faience

Inexpensive polychrome faience became increasingly popular during the first two-thirds of the eighteenth century. The height of popularity during the middle third of the century coincides almost exactly with the Tunica occupation of Trudeau, and it is no coincidence that all known examples came from that site. Two sherds from the same vessel, which exhibited green, yellow, and purple decoration on a white background, were found in V702A (see fig. 60c), while two more from another vessel with yellow, blue, and red decoration were among the artifacts from pit feature V710/711 (see fig. 65b–c). Two polychrome sherds were found on the surface. Four sherds with green-and-white decoration, from excavation unit B140B and the surface, may be broken from larger polychrome pieces.

Brown Faience

Faience brune, also commonly referred to as "Rouen faience," is distinguished by having a brown lead glaze on the exterior. The interior, however, has a white tin glaze and is usually decorated with floral designs and a trellis-and-dot border (Brain 1979, pp. 43–44).

One undecorated sherd was found in the excavations on the edge of the terrace at Bloodhound (A244A) (see fig. 156m). However, twenty-seven sherds were found at Trudeau (B106A; 112B; 117A; 118A; 121A; 127A; 141A; 142A; 180A; 181A; 182A; 190A; 191A; 192B; 193A; 203B; surface). The only vessel form identified is a deep platter.

Delft

Only two indisputable sherds of delft were found during the course of our investigations. They are pieces of English "powder purple" delftware, and both are from Trudeau: one from the bluff top (B93A), the other from the surface of the village area (see fig. 76e).

Majolica

The majolica is distinguished from the faience in this sample by the harder, brick red paste* and by glazes that tend to be so runny they are almost transparent. Insofar as the decorations can be reconstructed, they are distinctively different from faience and most closely resemble Mexican designs (Tunnell 1966; Goggin 1968; Barnes and May 1972; Barnes 1980). There are eight blue-and-white sherds (see figs. 76c–d, 122d), one green-

---

* A brick red paste is also known for faience, especially *faience brune*, but no examples are present in these collections.

and-blue-on-white (see fig. 65d), one black-and-blue-on-white (see fig. 65e), one with a light green interior and milky white exterior, and ten are undecorated. All are from Trudeau (V702A; 710/711; B111A; 124A1; 132A; 134A; 182A; 202A; 203A; surface). Simple bowls are the only forms identified.

LEAD-GLAZED EARTHENWARES

The lead-glazed earthenware has been divided into six types on the basis of differences in paste, slip, and glaze characteristics (Steponaitis 1979, pp. 44–73).

Type A

This type is distinguished by its buff to pink paste and dark green glaze.

Seventy-four sherds of Type A were found during the course of our excavations (see figs. 65f, 67a, 76k). All came from Trudeau (V710/711; B100B; 104A; 105A; 106A; 108A; 109A; 111A; 113B; 114A,B; 115A; 117A; 118A; 119A; 120B1; 121A; 123A1,2; 124A1; 125A1; 131A; 132A; 133A,B; 135A; 137A; 139A; 140A; 141A; 142A; 180A; 181A; 186A; 187A; 202A; 207A; 208A; surface). The only vessel forms recognized were pitchers and bowls.

Complete examples of Type A, Variety 1 jugs were found with burial 2 at Angola Farm and burial 1 at Bloodhound (see figs. 128a, 142). This form appears to have been popular in the late seventeenth and early eighteenth centuries. The type as a whole, however, seems to have been more common in the mid-eighteenth century.

Type B

Type B lead-glazed earthenware is characterized by a brick red paste and a transparent glaze that appears brown against the red background color. The glaze may be flecked with small dark spots (see figs. 60e, 65g–h, 67b, 76l–m, 122e–g).

One sherd, from a vessel of indeterminate shape, was found at Haynes Bluff (Y104G1). The principal provenience, however, was Trudeau, where 284 sherds were found (V702A,B; 706B; 708C2; 710/711; 723A; 727A; 729; 730A; B102A; 104B; 105A; 106A; 107A; 108A; 109A; 110A; 111A; 112B; 113B; 114A,B; 115A,B1; 116A; 117A; 118A; 119A,B1; 120B1; 121A,B1; 123A1,2; 124A1,2; 125A1; 127A; 128A; 129A; 130A; 131A; 132A; 135A; 137A; 138A; 139A; 140A,B; 141A,B; 142A; 158A; 165A; 178A; 180A,B; 181A,B1; 182A; 185A,B; 186A,B; 187A,B; 190A; 191A; 192A; 193A,B; 203A; 207A,C; surface). Basins, pitchers, and bowl forms, including Variety 2 slipware bowls (see figs. 76l, 122e), can be identified.

Type C

Type C lead-glazed earthenware has a reddish paste, a white underslip, and a bright green glaze.

Only one sherd, perhaps from a Variety 5 pitcher (see fig. 168l), was found at Haynes Bluff (Y102A2), but 114 sherds, plus 24 more from the same vessel, came from Trudeau (V702A; 710/711; 723A; 727A; B75A,B; 100A; 104C; 105A,B; 106A; 109B; 111A; 116A; 117A; 118A; 119A; 124A1,2; 127A; 129A; 130A; 135A; 139A; 140A; 141A,B; 144A; 180A; 181A; 182A; 185A; 186A; 190A,B; 191A; 193A,B; 202B; 203A; 207B; surface). Many of the sherds and the partial vessel are from Variety 1 bowls (see figs. 65i–j, 67c, 76n–p, 97t).

Type D

This type has a dark brick red paste and a greenish brown glaze.

Type D is known only from Trudeau, which has produced 113 sherds (V710/711; 727A; B105A; 109A; 116A; 117A; 119A; 121A; 123A1,2; 124A2; 125A2; 127A; 132A; 138A; 140B; 141A; 142A; 143A; 180A; 181A; 182A; 185A; 186A; 187A; 190A; 192A; 193A; 207A; surface). Vessel forms include Variety 1 pots, Variety 3 basins, and bowls of unspecified variety (see figs. 65k, 67d, 76q–r).

Type E

Type E lead-glazed earthenwares have a buff paste and a clear, or only slightly greenish, glaze.

This type is the rarest, twenty-eight sherds having been found only at Trudeau (V702B; 710/711; B107A; 115A; 116A; 121A; 123A2; 128A; 130B; 136A; 139A; 141A; 142A; 180B; 191A; 192A; surface). The only vessel forms recognized are bowls, the exact configurations of which are not determined (see figs. 65l, 76s).

Type F

This type is characterized by a brick red paste, a white underslip, and a dark green glaze.

Forty-seven sherds of this type were found at Trudeau (V702A; 708B; 710/711; 723A; 730A; B112A,B; 115A,B1; 116A; 119A; 121A; 124A2; 125A2; 129A; 130A; 134A; 137A; 139A; 140A; 141A,B; 143A; 144A; 181A; 182A; 185A,B2; 187A; 192B; surface). The only identifiable vessel shape is a large bowl or platter of unspecified variety (see fig. 65m).

Unglazed Earthenwares

Unglazed earthenware is the least diagnostic of all the European ceramics. Although it is possible that some vessels could have been made that were completely devoid of glaze, it is unlikely. Most, if not all, of these sherds, then, probably came from unglazed portions of partially glazed pieces. In all cases, vessel forms are indeterminable.

Only a single sherd of unusually coarse paste was turned up at Haynes Bluff (Y103A). Two sherds were found on the hill at Bloodhound (A84; A100A), and a third on the terrace (A184B) (see fig. 156n). However,

126 sherds came from Trudeau (V710/711; B75B; 101A; 106A; 107A; 108B2; 109A; 110A; 111A; 112A,B; 113B; 114B,C; 115A,B1; 116A; 118A,B1; 119B1; 121B1; 123A2; 124A1; 125A1; 127A; 128A; 132A; 133A; 135A; 136A; 138A; 139A; 141A; 143A; 144A; 180A; 181B1; 186A; 187A; 190A,B; 191B; 193A,B; 202A; surface).

STONEWARES

Stoneware is divided into salt-glazed and unglazed classes. The salt-glazed stoneware includes two very distinctive Rhenish types, a fine English type, and a more general type of French origin. Examples of the latter are only partially glazed. Five sherds of unglazed stoneware were found, all at Trudeau (B115A; surface).

Bellarmine

This type is distinguished by its hard gray-brown paste and brown salt glaze (Brain 1979, pp. 74–76). Decorations, when present, consist of stamped and molded motifs. The only known vessel form is the jug.

There are twenty-six undecorated sherds from Trudeau (V708B; B100A; 118A; 119A; 124A2; 128B; 175A; 187A; surface) (see figs. 67e, 76i–j, 122j).

Westerwald

This is the second major type of Rhenish stoneware. It is distinguished by a light to medium gray paste and clear salt glaze (Brain 1979, pp. 77–81). Vessels are invariably decorated with painted, stamped, incised, and/or molded designs.

Nine examples from Trudeau (V710/711; B141A; surface) include at least two mug fragments, one of which was in the "GR" style (see figs. 65n, 76h, 122h).

English White Salt-Glazed

This fine ceramic is characterized by a very hard, thin, white ware and clear salt glaze. It was made in England, mostly in Staffordshire, and was at the height of its popularity during the middle decades of the eighteenth century (1740–1770). This period coincides very closely with the Tunica occupation of Trudeau; however, only one sherd has been found at the site. Although the Tunica clearly were not a major market for this distinctive English product, they apparently treasured the lone example known to have been in their possession, since the sherd was found on the bluff top.

Grès

This type covers all stoneware presumed to be of French origin. All known examples are utilitarian, essentially undecorated, and have little glaze (Brain 1979, pp. 82–83).

There are two sherds from Trudeau (V710/711; B125A2). Both are from short-necked bottles (see figs. 65o, 122i).

PORCELAINS

Porcelains are very thin and hard ceramics that have been vitrified by firing at very high temperatures and are more or less translucent when held up to the light. Although European potters eventually learned the secret of making porcelain, the examples described here appear to be oriental in origin.

Only three sherds of porcelain were found during the course of our investigations, and all came from the surface of the village area at Trudeau. One is from a poor quality, blue-on-white underglaze Chinese export bowl (see fig. 76f). The other two, from the same vessel, have red-and-green overglaze decoration (see fig. 76g). These were the most common styles during the middle quarters of the eighteenth century (Miller and Stone 1970, pp. 82–88).

OTHER CERAMICS

The most important European ceramic artifacts other than vessels are tobacco pipes. Foremost among these are ones made of kaolin clay in the Netherlands and England.

Surprisingly, only seven bowl and stem fragments of kaolin pipes were found, all at Trudeau (V702C4; 710/711; B75B; 143A; 144A; 193B; surface). The example from pit feature V710/711 is decorated with a rouletted and stamped design (see fig. 65v). Stem bore diameters are approximately 2 mm or less.

Appendix E: Glass Artifacts

Glass artifacts may be separated into two basic groups: functional and ornamental. Functional artifacts are bottles and glasses; ornamental items are primarily beads, but also include pendants and buttons.

BOTTLES

Most early eighteenth-century glass bottles fall into two types distinguished on the basis of color: dark olive green and light blue-green. The olive green bottles are usually of the shape often referred to as "wine" bottles; the light blue-green bottles are found in many different forms and originally contained a variety of substances (Brain 1979, pp. 85–93). A third type, of unknown function and origin, is emerald green in color. A fourth type is amber.

Olive Green Bottle

French-made olive green bottles in the early eighteenth century were cylindrical, had long tapered necks with applied string lips, and a kickup in the base. While usually referred to as wine or rum bottles, they might have contained other spiritous liquors.

Twelve sherds from Haynes Bluff are all too small to contribute any information on shape or function, except that a couple seem to have the flat sides and sharp angles of a case bottle, which suggests that they, at least, might not be French in origin (see "Light Blue-Green Bottle"). All but one of the sherds were found on mound A (Y104H2; 111A; 140B1; 150A; 151A; 155A; 160A; 161A).

One bottle sherd was recovered from the excavations on the hill at Bloodhound (A111A), and eight more were found in the midden on the terrace (A177A; 185B; 229B,C; 231A; 242B) (see fig. 156u–w). One of the latter examples had been chipped into the form of an end scraper similar to the chert snub-nosed end scrapers (see fig. 156w).

At least 564 sherds of eighteenth-century* olive green glass were recovered from Trudeau. Insofar as can be determined, they all came from round bottles (e.g., see figs. 65t–u; 67h, j; 77a; 97q). The largest number (122) was found in pit feature V710/711. Other proveniences were V702A,B; 705A; 706A; 707A,B; 708B; 709A,C5; 715; 723A; 727A; 729A; B56A,B; 59B1; 75B; 93A,B; 100A,B; 101A,B2; 102A; 104A,B; 105A; 106A; 107A; 108A; 109A; 110A; 111A; 112A,B; 113A,B; 114A,B,C; 115A,B1; 116A; 117A; 118A; 119A,B1; 121A,B1;

123A1,2; 124A1,2; 125A1,2; 127A,B3; 128A,B; 129A,B; 130A,C; 131A; 132A; 133A; 134A; 135A; 137A; 138A; 139A; 140A,B; 141A; 142A; 143A; 144A; 154A; 160A; 163A; 166A; 170A; 176A; 180B; 181A,B1; 182A; 185A,B2; 186A; 187A; 190A,B; 191A,B; 192A,B; 193A,B; 202A,C1; 203A,B; 207A,C,D; 208A,B; surface.

Light Blue-Green Bottle

Light blue-green bottles are a characteristically French artifact. They could be cylindrical, in which case they varied greatly in form and size. Many, however, were square in cross section and of a fairly uniform size. These flat-sided bottles were meant to be packed together in a box and are referred to as case bottles. Case bottles were also made by the Dutch and the English, but those are easily distinguished by their dark olive green color.

Only one piece of light blue-green glass was found at Haynes Bluff (Y109A); it is from a case bottle. Two sherds were recovered from the excavations on the terrace at Bloodhound (A184B; 229B) (see fig. 156q–r). Trudeau, however, produced 297 sherds, although 110 of these represented two broken case bottles from looted burial V705C (see fig. 62o). Twenty-four pieces of both round (see fig. 65s) and square bottles were found in pit feature V710/711. The proveniences of the remaining sherds were V723A; 729A; B56A,B; 75B; 100A; 106A; 107A; 109A; 111A; 112A; 114A,B; 115A,B1; 116A; 117A; 118A; 119A; 121A,B1; 123A2; 124A1,2; 125A2; 127A; 128A; 129A,B; 131A; 132A; 134A; 135A; 136A,B; 140A,B1; 141A,B; 142A; 143A; 144A; 169A; 180A; 182A; 186A; 187A; 190B; 192A; 193A; 203A; 207A,B; 208A,B,D; surface (see figs. 67i, 77b, 97p).

Emerald Green Bottle

Only a few sherds of this type are known. They are too small for shapes to be reconstructed, and therefore it would be useless to speculate on the original contents or intended functions of the bottles.

Three sherds were found in the terrace midden at Bloodhound (A242B; 243B) (see fig. 156x), and three more were found in the village area at Trudeau (B115A; 139A; 190A).

Amber Bottle

A single sherd of amber-colored glass was found at Trudeau (B109A). It probably came from a small bottle or flask like the example in the Tunica Treasure (Brain 1979, pp. 94–95). There is no evidence of enameled decoration on this sherd, however.

---

* It is often difficult to distinguish eighteenth-century glass from early nineteenth-century glass which is also present on the site. When in doubt, we did not count the examples.

GLASSES

Sherds from water or wine glasses tend to be clear and therefore are usually easily recognizable. Often called lead glass, the material usually has fewer imperfections than bottle glass.

Two sherds were found in the midden on the terrace at Bloodhound (A175C; 242B). Both were too small to determine shape characteristics, but one had been reused by the Indians as a cutting or scraping tool (see fig. 156s–t).

A small chip of clear glass was found in the looted grave pit of burial V715 at Trudeau. Eleven sherds came from pit feature V710/711, among which can be recognized the base of a tumbler and fragments of at least one wine glass (see fig. 65p–r). Nine fragments of another wine glass (see fig. 97o) were found on the bluff top (B75B). Twenty-seven other miscellaneous fragments were scattered about the site (B75A; 105A; 109A; 115B1; 117A; 119A; 121A; 123A1; 124A2; 131A; 136A; 139A; 141B; 143A; 180A; 182A; 202C2; 207B; 208B; surface).

MIRRORS

Although mirrors have an obvious functional usage, they were also often used by the Indians as ornaments. An oval glass mirror was found with burial YB-2 at Haynes Bluff. A similar mirror apparently accompanied burial 1 at Bloodhound.

BEADS

Glass beads are the primary ornamental category of European artifacts. The variety, manufacture, and distribution of beads at eighteenth-century French contact sites have already been discussed (Brain 1979, pp. 96–133), and here it is necessary only to inventory the collections and describe a few new varieties.

At Haynes Bluff, all but one of the beads (a "gooseberry" [IVB1] from Y100A) (see fig. 175j) were found with the two burials at the summit of mound A (see table 49). Only 290 monochrome white beads (IIA1/IVA1) accompanied burial YB-1. Burial YB-2, however, was better endowed, with 1,460 turquoise beads (IIA7), a single dark blue (IIA6), a red/blue-on-white striped (IIB5), and more than a thousand white beads. All of these beads, and especially the preponderance of monochrome blue or white varieties, are typical of early eighteenth-century French contact sites.

Bloodhound produced a similar variety of drawn beads, and wire-wound examples are also present. For example, burial 1 apparently had IIA1, IIA7, IIB5, IIB16, IVB1, WIA7, WIIA2, and WIIB2. Burial 2, however, seems only to have had small monochrome white and "black" beads (IIA1/IVA1 and IIA6?), while the remains of burial 3 contained only IIA1 beads. Burial 4 also had a mass of IIA1 beads, plus one IIA7. Burial 5 had hundreds of small IIA7 beads, a IIA1, and a IIB7. Burial 6 was accompanied by hundreds more drawn beads (IIA1, IIA3, IIA7, and IIB7), while burial 7 had only one small IIA7. Scattered beads from the general excavations on the hill included the following varieties: IIA1, IIA6, IIA13, IIB5 (see table 43). The midden on the terrace produced seventy-one beads (see table 44), including two wire-wound and two new drawn varieties (see description below): IIA1, IIA4, IIA6, IIA7, IIA13, IIA14, IIA15, IIB2, IIB3, IIB5, IIB7, IIB15, IIB16, IIB17, IVA2, IVB3, IVB6, WIIIA1, and WIIIA2 (A174B2; 182B; 184B; 185B; 186B; 229B,C; 240A,B; 241B; 242A,B; 243B) (see fig. 156y–qq).

Most of the beads from Trudeau came from looted burials. At least 2,437 beads were recovered from grave pit V705C. These comprised twenty-one varieties, including two new wire-wound ones: IA1, IB2, IIA1, IIA5, IIA6, IIA7, IIIA1, IVA1, IVA2, WIA1, WIA2, WIB1, WIB3, WIC1, WIIA3, WIIA4, WIIA11, WIIB2, WIIC1, WIIC2, and WIIIA4 (see table 5). The most significant observation about this assemblage is that there are more wire-wound than drawn varieties. On the other hand, drawn beads are far more in evidence (numbers and varieties) in both burials Beta and Delta (burials V731 and Alpha did not have beads). Interestingly, there was no overlap of varieties between these two burials, except for the most common IIA1. Thus, in addition to IIA1, burial Beta had IIA10, IIB2, IIB10, IIB13, IVB2, IVB3, IVB4, WIA1, and WID1 (see fig. 103a–m), while burial Delta had IIA2, IIA5, IIA6, IIA7, WID4, and WIIA7. Together, these comprise quite a range of variation, but with the emphasis on drawn beads. Elsewhere on the site, drawn varieties also predominate overwhelmingly in scattered occurrences (see figs. 77c–l): IA2 (B113A), IA3 (B112A; 142A), IB2 (B143A; surface), IIA1/IVA1 (V702C4; 715; 727A; B144A; 185B; 186C; surface), IIA5 (B142A), IIA6 (B107A; 114B; 140B4; 143A; 185C1), IIA7 (V709C1; 723A; B111A; 112A; 123A1; 124B1; 128B; 142A; 144A; 181A; 187A; 190A; 207A; surface), IIA15 (surface), IIIA1 (B124A1; 125A1; 191B; 207A; surface), IVB1 (B113B), IVB2 (B144A), IVB3 (B117B1; surface), IVB4 (B109A), WIA1 (surface), WIC1 (surface), WID1 (B108A; 143A; 144A), and WIIA3 (surface). Even the thirteen beads in pit feature V710/711 are mostly drawn: IIA1, IIA6, IIA7, IIB1, IIB2, IIB10, IVB4, and WIIIA4 (see table 6).

Brief descriptions of new bead varieties—including five observed in the Angola Farm collections—are given on the next page.

PENDANTS

This class of artifacts is of considerable interest since it represents an innovation: a new technology was used to transform a European artifact into a new native-made form. Glass beads were pounded to powder, melted, and cast into flat triangular pendants (Ubelaker and Bass 1970; Brown 1972; Howard 1972; Perino 1975). One pair of these was found with burial YB-2 at Haynes Bluff (see fig. 167d).

BUTTONS

A simple round button made of wire-wound black (burgundy?) glass was found with burial YB-1 at Haynes Bluff (see fig. 166e). Nothing exactly like this button has been observed in other collections or described in the literature, so its significance is unknown.

Variety	Description	Provenience	Sample
IIA11	Small, opaque, greenish yellow (Kidd IIa21?)	Angola Farm	11
IIA16	Very small, translucent, medium blue (Kidd IIa44?)	Angola Farm	7
IIB9	Medium, opaque, bluish white, with three longitudinal dark blue stripes (Kidd IIb_)	Angola Farm	2
IIB11	Medium, opaque, yellow, with two dark red and two translucent green stripes (Kidd IIb46)	Angola Farm	23
IIB12	Medium, translucent, dark blue with three longitudinal white stripes (Kidd IIb56?)	Angola Farm	1
IIB15	Medium, opaque, light blue, with multiple alternating red, white, and dark blue stripes (Kidd IIb44?)	Bloodhound	1
IIB16	Medium, translucent, dark blue, with compound white-red-white stripes (Kidd IIbb25?)	Bloodhound	2
IIB17	Medium, translucent, burgundy, with compound white-red-white stripes (Kidd IIbb6?)	Bloodhound	1
WIIA11	Very large, translucent, aqua blue (Kidd WIIc7/8)	Trudeau	3
WIIC2	Large, translucent, amber (Kidd WIIf_)	Trudeau	1

Appendix F: Metal Artifacts

Metal artifacts are divided into four categories depending upon whether they were primarily made of iron, lead, silver, or copper/copper alloy. The kind of metal used was basic in determining the type and function of artifacts.

1. Iron

Iron artifacts constitute a very important category because functionally they probably had one of the greatest impacts upon the American Indian. In these collections, too, the sheer mass and weight of iron items bulk large. Unfortunately, however, the climate of Louisiana is especially detrimental to the preservation of iron, and many artifacts have corroded to the point that they are unidentifiable and can be assigned only to the miscellaneous category. Nevertheless, some basic classes—and even some distinctive types—are recognizable.

KETTLES

Large cast-iron kettles were made in many different shapes and sizes (Brain 1979, pp. 134–139). No whole examples have been found outside of the Tunica Treasure, however, and fragments are very difficult to classify.

One large fragment was found on the surface at Bloodhound Hill (A77). Seventeen more were recovered from Trudeau: seven from looted burial V705C (see fig. 62g), two from burial Delta, another from grave pit V707, one from excavation unit B191A, and six from the surface (see fig. 78a–b). Two fragments of a flat lid (see fig. 103n) were found near the impressions of a kettle in the grave of burial Beta.

AXES

Iron axes are among the most prominent items in the eighteenth-century trade and gift lists (e.g., Brain 1979, app. B). There is one basic type represented in the collections: the French *hache*. The standard French axe came in several grades and sizes, but it was fairly uniform in general shape characteristics (Brain 1979, pp. 140–143). Most noticeable is a flaring blade that makes the bit at least half as long as the total length of the axe, and a heavy haft that is expanded beyond the blade width at the neck.

Two medium-size axes of this type were found with burial 5 at Bloodhound (see fig. 145a). A third example

found nearby (A88) may also have been associated with this burial.

A large axe, 210 mm in length, was found discarded in pit feature V710/711 at Trudeau. It was bent, but whole (see fig. 65vv).

TOMAHAWKS

Tomahawks were a favored weapon of Indian warriors. Two distinctive types are present in these collections (H. L. Peterson 1965, pp. 22–26; Russell 1967, p. 276). The standard axe might also have been so used, but it was multifunctional and not specifically designed as a tomahawk.

Missouri War Hatchet

This lightweight axe made a perfect tomahawk. Although such an artifact could have had other uses, this one in fact had been hafted as a tomahawk and was found lying on the chest of the important male burial YB-2 at Haynes Bluff (see fig. 167i). Length from bit to top of haft is 190 mm.

Spontoon Tomahawk

This distinctive form of tomahawk is more closely related to the pike than to the axe. Unlike the pike described below, however, it was meant to be hafted transversely, like an axe—or, in this case, like a tomahawk.

A single example of the type was found lying on the chest of burial V731 at Trudeau (see fig. 69c). It is 300 mm long, 40 mm at the maximum width of the blade, and the internal diameter of the haft is 35 mm. The only other known specimen from the Lower Mississippi Valley was found with burial 7 at Angola Farm (see fig. 132b). This type of tomahawk seems to have enjoyed some popularity among the Tunica during the first half of the eighteenth century.

PIKES

As a military pole arm, pikes were phased out by the French in the mid-eighteenth century. At least two ended up in the hands of the Tunica at Trudeau: one is in the Tunica Treasure (Brain 1979, p. 158), and the other was excavated from pit feature V710/711 (see fig. 65rr). Both are simple in form, with leaf-shaped blades and round hafts 45 mm in diameter. The distal ends of the blades of both were broken off and missing, so the present length of the excavated specimen is only 210 mm.

HARPOONS

A harpoon point was found at Bloodhound Hill by local collectors. More than 400 mm in length, it has a single barb and socketed haft (see fig. 148r). Similar harpoons are represented in the Tunica Treasure (Brain 1979, p. 151).

SAWS

Considering the variety of tools found at the later Tunica sites, saws are a rare artifact. Apparently, axes and adzes were preferred for wood cutting and shaping purposes: in other words, traditional methods and tool forms prevailed.

Part of a saw blade was found in the excavations on the bluff top at Trudeau (B75B2). It is 105 mm in length and 22 mm wide (see fig. 97n).

KNIVES

Knives of all kinds were important articles in Indian trading and gifting. In fact, the first recorded European gift to an Indian in the southern part of the Lower Mississippi Valley was a knife presented to a Natchez "chief" by Tonti in 1682 (Margry 1879, vol. 1, p. 603).

Case Knife

The simplest form of knife, case knives had straight sturdy blades and wooden handles (Brain 1979, pp. 152–153). Although there was a considerable range in form and size, the common table or butcher knives seem to have been preferred. These were worn about the person (e.g., see Brain 1979, cover illustration).

Two pieces of a single case knife blade (see fig. 156a) were found in the midden on the terrace at Bloodhound (A229B). At Trudeau, an entire knife 240 mm long and 30 mm wide accompanied burial Alpha (see fig. 112), and part of another blade was found in the grave pit of looted burial V705C (see fig. 62j). Two probable fragments of a case knife blade were recovered from excavation unit B125A2 at Trudeau.

Folding Knife

Folding (or clasp) knives were especially popular items in the Indian trade (Brain 1979, p. 154).

A badly corroded blade accompanied burial YB-1 at Haynes Bluff (see fig. 166g); the reconstructed length of the blade is 110 mm. Two similar examples were found with burial 6 at Bloodhound, and fragments of a third were found in pit feature A73 (see fig. 148s). Pieces of two more (see fig. 156b–c) were found in the midden on the terrace (A229B; 240B). A blade missing only its tip and having a reconstructed length of approximately 100 mm came from pit feature V710/711 at Trudeau (see fig. 65ss), another with a length of 110 mm accompanied burial V731, and a broken blade was found on the surface (see fig. 78h).

HOOPS

Barrels were a common shipping container in the eighteenth century, and many must have ended up in the hands of the Indians. When disassembled, the barrel hoops must have been an important source of iron. In fact, in 1967 several reworked pieces of hoop were found at Haynes Bluff sticking out of a midden layer in the wall of the recently cut railroad grade. A complete, unmodified iron barrel hoop was found in another midden north of mound A (Y101C); it measured 50 cm in diameter. A bent strap, probably from a hoop, was one of the many artifacts discarded in pit feature V710/711 at Trudeau (see fig. 65tt).

PONTILS

Two possible pontils were found in excavation unit V708C at Trudeau. They are too badly corroded to identify details of size and form, and in fact could be merely bent spikes (see handwrought nails, Type V).

NAILS

Handwrought iron nails were made in a wide range of shapes and sizes. All have shanks that are roughly square in cross section and taper to a point. The most significant variation is in head form, differences in which are the defining criteria of the following typology.

Type I

This is the most common type of handwrought nail in Louisiana. It is distinguished by a head that has a relatively large diameter but is quite thin and has been struck with three or four shallow facets. Lengths range from 35 to 100 mm.

Ninety-one of these were found on the summit of mound A at Haynes Bluff (see fig. 168a–c), another at the base (Y141B). All of the nails found in the terrace midden at Bloodhound (A174B2; 181B; 184B; 185B; 229B; 240A,B; 241B) were probably of this type, but the advanced corrosion makes identification difficult (see fig. 156d–e). The same problems existed in the village area at Trudeau, where only forty-one of ninety-four nails from pit feature V710/711 could be definitely assigned to this type (see fig. 65ww), and one each from V702C4 and B202B. Classification is even more of a problem for the 120 nails collected from the surface of the site. At least 114 more, however, were identified from the bluff top at Trudeau (see fig. 97a–c), an interesting parallel to Haynes Bluff mound A. Many of the nails at both of these locations were uncorroded, apparently as a result of being subjected to prolonged or repeated heating which produced a coating of firescale that protected them from post-depositional corrosion (LaViolette 1982; Waldbaum 1982).

Type II

Type II nails have thick T-shaped heads that protrude from the shaft on only two sides. These range from 60 mm to at least 95 mm in length.

Two nails of this type were found on mound A at Haynes Bluff (Y155A) (see fig. 168d), and twenty-eight on the bluff top at Trudeau (B59A, 75B) (see fig. 97d–e), but none was identified from the village area.

Type III

This type includes the simplest and smallest nails. Heads are flat, thin, and unfaceted. Lengths range from approximately 30 to 60 mm.

Six of these nails were found at the summit of mound A at Haynes Bluff (see fig. 168e). At Trudeau, fourteen came from the bluff top and two from the village area (V710/711) (see figs. 65zz, 97f–g).

Type IV

These nails have thick heads in the form of a truncated pyramid: four steep facets sharply define the upper surface, and a fifth flattens the tip of the pyramid. These are relatively large nails, uniformly about 75 to 80 mm in length.

Four examples came from the summit of mound A at Haynes Bluff (see fig. 168f), and a fifth was found at the base of the mound (Y108A); ten were excavated from the bluff top at Trudeau, and fifteen came from the village area (V710/711; B121A) (see figs. 65yy, 97h).

Type V

This is the largest type of nail. In fact, examples are so large that they are really spikes (Brain 1979, p. 156). Heads are thick and have four prominent facets; lengths range from 120 to 150 mm. Five examples were found at the summit of mound A at Haynes Bluff (see fig. 168g); at Trudeau one came from the bluff top (see fig. 97i), but six were found in the village area (V710/711) (see figs. 60f, 65xx).

AWLS

Awls were a popular item of trading and gifting to the Indian (Brain 1979, app. B). Undoubtedly, these multifunctional tools were put to a variety of uses by the recipients.

Only one possible example of an awl was found in the excavations reported upon here. The evidence consists of a long, thin, pointed object that has a shank square in cross section. Presently it is 92 mm long and

measures 3 mm across each side of the shank. It was found with burial YB-1 at Haynes Bluff (see fig. 166b).

FISHHOOKS

A fishhook was recorded as having been found in pit feature V710/711 at Trudeau. Unfortunately, it was subsequently misplaced and cannot now be described.

STRIKE-A-LIGHTS

Strike-a-lights were a basic necessity in the eighteenth century for European and Indian alike. In 1733 alone, fifty gross were ordered for the Louisiana Colony (Brain 1979, app. B), and many of these must have ended up in the Indian trade.

Two strike-a-lights were found at Haynes Bluff among the possessions of the two individuals buried at the summit of mound A. An oval type was deposited with burial YB-2 (see fig. 167f), and a D-shaped type accompanied burial YB-1 (Brain 1979, p. 157).

BUTTONS

A possible button was collected from the surface of Trudeau in 1980. It is 20 mm in diameter and undecorated (see fig. 78d).

BUCKLES

A simple iron buckle was found with burial 7 at Bloodhound. From its shape and placement on the body it probably had been part of a belt. Three more rectangular buckles were recovered from Trudeau: one from looted burial V705C (see fig. 62l), another from pit feature V710/711, and the third from the surface (see fig. 78c). Reconstructed measurements range from approximately 25 × 30 mm to 30 × 40 mm.

BRACELETS

Bracelets of iron were not as popular as those made from brass or copper, and only a few survive archaeologically.

A single example was found in a gully on the south side of the terrace at Bloodhound (see fig. 156f). It may have come from a burial eroded by the gullying action. Although fragmentary, the inside diameter can be reconstructed at approximately 50 mm.

COILS

Coils of iron wire probably served a variety of functions among the Indians. Smaller ones, which actually were springs, are known to have been used as hair pluckers, and larger ones could have been ornaments (Brain 1979, pp. 157, 196).

Fragments of nine small coils or springs were found in the ditty bag that accompanied burial YB-1 at Haynes Bluff (see table 49). These springs had outside diameters of approximately 10 mm. Two large coils were interred with burial YB-2, one on each side of the head near the mastoids (see fig. 167). These coils could have been ear ornaments, but because of their size (outside diameter 55 mm) it is surmised that they were used to gather hanks or braids of hair. Five pieces of one or more small coils were found in the disturbed grave of burial Beta at Trudeau (see fig. 103o), while three additional fragments were recovered from middens in the village area (V710/711; B181A; B202B).

2. Lead

Most of the lead items in the collection are balls and shot, and the sprues and splashes left over from their casting. These, however, are more appropriately considered under guns and munitions (see app. G), where they are an integral part of a complex technological system.

Lead was sometimes used for other purposes, such as bale seals, and when alloyed was made into pewter utensils and ornaments.

BALE SEALS

A single, unmarked lead bale seal was found in the grave fill of burial 6 at Bloodhound. It was not definitely associated with the burial.

BUTTONS

A plain, pewter-sheathed bone button was found in the ditty bag placed beside the head of burial YB-1 at Haynes Bluff. A crude disc of lead, 22 mm in diameter and with a central perforation, may have been a button blank (see fig. 168m). It was found in the excavations at the summit of mound A at Haynes Bluff (Y151A).

3. Silver

Silver artifacts are rarely encountered in aboriginal sites of the first half of the eighteenth century. It was not until after 1760 that the great flood of silver ornaments entered the Indian trade. A few are known

from the Tunica Treasure (Brain 1979, p. 163), however, and the earring portions of two earbobs were found in the grave of looted burial V705C and excavation unit V729A at Trudeau (see figs. 62n, 67f).

4. Copper and Copper Alloys

Artifacts of copper and brass (no bronze has been recognized in these collections) are found in both utilitarian and ornamental function groups.

KETTLES

Fragments of sheet brass and copper kettles are present in the collections (see fig. 62h). These kettles were often cut up to make other artifacts—for example, tinkling cones. Only two whole kettles were found, both in burials.

Type A, Variety 1

This was the most common type of brass kettle in Louisiana during the eighteenth century (Brain 1979, pp. 166–172).

A single example was found inverted over the top of the head of burial YB-2 at Haynes Bluff (see fig. 167). This kettle is whole but has a hole in the bottom over which a rectangular patch has been riveted on the inside. It is 46 cm in diameter, approximately 20 cm in height (it has been crushed slightly, distorting the vertical dimension), and it weighs 2.7 kg. A smaller example accompanied burial 4 at Bloodhound (see fig. 144).

Type F, Variety 1

An iron lug from a Type F, Variety 1 copper kettle was found in pit feature V710/711 at Trudeau (see fig. 65uu).

Although no whole examples of this form of kettle were found in our excavations, one was supposedly recovered from burial 1 at Bloodhound (see fig. 142a). It differs from the Tunica Treasure kettles (Brain 1979, pp. 178–179) in that it apparently is made of sheet brass rather than copper. Like most of the examples from Trudeau, however, it is decorated with a complex hammered design, which seems to be characteristic of early eighteenth-century Louisiana, if not of the Tunica themselves. Kettles hammered in a simpler style may be more widespread in time and space—at least two are known from the seventeenth-century Grimsby site in Ontario (Kenyon 1982, pls. 55, 57, 58).

PINS

A single brass pin was recovered from pit feature V710/711 at Trudeau. Originally, it had been plated with silver or tin (Brain 1979, p. 189).

BUTTONS

Cast brass buttons were popular in the eighteenth century, and several types were common in Louisiana. One of the most distinctive has a flat, stamped edge and a wedge-shaped attachment with a drilled eye (Brain 1979, p. 189). This type seems to be a good marker for the French presence in Louisiana during the middle decades of the eighteenth century (ca. 1716–1763).

A single button was found with burial YB-1 at Haynes Bluff (see fig. 166a). Eight more large examples had accompanied burial Beta at Trudeau (see fig. 103q), and three were scattered elsewhere across the site (B59A; 128A; 208A) (see figs. 97k, 122k–l).

CRUCIFIXES

Crucifixes were given by missionary priests to Indians who were baptized. Thus, crucifixes were more than ornaments, although they may have been merely ornamental for many recipients who ignored their larger significance.

A small copper crucifix was found with burial 6 at Bloodhound (see fig. 146c). It is roughly cast and decorated with corpus and legend. A brass crucifix of slightly different form and decoration was recovered from excavation unit V706B at Trudeau (see fig. 60h).

PENDANTS

Ornamental pendants other than crucifixes were made in many different forms. Some were religious medals, but others were devoid of religious significance. An example of the latter is a hollow, sheet brass pendant from the summit of mound A at Haynes Bluff (Y160A). It is in the shape of a keystone, and is decorated with a stamped, raised border enclosing an etched floral design (see fig. 168i). It measures 32 mm from top to bottom.

A cast brass scallop shell was found in the midden on the terrace at Bloodhound (A185A). It was pierced for suspension and probably was worn as a pendant (see fig. 156j). A pair of triangular, sheet copper cut-outs (see fig. 156k–l), from a gully on the south side of the terrace (A52), were also probably pendants made by the Indians (see app. E, "Pendants," for homologous ornaments).

BELLS

Small brass or copper bells were, after glass beads, the most popular European ornaments among most Indian peoples (Brain 1975a). They were traded and gifted widely by most European nationalities, and many distinctive types and varieties are now recognized (Brown 1979b).

An interesting range of bells has been reported from Bloodhound and Trudeau, but only three types were found during the course of our excavations.

Type Key, Variety Fishkey

A fragment of this variety of cast brass bell was found at Trudeau (V729A). It came from a bell approximately 35 mm in diameter (see fig. 67g).

Type Key, Variety Flowerkey

Four examples of this variety of cast brass bell were excavated during the course of the investigations at Trudeau. Two small bells with diameters of only 25 mm were found in pit feature V710/711 (see fig. 65w), a third had accompanied disturbed burial Beta (see fig. 103p). A fragment of a large specimen approximately 50 mm in diameter was recovered from looted burial V705C (see fig. 62p).

Type Flush-Edge, Variety Flushloop

These sheet brass bells were among the most common in Louisiana.

Nine small bells of this variety accompanied burial 6 at Bloodhound (see fig. 146), and another specimen was recovered from the midden on the terrace (A185B) (see fig. 156i). At Trudeau, nine more small examples were found in the looted grave pit of burial Delta (see fig. 122m), and five bells of unusually large size (23 mm diameter) for the variety were discovered at the ankles of burial Alpha (see fig. 112).

Type Flanged-Edge, Variety Saturn

This variety of sheet brass bell is relatively rare in the Mississippi Valley. It is distinguished by the equatorial flange that joins the two hemispheres of the bell together.

Part of a single specimen was found in the grave pit of disturbed burial Beta at Trudeau.

RINGS

A brass finger ring was found at the summit of mound A at Haynes Bluff (Y152A). It is a simple ring with a flat, oval bezel that is decorated with a stylized engraved design (see fig. 168j). This ring is very small, having an internal diameter of only 12 mm. A similar ring is in the Tunica Treasure (Brain 1979, p. 192).

A simple ring of brass wire was recovered from the midden on the terrace at Bloodhound (A185B).

BRACELETS

Simple bracelets were probably manufactured for the Indian trade. In addition, bracelets were often made by the Indians from brass and copper wire or pieces of scrap (Brain 1979, p. 193).

Five simple copper wire bracelets were discovered on the left wrist of burial 6 at Bloodhound, and a fragment of a cast brass C-bracelet was found in the midden on the terrace (A185B) (see fig. 156g). Four fragments, comprising three different bracelets, were recovered from the grave pit of looted burial V705C at Trudeau (see fig. 62k). Three types are represented: a brass Type 4, a copper Type 5, and a brass Type 6 (ibid., p. 194).

TINKLING CONES

These conical objects were made by the Indians from sheet metal, cut-up kettles, or scrap. Such cones were decorative (conical metal arrow points were also made by many Indians, but none of these examples appears to have been made for this purpose): they were sewn on clothing or worn around the wrists or ankles. Movement caused them to rattle together and make a tinkling sound.

Two cones of sheet copper are from mound A at Haynes Bluff. One was collected from the surface (see fig. 175i), while the other was found in the excavations at the summit (Y110B). The latter is unusually large, being 52 mm in length (see fig. 168h); the former is more standard, having a length of 28 mm (Brain 1979, p. 195). A cone of sheet brass 30 mm in length (see fig. 156h) was recovered from the midden on the terrace at Bloodhound (A185B). Nine tinklers of brass and three of copper were found at Trudeau. Five of these came from pit feature V710/711, and the rest were scattered across the village area (B119A; 135A; 138A; 140B; 202C1,D1; 208A). The examples from Trudeau differ considerably in size and shape (see figs. 65y–cc, 122n–q).

COILS

A brass coil was found in the ditty bag that accompanied burial YB-1 at Haynes Bluff (see fig. 166f). It is made of solid wire that has a circular cross section and a diameter of just over 1 mm. The coil is 39 mm long and has an overall diameter of 15 mm. Similar coils are in the Tunica Treasure (Brain 1979, p. 196).

WIRES

Fragments of brass and copper wire were occasionally encountered in the excavations. In many instances, they may have been parts of larger artifacts.

Of special interest, but unknown function, are two thin (diameter approximately 0.5 mm) pieces of brass wire that have been bent to form identical semilunar outlines. These crescents are 25 mm in length and were found in the right shoulder area of burial YB-2 at Haynes Bluff. Three strands of double-twist copper wire were recovered from pit feature V710/711 at Trudeau (see fig. 65x). These possibly were part of a necklace.

BRAIDS

Strips of metallic braid, or galloon, were used to adorn clothing in the eighteenth century. Usually silver or gold colored, the wires of which they were made were predominantly copper or copper alloy. Several pieces ornamented with a simple woven design are present in the Tunica Treasure (Brain 1979, pp. 217–218).

A length of braid, but without any design, was sewn to the edge of a leather ditty bag that accompanied burial YB-1 at Haynes Bluff (see fig. 166). The surviving pieces of this braid add up to a total length of approximately 55 cm, so the bag had a theoretical diameter at the opening of at least 15 cm. Fragments of other strips of braid were found in pit features at Bloodhound (A108A; 111A) (see fig. 148w–x) and at Trudeau (V710/711).

Appendix G: Guns and Munitions

This appendix includes discussion of a variety of materials, but the artifacts are best treated together as parts of a single technological system.

During the course of our excavations, two fusils and a pistol were recovered from Haynes Bluff, one fusil was found at Bloodhound, and another was unearthed at Trudeau. Together with two more fusils discovered earlier at Bloodhound, these guns and the associated munitions are reported upon by T. M. Hamilton. First, however, a number of miscellaneous gun parts, balls, and flints found scattered around the sites will be described briefly.

1. Miscellaneous Gun Parts and Munitions

Identifiable gun parts from Haynes Bluff included an unbridled tumbler from a musket lock and part of an unclassified brass trigger guard, both from the base of mound A on the north side (Y140B2). A piece of brass butt plate was found in Y104B2 (see fig. 175l); it is similar to an example from burial 1 at Bloodhound (see fig. 142e) and would seem to be another version of Hamilton's Type C (Brain 1979, p. 212). Munitions were surprisingly rare, consisting only of one broken gunspall from Y161A (see fig. 168o) and two lead musket balls. One of the balls (Y104H2) was deformed but had a weight of 15 g (see fig. 175k), and the other, from the summit of mound A (Y159A), weighed 13.2 g and had a diameter of 13 mm (see fig. 168n).

From the Russell site (Y203A) there was only a single 32-*calibre* (diameter 13.5 mm, weight 14.6 g) lead musket ball.

At Bloodhound, there were fusils with burials 1 and 7 (app. G.2), and miscellaneous gun parts were found elsewhere on the hill by local collectors (see fig. 148a–q). Two butt plates were associated with burial 3. Both of these are examples of Type C (see fig. 143). Also present were other miscellaneous iron gun parts, lead shot, and a residue of gunpowder. In other excavations on the hill, a lock mainspring (see fig. 155b) and a flake from a gunflint were found (A75; 111B). From the midden on the terrace, a large number of gun parts and munitions were recovered (A174B1; 177A; 185B; 186D; 229A,B; 231C; 240A,B; 242B; 243A,B; surface). The gun parts consist of a musket lock mechanism (see fig. 155f), part of a brass trigger guard (see fig. 155e), a fragment of a Type C brass side plate (see fig. 155d), the heel of a Type C or D brass butt plate (see fig. 155a), and a brass escutcheon (see fig. 155c). The last is identical to an example from Fort Michilimackinac which is described by Hamilton (1976, p. 16, fig. 15b) as "similar to . . . a variation of Type D." Munitions include fifteen musket balls (see fig. 155g), which fall into a wide range of *calibres* since they have maximum diameters of 13 to 17 mm and weigh between 13 and 27.5 g. There are also twenty-one pieces of shot ranging from 4 to 7 mm in diameter (see fig. 155h). Of nine gunflints, seven are spalls and only two are the blade type (see fig. 155i–p). One, and possibly two, of the spalls were intended for pistols; the others were standard musket size, an unused spall having dimensions of 28 × 33 mm (see fig. 155n). All were made of the blond flint rather than the gray. Two pieces of unusual multicolored chalcedony are of special note: although unworked, they appear to be the same material later used for making gunflints in the nineteenth century (Mortillet Collection, Peabody Museum, Harvard University, cat. nos. 55923, 55924). Even if they are the same, the significance of their presence at Bloodhound remains obscure.

Miscellaneous gun parts and munitions were even more prevalent at Trudeau. Brass furniture includes two butt plate fragments (see fig. 122v–w), three ferrules (see fig. 122r–s), a plain tang probably from a trigger guard (see fig. 60g), a large part of a Type C trigger guard (see fig. 65dd), and three side plates, one each Type C, Type D, and unclassified (see figs. 65ee, 122t–u). There was one iron tang. Pieces of a Type C fusil were also found with the remains of burial Beta; the gun apparently had been fitted with both brass and iron furniture (see fig. 103r–t, y).

Other gun parts from Trudeau included pieces of lock mechanisms, such as a musket cock (see fig. 122x) and pan, and an entire pistol lock that was found on the surface (see fig. 78i). Segments of three musket barrels (see fig. 65qq) have measurable bores of approximately 14 mm, which are too small for the balls found (e.g., see table 39). Forty-three lead musket balls range from

14 to 15.5 mm in diameter, and 10.7 to 18 g (27.6 g if distorted balls are included) in weight (see figs. 60m–r, 65oo–pp, 67p–q, 78j–k, 97l, 122y). Thirteen of these were with burial Beta (see fig. 103x). They included the full range of sizes, which is of considerable interest if they were intended for use in the one gun that was evidenced in the grave. Four more balls found with burial Alpha had diameters of 18 to 19 mm (weights could not be ascertained since no artifacts were removed from the grave), which would mean that the only standard bore they could have fit was the English "Brown Bess" musket (Hamilton 1979, table 16), a most unexpected correlation. The measurements of four pistol balls, or large shot, are 7 to 13 mm and 1.3 to 8.6 g (see figs. 65oo, 97m). At least 155 pieces of shot averaged 5 mm in diameter and 0.7 g in weight (figs. 65nn, 122y). Of these, 147 came from the burial Beta grave pit (see fig. 103w); four more from burial Delta.

The sixty-seven gunflints and thirty-two flakes at Trudeau include gray spalls and blond blades of pistol size (measurable specimens range from 18 × 23 mm to 21 × 24 mm), as well as gray and blond spalls and blades for muskets (those that can be measured range from 19 × 25 mm to 33 × 37 mm, but the median is around 25/26 × 29/30 mm). There are also a small broken flint of dark gray material (intended for a pistol?) and three musket spalls of regulation size but made of an unfamiliar reddish flint. Most of these gunflints show considerable usage (many obviously with strike-a-lights), but some were discarded in pristine condition (figs. 60i–k, 65ff–mm, 67n, 78l–o, 97j, 103u–v, 122z–cc).

Proveniences of gun parts and munitions at Trudeau include all sections of the site: V702A,B,C4; 703B; 704B; 706A; 707A; 708B,C4; 710/711; 729A; 730A; B56B; 59A; 75B1,2,3; 93A2; 100A; 104A; 105A; 107A; 108A; 111A; 112A,B; 113A; 114B; 115A,B1; 117A; 118A,B1; 119A,B1; 120B1; 124A2; 125A1; 128A,B; 129A,E1; 130E1; 133A; 134A; 137A; 140A; 141A; 142A; 143A; 144A; 160A; 162A; 181A; 182A; 185C2; 187B; 202A; 207A,B; surface.

2. Guns and Munitions from Burials

by T. M. Hamilton

This appendix reports upon six fusils and one pistol found with burials at the Haynes Bluff, Bloodhound, and Trudeau sites. The reports were written between 1977 and 1979, and some of the results have been published separately (Hamilton 1980).

HAYNES BLUFF
Burial YB-1 Fusil

Barrel: The barrel was heavily encrusted with rust and sand concretions. After being cleaned in an electrolytic bath, it still was in one piece even though it was rusted through on one side 16.6 to 29.3 cm back from the muzzle. It is 116.7 cm long and measures 3.1 cm across the flats at the breech. The bottom flats on the fully octagonal breech are somewhat indistinct. The octagonal section was probably originally about 40 cm long, but the surface pitting is severe. The rear sight, which is broken off, was placed 10.2 cm from the breech. The front sight, also obliterated, was 3 cm back from the muzzle. The front mounting lug is placed 7.6 cm back from the muzzle, and the three others are placed back 36.8 cm, 65.6 cm, and 96.1 cm respectively. The breech screw was inserted through the tang. The barrel

was cut in two 8.9 cm from the breech, and the bore was found to be in perfect condition. The bore is 16.6 mm (.660 in.).

Lock: There is no lock with the gun.

Furniture: The side plate is of iron and is Type D (Hamilton 1968, fig. 6). It is too deeply pocked with rust to see any decorative details (see fig. 166k). The iron butt plate was a formalized torch finial with no evidence of a lug under the tang. It was held to the butt of the stock with one wood screw in the heel, which is most unusual (see fig. 166l). The trigger guard is of forged iron with Type D finials (Hamilton 1968, fig. 8d) front and back. It was held to the stock by two lugs, both of which still have their cross pins (see fig. 166m). There are three ram pipes (two front and one rear) of sheet iron with the pins still in place. Front pipes measure 3 cm long, the rear 7.6 cm. The internal diameter of the pipes is 1 cm.

Balls: There are twenty-seven balls and eight unformed lumps of lead. The eight lumps range from 4.3 to 28.3 g in weight. All the balls are pitted, but enough of the original surfaces remain to allow accurate measurement as follows:

Number	Maximum Diameter (mm)	Weight (g)
1	13.5[a]	13.8
2	14	14
1	14	14.3
1	14	14.8
2	14	15.1
1	14	15.2
1	14	15.4
1	14	16
2	14	16.5
2	14	16.8
2	14	17
1	14	17.2
1	14	17.3
1	14.5	16.5
1	14.5	16.6
2	14.5	17.2
1	14.5	17.4
1	14.5	17.5
1	14.5	17.6
1	14.5	18
1	15	15.8 (deformed)

[a] Most of these balls fall into the eighteenth-century French 26–28 calibres.

Gunflints: There are four spall gunflints. One is a pistol gunspall in near mint condition, measuring 20 mm long, 18 mm wide, and 6 mm thick. There is a fusil spall with one side broken off, now measuring approximately 22 mm long, 28 mm wide, and 8 mm thick. This is not a typical gunspall, for it is unusually narrow (long) from one side to the other. The two other gunspalls have been used as fire flints and their original dimensions cannot even be guessed. One has a grayish and the other a yellowish cast.

Comments: Until about 1750 the French naval musket had a 16.6 mm (.655 in.) bore and was designed to shoot a ball weighing 20 to the *livre* and having a diameter of 16 mm (.63 in.). For all practical purposes, this gun can be considered to have the same bore. Neither this gun nor the naval muskets had a stud for a bayonet, but this one does have a rear sight, which would rule it out as a naval gun. It is unfortunate that the lock used on this gun is not present since that might help in its identification. However, it is unquestionably French, and it has the earmarks of having been made in the early eighteenth century. I have examined the

butt plate carefully and can find no indication that it ever had a mounting lug under the tang. Butt plates of this sort with only one screw hole usually date from around 1700. The fact that the back mounting lug on the trigger guard was not hooked and that both lugs were drilled for a pin further indicates that the gun probably was made before 1710. There is much we do not know about French military muskets before they were standardized in 1717, but this gun looks as if it had been made in one of the French arsenals for either civilian use or the Indian trade. It may represent an early version of what came to be known as the Tulle fusil.

As for the bullets found with this gun, none was well suited to it. The largest would have left a windage of .05 inches, which would have been acceptable, but the smallest would have resulted in a blow-by of .120 inches, which seems to have been extreme even on the frontier where one often had to make do with whatever was available. The balls found with these old guns continue to puzzle me since they seldom seem to fit the gun with which they are found. I have often wondered if these mismatched balls were not included as grave offerings since they were practically useless in the guns of the living. The same principle may explain why no locks were found with either this gun or the one from YB-2: the locks may still have been in good condition and were saved for use on serviceable guns.

Burial YB-2 Fusil

Barrel: After cleaning, this barrel was found to be in fair condition. Its outer surface is deeply pocked with rust, but at no place is it rusted through. It is 123.8 cm long and measures 3.2 cm across the flats at the breech, 2.2 cm at the muzzle, and has a fully octagonal breech section approximately 26.7 cm long. There is a brass elongated bead front sight, 5 mm long, 3.5 cm back from the muzzle, and a Type C winged brass rear sight (Hamilton 1968, fig. 5g, h), 3.8 cm long by 2.2 cm wide, 7 cm in from the breech (see fig. 167o). The remains of three mounting lugs can be discerned equidistantly spaced along the bottom of the barrel. The tang on the breech plug is 4.4 cm long and is square. The tang screw went down to the trigger plate, which is missing. The bore measures 16 mm (.630 in.) at the muzzle, 2.5 cm in from the mouth. This is a reasonably accurate measurement, so the barrel was not cut in two.

Lock: There is no lock with this gun.

Furniture: A Type C brass trigger guard (Hamilton 1968, fig. 4a, b) was found with the gun but has since been lost.

Comments: The bore of 16 mm (.630 in.) cannot be definitely assigned. The square end on the breech plug tang is a characteristic of French guns around 1700. Since there is no lock nor butt plate and the trigger guard has disappeared, there is little to say other than that the barrel is probably French.

Burial YB-2 Pistol

Barrel: The barrel was heavily encrusted with rust and a sand concretion, as were all the parts. After cleaning, the muzzle section was found to be so badly eroded that the original length could not be determined, but it now measures 30 cm long, 2.5 cm across the flats at the breech, and has a half-octagon breech section. The barrel was cut in two 4.7 cm in front of the breech (see fig. 167n), fortunately where the original bore surfaces were still relatively intact. The bore diameter is 12.2 mm (.480 in.).

Lock: The lock was originally around 11.4 cm long overall, and has a rounded tail and a convex base on the cock. Very little else can be determined other than that the tumbler had no bridle (see fig. 167l).

Furniture: The side plate is of brass with a rather simple configuration at the rear. It was held by two side screws and was not engraved (see fig. 167k). The butt cap is of iron about 5 mm thick. It is a simple round cup with no side spurs and was held to the butt with a wood screw in its center (see fig. 167m). The trigger guard is of iron and so eroded that only two pieces could be recognized (see fig. 167j). The bow is spoon shaped, and the rear tang, at least, was held to the stock with a wood screw. There is one ram pipe made of sheet brass and held to the stock by flaring out the ends after inserting them through a slit in the stock. The bore of the pipe is 0.9 cm, length 2.3 cm. This ram pipe preserved a piece of the ramrod, now 2.3 cm long and 0.8 cm in diameter.

Gunflints: The gunflint in the lock is square and of native manufacture, nicely chipped, and could be the stem broken from an old straight-stemmed projectile point. It measures 18 × 16 mm and is 5 mm thick. Also associated are four gunflints of native manufacture and one European gunspall. The native gunflints are all nicely chipped and have a yellowish cast, which may be due to iron in the soil. They have the following dimensions: 20 × 18 × 6 mm; 21 × 18 × 5 mm; 22 × 16 × 8 mm; 22 × 18 × 6 mm. The gunspall is of gray-banded flint, 26 × 23 × 8 mm.

Comments: The side plate is of an entirely new design. If the rear half were eliminated, it would be similar to those used on French military arms after about 1717. This is not a military pistol, however, for the bore is only 12.2 mm and was intended to shoot a ball weighing about 50 or 52 to the *livre.* The small bore on the pistol, the round iron butt cap, and the native gunflint all point to an early 1700 date. The four native gunflints and the carefully reworked gunspall definitely show that the Indians had not yet become so acculturated that they had lost their skill in working flint.

BLOODHOUND
Burial 1 Fusils

Apparently, two guns accompanied burial 1. Although the parts had been mixed, the following combinations were reconstructed.

GUN A

Barrel: The barrel was originally about 113 cm long. The breech section is 68.6 cm long and the chase is 44.5 cm. It measures approximately 3 cm across the flats at the breech. The bore, which is surprisingly clean considering the condition of the exterior of the breech section, is 14.4 mm (.565 in.). The French classified this as a 34-*calibre* gun, by which they meant it was intended to shoot lead balls weighing 34 to the *livre.*

Furniture: The side plate (see fig. 142d) is the same as one found at the Fatherland site (Hamilton 1968, fig. 3b). The butt plate and trigger guard (see fig. 142e–f) are good examples of Type C. The escutcheon (see fig. 142c) is most interesting: the mask is similar to one from Fort Michilimackinac (Hamilton 1976, fig. 15d). I had thought that this mask was possibly English but now believe it to be French.

Comments: This is a typical Type C gun (Hamilton 1968, p. 9, fig. 5).

GUN B

Barrel: The barrel, originally about 124 cm long, is in five pieces. All except the breech section are in such sad shape that there is no reason to remove the rust, for there is little or no iron beneath. The breech measures about 3.4 cm across the flats, and the bore is in the neighborhood of 15.9 mm (.625 in.), or 26 *calibre.*

Lock: The lock appears to be a good French example, but is inverted so that it could be mounted on the left side of the barrel (see fig. 142i).

Furniture: The side plate is of brass and is similar to the French military side plates of that period, except for its fancy scroll-like rear end (see fig. 142h). No butt plate was found with this gun. Possibly it was removed by the Indians to make a hide scraper. The trigger guard (see fig. 142g) and the ram pipes are of cast brass, not made from rolled brass sheet as with trade guns. The escutcheon is in the form of a satyr's mask.

Comments: This is the only left-handed gun I know of that has been recovered archaeologically. It obviously was made on special order for someone who could afford to pay for it, since the lock and fittings are all special. Of course, it was a good quality gun, not a trade gun. The French called these fine quality guns *fusils fins.*

Burial 7 Fusil

Barrel: The only part of the barrel that can be salvaged is the breech section.

Lock: There is no lock.

Furniture: The iron furniture is greatly deteriorated. The butt plate fell apart in the bath: it was completely eaten through. Nothing much can be said other than that it had a long tang. The trigger guard also is flaking off and details are lacking. The other pieces are too far gone even to make a guess about them.

Comments: This gun is in extremely bad condition, and it can only be guessed from the iron furniture that it is an early model.

TRUDEAU
Burial V731 Fusil

Barrel: The barrel on this gun was exceptionally corroded (long since rusted in two) and encased in a rust and sand concretion. After cleaning, the rear portion was found to be fully octagonal and measured 3 cm across the flats at the breech. This section of the barrel was cut in two, approximately three inches in front of the breech. The bore was found to be in fair condition, and measured 14.9 mm (.587 in.). With a nominal bore of .59 inches, this gun was spoken of by the French as a 28 *calibre* and was designed to use bullets weighing 28 to the *livre* (diameter .56 in.). However, in practice the owner probably used whatever came to hand.

Furniture: The trigger guard is Type C (Hamilton 1968, fig. 4a), made of brass, and of very light construction. The bottom of the bow is decorated with what appears to be a knight's helmet with a plume and closed visor (see fig. 69a). The butt plate is also of brass, and is held to the butt by two wood screws, one at the toe and the other through the tang. The tang is decorated with an engraving of a man, but since the hole for the wood screw was drilled directly through his head, only his chin is decipherable (see fig. 69b).

Comments: The barrel is surprisingly heavy for a gun with such cheap furniture. I would have expected a barrel of not more than 32 *calibre*. Probably this gun was assembled from various pieces and then restocked by some frontier gunsmith. This supposition is strengthened further by the butt plate, which obviously had been taken from another gun and reworked to fit this one. In the process, the screw hole for the tang was drilled through the head of the figure decorating it.

Appendix H: Archaeozoology of a Trudeau Trash Pit

by Arthur Spiess

INTRODUCTION

Analysis of the faunal remains from a trash pit in excavation units V710/711 at Trudeau has revealed dependence on large mammals, in particular bison and white-tailed deer, as a major source of protein for the Tunica at Trudeau. A few remains of birds, including domestic chickens, and of fish and turtles also were recovered. Although preservation in the trash pit was quite good and the matrix was carefully screened through half-inch hardware cloth, no small mammal bones were found. This primary reliance on large mammals contrasts markedly with Mississippian subsistence patterns in southeastern Missouri, where small mammals and fish were more important than at Trudeau (Lewis 1974; Springer 1980). The Trudeau trash pit suggests a relative affluence, enabling the site's inhabitants to ignore many small species that could have been used for subsistence purposes.

The following taxa were represented in the Tunica trash pit:

Mammalia
  Artiodactyla
    Bison bison
    Odocoileus virgineanus (white-tailed deer)
  Carnivora
    Ursus Euarctos americanus (black bear)

Aves
    Aves; species indeterminate
    Gallus gallus (domestic chicken)
    Tympanuchus cupido (prairie chicken)
    Fulica americana (coot)
    Buteo sp.; two different-size species represented; one broad-winged-hawk-size species and one red-shouldered-hawk-size species

Pisces
    Lepisosteus spatula (alligator gar)
    Pisces; species indeterminate, medium-size teleost

Reptilia
  Chelonia
    Turtle species; one large species, one medium-size species

The number of identified bones from the trash pit is 324 and their combined weight is 4.64 kg. The weight of unidentified fragments of bone is 7.8 kg. The unidentified fragments are chiefly large mammal long bone flakes and pieces probably assignable to *Odocoileus*, *Bison*, and/or *Ursus*.

IDENTIFICATION

The final reference for mammal and bird species identification was the collection of Harvard University's Museum of Comparative Zoology. All the medium-size artiodactyl bones that could be identified to genus were found to be *Odocoileus*. It is assumed that the species represented is *Odocoileus virgineanus*, the white-tailed deer, on the basis of the present distributions of *O. virgineanus* and *O. hemoinus*. All medium-size artiodactyl bones that could not be identified to genus (rib fragments, pieces of vertebrae, etc.) were assigned to *O. virgineanus* on the basis that it was the only medium-size artiodactyl to be identified from the pit. All large artiodactyl bones that could be identified beyond the family Bovidae were shown to belong to *Bison bison*, rather than *Bos taurus*, by reference to Olsen (1960) and to Boessneck, Jequier, and Stampfli (1963). Large artiodactyl fragments not identifiable to species were assigned to *Bison bison* because it is the only identifiable large artiodactyl species from the site. Black bear (*Ursus Euarctos americanus*) and bird bones were also recovered from the trash pit. The author was particularly careful in the identification of the similar species *Gallus gallus* (domestic chicken) and *Tympanuchus cupido* (prairie chicken). The ranges of individual measurements for these species undoubtedly overlap, but *Gallus* has a noticeably more gracile build. For bones of the same length, *Gallus* is always less rugose, although the length of the same bone varies from individual to individual within each species. In addition, two skulls of *Gallus* were identified, and they are hard to confuse even with the prairie chicken.

QUANTIFICATION

In other faunal studies, quantification of the results has been expressed as (1) percentage representation of the taxa, (2) minimum number of individuals (MNI) for each taxon, or (3) a cumulative skeletal score of some kind.

Percentage representation is usually expressed as "x percent of species *a*," "y percent of species *b*," and so on, computed by totaling the number of identifiable bones for the whole site/stratum for each taxon and dividing by the grand total number of bones. Percentages are inaccurate for determining the original number of individuals (absolute or relative) of each taxon in the sample because they do not account for the possibility of different numbers of bones in the original skeleton of the different taxa, the possibility of breakage of one or more of those bones in differing numbers of identifiable pieces, and the differing resistance to destruction of those pieces. For example, a white-tailed deer has fewer carpal, tarsal, metacarpal, metatarsal, and phalangeal bones than a bear. If the bones are well preserved, in a mixed sample of these taxa the actual number of bears compared with deer would be misrepresented in bone percentage counts. On the other hand, some species' bones can be smashed into many more recognizable pieces and fragments than those of another species, chiefly because of size differential. A sample with prevalent bone breakage would tend to overrepresent the larger species in a percentage count.

MNI is a determination of the minimum number of different individuals of one taxon to which the bones from a given sample can be ascribed. Many levels of refinement can be introduced into the MNI, with diminishing returns in the identification of new individuals deriving from the introduction of each new level. Right versus left elements, and age as determined by tooth eruption or epiphyseal closure, are useful information, and measurements can be helpful in deciding whether left or right bones can be ascribed to the same individual. Finally, an extensive series of measurements taken on complete skeletons and regression analyses from one measurement to another for the size-range of a given species are useful in detecting whether two bones could have come from the same skeleton. All three techniques—right versus left, age, and measurements—were used in determining the MNIs given below for white-tailed deer. Measurements were not used for the other species.

A method of quantification called the cumulative skeletal score (CSS), developed by the author following ideas of Hesse and Perkins (1974), was also used for this work. The CSS is a relative measure and is essentially a bone count by taxon taking differing numbers of skeletal parts between taxa into consideration. Each bone is assigned a certain value depending on the number of bones in the original skeleton. For example, there is a high probability that three humeri in a sample of bear bones (2 per body) represent more original individuals than do three phalanges (56 per specimen); therefore, humeri are given a larger numerical value than phalanges when scoring them.

The Hesse and Perkins procedure consists of five steps:

1. Count the element type in the sample for each taxon (i.e., 28 humeri, 36 astragali, etc.).
2. Divide by the number of that element type found in one individual of the taxon to obtain corrected values (i.e., in the case of humeri and astragali, divide by 2, since each individual has 2 of each bone).
3. Sum these corrected values for each taxon.
4. Establish the arithmetic mean of all the element types for each taxon by dividing the sum obtained from step 3 by the number of element types (i.e., humeri, astragali, and femora constitute 3 element types in a hypothetical sample, so divide by 3).
5. Compare the arithmetic mean for each species.

Statistically, this type of method, which is a modification of the raw bone count, has the highest probability of truly representing the proportions between the original numbers of individuals from different taxa of any technique short of an extensive MNI count on a large sample (Hesse and Perkins 1974).

In computing CSS, the author transposes steps 1 and 2 of Hesse and Perkins. For example, there are 76 metacarpals, metatarsals, and phalanges in one bear, so each is counted as 1/76, or 0.0132 CSS units. If there are 12 such bones in a sample, the value assigned is $12 \times 0.0132 = 0.1584$ or 0.16 (recorded as significant to two decimal points). In a skeleton there are only 2 humeri, femora, tibia, and so on, so each is counted as 0.5 units if each bone type is a separate category. However, if we used long bones as a category, the CSS value assigned would be much less. In the CSS system, cranial vault and basicranial fragments (and some other bones) are arbitrarily assigned a value of 0.01, since the skull can be split into many pieces.

The next CSS step—summing the values for each species for each cultural (stratigraphic, etc.) unit—is entirely analogous to step 3 of Hesse and Perkins. This sum is the total CSS for that taxon for that sample, which can then be compared with other values from other samples. With the CSS, step 4 is unnecessary.

If one changes the scoring divisions from taxon to taxon, say from carpals, tarsals, metacarpals, metatarsals, and phalanges from bears to carpals, tarsals, metapodials, and phalanges in white-tailed deer, the scores are obviously no longer strictly comparable between taxa, although they are still comparable between sites for the same taxon. In any case, differential preservation and destruction of the bones from taxa with radically different bone architecture negates strict proportional intertaxa comparability.

Each method of faunal data quantification has its advantages and disadvantages. The straight percentage by bone count is a simple expression of which species is most frequently represented by identifiable bone fragments. For further analysis, however, it is almost useless.

MNI are most useful if a complete archaeological sample has been obtained—from a living floor, for example, or another limited occupation occurrence. An exhaustive MNI is then counted, using all the levels of refinement available in an effort to detect the actual number of individuals of each taxon represented in the refuse. The Trudeau trash pit is a complete sample, and it would be advantageous to know the number of individuals of the prey species represented.

MNI are also useful in the (statistically low) chance that an expectedly uncommon species is found to have a high CSS score in a given sample. MNI can then act as a check on CSS, and help determine whether a high CSS value is caused by the occurrence of a large portion of one skeleton in a sample or by the presence of more individuals. CSS is statistically a more accurate reflection of individual proportions in archaeological samples within taxa that have roughly comparable bone structure than are percentages or MNI, if the sample does not represent a complete occupation unit and includes fragmented bones.

Given below are the numbers of identified bones, CSS, and MNI for each taxon in the V710/711 trash pit at Trudeau.

Species	Number of Bones	CSS	MNI	Remarks
Odocoileus	205	39.5	8	2 less than 14–17 months old (Lewall and Cowan 1963); 2 30–35 months; 4 adult
Bison	12	2.29	2	1 between 1–4 years; 1 older than 5 years
Ursus	43	9.3	2	adult
Aves	7	3.0	1(?)	
Gallus	19	10.6	3	
Tympanuchus	4	2.0	2	
Fulica	3	1.5	1	
Buteo	6	3.0	5	4 broad-winged; 1 red-shouldered
Lepisosteus	1 (+ scales)	0.03	1	
Pisces	14	0.14	2	
Turtle	12	3.56	2	1 medium; 1 large

SEASONALITY

Season of death for many species is determinable directly from annual layers in teeth. This information is of immediate importance in the study of settlement patterns and can be used to verify seasonality determinations based on species presence and proportions as well as cultural criteria (Spiess 1976). In many mammalian species, growth of tooth dentin and/or cementum continues for many years after the tooth has erupted (Klevezal and Kleinenberg 1969). Detection and reading of the deposition layers is most commonly accomplished by decalcifying the tooth in an acid solution, cutting 10–20-micron-thick sections of the tooth, staining in hematoxylin, mounting on a slide, and viewing under the microscope (Miller 1974). The method was used successfully by the author on *Odocoileus* teeth from the Trudeau V710/711 trash pit and has been used successfully on the genus several times before in non-archaeological contexts (Erickson *et al.* 1970; Gilbert 1966; Ransom 1966). Annual layers are known to occur in bear teeth, but attempts to section the ones from the Trudeau site failed due to poor preservation of the organic material.

With the decalcification and staining techniques, each annual layer generally appears under transmitted light as a wider light-staining band and narrower dark-staining band. In white-tailed deer of the Lower Mississippi Valley, the dark-staining band is probably laid down from January to March and the light-staining band from March through December.

Wildlife management workers are usually interested in using this information to obtain ages accurate to within a half year, and it has been so used on archaeological samples (Saxon and Higham 1969), but we can interpret the data a little further. Using stained thin sections from white-tailed deer, one reads the outermost layer of the cementum to determine season of death. If deposition of the dark-staining layer was in progress at the time of death, then the animal was killed sometime between December and March; the remaining months of the year are represented by light-staining band formation. Determination of the date of death depends on a subjective judgment of the thickness of the bands. If the band is very thin compared with previous bands, then death occurred within a few weeks or months after the end of deposition of the previous band. Since the exact band widths vary slightly from year to year and generally tend to decrease with age, mathematical precision in the estimation of band width is unwarranted and would lend false precision to the results. The best we can do is "read" a tooth to a month or two span during which death occurred, but that is a considerable improvement over less precise seasonality determinations.

Organic material in the bone sample was generally poorly preserved, but four deer teeth were successfully decalcified and their annual layers read. A right lower third molar from V711D, the bottom of the trash pit, showed five or more dark-staining winter lines. Age of the animal based on tooth wear was estimated at eight to ten years, and since the third molar (M_3) erupts during the second year in *Odocoileus* (Severinghaus 1949), the number of dark lines visible is roughly correct. The layer forming at the time of death was a very thin light-staining layer, the very beginnings of spring growth.

Unfortunately we do not know the exact dates of formation of the dark and light layers in *Odocoileus*, although the light-staining layer is definitely well formed by August (Klevezal and Kleinenberg 1969). In caribou (*Rangifer tarandus*), the dark-staining layer is deposited between the first of December and sometime in April, the months of scarce food (plant protein) and slow animal growth. By analogy, the dark layer should form in

Odocoileus during the period of poor food availability, after the fall mast harvest is depleted or becomes inaccessible due to snow accumulation (in northern states) and before the appearance of new, protein-rich plant shoots in the spring. In southeastern Missouri we would expect dark-line formation in late December, January, February, and March, based on the reported ecology (Smith 1974). In southeastern Missouri the average date of the first killing frost is 21 October, and the average date of the last killing frost is 1 April, followed by expected new plant growth. In the Trudeau area of Louisiana, the average first killing frost occurs about November fifth and the last killing frost about March eleventh (Baker 1936). Thus, we would expect dark-line formation coincident with lowered food supply in January, February, and early March at Trudeau, after the fall mast harvest is eaten and before the new spring growth appears. The first V711D tooth is therefore from a kill in early spring, i.e., March or April.

The second successfully sectioned tooth from V711D was a left M_3 from a three-to-five-year-old deer's mandible. A second dark line was the deposition layer forming at the time of death, indicating an age of about four years and a death occurring in January, February, or early March.

A right lower second molar from V710C, the middle of the trash pit, yielded a section showing three dark-staining layers. Since M_2 erupts between two and seven months in white-tailed deer (Severinghaus 1949), the animal was probably in its third winter when killed. The dark layer forming at the time of death indicates that the individual was killed in January, February, or early March.

The fourth tooth with readable layers is an upper left second molar (M_2) from a very young individual; it was found in V711B, the top of the trash pit. The section revealed that the first dark layer in the cementum had not yet formed, and since there are no other layers to compare, we have no idea of the relative width of the light band that was forming. Thus, this individual was killed sometime between birth in late May or early June, and December.

In sum, it is possible that the deer teeth were deposited approximately in the chronological order of the animals' deaths: late winter/early spring, followed by the final deposition sometime later in the year. This sequence would suggest that the active use of the pit could have been limited to but a few months.

INTERPRETATION

Consideration of the amount of food represented by the carefully determined complete-pit MNI is complicated by several factors. We do not know how much of each animal was consumed by the household(s) contributing to the trash pit and how much was consumed by other households (if any). We do not know how many individuals comprised the household(s) contributing to the pit, nor the length of time represented by the refuse in the pit, although we could make order-of-magnitude guesses. More complete excavation of the village should provide some answers to these questions.

Some relative idea of how much of the skeleton of each taxon found its way into the trash pit, on the average, can be obtained by dividing the total CSS for each taxon by the MNI. A higher ratio is taken to mean inclusion in the trash pit of more of each skeleton per individual animal killed. These values, of course, are comparable only for groups of animals with roughly equivalent bone architecture, such as large mammals. Of the three large mammal species, *Bison* has less skeletal completeness per identified individual represented (1.14, versus 4.65 for *Ursus* and 4.94 for *Odocoileus*). This pattern would be expected if bison were partially butchered away from the village but bear and deer were brought in more or less intact, and it is not surprising in view of the weights of the species involved. It is possible to speculate that the bison meat was dried in the field before it was returned to the village.

The amount of food represented by an animal depends to a great extent on the time of year the animal was killed. Total muscle weight of an adult mammal does not vary much, but there is a definite seasonal fat storage cycle in most north-temperate mammals, and in many birds and fish. An adult male caribou, for example, may contain forty pounds more fat at the pre-rut peak of his fat cycle than during the lean early spring. Also, fat cycles are dependent on sex as well as season in many artiodactyls.

Comparisons of average weights of different species are, at best, comparisons of the relative amounts of fresh meat that can be obtained from individuals of different species. The decision to use that meat to fulfill protein or calorie requirements is dependent on the human consumer. With these words of warning, then, let us total the live weight represented by the various taxa from the Trudeau trash pit total MNI count.

Ursus Euarctos americanus averages about 135 kg (300 lbs.) live weight (Walker 1968). The adult bison bones at Trudeau are not large and are consequently considered to be female. Adult female bison average about 500 kg (1,100 lbs.) (ibid.). Since half-year-old bison weigh about 140 kg (300 lbs.) (Frison 1974), the immature animal at Trudeau may be assigned a juvenile intermediate weight of 300 kg (650 lbs.). Eighty-five kilograms (185 lbs.) is as good an average as any for the adult deer at Trudeau (Smith 1974, p. 34), with 53 kg (115 lbs.) a reasonable figure for the long yearlings and 67 kg (150 lbs.) for the three-year-olds. One kilogram per bird, 1 kg for the small turtle, 3 kg for the large turtle, 0.5 kg for each small fish, and 7 kg for the gar (a moderate-size individual) are reasonable estimates. The following are the calculated live weight totals and percentages:

Bison bison	800 kg (1,760 lbs.)	47.8%
Odocoileus virgineanus	580 kg (1,275 lbs.)	34.7%
Ursus	275 kg (600 lbs.)	16.4%
Birds, turtles, fish	18 kg (40 lbs.)	1.1%
Total	1,673 kg (3,675 lbs.)	

"Importance" in a diet is a function of fat content and seasonal availability, as well as gross weight. We can say, however, that white-tailed deer and bison provided the bulk of the meat represented in the Trudeau trash pit bones; bears were probably relished for their fat and as a change in diet; and birds, turtles, and fish were insignificant. It is of great interest, however, to note that the turtles were sea turtles and had to be imported.

As has been stated above, a large portion of the bone refuse from the Trudeau trash pit consisted of flakes and pieces of large-mammal long bones, averaging roughly 4 × 8 cm. Many of these pieces were partially charred, although few were calcined. Thus, many of the identified bones are epiphyseal ends left after the shafts had been broken up. Some of the long bone ends and other bones also were charred. Thus, the long bones were obviously broken to extract their marrow, and many of the resulting pieces were thrown into a fire—which was not hot enough to calcine them, however. Very few of the bird bones (2 specimens) showed signs of charring. Any reconstruction of the culinary habits of the Tunica at Trudeau must include breaking mammal long bones for their marrow and discarding the pieces in the general direction of a small open fire. Bird bones were generally not thrown into the fire, for some reason.

After removal of bone marrow, long bones still contain substantial amounts of fat, generally called "bone grease" in the literature (Leechman 1951). Many sub-arctic and north-temperate interior peoples whose diets were short of fats pounded mammal long bones into small pieces (averaging 2 × 3 cm) and then boiled them to extract the bone grease. The complete absence of this technique at Trudeau is another example of relative affluence, indicating that there were plenty of calories (fat or carbohydrate) in the diet.

The surfaces of many of the bones in the trash pit were beginning to disintegrate slightly; consequently, a search for the fine cuts and scratches marking the details of field and culinary butchery was futile. Relatively gross butchery marks were found, however, and in all cases they appear as a relatively thin and deep excavation into the bone that could only be made by a thin blade able to withstand considerable impact force. The author believes that such marks are the result of metal blades (axe, pike, or sword-like instrument) and could not have been made with chipped or ground stone or bone tools.

Thus, in the Trudeau trash pit we have evidence of a generally affluent adaptation marked by a mixture of pre- and post-contact technology and subsistence patterns.

Bibliography

Ackerman, Robert E., and Lillian A. Ackerman
1974 "Ethnoarcheological Interpretations of Territoriality and Land Use in Southwestern Alaska," *Ethnohistory*, vol. 20, no. 4, pp. 315–334.

Adair, James
1775 *The History of the American Indians; Particularly those Nations adjoining to the Mississippi, East and West Florida, Georgia, South and North Carolina, and Virginia.* Edward and Charles Dilly, London.

Adams, William H.
1974 "An Ethnoarchaeological Study of a Rural American Community: Silcott, Washington, 1900–1930," *Ethnohistory*, vol. 20, no. 4, pp. 335–346.
1976 *Silcott, Washington: Ethnoarchaeology of a Rural American Community.* Reports of Investigations, no. 54, Laboratory of Anthropology, Washington State University, Pullman.
1979 "Historical Archaeology: Science and Humanism," *North American Archaeologist*, vol. 1, no. 1, pp. 85–96.

Alberts, Robert C.
1953 "Trade Silver and Indian Silver Work in the Great Lakes Region," *The Wisconsin Archeologist*, vol. 34, no. 1, pp. 1–121.

Albrecht, Andrew C.
1945 "The Origin and Early Settlement of Baton Rouge, Louisiana," *The Louisiana Historical Quarterly*, vol. 28, no. 1, pp. 5–68.

Allen, Joel A.
1876 *The American Bisons, Living and Extinct.* Museum of Comparative Zoology, Memoir, vol. 4, no. 10, Harvard University, Cambridge.

Alvord, Clarence W., and Clarence E. Carter, eds.
1915 *The Critical Period, 1763–1765.* Collections of the Illinois State Historical Library, vol. 10, British Series, vol. 1, Springfield.
1916 *The New Regime, 1765–1767.* Collections of the Illinois State Historical Library, vol. 11, British Series, vol. 2, Springfield.

Anonymous
[1698] Map of the Mississippi River from the Illinois to the Taensa. Archives Nationales, Paris.
[1699] Map of the Mississippi River from the Illinois to below the Red River. Séminaire de Québec, Québec.
[1700] Map of the Lower Mississippi River. Bibliothèque Nationale, Paris.
1721 Map of the Ouachita River. Archives Nationales, Paris.
n.d. Map of the Mississippi Valley. Bibliothèque Nationale, Paris.

Arena, C. Richard
1974 "Land Settlement Policies and Practices in Spanish Louisiana," in *The Spanish in the Mississippi Valley, 1762–1804*, J. F. McDermott, ed. University of Illinois Press, Urbana.

Ashe, Thomas
1808 *Travels in America, performed in 1806, for the purpose of exploring the rivers Alleghany, Monongahela, Ohio, and Mississippi.* William Sawyer and Co., London.

Atkinson, James R.
1979 "An Historic Contact Indian Settlement in Oktibbeha County, Mississippi," *Journal of Alabama Archaeology*, vol. 25, no. 1, pp. 61–82.
1986 "The Origins of the Chickasaw Indians as Evidenced by Cultural Remains in the Upper Tombigbee River Valley in Northeast Mississippi." Manuscript, Natchez Trace Parkway, Tupelo, Mississippi.

Atkinson, James R., and Crawford H. Blakeman, Jr.
1975 "Archaeological Site Survey in the Tallahala Reservoir Area, Jasper County, Mississippi: 1975." Report to the National Park Service; Mississippi State University, Starkville.

Axtell, James
1981 *The European and the Indian: Essays in the Ethnohistory of Colonial North America.* Oxford University Press, New York.

Baerreis, David A.
1961 "The Ethnohistoric Approach and Archaeology," *Ethnohistory*, vol. 8, no. 1, pp. 49–77.

Baillargeon, Noël
1965 "The Seminary of Quebec: Resources for the History of the French in the Mississippi Valley," in *The French in the Mississippi Valley*, J. F. McDermott, ed. University of Illinois Press, Urbana.

Baird, W. David
1980 *The Quapaw Indians: A History of the Downstream People.* University of Oklahoma Press, Norman.

Baker, O. E.
1936 *Atlas of American Agriculture.* U.S. Department of Agriculture, Washington, D.C.

Baker, William S., and Clarence H. Webb
1976   "Catahoula Type Projectile Points," *Louisiana Archaeology*, no. 3, pp. 225–251.

Bamforth, Douglas B., and Albert C. Spaulding
1982   "Human Behavior, Explanation, Archaeology, History, and Science," *Journal of Anthropological Archaeology*, vol. 1, pp. 179–195.

Bandelier, Adolf F., ed.
1922   *The Journey of Alvar Nuñez Cabeza de Vaca.* Allerton Book Co., New York.

Barnes, Mark R.
1980   "Mexican Lead-Glazed Earthenwares," in *Spanish Colonial Frontier Research*, H. F. Dobyns, ed. Spanish Borderlands Research, no. 1, Center for Anthropological Studies, Albuquerque.

Barnes, Mark R., and Ronald V. May
1972   *Mexican Majolica in Northern New Spain.* Pacific Coast Archaeological Society Occasional Papers, no. 2, Costa Mesa, California.

Barron, Bill
1975   *The Vaudreuil Papers.* Polyanthos, New Orleans.

Barth, Fredrik
1969   "Introduction," in *Ethnic Groups and Boundaries*, F. Barth, ed. Little, Brown and Co., Boston.

Barthellon, Abbé
1731   Manuscript MG 1, F-562, pièce 42. Dépôt des Fortifications des Colonies, Archives des Colonies, Paris.

Baudier, R.
1939   *The Catholic Church in Louisiana.* Privately printed, New Orleans.

Bauxar, J. Joseph
1957   "Yuchi Ethnoarchaeology," *Ethnohistory*, vol. 4, no. 3, pp. 279–301; no. 4, pp. 369–464.

Beals, Ralph
1962   "Acculturation," in *Anthropology Today*, S. Tax, ed. The University of Chicago Press, Chicago.

Beaudoin, Kenneth L.
1951   "A Preliminary Report of Findings Made by Memphis Archaeological and Geological Society, Affiliated with the Tennessee Archaeological Society in the Northwestern Sector of the Carson Plantation Located in Coahoma County, Mississippi Six Miles South of Friars Point near Stovall, Mississippi." Memphis Archaeological and Geological Society, Publication no. 2, Memphis. Mimeo.
1952   "The Carson Site," *Tennessee Archaeologist*, vol. 8, no. 1, pp. 10–14.

Bee, Robert L.
1974   *Patterns and Processes: An Introduction to Anthropological Strategies for the Study of Sociocultural Change.* The Free Press, New York.

Beers, Henry Putney
1957   *The French in North America: A Bibliographical Guide to French Archives, Reproductions, and Research Missions.* Louisiana State University Press, Baton Rouge.

Bell, Robert E.
1960   *Guide to the Identification of Certain American Indian Projectile Points.* Oklahoma Anthropological Society, Special Bulletin no. 2, Norman.

Bellin, Jacques Nicolas
1744   "Carte de la Louisiane, cours du Mississipi et pais voisins," in *Histoire et Description Générale de la Nouvelle France . . .*, vol. 2, P. F. X. de Charlevoix. Ganeau, Paris. (Map reissued separately in 1744, 1750, and 1757.)
1764   "Suite du Cours du Fleuve St. Louis dupuis la Rivière d'Iberville jusqua celle des Yasous, et les Parties de la Rivière Rouge et la Rivière Noire." Map Collection, Harvard College Library, Cambridge.

Belmont, John S.
1961   "The Peabody Excavations, Coahoma County, Mississippi, 1901–1902." B.A. thesis, Harvard University, Cambridge.
1967   "The Culture Sequence at the Greenhouse Site, Louisiana," *Southeastern Archaeological Conference Bulletin*, no. 6, pp. 27–34.
1978   Contribution to "Archaeological Phases in the Lower Mississippi Valley." Document of the Avery Island Conference, Lower Mississippi Survey, Peabody Museum, Harvard University, Cambridge.
1981   "A Reconnaissance of the Boeuf Basin, Louisiana." Paper presented at the Southeastern Archaeological Conference, Asheville, North Carolina.

Belmont, John S., and Stephen Williams
1965   "The Foundation of American Archaeology." Manuscript, Department of Anthropology, Harvard University, Cambridge.

Bergier, Louis-Marc
1702   Letter. Archives du Séminaire de Québec, Québec.

Berquin-Duvallon, Pierre-Louis
1803   *Vue de la Colonie Espagnole du Mississipi, ou des Provinces de Louisiane et Floride occidentale, en l'année 1802.* L'Imprimerie Expéditive, Paris.

Berry, Brewton, and Carl Chapman
1942   "An Oneota Site in Missouri," *American Antiquity*, vol. 7, no. 3, pp. 290–305.

Berry, Jane M.
1917 "The Indian Policy of Spain in the Southwest, 1783–1795," *Mississippi Valley Historical Review*, vol. 3, pp. 462–477.

Berry, John W.
1980 "Acculturation as Varieties of Adaptation," in *Acculturation: Theory, Models, and Some New Findings*, A. M. Padilla, ed. American Association for the Advancement of Science, Selected Symposium no. 39, Westview Press, Boulder, Colorado.

BIA   *See* Bureau of Indian Affairs.

Binford, Lewis R.
1976 "Foreword," in *Method and Theory in Historical Archeology*, S. South. Academic Press, New York.
1978 *Nunamuit Ethnoarchaeology*. Academic Press, New York.

Bishop, Charles A., and Arthur J. Ray
1976 "Ethnohistoric Research in the Central Subarctic: Some Conceptual and Methodological Problems," *The Western Canadian Journal of Anthropology*, vol. 6, no. 1, pp. 116–144.

Bishop, Charles A., and M. Estellie Smith
1975 "Early Historic Populations In Northwestern Ontario: Archaeological and Ethnohistorical Interpretations," *American Antiquity*, vol. 40, pp. 54–63.

Bizzell, David W.
1981 "A Report on the Quapaw: The Letters of Governor George Izard to the American Philosophical Society, 1825–1827," *Pulaski County Historical Review*, vol. 29, pp. 66–79.

Bjork, David K.
1926 "Documents Regarding Indian Affairs in the Lower Mississippi Valley, 1771–1772," *Mississippi Valley Historical Review*, vol. 13, no. 3, pp. 398–410.

Black, Glenn A.
1967 *Angel Site: An Archaeological, Historical, and Ethnological Study*. Indiana Historical Society, Indianapolis.

Blitz, John Howard
1985 *An Archaeological Study of the Mississippi Choctaw Indians*. Mississippi Department of Archives and History, Archaeological Report no. 16, Jackson.

Boessneck, J., J. P. Jequier, and H. R. Stampfli
1963 *Seeberg, Burgäschissee-Süd; die Tierreste*. Acta Bernensia, vol. 2, part 3, Verlag Stämpfli & Cie, Bern.

Bohannan, Paul
1967 "Introduction," in *Beyond the Frontier: Social Process and Cultural Change*, P. Bohannan and F. Plog, eds. The Natural History Press, Garden City, New York.

Boimare, A.-L., ed.
1831 *Journal Historique de l'Etablissement des Français a la Louisiane*. Hector Bossange, Paris.

Bonne, M.
1788 "L'Ancien et le nouveau Méxique, avec la Floride et la basse Louisiane." Map Library, School of Geoscience, Louisiana State University, Baton Rouge.

Bossu, Jean-Bernard
1768 *Nouveaux Voyages aux Indes occidentales*. Le Jay, Paris.
1777 *Nouveaux Voyages dans l'Amérique Septentrionale*. Changuion, Amsterdam.

Boston, Barbara
1941 "The 'De Soto Map'," *Mid-America*, vol. 23, pp. 236–250.

Bourne, Edward G., ed.
1904 *Narratives of the Career of Hernando De Soto*. 2 vols. Trail Maker's Series, New York.

Bowen, Emanuel
1748 "A New Map of Georgia, with Part of Carolina, Florida and Louisiana." Map Collection, Harvard College Library, Cambridge.

Brackenridge, H. M.
1814 *Views of Louisiana; together with a Journal of a Voyage up the Missouri River in 1811*. Cramer, Spear and Eichbaum, Pittsburgh.

Bradbury, John
1904 "Travels in the Interior of America, in the Years 1809, 1810, and 1811," in *Early Western Travels, 1748–1846*, vol. 5, R. G. Thwaites, ed. A. M. Clark Co., Cleveland.

Brain, Jeffrey P.
1969 "Winterville: A Case Study of Prehistoric Culture Contact in the Lower Mississippi Valley." Ph.D. dissertation, Yale University, New Haven.
1970 *The Tunica Treasure*. Lower Mississippi Survey, Bulletin no. 2, Peabody Museum, Harvard University, Cambridge.
1971 "The Lower Mississippi Valley in North American Prehistory." Report to the National Park Service, Tallahassee; Manuscript, Arkansas Archeological Survey, Fayetteville.
1973 *Trudeau: An 18th Century Tunica Village*. Lower Mississippi Survey, Bulletin no. 3, Peabody Museum, Harvard University, Cambridge.
1974 "Cultural Dynamics in the Lower Mississippi Valley, A.D. 1000–1700: A Case Study of Missis-

sippian Impact on the Southern Periphery." Paper presented at the Advanced Seminar "Reviewing Mississippian Development," School of American Research, Santa Fe.

1975a   "Artifacts of the Adelantado," *The Conference on Historic Site Archaeology Papers*, vol. 8, pp. 129–138.

1975b   "The Archaeology of the Tunica (continued): Trial on the Yazoo." Report submitted to the National Geographic Society.

1976   "From the Words of the Living: The Indian Speaks," in *Clues to America's Past*, National Geographic Society Special Publication, Washington, D.C.

1977   *On the Tunica Trail*. Louisiana Archaeological Survey and Antiquities Commission, Anthropological Study no. 1, Department of Culture, Recreation and Tourism, Baton Rouge.

1978a   "Late Prehistoric Settlement Patterning in the Yazoo Basin and Natchez Bluffs Regions of the Lower Mississippi Valley," in *Mississippian Settlement Patterns*, B. Smith, ed. Academic Press, New York.

1978b   "The Archaeological Phase: Ethnographic Fact or Fancy?" in *Archaeological Essays in Honor of Irving B. Rouse*, R. C. Dunnell and E. S. Hall, eds. Mouton Publishers, The Hague.

1979   *Tunica Treasure*. Papers of the Peabody Museum, Harvard University, vol. 71. Published jointly by the Peabody Museum, Harvard University, Cambridge, and the Peabody Museum of Salem, Salem, Massachusetts.

1980   "Archaeological and Electronic Survey of the Trudeau Site." Final Report to the Louisiana Office of State Parks, Baton Rouge.

1981   "Tunica Archaeology," *Geoscience and Man*, vol. 22, pp. 43–50.

1982   "La Salle at the Natchez: An Archaeological and Historical Perspective," in *La Salle and His Legacy: Frenchmen and Indians in the Lower Mississippi Valley*, P. K. Galloway, ed. University Press of Mississippi, Jackson.

1983a   "Tunica Triumph," *Geoscience and Man*, vol. 23, pp. 45–51.

1983b   "The Archaeology of the Tunica: Trial on the Yazoo and Tunica Treasure II Projects," *National Geographic Society Research Reports*, no. 15, National Geographic Society, Washington, D.C.

1984   "The De Soto Entrada into the Lower Mississippi Valley," *Mississippi Archaeology*, vol. 19, no. 2, pp. 48–58.

1985   "Introduction: Update of De Soto Studies since the United States De Soto Expedition Commission Report," in *Final Report of the United States De Soto Expedition Commission*. Facsimile reprint of 1939 ed. Classics in Anthropology Series, Smithsonian Institution Press, Washington, D.C.

n.d.   *Winterville*. Mississippi Department of Archives and History, Archaeological Report no. 23, Jackson. Forthcoming.

Brain, Jeffrey P., and Ian W. Brown, eds.
1982   *Robert S. Neitzel: The Great Sun*. Lower Mississippi Survey, Bulletin no. 9, Peabody Museum, Harvard University, Cambridge.

Brain, Jeffrey P., Ian W. Brown, and Vincas P. Steponaitis
n.d.   "Archaeology of the Natchez Bluffs." Manuscript, Lower Mississippi Survey, Peabody Museum, Harvard University, Cambridge. Forthcoming.

Brain, Jeffrey P., Alan Toth, and Antonio Rodriguez-Buckingham
1974   "Ethnohistoric Archaeology and the De Soto Entrada into the Lower Mississippi Valley," *The Conference on Historic Site Archaeology Papers*, vol. 7, pp. 232–289.

Brasseaux, Carl A., ed. and trans.
1979   *A Comparative View of French Louisiana, 1699 and 1762: The Journals of Pierre Le Moyne d'Iberville and Jean-Jacques-Blaise d'Abbadie*. Center for Louisiana Studies, History Series, no. 13, University of Southwestern Louisiana, Lafayette.

Bridges, Katherine, and Jean Delanglez
1964   "The Journal of Pierre Vitry, S.J. (1738–1740)," *Louisiana Studies*, vol. 3, no. 3, pp. 247–309.

British West Florida Records
1775   Tunica Land Grant to John Thomas. British West Florida Records, 1763–1781, Great Britain Public Record Office, London.

Brose, David S.
1971   "The Direct Historic Approach to Michigan Archaeology," *Ethnohistory*, vol. 18, no. 1, pp. 51–61.

Brose, David S., Ned J. Jenkins, and Russel Weisman
1982   "Cultural Resources Reconnaissance Study of the Black Warrior–Tombigbee System Corridor, Alabama." Draft Report, Department of Geography and Geology, University of South Alabama, Mobile.

Broutin, Ignace François
1731   "Carte Particuliere du Cours du Fleuve Mississipi ou St. Louis a la Louisiane, depuis la Nouvelle Orleans jusqu'aux Natchez." Bibliothèque Nationale, Paris.

Broutin, Ignace François, Bernard de Vergés, and François Saucier
1740   "Carte Particuliere dune partie de la Louisianne." Bibliothèque Nationale, Paris.

Brown, Calvin S.
1926   *Archeology of Mississippi*. Mississippi Geological Survey, University, Mississippi.

Brown, Ian W.
1975   "Archaeological Investigations at the Historic
       Portland and St. Pierre Sites in the Lower Yazoo
       Basin, Mississippi, 1974." M.A. thesis, Brown
       University, Providence.
1976   "The Portland Site (22-M-12), an Early Eigh-
       teenth Century Historic Indian Site in Warren
       County, Mississippi," *Mississippi Archaeology*,
       vol. 11, no. 1, pp. 2–11.
1978a "An Archaeological Survey of Mississippi Period
       Sites in Coahoma County, Mississippi." Manu-
       script, Lower Mississippi Survey, Peabody Mu-
       seum, Harvard University, Cambridge.
1978b "An Archaeological Survey of the Tchula–Green-
       wood Bluffs Region, Mississippi." Manuscript,
       Lower Mississippi Survey, Peabody Museum,
       Harvard University, Cambridge.
1979a "Early 18th Century French-Indian Culture Con-
       tact in the Lower Mississippi Valley, as Revealed
       in the Study of Historic Archaeological Trade
       Materials." Ph.D. dissertation, Brown University,
       Providence.
1979b "Bells," in *Tunica Treasure*, J. P. Brain. Papers of
       the Peabody Museum, Harvard University, vol.
       71, Cambridge.
1979c "Historic Artifacts and Sociocultural Change:
       Some Warnings from the Lower Mississippi Val-
       ley," *The Conference on Historic Site Archaeol-
       ogy Papers*, vol. 13, pp. 109–121.
1979d "Functional Group Changes and Acculturation:
       A Case Study of the French and the Indian in the
       Lower Mississippi Valley," *Midcontinental Jour-
       nal of Archaeology*, vol. 4, no. 2, pp. 147–165.
1980   "Trade Bells," in *Burr's Hill, A 17th Century
       Wampanoag Burial Ground in Warren, Rhode Is-
       land*, S. G. Gibson, ed. The Haffenreffer Museum
       of Anthropology, Studies in Anthropology and
       Material Culture, vol. 2, Brown University, Prov-
       idence.
1982   "An Archaeological Study of Culture Contact
       and Change in the Natchez Bluffs Region," in *La
       Salle and His Legacy: Frenchmen and Indians in
       the Lower Mississippi Valley*, P. K. Galloway, ed.
       University Press of Mississippi, Jackson.
1983   "The O'Quinn Site: A Photohistoric/Historic In-
       dian Cemetery in the Natchez Bluffs Region,
       Mississippi." Manuscript, Lower Mississippi Sur-
       vey, Peabody Museum, Harvard University, Cam-
       bridge.
1984   "Natchez Indian Archaeology: Culture Change
       and Stability in the Lower Mississippi Valley."
       Manuscript, Lower Mississippi Survey, Peabody
       Museum, Harvard University, Cambridge.
1985   *Natchez Indian Archaeology: Culture Change
       and Stability in the Lower Mississippi Valley*.
       Mississippi Department of Archives and History,
       Archaeological Report no. 15, Jackson.

Brown, James A.
1977   "Current Directions in Midwestern Archaeol-
       ogy," *Annual Review of Anthropology*, vol. 6,
       pp. 161–179.

Brown, Margaret K.
1972   "Native Made Glass Pendants from East of the
       Mississippi," *American Antiquity*, vol. 37, no. 3,
       pp. 432–439.

Brown, Marley
1974   "The Use of Oral and Documentary Sources in
       Historical Archaeology: Ethnohistory at the Mott
       Farm," *Ethnohistory*, vol. 20, no. 4, pp. 347–360.

Buache, Philippe
1724   "Carte Reduite des Isles de l'Amerique et du
       Golfe du Mexique." Archives Nationales, Paris.

Bureau of Indian Affairs (BIA)
1980   "Documentation for Federal Acknowledgement
       of the Tunica-Biloxi Tribe of Louisiana: Memo-
       randum of December 4, 1980 and four previously
       prepared Technical Reports on the Anthropologi-
       cal (AR), Genealogical (GR), Historical (HR), and
       Demographic (DR) evidence." U.S. Department
       of the Interior, Washington, D.C.

Burke, R. P.
1936   "Origin of Certain Pottery Designs Attributed to
       the Muskogean Sites in Central Alabama," *Ar-
       row Points*, Alabama Anthropological Society,
       vol. 21, nos. 1–2, pp. 4–20.

Bushnell, David I., Jr.
1919   *Native Villages and Village Sites East of the Mis-
       sissippi*. Bureau of American Ethnology, Bulletin
       no. 69, Washington, D.C.
1920   *Native Cemeteries and Forms of Burial East of
       the Mississippi*. Bureau of American Ethnology,
       Bulletin no. 71, Washington, D.C.
1927   "Drawings by A. DeBatz in Louisiana, 1732–
       1735," *Smithsonian Miscellaneous Collections*,
       vol. 80, no. 5, pp. 1–15.

Butler, Louise
1924   "West Feliciana—A Glimpse of its History,"
       Louisiana Historical Quarterly, vol. 7, no. 1,
       pp. 90–120.

Butler, Madeleine L., producer
1978   *On the Tunica Trail*. WYES-TV, New Orleans.
       Documentary film.

Butler, Ruth Lapham, trans.
1934   *Journal of Paul du Ru*. The Caxton Club, Chicago.

Cain, Joan, Virginia Koenig, eds., and Glenn R. Conrad,
trans.
1971   *The Historical Journal of the Establishment of
       the French in Louisiana*. Center for Louisiana
       Studies, History Series, no. 3, University of
       Southwestern Louisiana, Lafayette.

Carmack, Robert M.
1972   "Ethnohistory: A Review of its Development,
       Definitions, Methods, and Aims," *Annual Re-
       view of Anthropology*, vol. 1, pp. 227–246.

Carmack, Robert M., and John M. Weeks
1981   "The Archaeology and Ethnohistory of Utatlan: A Conjunctive Approach," *American Antiquity*, vol. 46, no. 2, pp. 323–341.

Carpenter, W. M.
1847   "The Mississippi River in the Olden Time: A Genuine Account of the Present State of the River Mississippi and of the Land on Its Banks to the River Yasous, 1776," *De Bow's Review*, vol. 3.

Caruso, John Anthony
1966   *The Mississippi Valley Frontier: The Age of French Exploration and Settlement.* The Bobbs-Merrill Co., Indianapolis.

Caughey, John Walton
1934   *Bernardo de Gálvez in Louisiana, 1776–1783.* Publications of the University of California at Los Angeles in Social Science, vol. 4, University of California Press, Berkeley and Los Angeles.

Chaffers, William
1968   *Collector's Handbook of Marks and Monograms on Pottery and Porcelain.* William Reeves, London.

Chambers, M. E.
1900   Report to the Society. *Louisiana Historical Society Publication*, vol. 2, part 3, p. 34.

Chance, Norman A.
1960   "Culture Change and Integration: An Eskimo Example," *American Anthropologist*, vol. 62, no. 3, pp. 1,028–1,044.

Chang, K. C.
1967   *Rethinking Archaeology.* Random House, New York.
1978   "Some Theoretical Issues in the Archaeological Study of Historical Reality," in *Archaeological Essays in Honor of Irving B. Rouse*, R. C. Dunnell and E. S. Hall, eds. Mouton Publishers, The Hague.

Chapman, Carl H.
1959   *The Little Osage and Missouri Indian Village Sites, ca. 1727–1777 A.D.* The Missouri Archaeologist, vol. 21, no. 1, Columbia.

Chapman, Carl H., and Leo O. Anderson
1955   *The Campbell Site: A Late Mississippi Town Site and Cemetery in Southeast Missouri.* The Missouri Archaeologist, vol. 17, nos. 2–3, Columbia.

Chapple, Eliot D.
1977   "Biocultural Adaptation in Prehistoric America: An Anthropological Biologist's Perspective," in *Biocultural Adaptation in Prehistoric America*, R. L. Blakely, ed. The University of Georgia Press, Athens.

Charlevoix, P. F. X. de
1744   *Histoire et Description générale de la Nouvelle France avec le Journal Historique d'un Voyage fait par ordre du Roi dans l'Amérique Septentrionnale.* 3 vols. Ganeau, Paris.

Charrier, Leonard J.
1984   Deposition of 10 July. 20th Judicial District Court, West Feliciana Parish, St. Francisville, Louisiana.

Chartrand, René
1973   "The Troops of French Louisiana, 1699–1769," *Military Collector and Historian*, vol. 25, no. 2, pp. 58–73.

Chatelain, Henri A.
1719a   "Carte de la Nouvelle France." Map Library, School of Geoscience, Louisiana State University, Baton Rouge.
1719b   "Carte contenant le Royaume du Mexique et la Floride." Map Library, School of Geoscience, Louisiana State University, Baton Rouge.

Claiborne, J. F. H.
1880   *Mississippi, as a Province, Territory and State.* Power and Barksdale, Jackson, Mississippi.

Clausen, Carl
1932   Field Report. Museum of Anthropology, University of Michigan, Ann Arbor.

Cleland, Charles E., ed.
1971   *An Historic Burial Locality in Mackinac County, Michigan.* Publication of the Museum, Michigan State University, Anthropological Series, vol. 1, no. 1, East Lansing.

Coe, Michael D.
1978   "The Churches on the Green: A Cautionary Tale," in *Archaeological Essays in Honor of Irving B. Rouse*, R. C. Dunnell and E. S. Hall, eds. Mouton Publishers, The Hague.

Cohen, Morris Raphael
1953   *Reason and Nature: An Essay on the Meaning of Scientific Method.* Rev. ed. The Free Press, Glencoe, Illinois.

Collins, Henry B., Jr.
1927a   "Archaeological and Anthropometrical Work in Mississippi," *Smithsonian Miscellaneous Collections*, vol. 78, no. 1, pp. 89–95.
1927b   "Archaeological Work in Louisiana and Mississippi," *Smithsonian Miscellaneous Collections*, vol. 78, no. 7, pp. 200–207.
1927c   "Potsherds from Choctaw Village Sites in Mississippi," *Washington Academy of Sciences Journal*, vol. 17, no. 10, pp. 259–263.
1932a   "Excavations at a Prehistoric Indian Village Site in Mississippi," *Smithsonian Institution, United States National Museum, Proceedings*, vol. 79, pp. 1–22.

1932b "Archaeology of Mississippi," *Conference on Southern Pre-History*. National Research Council, Washington, D.C.

Connaway, John M.
1981 *Archaeological Investigations in Mississippi, 1969–1977*. Mississippi Department of Archives and History, Archaeological Report no. 6, Jackson.
1984 *The Wilsford Site (22-Co-516), Coahoma County, Mississippi: A Late Mississippi Period Settlement in the Northern Yazoo Basin of Mississippi*. Mississippi Department of Archives and History, Archaeological Report no. 14, Jackson.
1985 "Recent Radiocarbon Date Announcement," *Mississippi Archaeological Association Newsletter*, vol. 20, no. NL-1, p. 2.

Conrad, Geoffrey W., and Arthur A. Demarest
1984 *Religion and Empire: The Dynamics of Aztec and Inca Expansionism*. Cambridge University Press, Cambridge.

Coronelli, Marco Vincenzo
1688a "America Settentrionale." Newberry Library, Chicago.
1688b "Carta Geografica dell America Settentrionale." Map Library, School of Geoscience, Louisiana State University, Baton Rouge.

Cox, Isaac J., ed.
1922 *The Journeys of René Robert Cavelier, Sieur de LaSalle*. 2 vols. Allerton Book Co., New York.

Coxe, Daniel
1722 *A Description of the English Province of Carolana, by the Spaniards call'd Florida, and by the French La Louisiane*. B. Cowse, London.

Craig, Alan K., and Christopher S. Peebles
1974 "Ethnoecologic Change among the Seminoles, 1740–1840," *Geoscience and Man*, vol. 5, pp. 83–96.

Crane, Verner W.
1956 *The Southern Frontier, 1670–1732*. University of Michigan Press, Ann Arbor.

Crenay, Baron de, Sieur de Poilvilain
1733 "Carte de partie de la Louisianne." Archives Nationales, Paris.

Cuisenier, Jean
1971 "Perspectives pour une utilisation d'un système d'information automatique au Musée des arts et traditions populaires, Paris," *Museum*, vol. 23, no. 1, pp. 27–36.

Cumming, William P.
1958 *The Southeast in Early Maps*. Princeton University Press, Princeton.
1966 "Mapping of the Southeast: The First Two Centuries," *The Southeastern Geographer*, vol. 6, pp. 3–19.

Cushman, H. B.
1899 *History of the Choctaw, Chickasaw and Natchez Indians*. Headlight Printing House, Greenville, Texas.

D'Anville, Jean-Baptiste
1732 "Carte de la Louisiane." Map Collection, Harvard College Library, Cambridge.

Darby, William
1818 *The Emigrant's Guide to the Western and Southwestern States and Territories*. Kirk and Mercein, New York.

Dark, Philip
1957 "Methods of Synthesis in Ethnohistory," *Ethnohistory*, vol. 4, no. 3, pp. 231–278.

Davenport Academy of Science
1885 Accession Catalog. Putnam Museum, Davenport, Iowa.

Davis, Hester A.
1966 *An Introduction to Parkin Prehistory*. The Arkansas Archeologist, vol. 7, nos. 1–2, Fayetteville.

Davis, John, trans.
1806 *Travels in Louisiana and the Floridas in the Year 1802*. I. Riley and Co., New York. Translation of Berquin-Duvallon 1803.

DeBatz, Alexandre
[1732] Map of the Mississippi River from Natchez to the Gulf. Bibliothèque Nationale, Paris.
1747 "Carte General de toute la Côte de la Louisiane jusqu'a la Baye St. Bernard." Map Division, Library of Congress, Washington, D.C.

de Beauvilliers
1720 "Carte Nouvelle de la Partie de l'ouest de la Province de la Louisiane." Bibliothèque Nationale, Paris.

Deetz, James F.
1971 "Late Man in North America: Archaeology of European Americans," in *Man's Imprint from the Past: Readings in the Methods of Archaeology*, J. Deetz, ed. Little, Brown and Co., Boston.
1974 "A Cognitive Historical Model for American Material Culture: 1620–1835," in *Reconstructing Complex Societies*, C. Moore, ed. American Schools of Oriental Research, Bulletin Supplement no. 20, Cambridge, Massachusetts.
1977 *In Small Things Forgotten: The Archeology of Early American Life*. Anchor Press, Garden City, New York.
1983 "Scientific Humanism and Humanistic Science: A Plea for Paradigmatic Pluralism in Historical Archaeology," *Geoscience and Man*, vol. 23, pp. 27–34.

de Fer, Nicolas
1701   "Les costes aux environs de la riviere de Misi-
        sipi." Bibliothèque Nationale, Paris.

Delanglez, Jean
1935   *The French Jesuits in Lower Louisiana (1700–*
        1763). Loyola University, New Orleans.
1939   "Documents: Tonti Letters," *Mid-America*, vol.
        21, no. 3, pp. 209–238.
1943   "The Sources of the Delisle Map of America,
        1703," *Mid-America*, vol. 25, no. 4, pp. 275–298.
1945   *El Rio del Espíritu Santo: An Essay on the Car-*
        tography of the Gulf Coast and the Adjacent
        Territory during the Sixteenth and Seventeenth
        Centuries. U.S. Catholic Historical Society, Mono-
        graph Series, no. 21, New York.
n.d.   "Cartography of the Mississippi Valley, 1673–
        1703." Institute of Jesuit History Publications,
        Loyola University, Chicago.

De la Peña y Camara, Jose, Ernest J. Burrus, Charles E.
O'Neill, and Maria Teresa Garcia Fernandez
1968   *Catalogo de Documentos del Archivo General de*
        Indias (Seccion V, Gobierno. Audiencia de Santo
        Domingo) sobre la Epoca Española de Luisiana.
        2 vols. Dirección General de Archivos y Bibliote-
        cas, Madrid; Loyola University, New Orleans.

Delcourt, Hazel R., and Paul A. Delcourt
1974   "Primeval Magnolia-Holly-Beech Climax in Loui-
        siana," *Ecology*, vol. 55, pp. 638–644.
1975   "The Blufflands: Pleistocene Pathway into the
        Tunica Hills," *The American Midland Natural-*
        ist, vol. 94, no. 2, pp. 385–400.

Delcourt, Paul A., and Hazel R. Delcourt
1977   "The Tunica Hills, Louisiana-Mississippi: Late
        Glacial Locality for Spruce and Deciduous Forest
        Species," *Quaternary Research*, vol. 7, pp. 218–
        237.

Delisle, Guillaume
1701   "Carte des Environs du Missisipi." Bibliothèque
        Nationale, Paris.
1702   "Carte de la Riviere de Mississipi." Bibliothèque
        Nationale, Paris.
1703   "Carte du Mexique et de la Floride." Yale Uni-
        versity Library, New Haven.
1718   "Carte de la Louisiane et du Cours du Missis-
        sipi." Yale University Library, New Haven.

de Louvigny, Louis de la Porte
1697   "Carte du Fleuve Missisipi." Division of Maps,
        Library of Congress, Washington, D.C.

Demandeville, Antoine Philippe
1763   "Carte composée des differents ouvrages de Mrs.
        les Ingenieurs qui ont été a la Louisianne," Bib-
        liothèque Nationale, Paris.

de Rémonville, Antoine Alexandre
1715   Manuscript MG 1, F-562, pièce 27. Dépôt des
        Fortifications des Colonies, Archives des Colo-
        nies, Paris.

Des Barres, J. F. W.
1779   "Mississippi River from Iberville to Yazous."
        Map Collection, Harvard College Library, Cam-
        bridge.

DeVille, Winston
1974   *First Settlers of Pointe Coupée*. Polyanthros,
        New Orleans.

de Villiers, Marc
1907   "Rapport du chevalier de Kerlérec, gouverneur de
        la Louisiane française sur les peuplades des val-
        lées du Mississipi et du Missouri (1758),"
        Congrès International des Américanistes, XVe
        session, Québec, pp 61–86.
1919   "L'établissement de la Province de Loüisiane,
        Poème inédit de Dumont de Montigny," *Journal*
        de la Société des Américanistes de Paris, vol. 11,
        pp. 35–56.
1921   "Note sur deux Cartes dessinées par les Chika-
        chas en 1737," *Journal de la Société des Améri-*
        canistes de Paris, vol. 13, pp. 7–9.
1922   "Documents concernant l'histoire des indiens de
        la région orientale de la Louisiane," *Journal de la*
        Société des Américanistes de Paris, vol. 14,
        pp. 127–140.
1931   "L'établissement de la Province de la Louisiane,
        Poème composé de 1728 à 1742 par Dumont de
        Montigny," *Journal de la Société des Américan-*
        istes de Paris, vol. 23, pp. 273–440.

Devin
1721   "Carte de la Coste de la Louisiane." Newberry
        Library, Chicago.
1732   Detail of coastal map of Louisiana. Map Library,
        School of Geoscience, Louisiana State University,
        Baton Rouge.

De Vorsey, Louis, Jr.
1971   "Early Maps as a Source in the Reconstruction of
        Southern Indian Landscapes," in *Red, White, and*
        Black: Symposium on Indians in the Old South,
        C. M. Hudson, ed. Southern Anthropological So-
        ciety, Proceedings, no. 5, University of Georgia
        Press, Athens.
1982   "The Impact of the La Salle Expedition of 1682
        on European Cartography," in *La Salle and his*
        Legacy: Frenchmen and Indians in the Lower
        Mississippi Valley, P. K. Galloway, ed. Univer-
        sity Press of Mississippi, Jackson.

Dickinson, Samuel D.
1977   "Landmark of the Koroa," *Louisiana Folklife*,
        vol. 2, no. 2, pp. 1–3.
1980   "Historic Tribes of the Ouachita Drainage Sys-
        tem in Arkansas," *The Arkansas Archeologist*,
        vol. 21, pp. 1–11.
1984   "Lake Mitchegamas and the St. Francis," *The Ar-*
        kansas Historical Quarterly, vol. 43, pp. 197–207.

Dickinson, Samuel D., ed. and trans.
1982   *New Travels in North America by Jean-Bernard*
        Bossu, 1770–1771. Northwestern State Univer-
        sity Press, Natchitoches, Louisiana.

Dickinson, Samuel D., and S. C. Dellinger
1940 "A Survey of the Historic Earthenware of the Lower Arkansas Valley," *Texas Archeological and Paleontological Society*, vol. 12, pp. 76–97.

Diron d'Artaguiette, Bernard
1732 "Fleuve St. Louis cy devant Mississipy." Bibliothèque Nationale, Paris.
1916 "Journal of Diron D'Artaguiette, 1722–1723," in *Travels in the American Colonies*, N. D. Mereness, ed. The MacMillan Co., New York.

Dixon, Roland B.
1913 "Some Aspects of North American Archeology," *American Anthropologist*, vol. 15, no. 4, pp. 549–566.

Dobyns, Henry F.
1972 "Ethnohistory and Contemporary United States Social Problems," *Ethnohistory*, vol. 19, no. 1, pp. 1–12.
1983 *Their Number Become Thinned: Native American Population Dynamics in Eastern North America.* The University of Tennessee Press, Knoxville.

Donnan, Christopher B., and C. William Clewlow, Jr., eds.
1974 *Ethnoarchaeology.* University of California Institute of Archaeology, Monograph no. 4, Los Angeles.

Dorsey, James O., and John R. Swanton
1912 *A Dictionary of the Biloxi and Ofo Languages.* Bureau of American Ethnology, Bulletin no. 47, Washington, D.C.

Dorson, Richard M.
1961 "Ethnohistory and Ethnic Folklore," *Ethnohistory*, vol. 8, no. 1, pp. 12–30.

Downs, Ernest C.
1979 "The Struggle of the Louisiana Tunica Indians for Recognition," in *Southeastern Indians Since the Removal Era*, W. L. Williams, ed. The University of Georgia Press, Athens.

Drucker, Philip
1958 *The Native Brotherhoods: Modern Intertribal Organizations on the Northwest Coast.* Bureau of American Ethnology, Bulletin no. 168, Washington, D.C.

Dumont de Montigny, François
1753 *Mémoires Historiques sur la Louisiane.* 2 vols. J. B. Bauche, Paris.

Dunn, Mary Eubanks
1983 "Coquille Flora (Louisiana): An Ethnobotanical Reconstruction." *Economic Botany*, vol. 37, no. 3, pp. 349–359.

Dunnell, Robert C.
1979 "Trends in Current Americanist Archaeology," *American Journal of Archaeology*, vol. 83, no. 4, pp. 437–449.

Durnford, Elias
1770 "Plan of the River Mississippi from the Indian Village of the Tonicas to the River Ibberville shewing the lands surveyed thereon as also the Rivers Ibberville, Amit and Comit with the Situation of the New Town proposed at the Ibberville." Map Collection, Mississippi Department of Archives and History, Jackson.

Dymond, D. P.
1974 *Archaeology and History: A Plea for Reconciliation.* Thames and Hudson, London.

Eames, Warren B.
1950 Field Notes. Lower Mississippi Survey, Peabody Museum, Harvard University, Cambridge.

Eccles, W. J.
1972 *France in America.* Harper and Row, New York.

Eggan, Fred R.
1952 "The Ethnological Cultures and their Archeological Backgrounds," in *Archeology of the Eastern United States*, J. B. Griffin, ed. The University of Chicago Press, Chicago.

Eiseley, Loren
1973 *The Man Who Saw Through Time.* Charles Scribner's Sons, New York.

Ellicott, Andrew
1962 *The Journal of Andrew Ellicott.* Quadrangle Books, Chicago.

Erickson, James A., Allen E. Anderson, Dean E. Medin, and David C. Bowden
1970 "Estimating Ages of Mule Deer—an Evaluation of Technique Accuracy," *Journal of Wildlife Management*, vol. 34, pp. 523–531.

Essenpreis, Patricia Sue
1982 "The Anderson Village Site: Redefining the Anderson Phase of the Fort Ancient Tradition of the Middle Ohio Valley." Ph.D. dissertation, Harvard University, Cambridge.

Euler, Robert C.
1972 "Ethnohistory in the United States," *Ethnohistory*, vol. 19, no. 3, pp. 201–207.

Ewers, John C.
1974 "Symbols of Chiefly Authority in Spanish Louisiana," in *The Spanish in the Mississippi Valley, 1762–1804*, J. F. McDermott, ed. University of Illinois Press, Urbana.

Ezell, Paul H.
1961 *The Hispanic Acculturation of the Gila River Pimas.* American Anthropological Association, Memoir no. 90, Menasha, Wisconsin.

Faye, Stanley
1942 "The Forked River," *Louisiana Historical Quarterly*, vol. 25, no. 4, pp. 921–942.

Feiler, Seymour, ed. and trans.
1962   *Jean-Bernard Bossu's Travels in the Interior of North America, 1751–1762.* University of Oklahoma Press, Norman.

Fenton, William N.
1966   "Field Work, Museum Studies, and Ethnohistorical Research," *Ethnohistory*, vol. 13, nos. 1–2, pp. 71–85.

Fewkes, Jesse W.
1900   "Tusayan Migration Traditions," *Nineteenth Annual Report of the Bureau of American Ethnology*, pp. 577–633.

Fisk, Harold N.
1944   *Geological Investigation of the Alluvial Valley of the Lower Mississippi River.* War Department, U.S. Army Corps of Engineers, Mississippi River Commission, Publication no. 52, Vicksburg, Mississippi.

Fitting, James E.
1977   "The Structure of Historical Archaeology and the Importance of Material Things," in *Historical Archaeology and the Importance of Material Things*, L. Ferguson, ed. The Society for Historical Archaeology, Special Publication Series, no. 2, Washington, D.C.

Fitzhugh, William W., ed.
1985   *Cultures in Contact: The European Impact on Native Cultural Institutions in Eastern North America, A.D. 1000–1800.* Smithsonian Institution Press, Washington, D.C.

Flannery, Kent V.
1973   "Archeology with a Capital 'S'," in *Research and Theory in Current Archeology*, C. L. Redman, ed. John Wiley, New York.

Fontana, Bernard L.
1965   "On the Meaning of Historic Sites Archaeology," *American Antiquity*, vol. 31, no. 1, pp. 61–65.

Ford, James A.
1929   Field Notes. Mississippi Department of Archives and History, Jackson.
1934   Field Notes. Museum of Geoscience, Louisiana State University, Baton Rouge.
1936   *Analysis of Indian Village Site Collections from Louisiana and Mississippi.* Department of Conservation, Louisiana Geological Survey, Anthropological Study, no. 2, New Orleans.
1939   Site Index. Louisiana Archaeological Survey, Louisiana State University, Baton Rouge.
1961   *Menard Site: The Quapaw Village of Osotouy on the Arkansas River.* The American Museum of Natural History, Anthropological Papers, vol. 48, part 2, New York.

Ford, Richard I.
1973   "Archeology Serving Humanity," in *Research and Theory in Current Archeology*, C. L. Redman, ed. John Wiley, New York.

Fortier, Alcée
1972   *A History of Louisiana*, vol. 2, *The Spanish Domination and the Cession to the United States.* 2nd ed. J. A. Carrington, ed. Claitor's Publishing Division, Baton Rouge.

Foster, George M.
1960   *Culture and Conquest: America's Spanish Heritage.* Viking Fund Publications in Anthropology, no. 27, Wenner-Gren Foundation for Anthropological Research, New York.

Franquelin, Jean-Baptiste Louis
1684   "Carte de la Louisiane." Map Library, Lower Mississippi Survey, Peabody Museum, Harvard University, Cambridge.
1688   "Carte de l'Amerique Septentrionnalle." Division of Maps, Library of Congress, Washington, D.C.

French, B. F.
1846   *Historical Collections of Louisiana*, part 1. Wiley and Putnam, New York.
1850   *Historical Collections of Louisiana*, part 2. Daniels and Smith, Philadelphia.
1851   *Historical Collections of Louisiana*, part 3. D. Appleton and Co., New York.
1875   *Historical Collections of Louisiana and Florida.* 2nd ser. Albert Mason, New York.

Frison, George C.
1974   *The Casper Site.* Academic Press, New York.

Gallatin, Albert
1836   "A Synopsis of the Indian Tribes of North America," *Transactions and Collections of the American Antiquarian Society*, vol. 2, pp. 1–422.

Galloway, Patricia K.
1981   "Dearth and Bias: Issues in the Editing of Ethnohistorical Materials," *Newsletter of the Association for Documentary Editing*, vol. 3, no. 2, pp. 1–6.
1982   "Sources for the La Salle Expedition of 1682," in *La Salle and His Legacy: Frenchmen and Indians in the Lower Mississippi Valley*, P. K. Galloway, ed. University Press of Mississippi, Jackson.
1984   "Technical Origins for Chickachae Combed Ceramics: An Ethnohistorical Hypothesis," *Mississippi Archaeology*, vol. 19, no. 2, pp. 58–66.
1986   "The Direct Historical Approach and Early Historical Documents: The Ethnohistorian's View," in *The Protohistoric Period in the Mid-South: 1500–1700*, D. M. Dye and R. C. Brister, eds. Mississippi Department of Archives and History, Archaeological Report no. 18, Jackson.

Galloway, Patricia K., ed.
1982   *La Salle and His Legacy: Frenchmen and Indians in the Lower Mississippi Valley*. University Press of Mississippi, Jackson.

Garcilaso de la Vega, El Inca
1723   *La Florida del Inca. Historia del Adelantado, Hernando De Soto, Governador, y Capitan General del Reino de la Florida. Y de Otros Heroicos Caballeros Españoles, e Indios*. Nicolas Rodriguez Franco, Madrid.

Gardin, Jean-Claude
1980   *Archaeological Constructs: An Aspect of Theoretical Archaeology*. Cambridge University Press, Cambridge.

Gatschet, Albert S.
1884   *A Migration Legend of the Creek Indians*. D. G. Brinton, Philadelphia.
1889   "Sex-Denoting Nouns in American Languages," *Transactions of the American Philological Society*, vol. 20, pp. 159–171.

Gauld, George
1774   "Map of the British Settlements along the Mississippi River." Map Library, School of Geoscience, Louisiana State University, Baton Rouge. Listed under the date of 1768.

Gayarré, Charles
1885   *History of Louisiana*. F. S. Hansell and Brother, New Orleans.

Genêt, Nicole
1980   *Les collections archéologiques de la place Royale —la Faïence*. Ministère des Affaires Culturelles, Dossier 45, Québec.

Gentil
1699   "Carte de la Coste et des environs du Fleuve de Mississipi." Bibliothèque Nationale, Paris.

Giardino, Marco J.
1984   "Documentary Evidence for the Location of Historic Indian Villages in the Mississippi Delta," in *Perspectives On Gulf Coast Prehistory*, D. Davis, ed. Ripley P. Bullen Monographs in Anthropology and History, no. 5, University of Florida Press and Florida State Museum, Gainesville.

Gibson, Arrell M.
1971   "Chickasaw Ethnography: An Ethnohistorical Reconstruction," *Ethnohistory*, vol. 18, no. 2, pp. 99–118.

Gibson, Jon L.
1968   "Evaluation of the Geographical Potential of the Lower Ouachita River Valley with Regard to the De Soto-Moscoso Expedition," *Louisiana Studies*, pp. 203–212.
1977   *Archaeological Survey of Portions of Little River, Boeuf River, and Big Creek, East Central and Northeastern Louisiana*. Center for Archaeological Studies, University of Southwestern Louisiana, Lafayette.
1984   "Louisiana Archaeology, an Anecdotal History," in *Louisiana Archaeology and the Society: Celebration of a Decade of Achievement*, J. L. Gibson, ed. Louisiana Archaeological Society, Special Publication no. 2, Lafayette.

Gibson, Susan G.
1980   "Introduction," in *Burr's Hill, A 17th Century Wampanoag Burial Ground in Warren, Rhode Island*, S. G. Gibson, ed. The Haffenreffer Museum of Anthropology, Brown University, Studies in Anthropology and Material Culture, vol. 2, Providence.

Gilbert, F.
1966   "Aging White-Tailed Deer by Annuli in the Cementum of the First Incisor," *Journal of Wildlife Management*, vol. 30, pp. 200–202.

Giraud, Marcel
1953–   *Histoire de la Louisiane française*. 4 vols. Presses
1974   Universitaires de France, Paris. Vol. 1 translated by J. C. Lambert under the title *A History of French Louisiana*, vol. 1, *The Reign of Louis XIV, 1698–1715*. Louisiana State University Press, Baton Rouge, 1974.

Glassie, Henry
1975   *Folk Housing in Middle Virginia: A Structural Analysis of Historic Artifacts*. The University of Tennessee Press, Knoxville.

Godden, Geoffrey A.
1964   *Encyclopaedia of British Pottery and Porcelain Marks*. Bonanza Books, New York.

Goggin, John M.
1968   *Spanish Majolica in the New World: Types of the Sixteenth to Eighteenth Centuries*. Yale University Publications in Anthropology, no. 72, Department of Anthropology, Yale University, New Haven.

Gonichon
1731   "Carte du Cours du fleuve Mississipi ou de Saint Louis depuis la Nouvelle Orleans Jusqu'au Natchez." British Library pressmark K.Top CXXII.91, Map Library, British Library, London.

Goodyear, Albert C., III
1977   "The Historical and Ecological Position of Protohistoric Sites in the Slate Mountains, South Central Arizona," in *Research Strategies in Historical Archaeology*, S. South, ed. Academic Press, New York.

Gordon, Harry
1916   "Journal of Captain Harry Gordon, 1766," in
        Travels in the American Colonies, N. D. Mere-
        ness, ed. The MacMillan Co., New York.

Gould, Richard A.
1974   "Some Current Problems in Ethnoarchaeology,"
        in *Ethnoarchaeology*, C. B. Donnan and C. W.
        Clewlow, Jr., eds. University of California Insti-
        tute of Archaeology, Monograph no. 4, Los Ange-
        les.
1980   *Living Archaeology*. Cambridge University Press,
        Cambridge.
1985   "The Empiricist Strikes Back: Reply to Binford,"
        American Antiquity, vol. 50, no. 3, pp. 638–644.

Gould, Richard A., ed.
1978   *Explorations in Ethnoarchaeology*. University of
        New Mexico Press, Albuquerque.

Gould, Richard A., and Patty Jo Watson
1982   "A Dialogue on the Meaning and Use of Analogy
        in Ethnoarchaeological Reasoning," *Journal of
        Anthropological Archaeology*, vol. 1, pp. 355–
        381.

Green, Thomas J., and Cheryl A. Munson
1978   "Mississippian Settlement Patterns in South-
        western Indiana," in *Mississippian Settlement
        Patterns*, B. Smith, ed. Academic Press, New York.

Greer, John W.
1967   *A Description of the Stratigraphy, Features and
        Artifacts from an Archeological Excavation at
        the Alamo*. Texas State Building Commission,
        Archeological Program, Report no. 3, Austin.

Gregory, Hiram F.
1961   "Historic Tunica Burial in Avoyelles Ph., Louisi-
        ana." Field Report, Lower Mississippi Survey,
        Peabody Museum, Harvard University, Cam-
        bridge.
1973   "Eighteenth Century Caddoan Archaeology: A
        Study in Models and Interpretation." Ph.D. dis-
        sertation, Southern Methodist University, Dallas.
1975   Letter to Herman Viola, Native American Schol-
        ars Program, Smithsonian Institution. Depart-
        ment of Anthropology Archives, Smithsonian
        Institution, Washington, D.C.
1978   "A Historic Tunica Burial at the Coulee des
        Grues Site in Avoyelles Parish, Louisiana, " in
        Texas Archeology, K. D. House, ed. Southern
        Methodist University Press, Dallas.
1980   "Excavations: 1979. Presidio de Neustra Snra. del
        Pilar de Los Adaes." Contract Report, Division of
        State Parks, Louisiana Department of Culture,
        Recreation and Tourism, Baton Rouge.
1981   "Another Response to Perttula." *Louisiana Ar-
        chaeology*, no. 7, pp. 126–131.
1982   "Excavations: 1981–82. Presidio de Nuestra Snra.
        del Pilar de Los Adaes." Contract Report, Divi-
        sion of State Parks, Louisiana Department of
        Culture, Recreation and Tourism, Baton Rouge.

1985   " 'A Promise from the Sun': The Folklife Tradi-
        tions of Louisiana Indians," in *Louisiana Folk-
        life: A Guide to the State*, N. R. Spitzer, ed.
        Louisiana Department of Culture, Recreation and
        Tourism and the Center for Gulf South History
        and Culture, Baton Rouge.

Gregory, Hiram F., and Clarence H. Webb
1965   "European Trade Beads from Six Sites in Natchi-
        toches Parish, Louisiana," *The Florida Anthro-
        pologist*, vol. 18, no. 3, part 2, pp. 15–44.

Griffin, James B.
1960   "A Hypothesis for the Prehistory of the Winne-
        bago," in *Culture in History, Essays in Honor of
        Paul Radin*, S. Diamond, ed. Columbia Univer-
        sity Press, New York.

Guevin, Bryan L.
1985   "Grand Houmas Village: An Historic Houma In-
        dian Site (16AN35), Ascension Parish, Louisi-
        ana." Manuscript, Baton Rouge.

Gunnerson, James H.
1982   "Waldo R. Wedel, Archeologist: Perspectives that
        Grew in the Plains," in *Plains Indian Studies: A
        Collection of Essays in Honor of John C. Ewers
        and Waldo R. Wedel*, D. H. Ubelaker and H. J.
        Viola, eds. Smithsonian Contributions to Anthro-
        pology, no. 30, Smithsonian Institution Press,
        Washington, D.C.

Gursky, Karl-Heinz
1969   "A Lexical Comparison of the Atakapa, Chitama-
        cha, and Tunica Languages," *International Jour-
        nal of American Linguistics*, vol. 35, pp. 83–107.

Haag, William G.
1953   "Choctaw Archaeology," *Southeastern Archaeo-
        logical Conference Newsletter*, vol. 3, no. 3,
        pp. 25–28.
1965   "Louisiana in North American Prehistory," *Loui-
        siana Studies*, vol. 4, no. 3, pp. 279–323. (Re-
        printed in *Mélanges*, no. 1, 1971.)
1967   "The Identification of Archaeological Remains
        with Ethnic Groups," *Proceedings of the 2nd In-
        ternational Congress for the Study of Pre-Colum-
        bian Cultures in the Lesser Antilles*, pp. 121–
        124.

Haas, Mary R.
1940   "Tunica," in *Handbook of American Indian Lan-
        guages*, vol. 4. J. J. Augustin Publishers, New
        York.
1942   "The Solar Deity of the Tunica," *Papers of the
        Michigan Academy of Science, Arts and Letters*,
        vol. 28, part 4, pp. 531–535.
1950   *Tunica Texts*. University of California Publica-
        tions in Linguistics, vol. 6, no. 1, Berkeley and
        Los Angeles.
1953   *Tunica Dictionary*. University of California Pub-
        lications in Linguistics, vol. 6, no. 2, Berkeley
        and Los Angeles.

1971 "Southeastern Indian Linguistics," in *Red, White, and Black: Symposium on Indians in the Old South*, C. M. Hudson, ed. Southern Anthropological Society, Proceedings, no. 5, University of Georgia Press, Athens.

1973 "The Southeast," in *Current Trends in Linguistics*, vol. 10, *Linguistics in North America*, T. A. Sebeok, ed. Mouton Publishers, The Hague.

Hall, Robert L.
1977 "An Anthropocentric Perspective for Eastern United States Prehistory," *American Antiquity*, vol. 42, no. 4, pp. 499–518.

Hollowell, A. Irving
1963 "American Indians, White and Black: The Phenomenon of Transculturalization," *Current Anthropology*, vol. 4, no. 5, pp. 519–531.

Hally, David J.
1971 "The Archaeology of European-Indian Contact in the Southeast," in *Red, White, and Black: Symposium on Indians in the Old South*, C. M. Hudson, ed. Southern Anthropological Society, Proceedings, no. 5, University of Georgia Press, Athens.

1972 "The Plaquemine and Mississippian Occupations of the Upper Tensas Basin, Louisiana." Ph.D. dissertation, Harvard University, Cambridge.

Hamilton, T. M.
1968 *Early Indian Trade Guns: 1625–1775*. Contributions of the Museum of the Great Plains, no. 3, Lawton, Oklahoma.

1976 *Firearms on the Frontier: Guns at Fort Michilimackinac 1715–1781*. Mackinac Island State Park Commission, Reports in Mackinac History and Archaeology, no. 5, Williamson, Michigan.

1979 "Guns, Gunflints, Balls and Shot," in *Tunica Treasure*, J. P. Brain. Papers of the Peabody Museum, Harvard University, vol. 71, Cambridge.

1980 *Colonial Frontier Guns*. The Fur Press, Chadron, Nebraska.

Handler, Jerome S., and Frederick W. Lange
1978 *Plantation Slavery in Barbados: An Archaeological and Historical Investigation*. Harvard University Press, Cambridge.

Hanson, James A.
1982 "Laced Coats and Leather Jackets: The Great Plains Intercultural Clothing Exchange," in *Plains Indian Studies: A Collection of Essays in Honor of John C. Ewers and Waldo R. Wedel*, D. H. Ubelaker and H. J. Viola, eds. Smithsonian Contributions to Anthropology, no. 30, Smithsonian Institution Press, Washington, D.C.

Harley, J. B.
1968 "The Evaluation of Early Maps: Towards a Methodology," *Imago Mundi*, vol. 22, pp. 62–74.

Harrington, Jean C.
1952 "Historic Site Archeology in the United States," in *Archeology of Eastern United States*, J. B. Griffin, ed. The University of Chicago Press, Chicago.

1955 "Archaeology as an Auxiliary Science to American History," *American Anthropologist*, vol. 57, no. 6, part 1, pp. 1,121–1,130.

Hathcock, Roy
1983 *The Quapaw and their Pottery*. Hurley Press, Camden, Arkansas.

Heidenreich, C. E.
1976 "Seventeenth Century Maps of the Great Lakes and St. Lawrence Area as Ethnohistoric Material," *The Western Canadian Journal of Anthropology*, vol. 6, no. 1, pp. 12–29.

Hemmings, E. Thomas
1982 *Human Adaptation in the Grand Marais Lowland*. Arkansas Archeological Survey, Research Series, no. 17, Fayetteville.

Henige, David
1987 "The Context, Content, and Credibility of *La Florida del Ynca*," *The Americas*, vol. 43, pp. 1–23.

Henning, Dale R.
1970 *Development and Interrelationships of Oneota Culture in the Lower Missouri River Valley*. The Missouri Archaeologist, vol. 32, Columbia.

Herskovits, Melville J.
1938 *Acculturation: The Study of Culture Contact*. Augustin, New York. Reprint, Peter Smith, Gloucester, Massachusetts, 1958.

1952 "Introduction," in *Acculturation in the Americas*, S. Tax, ed. The University of Chicago Press, Chicago.

1964 *Cultural Dynamics*. Alfred A. Knopf, New York.

Hesse, Brian, and Dexter Perkins, Jr.
1974 "Faunal Remains from Karates-Semayük in Southwest Anatolia: An Interim Report," *Journal of Field Archaeology*, vol. 1, pp. 149–160.

Hickerson, Harold
1970 *The Chippewa and their Neighbors: A Study in Ethnohistory*. Holt, Rinehart and Winston, New York.

Hobler, Philip M.
1986 "Measures of the Acculturative Response to Trade on the Central Coast of British Columbia," *Historical Archaeology*, vol. 20, no. 2, pp. 16–26.

Hodder, Ian R.
1978 "Simple Correlations between Material Culture and Society: A Review," in *The Spatial Organization of Culture*, I. R. Hodder, ed. University of Pittsburgh Press, Pittsburgh.

1982a *Symbols in Action: Ethnoarchaeological Studies of Material Culture.* Cambridge University Press, Cambridge.

1982b *Symbolic and Structural Archaeology.* Cambridge University Press, Cambridge.

1983 *The Present Past: An Introduction to Anthropology for Archaeologists.* Pica Press, New York.

1984 "Burials, Houses, Women and Men in the European Neolithic," in *Ideology, Power and Prehistory,* D. Miller and C. Tilley, eds. Cambridge University Press, Cambridge.

Hodge, Frederick Webb
1910 *Handbook of American Indians North of Mexico,* part 2. Bureau of American Ethnology, Bulletin no. 30, Washington, D.C.

Hoffman, Michael P.
1975– "The Kinkead-Mainard Site, 3PU2: A Late Pre-
1977 historic Quapaw Phase Site Near Little Rock, Arkansas," *The Arkansas Archeologist,* vols. 16–18, pp. 1–41.

1985 "The Terminal Mississippian Period in the Arkansas River Valley and Quapaw Ethnogenesis." Paper presented at the Mississippian in the Memphis Area Symposium, Memphis State University, Memphis.

1986 "Protohistory of the Lower and Central Arkansas River Valley in Arkansas," in *The Protohistoric Period in the Mid-South: 1500–1700,* D. M. Dye and R. C. Brister, eds. Mississippi Department of Archives and History, Archaeological Report no. 18, Jackson.

Holmes, Jack D. L.
1963 "Maps, Plans and Charts of Louisiana in Spanish and Cuban Archives: A Checklist," *Louisiana Studies,* vol. 2, no. 4, pp. 183–203.

1965 "Maps, Plans, and Charts of Louisiana in Paris Archives: A Checklist," *Louisiana Studies,* vol. 4, no. 3, pp. 200–221.

Horvath, Steven M., Jr.
1983 "Ethnic Groups as Subjects of Archaeological Inquiry," in *Forgotten Places and Things: Archaeological Perspectives on American History,* A. E. Ward, ed. Center for Anthropological Studies, Contributions to Anthropological Studies, no. 3, Albuquerque.

House, John H.
1982 "SE Study Unit 9: The Kent and Old Town Phases, the Late Mississippian Period," in *A State Plan for the Conservation of Archeological Resources in Arkansas,* H. A. Davis, ed. Arkansas Archeological Survey, Research Series, no. 21, Fayetteville.

1983 "Noble Lake: Quapaw Phase Occupation in the Arkansas River Lowland, Eastern Arkansas." Paper presented at the Southeastern Archaeological Conference, Columbia, South Carolina.

1984 "Kent Phase Investigations in Eastern Arkansas, 1978–1984." Manuscript, Arkansas Archeological Survey, Monticello.

House, John H., and Henry McKelway
1982 "Study Unit 10: Mississippian and Quapaw on the Lower Arkansas," in *A State Plan for the Conservation of Archeological Resources in Arkansas,* H. A. Davis, ed. Arkansas Archeological Survey, Research Series, no. 21, Fayetteville.

Howard, James H.
1972 "Arikara Native-Made Glass Pendants: Their Probable Function," *American Antiquity,* vol. 37, no. 1, pp. 93–97.

Howell, Walter G.
1973 "The French in Mississippi, 1699–1763," in *A History of Mississippi,* R. A. McLemore, ed. University and College Press of Mississippi, Jackson.

Hudson, Charles
1966 "Folk History and Ethnohistory," *Ethnohistory,* vol. 13, nos. 1–2, pp. 52–70.

Hunter, Donald G.
1987 "Appalaches and 16RA335: A Summary of the History of the Appalache on Red River and of the Preliminary Archaeological Investigations at their Principal Village Site." Paper presented at the annual meeting of the Caddo Conference, Bossier City, Louisiana.

Hutchins, Thomas
1784 *An Historical Narrative and Topographical Description of Louisiana, and West-Florida.* Robert Aitken, Philadelphia. Facsimile reprint, University of Florida Press, Gainesville, 1968.

James, Charles D., III, and Alexander J. Lindsay, Jr.
1973 "Ethnoarchaeological Research at Canyon del Muerto, Arizona: A Navajo Example," *Ethnohistory,* vol. 20, no. 4, pp. 361–374.

Jaenen, Cornelius J.
1976 *Friend and Foe: Aspects of French-Amerindian Contact in the Sixteenth and Seventeenth Centuries.* Columbia University Press, New York.

Jelks, Edward B., ed.
1967 *The Gilbert Site: A Norteño Focus Site in Northeastern Texas.* Bulletin of the Texas Archeological Society, vol. 37, Dallas.

Jennings, Francis
1976 *The Invasion of America: Indians, Colonialism, and the Cant of Conquest.* W. W. Norton and Co., New York.

Jennings, Jesse D.
1941 "Chickasaw and Earlier Indian Cultures of Northeast Mississippi," *The Journal of Mississippi History,* vol. 3, no. 3, pp. 155–226.

Jeter, Marvin D.
1982a "The Archeology of Southeast Arkansas: An Overview for the 1980's," in *Arkansas Archeology in Review,* N. L. Trubowitz and M. D. Jeter, eds.

Arkansas Archeological Survey, Research Series, no. 15, Fayetteville.

1982b "The Protohistoric 'Tillar Complex' of Southeast Arkansas." Paper presented at the annual meeting of the Society for American Archaeology, Minneapolis.

1982c "SE Study Unit 8: The Bellaire Phase," in *A State Plan for the Conservation of Archeological Resources in Arkansas*, H. A. Davis, ed. Arkansas Archeological Survey, Research Series, no. 21, Fayetteville.

1986 "Tunicans West of the Mississippi: A Summary of Early Historic and Archaeological Evidence," in *The Protohistoric Period in the Mid-South: 1500–1700*, D. M. Dye and R. C. Brister, eds. Mississippi Department of Archives and History, Archaeological Report no. 18, Jackson.

Jeter, Marvin D., David B. Kelley, and George P. Kelley
1979 "The Kelley-Grimes Site: A Mississippi Period Burial Mound, Southeast Arkansas, Excavated in 1936," *The Arkansas Archeologist*, vol. 20, pp. 1 51.

Joffrion, Joseph
1870 General Government Confirmation Certificate, no. 1735, to Joseph Joffrion, filed 12 February 1870. Map Collection, Mississippi River Commission, Vicksburg, Mississippi.

Johnson, Glenn A.
n.d. "Field Notes: Burials Excavated at the Humber Site, 1969–1973." Manuscript, Cottonlandia Museum, Greenwood, Mississippi.

Jolliet, Louis
1679 Map of the Mississippi River to the Arkansas. Bibliothèque Nationale, Paris.

Jolly, Fletcher, III
1973 "A Catlinite Disk Pipe and Associated Vessels from Lowland Eastern Arkansas," *The Arkansas Archeologist*, vol. 14, no. 1, pp. 1–12.

Jones, Grant D.
1978 "The Ethnohistory of the Guale Coast through 1684," in *The Anthropology of St. Catherines Island*, vol. 1, *Natural and Cultural History*, D. H. Thomas, G. D. Jones, R. S. Durham, and C. S. Larsen. The American Museum of Natural History, Anthropological Papers, vol. 55, part 2, New York.

Judd, Neil M.
1929 "The Present Status of Archaeology in the United States," *American Anthropologist*, vol. 31, no. 3, pp. 401–418.

Juzan, Pierre Gabriel
1731a "Relation de ce qui c'est passé au fort françois des Natchez dans la Province de la Louisiane depuis le dixième de Mai 1731 jusqu'au premier juillet. . ." Dépôt des Fortifications des Colonies, Archives des Colonies, Paris.

1731b "Rapport de Sieur Juzan auz Thonicas, 29 Decembre 1731." Archives des Colonies, Louisiane, Archives Nationales, Paris.

Kappler, Charles J., ed.
1973 *Indian Treaties, 1778–1883*. Interland Publishing, New York.

Keesing, Felix M.
1939 *The Menomini Indians of Wisconsin: A Study of Three Centuries of Cultural Contact and Change*. American Philosophical Society, Memoirs, vol. 10, Philadelphia.

Kelly, Marsha C. S., and Roger E. Kelly
1980 "Approaches to Ethnic Identification in Historical Archaeology," in *Archaeological Perspectives on Ethnicity in America: Afro-American and Asian American Culture History*, R. Schuyler, ed. Baywood Publishing Co., Farmingdale, New York.

Kent, Susan
1983 "The Differential Acceptance of Culture Change: An Archaeological Test Case," *Historical Archaeology*, vol. 17, no. 2, pp. 56–63.

Kenyon, Walter A.
1982 *The Grimsby Site: A Historic Neutral Cemetery*. Royal Ontario Museum, Publications in Archaeology, Toronto.

Kernion, George C. H., trans.
1926 "Documents Concerning the History of the Indians of the Eastern Region of Louisiana," *Louisiana Historical Quarterly*, vol. 8, pp. 28–40.

Kidder, Tristram R.
1986 "Final Report on Archaeological Test Excavations in the Central Boeuf Basin, Louisiana, 1985." Report to the Louisiana Office of the State Archaeologist, Department of Culture, Recreation and Tourism, Baton Rouge.

1987 "Protohistoric and Early Historic Culture Dynamics in Southeast Arkansas and Northeast Louisiana, A.D. 1500–1700." Ph.D. dissertation, Harvard University, Cambridge.

Kidder, Tristram R., and Stephen Williams
1984 "Archaeological Survey of the Northern Boeuf Basin, Louisiana: A Preliminary Report." Paper presented at the annual meeting of the Louisiana Archaeological Society, Lafayette.

Kilmarx, John N.
1985 "A Comparison of Archaeological and Ethnohistoric Evidence for Material Acculturation in Northwest Alaska." M.A. thesis, State University of New York, Binghamton.

Kinnaird, Lawrence, ed.
1946a *Annual Report of the American Historical Association for the Year 1945*, vol. 3, *Spain in the Mississippi Valley, 1765–1794*, part 2, *Post War*

Decade, 1782–1791. Government Printing Office, Washington, D.C.

1946b *Annual Report of the American Historical Association for the Year 1945,* vol. 4, *Spain in the Mississippi Valley, 1765–1794,* part 3, *Problems of Frontier Defense, 1792–1794.* Government Printing Office, Washington, D.C.

1949 *Annual Report of the American Historical Association for the Year 1945,* vol. 2, *Spain in the Mississippi Valley, 1765–1794,* part 1, *The Revolutionary Period, 1765–1781.* Government Printing Office, Washington, D.C.

Klevezal, G., and S. Kleinenberg
1969 *Age Determination of Mammals from Annual Layers in Teeth and Bones.* Israel Program for Scientific Translations, Jerusalem.

Klinger, Timothy C.
1977 "Parkin Archeology: A Report on the 1966 Field School Test Excavations at the Parkin Site." *The Arkansas Archeologist,* vol. 16–18, pp. 45–80.

Kniffen, Fred B.
1935 "The Historic Indian Tribes of Louisiana," *Louisiana Conservation Review,* vol. 4, no. 7, pp. 5–12.

Kniffen, Fred B., and Henry Glassie
1966 "Building in Wood in the Eastern United States: A Time-Place Perspective," *The Geographical Review,* vol. 56, no. 1, pp. 40–66.

Knight, Vernon J., Jr.
1983 "The Institutional Organization of Mississippian Religion." Paper presented at the 40th annual Southeastern Archaeological Conference, Columbia, South Carolina.

1985a "Theme and Variation in Mississippian Ritual Expression," in *Indians, Colonists, and Slaves: Essays in Memory of Charles M. Fairbanks,* K. W. Johnson, J. M. Leader, and R. C. Wilson, eds. Florida Journal of Anthropology, Special Publication no. 4, Gainesville.

1985b "Symbolism of Mississippian Mounds." Paper presented at the 42nd annual Southeastern Archaeological Conference, Birmingham, Alabama.

Knight, Vernon J., Jr., and Sherée L. Adams
1981 "A Voyage to the Mobile and Tomeh in 1700, with Notes on the Interior of Alabama," *Journal of Alabama Archaeology,* vol. 27, no. 1, pp. 32–56.

Kramer, Carol, ed.
1979 *Ethnoarchaeology: Implications of Ethnography for Archaeology.* Columbia University Press, New York.

Krause, Bertram S.
1944 "Acculturation, a New Approach to the Iroquoian Problem," *American Antiquity,* vol. 9, no. 3, pp. 302–318.

Krause, Richard A.
1972 *The Leavenworth Site: Archaeology of an Historic Arikara Community.* University of Kansas, Publications in Anthropology, no. 3, Lawrence.

1985 *The Clay Sleeps: An Ethnoarchaeological Study of Three African Potters.* The University of Alabama Press, University, Alabama.

Kutsche, Paul, John R. Van Ness, and Andrew T. Smith
1976 "A Unified Approach to the Anthropology of Hispanic Northern New Mexico: Historical Archaeology, Ethnohistory, and Ethnography," *Historical Archaeology,* vol. 10, pp. 1–16.

Laguna, Frederica de
1960 *The Story of a Tlingit Community: A Problem in the Relationship between Archaeological, Ethnological, and Historical Methods.* Bureau of American Ethnology, Bulletin no. 172, Washington, D.C.

La Harpe, Bénard de
[1720] "Carte des Nouvelles découvertes faites en 1719." Bibliothèque Nationale, Paris.

Landry, Stuart O., trans.
1966 *Robin's Voyage to Louisiana, 1803–1805.* Pelican Publishing Co., New Orleans.

Larrabee, Edward McM.
1969 "Historic Site Archaeology in Relation to Other Archaeology," *Historical Archaeology,* vol. 3, pp. 67–74.

LaViolette, Adria
1982 "Metallographic Analysis of 18th Century Iron Nails from the Trudeau Site, West Feliciana Parish, Louisiana." Manuscript, Center for Materials Research in Archaeology and Ethnology, Massachusetts Institute of Technology, Cambridge.

Leechman, Douglas
1951 "Bone Grease," *American Antiquity,* vol. 16, pp. 355–356.

Leitch, Barbara A.
1979 *A Concise Dictionary of Indian Tribes of North America.* Reference Publications, Algonac, Michigan.

Le Maire, François
1716 "Carte nouvelle de la Louisiane et pais circonvoisins." Bibliothèque Nationale, Paris.

n.d. Manuscript. Fonds français, 12105, Bibliothèque Nationale, Paris.

Lemley, Harry J., and Samuel D. Dickinson
1937 "Archaeological Investigations on Bayou Macon in Arkansas," *Texas Archeological and Paleontological Society Bulletin,* vol. 9, pp. 11–47.

Leone, Mark P.
1972 "Issues in Anthropological Archaeology," in *Contemporary Archaeology*, M. P. Leone, ed. Southern Illinois University Press, Carbondale.
1982 "Some Opinions about Recovering Mind," *American Antiquity*, vol. 47, no. 4, pp. 742–760.

Le Page du Pratz, Antoine S.
1758 *Histoire de la Louisiane*. 3 vols. De Bure, La Veuve Delaguette, Lambert, Paris.
1774 *The History of Louisiana*. T. Becket, London. Facsimile reprint, Louisiana State University Press, Baton Rouge, 1975.

Le Sueur, Pierre Charles
[1700] *Journal du voyage de Lesueur Sur le Mississipi*. Archives Nationales, Paris.

Lewall, E. F., and I. McT. Cowan
1963 "Age Determination in Blacktail Deer by Degrees of Ossification of the Epiphyseal Plate in the Longbones," *Canadian Journal of Zoology*, vol. 41, pp. 629–636.

Lewis, R. Barry
1974 *Mississippian Exploitative Strategies: A Southeast Missouri Example*. Missouri Archaeological Society, Research Series, no. 11, Columbia.

Linton, Ralph, ed.
1940 *Acculturation in Seven American Indian Tribes*. D. Appleton Century Co., New York.

Longacre, William A.
1970 "Current Thinking in American Archeology," *American Anthropological Association Bulletin*, vol. 3, no. 3, part 2, pp. 126–138.

Louisiana Historical Quarterly
1921 "Records of the Superior Council of Louisiana," *The Louisiana Historical Quarterly*, vol. 4, no. 2, pp. 218–249, no. 4, pp. 481–526.

Lurie, Nancy Oestreich
1961 "Ethnohistory: An Ethnological Point of View," *Ethnohistory*, vol. 8, no. 1, pp. 78–92.
1971 "Indian Cultural Adjustment to European Civilization," in *The American Indian: Past and Present*, R. L. Nichols and G. R. Adams, eds. Xerox College Publishing, Waltham, Massachusetts.

McDermott, John Francis, ed.
1949 *Old Cahokia—A Narrative and Documents Illustrating the First Century of its History*. The St. Louis Historical Documents Foundation, St. Louis.
1965 *The French in the Mississippi Valley*. University of Illinois Press, Urbana.
1969 *Frenchmen and French Ways in the Mississippi Valley*. University of Illinois Press, Urbana.
1974 *The Spanish in the Mississippi Valley, 1762–1804*. University of Illinois Press, Urbana.

McGuire, Randall H.
1982 "The Study of Ethnicity in Historical Archaeology," *Journal of Anthropological Archaeology*, vol. 1, no. 2, pp. 159–178.
1983 "Ethnic Group, Status and Material Culture at the Rancho Punta de Agua," in *Forgotten Places and Things; Archaeological Perspective on American History*, A. Ward, ed. Center for Anthropological Studies, Contributions to Anthropological Studies, no. 3, Albuquerque.

McKay, Joyce
1976 "The Coalescence of History and Archaeology," *Historical Archaeology*, vol. 10, pp. 93–98.

McPherson, H. R.
1960 "Down the Mississippi," *Central States Archaeological Journal*, vol. 7, no. 1, p. 33.

McWilliams, Richebourg G., ed. and trans.
1953 *Fleur de Lys and Calumet: Being the Pénicaut Narrative of French Adventure in Louisiana*. Louisiana State University Press, Baton Rouge.
1981 *Iberville's Gulf Journals*. The University of Alabama Press, University, Alabama.

Maher, Thomas O.
1983 "Ceramic Exchange in the Southeastern United States: An Examination of Three Methods for Mineralogically Characterizing Aboriginal Ceramics from Archaeological Sites in Alabama, Louisiana and Mississippi." M.A. thesis, State University of New York, Binghamton.

Mainfort, Robert C., Jr.
1979 *Indian Social Dynamics in the Period of European Contact: Fletcher Site Cemetery, Bay County*. Michigan State University, Publications Series, vol. 1, no. 4, East Lansing.
1985 "Wealth, Space, and Status in an Historic Indian Cemetery," *American Antiquity*, vol. 50, no. 3, pp. 555–579.

Malinowski, Bronislaw
1945 *The Dynamics of Culture Change*. Yale University Press, New Haven.

Margry, Pierre
1879– *Mémoires et documents pour servir a l'histoire*
1888 *des origines françaises des pays d'outre-mer*. 6 vols. Maisonneuve et Cie, Paris.

Marquette, Jacques
1676 Map of the Mississippi, or Conception, River to the Arkansas. St. Mary's College, Montreal.

Marshall, Richard A.
1985 "Preliminary Archaeological Testing near Mound A, Buford (22TL501) Site, Tallahatchie County, Mississippi." Manuscript, Cobb Institute of Archaeology, Mississippi State, Mississippi; Cottonlandia Museum, Greenwood, Mississippi.

n.d. "Mississippian Phases at Lyon's Bluff Site (22OK1), East Central Mississippi." Manuscript, Lower Mississippi Survey, Peabody Museum, Harvard University, Cambridge.

Mason, Carol I.
1985 "Archaeological Analogy and Ethnographic Example: A Case from the Winnebago," in *Indians, Colonists, and Slaves: Essays in Memory of Charles H. Fairbanks*, K.W. Johnson, J.M. Leader, and R. C. Wilson, eds. Florida Journal of Anthropology, Special Publication no. 4, Gainesville.

Mason, Ronald J.
1976 "Ethnicity and Archaeology in the Upper Great Lakes," in *Cultural Change and Continuity: Essays in Honor of James Bennett Griffin*, C. E. Cleland, ed. Academic Press, New York.

Menier, Marie-Antoinette, Etienne Taillemite, and Gilberte de Forges
1976 *Inventaire des Archives Coloniales: Correspondance à l'arrivée en provenance de la Louisiane.* Archives Nationales, Paris.

Mereness, Newton D.
1916 *Travels in the American Colonies.* Macmillan Co., New York.

Merveilleux, François-Louis
n.d. "Relation de la Louisianne." Manuscript, Newberry Library, Chicago.

Milanich, Jerald T.
1978 "The Western Timucua: Patterns of Acculturation and Change," in *Tacachale*, J. T. Milanich and S. Proctor, eds. The University Presses of Florida, Gainesville.

Miller, Daniel, and Christopher Tilley, eds.
1984 *Ideology, Power and Prehistory.* Cambridge University Press, Cambridge.

Miller, Frank
1974 "Biology of the Kaminuriak Population of Barren-Ground Caribou, Part 2," *Canadian Wildlife Service*, Report Series, no. 31, pp. 1–88.

Miller, J. Jefferson, II, and Lyle M. Stone
1970 *Eighteenth-Century Ceramics from Fort Michilimackinac: A Study in Historical Archeology.* Smithsonian Studies in History and Technology, no. 4, Smithsonian Institution Press, Washington, D.C.

Milner, George R.
1980 "Epidemic Disease in the Postcontact Southeast: A Reappraisal," *Midcontinental Journal of Archaeology*, vol. 5, no. 1, pp. 39–56.

Minet
1685 "Carte de la Louisiane." Bibliothèque Nationale, Paris.

Mitchell, John
1755 "A Map of the British and French Dominions in North America." Map Collection, Yale University Library, New Haven.

Moll, Herman
1715 "A Map of the the West-Indies or the Islands of America in the North Sea; with ye adjacent countries." Facsimile ed., Historic Urban Plans, Ithaca, New York.

Moore, Clarence B.
1908 "Certain Mounds of Arkansas and of Mississippi," *Journal of the Academy of Natural Sciences of Philadelphia*, vol. 13, pp. 480–600.
1909 "Antiquities of the Ouachita Valley," *Journal of the Academy of Natural Sciences of Philadelphia*, vol. 14, pp. 1–170.
1911 "Some Aboriginal Sites on Mississippi River," *Journal of the Academy of Natural Sciences of Philadelphia*, vol. 14, pp. 365–480.
1913 "Some Aboriginal Sites in Louisiana and in Arkansas," *Journal of the Academy of Natural Sciences of Philadelphia*, vol. 16, pp. 5–102.

Moore, John Preston
1974 "Anglo-Spanish Rivalry on the Louisiana Frontier, 1763–68," in *The Spanish in the Mississippi Valley, 1762–1804*, J. F. McDermott, ed. University of Illinois Press, Urbana.

Morse, Dan F.
1982 "Regional Overview of Northeast Arkansas," in *Arkansas Archeology in Review*, N. L. Trubowitz and M. D. Jeter, eds. Arkansas Archeological Survey, Research Series, no. 15, Fayetteville.

Morse, Dan F., ed.
1973 *Nodena: An Account of 75 Years of Archeological Investigation in Southeast Mississippi County, Arkansas.* Arkansas Archeological Survey, Research Series, no. 4, Fayetteville.

Morse, Dan F., and Phyllis A. Morse
1983 *Archaeology of the Central Mississippi Valley.* Academic Press, New York.

Morse, Phyllis A.
1981 *Parkin: The 1978–1979 Archeological Investigations of a Cross County, Arkansas Site.* Arkansas Archeological Survey, Research Series, no. 13, Fayetteville.

Myer, William E.
1928 "Indian Trails of the Southeast," *Forty-second Annual Report of the Bureau of American Ethnology*, pp. 727–857.

Nadel, S. F.
1953 *The Foundations of Social Anthropology.* Cohen and West, London.

Nairne, Thomas
1708 "Capt. Thomas Nairne's Journalls to the Chicasaw and Talapoosies." Additional Manuscript 42,559, British Library, London.

Nasatir, A. P.
1974 "Commentary," *Louisiana Studies*, vol. 13, no. 1, pp. 5–8.

Neitzel, Robert S.
1965 *Archeology of the Fatherland Site: The Grand Village of the Natchez.* The American Museum of Natural History, Anthropological Papers, vol. 51, part 1, New York.
1983 *The Grand Village of the Natchez Revisited: Excavations at the Fatherland Site, Adams County, Mississippi, 1972.* Mississippi Department of Archives and History, Archaeological Report no. 12, Jackson.

Neuman, Robert W.
1984 *An Introduction to Louisiana Archaeology.* Louisiana State University Press, Baton Rouge.

Noël Hume, Ivor
1970 *A Guide to Artifacts of Colonial America.* A. A. Knopf, New York.

Northup, Solomon
1968 *Twelve Years a Slave.* Louisiana State University Press, Baton Rouge.

Nuttall, Thomas
1821 *Journal of Travels into the Arkansas Territory during the year 1819. With Occasional Observations on the Manners of the Aborigines.* T. H. Palmer, Philadelphia.

Olsen, Stanley J.
1960 *Postcranial Skeletal Characters of Bison and Bos.* Papers of the Peabody Museum, Harvard University, vol. 35, no. 4, Cambridge.

O'Neill, Charles E., ed.
1977 *Charlevoix's Louisiana: Selections from the History and the Journal, Pierre F. X. de Charlevoix.* Louisiana State University Press, Baton Rouge.

Orser, Charles E., Jr.
1979a "Ethnohistory, Analogy, and Historical Archaeology," *The Conference on Historic Site Archaeology Papers*, vol. 13, pp. 1–24.
1979b "Analogical Argumentation in Historical Archaeology." Manuscript, Lansing, Michigan.
1981 "Clues from the Recent Past: The Emergence and Development of American Historical Archaeology," in *A Guide for Historical Archaeology in Illinois*, C. E. Orser, ed. Mid-American Research Center, Loyola University, Chicago.

Ortiz, Fernando
1947 *Cuban Counterpoint: Tobacco and Sugar.* Knopf, New York.

Oswalt, Wendell H.
1974 "Ethnoarchaeology," in *Ethnoarchaeology*, C. B. Donnan and C. W. Clewlow, eds. University of California Institute of Archaeology, Monograph no. 4, Los Angeles.

Oswalt, Wendell H., and James W. VanStone
1967 *The Ethnoarchaeology of Crow Village, Alaska.* Bureau of American Ethnology, Bulletin no. 199, Washington, D.C.

Padilla, Amado M.
1980 *Acculturation: Theory, Models and Some New Findings.* American Association for the Advancement of Science, Selected Symposium no. 39, Westview Press, Boulder, Colorado.

Parkhurst, Helen
1945 "Don Pedro Favrot, A Creole Pepys," *Louisiana Historical Quarterly*, vol. 28, no. 3, pp. 679–734.

Patterson, L. W.
1976 "The Catahoula Projectile Point: A Distributional Study," *Louisiana Archaeology*, no. 3, pp. 217–223.

Peabody, Charles
1904 *Exploration of Mounds, Coahoma County, Mississippi.* Papers of the Peabody Museum, Harvard University, vol. 3, no. 2, Cambridge.

Penman, John T.
1977 *Archaeological Survey in Mississippi, 1974–1975.* Mississippi Department of Archives and History, Archaeological Report no. 2, Jackson.
1978 "Historic Choctaw Towns of the Southern Division," *Journal of Mississippi History*, vol. 40, no. 2, pp. 133–141.
1983 "Archaeology and Choctaw Removal," in *Southeastern Natives and Their Pasts*, D. G. Wyckoff and J. C. Hofman, eds. Oklahoma Archaeological Survey, Studies in Oklahoma's Past, no. 11; Cross Timbers Heritage Association, Contribution no. 2, Norman, Oklahoma.

Perino, Gregory
1966 *The Banks Village Site, Crittenden County, Arkansas.* Missouri Archaeological Society, Memoir no. 4, Columbia.
1975 "Some Indian-Made Glass Pendants," *Central States Archaeological Journal*, vol. 22, no. 4, pp. 158–161.

Peterson, Charles E.
1965 "The Houses of French St. Louis," in *The French in the Mississippi Valley*, J. F. McDermott, ed. University of Illinois Press, Urbana.

Peterson, Harold L.
1965 *American Indian Tomahawks.* Contributions from the Museum of the American Indian, Heye Foundation, vol. 19, New York.

Phillips, Philip
1939   "Introduction to the Archaeology of the Missis-
        sippi Valley." Ph.D. dissertation, Harvard Univer-
        sity, Cambridge.
1949   Field Notes. Lower Mississippi Survey, Peabody
        Museum, Harvard University, Cambridge.
1955   "American Archaeology and General Anthropo-
        logical Theory," *Southwestern Journal of Anthro-
        pology*, vol. 11, no. 3, pp. 246–250.
1958   Field Notes. Lower Mississippi Survey, Peabody
        Museum, Harvard University, Cambridge.
1970   *Archaeological Survey in the Lower Yazoo Basin,
        Mississippi, 1949–1955.* Papers of the Peabody
        Museum, Harvard University, vol. 60, Cambridge.

Phillips, Philip, James A. Ford, and James B. Griffin
1951   *Archaeological Survey in the Lower Mississippi
        Alluvial Valley, 1940–1947.* Papers of the Pea-
        body Museum, Harvard University, vol. 25, Cam-
        bridge.

Pittman, Phillip
1770   *The Present State of the European Settlements
        on the Mississippi.* J. Nourse, London. Facsimile
        reprint, University of Florida Press, Gainesville,
        1973.

Plog, Fred T.
1974   *The Study of Prehistoric Change.* Academic
        Press, New York.

Pollock, Oliver
1801   "Oliver Pollock, of Philadelphia, sells a tract of
        land in the Province of Louisiana to his brother,
        Jarret Pollock . . ." Deposition, West Feliciana
        Parish Courthouse, St. Francisville, Louisiana.

Popple, Henry
1733   "A Map of the British Empire in America with
        the French and Spanish Settlements adjacent
        thereto." Map Collection, Yale University Li-
        brary, New Haven.

Potts, Thomas D.
1975   "The French Site (22Ho565)." Manuscript, Mis-
        sissippi Department of Archives and History,
        Jackson.

Powell, J. W.
1891   "Indian Linguistic Families of America North of
        Mexico," *Seventh Annual Report of the Bureau
        of Ethnology*, pp. 1–142.

Price, Cynthia
1979   *Nineteenth Century Ceramics in the Eastern
        Ozark Border Region.* Center for Archaeological
        Research, Southwest Missouri State University,
        Monograph Series, no. 1, Springfield.

Quimby, George I.
1937   "Notes on Indian Trade Silver Ornaments in
        Michigan," *Papers of the Michigan Academy of
        Science, Arts and Letters*, vol. 22, pp. 15–24.

1942a   "Indian Trade Objects in Michigan and Louisi-
        ana," *Papers of the Michigan Academy of Sci-
        ence, Arts and Letters*, vol. 27, pp. 543–551.
1942b   "The Natchezan Culture Type," *American An-
        tiquity*, vol. 7, no. 3, pp. 255–275.
1953   "Natchez Archaeology: A Tribute to the Natchez
        for their Seeming Consistency in the Production
        of the Fictile Fabric," *Southeastern Archaeologi-
        cal Conference Newsletter*, vol. 3, no. 3, pp. 22–
        23.
1957   *The Bayou Goula Site, Iberville Parish, Louisi-
        ana.* Fieldiana: Anthropology, vol. 47, no. 2, Chi-
        cago Natural History Museum, Chicago.
1958   "Silver Ornaments and the Indians," *Miscellanea
        Paul Rivet, Octogenario Dicata*, Mexico.
1966   *Indian Culture and European Trade Goods.* Uni-
        versity of Wisconsin Press, Madison.

Quimby, George I., and Alexander Spoehr
1951   "Acculturation and Material Culture," *Fieldiana:
        Anthropology*, vol. 36, pp. 107–147.

Radin, Paul
1933   *The Method and Theory of Ethnology: An Essay
        in Criticism.* McGraw-Hill, New York.

Ramenofsky, Ann Felice
1982   "The Archaeology of Population Collapse: Native
        American Response to the Introduction of Infec-
        tious Disease." Ph.D. dissertation, University of
        Washington, Seattle.

Ransom, A.
1966   "Determining Age of White-Tailed Deer from
        Layers in Cementum of Molars," *Journal of
        Wildlife Management*, vol. 30, pp. 197–199.

Rea, Robert Right
1970a   "Redcoats and Redskins on the Lower Mississip-
        pi, 1763–1776: The Career of Lt. John Thomas,"
        Louisiana History, vol. 11, no. 1, pp. 5–35.
1970b   "Resources and Research Opportunities for Brit-
        ish West Florida, 1763–1781," in *In Search of
        Gulf Coast Colonial History*, E. F. Dibble and E.
        W. Newton, eds. Historic Pensacola Preservation
        Board, Pensacola, Florida.
1973a   "Assault on the Mississippi—the Loftus Expedi-
        tion, 1764," *The Alabama Review*, vol. 26, no. 3,
        pp. 173–193.
1973b   "Introduction," in *The Present State of the Euro-
        pean Settlements on the Mississippi*, P. Pittman.
        Facsimile reprint of 1770 ed., University of Flor-
        ida Press, Gainesville.

Redfield, Robert
1962   "Relations of Anthropology to the Social Sci-
        ences and to the Humanities," in *Anthropology
        Today*, S. Tax, ed. The University of Chicago
        Press, Chicago.

Redfield, Robert, Ralph Linton, and Melville J. Herskovits
1936   "Memorandum on the Study of Acculturation,"
        American Anthropologist, vol. 38, no. 1, pp. 149–
        152.

Rivas, Francisco
1786 Deposition of John Fitzpatrick relating to the loss of a scow loaded with tobacco belonging to Major John Ellis, which was sunk in the Mississippi River near Pointe Coupée in December 1784. Louisiana State Library, Baton Rouge.

Rodriguez Casado, Vicente
1942 *Primeros Años de Dominación Española en la Luisiana.* Consejo Superior de Investigaciones Cientificas, Instituto Gonzalo Fernandez de Oviedo, Madrid.

Rolingson, Martha A.
1971 "Lakeport: Initial Exploration of a Late Prehistoric Ceremonial Center in Southeastern Arkansas," *The Arkansas Archeologist,* vol. 12, no. 4, pp. 61–80.
1976 "The Bartholomew Phase: A Plaquemine Adaptation in the Mississippi Valley," in *Cultural Continuity and Change: Essays in Honor of James Bennett Griffin,* C. E. Cleland, ed. Academic Press, New York.

Rolingson, Martha A., and Frank F. Schambach
1981 *The Shallow Lake Site (3UN9/52) and its Place in Regional Prehistory.* Arkansas Archeological Survey, Research Series, no. 12. Fayetteville.

Romans, Bernard
1961 *A Concise Natural History of East and West Florida.* Pelican Publishing Co., New Orleans. Originally published in 1775.

Ross, John
1775 "Course of the River Mississippi, from the Balise to Fort Chartres; taken on an Expedition to the Illinois in the latter end of the Year 1765. By Lieut. Ross of the 54th Regiment: Improved from the Surveys of that River made by the French." Robert Sawyer, London; Map Library, Lower Mississippi Survey, Peabody Museum, Harvard University, Cambridge.

Rostlund, Erhard
1960 "The Geographic Range of the Historic Bison in the Southeast," *Association of American Geographers, Annals,* vol. 50, pp. 395–407.

Rouse, Irving
1962 "The Strategy of Culture History," in *Anthropology Today,* S. Tax, ed. The University of Chicago Press, Chicago.
1965 "The Place of 'Peoples' in Prehistoric Research," *The Journal of the Royal Anthropological Institute,* vol. 95, part 1, pp. 1–15.
1972 *Introduction To Prehistory: A Systematic Approach.* McGraw-Hill Book Co., New York.

Rowe, John H.
1965 "The Renaissance Foundations of Anthropology," *American Anthropologist,* vol. 67, no. 1, pp. 1–20.

Rowland, Dunbar
1925 *History of Mississippi: The Heart of the South,* vol. 1. S. J. Clarke Publishing Co., Chicago.
1931 Report of fieldwork in Mississippi. *American Anthropologist,* vol. 33, p. 470.

Rowland, Dunbar, comp. and ed.
1911 *Mississippi Provincial Archives, 1763–1766: English Dominion,* vol. 1. Press of Brandon Printing Company, Nashville.

Rowland, Dunbar, and Albert G. Sanders, eds. and trans.
1927– *Mississippi Provincial Archives: French Domin-*
1932 *ion,* vols. 1–3. Press of the Mississippi Department of Archives and History, Jackson.

Rowland, Dunbar, A. G. Sanders, and Patricia K. Galloway, eds. and trans.
1984 *Mississippi Provincial Archives: French Dominion,* vols. 4–5. Louisiana State University Press, Baton Rouge.

Rowland, Eron
1930 *Life, Letters and Papers of William Dunbar.* Press of the Mississippi Historical Society, Jackson.

Russell, C. P.
1967 *Firearms, Traps and Tools of the Mountain Men.* Knopf, New York.

Salmon, Merrilee H.
1982 *Philosophy and Archaeology.* Academic Press, New York.

Salter, Andrew H.
1977 "Catlinite Calumets: Artifactual Clues to Late Prehistoric and Historic Interactions in Eastern North America." B.A. thesis, Harvard University, Cambridge.

Santa Cruz, Alonso de
1544 Map of the Southeastern United States, containing information derived from the De Soto expedition. Archivo General de Indias, Seville.

Saucier, Corinne L.
1941 *A History of Avoyelles Parish.* Pelican Press, New Orleans.
1956 *Histoire et Geographie des Avoyelles en Louisiane.* Pelican Publishing Co., New Orleans.

Saxon, Andrew, and Charles Higham
1969 "A New Research Method for Economic Prehistorians," *American Antiquity,* vol. 34, pp. 303–311.

Schambach, Frank F., and John E. Miller
1984 "A Description and Analysis of the Ceramics," in *Cedar Grove: An Interdisciplinary Investigation of a Late Caddo Farmstead in the Red River Valley,* N. L. Trubowitz, ed. Arkansas Archeological Survey, Research Series, no. 23, Fayetteville.

Schiffer, Michael B., and John H. House, comps.
1975   *The Cache River Archeological Project: An Experiment in Contract Archeology.* Arkansas Archeological Survey, Research Series, no. 8, Fayetteville.

Schuetz, Mardith K.
1969   *The History and Archeology of Mission San Juan Capistrano, San Antonio, Texas*, vol. 2, *Description of the Artifacts and Ethno-History of the Coahuiltecan Indians.* Texas State Building Commission, Archeological Program, Report no. 11, Austin.

Schultz, Christian
1810   *Travels on an Inland Voyage through the States of New York, Pennsylvania, Virginia, Ohio, Kentucky, and Tennessee, and through the Territories of Indiana, Louisiana, Mississippi, and New Orleans; performed in the years 1807 and 1808.* I. Riley, New York.

Schuyler, Robert L.
1970   "Historical and Historic Sites Archaeology as Anthropology: Basic Definitions and Relationships," *Historical Archaeology*, vol. 4, pp. 83–89.

Schuyler, Robert L., ed.
1980   *Archaeological Perspectives on Ethnicity in America: Afro-American and Asian American Culture History.* Baywood Publishing Co., Farmingdale, New York.

Schwerin, Karl H.
1976   "The Future of Ethnohistory," *Ethnohistory*, vol. 23, no. 4, pp. 323–341.

Service, Elman R.
1962   *Primitive Social Organization: An Evolutionary Perspective.* Random House, New York.

Severinghaus, C. W.
1949   "Tooth Development and Wear as Criteria of Age in White-Tailed Deer," *Journal of Wildlife Management*, vol. 13, pp. 195–216.

Shea, John Gilmary
1852   *Discovery and Exploration of the Mississippi Valley.* J. McDonough, Albany.
1861   *Early Voyages Up and Down the Mississippi.* Joel Munsell, Albany.
1883   *History of the Catholic Missions among the Indian Tribes of the United States, 1529–1854.* E. Dunigan and Brother, New York.

Sibley, John
1832   "Historical Sketches of the Several Indian Tribes in Louisiana, South of the Arkansas and between the Mississippi and River Grande," *American State Papers, Indian Affairs*, vol. 1, Washington, D.C.

Simmons, William Scranton
1970   *Cautantowwit's House: An Indian Burial Ground on the Island of Conanicut in Narragansett Bay.* Brown University Press, Providence.

Skelton, R. A.
1965   *Looking at an Early Map.* University of Kansas Press, Lawrence.

Smith, Bruce D.
1974   "Predator-Prey Relationships in the Southeastern Ozarks—A.D. 1300," *Human Ecology*, vol. 2, pp. 31–44.

Smith, Bruce D., ed.
1978   *Mississippian Settlement Patterns.* Academic Press, New York.
n.d.   *Mississippian Emergence: The Evolution of Ranked Agricultural Societies in Eastern North America.* Smithsonian Institution Press, Washington, D.C.

Smith, Marvin T.
1981   "European and Aboriginal Glass Pendants in North America," *Ornament*, vol. 5, no. 2, pp. 21–23.
1984   "Depopulation and Culture Change in the Early Historic Period Interior Southeast." Ph.D. dissertation, University of Florida, Gainesville.

Social Science Research Council (SSRC)
1954   "Acculturation: An Exploratory Formulation," *American Anthropologist*, vol. 56, no. 3, pp. 973–1,002.

South, Stanley
1976   *Method and Theory in Historical Archeology.* Academic Press, New York.
1977   *Research Strategies in Historical Archeology.* Academic Press, New York.

South, Stanley, ed.
1968   *Historical Archaeology Forum on Theory and Method in Historical Archaeology.* The Conference on Historic Site Archaeology Papers, vol. 2, part 2, Raleigh, North Carolina.

Spector, Janet D.
1974   "Winnebago Indians, 1634–1829: An Archaeological and Ethnohistoric Investigation." Ph.D. dissertation, University of Wisconsin, Madison.
1975   "Crabapple Point (Je 93): An Historic Winnebago Indian Site in Jefferson County, Wisconsin," *The Wisconsin Archaeologist*, vol. 56, no. 4, pp. 270–345.
1977   "Winnebago Indians and Lead Mining: A Case Study of the Ethnohistoric Approach in Archeology," *Midcontinental Journal of Archaeology*, vol. 2, no. 1, pp. 131–137.

Spicer, Edward H.
1958   "Social Structure and the Acculturation Process: Social Structure and Cultural Process in Yaqui

Religious Acculturation," *American Anthropologist*, vol. 60, no. 3, pp. 433–441.
1961 "Types of Contact and Processes of Change," in *Perspectives in American Indian Culture Change*, E. H. Spicer, ed. The University of Chicago Press, Chicago.
1962 *Cycles of Conquest: The Impact of Spain, Mexico, and the United States on the Indians of the Southwest, 1533–1960*. The University of Arizona Press, Tucson.
1971 "Persistent Cultural Systems," *Science*, vol. 174, pp. 795–800.

Spiess, Arthur
1976 "Determining Season of Death of Archaeological Fauna by Analysis of Teeth," *Arctic*, vol. 29, no. 1, pp. 53–55.

Springer, James W.
1980 "An Analysis of Prehistoric Food Remains from the Bruly St. Martin Site, Louisiana, with a Comparative Discussion of Mississippi Valley Faunal Studies." Manuscript, Lower Mississippi Survey, Peabody Museum, Harvard University, Cambridge.

Springer, James Warren, and Stanley R. Witkowski
1982 "Siouan Historical Linguistics and Oneota Archaeology," in *Oneota Studies*, G. E. Gibbon, ed. University of Minnesota, Publications in Anthropology, no. 1, Minneapolis.

Squier, Ephraim G.
1851 *The Serpent Symbol, and the Worship of the Reciprocal Principles of Nature in America*. American Archaeological Researches, no. 1, George P. Putnam, New York.

Squier, Ephraim G., and E. H. Davis
1848 *Ancient Monuments of the Mississippi Valley*. Smithsonian Contributions to Knowledge, vol. 1, Washington, D.C.

SSRC   *See* Social Science Research Council.

Stanislawski, Michael B.
1974 "Ethnoarchaeology and Settlement Archaeology," *Ethnohistory*, vol. 20, no. 4, pp. 375–392.

Steponaitis, Vincas P.
1979 "Lead-Glazed Earthenware," in *Tunica Treasure*, J. P. Brain. Papers of the Peabody Museum, Harvard University, vol. 71, Cambridge.
n.d. "Analysis of Historic Ceramics from Sites in the Lower Mississippi Valley dated ca. 1760–1850." Manuscript, Lower Mississippi Survey, Peabody Museum, Harvard University, Cambridge.

Steponaitis, Vincas P., and Jeffrey P. Brain
1976 "A Portable Differential Proton Magnetometer," *Journal of Field Archaeology*, vol. 3, no. 4, pp. 455–463.

Steward, Julian H.
1942 "The Direct Historical Approach to Archaeology," *American Antiquity*, vol. 7, no. 4, pp. 337–343.
1955 *Theory of Culture Change*. University of Illinois Press, Urbana.

Stirling, Matthew W.
1932 "The Pre-Historic Southern Indians," *Conference on Southern Pre-History*, National Research Council, Washington, D.C.
1940 "The Historic Method as Applied to Southeastern Archeology," in *Essays in Historical Anthropology of North America*. Smithsonian Miscellaneous Collections, vol. 100, Washington, D.C.

Strong, William Duncan
1940 "From History to Prehistory in the Northern Great Plains," in *Essays in Historical Anthropology of North America*. Smithsonian Miscellaneous Collections, vol. 100, Washington, D.C.

Stubbs, John D., Jr.
1983 "Collection Data from Eight Sites in Clay County, Mississippi." Manuscript, Chickasaw Archaeological Survey, Mississippi Department of Archives and History, Jackson.
1984 "A Report Presenting the Results of Archaeological Survey in Lee County, Mississippi, June 1981 to June 1983." Manuscript, Chickasaw Indian Cultural Center Foundation, Tupelo, Mississippi.

Sturtevant, William C.
1966 "Anthropology, History, and Ethnohistory," *Ethnohistory*, vol. 13, nos. 1–2, pp. 1–51.

Suhm, Dee Ann, and Edward B. Jelks, eds.
1962 *Handbook of Texas Archeology: Type Descriptions*. The Texas Archeological Society, Special Publication no. 1; The Texas Memorial Museum, Bulletin no. 4, Austin.

Swanton, John R.
1911 *Indian Tribes of the Lower Mississippi Valley and Adjacent Coast of the Gulf of Mexico*. Bureau of American Ethnology, Bulletin no. 43, Washington, D.C.
1919 *A Structural and Lexical Comparison of the Tunica, Chitimacha, and Atakapa Languages*. Bureau of American Ethnology, Bulletin no. 68, Washington, D.C.
1921 "The Tunica Language," *International Journal of American Linguistics*, vol. 2, pp. 1–39.
1922 *Early History of the Creek Indians and their Neighbors*. Bureau of American Ethnology, Bulletin no. 73, Washington, D.C.
1931 *Source Material for the Social and Ceremonial Life of the Choctaw Indians*. Bureau of American Ethnology, Bulletin no. 103, Washington, D.C.
1932 "The Relation of the Southeast to General Culture Problems of American Pre-History," *Confer-*

ence on Southern Pre-History, National Research Council, Washington, D.C.

1939   *Final Report of the United States De Soto Expedition Commission.* 76th Congress, 1st Session, House Document no. 71, Government Printing Office, Washington, D.C.

1942   *Source Material on the History and Ethnology of the Caddo Indians.* Bureau of American Ethnology, Bulletin no. 132, Washington, D.C.

1946   *The Indians of the Southeastern United States.* Bureau of American Ethnology, Bulletin no. 137, Washington, D.C.

1952   "Hernando De Soto's Route through Arkansas," *American Antiquity*, vol. 18, no. 2, pp. 156–162.

Tardieu, P. F.
1796   "Map of the Course of the Mississippi, from the Missouri and the country of the Illinois to the mouth of this River." Map Collection, Harvard College Library, Cambridge.

Tax, Sol, ed.
1952   *Acculturation in the Americas.* The University of Chicago Press, Chicago.

Taylor, Walter W., Jr.
1948   *A Study of Archeology.* American Anthropological Association, Memoir no. 69, Menasha, Wisconsin.

Tesar, Louis D.
1976   *The Humber-McWilliams Site: A PreColumbian Indian Burial Ground, Coahoma County, Mississippi, Exploration and Analysis 1975–1976.* Port Caddo Press, Marshall, Texas.

Tesar, Louis D., and Donna L. Fichtner
1974   *A Preliminary Report on Archaeological Investigations Conducted at the Humber Site (22Co601) in Westcentral Coahoma County, Mississippi.* Cottonlandia Notes, vol. 1, no. 1, Greenwood, Mississippi.

Thomas, Cyrus
1894   "Report on the Mound Explorations of the Bureau of Ethnology," *Twelfth Annual Report of the Bureau of Ethnology*, pp. 1–742.

Thomassy, Marie Joseph Raymond
1860   "Cartographie de la Louisiane," in *Géologie Pratique de la Louisiane.* Lacroix et Baudry, Paris.

Thwaites, Rueben Gold, ed.
1900   *The Jesuit Relations and Allied Documents.* 73 vols. The Burrows Brothers Co., Cleveland.

Tilley, Christopher
1981   "Conceptual Frameworks for the Explanation of Sociocultural Change," in *Pattern of the Past: Studies in Honour of David Clarke*, I. Hodder, G. Isaac, N. Hammond, eds. Cambridge University Press, Cambridge.

Tollefson, Kenneth D.
1984   "Tlingit Acculturation: An Institutional Perspective," *Ethnology*, vol. 23, no. 3, pp. 229–247.

Tong, Enzeng
1982   "Slate Cist Graves and Megalithic Chamber Tombs in Southwest China: Archaeological, Historical, and Ethnographical Approaches to the Identification of Early Ethnic Groups," *Journal of Anthropological Archaeology*, vol. 1, no. 3, pp. 266–274.

Tonti, Henri de
1697   *Dernières découvertes dans l'Amérique septentrionale de M. De la Sale; mises au jour par M. le Chevalier Tonti, gouverneur du fort Saint Louis, aux Islinois.* Paris.

1700a   "Croquis du Mississipy." Map Collection, U.S. Army Corps of Engineers, Vicksburg, Mississippi. (Original believed to be in the Bibliothèque Nationale, Paris.)

1700b   "Carte du Mississipi." Map Collection, U.S. Army Corps of Engineers, Vicksburg, Mississippi. (A redrawing of Tonti 1700a by Jacques Bureau. Original in Chicago Historical Society.)

Toth, Alan
1974   *Archaeology and Ceramics at the Marksville Site.* Museum of Anthropology, Anthropology Papers, no. 56, University of Michigan, Ann Arbor.

Townsend, Joan B.
1974   "Ethnoarchaeology in Nineteenth Century Southern and Western Alaska: An Interpretive Model," *Ethnohistory*, vol. 20, no. 4, pp. 393–412.

Tregle, Joseph G., Jr.
1973   "Le Page du Pratz: Memoir of the Natchez Indians," in *The Colonial Legacy*, vol. 3, *Historians of Nature and Man's Nature*, L. H. Leder, ed. Harper and Row, New York.

Trigger, Bruce G.
1968   *Beyond History: The Methods of Prehistory.* Holt, Rinehart and Winston, New York.

1982   "Ethnohistory: Problems and Prospects," *Ethnohistory*, vol. 29, no. 1, pp. 1–19.

1984   "Archaeology at the Crossroads: What's New?" *Annual Review of Anthropology*, vol. 13, pp. 275–300.

Trudeau, Carlos
1788   "Parage Vulgaremente llamado, Aldea Biejo Tonica." Papeles de Cuba, Archivo General de Indias, Seville.

Tunnell, Curtis
1966   *A Description of Enameled Earthenware from an Archeological Excavation at Mission San Antonio de Valero (The Alamo).* Texas State Building

Commission, Archeological Program, Report no. 2, Austin.

Ubelaker, Douglas H., and William S. Bass
1970   "Arikara Glassworking Techniques at Leavenworth and Sully Sites," *American Antiquity*, vol. 35, no. 4, pp. 467–475.

Varner, John G., and Jeannette J. Varner
1951   *The Florida of the Inca*. University of Texas Press, Austin.

Vermale
1717   "Carte générale de la Louisiane ou du Miciscipi." Bibliothèque des Archives de la Marine, Paris.

Voegelin, Carl F.
1941   "Internal Relationships of Siouan Languages," *American Anthropologist*, vol. 43, no. 2, pp. 246–249.

Vogt, Evon Z.
1957   "The Acculturation of American Indians," *Annals of the American Academy of Political and Social Sciences*, vol. 311, pp. 137–146.

Wailes, B. L. C.
1853   Diaries. Mississippi Department of Archives and History, Jackson.

Waldbaum, Jane C.
1982   "Analysis of Iron Nails from Haynes Bluff: Final Report." Manuscript, Center for Materials Research in Archaeology and Ethnology, Massachusetts Institute of Technology, Cambridge.

Walker, Deward E., Jr.
1972   *The Emergent Native Americans: A Reader in Culture Contact*. Little, Brown and Co., Boston.

Walker, Ernest P.
1968   *Mammals of the World*. 2nd ed. Johns Hopkins Press, Baltimore.

Walker, Winslow M.
1935   "A Caddo Burial Site at Natchitoches, Louisiana," *Smithsonian Miscellaneous Collections*, vol. 94, no. 14, pp. 1–15.

Wallace, Anthony
1956   "Revitalization Movements," *American Anthropologist*, vol. 58, pp. 264–281.

Walthall, John A., and Elizabeth D. Benchley
1987   *The River L'abbé Mission: A French Colonial Church for the Cahokia Illini on Monks Mound*. Studies in Illinois Archaeology, no. 2, Illinois Historic Preservation Agency, Springfield.

Warden, D. B.
1819   *Statistical, Political, and Historical Account of the United States of North America*, vol. 2. Archibald Constable and Co., Edinburgh.

Ware, John D.
1982   *George Gauld: Surveyor and Cartographer of the Gulf Coast*. Revised and completed by Robert R. Rea. University of Florida/ University of South Florida Book, University Presses of Florida, Gainesville and Tampa.

Waselkov, Gregory A., and R. Eli Paul
1981   "Frontiers and Archaeology," *North American Archaeologist*, vol. 2, no. 4, pp. 309–329.

Washburn, Wilcomb E.
1961   "Ethnohistory: History 'in the Round'," *Ethnohistory*, vol. 8, no. 1, pp. 31–48.
1973   "James Adair's 'Noble Savages', " in *The Colonial Legacy*, vol. 3, *Historians of Nature and Man's Nature*, L. H. Leder, ed. Harper and Row, New York.

Watson, Patty J.
1979   "The Idea of Ethnoarchaeology: Notes and Comments," in *Ethnoarchaeology: Implications of Ethnography for Archaeology*, C. Kramer, ed. Columbia University Press, New York.

Wauchope, Robert, ed.
1956   "An Archaeological Classification of Culture Contact Situations," in *Seminars in Archaeology: 1955*. Society for American Archaeology, Memoir no. 11, Salt Lake City.

Webb, Clarence H.
1959   *The Belcher Mound: A Stratified Caddoan Site in Caddo Parish, Louisiana*. Society for American Archaeology, Memoir no. 16, Salt Lake City.
1962   "Early 19th Century Trade Material from the Colfax Ferry Site, Natchitoches Parish, Louisiana," *Southeastern Archaeological Conference Newsletter*, vol. 9, no. 1, pp. 30–33.

Webb, Clarence H., and Hiram F. Gregory
1978   *The Caddo Indians of Louisiana*. Louisiana Archaeological Survey and Antiquities Commission, Anthropological Study no. 2, Baton Rouge.

Wedel, Mildred Mott
1959   *Oneota Sites on the Upper Iowa River*. The Missouri Archaeologist, vol. 21, nos. 2–4, Columbia.
1971   "J.-B. Bénard, Sieur de la Harpe: Visitor to the Wichitas in 1719," *Great Plains Journal*, vol. 10, no. 2, pp. 37–70.
1974   "The Bénard de la Harpe Historiography on French Colonial Louisiana," *Louisiana Studies*, vol. 13, no. 1, pp. 9–67.
1976   "Ethnohistory: Its Payoffs and Pitfalls for Iowa Archeologists," *Journal of the Iowa Archeological Society*, vol. 23, pp. 1–44.
1979   "The Ethnohistoric Approach to Plains Caddoan Origins," *Nebraska History*, vol. 60, no. 2, pp. 183–196.
1981   *The Deer Creek Site, Oklahoma: A Wichita Village Sometimes Called Ferdinandina, an Ethno-*

historian's View. Oklahoma Historical Society, Series in Anthropology, no. 5, Oklahoma City.

1982 "The Wichita Indians in the Arkansas River Basin," in *Plains Indian Studies: A Collection of Essays in Honor of John C. Ewers and Waldo R. Wedel*, D. H. Ubelaker and H. J. Viola, eds. Smithsonian Contributions to Anthropology, no. 30, Smithsonian Institution Press, Washington, D.C.

Wedel, Mildred Mott, and Raymond J. DeMallie
1980 "The Ethnohistorical Approach in Plains Area Studies," in *Anthropology on the Great Plains*, W. R. Wood and M. Liberty, eds. University of Nebraska Press, Lincoln.

Wedel, Waldo R.
1938 "The Direct-Historical Approach in Pawnee Archeology," *Smithsonian Miscellaneous Collections*, vol. 97, no. 7, pp. 1–21.
1940 "Culture Sequences in the Central Great Plains," in *Essays in Historical Anthropology of North America*. Smithsonian Miscellaneous Collections, vol. 100, Washington, D.C.
1977 "The Education of a Plains Archeologist," *Plains Anthropologist*, vol. 22, no. 75, pp. 1–11.

Weinstein, Richard A.
1985 "Some New Thoughts on the De Soto Expedition through Western Mississippi," *Mississippi Archaeology*, vol. 20, no. 2, pp. 2–24.

Wells, Peter S.
1980 *Culture Contact and Culture Change: Early Iron Age Central Europe and the Mediterranean World*. Cambridge University Press, Cambridge.
1985 "Material Symbols and the Interpretation of Cultural Change," *Oxford Journal of Archaeology*, vol. 4, no. 1, pp. 9–17.

Wesolowski, Al B.
1974 "Investigations at Two Sites in Southeastern Arkansas," *The Arkansas Archeologist*, vol. 15, pp. 20–36.

Wheeler-Voegelin, Erminie
1954 "An Ethnohistorian's Viewpoint," *Ethnohistory*, vol. 1, pp. 106–172.

Whelan, James Patrick, Jr., and Charles E. Pearson
1983 "Cultural Resources Evaluation of Five Construction Areas Along Red River, Louisiana: Lac Amelia, Bertrand, and Lower Gin Lake Revetment, Once More Levee Setback and Pointfield Realignment." Contract Report, Coastal Environments, Inc., Baton Rouge.

White, John R.
1975 "Historic Contact Sites as Laboratories for the Study of Culture Change," *The Conference on Historic Site Archaeology Papers*, vol. 9, pp. 153–163.

1977 "Ethnoarchaeology, Ethnohistory, Ethnographic Analogy, and the Direct-Historical Approach: Four Methodological Entities Commonly Misconstrued," *The Conference on Historic Site Archaeology Papers*, vol. 11, pp. 98–110.

White, Leslie A.
1949 *The Science of Culture: A Study of Man and Civilization*. Grove Press, New York.

White, Patsy
1970 "Investigation of the Cemetery of the Gee's Landing Site, 3DR17," *The Arkansas Archeologist*, vol. 11, no. 1, pp. 1–20.

Wilhelm, Paul, Herzog von Württemberg
1835 *Erste Reise nach dem Nördlichen Amerika in den Jahren 1822 bis 1824*. J. O. Cotta'schen Buchhandlung, Stuttgart and Tübingen.

Willey, Gordon R.
1953 "A Pattern of Diffusion-Acculturation," *Southwestern Journal of Anthropology*, vol. 9, pp. 369–384.

Willey, Gordon R., and Jeremy A. Sabloff
1980 *A History of American Archaeology*. 2nd ed. W. H. Freeman and Co., San Francisco.

Williams, E. Russ, Jr.
1982 *Filhiol and the Founding of the Spanish Poste d'Ouachita: The Ouachita Valley in Colonial Louisiana, 1783–1804*. Monroe-Ouachita Valley Bicentennial Commission, Monroe, Louisiana.

Williams, Samuel Cole, ed.
1930 *Adair's History of the American Indians*. The Watauga Press, Johnson City, Tennessee. Reprint, Blue and Gray Press, Nashville, 1971.

Williams, Stephen
1956 "Settlement Patterns in the Lower Mississippi Valley," in *Prehistoric Settlement Patterns in the New World*, G. R. Willey, ed. Wenner-Gren Publications in Anthropology, no. 23, New York.
1962 "Historic Archaeology in the Lower Mississippi Valley," *Southeastern Archaeological Conference Newsletter*, vol. 9, no. 1, pp. 53–63.
1966 "Historic Archaeology, Past and Present," *Annual Report for 1966*, pp. 23–29, School of American Research, Santa Fe.
1967 "On the Location of the Historic Taensa Villages," *The Conference on Historic Site Archaeology Papers, 1965–1966*, vol. 1, pp. 3–13.
1971 "Nineteenth Century Tunica at the Pierite Site." Paper presented at the 28th Southeastern Archaeological Conference, Macon, Georgia.
1980 "Armorel: A Very Late Phase in the Lower Mississippi Valley," *Southeastern Archaeological Conference Bulletin*, no. 22, pp. 105–110.
1981a "Some Historic Perspectives on Southeastern Ceramic Traditions," *Geoscience and Man*, vol. 22, pp. 115–122.

1981b "Some Reflections on the Long, Happy, and Eventful Life of Robert Stuart Neitzel," *Southeastern Archaeological Conference Bulletin*, no. 24, pp. 7–9.

Williams, Stephen, and Jeffrey P. Brain
1983 *Excavations at the Lake George Site, Yazoo County, Mississippi, 1958–1960.* Papers of the Peabody Museum, Harvard University, vol. 74, Cambridge.

Willing, James
1772 Letter to General Haldimand dated 3 January 1772. Haldimand Papers, British Museum, London.

Willis, William S., Jr.
1980 "Fusion and Separation: Archaeology and Ethnohistory in Southeastern North America," in *Theory and Practice: Essays Presented to Gene Weltfish*, S. Diamond, ed. Mouton Publishers, The Hague.

Wilson, David
1975 *The New Archaeology.* Alfred A. Knopf, New York.

Wilson, Samuel, Jr.
1963 "Louisiana Drawings by Alexandre De Batz," *Journal of the Society of Architectural Historians*, vol. 22, pp. 75–89.
1969 "Ignace François Broutin," in *Frenchmen and French Ways in the Mississippi Valley*, J. F. McDermott, ed. University of Illinois Press, Urbana.

Wilton, William
1774 "Part of the River Mississippi from Manchac up to the River Yazous." Map Collection, Mississippi River Commission, Vicksburg, Mississippi.

Winsor, Justin, ed.
1887 *Narrative and Critical History of America*, vol. 5. Houghton, Mifflin and Co., Boston and New York.

Wood, W. Raymond, and Margot Liberty
1980 *Anthropology on the Great Plains.* University of Nebraska Press, Lincoln.

Woods, Patricia D.
1980 *French-Indian Relations on the Southern Frontier, 1699–1762.* University of Michigan Research Press, Studies in American History and Culture, no. 18, Ann Arbor.